The Works of Vincent van Gogh

The Works of Vincent van Gogh

J.-B. de la Faille

The Works of Vincent van Gogh

His Paintings and Drawings

Reynal & Company

In association with William Morrow & Company

Editorial Board for the revised, augmented and
annotated edition 1970: Abraham M. Hammacher,
President, Jan G. van Gelder, W. Jos de Gruyter
[till 1968], Jan Hulsker, Ellen Joosten, Horst
Gerson [secretary till 1965], Sturla J. Gudlaugsson
[secretary since 1965]
Preliminary work Mrs. Annet Tellegen-Hoogen-
doorn, Miss Martha M. Op de Coul [both from the
Netherlands Institute for Art History, The Hague]
and Evert van Uitert [from the Research Centre for
Art History, University of Utrecht]
Assistants Mrs. Louise A. de Leeuwe-Van Heel
[The Hague] and Miss Gera E. I. Hartog [Utrecht]

Catalogue styled and proofread by
Gary D. Schwartz
Translator of the essay of A. M. Hammacher
James Brockway
Design Frits Stoepman gvn

© Copyright 1970 by Meulenhoff International
Amsterdam

Library of Congress Card Catalogue Number
71-128116

Produced by Meulenhoff International Amsterdam
Printed in the Netherlands
All rights reserved. No part of this book may be
reproduced or utilized in any form or by any means,
electronic or mechanical, including photocopying,
recording or by any information storage and
retrieval system, without permission in writing
from the Publisher. Inquiries should be addressed
to William Morrow and Company Inc. 105 Madison
Avenue New York N. Y. 10016

Contents

Editorial Introduction

On September 18, 1961, the State Secretary of Education, Arts and Sciences at the Ministry of Education, Arts and Science in The Hague set up a Committee which had to report to him on the desirability and possibility of publishing the van Gogh manuscript of the late Dr J. B. de la Faille, which was in the possession of Mrs E. de la Faille-Fransen van de Putte.

The Committee consisted of Professor J.G. van Gelder, Dr W.Jos de Gruyter, Professor A.M.Hammacher, Dr Jan Hulsker and Dr H.Gerson, the director of the Netherlands Institute for Art History in The Hague, to which institution de la Faille's documentation material had been given and where the publication had to be prepared.

The Committee was unanimous in its opinion that, following the last significant van Gogh publication by Hyperion in 1939, which solely concerned his paintings, everywhere in the world where people were occupied with the personality of van Gogh, either because of exhibitions or studies, there was an urgent need for a complete and up-to-date edition of his works. Moreover, it would be an act of respect toward a pioneer in the field to bring out this new edition, which he had been busy preparing up to the time of his death in 1959, without any help, without even the assistance and the aids of the Netherlands Institute for Art History in The Hague, on which the Committee could rely.

In spite of a larger number of data to be rectified or corrected than was originally foreseen, and a number of partly already known problems concerning authenticity, it seemed only right to publish the author's own design and make a clear distinction where the Committee's share in the edition was concerned. An extensive account of this is given hereafter.

The many items to be changed might have tempted the Committee to a third numeration; but it was of the opinion that the drawback of numbers not consistently corresponding to the chronological sequence, compensated however by corrective annotations, was preferable to the disadvantage of a third numeration which would make the existing van Gogh literature more difficult to handle.

In 1962 the Committee's appointment under the chairmanship of A.M.Hammacher was officially announced. The Netherlands Institute for Art History in The Hague made available Mrs A.Tellegen-Hoogendoorn, and she was later joined by Miss M.M.Op de Coul. The preparatory work in conformity with the Committee's directives, which, except for the drawings, included a first critical arrangement of the data of the manuscript, supplemented with the data of the Netherlands Institute of History for Art, was done by this team. The preparation of the drawings (save 'Paris') was since 1966 in the hands of Evert van Uitert, Utrecht University, in conformity with the same directives. Wherever possible he verified measurements, materials and the paper of the drawings in the collections of the Kröller-Müller State Museum and the van Gogh Foundation. The results of the preparative work were submitted to the Committee for critical discussion in a series of sessions over a period of seven years. In 1965, Dr H.Gerson, who had been appointed Professor at Groningen, was replaced as director of the Netherlands Institute for Art History by Dr S.J.Gudlaugsson. To fill the gap caused by the long illness of Dr de Gruyter, Miss Ellen Joosten (deputy director of the Kröller-Müller State Museum in Otterlo) was since 1968 included in the Committee. F.Th.Gribling had made a critical selection from the van Gogh literature.

The Committee decided not to include the youth drawings in the oeuvre of the artist, drawings before the period when van Gogh, in the Borinage, became aware of his vocation as an artist. Yet, wherever possible, a reproduction was included with a separate Roman number. Professor J.G. van Gelder was prepared to revise his earlier publication and extend it, as a result of which this material, included in the appendix, has become a valuable addition to the catalogue.

CORRECTION OF AND ADDITIONS TO THE DE LA FAILLE MANUSCRIPT

The Committee has regarded de la Faille's work as the basis of all subsequent van Gogh study. Any new design, if ever feasible, will have to be based on what de la Faille accomplished, with limited means, in the first arrangement of the disorderly estate. The revisions and deletions which with admirable willingness he later considered necessary always had to be based on his first inventory. Because of its respect for and in recognition of this work, the Committee unanimously decided that the latest order, acknowledgments and attributions decided upon by him should in any case be published in full. Outright mistakes were corrected. However, where published data were available or new data had become known which de la Faille had not incorporated, they have been included in the supplement or in the editors' comment with the items in the catalogue, and clearly distinguished from de la Faille's presentation. In cases of a different opinion, they have been fully documented.

In the case of paintings and drawings that were discovered after de la Faille had completed his manuscript, the Committee included them in its supplement if the attribution seemed acceptable, in each case stating the source first responsible for the attribution.

Although for the sake of continuity titles were generally not changed, it nevertheless proved desirable to correct a number of them. In many cases the subject could be easily distinguished, whereas in others the use of nondescript titles had to be improved by adding adjectives and by otherwise clarifying the old title.

Wherever possible, measurements were revised when the available works could be measured again.

It was possible to base new dates on the improved chronology of van Gogh's letters published by Dr Jan Hulsker in the Dutch literary magazine *Maatstaf* 1958, 1959, 1960 and 1961 (vide bibliography). In these cases the new dates were made to agree with the datings of the cited letter without further comment. In those instances where stylistic, topographical, or other indications were found which rendered de la Faille's dating contestable, this has been stated. The consequence of this was that in maintaining the old numeration (which was also desirable for the sake of practicability in the literature), the numerous changes upset the numerical and visual order. Yet systematic references have, in practice, made everything traceable. The Hyperion numeration of the paintings can be found in the entries, although it has not been repeated everywhere.

Texts of letters were subjected to comprehensive study, resulting in corrections. The quotations were rigorously restricted to those which, actually or generally, related to a group of works or a specific work; wrong interpretations of texts were corrected. Only problems of chronology and authenticity were mentioned; observations which did not touch upon the authenticity or chronology were left out. Brief passages from letters were preferred to more comprehensive or longwinded quotations which can easily be found in the proper sources.

The difficulties in making excerpts from and interpretations of texts of letters translated from the Dutch or the French were sometimes caused by the uncertainty about the corrections of the translation of some passages or words. Blatant mistakes, however, were simply corrected. In a number of cases doubts could be resolved as far as the original letters were made available for comparison. Nevertheless, if the letters are to be republished in the near future, the Committee would like to recommend that the original texts be systematically collated with the translations and editions. This would be of great use for the detailed work of every advanced van Gogh study.

It was also evident on several occasions that the editions of the letters did not always provide an answer to the question whether illustrations were part of the letter or were added later, by Vincent himself or upon their publication. This fact too often proved of importance in being able to decide whether or not an illustration was related to the text of the letter with which it appeared. On this score the French edition of the letters produced a number of corrections. Owing to the willingness of Ir Dr V.W. van Gogh, grateful use was often made of the data in the archives of the van Gogh Foundation. Ir van Gogh attended some of the meetings of the Committee and gave verbal explanations. However, we had to respect his reservations for private research and publication of certain correspondence and notes concerning the French period and the transfer of works from the van Gogh estate.

Further, the archives of the Netherlands Institute for Art History in The Hague, and the catalogues of the Kröller-Müller State Museum of Otterlo have been important sources for this edition. Where the literature is concerned, the various editions of the letters were invaluable, and Dr Walter Vanbeselaere's comprehensive thesis was the principal source where the Dutch period is concerned.

Many owners have most generously provided us with information and photographs. For all this help we should like to express our gratitude to private collectors, art galleries, auction firms and museums. In view of the extent of Vincent's oeuvre, it is unfortunately not possible to list all names separately. Special mention is, however, due for manifold assistance received from the late Mr Myrtil Frank, New York, Mr Helmut Ripperger from Knoedler's New York and Dr Claus Virch of the Metropolitan Museum of Art, New York. Again and again it was necessary to appeal to the staff of the printroom and photographic service of the Stedelijk Museum in Amsterdam; we deeply appreciate the untiring help we received from this side.

In concluding our work, the officials of the Ministry of Culture, Recreation and Social Welfare in The Hague deserve special mention for their extra subsidy which made it possible to complete the work, particularly when the unforeseen long duration of the project called for patience as well. The management of the Netherlands Institute for Art History in The Hague should be mentioned because of its indefatigable hospitality and assistance in a task which has taken up more time and nerves from all those who were involved in it than could originally be foreseen.

The editors request that all those who can provide corrections of or additions to the here collected information, specially with reference to the present whereabouts of works by van Gogh, will notify the Netherlands Institute for Art History in The Hague.

January 1970, The Editorial Committee

Van Gogh and the Words

by A. M. Hammacher

I

When the world gradually became alive to Van Gogh a remarkable period of uncritical adulation began, extending over an ever wider field and becoming more and more specialized. It was accompanied by the inevitable abuse, which is normal but hardly interesting. The cult becomes fascinating only when, both as a human being and an artist, he begins to engage the minds of a number of creative personalities of exceptional stature and to have a fertilizing influence on art after his death in 1890. Between 1920 and 1930 this influence begins to show signs of wavering and flagging. During the 'twenties the psychiatrists begin to concern themselves with Vincent's case and philosophers, among them Heidegger and Bachelard, mention him in their writings. We are no longer far removed from an veneration and inter- pretive activity which extend to everything he touched in his life, an adoration *ad absurdum* which only Goethe before him had experienced.

In short, over a period of more than eighty years a number of reactions to what are the main sources – the letters, paintings and drawings – have been published which have created a dual image of Van Gogh. These reactions are in fact mirrors of all kinds, distorting mirrors included, misted-over, cracked and obscure mirrors – seldom indeed mirrors which do not distort in some way or other. In this environment of mirror images, to use a modish term, we can watch the myth evolving. As a rule, the period during which works of art exercise a fertilizing influence on the susceptible is a brief one. What happens afterwards – the growing attraction a name exerts in ever wider circles, the ever-higher prices the works fetch – may have its social significance but is of no importance at all as regards understanding, insight, revelation.

The acquirement of fame or popularity is an irresistible process. It in no way solves the well- known problem nor does it lend reality to the celebrated dream of 'art rooted in society'. We have, perhaps, arrived at the point – and the present publication bears witness to this – when the words and the letters should be freed from the swaddling clothes eighty years have wound about them and when we should try to arrive at greater accuracy regarding the true facts, the material facts, but equally those concerned with the creative process. In this respect, *Karl Jaspers,* at the time professor in philosophy at Heidelberg, was the first and only person to have grasped the importance of an *exact* chronology of the works to the study of Van Gogh and especially to what he at that time called a 'pathographic analysis'[1]. Jaspers completed his study in 1923. He had used the two-volume German translation of the *Letters* which Cassirer had published in 1914, the letters to Bernard, Mevrouw E. H. Du Quesne-van Gogh's personal recol- lections[2], illustrations in files and the impressions he had formed of Van Gogh in Cologne at the Sonderbund Exhibition of 1912, which contained no less than 108 works.

This Sonderbund Exhibition had a generative influence on numbers of artists from other countries and not merely on the German Expressionists. Artists made their way to it, both Cézanne and Van Gogh being its fascinating nuclei. That it made a deep and immediate impression on Karl Jaspers was to become apparent only eleven years later.

However, in order to grasp the entire process of Van Gogh's artistic career and the intensity with which he worked, Jaspers needed to determine the chronological order of his productions and the remarks he had confided to paper, yet he knew of no book which would supply him with this information. De la Faille's catalogue appeared in

Karl Jaspers, 1883-1969, see page 10

1928 and another nine years were to pass before the Scherjon-de Gruyter and Walther Vanbeselaere's emendations were published. Jaspers thought there was no further chance of determining their exact chronological sequence – [see notes to his pages 128 and 132]. There was a painful absence of certainty regarding the dates of the letters too, although he found these to be arranged in greater order than the paintings.

The work Jan Hulsker undertook to arrive at a more accurate dating of the letters – work of which we have been able to make good use in emending the chronology of the paintings – came too late for Jaspers to make use of it, yet it does in fact represent the first, though belated, response to a serious objection which had been constantly overlooked. Myth-forming, however, remains deaf and blind to such establishments of fact.

Unqualified to judge Jaspers' suspicions – advanced, for that matter, with a certain reserve – that Van Gogh was not an epileptic but a schizophrenic, I shall leave this question aside, but only to invite all the closer attention later on to his view of the letters' significance and their relation to the paintings. For anyone wishing to investigate the up-and-downs of Van Gogh's reputation and the relationship between these fluctuations and the date [and quality] of the reactions his work elicited will find the key to an understanding of Vincent as a personality in this connection between the letters and the paintings and drawings. It will become

apparent time and again how true appreciation, the revelation of the artist's essential nature, is hampered or assisted by the capacity of the author to understand or approach the exceptional aspects of the artist's dualistic creativity: in words and in images.

Those who had sufficient foresight to recognize and proclaim Van Gogh's importance deserve all praise. But such recognition forfeits much of its substance when it is not based on a genuine awareness of Van Gogh's significance, on true insight. On the other hand, it gains immediately in substance when there is evidence of an intuitive or somewhat more conscious insight into the complex character of this singular artistic gift. In other words, a critical survey of the various appraisals of Van Gogh must concern itself with both the chronological element [the time factor] and the quality of the inter- pretations. Any selection of these appraisals has of necessity to be limited to the most striking instances in the mainstream of eighty years of writing about Van Gogh.

II CRITICAL APPRAISALS BETWEEN 1888 AND 1898

The period during which Van Gogh came to be discovered covers a short span only: 1888-1892. It was in these years that his work appeared before the public eye. In 1888, three of his works were on exhibition at Les Indépendants, two in 1889, and ten at the Salon of 1890. Following on the Vingtistes in Brussels, an 'arrangement' held shortly after his death, in 1890, was organized by Emile Bernard in Theo's Paris home at the latter's request. The paintings were hung according to color, not chronologically.

Then follow ten works shown in the Pavillon de la Ville de Paris with Les Indépendants in the spring of 1891, the group of eight canvases and seven drawings to commemorate the artist at the xx. in Brussels, in February, 1891, and finally the exhibition organized by Emile Bernard at Le Barc de Boutteville at 47, rue le Peletier, which came about because Durand Ruel was not prepared to put at Theo's disposal the gallery the latter had asked for his brother [see Theo's letter to Aurier, August 27th, 1890]. Although no special exhibitions were organized during Van Gogh's lifetime, enthusiasts could view his works at Theo's home, at père Tanguy's shop in the rue Clauzel, and also at Thomas and Martin, the art dealer's. [See note* page 14 for exhibition details]. Theo in fact had rented a room at père Tanguy's [see his letter of 16th July, 1889–T 12] since he had insufficient space to hang all the canvases in his own home.

If Tanguy was able to sell any of the works–which were not his property–he had first to obtain either Theo's permission or, after his death, his widow's. He advertised as 'Maison Tanguy' in the weekly *L'Endehors* among other papers, and after his death his widow kept on his shop until mid-July, 1894. During this period she continued to render a scrupulous account of her situation and managed the financial affairs[3].

Vincent was not represented at the World Exhibition of 1889, nor at the special exhibition organized there in Volpini's café of works by artists who had not been invited to put works on show at the exhibition proper.

Among those visiting Theo's home during 1888 were the paintercritic Isaacson and Meyer de Haan [letters 555 and T 1 p 257], who came wishing to spend the winter in Paris.

Hart Nibbrig, later to become a Dutch pointillist, and Jan Veth, the Dutch portrait-painter and art critic, were there in 1889, as were also Saar de Swart [the sculptor], André Bonger [later to become Theo's brother-in-law], Julien Tanguy, Isaac Israels, van Rijsselberghe, Koning, Verenkiold, Octave Maus and Eugène Boch. The young painter Rappard, who lived in Paris between 1878-1881, was acquainted with Theo and at the latter's request Vincent, then in the Borinage, went to visit him in Brussels. When Vincent went to live at Theo's in Paris among the first visitors was Emile Bernard, and after 1889 Albert Aurier, the law student and literary critic, called too and continued to visit Theo after his essay on Van Gogh had appeared in the *Mercure de France*.

Johan de Meester, the literary journalist, had been the Paris correspondent of the Amsterdam daily the *Algemeen Handelsblad* from January 1886 until his appointment as arts editor of the *Nieuwe Rotterdamse Courant* on September 1st, 1891. De Meester did in fact visit Theo, but there are indications that Theo was not very kindly disposed to him, the Van Gogh family not being altogether happy about the articles he wrote.

Van Eeden, the Dutch author and poet, used to visit Paris now and then but showed no particular interest in modern French painting nor in Vincent van Gogh, with whom he was not acquainted. Strangely enough, Vincent must have read one of Van Eeden's books. From Arles, that is to say, he wrote to the painter Koning [letter 571a] and to his sister [letter w 4 ... the face of Death in Van Eeden's book or some such thing] and sought to explain the title he wanted to give to his BERCEUSE by alluding to Van Eeden's *Ons Wiegelied* ['Our Cradle Song'] or

Johan de Meester, 1860-1931, see page 11

De Wiegster ['The Woman at the Cradle'], writing that his style of writing seemed to him to run parallel to his style of painting, as regards color. But this matter is not clear. He gave a book of Van Eeden's to Koning to read. This must have been *De Kleine Johannes* ['Little John']. From October 1st, 1885 on it had been appearing in instalments in *De Nieuwe Gids* and was published in book form in 1887.

Theo did not read the *Nieuwe Gids* writers–at least he possessed none of their works–and though in the letters the brothers speak of French literature they do not mention the *Tachtigers* [Men of the 'Eighties], who represented the leading literary group of the day in the Netherlands. Vincent depended practically entirely on Theo for his reading matter. So Van Eeden must have been the only author of the *Nieuwe Gids* movement Van Gogh had read. That Theo possessed a copy of *De Kleine Johannes* has never been proved. Jo Bonger, later to become Theo's wife, had been befriended since her schooldays with Anna Dirks, whom Jan Veth married in Bussum. Through Veth and her Amsterdam circle she was aware of the significance of Van Eeden, the literary man and doctor, one of the first physicians in the Netherlands to practice and propagate psychotherapy. When in Paris, in the autumn of 1890, after Vincent's death, Theo became mentally unbalanced. Jo could think of nothing better to do than to call in Frederik van Eeden's help via her friend, Anna

Dirks, by then Mrs. Veth, living in Bussum. She asked him to come and see Theo in Paris and it was due to this delicate consultation that Van Eeden was confronted with Vincent's work–to which he reacted in his own manner, in a study which will be discussed later on. In recognition of his help, Theo's wife gave Van Eeden a painting, THE SOWER, as a result of which the Van Eedens were among the first ever to own a Van Gogh.

The publications which saw the light in France, Holland and Belgium between 1889 and 1892 owed their origin to a variety of stimuli and drew on sources which, though still inadequately registered, were very direct. The uneven quality of these writings, containing the germ of the Van Gogh literature which was to evolve later, is attributable not only to the individual characteristics and capacities of their authors but also to a difference in the level of aesthetic and cultural life in France, Belgium and the Netherlands.

In these countries, in the 1889-90 period, during which the first opinions on Van Gogh were published, there was a difference both as regards quantity and quality. France reigned supreme in literature in the other countries of Europe where French was read. 1889 saw a turning point in the admiration felt for the work of Emile Zola and the influence he exerted. In France, naturalism, which for some years had been the great source of inspiration to the young writers in Belgium and the

Emile Bernard, 1868-1941, portrait by Toulouse-
Lautrec, see page 14

Netherlands, began to lose its powers of inspiration.
The cry of 'le naturalisme est mort' was not
immediately replaced by any other device. Vague
group names such as 'Les Décadents' and 'Les
Symbolistes' – who were lumped together under the
term 'Les Idéistes' – indicated what the trend was,
but they also emphasized its complexity and lack of
definition.
A number of periodicals began to appear which
reported daily, weekly or monthly on the movement
which was afoot and which was not in fact confined
to art alone [*L'Endehors, L'Indépendant, La Revue
Indépendante, La Plume, Le Mercure de France,
L'Echo de Paris, Art et Critique*]. During this same
period we see the rise of the interview as a source of
information. In the *L'Echo de Paris* [1891], a
capable journalist, Jules Huret, presented a series of
conversations with literary figures on the controversial character of Zola's naturalism. The striking
thing about these pages is the significance attached
to anarchism. *L'Echo de Paris* was advanced but
L'Endehors seems even more anarchist. Anarchism
was studied as far back as its Russian background
[Bakunin, Kropotkin] – as, for instance, in the
writings of Octave Mirbeau, the literary critic, who
took a deep interest in Van Gogh and also discussed
the anarchist ideal. His *leitmotif* was 'L'heure que
nous vivons est hideuse'.
In Belgium there was an equally energetic campaign
for a new way of life, in which artists played a part,
side by side with politicians. Headed by Octave

Maus, the Vingtistes group in Brussels succeeded
for a time in rivalling Paris by organizing
exhibitions, since become famous, of work by the
avant-garde of Europe, accompanied by other
manifestations, including music.
In the Netherlands, however, activity of this sort
was at the time more restricted. The young writers
who had founded the *Nieuwe Gids* movement were
orientated to English and, to a still greater degree,
to French writing, yet their writing on aesthetics
was decidedly limited and only loosely concerned
with social issues. The writers were acquainted with
what was being done in art; sometimes they
numbered artists among their friends and now and
again commented on painting. But compared with
the French they produced a writer-partisan capable
of good art criticism only now and again. In the
Netherlands it was the painters themselves who
were the art critics – Jan Veth, R. N. Roland Holst,
M. van der Valk, Willem Steenhoff, Willem Witsen,
Eduard Karsen [for a brief period only], J. Isaacson
and Haverman.
The *Nieuwe Gids* acquired a reputation which was
not wholly justified where the fairly difficult period
between Zola and the Décadents and Symbolism
was concerned. Gerben Colmjon wrote a critical
study on the limitations of the *Nieuwe Gids* writers
and had sufficient insight to remark that Van
Gogh's letters showed that he had been more
avant-gardist in his appreciation of foreign authors
than had been the leading figures of the *Nieuwe*

Gids movement.
All the same, this praise of Vincent and his literary
interests requires some correction. Van Gogh read a
lot – the English, the French and even something of
the work of the great Russian authors who were
becoming more widely known at the time. He
continued to revere Zola and there is no sign during
the 1888-90 period that either he or Theo followed
the subsequent reaction in the work of the
Décadents, the Symbolists or the Idéistes with any
special interest. Yet they lived in their circles, a
milieu which was bristling with latent anarchism.
As late as 1905, Alphonse van Bever, Léautaud's
great friend, the secretary for literature at the
L'Oeuvre Theatre and later secretary of the
Mercure de France, was to censure Van Gogh in a
lecture[4], saying: 'he fell back on a secular avatar of
Religion, on the puerile and haughty doctrine of
Anarchy'.

The first critics to write about Van Gogh originated
from the three so very disparate yet interrelated
literary worlds of France, Belgium and the
Netherlands. The first to write on him was
J. J. Isaacson, a Dutch journalist-art critic and
painter [1859-1943] in *De Portefeuille* of August
17th, 1889. From this article J. Hulsker took
the title ['His name, Vincent, is for posterity'] he
used for his contribution to the commemorative
volume, *The Kingdom after 150 Years*, p 148 et seq.
Isaacson was a pupil of Meyer de Haan and had
studied at the Ecole des Beaux-Arts in Paris from
1888 to 1890. In 1906, as an art critic, he shows
himself to be a man who was seeking in art for a
king in the sense of St Paul's letter to the
Corinthians. He discerns two trends: the real, based
on ideas and understanding, and the mystical,
lyrical, magical trend. Van Gogh belonged to the
first. Vincent astonished but did not move him.
This must have come from his own long experience.
For that matter, he owned at least two important
Van Goghs, a SELF-PORTRAIT and a PIETÀ after
Delacroix. So he himself robbed his early
enthusiasm, which had had so prophetic a ring, of
its foundation. His values confused, and with a
pedantic self-overestimation – combined incidentally
with a gross underestimation of Vincent's power –
he declares that the professional critics in Holland
had listened to his words and had 'thereby learned
to see what I had pointed out to them'[5]. From what
I recollect of it at an exhibition held in the Pulchri
Studios at The Hague, his own painting was a
second-rate, exalted compound of late
Impressionism and symbolic biblical figures.
Isaacson lost his way and failed to live up to his
own prophetic utterances.
Likewise, on another level, a certain reserve is
necessary in mentioning the essay on Van Gogh by
the author-physician Frederik van Eeden, member
of the *Nieuwe Gids* circle. It was, indeed, the first
essay in the Netherlands[6]. Albert Aurier had written
the first important monograph earlier on, in 1889
–published in the *Mercure de France* in January,
1890 – though it is possible that Van Eeden, who did
not become acquainted with Van Gogh's work until
the year of the artist's death, was at the time still
unaware of Aurier's essay. He was unacquainted
with Monet and felt no appreciation for Degas,
Pissarro or Rafaelli, while for understandable
reasons he defended the views of the layman as
opposed to those of the professional critic. Van
Eeden actually lacked the requisite terminology to
formulate his impotent reactions to a painter such
as Van Gogh. He achieves no more than emotional
exclamations about the overwhelming power of his
work: *'To me it was a tremendous expression of the
uttermost despair'*. His sense of social superiority is
more questionable, where he remarks that, as a
man, Van Gogh belongs to the sort *'which the lower
classes call mad, but which people of our kind call*

holy'. He apparently knew nothing of the 'lower classes' to whom Van Gogh owed so much during his lifetime. His naïve, straightforward reaction, uninfluenced by any training, is laudable, and it is interesting to see how, as a psychiatrist, he pays more attention to the artist than to the work itself, while laying stress on the *ethical* aspect.

Thus, to begin with, appreciation for Van Gogh in the Netherlands is orthodox-ethical in character. Van Eeden is no more able to give depth or to sustain his admiration then Isaacson was. Years after this, he was to rank a not uninteresting but nevertheless second-rate painter like A. de Winter of Utrecht on the same level as Van Gogh, if not higher. He was unable to analyse Van Gogh and to see him against the background of his time. For all its honesty, what he had to say about him could not in any way bear comparison with what was being written in French nor with Hugo von Hofmannsthal's exclamatory reactions after he had been struck in 1901–as though by lightning–by Van Gogh's use of color in particular, recording these reactions in a complicated ultra-literary manner[7].

Johan de Meester, too, was among the first Dutchmen to draw attention to Van Gogh. His own difficult youth, involving a struggle to free himself from the constricting bonds of a severely religious environment in the Netherlands, and his interest in social problems must have given him a natural understanding of Van Gogh's life. He was a boyhood friend of the painter, Anton van Rappard, who became known throughout the world not for his own work, quite respectable and pure though it was, but for the publication of letters he exchanged with Van Gogh. So de Meester knew the kinds of problem painters came up against and, where terminology was concerned, was far more capable than many others.

He was an admirer of the de Concourts and Zola and had read *Germinal* when staying in the mining district of Charleroi. He was no liker of the vocabulary the 'Tachtigers'–the Men of the Eighties, as the *Nieuwe Gids* authors were often referred to–affected. The period he spent in Paris lasted from January 1886 to September 1891, after which he gave up his post as Paris correspondent of the *Algemeen Handelsblad* of Amsterdam to become Arts Editor of the *Nieuwe Rotterdamse Courant*. The situation between him and Theo van Gogh gave him little encouragement, but he did not allow this to stop him plunging with abandon into the work and writing about it at length–and in a didactic manner–in the Rotterdam paper. [See also letter of December 28th, 1890, in the *Algemeen Handelsblad* for December 31st, 1890 about the works Bernard hung in Theo's home].

De Meester's first visit to Theo's home took place in March, 1886 in the company of André Bonger. Presumably he saw little of Vincent's work on this occasion, for he had hardly got started in Paris at the time.

In 1891 de Meester discovered that the editor-in-chief at the *Nieuwe Rotterdamse Courant* had laid a taboo on the *Nieuwe Gids* writers, which also implied a repugnance for the things, literary, ethical and political, de Meester had associated himself with in Paris. Consequently, in view of the resistance of the editorial board and the paper's readership, his two articles in the *Nieuwe Rotterdamse Courant* of March 6th and 13th, 1892 represented something new and unexpected. It was a courageous act by a man who, unlike Van Eeden and Isaacson, remained loyal to this early admiration of his, as we see from his later studies, including articles in *Nederland*, March, 1891, the *Nederlandse Spectator*, 1892 and *De Gids* of May 1st, 1911 [p 285], in which he issued a strong warning against the memoirs which Mevrouw Du Quesne-van Gogh had published of Vincent's early years, terming them unreliable and of a well-bred

Octave Mirbeau, 1848-1917, see page 14

vacuity.

An article in the *Nieuwe Rotterdamse Courant* of April 4th, 1890–that is, when Vincent was still living–was assuredly not by de Meester, who at the time was still working for the *Algemeen Handelsblad*. It refers to Van Gogh's submissions to the exhibition of Les Indépandants in the Pavillon de la Ville de Paris, at which Seurat also put works on show. The anonymous correspondent, it is true, considers that this sort of painting took the bizarre to extremes. An interesting deviation from the average French reaction, represented, for example, by Georges Lecomte and Eugène Tardieu, who shortly afterwards was writing favourably of the work in *Le magazine francais illustré*. Of Van Gogh, Lecomte, in *Art et critique, revue littéraire, dramatique, musicale et artistique* for March 29, 1890, p 203, says, 'Monsieur Vincent van Gogh's ferocious impasto and his exclusive use of colors which harmonize easily result in powerful effects: the violet background of CYPRESSES and the symphony of green in a landscape make a vivid impression'. At this same exhibition there were works on show by the Belgian artists George Lemmen, van Rijsselberghe and Henry van de Velde, who, therefore, were already able to encounter works by Van Gogh there, which in turn had its influence on what the Vingtistes were to do for him in Brussels, with Octave Maus, who visited Theo van Gogh in Paris in 1889, as their spokesman.

The positive reaction of Georges Lecomte–who in 1892 delivered an address to the Vingtistes in Brussels among other things–is the earliest published appraisal of any significance, coming from a man who presumably had to depend on the exhibitions and did not visit Theo's home. Exhibiting was a difficult business for Vincent and perhaps even more so for Theo. He was already encountering opposition from the art dealers for whom he worked and hardly wished to make it still more difficult for himself by coming along with his brother's work. It should not, however, be supposed that Vincent seized every opportunity that came along to exhibit his work. On the contrary, he could be very exacting as to the suitability of the premises offered. For example, in 1888 the editors of *La Revue Indépendante* offered to arrange an exhibition for him, Eduard Dujardin acting as intermediary [see letter 561 from Arles].

I am not aware whether Theo and Vincent were fully aware of the reputation the review enjoyed. Dujardin was a well-known figure in literary circles and no less a figure than Fénéon had been its editor-in-chief in 1884. It had moved on from naturalism to symbolism [cf Jacques Lethève: *Impressionistes et symbolistes devant la presse*, Paris, 1959], and it was entirely in keeping with the growing interest in symbolism that they should have been especially interested at that juncture in putting work by Van Gogh on display. Vincent turned down their offer on the grounds that it was too dark a little hole and, moreover, generous though he otherwise was, when it came to giving his works away, he didn't feel inclined to relinquish one of his canvases in exchange for the cost of mounting the exhibition–which was often the practice, for that matter. He repeatedly returns to this subject: Theo was not authorized to do business without consulting the de Goupils; what's more Vincent wasn't so very interested, and, in his opinion, the few exhibitions there were not so very important. He mentions those organized at Tanguy's, later at Thomas's and finally at Martin's, a friend of Theo's with whom Theo was later to dine in Auvers at the end of May, 1890 [see letter T 35]. Thomas is often referred to as 'good old Thomas', with whom they [Theo, Vincent, Gauguin] wanted to do business, provide funds to finance Vincent's plans in Arles and to buy works of art [buying from Anquetin among others].

Thus there are at least nine to ten exhibitions known to us between 1887 and 1890 at which Van Gogh exhibited works in Paris besides shows at Theo's home, while the one projected by the *Revue Indépendante* was turned down*. What is certain is that these opportunities to exhibit were highly significant, if not to achieve immediate sales, at least for other painters, prospective customers and the art critics. The 'Maison Tanguy'–the name under which Julien Tanguy advertised his shop in the rue Clauzel–was particularly important, since that was where people met. *Octave Mirbeau* [1848-1917] often came there and he even helped Madame Tanguy in 1894, when she got into financial difficulties after her husband's death. It was here that *Emile Bernard* made Van Gogh's acquaintance and saw portfolios of drawings and sketches, mentioning among others LA FOSSE COMMUNE, the FORTIFICATIONS and the POTATO-EATERS, which he said was 'of a signal ugliness and of a disturbing life'. He had seen him at work before this at Cormon's, at no. 104, boulevard de Clichy, and recalled his departure from there. Emile Bernard knew *Albert Aurier,* the young poet, art-critic and lawyer, and claimed that he had drawn his attention to Van Gogh. It is in any case a fact that in an undated letter [in the Williame archives at Châteauroux] the envelope of which is date-stamped October 23rd, 1889, Bernard sent Aurier a short article about Van Gogh, asking him if he would expand it with a critical appraisal of the canvases Van Gogh had at Tanguy's.

And to it he adds: '*...and making one wish that his brother will not hesitate one day to put all his work on show at an exhibition to be organized by him–it could be at Goupil's. He seems to persist in refusing to believe in his brother Vincent's talent.*' This remark is an insinuation, but Bernard was aware neither of Theo's scruples nor of Vincent's unwillingness when it came to exhibiting.

As far as is known, Emile Bernard's article, which he offered Aurier for publication in the *Moderniste,* never saw print. Yet this prologue to Aurier's since celebrated essay in the *Mercure de France* for January, 1890 is of value, since it reveals the

*. 1. Restaurant la Fourche [on the corner of the avenue Saint-Ouen and the avenue de Clichy]. 2. Cabaret du Tambourin [La Segatori], boulevard de Clichy 62 [les peintres du petit boulevard]. 3.4.5. Les Indépendants, 22-3 March 1888, Pavillon de la Ville de Paris; 3 September-4 October 1889, Salle de la Société d'Horticulture, rue de Grenelle 84; 20 March-27 April 1890, Pavillon de la Ville de Paris. 6. Martin–mezzanine floor, rue Lafitte. 7. Thomas, boulevard Malesherbes. 8. Tanguy, rue Clauzel [letter 561]. 9. Les XX–7th exhibition, January-February 1890. 10. Théâtre Libre [letter 473 says that the 'jardin avec amoureux' canvas was hung there]. In any case, the first sale of a work we know of took place not at Brussels but at Tanguy's in Paris [see letter 506, which informs us that he received 20 francs for a portrait of a friend of Tanguy's]. It seems that E. Boch bought directly from Vincent Faille nr 622. In 1891, Mrs Bonger sold a drawing for 200 francs. The asking price for canvases put on exhibition in 1890 varies between 200 and 500 francs.

Albert Aurier, 1865-1892, see page 14

exchange of ideas among writing artists in the period 1888-89 on the exhibitions mentioned and their contacts with Vincent. In 1890 Alfred Vallette restyled and modernized the *Mercure* and it is understandable that in this new symbolist mood Aurier should have launched his series of articles on 'Les Isolés' with Van Gogh and none other. Emile Bernard sought in vain in what Aurier wrote for any mention of the role he himself had played in the genesis of Aurier's essay, and from then on his attitude to him is critical and derogatory–he even going as far as to deny him any feeling for painting. The reader is inclined to ask why, in that case, he should have encouraged him to write about Van Gogh in the first place and helped him to material. It did not improve matters when Aurier began to write about Gauguin and saw no reason at all why he should mention Bernard as his source of inspiration. What Octave Mirbeau, critical by nature, possessed of many gifts and one who was early to respond to Van Gogh as a painter [he saw his work at Tanguy's from 1888 on], thought of Bernard shows sharp-sightedness and suggests that he had good powers of observation and was well-informed. When reviewing the Van Gogh exhibition at Bernheim's in the *Figaro* for March 17th, 1901, he stressed Van Gogh's health of mind–which indicates remarkable insight in an age which found it a far more attractive proposition to lay the emphasis on the artist's abnormalities: '*there is no mind more balanced than his...he has nothing of the*

sectarian...As for literature, his ideas are, on the contrary, timid: he thinks that there is nothing to surpass de Maupassant...'
This last remark rightly counterbalances the exaggerated admiration attributed to Van Gogh for avant-garde writing [in the Netherlands Colmjon paid attention to this; also Carl Nordenfalk and Jean Seznek]. In the *Magazine of Art*, 1950, p 283 et seq, the latter wrote a survey of the works in which books appear as motifs–a thing Nordenfalk also did–and, moreover, quoted from letters concerning the relation between literature and painting. As has already been remarked, there is no sign that Theo or Vincent followed the numerous French avant-garde journals closely–papers which, under pressure from the Décadents and the Symbolists, were seeking to abandon naturalism à la Zola. After all, the brothers' main concern was painting.
Mirbeau, however, did not confine his remarks to Van Gogh but in this same article drew a portrait of Bernard: 'a very curious mind, very attractive, very inquiring, very erudite, of an unusual and lively intelligence, yet chimerical beyond limit and permeated by all manner of vague religious ideas, a mediocre painter, impotent even, had a great influence on Van Gogh's moral constitution, which at certain times could become troubled and obscure...He had none on his art, he had disturbed Gauguin's and that of several others who foundered in mysticism etc.' Finally: despite this 'mental equilibrium' Mirbeau regarded Bernard's further

evolution as a painter fatal.

Bernard was aware of Mirbeau's contact with Van Gogh's works and in 1891 he asked him for the loan of one of them for an exhibition to be held at le Barc de Boutteville, a 'magasin de vente' at 47, rue le Peletier, for mediocre painters, but one which nevertheless aimed to concentrate on the latest painters regardless of school. The entire exhibition consisted at the time of fourteen paintings.

Bernard's plan to put a portfolio on the market containing a dozen photographs of works by Van Gogh in order to publish the letters out of the proceeds is all but naïve and touching. [I discovered a sheet of notes on this project in Châteauroux, at the Williame home].

There can be no doubt that, whatever the ulterior motives, Bernard's admiration for Van Gogh was deep and genuine. It is to his credit that in his own work he should have resisted Van Gogh's influence, associating it rather with what Cézanne was doing. Bernard certainly culled more from the letters than the works and was sufficiently intelligent to comprehend the importance of the former, which were, in any case, based on a number of years of intensive intercourse[8, 9].

In *La Plume* of 1891, pp 300-301, – the year in which the magazine published a special issue on Jean Moréas' symbolism – Bernard drew the following portrait of Van Gogh: '*hair a russet-brown (goatee beard, primitive moustache, shaven bullet-head), eagle eyes, sharp mouth so to speak; of average stature, thickset, though not excessively, lively of gesture, irregular gait – there you had Van Gogh, and always with his pipe, a canvas or an engraving, or a piece of pasteboard. Vehement in argument, explaining things interminably and great at elaborating an idea; little inclined to enter into controversy – that was him as well; and dreams, ah! dreams! of gigantic exhibitions, philanthropic phalansteries of artists, the founding of colonies in le Midi, and besides all this – the progressive invasion of public circles in aid of the celebrated re-education of the masses, which had responded to art in the past*'.

La Plume was of great documentary value. Though not one-sided, it remained very lively. The character sketch of Van Gogh that its pages, particularly, provide us with is to be rated highly. Bernard's later introductions are not always correct, its repetitions are weaker, as for instance, the introduction to a new impression of the letters [*Editions de la Nouvelle Revue Belgique*, 1942]. Yet now and then one comes across useful notes, such as that about Dr. Gachet [p 22] 'whose portrait he made twice'; an argument in the dispute about the two portraits of Gachet [one in the former Kramarsky Collection in New York, the other – its authenticity disputed – in the Louvre]. The introduction to the 1911 edition by Vollard of the letters to Bernard about Vincent was already sour and offended in tone, too.

In artistic circles – which, when speaking of France, means first and foremost the literary coteries, a literary figure like Octave Mirbeau exercised more authority than Bernard. He won great respect, too. As a militant personality among the artists he enjoyed a *succès de scandale* in 1900 with his *Le Journal d'une femme de chambre* and again, in 1903, with his play *Les affaires sont les affaires*, in which he lambasted the morals of society with his own peculiar acerbity. Indeed, it was his militant spirit rather than his novels and plays themselves which earned him the respect that was his. His essays on art continued to find readers for a long time. It was he, too, who wrote enthusiastically in support of the auctioning of Gauguin's work to finance his departure to Tahiti, his essay, published in *Le Figaro* for February 16th, 1891, containing an excellent literary portrait of the artist.

De Meester knew Mirbeau too and records that it was he who later introduced Maeterlinck to Paris. But in the 'nineties we see him principally as a

August Vermeylen, 1872-1945, see page 19

vehement writer one of whose leading articles in *L'Endehors* of May, 1892 was devoted to Ravachol, the celebrated French anarchist, who was guilty of numerous outrages and who ended up on the guillotine. But Mirbeau was, in addition, an art critic, whose name was mentioned with that of Fénéon and Brunetière as being one of the revivers of art criticism. So the same man who had given vent to violent political feelings concerning Ravachol's execution – and this is characteristic, after all, of the types of person who were to be among Van Gogh's earliest defenders, typical, too, of the level on which they went to work – was to write a striking leading article in the *Echo de Paris* – 'a morning paper of literature and politics' – for March 31st, 1891, published on the *front page* next to a poem by Theodore de Banville[10]. What Dutch paper would have dared to do that?

The occasion for this article was provided by the canvases in Vincent's honor at the exhibition of Les Indépendants in the Pavillon de la Ville de Paris. It was wholly in the mood of mourning for Van Gogh, composed of fiery words and displaying great vision. There had been Aurier, whose essay in the *Mercure de France* had given the first important impulse, and now it was once again a considerable man of literature who recognized Van Gogh for what he was. Mirbeau was later to become the owner of several important works of Van Gogh's, including one of the portraits of père Tanguy, the IRISES and one of the SUNFLOWER canvases. In 1912 we find

Guillaume Apollinaire still mentioning this portrait of Tanguy and expressing the hope that Mirbeau will one day write Tanguy's story[11].

I shall quote below from this leading article in the *Echo de Paris*, one of my main reasons for doing so being that Mirbeau was not unknown in the Netherlands either and because his remarks concerning Vincent must have been of effect in Holland, although no mention was made of them. For, according to the daily newspaper the *Amsterdammer* of December 20th, 1892, his essay and that by Aurier were on exhibition on a table in the Panorama galleries in Amsterdam in 1892, when the great exhibition organized by the young painter R.N. Roland Holst was held there. The canvases were hung against a blue and green backcloth, kindly lent for the occasion by the Antwerp Association pour l'Art.

Mirbeau's reactions included the following: '*His was a restless, tormented mind, full of inspired ideas, vague and ardent, drawn perpetually towards the summits where the mysteries of human life reveal themselves. One never knew what force was active inside him – whether it was the apostle or the artist; he did not even know himself...*'

'*...he drowned himself in the apostle, losing himself in the evangelist, roamed through forests of dreams that were strange and obscure to him...*'

'*...He was not absorbed by nature either. He had absorbed nature into himself; he had forced it to unbend, to mould itself into the shapes of his thoughts,*

8e ANNÉE — N° 2507   Paris et Seine-et-Oise 10 cent. le Numéro — Départements 15 cent.   Mardi 31 Mars 1891

L'ÉCHO DE PARIS

JOURNAL LITTÉRAIRE ET POLITIQUE DU MATIN

VALENTIN SIMOND   VALENTIN SIMOND
DIRECTEUR   DIRECTEUR

ANNONCES, RÉCLAMES et FAITS DIVERS:
Chez MM. Lagrange, Cerf et Cie, 6, place de la Bourse
et dans les bureaux de l'Écho de Paris.
Les manuscrits non insérés ne sont pas rendus

RÉDACTION ET ADMINISTRATION : 16, RUE DU CROISSANT (Hôtel Colbert)

Publicité de première et deuxième page exclusivement aux bureaux de « L'ÉCHO DE PARIS », 16, rue du Croissant

L'ENFANT

PAR
THÉODORE DE BANVILLE

C'était au Luxembourg, par un matin brûlant
De Juillet, où le clair soleil étincelant
Versait partout les feux de ses apothéoses,
Jetait des taches d'or parmi les lauriers-roses
Et baignant de rayons leurs cœurs incendiés,
Embrasait, furieux, les fleurs des grenadiers.
De beaux enfants jouaient, montrant leurs jambes nues,
Gais, sérieux, ouvrant leurs bouches ingénues,
Et la course faisait voler dans l'air vermeil
Leurs cheveux frémissants, blonds comme le soleil.

Les beaux petits garçons et les petites filles
Jouaient à la madame, à la toupie, aux billes.
Ceux-ci, vite, emplissaient à la pelle du seaux
De sable, ou bien faisaient voltiger des cerceaux,
Ou se disputaient, fous et prompts à la riposte.
D'autres couraient ensemble et jouaient à la poste,
Faisant voler au vent leur petit cotillon.
L'un était le cheval, l'autre le postillon,
Et leurs petits amis avaient grand peine à suivre
Les claquements du fouet et les grelots de cuivre.
Tous, douces fleurs, charmante aurore du présent,
Allaient se bousculant, se battant, se baisant,
Et leurs grands yeux emplis d'espoir et de chimères
Faisaient s'épanouir les sourires des mères,
Et tout n'était que joie infinie à l'entour.

Mais, ô rêve ! ô sinistre enchantement du jour !
Comme s'il eût caché d'invisibles désastres,
Il sembla que l'azur, où sommeillent les astres,
S'allumait, et dans l'air fluide et paresseux,
Les spectres de midi, plus effrayants que ceux
De la nuit, au milieu des rayons apparurent,
Foules qui lentement s'enflèrent et s'accrurent,
Flottant dans la lumière et l'éblouissement ;
Et dans le lointain clair s'ébauchaient vaguement
Ces fantômes gardant leur sinistre posture,
Teints des couleurs du prisme et de la pourriture.

C'était le Meurtre ayant dans sa main son couteau,
Le Vol, cachant des sacs pleins d'or sous un manteau,
L'Usure avec des mains faites comme des serres,
La Débauche riante au sein rongé d'ulcères,
L'Avarice veillant auprès d'un coffre ouvert,
L'Ivresse avec son verre empli du poison vert,
La Colère acharnée à de hideux sévices,
Et toute la cohorte innombrable des Vices
Et des vils Appétits repus et triomphants.
Et tous, en regardant les beaux petits enfants,
Disaient : Vous serez les acteurs des sombres drames,
Les vivants. Vous serez des hommes et des femmes,
Nés de la fange, par le désir entraînés,
Abjects, vains ; c'est pourquoi vous nous appartenez.
Ivres et furieux, vous chercherez vos joies
Dans la chair pantelante, et vous êtes nos proies.

Mais un frisson d'horreur dans leur foule courut
Et tranquille, parmi les enfants apparut,
Avec une douceur amie et reposée,
Pareil au chaste lys que baigne la rosée,
Un enfant couronné d'épines, que ceignait
Une blanche auréole, et dont le front saignait.
Devant son clair regard, aussi doux que les baumes,
S'enfuirent, éperdus, les livides fantômes,
Les Vices, les Fureurs, les sanglants Appétits,
Et lui, le chaste Enfant, tandis que les petits
Le regardaient sans peur de leurs yeux téméraires,
Il leur disait : Jouez en paix, mes petits frères.

THÉODORE DE BANVILLE.

Mercredi, 5 janvier 188...

VINCENT VAN GOGH

A l'Exposition des indépendants, parmi quelques tentatives heureuses et, surtout, parmi beaucoup de banalité, et plus encore de fumisterie, éclatent les toiles du regretté Vincent Van Gogh. Et, devant elles, et, devant ce crêpe noir qui les endeuille et qui les désigne à la foule indifférente des passants, l'on se prend d'une grande tristesse à penser que ce peintre, si magnifiquement doué, que ce si frissonnant, si instinctif, si visionnaire artiste, fut parti de la vie en crucifié, en irréparable, que celle de M. Meissonier, bien que le peuple n'ait pas été convié à de fastueuses obsèques, et que le regretté Vincent Van Gogh, en qui s'est éteint une si belle flamme de génie, s'en soit allé dans la mort, aussi obscur, aussi ignoré, qu'il avait vécu, ignoré et obscur, dans l'injuste vie.

Encore ne le faudrait-il pas juger sur les quelques tableaux, exposés en ce moment, au pavillon de la Ville de Paris, quoiqu'ils paraissent très supérieurs, en richesse de vision, en richesse d'expression, en puissance de style, à tout ce qui les entoure. Certes, je ne suis pas insensible aux recherches de lumière de M. Georges Seurat, dont j'aime beaucoup les paysages maritimes, d'une blondeur exquise et profonde. Je trouve un charme rare aux fondoyantes atmosphères, aux grâces féminines, aux chairs élégances de M. Van Rysselberghe. Les petites compositions de M. Denis, d'un tor. si suave, d'une enveloppe mystique si tendre, m'attirent. Je reconnais au réalisme borné et sans idée de M. Armand Guillaumin, une belle patte, comme on dit, de probes et robustes qualités de métier. Et malgré les noirs dont il salit indûment ses figures, M. de Toulouse-Lautrec montre une force réelle, spirituelle et tragique, dans l'étude des physionomies et la pénétration des caractères. Les gravures de M. Lucien Pissarro ont de la verve, de la sobriété et de la distinction. Il n'est pas jusqu'à M. Anquetin qui, au milieu de réminiscences flagrantes, de conventions d'école, de bizarreries tatées, de caricaturales laideurs, ne nous offre, parfois, une jolie échappée de lumière, comme cet horizon parisien, dans la toile intitulée : Pont des Saint-Pères, et de savantes harmonies de gris, comme dans le portrait de femme. Mais aucun de ces incontestables artistes, avec lesquels il ne faudrait pas confondre M. Signac, dont la broyante, sèche, prétentieuse nullité agace, ne me suffisent autant que Vincent van Gogh. Je me sens, là, en présence de quelqu'un de plus haut, de plus maître, et qui m'inquiète, et qui m'émeut, et qui s'impose.

Ce n'est peut-être pas encore le moment de raconter Vincent van Gogh, comme il faudrait. Sa mort est trop proche et elle fut trop tragique. Les souvenirs que j'en évoquerais retiennent les douleurs, qui pleurent encore. Cette étude sera donc forcément incomplète, car ce qu'il y eut de grand et d'inattendu, d'aussi, parfois, de trop violent, d'excessif, dans l'âpre et délicieux talent de Van Gogh, est intimement lié aux fatalités cérébrales qui le prédestinèrent, jeune, à la mort.

Sa vie fut assez déconcertante. Il entra d'abord dans le commerce des tableaux, avec son frère, mort aussi de la même mort que lui, qui dirigeait la maison Goupil, au boulevard Montmartre. C'était un esprit inquiet, tourmenté, tout plein d'aspirations ingénues et ardentes, perpétuellement attiré sur les sommets où s'élucident les mystères humains. On ne savait alors ce qui s'agitait en lui, le l'apôtre ou de l'artiste ; il ne le savait pas lui-même. Il quitta bientôt le commerce, pour étudier la théologie. Il avait, paraît-il, une forte éducation littéraire, et une tendance naturelle vers le mysticisme. Ces nouvelles études semblèrent, un moment, avoir donné à son âme la direction qu'elle réclamait. Il paraissa. Sa voix retentit dans les chaires, parmi les foules. Mais il eut de rapides déboires. La prédication lui apparut tôt, comme une chose vaine. Il ne sentait pas assez près des âmes qu'il voulait conquérir, ses paroles enflammées d'amour se heurtaient aux murs des chapelles et des cœurs sans les pénétrer. Il pensa que l'enseignement serait plus efficace; et, abandonnant le prêche, il partit pour Londres, où il s'établit maître d'école. Durant quelques mois, il apprit aux petits enfants ce qui se passe en Dieu.

Évidemment, tout cela semble assez étrange et déconcertant. C'est pourtant bien explicable. L'artiste ingénieux qui couvait en lui s'ignorait encore; il se noyait dans l'apôtre, se perdait dans l'évangéliste, s'égarait, à travers des forêts de rêves, qui lui étaient étrangères et obscures. Pourtant il sentait qu'une force invincible l'appelait quelque part, mais où ?... qu'une lumière s'allumerait, quelque part, au bout de ces ténèbres, mais quand ? Le résultat un déséquilibre moral, qui l'incitait aux actions les plus disparates, et des fuites lointaines de lui. Ce fut à son retour de Londres que sa vocation éclata tout à coup. Il se mit à peindre, un jour, par hasard. Et il se trouva que, du premier coup, cette première toile fut presque un chef-d'œuvre. Elle révélait un instinct extraordinaire de peintre, de merveilleuses et fortes qualités de vision, une sensibilité aiguë, qui devinait la forme vivante et remuante, sous l'aspect rigide des choses, une éloquence, une abondance d'imagination, qui stupéfièrent ses amis. Alors Vincent van Gogh s'acharna. Le travail, sans trêves, le travail avec tous ses entêtements et toutes ses ivresses, s'empara de lui. Un besoin de produire, de créer, lui tenait au cœur, sans halte, sans repos, comme s'il eût voulu regagner le temps perdu. Cela dura sept ans. Et la mort vint, terrible, cueillir ce pauvre mort, avec toutes les espérances, qu'un tel artiste nous faisait concevoir, une œuvre considérable, près de quatre cents toiles, et une énorme quantité de dessins, dont beaucoup sont d'absolus chefs-d'œuvre.

Van Gogh était d'origine hollandaise, de la patrie de Rembrandt, qu'il semble avoir beaucoup aimé et beaucoup admiré. A un tempérament de cette originalité abondante, de cette fougue, de cette sensibilité hyperesthésiée, qui s'admettait comme guide, que ses impressions personnelles, si l'on peut donner une finalité artistique, on pourrait peut-être dire que Rembrandt fut son ancêtre de prédilection, celui en qui il se sentit mieux revivre. On retrouve dans ses dessins nombreux, non point des ressemblances, mais un culte exaspéré des mêmes formes, une richesse d'invention linéaire pareille. Van Gogh n'a pas toujours la correction, ni la sobriété du maître hollandais ; mais il atteint souvent à une puissance, à une prodigieuse faculté de rendre la vie. De la façon de sentir de Van Gogh, nous avons une indication très précise et très précieuse; ce sont les copies qu'il exécuta d'après divers tableaux de Rembrandt, de Delacroix, de Millet. Elles sont admirables. Mais ce ne sont pas, à proprement parler, des copies, ces exubérantes et grandioses restitutions. Ce sont plutôt des interprétations, par lesquelles le peintre arrive à recréer l'œuvre des autres, de la faire sienne, tout en lui conservant son esprit originel et son spécial caractère. Dans le Semeur, de Millet, rendu, si surhumainement beau par Van Gogh, le mouvement s'accentue, la vision s'élargit, la ligne s'amplifie jusqu'à la signification du symbole. Ce qu'il y a de Millet, demeure dans la copie; mais Vincent van Gogh y a introduit quelque chose à lui, et le tableau prend aussitôt un aspect de grandeur nouvelle. Il est bien certain qu'il apportait devant la nature les mêmes habitudes mentales, les mêmes dons supérieurs de création, que devant les chefs-d'œuvre de l'art. Il ne pouvait pas oublier sa personnalité, ni la contenir devant n'importe quel spectacle, et n'importe quel rêve extérieur. Elle débordait de lui ; elle s'imposait à la nature, la soumettait, la pliait aux formes de sa pensée, à la suivre dans ses envolées, à subir même ses déformations si caractéristiques. Van Gogh a eu, à un degré rare, ce par quoi un homme se différencie d'un autre : le style. Dans une foule de tableaux mêlés les uns aux autres, l'œil, sans nul doute, sûrement, reconnaît ceux de Vincent van Gogh, comme il reconnaît ceux de Corot, de Manet, de Degas, de Monet, de Monticelli, parce qu'ils ont un génie propre, qui ne peut être autre, et qui est le style, c'est-à-dire l'affirmation de la personnalité. Et tout, sous le pinceau de ce créateur étrange et puissant, s'anime d'une vie étrange, indépendante de celle des choses qu'il peint, et qui est en lui, et qui est lui. Il se dépense tout entier, au profit des arbres, des ciels, des fleurs, des champs, qu'il gonfle de la surprenante sève de son être. Ces formes se multiplient, s'échevèlent, se tordent, et jusque dans la toile formidable de ces ciels où les astres ivres tournoient et chancèlent, où les étoiles s'allongent en queues de comètes débraillées ; jusque dans le surgissement de ces fantastiques fleurs qui se dressent et se rêtent, semblables à des oiseaux déments, Van Gogh garde toujours ses admirables qualités de peintre, et une noblesse qui émeut, et une grandeur tragique qui épouvante. Et, dans les moments de calme, quelle sérénité dans les grandes plaines ensoleillées, dans les vergers fleuris, où les pruniers, les pommiers neigent de la joie, quel bonheur de vivre monte de la terre en frissons légers et s'épand dans les ciels pacifiques aux pâleurs tendres, aux rafraîchissantes brises. Ah ! comme il a compris l'âme exquise des fleurs. Comme sa main, qui promène les torches terribles dans les noirs firmaments, a été délicate pour en lier les gerbes parfumées et si frêles. Et quelles caresses ne trouve-t-il pas pour en exprimer l'inexprimable fraîcheur et les grâces infinies.

Et comme il a compris aussi ce qu'il y a de triste, d'inconnu et de divin, dans l'œil des pauvres fous et des malades fraternels!

OCTAVE MIRBEAU.

ÉCHOS

Aujourd'hui, lundi, à deux heures, courses à Longchamps.

GAGNANTS DE JEANNOT

La Bourse. — Barberousse, Laurier.
Prix de la Grotte. — Strawberry, Martinet.
Prix de Guiche. — Gosport, Laurier.
Prix de Lutèce. — Le Hardy, Chef-Lieu.
Prix du Cadran. — Mirabeau, Yellow.
Prix de Chevilly. — Pré-Catelan, Master Gillam.

(Voir l'article Sport, les pronostics raisonnés.)

Par suite des derniers mouvements de troupe, l'artillerie du 6e corps se trouve maintenant renforcée par les 7e, 8e et 9e batteries détachées du 15e régiment à Douai, du 24e régiment à Tarbes, du 35e régiment à Vannes et du 38e régiment à Nîmes.

Ces douze batteries sont destinées à accompagner les brigades d'infanterie de Saint-Mihiel, de Toul et de Verdun, plus spécialement affectées aux grands corps retranchés qui gardent la frontière.

L'insuffisance du casernement a fait précédemment maintenir au camp de Châlons les trois batteries du 24e d'artillerie.

Malgré les fêtes, les bureaux de la guerre ne chôment pas et nous devons reconnaître l'activité qu'ils déploient pour régler l'avancement de nos armées de seconde ligne. Aujourd'hui nous enregis-
trons dans l'infanterie, nomination de 2 lieutenants-colonels, 110 chefs de bataillon, 56 capitaines, 33 lieutenants et 141 sous-lieutenants territoriaux.

En plus, le ministre de la guerre a signé une promotion de 44 lieutenants de réserve.

Un de nos confrères pose diverses questions relativement aux Mémoires de Talleyrand. Nous y répondrons, puisque cela paraît l'intéresser.

Le gouvernement de Napoléon III n'a jamais fait apposer les scellés sur les papiers de l'ancien ambassadeur.

Un mot du prince de Talleyrand :

C'était en 1836. L'ancien diplomate, vieux et impotent, se faisait traîner en une petite voiture par son domestique. Il s'était arrêté en un endroit de Montmorency, second fils du duc de Valençay, l'autorisation de porter ce titre, à la grande colère du faubourg Saint-Germain.

Un brigadier de gendarmerie s'approche de lui :

— Que me voulez-vous, mon brave? demanda le prince. Je ne suis plus rien et ne peux vous être d'aucune utilité.

— C'est, riposta timidement le brigadier, que nous avons fait un pari. J'étais avec des amis : nous devisions de la campagne de Russie et chacun de nous de se demander pourquoi l'empereur nous avait emmené là-bas. Personne ne pouvait répondre. Alors, moi, j'ai dit : « Je vais demander au prince, et je parie qu'il me le dira...»

— Eh bien ! tu as eu raison, mon brave. Je vais te dire pourquoi Napoléon vous a emmenés en Russie : C'est le goût des voyages...

Autre mot, mais de Louis-Philippe, celui-là ?

Talleyrand disait un jour à ce roi :

— Cet oblélisque est bien laid au milieu de la place de la Concorde.

— Dépêchons-nous d'y mettre quelque chose, riposta mélancoliquement le roi, si nous ne voulons pas que les Parisiens y mettent la statue de la République...

Dans le monde.

Ce n'est pas seulement en France que le goût des gens du monde pour la comédie et la musique jouée et interprétée par des amateurs s'accroît de jour en jour ; nos compatriotes veulent l'y implanter jusque chez nos voisins.

Nous avons déjà signalé le succès de la soirée donnée par le prince Ferdinand de Bulgarie, dans son palais de Sofia. Son chambellan, un Parisien, le comte Robert de Bourboulon, a fait représenter une très jolie comédie, dans laquelle il remplissait le premier rôle. Pour lui donner la réplique, c'est encore une Française, Mlle de Grenaud, devenue Bulgare par son récent mariage, qui a été choisie et qui s'est acquittée de l'accueil et, dans l'autre, la noblesse de la ville et le plus grand succès.

A Madrid, il y a quelques jours, une grande soirée a été donnée à l'ambassade de France. Une grande salle de l'hôtel de la calle Royazza a été transformée en théâtre. Le spectacle a commencé par le monologue de notre confrère Abra..am Drey..us : Un monsieur en habit noir, admirablement dit par M. le comte d'Arlot de Saint-Sand, premier secrétaire d'ambassade.

On a représenté ensuite les Méprises d'un cabinet, un vieux vaudeville de Ludovic Halévy, dont les principaux rôles étaient tenus par la comtesse Wodgidka, la comtesse Stéfani, MM. Belle et d'Arlot.

Toute l'aristocratie madrilène assistait à cette fête dont les honneurs ont été faits avec beaucoup de tact par l'ambassadrice de France.

Enfin, c'est encore une Française, Mlle de Grandval, mariée au baron Marochetti, ambassadeur d'Italie à Pétersbourg, qui a dernièrement fait ses invitations à une grande soirée dramatique et musicale avec le concours d'artistes amateurs, au palais de l'ambassade. Un bal a suivi la représentation ; puis un souper de deux cents couverts auquel assistaient les grands ducs, les grandes duchesses, le corps diplomatique et toute la haute société de Pétersbourg.

Potins.

Dans un racontait, hier, à Auteuil, qu'une jolie petite comtesse blonde que l'on voit chaque jour au five o'clock du pâtissier à la mode, aurait reçu comme cadeau dans sa merveilleux œuf de Pâques en argent niellé une inscription de rente avec inscription de rente en Consolidés anglais.

C'est, paraît-il, un lord fort amoureux fou de la ravissante enfant, qui lui aurait fait cette agréable surprise.

Il était temps ; car le blason de la petite comtesse, que depuis la mort de son mari elle a quelque peu jeté par-dessus les moulins, commençait à être pitoyablement dédoré.

Petit dialogue entre deux dégrafées, surpris hier au paddock, après le prix Cheseka..

— Ma chère, on ne fait pas de ces choses-là. Je ne te présente pas mes amants pour que tu me les prennes.

— Oh ! ma foi, tu n'as pas à te plaindre... Il n'est pas si généreux.

— Quel pingre...

— A qui le dis-tu !!!

Et, réconciliées, nos deux dégrafées s'éloignent...

Pauvre Couche-à-Joue, comme on la calomnie !

Le cœur de la séduisante B... est assiégé
par trois gros amateurs de sport. Ils se la disputent, paraît-il, espèces sonnantes à la main ; aussi, n'appelle-t-on plus notre héroïne que Mlle Pari-Mutuel.

Dans le courant du mois prochain aura lieu, à la mairie du septième arrondissement, le mariage de Mlle de Chennevières-Pointel, fille du marquis de Chennevières-Pointel, directeur honoraire des Beaux-Arts, membre de l'Institut, avec M. de Chappotin, riche propriétaire de la Manche.

A la même époque aura lieu, à la mairie du huitième arrondissement, le mariage de M. Charles Léouzon-le-Duc, avocat à la Cour de Paris, ancien député, avec Mlle Louise Kiesner.

M. François Mortier, architecte de la Grande Chancellerie de la Légion d'honneur, a succombé hier à Auteuil à l'âge de quatre-vingt-trois ans.

M. Mortier avait reconstruit le palais de la Légion d'honneur après son incendie par la Commune en 1871 ; il avait été promu chevalier de la Légion d'honneur en récompense de ces travaux.

Ses obsèques auront lieu demain mardi à midi en l'église Notre-Dame d'Auteuil.

NOUVELLE A LA MAIN

A propos de la suppression des pièces. Chacun fait entrevoir les funestes conséquences de cette mesure.

— Jusqu'à cette brave madame X... qui ne va plus pouvoir sortir de chez elle.

— Pourquoi donc ?

— Avec ses boule de loto.

LE DIABLE AMOUREUX.

Demain matin, nous offrirons gratuitement à nos lecteurs un supplément illustré : le Concours Hippique, un supplément illustré par MM. H. Gerbault et A. de Clermont-Gallande, deux artistes dont l'éloge n'est plus à faire.

LA MACHINE A JUGER

Les journaux racontent que, samedi, dans une seule chambre correctionnelle, une affaire ont été jugées en cinq heures, ce qui fait vingt affaires à l'heure ou une affaire pour trois minutes. C'est la plus grande vitesse obtenue jusqu'à ce jour en matière de justice : l'honneur en revient tout entier à la ville de Paris dont l'initiative dans le genre a toujours été prépondérante.

De l'avis de certains personnes, il n'est guère probable que la vitesse de trois minutes puisse être dépassée, tant que la justice sera exercée par la main de l'homme. Mais on espère arriver avant peu à construire une machine assez délicate et assez précise à la fois pour obtenir un nombre de condamnations au moins décuple dans le même espace de temps. Le bruit court qu'Edison y travaille.

D'après les racontars, la machine à juger ressemblerait assez, extérieurement bien entendu, à ces machines automatiques que l'on rencontre dans les gares de chemins de fer, dans les établissements de bains qui vous respectent, et jusque dans certaines maisons qui auront contimé l'hygiène et le plaisir.

Le mouvement ne serait à peu près aboli que où on placerait une dans chaque salle du Palais de Justice, au-dessous de l'image du Christ. Les inculpés n'auraient qu'à tour et à leur suffirait de jeter dans un petit marque. immédiatement le nombre d'années et de mois et de journées de prison qu'ils mériterait selon l'automatisme de la machine à juger.

En tout mécanisme indiquerait les amendes afférentes.

Nous n'avons, d'ailleurs, aucun renseignement sur la constitution intérieure de la machine. Tout ce que l'on suppose, c'est qu'il y aura deux compartiments. Dans l'un, on mettra le dossier de l'accusé et, dans l'autre, un exemplaire du Code national. En trois ou quatre secondes, l'aiguille aura accompli sa besogne réparatrice.

Nous n'avons pas besoin d'insister sur les conséquences d'une pareille découverte. C'est la conscience des magistrats soulagée, l'inconnu qui ne va pas être confondu avec le malfaiteur, toutes les attaques dirigées contre la magistrature tombant d'elles-mêmes. C'est aussi la rapidité avec l'équité absolue.

Car maintenant, il est clair qu'on peut aller très vite, même si l'on prouve la statistique des affaires correctionnelles. Certes, trois ou quatre mois de prison de plus ou de moins ne sont rien pour un juge, mais l'accusé en éprouve toujours quelque désagrément ; et si, par surcroît, il est innocent, cela devient un chagrin véritable qu'il est plus humain de lui épargner.

GRAINDORGE.

CHRONIQUE

La ville de Paris est une heureuse personne civile, qui fait constamment des héritages et dont le patrimoine grossit sans cesse, grâce à de généreux donateurs. Il est vrai qu'elle est parfois embarrassée non des dons qu'on lui fait, car, comme disait César de Bazan :
De l'argent qu'on reçoit, d'abord, c'est toujours clair, mais des conditions qui sont mises à cette offre.

C'est ainsi que, cette semaine, elle a obtenu délivrance d'un gros cadeau testamentaire, dont l'acceptation a soulevé des scrupules au sein du Conseil municipal.

Un certain P... avait laissé à la Ville une vraie fortune, à condition qu'en perpétuerait à la fondation d'un établissement charitable qui porterait son nom. C'était bien le moins, et une telle clause ne soulève jamais de difficulté. Tout

*to follow him in his flights, even to submit to his
highly characteristic deformations...'*
*'He spares himself no effort, to the benefit of the
trees, skies, flowers, fields, which he inflates with the
astonishing dream of his being. And how he has
understood too how much sadness, how much that lies
unrevealed, how much divinity there is in the eyes of
the poor and his brother invalids.'*
*'In his numerous drawings we do not discover
resemblances but rather an aggravated cult of the
same shapes, a similar richness of linear invention.'*
Mirbeau is reminded of Rembrandt:
*'Van Gogh does not always achieve the accuracy nor
the sobriety of the Dutch master. THE SOWER after
Millet, rendered with such sublime beauty by Van
Gogh–the movement is accentuated, the vision
expands, the line expands, until it has the significance
of a symbol–a new grandeur.'*
And of Van Gogh's death he writes:
*'It is a cruel loss, infinitely more sad for art, and
irreparable, than that of Monsieur Meissonier, even
though the populace has not crowded to a magnificent
funeral and poor Vincent van Gogh, whose death
means the extinction of a beautiful flame of genius,
has gone to his death as obscure and neglected as he
had lived, neglected and obscure in this unjust life.'*
Later on, others were to judge these words
sentimental and dramatic, unaware, however, of
the circumstances which had given rise to them. An
élite consisting of French avant-garde artists living
in an age fired with anarchism, had been struck and
incensed by the official cult surrounding
Meissonier. Meissonier was, without doubt, the
Achilles heel of French painting at the time. But he
brought out a weak spot in Vincent too, for Vincent
admired him greatly, a fact which irritated the
avant-garde. We are able to grasp the degree of
irritation they felt only if we note that Meissonier
died shortly after Vincent, in 1891, but as a national
hero, who was given a magnificent funeral, or if we
recall the years of veneration he enjoyed on account
of the excellent service he rendered the Napoleon
cult and military circles in France with his anecdotal
canvases. Everyone reviewed his work [see Jules
Antoine in *L'Indépendant*, 1891, p 219: *'Contested
but honest...has understood nothing of modern
research...'*]. All this was given further emphasis by
the pompous funeral, which formed so striking a
contrast to the so much more genuine way in which
Vincent was laid to rest by a small circle of friends
who gathered together at Auvers.

The prologue to the role Aurier played in the first
years of Vincent's discovery was, as we saw, bound
up with the figure of Emile Bernard. Artists in the
Netherlands read both *La Plume* and the *Mercure*
so that they were aware of the way the French had
reacted to Van Gogh.
Aurier's article deserves closer attention, for his
vision was not without its effect. It represented a
first serious attempt to place Van Gogh in a cultural
and aesthetic framework: 'Les Isolés'. In this
Aurier was strongly influenced by the symbolism
which was gaining in importances at the time. Born
in 1865 and dying of fish-poisoning at the early age
of 27, as a law student Aurier had already shown
himself to be a poet and a novelist, who painted too
and went in for art criticism. What is more, he
attempted what, to my knowledge, no one else had
attempted at the time–i.e. to put his aesthetic
observations on a theoretical, purposeful basis. He
adopts a strict viewpoint and resists the attempt to
introduce scientific reasoning into the methods of
art criticism. He feels no sympathy for the
unconsidered application of rational concepts and
methods derived from the natural sciences in the
study of art, claiming that Taine–highly praised
and much followed at the time–was incapable of
penetrating to the work of art and the creative act.
Aurier considered it wrong to approach a work of

Julius Meier-Graefe, 1867-1935, see page 21

art as a product of a given period and milieu and
consequently to mention all manner of local and
domestic details which have nothing to do with the
work of art proper. What he was, in fact, doing,
was already taking up a stand against the evils of
academic art criticism, then still in its swaddling
clothes. As a result, he sought to concern himself
more and more directly with the work of art itself,
as opposed to the artist. This by no means excludes
scientific criticism, though it implies something
other than the reconstruction of a photographic
reality, such as Gustave Coquiot was later to
perform with his interest in topographical details
and Tralbaut after him in parts of his specialized
studies, and Pierre Leprohon.
Aurier's early death in 1892 prevented him from
completing his 'essai sur une nouvelle méthode de
critique'. It appeared in the *Oeuvres posthumes*
published by the *Mercure de France* in 1893,
together with a novel, verses and essays on Van
Gogh, Gauguin, Monticelli, etc. The attempt by
Rémy de Gourmont, who wrote the introduction,
to provide an unexpected end in the form of
fragments about love and mysticism [p 201 et seq]
seems unfortunate. They amount to pure lyricism
and are unsuited to form the closing item in a new
critical method. Aurier forecasted that in a hundred
years' time we should be brutes intent upon the
satisfaction of physical desires–people reduced by
the positive sciences to animals, pure and simple.
Art, not religion, which would no longer be
tolerated, would lead to a new exaltation. His
opposition to bourgeois art in expensive frames
which match the rest of the furniture was taken up
shortly after in Holland by young Richard
N. Roland Holst [1868-1938], when introducing
Van Gogh's work. Roland Holst also repeated
Aurier's warning against allowing the artist's life-
story to influence one's appreciation of the
paintings. Aurier's hatred of the man with the
'official' reputation was revelant now as well. But

his hankering after mysticism, his longing for an
'art of dreams and ideas' are as yet still unworked-
out expressions of the gifted poet in him who had
not yet arrived at clarity in his art criticism.
His character sketch of the painter accentuates both
the element of exaltation and the new, the
psychological element, in his realism. This interpretation is prompted by the discovery of the new
symbolic element, which appeals to the young. At
the same time he is fortunately not blind to the
striking pictorial characteristics. Vincent really did
appear as a painter who revealed his total being in
his personality:
*'The external, material side of his painting is
completely correlated with his temperament as an
artist. In all his works the execution is vigorous,
exalted, bold, intense. His drawing, passionate,
powerful, often maladroit and somewhat heavy-
handed, exaggerates the character of the subject,
simplifies, masters, conquers detail, attaining to a
grand synthesis, at times to the grand style, but by no
means always.*
*His color–we are all aware of that. It is improbably
dazzling. He is, as far as I know, the only painter to
perceive the chromatism of things with this intensity,
with this metallic, gem-like quality. His researches
into the color of shadows, of the influence of one tone
on another, of full sunshine, are highly unusual. He
does not always succeed in avoiding a certain
disagreeable crudity, certain dissonances, certain
disharmonies...As to his composition proper, his
immediate way of illuminating the canvas, like
everything else about him, these are impetuous, very
powerful, very nervous. His brush goes to work with
enormous thicknesses of paint in very pure tones,
with sweeping curves broken by rectilinear touches...
with accumulations, clumsy at times, of a highly
recticulated masonry, and all this lends some of his
canvases the solid appearance of dazzling murals
composed of crystals and sunlight.'* [p 264].
Of the work's future Aurier says, after all:

Rainer Maria Rilke, 1875-1926, see page 21

*of bourgeois sobriety and meticulous accuracy, a sort
of drunken giant, more apt at moving mountains than
at arranging gewgaws and knick-knacks, a mind in a
state of eruption irresistibly pouring out its lava into
the ravines of art, a terrible, mad genius, often
sublime, at times grotesque, always verging on the
pathological.'* [p 261]. Aurier foresees something of
the fame that was to be Vincent's in his final
question: *'This robust and genuine artist, a thorough-
bred, with the rough hands of a giant, with the
nervousness of a hysterical woman, with the soul of a
visionary, so original and so alone in the context of
the pitiful art of today, will he one day know—everything is possible—the joys of rehabilitation, the
repentant cajolery of fashion? Perhaps...'* [p 265].
When regarding Vincent as too simple and too
subtle for the present bourgeois spirit to appreciate
properly, he is already expressing doubts at this
early stage regarding the overwhelming bourgeois
appetite for Van Gogh products and the attendance
figures at popular exhibitions organized in the
USA, Europe and Japan after 1945.
There are a few more, brief, positive reactions to be
found in various French journals to the paintings
on display at the Indépendants Exhibition in the
spring of 1890. But these came nowhere near the
range of what Bernard, Aurier and Mirbeau felt
constrained to publish. This trio marked the true
beginning of the world's response to Van Gogh,
based on the data provided by his work, personal
impressions and partial knowledge of the letters.
In these three artists we find assembled both the
technical and mental elements and those characteristic of the general transition from naturalism
and neo-impressionism to a trend known by the
collective term of 'symbolism'. Thus began a
critical exposition of the phenomenon Van Gogh,
which was not a mere retrospect on the past but an
appraisal of a force which was still very much
present in the life of the time. The content of early
Dutch writing on Van Gogh [Isaacson, Van Eeden,
de Meester] cannot compete with this, although,
viewed historically, these positive voices did put the
Netherlands on the side of the admirers.
Of course, the understandable and consequently
always fairly easily ridiculed criticism by con-
formists, the conventional and by mediocre
professional critics, such as one encountered in
Belgium and the Netherlands, was not lacking in
France either. Generally speaking, such criticism is
of no interest and only convinced and well-founded
rejection is worth mentioning. The brothers Gaston
and Jules Costural were worthy representatives of
the resistance encountered in 1891. Under the title
Le fiasco symboliste [in *L'Indépendant*, 1891],
Aurier, too, comes in for criticism [he *'arouses our
serious distrust'*], Gauguin has *'very little talent'* and
Aurier *'goes from bad to worse, he falls into the
ridiculous and drowns in it'*. They attack Péladan,
but everything is motivated by a desire to protect
the Franco-Latin tradition from these anti-Latin
frauds. Alphonse Germain is of the same order. In
the impartial pages of *La Plume* [1891, p 290 et seq]
he was given an opportunity to attack the
'synthésophiles' who sang the praises of Cézanne,
Van Gogh and Gauguin.

Belgium, 1888-1893

Belgium's discovery of Van Gogh probably began
as early as 1889 when the painter Theo van Rijsselberghe [1862-1926] and Octave Maus, leader of the
Vingtistes in Brussels, visited Theo van Gogh. Close
contacts existed among the Belgians. Eugène Boch
[1855-1941] and likewise his sister Anna [1848-1936]
in Brussels, both painters with an uninhibited
interest in the new in their day and age, were well-
known personalities in art circles. Boch saw Vincent
repeatedly at Arles in 1888 and Vincent's work will
certainly have become known in Belgium thanks to

*'It will never be fully understood except by his
brothers, the artists who are wholly artists...and by
happy little people, the smallest of people who, by
chance, will have escaped the benevolent teachings of
the laity.'* [p 265].
Aurier had not yet read the letters to Theo at the
time—Vincent was still alive—but he probably had
read those to Bernard. He did not, however, wish to
make any use of what he knew of his life. In a
remarkable letter to Aurier after Vincent's death,
Theo was to suggest he should write a biography
and to promise him a sight of the letters—he had
only to ask for them [T 55, August 27th, 1890].
Aurier did visit Theo—he had known him since 1888
—and took letters away with him, which, however,
Theo was quick to have retrieved by the 'bonne'.
But Theo did resist others' attempts to do the same
—de Meester, for instance—since he rightly
considered Aurier to be the most suitable
biographer.
Later on, Aurier asked Theo's wife for the letters
once again when Theo was ill and after his death
André Bonger supplied him with autobiographical
particulars [February 28th, 1891]. Mevrouw van
Gogh then needed the letters back for publications
in magazines—the *Mercure* was to start publishing
them and the Flemish magazine *Van Nu en Straks*
was shortly to follow its example—and she asked
Aurier twice to bring them back [March 27th, 1892
being one date]. Aurier had been sounding
H. P. Boele van Hensbroek, the Hague publisher,

about a possible edition, and Boele van Hensbroek
in his turn had consulted Mesdag [1831-1915], the
Hague painter who had done such good work
collecting paintings by the Barbizon and early
Hague Schools. The outcome was negative. On
November 3rd, 1890 the publisher gave as his
opinion that he saw no prospects in a biography of
Vincent for publication in the Netherlands and that
Aurier would have a better chance of success with
this eccentric matter in Paris. Boele van Hensbroek's
description of Vincent suggests dislike: *'pinkish
face, rather reddish hair, neither important nor
attractive. He sat before an open fire and was very
calmly throwing page after page of an edifying book
he had received on New Year's Eve from his father,
who was a preacher, into the flames.'* [*Nederlandse
Spectator*, February 1895].
Nevertheless, it was to Boele van Hensbroek's
credit that he realized that someone should undertake an *unabridged* edition instead of publishing
mere fragments of the letters [*Nederlandse
Spectator*, August 1893].
It seems superfluous to go into the points made and
repeated *ad nauseam* by placid professional
criticism in later years—points which had been
made by Aurier in a far more militant, poetic and
timely fashion, as, for instance, in the following
passage:
*'What distinguishes his entire oeuvre is its excess,
excessive power, excessive nervousness, violence and
expressiveness... He is one of the exalted, an enemy*

Charles Mauron, and Roger Fry, 1866-1934,
see page 23

him, before anyone had a chance to see any of it, which was in 1889. In the spring of 1890 came the Indépendants Exhibition in Paris, to which a number of Belgian artists [including Van de Velde and Lemmen] submitted work as well as Vincent himself. Octave Maus, who made it possible for Vincent to exhibit with the Vingt [January-February 1890] engineered the first confrontation between his work and the Belgians. After his death in 1891, the Vingt organized the 'hommage à Vincent'. The voices raised in the Belgian press on these two occasions were largely of the well-known kind that ridicule what they do not understand or wat they will not, or cannot, make the effort to accept as being serious in its intentions. A great many of the reviews of the exhibition omit all reference to Van Gogh, whereas in most of them Seurat is discussed at length. Thus these critics either did not look at Vincent's canvases or, if they did, they were not even exacerbated by what they saw. José Hennebicq in *Les Jeunes* p 116, 1891 and Ernest Closson in *L'Impartial Bruxellois* [March 22nd, 1891] reacted positively or, at least, with respect. But the response is meagre.
Emile Verhaeren formed an exception, of course – but here we are dealing once again with a poet who studied painting keenly and who, moreover, played an important role as a symboliste on the international scene. In two lengthy articles in the *Nation* of February 10th and 14th, 1891, Verhaeren recorded his impressions of the exhibition, going deeply into the work of Seurat. Vincent's drawings enjoyed his fullest admiration, and he speaks of '*l'ensemble magistral*'. That he should have considered Van Gogh '*decorative above all*' eludes an explanation as long as we do not know what meaning he attributed to the word 'decorative' at the time. In La Société Nouvelle's *Chronique artistique* [1891, vol 1, no 7, p 248 et seq] he recapitulates. He goes seriously into Van Gogh even though we are obliged to note that he was

wrong on a number of points. But in this respect he was not alone among the supporters, who were, after all, very much impressed.
Verhaeren writes, for instance, of Van Gogh as follows:
'*One would say that he takes matches and engraves in broadly spread out paste with them. His composition is wild; in the* OLIVE PICKING *it is hasty; in the* IRISES *it is decided and thick; in the* CORNFIELD *it is deranged. His drawings are like those of a very practiced, very assured wood-engraver. They are marvellous–all of them. At times–in* THE SOWER, *for example, he achieves an almost epic vision and one asks oneself who, since Millet, has conveyed an impression of evening more simply and more grandly?*'

Yet Verhaeren, and others with him, named Guillaumin and Cézanne as the chief sources of inspiration for Gauguin. To my knowledge, Mirbeau [in *L'Echo de Paris*, March 31st, 1891] was the only critic in 1891 to write openly of Monsieur Armand Guillaumin's 'limited realism devoid of ideas' [though he had professional merit].
Verhaeren goes on to speak of '*Gauguin, from whom Van Gogh has developed, aesthetically*'. With all due respect for Verhaeren this genealogical tree was wide of the mark, yet Verhaeren was so much in earnest that he even expected this view to be borne out by historical evidence. We encounter the same genealogical tree in the writings of a former friend of Aurier's, Julien Leclercq, who arranged and introduced the celebrated exhibition at Bernheim's in 1901. At that date, Leclercq had still retained the following recollection of Van Gogh: '*a small, fair-haired man, nervous, with lively eyes, a broad fore-head and a chilly manner, who made one think vaguely of the attitude of a Spinoza concealing vehement mental activity behind a timid exterior*'. [from the Bernheim exhibition catalogue, 1901]. In later writings on Van Gogh, however, one finds

practically no mention of Guillaumin. Unjustly, for Van Gogh himself makes repeated and admiring mention of him. He was even a frequent visitor at his studio at 13, quai d'Anjou on the Île Saint-Louis in Paris, where Daubigny's old studio was. It is likely that Van Gogh made a number of sketches of Paris from this spot which cannot be brought into association with Theo's home or its surroundings, where most of his sketches were made. Then, too, as a critic, Mirbeau seems to have shown greater perspicacity than Verhaeren in placing Guillaumin.

Another Belgian, still a young student and essayist, one *August Vermeylen* [1872-1945], was involved in this nation's discovery of Van Gogh and the homage they paid to him during this same early incubatory period [1889-1891]. He was still at the grammar school when he experienced the first 'shock of recognition', and was later to recall particularly the SUNFLOWERS and THE SOWER. In 1892 he visited Theo's sister in Bussum and later, in 1893, he was one of the founders of the avant-garde magazine *Van Nu en Straks*, which devoted its third issue to Van Gogh, containing a drawing and fragments from letters chosen not by Vermeylen but by Mevrouw Van Gogh after Roland Holst had made use of them, while Henry Van de Velde did a little critical sifting. As a painter, Van de Velde had been deeply impressed by his style and it was he who wrote the introduction. Dr. E.Tralbaut's assertion that this was translated from the French could not be confirmed by reference to the Van de Velde archives in Brussels–no French manuscript having been discovered. So, in Belgium, the significance of the letters–equal to that of the paintings and drawings–was recognized. But the problem was not yet posed here either. The further part Vermeylen was to play in the admiration shown for Van Gogh also found expression in the Netherlands, but this was only three years later, in 1896.

The Netherlands, 1892-1898

Theo's widow was the heart and soul of the Dutch discovery of Van Gogh. She succeeded in convincing not merely Van Eeden but certainly Jan Veth [1864-1925] as well, who was no believer to begin with. Jan Toorop [1858-1928] was more independent, Roland Holst too, but no one as yet distinguished himself as a writer on the artist. Mevrouw Van Gogh was also the inspiring force behind most of the exhibitions designed to propagate Vincent's work after those at Brussels and Antwerp. According to Jan Hulsker and Ellen Joosten [Museum Journaal, no. 6 1968] and Drs. J. M. Joosten [Museum Journaal, nrs 3, 4, 5 and 6, 1969] the press was friendly, well-disposed and appreciative. One notices, however, an absence of the deeper penetration of the phenomenon, Van Gogh, which characterizes French articles on him. In these battle was joined in the political, social and aesthetic fields with an art of symbolist ideas in view. In Holland the ruling forces were the late Hague School, together with a powerful Amsterdam School [Breitner, Isaac Israëls, Witsen, Veth, Haverman, Suze Robertson and Floris Verster], and a monumental symbolist trend [der Kinderen, Verkade, Toorop, Holst, Prikker] sensitive to an emergent Art Nouveau. The more marked the concentration on architecture or the more obstinate the attack on Seurat's neo-impressionism [Hart Nibbrig, Aerts, Bremmer, Gestel, Vijlbrief], the more isolated Van Gogh became in an aura of admiration, without, however, growing genuine roots in the Dutch art world. It was not until the days of Dirk Nijland [1881-1955], Charley Toorop [1891-1955] and, to begin with, Jan Sluyters [1861-1957] and Mondriaan [1872-1944], too, that is

H. P. Bremmer, 1871-1956, see page 24

Schwabe's illustrations to *Le Rêve*, and he was moved deeply by them and very happy to have them[12]. This curious, high-flown, nineteenth century prose, at once symbolist and visionary, is of sufficient significance to quote extracts from it here to illustrate a reaction to the celebrated exhibition held at the Panorama gallery in Amsterdam, in December 1892.

Vincent van Gogh
'*These are not the actual impressions these works made on me but rather the thoughts that went through my head under the influence of my physical emotion, on recalling Van Gogh's colors, like forked lightning flashing through the sky as the bowels of the earth rumble. Art is the search for the infinite Self, the search for the infinite Non-self and for the equilibrium between these two.*
In this sense, Van Gogh is certainly not a master but a seeker, one, too, who has shown the most reckless daring. He has not spared himself. He walked naked into the world and allowed himself to be thrashed by the extra-I. He lay face downwards on the earth and it scared him to death. What he was seeking was the heart of his own being, not his spiritual being but the red and purple, bloody heart of flesh. He wrenched it out of the lukewarm living interior of his own body and spread it out across his canvases. This is madness and suicide, this painting was suicide, but all martyrs were suicides. – This work is a descent, it does not bear itself up through the universe, imbued with life eternal and itself life-giving, it falls. – But we shall bear it up, for he has suffered our anxieties and our passions. The deeper his descent into hell the higher the flights he forces our ascent to undertake. Every artist, every human being – but the greatest most of all – represents either a fall or an ascent for all mankind; it either bleeds to death through him and bears one more scar, or it triumphs through him; and it then partakes of that much extra life eternal.'
January 1893, A. de Graaf.
The second literary man and art critic who wrote passionately about Van Gogh in the pre-1900 period and who apparently based himself on notes he had made on him was Albert Plasschaert. Plasschaert was the first to publish a portfolio of ten reproductions accompanied by notes at his Arts and Crafts 'art nouveau' shop in The Hague. In 1898 Arts and Crafts held an exhibition, and Plasschaert was to continue to shown an interest in Van Gogh, though his subsequent publications appeared during the first five years of the twentieth century and later. His views will consequently be treated in a later section.

III IN THE SPOTLIGHT OF EXPRESSIONISM AND FAUVISM, 1900-1914–APOSTLES AND RENEGADES

Whereas in the era of discovery extending over approximately ten years subsequent to Vincent's death the emphasis had lain on France, Belgium and the Netherlands, after 1900 the Van Gogh cult shifts to Germany.
Despite the warnings Aurier and Roland Holst had issued at an early date, romanticized accounts of Van Gogh – of his life as well as his work – were now about to be written and chief among the authors of such work was Julius Meier-Graefe. But the writer who was to be the first to touch on the heart of the Van Gogh problem in his letters, even though his interest in the artist was of a less spectacular nature and even though he worked in seclusion, was the poet Rainer Maria Rilke.
One of the main features of this new phase was the publication of the Van Gogh letters by the artist's sister-in-law, Mevrouw Jo van Gogh-Bonger, who had become married again, this time to the painter J. H. G. Cohen Goschalk. It was this publication alone which made it possible to trace and study Van

to say, roughly the period 1907-1920, that there was any creative response to Van Gogh. In 1892 the example of Vincent shook others into awareness, they became fascinated, especially by the ethical aspects of his work; yet they were not truly alive to him.
It is remarkable that there should have been a positive response to Van Gogh among students. Proof of this is contained in a contribution signed J.v.V. in *Vox Gymnasii*, January 16th, 1893 [vol 4, no 10]. It was written with an undisciplined enthusiasm and it is said that the author's name was a pseudonym for Paul Scholten, who was later to become a celebrated professor of civil law. In 1896, Mutua Fides, a students' association in Groningen, was to show work by Van Gogh on the upper floor of the 'Harmonie', at an exhibition lasting six days: 'February 21 and the 5 days following'. It was here that August Vermeylen, the Fleming, came to give a lecture [in evening dress!] which made a deep impression on the professors, their wives and students. The *Nieuwe Rotterdamse Courant* of February 21st, 1896 reported at length on the lecture in an article which made Vermeylen's ecstatic views quite apparent. Vermeylen spoke of his university days, crossed swords with the 'social pathologists' and their theories, stressed the disharmony existing between society and the Church, recognized the power of Van Gogh's deformation and [cf Aurier] observed how ideas and movement were portrayed in his work. Vermeylen saw Van

Gogh in the context of a broad social and spiritual revival. He was a passionate believer in a happier future but did not look on science as the salvation of mankind. Like Aurier, he expected such salvation to come from deeper sources. In Van Gogh he discovered a love and a vision which society wrongly took to be those of a degraded creature, a madman.
In Holland, the harvest of literature on Van Gogh which succeeds in striking a deeper note than the numerous newspaper reviews of the exhibitions is actually a meagre one between the years 1892 and 1900. Two literary men of divergent quality but of remarkable penetration came forward, writing in the lofty and rather pathetic style of those years. One is *A. de Graaf,* the now almost forgotten friend of the monumental painter Antoon der Kinderen [1859-1925] and of the gifted and erudite composer and author, Alphons Diepenbrock. Diepenbrock was known in France from a reference in the *Mercure de France* in February 1893 to his essay on *Le Latin Mystique van de Gourmont.* He was not unacquainted with Van Gogh's work. In March 1891 he was in Paris at Saar de Swart's, the sculptress's, together with Bauk Mesdag and Van der Valk, the painter, who had attended Vincent's funeral at Auvers. In August 1892, Diepenbrock had visited Theo's widow in Bussum. In 1893 he bought Aurier's *Oeuvres posthumes.* A. de Graaf sent him two brief, exceedingly concise pieces about Van Gogh and

Albert Plasschaert, 1874-1941, portrait by
W. A. van Konijnenburg, see page 20

Gogh's struggle with his art in the letters he wrote to Van Rappard, Emile Bernard and in the almost uninterrupted series he wrote his brother Theo from his youth onward. This alone made the painter's complex character not clearer, it is true, but infinitely more absorbing and important. More important because it meant that a mine of information had been made available–one which it would take a very long time to exhaust in investigating the fundamental problem of Vincent's creative powers.

Theo, Emile Bernard, Albert Aurier and Jo van Gogh-Bonger had grasped intuitively and early on that a parallel and, indeed, simultaneous activity Van Gogh's claimed close attention in addition to painting and drawing–and this was writing. Bernard in the *Mercure de France*, followed by *Van Nu en Straks* and by Roland Holst set an example, by publishing extracts from the letters. Jo van Gogh-Bonger applied herself amid all her other activities to the task of preparing the material for publication, even undertaking the English translation herself– she had acquired a Dutch English-teaching diploma, In Berlin Cassirer published a number of editions but the first complete edition did not appear until 1914, in a translation by Leo Klein-Diepold, though this was immediately prior to the Dutch edition, published by the Wereldbibliotheek [World Library] in Amsterdam. Cassirer had published an edition, translated by Margarete Mauthner as early as 1906, which had gone into six editions by 1913.

It was not until 1923 that a second edition of the letters appeared in Holland, yet it is clear that between 1906 [or rather 1904–which saw their publication in *Kunst und Künstler*] and 1913 that Germany was simply devouring the letters. And this process went on, for by 1923 the Mauthner edition had reached its tenth impression. This German appetite for the letters was by no means fortuitous, for German expressionism discovered food in abundance for its own concepts in every aspect of Van Gogh's personality.

Although essentially a late impressionist and in Paris an active member of the Art Nouveau movement, *Julius Meier-Graefe* was the first to introduce a German expressionist note into writing on Van Gogh–in the form of a novel [1921] which did much to increase Vincent's popularity. As an art dealer and author he had observed Van Gogh's evolution and had been early to buy works during the days when he had his own Art Nouveau business, 'La Maison Moderne', in Paris in 1897. From 1906 onward he wrote frequently on Van Gogh.

It was Meier-Graefe who associated him with Dostoevski in his foreword to the revised edition of *Vincent*[13], a thing Just Havelaar was to do again in Holland. The evocation of Dostoevski [and none other] is indicative of the expressionist, fashionable and now and then highly exaggerated picture people had of Van Gogh. His works were now un-restrainedly associated with the melodrama of the torn, toiling, suffering artist.

According to Meier-Graefe Dostoevski foresaw Vincent's destiny, Vincent himself experiencing certain decisive aspects of Dostoevski's fate. Meier-Graefe and his age want to propagate the myth. He says so in so many words at the end of his book. They are in search of new symbols. For the 1906-1920 generations in Germany, Van Gogh became a topical subject. In Meier-Graefe, the words he wrote are already beginning to prevail over the paintings: '*Words count for more than many paintings. Many words have a power no painting achieves, at least in our time. Van Gogh had several such words. They existed inside him at a deeper level than the paintings, which were only a substitute for them!* [op cit note 13].

The question of the relation between the painter and the writer in Van Gogh is not posed. From this point on many skirt it by ranking 'Van Gogh the artist' above 'Van Gogh the painter'. Actually, Meier-Graefe betrays the latter. When he sees the paintings as a substitute [*Ersatz*] for the words, we have arrived at a nadir of deadly solemn but false, 'ethical-literary' appreciation.

German expressionism numbers at least as many literati as painters–it has already been said, and in his work *Lebendiger Expressionismus* [Living Expressionism], Kasimir Edschmid stressed once again that the term originally applied to a miscellany of things[14]. Thus in 1914 Paul Fechter[15] was able to write that Cézanne and Van Gogh were the early apostles of anti-impressionism. In this role Van Gogh represents an ecstatic identification with the world: '*he flings on to the canvas the very essence of these cornfields and trees, people and things, as he does his own soul, satisfying an almost erotic need for self-surrender in ornamental constraint.*'

'Rausch' [frenzy], 'Dionysus', 'Natureinfühlung' [empathy where Nature was concerned]–these are the expressions which occur again and again and which are typical of this interpretation. In his well-known address delivered in 1917 before the 'Deutsche Gesellschaft, 1914' Edschmidt states[14] that '*the word acquires a new authority*'. '*Description, scratching-about ceases. There is no longer any place for that. It becomes an arrow, pierces to the heart of the subject and is animated by it.*' The two extremes –of the written word and of painting–confronted one another and were reconciled. In a work on Expressionism[16] Heinrich Eduard Jakob states categorically that in Germany from 1908-1914 on Van Gogh had a unifying effect on this tension between the written word and the painting. In the same publication Ernst Blass[17] writes: '*Van Gogh: That was (for us) the courage to express oneself; Nietzsche: the courage to be oneself and have one's own experiences; Freud: the depths, the problems and the explosion (in penetrating insights).*'

Fauvism in France–no less in debt to Van Gogh for its inspiration–did not experience a similar blending of literary and pictorial values nor did it whisk Van Gogh up, as German expressionism had done, into such a maelstrom of ecstasy and inner laceration.

In these surroundings, this atmosphere, the figure of *Rainer Maria Rilke* stands aside, which is not to say that he remained unmoved. We are obliged to go to his letters to find out what Van Gogh meant to him, but what he contributed to a deeper under-standing of the 'Van Gogh problem'–which is concentrated around the relation between the letters and the paintings, i.e. his written words and his visual images–is quite a different matter and one which concerns us closely here.

It is well known that later in his life Rilke attributed far more significance to Cézanne's influence on him than to Van Gogh's, saying he had taken only a 'passing' interest in the latter. O. S. Fleischer's attempt in the *Germanic Review*[18] to demonstrate how it was via Van Gogh that he came to Cézanne, is wholly to the point. Yet everything persuades one that, when all was said and done, to Rilke Cézanne is 'the painter', whom he was able to interpret with the peculiar clairvoyance of a poet in whom the work of creation itself was preceded by a continually guarded preliminary process. Whether he wished it or not, this characteristic self-contemplation of Rilke's, which caused him to record everything going on inside himself *before* writing became possible to him, nevertheless brought him into very close contact with what went on in Van Gogh when he was writing letters and painting. Rilke, more than anyone else, sensed the weak and the strong [according to which view one takes] spot in Vincent's twofold, ambiguous activity.

In Rilke's hands what the Expressionists had done with ease – transformed Van Gogh into an amalgam of words and images, thereby making of him a symbol of tragic man – became an investigation. An investigation, because he himself was deeply involved in a process of creation in which he was fighting an importunate consciousness.

What did Rilke know of Van Gogh? What works of his had he seen? He owned one of the Cassirer editions of the letters. He saw some of the works in the private collection of G. Fayet at Igny, near Paris, which included some particularly fine specimens, including L'HOMME À LA PIPE. Mr. Bernheim showed him Van Goghs in his storehouse first, before he examined the Rodin drawings in the exhibition[19]. In 1907, at the home of Mathilde Vollmoeller, a painter friend of his, he saw a portfolio containing reproductions of a hundred drawings which she had brought with her from Holland[20, 21]. This demonstrates the importance of the reproductions at that time.

What engages Rilke's interest is the question – raised of course by his letters – of how disturbing and madly difficult it would have been for Van Gogh, if he had had to share the uniqueness of his vision, his motives, with anyone before transcribing them into his paintings: 'those characters who agree with him with all their hearts, take sides with him, swear by him.'[22] This was Rilke's central problem at the time – what he terms the 'individual madness', that which is incomprehensible to others, the extreme tribulation, must not be communicated to others around him, must not be exposed to others' eyes before the work of art has appeared. Rilke feels that Van Gogh's letters – and perhaps his own letters too – move in that direction. But they usually concern what has already been done. On this point Rilke is mistaken. Done, being done, to be done later – in Vincent's case these are subsumed in a single creative undulation. Rilke then thinks of Vincent's need to have Gauguin at his side. He then remarks that it was from artist to artist and it turned out badly too.

The second problem, related to the first, is the great importance of certain things remaining unconscious in a man and that it is precisely apparently pointless activities which perform the function of diverting the inquisitive intellect from processes of the spirit that can better remain unnoticed[23].

Rilke touches on the very heart of the matter, however, when, writing[24] to Clara Rilke about Cézanne's use of color, he refers to Van Gogh saying: '*The painter – like all artists generally – ought not to become aware of his flashes of insights, the advances he makes – mysterious even to himself – should come about in his work so rapidly, without any meditative detour, that at the moment of their transition he is unable to detect them.*'[19]

Rilke is afraid of this 'moment of transition.' If, at this juncture, something should not be right, the result is damage, loss. '*That Van Gogh's letters are so readable – that they contain so much – actually tells against him; as it tells against him as a painter*

Charles Mauron, 1899-1966, see page 29

(*compared with Cézanne) that he wanted, knew, experienced this, that and the other, that blue evoked orange, green red; that he – the inquisitive one – eavesdropping on his inner eye, had heard such things uttered within.*'

Elsewhere[24] Rilke says that '*insight is only safe within the work itself*'. 'Insight' outside the work itself occurs, in any case, more frequently, particularly among painters who write as well as paint. Work and insight then exist side by side. Here Rilke actually raises the question as to the significance of Vincent's existence as no one before him had done and practically no one has done since. That is to say: not the actual contents of the letters, not the actual contents of the works, but the inter-relation in the cycle of writing, painting and drawing, and living. Conscious activities which, he fears, impede one another and tear away their unconscious existence. The problem is reflected in Rilke's own life and work: the value of the letters as an activity running parallel to the poems.

Paul Klee was occupied by Van Gogh at this same period. He, too, possessed a selection of his letters published by Cassirer. Klee's diary reveals problems relating to consciousness as regards his work which are similar to Rilke's at this time. By 1908 he had become strongly fascinated by Van Gogh after first experiencing difficulty which went as far as actual dislike. In May of that year he saw an important exhibition, containing a large number of works from Mevrouw Van Gogh's collection, at

Brackl's, the Munich art dealer's. Even at this early date they were often being sold at prices which were high for the time. In December 1909 Brackl held another Van Gogh exhibition. Klee saw works of his at Zimmermann's too, including the ARLÉSIENNE[25]. '*His pathos is alien to me, particularly in my present phase, but he is quite certainly a genius. Pathos bordering on the pathological in someone imperilled in this way can endanger him who does not grasp it. Here is a mind suffering, burnt by a constellation. It breaks free from this just before his catastrophic end. Profoundest tragedy unfolds itself here, genuine tragedy, natural tragedy, exemplary tragedy. Allow me to register fright.*'

In 1911, as page 268 of the same diaries shows, Van Gogh still had a hold on him: '*I am realizing quite a few things about Van Gogh at the moment. Partly through his letters – a selection of which I have in my possession – I am gaining more and more confidence in him. He was capable of reaching down deep, deep into his heart. Nobody will lightly rush past such a landmark, for the historical clock ticks more insistently in the present than in the perspective of art historians; it never stands still, it merely seems to many a time on foggy days. Perhaps he had still not quite said all he had to say so that a few others might be called on to complete his work? It is extremely captivating to look back and watch Van Gogh's progress, to see how he emerged from impressionism without a break and then created a new one. His line*

Antonin Artaud, 1897-1948, selfportrait,
see page 29

The following extract from a rather obscure
translation comes from Malewich's writing[27]:
'*For him form was simply a tool through which
dynamic power passed. He saw that everything
trembles as the result of a simple, universal
movement; he was faced with conquering space, and
everything rushed into its depths. There was an
incredible tension of dynamic action in his brain
which he could see more clearly than in grasses,
flowers, people or the storm. The movement of his
brain's growths were locked in elemental striving in
his skull, and, perhaps, finding no outlet, were fated
to die in the furrows of his brain.
His landscapes, genre-paintings and portraits served
him as forms for expressing dynamic power, and he
hastened in the ragged, painted painterly textures to
express the movement of dynamism; it was as if a
current passed through every growth, and their form
made contact with world-unity. All the purely
impressionist aims that have been attributed to Van
Gogh are as false as in the case of the progenitor of
the Impressionists, Monet, who sought painterly
texture in light and shade as Van Gogh did dynamics
in the texture of color. But thanks to the fact that
with Van Gogh, Cézanne and Monet all these actions
were in the form of a sub-conscious germ they fell
into the all embracing junk of objectivity, a situation
that was worsened by the critics who attached to them
the collective label of Impressionism.
But in spite of all labels the subconscious and the
intuitive grew, and eventually Cézanne's
impressionism developed into the Cubist body, whilst
Van Gogh's became Futurist Dynamism. The latter
began to expel dynamics with great force ... and so
on... Van Gogh separated the textural waves from the
object, the latter being for him only form, saturated
with a maximum of dynamic power.*'

In France fauvism had been earlier to profit by Van
Gogh's work than expressionism had been in
Germany, but unlike the German movement
fauvism was not a literary phenomenon too and it
left scarcely a trace behind it in literary criticism.
Cubism, based on Seurat and Cézanne, did not
concern itself with Van Gogh. A man like
Apollinaire knew, of course, who and what Van
Gogh was and mentions him now and then, in
passing, but Van Gogh lay clearly outside his and
others' main sphere of interest. Futurism, with its
theory of movement, placed Van Gogh in a
diagram after Manet under the heading
'Impressionismo' in the 'Forma' group [intelletto][28].
Cézanne was their main object of attack, scarcely
any mention being made of Van Gogh.
Neither do art criticism and creative reactions to
Van Gogh in England and America contribute to a
Van Gogh cult or study of the artist. In London
Roger Fry was the first to organize an exhibition – a
famous one – in the Grafton Galleries in 1910. At a
time when France had already got over Van Gogh
and was busy absorbing cubism and futurism
England was still not ripe enough for him, where he
was described as a 'lunatic' and 'shocking'. Roger
Fry, in *The Nation* for November 19th and
December 3rd, 1910 was the sole person to go into
Van Gogh deeply, declaring painfully that the
exhibition was 'an insult'. It was not until 1923 that
a Van Gogh exhibition, in the Leicester Galleries,
was favorably received, but anything like a Van
Gogh cult was alien to the English character,
insensitive as it was to expressionism generally.
In 1915, New York was more Gauguin than Van
Gogh-minded [cf what Ir V. W. van Gogh has to say].
A very tentative exhibition in the Modern Gallery
was hardly epoch-maching. In 1920, the Montross
Gallery ['through arrangement with the artist's
family', as the Christian Science Monitor of October
25th, 1920 reports] received a good selection of the
works, and the newspapers printed large
reproductions and informative commentaries.

is new and at the same time very old, and,
fortunately, not a "pure" European affair. It is here
more a question of a reformation than of a
revolution. I find it extraordinarily exciting that
there should be a trend which draws upon
impressionism while at the same time transcending it.'
Here, once again, it is via another artist's [Klee's]
own creative process and his concern with his own
problems that Van Gogh's influence reaches us. I
reread these words now with greater reward and
pleasure than Meier-Graefe's or Just Havelaar's
pages, however infectious Meier-Graefe's
enthusiasm was in his day. Rilke and Klee take us
to 1907-8 and to 1911, and by then we are at least
rid of the exclamation marks. In 1909, Klee, who
did not look for Van Gogh outside the letters any
more than Rilke did, had, for that matter, uttered
this sight: '*Art is invaded by far too much biography,
no matter how engrossing it must be to investigate
such puzzles as Van Gogh and Ensor. This is due to
writers who are – precisely – writers.*' [p 247] Klee
wants the work itself, the work alone, to be the
point of departure.

In France, too, and in roughly the same period
[1905-1909], *Maurice Denis* was undertaking an
inquiry into Van Gogh. The negative verdict he
arrives at makes him a representative of the
traditional French-Latin reaction, contrasting with
that of enthusiasts like Aurier, Mirbeau and, at a
later date, Artaud. His rejections tell us more about

Denis himself [a source still often quoted today]
than they do about Van Gogh: '*Poor Van Gogh!
The victim of abstraction and anarchy, he attempted
to build with no other guide than the whims of his own
eyes and the fantasies of his brain; and, nevertheless,
he did compose; etc.*'[26] This critical reaction is
reprinted from *L'Ermitage*, May 15th, 1905:
'*...an incensed romantic; he is far more moved by the
picturesque and the pathetic than by plastic beauty
and order.*'
'*... Van Gogh's impetuous irregular execution.*'
'*... He attacks the canvas in the bad way the late
romantics considered a sign of genius; witness the
heavy burden of this type of painter which Zola has
fled from in L'Oeuvre ...His name is preserved by the
word temperament, with all it implies in the way of
bestiality. Van Gogh, that is, has brought about a
new decline into romanticism among the young ...*'[26]
In his veneration for Cézanne, distorted by his
decorative symbolism, Denis saw in Van Gogh and
Gauguin manifestations of a 'destructive and
negating anarchism.' Holding such views, how
could Denis ever hope to understand Van Gogh?
Nevertheless, he possessed a SELFPORTRAIT that
could have supplied him with an answer.
The Russian painter *K. S. Malewich* is livelier and
bores down to greater depths. His is a penetrating
psychological and kinetic vision, all the more
welcome since, for want of accessible information,
Russian reactions rarely reach us. The letters to
Bernard were available in Russian as from 1913.

Irving Stone, 1907- , see page 31

By 1935 one could no longer speak of a 'gesture' and Walter Pach admitted he had wondered whether the exhibition organized by the Museum of Modern Art in New York had not come too late, at a time when Van Gogh had lost some of his influence on art. Alfred Barr compiled a magnificent catalogue and the exhibition met with a triumphant reception as it travelled the country and went also to Canada. Society had clearly accepted Van Gogh as a symbol.

At the time when Rilke, Klee and Malewich were to all appearances intensely occupied with Van Gogh, one looks in vain in the Netherlands, Belgium and France for artist-authors or art critics who do proper justice to the Van Gogh problem in art. Cubism and futurism were not popular in the Netherlands, even though such work attracted attention. In art the monumental decorative school was in fashion, while the former worshippers at the shrine among the painters pursued another course, their attitude being actually more in line with the reservations uttered by Maurice Denis. There was nevertheless a number of serious art critics at work in the Netherlands who wrote reports on what they had seen of value to art history, among them: Willem Steenhoff, J. M. G. Cohen Goschalk, Julius de Boer, H. F. W. Jeltes, Willem Vogelsang, R. Jacobsen, H. P. Bremmer and Albert Plasschaert – to the last two of which I shall be returning.

The exhibitions continued to cultivate viewers, supporters and opponents, although the results achieved by the large representative exhibition of 1914, held at the Municipal [Stedelijk] Museum in Amsterdam – twenty-five visitors a day and fifty on the last day – could hardly be taken as a proof of popularity. Popularity, however, was on the way. Otherwise the publication of reproductions, definitely of interest to those working on Van Gogh, would not have been so prominent.
After Plasschaert's portfolio published for Arts and Crafts in 1898 came W. Versluys's 40 'photo-collographs' in Amsterdam, based on Van Gogh's paintings, drawings and letters with sketches. H. P. Bremmer wrote an introduction to 24 reproductions of drawings, likewise published by Versluys in 1907. It was he who had arranged the 100 drawings from the Hidde Nijland collection shown in the Dordrecht Museum in 1905. Versluys-reproductions became known internationally as a result.
Advertisements for these reproductions are to be found in *La Plume*. The French author, A. van Bever, who gave a lecture on Van Gogh in 1905[4] which attracted a fair amount of attention and who also wrote about him, used the reproductions Versluys had had made in 1904 among other material. 'Isografieën van Meurs', published by 'Van Meurs and Van Gogh', were excellent reproductions of drawings, sometimes offered as originals. In 1919 Piper in Munich published the

splendid and now celebrated facsimiles for the Marees Society.
In the Netherlands the crusader par excellence on Van Gogh's behalf was indisputably *H. P. Bremmer*, who came before the public eye through his publications and lectures from 1903 onward. No traces can be found of public activity by him in this field prior to 1900. His *chef d'oeuvre*, consisting of an introductory essay on Van Gogh, appeared in 1911[29]. As purchasing adviser to Mevrouw A. Kröller-Müller, he lent his encouragement to the building up of the celebrated Van Gogh collection which was later to form the nucleus of the National Kröller-Müller Museum at Otterlo in Holland. His commentaries continue to represent unique examples of that realistic, detailed discussion of works of art which is thoroughly Dutch. They took the form of imaginary dialogues with contrary infidels. The objections are composed of a cold-blooded intellectual or primitive mixture and could not be reprinted today. But what strikes one is Bremmer's rejection of exclamatory commentaries, abstract proofs and the art historian type of inter-pretation. He analyses purely on the basis of a mystical contact between himself and the work of art, an identification with it achieved by submerging himself in it, by believing in the artist's serious intention and, above all, in the human being first and only then the artist [see p 2 of his introductory essay].
Bremmer defends what he calls the 'pure and joyous harmony' of the world seen through Van Gogh's eyes, a vision acquired by his having known the depths of human suffering, and in this he is decidedly an opponent of the German expressionist view. He might have served as a healthy antidote to the tragic virus, to the 'kitsch' tragedy which thrived like a weed on the Van Gogh acres. How-ever, Bremmer puts forward the argument without going on to make it acceptable. Albert Verwey, the Dutch poet, accordingly attacks him on this point by raising doubts as to 'the peace and gaiety' Bremmer repeatedly observes. *'Did'*, he asked, *'the paleness of late blossoms express gaiety? Or was it the passionate brittleness of something which was to suffer the sun for so brief a period and then die?'*[30] [p 47]. Bremmer's vision is of the anthropocentric, actually atheistic variety [reminiscent of the 19th century Dutch author Multatuli] while being at the same time saturated in emotion and sentiment. Van Eeden had already clearly considered the human being in Van Gogh first and foremost, giving him pride of place even over the artist, while the artist preceded the painter. It is the same with Meier-Graefe and, after all, the conclusion to which Dr. G. Kraus, the psychiatrist, comes to as well. It really amounts to an unconscious reaction to what the *letters*, via words, add to the paintings or state in a different way. It is the unsolved problem of the relation between the letters and the paintings, which is not posed but merely sensed. It is an ethical evaluation of Van Gogh's life and, in Bremmer's case, a constant sensitivity to Van Gogh's growing awareness of the life story of things and people. Presented not as an anecdote or as something factual, but as an aspect, a visual, psychological aspect of life's wearing-down process. Doubt, too, regarding his being as a painter, since his being an artist, his being a human being, come first. Bremmer is also a champion of his dark, Dutch period, seeing it as preparatory to, a foundation for, his second, French, phase, an observation which reminds one of the mediaeval typological explanation of the Old Testament as being a forerunner of the New Testament. Another striking characteristic of Bremmer's work is that he should have assumed that it was the *human being* in Vincent that impelled him to make what he wanted to make rather than the artist. Here no account is taken of the function of the creative force, one

Henry Miller, 1891- , see page 31

which can never derive its driving power, its power to ignite, from typically 'human' sources.
In many respects *Albert Plasschaert* was Bremmer's exact opposite. As a critic, Plasschaert is the artist, the man of literature. In common with Aurier, Mirbeau and Rilke, his writing was literary, yet he used his senses to elucidate what painters do and the psychology of what they do. Plasschaert took 'the peace' of a work of art as his departure point. This explains why in discussing Vincent in 1905 he writes[31]: '...*not one of the greatest. He lacks the strange peace inherent in the greatest works of art.*'
In a small book about *19th Century Dutch Painting*, which bears no date[32], he writes: '*What distinguishes Van Gogh are the dimensions of his passion, its lack of moderation, the restlessness that results (rest is a prerequisite); and, in addition, the ethical element that is discernible even in the first heads of peasants he paints. All this makes of him the monstrosity of 19th century Dutch painting, the persona non grata, a phenomenon*' [p 81], and later on he writes: '*Our 19th century saw no figure of greater ethical passion than Van Gogh, than Vincent.*' Plasschaert regarded the letters as *necessary*. Furthermore, Vincent was '*too ethical, too moral in action*'. '*He has nothing about him of the complete artist.*' '*Vincent is always violent.*'
That which moved Bremmer to the surrender of the true believer, Plasschaert saw as a cause for reserve, but in the highest realms. He viewed the restlessness, the passion, the immoderation more realistically

than Bremmer. The ethics which Bremmer discounted in the 'human painting' troubled Plasschaert. But the ethics are more prominent in the letters than in the paintings and these ethics are not absent in the way the writers look at the paintings. *Herman F. E. Visser's* article on the literature concerning Van Gogh[33], recording, as it does, rather more and comprising a commentary, has probably done most to raise the level of Van Gogh studies. From the strictly historical point of view nothing of importance had yet been done. Visser discusses Theodore Duret's book on Van Gogh. He – wrongly – assumes that owing to his Dutch nature he has been best understood by Dutchmen and mostly fiercely attacked by them too. This attitude is seen to be untenable as soon as it is realized that Van Gogh's existence is not a specifically Dutch problem but a problem concerning the mechanism of the creative force as this manifested itself – in a divided form – in a late 19th century artist. Visser draws up a critical balance-sheet of Van Gogh. When he began his study after the Sonderbund Exhibition in 1912, Karl Jaspers, an expert researcher in a special field, had already found that he lacked exact date. Visser, working more theoretically, finds the same, and in 1917 he is the first to ask for a 'catalogue raisonné' of Van Gogh's works. He even goes as far as to visualize the form he would like to see it take and says that the phototype technique should be preferred for the reproductions. There are grounds

for supposing that J.-B. de la Faille hit on the idea of taking this great task on himself after having read Visser's words, and, indeed, Mevrouw E. de la Faille-Fransen van de Putte confirmed that this was so, when I approached her in the matter. There can be no doubt that the catalogue provided students of Van Gogh with a first basis for their work. Appreciation of Van Gogh in Holland, though it failed to produce any penetrating study of the Van Gogh problem in art, did at least provide three basic requisites for study: the publication of the letters, the preservation of the greater part of his oeuvre in a single accessible place, and the collection of scattered records and the registration of the oeuvre in an initial systematic catalogue.

IV IN SEARCH OF A SCIENTIFIC BASIS

The publication in 1928 of the de la Faille catalogue[34] was followed nine years later by an act which had a history leading up to it. Walter Vanbeselaere made a study of the Dutch period in Van Gogh's career, published by De Sikkel, Antwerp, in 1937[35]. After what has been written of the early enthusiasm which August Vermeylen – a genuine pioneer – had succeeded in firing among the public from 1893 on in the magazine *Van Nu en Straks*, his influence extending in 1896 even as far north as Groningen, it will come as no surprise to learn that after guiding his pupil Vanbeselaere's footsteps, he was happy to note his straightforward approach, hostile as he had become to all the literary arabesques which had been wound around Van Gogh's work. The architect Henry van de Velde, a leading figure in art circles, read through Vanbeselaere's manuscript, giving it minute attention and supplying the author with the notes he had made on it. Vanbeselaere does not spare de la Faille in criticising his work, saying that in his view it lacked a scientific basis. The analysis of the letters he finds inadequate, and now, more then thirty years later, we – the art historians included – are obliged to admit that much work still remains to be done on them. Vanbeselaere does not stop at the practical data that lay [and still lie] hidden in the letters, but states a principle – which is more important. It is: '*In the unravelling of their evolution lies the key to the work of cataloguing*' [p x]. He could, of course, have quoted Jaspers. For the art historian then, the question remains [to which I would reply in the affirmative] as to whether as much insight and truth was revealed via the potential knowledge that an important creative ability such as Aurier or Rilke possessed. Nevertheless, Vanbeselaere is chivalrous enough to recognize that the publication of the de la Faille catalogue was a gratifying event and formed '*the departure point for all further research*'.
With this, logically enough, the attack on the academic approach is brought into better perspective. Vanbeselaere did excellent work by supplying thorough going corrections to the de la Faille catalogue, and it has become clear that at a later date de la Faille took him as a guide. By doing so he at the same time put the Dutch period on a par with the popular French period–which, for that matter, H. P. Bremmer had already done in his own particular way.
With these principles Vanbeselaere also put an end to the expressionist image of Van Gogh, which had emphasized the unbalanced, torn human being in the artist. The old formula of the 'classical equilibrium between mind and the life-impulse, between thinking and feeling' [p x iv] comes to the surface again, which had also been present 'between the lines' in Bremmer's vision. It is a nineteenth rather than twentieth century view of things. There is no place for the irrational in it and the pathological element is excluded too. As a result, Van Gogh is reduced in stature as a transitional figure – the guise in which Malewich,

particularly, had seen him.
In addition to Vanbeselaere's work 1937 saw the publication of W. Scherjon's and W. Jos de Gruyter's *Vincent van Gogh's Great Period (Arles-Auvers)*[36] and was accordingly a productive year. Obviously inspired by their reaction to the inevitable mistakes in de la Faille's first great ordering of the work, they sought to do what he, too, had sought to do: to bring passages from the letters into relationship with the paintings etc.—but they improved upon him. They differed from de la Faille, however, in that their faith in the letters was all but absolute, believing, as they did, that they could provide 'an answer to nearly all the questions which can be raised with regard to Van Gogh's art, and the vivid descriptions make it possible, but for rare instances, to know with certainty which painting is implied'.

The relation between the texts of the letters and the paintings was so convincing that they as good as rejected any possible doubt as to this interpretation on the grounds of the improbability of any other contribution's deserving preference. The quantity of information yielded up by the letters on Vincent's activity certainly suggests that this is indeed so. Van Gogh found it difficult to relinquish a theme, making duplicates, variants, so that there are numerous instances in which one cannot say with certainty to which work he is referring. Questions of authenticity cannot, however, be solved by reference to the letters, despite the descriptions, though dating is considerably aided by them, even if it is necessary to use extra-textual data—for example, topographical, meteorological, botanical details—to clear up doubts as to subject-matter. The dating of the letters themselves, more-over, is mostly a matter of supposition, depending upon deduction. However much Vincent has to say about the watermills he painted, or about his models, about original works or duplicates, had it not been for the on the spot research done by such figures as Louis Pierard early on and by Marc Tralbaut and Leprohon at a later date, many questions would have remained. Even then authenticity continues to be contestable, for the canvases display features not found in the letters and which could never have appeared in them anyway, since they defied translation into another medium.

In this respect we are struck by the way in which *Vincent's words are always brought to a halt where questions of space, sensations of space, are involved.* At times he then has resort to rough sketches, squiggles. His conception of space is entirely his own and he invariably encounters difficulty with perspective. There are counterfeits in which everything seems right, but for the un-definable conception of space which was uniquely Vincent's. This special quality of the spatial in his work ought one day to be codified.
1937 also saw the emergence of a new feature in the presentation of his works at the exhibitions. This was the year in which René Huyghe organized a didactic, academic exhibition in Paris, which Frenchmen especially found difficult to digest. The presentation had been carefully thought out and was based on extracts from the letters, a system which till then had been adopted in catalogues only. The color of the frames and walls had been given consideration, too, just as Vincent himself had sometimes occupied himself deciding on frames and settings. The looking and reading problem was now transmitted to the public, the point of departure being the illustrative and informative character of the passages from the letters and of the knowledge drived from them.
In 1956 Dr. Marc Edo Tralbaut arranged a second exhibition on scientific principles at the Villa Hügel in Essen, three years after the Municipal

Gaston Bachelard, 1884-1962, see page 34

[Stedelijk] Museums in The Hague and Amsterdam and the Kröller-Müller Museum at Otterlo had included a documentary section in the exhibitions they had organized in 1953 to mark the hundredth anniversary of Van Gogh's birth—a method followed in Munich and Breda too. Tralbaut, however, applied the method practically without exception, making it the main constituent of his exhibition, so the works themselves became additional material. A photographic reconstruction of Van Gogh's subject matter and of the places where he worked has obvious limits and its value is relative, accentuating still further the gap that exists between the reality, nature, and the work of art.

V THE TURN OF THE TIDE

Growing popularity, growing interest on the part of the psychiatrists and art historians during the 'twenties went hand in hand with a turn in the tide as regards the manner in which the revival that Van Gogh had brought about in the world of artistic creation was assimilated.
Between cubism, futurism and abstraction an ageing latter-day expressionism was still orientated toward Van Gogh. This, too, however, was disappointing. In their early formative period, the Flemish Expressionists have little of remark to say of him—though the poet, Paul van Ostayen presents an exception. There is no ardent adulation such as

had been witnessed in earlier years among the Germans. A restricted view is sometimes taken even of his significance to 'les Fauves'. As Christian Zervos wrote[37]: '*Admittedly, this influence is not as general as some tried to make out. It is almost exclusively concerned with color. In all other respects Van Gogh is quite opposed to fauvism. What divides him from the fauvist painters is his concept of painting; more exactly: with Van Gogh spontaneity takes pride of place above the will.*'
This is going to extremes, yet Van Gogh's powerful attachment to the visual in nature—which meant that working from memory did not come easily to him—was to consistently widen the gap between his work and a twentieth century trend which gradually freed itself in more ways than one from its bondage to the visual. The distance dividing surrealism from Van Gogh is less easily explained. The psychiatric interest the Surrealists took in the category of the so-called insane among the artists— Hölderlin, Nietzsche—and in paranoia—Dali—hardly extended to cover Van Gogh. The violently eruptive poetry of Rimbaud, on the other hand, was quoted continuously. A great interest was taken in the way the artist conducted himself in society, especially in the psychological aspects of such behavior. Yet at the same time the Surrealists showed a dislike of deformity—at least, of the deformity of the Expressionists. Pure poetry, imagination, the invention of relations between things normally alien to one another, these chose to

leave the normal appearance of things untouched. Automatism, which was seen as a way of enabling unconscious forces in man that society had suppressed to operate unimpeded, was put into practice in general. The painter René Magritte, however, rejected it as far as he personally was concerned, even though he used concepts such as 'liberty', 'eternal youth', 'the marvellous', much employed by Breton in his argument. Pure poetry, which rejected the dominance of the intelligence and reason, also discarded symbolism and what the Surrealists called 'the mystery' [le mystère], which was to be distinguished from 'the marvellous' [le merveilleux].

Distinctions play a great part in this subtle terminology. The self-control and observation, the lucidity of Van Gogh, violent though he was, did not fit in with the irrational, nor with the ideal of free admittance to everything that came up out of the Unconscious.

In Van Gogh the Surrealists saw an old world that was dynamically dissolving, wasting away, burning itself out rather than the metamorphosis of a world experiencing a rejuvenation. They sensed the absence of their own dream of a world cleansed of taboos and returned to a state of original wonder. They failed to see the moments of lucidity and intensity which at times enabled Van Gogh to rise to great heights. They were put off by his delirious, destructive, frenzied actions. There is accordingly no mention of Van Gogh in the now famous surrealist magazine *Le Minotaure*. Magritte formulated a rejection of him which would, perhaps, not be tolerated by all Surrealists but which does make clear that Van Gogh could not fit into the surrealists' world[38]:

Van Gogh and Freedom
'...various techniques they (the Impressionists) inaugurated were employed by Van Gogh. But the uncertainty, the fever, the violence of Van Gogh's researches have left a painful mark on them... with him we are far removed from that atmosphere of freshness, of the fairylike, which conferred a new youth on the world the Impressionists represented. Van Gogh's delirious painting and actions exist on a level that is foreign to impressionism.
With Van Gogh we enter a domain of psychology and psychiatry. Aesthetics quit philosophy to be treated by the most "exact" sciences...
...The question posed by this "artistic" phenomenon and by him, who is responsible for it without wishing to be, is the question of freedom. The Impressionists conferred on freedom a sense of truth, for they tried to achieve purity. To do this, they needed a love of truth and intelligence, which punished them for having rid themselves of the problems to which the so-called "traditional" artists devoted themselves. Can one say that Van Gogh was liberated? It is hardly possible. He gave way to passions which granted him a blind force in exchange for his submission. Van Gogh makes me think of this blind force above all and I cannot attach a value to him which would oblige us to esteem and like him. I am of the opinion that violent feelings reduce the world to a rather vulgar place. Looking back on what remains of Van Gogh's frenzied activity, I see the memory of a delirious life, devoid of liberty.'

This verdict, which amounted to a condemnation, is based on the philosophical considerations of one who had adopted the surrealist attitude to life rather than on the actual components of Van Gogh's painting. Although Magritte did not possess all the characteristics of the surrealist according to Breton's conception of him, his alienation from Van Gogh is typical of this school. The change was already discernible in art criticism

Top: letter 82; bottom: letter 150

too, from 1927 onward. In that year Waldemar George was remarking how slow France had been to accept Van Gogh and how early and generous his reception in Germany was. '*She* [France] *has not submitted to it.*'[39] The rapid rise of cubism and futurism after the Fauves and the effect of Maurice Denis' not invariably correct theories had not done Vincent proper justice. Georges Duthuit is the first to ask himself seriously how far Vincent's works live on in us ['*si elles se prolongent dans notre recherche*'][40]. He rightly states that little of Van Gogh was to be seen in Paris. [There were no works by him in the public collections]. It was not until 1946 that donations and the bequests made by Paul Gachet and his sister were to fill up the gaps, and so until that year Vincent was not represented in the country that had been eager in its literature to annex him as a 'peintre français'. Duthuit is of the opinion that the paintings have 'aged badly' and he attempts to demonstrate that '*the man of literature prevails over the professional man*' [p 292] – thereby raising the problem of 'the words' once again, without, however, investigating it. Nevertheless, he remains what he had been for the critics of earlier times: 'the great forerunner'. Duthuit, of course, continues to see how he moulded us but his disappointment, which is really more of a turning point, remains latent.

VI THE PATHOLOGICAL SYNDROME

The incident involving his ear plays an important role in both Van Gogh's popularity among the public at large and the 'vie romancée' as well. It forms part of the endeavor to define the syndrome of his illness in the psychological studies which have been written since the 'twenties. This is no popular literature and I am naturally not competent to subject it to a critical examination. But in the works of some authors the subject has another side to it involving aesthetic and creative aspects in relation to his psychological stature. In 1923, following the studies Karl Jaspers published in 1922, came Victor Doiteau, who consulted Gachet in his quest for Van Gogh and in 1928 published *La Folie de Van Gogh* written together with Edgar Leroy[41]. In the Netherlands, in the psycho-analytical magazine *Imago*, A. J. Westerman Holstijn had provided a scientific basis in an article entitled *Die psychologische Entwicklung Vincent Van Gogh's*[42], followed by a concise and extremely useful critical summary by A. Hutter of *The five diagnoses of Vincent van Gogh's illness*[43]. Dr. Joachim Beer, however, tackles the problem of the relation of the clinical picture to his art [Strasbourg, 1936]. Between 1931 and 1967, with certain interruptions, J. A. M. Meerloo has been explaining Van Gogh's quest for identity to an uninitiated yet receptive audience[44].
A gifted trio consisting of G. Kraus, Françoise Minkowska and Charles Mauron, bringing an artistic touch to their professional specialization, have succeeded in placing the pathological syndrome in Van Gogh's total personality, as a result of which, taken together with the letters and the works themselves, it provides a practically complete introduction to his oeuvre.
Kraus warns us to proceed with all caution[45]. His own long experience had taught him that Van Gogh's personality, which he conceived of as a unit composed of his life, his letters and his works, produced phenomena that were unique. Van Gogh's illness formed no exception to this. Kraus never came across the same or even approximately similar symptoms in another. The data being insufficient, he did not venture to attach existing labels to them. What was more, the case was complicated by

Top: letter 268, see page 36; bottom: letter 271

Vincent's relationship with Theo. For that matter, Kraus regards his life, letters and works as so intertwined that he has difficulty in isolating one from the others, which as far as the paintings and drawings are concerned implies that limits have been set on their autonomous and future value. Kraus is one of the few psychiatrists capable of always applying his thorough, specialized knowledge to a warm, intensely human but also aesthetic penetration. He was the most cautious figure among his colleagues; not out of fear but rather out of a respect that know no bounds.

Dr. F. Minkowska resembled Kraus in taking as her departure point the principle of the unity of Van Gogh's life and work, his illness included, which she does not regard as an outside disorder working its way inward with destructive effect. She, too, was one of those who had been 'seized', one who had been inspired by Jaspers, but who carried out her own examination of the paintings, letters and studies, publishing her first study of Van Gogh in 1932, which was followed by a second in 1948[46]. She displays greater recklessness than Kraus in her analysis and conclusions, yet she remains true to Van Gogh, returns to him continually, with a scarcely suppressed passion and a daring artistic freedom, typical, too, of the admirer of Gaston Bachelard.

Charles Mauron succeeded in transforming and deepening his erudition in things literary and his close contacts with painting [including that of Seurat and Van Gogh] in one or two extraordinary studies of Van Gogh before blindness in 1940 called a halt to the extension of these contacts. He analysed the letters in *Psyche – Notes on the structure of the unconscious in Van Gogh*[48], which was succeeded by a lecture delivered in Amsterdam on March 31st, 1953 on 'Symbiosis – the relationship between Theo and Vincent'[47], and, finally, the deeply probing analysis of the Arles period: *Van Gogh au seuil de la Provence*[49]. This study is among the most illuminating ever conceived on Van Gogh.

Artaud – Van Gogh

In Artaud's writing the clinical picture of Van Gogh's illness is no longer subjected to an analysis by psychiatrists but to one carried out by a patient who rebels against them. In contrast to the psychiatrists and avoiding all clinical formulae, Artaud leads the problem of the illness back to the conflict with an oppressive society, and Artaud's own surrealist past has a word to add here. His own potent aesthetic gifts confer on this bias and subjectivity a significance which at times transcends the syndrome. At times the power of the creative in him causes his excessive subjectivity to attain to objectivity. When Artaud saw the Van Goghs at the Orangerie in Paris in 1946-7 Van Gogh became in a sense a character in Artaud's ideas concerning a 'theatre of cruelty'.

Van Gogh as the victim of the destructive forces in society – a society which is Artaud's too – becomes a myth once more, but a myth devoid of fables and divinity. Those surrounding him – Theo, Gachet, Gauguin, Bernard, are subjected to merciless criticism. Artaud tarnishes everything until a modern apocalypse results as a way to escape from the hell on earth. None of the other artists of Artaud's generation were concerning themselves with Van Gogh at the time, but his own years of crisis and the coincidence of the exhibition bring about Van Gogh's apocalyptic resurrection [for these crisis years, see the penetrating image Otto Hahn creates of Artaud in his *Portrait d'Antonin Artaud*[50]]. A few quotations from Artaud[51] will be sufficient to outline the violent picture he creates of himself and Van Gogh: '*I believe that Gauguin thought that the artist ought to search again for the symbol, the myth, enlarge the things of life to the*

Letter 307

proportions of the myth ...
Van Gogh, on the other hand, thought that it was necessary to deduce the myth from the most down to earth things of life. And in this, I think, he was damn well right. For reality is terribly superior to any and every story, every fable, every divinity, every surreality' [p 29].
'*And, for emerging from Hell, I prefer the landscapes of this quiet convulsionary to the seething compositions of Breughel the Elder or Jerome Bosch who, confronted with him, are nothing but artists where Van Gogh is simply a poor dunce endeavoring not to*

go wrong [p 41].
I don't know a single psychiatrist who would be able to scrutinize a man's face with such crushing power and to serve up its irrefutable psychology as though on a plate. Van Gogh's eye is that of a great genius, but in the way I see him desegregating me myself from the depths of the canvas where he has appeared, it is no longer the genius of a painter I sense alive in him at that moment but that of a certain philosopher whom I have never met in actual life. Socrates hadn't such an eye, perhaps the only one before him to possess this glance which can lay bare the spirit,

deliver the body from the spirit, to lay bare man's body and remove it from the subterfuges of the mind, was poor Nietzsche' [p 65].
'Simply a painter, Van Gogh, and nothing more, nothing of a philosopher, a mystic, no rites, "physcurgy" or liturgy, no history, literature, poetry about him, these sunflowers of bronzed gold have been painted: they have been painted like sunflowers and nothing else, yet to understand a real sunflower it is now necessary to return to a stormy sky, a plain in nature itself. One will no longer be able to avoid returning to Van Gogh' [p 52].
'...the marvellous thing is that this painter, who is a painter and nothing more, is also, of all painters ever born, the one who makes us forget more than any other that we are dealing with painting ...' [p 55].
'...but when one has seen Van Gogh, one can no longer believe there is anything harder to surpass than the subject matter: the simple motif of a bed-room candlestick standing alight on a chair of plaited straw in a purplish frame has more to tell us, when portrayed by Van Gogh, than all the Greek dramas put together, or the plays of Grille, Turner, Webster or Ford, which, for that matter, have remained unperformed to this day' [p 53].

At the beginning of the century Rilke had approached Van Gogh with the questions – but with the knowledge and wisdom too – which his own creative work had taught him. Looking became a process of absorption and in this way he discovered the point at which the writing and painting begin to suffer from the activity of the conscious mind, which led him to conclude that the letters actually contain too much. Artaud, too, looked at Van Gogh from the vantage point of his own spiritual and psychological existence. In view of the excess that was natural to him, his destructive suffering, Van Gogh's paint proved to have such an effect on him that the tables were turned: Van Gogh looked at Artaud, tore off layer after layer, made him lucid and intoxicated in his grasp.
The prose which resulted made Van Gogh once again, and perhaps for the last time, topical, alive. It was not a matter of contemplating him from a distance. It was rather the flaring-up of a consuming flame in a mind that interpreted Van Gogh's symbols according to its own psychological and aesthetic insights.

VII 'VIE ROMANCÉE'

For the most part the emotional interpretations of Van Gogh by the Fauves and the German Expressionists appeared prior to 1914. Malewich's rather later contribution [1915] and the latest of all, that of Artaud in 1947, are of the same order – image-forming involving the creative process. After 1908 interest broadened into a slowly but surely developing popularity, though it was to be 1935 before an unpredictable Van Gogh boom came about. As his popularity grew, an increasingly urgent demand developed for exacter information, a less distorted picture and greater insight into the complicated character of this artist. This demand was met, especially in the 1920-1937 period, when psychiatric studies were made of his syndrome, the works catalogued, and the Dutch period worked out in detail. The popularity trend – always some-what dubious – naturally accorded ill with the academic trend. Yet both implied a certain aloofness from the intuitive understanding that creative artists concerned with Van Gogh had once come forward with.

The pioneers of the initial period of discovery – Aurier, Mirbeau, Roland Holst, Vermeylen – were

Top: letter 339; bottom: letter 355

highly sensitive to the danger involved and from the very outset they warned against the confusion of values that a vulgar romanticization of Van Gogh's case would result in – at the expense of a proper understanding of his oeuvre. But there was nothing to be done about it. Those who, with the best intentions in the world for that matter, regarded the human being cum artist as a hero and saw him as the main object of interest, endeavoring to adapt painting to this conception of things, played into the hands of the writers of the 'vie romancée' – which at best is merely an interpretation of an artist's life.

Initially, it was still more or less in the hands of an art historian as long as Julius Meier-Graefe was involved. His essays and biographical study gradually evolved into the novel of a man in search of a god [*Der Roman eines Gottsuchers*, 1932[52]]. His respect for factual data was colored by the expressionist dramatics surrounding such a figure as Dostoevski, which were influential at the time in Holland, having been introduced into a more receptive atmosphere there by Dirk Coster and Just Havelaar. His audience consisted of the soi-disant artistic and intellectual circles. It is not until we come to *Irving Stone* that we enter the world of superlatives. From 1935 onward his book *Lust for Life*[53] enjoyed world fame, translations appearing everywhere. At all levels its story, written with undeniable élan, extends far beyond the circles to which Meier-Graefe had access. There is nothing against this so long as the matter treated is seen in its true light and within its true limits. Playing all the various registers of popularity in this way introduces a pseudo-intermediary. The 'vie romancée' has come to exist in its own right. It does not guide the reader toward the artist's works. These now inevitably become the illustrative material to the artist's life and lose their independent existence.

Van Gogh himself proves the necessary argument to justify all this. It was better to make children than paintings. He had actually missed out on life, marriage had avaded him, a family was lost to him. But whoever allows himself to be misguided by this forgets that he also saw the Fatum of his immoderate devotion to painting as the condition for his existence. He knew he would collapse, once his capacity to paint was threatened and became unstable.

When he proposed to paint really for sailors and for the poor, he endeavored to bore through the refined vision of the late Impressionists in his colors and subject matter to arrive at a primitivity, an archaism, which seemed rougher, more barbaric and which bubbled up from a different source. We do not know whether he had the popularity he enjoys today in mind at that time. Or, rather, we do know. He was *not* thinking of those thousands but of individuals, which to him meant Theo, his sister, his mother, an individual dealer, a friend, a sailor, a whore or an impoverished woman and her children. We do know actually. He never once thought at that time of the intermediaries, the priests, of middlemen like Irving Stone, of dealers as a group. He will have cherished the hope that people might stand and look at his works without any words having to be said, words which actually sell him to the publicity industry. Thousands went to look, incited to do so by the story of his life, drawn to his works by some one other than Van Gogh himself.

What *Henry Miller* did in *Plexus* also forms part of Van Gogh's assimilation into literature. Yet when, in writing his own 'vie romancée', Miller confesses the part Van Gogh played in forming his apocalyptic view of life, he does not go as far as to write a 'vie romancée' of the artist as well. Miller – who paints himself – is like von Hofmannsthal was in 1901 – ultra-sensitive to Van Gogh's color. His

Letter 405

interpretation is a mixture of intentions and values. The message Van Gogh's life has for him amounts to a passionately professed faith in which Van Gogh acts as a catalyst. Miller seems slightly ironical in dealing with his popularity:
'*Suddenly, due to the immense popularity of a sensational book, thousands upon thousands take to visiting the museums and galleries; they converge like a Niagara upon the intoxicating masterpieces of that despised and forlorn genius Vincent van Gogh*'[54].
The Viennese art historian, Fritz Novotny, a Van Gogh expert and enthusiast, attempts to explain

Van Gogh's popularity in an essay entitled *Die Popularität Van Gogh's in 1953*[55]. He sees in him the tension existing between two opposites: strict concentration on the individual life of things and people and his desire to express the super-individual in streams of movement. The former engages the interest of the masses sooner and more easily than does the second, the aspect of Van Gogh that Malewich understood so well. Van Gogh's ideal – to work for the people – a thing he did on a limited scale only for that matter – is best summed up in the words of Herkower, an illustrator much admired by

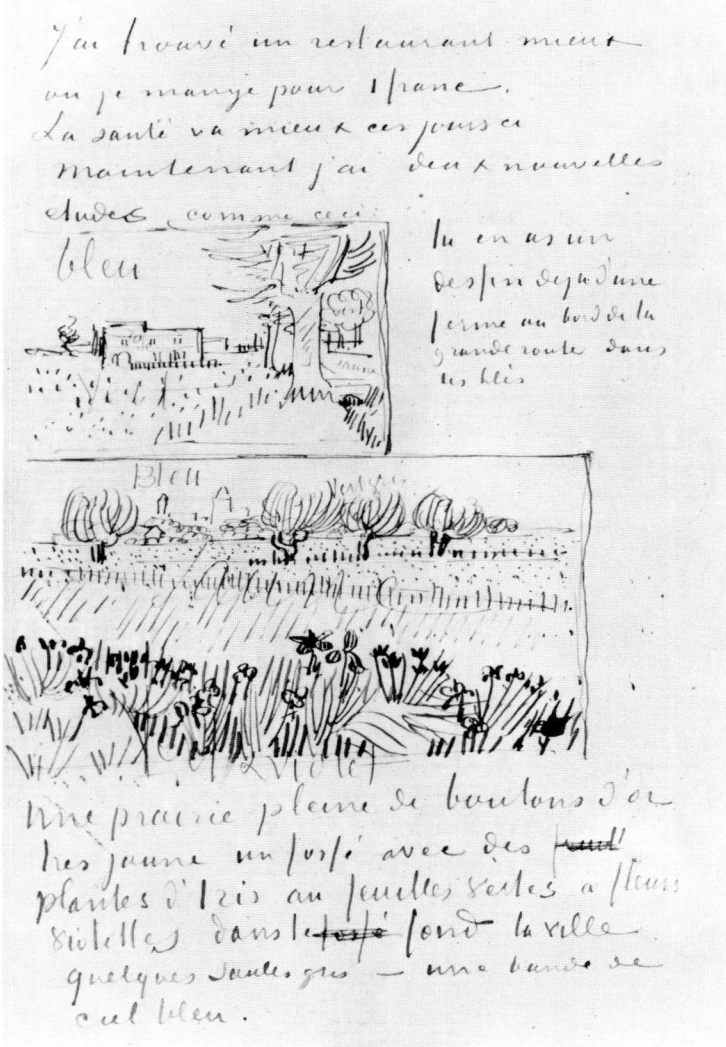

Van Gogh: *'For you – the public – it is really done.'*
And then Novotny sees the existence of things in
Vincent's works – so strangely direct and at the
same time narrative [not in the chronological sense,
but existentially] – as an explanation of the mass
response to his work.

Nevertheless – do we know sufficient about the
receptivity to art in the 20th century at all levels of
society and do we know Van Gogh – all aspects of
him – well enough still to be free of all doubts? Do
people go in crowds to queue for the exhibitions out
of love for the myth surrounding painting and
sculpture, out of love for a style, or is it, where Van
Gogh is concerned, the myth surrounding a
personality, aroused via the intermediary of the
Lust for Life? *Are the words, Vincent's and other
men's words, unavoidable on the way to his
paintings?*

All the same, the spectacle in Tokio 1958 of
Japanese coming from far and near in countless
numbers, the Emperor and the shoeshine, mothers
with their babies on their backs, who filed past Van
Gogh's works and stared at his works unhurriedly,
quietly – this had something of magic about it.
What is really going on as they stand there
absorbing him, slowly, silently? One may safely forget
the art slogans of 'democracy' and 'socialization'.

VIII THE POST-1945 BOOM

This boom formed no contradiction to the turn of
the tide – it confirmed it. The exhibitions which
began almost immediately after the war [in
Scandinavia, Belgium, France, England and the
USA] got the masses on the move. Yet had Van
Gogh not answered to something that fascinates the
man and woman who have nothing to do with art
in their daily lives it would have remained at this.
He was just far enough removed not to arouse the
difficulties encountered with the abstract and just
near enough to be regarded as belonging to the
present. In any event, he did not share in the favor
that fin de siècle art enjoyed as a result of a
nostalgic longing.

A kind of Van Gogh semiology developed, a socio-
aesthetic Van Gogh language, people beginning to
live according to Van Gogh symbols. These trends
manifest themselves in the lucrative industry of
producing books, booklets, calendars, illustrations
of all shapes and sizes, films, plays. It can be
claimed that exhibitions and this industry were the
reason for this semiology and consequently explain
it. But it is not so simple as that. The social
phenomenon, which has nothing to do with
understanding, revelation or study, or with the
violent wave of recognition of earlier times, is a
blend of sensation [interest in the artist's life], the
ethics of suffering, the powerful color [that is,
however, no longer savage to us today], the
figurative element, so charged with emotion, and
the irrefutable influence the books had – the Lust
for Life industry – as a result of which practically no
one was able any longer to come fresh and
unconditioned to the work itself.

As a symbol Van Gogh now lives in a society which
is still at odds with art, so that his symbol does not,
unfortunately, mean that art has now found roots
in the people [the people Klee was searching for].
He can disappear from society again as a token,
should the symbol show signs of wearing out. His
value, his significance, exist quite independently of
all this. Post-1945 writing on Van Gogh reflects this
situation – there is a flood of repetitive descriptions
and a small group of authors who make
contributions of importance, but in specialized
studies only. Research is limited but still proceeds.

Top: letter 487; bottom: letter 552, see page 37

We are obviously in the zone where only work on detail, smaller finds, or scarcely relevant local investigations are the order of the day. There is still room for improvement in our conception of Van Gogh's make-up as a painter cum writer, but not along the lines of prevailing art history disciplines. In the survey which follows, of necessity selective only, a number of contributions have been noted with this in view, contributions which keep the possibility of a new approach alive, though there are certain reservations.

General works intended for a broader but not uninitiated public are only interesting if they combine a personal vision with reliable, thorough study, which here and there throws new light on the image or revitalizes it. There are three such authors to be mentioned before all others: Carl Norde nalk, Jean Leymarie and Meyer Schapiro, who observe and know how to link one fact with another, experience the subject matter anew and succeed in avoiding clichés. John Rewald placed the 'Van Gogh happening' in the general context of art trends at the end of the 19th century. Direct approaches, such as that made by Frank Elgar, soundly based and written with critical point and warmth, remain rare[56]. The specialized studies of more general nature were concerned with color. Carl Derkert finally supplied insight into his palette in the Dutch period. Mark Buchman made a survey of the entire oeuvre in this light and in his *Die Farbenlehre van Goghs* [Van Gogh's Theory of Color] Kurt Badt[57] lay too great an emphasis on what was not a 'theory' at all, though latent as such in Van Gogh.

Among the studies which the art historian still treats warily or with distrust yet which approach the subject from an original angle is that contributed by J.Stellingwerff, *Werkelijkheid en grondmotief bij V. W. van Gogh* [Reality and Basic Subject Matter in V. W. van Gogh] in which he refers to the philosophers Heidegger and Jaspers[58]. Maurizio Bonicatti strikes the attention too and has things of fundamental importance to say about Van Gogh's mode of expression in his essay *La simbolica del linguaggio imaginativo dopo van Gogh* [The Symbolism of Imaginative Language after Van Gogh] in his book *Appunti sull' arte moderna ca. 1870-1900* [Notes on Modern Art, circa 1870-1900]–a field which certainly requires further investigation[59].

H. R. Graetz wrote *The Symbolic Language of Vincent van Gogh*[60], stating unequivocally that he had no wish to intrude on the territory of the art critics and historians. The question remains whether this is possible–even if one does not wish to–without setting bounds to the symbolic and psychological interpretation he had in view. The creative element continues, in any case, to be the untouched source. Nevertheless, Graetz's research, extending over a period of years, is potentially a method of guiding the interest taken in Van Gogh, the human being, and his own life–for this is what it amounts to in a refined way–back to the objects upon which Vincent had become fixated in his mind and in his work.

Less conspicuous is the work done to bring about an improvement in the compilation of catalogues for Van Gogh exhibitions. Douglas Cooper encouraged the move in this direction by designing his 1947 catalogue for the Tate Gallery Exhibition on scientific lines. This was followed in 1955 by his meticulous study of Van Gogh's drawings. In 1968/9, Alan Bowness followed Cooper's example when organizing the exhibition in the Hayward Gallery, which provided the stimulus for a

Top: letter 553b, see page 37; bottom: letter в 7, see page 36

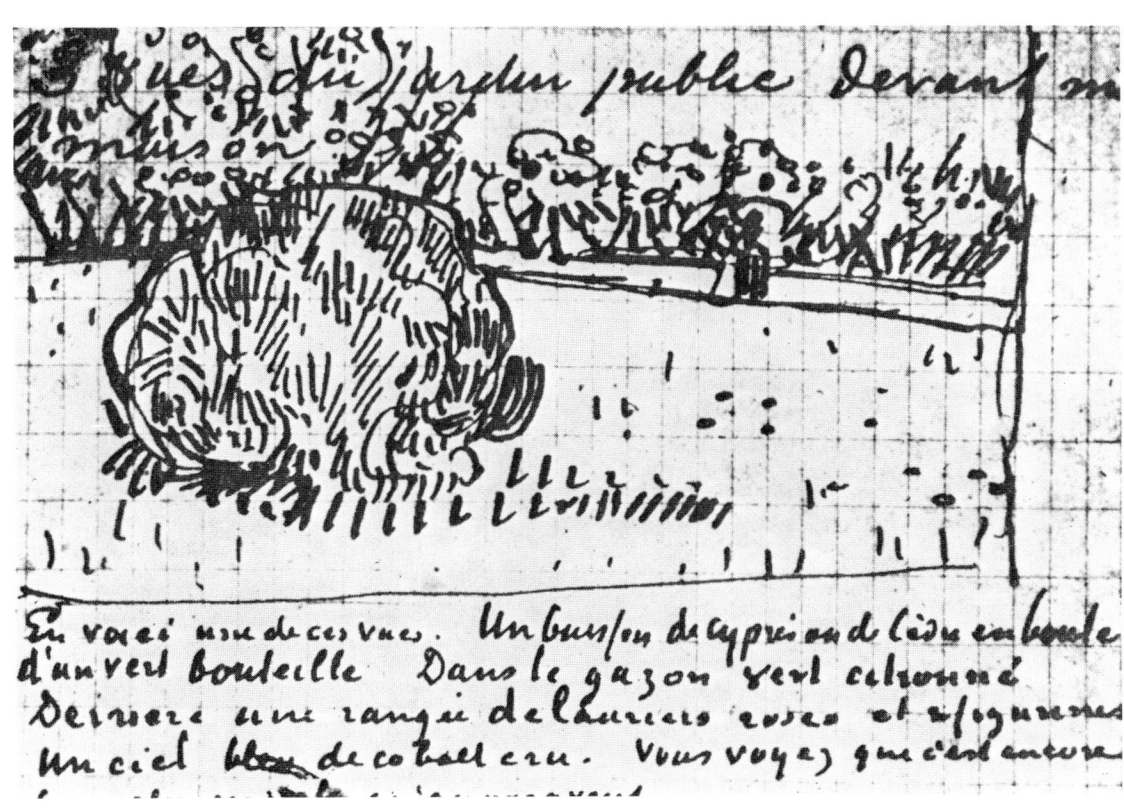

refreshing and critical re-assessment of established opinions in which students participated.

J. P. van Gelder demonstrated how in Van Gogh's case the creative process directed upon a single subject [the POTATO-EATERS, for example] always leads one to a history of a group of sketches and works which illuminate Vincent's way of going to work and conceiving his subject matter.

A curious study by Pierre Francastel[61] has remained in the shadows. It reunited Van Gogh with the tradition again, despite deviations, and does so in a lucid, critical manner, freeing him from the understandable hold that the Decadents and Symbolists had obtained on him.

From 1943 onward Marc Edo Tralbaut continued the Belgian contribution to the study of Van Gogh, which having been inaugurated by Vermeylen, became in the hands of Vanbeselaere a complete main work, and in Louis Pierard's on the spot research, enthusiastically undertaken. From 1943 onward, Tralbaut published no less than 73 studies of varying length apart from delivering 28 lectures, portions of which are to be found recorded in his publications. He added new shades of meaning to the conventional versions of the different phases by investigating Antwerp and Drenthe down to their topographical and other details and conferring a special value on them as a result. Like scarcely anyone before him, he acquired an almost encyclopaedic knowledge of Van Gogh, scattered across a large number of publications, which inevitably involved a certain lack of proportion in the relation between detail and his subject seen as a whole. The sifting and collation of all this scattered material would be welcome. To provide the necessary foundations for his work, Tralbaut collected everything relating to Van Gogh from all over the world, which certainly makes of him the last to have kept the cult [including the relics] alive. His work has borne permanent fruits in the Tralbaut Archives, which have become state property in the Netherlands and are now kept in the new state Van Gogh Museum, where they were not yet available for consultation when this was being written.

Bibliographical summaries represent useful work calling for a great deal of effort which, though not anonymous, is always performed with modesty. Marco Valsecchi made a first and gratifying attempt at this in 1936, his work being reprinted in another context in 1942. 1942 saw another publication – of 777 items, going as far as 1940, prepared by Charles Matoon Brooks. Additions and emendations would be welcome in the event of reprinting.

IX 'LIFE IS PROBABLY ROUND'

Artaud's words about Van Gogh: 'the only definite philosopher I have ever met in my life' apparently made a deep impression on *Gaston Bachelard* too. The point at issue with Bachelard is no longer the pathological syndrome but a discovery: that Vincent and three non-painters – Jaspers, Bourquet and La Fontaine – pronounce views concerning the 'roundness of life'. Under the title *La phénoméno-logie du Rond* in *La poétique de l'espace* Bachelard quotes Van Gogh as saying[62]: 'La vie est probable-ment ronde' – which should be compared with what the other three have to say. He particularly does not wish to explain this quotation by way of an illustration. The curves of the St. Rémy and Auvers periods immediately spring to mind. He is not inclined to see it as a metaphor nor does he wish to attempt a psycho-analytical explanation. Bachelard does not wish to pin it down visually or discuss it in an essay. He sees it as a strange experience, liberated from the past. Brief, hypnotic, sudden, pure – this is

Top: letter 651, see page 37; bottom: letter w 9

the effect of these pronouncements on the roundness of life. Primitive as well: '*They bear the stamp of primitivity. They are borne out of a body and behold, they are complete. He knows that that which isolates itself becomes round, assumes the shape of the being that is concentrated upon itself.*' Vincent's pronouncement should, however, be read in the light of the ideas from which it sprang. In a letter to Emile Bernard [B 8, end of June 1888, Arles], a letter full of curious ideas, he draws a distinction between the spoken word [of Christ] and the written word, which he rates less highly in civilization. It is in this letter that he likens the painter's existence to a larva, a caterpillar, that changes into a butterfly whose field of operation would be one of the countless stars, no less accessible after our death than the black dots on the geographical map of our earth. He expects scientific reasoning to have far-reaching results in the future: '*For look: the earth was supposed to be flat. It was true: it is still flat today, from Paris to Asnières, for instance. Only this does not prevent science from proving that the earth is actually round. A thing no one contests today. Now, at the moment, despite this, people believe that* life is flat *and progresses from birth to death.*
'*However,* that too, life, is probably round, *and much superior in extent and capacity to the hemisphere that is at present known to us. It is probable that future generations will explain this highly interesting matter to us; and then science, too, could – if it pleased – arrive at conclusions more or less parallel to those of Christ concerning the other half of existence. However this may be, the fact remains that we are painters in real life and that is a matter of whistling one's tune as long as one has the breath to do so ...*'

When brought back into the context of Vincent's imaginative thinking, the saying that Bachelard singled out is seen to signify a transcendental moment in his thought. He did not see his own existence as definite, fixed. He needed an image that would confer on him the power of a metamorphosis. Even now he had sufficient control over himself to be able to return to the very hub of his existence, his life as a painter. The ambivalent factor was preserved: he could not remain silent about this. He continued to reproduce it in words too so that there was always a great temptation to others to search for the narrative, illustrative element in the painting, which has accordingly been done – from Bremmer to Graetz.
Militating against this view is the fact that Van Gogh did, indeed, collect the English illustrations with passionate enthusiasm and wrote at length about them but never went any further than collecting them. All his plans for illustrating himself remained mere plans; he was unable to do anything creative about them. Writing never lost its grip on him. Taking a sober view of it, we can say that it was in part merely an example of the nineteenth century epistolary mode of communication. The letters are texts but not in the sense of literature. They represent information but at the same time discussions. In these discussions Theo is the listener, though no party to them. Vincent, the writer, is one with Theo, whom he seeks to remodel in his own image. Sometimes authors have asked themselves whether Theo really understood Vincent. There is no positively convincing answer to the reverse question: did Vincent really understand Theo, which is equally important from a human viewpoint – in view of Vincent's efforts to project himself upon Theo. One only obtains a picture of Theo from the letters after a great deal of retouching.
The letters are only indirectly autobiographical, since Vincent never stands back and sees himself from a distance. Their writing was as much a part

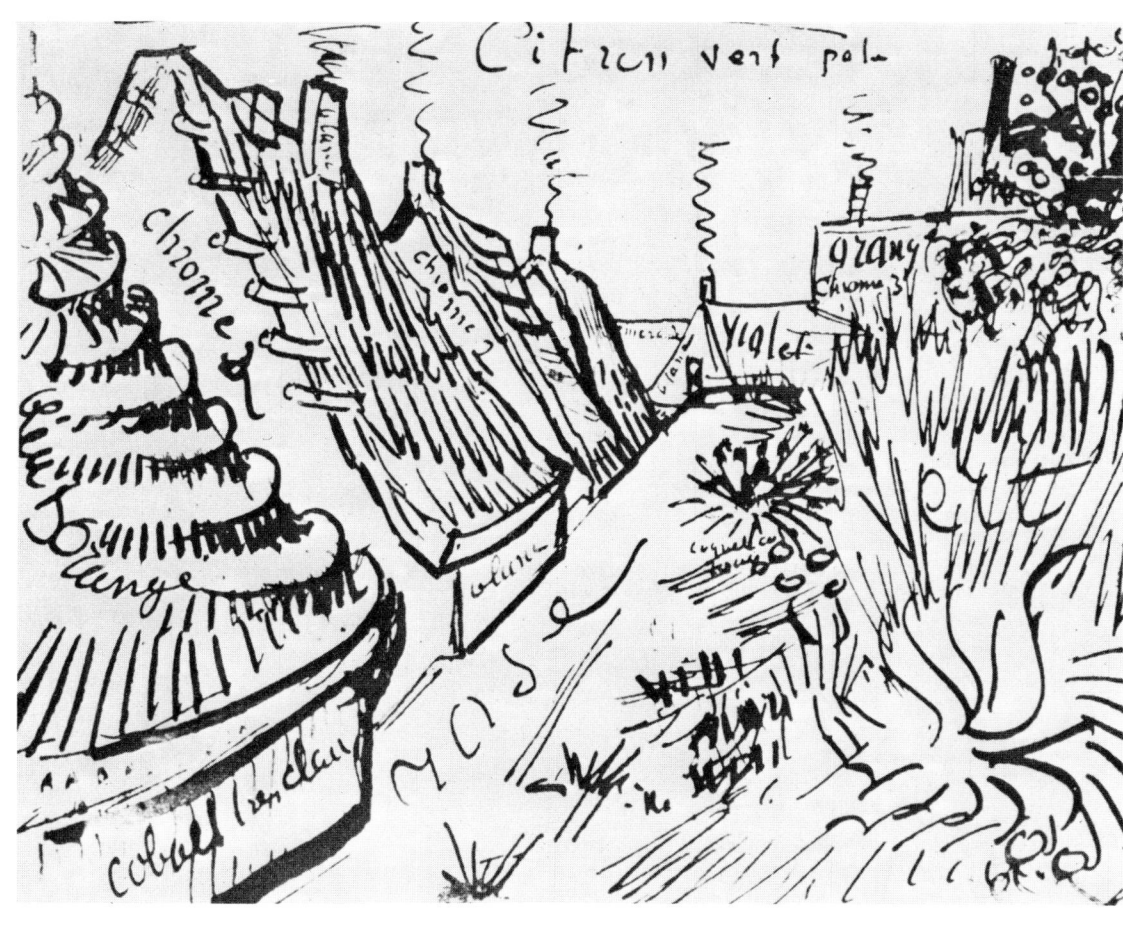

Letter B 6

of his life as his painting. He writes his way towards death.
The sketches the letters contain come about at points where words get stuck fast, impotent as they are to express the spatial. Lines, spatial symbols, take over their role from them. So his writing did not amount to conversation on paper – the letters can also be seen as monologues. It was an undulating stream, at times scarcely moving so deep is his thought, while at others it is vigorously ruffled as these thoughts come to the surface under pressure. They are constantly present: in debate, monologue, painting, writing.

It seems so simple that one can easily miss it while reading. In letter 604 to Theo he writes, four times in all, that he often writes away at the letter during pauses between painting: '*Ouf – the hay-maker is finished ...*' Sometimes he says that writing is a rest from days of drawing, but it is also the other way round – he sometimes relaxes from the exhausting job of writing by making a sketch. His ability repeatedly to interrupt his painter's élan in order to write, and vice versa, is, one realizes, actually far from being a simple thing, once one has experienced the violence, the intensity, of his works and his words. It tells us much about his awareness while he is painting. This is what Rilke had in mind. It cost him no mental effort to switch from the rhythm of painting to the rhythm of writing. This makes both activities complex – there is, of course, a factor, that is present in each though not in the other. Accordingly, there is a Van Gogh who is in each but not in each alone: he is contained in the writing and painting together.
His letters are often characterized by a frequently disjointed chronology – the logic of a narrative does not come easily to him. Viewed superficially, there is an incoherence, for instance, when in letter 8 to

Bernard [B 8] he is writing about a Monet exhibition his brother arranged for Goupil's gallery and then immediately asks Bernard if he has ever read a life of Luther, after which he mentions Louis XIV, whom he rejects, then going on to ask Bernard about his military service. He is, of course, obliged to accept the conventional use of words and grammar the same as any other man, but a comparative degree of incoherence causes one to sense a mind operating independently of words and intensely concerned with its own threatened existence. He often interrupts the descriptions, the relation of facts or of some event, the recollection or re-living of something he has done in order to listen to other sounds, belonging not to the past or the future but to the present. On such occasions the way in which he writes of his existence achieves a concentration and the unusual, shining truth to life which is only possible when the merciless unmasking, revelation, of which he was sometimes capable, is taking place. Such moments then become sublime fragments in the letters which when removed from their context and quoted as extracts lose their brilliance, for Van Gogh had been working his way to them all the time and the reader needs to follow the preliminaries, needs to follow him along the way that leads up to such moments, follow the undulations in order to appreciate the climaxes *as* climaxes.
The style of the letters is forceful and compulsive as a result. When he writes ordinary letters to Theo asking for paint, linen, paper, books, money, it is all bound up with this inescapable compulsion to work. He can never wait. The fatal, inexplicable compulsion the work exerts upon him is of inhuman proportions. His contacts with others are restricted by it, doomed to an irregular staccato, characteristic of his day to day activity but present, too, in the synchronous writing of the letters. The flow of

Letter 632, see page 37

element in the graphic art of draftsmanship. Listening to the articulation of sounds merges into the articulation of space.

X THE DRAWING AND THE WORDS [LETTERS]

The beginning lies in his childhood. As soon as words prove insufficient his pen obeys a different command from his brain. An illustration in the manner of a 19th century book or magazine illuminates the story. It has nothing to do with the writing. It is arbitrary. In line with the development that had taken place in the Middle Ages, the written text has become entirely separate from the visual. The aural and visual components of culture approach one another but are not united in a bond of marriage. Vincent's evolution as a painter also makes itself felt in the relation between his writing and drawing. During his Hague period it is even possible to pinpoint the moments at which he interrupts his writing to draw in order to explain something the better.

Letter 268 describes the distribution of light in front of a window. He goes on to say something about the blind and writes: '*Those blind people ...*', stops, leaves a space, draws a margin on the right and continues his letter lower down, begins to draw and finding he has insufficient room, draws lines over what he has written. This illustrates the synchronization of the two elements which go to make up his letter. It is almost always space that he is either unwilling or unable to describe in words, not an event, not, as it was earlier on, something that had to resemble English wood-cuts as illustrations or had to be in the spirit of Lancon or Boyd Houghton [see, inter alia, letters 140 and 262]. When he wants to keep his sketches more separate from what he writes, he draws a frame round them [letter 270]. At times the drawing must have been made first, before he began the letter, his writing then being carefully arranged to fit in with its limits [letter 333]. In this letter he tries persistently to persuade Theo to leave the art dealer's and become a painter himself and he becomes so dazed by his own argument that he has to make a little sketch *in order to put it out of his mind.* Listening to words ceases, changing into the sketching of an outdoor scene, but after this the argument resumed. In Arles the system is the same, but there is now a visible relationship between the hand that writes and the hand that draws, one that now and then becomes a fusion of the two. A letter to Russell [501a] is significant, providing, as it does, a curious example of the imperative compulsion in the drawing of objects observed, which he calls abstractions. He writes, however, without saying that he saw a little girl who looked like this or that, but interrupts the letter in order on the same paper to draw the little girl's head, not by way of communication but purely for the sake of making a drawing.

'*Well, instead of continuing the letter I began to draw on the very paper the head of a dirty little girl I saw this afternoon whilst I was painting a view of the river with a greenish yellow sky.*'

And further on he writes: '*I must hurry off this letter for I feel some more abstractions coming on and if I did not quickly fill up my paper, I would again set to drawing and you would not have your letter.*'

All the same he then draws THE SOWER [B 7]. The graphic art based on space prevails over the graphic art based on sound [writing] once the former exerts pressure on the latter. Thus again we meet with the stream that consists of two undulations in Vincent – and nothing of an illustrative nature dominates either in the writing or the drawing. The graphics of the drawing attract the letters to it like a magnet. The sound becomes almost wholly line, the vertical strokes of the t, p, f,

work demands this, is the cause of it – it is the only thing in him that does flow. In his life the tick-tock of time has been subordinated to a spatial continuity achieved in his work via the subjective perspective. In his letters 'later' and 'the future' are never concrete concepts but a perspective, shifted, or shifting, towards a far horizon. Like the fields, the roads, which lie stretched out in his drawings and paintings, like linear dimensions which converge only in infinity.

It is possible to trace an evolution in his letters. In his younger years the theological and ethical phrases lend his words a pathos that gives way later to the indecision, the groping towards clarity, indicative of a change going on inside him. A primitive philosophy of his own making blends here with the intentions of a painter and draftsman who proceeds to express himself both psychologically and graphically.

This evolution is discernible in the subtle change that comes about in the relation of the drawings in the letters to their actual texts. With Vincent there often comes a moment when the auditory element in the graphic art of writing changes into the spatial h, k are no longer distinguishable from the curves his hand draws to suggest clods of earth. The letters composing the words become alienated from their function as sounds. The arbitrary relation of the shape of the alphabetical letters to their sound is now absorbed into the no longer arbitrary order of space and rhythm. A highly telling example of this is provided by the sketch in letter 552 and that in letter 553b. By reason of the distinction between the letters and the short, angular lines of the drawing the first can be wholly separated from the sound and meaning of the words. A superb entity. Arles sees this interpenetration of letters and drawing reach its zenith. In these letters plus sketches the presence of an amazing lucidity and intensity of living [seeing, hearing, feeling, thinking] is so evident that it is difficult to find paintings of like value on this particular point. For their color –

which the letters lack – does not wholly make up for the process in which words become linear creations. The old distinction between the written word and the illustration, still so marked in the highly illustrative 19th century, of which Vincent was so fond, has been undermined. Unknown to himself, Vincent is here anticipating the 20th century. The strength that radiates from the undulations in the drawing onto the disintegrating handwriting is uncommonly powerful. For a moment a primitive, vital force, writing the auditory, oral and visual, makes its appearance. Impudent, primitive, brutish are the words his contemporaries used to describe it.

There is no further evolution in this coherence at St. Rémy and Auvers. It would be necessary to study all the letters with sketches written between 1889 and 1890 before one could draw more far-

reaching conclusions. Two examples from the Auvers period appear to be symptomatic: the sketch with the caption 'le jardin de Daubigny' beneath it [letter 651] and the sketch for LAZARUS [letter 632]. Both are literally separate from the written text, as earlier on. The Lazarus sketch is on the reverse side of the letter, while 'le jardin de Daubigny' forms a heading.

The superb dramatic sketch for the *Lazarus* is related to the text in which Vincent writes of his illness only as a literary symbol. The shape of the word is suspiciously regular, as in 'le jardin', where the drawing is not penetrated by the writing, whose pace is now tempered. The driving force is still exclusively confined to a succession of small curves which act like shorthand to translate the objects of a spatial world. With this, Vincent's own words die out and the words of other men about him begin.

NOTES

1. Jaspers, Karl, *Strindberg una Van Gogh, arbeiten zur angewandten Psychiatrie*, Berlin 1923
2. Du Quesne-Van Gogh, E. H., *Vincent van Gogh. Persoonlijke Herinneringen*, Baarn 1910; *Persönliche Erinnerungen an Vincent van Gogh*, Piper & Co., Munich 1911
3. Tralbaut, M. E., *Van Goghiana* I, Antwerp 1963 [p 28: 'André Bonger, l'ami des frères van Gogh']
4. Cerkez, Th. Dan., 'Report on Alphonse van Bever's lecture,' *Ecrits pour l'art, littéraires et philosophiques*, p 109, éditions Henri Jouve, 1905
5. Isaäcson, J. J., *Een nieuw standpunt in Kunst – Vincent van Gogh en D. B. Nanninga* [A new standpoint in Art – Vincent van Gogh and D. B. Nanninga], Amsterdam 1906
6. Eeden, Frederik, van, *De Nieuwe Gids*, p 263 et seq, 1 December 1890
7. Hofmannsthal, Hugo von, *Aus den Briefen des Zurück-gekehrten*, 'Die Farben', pp 206-219, Fischer Verlag, Berlin 1917
8. Bernard, Emile, *Les hommes d'aujourd'hui*, nr 390, Volume 8, Paris 1891
9. Bernard, Emile, *Vincent van Gogh. Lettres à Emile Bernard*, Vollard, Paris 1911. Reprint: Editions de la Nouvelle Revue, Brussels 1942 [with new introduction]
10. Mirbeau, Octave, *L'Echo de Paris – journal littéraire et politique du matin*, Bibliothèque Nationale, Paris, 31 Mars 1891. Reprint: Mirbeau – Des artistes, Paris 1922
11. Apollinaire, Guillaume, *Chroniques d'art*, p 259, Gallimard, Paris 1912
12. *Alphons Diepenbrock – brieven en documenten (bewerking Eduard Reeser)* [Letters of Diepenbrock], Volume 1, pp 366 and 422, The Hague 1962
13. Meier-Graefe, Julius, *Vincent*, Munich 1925
14. Edschmid, Kasimir, *Lebendiger Expressionismus*, p 20, Munich-Vienna-Basle 1964
15. Fechter, Paul, *Der Expressionismus*, p 8, Munich 1914
16. Jakob, Heinrich Eduard, *Expressionismus – Aufzeichnungen und Erinnerungen der Zeitgenossen*, p 15 Paul Raabe [ed], Walter Verlag, Olten and Freiburg im Breisgau 1965
17. Blass, Ernst, *Expressionismus* [op cit], p 38
18. Fleischner, O.S., 'Rilke und van Gogh', *The Germanic Review*, nr 20, pp 94-104, 1945
19. Rilke, Rainer Maria, *Briefe*, Letter 81, p 192-2, Insel Verlag, Wiesbaden, 17 October 1907. Reprint 1966
20. Rilke, Rainer Maria, *Brieven over Cézanne* [Letters about Cézanne], [note p 93 letter XXII], with an introduction by J. G. van Gelder, Stols, The Hague 1945
21. *De Hidde Nijland Collection, 40 reproductions after drawings and paintings*, W. G. Versluys, Amsterdam [without date]
22. Rilke, Rainer Maria, *Briefe*. Letter 64 to Clara Rilke, [op cit] p 163, Insel Verlag, Wiesbaden 1966
23. Letter 85 [op cit] p 199, Insel Verlag, Wiesbaden 1966
24. Letter 86 [op cit] 21 October 1907, p 201, Insel Verlag, Wiesbaden 1966. Letters [op cit] p 203, Insel Verlag, Wiesbaden 1966
25. *Tagebücher von Klee*, p 234, Cologne 1957
26. Denis, Maurice, *Théories*, 1890-1910, 3rd edition, pp 189 and 260-261, Paris 1913
27. Malewich, K.S., *Essays on Art*, 1915-1928, Volume 1, pp 109-112, essay 15 July 1919; Borgen-Copenhagen 1968
28. Boccioni, *Pittura Scultura Futuriste*, p 100, Milan 1914
29. Bremmer, H. P., *Vincent van Gogh, Inleidende Beschouwingen* [Introductory Essay], W. Versluys, Amsterdam 1911
30. Verwey, Albert, *Proza*, Volume IX, p 47, Amsterdam 1923. [Reprint of previous discussion]
31. Plasschaert, Albert [ed], *Kritiek van Beeldende Kunsten en Kunstnijverheid* [Critiques of the Arts and Crafts], 2nd volume 1905
32. Plasschaert, Albert, XIXe eeuwse Hollandse Schilderkunst [19th Century Dutch Painting], p 81, Wereldbibliotheek, Amsterdam [no date]
33. Visser, Herman F. E., 'Over de Literatuur over Van Gogh' [Concerning the Literature on Van Gogh], *De Beweging* [The Movement], edited by Albert Verwey, nr 1-2, 1917
34. Faille, Editions van Oest, Paris and Brussels 1928 [See bibliography Van Gogh]
35. Vanbeselaere, Walther, *De Hollandsche periode (1880-1885) in het werk van Vincent van Gogh* [The Dutch Period [1880-1885] in van Gogh's Work], De Sikkel, Antwerp 1937
36. Scherjon, W. and Gruyter, W. Jos de, *Vincent Van Gogh's Great Period (Arles-Auvers)*, Amsterdam 1937
37. Zervos, Christian, *Histoire de l'Art Contemporain*, p 87, Paris 1938
38. Magritte, René, 'Van Gogh et la Liberté', *Cahier de Nevelvlek – van Gogh*, May-June, Antwerp 1955 issue
39. George, Waldemar, *La revue mondiale*, pp 383-389, Paris 1927
40. Duthuit, Georges, *L'Amour de l'art*, VIII, 8 August 1927
41. Doiteau, Victor et Leroy, Edgar, *La Folie de Van Gogh*, Paris 1928
42. Westerman Holstijn, A.J., *Die psychologische Entwicklung van Gogh's Imago*, Volume 10, nr 4, 1924
43. Hutter, A., 'De Vijf Diagnoses van de ziekte van Vincent van Gogh' [The Five Diagnoses of Vincent van Gogh's Illness], *Het Nederlandsche Tijdschrift voor Geneeskunde* [Netherlands Medical Journal], 14 February 1931
44. Meerloo, J. A. M., *Creativity and Eternization*, Assen 1967
45. Kraus, G., *Symposium* issue, Reports nr 5 and 6, Municipal [Gemeente] Museum, The Hague 1953. Also *Lecture* of 25 October 1953, published jointly by the Kröller-Müller Foundation and J. M. Meulenhoff, Amsterdam
46. Minkowska, F., *Van Gogh, sa vie, sa maladie et son oeuvre*, Paris 1963
47. Mauron, Charles, *Vincent et Théo van Gogh, une symbiose*, Amsterdam 1953
48. Mauron, Charles, 'Notes sur la structure de l'inconscient chez Vincent van Gogh,' *Psyche*, nr 75-78, Paris 1953
49. Mauron, Charles, *Arles: Van Gogh au seuil de la Provence*, Saint Rémy de Provence 1959
50. Hahn, Otto, *Portrait d'Antonin Artaud*, Paris
51. Antonin Artaud, Van Gogh, *le suicédé de la Société*, u-éditeurs, Paris 1947
52. Meier-Graefe, Julius, *Der Roman eines Gottsuchers*, Vienna 1932
53. Stone, Irving, *Lust for Life, the novel of Vincent van Gogh*, London 1935
54. Miller, Henry, *Plexus*, pp 83-89, The Grove Press, New York 1965 [French edition, Paris 1952]
55. Novotny, Fritz, *Über das Elementare in der Kunstgeschichte und andere Aufsätze*, p 46, Vienna 1968
56. Elgar, Frank, *Van Gogh*, Fernand Hazan, Paris 1958; English version translated by James Cleugh, Thames and Hudson, London 1958; Revised edition, 1966
57. Badt, Kurt, *Die Farbenlehre van Goghs*, Cologne 1961
58. Stellingwerff, J., *Werkelijkheid en grondmotief bij Vincent Willem van Gogh*, [Reality and basic subject matter in V. W. van Gogh], Amsterdam 1959
59. Bonicatti, Maurizion, *Appunti sull'arte moderna ca 1870-1900*, Mario Bulzoni, Rome 1965
60. Graetz, H. R., *The Symbolic Language of Vincent van Gogh*, London 1963
61. Francastel, Pierre, *Nouveau dessin, nouvelle peinture*, pp 77-87, 100-2, Paris 1946
62. Bachelard, Gaston, *La poétique de l'espace*, pp 208 et seq, Paris 1958

Dr Jacob Baart de la Faille 1886-1959

At the University of Utrecht, J. B. de la Faille majored in Law and not in Art History. But his affinity to the world of art became clear when he included the following contention among the propositions required to accompany a Doctor's thesis in the Netherlands: 'It would be advisable if artists who exhibit portraits of persons without their consent were to be liable to punishment by law.'

After he completed his studies at the university, this early interest in the world of art became the predominant activity of his entire life. Even as a university student, he had, as actor, been an active member of the Utrecht Student Drama Troupe, and later maintained an advisory position to this group.

He oriented himself in the contemporary art of the time and, instead of becoming an active member of the Bar, he wrote articles in newspapers and magazines in the Netherlands and abroad, about art as well as about ethnographic and ethnological topics. At intervals, he also published works of fiction. He delivered lectures, in Europe and later in the United States as well, organized art exhibitions, and learned a great deal during a period of employment at the firm formerly renowned for its art auctions, Frederik Muller in Amsterdam. He took courses given by the well-known van Gogh expert, H. P. Bremmer. It is almost certain that an essay written by Herman F. E. Visser, which appeared in *De Beweging* in 1917, influenced him to take the bold initiative of drawing up a descriptive catalogue of all the work of Vincent van Gogh, which had hitherto never been systematically dealt with. H. P. Bremmer advised him on the project. It took eleven years before the work was ready for publication, in four volumes, at van Oest in Brussels in 1928. Considering the limited facilities and information available at the time, it can not be said that the project was not completed quickly. Certainly not when one considers the fact that the editing alone of his final revised manuscript took a group of experts more than eight years.

Ever since the publication of the van Gogh catalogue, of which the section on paintings was reprinted in 1939 by Hyperion in Paris, the hardly enviable role of van Gogh expert and author of the first classified description of his work has been ascribed to de la Faille, and as such he has often been disputed and criticized.

His judgment has often been called upon in falsification affairs, and sometimes disputed, in which case he never hesitated to humbly admit his mistakes and do justice to his adversaries.

His love for van Gogh was accompanied by a warm respect for French culture and the French spirit, which he expressed in deeds as well as words (chairman of the Verdun Committee, which presented Rodin's La Défense as Dutch homage in 1920).

Those who knew him remember him as an emotional, versatile author whose prolificacy in his field did not prevent him from being a passionate traveller as well. A man who, in addition to his mobility, possessed the qualities of endurance and perseverance so instrumental in the extensive task of drawing up a van Gogh catalogue.

Catalogue Paintings

INSTRUCTIONS FOR USE OF THE CATALOGUE

This edition in one volume follows a different system than the 1928 edition, which consisted of four volumes: two of text and two of plates [divided into paintings and drawings]. Illustrations and text are now in one volume, eliminating the need for descriptions, and the illustrations of paintings and drawings are also united in one volume.

NUMBERING

The numbers of the 1928 edition, preceded by the letter F, are in general use in the van Gogh literature. Van Gogh's paintings, though, have another 'Faille-number' in addition: their catalogue number in the 1939 Hyperion edition. These are preceded by an H. The drawings were not included in the 1939 edition, so that they have only F numbers. In publications from 1939 on it was always necessary to make it clear whether F or H numbers were being used, and the reader had to refer to the concordance in the 1939 edition to find the equivalent number in the other edition.

The problem involved in the third edition, this time including the drawings, is once again the numbering; since so many illustrations have been rearranged in order to obtain a better chronological order, the advantage of the numerical sequence was on the verge of disappearing. The obvious solution was to adopt a new numbering system, for the third time, but it was thought advisable to avoid the complications which this would lead to with respect to the international study of van Gogh and the process of drawing up new catalogues.

Dr J. B. de la Faille himself advocated a return to the original numbering system of 1928, but a method had to be found to deal with the inconsistencies caused by the rearrangement of the works.

The editors decided to meet with this problem by means of a system of references, eliminating the need for a concordance of F and H numbers. At the top of each page, the period and number are repeated, to facilitate finding specific works. De la Faille's original system of having the numbering of the drawings immediately follow that of the paintings has been left unchanged.

LITERATURE

References are restricted to works or studies in which the results were published of research having to do with factual data or the problems of dating and authenticity. Personal opinions and interpretations are not included, except in cases where they have led to factual conclusions. Variations in dating or repudiations of authenticity are mentioned in an EDITORS' COMMENT or under the heading LITERATURE, which also includes the original source of the dating adopted by the editors if it differs from that in de la Faille's manuscript.

PROVENANCE

These have been corrected and modified as accurately as possible. The name of the last known owner is to be found in the captions next to the illustrations.

In order to save space in the catalogue the full information has been moved to a separate section, EXHIBITIONS AND PROVENANCE.

EXHIBITIONS

Exhibitions, sometimes extremely extensive, are solely referred to in the section EXHIBITIONS AND PROVENANCE

DISSENTING VIEWS

Works that are now dated to another period than in the 1928 and 1939 editions are placed at the end of their *new* period, under the heading REDATED. In his manuscript for the present edition de la Faille added many works which first came to his attention since the appearance of the previous editions. He inserted these works between the existing catalogue numbers of the 1928 edition, giving them an F number followed by the word 'bis.' Since he sometimes added more than one work between two F numbers, the editors have replaced the work 'bis' with a, b, c, d and so on. Paintings and drawings which did not come to light until after the death of de la Faille and which the editors consider eligible to be included in the catalogue, are treated in a supplement. De la Faille left out of his manuscript for the present edition a number of works for which he had written certificates of authenticity in the past. Unless the editors had positive evidence that a particular piece was left out inadvertently, they considered the manuscript as de la Faille's last opinion.

ABBREVIATIONS

F precedes catalogue numbers of the 1928 edition and the present edition

H precedes catalogue numbers of the 1939 edition

Faille 1928: J. B. de la Faille, L'Oeuvre de Vincent van Gogh, Catalogue raisonné, Paris and Brussels 1928 [4 volumes]

Faille 1939: J. B. de la Faille, Vincent van Gogh, Paris 1939

Vanbeselaere 1937: W. Vanbeselaere, De hollandsche periode in het werk van Vincent van Gogh, Antwerp 1937

Scherjon and de Gruyter 1937: W. Scherjon and Jos de Gruyter, Vincent van Gogh's great period, Amsterdam 1937

SP: Supplementary Paintings

SD: Supplementary Drawings

LETTERS: The complete letters of Vincent van Gogh, Greenwich, Connecticut [3 volumes]. All references to the correspondence of van Gogh are given in the translation of this edition, unless otherwise indicated.

B: letters to Bernard

R: letters to van Rappard

T: letters from Theo van Gogh to Vincent

W: letters to Wilhelmina, Vincent's sister

Chetham: Ch. Scott Chetham, The role of Vincent van Gogh's copies in the development of his art, Cambridge, Massachusetts 1960 [thesis]

Tralbaut Antwerp 1948: M. E. Tralbaut, Vincent van Gogh in zijn Antwerpsche Periode, Amsterdam 1948

Tralbaut Drenthe 1959: M. E. Tralbaut, Vincent van Gogh in Drenthe, Assen 1959

Measurements are given first in centimeters, then [in brackets] in inches.

F 1

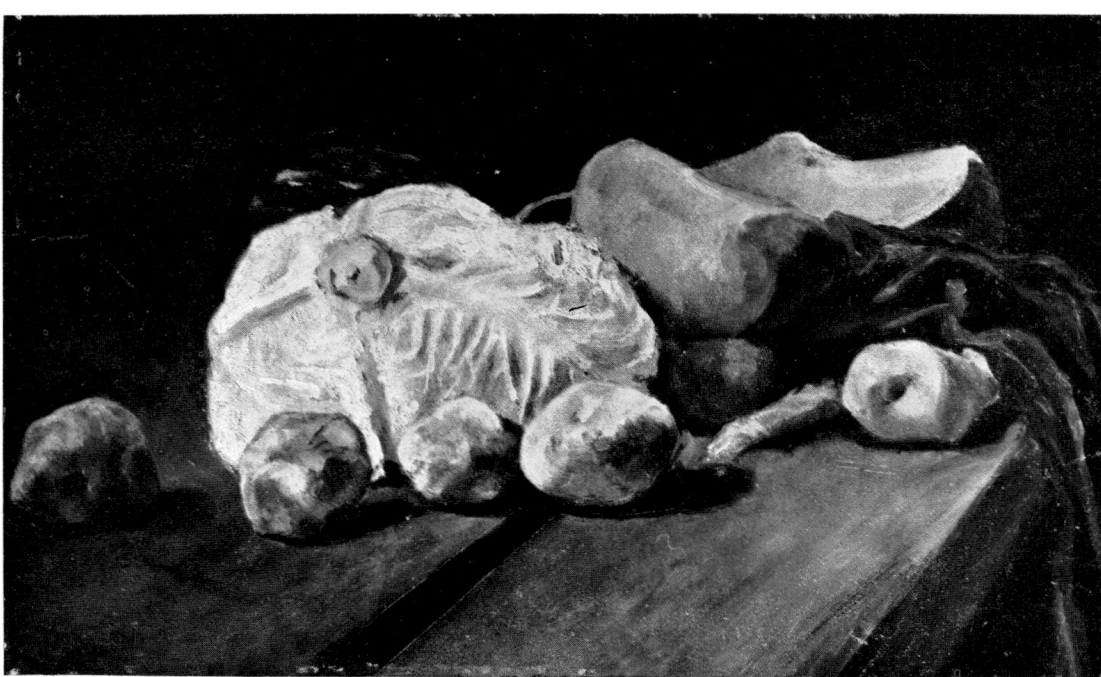

F 1a

F 1b

F 1c

F 3

ETTEN PERIOD

F 1 [H 2] STILL LIFE WITH CABBAGE

Paper on panel 34.5 × 55 [13½ × 21¾]
Compare sketch in letter 163 [reproduced only in
the Dutch editions of the letters]
The Hague [Etten period] December 1881
LETTER 163 [about 18 December] '*I still go to
Mauve's every day ... I have now painted five
studies ... The painted studies are still life ... These
are the subjects of two painted studies: ...and a white
cabbage with potatoes, etc.*'
LITERATURE R. Jacobsen, Onze Kunst 1903,
part 1, p 115. H. P. Bremmer, Moderne Kunstwerken 1903, nr 27. Not in Vanbeselaere 1937
COLLECTION Amsterdam, Rijksmuseum Vincent
van Gogh [Vincent van Gogh Foundation, inv
nr F 1]

F 1a [formerly F 1bis; H 1] STILL LIFE WITH BEER MUG AND FRUIT

Canvas 44.5 × 57.5 [17½ × 22¾]
The Hague [Etten period] December 1881
LETTER 163 [about 18 December] See F 1
LITERATURE Not in Faille 1928 or Vanbeselaere
1937
COLLECTION Wuppertal, Germany, Von der
Heydt-Museum der Stadt Wuppertal [acquired
1964; E. Baron von der Heydt bequest]

THE HAGUE PERIOD

F 1b LYING COW

Canvas 30 × 50 [11¾ × 19¾]
The Hague 1882
LITERATURE Not in Faille 1928, Vanbeselaere
1937 or Faille 1939
COLLECTION The Hague, A. Brandsma

F 1c LYING COW

Canvas 19 × 47.5 [7½ × 18¾]
Signed in lower left, under the hoof: Vincent
The Hague 1882
LITERATURE Not in Faille 1928, Vanbeselaere
1937 or Faille 1939
COLLECTION Sale New York [Parke-Bernet]
11 November 1959, nr 41
Present owner unknown

F 2 [H 7] BEACH AT SCHEVENINGEN IN CALM WEATHER

Paper on panel 35.5 × 49.5 [14 × 19½]
Compare sketch in letter 224
The Hague August 1882
LETTERS 224 [between 8 and 12 August] '*...and this
morning I marched to the beach and have just
returned from there with a rather large-sized painted
study of sand, sea and sky, a few fishing smacks, and
two men on the beach.*'
R 11 [13 August] '*Sunday evening ... Further, I have
a small marine ...*' [This quotation refers either to
F 2 or F 4]
LITERATURE R. Jacobsen, Onze Kunst 1903, part
1, p 116. H. P. Bremmer, Moderne Kunstwerken
1903, nr 30. Vanbeselaere 1937, pp 111, 153, 413
COLLECTION Aalst, Netherlands, Mrs H. van
Ogtrop-van Kempen [acquired 1929]

F 2a [formerly F 2bis; H 5] THE DUNE

Panel 36 × 58.5 [14¼ × 23]
The Hague August 1882
LETTERS R 11 [13 August] '*Sunday evening ..
Further I have ...patches of dune soil...*'
225 [14 August] '*Then I have painted a huge mass of*

F 2

dune ground – thickly painted and sticky.'
LITERATURE Vanbeselaere 1937, pp 111, 154, 413
COLLECTION Amsterdam, Private Collection

F 3 [H 4] DUNES, WITH FIGURES

Canvas on panel 24 × 32 [9½ × 12½]
Signed in lower right: Vincent
The Hague August 1882
LITERATURE Vanbeselaere 1937, pp 111, 413
COLLECTION Bern, H. R. Hahnloser

F 2a

F 4

F 7

F 5

F 6

F 4 [H 8] BEACH AT SCHEVENINGEN IN STORMY WEATHER

Canvas on pasteboard 34.5 × 51 [13½ × 20]
The Hague August 1882
LETTERS R 11 [13 August] See F 2
226 [19 August] '*Saturday evening … All during the week we have had a great deal of wind, storm and rain, and I went to Scheveningen several times to see it. I brought two small marines home from there …*'
LITERATURE De Kroniek 3 January 1903, pp 19-20. R. Jacobsen, Onze Kunst 1903, part 1, p 116. H. P. Bremmer, Moderne Kunstwerken 1903, nr 31. Vanbeselaere 1937, pp 111, 155, 413
COLLECTION Amsterdam, Stedelijk Museum [on loan from Miss E. Ribbius Peletier, Scheveningen]
Colorplate, p 57

F 5 [H 6] FISHERMAN ON THE BEACH

Canvas on panel 51 × 33.5 [20 × 13¼]
Compare companion piece F 6
The Hague August 1883
LITERATURE R. Jacobsen, Onze Kunst 1903, part 1, p 115. Vanbeselaere 1937, pp 112, 223-5, 413: August 1883; letters 308, 309
COLLECTION Otterlo, Rijksmuseum Kröller-Müller, inv nr 190-20, cat van Gogh 1970, nr 98

F 6 [H 3] FISHERMAN'S WIFE ON THE BEACH

Canvas on panel 52 × 34 [20½ × 13½]
Compare companion piece F 5
The Hague August 1883
LITERATURE R. Jacobsen, Onze Kunst 1903, part 1, p 115. Vanbeselaere 1937, pp 111, 223-4, 413: August 1883; letters 291, 308
COLLECTION Otterlo, Rijksmuseum Kröller-Müller, inv nr 191-20, cat van Gogh 1970, nr 97

F 7 [H 11] MENDING THE NETS

Paper on panel 42 × 62.5 [16½ × 24½]
The Hague August 1882
LETTER 227 [20 August] '*Sunday afternoon … something I saw at Scheveningen, a flat stretch … The grass was comparatively very green and the black nets were spread over it in enormous circles, giving the soil deep reddish-black and greenish-gray tones. On this somber ground, women in white caps and men spreading or repairing the nets were sitting or standing, or walking around like dark fantastic ghosts … I made a study of it on a sheet of oiled torchon.*'
LITERATURE Vanbeselaere 1937, pp 111, 156-7, 413
COLLECTION The Hague, Gemeente Museum, inv nr 5-X-1961, cat 1966, nr 131 [on loan since 1957 from Mrs L. Schokking-Ribbius Peletier, Doorn]

F 8 [H 10] GIRL IN WHITE IN THE WOODS

Canvas 39 × 59 [15¼ × 23¼]
Compare sketch in letter 229
The Hague August 1882
LETTERS 227 [20 August] '*Sunday afternoon … The other study in the wood is of some large green beech trunks on a stretch of ground covered with dry sticks, and the figure of a girl in white …*'
229 [9 September] '*Enclosed is another scribble of the woods. I made a large study of it.*'
LITERATURE Vanbeselaere 1937, pp 85, 111, 156-7, 413: letter R 12
COLLECTION Otterlo, Rijksmuseum Kröller-Müller, inv nr 220-20, cat van Gogh 1970, nr 96

F 8

F 8a [formerly F 8bis; H 12] GIRL IN THE WOODS

Panel 35 × 47 [13¾ × 18½]
The Hague August 1882
LETTER 227 [20 August] '*Sunday afternoon … This week I have painted some rather large studies in the wood …*'
LITERATURE Vanbeselaere 1937, pp 111, 156, 413
COLLECTION Netherlands, Private Collection

F 9 [H 9] POTATO DIGGING

Canvas 39.5 × 94.5 [15½ × 37¼]
Compare sketch in letter 296 and drawing F 1034
The Hague August 1883
LETTERS 308 [about 2 August] '*Theo, I am enormously eager to paint the potato diggers … Well, I made a few studies for it already, but I haven't been able to take enough models …*'
310 [about 10 August] '*All the time I am planning a large picture of the potato diggers, though it might not be finished until next year …*'
311 [14 August] '*I am working on a sketch in oils for the potato diggers …*'
LITERATURE Vanbeselaere 1937, pp 112, 215-7, 413: August 1883; letters 310, 311
COLLECTION New York, Mr and Mrs Julian J. Raskin

F 10 [H 16] A WIND-BEATEN TREE

Canvas 35 × 47 [13¾ × 18½]
The Hague August 1883
LITERATURE Vanbeselaere 1937, pp 112, 413
COLLECTION Formerly Zurich, Neupert Art Gallery [before 1964]
Present owner unknown

F 9

F 8a

F 10

F 11

F 12

F 13

F 16

F 11 [H 14] THE SOWER [sketch]

Panel 19 × 27.5 [7½ × 10¾]
The Hague 1883
LITERATURE Vanbeselaere 1937, pp 283, 413:
Nuenen August 1884
EDITORS' COMMENT See F 41. The date seems
uncertain.
COLLECTION Formerly Paris, E. Alexander
Present owner unknown

F 12 [H 13] MAN AT WORK

Paper on panel 31 × 29.5 [12¼ × 11½]
The Hague 1883
LITERATURE Vanbeselaere 1937, pp 112, 413:
August 1883. Not in Tralbaut Drenthe 1959
EDITORS' COMMENT The period seems uncertain,
and could have been Drenthe.
COLLECTION England, Private Collection

F 13 [H 18] A COACH STAND

Canvas on panel 42 × 53 [16½ × 20¾]
Signed in lower right: Vincent
The Hague 1883
LITERATURE Vanbeselaere 1937, pp 112, 210, 413:
August 1883
COLLECTION Winterthur, Switzerland, Mrs
L. Jäggli-Hahnloser

F 14 [H 19] THE GREEN PARROT
Nuenen period; see after F 203a

F 15 [H 15] COWS IN THE MEADOW

Canvas on panel 31.5 × 44 [12½ × 17¼]
The Hague 1883
LITERATURE Vanbeselaere 1937, pp 112, 413:
August 1883
COLLECTION Formerly Delft, H. Tutein Noltithenius
[until ca 1940]
Present owner unknown

F 15a [formerly F 15bis; H 17] IN THE DUNES

Panel 33.5 × 48.5 [13¼ × 19]
The Hague 1883
LITERATURE Vanbeselaere 1937, pp 112, 238, 413:
Drenthe September 1883. Tralbaut Drenthe 1959,
cat nr 6, chron nr 3, p 223: Drenthe September 1883
COLLECTION New York, Hirschl and Adler Art
Gallery

REDATED TO THE HAGUE

F 16 [H 21] OLD FARMS IN LOOSDUINEN AT
TWILIGHT

Canvas on panel 33 × 50 [13 × 19¾]
The Hague September 1883
LETTER 321 [about 7 or 8 September] 'I have found
beautiful things in Loosduinen – old farms – and in the
evening there are some splendid effects there.'
LITERATURE Faille 1928, nr 16: Drenthe October
1883; letter 330. Vanbeselaere 1937, pp 112, 228,
414: The Hague September 1883; letter 321. Faille
1939, nr 21: follows Vanbeselaere
COLLECTION Utrecht, Museum van Baaren
Foundation, inv nr 37

F 186 [H 20] BULB FIELDS

Canvas on pasteboard 48 × 65 [19 × 25½]
The Hague April 1883
LITERATURE Faille 1928, nr 186: Nuenen.
Vanbeselaere 1937, pp 282, 416: Nuenen May 1884
[p 282] and May 1885 [p 416: probably a misprint].
Faille 1939, nr 20: The Hague 1883
COLLECTION Upperville, Virginia, Mr and Mrs
Paul Mellon

F 15

F 15a

F 186

F 204

F 192

F 189 [H 206] FOOTBRIDGE ACROSS A DITCH

Canvas on panel 46×34 [18×13½]
The Hague August-September 1883
LITERATURE Faille 1928, nr 89: Nuenen.
Vanbeselaere 1937, pp 305, 400, 416: Nuenen
October-November 1885. Faille 1939, nr 206:
Nuenen 1885
EDITORS' COMMENT Dated to The Hague on
stylistic grounds
COLLECTION Chagrin Falls, Ohio, Mrs Gordon
Stouffer

F 192 [H 200] EDGE OF A WOOD

Canvas on panel 34.5×49 [13½×19¼]
The Hague September 1882
LITERATURE Faille 1928, nr 192: Nuenen.
Vanbeselaere 1937, pp 111, 416: The Hague. Faille
1939, nr 200: The Hague September 1882. Cat van
Gogh 1959, Rijksmuseum Kröller-Müller, nr 95:
autumn 1882; same motif as drawing F 903 of
Etten; same period as F 8
EDITORS' COMMENT F 192 is close in style to
F 8a of August
COLLECTION Otterlo, Rijksmuseum Kröller-
Müller, inv nr 223-09, cat van Gogh 1970, nr 95

F 204 [H 228] CLUSTER OF OLD HOUSES
WITH THE NEW CHURCH IN THE HAGUE

Canvas on pasteboard 35×25 [13¾×9¾]
Compare SD 1680 [nearby site]
The Hague probably first half of 1882
LITERATURE R. Jacobsen, Onze Kunst 1903,
part 2, p 60. A. Plasschaert, Onze Kunst 1904, part
2, p 152. Faille 1928, nr 204: Antwerp December
1885; letter 438. Faille 1939, nr 228: the same.
Tralbaut Antwerp 1948, pp 188-91, 283, nr 2:
identifies the church, unconvincingly, as the
Willebrordus Church in Antwerp and therefore
dates this painting to the Antwerp period, late
November-early December 1885; letter 438
EDITOR'S COMMENT Jacobsen had already
pointed out that the church depicted is probably
the New Church in The Hague.
COLLECTION Sale New York [Parke-Bernet]
20 November 1968, nr 59
Present owner unknown

DRENTHE PERIOD

F 16 OLD FARMS IN LOOSDUINEN AT
TWILIGHT
The Hague period; see after F 15a

F 17 [H 25] FARMHOUSES

Canvas on pasteboard 36×55.5 [14¼×21¾]
Drenthe September 1883
LETTER 330 [6 October] '... Before I left Hoogeveen,
I painted a few studies there, including one of a large
mossy-roofed farm.' [See also F 18]
LITERATURE Vanbeselaere 1937, pp 238, 414:
September 1883, letter 330. Tralbaut Drenthe 1959,
cat nr 7, p 210, chron nr 9, p 223: September 1883
COLLECTION Amsterdam, Rijksmuseum Vincent
van Gogh [Vincent van Gogh Foundation, inv
nr F 17]

F 18 [H 22] THE FARMHOUSE

Canvas on panel 29×39 [11½×15¼]
Drenthe September 1883
LETTER 330 [6 October] See F 17
LITERATURE Vanbeselaere 1937, pp 238, 243, 414:
September 1883; letter 330. Tralbaut Drenthe 1959,
cat nr 1, p 206, chron nr 10, p 223: 6 October 1883;
letter 330
COLLECTION Zurich, F. Meyer-Fierz

F 19 [H 23] TWO WOMEN DIGGING, AND A
WHEELBARROW

Canvas 27 × 35.5 [10¾ × 13¾]
Compare sketch in letter 331 [similar composition]
Drenthe October 1883
LETTER 331 [9 October] *'Here follows a scribble of
the peat fields ... I hope to make something of the
women on the moor on the scribble of the reverse
side, and I am going to the same field again ...'*
LITERATURE R. Jacobsen, Onze Kunst 1903,
part 1, pp 114-6. Vanbeselaere 1937, pp 238, 244,
397, 414: Drenthe September 1883; letter 331.
Tralbaut Drenthe 1959, cat nr 2, p 206, chron nr 19,
p 223: 9 October 1883; letter 331. Van Dantzig
1952, plate 9, pp 67-71
COLLECTION Amsterdam, Rijksmuseum Vincent
van Gogh [Vincent van Gogh Foundation, inv
nr F 19]

F 20 [H 24] PEASANT BURNING WEEDS

Panel 30.5 × 39.5 [12 × 15½]
Compare sketch in letter 335
Drenthe October 1883
LETTER 335 [31 October] *'These are two evening
effects; I am still working on that weed burner. The
oil sketch is better in tone than what I'd done before,
so that it renders more strongly the immensity of the
plain and the gathering twilight, the fire with a bit of
smoke being the only spot of light. I went again and
again to look at it in the evening ...'*
LITERATURE Vanbeselaere 1937, pp 238, 248, 414.
Tralbaut Drenthe 1959, cat nr 4, p 208, chron nr 29,
p 224: 31 October 1883; letter 335
COLLECTION Almelo, Netherlands, T. Bendien
[acquired 1941]

F 18

F 189

F 17

F 19

F 20

F 22

F 188

F 26

F 24

F 21 [H 26] THE PEAT BOAT

Canvas on panel 37 × 55.5 [14½ × 22]
Compare sketch in letter 335
Drenthe October 1883
LETTER 335 [31 October] '...they were loading peat, but I am afraid the scribbles are absolutely indecipherable.'
LITERATURE Vanbeselaere 1937, pp 239, 248, 414. Tralbaut Drenthe 1959, cat nr 3, p 207, chron nr 27, p 224: 31 October 1883
COLLECTION Rockanje, Netherlands, R. W. van Hoey Smith

F 22 [H 28] THE HUT

Canvas on pasteboard 37.5 × 55.5 [14¾ × 21¾]
Compare sketch in letter 339
Drenthe November 1883
LETTER 339 [14 November] 'I will just make a scribble of the landscapes which I have on the easel... The one at the bottom is a tender green wheatfield in the foreground, and withering grasses; behind the cottage, two piles of peat, again a glimpse of the heath, and a very light sky.'
358 [between 25 February and about 9 March] 'Let me take the studies from Drenthe... I am speaking now of... the largest of the sod huts, that is to say the one with the green plot in the foreground.'
LITERATURE Vanbeselaere 1937, pp 239, 248, 414: letter 339. Tralbaut Drenthe 1959, cat nr 5, pp 208-9, chron nr 36, p 224: 14 November 1883; letter 339
COLLECTION Amsterdam, Rijksmuseum Vincent van Gogh [Vincent van Gogh Foundation, inv nr F 22]

F 23 [H 27] WOMAN WITH STALKS OF WHEAT

Left out by Faille in his manuscript for the present edition
See REJECTED WORKS

REDATED TO DRENTHE

F 188 [H 207] LANDSCAPE WITH A CHURCH AT TWILIGHT

Pasteboard on panel 35 × 52 [13¾ × 20½]
Drenthe October 1883
LITERATURE R. Jacobsen, Onze Kunst 1903, part I, p 115 [?]. Faille 1928, nr 188: Nuenen. Vanbeselaere 1937, pp 239, 416: Drenthe September-October 1883. Faille 1939, nr 207: Drenthe or Nuenen 1883. Tralbaut Drenthe 1959, cat nr 8, p 210, chron nr 17, p 223: October 1883
COLLECTION Rotterdam, Private Collection

NUENEN PERIOD

F 24 [H 31] WEAVER WITH A VIEW OF THE NUENEN TOWER THROUGH A WINDOW: PART OF THE LOOM, FACING RIGHT

Canvas on pasteboard 68.5 × 93 [27 × 36½]
Compare drawing F 1118 and water color F 1119 [same interior]
Nuenen July 1884
LETTER 372 [about 1 July] '...just now I am quite absorbed again in two new large studies of weavers' interiors... As to these two pictures of weavers, one shows a part of the loom with the figure and a small window.'
LITERATURE Vanbeselaere 1937, pp 281, 318, 321, 414: July 1884; letter 372
EDITORS' COMMENT There must have existed a fairly similar painting with a baby chair on the right [see drawings F 1118 and F 1119], described in letter 355 [about 24 January 1884]: 'I am painting a loom of old, greenish, browned oak... Near that loom, in front of a little window which looks out on a green

plot, there is a baby chair...'
COLLECTION Berlin, Theodor Werner

F 25 [H 29] COMING OUT OF CHURCH IN
NUENEN

Canvas 41 × 32 [16¼ × 12½]
Compare sketch in letter 355 and drawing F 1117
Nuenen January 1884
LETTER 355 [about 24 January] '...*The other day I
painted for her the little church with the hedge and
the trees, something like this...'*
LITERATURE Vanbeselaere 1937, pp 281, 414
COLLECTION Amsterdam, Rijksmuseum Vincent
van Gogh [Vincent van Gogh Foundation, inv
nr F 25]

F 26 [H 30] WEAVER: FIGURE APART

Canvas 48 × 46 [19 × 18]
Compare drawing F 1122
Nuenen January 1884
LETTER 355 [about 24 January] '...*The last study I
made is the figure of a man sitting at the loom, just
the figure, the bust and hands...'*
LITERATURE Vanbeselaere 1937, pp 280, 316, 318,
320, 351, 414
COLLECTION Bern, H. R. Hahnloser

F 25

F 21

F 27

F 29

F 27 [H 32] WEAVER: FACING FRONT

Canvas on panel 48 × 61 [19 × 24]
Nuenen July 1884
LETTERS 372 [about 1 July] See F 24
373 [before 4 August] '*When you come, you will also see some new weavers.*'
LITERATURE Vanbeselaere 1937, pp 281, 318, 320, 414: July 1884; letter 373
COLLECTION Rotterdam, Museum Boymans-van Beuningen [acquired 1930; A. P. van Hoey Smith bequest], inv nr 1237, cat 1963, p 48
Colorplate, p 58

F 28 [H 39] THE KINGFISHER

Paris period; see after F 388 verso

F 29 [H 34] WEAVER WITH LOOM AND SPINNING WHEEL

Canvas 61 × 85 [24 × 33½]
Compare water color F 1107
Nuenen March and April 1884
LETTERS 364 [about 1 April] '*Besides those, I have a few painted studies…The one is a large study of a weaver, weaving a piece of red cloth.*'
367 [about 1 May] '*…another one, which I began last winter – a loom in which a piece of red cloth is being woven; there the loom is seen from aside.*'
LITERATURE A. Plasschaert, Onze Kunst 1903, part 2, p 173. Vanbeselaere 1937, pp 280, 320, 414: April 1884; letter 364. T. N. Maytham, Bulletin Museum of Fine Arts, Boston 1961, pp 4-12, with reproductions of the painting during and after cleaning: started in winter and finished in May 1884; letter 367; drawings F 1107 and F 1123 are preliminary studies
COLLECTION Boston, Museum of Fine Arts [acquired 1958; Arthur Gordon Tompkins Residuary Fund], acc nr 58.356

F 30 [H 33] THE WEAVER: THE WHOLE LOOM, FACING FRONT

Canvas 70 × 85 [27½ × 33½]
Nuenen May 1884
LETTER 367 [about 1 May] '*…I am working on a rather large picture of a weaver, the loom seen from the front – the little figure a dark silhouette against the white wall.*'
LITERATURE A. Plasschaert, Onze Kunst 1903, part 2, p 174. Vanbeselaere 1937, pp 280, 317-8, 320, 351, 414: letters 367, 368. Cat van Gogh 1959, Rijksmuseum Kröller-Müller, nr 166: compares Vincent's attitude to the motif of F 30 and that of an unidentified drawing sent to van Rappard, described in letter R 44
COLLECTION Otterlo, Rijksmuseum Kröller-Müller, inv nr 247-20, cat van Gogh 1970, nr 166

F 31 [H 38] POLLARD BIRCHES

Canvas on panel 43 × 58 [17 × 22¾]
Nuenen May 1884
LETTER 367 [about 1 May] '*And a landscape with pollard birches.*'
LITERATURE Vanbeselaere 1937, pp 282, 414: April-May 1884
EDITORS' COMMENT In the various editions of Vincent's letters the trees are wrongly called 'beeches.' This has been changed into 'pollard birches.' These trees are very rare, but they can be found in the region around Nuenen. In the original letter the word can be read either as 'knotberken' [pollard birches] or 'knotbeuken' [pollard beeches].
COLLECTION Paris, Private Collection

F 31

F 30

F 32

F 33

F 35
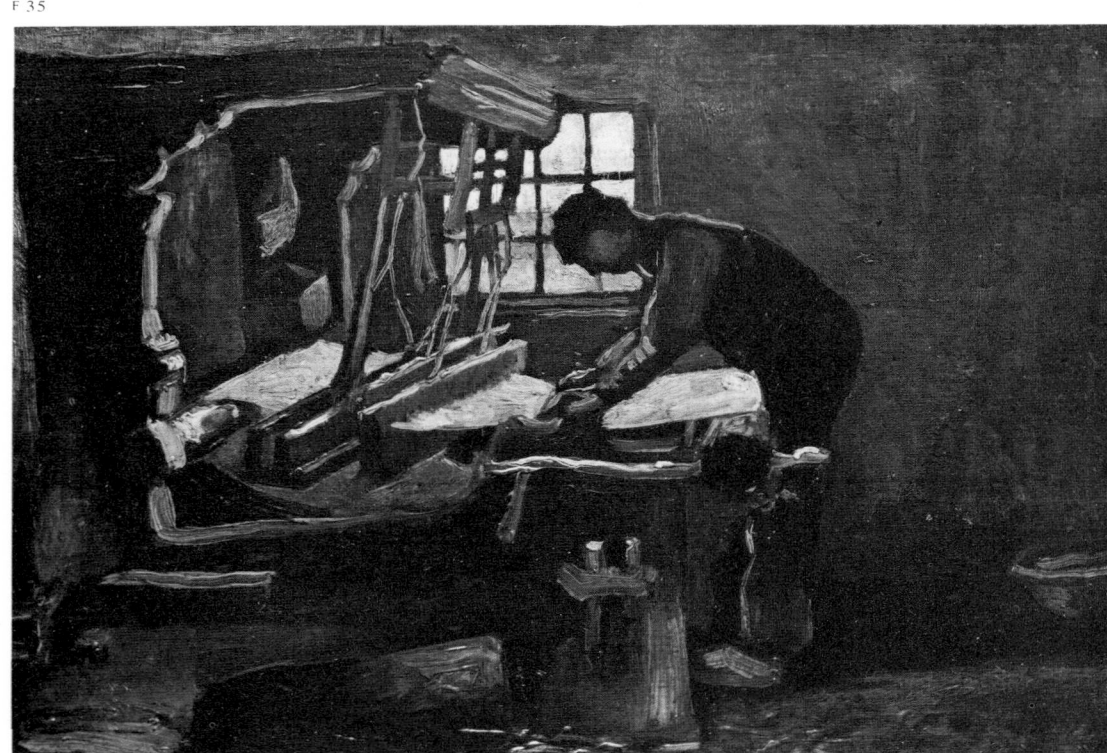

F 32 [H 36] WEAVER FACING LEFT STANDING

Panel 19.5 × 41 [7¾ × 16¼]
Compare F 35, drawing F 1134 and water color
SD 1688
Nuenen May 1884
LETTER 367 [about 1 May] '*Soon I hope to start on two others of weavers in which the figure comes quite differently, that is to say, the weaver is not sitting behind it, but is arranging the warp threads of the cloth.*'
LITERATURE Vanbeselaere 1937, pp 281, 317, 414: June 1884; letter 367
COLLECTION Munich, Karin Hielscher Art Gallery

F 33 [H 35] WEAVER STANDING: SEEN FROM THE BACK

Canvas on panel 55 × 79 [21¾ × 31]
Nuenen May 1884
LETTERS 367 [about 1 May] See F 32
369 [end May] '*I have just done a figure of a weaver standing in front of a loom, and one sees the machine behind him.*'
LITERATURE Vanbeselaere 1937, pp 281, 317, 414: June 1884; letter 367
COLLECTION London, Wildenstein Art Gallery

F 34 [H 37] THE OLD TOWER IN THE CEMETERY AT NUENEN, WITH A PLOWMAN

Canvas 34.5 × 42 [13½ × 16½]
Signed in lower left: Vincent
Nuenen second half of February 1884
LETTER 364 [about 1 April] '*Besides those, I have a few painted studies ... the little church in the wheat-fields ...*'
LITERATURE Vanbeselaere 1937, pp 281, 414: March 1884; letters 358, 364, R 40. S. Leurs and M. E. Tralbaut, Brabantia February 1957, pp 33-5: topographical history used for dating the different versions of this subject. Cat van Gogh 1959, Rijksmuseum Kröller-Müller, nr 192: February 1884; letters 358, R 40, 363a, 364
COLLECTION Otterlo, Rijksmuseum Kröller-Müller, inv nr 221-00, cat van Gogh 1970, nr 192

F 35 WEAVER FACING LEFT: WHOLE FIGURE

Canvas on panel 41 × 57 [16¼ × 22½]
Compare F 32, drawing F 1134 and water color
SD 1688
Nuenen April-May 1884
LETTER 367 [about 1 May] See F 32
LITERATURE Vanbeselaere 1937, pp 231, 317-8, 414: Nuenen June 1884; letter 369. Cat van Gogh 1966, Rijksmuseum Kröller-Muller, nr 165: April-May 1884; letter 367
COLLECTION Otterlo, Rijksmuseum Kröller-Muller, inv nr 228-12, cat van Gogh 1970, nr 165

F 36 [H 42] THE SPINNER

Canvas on pasteboard 41 × 32.5 [16¼ × 12¾]
Compare drawing F 1290a [same motif]
Nuenen 1885
LETTER 395 [1 March] '*Just now I paint not only as long as there is daylight, but even in the evening by the lamp in the cottages, when I can hardly distinguish anything on my palette, so as to catch, if possible, something of the curious effects of lamplight in the evening, with, for instance, a large shadow cast on the wall.*'
LITERATURE Vanbeselaere 1937, pp 294, 350-1, 354, 374, 414: March 1885; letter 395; close in style to THE POTATO EATERS [F 78 and F 82].

F 36

EDITORS' COMMENT Faille cites letter 395 on the authority of Vanbeselaere. This letter, however, does not refer to the present painting but – more likely – to F 365 recto. Close in style to THE POTATO EATERS.
COLLECTION Amsterdam, Rijksmuseum Vincent van Gogh [Vincent van Gogh Foundation, inv nr F 36]

F 37 [H 41] THE WEAVER: INTERIOR WITH THREE WINDOWS

Canvas 61 × 93 [24 × 36¾]
Compare water color F 1115
Nuenen last week of June 1884
LETTER 372 [about 1 July] '...*just now I am quite absorbed again in two new large studies of weavers' interiors...the other is an interior, with three small windows...*'
LITERATURE Vanbeselaere 1937, pp 281, 318, 320-1, 337, 414. Cat van Gogh 1959, Rijksmuseum Kröller-Müller, nr 164: many parallels with F 24, on which Vincent was working at the same time
COLLECTION Otterlo, Rijksmuseum Kröller-Müller, inv nr 234-20, cat van Gogh 1970, nr 164

F 34

F 37

F 38

F 39

F 40

F 43

F 38 [H 44] THE OX CART: RED AND WHITE OX

Canvas on panel 57 × 82.5 [22½ × 32½]
Nuenen July 1884
LETTER 373 [before 4 August] '*The last things I have done are two rather large studies of ox wagons, a black ox and a spotted red one.*'
LITERATURE Vanbeselaere 1937, pp 282, 323-4, 351, 414
COLLECTION Otterlo, Rijksmuseum Kröller-Müller, inv nr 229-18, cat van Gogh 1970, nr 182
Colorplate, p 75

F 39 [H 43] OX CART: SPOTTED BLACK OX

Canvas 60 × 80 [23½ × 31½]
Compare drawing F 1144
Nuenen July 1884
LETTER 373 [before 4 August] See F 38
LITERATURE De Kroniek 3 January 1903, pp 19-20. R. Jacobsen, Onze Kunst 1903, part 1, p 114. B.J. Stokvis 1926, p 8: the former owner Couvreur describes the painting from memory. Vanbeselaere 1937, pp 282, 323-4, 351, 414
COLLECTION USA, F. Julius Fohs

F 40 [H 47] THE OLD TOWER IN THE FIELDS

Canvas on pasteboard 35 × 47 [13¾ × 18½]
Nuenen early August 1884
LETTER 373 [before 4 August] '*I have also been working again on the old tower in the fields, in the evening, of which I made a larger study than the previous one, with the wheatfields around it.*'
LITERATURE R. Jacobsen, Onze Kunst 1903, part 2, p 60. Vanbeselaere 1937, pp 282, 347, 414: July 1884; close in style to F 70. S. Leurs and M.E. Tralbaut, Brabantia 1 February 1957, pp 35-8: May 1884; they reject letter 373 in favor of letter 368 as Vincent's description of the painting, since the dimensions of F 40 do not justify the designation 'larger study'
COLLECTION London, Brook Street Galleries

F 41 [H 46] POTATO PLANTING

Canvas 66 × 149 [26 × 58¾]
Compare drawing F 1141
Nuenen August 1884
LETTERS 374 [August] '*Last week I was in the fields every day during the wheat harvest, of which I made another composition. I made this for somebody in Eindhoven … There are six panels left on the longest wall, and for these I gave him preliminary sketches of a sower, a plower, shepherd, wheat harvest, potato digging, ox wagon in the snow.*'
R 47 [August] '*And, after a visit to my studio, I made six preliminary sketches for him of subjects from the country life – Sower, Plower, Wheat harvest, Potato planting, Shepherd, Winter scene with ox wagon. And now I am working on them.*'
R 48 [September] '*I very much enjoyed working on the six canvases I wrote you about … The subjects are: Potato planting, Ox Plow, Wheat Harvest, Sower, Shepherd (storm effect), Gatherers of dead wood (snow effect).*'
LITERATURE A. Plasschaert, Onze Kunst 1903, part 2, p 174. Vanbeselaere 1937, pp 283, 326, 414: painted study for a decoration by Hermans symbolizing the seasons. J. Leymarie, Van Gogh, 1951, pp 23, 28: probably inspired by a decoration made by Millet in 1864 of a dining room of a house in Paris, which portrayed the seasons as allegorical figures from mythology [A. Sensier, La Vie et l'Œuvre de J.F. Millet, Paris 1881, pp 286-7]. Cat van Gogh 1959, Rijksmuseum Kröller-Müller, nr 94: August-September 1884; letters 377, R 49
EDITORS' COMMENT The painting belongs to a series executed for the Eindhoven goldsmith Her-

mans. The other paintings in the series for Hermans
still in existence are F 42, F 43, F 172, S P 1669 and,
according to Vanbeselaere, F 11 [this is uncertain].
COLLECTION Otterlo, Rijksmuseum Kröller-
Müller, inv nr 233-20, cat van Gogh 1970, nr 94

F 42 [H 48] SHEPHERD: STORM EFFECT

Canvas on pasteboard 67 × 126 [26¾ × 49¾]
Nuenen August 1884
LETTERS 374 [August], R 47 [August] and R 48
[September] See F 41
LITERATURE B. J. Stokvis 1926 [quoted in the
Dutch edition of the letters under nr 435d]:
D. Gestel recalls that the subject was completed by
Vincent in the course of a single morning.
Vanbeselaere 1937, pp 283, 326, 414: painted study
for a decoration by Hermans symbolizing the
seasons
EDITORS' COMMENT See F 41
COLLECTION Sale London [Sotheby] 24 April
1968, nr 77
Present owner unknown

F 43 [H 45] WOOD GATHERERS IN THE SNOW

Canvas on panel 67 × 126 [26½ × 49½]
Compare drawings F 1081 and SD 1689 [partly the
same motif]
Nuenen September 1884
LETTER 377 [September] 'Last week I made a sketch
for the last of the six pictures for Hermans: wood
gatherers in the snow, so he has all six of them to
copy...'
LITERATURE Vanbeselaere 1937, pp 283, 326, 414:
painted study for a decoration by Hermans
symbolizing the seasons
EDITORS' COMMENT See F 41
COLLECTION Doorn, Netherlands, Mrs L. Schokking-Ribbius Peletier

F 44 [H 49] AUTUMN LANDSCAPE WITH FOUR TREES

Canvas 64 × 89 [25¼ × 35]
Compare drawing F 1129 [same trees]
Nuenen November 1885
LETTER 431 [November] 'You know those three
pollard oaks behind the garden at home; I have
plodded on them for the fourth time... But as he had a
fancy for it, I gave it to him, and he accepted it just as
I had intended, without many words...'
LITERATURE A. Kerssemakers, De Amsterdammer 14 and 21 April 1912 [reprinted in the
recent editions of Vincent's letters under nr 435c]:
'Before he set off he visited me once more to say
good-by, and as a souvenir he brought me a
beautiful autumn study, not yet entirely dry,
finished completely in the open air, and measuring
1 meter by 80 centimeters and took away with him
a little canvas as a souvenir in return. This autumn
picture is still in my possession; it is painted in a
very light range of colors, and the subject is very
simple.' Vanbeselaere 1937, pp 305, 384, 400, 414:
November 1885; letter 431
COLLECTION Otterlo, Rijksmuseum Kröller-
Müller, inv nr 1334-56, cat van Gogh 1970, nr 256

F 41

F 42

F 44

F 45

F 46

F 48

F 49

F 45 [H 50] LANE OF POPLARS NEAR NUENEN

Canvas 78 × 97.5 [30¾ × 38½]
Signed in lower left: Vincent
Compare sketch in letter 434 [erroneously
reproduced with letter 383 in the first Dutch edition
of Vincent's letters and with 384 in subsequent
Dutch and English editions; same view]
Nuenen autumn 1885, retouched in Paris 1886
LETTERS 430 [4 November] '*Shortly you will receive
two studies of the autumn leaves, one in yellow–
poplars…*'
434 [mid-November] '*Of course I shall take a few
pictures with me* [to Antwerp] *…and a view of the
village behind a row of poplars with yellow leaves…
The one landscape I am taking with me, and if
possible both, but the one with the yellow leaves… I
am enclosing a hasty scribble of it.*'
LITERATURE Vanbeselaere 1937, pp 283, 328, 414:
October 1884, retouched in Paris. M. E. Tralbaut,
exhib cat van Gogh Essen 1957, nr 176: letter 383
gives only a sketch and no description of this
painting. W. J. de Gruyter, Openbaar Kunstbezit
1964, nr 3. A. Tellegen, Bulletin Boymans-van
Beuningen 1967, pp 8-15: painted November 1885
and retouched in Paris; the sketch published in
letter 383 should be inserted in letter 434
COLLECTION Rotterdam, Museum Boymans-van
Beuningen [acquired 1903; gift of Friends of the
Museum] cat 1963, nr 1239
Colorplate, p 76

F 46 [H 53] WATER MILL AT GENNEP: STUDY OF THE WHEELS

Canvas 60 × 78.5 [23¾ × 31]
Compare F 47, F 125 and water color F 1144a [same
mill]
Nuenen November 1884
LITERATURE A. Plasschaert, De Kroniek 7 November 1903. Vanbeselaere 1937, pp 283, 330, 414:
November 1884. M. E. Tralbaut, De Toerist June
1955: identifies the motif of F 46 as the mill at
Gennep; disputes the authenticity of the painting.
A. Tellegen, Museumjournaal 1968, pp 117-22: the
authenticity of the painting is proved by its entry in
the exhibition of 1903, which contained only work
which Vincent had left in storage in Nuenen in 1885
COLLECTION Amsterdam, Stedelijk Museum [on
loan from Miss E. Ribbius Peletier, Scheveningen]

F 47 [H 54] WATER MILL AT GENNEP

Pasteboard 75 × 100 [29½ × 39½]
Signed in lower left: Vincent
Compare F 46, F 125 and water color F 1144a [same
mill]
Nuenen November 1884
LITERATURE A. Plasschaert, De Kroniek 7 No-
vember 1903. Vanbeselaere 1937, pp 283, 330, 414.
M. E. Tralbaut, De Toerist June 1955: identifies the
motif of F 47 as the mill at Gennep; disputes the
authenticity of the painting
COLLECTION New York, Private Collection

F 48 [H 52] WATER MILL AT OPWETTEN

Canvas on panel 45 × 58 [17¾ × 23]
Nuenen spring 1885
LITERATURE Vanbeselaere 1937, pp 284, 330, 414:
November 1884. M. E. Tralbaut, De Toerist June
1955: identifies the motif of F 48 as the mill at
Opwetten. A. Tellegen, Museumjournaal 1968, pp
117-22: spring 1885
COLLECTION London, Mr and Mrs A. T. Smith

F 48a [formerly F 48bis; H 51] WATER MILL AT KOL, NEAR NUENEN

Canvas on pasteboard 57.5 × 78 [22¾ × 30¾]
Nuenen May 1884
LETTER R 50 [end May] '*Since your departure I have been working on a water mill–the one I inquired about in that little bar near the station…It is the same motif as the other two water mills we went to look at together, but this one has* two red *roofs, and you see it right from the front–with poplars around it. In autumn it will be superb.*'
LITERATURE R. Jacobsen, Onze Kunst 1903, part I, p 115. Vanbeselaere 1937, pp 284, 330, 414: November 1884; letter R 50. M. E. Tralbaut, De Toerist June 1955: identifies the motif of F 48a as the mill at Kollen. A. Tellegen, Museumjournaal 1968, pp 117-22: redates both painting and letter R 50 to May 1884; the name of the village is Kol or Col, near the station of Eeneind, south of Nuenen
COLLECTION New York, Mr and Mrs S. J. Lefrak
Colorplate, p 93

F 49 [H 57] STILL LIFE WITH THREE BEER MUGS

Canvas on pasteboard 32 × 43 [12½ × 17]
Nuenen November 1884 or shortly later
LETTERS 385 [November] '*There are three people now at Eindhoven who want to learn painting and I teach them to do still life.*'
387 [before 20 November] '*Last week I painted still life day after day with the people who paint at Eindhoven.*'
LITERATURE Vanbeselaere 1937, pp 284-5, 330, 348, 414: on stylistic grounds to be dated March 1885
COLLECTION Amsterdam, Rijksmuseum Vincent van Gogh [Vincent van Gogh Foundation, inv nr F 49]

F 50 [H 58] STILL LIFE WITH FIVE BOTTLES AND CUP

Canvas 33 × 41 [13 × 16¼]
Compare F 56
Nuenen November 1884 or shortly later
LETTER 387 [before 20 November] See F 49
LITERATURE Vanbeselaere 1937, pp 284-5, 330, 347, 414: on stylistic grounds to be dated March 1885
COLLECTION Otterlo, Rijksmuseum Kröller-Müller, inv nr 232-20, cat van Gogh 1970, nr 188
Colorplate, p 94

F 47

F 48a

F 50

F 51

F 51 [H 55] STILL LIFE WITH BRASS BOWL

Canvas 65 × 80 [25½ × 31½]
Nuenen September 1885 [?]
LETTERS 424 [end September] *'The pictures I have for you are a few still lifes ... a brass kettle, etc, which I made especially with a view to modeling with different colors ...'*
427 [October] *'Today I forwarded post-paid a box marked V 4 containing the still lifes.'*
LITERATURE Vanbeselaere 1937, pp 300-1, 330, 346, 414: September-October 1885; letter 424
COLLECTION Amsterdam, Rijksmuseum Vincent van Gogh [Vincent van Gogh Foundation, inv nr F 51]

F 52 [H 56] STILL LIFE WITH COFFEE MILL, PIPE CASE AND JUG

Panel 34 × 43 [13½ × 17]
Nuenen November 1884 or shortly later
LETTER 387 [before 20 November] See F 49
LITERATURE A. Plasschaert, Onze Kunst 1903, part 2, p 174. Vanbeselaere 1937, pp 284-5, 330, 346-7, 414: November-December 1884; letters 385, 387; probably painted at Hermans' house
COLLECTION Otterlo, Rijksmuseum Kröller-Müller, inv nr 239-20, cat van Gogh 1970, nr 187

F 53 [H 65] STILL LIFE WITH CUPS, BOWLS AND THREE BOTTLES

Canvas on panel 39.5 × 56 [15½ × 22]
Nuenen first months of 1885
LITERATURE Vanbeselaere 1937, pp 284-6, 330, 347, 349, 414: on stylistic grounds March 1885
COLLECTION Amsterdam, Rijksmuseum Vincent van Gogh [Vincent van Gogh Foundation, inv nr F 53]

F 54 [H 60] STILL LIFE WITH CLOGS AND POTS

Canvas on panel 42 × 54 [16½ × 21¼]
Nuenen November 1884 or shortly later
LETTER 387 [before 20 November] See F 49
LITERATURE Wereldkroniek 1903, p 514 [with reproduction]. A. Plasschaert, Onze Kunst 1904, part 2, p 152. Vanbeselaere 1937, pp 284-5, 330, 346-7, 414: November-December 1884
COLLECTION Utrecht, Museum van Baaren Foundation, inv nr 63a

F 55 [H 59] STILL LIFE WITH A BOTTLE AND TWO BAGS

Canvas on panel 30.5 × 41 [12 × 16]
Nuenen November 1884 or shortly later
LETTER 387 [before 20 November] See F 49
LITERATURE R. Jacobsen, Onze Kunst 1903, part 2, p 60. Vanbeselaere 1937, pp 284-6, 330, 347, 349, 414: on stylistic grounds April 1885
COLLECTION The Hague, Heirs of H. P. Bremmer

F 56 [H 61] STILL LIFE WITH FIVE BOTTLES

Canvas 46.5 × 56 [18¼ × 22]
Compare F 50
Nuenen November 1884 or shortly later
LETTER 387 [before 20 November] See F 49
LITERATURE Vanbeselaere 1937, pp 284-6, 330, 347-8, 414: on stylistic grounds March 1885
COLLECTION The Hague, Heirs of H. P. Bremmer

F 57 [H 62] STILL LIFE WITH POTTERY AND TWO BOTTLES

Canvas 40 × 56 [15¾ × 22]
Nuenen November 1884 or shortly later
LETTER 387 [before 20 November] See F 49

F 52

F 55

F 53

F 57

F 54

F 59

LITERATURE Vanbeselaere 1937, pp 284-5, 330, 346, 414: November-December 1884
COLLECTION London, Arnold Hofland

F 58 [H 63] STILL LIFE WITH POTTERY, BEER GLASS AND BOTTLES

Canvas on panel 31 × 41 [12¼ × 16¼]
Compare F 178 recto
Nuenen November 1884 or shortly later
LETTER 387 [before 20 November] See F 49
LITERATURE R. Jacobsen, Onze Kunst 1903, part 1, p 116. Vanbeselaere 1937, pp 284-6, 330, 347, 349, 414: April 1885
COLLECTION USA, Private Collection

F 59 [H 68] STILL LIFE WITH TWO JARS AND TWO PUMPKINS

Canvas on panel 58 × 85 [22¾ × 33½]
Nuenen September 1885 [?]
LETTER possibly 424 [end September] 'The pictures I have for you are a few still lifes, a basket with potatoes in it, fruit, a brass kettle etc...'
LITERATURE A. Plasschaert, Onze Kunst 1903, part 2, p 174. Vanbeselaere 1937, pp 200-1, 330, 346, 414: September-October 1885
COLLECTION Zurich, Private Collection

F 60 [H 69] STILL LIFE WITH PAINTBRUSHES IN A POT

Canvas on panel 30.5 × 43 [12 × 17]
Nuenen November 1884 or shortly later
LETTER 387 [before 20 November] See F 49
LITERATURE Vanbeselaere 1937, pp 284-5, 330, 346-7, 414: on stylistic grounds January-March 1885
COLLECTION Formerly London, F. A. C. Guépin [until 1966]
Present owner unknown

F 61 recto [H 66] STILL LIFE WITH BOX AND OTHER OBJECTS

Canvas on pasteboard 31 × 42 [12¼ × 16½]
Nuenen November 1884 or shortly later
LETTER 387 [20 November] See F 49
LITERATURE Vanbeselaere 1937, pp 284-5, 330, 346-7, 414: January-March 1885; letters 385, 387
COLLECTION Amsterdam, Rijksmuseum Vincent van Gogh [Vincent van Gogh Foundation, inv nr F 61]

F 61 verso [H 410] SELF PORTRAIT
Paris period; see after F 388 verso

F 62 [H 70] STILL LIFE WITH STRAW HAT AND PIPE

Canvas 36 × 53.5 [14¼ × 21]
Nuenen probably summer 1885
LITERATURE Vanbeselaere 1937, pp 284-6, 330, 342, 346-8, 414: on stylistic grounds March 1885; letters 385, 387. C. Derkert, Konsthistorisk Tidskrift 1946, p 97, note 1: stylistically related to F 1. Cat van Gogh 1959, Rijksmuseum Kröller-Müller, nr 189: closely related to F 63
COLLECTION Otterlo, Rijksmuseum Kröller-Müller, inv nr 236-20, cat van Gogh 1970, nr 189

F 56

F 58

F 60

F 61 recto

F 62

F 64

F 63 [H 64] STILL LIFE WITH BOTTLE, CLOGS
AND POT WITH BRUSHES

Canvas on panel 39 × 41.5 [15¼ × 16¼]
Nuenen probably summer 1885
LITERATURE A. Plasschaert, Onze Kunst 1903,
part 2, p 174. Idem, De Kroniek 14 November
1903. Vanbeselaere 1937, pp 284-6, 330, 342, 346-8,
414: on stylistic grounds March 1885; letters 385,
387. C. Derkert, Konsthistorisk Tidskrift 1946, p 97:
compare F 62. Cat van Gogh 1959, Rijksmuseum
Kröller-Müller, nr 186: closely related to F 62 in its
careful, smooth painting and use of fine color
nuances
COLLECTION Otterlo, Rijksmuseum Kröller-
Müller, inv nr 222-12, cat van Gogh 1970, nr 186

F 64 [H 67] STILL LIFE WITH MANTELPIECE
ORNAMENT, COWRIE SHELL, INK BOTTLES
AND SMOKING SET

Canvas on panel 32 × 41 [12½ × 16¼]
Nuenen November 1884 or shortly later
LETTER 387 [before 20 November] See F 49
LITERATURE H. P. Bremmer, Moderne Kunstwerken 1908, nr 13: describes the motif as mantelpiece ornament. Vanbeselaere 1937, pp 284-5, 330,
346-7, 414: on stylistic grounds January-March
1885; letters 385, 387
COLLECTION Sale London [Sotheby] 3 July 1968,
nr 47
Present owner unknown

F 66

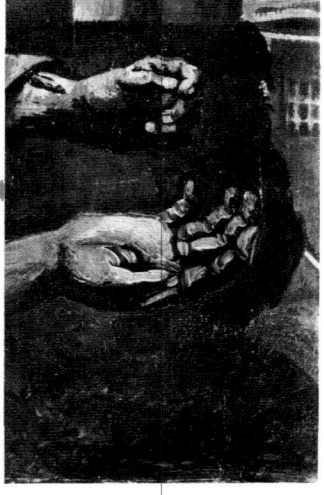

F 65

F 65 [H 71] PEASANT WOMAN WITH WHITE
CAP: HEAD, THREE QUARTERS LEFT

Canvas 38 × 30 [15 × 11¾]
Compare sketch in letter 392, reproduced with
letter 393, and SP 1667 [same model]
Nuenen January 1885
LETTER 392 [about 20 January] 'Enclosed are some
more quick scribbles of studies of heads.'
393 [about 24 January] 'I am working at various
heads and hands all the time.'
LITERATURE Vanbeselaere 1937, pp 286-9, 336-7,
414
COLLECTION Formerly Paris, M. Zetlin [1928 or
earlier]
Present owner unknown

F 66 [H 72] STUDY OF HANDS

Canvas on panel 29.5 × 19 [11½ × 7½]
Nuenen January 1885
LETTER 393 [about 24 January] See F 65
LITERATURE Vanbeselaere 1937, pp 295, 343, 414:
April 1885
COLLECTION The Hague, F. Bremmer

F 63

F 67a

F 67 [H 73] THE GARDEN OF THE VICARAGE
AT NUENEN

Canvas on panel 53 × 78 [21 × 30¾]
Nuenen January 1885
LETTER 394 [February] 'When there was snow, I also
painted a few studies of our garden.'
LITERATURE Vanbeselaere 1937, pp 294, 352, 414
COLLECTION Sale New York [Parke-Bernet]
20 November 1968, nr 37
Present owner unknown

F 67a THE STATION AT EINDHOVEN

Canvas 15 × 26 [6 × 10¼]
Nuenen December 1884-January 1885
LITERATURE A. Kerssemakers, De Amsterdammer
14 and 21 April 1912, reprinted in English edition of
Vincent's letters, nr 435 c: 'I still have a little study
as a souvenir of this unmanageable paint. He
painted it in a great hurry at my house, to instruct

me; it was a view from my window in winter with melting snow, and the thin white color ran all over the landscape.' Not in Faille 1928, Vanbeselaere 1937 or Faille 1939. Tralbaut Bildbiographie 1958, p 52 [reproduction]: described as the old station at Eindhoven
COLLECTION Otterlo, Rijksmuseum Kröller-Müller [on loan since 1964 from Mrs J. Hendrikx-Korting, Driel]

F 68 [H 75] PEASANT WOMAN WINDING BOBBINS
Nuenen period, drawings; see after F 1349 verso

F 69 [H 74] HEAD OF A PEASANT WOMAN: FULL FACE

Canvas on pasteboard 44 × 30.5 [17¼ × 12]
Compare sketch in letter 397 and F 160 [same model]
Nuenen January 1885 or shortly later
LETTERS 393 [about 24 January] See F 65
394 [February] '*I am very busy painting those heads … In this way I have already painted at least some thirty and drawn as many.*'
395 [1 March] '*…lately I have, as you know, painted heads almost exclusively.*'
396 [mid-March] '*Some of the heads I promised you are finished …*'
LITERATURE Vanbeselaere 1937, pp 286-9, 292, 335, 339, 342-3, 367-8, 414: on stylistic grounds April-May 1885; letters 397-8, 403, 408-9; one of the models from THE POTATO EATERS. J. G. van Gelder, Beeldende Kunst 1942, part 1, p 6 [English edition, 1946]: portrait of Stien de Groot; preliminary study for F 82, also used for F 78
COLLECTION Amsterdam, Rijksmuseum Vincent van Gogh [Vincent van Gogh Foundation, inv nr F 69]

F 69

F 67

F 70

F 70a

F 71

F 73

F 72

F 70 [H 76] HEAD OF A PEASANT WOMAN:
RIGHT PROFILE AGAINST A WINDOW

Canvas on pasteboard 41 × 32 [16¼ × 12½]
Compare two sketches in letter 396 [figure to the
left], F 71 and F 72 [same model]
Nuenen February-March 1885
LETTERS 394 [February] and 395 [1 March] See
F 69
396 [mid-March] '*I have studies of heads for it,
against the light as well as turned toward the light.*'
LITERATURE Vanbeselaere 1937, pp 286-9, 291,
334, 337-8, 339, 342, 347, 351, 353, 356, 414
COLLECTION Bergen, Netherlands, D. de Wolff
Peereboom [acquired 1943]

F 70a [formerly F 70bis; H 77] STUDY OF A
PEASANT WOMAN: FULL FACE, HALF
LENGTH AGAINST A WINDOW

Canvas 38.5 × 30.5 [15¼ × 12]
Compare sketch in letter 396 [figure to the right]
Nuenen February-March 1885
LETTERS 394 [February] and 395 [1 March] See
F 69
396 [mid-March] See F 70
LITERATURE Vanbeselaere 1937, pp 286-9, 291,
338-9, 356, 414
COLLECTION Amsterdam, Rijksmuseum Vincent
van Gogh [Vincent van Gogh Foundation, inv
nr F 70a]

F 71 [H 78] PEASANT WOMAN SEWING

Canvas on pasteboard 43.5 × 34.5 [17¼ × 13½]
Compare sketch in letter 396 [figure to the left],
F 70 and F 72 [same model]
Nuenen February-March 1885
LETTER 396 [mid-March] See F 70
LITERATURE Vanbeselaere 1937, pp 294, 351, 414
COLLECTION Amsterdam, Rijksmuseum Vincent
van Gogh [Vincent van Gogh Foundation, inv
nr F 71]

F 72 [H 80] PEASANT WOMAN TAKING HER
MEAL

Canvas 42 × 29 [16½ × 11½]
Compare sketch in letter 396 [figure to the left],
F 70 and F 71 [same model]
Nuenen February-March 1885
LETTER 396 [mid-March] '*I am brooding over a
couple of larger, more elaborate things…it would be,
for instance, something like this: namely figures
against the light of a window. I have studies of heads
for it, against the light as well as turned toward the
light, and I have worked several times already on the
complete figure…*'
LITERATURE Vanbeselaere 1937, pp 294, 351, 414.
Cat van Gogh 1959, Rijksmuseum Kröller-Müller,
nr 177: March 1885; refers to various other works
with the same motif
COLLECTION Otterlo, Rijksmuseum Kröller-
Müller, inv nr 242-20, cat van Gogh 1970, nr 177

F 73 [H 79] WOMAN SEATED BEFORE AN
OPEN DOOR, PEELING POTATOES

Canvas on panel 36.5 × 25 [14½ × 9¾]
Nuenen February-March 1885
LETTER 396 [mid-March] See F 72
LITERATURE Vanbeselaere 1937, pp 295, 351, 414
COLLECTION Switzerland, Doyer Family

F 74 [H 83] HEAD OF AN OLD PEASANT
WOMAN: FULL FACE, WITH DARK CAP

Canvas 37.5 × 28 [14¾ × 11]
Compare F 75, F 146, drawings F 1149 and F 1193a
[same model]

F 74

Nuenen February-March 1885
LETTERS 394 [February] and 395 [1 March] See
F 69
LITERATURE Faille 1928, nr 74: reproduction of
F 146 instead of F 74. Vanbeselaere 1937, pp 286-9,
292, 414: between April and June 1885; letters
397-8, 403, 408-10; stylistically close to F 160;
painted between F 69 of April-May and F 388 recto
of June. Cat van Gogh 1959, Rijksmuseum Kröller-
Müller, nr 170: May 1885
COLLECTION Otterlo, Rijksmuseum Kröller-
Müller, inv nr 231-20, cat van Gogh 1970, nr 170

F 75 [H 82] HEAD OF AN OLD PEASANT
WOMAN: FULL FACE, WITH WHITE CAP

Canvas 36.5 × 29.5 [14½ × 11¾]
Compare F 74, F 146, drawings F 1149 and F 1193a
[same model]
Nuenen February-March 1885
LETTERS 394 [February] and 395 [1 March] See
F 69
LITERATURE Vanbeselaere 1937, pp 286-9, 292,
414: April-June 1885; letters 397-8, 403, 408-10;
close to F 160; painted between F 69 of April-May
and F 388 recto of June
COLLECTION Wuppertal, Germany, Von der
Heydt-Museum der Stadt Wuppertal [acquired
1964; E. Baron von der Heydt bequest]

F 76 [H 81] STILL LIFE: SATIN FLOWERS AND
A BOWL WITH LEAVES AND FLOWERS

Canvas on pasteboard 42.5 × 32.5 [16¾ × 12¾]
Nuenen before 26 March 1885. Probably autumn
1884
LETTER 398 [early April 1885] '...a still life of satin
flowers similar to the one you took with you...'
LITERATURE Vanbeselaere 1937, pp 295, 335,
346-7, 414: March 1885; letter 398; painted before
the study reproduced with this letter
EDITORS' COMMENT Compare the stylistically
related still life F 200
COLLECTION Amsterdam, Rijksmuseum Vincent
van Gogh [Vincent van Gogh Foundation, inv
nr F 76]

F 76

F 75

F 77 recto

F 77a

F 80a

F 80

F 77 recto [H 91] INTERIOR OF A PEASANT'S HOUSE WITH FOUR PERSONS [first study for THE POTATO EATERS]

Canvas on pasteboard 33.5 × 45 [13¼ × 17¾]
Compare sketch in letter 399, F 77a, F 78, F 82, drawings F 1226, F 1227, F 1594 verso and lithograph F 1661
Nuenen February-March 1885
LETTER 398 [early April] See F 82
LITERATURE Vanbeselaere 1937, pp 295, 351, 356, 362-3, 414: April 1885; letter 398. J. G. van Gelder, Beeldende Kunst 1942, part 1, p 4 [English edition, 1946]: March 1885, before Theo's visit of the 26th; preliminary study done on the spot in the hut of peasant de Groot; first sketch for THE POTATO EATERS; letter R 57. L. Anfray, Art-Documents April 1953, p 1: Anfray supposes that after his visit to Nuenen Theo took this painting with him to Paris in April 1885 in order to show it to the art dealer Portier. A. Boime, Gazette des Beaux-Arts April 1966, pp 249-53: close parallel to sketch by J. Israels, published by Goupil & Co in 1884
EDITORS' COMMENT See F 82
COLLECTION Amsterdam, Rijksmuseum Vincent van Gogh [Vincent van Gogh Foundation, inv nr F 77]

F 77 verso [H VI] SELF PORTRAIT
Paris period; see after F 388 verso

F 77a THE POTATO EATERS

Canvas 65 × 92 [25½ × 36¼]
Compare sketch in letter 399, F 77 recto, F 78, F 82, drawings F 1226, F 1227, F 1594 verso and lithograph F 1661
Nuenen end April 1885. N.B. See EDITORS' COMMENT
LETTERS 401-410 are named by Faille in connection with this painting.
LITERATURE Not in Faille 1928, Vanbeselaere 1937 or Faille 1939. L. Anfray, Art-Documents December 1953, pp 4, 40; January 1954, pp 6-7: an original painting by van Gogh, discovered by Anfray at a broker's in 1944, proved authentic by examinations. H. Perruchot, L'Œil October 1955, pp 12-17: accepts authenticity of the painting. L. Gans, Museumjournaal December 1955, pp 98-103, 111: style-critical comparison shows F 77a to be a rather poor copy after F 78, possibly made by one of Vincent's pupils in Eindhoven. L. Anfray, Museumjournaal July 1956, pp 177-83, with final rebuttal of L. Gans, who maintains his original view: Anfray offers more details concerning the examination of the painting. J. Rewald, Post-Impressionism, 1956, p 577, nr 175: considers Gans' article an excellent refutation of Anfray. L. Anfray, Les Cahiers de Van Gogh 1958, p 20: identifies models, according to N. Eekman
EDITORS' COMMENT Authenticity rejected by the editors. See F 82, where the letters cited by Faille in connection with F 77a are quoted.
COLLECTION Cherbourg, Mme L. Anfray

F 78 [H 92] THE POTATO EATERS

Canvas [pasted on panel in 1946] 72 × 93 [28¼ × 36½]
Compare sketch in letter 399, F 77 recto, F 77a, F 82, drawings F 1226, F 1227, F 1594 verso and lithograph F 1661
Nuenen May-June 1885
LETTERS R 53 [second half of June] and R 57 [August] See F 82
LITERATURE Vanbeselaere 1937, pp 295, 351, 362-3, 369-70, 414: April 1885; letters 399, 400. J. G. van Gelder, Beeldende Kunst 1942, part 1, p 4 [English edition, 1946]: April 1885; second sketch, first composition for THE POTATO EATERS, painted in three days; the two figures on the left are

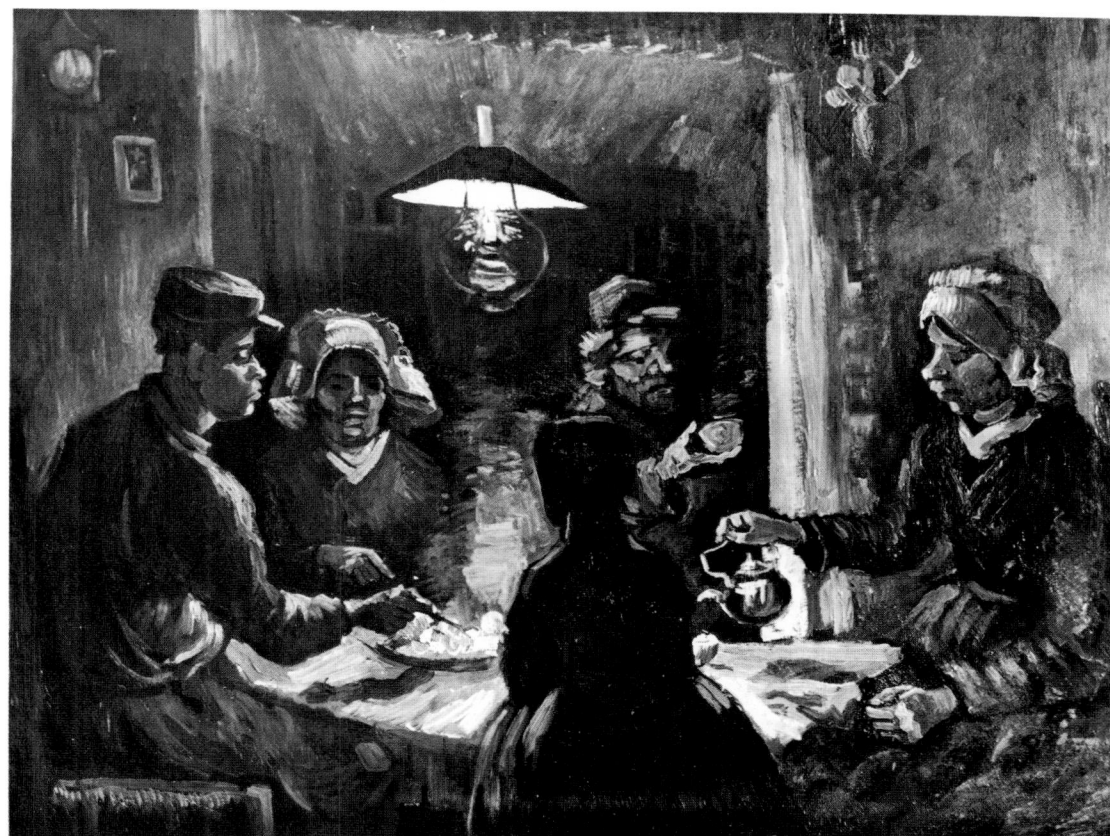

F 78

Gijsbert and Stien de Groot; earlier studies used for Gijsbert are the drawings F 1146 and F 1168, for Stien the paintings F 69, F 130 and F 138. Cat van Gogh 1959, Rijksmuseum Kröller-Müller, nr 167: April 1885; letters 399, 400, 401, 404, R 57; second version of THE POTATO EATERS, painted on the spot by lamplight; sketch for the definitive version of F 82
EDITORS' COMMENT See F 82
COLLECTION Otterlo, Rijksmuseum Kröller-Müller, inv nr·1145-46, cat van Gogh 1970, nr 167

F 79 [H 90] SUNSET

Canvas 27.5 × 41.5 [10¾ × 16¼]
Nuenen April 1885
LETTER 402 [end April] '*I am also working on a red sunset.*'
LITERATURE Vanbeselaere 1937, pp 297, 374, 414
COLLECTION Rüschlikon, Switzerland, R. Graber

F 80 [H 86] HEAD OF A PEASANT WOMAN WITH WHITE CAP: FACING RIGHT

Canvas on panel 41 × 31.5 [16¼ × 12½]
Compare F 80a and F 388 recto [probably the same model]
Nuenen December 1884 or shortly later
LETTERS 390 [mid-December] '*I'm working very hard on the series of heads from the people which I have set myself to make ...*'
394 [February 1885] and 395 [1 March] See F 69
LITERATURE Vanbeselaere 1937, pp 286-90, 297, 341, 414: January 1885; letter 394
COLLECTION Zurich, E. G. Bührle [acquired 1942], cat 1958, nr 235

F 80a [formerly F 80bis; H 84] HEAD OF A PEASANT WOMAN WITH WHITE CAP: FACING RIGHT

Canvas 42 × 35 [16½ × 13¾]
Compare F 80 and F 288 recto [probably the same model]
Nuenen December 1884 or shortly later
LETTERS 390 [mid-December] See F 80
394 [February 1885] and 395 [1 March] See F 69
LITERATURE Vanbeselaere 1937, pp 286-9, 292, 343-4, 376-7, 414: letters 397, 398, 403; close in technique to F 77 recto, the sketch for THE POTATO EATERS. J. G. van Gelder, Beeldende Kunst 1942, part 1 [English edition, 1946]
COLLECTION Amsterdam, Rijksmuseum Vincent van Gogh [Vincent van Gogh Foundation, inv nr F 80a]

F 81 [H 85] HEAD OF A PEASANT WOMAN WITH A WHITE CAP: FULL FACE

Canvas on panel 41 × 31.5 [16¼ × 12½]
Nuenen April 1885 or earlier
LITERATURE Vanbeselaere 1937, pp 286-9, 292, 297, 343-4, 414: April-June; letters 397-8, 403, 408-10; close in technique to F 77 recto
COLLECTION New York, J. K. Thannhauser Art Gallery

F 79

F 81

F 82

F 83

F 82 [H I] THE POTATO EATERS

Canvas 82 × 114 [32¼ × 45]

Signed in lower left, on the upper rung of the back of the chair: Vincent [discovered after 1960 by Mrs N. van Gogh-van der Goot]

Compare sketch in letter 399, F 77 recto, F 77a, F 78, drawings F 1226, F 1227, F 1594 verso and lithograph F 1661. Studies for and after details are F 160a, F 167, F 202, drawings F 1157, F 1161 recto and verso, F 1168, F 1194a, F 1198, F 1229, F 1349 recto and verso

Nuenen September-October 1885. N.B. See EDITORS' COMMENT

LETTERS 398 [early April] '*This week I intend to start that composition of those peasants around a dish of potatoes in the evening ... But whether it may succeed or not, I am going to begin the studies for the various figures.*'

399 [between 9 and 13 April] '*... I am again working on those peasants around a dish of potatoes ... This is what the composition has now become.*'

401 [between 13 and 17 April] '*By the same mail you will receive a few copies of a lithograph. I should like to make, with a few alterations, a definite picture of the sketch I painted in the cottage.*'

402 [end April] '*By the same mail you will receive a number of copies of the lithograph ... I hope to make some progress with that picture of the potato eaters.*'

403 [end April] '*I want to tell you that I am working on the potato eaters ...*'

404 [about 30 April] '*I should have liked to send you the picture of the potato eaters on that day* [1 May, Theo's birthday], *but though it is getting on well, it is not quite finished yet.*'

405 [early May] '*I think you will see what I mean in the picture of the potato eaters.*'

406 [early May] '*I am writing you a little note while waiting to send off the box ...*'

407 [6 May] '*Yesterday I sent you a number of painted studies by post, and today, Wednesday, a box marked V 1, post paid, containing the picture.*'

408 [after 8 May] '*I am anxious to hear if Portier has seen the potato eaters.*'

409 [after 10 May] '*What did Portier say about the potato eaters? I know quite well it has its faults, but just because I see that the heads I am doing now are becoming more vigorous, I dare maintain that the potato eaters will keep its value in relation to future pictures, too.*'

410 [1 June] '*I am very pleased to hear what you write about the picture, Portier's and Serret's remarks ...*'

R 53 [second half of June] '*Here is my explanation of the lithograph ... I thought a certain composition somewhat forced, and was using an altogether different process in an attempt to find a new idea to put it together. Besides, it was only an experiment and nothing more, and I used corrosives on the stone later on.*'

R 57 [August] '*As for my work, that scene of the potato eaters – you saw the lithograph of it – is a subject that I tried to paint, being inspired by the peculiar light effect in that grimy cottage ... the real picture differs in design from* both *the rough sketch for it, which I still have and which I made in that cottage by the light of a little lamp,* and *from the lithograph.*'

424 [end September] '*That the color of the Potato Eaters is not good is, partly at least, the fault of the paint.*'

LITERATURE Vanbeselaere 1937, pp 296-7, 362, 365, 369-72, 414: May 1885; letters 401-5, 407, 408; improved version of F 78, based on renewed study. J.G. van Gelder, De Aardappeleters, 1949: end April-early May; sequence of the works: F 78, F 1161, F 82. L. Anfray, L'Opinion du Dr de la Faille: Conférences à l'Institut culturel Néerlandais, Paris 8 and 9 February 1957: F 82 dates from September 1885. L. Anfray, Les Cahiers de Van Gogh 1957, pp 11-20: sequence of the works: F 77,

F 77a, F 78, F 82, F 1661. A. Boime, Gazette des Beaux-Arts April 1966, pp 249-53: motif probably derived from THE FRUGAL MEAL by J. Israëls, published in photogravure reproduction by Goupil & Co in 1884

EDITORS' COMMENT The sequence and dating of nrs F 77 recto, F 77a, F 78 and F 82 represent the thinking of Faille as found in the manuscript of the present work and in his published opinion [see LITERATURE]. Contrary to general scholarly opinion, he dated F 82, from a reference in letter 424 [end September] to September-October 1885, and with it the drawings directly connected with F 82 [F 1157, F 1161 recto and verso, F 1229, F 1349 recto and verso] as well as the lithograph F 1661. In this rearrangement F 77a takes the old place of F 82, being dated to the end of April 1885. The editors reject both theories and are unanimous in considering F 82 to be the finished painting [which Vincent therefore signed] that was sent from Nuenen to Paris on 6 May 1885 [letter 407]. Letter 424 offers no ground for another alternative: '*That the color of the Potato Eaters is not good is, partly at least, the fault of the paint. I was reminded of it because I painted a large still life in which I sought similar tones, and as I was not satisfied with it because I again got the same things as before, I painted it anew. Judging from this experience, it would have turned out much better with the mineral blue I have now than with what I had before.*' There can be no doubt that the first *it* in the last sentence refers to the still life, which was painted again, and the second *it* to THE POTATO EATERS, which was not. Moreover, there are no further references to THE POTATO EATERS in letter 424 or any following letter. Vincent does not mention sending it and makes no inquiry about Theo's opinion, neither does Theo seem to have referred to it [cf letters 427, 428]. All this makes it most improbable that a new version of the subject was painted in the months September-October 1885. On the contrary, the letters indicate unequivocally that Vincent was entirely wrapped up in still lifes in those months. The correct solution is indicated by the letters themselves, especially letters 400, 405, 408 and R 57. Vincent painted three pictures with THE POTATO EATERS as subject: F 77 recto [with four figures], F 78 and F 82. F 77 recto was presumably painted around 1 March, when Vincent wrote to Theo: '*Just now I paint not only as long as there is daylight, but even in the evening by the lamp in the cottages, when I can hardly distinguish anything on my palette, so as to catch, if possible, something of the curious effects of lamplight in the evening, with, for instance, a large shadow cast on the wall*' [letter 395]. We know that shortly after this he sent some studies to Theo, for he wrote in letter 397 '*I should like to hear whether those rolled-up things arrived safely.*' Later on, coming back to the poses in THE POTATO EATERS, he wrote, '*The finest thing I saw was when the woman was simply kneeling down, as in the* first *sketch I sent you*' [letter 408]. The editors identify F 77 recto as this 'first sketch.' Vincent must have come across it once again in Paris, for he painted a self portrait on the back of it.

He took the subject up again about a month later, this time with five figures. '*This week I intend to start that composition of those peasants around a dish of potatoes in the evening*' [letter 398]. Clearly he was referring here to something Theo already knew about; indeed, according to the above reference, Theo had already received F 77 recto. A sketch of the study that Vincent made subsequently appears in letter 399. An even clearer sketch is F 1226, which probably is the sketch mentioned in letter 400. The editors identify F 78 as the study referred to in letters 398-401. After Vincent had completed this study, he made the lithograph F 1661 from memory in a single day [letter R 53], coming very close to the study. The lithograph must have been made some-

time after 13 April, the day Vincent ordered the stone in Eindhoven [see letter 400]. A few days later [letter 401] some lithographs were sent to Paris. The date of F 1661 can therefore be taken to be the middle of April. In letter 401 Vincent wrote, '*I should like to make, with a few alterations, a definite picture of the sketch I painted in the cottage.*' Even though the word 'overwerken' in Vincent's Dutch text can be interpreted in different ways, the editors believe that what is meant here is the making of a *new* painting of the same motif. This is confirmed by various passages in letters 402, 403, 404 and 405, in which the progress of the work is described. In letter 407, finally, notice is given that the painting is being shipped.

A passage in letter 405, to take an example, illuminates this connection. Here Vincent describes how he began by painting the flesh tints fairly light and how he then rigorously painted them over with much darker colors. The editors identify this 'definite' version as F 82. x-ray photographs of the painting reveal heavy overpainting. Important changes in the final version are: altered directions of gaze, the left hand of the female figure on the right, her chair and the addition on the lower right of a small table with a kettle.

In letter 405 Vincent wrote of the painting, '*It is the same size as last year's Woman Spinning.*' The measurements of the latter, now lost, appear from letter 371 to have been 75 × 100 cm [29½ × 39½ in], approximating the dimensions of F 82 [82 × 114 cm] more nearly than those of either of the other pictures.

COLLECTION Amsterdam, Rijksmuseum Vincent van Gogh [Vincent van Gogh Foundation, inv nr F 82]

Colorplate, p 111

F 83 [H 93] COTTAGE AT NIGHTFALL

Canvas 64 × 78 [25¼ × 30¾]
Signed in lower left: Vincent
Nuenen May 1885
LETTERS 408 [after 8 May] '*Then I'm working on a large study of a cottage by night.*'
410 [1 June] '*I hope to send you this week a small box marked V 2, containing: 1 picture la Chaumière*

F 84

[Hovel with thatched roof]...'
411 [June] '*Today I sent off the small box in question...the cottage with the mossed roof reminds me of a wren's nest.*'
LITERATURE Vanbeselaere 1937, pp 297, 376-7, 395-6, 414: letters 408, 410, 411
COLLECTION Amsterdam, Rijksmuseum Vincent van Gogh [Vincent van Gogh Foundation, inv nr F 83]

F 84 [H 94] THE OLD CHURCH TOWER AT NUENEN

Canvas 63 × 79 [24¾ × 41]
Signed in lower right: Vincent
Nuenen May 1885
LETTERS 408 [after 8 May] '*The old tower will be pulled down next week! The spire has already gone. I'm working on a picture of it.*'
411 [June] '*Today I sent off the small box in question, containing, except what I mentioned already, another picture, Cimetière de Paysans.*'
LITERATURE Vanbeselaere 1937, pp 297-8, 354, 377, 401, 414: letters 408, 411, 414; in color and mood reminiscent of Millet's EGLISE DE CREVILLE
COLLECTION Amsterdam, Rijksmuseum Vincent van Gogh [Vincent van Gogh Foundation, inv nr F 84]

F 85

F 85a

F 87

F 90

F 85 [H 100] HEAD OF A PEASANT WOMAN WITH WHITE CAP: FULL FACE

Canvas 44 × 36 [17¼ × 14¼]
Compare sketches in letters 397 and 409, F 85a,
F 130, F 140, F 141 and SP 1668 [same model]
Nuenen May 1885
LETTER 409 [after 10 May] '*This is the sketch of a head, which I just brought home. There was the same one among the last studies I sent you, namely the largest of all. But painted smoothly. Now I have not smoothed down the brushstroke and in fact the color is quite different too.*'
LITERATURE Vanbeselaere 1937, pp 286-9, 293, 343-4, 414: May 1885; letters 409, 410. Cat van Gogh 1959, Rijksmuseum Kröller-Müller, nr 168: this is the version of April
EDITORS' COMMENT F 85, which is very much like the sketch in letter 409, is most likely the painting Vincent 'just brought home,' though this may have been F 141. The earlier study, 'painted smoothly,' may have been F 140.
COLLECTION Otterlo, Rijksmuseum Kröller-Müller, inv nr 226-17, cat van Gogh 1970, nr 168

F 85a HEAD OF A PEASANT WOMAN WITH WHITE CAP: FULL FACE

Canvas on panel 47 × 34.5 [18½ × 13½]
Compare sketches in letters 397 and 409, F 85,
F 130, F 140, F 141 and SP 1668 [same model]
Nuenen May 1885
LITERATURE Not in Faille 1928, Vanbeselaere 1937 or Faille 1937
COLLECTION Boston, R. M. Light

F 86 [H 95] HEAD OF A PEASANT WOMAN: LEFT PROFILE

Canvas 40.5 × 34 [16 × 13½]
Nuenen May 1885
LETTER 410 [1 June] '*You will find a variation among them – profile – a background of "the flat plain of sugar-beet fields under the starless night, dark and thick like ink." Standing out against this, the head of a hercheuse or sclôneuse with an expression as of a lowing cow, a person from: ...*' [there follows a passage from *Germinal*]
LITERATURE Vanbeselaere 1937, pp 286-9, 293, 343-4, 366, 376, 414: May 1885; letter 410; inspired by the reading of Zola's *Germinal*
COLLECTION Otterlo, Rijksmuseum Kröller-Müller, inv nr 245-20, cat van Gogh 1970, nr 174

F 87 [H 96] THE COUNTRY CEMETERY AT NUENEN IN THE SNOW

Canvas on pasteboard 30 × 41.5 [11¾ × 16¼]
Compare sketch in letter 385 [in the Dutch edition of the letters only] and F 88
Nuenen January 1885
LITERATURE Vanbeselaere 1937, pp 294, 352-3, 414: January 1885; close in style to F 67 and F 194, not to F 84
COLLECTION Athens, Stavros S. Niarchos, exhib cat 1957, nr 22

F 88 [H 97] THE OLD CHURCH TOWER AT NUENEN

Canvas on panel 47.5 × 55 [18¾ × 21¾]
Signed in lower right: Vincent
Compare F 87
Nuenen May 1884
LETTER 368 [mid-May] '*...and I have also started to paint the little tower, you know.*'
LITERATURE Vanbeselaere 1937, pp 282, 414: May 1884; letter 368
COLLECTION Zurich, E. G. Bührle [acquired 1945], cat 1958, nr 233

F 88

F 89 [H 103] COTTAGE WITH PEASANT
WOMAN DIGGING

Canvas on panel 30.5 × 40 [12 × 15¾]
Nuenen June 1885
LETTERS 414 [June] '*I also hope to send before the
harvest about three more cottages, painted studies,
like those last ones.*'
417 [15 July] '*Right now I need all my time, because
I am working two hours from here. What I want is to
have some more beautiful cottages on the heath. I
have four now, as large as the two I last sent you, and
a few smaller ones.*'
LITERATURE Vanbeselaere 1937, pp 298-9, 396,
415
COLLECTION Winnipeg, John A. MacAulay

F 90 [H 102] COTTAGE AND FIGURE WITH
GOAT

Canvas 60 × 85 [23½ × 33½]
Compare F 92 [same cottage]
Nuenen June-July 1885
LETTERS 414 [June] and 417 [15 July] See F 89
415 [end June] '*Then I showed him [Wenckebach]
that, as to color, I certainly do not want to always
paint dark. Some of the cottages are even quite light.*'
R 57 [August] '*When Wenckebach came to see me, I
had just finished painting some cottages.*'
LITERATURE Vanbeselaere 1937, pp 298-9, 396,
415: June-July 1885; letters 411-2, 414-5, 417-8;
belongs to the series of huts done shortly after F 83
COLLECTION Frankfurt, Städelsches Kunstinstitut
[acquired 1908], cat 1924, p 83 [Städelscher Museum-
verein, inv nr 1436]

F 89

F 86

F 91

F 92

F 96

F 91 [H 101] THE COTTAGE

Canvas 35.5 × 67 [14 × 26½]
Nuenen June 1885
LETTER 412 [June] '*I must tell you that I have another similar subject, a white clay cottage, the size more in the breadth.*'
LITERATURE Vanbeselaere 1937, pp 298-9, 396, 415: letter 412
COLLECTION Harrison, New York, John P. Natanson

F 92 [H 98] THE COTTAGE

Canvas 44 × 59.5 [17¼ × 23½]
Signed in lower left: Vincent
Compare F 90 [same cottage]
Nuenen June-July 1885
LETTERS 414 [June] and 417 [15 July] See F 89
LITERATURE Vanbeselaere 1937, pp 298-9, 396, 415: July 1885; letters 415, 417
COLLECTION Sale London [Sotheby] 28 June 1961, nr 28
Present owner unknown

F 92a THE COTTAGE

Canvas 22.5 × 34 [8¾ × 13½]
Nuenen June-July 1885
LETTERS 414 [June] and 417 [15 July] See F 89
LITERATURE Not in Faille 1928, Vanbeselaere 1937 or Faille 1939. First recognized by H. P. Bremmer 1943
COLLECTION Formerly Rotterdam, F. de Bry Art Gallery and Schipluiden, W. Brinkman [sold before 1965]
Present owner unknown

F 93 [H 99] THE FARM

Canvas on panel 32 × 46 [12½ × 18]
Nuenen June-July 1885
LETTERS 414 [June] and 417 [15 July] See F 89
LITERATURE Vanbeselaere 1937, pp 276, 299, 303, 393, 415: October 1885; not part of the series of cottages painted in July; close in style to F 117 and drawings F 1152, F 1215 and F 1217
COLLECTION Rotterdam, Mr and Mrs Plate-Elink Schuurman

F 94 [H 104] PEASANT WOMAN DIGGING: SEEN FROM THE BACK

Canvas on panel 36 × 25 [14¼ × 9¾]
Compare drawings F 1256 and F 1258 [similar motif]
Nuenen July-August 1885
LETTERS 416 [6 July] '*I have here before me some figures: a woman with a spade, seen from behind; another bending to glean the ears of wheat; another seen from the front, her head almost on the ground, digging carrots.*'
417 [15 July] '*But I hope you will bring those figure studies back when you come. For I am going to add others which I need for painting. I shall want them for figures that are definitely not larger than, for instance, a span and even less…*'
LITERATURE Vanbeselaere 1937, pp 299, 352, 415
COLLECTION Stockholm, Private Collection

F 95 [H 105] PEASANT WOMAN DIGGING

Canvas on panel 41.5 × 32 [16¼ × 12½]
Compare drawing F 1255 [similar motif]
Nuenen July 1885
LETTER 416 [6 July] See F 94
LITERATURE Vanbeselaere 1937, pp 300, 352, 415
COLLECTION Utrecht, G. Ribbius Peletier jr

F 95a PEASANT WOMAN DIGGING

Canvas on panel 42 × 32 [16½ × 12½]
Nuenen July 1885
LETTER 416 [6 July] See F 94
LITERATURE Not in Faille 1928, Vanbeselaere
1937 or Faille 1939
COLLECTION Birmingham, Barber Institute
[acquired 1961]

F 96 [H 106] TWO PEASANT WOMEN DIGGING, FACING EACH OTHER

Canvas on panel 41 × 56 [16¼ × 22]
Compare F 147 and drawing F 1296
Nuenen August 1885
LETTER 421 [August] 'I have painted three more
studies of women in the potato fields, of which you
already saw the first one.'
LITERATURE Vanbeselaere 1937, pp 304, 393, 415:
October-November 1885; conception of space new
in comparison with the more classical, static
composition of F 97 [September 1885]
COLLECTION Formerly Rotterdam, S. J. R. de
Monchy
Present owner unknown

F 97 [H 108] TWO PEASANT WOMEN DIGGING POTATOES, FACING RIGHT

Canvas on panel 31.5 × 42.5 [12½ × 16¾]
Compare sketch in letter R 57 and drawing F 1295
[similar motifs]
Nuenen August 1885
LETTERS 421 [August] See F 96
R 57 [August] 'Herewith a third scribble of a study I
did yesterday ... From my scribble you will see that I
take rather great pains to get action into my little
figures, to express their being at work, their doing
something.'
LITERATURE Vanbeselaere 1937, pp 300, 393,
396-7, 400, 415: September 1885; letter 421; composition similar to F 19. Cat van Gogh 1959, Rijksmuseum Kröller-Müller, nr 179: similar in composition to drawings F 1141, F 1295 and F 1299
COLLECTION Otterlo, Rijksmuseum Kröller-
Müller, inv nr 260-19, cat van Gogh 1970, nr 179

F 94

F 95

F 92a

F 93

F 95a

F 97

F 98

F 103

F 99

F 100

F 98 [H 107] PEASANT WOMAN DIGGING POTATOES: LEFT PROFILE

Paper on panel 31.5 × 38 [12½ × 15]
Nuenen August 1885
LETTER 421 [August] See F 96
LITERATURE R. Jacobsen, Onze Kunst 1903, part 1, p 114. Vanbeselaere 1937, pp 300, 415: September 1885; letter 421
COLLECTION Antwerp, Koninklijk Museum voor Schone Kunsten, inv nr 2889

F 99 [H 112] STILL LIFE: BASKET WITH APPLES

Canvas 43 × 59 [17 × 23¼]
Nuenen September 1885
LETTERS 424 [end September] and 427 [October] See F 51
LITERATURE Vanbeselaere 1937, pp 300-1, 415: September 1885; letters 424-427
COLLECTION Amsterdam, Rijksmuseum Vincent van Gogh [Vincent van Gogh Foundation, inv nr F 99]

F 100 [H 110] STILL LIFE: BASKET WITH POTATOES

Canvas 44.5 × 60 [17½ × 23½]
Nuenen September 1885
LETTER 424 [end September] See F 51
LITERATURE Vanbeselaere 1937, pp 300-1, 415: September 1885; letters 424, 427
COLLECTION Amsterdam, Rijksmuseum Vincent van Gogh [Vincent van Gogh Foundation, inv nr F 100]

F 101 [H 113] STILL LIFE: BASKET WITH APPLES

Canvas 33 × 43.5 [13 × 17¼]
Nuenen September 1885
LETTER 424 [end September] See F 51
LITERATURE Vanbeselaere 1937, pp 300-1, 415: September 1885; letters 424-427
COLLECTION Amsterdam, Rijksmuseum Vincent van Gogh [Vincent van Gogh Foundation, inv nr F 101]

F 102 [H 114] STILL LIFE: CABBAGES, POTATOES AND LEAVES

Canvas 75 × 93 [29½ × 36½]
Nuenen September 1885
LETTER 424 [end September] See F 51
LITERATURE Vanbeselaere 1937, pp 300-1, 415: September 1885; letters 424-427
COLLECTION Liège, F. C. Graindorge

F 103 [H 111] STILL LIFE: VEGETABLES AND FRUIT

Canvas on pasteboard 32.5 × 43 [12¾ × 17]
Nuenen September 1885
LETTER 424 [end September] See F 51
LITERATURE Vanbeselaere 1937, pp 300-2, 415: September 1885; letters 424-427
COLLECTION Amsterdam, Rijksmuseum Vincent van Gogh [Vincent van Gogh Foundation, inv nr F 103]

F 104 [H 109] STILL LIFE: GINGER POT AND APPLES

Canvas on panel 30.5 × 46.5 [12 × 18¼]
Nuenen September 1885
LETTER 424 [end September] See F 51
LITERATURE Vanbeselaere 1937, pp 300-2, 415: September 1885; letters 424-427
COLLECTION Toronto, Private Collection

F 101

F 104a STILL LIFE: GINGER POT AND ONIONS

Canvas 34 × 49.5 [13½ × 19½]
Signed in lower left: Vincent
Nuenen September 1885
LETTER 424 [end September] See F 51
LITERATURE Not in Faille 1928, Vanbeselaere
1937 or Faille 1939
COLLECTION Paris, Private Collection

F 105 [H 115] STILL LIFE: BOWL WITH PEARS

Canvas 33 × 43.5 [13 × 17¼]
Nuenen September 1885
LETTER 424 [end September] See F 51
LITERATURE Vanbeselaere 1937, pp 300-2, 415:
September 1885; letters 424-427
COLLECTION Utrecht, Museum van Baaren
Foundation, inv nr 35

F 106 [H 116] STILL LIFE: APPLES AND TWO
PUMPKINS

Canvas 59 × 84.5 [23¼ × 33¼]
Signed in lower left: Vincent
Nuenen September 1885
LETTER 424 [end September] See F 51
LITERATURE Vanbeselaere 1937, pp 300-2, 415:
September 1885; letters 424-427. Cat van Gogh 1959,
Rijksmuseum Kröller-Müller, nr 185: September-
October 1885
COLLECTION Otterlo, Rijksmuseum Kröller-
Müller, inv nr 240-20, cat van Gogh 1970, nr 185

F 102

F 105

F 106

F 104

F 104a

F 107

F 108

F 109 recto

F 110

F 107 [H 122] STILL LIFE: TWO BASKETS
WITH POTATOES

Canvas 66 × 79 [26 × 31]
Signed in lower left: Vincent
Nuenen September 1885
LETTERS 425 [probably 4 October] '*You will receive
a big still life of potatoes, in which I tried to get
corps, I mean, to express the material in such a way
that they become heavy, solid lumps which would
hurt you if they were thrown at you, for instance.*'
428 [October] '*Further, that one of the studies seemed
to you a variation on the brown-gray theme, well, that
certainly is the case, but all three potato studies are
like that, with this difference, that one is a study in
terre de Sienne, the second in terre de Sienne brûlée,
the third in yellow ocher and red ocher. The latter –
that is the large one – is* in my opinion *the best – notwithstanding the dull black background which I
purposely left dull because the ochers are also
naturally non- transparent colors. As to that study,
the largest one of the potatoes, it is made by changing,
by breaking, those untransparent ochers with a
transparent blue. As red ocher with yellow ocher
gives orange, their combination with blue is more
neutral, and against that neutral color, they become
either more red or more yellow. The highest light in
that whole picture is simply some pure yellow ocher.
The reason why this dull yellow stands out so is
because it is put in a wide field of, be it neutral, violet;
because ...red ocher with blue gives violet tones.*'
LITERATURE Vanbeselaere 1937, pp 300-2, 397-8,
415: October 1885; letters 424-427
COLLECTION Amsterdam, Rijksmuseum Vincent
van Gogh [Vincent van Gogh Foundation, inv
nr F 107]

F 108 [H 124] THREE BIRDS' NESTS

Canvas 33.5 × 50.5 [13¼ × 20]
Nuenen September 1885
LETTERS 425 [probably 4 October] '*I am now busy
painting still lifes of my birds' nests, four of which
are finished; I think some people who are good
observers of nature might like them because of the
colors of the moss, the dry leaves and grasses, clay,
etc.*'
428 [October] '*Well, the birds' nests were also
purposely painted against a black background,
because I want it to be obvious in these studies that
the objects do not appear in their natural surroundings, but against a conventional background.*'
LITERATURE Vanbeselaere 1937, pp 302-3, 398,
415: September 1885; letters 425, 428. Cat van
Gogh 1959, Rijksmuseum Kröller-Müller, nr 184:
September-October 1885
COLLECTION Otterlo, Rijksmuseum Kröller-
Müller, inv nr 249-20, cat van Gogh 1970, nr 184

F 109 recto [H 125] TWO BIRDS' NESTS

Canvas on pasteboard 31.5 × 43.5 [12½ × 17¼]
Nuenen September 1885
LETTERS 425 [probably 4 October] and 428
[October] See F 108
LITERATURE Vanbeselaere 1937, pp 302-3, 398,
415: September 1885; letters 425, 428
COLLECTION Amsterdam, Rijksmuseum Vincent
van Gogh [Vincent van Gogh Foundation, inv
nr F 109]

F 109 verso [H 411] SELF PORTRAIT
Paris period; see after F 388 verso

F 110 [H 128] THREE BIRDS' NESTS WITH
TREE TRUNK AND LEAVES

Canvas on panel 43 × 57 [17 × 22½]
Nuenen September 1885
LETTERS 425 [probably 4 October] and 428

[October] See F 108
LITERATURE A. Plasschaert, Onze Kunst 1903,
part 2, p 174. Vanbeselaere 1937, pp 302-3, 398,
415: September 1885; letters 425, 428
COLLECTION The Hague, Gemeente Museum, inv
nr 69-x-1947, cat 1962, nr 133 [on loan from
Wibbina Foundation, The Hague]

F 111 [H 127] FOUR BIRDS' NESTS AGAINST
A LIGHT BACKGROUND

Canvas 38.5 × 46.5 [15¼ × 18¼]
Signed in lower left: Vincent
Nuenen September-October 1885
LETTER 425 [probably 4 October] See F 108
LITERATURE Vanbeselaere 1937, pp 302, 304,
398-9, 415: October-November 1885; letters 425,
428; not painted against a black background as are
the other birds' nests but against a light one; close
to the 'mannerist' studies of October-November
COLLECTION Amsterdam, Rijksmuseum Vincent
van Gogh [Vincent van Gogh Foundation, inv
nr F 111]

F 112 [H 126] THREE BIRDS' NESTS

Canvas 33 × 42 [13 × 16½]
Signed in lower left: Vincent
Nuenen September 1885
LETTERS 425 [probably 4 October] and 428
[October] See F 108
LITERATURE Vanbeselaere 1937, pp 302-3, 398,
415: September 1885; letters 425, 428. Cat van
Gogh 1959, Rijksmuseum Kröller-Müller, nr 183:
September-October 1885
COLLECTION Otterlo, Rijksmuseum Kröller-
Müller, inv nr 248-00, cat van Gogh 1970, nr 183

F 113 [H 117] VIEW IN AMSTERDAM FROM
CENTRAL STATION

Panel 19 × 25.5 [7½ × 10]
Amsterdam [Nuenen period] October 1885
LETTER 426 [October] 'The two small panels I
painted in Amsterdam were done in a great hurry.
One even in the waiting room of the station, when I
was too early for the train, the other in the morning,
before I went to the museum at 10 o'clock. Yet I am
sending them to you, look upon them as "Dutch tiles,"
on which something is dashed off in a few strokes.'
LITERATURE A. Kerssemakers, De Amsterdammer
21 April 1912, reprinted in the English edition of
Vincent's letters under nr 435c: '...and there he was
sitting surrounded by this mob, in all tranquillity,
dressed in his shaggy ulster and his inevitable fur
cap, industriously making a few little city views...'
Vanbeselaere 1937, pp 303, 383, 415: October 1885;
letter 426
COLLECTION Amsterdam, P. and N. de Boer
Foundation

F 114 [H 129] LANDING STAGE AT
AMSTERDAM

Canvas on panel 35 × 47 [13¾ × 18½]
Signed in lower right: Vincent
Amsterdam [Nuenen period] October 1885
LITERATURE A. Kerssemakers, De Amsterdammer
21 April 1912, reprinted in the English edition of
Vincent's letters, under nr 435c: see F 113.
Vanbeselaere 1937, pp 303, 415: October 1885; not
the second sketch; F 114 is too large for a 'small
panel'
COLLECTION Bern, H. R. Hahnloser

F 111

F 112

F 113

F 114

F 115

F 116

F 117

F 120

F 115 [H 123] STILL LIFE: BASKET WITH APPLES

Canvas 30 × 47 [11¾ × 18½]
Nuenen September 1885
LETTER 424 [end September] See F 51
LITERATURE Vanbeselaere 1937, pp 300-2, 397-8, 415: October 1885; letter 428
COLLECTION The Hague, Gemeente Museum [since 1929], inv nr 55-x-1956, cat 1962, nr 134 [on loan originally from H.P. Bremmer, The Hague; after his death left on loan to the museum by his heirs]

F 116 [H 119] STILL LIFE: BASKET WITH POTATOES

Canvas 51 × 66 [20 × 26]
Nuenen September 1885
LETTER 428 [October] See F 107
LITERATURE Vanbeselaere 1937, pp 300-2, 415: October 1885; letter 428
COLLECTION Amsterdam, Rijksmuseum Vincent van Gogh [Vincent van Gogh Foundation, inv nr F 116]

F 117 [H 121] STILL LIFE WITH OPEN BIBLE, EXTINGUISHED CANDLE AND ZOLA'S JOIE DE VIVRE

Canvas 65 × 78 [25½ × 30¾]
Signed in lower left: Vincent
Nuenen October 1885
LETTER 429 [end October] 'In answer to your description of the study by Manet, I send you a still life of an open–so a broken white–Bible bound in leather, against a black background, with yellow-brown foreground, with a touch of citron yellow. I painted that in one rush, on one day.'
LITERATURE Vanbeselaere 1937, pp 303, 383, 393, 399, 415: October 1885; letter 429; compares F 117 with F 93 with regard to style; sees the same characteristics in F 1215 and F 1217. C. Nordenfalk, Journal of the Warburg and Courtauld Institutes 1947, pp 141-2: not solely a technical study of color tones–underlying it is a symbolic meaning; the Bible with a text from Isaiah and the burnt-out candle refer as a memento mori to the death of his father a half year earlier; Zola's novel La joie de vivre shows Vincent's right to adopt the ideas of the new times
COLLECTION Amsterdam, Rijksmuseum Vincent van Gogh [Vincent van Gogh Foundation, inv nr F 117]

F 118 [H 120] STILL LIFE: EARTHEN BOWL WITH POTATOES

Canvas 44.5 × 57 [17½ × 22½]
Nuenen September 1885
LETTER 428 [October] See F 107
LITERATURE R. Jacobsen, Onze Kunst 1903, part I, p 41. Vanbeselaere 1937, pp 300-2, 415: October 1885; letter 428
COLLECTION Groningen, Mrs.E. Brugmans-Beukema

F 119 [H 118] AUTUMN LANDSCAPE

Canvas on panel 64 × 87 [25¼ × 34¼]
Nuenen October 1885
LETTERS 429 [end October] 'Recently I painted a few studies out-of-doors, autumn landscapes.'
430 [4 November] 'Shortly you will receive two studies of the autumn leaves, one in yellow–poplars –the other in orange–oaks.'
LITERATURE Vanbeselaere 1937, pp 304, 400, 415: October-November 1885; letters 429, 430
COLLECTION London, Garman-Ryan Collection

F 120 [H 134] LANE IN AUTUMN

Canvas on panel 46 × 35 [18 × 13¾]
Nuenen October 1885
LETTER 429 [end October] See F 119
LITERATURE Vanbeselaere 1937, pp 304, 400, 415:
October-November 1885; letters 429, 430
COLLECTION Winterthur, Switzerland, Mrs
L. Jäggli-Hahnloser

F 118

F 119

F 122

F 121

F 126

F 124

F 126a

F 121 [H 130] THE CLOSE OF DAY IN AUTUMN: POPLARS

Canvas on panel 51 × 93 [20 × 36½]
Nuenen October-November 1885
LETTER 430 [4 November] See F 119
LITERATURE Onze Kunst 1904, part 2, p 28.
Vanbeselaere 1937, pp 304, 415: October-
November 1885; letters 429, 430
COLLECTION Utrecht, Centraal Museum
[acquired 1963; gift of the heirs of Mrs A. L. Ub-
bens-Ribbius Peletier]

F 122 [H 132] AVENUE OF POPLARS: AUTUMN

Canvas on panel 99 × 66 [39 × 26]
Nuenen October 1884
LETTER 383 [October] 'The last thing I made is a
rather large study of an avenue of poplars, with
yellow autumn leaves, the sun casting, here and there,
sparkling spots on the fallen leaves on the ground,
alternating with the long shadows of the trunks. At
the end of the road is a small cottage, and over it all
the blue sky through the autumn leaves.'
LITERATURE Vanbeselaere 1937, pp 304, 400, 415:
October-November 1885; no letter. M. E. Tralbaut,
exhib cat van Gogh Essen 1957, nr 176: letter 383,
with its 'avenue of poplars,' rather than letter 430
COLLECTION Rotterdam, Heirs of W. Nolst
Trénité

F 123 [H 133] AUTUMN LANE AT SUNSET

Canvas 46 × 33 [18 × 13]
Compare drawings F 1239 [same site] and F 1246
[similar motif and style]
Nuenen October-November 1885
LETTER 430 [4 November] See F 119
LITERATURE Vanbeselaere 1937, pp 304, 400, 415:
October-November 1885; no letter
COLLECTION Otterlo, Rijksmuseum Kröller-
Müller, inv nr 246-20, cat van Gogh 1970, nr 191

F 124 [H 131] THE POND IN THE VICARAGE
GARDEN AT NUENEN [destroyed]

Panel 92 × 104 [36¼ × 41]
Compare water color F 1234
Nuenen October-November 1885
LITERATURE Vanbeselaere 1937, pp 304-5, 400,
415: October-November 1885; letter 430; imaginary
landscape. D. Cooper, Zeichnungen und Aquarelle
von Vincent van Gogh, 1954, p 40: water color
F 1234 probably a preparatory study for F 124
COLLECTION Formerly Rotterdam, A. P. van Hoey
Smith Collection [destroyed in the battle of Arnhem
1944]

F 125 [H 135] WATER MILL AT GENNEP

Canvas on pasteboard 87 × 151 [34¼ × 59½]
Compare F 46, F 47 and water color F 1144a [same
mill]
Nuenen November 1884
LETTER 385 [November] 'Though it has been
freezing pretty hard here for the last few days, I am
still at work out-of-doors, on a rather large study
(more than 1 meter) of an old water mill at Gennep,
on the other side of Eindhoven. I want to do it
entirely out-of-doors, but it will certainly be the last
I shall paint out-of-doors this year.'
LITERATURE A. Plasschaert, Onze Kunst 1903,
part 2, p 174. Vanbeselaere 1937, pp 283, 415:
November 1884. Tralbaut, De Toerist June 1955:
identifies motif of F 125 as mill at Gennep
COLLECTION Private Collection [acquired 1947]

F 123

F 126 [H 150] PEASANT WOMAN SEATED

Panel 34 × 26 [13½ × 10¼]
Compare F 1167 recto [same hands]
Nuenen summer 1885
LITERATURE Vanbeselaere 1937, pp 300, 374, 415:
summer 1885; the style is based on the solidly
drawn figures of summer 1885
COLLECTION Formerly Paris, A. Loewy
Present owner unknown

F 126a [formerly F 126bis; H 149] PEASANT
WOMAN SEWING

Canvas 41 × 32 [16¼ × 12½]
Nuenen March 1885
LETTER 395 [1 March] See F 36
LITERATURE J. B. de la Faille, Der Cicerone 1927,
pp 101-2 [with reproduction]. Vanbeselaere 1937,
pp 291, 350-1, 415: March 1885; letter 395;
close in style to F 70. W. F. Douwes, Maandblad voor
Beeldende Kunsten 1929, pp 342-51: compares the
same motif as used by Jozef Israëls
COLLECTION Schweinfurth, Germany, Georg
Schäfer

F 127 [H 144] PEASANT WOMAN: HALF
FIGURE

Canvas on panel 45 × 27 [17¾ × 10¾]
Nuenen January 1885
LITERATURE Vanbeselaere 1937, pp 290, 415:
January 1885; close in style to F 132 and F 65 of
January
COLLECTION London, Leonard Slotover

F 127

F 125

F 128

F 131

F 132

F 133

F 130

F 128 [H 148] PEASANT WOMAN STANDING INDOORS

Canvas on panel 41 × 26 [16¼ × 10¼]
Nuenen March 1885
LITERATURE Vanbeselaere 1937, pp 291, 350-1, 415: March 1885; letter 395; the same direct approach to life as in F 36
COLLECTION Belgrade, Narodni Muzej

F 129 TWO PEASANT WOMEN DIGGING UP POTATOES, FACING RIGHT
This is the same painting as F 97

F 129a [formerly F 129bis; H 192] POTATO PLANTING: A MAN AND A WOMAN

Canvas 33 × 41 [13 × 16¼]
Compare sketch in postcard 399a and drawing F 1225 [similar motifs]
Nuenen April 1885
LETTER 399 [between 9 and 13 April] 'Enclosed you will find two scribbles of a few studies I made ...'
LITERATURE J. B. de la Faille, Der Cicerone 1927, pp 101-2 [with reproduction]. Vanbeselaere 1937, pp 297, 351-2, 374, 415: April 1885; letter 399; clear modelling of the volumes, as in F 148
COLLECTION Zurich, Kunsthaus [acquired 1927], inv nr 1860

F 130 [H 137] HEAD OF A PEASANT WOMAN WITH WHITE CAP: FRONT VIEW

Canvas on panel 45 × 36 [17¾ × 14¼]
Signed very indistinctly in upper right: Vincent
Compare sketches in letters 397 and 409, F 85, F 85a, F 140, F 141 and SP 1668 [same model]
Study for second figure from the left in THE POTATO EATERS [F 82]
Nuenen March 1885
LETTER 397 [early April] 'The head I painted today is, I think, as good as the one with the big white cap you have ...'
LITERATURE Vanbeselaere 1937, pp 290, 415: January-February 1885. J. G. van Gelder, De Aardappeleters, 1949: portrait of Stien de Groot; study used for F 78
EDITORS' COMMENT According to letter 397 Theo took some studies with him when he visited Nuenen, probably for his father's funeral, around 30 March. F 130 must be one of them. The other sketch in letter 397 – 'the head I painted today' – closely resembles F 160 [see there].
COLLECTION Amsterdam, Rijksmuseum Vincent van Gogh [Vincent van Gogh Foundation, inv nr F 130]

F 131 [H 162] HEAD OF A PEASANT WOMAN: LEFT PROFILE

Canvas, relined, formerly canvas on panel 41 × 34 [16¼ × 13½]
Nuenen probably April 1885
LITERATURE Vanbeselaere 1937, pp 293, 343-4, 415: April-June 1885; close in technique to F 77 recto of April
COLLECTION The Hague, Gemeente Museum [since 1963], inv nr 53-x-1963 [on loan from R. T. H. Steinmetz, The Hague]

F 132 [H 136] HEAD OF A PEASANT WOMAN: LEFT PROFILE

Canvas on panel 40 × 32.5 [15¾ × 12¾]
Compare sketch in letter 392, drawings F 1150 recto and F 1151 [same model]
Nuenen December 1884 or shortly later
LETTER 392 [about 20 January] See F 65
LITERATURE Vanbeselaere 1937, pp 289, 332, 336, 339, 340-1, 415: January 1885; letter 392; the first

of about 40 painted studies of heads
COLLECTION Sale London [Christie], 6-10
December 1968, nr 52
Present owner unknown

F 133 [H 160] HEAD OF A PEASANT WOMAN:
RIGHT PROFILE

Canvas on panel 39.5 × 30 [15½ × 11¾]
Compare F 153, drawings F 1178 and F 1185 [same
model]
Nuenen December 1884 or shortly later
LETTER 390 [mid-December] See F 80
LITERATURE Vanbeselaere 1937, pp 291, 342, 415:
March 1885; belongs to a series of heads against a
light background; close in style to F 70 of
February-March
COLLECTION The Hague, G. J. Nieuwenhuizen
Segaar Art Gallery [acquired 1946]

F 134 [H 143] HEAD OF A PEASANT WOMAN:
HALF PROFILE TO THE LEFT

Canvas on panel 38.5 × 26.5 [15¼ × 10½]
Compare F 135, F 136 and drawing F 1170 [same
model]
Nuenen December 1884 or shortly later
LETTERS 390 [mid-December] See F 80
394 [February 1885] and 395 [1 March] See F 69
LITERATURE Vanbeselaere 1937, pp 293, 344, 415:
April-June 1885; close in technique to the sketch
for THE POTATO EATERS, F 77 recto, of April
COLLECTION Paris, Musée National du Louvre,
inv nr RF 1954-20, cat Impressionistes 1959, nr 142

F 135 [H 142] HEAD OF A PEASANT WOMAN:
RIGHT PROFILE

Canvas on panel 37.5 × 24.5 [14¾ × 9¾]
Compare F 134, F 136 and F 1170 [same model]
Nuenen December 1884 or shortly later
LETTERS 390 [mid-December] See F 80
394 [February 1885] and F 395 [1 March] See F 69
LITERATURE Vanbeselaere 1937, pp 290, 342, 415:
March 1885
COLLECTION Cincinnati, The Cincinnati Art
Museum [gift of Mr and Mrs John J. Emery], inv
nr 1962-15

F 136 [H 141] HEAD OF A PEASANT WOMAN:
RIGHT PROFILE

Canvas on panel 40 × 30 [15¾ × 11¾]
Compare F 134, F 135 and drawing F 1170 [same
model]
Nuenen December 1884 or shortly later
LETTERS 390 [mid-December] See F 80
394 [February 1885] and 395 [1 March] See F 69
LITERATURE Vanbeselaere 1937, pp 293, 344, 415:
April-June 1885; close in technique to F 77 recto of
April. V. W. van Gogh, The Complete Letters of
Vincent van Gogh, 1958, letter 435a: the model is
identified as Sine de Groot
COLLECTION Paris, Dufresne Art Gallery

F 136a [formerly F 136bis; H 170] HEAD OF A
PEASANT WOMAN WITH DARK CAP: FULL
FACE

Canvas on panel 35 × 26 [13¾ × 10¼]
Compare drawing F 1176, reproduced with letter
389 [same model]
Nuenen December 1884
LETTER 389 [14 December] 'Enclosed you will find a
few scribbles of the heads I am working on...'
LITERATURE Not in Faille 1928 or Vanbeselaere
1937
COLLECTION Amsterdam, Private Collection

F 134

F 135

F 136

F 136a

F 129a

F 137

F 138

F 139

F 142

F 143

F 137 [H 157] BUST OF A PEASANT WOMAN:
FULL FACE, LIGHT BACKGROUND

Canvas 40 × 30.5 [15¾ × 12]
Compare F 138, drawings F 1172, F 1173 and F 1175
[same model]
Nuenen December 1884 or shortly later
LETTERS 390 [mid-December] See F 80
394 [February 1885] and 395 [1 March] See F 69
LITERATURE Vanbeselaere 1937, pp 290, 341, 415:
January-February 1885; possibly letter 394;
belongs to a group of smoothly painted heads in a
lighter tonality, painted between F 65 of January
and F 70 of February-March. C. Derkert, Konsthistorisk Tidskrift 1946, pp 107-9: analysis of the
colors as Prussian blue, burnt sienna, Naples
yellow and white, *no* black
COLLECTION Stockholm, Mrs H. Nordin

F 138 [H 158] HEAD OF A PEASANT WOMAN:
FULL FACE, LIGHT BACKGROUND

Canvas 33 × 23 [13 × 9]
Compare F 137, drawings F 1172, F 1173 and F 1175
[same model]
Nuenen December 1884 or shortly later
LETTER 390 [mid-December] See F 80
394 [February 1885] and 395 [1 March] See F 69
LITERATURE Vanbeselaere 1937, pp 290, 342, 337,
415: January-February 1885; belongs to a group of
smoothly painted studies of heads in a lighter
tonality, painted between F 65 of January and F 70
of February-March. J. G. van Gelder, Beeldende
Kunst 1942, p 5 [English edition, 1946]: portrait of
Stien de Groot
COLLECTION New York, Koetser Art Gallery

F 139 [H 172] PEASANT WOMAN RAKING

Canvas 38.5 × 26.5 [15¼ × 10½]
Compare drawing F 1277 [similar motif]
Nuenen July 1885
LETTER 418 [July] '*When I send you and Serret some
studies of diggers or peasant women weeding, glean-
ing, etc,* as the beginning *of a whole series of all
kinds of labor in the fields...*'
LITERATURE Vanbeselaere 1937, pp 300, 374, 415:
summer 1885; the style is based on the solidly
drawn figures of summer 1885
COLLECTION New York, Mr and Mrs
P. Schweitzer

F 140 [H 138] PEASANT WOMAN WITH A
WHITE CAP: LEFT THREE-QUARTER VIEW

Canvas on pasteboard 47.5 × 35.5 [18¾ × 14]
Compare sketches in letters 397 and 409, F 85, F 85a,
F 130, F 141 and SP 1668 [same model]
Nuenen March 1885
LETTER 409 [after 10 May] See F 85
LITERATURE Vanbeselaere 1937, pp 290, 415:
January 1885. Cat The Maitland Gift 1963, The
National Gallery of Scotland, p 34: presumably the
same model as in F 130
EDITORS' COMMENT See F 85
COLLECTION Edinburgh, National Gallery of
Scotland [acquired 1961; Maitland Gift], reg
nr 2216

F 141 [H 139] HEAD OF A PEASANT WOMAN
WITH A WHITE CAP: LEFT THREE-QUARTER
VIEW

Canvas 41 × 34.5 [16¼ × 13½]
Signed in upper left: Vincent
Compare sketches in letters 397 and 409, F 81, F 85,
F 85a, F 130, F 140 and SP 1668 [same model]
Nuenen May 1885
LETTER 409 [after 10 May] see F 85
LITERATURE Vanbeselaere 1937, pp 293, 343-4,

F 140

415: April-June 1885; close in technique to F 77 recto
COLLECTION Winnipeg, John A. MacAulay

F 142 [H 190] PEASANT WOMAN DIGGING IN
FRONT OF HER COTTAGE

Canvas on pasteboard 31 × 41 [12¼ × 16¼]
Nuenen June-July 1885
LETTERS 414 [June] and 417 [15 July] See F 89
LITERATURE Vanbeselaere 1937, pp 298-9, 396,
415: July 1885; letter 418
COLLECTION Chicago, The Art Institute of
Chicago [acquired 1968; bequest of John
J. Ireland], inv nr 1968.92

F 143 [H 151] PEASANT WOMAN SEATED
WITH ARMS CROSSED

Canvas on panel 36 × 26 [14¼ × 10¼]
Compare drawings F 1180, F 1189 and F 1192 [same
model]
Nuenen December 1884 or shortly later
LETTERS 390 [mid-December] See F 80
394 [February 1885] and 395 [1 March] See F 69
LITERATURE Vanbeselaere 1937, pp 289, 415:
before January 1885
COLLECTION Basle, Max Wirth

F 144 [H 154] HEAD OF A PEASANT WOMAN:
RIGHT PROFILE

Canvas on panel 40.5 × 30.5 [16 × 12]
Compare drawing F 1174 [same model]
Nuenen December 1884 or shortly later
LETTERS 390 [mid-December] See F 80
394 [February 1885] and 395 [1 March] See F 69
LITERATURE Vanbeselaere 1937, pp 290, 341-2,
415: January-February 1885; belongs to a series of
smoothly painted studies of heads in a lighter
tonality, painted between F 65 of January and F 70
of March 1885
COLLECTION Montreal, Miss Olive Hosmer

F 141

F 144

F 144a

F 145

F 144a [formerly F 144bis; H 153] PEASANT
WOMAN SEATED: RIGHT PROFILE

Paper on panel 36 × 27 [14¼ × 10¾]
Compare drawings F 1181 and F 1190 [same model]
Nuenen December 1884 or shortly later, in the
weeks before THE POTATO EATERS of April 1885
LITERATURE Not in Faille 1928 or Vanbeselaere
1937
COLLECTION The Hague, Ministry of Cultural
Affairs, Recreation and Social Welfare [on loan
from Dienst voor 's Rijks Verspreide Kunstvoor-
werpen]

F 145 [H 155] PEASANT WOMAN PEELING
POTATOES

Canvas on panel 42 × 32 [16½ × 12½]
Compare drawing F 1208
Nuenen March 1885
LETTER 395 [1 March] See F 69
LITERATURE Vanbeselaere 1937, pp 291, 350-1,
415: March 1885; letter 395
COLLECTION London, Jacques O'Hana Ltd
Collection

F 146 [H 145] HEAD OF AN OLD PEASANT
WOMAN WITH WHITE CAP: FULL FACE

Canvas on pasteboard 33 × 26 [13 × 10¼]
Compare F 74, F 75, drawings F 1149 and F 1193a
[same model]
Nuenen December 1884 or shortly later
LETTERS 390 [December] See F 80
394 [February 1885] and 395 [1 March] See F 69
LITERATURE Vanbeselaere 1937, pp 290, 415:
January-February 1885; painted between F 132 of
January and F 70 of March
COLLECTION Aalst, Netherlands, Mrs H. van
Ogtrop-van Kempen [acquired 1929]

F 146a [formerly F 146bis; H 146] HEAD OF A
PEASANT WOMAN WITH WHITE CAP: FULL
FACE

Canvas 43.5 × 37 [17¼ × 14½]
Compare drawings F 1148, F 1193 [same model] and
F 1224 [perhaps the same model]
Nuenen December 1884 or shortly later
LETTERS 390 [mid-December] See F 80
394 [February 1885] and 395 [1 March] See F 69
LITERATURE J. B. de la Faille, Der Cicerone 1927,
p 102 [with reproduction]. Vanbeselaere 1937, pp
293, 344, 415: April-June 1885; close in technique
to F 77 recto
COLLECTION Prague-New York, Paul Schmolka

F 147 [H 171] PEASANT WOMAN DIGGING
POTATOES

Canvas on panel 41 × 31 [16¼ × 12¼]
Compare F 96 and drawing F 1298 [left figure]
Nuenen August 1885
LETTER 421 [August] See F 96
LITERATURE Vanbeselaere 1937, pp 304, 374, 393,
415: October-November 1885; style based on the
solidly drawn figures of summer 1885
COLLECTION Amsterdam, Private Collection

F 148 [H 191] PEASANT WOMAN LAUNDERING

Canvas 29.5 × 36 [11½ × 14¼]
Nuenen summer 1885 [?]
LITERATURE Vanbeselaere 1937, pp 297, 352, 415:
April 1885; same pictorial qualities and clear
modelling of volumes as in F 69 and F 129a.
J. Leymarie, Van Gogh, 1951, p 98, nr 22:
composition taken over from A. Mauve's WOMAN
IN HER KITCHEN GARDEN [Rotterdam, Museum
Boymans-van Beuningen, inv nr 1499], though

F 146a

different in technique and in spirit
COLLECTION Hexham, Northumberland, Clive
Cookson

F 149 [H 156] WOMAN WITH A BOY ON HER
LAP

Canvas on pasteboard 43 × 34 [17 × 13½]
Nuenen March-April 1885, before THE POTATO
EATERS
LITERATURE Vanbeselaere 1937, pp 290, 415:
January 1885; close in style to F 132 and F 65;
mentioned in letter 392 of January 1885
COLLECTION London, Jacques O'Hana Ltd
Collection

F 148

F 146

F 147

F 149

F 48a [formerly F 48bis; H 51] WATER MILL
AT KOL, NEAR NUENEN
Nuenen May 1884

F 150

F 151

F 152

F 153

F 153a

F 154

F 155

F 156

F 150 [H 166] HEAD OF A PEASANT WOMAN:
LEFT HALF PROFILE, LIGHT BACKGROUND

Canvas 39 × 26 [15¼ × 10¼]
Nuenen December 1884 or shortly later
LETTERS 390 [mid-December] See F 80
394 [February 1885] and 395 [1 March] See F 69
LITERATURE Vanbeselaere 1937, pp 291, 342, 415:
March 1885; belongs to a series of monochrome
heads, mostly against a light background, close in
style to F 70 of March
COLLECTION Otterlo, Rijksmuseum Kröller-
Müller, inv nr 241-20, cat van Gogh 1970, nr 172

F 151 [H 152] HEAD OF A PEASANT WOMAN:
THREE QUARTERS TO THE LEFT

Canvas on panel 36 × 25.5 [14¼ × 10]
Nuenen December 1884 or shortly later
LETTERS 390 [mid-December] See F 80
394 [February 1885] and 395 [1 March] See F 69
LITERATURE Vanbeselaere 1937, pp 290, 342, 347,
415: January-February 1885; belongs to a series of
smoothly painted studies of heads in a lighter
tonality, painted between F 65 of January and F 70
of February-March
COLLECTION Otterlo, Rijksmuseum Kröller-
Müller, inv nr 237-20, cat van Gogh 1970, nr 169

F 152 [H 176] PEASANT WOMAN SWEEPING

Canvas on panel 41 × 27 [16¼ × 10¾]
Nuenen March 1885
LETTER 395 [1 March] See F 36
LITERATURE Vanbeselaere 1937, pp 291, 350-1,
415: March 1885; letter 395
COLLECTION Otterlo, Rijksmuseum Kröller-
Müller, inv nr 227-13, cat van Gogh 1970, nr 180

F 153 [H 165] HEAD OF A PEASANT WOMAN:
RIGHT PROFILE, LIGHT BACKGROUND

Canvas on panel 26 × 20 [10¼ × 8]
Compare F 133, drawings F 1178 and F 1185 [same
model]
Nuenen December 1884 or shortly later
LETTERS 390 [mid-December] See F 80
394 [February 1885] and 395 [1 March] See F 69
LITERATURE Vanbeselaere 1937, pp 291, 342, 415:
March 1885; belongs to a series of monochrome
heads, mostly against a light background, close in
style to F 70 of March
COLLECTION Otterlo, Rijksmuseum Kröller-
Müller, inv nr 224-13, cat van Gogh 1970, nr 173

F 153a [formerly F 153bis; H 161] HEAD OF A
PEASANT WOMAN: LEFT PROFILE, LIGHT
BACKGROUND

Canvas on panel 25 × 19 [9¾ × 7½]
Nuenen December 1884 or shortly later
LETTERS 390 [mid-December] See F 80
394 [February 1885] and 395 [1 March] See F 69
LITERATURE Not in Faille 1928 or Vanbeselaere
1937
COLLECTION New York, Mr and Mrs Donald
S. Stralem

F 154 [H 167] HEAD OF A PEASANT WOMAN:
THREE QUARTERS TO THE LEFT

Canvas 40 × 30 [15¾ × 11¾]
Compare drawing F 1177 [same model]
Nuenen December 1884 or shortly later
LETTERS 390 [mid-December] See F 80
394 [February 1885] and 395 [1 March] See F 69
LITERATURE Vanbeselaere 1937, pp 293, 344, 415:
April-June 1885; close in technique to F 77 recto
COLLECTION Otterlo, Rijksmuseum Kröller-
Müller, inv nr 225-17, cat van Gogh 1970, nr 171

F 158

F 155 [H 163] PEASANT WOMAN IN A MOSS-
GREEN SHAWL

Canvas 45 × 35 [17¾ × 13¾]
Compare F 161 [same model]
Nuenen May-June 1885 [?]
LITERATURE Vanbeselaere 1937, pp 293, 344,
376-7, 415: April-June 1885; letter 410; probably
painted after reading, in Zola's *Germinal*, a
description of a woman about to be executed;
close in technique to F 77 recto of April
COLLECTION Lyons, Musée de Lyon, inv nr
1937-34, cat VII La Peinture du XIXe et XXe Siècle
1956, nr 196, pp 248-50

F 156 [H 140] PEASANT WOMAN IN A WHITE
CAP: BUST, THREE QUARTERS TO THE LEFT

Canvas on panel 42.5 × 34 [16¾ × 13½]
Compare drawing F 1171 [same model]
Nuenen December 1884 or shortly later
LETTERS 390 [mid-December] See F 80
394 [February 1885] and 395 [1 March] See F 69
LITERATURE Vanbeselaere 1937, pp 292, 341, 343,
415: April-June 1885; compare drawings F 1171 and
F 1172; depicts one of the models from THE
POTATO EATERS, but done afterwards
COLLECTION Amsterdam, Rijksmuseum Vincent
van Gogh [Vincent van Gogh Foundation, inv
nr F 156]

F 157 [H 169] PEASANT WOMAN DARNING
STOCKINGS

Canvas on panel 28.5 × 18.5 [11¼ × 7¼]
Compare drawing F 1205
Nuenen February-March 1885
LETTER 396 [mid-March] '*But I do make* studies…
*I am brooding over a couple of larger, more elaborate
things…in that case I should keep the studies in
question here for the time being, because then I should
certainly need them – it would be, for instance, some-
thing like this: namely figures against the light of a
window…as well as turned toward the light.*'
LITERATURE Vanbeselaere 1937, pp 300, 415:
summer 1885
COLLECTION Formerly The Hague, Heirs of
H. P. Bremmer
Present owner unknown

F 158 [H 175] PEASANT WOMAN BY THE
FIREPLACE

Canvas on panel 29.5 × 40 [11½ × 15¾]
Compare F 176, drawings F 1211, F 1212, F 1288,
F 1291 [same model in same interior], F 1215,
F 1217 and F 1218 [same interior]
Nuenen March 1885 or shortly later
LITERATURE Vanbeselaere 1937, pp 291, 350-1,
415: March 1885; letter 395
COLLECTION Paris, Private Collection

F 157

F 159

F 160

F 160a

F 161

F 163

F 164

F 165

F 166

F 159 [H 168] SKETCH OF THE HEAD OF A
PEASANT WOMAN: FULL FACE, LIGHT
BACKGROUND

Canvas on panel 46 × 34 [18 × 13½]
Nuenen December 1884 or shortly later
LETTERS 390 [mid-December] See F 80
394 [February 1885] See F 69
LITERATURE Vanbeselaere 1937, pp 291, 342, 415:
March 1885; belongs to a series of monochrome
heads, mostly against a light background, close in
style to F 70 of March
COLLECTION Amsterdam, H. A. D. Thomas

F 160 [H 159] PEASANT WOMAN IN A RED
BONNET

Canvas 42.5 × 29.5 [16¾ × 11½]
Compare sketch in letter 397 and F 69 [same model]
Nuenen early April 1885, before THE POTATO
EATERS
LETTER 397 [early April] '...today's is a young girl's
almost a child's head... The head I painted today is,
I think, as good as the one with the big white cap you
have...'
LITERATURE Vanbeselaere 1937, pp 292, 335,
338-9, 342, 415: April 1885; letter 397; F 160 is
characteristic of the heads painted after F 70
EDITORS' COMMENT See F 130. The sketch in
letter 397 does closely resemble F 160, but the
painting can hardly be considered to depict 'a
young girl's, almost a child's head.'
COLLECTION Amsterdam, Rijksmuseum Vincent
van Gogh [Vincent van Gogh Foundation, inv
nr F 160]

F 160a PORTRAIT OF A PEASANT [study for
THE POTATO EATERS]

Canvas 39 × 30 [15¼ × 11¾]
Compare F 82 and drawing F 1198 [same model]
Nuenen April 1885
LITERATURE Not in Faille 1928, Vanbeselaere
1937 or Faille 1939
COLLECTION Aix-en-Provence, Mrs E. Mahé-
Williame

F 161 [H 164] HOODED PEASANT WOMAN:
HALF LENGTH

Canvas 45.5 × 33 [18 × 13]
Compare F 155 [same model]
Nuenen May-June 1885 [?]
LITERATURE Vanbeselaere 1937, pp 293, 343-4,
415: April-June 1885; close in technique to F 77
recto
COLLECTION Amsterdam, Rijksmuseum Vincent
van Gogh [Vincent van Gogh Foundation, inv
nr F 161]

F 162 [H 180] WEAVER: THE WHOLE LOOM,
FACING RIGHT

Canvas 37 × 45 [14½ × 17¾]
Compare water color F 1108 and drawing F 1121
Nuenen January 1884 or shortly later
LITERATURE Vanbeselaere 1937, pp 281, 317, 415:
May 1884
COLLECTION The Hague, Gemeente Museum, inv
nr 56-x-1956, cat 1962, nr 132 [on loan from the
heirs of H. P. Bremmer]

F 163 [H 183] HEAD OF A PEASANT

Canvas 39 × 30.5 [15¼ × 12]
Nuenen May 1885
LETTER 408 [after 8 May] 'Then I'm working on...
about six heads.'
LITERATURE Vanbeselaere 1937, pp 292, 343, 415:
April-June 1885; depicts one of the models from

THE POTATO EATERS, but done afterwards; letter
408; the other five heads spoken of in the letter are
F 69, F 80a, F 156, F 164 and F 388 verso
COLLECTION Brussels, Musée Royal des Beaux-
Arts [acquired 1931]

F 164 [H 184] HEAD OF A YOUNG PEASANT
WITH A PIPE

Canvas on panel 38 × 30 [15 × 11¾]
Nuenen May 1885 or shortly later
LETTER 408 [after 8 May] See F 163
LITERATURE Vanbeselaere 1937, pp 292, 343, 415:
April-June 1885; letter 408; depicts one of the
models from THE POTATO EATERS, but done
afterwards
COLLECTION Amsterdam, Rijksmuseum Vincent
van Gogh [Vincent van Gogh Foundation, inv
nr F 164]

F 165 [H 185] PORTRAIT OF A PEASANT

Panel 44.5 × 33.5 [17½ × 13¼]
Nuenen possibly February-March 1885
LITERATURE Vanbeselaere 1937, pp 290, 342, 415:
January-February 1885; belongs to a series of
studies of heads in a lighter tonality, painted
between F 65 of January and F 70 of March
COLLECTION Kansas City, The William Rockhill
Nelson Gallery of Art [acquired 1937], inv nr 37.1

F 166 [H 173] PEASANT DIGGING

Canvas 45.5 × 31.5 [18 × 12½]
Compare drawing F 1311 [same model]
Nuenen August 1885
LITERATURE Vanbeselaere 1937, pp 300, 415:
September 1885
COLLECTION Otterlo, Rijksmuseum Kröller-
Müller, inv nr 244-20, cat van Gogh 1970, nr 181

F 167 [H 179] PEASANT SEATED AT TABLE
[study for THE POTATO EATERS]

Canvas 44 × 32.5 [17¼ × 12¾]
Compare F 82
Nuenen March-April 1885
LITERATURE Vanbeselaere 1937, pp 291, 350-1,
415: March 1885; belongs to a series of studies with
the effect of a heavy shadow cast on a wall mentioned
in letter 395. Cat van Gogh 1959, Rijksmuseum
Kröller-Müller, nr 178: this figure was later
adapted to serve as the left corner figure in THE
POTATO EATERS [78]
COLLECTION Otterlo, Rijksmuseum Kröller-
Müller, inv nr 243-20, cat van Gogh 1970, nr 178

F 168 [H 189] HEAD OF A PEASANT: RIGHT
PROFILE

Canvas 47 × 30 [18½ × 11¾]
Nuenen December 1884 or shortly later
LETTERS 390 [mid-December] See F 80
394 [February 1885] See F 69
LITERATURE Vanbeselaere 1937, pp 290, 341, 415:
January-February 1885; belongs to a series of
studies of heads in a lighter tonality painted
between F 65 of January and F 70 of March. Cat van
Gogh 1959, Rijksmuseum Kröller-Müller, nr 175:
March 1885; the head is treated flatly to emphasize
its contour, as in F 70, F 70a and F 150; letter 396
COLLECTION Otterlo, Rijksmuseum Kröller-
Müller, inv nr 238-20, cat van Gogh 1970, nr 175

F 162

F 167

F 168

F 169

F 169a

F 171

F 171a

F 170

F 169 [H 182] HEAD OF A PEASANT WITH A PIPE: HALFPROFILE TO THE RIGHT

Canvas 44 × 32 [17¼ × 12½]
Nuenen November 1884
LETTER 385 [November] *'Since I wrote you, I have also been working on other studies, including two heads of polder workers.'*
LITERATURE Vanbeselaere 1937, pp 289, 331, 344: hesitates between November 1884-letter 386 [pp 289, 331] and April-June 1885 [pp 343-4, 416]; in any case considers it close to F 77 recto, the sketch for THE POTATO EATERS. Cat van Gogh 1959, Rijksmuseum Kröller-Müller, nr 176: November 1884; probably to be identified with one of the two 'heads of polder workers' mentioned in letter 385
COLLECTION Otterlo, Rijksmuseum Kröller-Müller, inv nr 235-20, cat van Gogh 1970, nr 176

F 169a HEAD OF A PEASANT

Canvas 35.5 × 26 [14 × 10¼]
Nuenen January-April 1885
LITERATURE Not in Faille 1928, Vanbeselaere 1937 or Faille 1939
COLLECTION Athens, Stavros S. Niarchos

F 170 [H 204] COTTAGE WITH PEASANT GOING HOME

Canvas 64 × 76 [25¼ × 30]
Signed in lower left: Vincent
Nuenen June-July 1885
LETTERS 414 [June] and 417 [15 July] See F 89
LITERATURE Vanbeselaere 1937, pp 298-9, 396, 415: July 1885; letters 414, 417; belongs to the series of huts done shortly after F 83
EDITORS' COMMENT Study of old photographs of the painting indicates that the trees have been repainted.
COLLECTION London, Mrs M. Q. Morris

F 171 [H 178] THE BASKET MAKER

Canvas 41 × 35 [16¼ × 13¾]
Compare F 171a
Nuenen March 1885
LETTER 395 [1 March] See F 36
LITERATURE Vanbeselaere 1937, pp 292, 350-1, 415: March 1885; letter 395
COLLECTION Switzerland, Private Collection

F 171a [formerly F 171b; H 810] THE BASKET MAKER

Canvas 41 × 33 [16¼ × 13]
Compare F 171
Nuenen March 1885
LETTER 395 [1 March] See F 36
LITERATURE Not in Faille 1928 or Vanbeselaere 1937. J. Rewald, L'Amour de l'Art 1938, pp 256-7
COLLECTION Formerly Aix-en-Provence, A. Bernheim
Present owner unknown

F 172 [H 177] THE PLOWER

Canvas 70.5 × 170 [27¾ × 67]
Compare drawing F 1142 and SP 1669
Nuenen August 1884
LETTERS 374 [August], R 47 [August] and R 48 [September] See F 41
LITERATURE Vanbeselaere 1937, pp 283, 326, 416: August 1884; the 'Plower' mentioned in letter 374, painted as a study for a decoration by Hermans, symbolizing the seasons, for Hermans' dining room in Eindhoven
EDITORS' COMMENT See F 41
COLLECTION Wuppertal, Von der Heydt Museum der Stadt Wuppertal [acquired 1962; gift of E. Baron

von der Heydt]

F 173 THE MIDWIFE

Left out by Faille in his manuscript for the present edition
See REJECTED WORKS

F 174 [H 147] THE MIDWIFE: HEAD WITH WHITE BONNET
Antwerp period; see after F 212a

F 175 [H 181] THE SPINNING WHEEL

Canvas on pasteboard 34 × 44 [13½ × 17¼]
Nuenen probably autumn 1885
LITERATURE Vanbeselaere 1937, pp 304, 393, 416: October-November 1885; new conception of space, as in F 96
COLLECTION Amsterdam, Rijksmuseum Vincent van Gogh [Vincent van Gogh Foundation, inv nr F 175]

F 176 [H 174] PEASANT WOMAN BY THE FIREPLACE

Canvas 44 × 38 [17¼ × 15]
Compare F 158, drawings F 1211, F 1212, F 1288, F 1291 [same model in same interior], F 1215, F 1217 and F 1218 [same interior]
Nuenen May 1885 or shortly later
LITERATURE Vanbeselaere 1937, pp 300, 416: September 1885
COLLECTION Norwalk, Connecticut, Mr and Mrs Mortimer Hays

F 175

F 176

F 172

F 177

F 183

F 182

F 178 recto

F 177 [H 205] TWO RATS

Panel 29.5 × 41.5 [11½ × 16¼]
Nuenen 1884 [?]
LITERATURE H. F. W. Jeltes, De Kroniek 6 April
1907. A. Plasschaert, Onze Kunst 1904, part 2,
p 152. Vanbeselaere 1937, p 416: Paris
COLLECTION Wassenaar, Mrs C. E. van Beuningen-
Fentener van Vlissingen

F 177a STUFFED KALONG
Paris period; see after F 388 verso

F 178 recto [formerly F 178 verso; H 217] STILL
LIFE WITH POTTERY, BEERGLASS AND
BOTTLES

Canvas 39.5 × 29.5 [15½ × 11½]
Compare F 58
Nuenen November 1884 or shortly later
LETTER 387 [20 November] See F 49
LITERATURE Cat 1935, Gemeente Museum,
nr 159: Nuenen 1885. Vanbeselaere 1937, pp 286,
347, 416: April 1885; close in style to F 69
COLLECTION The Hague, Gemeente Museum
[acquired 1918], inv nr 3-1918, cat 1962, nr 135

F 178 verso [formerly F 178; H 187] SELF
PORTRAIT
Paris period; see after F 388 verso

F 179 recto PORTRAIT OF A FARMER

Canvas 41.5 × 31 [16¼ × 12¼]
Nuenen 1885
LITERATURE Faille 1928, nr 179 verso: Nuenen.
Not in Vanbeselaere 1937 or Faille 1939
COLLECTION Amsterdam, Rijksmuseum Vincent
van Gogh [Vincent van Gogh Foundation, inv
nr F 179]

F 179 verso [formerly F 179; H 229] SELF
PORTRAIT
Paris period; see after F 388 verso

F 180 [H 188] SELF PORTRAIT
Paris period; see after F 388 verso

F 181 [H 186] SELF PORTRAIT BEFORE THE
EASEL
Paris period; see after F 388 verso

F 182 [H 199] THE VICARAGE AT NUENEN:
THE HOUSE OF VINCENT'S PARENTS, FRONT
VIEW

Canvas 33 × 43 [13 × 17]
Compare drawing F 1343a
Nuenen autumn 1885
LITERATURE Vanbeselaere 1937, pp 303, 393, 416:
October-November 1885; close in style to F 93 and
F 117
COLLECTION Amsterdam, Rijksmuseum Vincent
van Gogh [Vincent van Gogh Foundation, inv
nr F 182]

F 183 [H 195] THE VICARAGE AT NUENEN BY
MOONLIGHT: VIEW FROM THE GARDEN

Canvas 41 × 54.5 [16¼ × 21½]
Compare drawing F 1343
Nuenen November 1885
LITERATURE Vanbeselaere 1937, pp 304, 416:
October-November 1885
COLLECTION Cannes, Stoliar Galleries

F 184 [H 194] THE OLD TOWER AT NUENEN: TWO FIGURES IN THE FOREGROUND

Canvas on panel 33.5 × 44 [13¼ × 17¼]
Nuenen second half of February 1884
LETTERS R 40 [25 February] *'And during these last mild days I have been painting in the fields: a little country cemetery.'*
358 [between 25 February and about 9 March] *I have now painted the little old church ...'*
363a [about 17 March] *'...I wrote you I had yet ... and the painted study of the old tower, which at the time you said you were eager for.'*
LITERATURE Vanbeselaere 1937, pp 282, 416: May 1884
COLLECTION Amerongen, Netherlands, Mrs H. d'Audretsch-Krop

F 179 recto

F 184

F 185a

F 191

F 187

F 191a

F 185 [H 197] THE VICARAGE GARDEN AT NUENEN

Paper on panel 25 × 57 [9¾ × 22½]
Compare drawing F 1133
Nuenen end April 1884
LITERATURE Vanbeselaere 1937, pp 282, 416:
April-May 1884
COLLECTION Groningen, Groninger Museum voor
Stad en Ommelanden [acquired 1962], inv nr
1962-200

F 185a [formerly F 185bis; H 198] LANDSCAPE
WITH CHURCH

Canvas 22 × 37 [8¾ × 14½]
Nuenen [?] 1885 [?]
LITERATURE Not in Faille 1928 or Vanbeselaere
1937
COLLECTION Sale London [Christie] 6-10 December 1968, nr 67
Present owner unknown

F 186 [H 20] BULB FIELDS
The Hague period; see after F 15a

F 187 [H 193] COTTAGE UNDER THE TREES,
WITH A PEASANT WOMAN

Canvas 47.5 × 46 [18¾ × 18]
Nuenen June-July 1885
LETTERS 414 [June] and 417 [15 July] See F 89
LITERATURE De Kroniek 19 December 1903, pp
404-5. R. Jacobsen, Onze Kunst 1904, part 2, p 1
[with reproduction]. Vanbeselaere 1937, pp 299,
396, 416: July 1885; letters 417, 418; belongs to the
series of huts done shortly after F 83
COLLECTION Sale London [Sotheby] 6 July 1960,
nr 119
Present owner unknown

F 188 [H 207] LANDSCAPE WITH A CHURCH
AT TWILIGHT
Drenthe period; see after F 23

F 189 [H 206] FOOTBRIDGE ACROSS A DITCH
The Hague period; see after F 15a

F 190 [H 208] VILLAGE AT SUNSET

Canvas on pasteboard 57 × 82 [22½ × 32¼]
Nuenen 1884
LITERATURE R. Jacobsen, Onze Kunst 1903,
part 1, p 115. A. Plasschaert, Onze Kunst 1904,
part 1, p 152. Vanbeselaere 1937, pp 298-9, 396,
416: July 1885; letters 417, 418
COLLECTION Amsterdam, Rijksmuseum [gift of
Mr and Mrs D. A. J. Kessler-Hülsmann, nr 22], in v
nr A 3307, Annual report 1940, pp 14, 18

F 191 [H 201] LANDSCAPE WITH DITCH

Canvas on pasteboard 35 × 43 [13¾ × 17]
Nuenen October-November 1885
LITERATURE Vanbeselaere 1937, pp 305, 400, 416:
October-November 1885
COLLECTION Lugano-Castagnola, Switzerland,
Thyssen-Bornemisza Collection

F 191a [formerly F 191bis; H 202] COUNTRY
LANE WITH TWO FIGURES

Canvas on panel 30 × 38 [11¾ × 15]
Nuenen autumn 1885
LITERATURE Not in Faille 1928 or Vanbeselaere
1937
COLLECTION Formerly Amsterdam, B. Houthakker Art Gallery
Present owner unknown

F 185

F 190

F 193

F 195

F 192 [H 200] EDGE OF A WOOD
The Hague period; see after F 15a

F 193 [H 203] SHEAVES OF WHEAT

Canvas 40 × 30 [15¾ × 11¾]
Compare drawings F 1339, F 1340, F 1341 and F 1342
Nuenen August 1885
LITERATURE Vanbeselaere 1937, pp 300, 416:
August 1885
COLLECTION Otterlo, Rijksmuseum Kröller-
Müller, inv nr 230-20, cat van Gogh 1970, nr 190

F 194 [H 209] THE VICARAGE GARDEN UNDER
SNOW

Canvas, now pasted on panel 59 × 78 [23¼ × 30¾]
Compare sketch in letter 385 [reproduced in the
1955 Dutch edition of the letters–not in the English
edition]
Nuenen January 1885
LETTER 394 [February] See F 67
LITERATURE Vanbeselaere 1937, pp 294, 352-3,
416: January 1885; letter 394
COLLECTION Fullerton, California, Norton Simon
Foundation
Colorplate, p 145

F 195 [H 196] THE WILLOW

Panel 42 × 30 [16½ × 11¾]
Nuenen October-November 1885
LITERATURE Vanbeselaere 1937, pp 305, 400, 416:
October-November 1885
COLLECTION Ottawa, Haso Art Gallery

F 196 [H 211] A ROW OF TREES

Paper on panel 32 × 50 [12½ × 19¾]
Nuenen October-November 1885
LITERATURE Vanbeselaere 1937, pp 305, 400, 416:
October-November 1885
COLLECTION Formerly Rotterdam, P. Verschure
Present owner unknown

F 197 [H 210] STILL LIFE: BOUQUET OF
FLOWERS
Paris period; see after F 388 verso

F 198 [H 219] STILL LIFE: GINGER POT
FILLED WITH CHRYSANTHEMUMS

Canvas on panel 40 × 29.5 [15¾ × 11½]
Nuenen autumn 1885
LITERATURE Vanbeselaere 1937, p 416: Paris
COLLECTION New York, Howard J. Lepow

F 199 [H 212] STILL LIFE: HELLEBORES

Canvas on panel 31 × 22.5 [12¼ × 8¾]
Nuenen 1885
LITERATURE Vanbeselaere 1937, p 416: Paris
EDITORS' COMMENT The date seems uncertain.
COLLECTION Sale Geneva [Motte] 9-10 June 1967,
nr 54
Present owner unknown

F 200 [H 215] STILL LIFE: DEAD LEAVES

Canvas on panel 41.5 × 31 [16¼ × 12¼]
Nuenen probably autumn 1884
LITERATURE Vanbeselaere 1937, p 416: Paris
EDITORS' COMMENT Stylistically related to F 76.
Faille told Mr Brinkman that he felt this still life
was painted in Paris, but he left it in the Nuenen
period in his manuscript.
COLLECTION Netherlands, Private Collection

F 201 [H 218] STILL LIFE: GERANIUM IN A
POT
Paris period; see after F 388 verso

F 202 [H 216] STILL LIFE: COPPER COFFEE-
POT AND TWO WHITE BOWLS [study for THE
POTATO EATERS]

Panel 23 × 34 [9 × 13½]
Nuenen April 1885
LITERATURE Moderne Kunstwerken 1904, part 2,
nr 59 [with reproduction]. Vanbeselaere 1937, pp
286, 346-7, 349, 416: April 1885; study for THE
POTATO EATERS; close in style to F 69. J.G. van
Gelder, Beeldende Kunst 1942, p 6 [English edition,
1946]: study for a detail of THE POTATO EATERS
[F 82]
EDITORS' COMMENT The remnants of this
painting are in fetters. An attempt at restoration
before 1938 failed.
COLLECTION Utrecht, J.E. van der Meulen

F 203 [H 214] STILL LIFE: HERRINGS
Paris period; see after F 388 verso

F 203a [formerly F 203bis; H 213] STILL LIFE:
LEMONS
Antwerp period; see after F 212a

F 194

F 200

F 198

F 199

F 202

F 196

F 14

F 14 [H 19] THE GREEN PARROT

Canvas on panel 48 × 43 [19 × 17]
Nuenen 1885
LITERATURE H. P. Bremmer, Nieuws van den Dag
10 August 1905. H. F. W. Jeltes, De Kroniek
6 April 1907. Faille 1928, nr 14: The Hague.
Vanbeselaere 1937, pp 112, 413: Paris. Faille 1939,
nr 19: The Hague 1883
EDITORS' COMMENT The date and period seem
uncertain.
COLLECTION Rockanje, Netherlands, Mrs J. W.
van Hoey-Smith

F 210 [H 228] VIEW OF AN UNKNOWN TOWN
WITH DRAWBRIDGE

Panel 42 × 49.5 [16½ × 19½]
Probably Nuenen
LITERATURE Faille 1928, nr 210: Antwerp? Faille
1939, nr 227: Nuenen 1885. Tralbaut Antwerp
1948, p 211: not done in Antwerp
EDITORS' COMMENT The site could not be
identified. The style of the painting, which is close
to F 113, shows affinities with The Hague school.
COLLECTION The Hague, Mrs E. A. E. M. van
Meeteren-van Diemen Arbeiter

F 212a STILL LIFE: VEGETABLES

Canvas 35.5 × 45 [14 × 17¾]
Signed in lower right: Vincent
Nuenen September 1885
LITERATURE Not in Faille 1928, Vanbeselaere
1937 or Faille 1939
COLLECTION Landsberg, Germany, Anneliese
Brand

F 210

F 212a

F 269 recto [formerly F 269 verso; H 88] STUDY
OF A PEASANT WOMAN

Canvas 41 × 33 [16¼ × 13]
Nuenen April 1885
LITERATURE Faille 1928, nr 269 verso: Nuenen.
Vanbeselaere 1937, pp 343-4: close in technique to
F 77 recto of March
COLLECTION Amsterdam, Rijksmuseum Vincent
van Gogh [Vincent van Gogh Foundation, inv
nr F 269]

F 365 recto [formerly F 365 verso; H 87]
PEASANT WOMAN SEATED

Canvas 41 × 31.5 [16¼ × 12½]
Nuenen February-March 1885
LITERATURE J. B. de la Faille, Der Cicerone 1927,
p 102 [with reproduction]. Faille 1928, nr 365 verso:
Nuenen. Vanbeselaere 1937, p 362: the model is the
same woman seen seated at the right of THE
POTATO EATERS [F 77 recto]. J. G. van Gelder, De
Aardappeleters, 1949, p 9: study for THE POTATO
EATERS [F 78]; F 365 recto is not mentioned in the
1946 English edition of this publication
COLLECTION New York, The Metropolitan
Museum of Art [on loan since 1936 from, Miss
Adelaide Milton de Groot; acquired 1967; Miss
Adelaide Milton de Groot bequest], inv nr
67.187.70a

F 388 recto [formerly F 388 verso; H 89] HEAD
OF A PEASANT WOMAN

F 365 recto

F 388 recto

Canvas 42.5 × 35.5 [16¾ × 14]
Compare F 80 and F 80a [probably the same model]
Nuenen May 1885
LETTER 410 [1 June] 'I hope to send you this week a
small box marked V 2, containing ... 12 painted
studies ...'

LITERATURE Faille 1928, nr 388 verso: Nuenen.
Vanbeselaere 1937, pp 293, 343-4, 366: June 1885;
letter 410; depicts one of the models from THE
POTATO EATERS, but painted afterwards
COLLECTION Amsterdam, Rijksmuseum Vincent
van Gogh [Vincent van Gogh Foundation, inv
nr F 388]

ANTWERP PERIOD

F 204 [H 228] CLUSTER OF OLD HOUSES
WITH THE NEW CHURCH AT THE HAGUE
The Hague period; see after F 15a

F 205 [H 225] HEAD OF AN OLD MAN: LEFT
PROFILE

Canvas 44 × 33.5 [17¼ × 13¼]
Antwerp December 1885
LETTERS 438 [first half of December] '*For tomorrow
I have an appointment with a splendid old man – will
he come??*'
439 [first half of December] '*I have made two fairly
big heads, by way of trial for a portrait. First, that
old man whom I wrote you about, a kind of head of
the type of Victor Hugo's ...*'
LITERATURE Tralbaut Antwerp 1948, pp 192-5,
283, nr 13
COLLECTION Amsterdam, Rijksmuseum Vincent
van Gogh [Vincent van Gogh Foundation, inv
nr F 205]

F 206 [H 222] HEAD OF A WOMAN: NEARLY
FULL FACE

Canvas 35 × 24 [13¾ × 9½]
Antwerp December 1885
LETTER 439 [first half of December] '*I have made
two fairly big heads ... then also a study of a woman.
In the woman's portrait I have brought lighter tones
into the flesh, white tinted with carmine, vermilion,
yellow and a light background of gray-yellow, from
which the face is separated only by the black hair.
Lilac tones in the dress.*'
LITERATURE Tralbaut Antwerp 1948, pp 195-9,
283, nr 11
COLLECTION Amsterdam, Rijksmuseum Vincent
van Gogh [Vincent van Gogh Foundation, inv
nr F 206]

F 269 recto

F 205

F 206

F 207

F 212

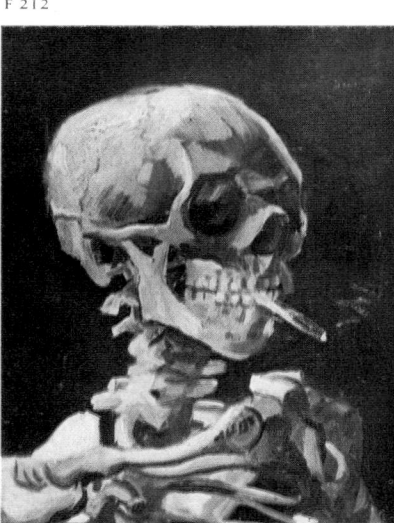

F 203a

F 211

F 207 [H 223] PORTRAIT OF A WOMAN: BUST,
LEFT PROFILE

Canvas 60 × 50 [23¾ × 19¾]
Antwerp December 1885
LETTER 442 [28 December] '...*I took a beautiful
model and painted her head life-size... Here follows
the color scheme—a well-toned flesh color, in the neck
rather bronze-like, jet-black hair...dingy white for
the little jacket... A scarlet note in the jet-black hair
and another scarlet ribbon in the dullish white. She is
a girl from a café-chantant...I began a second study
of the same model in profile.*'
LITERATURE Tralbaut Antwerp 1948, pp 200-2,
284, nr 29
COLLECTION New York, Alfred Wyler
Colorplate, p 146

F 207a PORTRAIT OF A WOMAN IN BLUE:
THREE QUARTERS TO THE RIGHT
Paris period; see after F 388 verso

F 208 SELF PORTRAIT WITH PIPE: THREE
QUARTERS TO THE RIGHT
Paris period; see after F 388 verso

F 208a SELF PORTRAIT WITH FELT HAT
Paris period; see after F 388 verso

F 209 [H 220] HEAD OF A MAN: THREE
QUARTERS TO THE LEFT
Paris period; see after F 388 verso

F 210 [H 227] VIEW OF AN UNKNOWN TOWN
WITH DRAWBRIDGE
Nuenen period; see after F 203a

F 211 [H 226] THE ANTWERP QUAY

Panel 20.5 × 27 [8 × 10¾]
Antwerp December 1885
LETTER 438 [first half of December] '*At a fourth
[art dealer] I can exhibit a view of the quay as soon
as the weather permits me to make it...*'
LITERATURE Tralbaut Antwerp 1948, pp 211-4,
283, nr 5: early December 1885; letter 438; the style
seems to be influenced by Japanese woodcuts; the
site can be located near the present pilot office,
facing the left bank of the Scheldt
COLLECTION Amsterdam, Rijksmuseum Vincent
van Gogh [Vincent van Gogh Foundation, inv
nr F 211]

F 212 [H 221] SKULL WITH A BURNING
CIGARETTE

Canvas 32.5 × 24 [12¾ × 9½]
Antwerp December 1885
LITERATURE Tralbaut Antwerp 1948, pp 223-9,
284, nr 35
COLLECTION Amsterdam, Rijksmuseum Vincent
van Gogh [Vincent van Gogh Foundation, inv
nr F 212]

F 212a STILL LIFE: VEGETABLES
Nuenen period; see after F 203a

REDATED TO ANTWERP

F 174 [H 147] THE MIDWIFE: HEAD WITH
WHITE BONNET

Canvas 50 × 40 [19¾ × 15¾]
Antwerp December 1885
LITERATURE Faille 1928, nr 174: Nuenen. Van-
beselaere 1937, p 416: Antwerp. Faille 1939, nr 147:
Nuenen or Antwerp. Tralbaut Antwerp 1948, p 284,
nr 33: December 1885

COLLECTION Amsterdam, Rijksmuseum Vincent van Gogh [Vincent van Gogh Foundation, inv nr F 174]

F 203a [formerly F 203bis; H 213] STILL LIFE: LEMONS

Canvas on panel 34.5 × 50 [13¼ × 19¾]
Antwerp-Paris 1886
LITERATURE Faille 1928, nr 203bis: Nuenen. Vanbeselaere 1937, p 416; Paris. Faille 1939, nr 213: Antwerp 1885
EDITORS' COMMENT The attribution seems doubtful.
COLLECTION Berkeley Heights, New Jersey, H.E.Hirschland

F 260 [H 260] HOUSES IN ANTWERP

Canvas 44 × 33.5 [17¼ × 13¼]
Antwerp early December 1885
LETTER 438 [first half of December] '*Last week I painted three more studies, one with backs of old houses, seen from my window…*'
LITERATURE Faille 1928, nr 260: Paris. Faille 1939, nr 260: Antwerp December 1885; letter 438. Tralbaut Antwerp 1948, pp 110, 180-7, 283: late November or early December 1885; identified as the site behind Vincent's house in the Beeldekens-straat; technique influenced by Japanese color prints
COLLECTION Amsterdam, Rijksmuseum Vincent van Gogh [Vincent van Gogh Foundation, inv nr F 260]

64b

F 174

F 260

F 213

F 214

F 215a

F 215b

F 215c

PARIS PERIOD

F 213 [H 298] STILL LIFE: FRITILLARIES IN A COPPER VASE

Canvas 73.5 × 60.5 [29 × 23¾]
Signed in upper left: Vincent
Paris summer 1887
LITERATURE P. Gachet, Deux amis des Impressionistes, 1956, p 177: one of the two paintings that belonged to Mürer and were sold in 1897 to Vollard
EDITORS' COMMENT Flower pieces from the Paris period are only mentioned in three letters:
460 [postscript by A. Bonger to letter by Vincent; before 26 August 1886] '*He has made a number of very beautiful things; those on a yellow background are quite striking. The flower pieces are most gay and colorful as a whole; but some pictures are flat, a thing I am unable to convince him of. He persists in replying, But I wanted to introduce this or that color contrast ... As for my work, I painted the pendant to those flowers you have. A branch of white lilies – white, pink, green – against black, something like black Japanese lacquer inlaid with mother-of-pearl, which you know – then a bunch of orange tiger lilies against a blue background, then a bunch of dahlias, violet against a yellow background, and red gladioli in a blue vase against light yellow.*'
459a [to Mr Levens; August-October 1886; in English] '*But I have made a series of colour studies in painting, simply flowers, red poppies, blue corn-flowers and myosotys, white and rose roses, yellow chrysantemums – seeking oppositions of blue with orange, red and green, yellow and violet seeking* les tons rompus et neutres *to harmonise brutal extremes. Trying to render intense colour and not a grey harmony.*'
W 1 [summer or autumn 1887] '*Last year I painted hardly anything but flowers in order to get accustomed to using a scale of colors other than gray – namely pink, soft and vivid green, light blue, violet, yellow, orange, rich red.*'
Since no existing painting can be identified with those mentioned in these letters [with the possible exception of F 247], the flower pieces of the Paris period have to be dated stylistically.
COLLECTION Paris, Musée National du Louvre [acquired 1908; bequest of Is. de Camondo], inv nr R F 1989, cat 1959, nr 143

F 214 [H 297] STILL LIFE WITH FRITILLARIES

Canvas 38 × 55 [15 × 21¾]
Paris late summer 1886
LETTERS 459a [August-October], 460a [before 26 August] and W 1 [summer or autumn 1887] See EDITORS' COMMENT under F 213
LITERATURE P. Gachet, Deux amis des Impressionistes, 1956, p 177: perhaps one of the two paintings that belonged to Mürer and were sold to Vollard in 1897
COLLECTION Formerly Paris, Duret Art Gallery
Present owner unknown

F 215 [H 247] NUDE STUDY: LITTLE GIRL SEATED

Canvas 27 × 22 [10¾ × 8¾]
Compare drawings F 1366 recto and verso [same composition] and F 1367 [same model]
Paris 1886
EDITORS' COMMENT Model in Cormon's studio. See LITERATURE under F 1367: A. Bowness, exhib cat van Gogh London [Hayward Gallery] 1968-9, nr 67.
COLLECTION Amsterdam, Rijksmuseum Vincent van Gogh [Vincent van Gogh Foundation, inv nr F 215]

F 216

F 216g [H p 557] PLASTER STATUETTE:
FEMALE TORSO ON PEDESTAL, SEEN FROM
THE BACK

Canvas 40.5 × 27 [16 × 10½]
Compare numbers noted under F 216a [same
statuette]
Paris 1886-7
COLLECTION Amsterdam, Rijksmuseum Vincent
van Gogh [Vincent van Gogh Foundation, inv
nr F 216g]

F 216i

F 216j

F 217

F 218

F 219

F 216h [H 239] PLASTER STATUETTE: FEMALE TORSO ON PEDESTAL, SEEN FROM THE FRONT

Canvas 41 × 32.5 [16¼ × 12¾]
Compare numbers noted under F 216a [same statuette]
Paris late 1886
EDITORS' COMMENT Not reproduced in former editions. The painting reproduced in Faille 1928 and Faille 1939 above this number is F 216b.
COLLECTION Amsterdam, Rijksmuseum Vincent van Gogh [Vincent van Gogh Foundation, inv nr F 216h]

F 216i [H 244] PLASTER STATUETTE: FEMALE TORSO WITH ONE LEG, SEEN FROM THE SIDE

Pasteboard 32.5 × 24 [12¾ × 9½]
Compare F 216d, F 360 and drawing F 1363c recto [same statuette]
Paris 1887
COLLECTION Amsterdam, Rijksmuseum Vincent van Gogh [Vincent van Gogh Foundation, inv nr F 216i]

F 216j [H p 557] PLASTER STATUETTE: FEMALE TORSO ON PEDESTAL, SEEN FROM THE FRONT

Pasteboard 35 × 27 [13¾ × 10¾]
Compare numbers noted under F 216a [same statuette]
Paris 1886-7
EDITORS' COMMENT In former editions erroneously reproduced as F 216b [H 238].
COLLECTION Amsterdam, Rijksmuseum Vincent van Gogh [Vincent van Gogh Foundation, inv nr F 216j]

F 217 [H p 557] STILL LIFE: BOWL WITH CHRYSANTHEMUMS

Canvas 46 × 61 [18 × 24]
Paris autumn 1886
COLLECTION Formerly New York, Wildenstein Art Gallery
Present owner unknown

F 218 [H 344] STILL LIFE: VASE WITH ROSES

Pasteboard 35 × 27 [13¾ × 10¾]
Paris summer 1886
COLLECTION Amsterdam, Rijksmuseum Vincent van Gogh [Vincent van Gogh Foundation, inv nr F 218]

F 219 [H 311] STILL LIFE: BASKET WITH APPLES, MEAT AND A BREADROLL

Canvas 46 × 55 [18 × 21¾]
Paris 1886
COLLECTION Otterlo, Rijksmuseum Kröller-Müller, inv nr 270-12, cat van Gogh 1970, nr 194

F 220 [H 340] STILL LIFE: VASE WITH CARNATIONS

Canvas 40 × 32.5 [15¾ × 12¾]
Paris summer 1886
COLLECTION Rotterdam, Willem van der Vorm Foundation, cat 1962, nr 30

F 221 [H 389] THE PONT DU CARROUSEL AND
THE LOUVRE

Canvas 31×44 [12¼×17½]
Paris early summer 1886
EDITORS' COMMENT Site identified by
P. Leprohon [written communication].
COLLECTION Los Angeles, F. Herman

F 220

F 221

F 216h

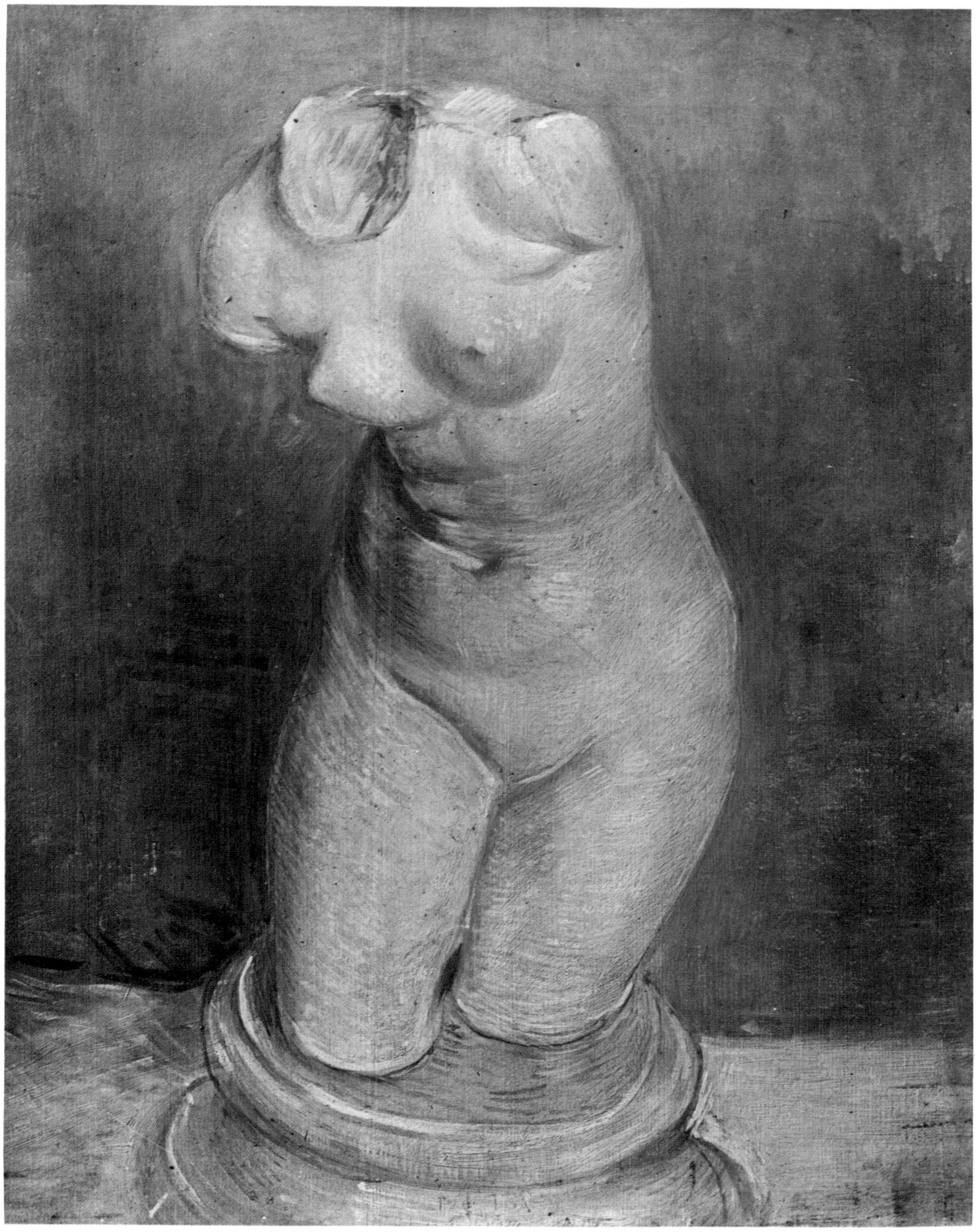

F 222

F 224

F 221a [formerly F 221b: H 395] THE TRAMP

Canvas 33 × 24.5 [13 × 9½]
Paris 1886. N.B. See EDITORS' COMMENT
LITERATURE Not in Faille 1928. J. B. de la Faille,
Les Faux van Gogh, 1930, nr 141, plate XL: false.
H. P. Bremmer, Beeldende Kunst November 1937:
genuine; probably early in the Paris period;
represents van Gogh himself in the garden of the
Moulin de la Galette
EDITORS' COMMENT Expertised by M. E. Tralbaut
and H. L. C. Jaffé in 1954: not by van Gogh. The
editors also doubt the attribution to van Gogh.
Faille accepts it in his manuscript for the present
edition.
COLLECTION London, A. Tooth Art Gallery

F 222 [H 387] THE FOURTEENTH OF JULY
CELEBRATION IN PARIS

Canvas 44 × 39 [17¼ × 15¼]
Paris second half of 1886
LITERATURE J. Leymarie, Van Gogh, 1951, p 103,
nr 56: Paris 1887. Het Vrije Volk 8 August 1953:
according to M. M. van Dantzig not a work of van
Gogh. R. Shikiba, Vincent van Gogh, 1954 [in
Japanese; English translation in the library of the
Rijksmuseum Kröller-Müller]: left out on advice of
M. E. Tralbaut, who does not accept the author-
ship of van Gogh. K. Bromig-Kolleritz, Die Selbst-
bildnisse Vincent van Goghs, 1955, pp 96-100:
brush strokes similar to those in SELF PORTRAIT
F 267; both to be dated July 1886
EDITORS' COMMENT Difficult to date exactly.
Influenced by Monet's painting RUE
MONTORGUEIL of 1878 [Rouen].
COLLECTION Winterthur, Switzerland,
Mrs L. Jäggli-Hahnloser

F 223 [H 388] THE TERRACE AT THE
TUILERIES

Canvas 27.5 × 46 [10¾ × 18]
Compare drawing F 1383 [same site]
Paris spring 1886
COLLECTION Formerly London, Leicester Art
Galleries
Present owner unknown

F 224 [H 390] IN THE BOIS DE BOULOGNE

Canvas 46.5 × 37 [18¼ × 14½]
Signed in lower right: Vincent
Paris early summer 1886
COLLECTION Zurich, Mrs Dora Hahnloser-
Gassmann

F 225 [H 254] A PUBLIC GARDEN IN PARIS

Canvas 37.5 × 45.5 [14¾ × 18]
Paris early summer 1886
COLLECTION USA, Private Collection

F 226 [H 270] THE MILL LE RADET, RUE
LEPIC [?]

Canvas 38 × 46 [15 × 18]
Inscription on the mill: Moulin Galette
Inscription on the café: commerce vins – buvette
Moulin Galette – vins lique...
Compare F 227 and F 228
Paris spring 1886
EDITORS' COMMENT Faille, quoted in cat van
Gogh 1970, Rijksmuseum Kröller-Müller, nr 199,
identified the mill as 'le Radet' in the Rue Lepic, an
identification that could not be verified and is
probably erroneous.
COLLECTION Baden, Switzerland, John Brown

F 223

F 226

F 225

F 221a

F 227

F 228

F 229

F 231

F 227 [H 267] THE MILL LE RADET, RUE LEPIC [?]

Canvas 38.5×46 [15¼×18]
Inscription on the mill: Moulin de Galette
Inscription on the café: commerce de vins – buvette
Moulin [de] Galette – vins liqueurs
Compare F 226 and F 228
Paris spring 1886
EDITORS' COMMENT See F 226
COLLECTION Otterlo, Rijksmuseum Kröller-
Müller, inv nr 268-12, cat van Gogh 1970, nr 199

F 228 [H 268] THE MILL LE RADET, RUE LEPIC [?]

Canvas 38×46.5 [15×18¼]
Inscription on the mill: Moulin d. Galette
Inscription on the café: commerce de vins – buvette
Moulin de Galette – vins lique...
Compare F 226 and F 227
Paris spring 1886
LITERATURE Exhib cat van Gogh Paris 1960,
nr 30: Moulin de la Galette, seen from the Rue
Girardon
EDITORS' COMMENT See F 226
COLLECTION Berlin, Nationalgalerie [acquired
1929], inv. nr NG 1616, cat 1968, p 83

F 229 [H 261] MONTMARTRE: QUARRY, GENERAL VIEW

Canvas 32×41 [12½×16¼]
Signed in lower left: Vincent
Compare F 230 [nearby site]
Paris October 1886
COLLECTION Amsterdam, Rijksmuseum Vincent
van Gogh [Vincent van Gogh Foundation, inv
nr F 229]

F 230 [H 262] MONTMARTRE: QUARRY, THE MILLS

Canvas 56×62 [22×24½]
Compare F 229 [nearby site]
Paris October 1886
COLLECTION Amsterdam, Rijksmuseum Vincent
van Gogh [Vincent van Gogh Foundation, inv
nr F 230]

F 231 VIEW OF ROOFTOPS IN PARIS

Pasteboard 30×41 [11¾×16¼]
Paris May-June 1886
COLLECTION Amsterdam, Rijksmuseum Vincent
van Gogh [Vincent van Gogh Foundation, inv
nr F 231]

F 232 [H 356] MONTMARTRE

Pasteboard 22×16 [8¾×6¼]
Paris spring 1886
COLLECTION Amsterdam, Rijksmuseum Vincent
van Gogh [Vincent van Gogh Foundation, inv
nr F 232]

F 233 [H 253] MONTMARTRE: QUARRY

Canvas 22×33 [8¾×13]
Paris September-October 1886
COLLECTION Amsterdam, Rijksmuseum Vincent
van Gogh [Vincent van Gogh Foundation, inv
nr F 233]

F 230

F 233

F 232

F 235

F 234 [H 300] STILL LIFE: ONE-EARED VASE
WITH ASTERS AND PHLOX

Canvas 61 × 46 [24 × 18]
Signed in lower left: Vincent
Paris August-September 1886
COLLECTION Amsterdam, Rijksmuseum Vincent
van Gogh [Vincent van Gogh Foundation, inv
nr F 234]

F 235 [H 334] STILL LIFE: ONE-EARED VASE
WITH HOLLYHOCKS

Canvas 94 × 51 [37 × 20]
Signed in lower left: Vincent
Paris summer 1886
LITERATURE P. Fechter, Kunst und Künstler
1909-10, pp 346-55 [with reproduction].
M. E. Tralbaut, exhib cat van Gogh Essen 1957,
nr 230: Paris August-October 1886; letter 459a
COLLECTION Zurich, Kunsthaus, inv nr 2414, cat
1958, p 27

F 235a [formerly F 235bis; H 327] STILL LIFE:
BOUQUET OF FLOWERS

Canvas 75 × 44.5 [29½ × 17½]
Signed in lower right: Vincent
Paris 1886. N.B. See EDITORS' COMMENT
LITERATURE Not in Faille 1928
EDITORS' COMMENT The editors do not agree
with Faille about the status of this painting. They
do not accept it as an authentic work by van Gogh.
COLLECTION Zurich, E. G. Bührle [acquired 1938]

F 236 [H 301] STILL LIFE: ONE-EARED VASE
WITH DIANTHUS

Canvas 58 × 45.5 [22¾ × 18]
Paris summer 1886
COLLECTION Formerly New York, A. Ball Art
Gallery
Present owner unknown

F 237 [H 302] STILL LIFE: ONE-EARED VASE
WITH PHYSOSTEGIA, GLADIOLUS AND
LYCHNIS

Canvas 65.5 × 35 [25¾ × 13¾]
Signed and dated in upper left: Vincent 86
Paris late summer 1886
LITERATURE Cat 1963, Museum Boymans-van
Beuningen, p 50: summer 1886; influence of
Monticelli
COLLECTION Rotterdam, Museum Boymans-van
Beuningen [acquired 1958], inv nr 2607, cat 1963, p 50

F 238 [H 393] LA GUINGUETTE

Canvas 49 × 64 [19¼ × 25¼]
Signed in lower left: Vincent
Compare drawing F 1407 [same site]
Paris October 1886
LITERATURE W. J. de Gruyter, Tekeningen van
Vincent van Gogh, 1962, p 103, nr 34: painted some
weeks after drawing F 1407, which was drawn
shortly after Vincent's arrival in Paris on
27 February 1886
COLLECTION Paris, Musée National du Louvre
[acquired 1929], inv nr RF 2243, cat 1959, nr 144
Colorplate, p 163

F 239 [H 385] THE VIADUCT

Canvas 31.5 × 40.5 [12½ × 16]
Paris early summer 1887
LITERATURE J. B. de la Faille, Der Cicerone 1927,
p 102 [with reproduction]
COLLECTION New York, Justin K. Thannhauser
Foundation

F 234

F 235a

F 236

F 238

F 239

F 237

F 241

F 242

F 243

F 243a

F 244

F 240 [H 386] THE PONT ROUTE AT
ASNIÈRES

Canvas 53 × 73 [21 × 28¾]
Paris early summer 1887
COLLECTION New York-Houston, Mr and Mrs
John de Menil

F 241 [H 294] STILL LIFE: VASE WITH
ZINNIAS AND GERANIUMS

Canvas 63 × 46 [24¾ × 18]
Signed in lower right: Vincent
Paris late summer 1886
COLLECTION Ottawa, National Gallery of Canada
[acquired 1950], inv nr 5045, cat Paintings and
Sculpture 1959, volume 2, p 29

F 242 [H 335] STILL LIFE: VASE WITH
ONOETHERA AND ALSTROEMERIA

Canvas 78.5 × 40.5 [31 × 16]
Paris late summer 1886
COLLECTION Riggisberg, Switzerland, Abegg-
Stiftung Bern

F 243 [H 317] STILL LIFE: VASE WITH
CARNATIONS

Canvas 46 × 38 [18 × 15]
Paris late summer 1886
COLLECTION New York, Mrs Charles B. Murphy

F 243a [formerly F 243bis; H 337] STILL LIFE:
VASE WITH MYOSOTIS AND PEONIES

Pasteboard 34.5 × 27.5 [13½ × 10¾]
Paris June 1886
COLLECTION Amsterdam, Rijksmuseum Vincent
van Gogh [Vincent van Gogh Foundation, inv
nr F 243a]

F 244 [H 286] STILL LIFE: BOWL WITH
PANSIES

Canvas 46 × 55 [18 × 21¾]
Signed in lower left: Vincent
Paris spring 1886
COLLECTION Amsterdam, Rijksmuseum Vincent
van Gogh [Vincent van Gogh Foundation, inv
nr F 244]

F 245 [H 338] STILL LIFE: VASE WITH
CARNATIONS

Canvas 46 × 37.5 [18 × 14¾]
Signed in lower left: Vincent
Paris summer 1886
COLLECTION Amsterdam, Stedelijk Museum, inv
nr A 2235

F 246 [H 312] STILL LIFE: ONE-EARED VASE
WITH CARNATIONS AND ROSES AND A
BOTTLE

Canvas 40 × 32 [15¾ × 12½]
Signed in lower right: Vincent
Paris early summer 1886
LITERATURE E. Joosten, Museumjournaal 1959,
part 2, pp 73-6: influence of Monticelli
COLLECTION Otterlo, Rijksmuseum Kröller-
Müller, inv nr 266-13, cat van Gogh 1970, nr 196

F 240

F 245

F 246

F 246a

F 248

F 247

F 246a STILL LIFE: FLOWERS

Canvas 35.5 × 40.5 [14 × 16]
Paris 1886. N.B. See EDITORS' COMMENT
LITERATURE Not in Faille 1928 or Faille 1939
EDITORS' COMMENT The editors do not agree
with Faille about the status of this painting. They
do not accept it as an authentic work by van Gogh.
COLLECTION Netherlands, Private Collection

F 247 [H V] STILL LIFE: VASE WITH
GLADIOLI

Canvas 65 × 40 [25½ × 15¾]
Signed in lower right: Vincent
Paris late summer 1886
COLLECTION Short Hills, New York, Albert
W. Blum

F 248 [H 343] STILL LIFE: VASE WITH RED
GLADIOLI

Canvas 50.5 × 39.5 [20 × 15½]
Signed in lower right: Vincent
Paris late summer 1886
COLLECTION Formerly Paris, Alden Brooks
[before 1928]
Present owner unknown

F 248a STILL LIFE: VASE WITH GLADIOLI

Canvas 48.5 × 40 [19 × 15¾]
Paris late summer 1886
LITERATURE Not in Faille 1928 or Faille 1939
COLLECTION Amsterdam, Rijksmuseum Vincent
van Gogh [Vincent van Gogh Foundation, inv
nr F 248a]

F 248b STILL LIFE: ONE-EARED VASE WITH
RED GLADIOLI

Canvas 65 × 35 [25½ × 13¾]
Signed in lower left: Vincent
Paris late summer 1886
LITERATURE Not in Faille 1928 or Faille 1939
COLLECTION Morges, Switzerland – Paris,
J. Planque [acquired 1956]

F 249 [H 288] STILL LIFE: BOWL WITH
PEONIES AND ROSES

Canvas 59 × 71 [23¼ × 28]
Signed in lower right: Vincent
Paris autumn 1886
LETTER W I [summer or autumn 1887] See
EDITORS' COMMENT under F 213
LITERATURE L. Gans, Museumjournaal 1958,
part I, p 85: painted in the first half of the Paris
period. Cat van Gogh 1966, Rijksmuseum Kröller-
Müller, nr 197: about 1886
COLLECTION Otterlo, Rijksmuseum Kröller-
Müller, inv nr 1106-41, cat van Gogh 1970, nr 197

F 248b

F 248a

F 249

F 250

F 251

F 250 [H 289] STILL LIFE: BOWL WITH
SUNFLOWERS AND OTHER FLOWERS

Canvas 50 × 61 [19¾ × 24]
Signed in lower left: Vincent
Paris autumn 1886
LITERATURE Cat Gemäldesammlung 1957,
Städtische Kunsthalle, nr 59: about 1887
COLLECTION Mannheim, Städtische Kunsthalle
[acquired 1911], cat Gemäldesammlung 1957, nr 59

F 251 [H 295] STILL LIFE: BOWL WITH
SUMMER FLOWERS [HELIOPSIS AND
GYPSOPHILA?]

Canvas 49.5 × 61 [19½ × 24]
Signed in lower right: Vincent
Paris summer 1886
LITERATURE Cat Paintings and Sculpture 1959,
National Gallery of Canada, volume 2, p 30:
about 1887
COLLECTION Ottawa, National Gallery of Canada
[acquired 1951], inv nr 5808, cat Paintings and
Sculpture 1959, volume 2, p 30

F 252 [H 293] STILL LIFE: BOWL WITH
ZINNIAS

Canvas 61 × 45.5 [24 × 18]
Signed in lower right: Vincent
Paris late summer 1886
COLLECTION Sale New York [Parke-Bernet]
15 October 1969, nr 4
Present owner unknown

F 253 [H 308] STILL LIFE: A BOTTLE, TWO
GLASSES AND A PLATE OF BREAD

Canvas 37.5 × 46 [14¾ × 18]
Paris first half of 1886
COLLECTION Amsterdam, Rijksmuseum Vincent
van Gogh [Vincent van Gogh Foundation, inv
nr F 253]

F 252

F 253

F 253a

F 255

F 253a [formerly 253bis; H 284] STILL LIFE: PLATE WITH ROLLS

Canvas 31.5×40 [12½ × 15¾]
Paris early 1887
COLLECTION Amsterdam, Rijksmuseum Vincent van Gogh [Vincent van Gogh Foundation, inv nr F 253a]

F 254 [H 281] STILL LIFE: APPLES

Canvas 45.5 × 61 [18 × 24]
Paris July-September 1887
LITERATURE A. Bowness, exhib cat van Gogh London [Hayward Gallery] 1968-9: the pattern of radiating brushstrokes around the center suggests 1887 as a likely date; the dark underpainting may, however, mean that Vincent added this brushwork to an earlier painting; Vincent was painting apples at Nuenen in the late summer of 1885
COLLECTION Amsterdam, Rijksmuseum Vincent van Gogh [Vincent van Gogh Foundation, inv nr F 254]

F 255 [H 248] A PAIR OF SHOES

Canvas 37.5 × 45.5 [14¾ × 18]
Signed in upper left: Vincent
Paris late 1886
LITERATURE C. Nordenfalk, Ord och Bild 1944, p 293: the theme possibly suggested by a painting made by Nils Kreuger in Paris in 1882 rather than by Millet's drawing of wooden shoes reproduced in Sensier's monograph. Idem, Journal of the Warburg and Courtauld Institutes 1947, p 136: Nuenen or possibly Antwerp 1885. A. Bowness, exhib cat van Gogh London [Hayward Gallery] 1968-9, nr 52: Nuenen end 1885
EDITORS' COMMENT The painting must be from the Paris period. Compare the pair of shoes to the left on F 332 and F 333, which is dated by Vincent 1887.
COLLECTION Amsterdam, Rijksmuseum Vincent van Gogh [Vincent van Gogh Foundation, inv nr F 255]

F 256 [H 287] MUSSELS AND SHRIMPS

Canvas 27 × 34 [10½ × 13½]
Paris autumn 1886
COLLECTION Amsterdam, Rijksmuseum Vincent van Gogh [Vincent van Gogh Foundation, inv nr F 256]

F 257 [H 341] STILL LIFE: PLATE, VASE AND FLOWERS

Canvas 54 × 45 [21¼ × 17¾]
Paris 1886. N.B. See EDITORS' COMMENT
EDITORS' COMMENT The editors do not agree with Faille about the status of this painting. They do not accept it as an authentic work by van Gogh.
COLLECTION São Paolo, Museu de Arte, cat 1963, nr 111

F 258 [H 330] STILL LIFE: WHITE VASE WITH ROSES AND OTHER FLOWERS

Canvas 37 × 25.5 [14½ × 10]
Annotated in lower left: V
Paris summer 1886
COLLECTION Formerly Berlin, Private Collection
Present owner unknown

F 256

F 259 [H 331] STILL LIFE: VASE WITH
CARNATIONS AND ZINNIAS

Canvas 61 × 49 [24 × 19¼]
Paris summer 1886
COLLECTION Formerly New York, M. Frank
[acquired 1960]
Present owner unknown

F 254

F 257

F 259

F 258

F 261

F 264

F 260 [H 260] HOUSES IN ANTWERP
Antwerp period; see after F 212a

F 261 [H 259] VIEW OF PARIS

Canvas 54 × 72 [21¼ × 28¼]
Compare drawing F 1387
Paris late summer-autumn 1886
LETTER T 1a [to Mrs van Stockum-Haanebeek;
10 July 1887] 'The remarkable thing about our
dwelling is that one has a magnificent view of the
whole town from its windows, with the hills of
Meudon, St Cloud and so on on the horizon, and over
it an expanse of sky nearly as large as when one is
standing on the top of a dune.'
COLLECTION Amsterdam, Rijksmuseum Vincent
van Gogh [Vincent van Gogh Foundation, inv
nr F 261]

F 262 [H 258] VIEW FROM MONTMARTRE

Canvas 38.5 × 61.5 [15¼ × 24¼]
Signed in lower left: Vincent
Paris late summer-autumn 1886
LETTER T 1a [10 July 1887] See F 261
COLLECTION Basle, Öffentliche Kunstsammlung
[acquired 1946], inv nr 1982, cat 1961, p 12

F 263 [H 416] PORTRAIT OF PÈRE TANGUY

Canvas 47 × 38.5 [18½ × 15¼]
Signed and dated in lower left: Vincent janvier 87
Annotated by Vincent in upper left: Tanguy
Compare F 363, F 364 and drawing F 1412 [same
model]
Paris January 1887
COLLECTION Copenhagen, Ny Carlsberg
Glyptotek [acquired 1923; gift of Ny Carlsberg-
fondet], inv nr 1908, cat 1961, nr 944

F 263a [formerly F 263bis; H 414] SELF
PORTRAIT WITH PIPE AND GLASS

Canvas 61 × 50 [24 × 19¾]
Signed and dated in upper left: Vincent 87
Paris 1886, reworked in the beginning of 1887
LITERATURE K. Bromig-Kolleritz, Die Selbstbildnisse Vincent van Goghs, 1955, pp 102-3: very
early 1887. F. Erpel, Die Selbstbildnisse Vincent
van Goghs, 1963, nr 24: signature and date of
F 263a may be false
EDITORS' COMMENT The editors accept the
authenticity of the signature and date of F 263a.
The painting could have been executed in 1886,
then reworked in 1887.
COLLECTION Amsterdam, Rijksmuseum Vincent
van Gogh [Vincent van Gogh Foundation, inv
nr F 263a]

F 264 [H 256] THE OUTSKIRTS OF PARIS

Canvas on pasteboard 46.5 × 54.5 [18¼ × 21½]
Paris autumn 1886
COLLECTION Sale London [Christie] 1 December
1967, nr 42
Present owner unknown

F 264a [formerly F 264bis; H 394] SHELTER ON
THE HILL OF MONTMARTRE

Canvas 35.5 × 27 [14 × 10½]
Compare water color F 1411 [same site]
Paris late summer 1886
LITERATURE D. Cooper, Zeichnungen und
Aquarelle von Vincent van Gogh, 1954, p 58: water
color F 1411 could have been a study for this
painting
COLLECTION San Francisco, California Palace of
the Legion of Honor [Mr and Mrs Frederick
J. Hellman Collection]

F 263

F 265 [H 257] VIEW OF PARIS IN THE
NEIGHBORHOOD OF MONTMARTRE

Canvas 44.5 × 37 [17½ × 14½]
Signed in lower left: Vincent
Paris late summer-autumn 1886
LETTER T 1a [10 July 1887] See F 261
COLLECTION West Germany, Private Collection

F 262

F 264a

F 263a

F 265

F 267

F 268

F 266 [H 271] THE HILL OF MONTMARTRE

Canvas 36 × 61 [14¼ × 24]
Compare drawings F 1394 and F 1398 [same site]
Paris autumn 1886
LITERATURE Cat van Gogh 1959, Rijksmuseum
Kröller-Müller, nr 200: 1887; the same view of the
hill of Montmartre as F 229, F 230 and F 350
COLLECTION Otterlo, Rijksmuseum Kröller-
Müller, inv nr 262-12, cat van Gogh 1970, nr 200

F 266a [formerly F 266bis; H 255] FACTORIES
SEEN FROM A HILLSIDE IN MOONLIGHT

Canvas 20.5 × 46 [8 × 18]
Paris February-March 1887
COLLECTION Amsterdam, Rijksmuseum Vincent
van Gogh [Vincent van Gogh Foundation, inv
nr F 266a]

F 267 [H 418] SELF PORTRAIT: THREE
QUARTERS TO THE LEFT

Pasteboard 19 × 14 [7½ × 5½]
Paris summer 1887
LITERATURE K. Bromig-Kolleritz, Die Selbstbildnisse Vincent van Goghs, 1955, pp 99-100: July
1886. A. M. Hammacher, Van Gogh: Selbstbildnisse, 1960, p 12: very close in style to F 380.
F. Erpel, Die Selbstbildnisse Vincent van Goghs,
1963, nr 17
COLLECTION Amsterdam, Rijksmuseum Vincent
van Gogh [Vincent van Gogh Foundation, inv
nr F 267]

F 268 [H 417] SELF PORTRAIT: THREE
QUARTERS TO THE RIGHT

Canvas 41 × 33.5 [16¼ × 13¼]
Paris summer 1887
LITERATURE K. Bromig-Kolleritz, Die Selbstbild-
nisse Vincent van Goghs, 1955, p 105. C. Cunning-
ham, Wadsworth Atheneum Bulletin January 1955,
p 1: gives provenance. F. Erpel, Die Selbstbildnisse
Vincent van Goghs, 1963, nr 35
COLLECTION Hartford, Connecticut, Wadsworth
Atheneum [acquired 1954; gift of Philip L. Good-
win], acc nr 1954.189, handbook 1958, nr 134

F 269 recto [formerly F 269 verso; H 88] STUDY
OF A PEASANT WOMAN
Nuenen period; see after F 203a

F 266

F 266a

F 269 verso

F 270

F 269 verso [formerly F 269; H 419] SELF PORTRAIT: FULL FACE

Canvas 41 × 33 [16¼ × 13]
Paris summer 1887
LITERATURE K. Bromig-Kolleritz, Die Selbstbildnisse Vincent van Goghs, 1955, p 105. A. M. Hammacher, Van Gogh: Selbstbildnisse, 1960, p 12. F. Erpel, Die Selbstbildnisse Vincent van Goghs, 1963, nr 28
COLLECTION Amsterdam, Rijksmuseum Vincent van Gogh [Vincent van Gogh Foundation, inv nr F 269]

F 270 [H 404] PORTRAIT OF ALEXANDER REID

Pasteboard 41 × 33 [16¼ × 13]
Compare F 343 [same model]
Paris early 1887
LITERATURE T. J. Honeyman, Scottish Art Review 1948, part 2, pp 16-20: Vincent painted at least three and possibly four portraits of his friend Alexander Reid, who later became an art dealer in Glasgow. Only F 270 and F 343 have been identified as portraits of Reid
COLLECTION Oklahoma City, A. M. Weitzenhoffer

F 270a [formerly F 270bis; H 359] CHESTNUT TREE IN FLOWER

Canvas 56 × 46 [22 × 18]
Paris May 1887
COLLECTION Amsterdam, Rijksmuseum Vincent van Gogh [Vincent van Gogh Foundation, inv nr F 270a]

F 271 [H 376] WINDMILL ON MONTMARTRE [destroyed]

Canvas 46.5 × 38 [18¼ × 15]
Signed in lower left: Vincent
Compare drawings F 1395 and F 1396a and the painting by A. H. Koning in exhib cat Theo van Gogh Amsterdam-Otterlo 1960, nr 70 [same site]
Paris early winter 1886
LITERATURE Sale cat W. A. Cargill, London [Sotheby] 11 June 1963, nr 49: spring 1887; compare painting by A. H. Koning, which Vincent may have acquired in exchange for two drawings, as mentioned in letter 478 of April 1888
COLLECTION Sale W. A. Cargill, London [Sotheby] 11 June 1963, nr 49
Destroyed by fire [1967]

F 272 [H 370] MONTMARTRE NEAR THE UPPER MILL

Canvas on masonite 44 × 33.5 [17¼ × 13¼]
Compare F 274, F 346, F 348, F 348a and drawing F 1396 [same site]
Paris winter 1886
LITERATURE J. Leymarie, Van Gogh, 1951, p 99, nr 30: Paris 1886
COLLECTION Chicago, The Art Institute of Chicago [acquired 1926; Helen Birch Bartlett Memorial Collection], inv nr 26.202, cat 1961, p 181

F 271

F 270a

F 272

F 273

F 274

F 273 [H 263] WINDMILLS ON MONTMARTRE

Canvas 46.5 × 38 [18¼ × 15]
Signed in lower right: Vincent
Paris summer 1886
COLLECTION New York, J. S. Lasdon

F 274 [H 272] MOULIN DE LA GALETTE

Canvas 46 × 38 [18 × 15]
Signed in lower right: Vincent
Compare F 272, F 346, F 348, F 348a and drawing
F 1396 [same site]
Paris summer 1886
COLLECTION Glasgow, Glasgow Art Gallery
[acquired 1944; McInnes bequest], inv nr 2425, cat
1967, pp 15, 63

F 275 [H 354] VIEW IN VOYER-D'ARGENSON
PARK AT ASNIÈRES

Canvas on pasteboard 32.5 × 42 [12¾ × 16½]
Compare F 276 [same site]
Paris May 1887
COLLECTION Amsterdam, Rijksmuseum Vincent
van Gogh [Vincent van Gogh Foundation, inv
nr F 275]

F 276 [H 353] CORNER IN VOYER-D'ARGEN-
SON PARK AT ASNIÈRES

Canvas 59 × 81 [23¼ × 32]
Compare F 275 [same site]
Paris May 1887
LITERATURE Yale University Art Gallery Bulletin
April 1959, p 28: a corner in the Montsouris Park.
P. Leprohon, Tel fut van Gogh, 1964, p 414: Paris
1887; the site is Voyer-d'Argenson Park on the
Seine at Asnières
COLLECTION New Haven, Yale University Art
Gallery [gift of H. R. Luce], inv nr 1958.59, cat 1968,
p 11

F 277 [H 352] THE AVENUE IN VOYER-
D'ARGENSON PARK AT ASNIÈRES

Canvas 55 × 67 [21¾ × 26¼]
Paris summer 1887
LITERATURE P. Leprohon, Tel fut van Gogh, 1964,
p 414: the Parc Voyer-d'Argenson on the Seine at
Asnières
COLLECTION New York, Mrs Charles Gilman

F 278 [H 329] STILL LIFE: VASE WITH
DAISIES AND DAHLIAS

Canvas 99 × 79 [39 × 31]
Compare F 197
Signed in upper right: Vincent
Paris autumn 1886
COLLECTION Eindhoven, Netherlands,
Mrs A. H. E. M. Philips-de Jongh

F 276

F 278

F 277

F 275

F 279

F 281

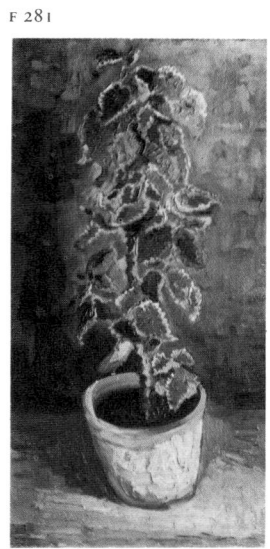

F 283

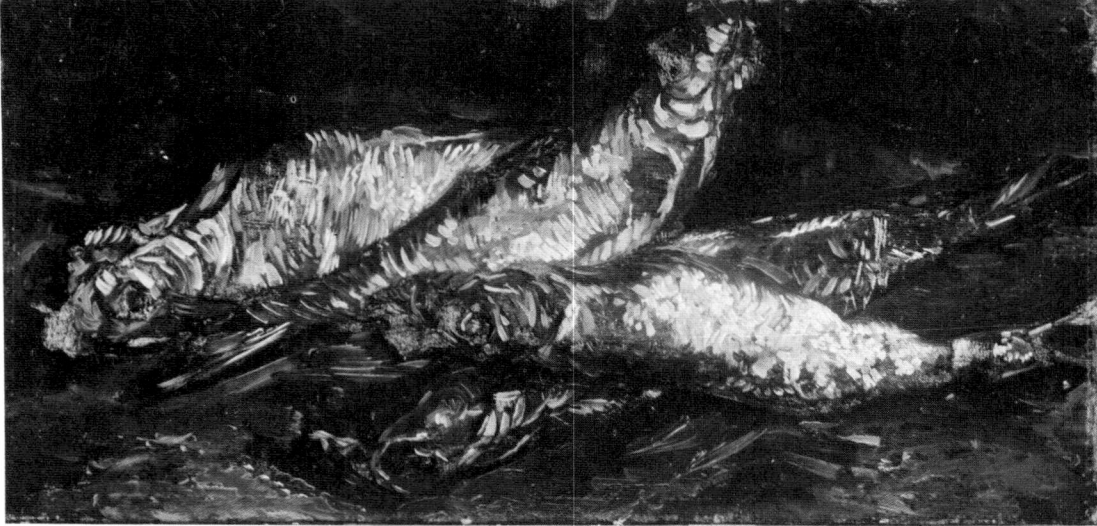

F 283a

F 279 [H 342] STILL LIFE: RED POPPIES

Canvas 56 × 46.5 [22 × 18¼]
Paris autumn 1886
COLLECTION Hartford, Wadsworth Atheneum
[gift of Mr and Mrs Audrey G. Carey], inv nr
1957.617

F 280 [H 325] STILL LIFE: VASE WITH DAISIES
AND POPPIES
Auvers period; see after F 824

F 281 [H 324] STILL LIFE: COLEUS PLANT IN
A FLOWER POT

Canvas 42 × 22 [16½ × 8¾]
Paris late summer 1886
COLLECTION Amsterdam, Rijksmuseum Vincent
van Gogh [Vincent van Gogh Foundation, inv
nr F 281]

F 282 [H 345] STILL LIFE: CINERARIA IN A
FLOWERPOT

Canvas 54.5 × 46 [21½ × 18]
Signed in lower left: Vincent
Paris autumn 1886
LITERATURE Cat 1963, Museum Boymans-van
Beuningen, p 50: Paris summer 1886
COLLECTION Rotterdam, Museum Boymans-van
Beuningen [acquired 1951; gift of Mrs E. Y. van
Beek-van Hoorn Janssen and children], inv nr St.
92, cat 1963, p 50

F 283 [H 313] STILL LIFE: RED HERRINGS

Canvas 21 × 42 [8¼ × 16½]
Paris late spring 1886
LETTER 581 [Arles 24 March 1889] 'You remember
that I did this same still life [two herrings, given in
Arles to Signac: editors] two or three times in Paris,
and exchanged it once for a carpet in the old days.'
COLLECTION Basle, Rudolf Staechelin Foundation
[acquired 1931]

F 283a STILL LIFE: TWO HERRINGS

Canvas 33 × 47 [13 × 18½]
Signed in lower center: Vincent
An x-ray photograph made by the Institut Royal
du Patrimoine Artistique in Brussels shows a copy
of a detail from Delacroix' LES FEMMES D'ALGER
under the two herrings. The copy may be by van
Gogh
Paris first half of 1887
LETTER 581 [Arles 24 March 1889] See F 283
LITERATURE Not in Faille 1928 or Faille 1939
COLLECTION France, Francis Junker [acquired
1958]

F 283b STILL LIFE: HERRINGS WITH A
GARLIC

Canvas 37 × 44.5 [14½ × 17½]
Signed in lower left: Vincent
Paris 1887
LETTER 581 [Arles 24 March 1889] See F 283
LITERATURE Not in Faille 1928 or Faille 1939
EDITORS' COMMENT The dating seems doubtful
COLLECTION Tokyo, Shojiro Ishibashi
[Bridgestone Museum of Art], cat 1959, nr 61

F 284 [H 310] STILL LIFE: HERRINGS AND
ONIONS

Left out by Faille in his manuscript for the present
edition
See REJECTED WORKS

F 285 [H 314] STILL LIFE: HERRINGS,
LEMONS AND TOMATOES

Canvas 39 × 56.5 [15¼ × 22¼]
Signed in lower right: Vincent
Paris 1886
LETTER 581 [Arles 24 March 1889] See F 283
LITERATURE J. Leymarie, Van Gogh, 1951, p 103,
nr 54: Paris 1886-7; letter 581; very likely not
mackerels but herrings, as on F 203, F 283 and F 510
COLLECTION Winterthur, Switzerland, Oskar
Reinhart

F 283b

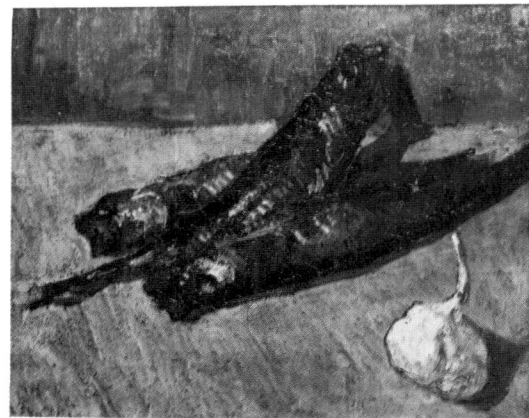

F 285

F 282

F 286

F 286a

F 286b

F 286 [H 323] STILL LIFE: VASE WITH
DELPHINIUM, ASTER, SALVIA AND SPIRAEA

Canvas 70.5 × 34 [27¾ × 13½]
Compare F 286a
Paris summer 1886
LITERATURE M. E. Tralbaut, exhib cat van Gogh
Essen 1957, nr 228: summer 1886; letter 459a;
earlier than F 286a, because less influenced by
Monticelli
COLLECTION The Hague, Gemeente Museum
[acquired 1920], inv nr 2-1920, cat 1962, nr 136

F 286a STILL LIFE: VASE WITH GLADIOLI
AND LILACS

Canvas 69 × 33.5 [27¼ × 13¼]
Compare F 286
Paris summer 1886
LITERATURE Not in Faille 1928 or Faille 1939.
Expertised under the auspices of the Expertise
Instituut, Amsterdam [1955]. M. E. Tralbaut, exhib
cat van Gogh Essen 1957, nr 229: summer 1886;
letter 459a; later than F 286, because of more
pronounced influence of Monticelli
COLLECTION Saint Louis, Mr and Mrs Edwin
McClellan Johnston

F 286b [formerly F 286bis; H 296] STILL LIFE:
LILAC

Canvas 27 × 34.5 [10¾ × 13½]
Signed in lower left: Vincent
Paris spring 1887
LITERATURE Not in Faille 1928
COLLECTION Zurich, Fritz and Peter Nathan

F 287 [H 316] STILL LIFE: VASE WITH
FLOWERS, COFFEEPOT AND FRUIT

Canvas 41 × 38 [16¼ × 15]
Paris early 1887
LITERATURE Cat 1964, Von der Heydt-Museum
der Stadt Wuppertal, p 26: 1886
COLLECTION Wuppertal, Von der Heydt-Museum
der Stadt Wuppertal [acquired 1952; gift of
E. Baron von der Heydt], cat 1964, p 26

F 288 [H 413] PORTRAIT OF A MAN

Canvas 55 × 41 [21¾ × 16¼]
Signed in lower left: Vincent
Paris late 1886
EDITORS' COMMENT In his manuscript for the
present edition Faille dates F 288 to 1887.
COLLECTION Formerly Paris, Allard Art Gallery
Present owner unknown

F 289 [H 415] MAN IN A SKULL CAP

Canvas 65.5 × 54 [25¾ × 21¼]
Paris late 1887
COLLECTION Amsterdam, Rijksmuseum Vincent
van Gogh [Vincent van Gogh Foundation, inv
nr F 289]

F 290 [H 371] LANDSCAPE WITH SNOW
Arles period; see after F 607

F 291 [H 372] TREES IN A FIELD ON A SUNNY
DAY

Canvas 37 × 45.5 [14½ × 18]
Paris summer 1887
COLLECTION Amsterdam, P. and N. de Boer
Foundation

F 288

F 291

F 287

F 289

F 194 [H 209] THE VICARAGE GARDEN UNDER SNOW
Nuenen January 1885

F 294

F 295

F 292 [H 374] BOULEVARD DE CLICHY

Canvas 46.5 × 55 [18¼ × 21¾]
Compare drawing F 1393
Paris February-March 1887
LITERATURE D. Cooper, Zeichnungen und
Aquarelle von Vincent van Gogh, 1954, p 50: a
preliminary study for this painting is drawing
F 1393 of winter 1886-7. A. Bowness, exhib cat van
Gogh London [Hayward Gallery] 1968-9, nr 70:
Paris December 1886-January 1887
COLLECTION Amsterdam, Rijksmuseum Vincent
van Gogh [Vincent van Gogh Foundation, inv
nr F 292]

F 293 [H 379] THE BANKS OF THE SEINE

Canvas 32 × 45.5 [12½ × 18]
Paris May 1887
LITERATURE P. Leprohon, Tel fut van Gogh, 1964,
p 414: Paris spring 1887; probably the bank of the
Seine at Asnières, between the Pont d'Asnières and
the Pont de Clichy, where there is now a public park
COLLECTION Amsterdam, Rijksmuseum Vincent
van Gogh [Vincent van Gogh Foundation, inv
nr F 293]

F 294 [H 420] SELF PORTRAIT WITH STRAW
HAT: THREE QUARTERS TO THE LEFT

Pasteboard 19 × 14 [7½ × 5½]
Paris summer 1887
LITERATURE K. Bromig-Kolleritz, Die Selbstbildnisse Vincent van Goghs, 1955, p 98: early Paris
period, 1886. A. M. Hammacher, Van Gogh:
Selbstbildnisse, 1960, pp 10-1: summer 1887; all
the self portraits with straw hat were painted at the
same period, and were influenced by admiration for
Monticelli. F. Erpel, Die Selbstbildnisse Vincent
van Goghs, 1963, nr 12
COLLECTION Amsterdam, Rijksmuseum Vincent
van Gogh [Vincent van Gogh Foundation, inv
nr F 294]

F 295 [H 422] SELF PORTRAIT WITH GRAY
FELT HAT: BUST, FULL FACE

Pasteboard 41 × 32 [16 × 12½]
Paris summer 1887
LITERATURE K. Bromig-Kolleritz, Die Selbstbild-
nisse Vincent van Goghs, 1955, p 96: 1886.
F. Erpel, Die Selbstbildnisse Vincent van Goghs,
1963, nr 9
COLLECTION Amsterdam, Stedelijk Museum [on
loan since 1950 from the Rijksmuseum; gift of
Mrs F. Bonger, 1936], inv nr B 855

F 292

F 293

F 296

F 298

F 296 [H 421] SELF PORTRAIT WITH GRAY
FELT HAT: FULL FACE

Pasteboard 19 × 14 [7½ × 5½]
Paris 1887
LITERATURE K. Bromig-Kolleritz, Die Selbstbildnisse Vincent van Goghs, 1955, pp 95-6: Paris 1886.
J. B. de la Faille, Les Cahiers de van Gogh 1958,
pp 3-4: identified with the PORTRAIT DE
THÉODORE VAN GOGH mentioned as nr 11 in
exhib cat van Gogh Paris [Bernheim jeune] 1901.
A. M. Hammacher, Van Gogh: Selbstbildnisse,
1960, pp 9-10: rejects Faille's identification of the
sitter as Theo, considering F 296 a self portrait
[this opinion is supported by Dr V. W. van Gogh].
F. Erpel, Die Selbstbildnisse Vincent van Goghs,
1963, nr 8
COLLECTION Amsterdam, Rijksmuseum Vincent
van Gogh [Vincent van Gogh Foundation, inv
nr F 296]

F 297 [H 402] THE SKULL

Canvas 42.5 × 30.5 [16¾ × 12]
Paris 1887
LITERATURE Tralbaut Antwerp 1948, pp 228-9:
Paris; probably the same skull as on F 297a and
F 212 of the Antwerp period
COLLECTION Amsterdam, Rijksmuseum Vincent
van Gogh [Vincent van Gogh Foundation, inv
nr F 297]

F 297a [formerly F 297bis; H 403] THE SKULL

Canvas 41.5 × 31.5 [16¼ × 12½]
Paris 1887
LITERATURE Tralbaut Antwerp 1948, pp 228-9:
Paris; probably the same skull as on F 297 and
F 212 of the Antwerp period
COLLECTION Amsterdam, Rijksmuseum Vincent
van Gogh [Vincent van Gogh Foundation, inv
nr F 297a]

F 298 THE SEINE

Canvas 55 × 65 [21¾ × 25½]
Paris May-June 1887
LITERATURE Faille 1928, nr 298: Paris. Not in
Faille 1939 or the manuscript for the present
edition
EDITORS' COMMENT For unspecified reasons left
out by Faille in the Hyperion edition and in his
manuscript. The editors accept the authenticity of
F 298 after having seen the picture in 1968.
COLLECTION Paris, Private Collection [acquired
1934]

F 299 [H 383] RIVERSIDE WALK NEAR
ASNIÈRES

Canvas 49 × 66 [19¼ × 26]
Paris early summer 1887
LITERATURE P. Leprohon, Tel fut van Gogh, 1964,
pp 413-4: Paris spring 1887; painted at Asnières on
the Seine between the Pont d'Asnières and the Pont
de Clichy
COLLECTION Amsterdam, Rijksmuseum Vincent
van Gogh [Vincent van Gogh Foundation, inv
nr F 299]

F 300 [H 384] MOORED WHERRIES

Canvas 52 × 65 [20½ × 25½]
Paris summer 1887
COLLECTION Aberdeen, Scotland, Mr Middleton

F 301 [H 380] THE BRIDGES AT ASNIÈRES

Canvas 52 × 65 [20½ × 25½]
Paris summer 1887

LITERATURE J. Rewald, Post Impressionism:
From van Gogh to Gauguin, 1956, p 60: 'BRIDGE
AT ASNIÈRES.' Exhib cat van Gogh Paris 1960,
nr 327: compares the bridge depicted here with a
photograph of the Pont de Chatou, ascribing the
considerable differences to van Gogh's creative
imagination and possible changes made on the
bridge since he painted it. L. Reidemeister, Auf den
Spuren der Maler der Ile de France, 1963, p 116
[with a photograph of the bridge as it is today]: the
bridges at Asnières. P. Leprohon, Tel fut van Gogh,
1964, pp 409-11; also in La Vie du Rail 9 February
1964, pp 22-3: railway bridge at Asnières seen from
the Quai d'Asnières looking towards Courbevoie;
erroneously identified in older literature as the
Pont de Chatou
COLLECTION Zurich, E. G. Bührle [acquired 1951],
cat 1958, nr 237

F 297

F 297a

F 300

F 301

F 299

F 304

F 305

F 302 [H 381] PONT DE CLICHY

Pasteboard 30.5 × 39 [12 × 15¼]
Compare sketch in letter 471 and F 303 [same site]
Paris summer 1887
LITERATURE P. Leprohon, Tel fut van Gogh, 1964,
pp 411-2: the bridge is the Pont de Clichy; in the
house on the left was a small restaurant mentioned
by Vincent in letter 489 from Arles; erroneously
identified in older literature as the bridge at
Asnières
COLLECTION Athens, Stavros S. Niarchos, exhib
cat 1957, nr 24

F 303 [H 373] PONT DE CLICHY

Canvas 55 × 46 [21½ × 18]
Compare sketch in letter 471 and F 302 [same site]
Paris summer 1887
LETTER 471 [Arles about 24 March 1888] 'It would
not be a bad idea for you to send Tersteeg one of my
studies: would you say the bridge at Clichy with the
yellow sky and two houses reflected in the water?...'
LITERATURE P. Cabanne, Van Gogh, 1961, p 276,
nr 153: M. E. Tralbaut discovered a reference to a
Pont de Clichy by van Gogh in the livre de vente of
Boussod et Valadon, on 8 June 1888 [Inventory
1888-9, in the Goupil archives, kept at the Rijksbureau voor Kunsthistorische Documentatie, The
Hague]. P. Leprohon, Tel fut van Gogh, 1964, p 411:
the bridge is the Pont de Clichy; erroneously
identified by Faille as the bridge at Asnières
COLLECTION Harrison, New York, F. H. Hirschland

F 304 [H 382] PONT DE LA GRANDE JATTE

Canvas 32 × 40.5 [12½ × 16]
Paris summer 1887
EDITORS' COMMENT According to the results of
research conducted in Paris by Mrs B. Welsh, the
bridge depicted is the Pont de la Grande Jatte, also
called the Pont Bineau or Pont de Courbevoie,
situated between Neuilly and Courbevoie. It was
built in 1870-7 and was replaced by a new bridge in
1965.
COLLECTION Amsterdam, Rijksmuseum Vincent
van Gogh [Vincent van Gogh Foundation, inv
nr F 304]

F 305 [H 351] ENTRANCE OF VOYER-
D'ARGENSON PARK AT ASNIÈRES

Canvas 55 × 67 [21½ × 26¼]
Paris May 1887
LITERATURE P. Leprohon, Tel fut van Gogh, 1964,
p 414: Voyer-d'Argenson Park at Asnières; 1887
COLLECTION New York, Mrs Charles Gilman

F 306 [H 346] UNDERGROWTH

Canvas 32 × 46 [12½ × 18]
Paris summer 1887
COLLECTION Utrecht, Museum van Baaren
Foundation, inv nr 56

F 307 [H 349] UNDERGROWTH

Canvas 46 × 38 [18 × 15]
Paris summer 1887
COLLECTION Amsterdam, Rijksmuseum Vincent
van Gogh [Vincent van Gogh Foundation, inv
nr F 307]

F 303

F 302

F 306

F 307

F 308

F 309a

F 308 [H 350] UNDERGROWTH

Canvas 46 × 38 [18 × 15]
Paris summer 1887
COLLECTION Amsterdam, Rijksmuseum Vincent
van Gogh [Vincent van Gogh Foundation, inv
nr F 308]

F 309 [H 348] A PATH IN THE WOODS

Canvas 46 × 38.5 [18 × 15¼]
Paris summer 1887
COLLECTION Amsterdam, Rijksmuseum Vincent
van Gogh [Vincent van Gogh Foundation, inv
nr F 309]

F 309a [formerly F 309bis; H 347] UNDER-
GROWTH

Canvas 46 × 55.5 [18 × 21¾]
Paris summer 1887
COLLECTION Amsterdam, Rijksmuseum Vincent
van Gogh [Vincent van Gogh Foundation, inv
nr F 309a]

F 310 [H 360] A WHEATFIELD WITH A LARK

Canvas 54 × 64.5 [21¼ × 25½]
Paris summer 1887
LITERATURE J. Leymarie, Van Gogh, 1951, p 103,
nr 53: Paris 1887
EDITORS' COMMENT Fred Orton [oral
communication] has found traces on the painting
that indicate the use of a perspective frame.
COLLECTION Amsterdam, Rijksmuseum Vincent
van Gogh [Vincent van Gogh Foundation, inv
nr F 310]

F 310a [formerly F 310bis; H 355] EDGE OF A
WHEATFIELD

Canvas on pasteboard 40 × 32.5 [15¾ × 12¾]
Paris summer 1887
COLLECTION Boston, Mrs William Herman

F 311 [H 378] BATHING PLACE ON THE SEINE
AT ASNIÈRES

Canvas 19 × 27 [7½ × 10½]
Paris summer 1887
COLLECTION Upperville, Virginia, Mr and Mrs
Paul Mellon

F 309

F 310

F 310a

F 311

F 312

F 313

F 312 [H 377] RESTAURANT DE LA SIRÈNE AT ASNIÈRES

Canvas 51.5 × 64 [20¼ × 25¼]
Compare F 313 and drawing F 1408 [same site]
Paris early summer 1887
LITERATURE G. Coquiot, Vincent van Gogh, 1923,
p 145: Restaurant de la Sirène at Asnières.
P. Leprohon, Tel fut van Gogh, 1964, p 412
COLLECTION Formerly Berlin, Mrs Paret [1928 or
later]
Present owner unknown

F 313 [H 375] RESTAURANT DE LA SIRÈNE AT ASNIÈRES

Canvas 57 × 68 [22½ × 26¾]
Compare F 312 and drawing F 1408 [same site]
Paris early summer 1887
LITERATURE R. Jacobsen, Onze Kunst 1904, part
2, p 1 [with reproduction]. G. Coquiot, Vincent van
Gogh, 1923, p 145: Restaurant de la Sirène at
Asnières. J. Leymarie, Van Gogh, 1951, p 102,
nr 47: Paris 1887. P. Leprohon, Tel fut van Gogh,
1964, p 412
COLLECTION Paris, Musée National du Louvre
[acquired 1929], inv nr R F 2325, cat Impressionistes
1959, nr 145

F 314 [H 368] VOYER-D'ARGENSON PARK AT ASNIÈRES

Canvas 75.5 × 113 [29¾ × 44½]
Paris May 1887
LITERATURE P. Leprohon, Tel fut van Gogh, 1964,
p 414: Voyer-d'Argenson Park at Asnières
COLLECTION Amsterdam, Rijksmuseum Vincent
van Gogh [Vincent van Gogh Foundation, inv
nr F 314]
Colorplate, p 164

F 315 [H 361] CORNER OF VOYER-D'ARGEN-SON PARK AT ASNIÈRES

Canvas 49 × 65 [19¼ × 25½]
Paris 1887
LITERATURE P. Leprohon, Tel fut van Gogh, 1964,
p 414: Voyer-d'Argenson Park at Asnières
COLLECTION Formerly Copenhagen, Chr. Tetzen-
Lund
Present owner unknown

F 316 [H 364] VIEW FROM MONTMARTRE

Canvas 81 × 100 [32 × 39¼]
Paris summer 1887
LETTER 497 [Arles 12 June 1888] '*I am working on
a landscape with wheatfields...it is in the style of the
two landscapes of the Butte Montmartre which were
at the Indépendants.*'
LITERATURE M. E. Tralbaut, exhib cat van Gogh
Essen 1957, nr 236: one of the two views of the
Butte Montmartre exhibited in 1888 at the
Indépendants and mentioned in letter 497; the
other is F 350
COLLECTION Amsterdam, Rijksmuseum Vincent
van Gogh [Vincent van Gogh Foundation, inv
nr F 316]

F 317 [H 397] FACTORIES AT ASNIÈRES, SEEN FROM THE QUAI DE CLICHY

Canvas 54 × 72 [21¼ × 28¼]
Paris summer 1887
LITERATURE P. Leprohon, Tel fut van Gogh, 1964,
p 414: factories in Asnières, near the Pont de
Clichy, opposite the Quai de Clichy
COLLECTION Saint Louis, City Art Museum
[acquired December 1958]

F 316

F 314

F 317

F 315

F 319

F 318

F 318 [H 396] THE FACTORY AT ASNIÈRES

Canvas 46.5 × 54 [18¼ × 21¼]
Paris summer 1887
LITERATURE P. Leprohon, Tel fut van Gogh,
1964, p 414: factory at Asnières, near the Pont de
Clichy
COLLECTION Merion, Pennsylvania, The Barnes
Foundation [acquired 1922]

F 319 [H 399] SELF PORTRAIT WITH A
JAPANESE PRINT

Canvas 44 × 35 [17¼ × 13¾]
Paris end 1887
LITERATURE K. Bromig-Kolleritz, Die Selbstbild-
nisse Vincent van Goghs, 1955, p 106. F. Erpel, Die
Selbstbildnisse Vincent van Goghs, 1963, nr 30:
anticipates F 522 in manner of painting
COLLECTION Basle, Emile Dreyfus

F 320 [H 400] SELF PORTRAIT: THREE
QUARTERS TO THE LEFT

Canvas 47 × 35 [18½ × 13¾]
Paris autumn 1887
LITERATURE K. Bromig-Kolleritz, Die Selbstbild-
nisse Vincent van Goghs, 1955, p 106. F. Erpel, Die
Selbstbildnisse Vincent van Goghs, 1963, nr 29
COLLECTION Paris, Musée National du Louvre
[acquired 1947; gift of H. J. Laroche], inv nr R F
1947-28, cat Impressionistes 1959, p 247

F 321 [H 365] RESTAURANT AT ASNIÈRES

Canvas 19 × 26.5 [7½ × 10½]
Paris summer 1887
LITERATURE J. Leymarie, Van Gogh, 1951, p 100,
nr 38: summer 1887
COLLECTION Amsterdam, Rijksmuseum Vincent
van Gogh [Vincent van Gogh Foundation, inv
nr F 321]

F 322 [H 333] STILL LIFE: VASE WITH
LILACS, DAISIES AND ANEMONES

Canvas 46.5 × 37.5 [18¼ × 14¾]
Signed in middle, to the left: Vincent
Paris summer 1887
COLLECTION Switzerland, Private Collection

F 323 [H 328] STILL LIFE: VASE WITH
DAISIES AND ANEMONES

Canvas 61 × 38 [24 × 15]
Paris summer 1887
LITERATURE L. Gans, Museumjournaal 1958,
part 1, p 85: first half of the Paris period; continues
Dutch style in composition and manner of painting
COLLECTION Otterlo, Rijksmuseum Kröller-
Müller, inv nr 263-14, cat van Gogh 1970, nr 204

F 324 [H 332] STILL LIFE: VASE WITH
CORNFLOWERS AND POPPIES

Canvas 80 × 67 [31½ × 26½]
Signed in upper left: Vincent
Paris summer 1887
COLLECTION Formerly Berlin-Grunewald,
Mrs H. Harries-von Siemens [1928 or earlier]
Present owner unknown

F 324a [formerly F 324bis; H 336] STILL LIFE:
VASE WITH VISCARIA

Canvas 65 × 54 [25½ × 21¼]
Signed in lower left: Vincent
Paris summer 1886
LITERATURE Not in Faille 1928

COLLECTION Republic of Egypt [acquired 1960; bequest of the widow of Mohammed Mahmoud Bey Khalil]

F 325 STILL LIFE: VASE WITH DAISIES AND POPPIES

Left out by Faille in his manuscript for the present edition
See REJECTED WORKS

F 326 [H 339] STILL LIFE: CORNFLOWERS

Canvas 46 × 38 [18 × 15]
Signed in lower right: Vincent
Paris 1886-7. N.B. See EDITORS' COMMENT
EDITORS' COMMENT The editors do not agree with Faille about the status of this painting. They do not accept it as an authentic work by van Gogh.
COLLECTION Mamaroneck, New York, Private Collection

F 320

F 321

F 322

F 323

F 324

F 324a

F 326

F 328

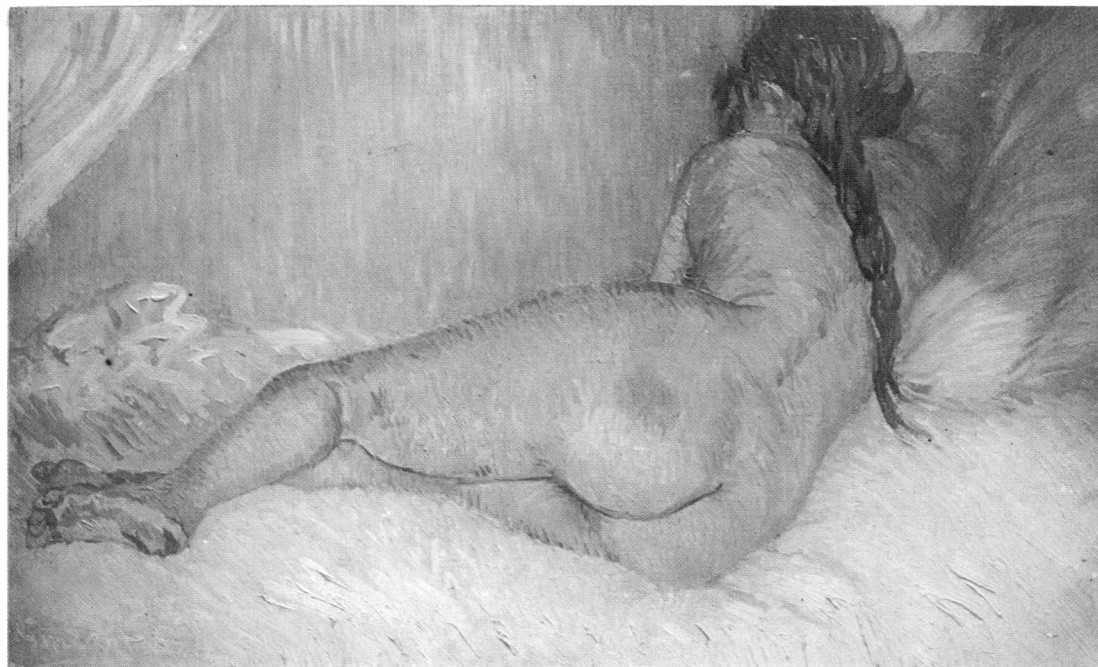

F 329

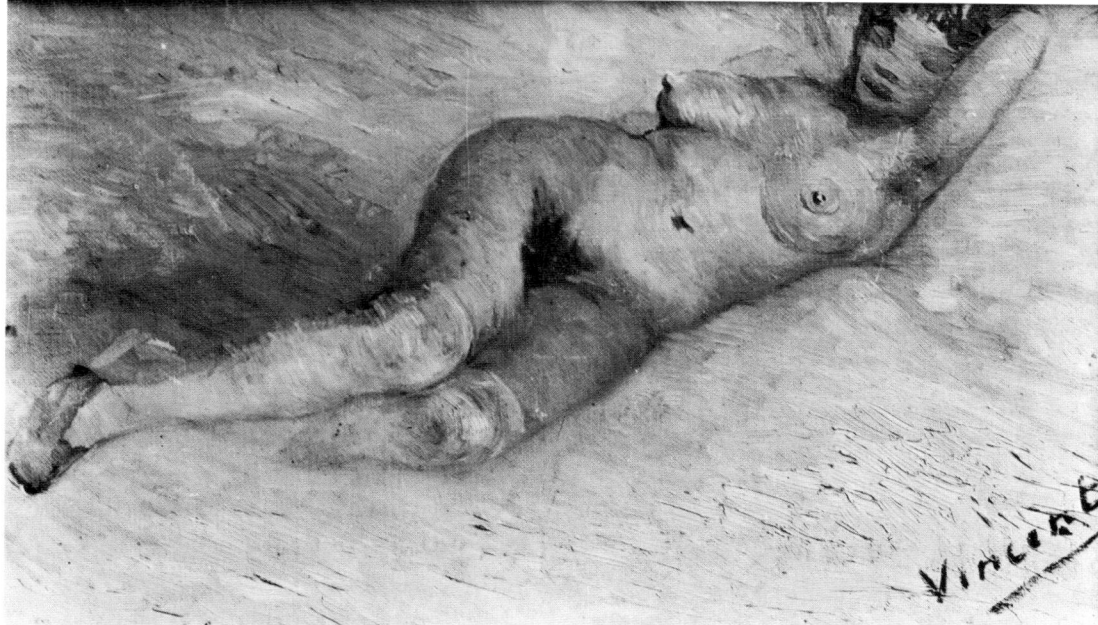

F 332

F 327 [H 290] STILL LIFE: ONE-EARED VASE
WITH CARNATIONS

Canvas 40 × 52 [15¾ × 20½]
Paris early summer 1886
LITERATURE Cat van Gogh 1959, Rijksmuseum
Kröller-Müller, nr 201: red and white carnations;
spring 1887
COLLECTION Otterlo, Rijksmuseum Kröller-
Müller, inv nr 273-20, cat van Gogh 1970, nr 201

F 328 [H 236] NUDE WOMAN RECLINING:
SEEN FROM THE BACK

Canvas 38 × 61 [15 × 24]
Signed and dated in lower left: Vincent 87
Paris first half of 1887
COLLECTION Paris, Private Collection

F 329 [H 111] NUDE WOMAN RECLINING

Canvas 24 × 41 [9½ × 16]
Signed in lower right: Vincent
Compare F 330, F 357 and drawing F 1404
[probably the same model]
Paris first half of 1887
LITERATURE C. Veth, Schoon schip!, 1932, p 40
COLLECTION De Steeg, Netherlands-Oberägeri,
Switzerland, S. van Deventer

F 330 [H 235] NUDE WOMAN ON A BED

Canvas 59.5 × 73 [23½ × 28¾] Oval
Compare F 329, F 357 [probably the same model]
and drawing F 1404 [same composition]
Paris first half of 1887
LITERATURE J. Leymarie, Van Gogh, 1951,
pp 98-9, nr 27: Paris 1886
COLLECTION Merion, Pennsylvania, The Barnes
Foundation

F 331 [H 249] A PAIR OF SHOES

Pasteboard 33 × 41 [13 × 16¼]
Signed in upper left: Vincent
Paris first half of 1887
COLLECTION Amsterdam, Rijksmuseum Vincent
van Gogh [Vincent van Gogh Foundation, inv
nr F 331]

F 332 [H 250] THREE PAIRS OF SHOES

Canvas 49 × 72 [19¼ × 28¼]
Paris winter 1886-7
COLLECTION Cambridge, Massachusetts, Fogg
Art Museum [acquired 1951; bequest of Maurice
Wertheim], inv nr 1951.66

F 332a A PAIR OF SHOES

Canvas 37.5 × 45.5 [14¾ × 18]
Signed in upper left: Vincent
Paris winter 1886-7
LITERATURE Not in Faille 1928 or Faille 1939
COLLECTION Brussels, E. Schumacher

F 333 [H 251] A PAIR OF SHOES

Canvas 34 × 41.5 [13½ × 16¼]
Signed and dated in lower right: Vincent 87
Paris first half of 1887
COLLECTION Baltimore, The Baltimore Museum
of Art [acquired 1949 with the Cone Collection],
cat The Cone Collection 1967, nr 26

F 334 [H 277] STILL LIFE: A BASKET OF
CROCUSES

Canvas 32.5 × 41 [12¾ × 16]
Signed in lower left: Vincent
Paris early spring 1887
COLLECTION Amsterdam, Rijksmuseum Vincent
van Gogh [Vincent van Gogh Foundation, inv
nr F 334]

F 331

F 327

F 330

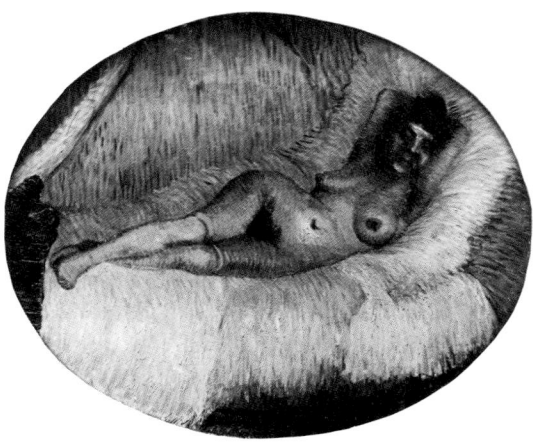

F 332a

F 333

F 334

F 335

F 336

F 338

F 340

F 335 [H 246] STILL LIFE: THREE BOOKS [Emile Zola, *Au Bonheur des Dames*; Jean Richepin, *Braves Gens*; Jules and Edmond de Goncourt, *Fille Elisa*]

Panel 31×48.5 [12¼×19] Oval. Painted on the lid of a Japanese teabox, as is F 336
Dated in upper right: 87
Paris early spring 1887
LETTER W 1 [summer or autumn 1887] *'If...one wants truth, life as it is, then there are for instance de Goncourt in* Germinie Lacerteux, la Fille Elisa, *Zola in* La joie de vivre *and* L'assommoir *and so many other masterpieces; they paint life as we feel it ourselves, and thus they satisfy the need we feel of having told the truth. The work of the French naturalists, Zola, Guy de Maupassant, de Goncourt, Richepin, Daudet, Huysmans, is magnificent, and one can hardly be said to belong to one's time if one has paid no attention to it. Maupassant's masterpiece is* Bel Ami...'
LITERATURE A. M. Hammacher, exhib cat van Gogh-Signac London [Marlborough] 1962, p 92: Paris 1886; earlier than F 358 and F 359; inspired by Signac's picture with the novel *Au soleil* of 1883; the bird's-eye perspective, the number of books shown and the folds of the tablecloth also show resemblance to similar themes painted by Signac between 1883 and 1887
COLLECTION Amsterdam, Rijksmuseum Vincent van Gogh [Vincent van Gogh Foundation, inv nr F 335]

F 336 [H 276] STILL LIFE: BASKET OF BULBS

Panel 31.5×48 [12½×19] Oval. Painted on the lid of a Japanese teabox, as is F 335
Paris early spring 1887
COLLECTION Amsterdam, Rijksmuseum Vincent van Gogh [Vincent van Gogh Foundation, inv nr F 336]

F 337 [H 315] STILL LIFE: POT WITH CHIVE

Canvas 32×22 [12½×8½]
Paris spring 1887
COLLECTION Amsterdam, Rijksmuseum Vincent van Gogh [Vincent van Gogh Foundation, inv nr F 337]

F 338 [H 309] STILL LIFE: LEMONS ON A PLATE

Canvas 21×26.5 [8¼×10½]
Paris early spring 1887
COLLECTION Amsterdam, Rijksmuseum Vincent van Gogh [Vincent van Gogh Foundation, inv nr F 338]

F 339 [H 306] STILL LIFE: ABSINTHE

Canvas 46.5×33 [18¼×13]
Paris early spring 1887
LITERATURE J. Leymarie, Van Gogh, 1951, p 103, nr 55: Paris 1886-7; subject and composition probably inspired by Degas
COLLECTION Amsterdam, Rijksmuseum Vincent van Gogh [Vincent van Gogh Foundation, inv nr F 339]

F 340 [H 307] STILL LIFE: DECANTER AND LEMONS ON A PLATE

Canvas 46×38 [18×15]
Signed and dated in lower right: Vincent 87
Paris early spring 1887
COLLECTION Amsterdam, Rijksmuseum Vincent van Gogh [Vincent van Gogh Foundation, inv nr F 340]

F 337

F 341 [H 392] VIEW FROM VINCENT'S ROOM
IN THE RUE LEPIC

Canvas 46 × 38 [18 × 15]
Compare F 341a and drawing F 1391
Paris early spring 1887
COLLECTION Amsterdam, Rijksmuseum Vincent
van Gogh [Vincent van Gogh Foundation, inv
nr F 341]

F 341a [formerly F 341bis; H 398] VIEW FROM
VINCENT'S ROOM IN THE RUE LEPIC

Pasteboard 46 × 38 [18 × 15]
Compare F 341 and drawing F 1391
Paris early spring 1887
LITERATURE Not in Faille 1928. Exhib cat van
Gogh Houston 1951, nr 4: van Gogh had rented
the studio from Toulouse Lautrec and gave him
this painting
EDITORS' COMMENT This view is taken from a
slightly different angle than F 341 and drawing
F 1391.
COLLECTION New York, Miss Millicent Rogers

F 341

F 341a

F 339

F 342

F 342 [H 369] INTERIOR OF A RESTAURANT

Canvas 45.5 × 56.5 [18 × 22¼]
Paris summer 1887
LITERATURE G. Schmidt, Van Gogh, 1947, reproduction nr 14: autumn 1886. M. Buchmann, Die Farbe bei Vincent van Gogh, 1948, pp 24-30, 50: color analysis of the picture. Exhib cat van Gogh Munich 1956, nr 103: end 1886 or early 1887. M. E. Tralbaut, Exhib cat van Gogh Essen 1957, nr 244: spring 1887. Cat van Gogh 1959, Rijksmuseum Kröller-Müller, nr 205: 1887; the restaurant is thought to be Chez Bataille, not far from the Rue Lepic
COLLECTION Otterlo, Rijksmuseum Kröller-Müller, inv nr 271-12, cat van Gogh 1970, nr 205

F 343 [H 401] PORTRAIT OF ALEXANDER REID

Pasteboard 41.5 × 33.5 [16¼ × 13¼]
Signed in lower right: Vincent
Compare F 270 [same model]
Paris summer 1887
LITERATURE T. J. Honeyman, Scottish Art Review 1948, pp 16-20: Vincent painted at least three and possibly four portraits of his friend Alexander Reid, who later became an art dealer in Glasgow. Only F 270 and F 343 have been identified as portraits of Reid
COLLECTION Graham H. Reid

F 346

F 344 [H VII] SELF PORTRAIT IN A GRAY FELT HAT: THREE QUARTERS TO THE LEFT

Canvas 44 × 37.5 [17¼ × 14¾]
Paris late summer 1887
LITERATURE J. Leymarie, Van Gogh, 1951, nr 45, pp 101-2: Paris 1887. K. Bromig-Kolleritz, Die Selbstbildnisse Vincent van Goghs, 1955, pp 49, 106. F. Erpel, Die Selbstbildnisse Vincent van Goghs, 1963, nr 10. A. Bowness, exhib cat van Gogh London [Hayward Gallery] 1968-9, nr 96: Paris September-December 1887
COLLECTION Amsterdam, Rijksmuseum Vincent van Gogh [Vincent van Gogh Foundation, inv nr F 344]

F 345 [H 406] SELF PORTRAIT: THREE QUARTERS TO THE LEFT

Pasteboard 42 × 33.7 [16½ × 13¼]
Paris spring 1887
LITERATURE K. Bromig-Kolleritz, Die Selbstbildnisse Vincent van Goghs, 1955, pp 101-2: autumn 1886. F. Erpel, Die Selbstbildnisse Vincent van Goghs, 1963, nr 22
COLLECTION Chicago, The Art Institute of Chicago [acquired 1954; J. Winterbotham bequest], inv nr 54.326, cat 1961, pp 181-2

F 346 [H 265] VIEW OF KITCHEN GARDENS ON MONTMARTRE

Canvas 43 × 80 [17 × 31½]
Signed in lower left: Vincent
Compare F 272, F 274, F 348, F 348a and drawing F 1396 [same site]
Paris early spring 1887
COLLECTION Amsterdam, Rijksmuseum Vincent van Gogh [Vincent van Gogh Foundation, inv nr F 346]

F 347 [H 264] A CORNER OF MONTMARTRE

Canvas 35 × 64.5 [13¾ × 25½]
Signed in lower left: Vincent
Annotated by Vincent in middle left: Point de vue
Paris early spring 1887
COLLECTION Amsterdam, Rijksmuseum Vincent

F 347

van Gogh [Vincent van Gogh Foundation, inv
nr F 347]

F 348 [H 266] THE MOULIN DE LA GALETTE

Canvas 61 × 50 [24 × 19¾]
Compare F 272, F 274, F 346, F 348a and drawing
F 1396 [same site]
Paris winter 1886-7
COLLECTION Buenos Aires, Museo nacional de
bellas artes

F 344

F 343

F 348

F 345

F 348a

F 350

F 348a [formerly F 348bis; H 269] THE MOULIN
DE LA GALETTE

Canvas 46 × 38 [18 × 15]
Compare F 272, F 274, F 346, F 348 and drawing
F 1396 [same site]
Paris February-March 1887
COLLECTION Pittsburgh, Carnegie Institute [gift of
the Sarah Mellon Scaife family]

F 349 [H 273] THE MOULIN DE LA GALETTE

Canvas 55 × 38.5 [21½ × 15¼]
Paris early winter 1886
COLLECTION Newark, New Jersey, Mr and Mrs
Charles W. Engelhard

F 350 [H IV] KITCHEN GARDENS ON
MONTMARTRE

Canvas 96 × 120 [37¾ × 47¼]
Paris summer 1887
LETTER 497 [Arles 12 June 1888] See F 316
LITERATURE Exhib cat van Gogh Essen 1957,
nr 236: Tralbaut identifies F 350 as one of the two
views of Montmartre exhibited in 1888 at the
Indépendants and mentioned in letter 497; the
other is F 316
COLLECTION Amsterdam, Stedelijk Museum
[acquired 1913], cat 1914, nr 126

F 351 [H 362] IN THE OUTSKIRTS OF PARIS

Canvas 38 × 46 [15 × 18]
Paris early summer 1887
COLLECTION Scarsdale, New York, Mrs Salman
Schocken

F 352 [H 363] THE RIVERSIDE IN SPRING:
PONT DE CLICHY

Canvas 50 × 60 [19¾ × 23½]
Paris summer 1887
LITERATURE P. Leprohon, Tel fut van Gogh, 1964,
p 414: Pont de Clichy, linking the Ile des Ravageurs
and the Ile de Robinson
COLLECTION Texas, Private Collection
Colorplate, p 181

F 353 [H 366] BOAT MOORED TO THE BANK

Canvas 48 × 55 [19 × 21½]
Compare F 1375
Paris early summer 1887
COLLECTION New York, Farkas Foundation

F 354 [H 367] FISHING IN SPRING, PROBABLY
NEAR THE PONT LEVALLOIS

Canvas 49 × 58 [19¼ × 22¾]
Paris spring 1887
LITERATURE J. Leymarie, Van Gogh, 1951, nr 40,
p 101: 1887. P. Leprohon, Tel fut van Gogh, 1964,
p 414: Pont Levallois seen from the island La
Grande Jatte
COLLECTION Chicago, The Art Institute of
Chicago [acquired 1965; gift of Charles Deering
McCormick, Brooks McCormick and Roger
McCormick]
Colorplate, p 182

F 355 [H 391] RESTAURANT RISPAL AT
ASNIÈRES

Canvas 72 × 60 [28¼ × 23½]
Paris May 1887
LITERATURE P. Leprohon, Tel fut van Gogh, 1964,
p 413: the restaurant was at 117 Boulevard de
Seine, now called Quai Aulagnier
COLLECTION New York, Mrs Hugo L. Moser

F 349

F 351

F 352

F 354

F 353

F 355

F 356

F 358

F 356 [H 412] SELF PORTRAIT: THREE QUARTERS TO THE RIGHT

Canvas 41 × 33 [16 × 13]
Paris summer 1887
LITERATURE K. Bromig-Kolleritz, Die Selbstbildnisse Vincent van Goghs, 1955, pp 100-1: 1886.
F. Erpel, Die Selbstbildnisse Vincent van Goghs, 1963, nr 19. A. Bowness, exhib cat van Gogh London [Hayward Gallery] 1968-9, nr 94: Paris September-December 1887
COLLECTION Amsterdam, Rijksmuseum Vincent van Gogh [Vincent van Gogh Foundation, inv nr F 356]

F 357 [H 232] HEAD OF A WOMAN [MRS TANGUY?]

Canvas 42 × 35 [16¼ × 13¾]
Signed and dated in upper right: Vincent 87
Compare F 329, F 330 and drawing F 1404 [probably the same model]
Paris spring 1887
EDITORS' COMMENT There is no evidence that the model is Mrs Tanguy.
COLLECTION Basle, Öffentliche Kunstsammlung [on loan since 1947 with the Rudolf Staechelin Collection], cat 1961, p 12

F 358 [H 230] STILL LIFE: ROMANS PARISIENS

Canvas 53 × 72.5 [20¾ × 28½]
Compare F 359 [same motif]
Paris autumn 1887
LETTER W 3 [Arles probably 30 March 1888]
'I will set aside for you a little study of a book and a flower. In a larger size with a whole lot of books with pink, yellow, green covers and bright red ones – my painting Parisian novels was the same subject – Theo will take it along for you...'
LITERATURE C. Nordenfalk, Journal of the Warburg and Courtauld Institutes 1947, p 143: autumn 1888; a repetition from memory of F 359. J. Seznec, Magazine of Art 1950
EDITORS' COMMENT The text of the letter has been corrected by the editors. The painting intended for Wilhelmina mentioned in letter W 3 was probably F 393.
COLLECTION Amsterdam, Rijksmuseum Vincent van Gogh [Vincent van Gogh Foundation, inv nr F 358]

F 359 [H 231] STILL LIFE: ROMANS PARISIENS WITH A ROSE

Canvas 73 × 93 [28¾ × 36½]
Compare F 358 [same motif]
Paris autumn 1887
LETTER 468 [Arles 10 March 1888] 'I quite approve of your exhibiting the 'Livres' with the Indépendants; its title ought to be 'Romans Parisiens.'
LITERATURE G. Coquiot, Vincent van Gogh, 1923, p 136: Guillaumin and the art dealer Portier found Vincent working on this painting when they visited him at his studio in the Rue Lepic. C. Nordenfalk and Å. Meyerson, Konsthistorisk Tidskrift 1946, p 133: to judge by the technique executed in the first half of 1887; also mentioned in letter 555 [Arles October 1888]. Exhib cat Collections Suisses Lausanne 1964, nr 112: letters 468 and 555
EDITORS' COMMENT It cannot be determined which of the two versions of ROMANS PARISIENS was exhibited at the Indépendants.
COLLECTION Baden, Switzerland, Private Collection

F 360 [H 237] STILL LIFE: PLASTER
STATUETTE AND BOOKS [G. de Maupassant,
Bel Ami; Jules and Edmond Goncourt,
Germinie Lacerteux]

Canvas 55 × 46.5 [21½ × 18¼]
Compare F 216d, F 216i and drawing F 1363c recto
[same statuette]
Paris summer or autumn 1887
LETTER W I [summer or autumn 1887] See F 335
LITERATURE M. Buchmann, Die Farbe bei Vincent
van Gogh, 1948, pp 31-3: color analysis; compared
to the impressionist style of F 342 further developed;
the colors are used here in a more decorative way
COLLECTION Otterlo, Rijksmuseum Kröller-
Müller, inv nr 265-12, cat van Gogh 1970, nr 203
Colorplate, p 199

F 361 [H 357] OUTSKIRTS OF PARIS: ROAD
WITH PEASANT SHOULDERING A SPADE

Canvas 48 × 73 [19 × 28¾]
Paris spring 1887
COLLECTION Fort Worth, Texas, Miss Karen
Carter Johnson

F 359

F 361

F 357

F 360

F 362

F 363

F 362 [H 358] A PARK IN SPRING

Canvas 50 × 65 [19¾ × 25½]
Paris May 1887
LITERATURE Bulletin J. H. de Bois Art Gallery,
Haarlem, 1918, pp 2-3: wrongly called SUMMER
AT ARLES
COLLECTION Laren, Netherlands, R. F. Volz

F 363 [H 304] PORTRAIT OF PÈRE TANGUY

Canvas 92 × 75 [36¼ × 29½]
Compare F 263, drawing F 1412 [same model] and
F 364 [same composition]
Paris autumn 1887
LITERATURE C. Nordenfalk, Vincent van Gogh,
1948, p 83: end 1887-early 1888. J. Leymarie, Van
Gogh, 1951, p 100, nr 33: tries to identify the
Japanese prints; the print in the lower right,
depicting a standing actor in the style of Kesaï
Yeisen, appears in F 373 as well; the prints in the
background, from upper left to lower right, are:
[1] WINTER LANDSCAPE in the style of Hiroshige
[2] one of the 36 VIEWS OF THE FUJIYAMA by
Hokusai [3] FLOWERING TREE after Hiroshige
[the landscape is by van Gogh] [4] BUST OF AN
ACTOR in the style of Toyokuni or Kuniyoshi
[5] FLOWERS in the style of Hokusai [6] STANDING
ACTOR in the style of Kesaï Yeisen. M. E. Tralbaut,
Mededelingen van de Dienst voor Schone Kunsten
der Gemeente 's-Gravenhage 1954, pp 6-40: the
print in the lower right was also used on the cover
of a special double number of Paris Illustré devoted
to Japan [1 May 1886]; a copy of this issue was
part of the estate of van Gogh
EDITORS' COMMENT In his M.A. thesis for the
Courtauld Institute, University of London, Fred
Orton suggests the following identifications for the
Japanese prints in F 363: left row [1] Hiroshige I
[2] Toyokuni III, Miyrayano Takao AN OIRAN
[3] untraceable; in the middle row is a composite
print; right row [1] probably a composite [2] from
the cover of Paris Illustré, 1 May 1886.
COLLECTION Paris, Musée Rodin, cat 1938, nr 386
Colorplate, p 200

F 364 [H 305] PORTRAIT OF PÈRE TANGUY

Canvas 65 × 51 [25½ × 20]
Compare F 263, drawing F 1412 [same model] and
F 366 [same composition]
Paris late 1887
EDITORS' COMMENT In his M.A. thesis for the
Courtauld Institute, University of London, Fred
Orton suggests these identifications of the wall
decoration: left row [1] F 283 [2] Toyokuni III,
Miyrayano Takao AN OIRAN [3] untraceable; the
print in the middle row is untraceable and is
probably an invention; right row [1] Yoshitora
[2] Hiroshige II? GOJN SAN TSUGI MEI SHO QUÉ
[3] Toyokuni III
EDITORS' COMMENT F 364 is later than F 363.
COLLECTION Athens, Stavros S. Niarchos, exhib
cat 1957, nr 23

F 365 recto [formerly F 365 verso; H 87]
PEASANT WOMAN SEATED
Nuenen period; see after F 203a

F 365 verso [formerly F 365 recto; H 409] SELF
PORTRAIT WITH STRAW HAT

Canvas 41 × 31.5 [16 × 12½]
Paris 1887
LITERATURE J. B. de la Faille, Der Cicerone 1927,
p 101 [with reproduction]. H. B. Wehle, Bulletin of
the Metropolitan Museum of Art 1948, pp 264-71:
on loan since 1936. K. Bromig-Kolleritz, Die
Selbstbildnisse Vincent van Goghs, 1955, p 102:
1886. F. Erpel, Die Selbstbildnisse Vincent van

Goghs, 1963, nr 15: possibly end of the Paris period
COLLECTION New York, The Metropolitan
Museum of Art [on loan since 1936 from Miss
Adelaide Milton de Groot; acquired 1967 with
Adelaide Milton de Groot bequest], inv nr
67.187.70a

F 366 [H 405] SELF PORTRAIT: NEARLY FULL
FACE

Canvas 46.5 × 35.5 [18¼ × 14]
Paris autumn 1887
LITERATURE K. Bromig-Kolleritz, Die Selbstbildnisse Vincent van Goghs, 1955, pp 103-4: painted
between autumn 1886 and early 1887, before the
dated [1887] portrait F 263a; the background still
shows traces of the pointillist method. F. Erpel, Die
Selbstbildnisse Vincent van Goghs, 1963, nr 23
EDITORS' COMMENT Faille connects this painting,
without giving any reason, with letter 553, in which
mention is made of a self portrait Vincent gave to
Emile Bernard.
COLLECTION Zurich, E. G. Bührle [acquired 1945],
cat 1958, nr 238

F 367 [H 292] WOMAN SEATED IN THE GRASS

Canvas 41.5 × 34.5 [16¼ × 13½]
Paris spring 1887
COLLECTION New York, Private Collection

F 364

F 366

F 367

F 365 verso

F 368

F 370

F 368 [H 291] A WOMAN WALKING IN A GARDEN

Canvas 48 × 60 [19 × 23½]
Paris spring 1887
COLLECTION USA, E. J. Bowes

F 369 [H 318] WOMAN WITH CRADLE

Canvas 61 × 46 [24 × 18]
Paris spring 1887
LITERATURE A. Bowness, exhib cat van Gogh
London [Hayward Gallery] 1968-9, nr 71: Paris
December 1886-January 1887: color and handling
of this portrait closest to F 292 and drawing F 1393;
stylistically a little earlier than F 370
COLLECTION Amsterdam, Rijksmuseum Vincent
van Gogh [Vincent van Gogh Foundation, inv
nr F 369]
Colorplate, p 233

F 370 [H 299] WOMAN SITTING IN THE CAFÉ
DU TAMBOURIN [Avenue de Clichy, Paris]

Canvas 55.5 × 46.5 [21¾ × 18¼]
Paris February 1887
LITERATURE J. Leymarie, Van Gogh, 1951, p 102,
nr 48: spring 1887. M.E. Tralbaut, Mededelingen
van de Dienst voor Schone Kunsten der Gemeente
's-Gravenhage 1954, p 20: the woman may be 'La
Segattori,' the owner of the Café du Tambourin.
A. M. Hammacher, exhib cat van Gogh-Signac
London [Marlborough] 1962, p 93: closely
connected with cat nr 79, Signac's SEATED
WOMAN PUTTING ON HER STOCKINGS of 1883.
COLLECTION Amsterdam, Rijksmuseum Vincent
van Gogh [Vincent van Gogh Foundation, inv
nr F 370]

F 371 [H 11] JAPONAISERIE: THE FLOWERING
PLUMTREE [after Hiroshige]

Canvas 55 × 46 [21¾ × 18]
Paris first half of 1887
LITERATURE M. E. Tralbaut, Mededelingen van de
Dienst voor Schone Kunsten der Gemeente
's-Gravenhage 1954, pp 22, 30-3: the painting is
one-and-a-half times enlarged from the Hiroshige
print [reproduction IX] by means of a transfer
[reproduction XI] divided in squares, still preserved
in the Vincent van Gogh Foundation in
Amsterdam; the Japanese characters are added for
their decorative value, and do not correspond with
those on Hiroshige's print
EDITORS' COMMENT The title of the print, one of
the HUNDRED FAMOUS VIEWS OF EDO, 1857, is
UAMEIDO UMEYASHIKI [Flowering Plumtree].
The view is taken from the veranda of the teahouse
at Kameido.
COLLECTION Amsterdam, Rijksmuseum Vincent
van Gogh [Vincent van Gogh Foundation, inv
nr F 371]

F 372 [H 233] JAPONAISERIE: THE BRIDGE
IN THE RAIN [after Hiroshige]

Canvas 73 × 54 [28¾ × 21¼]
Paris summer 1887
LITERATURE M. E. Tralbaut, Mededelingen van de
Dienst voor Schone Kunsten der Gemeente
's-Gravenhage 1954, pp 33-4 [reproduction XIII]:
the painting is one-and-three-quarters times
enlarged from the Hiroshige print BRIDGE IN THE
RAIN [reproduction XII]; the imitation Japanese
characters along the edge are an addition of
Vincent's; the transfer we may assume Vincent to
have used, as in F 371 and F 373, is not known to
have survived

COLLECTION Amsterdam, Rijksmuseum Vincent van Gogh [Vincent van Gogh Foundation, inv nr F 372]

F 373 [H 234] JAPONAISERIE OIRAN [after Kesaï Yeisen]

Canvas 105×61 [41¼×24]
Paris summer 1887
LITERATURE J. Leymarie, Van Gogh, 1951, p 100, nr 33, p 102, nr 50: Paris 1887; the same print is copied in the background of F 363. M. E. Tralbaut, Mededelingen van de Dienst voor Schone Kunsten der Gemeente 's-Gravenhage 1954, pp 22-30: painted after a reproduction of the print THE ACTOR by Kesaï Yeisen on the front cover of a special Japanese number [May 1886] of Paris Illustré [reproduction III], a copy of which belonged to Vincent; from a transfer [reproduction V] divided in squares he made an enlargement for the painting, doubling the height and breadth; the motifs in the border are derived from various sources: the reeds were inspired by another page in the Japan number of Paris Illustré [reproduction VI], the frogs were copied from a Japanese print in Vincent's possession [reproductions VII and VIII] and the cranes from a page with bird studies in Hokusai's MANGWA. A. Bowness, exhib cat van Gogh London [Hayward Gallery] 1968-9, nr 78: Paris March-May 1887 [or October-December 1887?]
COLLECTION Amsterdam, Rijksmuseum Vincent van Gogh [Vincent van Gogh Foundation, inv nr F 373]

F 374 [H 274] STILL LIFE: RED CABBAGES AND ONIONS

Canvas 50×65 [19¾×25½]
Paris autumn 1887
COLLECTION Amsterdam, Rijksmuseum Vincent van Gogh [Vincent van Gogh Foundation, inv nr F 374]

F 371

F 369

F 372

F 374

F 373

F 375

F 376

F 375 [H 278] STILL LIFE: SUNFLOWERS

Canvas 43 × 61 [17 × 24]
Signed and dated in lower left: Vincent 87
Compare F 377
Paris late summer 1887
LITERATURE A. Tellegen, Museumjournaal 1966,
p 42: the two paintings of sunflowers F 375 and
F 376 belonged to Gauguin as early as 1887, as a
result of an exchange of works between van Gogh
and Gauguin in Paris; letter w 5 and 571
EDITORS' COMMENT F 377 is a study for F 375.
COLLECTION New York, The Metropolitan
Museum of Art [acquired 1949; purchase, Rogers
Fund], inv nr 49.41, cat French Paintings 1967,
volume 3, p 182

F 376 [H 279] STILL LIFE: SUNFLOWERS

Canvas 50 × 60 [19¾ × 23½]
Signed and dated in lower right: Vincent 87
Paris late summer 1887
LETTERS W 5 [Arles about 1 August 1888] 'We have
a second painting of his [Gauguin's] besides, which he
did exchange for one of my studies.'
571 [Arles 19 January 1889] 'If he is not content with
the exchange ... he can take back his little canvas ...
and his portrait, giving me back my portrait and my
two canvases of sunflowers which he took in Paris.'
LITERATURE A. Vollard, Souvenirs d'un marchand
de tableaux, 1937, p 196. A. Tellegen, Museumjournaal 1966, p 42: Vollard recalls having seen
two of van Gogh's SUNFLOWERS at Gauguin's,
the ones that were so much admired at the Degas
sale; in fact F 375 and F 376 belonged to Gauguin
as early as 1887, as a result of an exchange of works
between van Gogh and Gauguin in Paris; letters
W 5 and 571
EDITORS' COMMENT The translation of the
passage from letter w 5 has been corrected by the
editors.
COLLECTION Bern, H. R. Hahnloser

F 377 [H 275] STILL LIFE: SUNFLOWER

Canvas 20.5 × 26.5 [8 × 10½]
Compare F 375
Paris late summer 1887
EDITORS' COMMENT See F 375.
COLLECTION Amsterdam, Rijksmuseum Vincent
van Gogh [Vincent van Gogh Foundation, inv
nr F 377]

F 378 [H 319] STILL LIFE: BASKET OF APPLES

Canvas 50 × 61 [19¾ × 24]
Signed and annotated in lower left: à l'ami Lucien
Pissaro – Vincent
Compare F 379 and F 395
Paris autumn 1887
LETTERS 467 [Arles between 4 and 9 March 1888]
'I have just finished a study like the one Lucien
Pissarro has of mine ...'
473 [Arles about 1 April] 'Suppose I dedicate a study
to Breitner (I have one of oranges, foreground white,
background blue, exactly like the study which I
exchanged with L. Pissarro and the one Reid has) ...'
LITERATURE W. Weisbach, Vincent van Gogh,
1951, volume 2, pp 41-2, 137: the view from above
and the color composition are not Impressionistic
but influenced by Japanese woodcuts; F 378 fore-
shadows the direction Vincent's art was to take in
Arles
COLLECTION Otterlo, Rijksmuseum Kröller-
Müller, inv nr 216-12, cat van Gogh 1970, nr 217

F 379 [H 322] STILL LIFE: BASKET OF APPLES

Canvas 46 × 55 [18 × 21¾]
Signed and dated in lower left: Vincent 87
Compare F 378 and F 395
Paris autumn 1887
LETTER 473 [Arles about 1 April 1888] See F 378
COLLECTION Saint Louis, Mr and Mrs Sydney
M. Schoenberg

F 380 [H 407] SELF PORTRAIT: THREE
QUARTERS TO THE LEFT

Paper 34.2 × 25.5 [13½ × 10]
Compare drawing F 1378 recto
Paris summer 1887
LITERATURE K. Bromig-Kolleritz, Die Selbstbild-
nisse Vincent van Goghs, 1955, p 100. F. Erpel, Die
Selbstbildnisse Vincent van Goghs, 1963, nr 18
COLLECTION Otterlo, Rijksmuseum Kröller-
Müller, inv nr 274-19, cat van Gogh 1970, nr 198

F 381 [H 285] THE ITALIAN WOMAN WITH
CARNATIONS [LA SEGATORI?]

Canvas 81 × 60 [32 × 23½]
Paris end 1887 or January 1888
COLLECTION Paris, Musée National du Louvre
[acquired 1965; gift of Baronne Gourgaud]

F 380

F 377

F 378

F 379

F 381

F 383

F 388 verso

F 382 [H 321] STILL LIFE: APPLES, GRAPES AND PEARS

Canvas 44 × 58.7 [17¼ × 23]
Paris autumn 1887
COLLECTION Chicago, The Art Institute of Chicago [acquired 1949; gift of Kate L. Brewster], inv nr 49.215, cat 1961, p 182

F 383 [H 320] STILL LIFE: LEMONS, PEARS AND GRAPES

Canvas 49 × 65 [19¼ × 25½] Picture continues onto frame
Signed, dated and annotated by Vincent in lower left: Vincent 87 A mon frère Théo
Paris autumn 1887
COLLECTION Amsterdam, Rijksmuseum Vincent van Gogh [Vincent van Gogh Foundation, inv nr F 383]

F 384 [H 589] STILL LIFE: A BASKET OF LEMONS
Arles period; see after F 607

F 385 [H 812] SELF PORTRAIT

Left out by Faille in his manuscript for the present edition
See REJECTED WORKS

F 386 [H 283] STILL LIFE: POTATOES
Arles period; see after F 607

F 387 STILL LIFE WITH BREADROLLS

Left out by Faille in his manuscript for the present edition
See REJECTED WORKS

F 388 recto [formerly F 388 verso; H 89] HEAD OF A PEASANT WOMAN
Nuenen period; see after F 203a

F 388 verso [formerly F 388; H 282] GARDEN WITH SUNFLOWER

Canvas 42.5 × 35.5 [16¾ × 14]
Paris summer 1887
COLLECTION Amsterdam, Rijksmuseum Vincent van Gogh [Vincent van Gogh Foundation, inv nr F 338]

REDATED TO PARIS

F 28 [H 39] THE KINGFISHER

Canvas 19 × 26.5 [7½ × 10½]
Signed in lower left: Vincent
Paris 1886
LITERATURE Faille 1928, nr 28: Nuenen May 1884; letter 364. Vanbeselaere 1937, pp 282, 414: Paris. Faille 1939, nr 39: Nuenen May 1884; letter 364
EDITORS' COMMENT The motif is mentioned in letters 363a and 364 [March-April 1884] as the subject of a drawing, not yet identified. F 28 does not fit readily into the Nuenen period, however; Paris seems more probable. Moreover, V. W. van Gogh has identified the kingfisher as a stuffed bird, still in his possession, which Vincent bought in Paris.
COLLECTION Amsterdam, Rijksmuseum Vincent van Gogh [Vincent van Gogh Foundation, inv nr F 28]

F 382

F 28

F 61 verso

F 77 verso

F 61 verso [H 410] SELF PORTRAIT WITH STRAW HAT

Canvas on pasteboard 42 × 31 [16½ × 12¼]
Paris summer 1887
LITERATURE Not in Faille 1928. K. Bromig-
Kolleritz, Die Selbstbildnisse Vincent van Goghs,
1955, pp 47-8, 105. A. M. Hammacher, Van Gogh:
Selbstbildnisse, 1958, p 10, reproduction nr 6.
F. Erpel, Die Selbstbildnisse Vincent van Goghs,
1963, nr 16
COLLECTION Amsterdam, Rijksmuseum Vincent
van Gogh [Vincent van Gogh Foundation, inv
nr F 61]

F 77 verso [H VI] SELF PORTRAIT: FULL FACE

Canvas 41 × 33 [16¼ × 13]
Paris summer 1887
LITERATURE Not in Faille 1928. K. Bromig-
Kolleritz, Die Selbstbildnisse Vincent van Goghs,
1955, pp 47-8, 105. F. Erpel, Die Selbstbildnisse
Vincent van Goghs, 1963, nr 27
COLLECTION Amsterdam, Rijksmuseum Vincent
van Gogh [Vincent van Gogh Foundation, inv
nr F 77]

F 109 verso [H 411] SELF PORTRAIT: FULL FACE

Canvas on pasteboard 43.5 × 31.5 [17¼ × 12½]
Paris summer 1887
LITERATURE Not in Faille 1928. K. Bromig-
Kolleritz, Die Selbstbildnisse Vincent van Goghs,
1955, pp 47-8, 105. A. M. Hammacher, Van Gogh:
Selbstbildnisse, 1958, p 10: belongs to the middle of
the Paris period. F. Erpel, Die Selbstbildnisse
Vincent van Goghs, 1963, nr 26
COLLECTION Amsterdam, Rijksmuseum Vincent
van Gogh [Vincent van Gogh Foundation, inv
nr F 109]

F 177a STUFFED KALONG

Canvas 41 × 79 [16¼ × 31]
Paris 1886
LITERATURE Not in Faille 1928, Vanbeselaere
1937 or Faille 1939
EDITORS' COMMENT Zoologist Dr J. W. Sluiter of
Utrecht kindly informed us that the bat painted
here by van Gogh is a kalong or flying dog, a genus
living in Africa and in the Indo-Australian tropical
and subtropical territories.
COLLECTION Eindhoven, Netherlands,
Mrs A. H. E. M. Philips-de Jongh
Colorpate, p 112

F 178 verso [formerly F 178; H 187] SELF PORTRAIT

Canvas 39.5 × 29.5 [15½ × 11½]
Compare drawing F 1378 recto
Paris first half of 1886
LITERATURE Faille 1928, nr 178: Nuenen. Cat
1935, Gemeente Museum, nr 159: Paris. Not in
Vanbeselaere 1937. Faille 1939, nr 187: Nuenen
1885. C. Zervos, Cahiers d'Art 1947, p 171: Paris.
K. Bromig-Kolleritz, Die Selbstbildnisse Vincent
van Goghs, 1955, pp 93-4: late Antwerp. F. Elgar,
Van Gogh, 1958, cat nr 71 [index]: Paris 1887.
F. Erpel, Die Selbstbildnisse Vincent van Goghs,
1963, nr 3: early Paris March-April 1886
COLLECTION The Hague, Gemeente Museum, inv
nr 3-1918, cat1962, nr 135

F 178 verso

F 179 verso [formerly F 179; H 229] SELF PORTRAIT

Canvas 41.5 × 31 [16¼ × 12½]
Paris summer 1887
LITERATURE Faille 1928, nr 179: Nuenen. Faille 1939, nr 229: Paris 1886. K. Bromig-Kolleritz, Die Selbstbildnisse Vincent van Goghs, 1955, pp 43, 44, 97, 98. F. Erpel, Die Selbstbildnisse Vincent van Goghs, 1963, nr 11
COLLECTION Amsterdam, Rijksmuseum Vincent van Gogh [Vincent van Gogh Foundation, inv nr F 179]

F 180 [H 188] SELF PORTRAIT

Canvas 46 × 38 [18 × 15]
Signed in upper left: Vincent
Compare F 208
Paris first half of 1886
LITERATURE Faille 1928, nr 180: Nuenen. Vanbeselaere 1937, p 416: Antwerp, not Nuenen. Faille 1939, nr 188: Nuenen or Antwerp 1885-6. Tralbaut Antwerp 1948, p 283, nr 17: Antwerp early December 1885. K. Bromig-Kolleritz, Die Selbstbildnisse Vincent van Goghs, 1955, pp 90 ff: Antwerp F. Erpel, Die Selbstbildnisse Vincent van Goghs, 1963, nr 3: Antwerp A. Bowness, exhib cat van Gogh London [Hayward Gallery] 1968-9, nr 49: Nuenen August-November 1885
COLLECTION Amsterdam, Rijksmuseum Vincent van Gogh [Vincent van Gogh Foundation, inv nr F 180]

F 181 [H 186] SELF PORTRAIT IN FRONT OF THE EASEL

Canvas 45.5 × 37.5 [18 × 14¾]
Paris early 1886 [?]
LITERATURE Faille 1928, nr 181: Nuenen. Vanbeselaere 1937, p 416: Antwerp. Faille 1939, nr 186: Nuenen or Antwerp 1885-6. Tralbaut Antwerp 1948, p 220: not Antwerp but Nuenen. K. Bromig-Kolleritz, Die Selbstbildnisse Vincent van Goghs, 1955, pp 88-9: Nuenen early November 1885. F. Erpel, Die Selbstbildnisse Vincent van Goghs, 1963, nr 1: Nuenen end 1885
EDITORS' COMMENT In too poor condition to be judged properly; closest to F 208a of the Paris period.
COLLECTION Amsterdam, Rijksmuseum Vincent van Gogh [Vincent van Gogh Foundation, inv nr F 181]

F 109 verso

F 179 verso

F 177a

F 180

F 181

F 197

F 203

F 197 [H 210] STILL LIFE: BOUQUET OF
DAISIES

Paper on panel 40 × 56 [15¾ × 22]
Compare F 278
Paris autumn 1886
LITERATURE De Kroniek 3 January 1903,
pp 19-20. De Kroniek 7 February 1903, pp 45-6.
Faille 1928, nr 197: Nuenen. Vanbeselaere 1937,
p 416: Paris. Faille 1939, nr 210: Nuenen 1885
COLLECTION Saint David's, Pennsylvania, Mr and
Mrs William Coxe Wright

F 201 [H 218] STILL LIFE: GERANIUM IN A
POT

Canvas 46 × 38 [18 × 15]
Signed in lower left: Vincent
Paris summer 1886
LITERATURE Faille 1928, nr 201: Nuenen.
Vanbeselaere 1937, p 416: Paris. Faille 1939,
nr 218: Paris 1886. L. Gans, exhib cat van Gogh
Munich 1956, nr 98: summer 1886; letter W 1.
M. E. Tralbaut, exhib cat van Gogh Essen 1957,
nr 231: summer 1886; letter 459a
COLLECTION Otterlo, Rijksmuseum Kröller-
Müller [on loan from the heirs of Mrs A. T. Scholte-
van Houten, Netherlands]

F 203 [H 214] STILL LIFE: HERRINGS

Canvas 45 × 38 [17¾ × 15]
Signed in upper left: Vincent
Paris late spring 1886
LETTER 581 [24 March 1889] See F 283
LITERATURE Faille 1928, nr 203: Nuenen.
Vanbeselaere 1937, p 305: Nuenen November 1885;
p 416: Nuenen September-November 1885. Faille
1939, nr 214: Nuenen 1885. Cat van Gogh 1959,
Rijksmuseum Kröller-Müller, nr 195: certainly
Paris period; compare F 283 and F 285 of the Paris
period and F 510 of the Arles period
COLLECTION Otterlo, Rijksmuseum Kröller-
Müller, inv nr 258-12, cat van Gogh 1970, nr 195

F 207a PORTRAIT OF A WOMAN IN BLUE:
THREE QUARTERS TO THE RIGHT

Canvas 46 × 38 [18 × 15]
Paris summer 1886
LITERATURE Not in Faille 1928 or Faille 1939.
Tralbaut Antwerp 1948, pp 205-10, 284, nr 31:
Antwerp December 1885; letter 443
COLLECTION Amsterdam, Rijksmuseum Vincent
van Gogh [Vincent van Gogh Foundation, inv
nr F 207a]

F 208 [H 224] SELF PORTRAIT WITH PIPE:
THREE QUARTERS TO THE RIGHT

Canvas 27 × 19 [10½ × 7½]
Compare F 180
Paris first half of 1886
LITERATURE Faille 1928, nr 208: Antwerp. Faille
1939, nr 224: Antwerp 1885. Tralbaut Antwerp
1948, pp 215-7: painted very shortly after arrival in
Antwerp; p 283, nr 16: December 1885. K. Bromig-
Kolleritz, Die Selbstbildnisse Vincent van Goghs,
1955, pp 89-90: early December 1885. F. Erpel, Die
Selbstbildnisse Vincent van Goghs, 1963, nr 2
COLLECTION Amsterdam, Rijksmuseum Vincent
van Gogh [Vincent van Gogh Foundation, inv
nr F 208]

F 207a

F 208a SELF PORTRAIT WITH FELT HAT

Canvas 41 × 32.5 [16¼ × 12¾]
Paris early 1886
LITERATURE Not in Faille 1928 or 1939.
A. Bowness, exhib cat van Gogh London [Hayward
Gallery] 1968-9, nr 95: Paris September-December
1887
EDITORS' COMMENT In his manuscript for the
present edition Faille dates F 208a Antwerp 1885.
COLLECTION Amsterdam, Rijksmuseum Vincent
van Gogh [Vincent van Gogh Foundation, inv
nr F 208a]

F 201

F 208a

F 208

F 209

F 469

F 209 [H 220] HEAD OF A MAN: THREE
QUARTERS TO THE LEFT

Canvas on panel 31 × 39.5 [12¼ × 15½]
Paris summer 1886
LITERATURE Faille 1928, nr 209: Antwerp. Faille
1939, nr 220: Antwerp January 1886. Tralbaut
Antwerp 1938, pp 222-3, 284, nr 40: the style
indicates the Paris period, but Faille assured
Tralbaut that the Dutch painter A. H. C. Briët
remembers the model from the time he studied in
Antwerp
EDITORS' COMMENT The sitter has been called,
erroneously, the painter Meyer de Haan.
Stylistically there is no reason to place F 209 in
Antwerp; it is connected with the still lifes and
flower pieces of summer 1886. This is the only
known portrait in horizontal format.
COLLECTION Melbourne, National Gallery of
Victoria [acquired 1939; Felton bequest], cat 1948,
nr 57

F 452 [H 280] SUNFLOWERS

Canvas 60 × 100 [23½ × 39½]
Paris late summer 1887
LITERATURE R. Jacobsen, Onze Kunst 1904,
part 2, pp 6-7 [with reproduction]. Faille 1928,
nr 452: Arles August 1888; letter 526. Scherjon and
de Gruyter 1937, p 28: Paris, not Arles. Faille 1939,
nr 280: Paris. Cat van Gogh 1959, Rijksmuseum
Kröller-Müller, nr 202: summer 1887; very similar
to F 375 and F 376
COLLECTION Otterlo, Rijksmuseum Kröller-
Müller, inv nr 279-08, cat van Gogh 1970, nr 202
Colorplate, p 270

F 469 [H 408] SELF PORTRAIT WITH STRAW
HAT

Pasteboard 41 × 33 [16¼ × 13]
Paris summer 1887
LITERATURE Faille 1928, nr 469: Arles September
1888; letter 537. Scherjon and de Gruyter 1937,
p 28: Paris, not Arles. Faille 1939, nr 408: Paris.
K. Bromig-Kolleritz, Die Selbstbildnisse Vincent
van Goghs, 1955, p 99: 1886. A. M. Hammacher,
Van Gogh: Selbstbildnisse, 1960, pp 10-1: summer
1887; belongs to the third period, with the neo-
Impressionistic influence of Seurat and Signac.
F. Erpel, Die Selbstbildnisse Vincent van Goghs,
1963, nr 13. A. Bowness, exhib cat van Gogh
London [Hayward Gallery] 1968-9, nr 93: Paris
September-December 1887
COLLECTION Amsterdam, Rijksmuseum Vincent
van Gogh [Vincent van Gogh Foundation, inv
nr F 469]

F 522 [H 425] SELF PORTRAIT IN FRONT OF
THE EASEL

Canvas 65 × 50.5 [25½ × 20]
Signed and dated in lower right: Vincent 88
Paris early 1888
LETTER W 4 [Arles June-July 1888] 'Here I give a
conception of mine, which is the result of a portrait I
painted in the mirror, and which is now in Theo's
possession. A pinkish-gray face with green eyes, ash-
colored hair, wrinkles on the forehead and around the
mouth, stiff, wooden, a very red beard, considerably
neglected and mournful, but the lips are full, a blue
peasant's blouse of coarse linen, and a palette with
citron yellow, vermilion, malachite green, cobalt
blue, in short all the colors on the palette except the
orange beard, but only whole colors. The figure
against a grayish-white wall. You will say that this
resembles somewhat, for instance, the face of – Death
– in Van Eeden's book or some such thing – all right,
but it is a figure like this – and it isn't an easy job to
paint oneself – at any rate if it is to be different from a

photograph. And you see – this, in my opinion, is the advantage that impressionism possesses over all the other things; it is not banal, and one seeks after a deeper resemblance than the photographer's. However, at the present moment I look different, insofar as I am wearing neither hair nor beard, the same having been shaved off clean.'

LITERATURE Faille 1928, nr 522: Arles. Scherjon and de Gruyter 1937, p 28: not Arles but Paris. Faille 1939, nr 425: Paris. C. Nordenfalk, Vincent van Gogh, 1948, p 86: Vincent's last self portrait from the Paris period. K. Bromig-Kolleritz, Die Selbstbildnisse Vincent van Goghs, 1955, pp 31, 105, 107. A. M. Hammacher, Van Gogh: Selbstbildnisse, 1960, pp 10, 12-3: end of Paris period. F. Erpel, Die Selbstbildnisse Vincent van Goghs, 1963, nr 31. A. Bowness, exhib cat van Gogh London [Hayward Gallery] 1968-9, nr 99: Paris January-February 1888
COLLECTION Amsterdam, Rijksmuseum Vincent van Gogh [Vincent van Gogh Foundation, inv nr F 522]
Colorplate, p 357

F 526 [H 424] SELF PORTRAIT WITH STRAW HAT

Canvas on panel 35.5 × 27 [14 × 10½]
Paris summer 1887
LITERATURE Faille 1928, nr 526: Arles. Scherjon and de Gruyter 1937, p 28: Paris. Faille 1939, nr 424: Paris. K. Bromig-Kolleritz, Die Selbstbildnisse Vincent van Goghs, 1955, pp 45, 99. F. Erpel, Die Selbstbildnisse Vincent van Goghs, 1963, nr 14
COLLECTION Detroit, The Detroit Institute of Arts [acquired 1922; city appropriation], acc nr 22.13, cat 1944, nr 87

F 583 [H 584] PASTURE IN BLOOM

Canvas 31.5 × 40.5 [12½ × 16]
Paris spring 1887
LITERATURE Faille 1928, nr 583: Arles. A. H. Barr, exhib cat van Gogh USA-Canada 1935-6, nr 43: possibly Paris period. Scherjon and de Gruyter 1937: Arles nr 185. Faille 1939, nr 584: Paris 1887; letter T 33
COLLECTION Otterlo, Rijksmuseum Kröller-Müller, inv nr 264-14, cat van Gogh 1970, nr 213

F 526

F 452

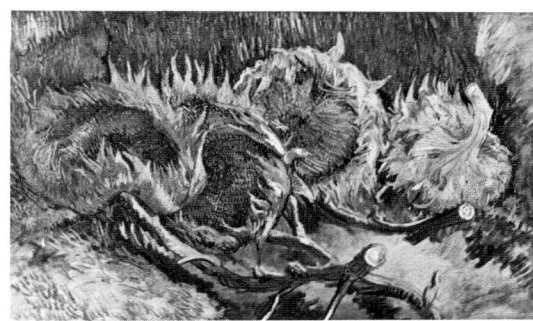

F 583

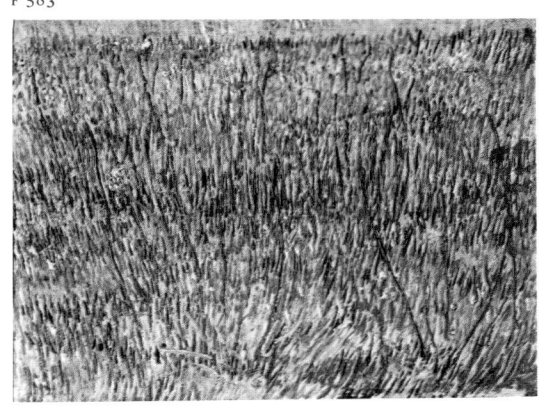

F 596

F 603

F 596 [H 303] STILL LIFE: VASE WITH
KENTRANTHUS, LYCHNIS AND DIANTHUS

Canvas 61 × 38 [24 × 15]
Signed in lower right: Vincent
Paris summer 1886
LITERATURE Faille 1928, nr 596: Arles. Scherjon
and de Gruyter 1937, p 28: Paris, not Arles. Faille
1939, nr 303: Paris. J. Leymarie, Van Gogh, 1951,
pp 102-3, nr 51: Paris 1886
COLLECTION Washington, DC, Mr and Mrs
D. L. Kreeger [acquired 1960]

F 603 [H 326] STILL LIFE: GRAPES

Canvas 34 × 47.5 [13¼ × 18¾]
Paris autumn 1887
LITERATURE Faille 1928, nr 603: Arles. Scherjon
and de Gruyter 1937, p 28, note 3: Paris. Faille
1939, nr 326: Paris
COLLECTION Amsterdam, Rijksmuseum Vincent
van Gogh [Vincent van Gogh Foundation inv
nr F 603]

F 666 [H 652] STILL LIFE: SCABIOSA AND
RANUNCULUS

Canvas 26 × 20 [10¼ × 8]
Paris early summer 1886
LITERATURE Faille 1928, nr 666: Saint Rémy
January 1890; letter 622. Scherjon and de Gruyter
1937, Saint Rémy nr 46: letter 607. Faille 1939,
nr 652: Saint Rémy October 1889; letter 607
EDITORS' COMMENT Faille accepted F 666–
without having seen it–probably on the basis of an
erroneous quotation from letter 622: 'And I gave
Mr Salles a little canvas with some pink and red
geraniums against a perfectly black background...'
This passage is also mentioned by B. Stokvis,
Kunst und Künstler 1929, p 474: 'The daughter of
Mr Salles, Mrs Lasargue, sold the work for 200 frs.'
The background of the present painting is, however,
light green and the flowers are not geraniums. This
painting cannot, then, be identified as the piece
given to Mr Salles in Arles, later sold by his
daughter Mrs Lasargue. In the 1939 edition
[Hyperion] and in his manuscript for the present
edition Faille connected the painting with letter
607: 'I am adding a study of flowers to the roll of
canvases–nothing much but after all I do not want to
tear it up.' In this letter, however, no mention of
Mr Salles is made. According to the editors, the
picture cannot be placed in the Arles, Saint Rémy
or Auvers periods.
COLLECTION Stuttgart, F. C. Valentien

F 666a STILL LIFE: PEONIES

Canvas 55 × 46 [21¾ × 18]
Signed and dated in lower left: Vincent 89 N. B. See
EDITORS' COMMENT
Paris summer 1886
LITERATURE Not in Faille 1928, Scherjon and de
Gruyter 1937 or Faille 1939
EDITORS' COMMENT In his manuscript for the
present edition Faille dated this painting to Saint
Rémy October 1889. The editors do not accept the
authenticity of the date inscribed on the painting.
They date the painting to the Paris period.
COLLECTION Sale London [Sotheby] 28 June 1967,
nr 48
Present owner unknown

ARLES PERIOD

F 389 [H 428] A PORK-BUTCHER'S SHOP

Canvas on pasteboard 39.5 × 32.5 [15½ × 12½]
Arles February 1888
LETTER 464 [about 25 February] '...but still I have

finished three studies…The studies I've done are…a view of a bit of a pavement with a pork-butcher's shop.'
LITERATURE Scherjon and de Gruyter 1937, Arles nr 3
COLLECTION Amsterdam, Rijksmuseum Vincent van Gogh [Vincent van Gogh Foundation, inv nr F 389]

F 390 [H 429] AN OLD ARLESIAN WOMAN

Canvas 55 × 43 [21¾ × 17]
Arles February 1888
LETTER 464 [about 25 February] *'…but still I have finished three studies…The studies I've done are – an old Arlesian woman…'*
LITERATURE Scherjon and de Gruyter 1937, Arles nr 1 : letter 464
COLLECTION Amsterdam, Rijksmuseum Vincent van Gogh [Vincent van Gogh Foundation, inv nr F 390]

F 391 [H 430] SNOWY LANDSCAPE WITH ARLES IN THE BACKGROUND

Canvas 50 × 60 [19¾ × 23½]
Arles February-March 1888
LETTER 466 [probably 3 March] *'Down here it is freezing hard and there is still some snow left in the country. I have a study of a landscape in white with the town in the background.'*
LITERATURE Scherjon and de Gruyter 1937, Arles nr 2 : letters 464 and 466
COLLECTION Basle, Private Collection

F 392 [H 427] STILL LIFE: BLOSSOMING ALMOND BRANCH IN A GLASS

Canvas 24 × 19 [9½ × 7½]
Signed in upper left: Vincent
Compare F 393
Arles February-March 1888
LETTER 466 [probably 3 March] *'Down here it is freezing hard and there is still some snow left in the country…Then two little studies of an almond branch already in flower in spite of it.'*
LITERATURE Scherjon and de Gruyter 1937, Arles nr 4
COLLECTION Amsterdam, Rijksmuseum Vincent van Gogh [Vincent van Gogh Foundation, inv nr F 392]

F 389

F 666

F 666a

F 390

F 391

F 392

F 394

F 396

F 393 [H 426] STILL LIFE: BOOK AND
BLOSSOMING ALMOND BRANCH IN A GLASS

Canvas 24 × 19 [9½ × 7½]
Signed in upper left: Vincent
Compare F 392
Arles February-March 1888
LETTERS 466 [probably 3 March] See F 392
w 3 [probably 30 March] '...*as I should very much
like to give you something of my work that will please
you, I will set aside for you a little study of a book
and a flower.*'
LITERATURE Scherjon and de Gruyter 1937, Arles
nr 5
EDITORS' COMMENT None of the known paintings
answers precisely to the description in letter w 3,
but it is not impossible that Vincent was thinking of
F 393 when he wrote that passage.
COLLECTION Switzerland, Private Collection

F 394 [H 431] PINK PEACH TREE IN BLOSSOM
[SOUVENIR DE MAUVE]

Canvas 73 × 59.5 [28¾ × 23½]
Signed and annotated by Vincent in lower left:
Souvenir de Mauve Vincent
Compare sketch in letter 477, F 404 and water color
F 1469
Arles March 1888
LETTERS W 3 [probably 30 March] '*And what I
brought home today would probably please you – it is
a dug-up square of earth in an orchard with a fence of
rushes and two peach trees in full bloom. Pink against
a scintillating blue sky with white clouds, and in the
sunshine. It is possible you will see it, for I have
finally decided to set it aside for Jet Mauve. I have
written on it "Souvenir de Mauve, Vincent & Theo."*'
472 [about 31 March] '*I have been working on a size
20 canvas in the open air in an orchard, lilac plowland,
a reed fence, two pink peach trees against a sky of
glorious blue and white. Probably the best landscape
I have done. I had just brought it home when I
received from our sister a Dutch notice in memory of
Mauve, with his portrait (the portrait, very good),
the text, poor and nothing in it, a pretty etching.
Something – I don't know what – took hold of me and
brought a lump to my throat, and I wrote on my
picture "Souvenir de Mauve Vincent & Theo" and if
you agree we two will send it, such as it is, to
Mrs Mauve.*'
473 [about 1 April] '*Suppose that first of all we give
the Souvenir de Mauve to Jet Mauve.*'
474 [probably 9 April] '*Mauve's death was a terrible
blow to me. You will see that the pink peach trees
were painted with a sort of passion.*'
486 [probably 10 May] '*The first thing you will find
in the case are the pictures I did for Jet Mauve and
Tersteeg... As for the copies of these two studies, I
think that the bridge is better than Tersteeg's, but
that the study for Jet Mauve is simpler than the copy.
Perhaps this copy will improve with time. I have
worked on it a lot.*'
492 [probably 29 May] '*If you think the Souvenir
de Mauve tolerable, you should put it in the next lot
for The Hague, in a plain white frame.*'
524 [14 or 15 August] '*What has happened to the
Souvenir de Mauve? Not having heard any word
about it, I have been inclined to think that Tersteeg
must have said something disagreeable to you about
it, to the effect that it would be refused, or some such
unpleasantness.*'
562 [November or December] '*I know you will be
pleased that I have had a letter from Jet Mauve,
thanking us for the picture.*'
LITERATURE Scherjon and de Gruyter 1937, Arles
nr 11. D. Cooper, Zeichnungen und Aquarelle von
Vincent van Gogh, 1954, p 64: dates from the same
time as water color F 1469. Cat van Gogh 1959,
Rijksmuseum Kröller-Müller, nr 206: letters 486,
492, 524, 562 and w 3; in contrast to what Vincent

says in letters w 3 and 472 about signing the painting Vincent & Theo, it is signed only Vincent
COLLECTION Otterlo, Rijksmuseum Kröller-Müller, inv nr 302-18, cat van Gogh 1970, nr 206

F 395 [H 433] STILL LIFE: BASKET WITH SIX ORANGES

Canvas 45 × 54 [17¾ × 21¼]
Signed in lower left: Vincent
Compare F 378 and F 379
Arles March 1888
LETTERS 467 [between 4 and 9 March] *I have just finished a study like the one of mine that Lucien Pissarro has, but this time it is oranges.'*
473 [about 1 April] *'...suppose I dedicate a study to Breitner (I have one of oranges, foreground white, background blue, exactly like the study which I exchanged with L. Pissarro and the one Reid has) ...'*
LITERATURE Scherjon and de Gruyter 1937, Arles nr 6: letters 467 and 473
COLLECTION New York, Mr and Mrs Basil Goulandris

F 396 [H 438] THE GLEIZE BRIDGE OVER THE VIGUEYRET CANAL, NEAR ARLES

Canvas 46 × 49 [18 × 19¼]
Signed in lower left: Vincent
Arles March 1888
LETTER 469 [about 17 March] *'And another landscape with a little country bridge and more women washing linen ... I made my last three studies with the perspective frame I told you about.'*
LITERATURE Scherjon and de Gruyter 1937, Arles nr 8: letter 469
EDITORS' COMMENT The three studies mentioned in letter 469 are F 396, F 397 and F 398.
COLLECTION Private Collection

F 397 [H 435] THE LANGLOIS BRIDGE WITH WOMEN WASHING

Canvas 54 × 65 [21¼ × 25½]
Signed in lower left: Vincent
Compare F 571, water color F 1480 [same composition], F 400, F 570, drawings F 1470 and F 1471 [same site]
Arles March 1888
LETTERS 469 [about 17 March] *'As for my work, I brought back a size 15 canvas today. It is a drawbridge with a little cart going over it, outlined against a blue sky – the river blue as well, the banks orange colored with green grass and a group of women washing linen in smocks and multicolored caps ... I made my last three studies with the perspective frame I told you about.'*
B 2 [March] *'I have another study of the same drawbridge with a group of women washing.'* [F 544]
473 [about 1 April] *'Well, he [Tersteeg] shall have a picture of mine in his own collection ... It is the drawbridge with the little yellow cart and the group of women washing linen, a study in which the ground is bright orange, the grass bright green and the sky and water blue.'*
474 [probably 9 April] *'I have a great mind to do a second one like Tersteeg's, ...'*
486 [probably 10 May] *'The first thing you will find in the case are the pictures I did for Jet Mauve and Tersteeg. If meanwhile you have come to the conclusion that Tersteeg would be offended by it, if in short I had better have nothing to do with him, then keep it yourself and you can scrape off the dedication, and we can exchange it for something by one of the comrades.'*
492 [probably 29 May] *'If you think the Souvenir de Mauve tolerable, you should put it in the next lot for The Hague, in a plain white frame. If you find among them a study that seems to you more suitable for Tersteeg, you can put it in without any dedication and*

keep the one with his dedication, which you can then scrape off.'
LITERATURE Scherjon and de Gruyter 1937, Arles nr 7. Cat van Gogh 1959, Rijksmuseum Kröller-Müller, nr 208: this work, the first of four variations, was sent to Tersteeg, the director of the Goupil art gallery in The Hague; the other three are F 400, F 570 and F 571. P. Leprohon, Tel fut van Gogh, 1964, pp 416-7 [with photographs of the modern bridges on p 267]: the name of the bridge is derived from the name of the former bridge guard, Langlois; the original bridge does not exist anymore, but has been replaced by a modern one; a reconstruction of the old bridge was erected in 1962 on another spot, about three kilometers from

Arles; the bridge painted by Vincent spanned the canal from Arles to Port-de-Bouc and was situated nearby the town, 300 meters from the crossing of Avenue Sadi-Carnot and the road to Port St Louis
EDITORS' COMMENT There is no evidence that this painting was ever in the Tersteeg Collection, or that it had a dedication to Tersteeg that was scratched out. The sequence of the views of the Langlois bridge, according to the editors, is: F 397, F 544 [now a fragment; compare sketch in letter B 2], F 400, F 571 and F 570. See EDITORS' COMMENT to F 396.
COLLECTION Otterlo, Rijksmuseum Kröller-Müller, inv nr 290-12, cat van Gogh 1970, nr 208

F 393

F 395

F 397

F 399

F 400

F 398 [H 439] AVENUE OF PLANE TREES NEAR THE STATION

Canvas 45 × 49 [17¾ × 19¼]
Signed in lower left: Vincent
Arles March 1888
LETTER 469 [about 17 March] '*Also an avenue with plane trees near the station…I made my last three studies with the perspective frame I told you about.*'
LITERATURE Scherjon and de Gruyter 1937, Arles nr 9
EDITORS' COMMENT See F 396
COLLECTION Paris, Musée Rodin, cat 1938, nr 388

F 399 [H 437] APRICOT TREES IN BLOSSOM

Canvas 41 × 33 [16¼ × 13]
Compare left part of sketch in letter B 3, F 513 and F 554 [same orchard]
Arles April 1888
LETTER 478 [20 April] '*I have ten orchards now, not counting three little studies.*'
LITERATURE Scherjon and de Gruyter 1937, Arles nr 24
EDITORS' COMMENT The '*three little studies*' mentioned in letter 478 are most probably F 399, F 554 [12¾ × 15¾] and F 557 [20 × 15¾]. All the other orchards are considerably larger.
COLLECTION Johannesburg, Mrs L. Fürstenberg-Cassirer

F 400 [H 436] THE LANGLOIS BRIDGE WITH ROAD ALONGSIDE THE CANAL

Canvas 58.5 × 73 [23 × 28¾]
Signed in lower left: Vincent
Compare F 397, F 570, F 571, drawings F 1470, F 1471 and water color F 1480 [same site]
Arles March 1888
LETTER 471 [about 24 March] '*However, I at once began the same subject again on another canvas, but, as the weather was quite different, in gray tones and without figures.*'
LITERATURE Scherjon and de Gruyter 1937, Arles nr 10: letters 470, 471 and B 2 [with sketch].
P. Leprohon, Tel fut van Gogh, 1964, pp 416-7: see under F 397
EDITORS' COMMENT See F 397
COLLECTION Amsterdam, Rijksmuseum Vincent van Gogh [Vincent van Gogh Foundation, inv nr F 400]

F 401 THE LANGLOIS BRIDGE

Left out by Faille in his manuscript for the present edition
See REJECTED WORKS

F 402 [H 705] TWO WHITE BUTTERFLIES
Saint Rémy period; see after F 749

F 403 [H 432] THE WHITE ORCHARD

Canvas 60 × 80 [23½ × 31½]
Signed in lower left: Vincent
Compare sketch in letter 477 and drawing F 1414
Meant to form part of a series with F 404 and F 555
Arles April 1888
LETTERS 477 [between 10 and 14 April] '*Now I must tell you that I am working on the two pictures which I want to make copies of. The pink peach tree gives me the most trouble. You see from the three squares on the other side of this page that the three orchards make a series, more or less. As soon as the Pont de Langlois and the copy of the other picture, the pink peach tree, are dry, I'll send them off.*'
485 [10 May] '*In this batch there are the pink orchard on coarse canvas, and the white orchard, lengthways, and the bridge.*'

486 [probably 10 May] '*Next the series of orchards –
I think that the white orchard which I'm sending you
a pen drawing of…*'
576 [3 February 1889] '*As for the Indépendants, I
think that six pictures is too much by half. To my
mind the "Harvest" and the "White Orchard" are
enough…*'
LITERATURE Scherjon and de Gruyter 1937, Arles
nr 15: letters 473, 477, 485, 486 and 576: belongs
with F 404 and F 555 to the first decoration scheme
of three orchards in bloom
COLLECTION Amsterdam, Rijksmuseum Vincent
van Gogh [Vincent van Gogh Foundation, inv
nr F 403]

F 404 [H VIII] ORCHARD IN BLOSSOM

Canvas 81 × 62 [32 × 24½]
Compare sketch in letter 477, F 394 and water color
F 1469
Meant to form part of a series with F 403 and F 555
Arles between 14 April and 10 May 1888
LETTERS 476 [between 10 and 14 April] '*And I have
a good mind to make a replica of the one for Jet
Mauve as well…*'
477 [between 10 and 14 April] See F 403
486 [probably 10 May] See F 394
LITERATURE Scherjon and de Gruyter 1937, Arles
nr 14: letters 477 and 486; belongs with F 403 and
F 555 to the first decoration scheme of three
orchards in bloom
COLLECTION Amsterdam, Rijksmuseum Vincent
van Gogh [Vincent van Gogh Foundation, inv
nr F 404]

F 403

F 404

F 398

F 405

F 407

F 409

F 408

F405 [H 434] PEAR TREE IN BLOSSOM

Canvas 73 × 46 [28¾ × 18]
Signed in lower left: Vincent
Compare sketch in letter 477 [not reproduced in the English edition of the letters]
Meant to form part of a series, presumably with F 553 and F 556
Arles April 1888
LETTER 477 [between 10 and 14 April] '*I have also just now a little pear tree, vertical, between two horizontal canvases ... Here is the other middle piece of the size 12 canvas. The ground violet, in the background a wall with straight poplars and a very blue sky. The little pear tree has a violet trunk and white flowers, with a big yellow butterfly on one of the clusters. To the left in the corner, a little garden with a fence of yellow reeds and green bushes, and a flower bed. A little pink house. There now, you have the details of this decoration scheme of orchards in bloom that I have planned for you.*'
LITERATURE Scherjon and de Gruyter 1937, Arles nr 17: letter 477; belongs with F 553 and F 556 to the second decoration scheme of three orchards in bloom. J.Leymarie, Van Gogh, 1951, p 103, nr 58: Arles April 1888; letters 477 and B 3. M. E. Tralbaut, Mededelingen van de Dienst voor Schone Kunsten der Gemeente 's Gravenhage 1954, pp 36-7; inspired by a Hiroshige print of a view of the Fuji seen through two pear trees [collection of V. W. van Gogh]. V.W. van Gogh, Openbaar Kunstbezit 1957, nr 2
EDITORS' COMMENT According to letter 477, F 405 formed the central piece of a triptych. F 553 and F 556 are assumed to be the wings, although no proof for this can be found in the letters.
COLLECTION Amsterdam, Rijksmuseum Vincent van Gogh [Vincent van Gogh Foundation, inv nr F 405]

F 406 [H 440] ORCHARD IN BLOSSOM

Canvas 72 × 58 [28¼ × 22¾]
Signed in lower left: Vincent
Compare sketches in letters 478 and B 4
Arles April 1888
LETTERS 478 [20 April] '*Here is a sketch of an orchard that I planned more particularly for you to celebrate May 1. It is absolutely clear, and done all at once. A frenzy of impastos of the faintest yellow and lilac on the original white mass.*'
B 4 [about 20 April] '*Here is another orchard, rather simple as a composition: a white tree, a small green tree, a square patch of green, lilac soil, an orange roof, a large blue sky.*'
480 [May] '*You will soon be getting a picture I painted for you for the first of May.*'
LITERATURE Scherjon and de Gruyter 1937, Arles nr 23: letters 478, 480 and B 4
COLLECTION Manchester, Mrs E. Friedlaender

F 407 [H 443] PATH THROUGH A FIELD WITH WILLOWS

Canvas 31 × 38.5 [12¼ × 15¼]
Compare drawing F 1499
Arles May 1888
LETTER 484 [7 May] '*There is a little landscape with a hovel, white, red and green, and a cypress beside it; you have the drawing of it, and I did the whole painting of it in the house. This will show you that, if you like, I can make little pictures like the Japanese prints of all these drawings.*'
LITERATURE Scherjon and de Gruyter 1937, Arles nr 26: letter 484
COLLECTION Formerly Glarus, Switzerland, Mrs I. Schuler-Ganzoni
Present owner unknown

F 408 [H 441] THE FARMHOUSE IN THE WHEATFIELD

Canvas 45 × 50 [17¾ × 19¾]
Compare sketches in letters 487 and B 6 and drawing F 1415
Arles May 1888
LETTER 487 [about 12 May] '*Just now I have done two new studies like these* [i.e. the enclosed sketches]: *you have a drawing of one of them already, a farm by the highroad among wheatfields.*'
B 6 [about 24 June] '*…I myself am still doing nothing but landscapes – enclosed is a sketch…*'
LITERATURE Scherjon and de Gruyter 1937, Arles nr 27
COLLECTION Amsterdam, Rijksmuseum Vincent van Gogh [Vincent van Gogh Foundation, inv nr F 408]

F 409 [H 442] VIEW OF ARLES WITH IRISES IN THE FOREGROUND

Canvas 54 × 65 [21¼ × 25½]
Compare sketch in letter 487 and drawing F 1416 recto
Arles May 1888
LETTERS 487 [about 12 May] '*Just now I have done two new studies… A meadow full of very yellow buttercups, a ditch with irises, green leaves and violet flowers, the town in the background, some gray willows, and a strip of blue sky. If the meadow does not get mowed, I'd like to do this study again, for the subject was very beautiful, and I had some trouble getting the composition.*'
B 5 [second half of May] '*Further a view of Arles. Of the town itself one sees only some red roofs and a tower, far away in the background, and a narrow strip of blue sky above it. The town is surrounded by immense meadows all abloom with countless buttercups – a sea of yellow – in the foreground these meadows are divided by a ditch full of violet irises. They were mowing the grass while I was painting, so it is only a study and not the finished picture that I had intended to do.*'
LITERATURE Scherjon and de Gruyter 1937, Arles nr 28
COLLECTION Amsterdam, Rijksmuseum Vincent van Gogh [Vincent van Gogh Foundation, inv nr F 409]

F 410 [H IX] STILL LIFE: BLUE ENAMEL COFFEEPOT, EARTHENWARE AND FRUIT

Canvas 65 × 81 [25½ × 32]
Signed in upper left: Vincent
Compare sketches in letters 489 and B 5 [same composition], F 592, F 593, F 594 [same vase] and F 600 [same vase and cup]
Arles May 1888
LETTERS 489 [probably 19 May] '*I have done two still lifes this week. A blue enamel coffeepot, a cup (on the left), royal blue and gold, a milk jug in squares of pale blue and white, a cup – on the right – of white with a blue and orange pattern, on an earthen tray of grayish yellow, a jug in earthenware or majolica, blue with a pattern in reds, greens and browns, and lastly two oranges and three lemons; the table is covered with a blue cloth, the background is greenish-yellow, so that there are six different blues and four or five yellows and oranges.*'
B 5 [second half of May] '*As for me, I have done a still life of a blue-enameled iron coffeepot, a royal-blue cup and saucer, a milk jug with pale cobalt and white checks, a cup with orange and blue patterns on a white ground, a blue majolica jug decorated with green, brown and pink flowers and leaves. The whole on a blue tablecloth, against a yellow background, and among this crockery two oranges and three lemons. So it is a variation of blues, livened up by a series of yellows that go as far as orange.*'

497 [12 June] '*The last canvas* [F 425] *absolutely kills all the others; there is only one other that can hold its own next to it – a still life, with coffeepots and cups and plates in blue and yellow. This must be owing to the design.*'
LITERATURE Scherjon and de Gruyter 1937, Arles nr 32: letter 497
COLLECTION France, Marquise de Chabannes

F 411 [H 444] WHEATFIELD WITH THE ALPINE FOOTHILLS IN THE BACKGROUND

Canvas on pasteboard 54 × 65 [21¼ × 25½]
Compare drawing F 1481
Arles June 1888
LETTER 501 [about 29 June] '*I have had a week's hard, close work among the wheatfields in the full sun. The result is some studies of wheatfields, landscapes…*'
LITERATURE Scherjon and de Gruyter 1937, Arles nr 167: letter 501. A. Bowness, exhib cat van Gogh London [Hayward Gallery] 1968-9, nr 124: Arles 23-30 June 1888
COLLECTION Amsterdam, Rijksmuseum Vincent van Gogh [Vincent van Gogh Foundation, inv nr F 411]

F 406

F 410

F 411

F 412

F 416

F 412 [H X] HARVEST AT LA CRAU, WITH
MONTMAJOUR IN THE BACKGROUND

Canvas 72.5 × 92 [28½ × 36¼]
Signed in lower left: Vincent
Compare water colors F 1483, F 1484, drawings
F 1485 and F 1486
Arles June 1888
LETTERS 496 [12 June] '*I am working on a new
subject, fields green and yellow as far as the eye can
reach. I have already drawn it twice, and I am
starting it again as a painting; it is exactly like a
Salomon* [sic] *Konink – you know, the pupil of
Rembrandt who painted vast level plains.*'
497 [12 June] '*I am working on a landscape with
wheatfields…*'
498 [about 16 June] '*That is the subject I have
worked on this week on a size 30 canvas; it isn't at all
finished, but it kills everything else I have, except a
still life which I patiently worked out.*'
519 [8 August] '*Now the Harvest…are sketches after
painted studies.*'
531 [3 September] '*I beg you to keep my studies of
this place as well aired as possible, because they are
not yet thoroughly dry…So it would be a good thing
if you could put…"The Harvest" (a wide landscape
with the ruin in the background and the line of the
Alpilles) on stretchers.*'
576 [3 February 1889] See F 403
LITERATURE Scherjon and de Gruyter 1937, Arles
nr 35: letters 496, 497 and 531. J. Leymarie, Van
Gogh, 1951, p 106, nr 65: preparatory drawings are
F 1483-6. M. Roskill, Oud Holland 1966, pp 5-21:
mid-June 1888; based upon F 1484 [first sketch] and
F 1483 [cartoon]; F 1486 and F 1485 postdate the
painting, having been done towards the end of July
and August, respectively
COLLECTION Amsterdam, Rijksmuseum Vincent
van Gogh [Vincent van Gogh Foundation, inv
nr F 412]

F 413 [H 451] BOATS ON THE BEACH AT
SAINTES-MARIES

Canvas 64.5 × 81 [25½ × 32]
Signed on a chest in the foreground: Vincent
Compare sketch in letter B 6, drawing F 1428 and
water color F 1429
Saintes-Maries [Arles period] June 1888
LETTERS 500 [about 23 June] '*I made the drawing of
the boats just as I was going to leave* [Saintes-Maries]
*in the morning, very early, and I am working on the
picture after it, a size 30 canvas with more sea and
sky on the right.*'
B 6 [about 24 June] See F 408
LITERATURE Scherjon and de Gruyter 1937, Arles
nr 40: letter 500. J. Leymarie, Van Gogh, 1951,
p 104, nr 60: preparatory drawings are F 1428 and
F 1429
COLLECTION Amsterdam, Rijksmuseum Vincent
van Gogh [Vincent van Gogh Foundation, inv
nr F 413]

F 414 BOATS AT SAINTES-MARIES

Left out by Faille in his manuscript for the present
edition
See REJECTED WORKS

F 415 [H 454] SEASCAPE

Canvas 51 × 64 [20 × 25¼]
Signed in lower left: Vincent
Compare drawings F 1431 and F 1433
Saintes-Maries [Arles period] June 1888
LETTERS 499 [probably 22 June] '*The Mediterranean
has the colors of mackerel, changeable I mean. You
don't always know if it is green or violet, you can't
even say it's blue, because the next moment the
changing light has taken on a tinge of pink or gray…*

I brought three canvases and have covered them – two seascapes, a view of the village...'
524 [14 or 15 August] *'On one seascape there is an excessively red signature, because I wanted a red note in the green.'*
LITERATURE Scherjon and de Gruyter 1937, Arles nr 38. A. Bowness, exhib cat van Gogh London [Hayward Gallery] 1968-9, nr 119: 17-23 June 1888
COLLECTION Amsterdam, Rijksmuseum Vincent van Gogh [Vincent van Gogh Foundation, inv nr F 415]

F 416 [H 456] VIEW OF SAINTES-MARIES

Canvas 64 × 53 [25¼ × 20¾]
Compare drawing F 1439
Saintes-Maries [Arles period] June 1888
LETTER 499 [probably 22 June] See F 415
LITERATURE Scherjon and de Gruyter 1937, Arles nr 39. J. Leymarie, Van Gogh, 1951, nr 61, p 104: preparatory drawing is F 1439. W. Weisbach, Vincent van Gogh, volume 2, 1951, p 68: the drawing of the same subject is taken from a somewhat different point
COLLECTION Otterlo, Rijksmuseum Kröller-Müller, inv nr 287-12, cat van Gogh 1970, nr 209

F 417 [H 455] SEASCAPE AT SAINTES-MARIES

Canvas 44 × 53 [17¼ × 20¾]
Signed in lower right: Vincent
Compare sketch in letter B 6, drawings F 1430, F 1430a and F 1430b
Saintes-Maries [Arles period] June 1888
LETTER 499 [probably 22 June] See F 415
B 6 [about 24 June] See F 408
LITERATURE Scherjon and de Gruyter 1937, Arles nr 37
COLLECTION Moscow, Pushkin Museum [acquired 1948, from the Museum of Modern Western Art], inv nr 3438, cat 1961, p 53

F 418 [H 814] THE SEA AT SAINTES-MARIES

Left out by Faille in his manuscript for the present edition
See REJECTED WORKS

F 418a [formerly F 418bis] BOATS AT SAINTES-MARIES

Left out by Faille in his manuscript for the present edition
See REJECTED WORKS

F 419 [H 445] WHITE MAS AT SAINTES-MARIES

Canvas 33.5 × 41.5 [13¼ × 16¼]
Compare drawings F 1438 [same composition] and F 1440 [same site]
Saintes-Maries [Arles period] June 1888 or shortly later
LETTER W 7 [9 and 16 September] *'I am inclined to think that you took the white cottages surrounded by green plants under a blue sky, which I made at Saintes-Maries on the coast of the Mediterranean.'*
LITERATURE J.-G. Goulinat, l'Amour de l'Art April 1925, pp 131-42. Scherjon and de Gruyter 1937, Arles nr 41
COLLECTION San Francisco, Henry P. Russell

F 420 [H 446] MAS AT SAINTES-MARIES

Canvas 36.5 × 44 [14½ × 17¼]
Compare sketch in letter B 6, drawings F 1434 and F 1435
Saintes-Maries [Arles period] June 1888
LETTER B 6 [about 24 June] See F 408
LITERATURE Scherjon and de Gruyter 1937, Arles

F 420

F 413

F 415

F 417

F 419

nr 42: letter 500
COLLECTION Formerly Copenhagen, Ernst Goldschmidt
Present owner unknown

F 421 MAS AT SAINTES-MARIES

Left out by Faille in his manuscript for the present edition
See REJECTED WORKS

F 423

F 424

F 422 [H 448] THE SOWER

Canvas 64 × 80.5 [25¼ × 31¾]
Signed in lower left: Vincent
Compare sketches in letters 501a and B 7, drawings
F 1441 and F 1442
Arles June 1888
LETTERS 501a [to John Russell; about 27 June; in
English] '*Am working at a Sower: the great field all
violet the sky & sun very yellow, it is a hard subject to
treat.*'
B 7 [about 28 June] '*Here is a sketch of a sower:
large plowed field with clods of earth, for the most
part frankly violet. A field of ripe wheat, yellow ocher
in tone with a little carmine. The sky, chrome yellow,
almost as bright as the sun itself, which is chrome
yellow No. 1 with a little white, whereas the rest of
the sky is chrome yellow Nos. 1 and 2 mixed. So very
yellow. The Sower's shirt is blue and his trousers
white. Size 25 canvas, square.*'
501 [about 29 June] '*The result is some studies of
wheatfields, landscapes, and a sketch of a sower. A
plowed field, a big field with clods of violet earth –
climbing toward the horizon, a sower in blue and
white. On the horizon a field of short ripe wheat. Over
it all a yellow sky with a yellow sun ... And the sketch,
such as it is – a size 25 canvas – torments me ...*'
503 [about 6 July] '*Yesterday and today I worked on
the sower, which is done completely differently. The
sky is yellow and green, the ground violet and
orange ... I hope to send you this attempt along with
some others soon.*'
533 [8 September] '*Has Pissarro said anything about
the "Sower"? Afterward, when I have carried these
experiments even further, the "Sower" will still be
the first attempt in that style.*'
535 [10 September] '*The idea of the "Sower"
continues to haunt me all the time. Exaggerated
studies like the "Sower" ... usually seem to me
atrociously ugly and bad ...*'
576 [3 February 1889] '*As for the Indépendants ...
To my mind the "Harvest" and the "White Orchard"
are enough, with the little "Provençal Girl" or the
"Sower" if you like.*'
LITERATURE Scherjon and de Gruyter 1937, Arles
nr 44: letters 533, 535, 576 and B 7. H. Thannhauser,
Burlington Magazine 1938, part 2, pp 94-104:
publishes letter 501a as nr 2 of the unknown letters
to Russell. J. Leymarie, Van Gogh, 1951, p 108,
nr 69: compare drawings F 1441 and F 1442. Cat
van Gogh 1959, Rijksmuseum Kröller-Müller,
nr 214: description and sketches in letters 501, 501a
and B 7 show a sower who is dressed differently
from the figure in this picture; see letter 503 and
drawing F 1442, done after this painting
EDITORS' COMMENT The trousers in this picture
are blue, whereas in the letters 501 and B 7 white
trousers are mentioned
COLLECTION Otterlo, Rijksmuseum Kröller-
Müller, inv nr 303-18, cat van Gogh 1970, nr 214
Colorplate, p 234

F 423 [H 449] A BUGLER OF THE ZOUAVE
REGIMENT

Canvas 65 × 54 [25½ × 21¼]
Compare F 424, drawing F 1443 [same model],
water color F 1482 and drawing F 1482a [same
composition]
Arles June 1888
LETTERS 501 [about 29 June] '*I have a model at last
– a Zouave – a boy with a small face, a bull neck, and
the eye of a tiger, and I began with one portrait, and
began again with another; the half-length I did of him
was horribly harsh, in a blue uniform, the blue of
enamel saucepans, with braids of a faded reddish-
orange, and two stars on his breast, an ordinary blue,
and very hard to do. That bronzed, feline head of his
with the reddish cap, against a green door and the
orange bricks of a wall. So it's a savage combination*

*of incongruous tones, not easy to manage. The study
I made of it seems to me very harsh, but all the same
I'd like always to be working on vulgar, even loud
portraits like this. It teaches me something, and
above all that is what I want of my work.'*
502 [about 30 June] *'I should not be surprised if he
[Bernard] wanted to make an exchange with me for
the Zouave's head, though it is very ugly.'*
B 8 [about 1 July] *'What I have dashed off is very
ugly; a drawing of a seated Zouave ... and finally his
portrait against a green door and some orange bricks
of a wall.'*
W 5 [about 1 August] *'Also a portrait bust of a
Zouave, in a blue uniform with red and yellow
trimmings, with a sky-blue sash, a blood-red cap with
a blue tassel, the face sunburned – black hair cropped
short – eyes leering like a cat's – orange and green – a
small head on a bull's neck. In this one the background is a harshly green door and some orange
bricks of the wall and the white stucco.'*
LITERATURE Scherjon and de Gruyter 1937, Arles
nr 45: not only letter 501 but also 502; the name of
the officer of the Zouaves was Milliet. A. Bowness,
exhib cat van Gogh London [Hayward Gallery]
1968-9, nr 125: Arles 23-30 June 1888
COLLECTION Amsterdam, Rijksmuseum Vincent
van Gogh [Vincent van Gogh Foundation, inv
nr F 423]

F 424 [H 450] THE ZOUAVE

Canvas 81 × 65 [32 × 25½]
Compare F 423, drawing F 1443, watercolor F 1482
and drawing F 1482a [same model]
Arles June and August 1888
LETTERS 501 [about 29 June] *'The second portrait
will be full length, sitting against a white wall.'*
B 8 [about 1 July] *'What I have dashed off is very
ugly: a drawing of a seated Zouave, a painted sketch
of the Zouave against a completely white wall ...'*
519 [8 August] *'I have again worked on a portrait of a
Zouave sitting on a bench against a white wall, which
makes a fifth figure.'*
LITERATURE Scherjon and de Gruyter 1937, Arles
nr 58. J. Leymarie, Van Gogh, 1951, pp 113-4, nr 85:
June 1888; preparatory drawings for this painting
of an anonymous Zouave [not to be confused with
the officer of the Zouaves, Milliet, depicted in F 473],
are F 1143 and F 1482; is the portrait mentioned in
letter 519 an unknown replica, or a new attack on
the portrait of a month earlier mentioned in letters
501 and 519?
COLLECTION New York, Mrs Albert D. Lasker

F 425 [H 447] HAYSTACKS IN PROVENCE

Canvas 73 × 92.5 [28¾ × 36½]
Signed in lower right: Vincent
Compare F 565, drawings F 1478 [same houses],
F 1425, F 1426, F 1427 [same composition]
Arles June 1888
LETTERS 497 [12 June] *'And I have another subject,
a farm and some ricks, which will probably be a
pendant.'*
498 [about 16 June] *'Today I am sending you 3
drawings by post. You will think the one with the ricks
in a farmyard too bizarre, but it was done in a great
hurry as a cartoon for a picture and it is to show you
the idea.'*
501 [about 29 June] *'Among the studies of wheat
fields there is the one of the stacks, of which I sent
you the first sketch; it is on a square size 30 canvas.'*
LITERATURE Scherjon and de Gruyter 1937, Arles
nr 36: letters 497 and 498; pendant of F 412.
W. Weisbach, Vincent van Gogh, volume 2, 1951,
pp 66-7: preparatory drawings are F 1425-7. Cat van
Gogh 1959, Rijksmuseum Kröller-Müller, nr 226:
drawing F 1425 could be a preliminary study,
whereas it seems that F 1426 and F 1427 were done
after completion of the painting

F 422

F 425

F 426

COLLECTION Otterlo, Rijksmuseum Kröller-
Müller, inv nr 305-20, cat van Gogh 1970, nr 226

F 426 [H 452] THE BRIDGE AT TRINQUETAILLE

Canvas 65 × 81 [25½ × 32]
Compare drawing F 1507
Arles June-July 1888
LETTERS 503 [about 6 July] *'I have a view of the
Rhône – the iron bridge at Trinquetaille – in which the
sky and the river are the color of absinthe; the
quays, a shade of lilac; the figures leaning on their
elbows on the parapet, blackish; the iron bridge, an
intense blue, with a note of vivid orange in the blue
background, and a note of intense malachite green.'*
524 [14 or 15 August] *'There is a view of the Rhône
in which the sky and the water are the color of
absinthe, with a blue bridge and figures of little black
urchins ...'*
LITERATURE R. Jacobsen, Onze Kunst 1904, part
2, pp 1 ff [with reproduction]. Scherjon and de
Gruyter 1937, Arles nr 49: letters 503 and 524
COLLECTION New York, André Meyer

F 430

F 431

F 360 [H 237] STILL LIFE: PLASTER STATUETTE
AND BOOKS
Paris summer or autumn 1887

F 427 [H 453] THE CANAL LA ROUBINE DU
ROI WITH WASHERWOMEN

Canvas 74 × 60 [29 × 23½]
Compare drawings F 1444 and F 1473 [same site]
Arles July 1888
LETTERS 504 [about 7 July] '*Do you remember
among the little drawings a wooden bridge with a
washing place, and a view of the town in the distance?*
[probably F 1444]. *I have just painted that subject in
a large size.*'
524 [14 or 15 August] '*…there is the sower, and a
washing place and others as well, which have not come
off at all and are unfinished, especially one big
landscape with brushwood.*'
LITERATURE Scherjon and de Gruyter 1937, Arles
nr 50: letters 504 and 524. Tralbaut Bildbiographie
1958, p 88
COLLECTION New York, Private Collection
[acquired 1943]

F 428 [H 457] SUNNY LAWN IN A PUBLIC
PARK

Canvas 60.5 × 73.5 [23¾ × 29]
Compare sketches in letters 508 [same composition]
and 553b [in the English edition of the letters only],
F 468, drawings F 1421, F 1449, F 1450, F 1451 and
F 1465 [same site]
Arles July 1888
LETTERS 508 [12 July] '*Here is a new subject. A
corner of a park with clipped shrubs and a weeping
tree, and in the background some clumps of oleanders.
And the lawn just cut with long trails of hay drying in
the sun, and a little corner of blue sky at the top.*'
W 5 [about 1 August] '*I have also got a garden
without flowers, that is to say a lawn, newly mown,
bright green with the gray hay spread in long streaks.
A weeping ash and a number of cedars and cypresses,
the cedars yellowish and spherical in form, the
cypresses rising high into the air, blue-green. At the
back, oleander and a patch of green-blue sky. The
blue shadows of the shrubs on the grass.*'
531 [3 September] '*So…the park with the weeping
trees and clumps of conifers – it would be a good thing
if you could put these on stretchers.*'
LITERATURE Scherjon and de Gruyter 1937, Arles
nr 52: letters 508 and 531; study for the final F 468
COLLECTION Zurich, Kunsthaus [deposited by
B. Mayer]

F 429 [H 458] FLOWERING GARDEN WITH
PATH

Canvas 72 × 91 [28¼ × 35¾]
Compare sketch in letter 512, F 430, drawings
F 1455 [same site] and F 1454 [same composition]
Arles July 1888
LETTERS 512 [about 24 July] '*I have a new drawing
of a garden full of flowers, and two painted studies as
well…You will see from this sketch the subject of the
new studies. There is one vertical and another
horizontal of the same subject, size 30 canvases.*'
513 [about 26 July] '*Yesterday McKnight broke his
silence a little by saying that he liked my last two
studies (the garden of flowers) very much, and talked
about them for a very long time.*'
W 5 [about 1 August] '*I have a study of a garden one
meter wide, poppies and other red flowers surrounded
by green in the foreground, and a square of blue
campanulas…*'
516 [about 1 August] '*McKnight came again
yesterday to see me, and…said that he liked my
Garden.*'
LITERATURE Scherjon and de Gruyter 1937, Arles
nr 54: letters 512, 513 and 516
COLLECTION The Hague, Gemeente Museum
[on loan from the Dienst voor 's Rijks Verspreide
Kunstvoorwerpen; acquired 1962]
Colorplate, p 251

F 430 [H 459] FLOWERING GARDEN

Canvas 95 × 73 [37½ × 28¾]
Compare sketch in letter 512 [same composition],
F 429, drawings F 1454 and F 1455 [same site]
Arles July 1888
LETTERS 512 [about 24 July] and 513 [about
26 July] See F 429
LITERATURE Scherjon and de Gruyter 1937, Arles
nr 53: letters 512 and 513
COLLECTION Zurich, Private Collection

F 431 [H 460] LA MOUSMÉ

Canvas 74 × 60 [29¼ × 23½]
Compare drawings F 1503 [same model], F 1504 and
SD 1722 [same composition]
Arles July 1888
LETTERS B 12 [28 July] '*I have just finished a portrait
of a girl of twelve, brown eyes, black hair and eyebrows, gray-yellowish flesh, the background heavily
tinged with malachite green, the bodice blood red
with violet stripes, the skirt blue with large orange
polka dots, an oleander flower in the charming little
hand.*'
514 [29 July] '*And now, if you know what a
"mousmé" is (you will know when you have read
Loti's* Madame Chrysanthème*), I have just painted
one. It took me a whole week, I have not been able to
do anything else, not having been very well either...
A mousmé is a Japanese girl – Provençal in this case –
12 to 14 years old... The portrait of the girl is against
a background of white strongly tinged with malachite
green, her bodice of striped blood red and violet, the
skirt is royal blue, with large yellow-orange dots. The
mat flesh tones are yellowish-gray; the hair tinged
with violet; the eyebrows and the eyelashes are black;
the eyes, orange and Prussian blue. A branch of
oleander in her fingers, for the two hands are
showing.*'
W 5 [about 1 August] '*I also have a portrait of a
twelve-year-old girl, brown eyes, black hair and
eyebrows, yellowish mat complexion. She is sitting in
a cane chair, a blood-red-and-violet-striped bodice, a
deep blue skirt with little orange dots, a branch of
oleander in her hand. The background light green,
nearly white.*'
516 [about August] '*McKnight came again yesterday
to see me, and he also liked the portrait of the girl...*'
533 [8 September] '*I am greatly pleased that Pissarro
found something in the Young Girl.*'
LITERATURE Scherjon and de Gruyter 1937, Arles
nr 55: letters 514, 516 and 533. J. Leymarie, Van
Gogh, 1951, p 116, nr 91: this portrait shows the
influence of Japan and of literature
COLLECTION Washington, National Gallery of
Art, inv nr 1815, cat Chester Dale Collection 1965,
p 125

F 432 [H 461] THE POSTMAN JOSEPH ROULIN: HALF LENGTH, SITTING AT A TABLE

Canvas 81 × 65 [32 × 25½]
Compare F 433, F 434, F 435, F 436, F 439, drawings
F 1458 [same model], F 1459 and SD 1723 [same
composition]
Arles August 1888
LETTERS W 5 [about 1 August] '*I am now engaged
on a portrait of a postman in his dark-blue uniform
with yellow. A head somewhat like Socrates, hardly
any nose at all, a high forehead, bald crown, little
gray eyes, bright red chubby cheeks, a big pepper-
and-salt beard, large ears. This man is an ardent
republican and socialist, reasons quite well, and
knows a lot of things.*'
517 [3 August] '*So now I am working on two figures,
one the head, and one a half length with the hands, of
an old postman in a dark blue uniform. He has a head
like Socrates, interesting to paint.*'
B 14 [4 or 5 August] '*I have just done a portrait of a*

postman, or rather even two portraits. A Socratic
type, none the less Socratic for being somewhat
addicted to liquor and having a high color as a result.*'
518 [6 August] '*Last week I did not only one but two
portraits of my postman, a half length with the hands,
and a head, life size.*'
LITERATURE Scherjon and de Gruyter 1937, Arles
nr 56: letters 516, 518, 520, 560 and B 15 [the last
two mentioned on p 154]. C. C. Cunningham,
Bulletin of the Museum of Fine Arts [Boston] 1936,
pp 2-3: influence of Japanese prints in the
silhouette and of Delacroix in the arbitrary use of
color. J. Leymarie, Van Gogh, 1951, p 114, nr 86:
letter 517
COLLECTION Boston, Museum of Fine Arts
[Robert Treat Paine II bequest], inv nr 35. 1982, cat
1955, p 29

F 427

F 428

F 432

F 429

F 433

F 434

F 435

F 436

F 437

F 433 [H 466] HEAD OF THE POSTMAN JOSEPH ROULIN

Canvas 64 × 48 [25¼ × 19]
Compare F 432, drawings F 1459, SD 1723 [same model], F 434, F 435, F 436, F 439 and drawing F 1458 [same composition]
Arles August 1888
LETTERS 517 [3 August] and 518 [6 August]
See F 432
LITERATURE Not in Scherjon and de Gruyter 1937
EDITORS' COMMENT Faille states in the Hyperion edition 1939: 'Après maintes considérations d'ordre esthétique et m'appuyant sur ce que van Gogh a écrit au sujet des portraits du postier, je trouve ce tableau fort douteux.' This statement seems in contradiction with the fact that this painting belonged to Mrs van Gogh-Bonger. In his manuscript Faille inserted this painting without any comment.
COLLECTION Detroit, Private Collection

F 434 [H 463] HEAD OF THE POSTMAN JOSEPH ROULIN

Canvas 65 × 54 [25½ × 21¼]
Compare F 432, drawings F 1459 and SD 1723 [same model], F 433, F 435, F 436, F 439 and drawing F 1458 [same composition]
Arles August 1888
LETTERS 517 [3 August] and 518 [6 August]
See F 432
LITERATURE Scherjon and de Gruyter 1937, Arles nr 57: letters 517, 525, 560 and B 15 [the last two mentioned on p 154]
EDITORS' COMMENT Faille connects F 434 with letters 517 and 518. For stylistic reasons, however, this painting does not seem to fit in the series of the Roulin portraits.
COLLECTION Winterthur, Kunstmuseum [acquired 1955; gift of the heirs of G. Reinhart], inv nr 868, cat 1958, nr 178

F 435 [H 462] HEAD OF THE POSTMAN JOSEPH ROULIN AGAINST A FLOWERY BACKGROUND

Canvas 67.5 × 56 [26½ × 22]
Signed in upper left: Vincent
Compare F 432, drawings F 1459, SD 1723 [same model], F 433, F 434, F 436, F 439 and drawing F 1458 [same composition]
Arles December 1888-January 1889
LETTER 560 [November or December 1888] 'But I have made portraits of a whole family, that of the postman whose head I had done previously – the man, his wife, the baby, the little boy, and the son of sixteen…Size 15 canvases.'
LITERATURE Scherjon and de Gruyter 1937, Arles nr 162: painted in the first months of 1889, but not mentioned in Vincent's letters; closely related in style to several versions of LA BERCEUSE and to F 500, the portrait of Dr Rey
EDITORS' COMMENT To judge by the style, the sequence seems to be F 435, F 439 and F 436.
COLLECTION Merion, Pennsylvania, Barnes Foundation [acquired 1912]

F 436 [H 464] HEAD OF THE POSTMAN JOSEPH ROULIN AGAINST A FLOWERY BACK-GROUND

Canvas 64 × 54.5 [25¼ × 21½]
Compare F 432, drawings F 1459, SD 1723 [same model], F 433, F 434, F 435, F 439 and drawing F 1458 [same composition]
Arles January-February 1889
LETTERS 560 [November or December 1888]
See F 435
563 [after 13 November] 'I am beginning to compose

from memory...'
LITERATURE Scherjon and de Gruyter 1937, Arles
nr 163: painted in the first months of 1889, but not
mentioned in Vincent's letters; closely related in
style to several versions of LA BERCEUSE and to
F 500, the portrait of Dr Rey
EDITORS' COMMENT See F 435
COLLECTION Zurich/Ascona, Private Collection

F 437 [H 483] THE STEVEDORES

Canvas 71 × 95 [28 × 37½]
Compare F 438 [same site]
Arles end August 1888
LETTERS 516 [about 1 August] *'I saw a magnificent
and strange effect this evening. A very big boat loaded
with coal on the Rhône, moored to the quay. Seen
from above it was all shining and wet with a shower;
the water was yellowish-white and clouded pearl gray;
the sky, lilac, with an orange streak in the west; the
town, violet. On the boat some poor workmen in
dirty blue and white came and went carrying the cargo
on shore. It was pure Hokusai. It was too late to do
it, but one day when that coal boat comes back, I
must give it a try.'*
526 [about 21 August] *'I saw again today the same
coal boat with the workmen unloading it that I told
you about before, at the same place as the boats
loaded with sand which I sent you the drawing of. It
would be a splendid subject.'* [The last sentence but
one refers to drawing F 1462 and the sketch in letter
524]
LITERATURE Scherjon and de Gruyter 1937, Arles
nr 59: letters 516 and 526
EDITORS' COMMENT Letters B 18 and B 19, which
Faille mentions in connection with this picture,
refer to F 449.
COLLECTION Annapolis, Maryland, Mr and Mrs
Carleton Mitchell

F 438 [H 484] THE STEVEDORES

Canvas 53.5 × 64 [21 × 25¼]
Compare F 437 [same site]
Arles end August 1888
LETTERS 516 [about 1 August] and 526 [about
21 August] See F 437
LITERATURE Scherjon and de Gruyter 1937, Arles
nr 60: letters 516 and 526; this painting may be a
preliminary study for the final painting [F 437]
COLLECTION Lugano-Castagnola, Switzerland,
Thyssen-Bornemisza Collection

F 439 [H 465] HEAD OF THE POSTMAN
JOSEPH ROULIN AGAINST A FLOWERY
BACKGROUND

Canvas 65 × 54 [25½ × 21¼]
Compare F 432, drawings F 1459, SD 1723 [same
model], F 433, F 434, F 435, F 436 and drawing
F 1458 [same composition]
Arles January-February 1889
LETTERS 560 [November or December 1888]
See F 435
563 [after 13 November] See F 436
LITERATURE Scherjon and de Gruyter 1937, Arles
nr 161: painted in the first months of 1889, but not
mentioned in Vincent's letters; closely related in
style to several versions of LA BERCEUSE and to
F 500, the portrait of Dr Rey. M. Buchmann, Die
Farbe bei Vincent van Gogh, 1948, pp 33-6
EDITORS' COMMENT See F 435
COLLECTION Otterlo, Rijksmuseum Kröller-
Müller, inv nr 286-12, cat van Gogh 1970, nr 218

F 440 [H 475] THE BABY MARCELLE ROULIN

Canvas 35 × 24 [13¾ × 9½]
Compare F 441 and F 441a [same baby]
Arles November-December 1888

F 438

F 439

F 440

LETTER 560 [November or December] See F 435
LITERATURE G. Coquiot, Vincent van Gogh, 1923,
p 179: the baby is Marcelle Roulin, a daughter of
the postman. Scherjon and de Gruyter 1937, Arles
nr 128: letters 560 and B 15. J. Leymarie, Van Gogh,
1951, pp 119-20, nr 102: letters T 11 and T 19
EDITORS' COMMENT In F 440 the directness of
certain touches points to immediate visual
observation. F 441 and F 441a are more elaborate
repetitions.
COLLECTION Washington, National Gallery of
Art, inv nr 1695, cat Chester Dale Collection 1965,
p 126

F 441

F 441a

F 443

F 444

F 446

F 447

F 447a

F 448

F 441 [H 476] THE BABY MARCELLE ROULIN

Canvas 35.5 × 24.5 [14 × 9½]
Compare F 440 and F 441a [same baby]
Arles November-December 1888
LETTERS 560 [November or December] See F 435
T 11 [5 July 1889] '*Do you remember the portrait of the Roulin baby you sent to Theo? Everybody admires it greatly … from my place at the table I can just see the big blue eyes and the pretty little hands and the round cheeks of the baby …*'
LITERATURE Scherjon and de Gruyter 1937, Arles nr 126: letters 560 and B 15
EDITORS' COMMENT See F 440
COLLECTION Amsterdam, Rijksmuseum Vincent van Gogh [Vincent van Gogh Foundation, inv nr F 441]

F 441a [formerly F 441bis; H 477] THE BABY MARCELLE ROULIN

Canvas 36 × 25 [14¼ × 9¾]
Compare F 440 and F 441 [same baby]
Arles November-December 1888
LETTER 560 [November or December] See F 435
LITERATURE Not in Faille 1928. Scherjon and de Gruyter 1937, Arles nr 127: letters 560 and B 15
EDITORS' COMMENT See F 440. From a letter of J. Rewald to A. M. Hammacher, 29 April 1962: 'Lorsque j'ai montré le volume Hypérion à la fille de Roulin à Arles, elle a désigné les tableaux suivants comme ayant appartenu à ses parents et ayant été vendus à Vollard vers 1895: Nos 477 [F 441a], 544 [F 537], 594 [F 593], XIII [F 492] et XIV [F 505].' See also J. N. Priou in Revue des PTT de France 1955, nr 3
EDITORS' COMMENT See F 440
COLLECTION Gstaad, Switzerland, Louis Franck

F 442 THE SMALL GARDEN

Left out by Faille in his manuscript for the present edition
See REJECTED WORKS

F 443 [H 478] PORTRAIT OF PATIENCE ESCALIER, SHEPHERD IN THE PROVENCE

Canvas 64 × 54 [25¼ × 21¼]
Signed in upper left: Vincent
Compare F 444, drawings F 1460 and F 1461 [same model]
Arles August 1888
LETTERS 520 [11 August] '*You are shortly to make the acquaintance of Master Patience Escalier, a sort of "man with a hoe," formerly cowherd of the Camargue, now gardener at a house in the Crau.*'
522 [about 13 August] '*I think that the picture of the old peasant's head is as strange in color as the Sower …*'
528 [about 27 August] '*This week I have had the old peasant once again.*'
529 [about 29 August] '*I have two models this week: … and the old peasant.*'
LITERATURE Scherjon and de Gruyter 1937, Arles nr 62: letters 519, 520, 522, 528, 529 and 534 are related to both F 443 and F 444
COLLECTION New York, Mrs H. Harris Jonas

F 444 [H 479] PORTRAIT OF PATIENCE ESCALIER, SHEPHERD IN THE PROVENCE

Canvas 69 × 56 [27¼ × 22]
Compare F 443, drawings F 1460 and F 1461 [same model]
Arles August 1888
LETTERS See under F 443
LITERATURE Scherjon and de Gruyter 1937, Arles nr 61: letters 519, 520, 522, 528, 529 and 534 are related to both F 443 and F 444. J. Leymarie, Van

Gogh, 1951, pp 115-6, nr 90: letter B 15
COLLECTION London, Heirs of A. Chester Beatty
Colorplate, p 252

F 445 [H 487] ENCAMPMENT OF GYPSIES
WITH CARAVANS

Canvas 45 × 51 [17¾ × 20]
Compare drawing SD 1721 [same motif]
Arles August 1888
LETTER 522 [about 13 August] '*Then a little study of
a roadside inn, with red and green carts...these last
two studies have been approved of as having "quite
the modern touch" by the young rival of good old
General Boulanger, the very resplendent 2nd
lieutenant of Zouaves.*'
LITERATURE Scherjon and de Gruyter 1937, Arles
nr 68
COLLECTION Paris, Musée National du Louvre
[acquired 1931; Koechlin bequest], inv nr RF 3670,
cat Impressionistes 1959, nr 146

F 446 [H 486] RAILWAY CARRIAGES

Canvas 45 × 50 [17¾ × 19¾]
Signed in lower right: Vincent
Arles August 1888
LETTER 522 [about 13 August] '*...and also a little
study of Paris-Lyons-Méditerranée carriages; these
last two studies have been approved of as having
"quite the modern touch" by the young rival of good
old General Boulanger, the very resplendent 2nd
lieutenant of Zouaves.*'
LITERATURE Scherjon and de Gruyter 1937, Arles
nr 69
COLLECTION Formerly Paris, Jacques Doucet
Present owner unknown

F 447 [H 482] THE THISTLES

Canvas 59 × 49 [23¼ × 19¼]
Arles August 1888
LETTERS 522 [about 13 August] '*As to studies, I
have two studies of thistles in a vague field, thistles
white with the fine dust of the road.*'
B 18 [about 29 September] '*Moreover I should have...
a study of gray and dusty thistles...*'
LITERATURE Scherjon and de Gruyter 1937, Arles
nr 66
COLLECTION Athens, Stavros S. Niarchos, exhib
cat 1957, nr 25

F 447a TWO THISTLES

Canvas 55 × 45 [21¾ × 17¾]
Arles August 1888
LETTER 522 [about 13 August] See F 447
LITERATURE Not in Faille 1928, Scherjon and
de Gruyter 1937 or Faille 1939. According to a note
in Faille's manuscript for this edition Paul Signac
wrote in a letter of March 1921 to Mr L. Marseille:
'Not being one of the most emotional van Goghs,
it is certainly a van Gogh which can have its right
place in a good collection.' Expertised under the
auspices of the Expertise Instituut, Amsterdam
[1964, 1968]
COLLECTION Sale London [Christie] 28 June 1968,
nr 76
Present owner unknown

F 448 [H 474] THE PAINTER ON THE ROAD TO
TARASCON [destroyed]

Canvas 48 × 44 [19 × 17¼]
Compare drawings F 1502, F 1502a and F 1518
[same site]
Arles August 1888
LETTER 524 [14 or 15 August] '*The roll he [Milliet]
is bringing contains 35 studies...For instance, there is
a rough sketch I made of myself laden with boxes,*

F 445

F 449

props and canvas on the sunny road to Tarascon.'
LITERATURE R. Jacobsen, Onze Kunst 1903, part
I, p 114. Scherjon and de Gruyter 1937, Arles nr 70.
J. Leymarie, Van Gogh, 1951, pp 106-7, nr 66:
the theme is related to F 361 of the Paris period.
K. Bromig-Kolleritz, Die Selbstbildnisse Vincent
van Goghs, 1955, pp 18 and 109: first half of
August 1888; connected with drawing F 1502.
F. Erpel, Die Selbstbildnisse Vincent van Goghs,
1963, nr 34. M. Bernhard, Verlorene Werke der
Malerei, 1965, p 148 [with color reproduction].
R. M. Dippel, Museumjournaal 1969, pp 100 ff
COLLECTION Formerly Magdeburg, Kaiser
Friedrich Museum [acquired 1912], inv nr GK 558
The painting was destroyed by fire in May 1945
together with the whole collection of the museum

F 449 [H 485] BOATS WITH MEN UNLOADING
SAND

Canvas 55 × 66 [21¾ × 26]
Signed in lower right: Vincent
Compare sketch in letter 524 and drawing F 1462
Arles August 1888
LETTERS 524 [14 or 15 August] '*Just now I am
working on a study like this, of boats seen from the
quay above, the two boats are pink tinged with violet,
the water is bright green, no sky, a tricolor on the*

*mast. A workman with a barrow is unloading sand. I
have a drawing of it as well.*'
525 [15 August] '*I have put in this package a drawing
after a picture which I am working on now – the boats
with men unloading sand.*'
B 15 [about 18 August] '*I also have "Men Unloading
a Sand Barge" – that is to say, there are two vessels,
violet-pink in a malachite green with gray sand,
wheelbarrows, planks and a little blue-and-yellow
fellow. All of it seen from the quay above, looking
down at a bird's-eye view. No sky; it is only a sketch
or rather a scribble, done during the full violence of
the mistral.*'
B 18 [about 29 September] '*If, when it is exposed
tomorrow to the sun, it gets sufficiently dry to be
rolled up, I shall add a landscape of "Men Unloading
Sand," also a project for and an attempt at a picture,
in which there is a more mature purposefulness.*'
B 19 [about 8 October] '*Of course, if you should
prefer another study in this batch to the "Men
Unloading Sand," you can take it and erase the
dedication, if someone else will have it.*'
LITERATURE Scherjon and de Gruyter 1937, Arles
nr 72: letters 525, B 18 and B 19. M. E. Tralbaut,
exhib cat van Gogh Essen 1957, nr 297: letter 526;
drawing F 1462 was probably done before the
painting
EDITORS' COMMENT Apparently the dedication
mentioned in letter B 19 was erased.
COLLECTION Essen, Museum Folkwang
[acquired 1912], inv nr G 61, cat 1961, nr 60
Colorplate, p 269

F 450

F 453

F 451

F 454

F 455

F 450 [H 481] THE SOWER

Burlap on canvas 73.5 × 93 [29 × 36½]
Signed in lower right: Vincent
Compare sketch in letter 558a [in the English
edition of the letters only] and F 451
Arles autumn 1888
LETTERS 558a [between 28 October and 12
November] '*This is a sketch of the latest canvas I am
working on, another Sower. An immense citron-
yellow disk for the sun. A green-yellow sky with pink
clouds. The field violet, the sower and the tree
Prussian blue. Size 30 canvas.*'
560 [November or December] '*From time to time
there's a canvas which will make a picture, such as
the "Sower" in question, which I myself think better
than the first.*'
LITERATURE Scherjon and de Gruyter 1937, Arles
nr 114: letters 558 and 560; this is the final painting,
F 451 is the study. W. Weisbach, Vincent van Gogh,
volume 2, 1951, p 79: composition probably
borrowed from Gauguin's THE VISION AFTER
THE SERMON. J. Hulsker, Maatstaf 1960, part 1,
p 333: letter 558a. D. Cooper, exhib cat Bührle
Collection Edinburgh-London 1961, nr 59: painted
during the first fortnight of December 1888, as
letter 558a should be dated on internal evidence
early December and not end October 1888
EDITORS' COMMENT Faille mentions letters
558, 558a, 560 and T 9 in connection with this
number. The cited passages refer to four versions,
however. The later, '*size 30*' version mentioned in
letter 558a corresponds in dimensions with F 450.
Letter 558 refers to F 494 [mentioned and sketched
in letter 558b]. Letter 560 refers to F 450. The words
'*better than the first*' must refer to F 422, the version
of June. Finally, letter T 9 refers to F 451: '*The little
sower with the tree.*'
COLLECTION Zurich, E. G. Bührle, cat 1958,
nr 241

F 451 [H 480] THE SOWER

Canvas 32 × 40 [12½ × 15¾]
Compare sketch in letter 558a [in the English
edition of the letters only] and F 450
Arles autumn 1888
LETTER T 9 [21 May 1889] '*Some days ago I got
your consignment ... the little sower with the tree.*'
LITERATURE Scherjon and de Gruyter 1937, Arles
nr 113: letter 558; study for F 450. W. Weisbach,
Vincent van Gogh, volume 2, 1951, p 79:
composition probably borrowed from Gauguin's
THE VISION AFTER THE SERMON. A. Bowness,
exhib cat van Gogh London [Hayward Gallery]
1968-9, nr 140: Arles late November 1888
EDITORS' COMMENT See F 450
COLLECTION Amsterdam, Rijksmuseum Vincent
van Gogh [Vincent van Gogh Foundation, inv
nr F 451]

F 452 [H 280] SUNFLOWERS
Paris period; see after F 388 verso

**F 453 [H 473] STILL LIFE: VASE WITH THREE
SUNFLOWERS**

Canvas 73 × 58 [28¾ × 22¾]
Arles August 1888
LETTERS B 15 [about 18 August] '*I am thinking of
decorating my studio with half a dozen pictures of
"Sunflowers," a decoration in which the raw or
broken chrome yellows will blaze forth on various
backgrounds – blue, from the palest malachite green
to royal blue ...*'
526 [about 21 August] '*I have three canvases going
– 1st, three huge flowers in a green vase, with a light
background, a size 15 canvas;* [F 453] *2nd, three
flowers, one gone to seed, having lost its petals, and
one a bud against a royal-blue background, size 25*

canvas; [F 459] *3rd, twelve flowers and buds in a yellow vase (size 30 canvas). The last one is therefore light on light, and I hope it will be the best.'* [F 456]
W 6 [second half of August] *'At the moment I am working on a bunch of twelve sunflowers in a yellow earthenware pot, and I intend to decorate the whole studio with nothing but sunflowers... I am very busy working on my sunflowers...'*
527 [about 24 August] *'I am now on the fourth picture of sunflowers. This fourth one is a bunch of 14 flowers, against a yellow background* [F 454], *like a still life of quinces and lemons...One of the decorations of sunflowers on royal blue ground has "a halo," that is to say each object is surrounded by a glow of the complementary color of the background against which it stands out.'* [F 459]
528 [about 27 August] *'The sunflowers are getting on, there is a new bunch of 14 flowers on a greenish-yellow ground* [F 554], *so it is exactly the same effect—but in a larger size, a 30 canvas—as the still life of the quinces and lemons, which you already have—but in the sunflowers the painting is much more simple.'*
529 [about 29 August] *'I am also working on a bunch of flowers...'*
W 7 [9 and 16 September] *'In this very little room* [the guestroom] *I want to put in the Japanese manner, at least six very large canvases, particularly the enormous bouquets of sunflowers.'* [F 454 and F 456]
W 8 [first half of October, before Gauguin's arrival] *'So I myself too have already finished a picture all in yellow—of sunflowers (fourteen flowers in a yellow vase and against a yellow background...'* [F 454]
575 [30 January 1889] *'When Roulin came I had just finished the duplicate of my sunflowers...'* [F 455, F 457, F 458]
T 9 [21 May] *'Some days ago I got your consignment ...the sunflowers...'*
T 12 [16 July] *'In general people like the night effect and the sunflowers.'*
626a [to Aurier; 11 February 1890] *'Suppose that the two pictures of sunflowers, which are now at the Vingtistes' exhibition* [F 454, F 456], *have certain qualities of color, and that they also express an idea symbolizing "gratitude."'*
LITERATURE Scherjon and de Gruyter 1937, Arles nr 73
EDITORS' COMMENT In a few days at the end of August 1888, Vincent made four paintings of bouquets of sunflowers, meant as a decoration for his studio. In letter 526 [about 21 August] he describes three of them which he is working on: one of three flowers in a green vase with light background, one with five flowers with a royal blue background, and one with twelve flowers in a yellow vase and light background. The first two can easily be identified as F 453 and F 459. The third one might be either F 455 or F 456, as both correspond to the description *'twelve flowers in a yellow vase with light background.'*
In letter 527 [about 22 August], Vincent describes his fourth bouquet of sunflowers as one of fourteen flowers with a yellow background [or greenish yellow, as he puts it in letter 528]. This one might be either F 454, F 457 or F 458, as these three almost identical paintings all correspond to the description of *'fourteen flowers with a yellow or greenish yellow background.'* [One might count fifteen flowers, but Vincent himself spoke of fourteen flowers in various letters.]
Two or three of these paintings must have been executed in January 1889, when Vincent produced replicas of the two paintings with twelve and fourteen flowers he had made in August [see letter 575 [30 January]: *'When Roulin came I had just finished the duplicate of my sunflowers, and I showed him the two canvases of "La Berceuse" between the four bunches of flowers.'*]
It has not been possible to identify with certainty on the evidence of the letters alone which were the

third and fourth paintings of sunflowers, made in August, and which were the replicas, made in January. On stylistic grounds, however, the editors think that as far as the two paintings with twelve flowers are concerned, F 456 was the original painting and F 455 was the replica, and that as far as the three paintings with fourteen flowers are concerned, F 454 is the original one, and F 457 and F 458 are the replicas.
There is another problem in respect to the three paintings mentioned in letter 526. Vincent refers to the painting with three flowers as a *'size 15 canvas,'* the one with five flowers as a *'size 25 canvas,'* and the one with twelve flowers as a *'size 30 canvas.'* Now the sizes of F 453 and F 459 are $28\frac{3}{4} \times 22\frac{3}{4}$ inches and $38\frac{1}{2} \times 27\frac{1}{4}$ inches respectively, and F 455 and F 456 are $36\frac{1}{4} \times 28\frac{1}{2}$ inches and $35\frac{3}{4} \times 28$ inches respectively.
Not only should the first two rather be called size 20 and size 30 respectively [F 459 might even be called larger than size 30], but F 455 and F 456 [which are indeed size 30 canvases] are not even as large as F 459, which Vincent called a *'size 25 canvas.'* If Vincent erroneously used the wrong indications for the first two paintings he mentioned in letter 526, one would at least have expected the third picture, called *'size 30 canvas,'* to be a bigger one than the second one which he called a *'size 25 canvas.'* The editors have not found a solution to this problem.
COLLECTION USA, Private Collection

F 454 [H 467] STILL LIFE: VASE WITH FOURTEEN SUNFLOWERS

Canvas 93×73 [$36\frac{1}{2} \times 28\frac{3}{4}$]
Signed on the vase at the left: Vincent
Compare F 457 and F 458
Arles August 1888
LETTERS See under F 453, especially letters 527, 528, W 7, W 8, and 626a
LITERATURE Scherjon and de Gruyter 1937, Arles nr 76. D. Cooper, The Courtauld Collection, 1954, nr 83: letters 526-9 and B 15; compare F 457 and F 458. J. J. Gillon, Le concours médical 1 January 1955, pp 73-9. A. Wagner, Museumjournaal 1961-2, pp 131-5; the painter Israëls had this still life on loan from 1917 until 1920 and used it in the background of at least three figure studies
EDITORS' COMMENT See F 453
COLLECTION London, Tate Gallery [acquired 1924; Courtauld Fund], cat The Courtauld Collection, 1954, nr 83

F 455 [H 469] STILL LIFE: VASE WITH TWELVE SUNFLOWERS

Canvas $92 \times 72\frac{1}{2}$ [$36\frac{1}{4} \times 28\frac{1}{2}$]
Signed on the vase: Vincent
Compare F 456
Arles January 1889
LETTERS See under F 453, especially letters 526, W 6 and 575
LITERATURE Scherjon and de Gruyter 1937, Arles nr 78
EDITORS' COMMENT See F 453
COLLECTION Philadelphia, The Philadelphia Museum of Art [acquired 1963; Mrs C. S. Tyson bequest], inv nr 63-116-19, check list of paintings 1 January 1965, p 28

F 456 [H 468] STILL LIFE: VASE WITH TWELVE SUNFLOWERS

Canvas 91×71 [$35\frac{3}{4} \times 28$]
Signed on the vase: Vincent
Compare F 455
Arles August 1888
LETTERS See under F 453, especially letters 526, W 6 and 626a

F 456

F 457

LITERATURE H. Uhde, Kunst und Künstler 1911-2, pp 379-88 [with reproduction]. Scherjon and de Gruyter 1937, Arles nr 75
EDITORS' COMMENT See F 453
COLLECTION Munich, Bayerische Staatsgemälde-sammlungen [acquired 1912; gift of a collector in memory of H. von Tschudi], inv nr 8672, cat 1966, p 43

F 457 [H 470] STILL LIFE: VASE WITH FOURTEEN SUNFLOWERS

Canvas 100×76 [$39\frac{1}{2} \times 30$]
Compare F 454 and F 458
Arles January 1889
LETTERS See under F 453, especially letters 527, 528, W 8, 575
LITERATURE Scherjon and de Gruyter 1937, Arles nr 153: the duplicate from January 1889 mentioned in letter 575
EDITORS' COMMENT See F 453
COLLECTION London, Miss Edith Beatty

F 458

F 459

F 460

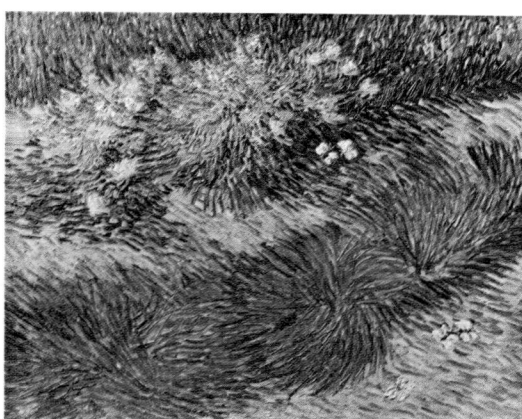

F 462

F 461

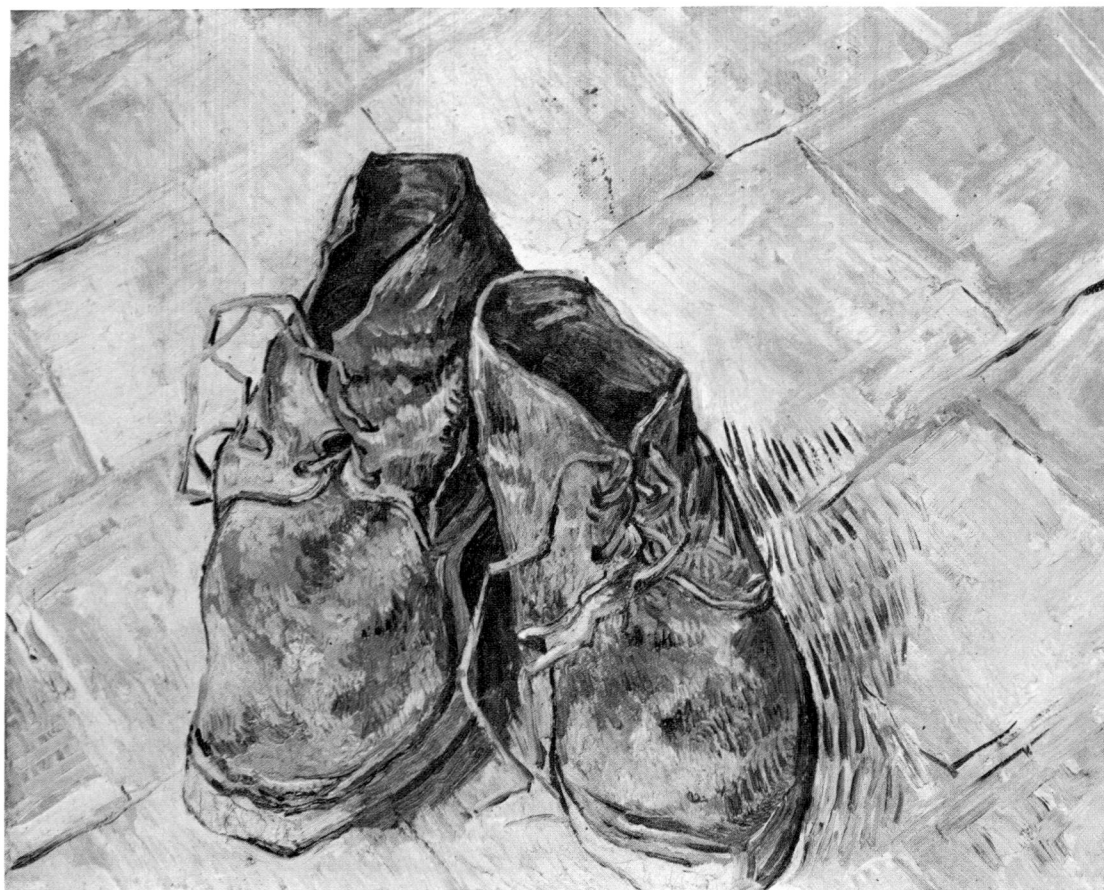

F 458 [H 471] STILL LIFE: VASE WITH FOURTEEN SUNFLOWERS

Canvas 95 × 73 [37½ × 28¾]
Signed on the vase: Vincent
Compare F 454 and F 457
Arles January 1889
LETTERS See under F 453, especially letters 526, 527 and w 8 and 575
EDITORS' COMMENT See F 453
COLLECTION Amsterdam, Rijksmuseum Vincent van Gogh [Vincent van Gogh Foundation, inv nr F 458]

F 459 [H 472] STILL LIFE: VASE WITH FIVE SUNFLOWERS [destroyed]

Panel 98 × 69 [38½ × 27¼]
Arles August 1888
LETTERS See under F 453, especially letters 526, 527
LITERATURE Scherjon and de Gruyter 1937, Arles nr 74
EDITORS' COMMENT See F 453
COLLECTION Formerly Yokohama, Japan, Koyata Yamamoto [acquired 1920; destroyed by fire during the Second World War]

F 460 [H 704] CORNER OF A GARDEN WITH BUTTERFLIES

Canvas 51 × 61 [20 × 24]
Probably Arles spring 1889
LITERATURE Faille 1928, nr 460: Arles August 1888; letter 526. Scherjon and de Gruyter 1937, Arles nr 186. Faille 1939, nr 704: Saint Rémy 1889
COLLECTION Paris, Private Collection

F 461 [H 488] STILL LIFE: A PAIR OF SHOES

Canvas 44 × 53 [17¼ × 20¾]
Signed in lower left: Vincent
Arles August 1888
LETTERS 529 [about 29 August] '*I am also working on...a still life of an old pair of shoes.*'
B 18 [about 29 September] '*As for exchanges,...I should have...a still life of a peasant's old boots...*'
LITERATURE Scherjon and de Gruyter 1937, Arles nr 81
COLLECTION USA, S. Kramarsky Trust Fund

F 462 [H 490] PORTRAIT OF EUGÈNE BOCH, A BELGIAN PAINTER

Canvas 60 × 45 [23½ × 17¾]
Arles September 1888
LETTERS 531 [3 September] '*Well, thanks to him I at last have a first version of that picture which I have dreamed of for so long – the poet. He posed for me. His fine head with that keen gaze stands out in my portrait against a starry sky of deep ultramarine; for clothes, a short yellow coat, a collar of unbleached linen, and a spotted tie. He gave me two sittings in one day.*'
w 7 [9 and 16 September] '*I already have one to begin with, namely the portrait of a young Belgian impressionist. I have painted him a little like a poet, the fine nervous head standing out against a back-ground of a deep ultramarine night sky with sparkling stars.*'
LITERATURE Scherjon and de Gruyter 1937, Arles nr 63: letters 520, 533 and B 19. J. Leymarie, Van Gogh, 1951, p 113, nr 83: this portrait was the study for a destroyed composition LE POÈTE
EDITORS' COMMENT The version which was destroyed by Vincent is mentioned in letter B 19 [Arles about 8 October 1888].
COLLECTION Paris, Musée National du Louvre [acquired 1941; Eugène Boch bequest], inv nr RF 1944-9, cat Impressionnistes 1959, nr 147
Colorplate, p 287

F 463 [H 491] THE NIGHT CAFÉ [now Café de l'Alcazar] ON THE PLACE LAMARTINE, ARLES

Canvas 70 × 89 [27½ × 35]
Signed and annotated by Vincent in lower right:
Vincent, Le café de nuit
Compare water color F 1463
Arles September 1888
LETTERS 518 [6 August] '*Today I am probably going to start on the interior of the café where I eat, by gaslight, in the evening. It is what they call here a "café de nuit" (they are fairly common here), staying open all night. Night prowlers can take refuge there when they have no money to pay for a lodging or are too tight to be taken in.*'
521 [about 12 August] '*This restaurant where I am is very queer; it is gray all over; the floor is of gray bitumen like a street pavement, gray paper on the walls, green blinds always drawn, a big green curtain in front of the door which is always open, to stop the dust coming in.*'
533 [8 September] '*Then to the great joy of the landlord, ... of the visiting night prowlers and of myself, for three nights running I sat up to paint and went to bed during the day ... I have tried to express the terrible passions of humanity by means of red and green ... The "Night Café" carries on the style of the "Sower," as do the head of the old peasant and of the poet also ...*'
534 [9 September] '*I have just mailed the sketch [F 1463] of the new picture, the "Night Café" ... In my picture of the "Night Café" I have tried to express the idea that the café is a place where one can ruin oneself ...*'
W 7 [9 and 16 September] '*I have just finished a canvas representing the interior of a night café lighted with lamps. A number of poor wanderers are asleep in a corner. The room is painted red, and in it, under the gaslight, a green billiard table casts an immense shadow on the boarded floor. There are six or seven different reds in this canvas, from blood red to delicate pink, contrasting with as many pale or deep greens.*'
539 [18 September] '*That makes ... Then the two cafés ...*'
B 16 [about 20 September] '*... it is true that I have just done that study of the "Night Café" ...*'
B 18 [about 29 September] '*I cannot send a replica of the "Night Café" yet because it has not even been begun, but I shall be delighted to do one for you.*'
553b [to Eugène Boch; 4 October] '*I am also working on seven square size 30 canvases. In the first place the night café where I have stayed with lamp light effect, painted in the night-time.*'
B 19 [about 8 October] '*... that my night café isn't a brothel; it is a café where night prowlers cease to be night prowlers ...*'
605 [between 6 and 10 September 1889] '*I shall make duplicates ... and especially of the "Red Cabaret," that night café which is the most characteristic of all in its color.*'
LITERATURE Scherjon and de Gruyter 1937, Arles nr 83: letters 518, 534, 539 and 605. A. Meyerson, Konsthistorisk Tidskrift 1946, 3-4, pp 135-49: Vincent finished the painting on 8 September 1888; the same interior has been painted by Gauguin. J. Leymarie, Van Gogh, 1951, nr 96: water color F 1463 is a preparatory study. P. Leprohon, Tel fut van Gogh, 1964, pp 415-5: the café is probably not the Café de l'Alcazar as presumed by Faille
COLLECTION New Haven, Yale University Art Gallery [acquired October 1961; Clark bequest], inv nr 1961.18.34
Colorplate, p 288

F 464 [H 489] VINCENT'S HOUSE ON THE PLACE LAMARTINE, ARLES

Canvas 76 × 94 [30 × 37]
Compare water color F 1413, drawings F 1453 [same composition] and F 1513 [same house]
Arles September 1888
LETTERS 534 [9 September] '*Someday or other you shall have a picture of the little house itself in bright sunshine, or else with the window lit up, and a starry sky.*'
543 [probably 28 September] '*Also a sketch of a size 30 canvas representing the house and its surroundings in sulphur-colored sunshine, under a sky of pure cobalt.*' [The letter continues with a description of this painting]
B 18 [about 29 September] '*I am terribly absorbed in decorating my house ... Well, I myself have ... then the view of the house, which might be called "The Street."*'

553b [to E. Boch; 4 October] '*I am also working on seven square size 30 canvases ... Further a view of my house and its surroundings in a sulphur sun. The sky a hard and bright cobalt. – A difficult job, I tell you!*'
LITERATURE Scherjon and de Gruyter 1937, Arles nr 84. J. Leymarie, Van Gogh, 1951, nr 75: see F 1413, F 1453 and F 1513; description of the house in letter 480. D. Cooper, Mededelingen van de Dienst voor Schone Kunsten der Gemeente 's-Gravenhage 1953, pp 94-106
COLLECTION Amsterdam, Rijksmuseum Vincent van Gogh [Vincent van Gogh Foundation, inv nr F 464]

F 463

F 464

F 465

F 466

F 465 [H 492] SUMMER EVENING

Canvas 74 × 91 [29 × 35¾]
Signed in lower left: Vincent
Compare sketch in letter B 7 and drawing F 1514
Arles end June 1888
LETTERS B 7 [about 28 June] '*Herewith another landscape. Sunset? Rising Moon? In any case a summer evening. The town violet, the orb yellow, the sky blue-green. The wheat has all the tones of old gold, copper, gold-green or gold-red, gold-yellow, bronze-yellow, green-red. Size 30 canvas, square. I painted it with the mistral raging. My easel was fixed in the ground with iron stakes…*'
B 9 [end June] '*For instance, I painted a size 30 canvas, the "Summer Evening," at a single sitting.*'
535 [10 September] '*I have a third study now, of a landscape with a factory, and a huge sun in a red sky above red roofs, a day with a wicked mistral when nature seems to be in a fury.*'
539 [18 September] '*That makes…Then the red sun over the factory…*'
B 19 [about 8 October] '*The sun in the "Red Sunset" should be imagined higher up, outside the picture, let's say on a level with the frame. In this way, an hour or an hour and a half before sunset, the things on earth still keep their color. Later on the blue and violet make them look blacker…*'
LITERATURE Scherjon and de Gruyter 1937, Arles nr 87. W. Hausenstein, Hauptwerke des Kunst-museums Winterthur, 1949, p 83-7
EDITORS' COMMENT The text of letter B 7 is visible on the letter sketch and reads: '*En tout cas soir d'été*' and not, as printed in the earlier editions, '*Soleil d'été en tout cas.*'
COLLECTION Winterthur, Switzerland, Kunst-museum [acquired 1922; gift of Emil Hahnloser], inv nr 469, cat 1958, nr 179

F 466 [H 494] THE ROCKS

Canvas 54 × 65 [21¼ × 25½]
Compare drawing F 1554
Arles May-August 1888
LETTER 535 [10 September] '*I have a study of an old mill painted in broken tones like the oak tree on the rock, that study you were saying you had had framed along with the "Sower."*'
LITERATURE Scherjon and de Gruyter 1937, Arles nr 85
EDITORS' COMMENT F 466 is mentioned for the first time in letter 535 of 10 September. According to the text it was already in Theo's possession at that date. It is probably one of 35 works sent to Theo by means of Milliet on 15 August [letter 524]. The first sending of 26 works from Arles [flowering gardens and earlier work] took place on 10 May. Hence our dating of F 466 between May and August.
COLLECTION Houston, Texas, John A. Beck

F 467 [H 493] THE CAFÉ TERRACE ON THE PLACE DU FORUM, ARLES, AT NIGHT

Canvas 81 × 65.5 [32 × 25¾]
Compare drawing F 1519
Arles September 1888
LETTERS W 7 [9 and 16 September] '*In point of fact I was interrupted these days by my toiling on a new picture representing the outside of a night café. On the terrace there are the tiny figures of people drinking. An enormous yellow lantern sheds its light on the terrace, the house front and the sidewalk, and even casts a certain brightness on the pavement of the street, which takes a pinkish violet tone. The gable-topped fronts of the houses in a street stretching away under a blue sky spangled with stars are dark blue or violet and there is a green tree. Here you have a night picture without any black in it, done with nothing but beautiful blue and violet and green, and in these*'

surroundings the lighted square acquires a pale
sulphur and greenish citron-yellow color. It amuses
me enormously to paint the night right on the spot.'
537 [16 September] *'The second represents the out-*
side of a café, with the terrace lit up by a big gas
lamp in the blue night, and a corner of a starry blue
sky.'
553b [4 October] See F 463
LITERATURE Scherjon and de Gruyter 1937, Arles
nr 89. J. Leymarie, Van Gogh, 1951, p 109, nr 74:

compare drawing F 1519. L. Gans, Museumjournaal December 1958, p 92: the influence of
Anquetin's AVENUE DE CLICHY IN THE EVENING
[reproduction nr 15] is visible in the motif and the
composition of F 467
COLLECTION Otterlo, Rijksmuseum Kröller-
Müller [acquired before 1917 from the heirs of
A. Aurier], inv nr 289-00, cat van Gogh 1970,
nr 212

F 467

F 468

F 468 [H 497] SUNSHINE IN THE PARK: THE POET'S GARDEN

Canvas 73 × 92 [28¾ × 36¼]
Arles September 1888
Compare sketches in letters 508 and 553b [in the English edition of the letters only], F 428, drawings F 1421, F 1449, F 1450, F 1451 and F 1465 [same site]
LETTERS 537 [16 September] 'In this last category there is a square size 30 canvas, a corner of a garden with a weeping tree, grass, round clipped cedar shrubs and an oleander bush. The same corner of the park, that is, which you have already had a study of in the last parcel. But as this one is bigger, there is a citron sky over everything, and also the colors have the richness and intensity of autumn. And besides it is in even heavier paint than the other one, plain and thick.'
538 [17 September] 'At the moment I am working on another square size 30 canvas, another garden or rather a walk under plane trees, with the green turf, and black clumps of pines.'
538a [18 September] 'Very soon the hour will come for me to resume my painting in the garden.'
539 [18 September] 'I wrote to you already, early this morning, then I went away to go on with a picture of a garden in the sunshine. Then I brought it back and went out again with a blank canvas, and that also is finished. ...That makes three pictures of the gardens opposite the house...The last picture, done with the last tubes of paint on the last canvas, of a garden, green of course, is painted without pure green, nothing but Prussian blue and chrome yellow. [F 471] ...This side of the garden is also, for the same reason of chastity or morality, destitute of any flowering bushes such as oleanders. There are ordinary plane trees, pines in stiff clumps, a weeping tree, and the green grass. But it is all so intimate. Manet has gardens like this...Tomorrow I am going to draw, until the paints come. But I have deliberately arrived at the point where I will not draw a picture with charcoal.' [drawings F 1476 and F 1477]
541 [about 23 September] 'Since seven o'clock this morning I have been sitting in front of something which after all is no great matter, a clipped round bush of cedar or cypress growing amid grass. You already know this clipped bush, because you have had a study of the garden. Enclosed also a sketch of my canvas, again a square size 30 canvas [drawing F 1465]. The bush is green, touched a little with bronze and various other tints...This makes a pendant to another size 30 canvas of the same spot, only from a totally different angle, in which the whole garden is in quite different greens, under a sky of pale citron. But isn't it true that this garden has a fantastic character which makes you quite able to imagine the poets of the Renaissance, Dante, Petrarch, Boccaccio, strolling among these bushes and over the flowery grass? It is true that I have left out some trees, but what I have kept in the composition is really there just as you see it. Only it has been overcrowded with some shrubs which are not in character. And to get at that character, the fundamental truth of it: that's three times now that I've painted the same spot. It happens to be the garden just in front of my house. But this corner of the garden is a good example of what I was telling you, that to get at the real character of things here, you must look at them and paint them for a long time.'
544a [in Dutch edition 553a; to Gauguin; about 29 September] 'I have expressly made a decoration for the room you will be staying in, a poet's garden (among the sketches Bernard has there is a first rough draft of it, later simplified). The ordinary public garden contains plants and shrubs that make one dream of landscapes in which one likes to imagine the presence of Botticelli, Giotto, Petrarch, Dante and Boccaccio. In the decoration I have tried to disentangle the essential from what constitutes the

immutable character of the country. And what I wanted was to paint the garden in such a way that one would think of the old poet from here (or rather from Avignon), Petrarch, and at the same time of the new poet living here – Paul Gauguin ...'
B 18 [about 29 September] '*Well, I myself have the "Poet's Garden" (2 canvases; among the sketches you have there is the first conception of it, done after a smaller study that is already at my brother's).'*
553b [to E. Boch; 4 October] '*Three views of the public garden in front of the house. This is one of these views. A cypress or cedar shrub in a bottle-green tub on a citron hued green lawn. In the background a row of oleanders and two statuettes. The sky a raw cobalt blue. You see, it is even a lot simpler than formerly.'* [drawing F 1465]
546 [8 October] '*I have had walnut frames made for the two pictures of "The Poet's Garden,"*...'
549 [9 or 10 October] '*I have done a new size 30 canvas, and I expect to begin a new one this evening, when the gas is lit. The one I have just done is another garden'* [possibly F 470].
551 [10 or 11 October] '*I have done another size 30 canvas, "An Autumn Garden," with two cypresses, bottle green, shaped like bottles, and three little chestnut trees with tobacco and orange-colored leaves. And a little yew tree with pale citron foliage and a violet trunk, and two little bushes, blood-red and scarlet purple leaves. And some sand, some grass, and some blue sky.'*
552 [13 October] '*Now imagine an immense pine tree of greenish-blue, spreading its branches horizontally over a bright green lawn, and gravel splashed with light and shade. Two figures of lovers in the shade of the great tree: size 30 canvas. This very simple patch of garden is brightened by beds of geraniums, orange in the distance under the black branches* [F 479] *...That makes 5 canvases I have started this week, which brings the number of these size 30 canvases up to 15, I think ...2 canvases of the other garden ...'*
556 [22 October] '*Here is a very rough sketch of my last canvas, a row of green cypresses against a pink sky with a crescent moon in pale citron. An indefinite foreground, sand and some thistles. Two lovers, the man in pale blue with a yellow hat, the woman with a pink bodice and a black skirt. That makes the fourth canvas of "The Poet's Garden," which is the scheme of decoration for Gauguin's room.'*
LITERATURE Scherjon and de Gruyter 1937, Arles nr 88: letter 541; F 428 is a study for this painting
EDITORS' COMMENT The letters between 16 September and 22 October 1888 [537-43, 544a, 546, 549, 551, 552, 556 and B 18] speak of the impression made on Vincent by the public garden in Arles in front of the Yellow House. There is no certainty that this subject is the same as the four POET'S GARDENS he mentions on 22 October [letter 556]. Only in letter 539 [18 September] does he try to define his poetic feelings about the garden, naming for the first time Boccaccio and Dante, Petrarch, Giotto and Botticelli, though without giving a special title to his garden subjects.
About 29 September [letter 544a to Gauguin] he mentions THE POET'S GARDEN, a decoration for Gauguin's room, thinking of two poets: Petrarch and the new poet Paul Gauguin. It is uncertain whether he means one of the former garden pictures or a new one.
Bernard receives a sketch of his first idea [letter B 18] and he speaks then of *two* pictures called THE POET'S GARDEN. The first idea could be drawing F 1465, included in letter 541 [about 23 September] to Theo, but from the letter to Bernard B 18 [about 29 September] one knows that Theo must also have a small painted study, no longer traceable. A similar sketch [but without the tall and dark cypress] is included in letter 553b to Eugène Boch. Vincent speaks about '*ce buisson en boules,' 'un buisson de cèdre ou de cyprès en boule,'* well known to Theo through the drawing [F 1465] and the small

painted study.
On 13 October he has three POET'S GARDENS [letter 552] and on 22 October [letter 556] *four,* without reference to any particular poets. The conclusion must be that only a first idea can be identified [drawing F 1465]; but the pictures of the garden between 16 September and 22 October all deal with that poetic ambiance to which he gives the special title of 'Poet's Garden' only in the pieces intended for the decorations of Gauguin's room. Drawings F 1449 and F 1451 are views of the same spot from other viewpoints, F 1476 has an '*arbre pleureur',* and so does F 1468, though a different tree. The same '*arbre pleureur'* is in the sketch in letter 508 as well as in the drawings F 1449 and F 1451. In the background of drawing F 1513 we see the Yellow House.
COLLECTION Chicago, The Art Institute of Chicago [acquired 1933; Mr and Mrs Lewis L. Coburn Memorial Collection], inv nr 33.433, cat 1961, p 182

F 469 [H 408] SELF PORTRAIT WITH STRAW HAT
Paris period; see after F 388 verso

F 470 [H 498] THE CEDAR WALK

Canvas 73 × 92 [28¾ × 36¼]
Arles September 1888
LETTERS See under F 468, especially letter 549
LITERATURE Scherjon and de Gruyter 1937, Arles

nr 95: letter 541. Cat van Gogh 1959, Rijksmuseum Kröller-Müller, nr 211: letters 541, 546 and 544a [in Dutch edition 553a]; belongs to a series of similar motifs, which Vincent called 'Jardin du Poète.' Cat van Gogh 1966, Rijksmuseum Kröller-Müller, nr 211: October 1888; no letters; the title has been changed into 'The Cedar Walk,' as the painting is no longer considered to belong to the series of the 'Jardin du Poète'; closely related to F 472
EDITORS' COMMENT See F 468. The '*other garden'* mentioned in letter 549 may be F 470, the third of the POET'S GARDENS.
COLLECTION Otterlo, Rijksmuseum Kröller-Müller, inv nr 299-20, cat van Gogh 1970, nr 211

F 471 [H 496] THE PARK WITH THE ENTRANCE SEEN THROUGH THE TREES

Canvas 74 × 62 [29¼ × 24½]
Arles 18 September 1888
LETTERS See under F 468, especially letter 539
LITERATURE Scherjon and de Gruyter 1937, Arles nr 92
EDITORS' COMMENT See F 468. In the publication of the French text of letter 539, the editor has wrongly printed '*dans vert,'* in green, instead of '*sans vert,'* without green. See J. Hulsker, Maatstaf 1960, footnote on p 324.
COLLECTION Berlin, Eduard Arnhold [according to M. Frank the painting was destroyed in the Second World War]

F 471

F 472

F 476

F 472 [H 495] THE PUBLIC PARK

Canvas 72 × 93 [28¼ × 36½]
Arles October 1888
LETTERS 549 [9 or 10 October] '*I have done a new size 30 canvas, and I expect to begin a new one this evening*, when the gas is lit. *The one I have just done is another garden.*'
551 [11 or 12 October] '*I have another size 30 canvas, "An Autumn Garden," with two cypresses, bottle green, shaped like bottles, and three little chestnut trees with tobacco and orange-colored leaves. And a little yew tree with pale citron foliage and a violet trunk, and two little bushes, blood-red and scarlet purple leaves. And some sand, some grass, and some blue sky.*'
LITERATURE Scherjon and de Gruyter 1937, Arles nr 106: letters 549 and 551
EDITORS' COMMENT Faille lost track of F 472 until shortly before his death, when A. M. Hammacher put him in touch with a Paris art gallery that was able to tell him that a similar picture was in a private collection in Paris. A careful comparison with the photograph Faille had used for his catalogue of 1928 and a few other documents made it seem credible that the lost picture had been rediscovered. No one had ever heard of the existence of a replica. Then other sources of information turned up, and some very small differences were discovered between details of the old photo and that of the Paris picture, making it appear likely that we had to do with an exact copy, made directly after the original. As the differences were very slight, and had been observed only in photographs, a confrontation of the two originals was highly desirable. It was hoped that this could be arranged when, in 1967, the hitherto missing F 472 was sold in New York by the Rosenberg and Stiebel Art Gallery. Unfortunately, permission to compare the two paintings was withheld, so the issue could not be settled. Our reproduction is taken from the same old photograph used in the 1928 edition.
COLLECTION Formerly New York, Rosenberg & Stiebel Art Gallery [sold 1967]
Present owner unknown

F 473 [H 499] PORTRAIT OF MILLIET

Canvas 60 × 49 [23½ × 19¼]
Arles September-October 1888
LETTERS B 16 [about 20 September] '*One of these days I am going to do the portrait of the second lieutenant of the Zouaves whom I told you about, and who is on the point of leaving for Africa.*'
541 [about 23 September] '*Milliet today was pleased with what I had done ... If he posed better, he would give me great pleasure, and he would have a more distinctive portrait than I can manage now, though the subject is good – the mat pale tints of his face, the red soldier's cap against an emerald background.*'
553b [to E. Boch; 4 October] '*Your portrait is in my bedroom along with that of Milliet, the Zouave, which I have just finished.*'
LITERATURE Scherjon and de Gruyter 1937, Arles nr 98. J. Leymarie, Van Gogh, 1951, pp 112-3, nr 82: letters 506, 516, 522, 524, 525, 539-542, 561, B 7 and B 16; a letter of Milliet to Vincent is in possession of V. W. van Gogh, Laren. Cat van Gogh 1966, Rijksmuseum Kröller-Müller, nr 221
COLLECTION Otterlo, Rijksmuseum Kröller-Müller, inv nr 280-12, cat van Gogh 1970, nr 221

F 474 [H 500] THE STARRY NIGHT

Canvas 72.5 × 92 [28½ × 36¼]
Compare sketch in letter 553b [in the English edition of the letters only], drawings F 1515 [same composition] and F 1472 [same site]
Arles September 1888

LETTERS B 3 [probably 9 April] '*A starry sky, for instance – look, that is something I should like to try to do, just as in the daytime I am going to try to paint a green meadow spangled with dandelions.*'
W 7 [9 and 16 September] '*So far you have not told me whether you have read* Bel Ami *by Guy de Maupassant, and what in general you think of his talent now. I say this because the beginning of* Bel Ami *happens to be a description of a starlit night in Paris with the brightly lighted cafés of the Boulevard, and this is approximately the same subject I just painted.*'
543 [probably 28 September] '*Enclosed a little sketch of a square size 30 canvas, the starry sky actually painted at night under a gas jet.*'
[A description of the painting follows]
B 18 [about 29 September] '*Then the "Starry Night," further the "Vineyard," then the "Furrows"...*'
553b [to E. Boch; 4 October] '*I am also working on seven square size 30 canvases... And lastly a study of the Rhône – of the town lighted with gas reflected in the blue river. Over it the starry sky with the Great Bear – a sparkling of pink and green on the cobalt blue field of the night sky, whereas the lights of the town and its ruthless reflections are red gold and bronzed green.*'
547 [8 October] '*So if you happen to see him* [Bague] *– and if you don't, then go on purpose – let him know that I have told you I have a "Starry Night"...*'
552 [13 October] '*That makes 5 canvases I have started this week, which brings the number of these size 30 canvases up to 15, I think...1 canvas of the starry night.*'
T.9 [21 May 1889] '*Everything arrived in good condition...the starry night...are the ones I prefer so far.*'
T 16 [5 September] '*Now I still have to tell you that the exhibition of the Indépendants is open, and that your two pictures are there, the "Irises" and "The Starry Night."*'
LITERATURE Scherjon and de Gruyter 1937, Arles nr 99: letter 541
COLLECTION Formerly Paris, F. Moch
Present owner unknown

F 475 [H 501] THE GREEN VINEYARD

Canvas 72 × 92 [28¼ × 36¼]
Arles September 1888
LETTERS 544 [29 September] '*Oh! My study of vineyards, I have worked like a slave over it, but I have got it, again a square size 30 canvas...*'
544a [to Gauguin; about 29 September] '*These days I have an extraordinary feverish energy; at the moment I am struggling with a landscape that has a blue sky over an immense vine...*' [A description of the painting follows]
B 18 [about 29 September] See F 474
546 [8 October] '*Pine* [for a frame] *also goes well with the "Furrows" and the "Vineyard."*'
547 [8 October] '*And if you see him, do give Bague my kind regards, and tell him that I recommend him my "Vineyard" and my "Starry Night."*'
552 [13 October] '*That makes 5 canvases I have started this week, which brings the number of these size 30 canvases up to 15, I think...1 canvas of the vineyard*'.
589 [2 May 1889] '*Here are the ones I think worth putting on stretchers out of the batch I'm sending: The Night Café, The Green Vineyard...*'
LITERATURE Scherjon and de Gruyter 1937, Arles nr 102. Cat van Gogh 1959, Rijksmuseum Kröller-Müller, nr 225: October 1888
COLLECTION Otterlo, Rijksmuseum Kröller-Müller [acquired 1920], inv nr 300-20, cat van Gogh 1970, nr 225
Colorplate, p 321

F 476 [H 505] SELF PORTRAIT [Dedicated to Paul Gauguin]

Canvas 62 × 52 [24½ × 20½]
Signed in lower right: Vincent
Annotated by Vincent in upper left: A mon ami Paul G.
Arles September 1888
LETTERS W 7 [9 and 16 September] '*I also made a new portrait of myself, as a study, in which I look like a Japanese.*'
537 [16 September] '*The third picture this week is a portrait of myself, almost colorless, in gray tones against a background of pale malachite.*'
544a [to Gauguin; about 29 September] '*I have a portrait of myself, all ash-colored. The ashen-gray color is the result of mixing malachite green with an orange hue, on pale malachite ground, all in harmony with the reddish-brown clothes. But as I also exaggerate my personality, I have in the first place aimed at the character of a simple bonze worshiping the Eternal Buddha. It has cost me a lot of trouble, yet I shall have to do it all over again if I want to succeed in expressing what I mean. It will even be necessary for me to recover somewhat more from the stultifying influence of our so-called state of civilization in order to have a better model for a better picture.*'
545 [7 October] '*My portrait, which I am sending to Gauguin in exchange, holds its own, I am sure of that. I have written to Gauguin in reply to his letter that if I might be allowed to stress my own personality in a portrait, I had done so in trying to convey in my portrait not only myself but an impressionist in general, had conceived it as the portrait of a bonze, a simple worshiper of the eternal Buddha.*'
LITERATURE Scherjon and de Gruyter 1937, Arles nr 90: letter 537. Åke Meyerson, Konsthistorisk Tidskrift 1946, p 137: probably the first self portrait of the Arles period. J. Leymarie, Van Gogh, 1951, p 112, nr 80: letter B 18. K. Bromig-Kolleritz, Die Selbstbildnisse Vincent van Goghs, 1955, pp 19, 110: painted about 15 September 1888. F. Erpel, Die Selbstbildnisse Vincent van Goghs, 1963, nr 35: letters 539 and 544a to P. Gauguin
COLLECTION Cambridge, Massachusetts, Fogg Art Museum [acquired 1951; Maurice Wertheim Collection], inv nr 1951.65

F 473

F 475

F 474

F 478a

F 479

F 476a STUDY BY CANDLELIGHT

Canvas 81 × 60 [32 × 23½]
Signed and dated in the left middle: Vincent 88
N.B. See EDITORS' COMMENT
Annotated in lower right: étude à la bougie
Arles September 1888 N.B. See EDITORS'
COMMENT
LETTERS 540 [about 22 September] '*Milliet also
came this morning, bringing me the package of
Japanese prints and other things.*'
W 7 [9 and 16 September] See F 476
LITERATURE Not in Faille 1928, Scherjon and
de Gruyter 1937 or Faille 1939. M. M. van Dantzig,
Vincent?, 1952, pp 107, 112-8: false; probably
painted around 1920. L. Anfray, Les Cahiers de
van Gogh 1957, pp 3-22
EDITORS' COMMENT This case gave rise to many
controversial opinions in the years 1948-50. Since
many of these were published only in Dutch newspaper articles, the editors, who do not share Faille's
opinion, thought it useful to provide a selective
survey of the main items:
1942. 7 August: Paul Gachet reacts positively
1947. 6 October: Faille finds F 476a genuine
1948. 9 October: Article by Faille in Phoenix, p 12
1949. 28 and 30 May: Announcement in Het Parool
of the official complaint entered in court by
W. Sandberg, director of the Stedelijk Museum in
Amsterdam, with supporting statements by
M. M. van Dantzig and H. Jaffé, declaring the
picture false
– 1 June: H. P. Bremmer refuses to comment to the
press
– 8 July: Irving Stone, writing in De Waarheid,
gives his opinion, admittedly not that of an expert,
that the painting is genuine
– 26 October: Nieuwe Rotterdamse Courant reports
that experts Sheldon Keck, Alfred Barr, George
Stout and James Plant, invited by the director of
the Metropolitan Museum, New York, to study and
analyze the painting, abstained from a statement of
authenticity
1950. 4 October: C. E. Geyer, customs agent, and
C. K. Wyatt, supervisor, of the US Customs Office in
the Port of New York, find the painting genuine
– 4 October: Het Parool reports that a committee
consisting of Faille, C. H. de Stuers, A. C. Willink,
W. C. Feltkamp, C. W. Huinck and André Schoeller
finds the painting genuine
– 14 October: Article in Elseviers Weekblad on the
findings of the committee
– 28 October: Article by W. J. de Gruyter in Nieuwe
Courant [Het Vaderland] expressing doubts as to
the authenticity of the painting
1957. 22 January: Article in Look, 'The mystery of
study by candlelight.' Survey of the affair
The reference to letters 540 and W 7 is from Faille's
manuscript for the present edition.
COLLECTION Los Angeles, California, Mr and
Mrs William Goetz [acquired 1948]

F 477 [H 502] PORTRAIT OF THE ARTIST'S
MOTHER [after a photograph]

Canvas 40.5 × 32.5 [16 × 12¾]
Arles October 1888
LETTERS 546 [8 October] '*I write in haste, I am
working on a portrait. That is to say, I am doing a
portrait of Mother for myself. I cannot stand the
colorless photograph, and I am trying to do one in a
harmony of color, as I see her in my memory.*'
548 [9 October] '*I am working on a portrait of
Mother, because the black-and-white photograph
annoys me so…That of Mother, a size 8 canvas, will
be ashen gray, against a green background, the dress
carmine. I do not know if it will be like her, but
anyhow I want to give the impression of a blonde
coloring.*'
LITERATURE Scherjon and de Gruyter 1937, Arles

nr 104

EDITORS' COMMENT F 477 can be seen hanging on the wall of Carl Moll's studio in his painting of 1906, DER KÜNSTLER IN SEINEM ATELIER, in the Gemälde Sammlung der Bildenden Künste, Vienna [exhibited in Ostende 1967, cat nr 67].
COLLECTION Fullerton, California, Norton Simon Inc Museum of Art

F 478 [H 509] THE BROTHEL

Canvas 33 × 41 [13 × 16¼]
Arles October 1888
LETTERS 548 [9 October] '...I am doing a brothel study from memory for Bernard.'
561 [between 29 October and 12 November] 'I have done a rough sketch of the brothel, and I quite intend to do a brothel picture.'
LITERATURE Vincent van Gogh, Lettres à Bernard, 1911, plate LXXXIV. Scherjon and de Gruyter 1937, Arles nr 105
EDITORS' COMMENT It is not certain that the rough sketch mentioned in letter 561 is the same as the study from memory mentioned in letter 548.
COLLECTION Merion, Pennsylvania, The Barnes Foundation

F 478a [H 811] THE TARASCON COACHES

Canvas 72 × 92 [28¼ × 36¼]
Compare sketch in letter 552
Arles October 1888
LETTERS 552 [13 October] 'Well, I have just painted that red and green vehicle in the courtyard of the inn. You will see it. This hasty sketch gives you the composition, a simple foreground of gray gravel, a very, very simple background too, pink and yellow walls, with windows with green shutters, and a patch of blue sky. The two carriages very brightly colored, green and red, the wheels – yellow, black, blue and orange. Again a size 30 canvas. The carriages are painted like a Monticelli with spots of thickly laid on paint. You used to have a very fine Claude Monet showing four colored boats on a beach. Well, here they are carriages, but the composition is in the same style.'
571 [17 January 1889] 'At the time of your visit here, were you able to notice the study I painted of the Tarascon diligence, which as you know is mentioned in Tartarin the lion hunter?'
LITERATURE Not in Faille 1928 or Scherjon and de Gruyter 1937. Margaret Barr, Medardo Rosso, 1963, p 75 [note 134]
COLLECTION New York, Mr and Mrs Henry Pearlman [acquired 1950]

F 479 [H 504] PARK: THE POET'S GARDEN

Canvas 73 × 92 [28¾ × 36¼]
Arles October 1888
Compare sketch in letter 552
LETTERS See under F 468, especially letters 552 and 556
LITERATURE J. F. Goulinat, l'Amour de l'Art April 1925, pp 131-42. Scherjon and de Gruyter 1937, Arles nr 111
EDITORS' COMMENT See F 468
COLLECTION Formerly New York, Rosenberg and Stiebel Art Gallery
Present owner unknown

F 480 [H 507] THE RAILWAY BRIDGE OVER AVENUE MONTMAJOUR, ARLES

Canvas 71 × 92 [28 × 36¼]
Compare sketch in letter 552
Arles October 1888
LETTER 552 [13 October] Then two more size 30 canvases...and another bridge, where the railway passes over the road.'

LITERATURE Scherjon and de Gruyter 1937, Arles nr 108
COLLECTION Zurich, Kunsthaus [on loan since 1958], inv nr 1958/21

F 478

F 476a

F 477

F 480

F 481

F 482

F 486

F 487

F 481 [H 506] THE IRON BRIDGE AT
TRINQUETAILLE

Canvas 73.5 × 92.5 [29 × 36½]
Compare sketch in letter 552
Arles October 1888
LETTER 552 [13 October] '*Then two more size 30
canvases, the Trinquetaille bridge and another bridge,
where the railway passes over the road. This canvas is
a little like a Bosboom in color. The Trinquetaille
bridge with all these steps is a canvas done on a gray
morning, the stones, the asphalt, the pavements are
gray; the sky, pale blue; the figures, colored; and
there is a sickly tree with yellow foliage.*'
LITERATURE Scherjon and de Gruyter 1937, Arles
nr 107. J. Leymarie, Van Gogh, 1951, p 119, nr 99:
the bridge connects Arles and the suburb of
Trinquetaille
COLLECTION Brooklyn, New York, Mrs S. Binkhorst-Kramarsky

F 482 [H 627] VINCENT'S BEDROOM IN
ARLES

Canvas 72 × 90 [28¼ × 35½]
Compare sketch in letter B 22, F 483, F 484 and
drawing F 1508 verso [faint traces of the bedroom]
Arles October 1888
LETTERS 554 [about 17 October] '*This time it is just
simply my bedroom, only here color is to do everything and giving by its simplification a grander style
to things, is to be suggestive here of* rest *or of sleep in
general. In a word, looking at the picture ought to
rest the brain, or rather the imagination. The walls
are pale violet. The floor is red tiles. The wood of the
bed and chairs is the yellow of fresh butter, the sheets
and pillows very light greenish-citron. The coverlet
scarlet. The window green. The toilet table orange,
the basin blue. The doors lilac. And that is all – there
is nothing in this room with its closed shutters. The
broad lines of the furniture again must express
inviolable rest. Portraits on the walls, and a mirror
and a towel and some clothes. The frame – as there is
no white in the picture – will be white.*'
555 [about 18 October] '*I am adding a line to tell you
that this afternoon I finished the canvas representing
the bedroom.*'
B 22 [to Gauguin; shortly before 20 October] '*I have
done, still for my decoration, a size 30 canvas of my
bedroom...*'
T 10 [16 June 1889] '*I shall send you back the bedroom, but you must not think of retouching this
canvas if you can repair the damage.*'
W 15 [Saint Rémy October 1889] '*Within a very
short time, I shall send Theo the painted studies I
promised you, and he will see to it that they are sent
on to you at Leyden...You will probably think the
interior, an empty bedroom with a wooden bedstead,
the most unbeautiful thing of all – and notwithstanding this I have painted it twice on a large scale.*'
LITERATURE Faille 1928, nr 482: Arles October
1888; letters 554, 555 and B 22. Scherjon and de
Gruyter 1937, Saint Rémy nr 26: letters 604 and
617. Faille 1939, nr 627: Saint Rémy September
1889; letters 604, 617, T 10, T 22 and B 22
EDITORS' COMMENT According to the letters there
are two paintings which were executed at Saint
Rémy, the smaller of which was given to
Wilhelmina. The version destined for Theo was
executed at Arles. It must be identical with F 482.
The smaller version is F 483.
COLLECTION Amsterdam, Rijksmuseum Vincent
van Gogh [Vincent van Gogh Foundation, inv
nr F 482]

F 483 [H 628] VINCENT'S BEDROOM IN ARLES
Saint Rémy period; see after F 749

F 484 [H 510] VINCENT'S BEDROOM IN ARLES
Saint Rémy period; see after F 749

F 485 [H 503] THE LOVERS: THE POET'S GARDEN

Canvas 75 × 92 [29½ × 36¼]
Compare sketch in letter 556
Arles October 1888
LETTER 556 [22 October] '*Here is a very rough sketch of my last canvas, a row of green cypresses against a pink sky with a crescent moon in pale citron…That makes the fourth canvas of "The Poet's Garden," which is the scheme of decoration for Gauguin's room.*'
LITERATURE Scherjon and de Gruyter 1937, Arles nr 117
EDITORS' COMMENT See F 486
COLLECTION Formerly Berlin, National Galerie [confiscated by the German government in 1937] Present owner unknown

F 486 [H 513] LES ALYSCAMPS

Canvas 73 × 92 [28¾ × 36¼]
Compare F 487 [same subject], F 568 and F 569 [same site]
Arles end October 1888
LETTERS 559 [between 29 October and 12 November] '*I have done two canvases of the falling leaves…The second canvas is the same avenue but with an old fellow and a woman as fat and round as a ball.*'
B 19a [after 1 November] '*I myself have done two studies of falling leaves in an avenue of poplars and the third study of this whole avenue entirely yellow.*'
LITERATURE Scherjon and de Gruyter 1937, Arles nr 116: letter 559. Cat van Gogh 1959, Rijksmuseum Kröller-Müller, nr 224: painted directly after Gauguin's arrival in Arles on 23 October; Gauguin made two paintings of 'Les Alyscamps'
EDITORS' COMMENT F 486 is the second version of this composition; the third version, mentioned in letter B 19a, is F 568 or F 569.
COLLECTION Otterlo, Rijksmuseum Kröller-Müller, inv nr 277-12, cat van Gogh 1970, nr 224

F 487 [H 514] LES ALYSCAMPS

Canvas 72 × 91 [28¼ × 35¾]
Compare F 486 [same subject], F 568 and F 569 [same site]
Arles end October 1888
LETTERS 559 [between 29 October and 12 November] '*I have done two canvases of the falling leaves, which Gauguin liked…And in the avenue, little black figures of lovers.*'
B 19a [after 1 November] '*I myself have done two studies of the fall of leaves in an avenue of poplars…*'
LITERATURE Scherjon and de Gruyter 1937, Arles nr 115: letter 559
COLLECTION Athens, Stavros S. Niarchos, exhib cat 1957, nr 26

F 488 [H 515] L'ARLÉSIENNE: MADAME GINOUX WITH BOOKS

Canvas 90 × 72 [35½ × 28¼]
Arles November 1888
Compare F 489 [same model]
LETTERS 559 [between 29 October and 12 November] '*Then I have an Arlésienne at last, a figure (size 30 canvas) slashed on in an hour, background pale citron…*'
573 [23 January 1889] '*During your hasty visit did you see the portrait of Mme Ginoux in black and yellow? That portrait was painted in three-quarters of an hour.*'
T 10 [16 June] '*I am also very fond of that figure of a woman in vertical format.*'
595 [18 June] '*I am glad to hear that Isaäcson has found some things that please him in my consignment. He and de Haan seem very faithful, and that is so rare nowadays that one must appreciate it. And I am*

also glad to hear that someone else has turned up who actually saw something in the woman's figure in black and yellow.'
LITERATURE Scherjon and de Gruyter 1937, Arles nr 118: letters 582, 590 and 595. Åke Meyerson, Konsthistorisk Tidskrift 1946, p 143: early November

F 485

F 488

EDITORS' COMMENT In the letters only one version is mentioned.
COLLECTION New York, The Metropolitan Museum [acquired 1951; Samuel A. Lewisohn bequest], inv nr 51.112.3, cat European Paintings 1954, p 43

F 489 [H XI] L'ARLÉSIENNE: MADAME
GINOUX WITH GLOVES AND UMBRELLA

Canvas 93 × 74 [36½ × 29¼]
Compare F 488 [same model]
Arles November 1888
LETTERS 559 [between 29 October and 12
November] and 573 [23 January 1889] See F 488
LITERATURE Not in Scherjon and de Gruyter 1937
COLLECTION Paris, Musée National du Louvre
[gift of Mrs. R. von Goldschmidt-de Rothschild,
held in usufruct], inv nr R F 1952.6

F 490 [H 520] MOTHER ROULIN WITH HER
BABY

Canvas 92 × 73.5 [36¼ × 29]
Compare F 491 [same models]
Arles November-December 1888
LITERATURE Scherjon and de Gruyter 1937, Arles
nr 129: letter B 15
COLLECTION Philadelphia, The Philadelphia
Museum of Art [acquired 1950; Lisa Norris Elkins
bequest], inv nr 50-92-22, [cat] check list of paintings
1 January 1965, p 28

F 491 [H 519] MOTHER ROULIN [IN PROFILE]
WITH HER BABY

Canvas 63.5 × 51 [25 × 20]
Compare F 490 [same models]
Arles November-December 1888
LETTER 560 [November or December] See F 435
LITERATURE Scherjon and de Gruyter 1937, Arles
nr 130: letter B 15
COLLECTION New York, Estate of Robert
Lehman [bequeathed to Metropolitan Museum,
1969]

F 492 [H XIII] PORTRAIT OF ARMAND
ROULIN

Canvas 66 × 55 [26 × 21¾]
Compare F 493 [same model]
Arles November 1888
LETTER 560 [November or December] See F 435
LITERATURE Scherjon and de Gruyter 1937, Arles
nr 131: letter B 15
COLLECTION Essen, Museum Folkwang, inv
nr G 63, cat 1961, nr 61

F 493 [H 518] PORTRAIT OF ARMAND
ROULIN: FACING LEFT

Canvas 65 × 54 [25½ × 21¼]
Compare F 492 [same model]
Arles November 1888
LETTER 560 [November or December] See F 435
LITERATURE Scherjon and de Gruyter 1937, Arles
nr 132: letter B 15
COLLECTION Rotterdam, Museum Boymans-Van
Beuningen, inv nr 2608, cat 1963, p 51

F 494 [H 511] THE SOWER

Canvas 72 × 91.5 [28¼ × 36]
Compare sketch in letter 558b [in the English
edition of the letters only]
Arles October 1888
LETTERS 558b [28 October] 'This week I made a
new study of a sower, the landscape quite flat, the
figure small and vague.'
558 [28 October] 'I venture to think that you will like
the new "Sower."'
LITERATURE Scherjon and de Gruyter 1937, Arles
nr 43: letters 501, 503, 533, 535 and 576; this
painting is the sketch for F 422
EDITORS' COMMENT Letters 558b and 558 were
written on the same day in this order.

COLLECTION Winterthur, Switzerland, Mrs
L. Jäggli-Hahnloser

F 495 [H 512] THE RED VINEYARD:
MONTMAJOUR

Canvas 75 × 93 [29½ × 36½]
Arles November 1888
LETTERS 559 [between 29 October and 12
November] '*...and I'm working now on a vineyard
all purple and yellow.*'
561 [between 29 October and 12 November] '*I too
have finished a canvas of a vineyard all purple and
yellow, with small blue and violet figures and yellow
sunlight.*'
589 [2 May 1889] '*Here are the ones I think worth
putting on stretchers out of the batch I'm sending:
...The Red Vineyard...*'
T 10 [16 June] '*The red vine is very beautiful; I have
hung it in one of our rooms.*'
614 [after 16 November] '*As for the Vingtistes, here
is what I'd like to exhibit: ... 5. The Red Vineyard.*'
614b [to Octave Maus; 20 November] '*It's a
pleasure to accept your invitation to exhibit with the
Vingtistes. Here you have the list of paintings I am
reserving for you: ... 5. The Red Vineyard
(Montmajour).*'
LITERATURE Scherjon and de Gruyter 1937, Arles
nr 119: letters 559 and 614. T. Faider-Thomas,
Miscellanea Jozef Duverger, volume 1, 1968,
pp 402-10: in the van Gogh literature F 495 is
generally assumed to be the painting bought by
Miss Anna Boch at the exhibition of the Vingt in
Brussels in February 1890; according to the family,
it is certain that Miss Boch did buy THE RED
VINEYARD, which was in the possession of the
family for many years; a letter by Octave Maus of
29 June 1891 makes it clear that Miss Boch bought
a van Gogh painting [and others] through the Paris
dealer Tanguy for 350 francs in May 1891
EDITORS' COMMENT The information published
by Faider-Thomas [see LITERATURE] makes it
seem probable that the picture sold in Brussels in
February 1890 for 400 francs [as mentioned by
Vincent in letter 627] was not F 495. It might have
been one of the SUNFLOWERS, two of which were
represented among the six van Goghs in the
Brussels exhibition, while only one was sent on to a
following exhibition in Paris at the Indépendants
[20 March-27 April], together with the three other
van Goghs from the Brussels exhibition.
COLLECTION Moscow, Museum Pushkin
[acquired 1948], inv nr 3372, cat 1961, p 53

F 496 [H 516] MEMORY OF THE GARDEN AT
ETTEN

Canvas 73.5 × 92.5 [29 × 36½]
Compare sketch in letter w 9 and Gauguin's
painting ARLÉSIENNES IN THE PARK of the same
period in the Art Institute of Chicago [L. L. Coburn
Memorial Collection]
Arles November 1888
LETTERS W 9 [November or December] '*I have just
finished painting, to put in my bedroom, a memory of
the garden at Etten; here is a scribble of it... All the
same, let us suppose that the two ladies out for a walk
are you and our mother...*'
562 [November or December] '*I have been working
on two canvases. A memory of our garden at Etten,
with cabbages, cypresses, dahlias and figures...*'
LITERATURE Scherjon and de Gruyter, Arles
nr 135. Åke Meyerson, Konsthistorisk Tidskrift
1946, pp 145-6: close connection with the picture of
Paul Gauguin, ARLÉSIENNES IN THE PARK.
M. E. Tralbaut, 8 × van Gogh, 1962, pp 16-28: the
left figure must be Vincent's cousin Kee Vos-
Stricker
COLLECTION Leningrad, Hermitage [acquired
1948], inv nr 9116, cat 1967, nrs 65-66

F 495

F 496

F 494

F 497

F 498

F 499

F 500

F 501

F 497 [H 517] THE NOVEL READER

Canvas 73 × 92 [28¾ × 36¼]
Compare sketch in letter w 9
Arles November 1888
LETTERS W 9 [November or December] '*I have also painted "Une Liseuse de Romans," the luxuriant hair very black, a green bodice, the sleeves the color of wine lees, the skirt black, the background all yellow, bookshelves with books. She is holding a yellow book in her hands.*'
562 [November or December] '*I have been working on two canvases…then a woman reading a novel in a library like the Lecture Française, a woman all in green.*'
B 21 [Saint Rémy between 16 November and 8 December 1889] '*As you know, once or twice, while Gauguin was in Arles, I gave myself free rein with abstractions, for instance in the "Woman Rocking," in the "Woman Reading a Novel," black in a yellow library; and at the time abstraction seemed to me a charming path. But it is enchanted ground, old man, and one soon finds oneself up against a stone wall.*'
LITERATURE Scherjon and de Gruyter, Arles nr 136: letter 590
COLLECTION London, Mr and Mrs Louis Franck

F 498 [H 521] VINCENT'S CHAIR WITH HIS PIPE

Canvas 93 × 73.5 [36½ × 29]
Signed on the chest at the left: Vincent
Compare the companion painting F 499
Arles December 1888-January 1889
LETTERS 563 [after 13 November 1888] '*…the last two studies are odd enough. Size 30 canvases, a wooden rush-bottomed chair all yellow on red tiles against a wall (daytime).*'
571 [17 January 1889] '*I have just been working again today on its pendant, my own empty chair, a white deal chair with a pipe and a tobacco pouch.*'
T 9 [21 May] '*Everything arrived in good condition and without any damage…and the chair with the pipe and tobacco pouch are the ones I prefer so far.*'
LITERATURE Scherjon and de Gruyter 1937, Arles nr 137: painted as 'day-effect.' D. Cooper, cat The Courtauld Collection, 1954, nr 84
COLLECTION London, Tate Gallery [acquired 1924; Courtauld Fund], cat The Courtauld Collection, 1954, nr 84

F 499 [H 522] GAUGUIN'S ARMCHAIR, CANDLE AND BOOKS [HIS EMPTY CHAIR]

Canvas 90.5 × 72 [35¾ × 28¼]
Compare the companion painting F 498
Arles December 1888
LETTERS 563 [after 13 November] '*…the last two studies are odd enough. Size 30 canvases…Then Gauguin's armchair, red and green night effect, walls and floor red and green again, on the seat two novels and a candle, on thin canvas with a thick impasto.*'
571 [17 January 1889] '*I should like de Haan to see a study of mine of a lighted candle and two novels (one yellow, the other pink) lying on an empty armchair (really Gauguin's chair), a size 30 canvas, in red and green.*'
626a [to A. Aurier; 11 February 1890] '*A few days before parting company…I tried to paint "his [Gauguin's] empty seat." It is a study of his armchair of somber reddish-brown wood, the seat of greenish straw, and in the absent one's place a lighted torch and modern novels.*'
LITERATURE Scherjon and de Gruyter 1937, Arles nr 138: letters 563 and 571: painted as 'night effect.' J. Leymarie, Van Gogh, 1951, pp 110-11, nr 77
EDITORS' COMMENT For the motif of the empty chair see letter 252 [about 10 December 1882].

COLLECTION Amsterdam, Rijksmuseum Vincent
van Gogh [Vincent van Gogh Foundation, inv
nr F 499]

F 500 [H 526] PORTRAIT OF DOCTOR FÉLIX
REY

Canvas 64 × 53 [25¼ × 21]
Signed and dated in lower right: Vincent Arles 89
Arles January 1889
LETTER 568 [7 January] '*I now intend to do a portrait
of M. Rey…*'
571 [17 January] '*Nevertheless I have started work
again, and I already have…the portrait of Dr Rey,
which I gave him as a keepsake.*'
LITERATURE Cat de la collection Stchoukine,
1913, nr 33. J. Touguenhold, La collection
Stchoukine, Apollon 1914, nr 1-2, p 39 [reproduced
in color]. Scherjon and de Gruyter 1937, Arles
nr 144: letters 568, 569 and 571. V. Doiteau and
E. Leroy, Aesculape 1939, pp 42-7 and 50-5.
J. Leymarie, Van Gogh, 1951, nr 109, pp 122-3:
gives heretofore unknown details on the provenance
COLLECTION Moscow, Pushkin Museum
[acquired 1948], inv nr 3272, cat 1961, p 53

F 501 [H 523] SELF PORTRAIT

Canvas 46 × 38 [18 × 15]
Signed and annotated by Vincent in lower right: à
l'ami Laval, Vincent
Arles November-December 1888
LETTER 571 [17 January 1889] '*If you have the
address of Gauguin's friend Laval, you can tell Laval
that I am very surprised that his friend Gauguin did
not take along and deliver to Laval a self portrait I
intended for him.*'
LITERATURE Scherjon and de Gruyter 1937, Arles
nr 139. J. Leymarie, Van Gogh, 1951, p 121, nr 105:
November-December 1888; painted after Vincent
received Laval's portrait. K. Bromig-Kolleritz, Die
Selbstbildnisse Vincent van Goghs, 1955, pp 19-20,
112: letter 540; September-November 1888;
painted before Vincent received Laval's portrait.
F. Erpel, Die Selbstbildnisse Vincent van Goghs,
1963, nr 38
COLLECTION New York, Estate of Robert Lehman
[bequeathed to Metropolitan Museum, 1969]

F 502 [H 525] STILL LIFE WITH ORANGES,
LEMONS AND BLUE GLOVES

Canvas 48 × 62 [19 × 24½]
Signed and dated in lower right: Vincent Arles 89
Arles January 1889
LETTER 573 [23 January] '*I have just finished a new
canvas which has almost what you would call* chic, *a
wicker basket with lemons and oranges, a cypress
branch and a pair of blue gloves.*'
LITERATURE Scherjon and de Gruyter 1937, Arles
nr 147
COLLECTION Upperville, Virginia, Mrs and Mrs
Paul Mellon

F 503 [H 524] MME AUGUSTINE ROULIN

Canvas 55 × 65 [21¾ × 25½]
Compare sketch in letter 592, F 504, F 505, F 506,
F 507, F 508 [same model] and F 547 [the head on the
right: same model]
Arles November or December 1888
LETTER 560 [November or December] See F 435
LITERATURE Scherjon and de Gruyter 1937, Arles
nr 125: letters 560 and B 15. V. W. van Gogh,
Museumjournaal October 1955, pp 47-8: compares
it with the portrait of Mme Roulin by Gauguin
COLLECTION Winterthur, Switzerland, Oskar
Reinhart

F 502

F 503

F 505

F 504

F 506

F 507

F 508

F 504 [H 528] LA BERCEUSE: MME AUGUSTINE ROULIN

Canvas 92 × 73 [36¼ × 28¾]
Signed on the arm of the chair: Vincent
Annotated by Vincent to the right of the signature:
la Berceuse
Compare sketch in letter 592, F 505, F 506, F 507,
F 508 [same composition], F 503 [same model] and
F 547 [the head on the right: same model]
Arles January 1889
LETTERS 571a [to A. H. Koning; between 7 and 17
January] 'At present I have…on my easel, the portrait
of a woman. I call it "La Berceuse"…'
573 [23 January] 'I am working on the portrait of
Roulin's wife, which I was working on before I was
ill.'
574 [28 January] 'I have just put the finishing touches
to copies, absolutely identical replicas of them. I
think I have already told you that besides these I have
a canvas of "La Berceuse," the very one I was
working on when my illness interrupted me. I now
have two copies of this one too.'
575 [30 January] 'When Roulin came…I showed him
the two canvases of "La Berceuse"…I could just
show him the two copies of the portrait of his wife,
which pleased him very much.'
576 [3 February] 'I have done "La Berceuse" three
times, and as Mme Roulin was the model and I only
the painter, I let her choose between the three, her
and her husband, but on condition that I should make
another duplicate for myself of the one she chose, and
I am working on this now.'
578 [22 February] 'When Mme Roulin also left to go
and live temporarily with her mother in the country,
she took "La Berceuse" with her. I had a sketch of it
and two duplicates. She had a good eye and took the
best, only I am doing it again at the moment and I do
not want it to be inferior.'
582 [29 March] 'And now I am returning to my
portrait of "La Berceuse" for the fifth time.'
592 [22 May] 'What you say about "La Berceuse"
pleases me…If he will accept it, give Gauguin the
copy of "La Berceuse" that was not mounted on a
stretcher, and another to Bernard as a token of
friendship…You must realize that if you arrange
them this way, say "La Berceuse" in the middle and
the two canvases of sunflowers to the right and left, it
makes a sort of triptych. And then the yellow and
orange tones of the head will gain in brilliance by the
proximity of the yellow wings.'
LITERATURE Scherjon and de Gruyter 1937, Arles
nr 148: letter B 21. E. Joosten, Museumjournaal
June 1957, pp 36-7. Cat van Gogh 1966, Rijksmuseum Kröller-Müller, nr 222: December 1888-
March 1889; letter T 9 and letter to Gauguin in:
Vincent van Gogh, Briefe an Emile Bernard und
Paul Gauguin, 1921, p 105
EDITORS' COMMENT The version which Mme
Roulin took is F 505. This version differs from the
others in the position of the hands. F 504 and F 505
seem to be from January. For stylistic reasons,
especially with regard to the backgrounds, the
chronological order of the other three versions is
likely F 506, F 508 and F 507.
COLLECTION Otterlo, Rijksmuseum Kröller-
Müller, inv nr 293-12, cat van Gogh 1970, nr 222
Colorplate, p 322

F 505 [H XIV] LA BERCEUSE: MME
AUGUSTINE ROULIN

Canvas 93 × 74 [36½ × 29¼]
Signed and dated to the right: Vincent Arles 89
Annotated by Vincent to the right of the signature:
La Berceuse
Compare sketch in letter 592, F 504, F 506, F 507,
F 508 [same composition], F 503 [same model] and
F 547 [the head on the right: same model]
Arles January 1889

LETTERS See under F 504
LITERATURE Scherjon and de Gruyter 1937, Arles
nr 149. W. Weisbach, Vincent van Gogh, volume 2,
1951, pp 130-4: the first version of the series LA
BERCEUSE, because the position of the hands is
different from all the other versions. J. N. Priou,
Revue des PTT de France 1955, pp 26-32: according
to the daughter, Marcelle Roulin, the art dealer
Ambroise Vollard bought all the van Goghs owned
by Joseph Roulin in 1895 for 450 francs; the
collection consisted of six paintings: the portraits of
her father, her mother, both her brothers Armand
and Camille, of herself and finally a still life of
oleander flowers in a vase
EDITORS' COMMENT See F 504
COLLECTION London, Walter H. Annenberg

F 506 [H 530] LA BERCEUSE: MME AUGUSTINE ROULIN

Canvas 93 × 73.4 [36½ × 29]
Signed and dated to the right: Vincent Arles 89
Annotated by Vincent to the right of the signature:
la Berceuse
Compare sketch in letter 592, F 504, F 505, F 507,
F 508 [same composition], 503 [same model] and
F 547 [the head on the right: same model]
Arles end January 1889
LETTERS See under F 504, especially letters 575, 576
and 592
LITERATURE Scherjon and de Gruyter 1937, Arles
nr 150
EDITORS' COMMENT See F 504
COLLECTION Chicago, The Art Institute of Chicago
[acquired 1926; Helen Birch Bartlett Memorial
Collection], inv nr 26.200, cat 1961, p 198

F 507 [H 527] LA BERCEUSE: MME AUGUSTINE ROULIN

Canvas 91 × 71.5 [35¾ × 28¼]
Compare sketch in letter 592, F 504, F 505, F 506,
F 508 [same composition], F 503 [same model] and
F 547 [the head on the right: same model]
Arles March 1889
LETTERS See under F 504, especially letter 582
LITERATURE Scherjon and de Gruyter 1937, Arles
nr 151
EDITORS' COMMENT See F 504
COLLECTION Amsterdam, Stedelijk Museum
[acquired 1945; gift of V. W. van Gogh], inv nr
A 965

F 508 [H 529] LA BERCEUSE: MME AUGUSTINE ROULIN

Canvas 92 × 72 [36¼ × 28¼]
Annotated by Vincent in lower right: la Berceuse
Compare sketch in letter 592, F 504, F 505, F 506,
F 507 [same composition], F 503 [same model] and
F 547 [the head on the right: same model]
Arles February-March 1889
LETTERS See under F 504
LITERATURE Scherjon and de Gruyter 1937, Arles
nr 152: letter B 21
EDITORS' COMMENT See F 504
COLLECTION Boston, Museum of Fine Arts
[acquired 1948; J. T. Spaulding bequest], inv
nr 48.548, cat 1955, p 29

F 509 LA BERCEUSE

Left out by Faille in his manuscript for the present
edition
See REJECTED WORKS

F 510

F 511

F 510 [H 532] BLOATERS ON A PIECE OF YELLOW PAPER

Canvas 33 × 41 [13 × 16¼]
Arles March 1889
LETTER 581 [24 March] 'I gave him [Signac] as a
keepsake a still life which had annoyed the good
gendarmes of the town of Arles, because it represented
two bloaters [harengs fumés], and as you know they,
the gendarmes, are called that.'
LITERATURE Scherjon and de Gruyter, Arles
nr 154
COLLECTION Paris, Mrs G. Signac

F 511 [H 709] ORCHARD IN BLOSSOM

Canvas 72.5 × 92 [28½ × 36¼]
Arles spring 1888
LITERATURE Scherjon and de Gruyter 1937, Saint
Rémy nr 24
EDITORS' COMMENT In the manuscript for this
edition Faille dated the painting Saint Rémy
September 1889 and connected it with letters
584, 603, 607 and 618. For stylistic reasons the
editors put it back in Arles and date it spring 1888.
COLLECTION Amsterdam, Rijksmuseum Vincent
van Gogh [Vincent van Gogh Foundation, inv
nr F 511]

F 513

F 518

F 512 ORCHARD IN BLOSSOM

Left out by Faille in his manuscript for the present edition
See REJECTED WORKS

F 513 [H 535] ORCHARD SURROUNDED BY CYPRESSES

Canvas 65 × 81 [25½ × 32]
Compare sketch in letter B 3, F 554 [same composition], F 399 [same orchard] and F 551 [companion piece]
Arles April 1888
LETTERS B 3 [probably 9 April] *'For that matter here is a sketch, the entrance to a Provençal orchard with its yellow fences, its enclosure of black cypresses (against the mistral), its characteristic vegetables of varying greens: yellow lettuces, onions, garlic, emerald leeks.'*
486 [probably 10 May] *'A big study without stretchers and another one on stretchers, in which there is a lot of stippling, are unfinished, which I regret, for the composition gave the general effect of the big orchards here surrounded by cypresses.'*
492 [probably 29 May] *'The study of the orchard you speak of – where there is a lot of stippling – is half of the principal subject for the scheme of decoration. The other half is the study of the same size, without stretchers.'*
LITERATURE Scherjon and de Gruyter 1937, Arles nr 19: letter B 3; belongs with F 551 and F 557 to the third decoration scheme of three orchards in bloom
COLLECTION Otterlo, Rijksmuseum Kröller-Müller, inv nr 298-17, cat van Gogh 1970, nr 207

F 514 [H 531] THE PLAIN OF LA CRAU WITH ORCHARD OF PEACH TREES

Canvas 65.5 × 81.5 [25¾ × 32]
Compare sketch in letter 583b
Arles April 1889
LETTERS 583 [early April] *'Just now I have on the easel an orchard of peach trees beside a road with the Alpille foothills in the background.'*
583b [to Signac; between 5 and 11 April] *'I have just come back with two studies of orchards. Here is a crude sketch of them – the big one is a poor landscape with little cottages, blue skyline of the Alpille foothills, sky white and blue. The foreground, patches of land surrounded by cane hedges, where small peach trees are in bloom – everything is small there, the gardens, the fields, the orchards, and the trees, even the mountains, as in certain Japanese landscapes, which is the reason why the subject attracted me.'*
584 [between 13 and 16 April] *'I have six studies of the spring, two of them big orchards.'*
600 [Saint Rémy about 9 July] *'Now for the subjects of these seven studies: ... "Peach Trees in Bloom" (Arles) ...'*
T 13 [29 July] *'I received your last consignment, which was in perfect condition ... the fields with the gardens in spring are very beautiful.'*
LITERATURE Scherjon and de Gruyter 1937, Arles nr 155: letter 583. D. Cooper, Zeichnungen und Aquarelle von Vincent van Gogh, 1954, nr 22: the same site as in drawing F 1484. D. Cooper, cat The Courtauld Collection, 1954, nr 86
COLLECTION London, Courtauld Institute Galleries [acquired 1932; The Home House Trustees], cat 1962, nr 33

F 515 [H 533] THE ORCHARD WITH VIEW OF ARLES

Canvas 50.5 × 65 [20 × 25½]
Compare sketch in letter 583b [same composition]
Arles April 1889
LETTERS 583b [to Signac; between 5 and 11 April] *'I have just come back with two studies of orchards.*

Here is a crude sketch of them ... The other landscape is nearly all green with a little lilac and gray – on a rainy day.'
600 [Saint Rémy about 9 July] *'I am putting in with them some more studies which are dry, but which are more studies from nature than subjects for pictures ... Now for the subjects of these seven studies: ... "Peach Trees in Bloom" (Arles) ...'*
LITERATURE Scherjon and de Gruyter 1937, Arles nr 158
COLLECTION Amsterdam, Rijksmuseum Vincent van Gogh [Vincent van Gogh Foundation, inv nr F 515]

F 516 [H 534] A VIEW OF ARLES

Canvas 72 × 92 [28¼ × 36¼]
Arles April 1889
LETTERS 600 [Saint Rémy about 9 July] *'Tomorrow I shall send a small roll of canvases by goods train. There are four, namely the following: 1. View of Arles – Orchards in Bloom ...'*
614 [after 16 November] *'As for the Vingtistes, here is what I'd like to exhibit: ...4. Orchard in Bloom (the one Tanguy is exhibiting just now), with a row of poplars across the canvas.'*
T 20 [16 November] *'At the moment there is one in the show window at Tanguy's, a view of the countryside in spring with poplars that run across the canvas in such a way that one can see neither the bottoms nor the tops of the trees.'*
614b [to Octave Maus; 20 November] *'It's a pleasure to accept your invitation to exhibit with the Vingtistes. Here you have the list of paintings I am reserving for you: ... 4. orchard in bloom (Arles) ...'*
LITERATURE Scherjon and de Gruyter 1937, Arles nr 159: letters 600 and 614. M.E. Tralbaut, Van Goghiana 1963, p 43: appears as nr 14 in the list of paintings of Vincent van Gogh owned by Mrs van Gogh-Bonger that were deposited with the widow of Tanguy in Paris, April 1894
COLLECTION Munich, Bayerische Staatsgemälde-sammlungen [acquired 1912; gift of Miss Amy Roth in memory of H. von Tschudi], inv nr 8671, cat 1966, p 43
Colorplate, p 339

F 517 [H 537] RED CHESTNUTS IN THE PUBLIC GARDEN AT ARLES

Canvas 72.5 × 92 [28½ × 36¼]
Arles May 1889
LETTERS 589 [2 May] *'I am doing an avenue of pink flowering chestnuts and a little cherry tree in flower and a wisteria plant and a path in the park splashed with light and shade.'*
600 [Saint Rémy about 9 July] *'Tomorrow I shall send a small roll of canvases by goods train. There are four, namely the following: ... 4. Red Chestnuts in the Jardin des Plantes in Arles ...'*
LITERATURE Scherjon and de Gruyter 1937, Arles nr 156
COLLECTION USA, Private Collection

F 518 [H 539] PORTRAIT OF A YOUNG GIRL AGAINST A PINK BACKGROUND

Canvas 51 × 49 [20 × 19¼]
Arles second half of 1888
LITERATURE Scherjon and de Gruyter 1937, Arles nr 65. Cat van Gogh 1966, Rijksmuseum Kröller-Müller, nr 220: the style of the portrait – similar to Miss Gachet at the piano [F 772] – points to Auvers; the description in letter 521 doesn't correspond very well with this painting. Cat van Gogh 1970, Rijks-museum Kröller-Müller, nr 220: Arles
EDITORS' COMMENT Faille connected this painting with passages in letters 521 and 529; which the editors do not agree.
COLLECTION Otterlo, Rijksmuseum Kröller-

F 517

F 514

F 515

F 516

F 519

Müller, inv nr 296-10, cat van Gogh 1970, nr 220

F 519 [H 536] THE COURTYARD OF THE HOSPITAL AT ARLES

Canvas 73 × 92 [28¾ × 36¼]
Compare drawing F 1467 [same site]
Arles April 1889
LETTERS W 11 [30 April] *'Notwithstanding this I am working, and I have just finished two pictures of the hospital, one of a ward ... And then, as a pendant, the inner court.'*
597 [between 30 June and 6 July] *'I still have some*

canvases in Arles which were not dry when I left ... The drawings seem to have little color this time, and the too-smooth paper is a little responsible for that. The "Weeping Tree" and the courtyard of "Hospital at Arles" have more color ...'
LITERATURE Scherjon and de Gruyter 1937, Arles nr 157
EDITORS' COMMENT The 'weeping tree' and hospital courtyard referred to in letter 597 were probably water colors, but water colors of these subjects have never been found.
COLLECTION Winterthur Oskar Reinhart
Colorplate, p 340

F 520

F 524

F 527

F 525

F 529

F 520 [H 538] THE OLD WILLOWS

Canvas 55 × 65 [21¾ × 25½]
Arles before May 1889
LETTER 600 [Saint Rémy about 9 July] '*I am putting
in with them some more studies which are dry, but
which are more studies from nature than subjects for
pictures…Now for the subjects of these seven
studies:…"Old Willows" (Arles)…*'
LITERATURE Scherjon and de Gruyter 1937, Arles
nr 160
COLLECTION Athens, Stavros S. Niarchos, exhib
cat 1957, nr 27

F 521 SELF PORTRAIT

Left out by Faille in his manuscript for the present
edition
See REJECTED WORKS

F 522 [H 425] SELF PORTRAIT IN FRONT OF
THE EASEL
Paris period; see after F 388 verso

F 523 [H 813] SELF PORTRAIT BEFORE HIS
EASEL

Left out by Faille in his manuscript for the present
edition
See REJECTED WORKS

F 524 [H 423] SELF PORTRAIT WITH PIPE
AND STRAW HAT

Canvas on pasteboard 42 × 31 [16½ × 12¼]
Arles summer 1888
LITERATURE Scherjon and de Gruyter 1937, p 28,
note 3: Paris, not Arles. Faille 1939, nr 432: Paris.
K. Bromig-Kolleritz, Die Selbstbildnisse Vincent
van Goghs, 1954, pp 108-9: Arles end of spring
1888. A. M. Hammacher, Vincent van Gogh:
Selbstbildnisse, 1960, p 11: Arles. F. Erpel, Die
Selbstbildnisse Vincent van Goghs, 1963, nr 33:
Arles
EDITORS' COMMENT In his manuscript for the
present edition Faille dates F 524 Paris 1887
COLLECTION Amsterdam, Rijksmuseum Vincent
van Gogh [Vincent van Gogh Foundation, inv
nr F 524]

F 525 [H 545] SELF PORTRAIT WITHOUT
BEARD

Canvas 40 × 31 [15¾ × 12¼]
Compare F 483 [this self portrait is hanging on the
wall there]
Arles September 1888
LETTER 540 [about 22 September] '*Mother's
photograph gave me very great pleasure, because you
can see that she is well, and because she still has such
a lively expression. But I do not care for it at all as a
real likeness; I have just painted my own portrait, in
my own ashen coloring, and unless we are painted in
color, the result is nowhere near a speaking likeness.
Just because I had taken a terrific amount of trouble
to get the combination of ashen and gray-pink tones,
I could not like the portrait in black and white.*'
LITERATURE Scherjon and de Gruyter 1937, Arles
nr 94. K. Bromig-Kolleritz, Die Selbstbildnisse
Vincent van Goghs, 1955, pp 22-4, 114: Saint Rémy
September 1889; portrait sent to his mother and
sister; letters 608, 612 and 618. A. M. Hammacher,
Vincent van Gogh: Selbstbildnisse, 1960, p 11.
F. Erpel, Die Selbstbildnisse Vincent van Goghs,
1963, nr 43
COLLECTION Bolligen, Switzerland, J. Körfer

F 526 [H 424] SELF PORTRAIT WITH STRAW
HAT
Paris period; see after F 388 verso

F 527 [H 547] SELF PORTRAIT WITH
BANDAGED EAR

Canvas 60 × 49 [23½ × 19¼]
Compare F 529 [also a self portrait with bandaged
ear]
Arles January 1889
LETTER 571 [17 January] '*I have another new one*
[self portrait] *for you too.*'
LITERATURE Scherjon and de Gruyter, Arles
nr 146: painted before the other version, F 529.
K. Bromig-Kolleritz, Die Selbstbildnisse Vincent
van Goghs, 1954, pp 21, 62, 113: painted between
7 and 17 January. D. Cooper, cat The Courtauld
Collection, 1955, nr 85. D. Cooper, Burlington
Magazine 1957, p 204; Cooper discovered in Paris
two Japanese prints, certified by Paul Gachet to
have belonged to Vincent van Gogh; one of these, a
print by Sato Torakiyo, has been used – though in a
very free way – in the background of the portrait;
this seems to dissipate the doubt expressed by some
students in 1955 about the authenticity of this
painting
EDITORS' COMMENT There is no evidence to
decide which of the two versions could be the first
one.
COLLECTION London, Courtauld Institute
Galleries, cat The Courtauld Collection, 1954,
nr 85

F 527a [formerly F 527bis] SELF PORTRAIT
WITH BANDAGED EAR

Left out by Faille in his manuscript for the present
edition
See REJECTED WORKS

F 528 [H 546] SELF PORTRAIT
Saint Rémy period; see after F 749

F 529 [H XII] SELF PORTRAIT WITH
BANDAGED EAR AND PIPE

Canvas 51 × 45 [20 × 17¾]
Compare F 527 [also a self portrait with bandaged
ear]
Arles January 1889
LETTER 571 [17 January] See F 527
LITERATURE J. G. Goulinat, l'Amour de l'Art
1925, pp 131-42. Scherjon and de Gruyter 1937,
Arles nr 145: second version; the first is F 527,
which still shows Vincent's shaken state of health as
described in letter 571. K. Bromig-Kolleritz, Die
Selbstbildnisse Vincent van Goghs, 1955, p 113.
D. Cooper, Burlington Magazine 1957, p 204:
affirms the opinion of Scherjon and de Gruyter.
F. Erpel, Die Selbstbildnisse Vincent van Goghs,
1963, nr 40
EDITORS' COMMENT See F 527
COLLECTION Chicago, Mr and Mrs Leigh
B. Block
Colorplate, p 358

F 530 [H 508] SELF PORTRAIT

Left out by Faille in his manuscript for the present
edition
See REJECTED WORKS

F 531 [H 778] THE PEASANT
Saint Rémy period; see after F 749

F 532 [H 559] THE ONE-EYED MAN

Canvas 56 × 36 [22 × 14¼]
Arles second half of 1888
LITERATURE Scherjon and de Gruyter 1937, Arles
nr 176. A. Bowness, exhib cat van Gogh London
[Hayward Gallery] 1968-9, nr 173: Saint Rémy
October 1889 [?]

COLLECTION Amsterdam, Rijksmuseum Vincent
van Gogh [Vincent van Gogh Foundation, inv
nr F 532]

F 533 [H 558] PORTRAIT OF A MAN

Canvas 65 × 54.5 [25½ × 21½]
Arles November 1888
LITERATURE Scherjon and de Gruyter 1937, Arles
nr 175. Cat van Gogh 1959, Rijksmuseum Kröller-
Müller, nr 219: Saint Rémy; letter T 33. Exhib cat
van Gogh Aix-en-Provence 1959, nr 48: Arles
winter 1888-9. D. Cooper remarked that the same
man also sat for Gauguin [cat collection Theo van
Gogh Amsterdam 1953, nr 92, as anonymous
portrait]. Cat van Gogh 1966, Rijksmuseum
Kröller-Müller, nr 219: Arles; the text of letter
T 33 is not decisive
EDITORS' COMMENT In his manuscript for the
present edition Faille dates F 533 Saint Rémy winter
1889-90. C. Nordenfalk, Konsthistorisk Tidskrift
1946, p 92 suggests that F 533 is identical with a
man's portrait exhibited in Christiania [Oslo] etc
1898, nr 63. The title AN ACTOR was given to this
picture for the first time in the catalogue of the
Sonderbund exhibition, Cologne 1912.
COLLECTION Otterlo, Rijksmuseum Kröller-
Müller [acquired 1912], inv nr 267-12, cat van Gogh
1970, nr 219
Colorplate, p 375

F 534 [H 549] THE SMOKER

Canvas 62 × 47 [24½ × 18½]
Arles summer 1888
LITERATURE Scherjon and de Gruyter 1937, Arles
nr 173
COLLECTION Merion, Pennsylvania, The Barnes
Foundation [acquired 1912]

F 535 [H 560] THE GIRL WITH THE RUFFLED
HAIR

Canvas 35.5 × 24.5 [14 × 9¾]
Compare drawing F 1507a [included in letter 501a:
same model]
Arles June 1888
LETTER 501a [to John Russell; about 27 June; in
English] '...*I began to draw on the very paper the
head of the dirty little girl...This dirty "mudlark" I
thought yet had a vague Florentine sort of figure like
the heads in the Monticelli pictures...*'
LITERATURE Scherjon and de Gruyter 1937, Arles
nr 177
COLLECTION Switzerland, Private Collection

F 532

F 533

F 534

F 535

F 536

F 537

F 538

F 544

F 548

I've worked at home on the study which I made a sketch of in Bernard's letter. I want to manage to get colors into it like stained glass windows, and a good, bold design.'
471 [about 24 March] *'I've had a setback with the sunset with figures and a bridge that I spoke of to Bernard. The bad weather prevented my working on the spot, and I've completely ruined it by trying to finish it at home.'*
LITERATURE Scherjon and de Gruyter 1937, Arles nr 181
EDITORS' COMMENT See F 397
COLLECTION Lysaker, Norway, J. E. Werenskiold

F 545 [H 562] THE MOWERS, ARLES IN THE BACKGROUND

F 545

Canvas 73 × 54 [28¾ × 21¼]
Compare drawings F 1490, F 1491 and F 1492 [same site]
Arles August 1888
LITERATURE Scherjon and de Gruyter 1937, Arles nr 166; letter 501. J. Rewald, Post-Impressionism, 1956, p 32: L. Anquetin's LANDSCAPE WITH A MOWER, painted in 1887 [reproduced p 35] inspired van Gogh to paint this composition. L. Gans, Museumjournaal December 1958, pp 85-93: Vincent wrote about his admiration for Anquetin's HARVEST to E. Bernard in letter B 7 from June 1888
COLLECTION Paris, Musée Rodin, cat 1938, nr 387

F 546 PORTRAIT OF PAUL GAUGUIN

Left out by Faille in his manuscript for the present edition
See REJECTED WORKS

F 547 [H 555] THE DANCE HALL

Canvas 65 × 81 [25½ × 32]
Arles October-November 1888
Compare sketch in letter 592, F 503, F 504, F 505, F 506, F 507 and F 508 [head on the right: same model]
LITERATURE Scherjon and de Gruyter 1937, Arles nr 93: letter 539. Åke Meyerson, Konsthistorisk Tidskrift 1947, p 141: the style of this painting is influenced by Bernard's BRETON WOMEN IN THE MEADOW [Musée d'Art Moderne, Paris], which Gauguin brought to Arles; the head on the right in three-quarter profile is that of Mme Roulin [note 7]. J. Leymarie, Van Gogh, 1951, p 117, nr 94: painted in the Folies Arlésiennes
COLLECTION Paris, Musée National du Louvre, inv nr RF 1950-9, cat Impressionnistes 1959, p 248

F 548 [H 556] A VIEW OF THE ARENA IN ARLES

Canvas 73 × 92 [28¾ × 36¼]
Arles October-November 1888
LITERATURE Iskusstwo 1905, 2. J. Touguenhold, Apollon 1914, p 39. Scherjon and de Gruyter 1937, Arles nr 101: letter B 3
COLLECTION Leningrad, Hermitage [acquired 1931], inv nr 6529, cat 1967, nr 64

F 547

F 549

F 549a

F 552

F 551

F 553

F 549 [H 554] INTERIOR OF A RESTAURANT
IN ARLES

Canvas 54 × 64.5 [21¼ × 25½]
Compare the sketchy version F 549a
Arles summer 1888
LITERATURE Scherjon and de Gruyter, Arles
nr 64: letters 521, 534 and 539. J. Leymarie, Van
Gogh, 1951, p 117, nr 95: this has been wrongly
called Restaurant Carrel. P. Leprohon, Tel fut van
Gogh, 1964, pp 414-5: probably the interior of the
restaurant next door to Vincent's 'yellow house'
COLLECTION Providence, Rhode Island, Murray
S. Danforth jr

F 549a INTERIOR OF A RESTAURANT IN
ARLES

Canvas 65.5 × 81 [25¾ × 32]
Compare the more finished version F 549
Arles summer 1888
LITERATURE Not in Faille 1928 or Scherjon and
de Gruyter 1937
COLLECTION Zurich, V. Margutti and Neuchâtel,
H. Vaucher

F 550 [H 561] THE OLD MILL IN THE RUE
MIREILLE, ARLES

Canvas 64.5 × 54 [25½ × 21¼]
Signed in lower right: Vincent
Arles September 1888
LETTER 535 [10 September] 'I have a study of an old
mill painted in broken tones like the oak tree on the
rock, that study you were saying you had had framed
along with the "Sower."'
LITERATURE Scherjon and de Gruyter 1937, Arles
nr 86. A. Tellegen, Museumjournaal January 1966,
p 45: Vincent seems to have exchanged this painting
for a water color by de Chamaillard now in the
Theo van Gogh Collection; letters B 18 and B 19
COLLECTION Buffalo, Albright-Knox Art Gallery
[acquired 1964; gift of A. Conger Goodyear]

F 551 [H 575] ORCHARD IN BLOSSOM WITH
YELLOW ENCLOSURE

Canvas 65 × 81 [25½ × 32]
Arles April 1888
Compare F 513 [companion piece]
LETTERS 486 [probably 10 May] and 492 [probably
29 May] See F 513
LITERATURE Scherjon and de Gruyter 1937, Arles
nr 21: letters 486, 492 and B 3: belongs with F 557
and F 513 to the third decoration scheme of three
orchards in bloom
COLLECTION New York, Private Collection

F 552 [H 577] THE ORCHARD: WHITE
BLOSSOMS AND VIOLET BRANCHES

Canvas 74 × 55 [29¼ × 21¾]
Signed in lower left: Vincent
Arles April 1888
LETTERS 478 [20 April] 'I have ten orchards now,
not counting three little studies, and one big one of a
cherry tree, which I've spoiled.'
B 4 [about 20 April] 'Yesterday I overpainted one
[canvas] of a cherry tree against a blue sky; the
young leaf shoots were orange and gold, the clusters
of flowers white, and that against the green-blue of
the sky was wonderfully glorious. Unfortunately
there is rain today which prevents my returning to the
charge.'
LITERATURE Scherjon and de Gruyter 1937, Arles
nr 22: letters 478 and B 4
COLLECTION New York, Metropolitan Museum
of Art [acquired 1956; Mr and Mrs Henry
Ittleson jr Purchase Fund]

F 553 [H 576] A CORNER OF THE ORCHARD

Canvas 55×65 [21¾×25½]
Signed in lower left: Vincent
Meant to form part of a series, presumably with
F 405 and F 556
Arles April 1888
LETTER 474 [probably 9 April] '*At the moment I am
working on some plum trees, yellowish-white, with
thousands of black branches.*'
LITERATURE Scherjon and de Gruyter 1937, Arles
nr 16: letters 474 and 476
EDITORS' COMMENT See F 405
COLLECTION Edinburgh, National Gallery of
Scotland [acquired 1960; The Maitland Gift], inv
nr 2217, cat The Maitland Gift 1963, p 36

F 554 [H 581] THE ORCHARD IN FLOWER

Canvas 32×40 [12¾×15¾]
Compare sketch in letter B 3, F 513, F 554 [same
composition] and F 397 [same orchard]
Arles early April 1888
LETTERS B 3 [probably 9 April] See F 513
478 [20 April] See F 399
LITERATURE Scherjon and de Gruyter 1937, Arles
nr 25: letter 478
EDITORS' COMMENT See F 399
COLLECTION New York, Mrs Richard J. Bernhard

F 555 [H 578] THE PINK ORCHARD

Canvas 65.5×80.5 [24¾×31¾]
Signed in lower right: Vincent
Meant to form part of a series with F 403 and F 404
Arles March-April 1888
LETTERS 471 [about 24 March] '*I have just finished
a group of apricot trees in bloom in a little orchard of
fresh green.*'
477 [between 10 and 14 April] See F 403
485 [10 May] '*In this batch there are the pink orchard
on coarse canvas...*'
LITERATURE Scherjon and de Gruyter 1937, Arles
nr 13: letter 471
COLLECTION Amsterdam, Rijksmuseum Vincent
van Gogh [Vincent van Gogh Foundation, inv
nr F 555]

F 556 [H 579] APRICOT TREES IN BLOSSOM

Canvas 55×65.5 [21¾×25¾]
Signed in lower right: Vincent
Meant to form part of a series, presumably with
F 405 and F 553
Arles March-April 1888
LETTER 474 [probably 9 April] '*I have another
orchard, as good as the pink peach trees, apricot trees
of a very pale pink.*'
LITERATURE Scherjon and de Gruyter 1937, Arles
nr 18: letter 474
EDITORS' COMMENT See F 405
COLLECTION Private Collection

F 557 [H 580] ALMOND TREE IN BLOSSOM

Canvas 50.5×38 [20×15]
Arles March-April 1888
LITERATURE Scherjon and de Gruyter 1937, Arles
nr 20: letter 477
EDITORS' COMMENT See F 399
COLLECTION Amsterdam, Rijksmuseum Vincent
van Gogh [Vincent van Gogh Foundation, inv
nr F 557]

F 550

F 554

F 555

F 556

F 557

F 558

F 561

F 558 [H 563] HARVEST IN PROVENCE

Canvas 50 × 60 [19¾ × 23½]
Arles summer 1888
LITERATURE Scherjon and de Gruyter 1937, Arles
nr 171
COLLECTION Jerusalem, The Israel Museum
[acquired 1966; gift of Hanadiv, a Rothschild
Foundation], inv nr IM 504/135

F 559 [H 564] WHEAT STACKS WITH REAPER

Canvas 73 × 93 [28¾ × 36½]
Compare F 560
Arles summer 1888
LITERATURE J. G. Goulinat, l'Amour de l'Art
1925, pp 131-42. Scherjon and de Gruyter 1937,
Arles nr 47: letter 501; final study, the first draft
being F 560. C. Derkert, H. Eklund and
O. Reutersvärd, Konsthistorisk Tidskrift 1946,
pp 121-30: study which served as example for F 560.
Museum News [Toledo] 1969, p 80
COLLECTION Toledo, Ohio, Toledo Museum of
Art [acquired 1935; gift of Edward Drummond
Libbey], cat 1939, p 250

F 560 [H 565] WHEAT STACKS WITH REAPER AND PEASANT WOMAN

Canvas 53 × 66 [21 × 26]
Arles summer 1888
Compare F 559
LITERATURE Scherjon and de Gruyter 1937, Arles
nr 46: letter 501; first draft, the final study being
F 559. C. Derkert, H. Eklund and O. Reutersvärd,
Konsthistorisk Tidskrift 1946, pp 121-30: a replica
of F 559, of much weaker quality, possibly executed
two years later at Auvers. C. Nordenfalk and
Å. Meyerson, Konsthistorisk Tidskrift 1946, pp
130-3: done presumably soon after the middle of
December 1888 under direct influence of Gauguin.
M. M. van Dantzig, Vincent?, 1952, pp 102-7: a
fake from about 1900
EDITORS' COMMENT The editors accept the
possibility of doubt as to the painting's authenticity,
a suggestion rejected by Derkert.
COLLECTION Stockholm, National Museum
[acquired 1914], inv nr 1802, cat 1958, p 80

F 561 [H 566] THE WHEATFIELD

Canvas 52.7 × 64.2 [20¾ × 25¼]
Compare drawings F 1488 and F 1489
Arles summer 1888
LITERATURE Scherjon and de Gruyter 1937, Arles
nr 168: letter 501
COLLECTION Honolulu, Academy of Arts
[acquired 1946; gift of Mrs Richard A. Cooke]

F 562 [H 567] GREEN EARS OF WHEAT

Canvas 54 × 65 [21¼ × 25½]
Arles summer 1888
LITERATURE Scherjon and de Gruyter 1937, Arles
nr 169: letter 501
EDITORS' COMMENT Left out by Faille in his
manuscript for the present edition. The editors do
not doubt the authenticity of F 562.
COLLECTION Jerusalem, The Israel Museum
[acquired 1966; gift of Hanadiv, a Rothschild
Foundation]

F 563 [H 550] LANDSCAPE WITH A STRAW-HEAP

Canvas 64 × 52.5 [25¼ × 20¾]
Arles June 1888
LITERATURE Scherjon and de Gruyter 1937, Arles
nr 48: letter 501. Cat van Gogh 1959, Rijksmuseum
Kröller-Müller, nr 227: Saint Rémy. Cat van Gogh

F 566

1970, Rijksmuseum Kröller-Müller, nr 227: difficult to decide whether F 563 is from Arles or Auvers
EDITORS' COMMENT Possibly painted in Saint Rémy a year later than June 1888.
COLLECTION Otterlo, Rijksmuseum Kröller-Müller [acquired before 1919], inv nr 301-00, cat van Gogh 1970, nr 227

F 564 [H 541] THE WHEATFIELD

Canvas 50 × 61 [19¾ × 24]
Arles early summer 1888
LITERATURE Scherjon and de Gruyter 1937, Arles nr 165: letter 501
COLLECTION Amsterdam, P. and N. de Boer Foundation

F 565 [H 542] THE FARM GATE

Canvas 46 × 61 [18 × 24]
Compare F 425, drawings F 1478 [same composition]
Arles June 1888
LITERATURE Scherjon and de Gruyter 1937, Arles nr 170
COLLECTION New York, Estate of Mrs Ailsa Mellon Bruce

F 566 [H 553] THE ENTRANCE OF THE PUBLIC GARDEN

Canvas 72.5 × 91 [28½ × 35¾]
Arles September 1888
LETTERS 538 [18 September] '*At the moment I am working on another square size 30 canvas, another garden or rather a walk under plane trees, with the green turf, and black clumps of pines.*'
539 [18 September] '*I wrote to you already, early this morning, then I went away to go on with a picture of a garden in the sunshine.*'
LITERATURE Scherjon and de Gruyter 1937, Arles nr 91: letters 538 and 539
EDITORS' COMMENT The passages from letters 538 and 539, cited by Faille, do not necessarily refer to this picture.
COLLECTION Washington, DC, The Phillips Collection, cat 1952, p 42

F 559

F 562

F 560

F 563

F 564

F 565

F 567

F 569

F 568

F 572

F 573

F 567 [H 571] A WALK NEAR ARLES

Canvas 61 × 50 [24 × 19¾]
Compare sketch in letter B 6 and drawing F 1518a
[same site]
Arles second half of June 1888
LETTER B 6 [about 24 June] '*I am very eager to
know what you have been working at lately – I myself
am still doing nothing but landscapes – enclosed a
sketch...*'
LITERATURE Scherjon and de Gruyter 1937, Arles
nr 164: letter 501
COLLECTION West Germany, The City of Coburg

F 568 [H 551] THE ALLEY OF LES ALYSCAMPS

Canvas 89 × 72 [35 × 28¼]
Compare F 486, F 487 [same site] and F 569 [same
subject]
Arles end October 1888
LETTERS B 19a [after 1 November] See F 486
589 [2 May 1889] '*Here are the ones I think worth
putting on stretchers out of the batch I'm sending:
... Les Aliscamps (Alley of the tombs), Ditto...*'
LITERATURE Scherjon and de Gruyter 1937, Arles
nr 124: letter 589
EDITORS' COMMENT See F 486
COLLECTION New York, Mr and Mrs Edwin
C. Vogel

F 569 [H 552] THE ALLEY OF LES ALYSCAMPS

Canvas 92 × 73.5 [36¼ × 29]
Compare F 486, F 487 [same site] and F 568 [same
subject]
Arles end October 1888
LETTERS B 19a [after 1 November] See F 486
589 [2 May 1889] See F 568
LITERATURE Scherjon and de Gruyter 1937, Arles
nr 123: letter 589
EDITORS' COMMENT See F 486
COLLECTION Zollikon, Switzerland, Mrs
A. Mettler-Weber

F 570 [H 588] THE LANGLOIS BRIDGE

Canvas 49.5 × 64 [19½ × 25¼]
Compare F 397, F 400, F 571, drawing F 1470, water
color F 1480 [same site] and drawing F 1471 [same
composition]
Arles May 1888
LETTER 488 [13 May] '*I have done two new studies, a
bridge and the side of a high road.*'
LITERATURE Scherjon and de Gruyter, Arles
nr 31: letter 488
EDITORS' COMMENT See F 397
COLLECTION Cologne, Wallraf-Richartz Museum
[acquired 1911], inv nr WRM 1197, cat 1964, p 45

F 571 [H 587] THE LANGLOIS BRIDGE

Canvas 60 × 65 [23¼ × 25½]
Signed in lower left: Vincent, Pont de l'Anglois
Compare F 397, water color F 1480 [same
composition], F 400, F 570, drawings F 1470 and
F 1471 [same site]
Arles April 1888
LETTERS 474 [probably 9 April] See F 397
476 [between 10 and 14 April] '*Then after dinner I
set to work on the same picture that Tersteeg is to
have* [the 'Pont de l'Anglais'] *for you.*'
477 [between 10 and 14 April] '*The Pont de l'Anglais
for you is coming along well, and will be better than
the study, I think.*'
486 [probably 10 May] '*As for the copies of these
two studies, I think that the bridge is better than
Tersteeg's...*'
LITERATURE Scherjon and de Gruyter 1937, Arles
nr 12: letters 476, 477 and 486; repetition of F 397.
J. Lassaigne, Arts 19 July 1946, p 8: review of the

F 571

exhibition Paris 1946, where F 571 was exhibited.
F. Elgar, Le Pont de l'Anglois, 1948. J. Leymarie,
Van Gogh, 1951, p 109, nr 72: the name of the
bridge is derived from the name of the former
bridge-guard, Langlois
EDITORS' COMMENT See F 397
COLLECTION Paris, Private Collection

F 572 [H 540] WILLOWS AT SUNSET

Canvas on cardboard 31.5 × 34.5 [12½ × 13½]
Arles autumn 1888
LETTER possibly 545 [7 October] '*Yesterday I
painted a sunset.*'
LITERATURE Scherjon and de Gruyter 1937, Arles
nr 103: letter 545
COLLECTION Otterlo, Rijksmuseum Kröller-
Müller, inv nr 291-10, cat van Gogh 1970, nr 228

F 573 [H 570] TRUNK OF AN OLD YEW TREE

Canvas 91 × 71 [35¾ × 28]
Compare sketch in letter 558b [in the English
edition of the letters only]
Arles October 1888
LETTER 558b [28 October] '*Further I have made
another study of a plowed field with the stump of an
old yew tree.*'
LITERATURE Scherjon and de Gruyter 1937, Arles
nr 97: letter 589 [2 May 1889]
COLLECTION Upperville, Virginia, Mr and Mrs
Paul Mellon

F 574 [H 568] PLOWED FIELDS [THE
FURROWS]

Canvas 72.5 × 92 [28½ × 36¼]
Compare sketch in letter 541a [in the English
edition of the letters only]
Arles September 1888
LETTERS 541 [about 23 September] '*Milliet today
was pleased with what I had done – the "Plowed
Fields"; generally he does not like what I do, but
because the color of the lumps of earth is as soft as a
pair of sabots, it did not offend him, with the forget-
me-not blue sky flecked with white clouds.*'
541a [about 26 or 27 September] '*... but all the same
I have just finished a size 30 canvas representing a
plowed field, done in the sunny intervals.*'
543 [about 29 September] '*I should not be surprised
if you liked the "Starry Night" and the "Plowed
Fields," there is a greater quiet about them than in
the other canvases.*'
B 18 [about 29 September] '*I am terribly absorbed in
decorating my house; ... Then the "Starry Night,"
further the "Vineyard," then the "Furrows."*'
553b [to E. Boch; 4 October] '*Then plowed fields; a
scenery with nothing but lumps of earth, the furrows
the color of an old wooden shoe under a forget-me-not
blue sky with white cloud flocks.*'
LITERATURE Scherjon and de Gruyter 1937, Arles
nr 96: letters 541, 543 and B 18
COLLECTION Amsterdam, Rijksmuseum Vincent
van Gogh [Vincent van Gogh Foundation, inv
nr F 574]

F 570

F 574

F 575

F 576

F 575a

F 580

F 575 [H 585] LANDSCAPE UNDER A STORMY SKY

Canvas 60 × 73 [23½ × 28¾]
Arles spring 1888
LITERATURE Scherjon and de Gruyter 1937, Arles
nr 100: letters 600 and B 3
COLLECTION Gstaad, Switzerland, Louis Franck

F 575a THE SOWER: OUTSKIRTS OF ARLES
IN THE BACKGROUND

Canvas 33 × 40 [13 × 15¾]
Arles September 1888
LITERATURE Not in Faille 1928, Scherjon and de
Gruyter 1937 or Faille 1939
EDITORS' COMMENT The editors hesitated to
include this painting before some doubts concerning
its provenance could be cleared up. Research by
V. W. van Gogh finally determined, however, that
the painting was in fact sold in 1920 by Mrs van
Gogh-Bonger to the Montross Gallery.
COLLECTION Los Angeles, California, Armand
Hammer

F 576 [H 569] LANDSCAPE NEAR ARLES

Canvas 23 × 34 [9 × 13½]
Compare drawing F 1474
Arles September 1888
LETTER B 18 [about 29 September] 'Moreover I
should have ... last of all a little landscape of nothing
at all, in which there is only some space.'
LITERATURE Scherjon and de Gruyter 1937, Arles
nr 109: letter B 18. A. Bowness, exhib cat van Gogh
London [Hayward Gallery] 1968-9, nr 126: June
1888
COLLECTION Amsterdam, Rijksmuseum Vincent
van Gogh [Vincent van Gogh Foundation, inv
nr F 576]

F 577 THE GARDEN

Left out by Faille in his manuscript for the present
edition
See REJECTED WORKS

F 578 [H 572] GARDEN BEHIND A HOUSE

Canvas 65 × 54 [25½ × 21¼]
Signed in lower left: Vincent
Compare drawing F 1456
Arles August 1888
LETTER 519 [8 August] 'The little cottage garden
in vertical format has in itself amazing colors: the
dahlias are a rich and somber purple; the double row
of flowers is pink and green on one side, and orange
with hardly any leaves on the other. In the midst a
white dwarf dahlia, and a little pomegranate with
flowers of the most vivid reddish-orange, with
yellowish-green fruits. The ground gray, the tall
reeds, "canes," blue-green, the fig trees emerald, the
sky blue, the houses white with green windows and
red roofs, in the morning full in the sunshine, in the
evening drowned in the shadows thrown by the fig
trees and the reeds.'
B 18 [about 29 September] 'Moreover I should have
a study of a little garden with multicolored flowers ...'
LITERATURE Scherjon and de Gruyter 1937, Arles
nr 120: letters 593 and B 18
COLLECTION Paris, Private Collection

F 579 [H 582] BUSHES

Canvas 73 × 92 [28¾ × 36¼]
Signed in lower left: Vincent
Arles August 1888
LETTER 524 [14 or 15 August] 'There is ... and others
as well, which have not come off at all and are
unfinished, especially one big landscape with

F 579

brushwood.'
LITERATURE Scherjon and de Gruyter 1937, Arles
nr 71: letter 524. Meisterwerke aus der Eremitage,
Französische Malerei des 19. und 20. Jahrhunderts,
1967, nr 67: Saint Rémy May 1889; letter 591
COLLECTION Leningrad, Hermitage [acquired
1930], inv nr 6511, cat 1967, nrs 67 and 68
Colorplate, p 376

F 580 [H 592] ROSEBUSHES IN FLOWER

Canvas 33 × 42 [13 × 16½]
Compare water color F 1526
Arles 1888
LITERATURE Scherjon and de Gruyter 1937, Arles
nr 29: letters 488 and 519
COLLECTION Tokyo, National Museum of
Western Art [acquired 1959; gift of the French
government], inv nr P-299, cat 1961

F 581 [H 696] POPPIES IN THE FIELD
Saint Rémy period; see after F 749

F 582 [H 586] A GRASSY NOOK

Canvas 44.5 × 49 [17½ × 19¼]
Arles April 1889
LITERATURE Scherjon and de Gruyter 1937, Arles
nr 187
COLLECTION Formerly Ascona, Werner von der
Schulenburg [acquired 1923]
Present owner unknown

F 583 [H 584] PASTURE IN BLOOM
Paris period; see after F 388 verso

F 584 [H 583] A FIELD OF YELLOW FLOWERS

Canvas on pasteboard 34.5 × 53 [13¼ × 20¾]
Arles April 1889
LITERATURE Scherjon and de Gruyter 1937, Arles
nr 188
COLLECTION Formerly Zurich, Fritz and Peter
Nathan Art Gallery
Present owner unknown

F 585 [H 708] OLIVE YARD: BLUE SKY
Saint Rémy period; see after F 749

F 582

F 584

F 578

F 588

F 592

F 591

F 594

F 600

F 586 [H 651] OLIVE YARD: ORANGE SKY
Saint Rémy period; see after F 749

F 587 [H 650] OLIVE PICKING IN ORCHARD:
ORANGE SKY
Saint Rémy period; see after F 749

F 588 [H 602] STILL LIFE: WILD FLOWERS IN
A VASE

Canvas 65 × 54 [25½ × 21¼]
Arles 1888
LITERATURE Scherjon and de Gruyter 1937, Arles
nr 193
EDITORS' COMMENT Date and period uncertain.
Possibly painted in Saint Rémy.
COLLECTION New York, Mr and Mrs Averell
Harriman

F 589 [H 601] STILL LIFE: FLOWERS IN A VASE
Auvers period; see after F 824

F 590 STILL LIFE: ASTERS

Left out by Faille in his manuscript for the present
edition
See REJECTED WORKS

F 591 [H 593] STILL LIFE: BASKET WITH
DAISIES

Canvas 33 × 42 [13 × 16½]
Signed in lower left: Vincent
Arles summer 1888
LITERATURE Scherjon and de Gruyter 1937, Arles
nr 192
COLLECTION Upperville, Virginia, Mr and Mrs
Paul Mellon

F 592 [H 604] STILL LIFE: ONE-EARED VASE
WITH ZINNIAS

Canvas 64 × 49.5 [25¼ × 19½]
Compare sketches in letters 409 and B 5, F 410,
F 593, F 594 and F 600 [same vase]
Arles summer 1888
LITERATURE Scherjon and de Gruyter 1937, Arles
nr 121: autumn 1888; letter 589 [of 1889].
M.E.Tralbaut, Vincent en de keramiek, 1955, p 26
COLLECTION California, Private Collection

F 593 [H 594] STILL LIFE: ONE-EARED VASE
WITH OLEANDERS AND BOOKS

Canvas 60 × 73 [23½ × 28¾]
Compare sketches in letters 489 and B 5, F 410,
F 592, F 594 and F 600 [same vase]
The book on top is Zola's La Joie de Vivre
Arles August 1888
LETTER 524 [14 or 15 August] 'One of these days I
hope to make a study of oleanders.'
LITERATURE Scherjon and de Gruyter, Arles
nr 80: letter 524 [this painting or F 594]
COLLECTION New York, The Metropolitan
Museum of Art [Metropolitan Museum and Mr
and Mrs John L. Loeb], inv nr 62.24

F 594 [H 605] STILL LIFE: VASE WITH
OLEANDERS

Canvas 56 × 36 [22 × 14¼]
Signed in lower left: Vincent
Compare sketches in letters 489 and B 5, F 410,
F 592, F 593 and F 600 [same vase]
Arles August 1888
LETTER 524 [14 or 15 August] See F 593
LITERATURE Scherjon and de Gruyter, Arles
nr 79: letter 524 [this painting or F 593]. M.E.Tral-
baut, Vincent van Gogh en de keramiek, 1955, p 26

COLLECTION Formerly La Bachellerie, France, Jean Dauberville
Present owner unknown [painting probably stolen in 1944]

F 595 [H 595] STILL LIFE: PINK ROSES
Saint Rémy-Auvers period; see after F 824

F 596 [H 303] STILL LIFE: VASE WITH KENTRANTHUS, LYCHNIS AND DIANTHUS
Paris period; see after F 388 verso

F 597 [H 805] DOG-ROSES OR BRANCHES OF WILD-BRIAR
Saint Rémy-Auvers period; see after F 824

F 598 [H 600] STILL LIFE: VASE WITH CARNATIONS
Auvers period; see after F 824

F 599 [H 804] STILL LIFE: VASE WITH THISTLES
Auvers period; see after F 824

F 600 [H 603] STILL LIFE: ONE-EARED VASE WITH WILD FLOWERS

Canvas 55 × 46 [21¾ × 18]
Compare sketches in letters 489 and B 5, F 410 [the same vase and cup], F 592, F 593 and F 594 [the same vase]
Arles May 1888
LETTER 489 [probably 19 May] 'I have done two still lifes this week ... The other still life is the majolica pot with wild flowers.'
LITERATURE Vincent van Gogh, Lettres à Bernard, 1911, plate XCII. M.E. Tralbaut, Vincent van Gogh en de keramiek, 1955, p 26
COLLECTION Merion, Pennsylvania, The Barnes Foundation

F 601 [H 591] STILL LIFE: THE IRIS

Paper mounted on canvas 62.5 × 48 [24¾ × 19]
Arles April 1889
LITERATURE Scherjon and de Gruyter 1937, Arles nr 183
COLLECTION Ottawa, National Gallery of Canada [acquired 1955], inv nr 6294, cat Paintings and Sculpture 1959, volume 2, p 30

F 593

F 601

F 602

F 604

F 602 [H 599] STILL LIFE: QUINCE PEARS

Canvas 46 × 59.5 [18 × 23½]
Arles autumn 1888
LITERATURE Scherjon and de Gruyter 1937, Arles
nr 141: letters 569 and 571
COLLECTION Dresden, Staatliche Gemäldegalerie
[acquired 1920], inv nr 2593, cat 1966, p 56

F 603 [H 326] STILL LIFE: GRAPES
Paris period; see after F 388 verso

F 604 [H 596] STILL LIFE: DRAWING BOARD
WITH ONIONS ETC

Canvas 50 × 64 [19¾ × 25¼]
Arles January 1889
LETTER 569 [7 January] '*I am going to set to work
again tomorrow. I shall begin by doing one or two
still lifes so as to get back into the habit of painting.*'
LITERATURE Scherjon and de Gruyter 1937, Arles
nr 140: letters 569 and 571. C. Nordenfalk, Journal
of the Warburg and Courtauld Institute 1947,
pp 139 ff: the date of the painting can be fixed
shortly after Vincent's return from the hospital by
the objects rendered in this still life; the book,
F. V. Raspail's *Annuaire de la Santé*, gives a
prescription which in letter 570 of 9 January 1889
Vincent mentions as being very useful against
insomnia
COLLECTION Otterlo, Rijksmuseum Kröller-
Müller, inv nr 288-13, cat van Gogh 1970, nr 223
Colorplate, p 427

F 605 [H 589] A CRAB UPSIDE DOWN

Canvas 38 × 45.5 [15 × 18]
Compare F 606 [same motif]
Arles winter 1888-9
LITERATURE Scherjon and de Gruyter 1937, Arles
nr 143: letters 569 and 571
COLLECTION Amsterdam, Rijksmuseum Vincent
van Gogh [Vincent van Gogh Foundation, inv
nr F 605]

F 606 [H 590] TWO CRABS [probably one crab,
seen from above and below]

Canvas 47 × 61 [18½ × 24]
Compare F 605 [same motif]
Arles winter 1888-1889
LITERATURE Scherjon and de Gruyter 1937, Arles
nr 142: letters 569 and 571
COLLECTION Formerly Paris, Marquis de Ganay
Present owner unknown

F 607 [H 597] A PAIR OF WOODEN SHOES

Canvas 32.5 × 40.5 [12¾ × 16]
Arles end 1888
LITERATURE Scherjon and de Gruyter 1937, Arles
nr 179. A. Bowness, exhib cat van Gogh London
[Hayward Gallery] 1968-9, nr 143: Arles January
1889 [?]
COLLECTION Amsterdam, Rijksmuseum Vincent
van Gogh [Vincent van Gogh Foundation, inv
nr F 607]

F 606

REDATED TO ARLES

F 290 [H 371] LANDSCAPE WITH SNOW

Canvas 38 × 46 [15 × 18]
Arles February 1888
LITERATURE J. B. de la Faille, Der Cicerone 1927,
pp 101-2 [with reproduction]. Faille 1928, nr 290:
Paris. Faille 1939, nr 371: Paris. F. Elgar, Van
Gogh, 1958, pp 77, 306: Arles February 1888
EDITORS' COMMENT See F 126a
COLLECTION New York, J. K. Thannhauser
Foundation

F 384 [H 598] STILL LIFE: A BASKET OF LEMONS

Canvas 53 × 63 [20¾ × 24¾]
Arles May 1888
LETTER B 5 [second half of May] *'Then I have
another still life, lemons in a basket against a yellow
background.'*
LITERATURE A. Plasschaert, Onze Kunst 1904,
part 2, p 152. Faille 1928, nr 384: Paris. Scherjon
and de Gruyter 1937, Arles nr 34 letter B 5. Faille
1939, nr 598: Arles May 1888; letter B 5. Cat van
Gogh 1966, Rijksmuseum Kröller-Müller, nr 216:
letter B 5 probably does not refer to F 384, which has
a green background and shows more fruits than
just lemons
COLLECTION Otterlo, Rijksmuseum Kröller-
Müller, inv nr 268-09, cat van Gogh 1970, nr 216

F 386 [H 283] STILL LIFE: POTATOES

Canvas 39 × 47 [15¼ × 18½]
Arles March 1888
LITERATURE Faille 1928, nr 386: Paris. Scherjon
and de Gruyter 1937, Arles nr 182. Faille 1939,
nr 283: Arles 1888. Cat van Gogh 1959, Rijks-
museum Kröller-Müller, nr 215: Arles spring 1888
COLLECTION Otterlo, Rijksmuseum Kröller-
Müller, inv nr 272-17, cat van Gogh 1970, nr 215

F 290

F 605

F 607

F 384

F 386

F 608

F 610

F 611

F 612

F 613

SAINT RÉMY PERIOD

F 608 [H 606] IRISES

Canvas 71 × 93 [28 × 36¾]
Signed in lower right: Vincent
Saint Rémy May 1889
LETTERS 591 [mid-May] *'I am working on two others – some violet irises … two subjects taken from the garden.'*
600 [about 9 July] *'I am putting in with them some more studies which are dry … Now for the subjects of these seven studies: "Irises" – … size 30 canvases.'*
T 16 [5 September 1889] *'Now I still have to tell you that the exhibition of the Indépendants is open, and that your two pictures are there, the "Irises" and "The Starlit Night."'*
T 19 [22 October] *'The exhibition of the Indépendants is over and I've got your Irises back; it is one of your good things.'*
LITERATURE Scherjon and de Gruyter 1937, Saint Rémy nr 1. J. Leymarie, Van Gogh, 1951, p 124, nr 114: letters 593 and T 20
COLLECTION New York, Private Collection

F 609 [H 607] A CORNER IN THE GARDEN OF SAINT PAUL'S HOSPITAL: IVY

Canvas 92 × 72 [36¼ × 28¼]
Signed in lower left: Vincent
Compare sketch in letter 592 and drawing F 1522
Saint Rémy May-June 1889
LETTERS 592 [22 May] *'Here is a new size 30 canvas, once again as commonplace as a chromo in the little shops, which represents the eternal nests of greenery for lovers. Some thick tree trunks covered with ivy …'*
594 [9 June] *'The shrubbery with the ivy is completely finished.'*
600 [about 9 July] *'Tomorrow I shall send a small roll of canvases by goods train. There are four, namely the following: …2. Ivy …'*
T 13 [29 July] *'I received your last consignment, which was in perfect condition, and which I think extremely beautiful … The one with the underbrush and the trees overgrown with ivy … very beautiful.'*
T 19 [22 October] *'It seems to me that you are stronger when you paint true things like that … or the underbrush with the ivy …'*
614 [after 16 November] *'As for the Vingtistes, here is what I'd like to exhibit: …3. The Ivy, perpendicular.'*
614b [to Octave Maus; 20 November] *'It's a pleasure to accept your invitation to exhibit with the Vingtistes. Here you have the list of paintings I am reserving for you: …3. Ivy.'*
LITERATURE Scherjon and de Gruyter 1937, Saint Rémy nr 3: letter 600
COLLECTION Formerly Paris, Baron de Rothschild
Present owner unknown

F 610 [H 608] DEATH'S-HEAD MOTH

Canvas 33 × 24 [13 × 9½]
Compare sketch in letter 592, drawings F 1523 [same moth], F 1613 and F 1650 recto [same plants]
Saint Rémy May-June 1889
LETTERS 592 [22 May] *'Yesterday I drew a very big, rather rare night moth, called the death's-head, its coloring of amazing distinction, black, gray, cloudy white tinged with carmine or vaguely shading off into olive-green; it is very big. In order to paint it I should have had to kill it, and that would have been a pity, it was such a beautiful creature. I will send you the drawing along with some other drawings of plants.'*
T 12 [16 July] *'I thank you for your letters and the fine drawings you sent me … the butterfly and the branch of eglantine are very beautiful too; simple in color and very beautifully drawn.'*
LITERATURE Scherjon and de Gruyter 1937, Saint

F 609

Rémy nr 5. A. Bowness, exhib cat van Gogh London [Hayward Gallery] 1968-9; nr 153: clearly the emperor moth, and not the death's-head, as Vincent calls it
EDITORS' COMMENT F 610 must have been executed after drawing F 1523, as Vincent suggests in letter 592.
COLLECTION Amsterdam, Rijksmuseum Vincent van Gogh [Vincent van Gogh Foundation, inv nr F 610]

F 611 [H 609] MOUNTAINOUS LANDSCAPE BEHIND SAINT PAUL'S HOSPITAL

Canvas 70.5 × 88.5 [27¾ × 34¾]
Compare F 722 and drawing F 1547
Saint Rémy June 1889
LETTERS 594 [9 June] '*I am working on two landscapes (size 30 canvases), views taken in the hills, one is the country that I see from the window of my bedroom. In the foreground, a field of wheat ruined and hurled to the ground by the storm. A boundary wall and beyond the gray foliage of a few olive trees, some huts and the hills. Then at the top of the canvas a great white and gray cloud floating in the azure.*'
607 [19 September] '*In return I am sending you with the portrait the following canvases:... Field of Green Wheat... Altogether I think nothing in it at all good except the "Field of Wheat"...*'
LITERATURE Scherjon and de Gruyter 1937, Saint Rémy nr 6: letter 607. J. Rohde, Journal fra en Rejse i 1892, 1955, pp 104-12, 196: the author bought the painting in 1892 at the exhibition in The Hague
COLLECTION Copenhagen, Ny Carlsberg Glyptotek [on loan since 1915 from Statens Museum for Konst; acquired 1905], cat 1961, nr 945

F 612 [H 612] THE STARRY NIGHT

Canvas 73 × 92 [28¾ × 36¼]
Compare drawings F 1540 [same composition] and F 1541 verso [same church]
Saint Rémy June 1889
LETTERS 595 [18 June] '*Enfin, I have... also a new study of a starry sky.*'
607 [19 September] '*In return I am sending you with the portrait the following canvases:... Study of Night... The "Olives" with a white cloud... and the night effect are exaggerations from the point of view of arrangement, their lines are warped as in old wood.*'
T 19 [22 October] '*I understand quite well what it is which preoccupies you in your new canvases, like the village in the moonlight...*'
LITERATURE Scherjon and de Gruyter 1937, Saint Rémy nr 9: letter 607
COLLECTION New York, Museum of Modern Art [acquired 1941; L. P. Bliss bequest], inv nr 472.41, cat 1948, nr 280
Colorplate, p 428

F 613 [H 616] THE CYPRESSES

Canvas 95 × 73 [37½ × 28¾]
Compare sketch in letter 596 and drawing F 1525
Saint Rémy June 1889
LETTERS 596 [25 June] '*Two studies of cypresses of that difficult bottle-green hue; I have worked their foregrounds with thick layers of white lead, which gives firmness to the ground... I think that of the two canvases of cypresses, the one I am making this sketch of will be the best.*'
608 [28 September] '*So I will send them at the next opportunity – or rather they are leaving today with other canvases – as follows: Wheat Field, Study of Cypresses...*'
LITERATURE Scherjon and de Gruyter 1937, Saint

F 615

Rémy nr 10: letter 608. M. M. van Dantzig, Vincent?, 1952, pp 95-6: genuine. M. Pease, Art News Annual 1950, pp 91-6: careful analysis of the technique and of the structure of the paint medium
COLLECTION New York, Metropolitan Museum of Art [acquired 1949; Rogers Fund], inv nr 49.30, cat European Paintings 1954, p 43

F 614 [H 816] THE CYPRESSES

Left out by Faille in his manuscript for the present edition
See REJECTED WORKS

F 615 [H 611] WHEATFIELD WITH CYPRESSES

Canvas 72.5 × 91.5 [28½ × 36]
Compare F 717, F 743 and drawing F 1538
Saint Rémy July 1889

LETTER 608 [28 September] '*So I will send them at the next opportunity – or rather they are leaving today with other canvases – as follows:... Wheat Field and Cypresses, ditto...*'
LITERATURE Scherjon and de Gruyter 1937, Saint Rémy nr 47: letter 608. D. Cooper, cat The Courtauld Collection, 1954, nr 87: September-October 1889
COLLECTION London, National Gallery [on loan since 1961 from the Tate Gallery; acquired 1923], cat The Courtauld Collection, 1954, nr 87
Colorplate, p 445

F 616 THE CYPRESSES

Left out by Faille in his manuscript for the present edition
See REJECTED WORKS

F 620

F 622

F 617 [H 614] THE WHEATFIELD BEHIND
SAINT PAUL'S HOSPITAL WITH A REAPER

Canvas 72 × 92 [28¼ × 36¼]
Compare F 618, F 619 and drawing F 1546
Saint Rémy September 1889
LETTERS 604 [4 or 5 September] *'Work is going
pretty well – I am struggling with a canvas begun some
days before my indisposition, a "Reaper"; the study
is all yellow, terribly thickly painted, but the subject
was fine and simple. For I see in this reaper – a vague
figure fighting like a devil in the midst of the heat to
get to the end of his task – I see in him the image of
death, in the sense that humanity might be the wheat
he is reaping. So it is – if you like – the opposite of that
sower I tried to do before. But there's nothing sad in
this death, it goes its way in broad daylight with a sun
flooding everything with a light of pure gold. Look,
there I am at it again, but I don't let go my hold, and
with a new canvas I shall try again.'*
607 [19 September] *'The other canvases, the
"Reaper," etc, are not dry.'*
608 [28 September] *'So I will send them at the next
opportunity – or rather they are leaving today with
other canvases – as follows: ... Reaper ditto ...'*
LITERATURE Scherjon and de Gruyter 1937, Saint
Rémy nr 21 : letters 600, 604, 607, 608 and B 21. Cat
van Gogh 1959, Rijksmuseum Kröller-Müller,
nr 244 : begun in June and completed in September;
letter 596
COLLECTION Otterlo, Rijksmuseum Kröller-
Müller, inv nr 308-12, cat van Gogh 1970, nr 244

F 618 [H 613] THE WHEATFIELD BEHIND
SAINT PAUL'S HOSPITAL AT THE FALL OF
THE DAY WITH A REAPER

Canvas 74 × 92 [29¼ × 36¼]
Compare F 617, F 619 and drawing F 1546
Saint Rémy early July 1889
LETTERS 597 [between 30 June and 4 July] *'The
latest one I've started is the "Wheat Field," in which
there is a little reaper and a big sun. The canvas is all
yellow except for the wall and the background of
violet-tinted hills.'*
600 [about 9 July] *'I'm sorry not to be able to put the
wheat field with the reaper into this package.'*
608 [28 September] *'Now as for the "Reaper" – first I
thought that the large-sized duplicate that I am
sending you was not bad – but afterwards, when the
days of mistral and rain came, I preferred the canvas
done from nature, which seemed rather strange to me.'*
B 21 [between 16 November and 8 December] *'Have
you seen a study of mine with a little reaper, a yellow
wheat field and a yellow sun? It isn't it yet, however, I
have attacked that devilish problem of the yellows in
it again. I'm speaking of the one with the heavy
impasto, done on the spot, and not of the replica with
hatchings, in which the effect is weaker.'*
LITERATURE Scherjon and de Gruyter 1937, Saint
Rémy nr 20. J. Leymarie, Van Gogh, 1951, p 127,
nr 121 : F 619 is a replica of F 618. A. Bowness,
exhib cat van Gogh London [Hayward Gallery]
1968-9, nr 158 : late June-early July 1889
EDITORS' COMMENT The passage in letter 608
proves that Vincent did one of the reapers at the
site and that the other ones are duplicates. F 618
makes the impression of being the one done
directly from nature.
COLLECTION Amsterdam, Rijksmuseum Vincent
van Gogh [Vincent van Gogh Foundation, inv
nr F 618]
Colorplate, p 446

F 619 [H 632] THE WHEATFIELD BEHIND
SAINT PAUL'S HOSPITAL WITH A REAPER

Canvas 59.5 × 73 [23½ × 28¾]
Compare F 617, F 618 and drawing F 1546
Saint Rémy before 28 September 1889

LETTER 608 [28 September] '*So I will send them at the next opportunity – or rather they are leaving today with other canvases – as follows: ... Reaper, ditto ... Soon I shall send you some smaller canvases with the four or five studies that I want to give Mother and our sister. These studies are drying now, they are size 10 and 12 canvases, small copies of ... the "Reaper" ...*'
LITERATURE Scherjon and de Gruyter 1937, Saint Rémy nr 22: letter 608; larger replica of F 618.
M. E. Tralbaut, exhib cat van Gogh Essen 1957, nr 338: letter B 21
EDITORS' COMMENT Vincent made a smaller copy of one of the REAPERS before 28 September to give to his mother or his sister, but he speaks of size 10 and 12 canvases, whereas F 619 is size 20. It remains uncertain, therefore, whether this is the painting for his mother or sister.
COLLECTION Essen, Museum Folkwang [acquired 1922], inv nr G 62, cat 1961, nr 62

F 620 [H 617] THE CYPRESSES

Canvas 92 × 73 [36¼ × 28¾]
Compare F 621, drawings F 1524 and F 1525a
Saint Rémy June 1889, finished February 1890
LETTERS 596 [25 June] See F 613
597 [between 30 June and 4 July] '*I have a canvas of cypresses with some ears of wheat, some poppies, a blue sky like a piece of Scotch plaid, the former painted with a thick impasto like the Monticellis, and the wheat field in the sun, which represents the extreme heat, very thick too ...*'
B 21 [between 16 November and 8 December] '*My ambition is limited to ... a cypress – the latter, for instance, by no means easy to do.*'
626 [11 February 1890] '*I think you will like the canvas for Mr Aurier; it is in a terribly thick impasto and worked over like some Monticellis; I have kept it for almost a year.*'
626a [to Albert Aurier; 11 February] '*In the next batch that I send to my brother, I shall include a study of cypresses for you, if you will do me the favor of accepting it in remembrance of your article. I am still working on it at the moment, as I want to put in a little figure ... The study I have set aside for you represents a group of them in the corner of a wheat field during a summer mistral ... You will see that this constitutes something like the combination of tones in those pretty Scotch tartans of green, blue, red, yellow, black ...*'
629 [29 April] '*Then the cypresses are for Mr Aurier.*'
T 33 [3 May] '*The picture for Aurier is one of the finest you have done so far; it has the richness of a peacock's tail.*'
LITERATURE Scherjon and de Gruyter 1937, Saint Rémy nr 11: letters 596, 626 and 629. Cat van Gogh 1959, Rijksmuseum Kröller-Müller, nr 233: letters 626a and T 33
COLLECTION Otterlo, Rijksmuseum Kröller-Müller, inv nr 307-00, cat van Gogh 1970, nr 233

F 621 [H 618] THE CYPRESSES

Canvas 42 × 26 [16½ × 10¼]
Compare F 620, drawings F 1524 and F 1525a
Saint Rémy February 1890
LITERATURE Scherjon and de Gruyter 1937, Saint Rémy nr 163. A. Bowness, exhib cat van Gogh London [Hayward Gallery] 1968-9, nr 169: Saint Rémy late September-October 1889 [?]
EDITORS' COMMENT This work seems to be a small copy of F 620, which was sent to Aurier. It was executed after the two figures had been added to F 620.
COLLECTION Amsterdam, Rijksmuseum Vincent van Gogh [Vincent van Gogh Foundation, inv nr F 621]

F 622 [H 619] THE ALPILLES WITH DARK HUT

Canvas 73 × 93 [28¾ × 36¾]
Saint Rémy July 1889
LETTERS 600 [about 9 July] '*The last canvas I have done is a view of mountains with a dark hut at the bottom among some olive trees.*'
601 [about 17 August] '*While I have no extravagant liking for Rod's book, all the same I have made a canvas of the passage where he speaks of the mountains and the dark huts.*'
602 [probably 3 or 4 September] '*You will soon see a canvas of a hovel in the mountains, which I did under the influence of that book of Rod's.*'
607 [19 September] '*In return I am sending you with the portrait the following canvases: ... The Mountain... there is something sad in it which is healthy, and that is why it does not bore me. Perhaps that is true of the "Mountain" too. They will tell me that mountains are not like that and that there are black outlines of a finger's width. But after all it seemed to me it expressed the passage in Rod's book – one of the very rare passages of his in which I found something good – about a desolate country of somber mountains, among which are some dark goatherds' huts where sunflowers are blooming.*'
T 38 [23 June 1890] '*In the first place I went to the Salon with De Bock [a slip of the pen for Eugène Boch] yesterday; he came to lunch with us, and then we looked at your pictures. He likes them very much, and he gives me the impression of understanding them. As you told me that you would be glad to exchange a picture with him, when I saw that he preferred the canvas you did after reading the book by Rod, I told him he could take that one in exchange for a picture of his.*'
644 [Auvers 24 June] '*I am glad that Bock [here too Boch is intended] made that exchange with me, for I thought that, being friends, they really paid a comparatively big price for the other canvas.*'
LITERATURE Scherjon and de Gruyter 1937, Saint Rémy nr 14: letters 601, 602 and 607
EDITORS' COMMENT The title of the book by Rod is *Le sens de la vie* [see letter W 13]. The painting which Vincent got in exchange from Eugène Boch is LA NUIT DE L'AGRAPPE À FRAMERIES, BORINAGE, exhib cat Theo van Gogh, Amsterdam-Otterlo 1960, nr 16
COLLECTION New York, Thannhauser Foundation

F 623 [H 620] WOODEN SHEDS

Canvas 45.5 × 60 [18 × 23¾]
Saint Rémy August 1889
LITERATURE Scherjon and de Gruyter 1937, Saint Rémy nr 178
COLLECTION Formerly Paris, Georges Renand Present owner unknown

F 617

F 618

F 619

F 621

F 623

F 624

F 624 [H 621] HALF-LENGTH OF AN ANGEL

Canvas 54 × 64 [21¼ × 25¼]
Saint Rémy November 1889
LETTERS T 10 [16 June] *'The other day a sketch by Rembrandt was sold at a public auction; I wish you could have seen it. It is the figure of the angel Gabriel, standing, as he is in the heaven of his etching "The Annunciation to the Shepherds." What a marvel! The color has remained quite clear ...'*
601 [about 17 August] *'Thank you especially for that etching after Rembrandt.'*
602 [probably 3 or 4 September] *'Thank you once more for the lovely etching after Rembrandt. I would very much like to know the picture and to know in which period of his life he painted it.'*
LITERATURE Scherjon and de Gruyter 1937, Saint Rémy nr 166. Exhib cat van Gogh Munich 1956, nr 147: letters 596 and 601; the original was in the Sellar collection in London, sold in Paris 6 June 1889, cat nr 57, L'ANGE RAPHAEL, a painting ascribed to Rembrandt. Vincent painted his work from the reproduction in the catalogue, engraved by C. Courtry
EDITORS' COMMENT The picture of the angel is described in C. Hofstede de Groot, Kritisches Verzeichnis, volume 6, 1915: Rembrandt nr 28. The original is not by Rembrandt.
COLLECTION Formerly London, Knoedler Art Gallery
Present owner unknown

F 625

F 626

F 625 [H 622] LANDSCAPE WITH PLOWMAN

Canvas 49 × 62 [19¼ × 24½]
Compare sketch in letter 602
Saint Rémy early September 1889
LETTERS 602 [probably 3 or 4 September]
'Yesterday I began to work a little again – on a thing that I see from my window – a field of yellow stubble that they are plowing, the contrast of the violet-tinted plowed earth with the strips of yellow stubble, background of hills.'
618 [before 8 December] *'Among the studies you will find the following which are for Mother and our sister:..."Plowing"...'*
LITERATURE Scherjon and de Gruyter 1937, Saint Rémy nr 16: letter 618

EDITORS' COMMENT There is no evidence that F 625 is to be identified with the study mentioned in letter 618.
COLLECTION Sale New York [Parke-Bernet] 25 February 1970, nr 13
Present owner unknown

F 625a [formerly F 625bis; H 630] RISING MOON: HAYCOCKS

Left out by Faille in his manuscript for the present edition
See REJECTED WORKS

F 627

F 629

F 626 [H 624] SELF PORTRAIT

Canvas 57 × 43.5 [22½ × 17¼]
Saint Rémy September 1889
LETTERS 604 [4 or 5 September] *'I am working on two portraits of myself at this moment – for want of another model – because it is more than time I did a little figure work. One I began the day I got up; I was thin and pale as a ghost. It is dark violet-blue and the head whitish with yellow hair, so it has a color effect.'*
607 [19 September] *'I have another one [self portrait] which is an attempt made when I was ill...I have tried to make it simple. Show it to old Pissarro when you see him.'*
W 14 [19 September] *'I painted two pictures of myself lately, one of which has rather the true character, I think, although in Holland they would probably scoff at the ideas about portrait painting that are*

germinating here.'
LITERATURE Scherjon and de Gruyter 1937, Saint Rémy nr 28: letter 607. K. Bromig-Kolleritz, Die Selbstbildnisse Vincent van Goghs, 1955, pp 21-2, 113: letter 605. A. M. Hammacher, Vincent van Gogh: Selbstbildnisse, 1960, pp 18-9. F. Erpel, Die Selbstbildnisse Vincent van Goghs, 1963, nr 41
COLLECTION New York, John Hay Whitney
Colorplate, p 463

F 627 [H 748] SELF PORTRAIT

Canvas 65 × 54 [25½ × 21¼]
Saint Rémy September 1889
LETTERS 604 [4 or 5 September] *'I am working on two portraits of myself at this moment – for want of another model ... But since then I have begun another one, three-quarter length on a light background.'*
605 [between 6 and 10 September] *'I have done the portrait of the attendant ... This makes a rather curious contrast with the portrait I have done of myself, in which the look is vague and veiled, whereas he has something military in his small quick black eyes.'*
607 [19 September] *'I am sending you my own portrait today, you must look at it for some time; you will see, I hope, that my face is much calmer, though it seems to me that my look is vaguer than before. I have another one which is an attempt made when I was ill, but I think this will please you more, and I have tried to make it simple. Show it to old Pissarro when you see him.'*
W 14 [19 September] See F 626
638 [3 June 1890] *'I am working at his portrait ... It has the same sentiment as the self portrait I took when I left for this place.'*
LITERATURE Scherjon and de Gruyter 1937, Saint Rémy nr 116 and p 24: early May 1890; letter 638. M. Florisoone, Musées de France 1949, pp 143-9: dates the portrait September 1889 for reasons of style; not mentioned in the letters. Otto Kurz, Burlington Magazine 1950, p 240: discusses the confusion concerning the date. J. Leymarie, Van Gogh, 1951, p 135, nr 150: possibly painted in Paris between 17 and 21 May 1890. K. Bromig-Kolleritz, Die Selbstbildnisse Vincent van Goghs, 1955, pp 24, 25, 114: Saint Rémy May 1890. A. M. Hammacher, Vincent van Gogh: Selbstbildnisse, 1960, pp 20-2: mentions the controversy in dating this portrait; the opinions vary from Paris to Saint Rémy and Auvers; he rejects Paris in favor of Saint Rémy. F. Erpel, Die Selbstbildnisse Vincent van Goghs, 1963, nr 45
COLLECTION Paris, Musée National du Louvre [acquired 1949; gift of Paul and Marguerite Gachet], inv nr RF 1949-17, cat Impressionnistes 1959, nr 156
Colorplate, p 464

F 628 HARVEST

Left out by Faille in his manuscript for the present edition
See REJECTED WORKS

F 629 [H 623] PORTRAIT OF TRABU, AN ATTENDANT OF SAINT PAUL'S HOSPITAL

Canvas 61 × 46 [24 × 18¼]
Saint Rémy between 4 and 10 September 1889
LETTERS 604 [4 or 5 September] *'Yesterday I began the portrait of the head attendant, and perhaps I shall do his wife too, for he is married and lives in a little house a few steps away from the establishment. A very interesting face, there is a fine etching by Legros, representing an old Spanish grandee, if you remember it, that will give you an idea of the type ... This afternoon I have been working on the portrait of the attendant, which is getting on.'*
605 [between 6 and 10 September] *'I have done the*

portrait of the attendant, and I have a duplicate of it for you.'
T 33 [3 May 1890] *'The guard and the other fellow with his swollen face are extraordinary ...'*
LITERATURE Scherjon and de Gruyter 1937, Saint Rémy nr 31. J. Leymarie, Van Gogh, 1951, p 128, nr 125: letter T 33, only replicas are known of the paintings of Trabu and his wife [F 631]; the originals seem to be lost
EDITORS' COMMENT The first version is unknown.
COLLECTION Solothurn, Switzerland, Mrs G. Dübi-Müller [acquired April 1908]
Colorplate, p 481

F 630 [H 625] PIETÀ [after Delacroix]

Canvas 73 × 60.5 [28¾ × 23¾]
Compare F 757
Saint Rémy September 1889
LETTERS 605 [between 6 and 10 September] *'So this last time during my illness an unfortunate accident happened to me – that lithograph of Delacroix's "Pietà," along with some other sheets, fell into some oil and paint and was ruined. I was very distressed – then in the meantime I have been busy painting it, and you will see it someday. I made a copy of it on a size 5 or 6 canvas; I hope it has feeling ... if you could see me working, my brain so clear and my fingers so sure that I have drawn that "Pietà" by Delacroix without taking a single measurement, and yet there are those four hands and arms in the foreground in it – gestures and twisted postures not exactly easy or simple.'*
607 [19 September] *'It is odd, just when I was making that copy of the "Pietà" by Delacroix ...'*
W 14 [19 September] *'... which is why I copied one picture by Delacroix and some others by Millet. The Delacroix is a "Pietà" ...'*
LITERATURE Scherjon and de Gruyter 1937, Auvers nr 189. D. Cooper, exhib cat van Gogh London 1947-8, nr 90: Auvers. P. Gachet, Deux amis des impressionistes, 1956, p 119
EDITORS' COMMENT F 630 and F 757 are done from the lithograph by C. Nanteuil after a painting by Delacroix of 1850 [Robaut nr 1173]. In his manuscript Faille accepted Cooper's dating of this version to Auvers. For stylistic reasons the editors leave the painting in the Saint Rémy period, however.
COLLECTION Amsterdam, Rijksmuseum Vincent van Gogh [Vincent van Gogh Foundation, inv nr F 630]
Colorplate, p 482

F 631 [H 637] PORTRAIT OF THE WIFE OF THE ATTENDANT TRABU

Canvas on panel 64 × 49 [25¼ × 19¼]
Saint Rémy September 1889
LETTERS 605 [between 6 and 10 September] *'I have done the portrait of the attendant, and I have a duplicate of it for you ... I have made him a present of it and I shall do his wife too if she wants to sit. She is a faded woman, an unhappy, resigned creature of ·small account, so insignificant that I have a great longing to paint that dusty blade of grass.'*
607 [19 September] *'I have done a woman's portrait – the attendant's wife – which I think you would like. I have done a duplicate of it which is less good than the one from life. And I am afraid they will take the latter; I should have liked you to have it. It is pink and black.'*
W 14 [19 September] *'The other day I finished the portrait of a woman upward of forty years old, an insignificant woman. The withered face is tired, pockmarked – a sunburned, olive-colored complexion, black hair. A faded black dress relieved by a geranium of a delicate pink, and the background in a neutral tone, between pink and green.'*
LITERATURE Scherjon and de Gruyter 1937, Saint Rémy nr 34. J. Leymarie, Van Gogh, 1951, nr 125:

see under F 629
EDITORS' COMMENT One version is lost. It is uncertain whether this is the original or the replica.
COLLECTION Formerly Otto Krebs, Holzdorf
Present owner unknown

F 630

F 631

F 633

F 634

F 638

F 639

F 640

F 632 [H 686] THE PLOW AND THE HARROW
[after Millet]

Canvas 72 × 92 [28¼ × 36¼]
Saint Rémy January 1890
LETTERS 623 [about 10 January] '*This week I am going to start on Millet's snow-covered field...Then there will be six canvases in a series, and I can tell you, I have put much thought into the disposition of the colors while working on these last three of the "Hours of the Day"...For the moment I am busy with the Millets, but this means that I shall not lack things to work on.*'
629 [29 April] '*You will see that first of all there are canvases after Millet.*'
T 33 [3 May] '*The copies after Millet are perhaps the best things you have done yet...*'
LITERATURE Scherjon and de Gruyter 1937, Saint Rémy nr 92: letter 623. J. Leymarie, Van Gogh, 1951, p 131, nr 135: letters 629 and T 33. F. Novotny, Alte und neue Kunst, 1953, nr 2: reproduction of Delauney's print in the van Gogh collection, divided in squares by Vincent. Idem, Festschrift Kurt Badt, 1961, pp 224-5: the snow is Vincent's invention; the original Millet painting in Vienna shows only bluish frost
EDITORS' COMMENT Copied from an etching by A. Delauney, after the painting LA HERSE by J. F. Millet, of which one version is in the National Galerie in Berlin, the other in the Kunsthistorisches Museum in Vienna, cat 1966, nr 89.
COLLECTION Amsterdam, Rijksmuseum Vincent van Gogh [Vincent van Gogh Foundation, inv nr F 632]

F 633 [H 698] THE GOOD SAMARITAN
[after Delacroix]

Canvas 73 × 60 [28¾ × 23½]
Saint Rémy May 1890
LETTER 632 [between 5 and 8 May] '*I have also tried a copy of the "Good Samaritan" by Delacroix.*'
LITERATURE Scherjon and de Gruyter 1937, Saint Rémy nr 109. F. Novotny, Festschrift Kurt Badt, 1961, p 219: letter 626
EDITORS' COMMENT Copied from a lithograph by J. Laurens after Delacroix' painting of 1850 [Robaut nr 1168].
COLLECTION Otterlo, Rijksmuseum Kröller-Müller, inv nr 311-12, cat van Gogh 1970, nr 250

F 634 [H 646] SHEEP SHEARERS [after Millet]

Canvas 43 × 29 [17 × 11½]
Saint Rémy about 19 September 1889
LETTERS 607 [19 September] '*I have now seven copies out of the ten of Millet's "Travaux des Champs." I can assure you that making copies interests me enormously...Today I tried the "Women Shearing Sheep" in a color scheme ranging from lilac to yellow. They are little canvases of about size 5.*'
623 [about 10 January 1890] '*For you know that I already did the "Travaux des Champs" last summer. Now I haven't sent these reproductions–you'll see them someday–because they were more groping attempts than these, but all the same they have been very useful to me for the "Hours of the Day."*'
629 [29 April] See F 632
LITERATURE Scherjon and de Gruyter 1937, Saint Rémy nr 37: cite letters 607, 623 and 629 for all the copies after Millet. F. Novotny, Festschrift Kurt Badt, 1961, pp 213-30
EDITORS' COMMENT Copied from a wood-engraving by J. A. Lavieille after Millet's series LES TRAVAUX DES CHAMPS. The other paintings of Vincent's series after Millet are F 670, F 687, F 688, F 692, F 693, F 696, F 697, F 698 and F 700. As follows from letter 607, F 634 was the eighth of the series. Of the ten small copies after the TRAVAUX DES CHAMPS two are later than 19 September 1889, and

one of them, F 670, dates from February 1890 [see letter 626].
COLLECTION Amsterdam, Rijksmuseum Vincent van Gogh [Vincent van Gogh Foundation, inv nr F 634]

F 635 [H 644] QUARRY NEAR SAINT RÉMY

Canvas 52 × 64 [20½ × 25¼]
Saint Rémy July 1889
LETTERS 601 [about 17 August] '*This new attack, my boy, came on me in the fields, on a windy day, when I was busy painting. I will send you the canvas. I finished it in spite of it.*'
607 [19 September] '*In return I am sending you with the portrait the following canvases: ...Entrance to a Quarry...I rather like the "Entrance to a Quarry" – I was doing it when I felt this attack coming on – because to my mind the somber greens go well with the ocher tones; there is something sad in it which is healthy, and that is why it does not bore me.*'
LITERATURE Scherjon and de Gruyter 1937, Saint Rémy nr 15: letter 601. J. Leymarie, Van Gogh, 1951, pp 125-6, nr 117: July 1889
COLLECTION New York, Mrs Morton Palmer and George A. Forman

F 636 [H 755] FIELD WITH POPPIES IN ALFALFA
Auvers period; see after F 824

F 637 [H 640] THE MULBERRY TREE

Canvas 54 × 65 [21¼ × 25½]
Saint Rémy October 1889
LETTERS 609 [about 5 or 6 October] '*I have some studies, among others a mulberry tree all yellow on stony ground, outlined against the blue of the sky, in which study I hope you will see that I am on Monticelli's track.*'
618 [before 8 December] '*The rest are mostly studies of autumn, and I think that the best is the yellow mulberry tree against a bright blue sky...*'
W 16 [after 8 December] '*As for mulberry trees, there are a good many of them here. I painted one some time ago, when its dense foliage was of a magnificent yellow color against a very blue sky. On a white stony field with the sunshine from behind.*'
LITERATURE Scherjon and de Gruyter 1937, Saint Rémy nr 53: letter 618
COLLECTION Los Angeles, California, Mr and Mrs Norton Simon

F 638 [H 643] TWO POPLARS ON A ROAD THROUGH THE HILLS

Canvas 61 × 45.5 [24 × 18]
Compare F 639
Saint Rémy October 1889 or shortly later
LETTERS 609 [about 5 or 6 October] '*I have a study of two yellowing poplars against a background of mountains...*'
630 [1 or 2 May 1890] '*So Gauguin and Guillaumin, both of them, want to exchange something for the landscape of the Alpilles. Well, there are two of them, only I think that the one done last, which I have just sent you, is done with more decision and is truer in expression.*'
LITERATURE Scherjon and de Gruyter, Saint Rémy nr 57: letters 617 and 630
COLLECTION Cleveland, The Cleveland Museum of Art [acquired 1958; Leonard C. Hanna bequest], inv nr 58.32, cat In memoriam L. C. Hanna jr 1958, nr 15

F 639 [H 817] TWO POPLARS ON A ROAD THROUGH THE HILLS

Canvas 55 × 45 [21¾ × 17¾]
Compare F 638

Saint Rémy October 1889
LITERATURE Faille 1928, nr 639 [in Corrigenda, on an insert]: false. J. B. de la Faille, Les faux van Gogh, 1930, p 8, nr 26, plate VIII: false; compare F 638. W. J. de Gruyter, Elsevier's Geïllustreerd Maandschrift 1930, pp 65-7: genuine; the painting has certificates of authenticity by J. Meier-Graefe, H. P. Bremmer and J. Havelaar. W. Scherjon, Art News 1930, pp 14-5: genuine. H. A. Bull, International Studio August 1931, p 50. C. Veth, Schoon Schip!, [1932], pp 37, 53-64: judged authentic by H. P. Bremmer, W. Steenhoff, J. Havelaar, W. J. de Gruyter, J. Meier-Graefe [with reproductions of the certificates], the restorers A. M. de Wild and J. C. Traas; photocopy of the result of a dactyloscopic investigation by C. M. Garnier reproduced. W. Scherjon, Catalogue des Tableaux par Vincent van Gogh décrits dans ses Lettres, 1932, nr 56: letters 610 and 622. Scherjon and de Gruyter 1937, Saint Rémy nr 56. Faille 1939, nr 817: Saint Rémy October 1889; letters 609, 622 and 630
EDITORS' COMMENT None of the editors but W. J. de Gruyter agree with Faille, who accepted F 639 in the 1939 edition and in his manuscript for the present edition. The other editors do not consider the painting an authentic work by van Gogh. The only editors who have seen the painting are W. J. de Gruyter and A. M. Hammacher, who saw it in 1930.
COLLECTION Kurashiki, Japan, Museum of Fine Arts of Ohara

F 640 [H 642] THE PARK OF SAINT PAUL'S HOSPITAL

Canvas 64.5 × 49 [25½ × 19¼]
Compare F 731 and water color F 1535 [same site]
Saint Rémy October 1889
LETTER 610 [mid-October] '*I also have two views of the park and the asylum, where this place looked very pleasing. I tried to reconstruct the thing as it might have been, simplifying and accentuating the haughty, unchanging character of the pines and cedar clumps against the blue.*'
LITERATURE Scherjon and de Gruyter 1937, Saint Rémy nr 152: cite letters 608 and 609 for all the studies of autumn effects
EDITORS' COMMENT Faille connected this painting with a passage from letter 609, which the editors, however, refer to F 642.
COLLECTION Geneva, Private Collection [acquired 1963]

F 632

F 635

F 637

F 641

F 642

F 645

F 646

F 648

F 641 [H 649] WHEATFIELD WITH PEASANT
BEARING A SHEAF

Canvas 73 × 92 [28¾ × 36¼]
Saint Rémy October 1889
LETTERS B 20 [first half of October] 'For instance,
there is also a size 30 canvas with plowed fields,
broken lilac, and a background of mountains rising
to the very height of the picture; so nothing but rough
fields and rocks, with a thistle and dried grass in a
corner, and a little fellow, violet and yellow.'
610 [mid-October] 'I have just brought back a canvas
on which I have been working for some time,
representing the same field again as in the "Reaper."
Now it is clods of earth and the background of
parched land, then the rocks of the Alps. A bit of
green-blue sky with a little white and violet cloud. In
the foreground a thistle and some dry grass. A
peasant dragging a truss of straw in the middle. It is
again a harsh study, and instead of being almost
entirely yellow, it makes a picture almost entirely
violet. Broken violet and neutral tints. But I am
writing you because I think this will complement the
"Reaper" and will make clearer what that is. For the
"Reaper" looks as though it were done at random,
and this will give it balance.'
621 [3 January 1890] 'Today I sent off some canvases,
as follows: "Plowed field" with background of
mountains – it is the same field as the reaper's of last
summer and can be a pendant to it; I think that one
will set off the other.'
LITERATURE Scherjon and de Gruyter 1937, Saint
Rémy nr 58: letter 621
COLLECTION Indianapolis, Indianapolis Museum
of Art [gift in memory of Daniel W. and Elizabeth
C. Marmon], cat The Marmon Memorial
Collection 1948, pp 32-5

F 642 [H 647] THE GARDEN OF SAINT PAUL'S
HOSPITAL

Canvas 73 × 60 [28¾ × 23¾]
Saint Rémy October 1889
LETTER 609 [about 5 or 6 October] 'That said, I tell
you that we are having some superb autumn days and
that I am taking advantage of them…I have a study
of two yellowing poplars against a background of
mountains and a view of the park here, an autumn
effect in which the drawing is a little more naïve and
more – home-felt.'
LITERATURE Scherjon and de Gruyter 1937, Saint
Rémy nr 156
EDITORS' COMMENT See F 640
COLLECTION Switzerland, Private Collection

F 643 [H 648] SAINT PAUL'S HOSPITAL

Canvas 90 × 71 [35½ × 28]
Saint Rémy October 1889
LITERATURE Scherjon and de Gruyter 1937, Saint
Rémy nr 4: letter 600
EDITORS' COMMENT The style of the painting is
close to F 642 and the colors of the trees likewise
indicate a probable dating in autumn [1889].
COLLECTION Los Angeles, California, Mr and
Mrs Norton Simon

F 644 [H 654] THE MAN IS AT SEA [after
Virginie Demont-Breton]

Canvas 66 × 51 [26 × 20]
Saint Rémy October 1889
LETTER 610 [mid-October] 'I have copied that
"Woman with a Child sitting by a Hearth," by
Mme Dumont [sic]-Breton, almost all in violet. I am
certainly going on copying, that will give me a
collection of my own, and when this is large and
complete enough I shall give the whole to a school.'
LITERATURE Scherjon and de Gruyter 1937, Saint
Rémy nr 86. F. Novotny, Festschrift Kurt Badt,

1961, pp 213-30
EDITORS' COMMENT Copied from a reproduction of Demont-Breton's painting L'HOMME EST EN MER, exhibited in the Salon of 1889, nr 796.
COLLECTION Sale London [Sotheby] 29 April 1964, nr 52
Present owner unknown

F 645 [H 727] LES PEIROULETS

Canvas 31 × 40 [12¼ × 15¾]
Compare F 661 and F 662 [same site]
Saint Rémy October 1889
LITERATURE Scherjon and de Gruyter 1957, Saint Rémy nr 176
COLLECTION Amsterdam, Rijksmuseum Vincent van Gogh [Vincent van Gogh Foundation, inv nr F 645]

F 646 [H 645] THE HOSPITAL IN ARLES

Canvas 74 × 92 [29¼ × 36¼]
Saint Rémy October 1889 [begun in Arles April 1889]
LETTERS W 11 [Arles 30 April] *'Notwithstanding this I am working, and I have just finished two pictures of the hospital, one of a ward, a very long ward, with rows of beds with white curtains, in which some figures of patients are moving.'*
611 [Saint Rémy about 25 October] *'I have worked on a study of the mad ward at the Arles Hospital...'*
W 15 [October] *'I am now working on a ward in the hospital. In the foreground a big black stove surrounded by a number of gray and black figures of patients, behind this the very long room with a red tile floor, with two rows of white beds, the walls white, but a white which is lilac or green, and the windows with pink and green curtains, and in the background the figures of two sisters in black and white. The ceiling is violet with big beams. I had read an article about Dostoevski, who wrote a book Souvenirs de la maison des morts, and this induced me to resume a large study I had begun in the fever ward at Arles. But it is annoying to paint figures without models.'*
LITERATURE M. Braumann, Kunst und Künstler 1928, pp 451-4: Félix Rey informed Braumann that Vincent gave him three works: a portrait of Rey [F 500], the garden of the hospital [F 519] and the hospital at Arles [F 646]; Rey offered the last work to the director of the hospital, who presented it to the secretary, Rousseau; Rousseau in his turn gave it to the chemist, Nivière. Scherjon and de Gruyter 1937, Saint Rémy nr 62. M. Buchmann, Die Farbe bei Vincent van Gogh, 1948, pp 15-9: analysis of the color. K. Bromig-Kolleritz, Die Selbstbildnisse Vincent van Goghs, 1955, pp 26, 118-9: the third figure from the left could be the painter
EDITORS' COMMENT The painting of the Arles hospital Braumann reports to have been given by Vincent to Félix Rey in Arles cannot have been F 646, which was still in Vincent's possession in Saint Rémy, as we know from letter W 15 [*'...resume a large study I had begun in the fever ward at Arles.'*]
COLLECTION Winterthur, Switzerland, Oscar Reinhart
Colorplate, p 499

F 647 [H 655] NIGHT: THE WATCH [after Millet]

Canvas 72.5 × 92 [28½ × 36¼]
Saint Rémy October 1889
LETTERS 613 [about 26 October] *'I have finished the "Veillée" and am working on the "Diggers" and the "Man Putting on his Jacket," size 30 canvases...'*
621 [3 January 1890] *'Today I sent off some canvases, as follows: ... Copy after Millet: "La Veillée."'*
T 24 [8 January] *'Do you know, one of the things I*

like most is that "Evening" after Millet.'
623 [about 10 January] *'I am pleased with what you say of the copy after Millet, "La Veillée."'*
LITERATURE Scherjon and de Gruyter 1937, Saint Rémy nr 91. F. Novotny, Festschrift Kurt Badt, 1961, pp 213-30
EDITORS' COMMENT Copied from LA NUIT, a wood engraving by A. Lavieille after one of the paintings of Millet's series LES QUATRE HEURES DU JOUR. The other paintings copied from this series are F 649 [LE SOIR], F 684 [LE MATIN] and F 686 [LE MIDI].
COLLECTION Amsterdam, Rijksmuseum Vincent van Gogh [Vincent van Gogh Foundation, inv nr F 647]

F 648 [H 658] TWO PEASANTS DIGGING [after a reproduction of a Millet etching: Delteil nr 13]

Canvas 72 × 92 [28¼ × 36¼]
Compare drawings F 828 and F 829
Saint Rémy October-November 1889
LETTERS 611 [about 25 October] *'I began the "Diggers" this morning on a size 30 canvas...I am going to work again at the "Diggers"...'*
613 [about 26 October] See F 647
618 [before 8 December] *'I have also finished the copy of the "Diggers," or nearly so.'*
621 [3 January 1890] *'Today I sent off some canvases as follows: ...Copy after Millet: "The Diggers."'*
LITERATURE Scherjon and de Gruyter 1937, Saint Rémy nr 87: letter 621. F. Novotny, Festschrift Kurt Badt, 1961, pp 213-30
COLLECTION Amsterdam, Stedelijk Museum [acquired 21 January 1927], inv nr A 411

F 643

F 644

F 647

F 651

F 653

F 652

F 654

F 655

F 649 [H 659] EVENING: THE END OF THE
DAY [after Millet]

Canvas 72 × 92 [28¼ × 36¼]
Saint Rémy probably October 1889, finished
January 1890
LETTERS 613 [about 26 October] See F 647
623 [about 10 January 1890] *'So I have just finished
the three other "Hours of the Day," after the
woodcuts by Lavieille. It has taken me a lot of time
and trouble.'*
LITERATURE Scherjon and de Gruyter 1937, Saint
Rémy nr 90. F. Novotny, Festschrift Kurt Badt,
1961, pp 213-30
EDITORS' COMMENT See F 647. The painting was
probably finished in January 1890, as Vincent
writes in letter 623: *'So I have just finished the three
other "Hours of the day"...'*
COLLECTION New York, Walter P. Chrysler jr
[acquired 1955]

F 650 [H 656] RAIN EFFECT: BEHIND THE
HOSPITAL

Canvas 73.5 × 92.5 [29 × 36½]
Compare F 720, F 737, drawings F 1552, SD 1728
[same site], F 1550 and F 1551 recto [landscapes in
the rain]
Saint Rémy October 1889
LETTERS 613 [about 26 October] *'Besides that, I
have a rain effect going ...'*
621 [3 January 1890] *'Today I sent off some canvases,
as follows: ... I must not forget "Rain."'*
LITERATURE Scherjon and de Gruyter 1937, Saint
Rémy nr 65: letters 613 and 621
COLLECTION Philadelphia, Henry P. McIlhenny

F 651 [H 657] THE WALK: FALLING LEAVES

Canvas 73.5 × 60 [29 × 23¾]
Saint Rémy October 1889
LETTER 613 [about 26 October] *'And also one of the
falling leaves.'*
LITERATURE Scherjon and de Gruyter 1937, Saint
Rémy nr 67
COLLECTION Amsterdam, Rijksmuseum Vincent
van Gogh [Vincent van Gogh Foundation, inv
nr F 651]

F 652 [H 573] FIR WOODS AT THE FALL OF
DAY

Canvas 92 × 73 [36¼ × 28¾]
Signed in lower right: Vincent
Saint Rémy between October and December 1889
LETTERS 613 [about 26 October] *'Besides that, I
have a rain effect going and an evening effect with
some big pines.'*
W 16 [after 8 December] *'I am working on twelve
large canvases ... Moreover, tall weather-beaten fir
trees against a red evening sky ... While I was writing
this letter I got up in order to put a few brushstrokes
on a canvas I'm working on – the very picture of those
weather-beaten fir trees against a red, orange, yellow
sky ...'*
617 [about 9 December] *'I am again going to work a
little outside: there is a mistral. Toward sunset it
generally grows a little calmer, then there are superb
sky effects of pale citron, and the mournful pines with
their silhouettes standing out in relief against it with
exquisite black lace effects.'*
LITERATURE Scherjon and de Gruyter 1937, Saint
Rémy nr 150. Cat van Gogh 1959, Rijksmuseum
Kröller-Müller, nr 240: Saint Rémy; letters 613,
617 and W 16
COLLECTION Otterlo, Rijksmuseum Kröller-
Müller, inv nr 276-12, cat van Gogh 1970, nr 240

F 653 [H 666] SAINT PAUL'S HOSPITAL

Canvas 58 × 45 [22¾ × 17¾]
Saint Rémy October 1889
LETTER 613 [about 26 October] '*I have also done a canvas for Mr Peyron; a view of the house with a big pine.*'
LITERATURE Scherjon and de Gruyter 1937, Saint Rémy nr 68: letter 617. J. Rewald, Post-Impressionism, 1956, p 329: Dr Peyron [?] in front of the asylum
COLLECTION Switzerland, Private Collection [until 1966 on loan to the Kunstmuseum, Bern]

F 654 [H 664] OLIVE PICKING

Canvas 73 × 92 [28¾ × 36¼]
Compare F 655, F 656 and drawing SD 1729
Saint Rémy November 1889
LETTERS 617 [about 9 December] '*For instance, I am working on a picture this moment, women gathering olives ... These are the colors: the ground is violet, and farther off, yellow ocher; the olives with bronze trunks have gray-green foliage, the sky is entirely pink, and three small figures pink too. The whole is a very discreet color scheme. It is a canvas done from memory after the study of the same size made on the spot ...*'
619 [to his mother; end December] '*I hope Theo has sent you my studies, but I started still another rather big picture for you of women gathering olives.*'
621 [3 January 1890] '*Today I sent off some canvases, as follows: ..."The Women Gathering Olives" – I had intended this picture for Mother and sister, so that they should have something a little studied. I also have a copy of it for you, and the study (more colored, with deeper tones) from nature.*'
W 17 [January] '*I sent a number of pictures to Paris, yesterday. I designated the one with the olive trees for you and Mother.*'
W 18 [January] '*I hope you will like the canvas for you and Mother which I am working on at present a little. It is a repetition of a picture for Theo, women gathering olives.*'
W 19 [January] '*I hope that the picture of the women in the orchard of olive trees will be a little to your liking ...*'
LITERATURE Scherjon and de Gruyter 1937, Saint Rémy nr 69. M. E. Tralbaut, De Tafelronde 1955, nr 8-9, pp 6-9: F 654 is '*the study made on the spot*'; F 655 and F 656 are the two repetitions. Bulletin Metropolitan Museum of Art April 1956, pp 198-204
EDITORS' COMMENT The editors agree with Tralbaut that this is the original picture.
COLLECTION New York, Metropolitan Museum of Art [acquired 1956 with funds provided by Mr and Mrs Richard J. Bernhard, New York]

F 655 [H 665] OLIVE PICKING

Canvas 73 × 89 [28¾ × 35]
Compare F 654, F 656 and drawing SD 1729
Saint Rémy December 1889
LETTERS 617 [about 9 December], 619 [end December] and 621 [3 January 1890] See F 654
LITERATURE Scherjon and de Gruyter 1937, Saint Rémy nr 70. M. E. Tralbaut, De Tafelronde 1955: see under F 654
EDITORS' COMMENT See F 654
COLLECTION USA, Enid A. Haupt

F 656 [H 661] OLIVE PICKING

Canvas 73 × 92 [28¾ × 36¼]
Compare F 654, F 655 and drawing SD 1729
Saint Rémy December 1889
LETTERS 617 [about 9 December], 619 [end December] and 621 [3 January 1890] See F 654
LITERATURE Scherjon and de Gruyter 1937, Saint

Rémy nr 71. M. E. Tralbaut, De Tafelronde 1955: see under F 654
EDITORS' COMMENT See F 654
COLLECTION Washington, National Gallery of Art, inv nr 1816, cat Chester Dale Collection 1965, p 127

F 657 [H 667] THE ROAD MENDERS AT BOULEVARD VICTOR HUGO IN SAINT RÉMY

Canvas 74 × 93 [29¼ × 36½]
Compare F 658
Saint Rémy December 1889
LETTERS 621 [3 January 1890] '*Today I sent off some canvases, as follows: ... The big plane trees – the chief street or boulevard of Saint Rémy, study from nature – I have a repetition of this subject which is perhaps more finished here.*'
T 24 [8 January] '*As for the other canvases, I very much like ... the highway with the road menders.*'
LITERATURE J. G. Goulinat, L'Amour de l'Art April 1925, pp 131-42. Scherjon and de Gruyter 1937, Saint Rémy nr 77: this work is the study from nature and F 658 the replica. J. Leymarie, Van Gogh, 1951, p 128, nr 123: letter T 24
EDITORS' COMMENT As it is certain that F 658 was sent to Theo, the editors consider this picture to be the original one. F 657 would then be the replica, mentioned in letter 621 as '*perhaps more finished,*' kept by Vincent when he sent off the other one to his brother.
COLLECTION Cleveland, The Cleveland Museum of Art [acquired 1947; gift of Hanna Fund], inv nr 47.209, cat In memoriam L. C. Hanna 1958, nr 53

F 649

F 650

F 657

F 656

F 658

F 660

F 658 [H 668] THE ROAD MENDERS

Canvas 73.5 × 92.5 [29 × 36½]
Compare F 657
Saint Rémy December 1889
LETTERS 618 [before 8 December] '*The last study I did is a view of the village, where they were at work – under some enormous plane trees – repairing the pavements. So there are heaps of sand, stones and the gigantic trunks – the leaves yellowing and here and there you get a glimpse of a house front and small figures.*'
621 [3 January 1890] and T 24 [8 January] See F 657
LITERATURE Scherjon and de Gruyter 1937, Saint Rémy nr 78: this work is the replica of F 657
EDITORS' COMMENT See F 657
COLLECTION Washington, The Phillips Collection, cat 1952, p 43

F 659 [H p 557] THE GARDEN OF SAINT PAUL'S HOSPITAL IN AUTUMN

Canvas 71.5 × 90.5 [28¼ × 35¾]
Compare F 660 and drawing F 1545
Saint Rémy October 1889
LETTERS 610 [mid-October] See F 640
B 21 [between 16 November and 8 December] '*Here is the description of a canvas which is in front of me at the moment. A view of the park of the asylum where I am staying; on the right a gray terrace and a side wall of the house. Some deflowered rose bushes, on the left a stretch of the park – red ocher – the soil scorched by the sun, covered with fallen pine needles.*'
618 [before 8 December] '*Among the studies you will find the following which are for Mother and our sister: … then the study of the house and the park, of which there are two variations.*'
619 [to his mother; end December] '*Well, I believe that Jules Bakhuysen, for instance, would quite well understand what I am painting these days – … and another picture of the hospital park – big fir trees against an evening sky.*'
LITERATURE Scherjon and de Gruyter 1937, Saint Rémy nr 55: letters 610, 618 and B 21; the variant is F 660
EDITORS' COMMENT This painting was presented to the Vincent van Gogh Foundation by Paul Gachet. Dr V. W. van Gogh does not consider it to have been painted by Vincent.
COLLECTION Amsterdam, Rijksmuseum Vincent van Gogh [Vincent van Gogh Foundation, inv nr F 659]

F 660 [H 669] THE GARDEN OF SAINT PAUL'S HOSPITAL

Canvas 73.5 × 92 [29 × 36¼]
Compare F 659 and drawing F 1545
Saint Rémy October 1889
LETTERS 610 [mid-October] See F 640
B 21 [between 16 November and 8 December], 618 [before 8 December] and 619 [end December]
See F 659
LITERATURE Scherjon and de Gruyter 1937, Saint Rémy nr 54: letters 610 and 618; most probably the second painting is F 659
EDITORS' COMMENT Drawing F 1545 is closer to this version than to F 659.
COLLECTION Essen, Folkwang Museum [acquired 1922], inv nr G 64, cat 1961, nr 63

F 661 [H 670] LES PEIROULETS: THE RAVINE

Canvas 72 × 92 [28¼ × 36¼]
Compare F 645 [same site] and F 662 [same composition]
Saint Rémy December 1889
LETTERS B 20 [first half of October] '*I am working on a large canvas of a "Ravine"; it is quite the same motif as your study with a yellow tree, which I still*'

have; two bases of extremely solid rocks, between which there flows a rivulet; a third mountain blocking the ravine.'
610 [mid-October] '*I have a sterner study than the previous one of the mountains. A very wild ravine where a small stream winds its way along its bed of rocks. It is all violet.'*
619 [to his mother; end December] '*For the moment I am working on a picture of a path between the mountains and a little brook forcing its way between the stones. The rocks are of a plain violet-gray or pink, with here and there palm bushes and a kind of broom, which has all kinds of colors, green, yellow, red, brown, all through the autumn. And the brook in the foreground, white and foaming like soapsuds, and farther on, reflecting the blue of the sky. Well, I believe that Jules Bakhuysen, for instance, would quite well understand what I am painting these days – this ravine with the brook ...'*
621 [3 January 1890] '*Today I sent off some canvases, as follows: ..."The Ravine" – it is the study during the mistral – I had secured my easel with big stones. The picture of this is not dry; it has a closer drawing and there is more controlled passion and more color in it.'*
622 [4 January] '*I must do more canvases of cypresses and mountains to give an idea of Provence. The "Ravine" and ... are typical for it. And the "Ravine" especially, which I still have here because it is not dry.'*
T 24 [8 January] '*As for the other canvases, I very much like the one of those women clambering over the rocks ...'*
LITERATURE Scherjon and de Gruyter 1937, Saint Rémy nr 61: painted after the study F 662.
Å. Meyerson, Konsthistorisk Tidskrift 1946, pp 141-2: letter B 20; Vincent had been inspired by a study of Bernard's of a yellow tree. M. Buchmann, Die Farbe bei Vincent van Gogh, 1948, pp 36-9, 50: analysis of the color scheme. J. Leymarie, Van Gogh, 1951, p 126, nr 119; according to Dr E. Leroy the site depicted is 'Les Peiroulets' [the devil's kettles], 1.5 kilometers southwest of the hospital. Cat van Gogh 1966, Rijksmuseum Kröller-Müller, nr 239: compare a pencil sketch of the same motif in a sketchbook in the Vincent van Gogh Foundation, Amsterdam
EDITORS' COMMENT One of the paintings F 661 and F 662 was considered by Vincent a '*study,'* the other – painted in December – a '*picture'* [see letter 621]. On stylistic grounds the editors consider F 662 to be the study, made in October and sent to Theo in December [see the same letter], as this shows '*closer drawing'* and '*more controlled passion.'*
COLLECTION Otterlo, Rijksmuseum Kröller-Müller, inv nr 314-12, cat van Gogh 1970, nr 239

F 662 [H 671] LES PEIROULETS: THE RAVINE

Canvas 73 × 92 [28¾ × 36¼]
Compare F 645 [same site] and F 661 [same composition]
Saint Rémy October 1889
LETTERS B 20 [first half of October], 610 [mid-October], 619 [end December], 621 [3 January 1890], 622 [4 January] and T 24 [8 January] See F 661
LITERATURE Scherjon and de Gruyter 1937, Saint Rémy nr 60: letter 610; study for F 661. Å Meyerson 1946: see under F 661. J. Leymarie, Van Gogh, 1951: see under F 661. J. Rewald, Post-Impressionism, 1956, p 378: mentions an un-published letter of Gauguin, which connects this subject with the painting shown in 1890 in Paris at the Indépendants under nr 833, 'PAYSAGE MONTAGNEUX EN PROVENCE,' which Gauguin wants to '*exchange for anything of mine you choose.'*
EDITORS' COMMENT See F 661
COLLECTION Boston, Museum of Fine Arts [acquired 1952; bequest of Keith McLeod], inv nr 52.1524, cat 1955, p 29

F 659

F 662

F 661

F 663

F 663 [H 672] LANDSCAPE WITH OLIVE TREE AND MOUNTAINS IN THE BACKGROUND

Canvas 45 × 55 [17¾ × 21¾]
Saint Rémy January 1890
LETTER 622 [4 January] '*Yesterday I sent two canvases to Marseilles, that is to say, I made a present of them to my friend Roulin: a white house among the olives, and a wheat field with a background of lilac mountains and a black tree, as in the big canvas I sent you.'*
LITERATURE Scherjon and de Gruyter 1937, Saint Rémy nr 82bis: the big canvas mentioned in letter 622 is nr 82, F 721. Cat van Gogh 1959, Rijksmuseum Kröller-Müller, nr 247: doubts that F 721 is the painting described in letter 622 or that it is connected with F 663
COLLECTION Formerly France, P. Pompidor [acquired 1901]
Present owner unknown

F 664

F 665

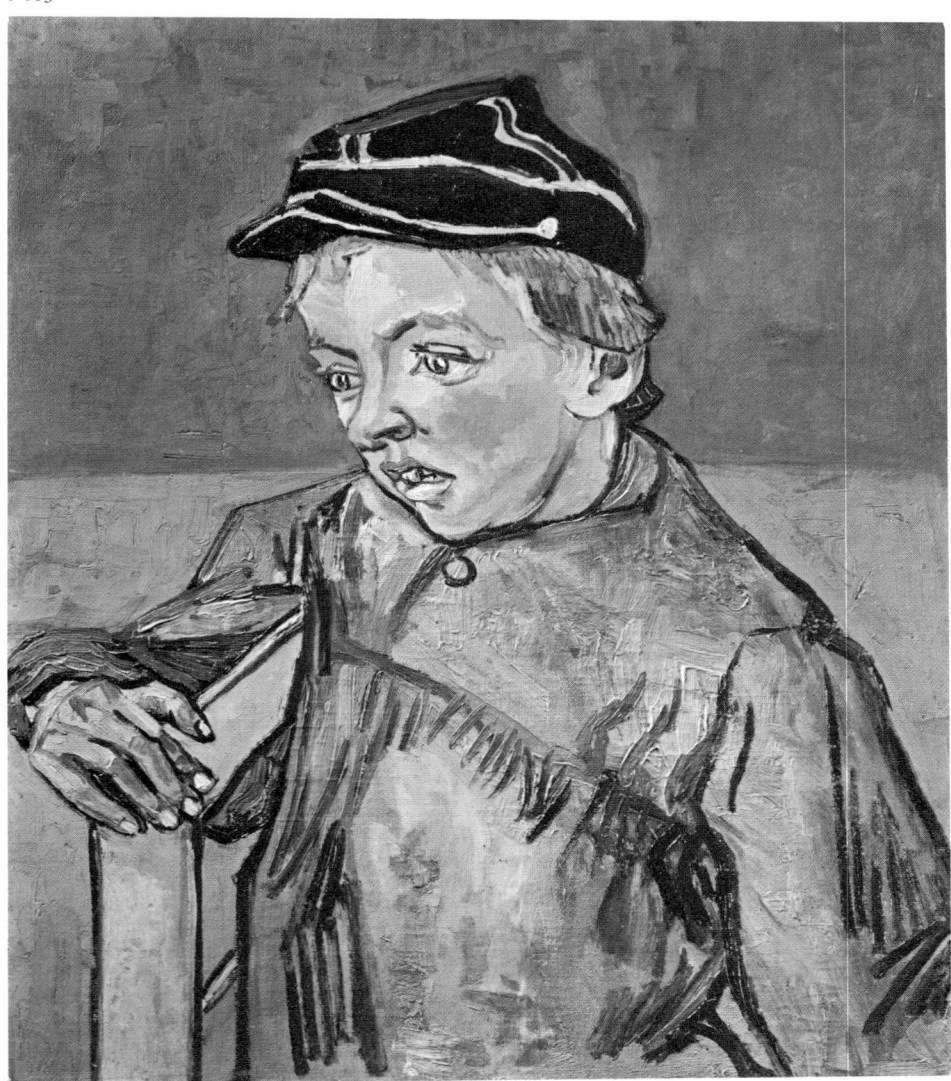

F 664 [H 673] THE WHITE MAS AMONG THE OLIVE TREES

Canvas 70 × 60 [27½ × 23½]
Signed in lower right: Vincent
Saint Rémy winter 1889-90
LETTER 622 [4 January] See F 663
LITERATURE Scherjon and de Gruyter 1937, Saint Rémy nr 81: letter 622
COLLECTION Formerly France, P. Pompidor [acquired 1903]
Present owner unknown

F 665 [H 678] THE SCHOOLBOY

Canvas 63.5 × 54 [25 × 21¼]
Saint Rémy January 1890
LETTER 622 [4 January] '*Just now I have done a little portrait of one of the boys here, which he wanted to send to his mother.*'
LITERATURE Scherjon and de Gruyter 1937, Saint Rémy nr 84. Cat São Paulo 1963, nr 112: model identified as Camille Roulin
EDITORS' COMMENT There is no reason to accept the São Paolo catalogue's identification of the model as Camille Roulin [see F 538, F 544]. While the style is close to the portraits executed at Arles, the passage from letter 622 makes it more probable that this painting was executed at Saint Rémy.
COLLECTION São Paulo, Museu de Arte, cat 1963, nr 112

F 666 [H 652] STILL LIFE: FLOWERS SCABIOSA AND RANUNCULUS
Paris period; see after F 388 verso

F 666a STILL LIFE: PEONIES
Paris period; see after F 388 verso

F 667 [H 687] THE TOPERS [after Daumier]

Canvas 60 × 73 [23½ × 28¾]
Saint Rémy January-February 1890
LETTERS 623 [about 10 January] '*So what I think I shall do in painting is the "Men Drinking" by Daumier...*'
626 [11 February] '*I have tried to copy the "Men Drinking" by Daumier...it is very difficult.*'
LITERATURE Scherjon and de Gruyter, Saint Rémy nr 97
EDITORS' COMMENT Copied from a wood engraving by G. Maurand after Daumier's LES QUATRE ÂGES. PHYSIOLOGIE DU BUVEUR [E. Bouvy, Daumier, *L'Oeuvre gravé du maître*, Paris 1933, volume 2, nr 935]
COLLECTION Chicago, The Art Institute of Chicago [acquired 1953; bequest of Joseph Winterbotham], inv nr 53.178, cat 1961, p 199

F 668 [H 685] THE FIRST STEPS [after Millet]

Canvas 73 × 92 [28¾ × 36¼]
Saint Rémy January 1890
LETTERS 611 [about 25 October 1889] '*...last night the canvas arrived and the Millet reproductions... You know it might be interesting to try to do Millet's drawings in painting, that would be quite a special collection of copies... How beautiful that Millet is, "A Child's First Steps"!*'
623 [about 10 January] '*This week I am going to start on the snow-covered field and Millet's "The First Steps," in the same size as the others. Then there will be six canvases in a series, and I can tell you, I have put much thought into the disposition of the colors while working on these last three of the "Hours of the Day."*'
LITERATURE Scherjon and de Gruyter 1937, Saint Rémy nr 93. Cat French Paintings, vol 3, 1967, Metropolitan Museum of Art, pp 190-1: probably copied after the drawing by Millet in the collection

of Georges Petit, reproduced by A. Sensier,
J. F. Millet, Paris 1881, p 345
COLLECTION New York, Metropolitan Museum
of Art [gift of George N. Richard and Helen
M. Richard], inv nr 64.165.2, cat French Paintings,
volume 3, 1967, pp 190-1

F 669 [H 690] THE PRISON COURT-YARD
[after Gustave Doré]

Canvas 80 × 64 [31½ × 25¼]
Saint Rémy February 1890
LETTERS 623 [about 10 January] *'So what I think I
shall do in painting is the "Men Drinking" by
Daumier and the "Convict Prison" by Régamey. You
will find them among the wood engravings.'*
626 [11 February] *'I have tried to copy the "Men
Drinking" by Daumier and the "Convict Prison" by
Doré; it is very difficult.'*
LITERATURE B. Ternovitz, Sredi Kollektzionerov
1922, pp 11-7 [in Russian]. Scherjon and de
Gruyter 1937, Saint Rémy nr 96. F. Novotny,
Festschrift Kurt Badt, 1961, p 215: notes the exact
example for the painting
EDITORS' COMMENT Obviously not after
Régamey but copied after a wood engraving in
London, a Pilgrimage by Gustave Doré and
Blanchard Jerrold, London 1872, representing
'Newgate – The Exercise Yard.' Blanchard Jerrold
wrote the text and Doré made the engravings.
COLLECTION Moscow, Pushkin Museum
[acquired 1948], inv nr 3373, cat 1961, p 53

F 667

F 669

F 668

F 671

F 672

F 670 [H 689] THE WOOD-CUTTER [after Millet]

Canvas 43.5 × 25 [17¼ × 9¾]
Saint Rémy February 1890
LETTERS 607 [19 September 1889] See F 634
623 [about 10 January 1890] See F 632
626 [11 February] 'One of these days I hope to start on the "Good Samaritan" by Delacroix and the "Woodcutter" by Millet.'
629 [29 April] See F 634
LITERATURE Scherjon and de Gruyter 1937, Saint Rémy nr 41 : cite letters 607, 623 and 629 for the whole series. F. Novotny, Festschrift Kurt Badt, 1961, pp 213-30
EDITORS' COMMENT See F 634
COLLECTION Amsterdam, Rijksmuseum Vincent van Gogh [Vincent van Gogh Foundation, inv nr F 670]

F 671 [H 688] BRANCH OF AN ALMOND TREE IN BLOSSOM

Canvas 73 × 92 [28¾ × 36¼]
Saint Rémy February 1890
LETTERS W 20 [15 February] 'Well, the result is after all that the child is there – and as I am writing to his grandmother – a few days ago I started painting a big canvas for him of a blue sky with branches full of blossoms standing out against it.'
627 [to his mother; 15 February] '...I started right away to make a picture for him, to hang in their bedroom, big branches of white almond blossom against a blue sky.'
628 [mid-April] 'My work was going well, the last canvas of branches in blossom – you will see that it was perhaps the best, the most patiently worked thing I had done, painted with calm and with a greater firmness of touch.'
629 [29 April] 'I felt ill at the time I was doing the almond blossoms.'
T 33 [3 May] 'Your consignment of pictures arrived too ... the branch of almond blossoms shows that for these themes you have missed the time of blooming of the trees and flowers.'
W 22 [Auvers between 3 and 8 June] 'I brought along a relatively large picture for Theo's and Jo's little boy – which they hung over the piano – white almond blossoms – big branches against a sky-blue background ...'
LITERATURE Scherjon and de Gruyter 1937, Saint Rémy nr 85 : letters 628 and 629
EDITORS' COMMENT The passage from letter W 20 was wrongly translated in the English edition of the letters and has been corrected by the editors.
COLLECTION Amsterdam, Rijksmuseum Vincent van Gogh [Vincent van Gogh Foundation, inv nr F 671]

F 672 [H 694] THE MEADOW WITH BUTTERFLIES

Canvas 64.5 × 81 [25½ × 32]
Saint Rémy April 1890
LETTER 631 [4 May] '...I have done two canvases of the fresh grass in the park ...'
LITERATURE Cat Modern Foreign School 1926, National Gallery, London nr 4169 : Arles period. Scherjon and de Gruyter 1937, Saint Rémy nr 106 : letter 631. D. Cooper, cat The Courtauld Collection, 1954, nr 88 : April-May 1890; painted in the park of the Saint Paul's Hospital, Saint Rémy
EDITORS' COMMENT The other picture referred to in letter 631 is F 676.
COLLECTION London, National Gallery [on loan since June 1961 from the Tate Gallery]

F 676

F 673 [H 691] HUTS: REMINISCENCE OF THE
NORTH

Canvas 45.5 × 43 [18 × 17]
Compare F 674 [same composition] and drawing
F 1591 verso [similar motif]
Saint Rémy March-April 1890
LETTERS 629 [29 April] '*While I was ill I nevertheless
did some little canvases from memory which you will
see later, memories of the North...*'
629a [to his mother and sister; 29 April] '*I continued
painting even when my illness was at its height,
among other things a memory of Brabant, hovels
with moss-covered roofs and beech hedges on a
autumn evening with a stormy sky, the sun setting
amid ruddy clouds.*'
LITERATURE Scherjon and de Gruyter 1937, Saint
Rémy nr 102. P. Gachet, Deux amis des
impressionistes, 1956, pp 71-2: March 1890; gift of
Theo to Mrs Chevalier after Vincent's death
COLLECTION Switzerland, Private Collection
[acquired April 1956]

F 674 [H 692] THATCHED HUTS IN THE
SUNSHINE: REMINISCENCE OF THE NORTH

Canvas 50 × 39 [19¾ × 15¼]
Compare F 673 [same composition] and drawing
F 1591 verso [similar motif]
Saint Rémy March-April 1890
LETTERS 629 [29 April] and 629a [29 April]
See F 673
LITERATURE Scherjon and de Gruyter 1937, Saint
Rémy nr 103
COLLECTION Merion, Pennsylvania, The Barnes
Foundation [acquired 1922]

F 675 [H 693] WINTER LANDSCAPE:
REMINISCENCE OF THE NORTH

Canvas on panel 29 × 36.5 [11½ × 14½]
Saint Rémy March-April 1890
LETTERS 629 [29 April] and 629a [29 April]
See F 673
LITERATURE Scherjon and de Gruyter 1937, Saint
Rémy nr 104
COLLECTION Amsterdam, Rijksmuseum Vincent
van Gogh [Vincent van Gogh Foundation, inv
nr F 675]

F 676 [H 697] TREE TRUNKS

Canvas 72 × 90 [28¼ × 35½]
Compare sketch in letter 631
Saint Rémy April 1890
LETTERS 629 [29 April] '*...now I have just finished a
corner of a sunny meadow, which I think is fairly
vigorous.*'
629a [to his mother and sister; 29 April] '*These last
few days I have been working on the picture of a lawn
in the blazing sun with yellow dandelions.*'
631 [4 May] '*...I have done two canvases of the fresh
grass in the park, one of which is extremely simple,
here is a hasty sketch of it. The trunk of a pine violet-
pink and then the grass with white flowers and
dandelions, a little rose tree and other tree trunks in
the background right at the top of the canvas.*'
LITERATURE Scherjon and de Gruyter 1937, Saint
Rémy nr 105
EDITORS' COMMENT The other picture referred to
in letter 631 is F 672.
COLLECTION Otterlo, Rijksmuseum Kröller-
Müller, inv nr 275-22, cat van Gogh 1970, nr 241

F 670

F 673

F 674

F 675

F 677

F 678

F 677 [H 699] THE RAISING OF LAZARUS
[after Rembrandt]

Canvas 48.5 × 63 [19 × 24¾]
Compare sketch in letter 632
Saint Rémy May 1890
LETTER 632 [between 5 and 8 May] *'The etchings
which you sent me are very fine! On the back of this
page I have scribbled a sketch after a painting I have
done of three figures which are in the background of
the etching of "Lazarus": the dead man and his two
sisters. The cave and the corpse are white-yellow-
violet. The woman who takes the handkerchief away
from the face of the resurrected man has a green
dress and orange hair, the other has black hair and a
gown of striped green and pink. In the background a
countryside of blue hills, a yellow sunrise. Thus the
combination of colors would itself suggest the same
thing which the chiaroscuro of the etching expresses.'*
LITERATURE Scherjon and de Gruyter 1937, Saint
Rémy nr 107. J. Leymarie, Van Gogh, 1951, p 130,
nr 132: copy of a detail of Rembrandt's etching
[Bartsch nr 73]; the figure of Christ has been
replaced by the sun. F. Novotny, Festschrift Kurt
Badt, 1961, pp 213-30
COLLECTION Amsterdam, Rijksmuseum Vincent
van Gogh [Vincent van Gogh Foundation, inv
nr F 677]

F 678 [H 700] STILL LIFE: VASE WITH IRISES
AGAINST A YELLOW BACKGROUND

Canvas 92 × 73.5 [36¼ × 29]
Saint Rémy May 1890
LETTERS 633 [11 or 12 May] *'I am doing...two
canvases representing big bunches of violet irises...
On the other hand, the other violet bunch (ranging
from carmine to pure Prussian blue) stands out
against a startling citron background, with other
yellow tones in the vase and the stand on which it
rests, so it is an effect of tremendously disparate
complementaries, which strengthen each other by
their juxtaposition.'*
614a [to Isaäcson; Auvers between 16 and 20 May]
*'These canvases, together with a number of flower
studies, are all that I have done since our last
correspondence. These flowers are an avalanche of
roses against a green background, and a very big
bouquet of irises, violet against a yellow
background...'*
w 21 [Auvers between 3 and 8 June] *'And those last
days at Saint Rémy I still worked as in a frenzy.
Great bunches of flowers, violet irises...'*
w 22 [Auvers between 3 and 8 June] *'But during the
last weeks at Saint Rémy I worked like a man in a
frenzy, especially on bunches of flowers, roses and
violet irises.'*
644 [Auvers 24 June] *'The canvases have arrived now
from there; the irises are quite dry and I hope you
will see something in it...'*
LITERATURE Scherjon and de Gruyter 1937, Saint
Rémy nr 112: letter 644
EDITORS' COMMENT The other canvas of irises
referred to in letters 614a and 633 is F 680.
COLLECTION Amsterdam, Rijksmuseum Vincent
van Gogh [Vincent van Gogh Foundation, inv
nr F 678]

F 679 STILL LIFE: BOUQUET OF IRISES

Left out by Faille in his manuscript for the present
edition
See REJECTED WORKS

F 680 [H 701] STILL LIFE: VASE WITH IRISES
AGAINST A PINK BACKGROUND

Canvas 73 × 93 [28¾ × 36½]
Saint Rémy May 1890
LETTERS 633 [11 or 12 May] *'I am doing...two*

canvases representing big bunches of violet irises, one lot against a pink background in which the effect is soft and harmonious because of the combination of greens, pinks, violets.'

614a [Auvers between 16 and 20 May], W 21 [Auvers between 3 and 8 June], W 22 [Auvers between 3 and 8 June] and 644 [Auvers 24 June] See F 678

LITERATURE Scherjon and de Gruyter, Saint Rémy nr 111: letter 644

EDITORS' COMMENT The other canvas of irises referred to in letters 614a and 633 is F 678

COLLECTION New York, The Metropolitan Museum of Art [acquired 1958; gift of Adele R. Levy], inv nr 58.187, cat French Paintings, volume 3, 1967, pp 191-2

F 681 [H 702] STILL LIFE: ROSES IN A TERRACOTTA POT

Canvas 71 × 90 [28 × 35½]
Saint Rémy May 1890
LETTERS 633 [11 or 12 May] *'I am doing a canvas of roses with a light green background…'*
614a [to Isaäcson; Auvers between 16 and 20 May] *'These canvases, together with a number of flower studies, are all that I have done since our last correspondence. These flowers are an avalanche of roses against a green background…'*
W 21 [Auvers between 3 and 8 June] *'And those last days at Saint Rémy I still worked as in a frenzy. Great bunches of flowers…big bouquets of roses…'*
W 22 [Auvers between 3 and 8 June] *'But during the last weeks at Saint Rémy I worked like a man in a frenzy, especially on bunches of flowers, roses…'*
644 [Auvers 24 June] *'The canvases have arrived now from there…and there are also the roses…'*
LITERATURE Scherjon and de Gruyter 1937, Saint Rémy nr 110: letter 644
COLLECTION New York, Mr and Mrs William Averell Harriman

F 681a STILL LIFE: ROSES

Left out by Faille in his manuscript for the present edition
See REJECTED WORKS

F 682 [H 703] STILL LIFE: ROSES IN GREEN POT

Canvas 93 × 72 [36½ × 28¼]
Saint Rémy May 1890
LETTERS 634 [13 May] *'I have just finished another canvas of pink roses against a yellow-green background in a green vase.'*
614a [Auvers between 16 and 20 May], W 21 [Auvers between 3 and 8 June], W 22 [Auvers between 3 and 8 June] and 644 [Auvers 24 June] See F 681
LITERATURE Scherjon and de Gruyter 1937, Saint Rémy nr 113: letter 644
COLLECTION New York, Mrs Albert D. Lasker

F 680

F 682

F 681

F 449 [485] BOATS WITH MEN UNLOADING
SAND
Arles August 1888

F 683

F 687

F 683 [H 695] ROAD WITH CYPRESS AND
STAR

Canvas 92 × 73 [36¼ × 28¾]
Compare sketch in letter 643 [same composition],
F 760, drawings F 1587 recto, F 1609 recto and
F 1610 recto [motif of horse and cart]
Saint Rémy May 1890
LETTERS 643 [to Gauguin; Auvers between 16 and
23 June] 'I still have a cypress with a star from down
there, a last attempt – a night sky with a moon
without radiance, the slender crescent barely
emerging from the opaque shadow cast by the earth –
one star with an exaggerated brilliance, if you like, a
soft brilliance of pink and green in the ultramarine
sky, across which some clouds are hurrying. Below, a
road bordered with tall yellow canes, behind these the
blue Basses Alpes, an old inn with yellow lighted
windows, and a very tall cypress, very straight, very
somber. On the road, a yellow cart with a white horse
in harness, and two late wayfarers. Very romantic, if
you like, but also Provence, I think. I shall probably
etch this and also other landscapes and subjects,
memories of Provence ...'
644 [Auvers 24 June] 'The canvases have arrived now
from there ... and finally a cypress with a star.'
LITERATURE Scherjon and de Gruyter 1937, Saint
Rémy nr 115: letter 644. Cat van Gogh 1959,
Rijksmuseum Kröller-Müller, nr 243: compares
several drawings and sketches in a sketch book in
the Vincent van Gogh Foundation related to the
motif of horse, carriage and people walking
COLLECTION Otterlo, Rijksmuseum Kröller-
Müller, inv nr 312-12, cat van Gogh 1970, nr 243

F 684 [H 676] MORNING: GOING OUT TO
WORK [after Millet]

Canvas 73 × 92 [28¾ × 36¼]
Saint Rémy January 1890
LETTER 623 [about 10 January] See F 649
LITERATURE Scherjon and de Gruyter 1937, Saint
Rémy nr 88: letter 623. F. Novotny, Festschrift
Kurt Badt, 1961, pp 213-30
EDITORS' COMMENT See F 647 and F 649
COLLECTION Formerly Holzdorf, Otto Krebs
Present owner unknown

F 685 PEASANT WITH HAY-FORK [after
Millet; detail from the composition F 684]

Left out by Faille in his manuscript for the present
edition
See REJECTED WORKS

F 686 [H 677] NOON: REST FROM WORK
[after Millet]

Canvas 73 × 91 [28¾ × 35¾]
Saint Rémy January 1890
LETTER 623 [about 10 January] See F 649
LITERATURE Scherjon and de Gruyter 1937, Saint
Rémy nr 89: letter 623. F. Novotny, Festschrift
Kurt Badt, 1961, pp 213-30
EDITORS' COMMENT See F 647 and F 649
COLLECTION Paris, Musée National du Louvre
[acquired 1952; gift of Mrs F. Halphen], inv nr RF
1952-17, cat Impressionnistes 1959, p 247

F 687 [H 674] THE REAPER [after Millet]

Canvas 43.5 × 33.5 [17 × 13¼]
Compare drawing SD 1674
Saint Rémy September 1889
LETTERS 607 [19 September] and 623 [about
10 January 1890] See F 634
LITERATURE Scherjon and de Gruyter 1937, Saint
Rémy nr 38: cite letters 607, 623 and 629 for all the
copies after Millet's work IN THE FIELDS.
F. Novotny, Festschrift Kurt Badt, 1961, pp 213-30

EDITORS' COMMENT See F 634
COLLECTION Amsterdam, Rijksmuseum Vincent
van Gogh [Vincent van Gogh Foundation, inv
nr F 687]

F 688 [H 684] THE MOWER [after Millet]

Canvas 43.5 × 25 [17 × 9¾]
Saint Rémy September 1889
LETTERS 607 [19 September] and 623 [about
10 January 1890] See F 634
LITERATURE Scherjon and de Gruyter 1937, Saint
Rémy nr 43: cite letters 607, 623 and 629 for all the
copies after Millet's WORK IN THE FIELDS.
F. Novotny, Festschrift Kurt Badt, 1961, pp
213-230
EDITORS' COMMENT See F 634
COLLECTION USA, Property of trustees under the
will of the late Georg S. Hirschland

F 689 [H 660] THE SOWER [after Lerat's etching
of Millet's Sower]

Canvas 64 × 55 [25¼ × 21¾]
Compare F 690 and drawing F 830
Saint Rémy October 1889
LETTERS 607 [19 September] 'I should also like to
copy "The Sower"...And there is Lerat's etching of
"The Sower" at Durand Ruel's.'
613 [about 26 October] '...and am working on...
size 30 canvases, and the "Sower," smaller.'
LITERATURE Scherjon and de Gruyter 1937, Saint
Rémy, nr 94: letter 613. Cat van Gogh 1959,
Rijksmuseum Kröller-Müller, nr 249: compare
drawing F 830 and the replica F 690; probably done
after an engraving of Millet's painting. F. Novotny,
Festschrift Kurt Badt, 1961, pp 213-30
COLLECTION Otterlo, Rijksmuseum Kröller-
Müller, inv nr 309-09, cat van Gogh 1970, nr 249

F 690 [H 675] THE SOWER [after Millet]

Canvas 81 × 65 [31 × 25½]
Compare F 689 and drawing F 830
Saint Rémy January-February 1890
LETTER 625 [2 February] 'I am stopping at the
"Sower," which I am working on, and which is not
coming off as I should wish.'
LITERATURE Scherjon and de Gruyter 1937, Saint
Rémy nr 95: letter 625; this second canvas
remained in a unfinished state. F. Novotny,
Festschrift Kurt Badt, 1961, pp 213-30
COLLECTION Athens, Stavros S. Niarchos

F 691 THE SOWER

Left out by Faille in his manuscript for the present
edition
See REJECTED WORKS

F 686
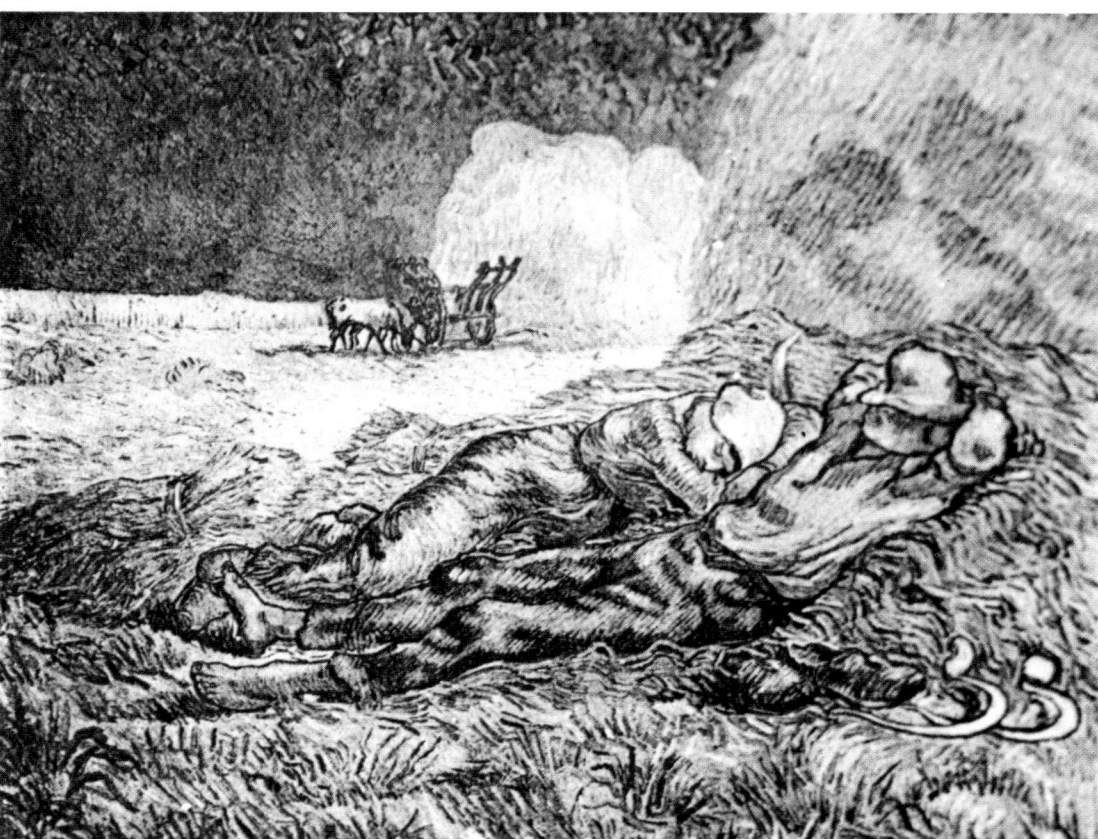

F 684

F 688

F 689

F 690

F 692

F 694

F 693

F 696

F 697

F 692 [H 683] THE THRESHER [after Millet]

Canvas 44 × 27 [17¼ × 10¾]
Saint Rémy September 1889
LETTERS 607 [19 September] and 623 [about 10
January 1890] See F 634
LITERATURE Scherjon and de Gruyter 1937, Saint
Rémy nr 40: cite letters 607, 623 and 629 for all the
copies after Millet's WORK IN THE FIELDS.
F. Novotny, Festschrift Kurt Badt, 1961, pp 213-30
EDITORS' COMMENT See F 634
COLLECTION Amsterdam, Rijksmuseum Vincent
van Gogh [Vincent van Gogh Foundation, inv
nr F 692]

F 693 [H 681] THE SHEAF-BINDER [after
Millet]

Canvas 44 × 32.5 [17¼ × 12¾]
Saint Rémy September 1889
LETTERS 607 [19 September] and 623 [about 10
January 1890] See F 634
LITERATURE Scherjon and de Gruyter 1937, Saint
Rémy nr 39: cite letters 607, 623 and 629 for all the
copies after Millet's WORK IN THE FIELDS.
F. Novotny, Festschrift Kurt Badt, 1961, pp 213-30
EDITORS' COMMENT See F 634
COLLECTION Amsterdam, Rijksmuseum Vincent
van Gogh [Vincent van Gogh Foundation, inv
nr F 693]

F 694 [H 717] PEASANTS DIGGING UP
POTATOES [after Millet]

Canvas 32 × 40.5 [12½ × 16]
Compare F 1649 recto
Saint Rémy March-April 1890
LITERATURE Scherjon and de Gruyter 1937, Saint
Rémy nr 168. F. Novotny, Festschrift Kurt Badt,
1961, pp 213-30
COLLECTION New York, J. K. Thannhauser

F 695 [H 718] WOMEN DIGGING IN FIELD
WITH SNOW

Canvas 50 × 64 [19¾ × 25¼]
Compare drawing F 1586 verso [similar motif]
Saint Rémy March-April 1890
LETTER 629a [to his mother and sister; 29 April]
*'I continued painting even when my illness was at its
height, among other things … Also a turnip field with
women gathering green stuff in the snow.'*
LITERATURE Scherjon and de Gruyter 1937, Saint
Rémy nr 167. J. Rewald, Post-Impressionism, 1956,
p 375: March-April 1890; letter 629a. F. Novotny,
Festschrift Kurt Badt, 1961, pp 213-30
EDITORS' COMMENT Faille called the work a copy
after Millet, for which no evidence can be found.
COLLECTION Zurich, E. G. Bührle, cat 1958, nr 245
Colorplate, p 500

F 696 [H 716] THE SPINNER [after Millet]

Canvas 40 × 25.5 [15¾ × 10]
Saint Rémy September 1889
LETTERS 607 [19 September] and 623 [about 10
January 1890] See F 634
LITERATURE Scherjon and de Gruyter 1937, Saint
Rémy nr 44: cite letters 607, 623 and 629 for all the
copies after Millet's WORK IN THE FIELDS.
F. Novotny, Festschrift Kurt Badt, 1961, pp 213-30
EDITORS' COMMENT See F 634
COLLECTION Mrs L. Wolf

F 697 [H 680] PEASANT WOMAN CUTTING
STRAW [after Millet]

Canvas 40.5 × 26.5 [16 × 10½]
Saint Rémy September 1889
LETTERS 607 [19 September] and 623 [about 10

January 1890] See F 634
LITERATURE Scherjon and de Gruyter 1937, Saint Rémy nr 45: cite letters 607, 623 and 629 for all the copies after Millet's WORK IN THE FIELDS.
F. Novotny, Festschrift Kurt Badt, 1961, pp 213-30
EDITORS' COMMENT See F 634
COLLECTION Amsterdam, Rijksmuseum Vincent van Gogh [Vincent van Gogh Foundation, inv nr F 697]

F 698 [H 679] PEASANT WOMAN MOWING [after Millet]

Canvas 39 × 24 [15¼ × 9½]
Saint Rémy September 1889
LETTERS 607 [19 September] and 623 [about 10 January 1890] See F 634
LITERATURE Scherjon and de Gruyter 1937, Saint Rémy nr 42: cite letters 607, 623 and 629 for all the copies after Millet's WORK IN THE FIELDS.
F. Novotny, Festschrift Kurt Badt, 1961, pp 213-30
EDITORS' COMMENT See F 634
COLLECTION Sale Geneva [Galerie Motte] 9-10 June 1967, nr 55
Present owner unknown

F 699 [H 714] THE SHEPHERDESS [after Millet]

Canvas 53 × 41.5 [21 × 16¼]
Saint Rémy August-November 1889
LITERATURE Scherjon and de Gruyter 1937, Saint Rémy nr 164. F. Novotny, Festschrift Kurt Badt, 1961, pp 213-30
EDITORS' COMMENT Presumably done from a reproduction of Millet's wood engraving LA GRANDE BERGÈRE ASSISE [Delteil nr 33].
COLLECTION Basle, Robert von Hirsch

F 699a [formerly F 699bis; H 715] PEASANT WOMAN WALKING IN THE FIELDS

Canvas 46 × 38 [18 × 15]
Saint Rémy August-November 1889. N.B. See EDITORS' COMMENT
LITERATURE Scherjon and de Gruyter 1937, Saint Rémy nr 165. F. Novotny, Festschrift Kurt Badt, 1961, pp 213-30
EDITORS' COMMENT Faille called the work a copy after Millet, for which no evidence can be found. The work shows similarities with F 685. As in that case the editors do not accept the authenticity of F 699a.
COLLECTION Sale London [Sotheby] 1 July 1964, nr 79
Present owner unknown

F 700 [H 682] PEASANT WOMAN BINDING WHEAT IN SHEAVES [after Millet]

Canvas 43.5 × 33.5 [17¼ × 13¼]
Saint Rémy September 1889
LETTERS 607 [19 September] and 623 [about 10 January 1890] See F 634
LITERATURE Scherjon and de Gruyter 1937, Saint Rémy nr 36: cite letters 607, 623 and 629 for all the copies after Millet's WORK IN THE FIELDS.
F. Novotny, Festschrift Kurt Badt, 1961, pp 213-30
EDITORS' COMMENT See F 634
COLLECTION Amsterdam, Rijksmuseum Vincent van Gogh [Vincent van Gogh Foundation, inv nr F 700]

F 695

F 698

F 699

F 699a

F 700

F 701 [H 721] THE DIGGERS

Canvas 62 × 44 [24½ × 17¼]
Saint Rémy autumn 1889
LITERATURE Scherjon and de Gruyter 1937, Saint
Rémy nr 184. F. Novotny, Festschrift Kurt Badt,
1961, pp 213-30
EDITORS' COMMENT Faille dated F 701 to April
1890 without giving any reason. The editors date it
autumn 1889 especially on account of the
resemblance of the trees to landscapes of autumn
1889. Faille called the work a copy after Millet, for
which there is no evidence.
COLLECTION Detroit, Institute of Arts [Robert
H. Tannahill bequest]

F 702 [H 719] WORN OUT: AT ETERNITY'S
GATE

Canvas 81 × 65 [32 × 25½]
Compare drawings F 997, F 998 and lithograph
F 1662
Saint Rémy May 1890
LITERATURE Scherjon and de Gruyter 1937, Saint
Rémy nr 185: compare drawing F 997. W. Weisbach,
Vincent van Gogh, volume I, 1951, p 155: done
after lithograph F 1662
COLLECTION Otterlo, Rijksmuseum Kröller-
Müller, inv nr 313-12, cat van Gogh 1970, nr 251

F 703 [H 653] HEAD OF A PATIENT OF THE
HOSPITAL AT SAINT RÉMY

Canvas 32 × 23.5 [12½ × 9¼]
Saint Rémy October 1889
LETTER 612 [to his mother; end October] 'At the
moment I am working on a portrait of one of the
patients here.'
LITERATURE Scherjon and de Gruyter 1937, Saint
Rémy nr 64: letter 612
COLLECTION Amsterdam, Rijksmuseum Vincent
van Gogh [Vincent van Gogh Foundation, inv
nr F 703]

F 704 [H 720] THE EVENING WALK

Canvas 49.5 × 45.5 [19½ × 18]
Saint Rémy October 1889
LITERATURE Scherjon and de Gruyter 1937, Saint
Rémy nr 186
COLLECTION São Paulo, Museu de Arte, cat 1963,
nr 113

F 705 THE SOWER

Left out by Faille in his manuscript for the present
edition
See REJECTED WORKS

F 706 [H 722] LANDSCAPE AT FONTVIEILLE,
WITH PLOWMAN AND MILLS IN THE
BACKGROUND

Canvas 54 × 67 [21¼ × 26½]
Saint Rémy September 1889
LITERATURE Scherjon and de Gruyter 1937, Saint
Rémy nr 182
COLLECTION Cambridge, Massachusetts,
W. A. Coolidge [acquired about 1936]

F 707 [H 639] OLIVE TREES: PINK SKY

Canvas 73 × 92.5 [28¾ × 36½]
Saint Rémy September-December 1889
LETTERS 608 [28 September] '...they are leaving
today with other canvases–as follows:...Olives...'
615 [between 16 November and 8 December] 'The
thing is that this month I have been working in the
olive groves...I have been knocking about in the
orchards, and the result is five size 30 canvases, which

along with the three studies of olives that you have, at least constitute an attack on the problem.'
B 21 [between 16 November and 8 December] *'So I am working at present among the olive trees, seeking after the various effects of a gray sky against a yellow soil, with a green-black note in the foliage; another time the soil and the foliage all of a violet hue against a yellow sky; then again a red-ocher soil and a pinkish green sky.'*
621 [3 January 1890] *'Today I sent off some canvases, as follows: ... ''Olive Trees'' ... Ditto. Neutral effect.'*
629 [29 April 1890] *'At the same time I beg you to accept the various pictures I am sending you ... You will find that the olives with the pink sky are the best, and the mountains, I imagine; the first would go well as a pendant to those with the yellow sky.'*
LITERATURE Scherjon and de Gruyter 1937, Saint Rémy nr 75 and p 268: letter 615; it is impossible to determine the precise period in which it was done or sent off
EDITORS' COMMENT With the exception of F 712 the paintings of olive trees are difficult to date, since the references in the letters are vague.
COLLECTION Amsterdam, Rijksmuseum Vincent van Gogh [Vincent van Gogh Foundation, inv nr F 707]

F 708 [H 723] OLIVE TREES: PALE BLUE SKY

Canvas 73.5 × 91.5 [29 × 36]
Saint Rémy September-November 1889
LETTERS 608 [28 September], 615 [between 16 November and 8 December], B 21 [between 16 November and 8 December], 621 [3 January 1890] and 629 [29 April] See F 707
LITERATURE Scherjon and de Gruyter 1937, Saint Rémy nr 8 and p 268: June 1889; letters 595, 600 and 615; it is impossible to determine the precise period in which it was done or sent off
EDITORS' COMMENT See F 707
COLLECTION London, Mr and Mrs W.H. Annenberg

F 709 [H 725] OLIVE TREES: BRIGHT BLUE SKY

Canvas 44 × 59 [17¼ × 23¼]
Saint Rémy September-November 1889
LETTERS 608 [28 September], 615 [between 16 November and 8 December], B 21 [between 16 November and 8 December], 621 [3 January 1890] and 629 [29 April] See F 707
LITERATURE Scherjon and de Gruyter 1937, Saint Rémy nr 171
EDITORS' COMMENT See F 707
COLLECTION Amsterdam, Rijksmuseum Vincent van Gogh [Vincent van Gogh Foundation, inv nr F 709]

F 704

F 706

F 709

F 710

F 711

F 714

F 715

F 716

F 710 [H 638] OLIVE TREES: YELLOW SKY WITH SUN

Canvas 74 × 93 [29 × 36½]
Saint Rémy September-November 1889
LETTERS 608 [28 September], 615 [between 16 November and 8 December], B 21 [between 16 November and 8 December], 621 [3 January 1890] and 629 [29 April] See F 707
LITERATURE Scherjon and de Gruyter 1937, Saint Rémy nr 74: letters 615, 621 and 629
EDITORS' COMMENT See F 707
COLLECTION Minneapolis, The Minneapolis Institute of Arts [acquired 1951; Dunwoody Fund], Bulletin of the Minneapolis Institute of Arts 1951, pp 113-20

F 710a OLIVE TREES

Left out by Faille in his manuscript for the present edition
See REJECTED WORKS

F 711 [H 724] THE OLIVE PLANTATION

Canvas 53.5 × 64.5 [21 × 25½]
Saint Rémy September-November 1889
LETTERS 608 [28 September], 615 [between 16 November and 8 December], B 21 [between 16 November and 8 December], 621 [3 January 1890] and 629 [29 April] See F 707
LITERATURE Scherjon and de Gruyter 1937, Saint Rémy nr 172
EDITORS' COMMENT See F 707
COLLECTION Switzerland, Private Collection

F 712 [H 635] OLIVE TREES: BLUE SKY WITH LARGE WHITE CLOUD

Canvas 72.5 × 92 [28½ × 36¼]
Compare drawing F 1544
Saint Rémy June-July 1889
LETTER 607 [19 September] *'In return I am sending you with the portrait the following canvases: ...Study of Olives...Olives... ...The "Olives" with a white cloud and a background of mountains, as well as the "Moonrise" and the night effect, are exaggerations from the point of view of arrangement, their lines are warped as in old wood...
Altogether I think nothing in it at all good except the..."Olives" with the blue hills...where these lines are close and deliberate it begins to be a picture, even if it is exaggerated.'*
LITERATURE Scherjon and de Gruyter 1937, Saint Rémy nr 50: letters 607 and 615. J. Leymarie, Van Gogh, 1951, p 124, nr 113: June-July; in style and composition close to F 622; to the right the Massif du Gaussier, to the left the 'Tunnel'
COLLECTION New York, Mr and Mrs John Hay Whitney

F 713 OLIVE TREES

Left out by Faille in his manuscript for the present edition
See REJECTED WORKS

F 714 [H 726] OLIVE TREES: BRIGHT BLUE SKY

Canvas 49 × 63 [19¼ × 24¾]
Compare drawing F 1555
Saint Rémy September-November 1889
LETTERS 608 [28 September], 615 [between 16 November and 8 December], B 21 [between 16 November and 8 December], 621 [3 January 1890] and 629 [29 April] See F 707
LITERATURE Scherjon and de Gruyter 1937, Saint Rémy nr 169
EDITORS' COMMENT See F 707

COLLECTION Edinburgh, National Gallery of
Scotland [acquired 1934], inv nr 1803, cat 1957,
p 108

F 715 [H 641] OLIVE TREES

Canvas 73 × 93 [28¾ × 36½]
Saint Rémy September-November 1889
LETTERS 608 [28 September], 615 [between 16
November and 8 December], B 21 [between 16
November and 8 December], 621 [3 January 1890]
and 629 [29 April] See F 707
LITERATURE Scherjon and de Gruyter 1937, Saint
Rémy nr 76 and p 268; letter 615; it is impossible to
determine the precise period in which it was done
or sent off
EDITORS' COMMENT See F 707
COLLECTION Kansas City, Nelson Gallery-Atkins
Museum [acquired 1932; Nelson Fund], inv nr 32.2,
Handbook 1959, p 125

F 715a OLIVE TREES

Left out by Faille in his manuscript for the present
edition
See REJECTED WORKS

F 716 [H 728] OLIVE TREES AGAINST A SLOPE OF A HILL

Canvas 33 × 40 [13 × 15¾]
Saint Rémy September-November 1889
LETTERS 608 [28 September], 615 [between 16
November and 8 December], B 21 [between 16
November and 8 December], 621 [3 January 1890]
and 629 [29 April] See F 707
LITERATURE Scherjon and de Gruyter 1937, Saint
Rémy nr 170
EDITORS' COMMENT See F 707
COLLECTION Amsterdam, Rijksmuseum Vincent
van Gogh [Vincent van Gogh Foundation, inv
nr F 716]

F 717 [H 633] WHEATFIELD WITH CYPRESS, AT THE HAUTE GALLINE, NEAR EYGALIÈRES

Canvas 73 × 93.5 [28¾ × 36¾]
Compare F 615, F 743 and drawing F 1538
Saint Rémy June-July 1889
LETTER 608 [29 September] *'So I will send them at
the next opportunity – or rather they are leaving
today with other canvases – as follows: ... Wheat
Field and Cypresses ...'*
LITERATURE Scherjon and de Gruyter 1937, Saint
Rémy nr 48: letter 608
COLLECTION Switzerland, Private Collection

F 712

F 717

F 718

F 719

F 722

F 724

F 718 [H 615] THE GREEN WHEATFIELD
BEHIND THE ASYLUM

Canvas 73 × 92 [28¾ × 36¼]
Saint Rémy June 1889
LETTERS 594 [9 June] 'I am working on two
landscapes (size 30 canvases), views taken in the
hills...'
608 [28 September] 'So I will send them at the next
opportunity – or rather they are leaving today with
other canvases – as follows: Wheat Fields...'
LITERATURE Scherjon and de Gruyter 1937, Saint
Rémy nr 7: letters 594, 596 and 608
COLLECTION Formerly Hugo Moser
Present owner unknown

F 719 [H 610] GREEN WHEAT

Canvas 73.5 × 92.5 [29 × 36½]
Compare drawing F 1548
Saint Rémy June 1889
LITERATURE Volne Smery XXII, 6-8 [year
unknown], p 157. A. Volavka, La peinture française
au musée d'art moderne de Prague, 1934. Scherjon
and de Gruyter 1937, Saint Rémy nr 12: letters 597
and 608. Carl Nordenfalk, Konsthistorisk Tidskrift
1946, p 94, note 1
COLLECTION Prague, Národní Galerie [acquired
1923], inv nr 0-3208, cat Sbírka francouzského
umění 1962, nr 59

F 720 [H 662] THE FIELD ENCLOSURE

Canvas 72 × 92 [28¼ × 36¼]
Compare F 650, F 737, drawings F 1552 and SD 1728
[same site]
Saint Rémy spring 1890
LITERATURE Scherjon and de Gruyter 1937, Saint
Rémy nr 79: letters 614, 617 and B 21. Tralbaut
Bildbiographie 1958, pp 112-3: March or April
1890. Cat van Gogh 1959, Rijksmuseum Kröller-
Müller, nr 235: accepts neither of the former letters,
which are related to F 737; F 720 however has
affinities to F 724 and should be dated May 1890
EDITORS' COMMENT The young wheat and the
flowers indicate a dating in spring [1890]. The
letters given in the cat Kröller-Müller refer to F 737.
COLLECTION Otterlo, Rijksmuseum Kröller-
Müller, inv nr 284-12, cat van Gogh 1970, nr 235

F 721 [H 730] A MEADOW IN THE MOUNTAINS:
LE MAS DE SAINT PAUL, CALLED LE MAS
DE GEORGE

Canvas 73 × 91.5 [28¾ × 36]
Saint Rémy December 1889
LETTERS 621 [3 January 1890] 'Today I sent off
some canvases, as follows: ..."The Fields." Fields of
young wheat with background of lilac mountains and
yellowish sky.'
622 [4 January] See F 663
LITERATURE Scherjon and de Gruyter 1937, Saint
Rémy nr 82: letter 622; the small canvas mentioned
in letter 622 is nr 82bis, F 663. Cat van Gogh 1959,
Rijksmuseum Kröller-Müller, nr 247: doubts that
F 721 is the painting described in letter 622
EDITORS' COMMENT It is uncertain whether the
passages from letters 621 and 622 are to be
connected with this painting. If this is the painting
mentioned in the letters, Roulin must have been its
first owner.
COLLECTION Otterlo, Rijksmuseum Kröller-
Müller, inv nr 282-12, cat van Gogh 1970, nr 247

F 722 [H 729] THE MEADOW BEHIND SAINT
PAUL'S HOSPITAL

Canvas 21.5 × 32.5 [8½ × 12¾]
Compare F 611 and drawing F 1547
Saint Rémy November-December 1889

LITERATURE Scherjon and de Gruyter 1937, Saint Rémy nr 161
COLLECTION Formerly The Hague, Heirs of H. P. Bremmer
Present owner unknown

F 723 [H 731] AT THE FOOT OF THE MOUNTAINS

Canvas 37.5 × 30.5 [14¾ × 12]
Compare drawing F 1549 verso
Saint Rémy June 1889
LITERATURE Scherjon and de Gruyter 1937, Saint Rémy nr 175
COLLECTION Scheveningen, Netherlands, Miss E. Ribbius Peletier

F 724 [H 732] ON THE BORDER OF THE ALPILLES

Canvas 59 × 72 [23¼ × 28¼]
Saint Rémy April 1890
LITERATURE Scherjon and de Gruyter 1937, Saint Rémy nr 114: letter 644. J. Leymarie, Van Gogh, 1951, pp 127-8, nr 122: May 1890; letters 615 and 622; represented are 'Les Alpilles,' a range of small mountains to the south of Saint Rémy. Cat van Gogh 1966, Rijksmuseum Kröller-Müller, nr 248
EDITORS' COMMENT Neither the quotations from letter 630, cited by Faille in his manuscript for the present edition in connection with this painting, nor those cited by other scholars refer to it.
COLLECTION Otterlo, Rijksmuseum Kröller-Müller, inv nr 278-12, cat van Gogh 1970, nr 248

F 725 [H 734] LE MONT GAUSSIER WITH THE MAS DE SAINT PAUL

Canvas 53 × 70 [21 × 27½]
Saint Rémy May 1890
LITERATURE Scherjon and de Gruyter 1937, Saint Rémy nr 179
COLLECTION London, Private Collection

F 723

F 725

F 720

F 721

F 726

F 727

F 728

F 731

F 730

F 726 [H 733] LANDSCAPE IN THE
NEIGHBORHOOD OF SAINT RÉMY

Canvas 33 × 41 [13 × 16¼]
Saint Rémy spring 1890
LETTER 644 [Auvers 24 June] *'The canvases have
arrived now from there ... a little canvas with
mountains ...'*
LITERATURE Not in Scherjon and de Gruyter 1937
COLLECTION New York, Museum of Modern Art
[gift of A. Conger Goodyear]

F 727 [H p 557] A SPOT OF GREENERY:
VALLEY WITH PLOWMAN SEEN FROM
ABOVE

Canvas 33 × 41 [13 × 16¼]
Saint Rémy early spring 1890
LITERATURE Scherjon and de Gruyter 1937, Saint
Rémy nr 183
EDITORS' COMMENT The editors are not
convinced that the passage from letter 632 which
Faille connects with F 727 really concerns this
painting.
COLLECTION Formerly Holzdorf, Otto Krebs
Present owner unknown

F 728 [H 735] A ROAD AT SAINT RÉMY WITH
A FIGURE

Canvas 32.5 × 40.5 [12¾ × 16]
Saint Rémy May 1890
LITERATURE Scherjon and de Gruyter 1937, Saint
Rémy nr 183
COLLECTION Lausanne, Private Collection

F 729 LANDSCAPE AT SUNRISE

Left out by Faille in his manuscript for the present
edition
See REJECTED WORKS

F 730 [H 736] THE GARDEN OF SAINT PAUL'S
HOSPITAL

Canvas 50 × 63 [19¾ × 24¾]
Saint Rémy October 1889
LITERATURE Scherjon and de Gruyter 1937, Saint
Rémy nr 158
COLLECTION Private Collection

F 731 [H 738] TREES IN THE GARDEN OF
SAINT PAUL'S HOSPITAL

Canvas 42 × 32 [16½ × 12½]
Compare F 640 and water color F 1535 [same site]
Saint Rémy October-November 1889
LITERATURE Scherjon and de Gruyter 1937, Saint
Rémy nr 151
COLLECTION Switzerland, Private Collection

F 732 [H 737] THE STONE BENCH IN THE
GARDEN OF SAINT PAUL'S HOSPITAL

Canvas 39 × 46 [15¼ × 18]
Saint Rémy October 1889
LITERATURE Scherjon and de Gruyter 1937, Saint
Rémy nr 157
COLLECTION São Paulo, Museu de Arte, cat 1963,
nr 115

F 733 [H 663] THE GARDEN OF SAINT PAUL'S
HOSPITAL WITH FIGURE

Canvas 61 × 50 [24 × 19¾]
Saint Rémy November 1889
LITERATURE Scherjon and de Gruyter 1937, Saint
Rémy nr 66: letter 613. Cat van Gogh 1959,
Rijksmuseum Kröller-Müller, nr 238: incorrectly
identified by Scherjon and de Gruyter as mentioned

in letter 613; this reference applies to F 652
COLLECTION Otterlo, Rijksmuseum Kröller-
Müller, inv nr 315-17, cat van Gogh 1970, nr 238

F 734 [H 741] THE GARDEN OF SAINT PAUL'S
HOSPITAL

Canvas 95 × 75.5 [37½ × 29¾]
Signed in lower right: Vincent
Saint Rémy May-June 1889
LITERATURE Scherjon and de Gruyter 1937, Saint
Rémy nr 155
COLLECTION Otterlo, Rijksmuseum Kröller-
Müller, inv nr 304-20, cat van Gogh 1970, nr 232

F 735 [H 631] RISING MOON: HAYCOCKS

Canvas 72 × 92 [28¼ × 36¼]
Saint Rémy July 1889
LETTERS 603 [6 July] '*Anyway, meanwhile the only
thing I can do is plod a little at my pictures. I have
one going of a moonrise over the same field as the
sketch in Gauguin's letter, but in it some stacks take
the place of the wheat. It is dull yellow-ocher and
violet.*'
607 [19 September] '*In return I am sending you with
the portrait the following canvases: Moonrise
(ricks) ... as well as the "Moonrise" and ... are
exaggerations from the point of view of arrangement,
their lines are warped as in old wood ... where these
lines are close and deliberate it begins to be a picture
even if it is exaggerated.*'
LITERATURE Scherjon and de Gruyter 1937, Saint
Rémy nr 17: letters 603 and 607. Cat van Gogh
1959, Rijksmuseum Kröller-Müller, nr 246: F 625a
is a forgery with the same motif. Cat van Gogh
1966, Rijksmuseum Kröller-Müller, nr 246: July
1889; letter 608
COLLECTION Otterlo, Rijksmuseum Kröller-
Müller, inv nr 310-12, cat van Gogh 1970, nr 246

F 736 [H 815] RISING MOON: HAYCOCKS

Left out by Faille in his manuscript for the present
edition
See REJECTED WORKS

F 732

F 733

F 734

F 735

F 737

F 743

F 737 [H 739] LANDSCAPE WITH RISING SUN

Canvas 71 × 90.5 [28 × 35¾]
Compare F 650, F 720, drawings F 1552 and SD 1728
[same site]
Saint Rémy November 1889
LETTERS W 16 [after 8 December] '*I think I shall
send to Brussels: ...and finally a field of young wheat
at sunrise.*'
614 [after 16 November] '*As for the Vingtistes, here
is what I'd like to exhibit: ...6. Wheat Field at
Sunrise, on which I am working at the moment.*'
614b [to Octave Maus; 20 November] '*It's a
pleasure to accept your invitation to exhibit with the
Vingtistes. Here you have the list of paintings I am
reserving for you: ...5. Wheatfield at Sunrise (Saint
Rémy)...*'
B 21 [between 16 November and 8 December] '*Another canvas shows the sun rising over a field of
young wheat; lines fleeting away, furrows rising up
high into the picture toward a wall and a row of lilac
hills. The field is violet and yellow-green. The white
sun is surrounded by a great yellow halo. Here, in
contrast to the other canvas, I have tried to express
calmness, a great peace.*'
617 [about 9 December] '*Perhaps you will also see it
in the canvas for the Vingtistes, which I sent off
yesterday; the field of wheat at sunrise ...I am curious
to know what you will say about the "Wheat
Field"...*'
T 22 [Paris 22 December] '*I received the package
containing your wheat field and ...The wheat field has
perhaps more poetry in it; it is like a memory of
something one has once seen.*'
LITERATURE Scherjon and de Gruyter 1937, Saint
Rémy nr 181. Cat van Gogh 1959, Rijksmuseum
Kröller-Müller, nr 235: this work, rather then F 720,
is probably the one described in the above-
mentioned letters, as the '*wheatfield at sunrise*'
COLLECTION Princeton, New Jersey, Mrs Robert
Oppenheimer

F 738 [H 740] LANDSCAPE AT SUNSET

Left out by Faille in his manuscript for the present
edition
See REJECTED WORKS

F 739 [H 742] LANDSCAPE WITH RABBITS

Canvas 33 × 40.5 [13 × 16]
Saint Rémy October 1889
LITERATURE Scherjon and de Gruyter 1937, Saint
Rémy nr 180
COLLECTION Amsterdam, Rijksmuseum Vincent
van Gogh [Vincent van Gogh Foundation, inv
nr F 739]

F 740 [Hp 557] THE LITTLE STREAM
Auvers period; see after F 824

F 741 THE CYPRESSES

Left out by Faille in his manuscript for the present
edition
See REJECTED WORKS

F 741a THE CYPRESSES

Left out by Faille in his manuscript for the present
edition
See REJECTED WORKS

F 742 [H 744] A CLUMP OF TREES IN THE
GARDEN OF SAINT PAUL'S HOSPITAL

Canvas 46 × 51 [18 × 20]
Saint Rémy autumn 1889
LITERATURE Scherjon and de Gruyter 1927, Saint
Rémy nr 154. Cat van Gogh 1959, Rijksmuseum

Kröller-Müller, nr 237: November 1889
COLLECTION Otterlo, Rijksmuseum Kröller-
Müller, inv nr 316-00, cat van Gogh 1970, nr 237

F 743 [H 634] THE CYPRESS AND THE FLOWERING TREE

Canvas 52 × 65 [20½ × 25½]
Compare F 615, F 717 and drawing F 1538
Saint Rémy June-July 1889
LETTERS 608 [28 September] *'Soon I shall send you some smaller canvases with the four or five studies that I want to give Mother and our sister. These studies are drying now, they are size 10 and 12 canvases, small copies of the "Wheat Field and Cypresses"...'*
618 [before 8 December] *'Yesterday I sent off by post three packages, containing studies, which I hope will reach you safely... Among the studies you will find the following which are for Mother and our sister: ... "Wheat Field with Cypresses"...'*
LITERATURE J. G. Goulinat, L'Amour de l'Art April 1925, pp 131-42. Scherjon and de Gruyter 1937, Saint Rémy nr 49: letters 608 and 618
COLLECTION Sale New York [Parke-Bernet] 25 February 1970, nr 10
Present owner unknown

F 744 [H 636] THE QUARRY

Canvas 60 × 72.5 [23½ × 28½]
Saint Rémy October 1889
LETTERS 610 [mid-October] *'Then this week I have also done the "Entrance to a Quarry," which is like something Japanese...'*
B 20 [first half of October] *'Among these studies there is an "Entrance to a Quarry": pale lilac rocks in reddish fields, as in certain Japanese drawings.'*
LITERATURE Scherjon and de Gruyter 1937, Saint Rémy nr 59: letters 610 and B 20
COLLECTION Amsterdam, Rijksmuseum Vincent van Gogh [Vincent van Gogh Foundation, inv nr F 744]

F 745 [H 745] UNDERGROWTH

Canvas 47 × 61 [18½ × 24]
Saint Rémy July 1889
LITERATURE Scherjon and de Gruyter 1937, Saint Rémy nr 159
EDITORS' COMMENT Stylistically closely linked with F 746 and accordingly to be dated July 1889; Faille dated the painting in September
COLLECTION Amsterdam, Rijksmuseum Vincent van Gogh [Vincent van Gogh Foundation, inv nr F 745]

F 746 [H 629] UNDERGROWTH

Canvas 74 × 92 [29¼ × 36¼]
Compare F 747
Saint Rémy July 1889
LETTERS 603 [6 July] *'I am also working on a new one with ivy.'*
608 [28 September] *'So I will send them at the next opportunity – or rather they are leaving today with other canvases – as follows: ... Ivy ...'*
T 30 [29 March 1890; postscript written by Theo's wife, Mrs J. van Gogh-Bonger] *'... but I managed to escape for a little while at the opening of the Indépendants to see your pictures there ... and while Theo was talking to all sorts of people I sat there for a whole fifteen minutes enjoying the delicious coolness and freshness of the "Undergrowth"...'*
LITERATURE Scherjon and de Gruyter 1937, Saint Rémy nr 19: letters 603 and 608
COLLECTION Amsterdam, Rijksmuseum Vincent van Gogh [Vincent van Gogh Foundation, inv nr F 746]

F 739

F 742

F 744

F 745

F 746

F 747

F 484

F 747 [H 743] UNDERGROWTH

Canvas 45 × 60 [17¾ × 23½]
Compare F 746
Saint Rémy July 1889
LETTERS 603 [6 July] and 608 [28 September]
See F 746
LITERATURE Scherjon and de Gruyter 1937, Saint Rémy nr 160
COLLECTION Otterlo, Rijksmuseum Kröller-Müller, inv nr 295-10, cat van Gogh 1970, nr 242

F 748 [H 706] BUTTERFLIES AND POPPIES
Auvers period; see after F 824

F 749 [H 707] ROSES AND A BEETLE
Auvers period; see after F 824

REDATED TO SAINT RÉMY

F 402 [H 705] TWO WHITE BUTTERFLIES

Canvas 54 × 46 [21¼ × 18]
Saint Rémy spring 1890
LITERATURE Faille 1928, nr 402: Arles March-April 1888; letter 471. Scherjon and de Gruyter 1937, Arles nr 184. Faille 1939, nr 705: Saint Rémy 1889. A. Bowness, exhib cat van Gogh London [Hayward Gallery] 1968-9, nr 190a: Saint Rémy May 1890
EDITORS' COMMENT Stylistically closely related to F 672.
COLLECTION Amsterdam, Rijksmuseum Vincent van Gogh [Vincent van Gogh Foundation, inv nr F 402]

F 483 [H 628] VINCENT'S BEDROOM IN ARLES

Canvas 56.5 × 74 [22¼ × 29]
Compare F 482, F 484 [same subject] and F 525 [portrait on the wall]
Saint Rémy September 1889
LETTERS 608 [28 September] '*Soon I shall send you some smaller canvases with the four or five studies that I want to give Mother and our sister. These studies are drying now, they are size 10 and 12 canvases, small copies of ... and the "Bedroom" ...*'
W 15 [October] See F 482
LITERATURE Faille 1928, nr 483: Arles October 1888; letters 554 and 555. Scherjon and de Gruyter 1937, Saint Rémy nr 27: letters 608, 610 and 618. Faille 1939, nr 628: Saint Rémy September 1889; letters 608, 610, 618 and T 22
EDITORS' COMMENT See F 482
COLLECTION Paris, Musée National du Louvre [acquired 1952], inv nr RF 1959-2, cat Impressionnistes 1959, nr 153

F 484 [H 510] VINCENT'S BEDROOM IN ARLES

Canvas 73 × 92 [28¾ × 36¼]
Compare F 482 and F 483
Saint Rémy September 1889
LETTERS 604 [4 or 5 September] '*So I have gone over the canvas of my bedroom.*'
W 15 [October] See F 482
B 22 [to Gauguin; shortly before 20 October 1888] '*I have done, still for my decoration, a size 30 canvas of my bedroom ...*'
617 [about 9 December] '*You will get the "Bedroom" at the same time.*'
T 22 [22 December] '*I received the package containing ... and the two bedrooms.*'
LITERATURE Faille 1928, nr 484: Arles October 1888 or Saint Rémy September 1889; letters 554, 555 and 604. Scherjon and de Gruyter 1937, Arles nr 112: letters 573 and B 22. Faille 1939, nr 510: Arles October 1888; letters 554, 555, B 22 and T 10. K. Bromig-Kolleritz, Die Selbstbildnisse Vincent van Goghs, 1955, pp 26-7, 115: the portrait on the

wall is probably a lost self portrait
EDITORS' COMMENT See F 482
COLLECTION Chicago, The Art Institute of
Chicago [acquired 1926; Helen B. Bartlett Memorial
Collection], inv nr 26.417, cat 1961, p 198

F 528 [H 546] SELF PORTRAIT

Canvas 51 × 45 [20 × 17¾]
Saint Rémy September 1889
LETTERS 608 [28 September] '*Soon I shall send you
some smaller canvases with the four or five studies
that I want to give Mother and our sister. These
studies are drying now, they are all size 10 and 12
canvases, small copies of ... and a little self portrait.*'
612 [to his mother; end October] '*Now I can tell you
what I promised you is quite ready – ... and a small
self portrait ... You will see from the self portrait I
add that ... I keep looking more or less like a peasant
of Zundert ...*'
LITERATURE Faille 1928, nr 528: Arles. Scherjon
and de Gruyter 1937, Auvers nr 220. Faille 1939,
nr 546: Auvers. K. Bromig-Kolleritz, Die Selbstbildnisse Vincent van Goghs, 1955, pp 25-6, 72-4,
114: Auvers F. Erpel, Die Selbstbildnisse Vincent
van Goghs, 1963, nr 44: Auvers; close in style to
F 779; the expression is morbid, near to death
COLLECTION Oslo, Nasjonal Galleriet, inv nr 943

F 531 [H 778] THE PEASANT

Canvas 61 × 50 [24 × 19¾]
Saint Rémy spring 1889
LITERATURE Faille 1928, nr 531: Arles. Scherjon
and de Gruyter 1937, Arles nr 174. Faille 1939,
nr 778: Saint Rémy May 1889. J. Leymarie, Van
Gogh, 1951, p 132, nr 136: Saint Rémy June 1889
COLLECTION Milan, Civica Galleria d'Arte
Moderna di Milano [Grassi Collection]

F 528

F 531

F 402

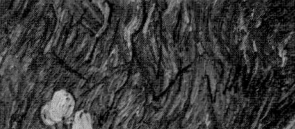

F 483

F 540

F 541

F 543

F 542

F 540 [H 712] L'ARLÉSIENNE, MADAME GINOUX: AGAINST A CHERRY-COLORED BACKGROUND [after a drawing by Paul Gauguin]

Canvas 60 × 50 [23½ × 19¾]
Compare F 541, F 542 and F 543
The titles of the books are: H. Beecher Stowe, *Uncle Tom's Cabin* and C. Dickens, *A Christmas Carol*
Saint Rémy January-February 1890
LETTERS 629 [29 April] '*At the same time I beg you to accept the various pictures I am sending you ... As for the portrait of the Arlésienne, you know that I have promised a copy of it to our friend Gauguin, and you must send it to him.*'
638 [3 June] '*He [Gachet] has now got so far as to understand the last portrait of the Arlésienne, of which you have one in pink ... What did Gauguin say of the last portrait of the Arlésienne, which is done after his drawing?*'
642 [17 June] '*Very glad too that he [Gauguin] thinks well of the head of the Arlésienne in question.*'
643 [to Gauguin; between 16 and 23 June] '*And it gives me enormous pleasure when you say the Arlésienne's portrait, which was based strictly on your drawing, is to your liking.*'
LITERATURE Faille 1928, nr 540: Arles. Scherjon and de Gruyter 1937, Saint Rémy nr 98: it is difficult to determine from the several letters the number of canvases that Vincent painted at Saint Rémy after Gauguin's drawing of an Arlésienne. Faille 1939, nr 712: Saint Rémy January-February 1890; letters 629, 638, 642 and 643. C. Nordenfalk, Journal of the Warburg and Courtauld Institutes 1947, p 138: the two books are mentioned in letters 582 [29 March 1889] and 583 [early April 1889], from Arles. F. Cachin, Gauguin, 1968, p 133: one of the painted portraits of van Gogh must have been painted not after a drawing but directly from life, while Gauguin was at work in his studio painting from drawings
EDITORS' COMMENT After Gauguin's drawing [Hanley Collection, Bradford, Pennsylvania; reproduced in J. Rewald, Post-Impressionism, 1956, p 356] and his painting AU CAFÉ [Wildenstein, nr 305]. According to letter 629 two versions were sent to Theo, one of them – it is not certain which – intended for Gauguin. Letter W 22 states that Theo had a version with a pink dress and a white background [F 543]. In none of the letters is a fourth version mentioned. It is possible that one of the paintings of van Gogh was done directly from life, as F. Cachin says, since Vincent writes only of two pictures done after the Gauguin drawing.
COLLECTION Rome, Galleria Nazionale d'Arte Moderna [acquired 1962]

F 541 [H 710] L'ARLÉSIENNE, MADAME GINOUX: AGAINST A LIGHT VIOLET-PINK BACKGROUND [after a drawing by Paul Gauguin]

Canvas 65 × 49 [25½ × 19¼]
Compare F 540, F 542 and F 543
The titles of the books are: H. Beecher Stowe, *Uncle Tom's cabin* and C. Dickens, *A Christmas Carol*
Saint Rémy January-February 1890
LETTERS 629 [29 April], 638 [3 June], 642 [17 June] and 643 [between 16 and 23 June] See F 540
W 22 [between 3 and 8 June] '*The portrait of the Arlésienne has a drab and lusterless flesh color, the eyes calm and very simple, a black dress, the background pink, and with her elbow she is leaning on a green table with green books.*'
LITERATURE Faille 1928, nr 541: Arles. Scherjon and de Gruyter 1937, Saint Rémy nr 99. Faille 1939, nr 710: Saint Rémy January-February 1890; letters 629, 638, 642 and 643. Cat van Gogh 1966, Rijksmuseum Kröller-Müller, nr 245: between February and April; letters T 37, W 20 and W 22. F. Cachin,

Gauguin, 1968: see under F 540
EDITORS' COMMENT See F 540
COLLECTION Otterlo, Rijksmuseum Kröller-
Müller, inv nr 292-14, cat van Gogh 1970, nr 245

F 542 [H 713] L'ARLÉSIENNE, MADAME
GINOUX: AGAINST A ROSE-COLORED
BACKGROUND [after a drawing by Paul
Gauguin]

Canvas 65 × 54 [25½ × 21¼]
Compare F 540, F 541 and F 543
The titles of the books are: H. Beecher Stowe, *Uncle
Tom's Cabin* and C. Dickens, *A Christmas Carol*
Saint Rémy January-February 1890
LETTERS 629 [29 April], 638 [3 June], 642 [17 June]
and 643 [between 16 and 23 June] See F 540
W 22 [between 3 and 8 June] '...*and they* [Theo and
Jo] *also have a new portrait of the Arlésienne in their
apartment. My friend Dr. Gachet is decidedly
enthusiastic about the latter portrait of the
Arlésienne, which I have made a copy of for myself
...The portrait of the Arlésienne has a drab and
lusterless flesh color, the eyes calm and very simple,
a black dress, the background pink, and with her
elbow she is leaning on a green table with green
books.*'
LITERATURE Faille 1928, nr 542: Arles. Scherjon
and de Gruyter 1937, Saint Rémy nr 100. Faille
1939, nr 713: Saint Rémy January-February 1890;
letters 629, 638, 642 and 643. C. Nordenfalk,
Journal of the Warburg and Courtauld Institutes
1947, pp 132-47: see under F 540. F. Cachin,
Gauguin, 1968: see under F 540
EDITORS' COMMENT See F 540
COLLECTION São Paulo, Museu de Arte, cat 1963,
nr 114

F 543 [H 711] L'ARLÉSIENNE, MADAME
GINOUX, IN A LIGHT DRESS: AGAINST A
CREAM-COLORED BACKGROUND WITH
FLOWERS

Canvas 66 × 54 [26 × 21¼]
Signed in lower right: Vincent
Compare sketch in letter W 22, F 540, F 541 and
F 542
The titles of the books are: H. Beecher Stowe, *Uncle
Tom's Cabin* and C. Dickens, *A Christmas Carol*
Saint Rémy April 1890
LETTERS 629 [29 April], 638 [3 June], 642 [17 June]
and 643 [between 16 and 23 June] See F 540
W 22 [between 3 and 8 June] '*But in the copy which is
in Theo's possession the dress is pink, the background
yellowish white, and the front of the open bodice is of
muslin of a white color merging into green. Among all
these colors only the hair, the eyebrows and the eyes
form black spots.*'
LITERATURE Faille 1928, nr 543: Arles. Scherjon
and de Gruyter 1937, Saint Rémy nr 101. Faille
1939, nr 711: Saint Rémy January-February 1890;
letters 629, 638, 642 and 643. C. Nordenfalk,
Journal of the Warburg and Courtauld Institutes
1947, p 138: Arles spring 1889; earliest of the four
versions of the Arlésienne; letters 582 and 583,
where Vincent mentions the titles of both the books
depicted in all four versions
EDITORS' COMMENT See F 540. This is the only
one of the four ARLÉSIENNES where the topmost
book lies backwards. The writing on the books does
not look like Vincent's usual writing.
COLLECTION New York, Mr and Mrs Harry
Bakwin, New York

F 581 [H 696] POPPIES IN THE FIELD

Canvas 71 × 91 [28 × 35¾]
Compare drawing F 1494
Saint Rémy April 1890
LITERATURE Faille 1928, nr 581: Arles. Scherjon

and de Gruyter 1937, Saint Rémy nr 108: letters 629
and 632. Faille 1939, nr 696: Saint Rémy April 1890
COLLECTION Bremen, Kunsthalle [acquired 1911],
cat 1935, p 37
Colorplate, p 409

F 585 [H 706] OLIVE YARD: BLUE SKY

Canvas 72 × 92 [28¼ × 36¼]
Signed in lower left: Vincent
Saint Rémy September-December 1889
LETTERS 607 [19 September] '...*I am sending you...
the following canvases:... Study of Olives...Olives*
[F 712]...'
608 [28 September], 615 [between 16 November and
8 December], B 21 [between 16 November and
8 December], 621 [3 January 1890] and 629 [29
April] See F 707
T 25 [22 January] '*Do you know, when I saw your
olive trees again, I admired them more and more...*'
LITERATURE Faille 1928, nr 585: Arles. Scherjon
and de Gruyter 1937, Saint Rémy nr 51 and p 268:
letters 608 and 615; impossible to determine the
precise period in which it was done or sent off.
Faille 1939, nr 708: Saint Rémy September-October
1889. Cat van Gogh 1959, Rijksmuseum Kröller-

Müller, nr 234: September-November 1889, on
grounds of stylistic similarity to F 710
EDITORS' COMMENT See F 707
COLLECTION Otterlo, Rijksmuseum Kröller-
Müller, inv nr 283-12, cat van Gogh 1970, nr 234
Colorplate, p 410

F 586 [H 651] OLIVE YARD: ORANGE SKY

Canvas 74 × 93 [29¼ × 36½]
Compare F 587
Saint Rémy September-December 1889
LETTERS 607 [19 September] and T 25 [22 January
1890] See F 585
608 [28 September 1889], 615 [between 16 November and 8 December], B 21 [between 16 November
and 8 December], 621 [3 January 1890] and 629
[29 April] See F 707
LITERATURE Faille 1928, nr 586: Arles. Scherjon
and de Gruyter 1937, St Rémy nr 73: letters 615,
621 and 629; a variant of F 587, with figures. Faille
1939, nr 651: Saint Rémy September-October 1889
EDITORS' COMMENT See F 707
COLLECTION Göteborg, Konstmuseum [acquired
1917], cat 1945, p 106

F 581

F 585

F 586

F 587

F 751

F 587 [H 650] OLIVE PICKING IN ORCHARD: ORANGE SKY

Canvas 73 × 92 [28¾ × 36¼]
Compare F 586
Saint Rémy September-December 1889
LETTERS 607 [19 September] and T 25 [22 January 1890] See F 585
608 [28 September 1889], 615 [between 16 November and 8 December], B 21 [between 16 November and 8 December], 621 [3 January 1890] and 629 [29 April] See F 707
LITERATURE Faille 1928, nr 587: Arles. Scherjon and de Gruyter 1937, Saint Rémy nr 72: letters 615, 621 and 629; a variant of F 586, without figures. Faille 1939, nr 650: Saint Rémy September-October. Cat van Gogh 1959, Rijksmuseum Kröller-Müller, nr 236: November 1889
EDITORS' COMMENT See F 707
COLLECTION Otterlo, Rijksmuseum Kröller-Müller, inv nr 285-12, cat van Gogh 1970, nr 236

F 818 [H 802] LANDSCAPE WITH TREES AND FIGURES

Canvas 50 × 65.5 [19¾ × 25¾]
Saint Rémy spring 1890
LITERATURE Faille 1928, nr 818: Auvers. Scherjon and de Gruyter 1937, Saint Rémy nr 153: letter 609. Faille 1939, nr 802: Auvers June 1890
EDITORS' COMMENT In his manuscript for the present edition Faille dated F 818 to October 1889. The pine trees do seem to indicate Saint Rémy, but the style is already quite close to that of the Auvers period.
COLLECTION Baltimore, The Baltimore Museum of Art, cat The Cone Collection 1967, nr 27

AUVERS PERIOD

F 750 [H 746] COTTAGES WITH THATCHED ROOFS

Canvas 60 × 73 [23½ × 28¾]
Compare water color F 1640 recto
Auvers May 1890
LETTER 636 [about 21 May] 'Now I have one study of old thatched roofs with a field of peas in flower in the foreground and some wheat, background of hills, a study which I think you will like.'
LITERATURE Vincent van Gogh, Lettres à Bernard, 1911, plate XCVI. S. Makowski, Apollon 1912, p 19 [with reproduction]. Cat Musée d'Art Moderne Occidental 1928, Moscow, nr 84. Scherjon and de Gruyter 1937, Auvers nr 117: letter 636
COLLECTION Leningrad, Hermitage [acquired 1930 from Museum of Modern Western Art, Morosov Collection], inv nr 9117, cat 1967, nr 69

F 751 [H 749] CHESTNUT TREES IN FLOWER: PINK AND WHITE BLOSSOMS

Canvas 70 × 58 [27½ × 22¾]
Auvers May 1890
LETTER 637 [25 May] 'I have ... a study of pink chestnuts and one of white chestnuts.'
LITERATURE Scherjon and de Gruyter 1937, Auvers nr 196. W. Eckhardt, Van Gogh und Deutschland, 1956, p 58: the painting was bought in 1896 by S. Fischer from Vollard, Paris
COLLECTION New York, Mrs. H. Harris-Jonas

F 752 [H 574] CHESTNUT TREE IN FLOWER: WHITE BLOSSOMS

Canvas 63 × 50.5 [24¾ × 20]
Auvers May 1890
LETTER 637 [25 May] See F 751
LITERATURE Scherjon and de Gruyter 1937, Auvers nr 195

COLLECTION Otterlo, Rijksmuseum Kröller-Müller, inv nr 294-10, cat van Gogh 1970, nr 253

F 753 [H 752] PORTRAIT OF DR GACHET

Canvas 66 × 57 [26 × 22½]
Compare sketch in letter 638 and F 754 [same model]
Auvers June 1890
LETTERS 638 [3 June] '*I am working at his
[Gachet's] portrait, the head with a white cap, very
fair, very light, the hands also a light flesh tint, a blue
frock coat and a cobalt blue background, leaning on a
red table, on which are a yellow book and a foxglove
plant with purple flowers. It has the same sentiment
as the self-portrait I did when I left for this place.*'
W 22 [between 3 and 8 June] '*I painted his [Gachet's]
portrait the other day... So the portrait of Dr Gachet
shows you a face the color of an overheated brick, and
scorched by the sun, with reddish hair and a white cap,
surrounded by a rustic scenery with a background of
blue hills; his clothes are ultramarine – this brings out
the face and makes it paler ...*'
W 23 [between 10 and 14 June] '*I painted a portrait
of Dr Gachet with an expression of melancholy,
which would seem to look like a grimace to many who
saw the canvas.*'
643 [to Gauguin; between 16 and 23 June] '*Meanwhile I have a portrait of Dr Gachet with the heart-
broken expression of our time.*'
LITERATURE Scherjon and de Gruyter 1937,
Auvers nr 120: letters 638 and 643. C. Nordenfalk,
Journal of the Warburg and Courtauld Institutes
1947, p 138: the books lying on the table, *Manette
Salomon* and *Germinie Lacerteux*, are both by J. and
E. de Goncourt. Exhib cat van Gogh et les peintres
d'Auvers-sur-Oise, Paris 1954-5, nr 46: around
4 June
COLLECTION New York, S. Kramarsky Trust
Fund

F 752

F 753

F 818

F 750

F 754

F 755

F 756

F 757

F 759

F 754 [H 753] PORTRAIT OF DR GACHET

Canvas 68 × 57 [26¾ × 22½]
Compare sketch in letter 638, F 753 and etching
F 1664 [same model]
Auvers early June 1890
LITERATURE Dr Doiteau, Aesculape November-
December 1923: cites letters 638 and 643 to show
that Vincent made two portraits of Dr Gachet.
Scherjon and de Gruyter 1937, Auvers nr 121:
letter 638; second version of F 753 done again
directly from the sitter. J. Leymarie, Van Gogh,
1951, pp 134-5, nr 149: letters 638 and 643. Exhib
cat Van Gogh et les peintres d'Auvers-sur-Oise,
Paris 1954-5, nr 46: between 4 and 14 June; letter
W 23. L. Anfray, Art-Documents April 1954, pp 4-6:
the text in letter 638 does not say that Dr Gachet
wanted to have a second version of his own portrait
but one of Vincent. M. E. Tralbaut, Vincent le mal
aimé, 1969, pp 316, 321: between 4 and 7 June
EDITORS' COMMENT Faille noted in his
manuscript: 'We consider this painting a very weak
replica of the preceding one, missing the piercing
look of F 753 and *"the grieving expression of our
time"* [letter 643].' The editors do not agree with
Faille's interpretation of the expression and regard
both pictures as works of high quality.
COLLECTION Paris, Musée National du Louvre
[acquired 1949; gift of Paul and Marguerite
Gachet], inv nr RF 1949-16, cat Impressionnistes
1959, nr 155

F 755 [Hp 557] DR GACHET'S GARDEN

Canvas 73 × 51.5 [28¾ × 20¼]
Auvers end May 1890
LETTERS 638 [3 June] '*Then I have painted two
studies at his house, which I gave him last week, an
aloe with marigolds and cypresses...*'
W 22 [between 3 and 8 June] '*...and every week I
shall go stay at his house one or two days in order to
work in his garden, where I have already painted two
studies, one with southern plants, aloes, cypresses,
marigolds...*'
LITERATURE Scherjon and de Gruyter 1937,
Auvers nr 123 [not reproduced]: letter 638. Exhib
cat Van Gogh et les peintres.d'Auvers, Paris 1954-5,
nr 43: 27 May 1890
COLLECTION Paris, Musée National du Louvre
[acquired 1954; gift of P. Gachet], inv nr RF 1954-15,
cat Impressionnistes 1959, nr 148
Colorplate, p 517

**F 756 [Hp 557] MARGUERITE GACHET IN
THE GARDEN**

Canvas 46 × 55 [18 × 21¾]
Auvers 1 June 1890
LETTERS 638 [3 June] '*Then I have painted two
studies at his* [Gachet's] *house, which I gave him last
week...then last Sunday some white roses, vines and
a white figure in it.*'
W 22 [between 3 and 8 June] '*...and every week I
shall go stay at his* [Gachet's] *house one or two days
in order to work in his garden, where I have already
painted two studies...the other with white roses, some
vines and a figure...*'
LITERATURE Scherjon and de Gruyter 1937,
Auvers nr 124 [not reproduced]: letter 638
COLLECTION Paris, Musée National du Louvre
[acquired 1954; gift of P. Gachet], inv nr RF 1954-13,
cat Impressionnistes 1959, nr 149

F 757 [H 626] PIETÀ [after Delacroix]

Canvas 42 × 34 [16½ × 13½]
Signed and annotated by Vincent in lower right:
d'après Eug Delacroix a apartenu à Diaz Vincent
Compare F 630
Auvers June 1890

LETTER 638 [3 June] '*Gachet also told me, that if I wished to give him great pleasure, he would like me to do again the "Pietà" by Delacroix for him, he looked at it for a long time.*'
LITERATURE J. F. Goulinat, L'Amour de l'Art April 1925, pp 131-42. Scherjon and de Gruyter 1937, Saint Rémy nr 33: letter 605. P. Gachet, Deux amis des impressionistes, 1956, p 119
EDITORS' COMMENT See F 630
COLLECTION Los Angeles, Private Collection

F 758 [HP 557] THE THATCH-ROOFED COTTAGES OF JORGUS

Canvas 33 × 40.5 [13 × 16]
Auvers June 1890
LETTER 640 [10 June] '*Since Sunday I have done two studies of houses among the trees.*'
LITERATURE Scherjon and de Gruyter 1937, Auvers nr 194 [not reproduced]
COLLECTION New York, Reader's Digest Collection

F 759 [H 754] HOUSES AT AUVERS

Canvas 61 × 73 [24 × 28¾]
Auvers June 1890
LETTER 640 [10 June] See F 758
LITERATURE Scherjon and de Gruyter 1937, Auvers nr 125: letter 640 concerns paintings F 759 and F 792. L. Reidemeister, Auf den Spuren der Maler der Ile de France, 1963, p 165: reproduces a photograph of the site at 5 rue de Gré in Auvers
COLLECTION Toledo, Ohio, The Toledo Museum of Art [acquired 1935; gift of Edw. Drummond Libbey], cat 1939, p 252

F 760 [H 756] LANDSCAPE WITH CARRIAGE AND TRAIN

Canvas 72 × 90 [28¼ × 35½]
Compare sketch in letter 643, F 683, drawings F 1587 recto, F 1609 recto and F 1610 recto [motif of horse and carriage]
Auvers June 1890
LETTERS 641 [14 June] '*I have another study in the style of the "Harvest," which is in your room where the piano is. Some fields seen from a height, with a road and a little carriage on it ...*'
W 23 [between 10 and 14 June] '*Yesterday in the square I painted a large landscape, showing fields as far as one can see, looked at from a height, different kinds of green growth, a potato field of a somber green color, between the regular beds the rich violet earth ...*'
LITERATURE Scherjon and de Gruyter 1937, Auvers nr 127; letter 641
COLLECTION Moscow, Pushkin Museum [acquired 1948], inv nr 3374, cat 1961, p 53

F 761 THE FIELDS

Canvas 50 × 65 [19¾ × 25½]
Auvers June-July 1890
LITERATURE Not in Scherjon and de Gruyter 1937. Not in Faille 1939
EDITORS' COMMENT Faille refers to letter 641. The passage about the '*poppies in alfalfa,*' however, apparently refers to F 636.
COLLECTION Zurich, Private Collection

F 760

F 761

F 758

F 762

F 763

F 762 [H 751] VINEYARDS AT AUVERS

Canvas 64 × 80 [25¼ × 31½]
Auvers June 1890
LETTERS 641 [14 June] '*I have a vineyard study,
which Mr Gachet liked very much the last time he
came to see me.*'
W 23 [between 10 and 14 June] '*There is another
landscape with vines and meadows in the foreground,
and behind them the roofs of the village.*'
LITERATURE Scherjon and de Gruyter 1937,
Auvers nr 129: letter 641
COLLECTION Saint Louis, City Art Museum [gift
of Mrs Mark C. Steinberg]

F 763 [H XV] STILL LIFE: VASE WITH FIELD
FLOWERS AND THISTLES

Painted on paper and subsequently lined with
canvas 66 × 45 [26 × 17¾]
Auvers June 1890
LETTER 642 [17 June] '*At the moment I am working
on two studies, one a bunch of wild plants, thistles,
ears of wheat, and sprays of different kinds of leaves –
the one almost red, the other bright green, the third
turning yellow.*'
LITERATURE Scherjon and de Gruyter 1937,
Auvers nr 130: letter 642
EDITORS' COMMENT The second painting
mentioned in the cited passage in letter 642 is F 766.
COLLECTION New York, André Meyer

F 764 [H p 557] STILL LIFE: JAPANESE VASE
WITH ROSES AND ANEMONES

Canvas 51 × 51 [20 × 20]
Auvers June 1890
LITERATURE Scherjon and de Gruyter 1937,
Auvers nr 192 [not reproduced]. P. Gachet,
Souvenirs de Cézanne et de Van Gogh, 1953: with
reproductions of the painting and of the Japanese
vase from his father's collection
COLLECTION Paris, Musée National du Louvre
[acquired 1954; gift of P. Gachet], inv nr RF
1954-12, cat Impressionnistes 1959, nr 151

F 764a STILL LIFE: VASE WITH ROSE-
MALLOWS

Canvas 42 × 29 [16¼ × 11½]
Auvers June 1890
LITERATURE Not in Faille 1928, Scherjon and de
Gruyter 1937 or Faille 1939
COLLECTION Amsterdam, Rijksmuseum Vincent
van Gogh [Vincent van Gogh Foundation, inv
nr F 764a]

F 765 [H 760] CORNER IN THE GARDEN OF
DAUBIGNY

Canvas 51 × 51 [20 × 20]
Compare sketch in letter 651, F 776 and F 777 [same
site]
Auvers before 17 June 1890
LETTER 642 [17 June] '*I am planning to make a
more important canvas of Daubigny's house and
garden, of which I already have a little study.*'
LITERATURE Scherjon and de Gruyter 1937,
Auvers nr 133: letter 642
COLLECTION Amsterdam, Rijksmuseum Vincent
van Gogh [Vincent van Gogh Foundation, inv
nr F 765]

F 766 [H 763] THE WHITE HOUSE AT NIGHT

Canvas 59.5 × 73 [23½ × 28¾]
Auvers June 1890
LETTER 642 [17 June] '*At the moment I am working
on two studies... The second study, a white house
among the trees, with a night sky and an orange light*'

in the window and dark greenery and a note of somber pink.'
LITERATURE Scherjon and de Gruyter 1937, Auvers nr 132: letter 642
EDITORS' COMMENT The first painting referred to in letter 642 is F 763.
COLLECTION Formerly Holzdorf, Otto Krebs Present owner unknown

F 767 [H 761] EARS OF WHEAT

Canvas 64.5 × 47 [25½ × 18½]
Compare sketch in letter 643
Auvers June 1890
LETTER 643 [to Gauguin; between 16 and 23 June]
'Look, here's an idea which may suit you, I am trying to do some studies of wheat like this, but I cannot draw it – nothing but ears of wheat with green-blue stalks, long leaves like ribbons of green shot with pink, ears that are just turning yellow, edged with the pale pink of the dusty bloom – a pink bindweed at the bottom twisted round a stem.'
LITERATURE Scherjon and de Gruyter 1937, Auvers nr 134: letter 643
COLLECTION Amsterdam, Rijksmuseum Vincent van Gogh [Vincent van Gogh Foundation, inv nr F 767]

F 768 [H 767] PORTRAIT OF MISS ADELINE RAVOUX, THE INNKEEPER'S DAUGHTER

Canvas 67 × 55 [26½ × 21¾]
Signed in lower left: Vincent
Compare F 769 and F 786 [same model]
Auvers June 1890
LETTER 644 [24 June] *'Last week I did a portrait of a girl of about sixteen, in blue against a blue back-ground, the daughter of the people with whom I am staying. I have given her this portrait ...'*
LITERATURE Scherjon and de Gruyter 1937, Auvers nr 136: letter 644. J. Leymarie, Van Gogh, 1951, p 136, nr 156: F 768 is the first version.
L. Anfray, Les Cahiers de Van Gogh 1957, pp 7-15: painted in one afternoon when Adeline was 13 years old; the other two portraits of Adeline were unknown to her; she thinks the painting was sold by her father Gustave about 1905 together wit F 790
COLLECTION Switzerland, Private Collection

F 768

F 764

F 764a

F 765

F 767

F 766

F 769

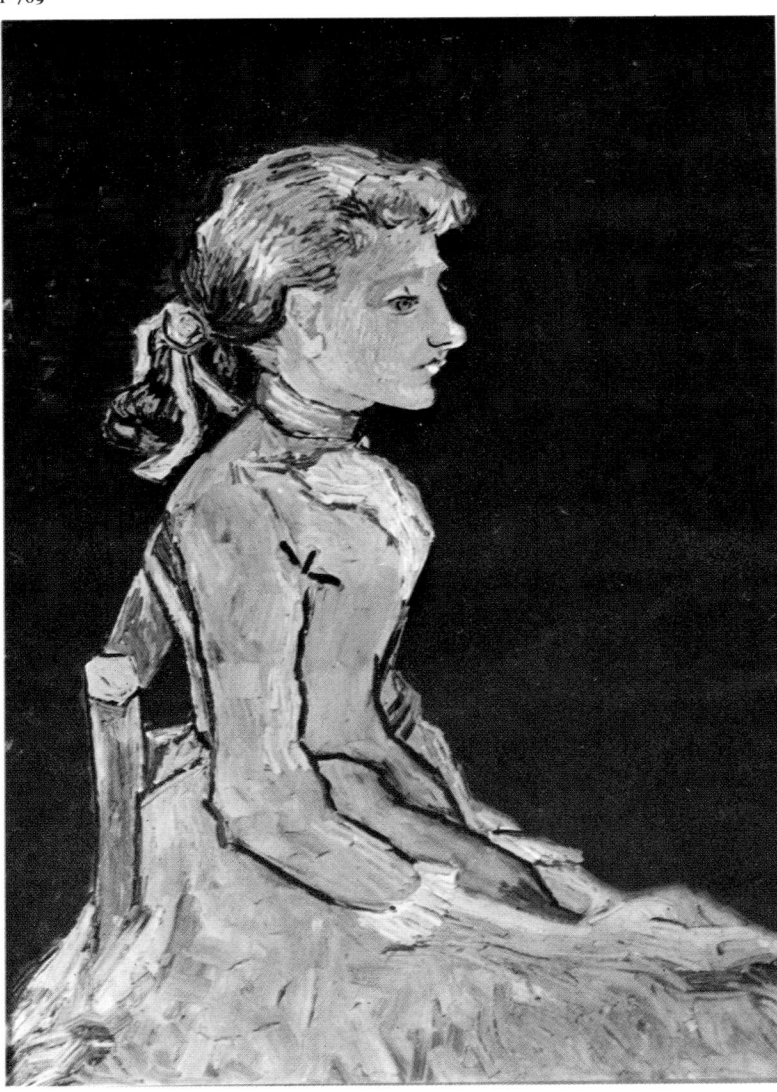

F 774

F 769 [H 768] PORTRAIT OF MISS ADELINE
RAVOUX, THE INNKEEPER'S DAUGHTER

Canvas 71.5 × 53 [28¼ × 21]
Compare F 768 and F 786 [same model]
Auvers June 1890
LITERATURE Scherjon and de Gruyter 1937,
Auvers nr 137: letter 644; this portrait is the replica
of F 768. J.Leymarie, Van Gogh, 1951, p 136,
nr 156: F 786 rather than the replica, F 769, is the
version sent to Theo. L.Anfray, Les Cahiers de van
Gogh 1957, pp 7-15: this painting and F 786 were
unknown to Adeline Ravoux
EDITORS' COMMENT Faille connected the variant
mentioned in letter 644 both with this painting and
with F 786. To the editors it seems more likely that
this passage refers to F 786 alone.
COLLECTION Lausanne, Private Collection

F 770 [H 762] THE CHÂTEAU D'AUVERS

Canvas 50 × 100 [19¾ × 39½]
Auvers June 1890
LETTER 644 [24 June] 'Then I have a canvas 40
inches long and only 20 inches high, of wheat fields,
and one which is a pendant to it, of undergrowth...
Lastly, an evening effect – two pear trees quite black
against a yellowing sky, with some wheat, and in the
violet background the château surrounded by somber
greenery.'
LITERATURE Scherjon and de Gruyter 1937,
Auvers nr 140: letters 644 and 646
COLLECTION Amsterdam, Rijksmuseum Vincent
van Gogh [Vincent van Gogh Foundation, inv
nr F 770]

F 771 [H 757] SHEAVES OF WHEAT

Canvas 50.5 × 101 [20 × 39¾]
Auvers July 1890
LITERATURE Scherjon and de Gruyter 1937,
Auvers nr 224
COLLECTION London, Mrs Charles Beatty

F 772 [H 769] MARGUERITE GACHET AT THE
PIANO

Canvas 102 × 50 [40¼ × 19¾]
Compare sketches in letter 645 [reproduced in the
Dutch edition of the letters only] and drawing
F 1623 recto
Auvers late June 1890
LETTERS W 22 [between 3 and 8 June] 'I painted his
[Gachet's] portrait the other day, and I am also
going to paint a portrait of his daughter, who is
nineteen years old.'
645 [27, 28 or 29 June] 'Yesterday and the day before
I painted Mlle Gachet's portrait, which I hope you
will see soon; the dress is red, the wall in the background green with orange spots, the carpet red with
green spots, the piano dark violet; it is 40 inches high
by 20 inches wide. It is a figure that I enjoyed
painting – but it is difficult ... I have noticed that this
canvas goes very well with another horizontal one of
the wheat, as one canvas is vertical and in pink tones,
the other pale green and greenish-yellow, the
complementary of pink ...'
T 39 [30 June] 'Your portrait of Mlle Gachet must be
admirable, and I shall be happy to see it with those
spots of orange in the background.'
LITERATURE Scherjon and de Gruyter 1937,
Auvers nr 141. J.Leymarie, Van Gogh, 1951, p 134,
nr 147: letters 638 and 649: the composition recalls
a contemporary painting by Lautrec,
MADEMOISELLE DIHAU AU PIANO [Musée
d'Albi, nr 46] which Vincent only saw later, in July
1890, at the Salon des Indépendants in Paris.
P.Gachet, Van Gogh à Auvers, 1953: Vincent
completed this work in two sessions on 28 and 29
June with his own palette and one borrowed from

Dr Gachet, the author's father
COLLECTION Basle, Öffentliche Kunstsammlung [acquired 1934], inv nr 1635, cat 1961, p 13

F 773 [H 764] UNDERGROWTH WITH TWO FIGURES

Canvas 50 × 100 [19¾ × 39½]
Compare sketch in letter 646
Auvers late June 1890
LETTERS 644 [24 June] '*Then I have a canvas 40 inches long and only 20 inches high, of wheat fields, and one which is a pendant to it, of undergrowth, lilac poplar trunks and at their foot, grass with flowers, pink, yellow, white and various greens.*'

646 [about 1 July] '*Here are three sketches ... Then the undergrowth around poplars, violet trunks running across the landscape, perpendicular like columns; the depths of the wood are blue and at the bottom of the big trunks, the grassy ground full of flowers, white, pink, yellow and green, long grass turning russet, and flowers.*'
LITERATURE Scherjon and de Gruyter 1937, Auvers nr 139. Tralbaut, Van Goghiana 1963, p 43: this painting was still deposited with Tanguy's widow in April 1894 under nr 286 of an old inventory list: toile en longueur [bois avec 2 figures au milieu]
COLLECTION Cincinnati, Cincinnati Museum [on loan from Miss Mary E. Johnston, Glendale, Ohio]

F 774 [H 766] PEASANT WOMAN AGAINST A BACKGROUND OF WHEAT

Canvas 92 × 73 [36¼ × 28¾]
Compare sketch in letter 646 and F 788
[same model]
Auvers late June 1890
LETTER 646 [about 1 July] '*Here are three sketches – one of a peasant woman, big yellow hat with a knot of sky-blue ribbons, very red face, rich blue blouse with orange spots, background of ears of wheat. It is a size 30 canvas, but I'm afraid it's really a bit coarse.*'
LITERATURE Scherjon and de Gruyter 1937, Auvers nr 143
COLLECTION Bern, H. R. Hahnloser

F 772

F 770

F 771

F 773

F 775

F 776

F 777

F 775 [H 808] THE PLAIN OF AUVERS

Canvas 50 × 101 [19¾ × 39¾]
Compare sketches in letters 645 [reproduced in the
Dutch edition of the letters only] and 646
Auvers June 1890
LETTERS 644 [24 June] See F 773
645 [27, 28 or 29 June] See F 772
646 [about 1 July] *'Then the horizontal landscape
with fields, like one of Michel's, but then the color is
soft green, yellow and green-blue.'*
LITERATURE Scherjon and de Gruyter 1937,
Auvers nr 138: letters 644 and 645. F. Novotny,
Art Bulletin March 1953, pp 37 and 43: compares
the aesthetic function of this painting with that of
drawing F 1500. Exhib cat Van Gogh et les peintres
d'Auvers, Paris 1954-5, nr 54: about 24 June
COLLECTION Vienna, Oesterreichische Staatsgalerie [acquired 1903; gift of the Society of the
Artists of the Austrian Secession], inv nr MG 301,
cat 1967, p 19
Colorplate, p 518

F 776 [H 758] THE GARDEN OF DAUBIGNY

Canvas 53 × 104 [20¾ × 41]
Compare sketch in letter 651, F 777 [same
composition] and F 765 [same site]
Auvers between 17 June and 23 July 1890
LETTERS 642 [17 June] See F 765
649 [about 9 July] *'Now the third canvas is
Daubigny's garden, a picture I have been thinking
about since I came here.'*
651 [23 July] *'Perhaps you will look at this sketch of
Daubigny's garden ... Daubigny's garden, foreground
of grass in green and pink. To the left a green and
lilac bush and the stem of a plant with whitish leaves.
In the middle a border of roses, to the right a wicket,
a wall, and above the wall a hazel tree with violet
foliage. Then a lilac hedge, a row of rounded yellow
lime trees, the house itself in the background, pink,
with a roof of bluish tiles. A bench and three chairs, a
figure in black with a yellow hat and in the foreground
a black cat. Sky pale green.'*
LITERATURE L. Justi, Museum der Gegenwart
1932, pp 220-7: both F 776 and F 777 are genuine.
M. J. Schretlen, Maandblad voor Beeldende
Kunsten 1933, pp 44-9: doubts F 776. K. Scheffler,
Kunst und Künstler 1933, pp 141-4: proposes to
bring F 776 and F 777 together for comparison.
A. Pfannstiel, Maandblad voor Beeldende Kunsten
1935, pp 140-2: both paintings are authentic; F 776
might be done after nature; F 777 is somewhat later.
M. J. Schretlen, Maandblad voor Beeldende
Kunsten 1935, pp 142-5: originally there was also a
cat in the foreground of F 776; it was scratched out
after 1900. A. Hentzen, Zeitschrift für Kunstgeschichte 1936, pp 252-9: gives a survey of the
history and opinions of both paintings with a color
analysis; he thinks F 776 to be genuine and F 777 to
be a forgery. W. Ueberwasser, Le Jardin de
Daubigny, 1936: critical study with x-ray
photographs; both paintings are authentic; F 776
might be done after nature; F 777 is somewhat
later. Not in Scherjon and de Gruyter 1937.
P. O. Rave, Kunst und Diktatur im Dritten Reich,
1949, p 65: history of the painting during Nazi era.
F. Roh, 'Entartete' Kunst, Kunstbarbarei im
Dritten Reich, 1962, pp 52 and 128: ditto.
L. Reidemeister, Auf den Spuren der Maler der Ile
de France, 1963, p 168: reproduces a photograph
of the garden of the house formerly inhabited by
Daubigny, 24 rue Général de Gaulle at Auvers
EDITORS' COMMENT The cat mentioned in letter
651 can be made out on x-rays of the painting. The
two other paintings mentioned in letter 649 are
F 778 and F 779. See also EDITORS' COMMENT
under F 777.
COLLECTION New York, S. Kramarsky Trust
Fund

F 777 [H 765] THE GARDEN OF DAUBIGNY WITH THE BLACK CAT

Canvas 56 × 101.5 [22 × 40]
Annotated by Vincent [?] in lower right: le jardin de Daubigny
Compare sketch in letter 651, F 776 [same composition] and F 765 [same site]
Auvers between 17 June and 23 July 1890
LITERATURE Scherjon and de Gruyter 1937, Auvers nr 146. For complete references see F 776
EDITORS' COMMENT There was an opportunity to compare F 776 and F 777 at Basle in 1967. Many differences were observed in brush strokes and color. Generally speaking F 777 had many weaker and on the other hand only a few stronger structural details than F 776. Comparison with F 776 left no doubt of the authenticity of F 776, the most harmonious painting of the two. F 777, being unequal in values, must have been painted with less

control.
COLLECTION Basle, Öffentliche Kunstsammlung [acquired 1968]

F 778 [H 806] FIELD UNDER THUNDER-CLOUDS

Canvas 50 × 100 [19¾ × 39½]
Auvers before 9 July 1890
LETTER 649 [about 9 July] '...I have painted three more big canvases since. They are vast fields of wheat under troubled skies, and I did not need to go out of my way to try to express sadness and extreme loneliness. I hope you will see them soon–for I hope to bring them to you in Paris as soon as possible, since I almost think that these canvases will tell you what I cannot say in words, the health and restorative forces that I see in the country.'
LITERATURE Scherjon and de Gruyter 1937,

Auvers nr 144
EDITORS' COMMENT The two other paintings mentioned in letter 649 are F 776 and F 779.
COLLECTION Amsterdam, Rijksmuseum Vincent van Gogh [Vincent van Gogh Foundation, inv nr F 778]

F 779 [H 809] CROWS IN THE WHEATFIELDS

Canvas 50.5 × 100.5 [20 × 39½]
Auvers before 9 July 1890
LETTER 649 [about 9 July] see F 778
LITERATURE Scherjon and de Gruyter 1937, Auvers nr 145. M. Roskill, Oud Holland 1966, pp 18-9
EDITORS' COMMENT See F 778
COLLECTION Amsterdam, Rijksmuseum Vincent van Gogh [Vincent van Gogh Foundation, inv nr F 779]

F 778

F 779

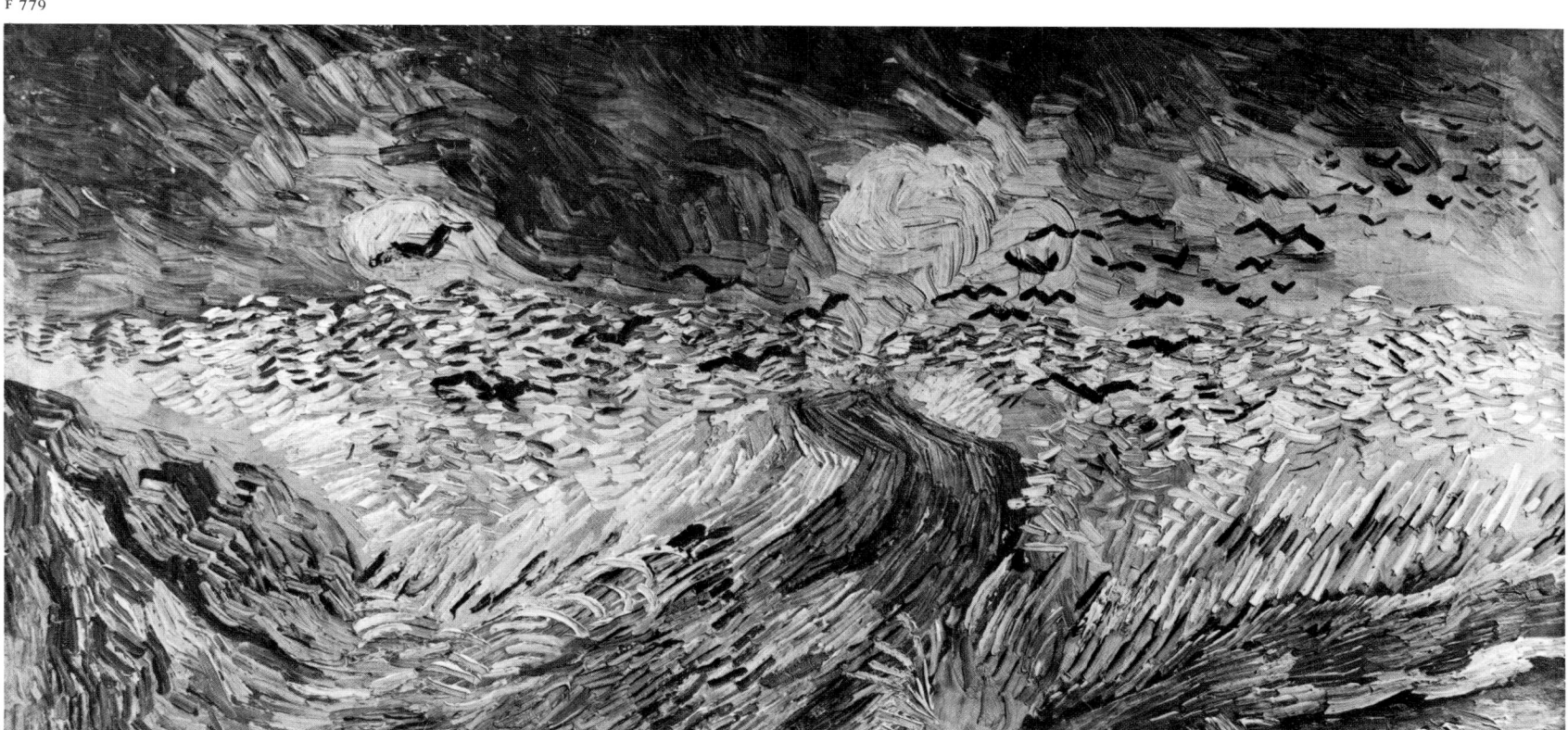

F 780

F 781

F 780 [H 770] THATCHED SANDSTONE
COTTAGES AT CHAPONVAL

Canvas 65 × 81 [25½ × 32]
Compare sketch in letter 651
Auvers July 1890
LETTER 651 [23 July] '*I add a sketch of some old
thatched roofs …*'
LITERATURE Scherjon and de Gruyter 1937,
Auvers nr 147
COLLECTION Zurich, Kunsthaus [acquired 1920;
bequest of H. Schuler], inv nr 1398

F 781 [H 807] THE PLAIN OF AUVERS

Canvas 73 × 92 [28¾ × 36¼]
Compare sketch in letter 651 and F 812
Auvers July 1890
LETTERS 650 [to his mother and sister; 9 or 10
July] '*I myself am quite absorbed in the immense
plain with wheatfields against the hills, boundless as a
sea, delicate yellow, delicate soft green, the delicate
violet of a dug-up and weeded piece of soil, checkered
at regular intervals with the green of flowering potato
plants, everything under a sky of delicate blue, white,
pink, violet tones.*'
651 [23 July] '*I add a sketch of some old thatched
roofs and the sketches of two size 30 canvases
representing vast fields of wheat after the rain.*'
LITERATURE Scherjon and de Gruyter 1937,
Auvers nr 149
COLLECTION Pittsburgh, Carnegie Institute
[donated by the family of Sarah Mellon Scaife]

F 782 [H 759] THE PLAIN WITH FARM NEAR
AUVERS

Canvas 73.5 × 92 [29 × 36¼]
Compare sketch in letter 651
Auvers July 1890
LETTERS 650 [9 or 10 July] and 651 [23 July]
See F 781
LITERATURE Scherjon and de Gruyter 1937,
Auvers nr 148: letter 650
COLLECTION Munich, Bayerische Staatsgemälde-
sammlungen [acquired 1929], inv nr 9584, cat 1966,
p 44
Colorplate, p 535

F 783 [H 773] TWO CHILDREN

Canvas 51.5 × 51.5 [20¼ × 20¼]
Compare F 784
Auvers June 1890
LITERATURE Vincent van Gogh, Lettres à
Bernard, 1911, plate LXXXVIII. Scherjon and de
Gruyter 1937, Auvers nr 218
COLLECTION Paris, Musée National du Louvre
[acquired 1954; gift of Paul Gachet], inv nr RF
1954-16, cat Impressionnistes 1959, nr 152

F 784 [H 774] TWO CHILDREN

Canvas 51.5 × 46.5 [20¼ × 18¼]
Compare F 783
Auvers June 1890
LITERATURE Scherjon and de Gruyter 1937,
Auvers nr 219
EDITORS' COMMENT Of F 783 and F 784 the latter
seems to be more finished.
COLLECTION France, Private Collection

F 785 [H 777] LEVERT'S DAUGHTER WITH
ORANGE

Canvas 50 × 51 [19¾ × 20]
Auvers June 1890
LITERATURE Scherjon and de Gruyter 1937,
Auvers nr 217. A. Carrié, Les Cahiers de van Gogh
1957, p 15: the child is the little daughter of the

carpenter Levert, neighbour of Ravoux
COLLECTION Winterthur, Switzerland, Mrs
L. Jäggli-Hahnloser

F 786 [H 776] PORTRAIT OF MISS ADELINE
RAVOUX, THE INNKEEPER'S DAUGHTER

Canvas 52 × 52 [20½ × 20½]
Compare F 768 and F 769 [same model]
Auvers June 1890
LETTER 644 [24 June] '*Last week I did a portrait of a
girl of about sixteen, in blue against a blue background, the daughter of the people with whom I am
staying. I have given her this portrait, but I made a
variant of it for you, a size 15 canvas.*'
LITERATURE Scherjon and de Gruyter 1937,
Auvers nr 222. J. Leymarie, Van Gogh, 1951, p 136,
nr 156: the original portrait of Miss Ravoux is
F 768; F 769 is a replica of poor quality; it may
therefore be assumed that F 786, though not
exactly a size-15 canvas, was the variant done for
Theo. L. Anfray, Les Cahiers de Van Gogh
1957, pp 7-15: this painting and F 769 were
unknown to Adeline Ravoux
EDITORS' COMMENT The editors agree with the
statement of Leymarie.
COLLECTION Cleveland, The Cleveland Museum
of Art [acquired 1958; bequest of L. C. Hanna], inv
nr 58.31, cat In memoriam L. C. Hanna 1958, nr 16

F 787 [H 772] YOUNG MAN WITH CORN-
FLOWER

Canvas 39 × 30.5 [15¼ × 12]
Auvers June 1890
LITERATURE Scherjon and de Gruyter 1937,
Auvers nr 221
COLLECTION Formerly Berlin, Paul von
Mendelssohn-Bartholdy
Present owner unknown

F 786

F 782

F 783

F 784

F 785

F 787

F 788

F 789

F 788 [H 775] YOUNG GIRL STANDING
AGAINST BACKGROUND OF WHEAT

Canvas 66 × 45 [26 × 17¾]
Compare sketch in letter 646 and F 774 [same model]
Auvers second half of June 1890
LETTER 643 [to Gauguin; between 16 and 23 June]
'Look, here's an idea which may suit you, I am
trying to do some studies of wheat like this, but I
cannot draw it – nothing but ears of wheat with green-
blue stalks, long leaves like ribbons of green shot
with pink, ears that are just turning yellow, edged
with the pale pink of the dusty bloom – a pink
bindweed at the bottom twisted round a stem. On this
very vivid yet tranquil background I would like to
paint some portraits. There are the greens of a
different quality, but of the same value, so as to form
a whole of green tones, which by its vibration will
make you think of the gentle rustle of the ears
swaying in the breeze: it is not at all easy as a color
scheme.'
LITERATURE Scherjon and de Gruyter 1937,
Auvers nr 190
COLLECTION Washington, National Gallery of
Art, inv nr 1694, cat Chester Dale Collection 1965,
p 129

F 789 [H p 557] THE CHURCH AT AUVERS

Canvas 94 × 74 [37 × 29¼]
Auvers first week of June 1890
LETTER W 22 [between 3 and 8 June] 'Apart from
these I have a larger picture of the village church – an
effect in which the building appears to be violet-hued
against a sky of a simple deep blue color, pure cobalt;
the stained-glass windows appear as ultramarine
blotches, the roof is violet and partly orange. In the
foreground some green plants in bloom, and with the
pink glow of sunshine on it.'
LITERATURE Scherjon and de Gruyter 1937,
Auvers nr 191 [not reproduced]. Exhib cat Van
Gogh et les peintres d'Auvers, Paris 1954-5, nr 45:
letter W 22, to be dated between 4 and 8 June.
L. Reidemeister, Auf den Spuren der Maler der Ile
de France, 1963, p 167: reproduces a photograph of
the site
COLLECTION Paris, Musée National du Louvre
[acquired 1951; gift of Paul Gachet], inv nr RF
1951-42, cat Impressionnistes 1959, nr 150
Colorplate, p 536

F 790 [H XVI] THE TOWN HALL IN AUVERS
ON THE 14TH OF JULY

Canvas 72 × 93 [28¼ × 36½]
Compare drawing F 1630 recto [same site]
Auvers middle of July 1890
LITERATURE Vincent van Gogh, Lettres à Bernard,
1911, plate XCIX. Scherjon and de Gruyter 1937,
Auvers nr 197. J. Leymarie, Van Gogh, 1951, p 136,
nr 155: compare drawing F 1630. M. E. Tralbaut,
Mededelingen van de Dienst voor Schone Kunsten
der gemeente 's-Gravenhage 1954, p 39: the
structure of the painting is related to the Japanese
print BOYS' HOLIDAY in the V.W. van Gogh
collection. A. Carrié, Les cahiers de van Gogh
1957, pp 7-15: the painting had been given to
Ravoux who sold it about 1905 for 10 francs
together with the portrait of Miss Ravoux [F 768] to
some painters in Meulan, one of them an American
named Harry Harronson. L. Reidemeister, Auf den
Spuren der Maler der Ile de France, 1963, p 163:
reproduces a photograph of the site
COLLECTION Mr and Mrs Leigh B. Block
[acquired 1944]

F 791 [H 771] THE HOUSE OF PÈRE PILON

Canvas 49 × 70 [19¼ × 27½]
Compare drawing F 1638 recto [same site]

Auvers May-early June 1890
LITERATURE Scherjon and de Gruyter 1937,
Auvers nr 201. L. Reidemeister, Auf den Spuren der
Maler der Ile de France, 1963, p 166: reproduces a
photograph of the site at 18 rue François Villon,
Auvers
EDITORS' COMMENT The title is first found in
Faille 1928, and apparently is based on information
since lost.
COLLECTION Athens, Stavros S. Niarchos, exhib
cat 1957, nr 28

F 792 [H 779] THATCH-ROOFED COTTAGES AT CORDEVILLE

Canvas 72 × 91 [28¼ × 35¾]
Compare drawing F 1637 recto [similar houses]
Auvers June 1890
LETTER 640 [10 June] See F 758
LITERATURE Faille 1928: Chaumes de Montcel.
Scherjon and de Gruyter 1937, Auvers nr 126: letter
640 concerns F 759 and F 792. Faille 1939: Chaumes
de Montcel. Exhib cat Van Gogh et les peintres
d'Auvers, Paris 1954-5, nr 47: according to Paul
Gachet the houses are situated in Cordeville and
not in Montcel
COLLECTION Paris, Musée National du Louvre
[acquired 1954; gift of P. Gachet], inv nr RF 1954-14,
cat Impressionnistes 1959, nr 154

F 793 [H 781] FARMS NEAR AUVERS

Canvas 50 × 100 [19¾ × 39½]
Compare F 806 [same site]
Auvers July 1890
LITERATURE Scherjon and de Gruyter 1937,
Auvers nr 223. Ronald Alley, cat Tate Gallery 1959,
p 273: letter W 21; probably one of the first
paintings of mossy thatched roofs executed at
Auvers; it appears to be unfinished
COLLECTION London, Tate Gallery [acquired
1933; bequest of F. Stoop], inv nr 4713, cat 1959,
p 273
Colorplate, p 553

F 794 [H 780] THE HOUSE OF PÈRE ÉLOI

Canvas 51 × 58 [20 × 22¾]
Auvers June-July 1890
LITERATURE Scherjon and de Gruyter 1937,
Auvers nr 202
EDITORS' COMMENT The title is first found in
Faille 1928, and apparently is based on information
since lost.
COLLECTION Formerly London, F. H. Herrmann
Present owner unknown

F 790

F 791

F 792

F 793

F 794

F 795

F 796

F 797

F 799

F 800

F 795 [H 783] THE AUVERS STAIRS WITH
FIVE FIGURES

Canvas 51 × 71 [20 × 28]
Compare F 796 [same site] and drawing F 1652 recto
[same figures]
Auvers July 1890
LITERATURE Scherjon and de Gruyter 1937,
Auvers nr 203. J. Leymarie, Van Gogh, 1951, p 133,
nr 144: the other version is F 796. R. M. Rogers,
Saint Louis Museum Bulletin April 1935, pp 20-2
EDITORS' COMMENT F 795 is more elaborate than
the other version, F 796.
COLLECTION Saint Louis, City Art Museum
[acquired 1935], Handbook 1953, p 144

F 796 [H 782] THE AUVERS STAIRS WITH
TWO FIGURES

Canvas 20.5 × 26 [8 × 10¼]
Compare F 795
Auvers July 1890
LITERATURE Scherjon and de Gruyter 1937,
Auvers nr 204
EDITORS' COMMENT See F 795
COLLECTION Tiegenhof, East Germany, Mr Loebb

F 797 [H 784] THE VESSENOTS AT AUVERS

Canvas 55 × 65 [21¾ × 25½]
Auvers early July 1890
LITERATURE Scherjon and de Gruyter 1937,
Auvers nr 206. J. Leymarie, Van Gogh, 1951, p 136,
nr 157: the house of Dr Gachet was situated in the
district of the Vessenots
COLLECTION Zurich, Mrs Dora Hahnloser-
Gassmann

F 798 [H 785] THE BANK OF THE OISE

Canvas 72 × 92 [28¼ × 36¼]
Auvers June 1890
LITERATURE Not in Scherjon and de Gruyter
1937. P. Leprohon, Tel fut Van Gogh, 1964, p 418:
Auvers; Faille's title 'LA GRENOUILLÈRE' is
wrong; The island 'La Grenouillère' is situated at
Rueil not far from the Chatou bridge; Vincent
never visited there during his stay at Auvers
EDITORS' COMMENT The possibility must not be
excluded that this work was executed in Paris
during the summer of 1887.
COLLECTION Detroit, The Detroit Institute of Arts

F 799 [H 787] VIEW AT AUVERS

Canvas 50 × 52 [19¾ × 20½]
Auvers June-July 1890
LITERATURE Scherjon and de Gruyter 1937,
Auvers nr 207
COLLECTION Amsterdam, Rijksmuseum Vincent
van Gogh [Vincent van Gogh Foundation, inv
nr F 799]

F 800 [H 788] VIEW OF AUVERS WITH
CHURCH

Canvas 34 × 42 [13½ × 16½]
Auvers June 1890
LITERATURE Scherjon and de Gruyter 1937,
Auvers nr 205
COLLECTION Providence, Rhode Island, Museum
of Art, Rhode Island School of Design [acquired
1948; donated in memory of Miss Dorothy Sturges]

F 801 [H 786] WHEATFIELDS WITH AUVERS
IN THE BACKGROUND

Canvas 43 × 50 [17 × 19¾]
Auvers June 1890
LITERATURE Scherjon and de Gruyter 1937,

Auvers nr 209
COLLECTION Switzerland, Private Collection

F 802 [H 790] ROAD AT AUVERS

Canvas 73 × 92 [28¾ × 36¼]
Auvers July 1890
LITERATURE Scherjon and de Gruyter 1937,
Auvers nr 210. Exhib cat van Gogh Munich 1956,
nr 161 : June 1890
COLLECTION Helsinki, Konstsammlingarna I
Atheneum [acquired 1903], cat 1962, p 40

F 803 [H 791] VIEW OF THE CHURCH OF
LABBEVILLE NEAR AUVERS

Canvas 44.5 × 60 [17½ × 23¾]
Auvers end June 1890
LITERATURE Faille 1928, nr 803 : Auvers. Scherjon
and de Gruyter 1937, Auvers nr 208. Faille 1939,
nr 791 : Auvers June 1890. J. Rewald, note in sales
cat London 24 April 1963 : identifies subject as the
chapel of Saint Paul's Hospital at Saint Rémy.
P. Leprohon, Tel fut Van Gogh, 1964, p 418 : the
picture represents the church of Labbeville, a
village in the neighbourhood of Auvers
EDITORS' COMMENT Dated by Faille in his
manuscript to Saint Rémy October-November
1889. He calls it the chapel of Saint Paul's Hospital
at Saint Rémy.
COLLECTION Elizabeth Taylor

F 804 [H 793] HOUSE AT AUVERS

Canvas 48.5 × 63 [19 × 24¾]
Auvers mid-June 1890
LETTER W 23 [between 10 and 14 June] '*Yesterday
...I painted a large landscape...And another one with
nothing but a green field of wheat, stretching away to
a white country house, surrounded by a white wall
with a single tree.*'
LITERATURE Scherjon and de Gruyter 1937,
Auvers nr 213
COLLECTION Washington, The Phillips Collection

F 798

F 802

F 801

F 803

F 804

F 805

F 806

F 807

F 808

F 810

F 805 [H 789] HOUSES AT AUVERS WITH ONE FIGURE

Canvas 73 × 60.5 [28¾ × 23¾]
Auvers June–July 1890
LITERATURE Scherjon and de Gruyter 1937,
Auvers nr 198. L. Reidemeister, Auf den Spuren der
Maler der Ile de France, 1963, p 164: reproduces a
photograph of the site, at 2 rue Marceau, Auvers
COLLECTION Boston, Museum of Fine Arts
[bequest of John T. Spaulding], inv nr 48.549, cat
1955, p 29

F 806 [H 792] FARM NEAR AUVERS WITH
TWO FIGURES

Canvas 38 × 45 [15 × 17¾]
Compare F 793 [same site]
Auvers July 1890
LITERATURE Scherjon and de Gruyter 1937,
Auvers nr 199
COLLECTION Amsterdam, Rijksmuseum Vincent
van Gogh [Vincent van Gogh Foundation, inv
nr F 806]

F 807 [H 794] FIELD OF GREEN WHEAT

Canvas 73 × 93 [28¾ × 36½]
Auvers early July 1890
LITERATURE Scherjon and de Gruyter 1937,
Auvers nr 212
COLLECTION Upperville, Virginia, Mr and Mrs
Paul Mellon

F 808 [H 796] WHEATFIELD WITH
CORNFLOWERS

Canvas 60 × 81 [23½ × 32]
Auvers first half of July 1890
LITERATURE Scherjon and de Gruyter 1937,
Auvers nr 211
COLLECTION Private Collection

F 809 [H 795] WHEAT STACKS

Canvas 50 × 100 [19¾ × 39½]
Auvers July 1890
LITERATURE Scherjon and de Gruyter 1937,
Auvers nr 225
COLLECTION Bern, H. R. Hahnloser

F 810 [H 799] HOUSES WITH SUNFLOWERS

Panel 31.5 × 41 [12½ × 16¼]
Auvers June 1890
LITERATURE Scherjon and de Gruyter 1937,
Auvers nr 200
COLLECTION Paris, A. C. M. Baronesse de
Rothschild

F 811 [H 798] LANDSCAPE AT AUVERS IN
THE RAIN

Canvas 50 × 100 [19¾ × 39½]
Auvers July 1890
LITERATURE Scherjon and de Gruyter 1937,
Auvers nr 226
COLLECTION Cardiff, National Museum of Wales
[acquired 1952; bequest of Gwendoline E. Davies],
cat The Davies Collection of French Art 1967,
pp 87-8

F 812 THE FIELDS

Canvas 50 × 40 [19¾ × 15¾]
Compare sketch in letter 651 and F 781
Auvers July 1890
LITERATURE Faille 1928, nr 812: Auvers. J. B. de
la Faille, Les faux van Gogh, 1930, p 10, nr 46,
plate XIII. Not in Scherjon and de Gruyter 1937 or

Faille 1939
EDITORS' COMMENT Left out by Faille in his
manuscript for the present edition, but accepted as
authentic by the editors.
COLLECTION Washington, The Phillips Collection

F 813 THE FIELDS

Left out by Faille in his manuscript for the present
edition
See REJECTED WORKS

F 814 [H 797] GARDEN AT AUVERS

Canvas 64 × 80 [25¼ × 31½]
Auvers July 1890
LITERATURE Scherjon and de Gruyter 1937,
Auvers nr 214
COLLECTION Paris, Jacques Walter

F 815 [H 800] THREE TREES

Canvas 64 × 78 [25¼ × 30¾]
Auvers July 1890
LITERATURE Scherjon and de Gruyter 1937,
Auvers nr 215
COLLECTION Otterlo, Rijksmuseum Kröller-
Müller, inv nr 317-13, cat van Gogh 1970, nr 254

F 816 [H 801] TREES, ROOTS AND BRANCHES

Canvas 50.5 × 100.5 [20 × 39½]
Auvers July 1890
LITERATURE Scherjon and de Gruyter 1937,
Auvers nr 227
COLLECTION Amsterdam, Rijksmuseum Vincent
van Gogh [Vincent van Gogh Foundation, inv
nr F 816]
Colorplate, p 554

F 809

F 812

F 811

F 814

F 815

F 816

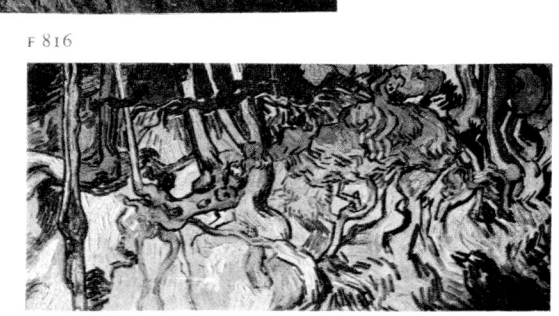

F 817

F 819

F 280

F 589

F 817 [H 803] THE GROVE

Canvas 73 × 92 [28¾ × 36¼]
Auvers June 1890
LITERATURE Scherjon and de Gruyter 1937,
Auvers nr 216
EDITORS' COMMENT The possibility must not be
excluded that this work was executed in Paris
during the summer of 1887.
COLLECTION New York, Mr and Mrs Joseph
H. Hazen

F 818 [H 802] LANDSCAPE WITH FIGURES
Saint Rémy period; see after F 749

F 819 [H 750] WOMEN WALKING ALONG THE
FIELDS

Canvas 32 × 61 [12½ × 24]
Auvers July 1890
LITERATURE Scherjon and de Gruyter 1937,
Auvers nr 142: letter 645
EDITORS' COMMENT Faille refers to a description
in letter 645 [27, 28 or 29 June] of a similar scene
which Vincent describes from reality. The colors
mentioned there, however, differ from this picture,
which might be a recollection of the impression
described in this letter. The style seems to be later
than June.
COLLECTION San Antonio, Texas, Marion
Koogler MacNay Art Institute, inv nr 1950.49

F 820 [H 747] BLOSSOMING CHESTNUT
BRANCHES

Canvas 72 × 91 [28¼ × 35¾]
Compare drawing F 1611 recto [similar motif]
Auvers before 25 May 1890
LETTER 637 [25 May] See F 751
LITERATURE Scherjon and de Gruyter 1937,
Auvers nr 118: letter 637
COLLECTION Zurich, E. Bührle, cat 1958, nr 246

F 821 [Hp 557] BRANCHES OF A WHITE
FLOWERING ACACIA TREE

Canvas 33 × 24.2 [13 × 9½]
Auvers 7 June 1890
LITERATURE Scherjon and de Gruyter 1937,
Auvers nr 193 [not reproduced]. M. E. Tralbaut,
Van Goghiana 1967. Idem, Van Gogh, le mal aimé,
1969, pp 316, 321 [with reproduction]: 7 June 1890
EDITORS' COMMENT Left out by Faille in his
manuscript for the present edition, but accepted as
authentic by the editors.
COLLECTION Stockholm, Nationalmuseum
[acquired 1966], inv nr NM 5939

F 822 [Hp 557] THE COWS [after a dry point by
Dr Gachet from Jordaens' painting in the
Musée des Beaux-Arts, Lille]

Canvas 55 × 65 [21¾ × 25½]
Auvers June-July 1890
LITERATURE Not in Scherjon and de Gruyter 1937.
P. Gachet, 'Les vaches'de J. Jordaens, 1954
EDITORS' COMMENT Left out by Faille in his
manuscript for the present edition, but accepted as
authentic by the editors.
COLLECTION Lille, Musée des Beaux-Arts
[acquired 1950; gift of P. Gachet]

F 823 THE WHEATFIELD

Left out by Faille in his manuscript for the present
edition
See REJECTED WORKS

F 824 LANDSCAPE

Left out by Faille in his manuscript for the present
edition
See REJECTED WORKS

REDATED TO AUVERS

F 280 [H 325] STILL LIFE: VASE WITH
DAISIES AND POPPIES

Canvas 65 × 50 [25½ × 19¾]
Auvers June 1890
LITERATURE Faille 1928, nr 280: Paris. Not in
Scherjon and de Gruyter 1937. Faille 1939, nr 325:
Paris
EDITORS' COMMENT In his manuscript for the
present edition Faille dates F 280 Paris 1886. For
stylistic reasons the editors place it in Auvers.
COLLECTION Buffalo, New York, George
F. Goodyear

F 589 [H 601] STILL LIFE: FIELD FLOWERS IN
A VASE

Canvas 41 × 34 [16¼ × 13½]
Auvers June 1890
LITERATURE Faille 1928, nr 589: Arles. Scherjon
and de Gruyter 1937, Arles nr 189. Faille 1939,
nr 601: Arles 1888
EDITORS' COMMENT In his manuscript for the
present edition Faille dates F 589 Arles 1889. For
stylistic reasons the editors place it in Auvers.
COLLECTION Formerly New York, Paul Rosenberg Art Gallery
Present owner unknown

F 820

F 822

F 821

F 595

F 597

F 598

F 599

F 636

F 595 [H 595] STILL LIFE: PINK ROSES

Canvas 32 × 40.5 [12½ × 16]
Saint Rémy-Auvers May 1890
LITERATURE Faille 1928, nr 595: Arles; Scherjon
and de Gruyter 1937, Arles nr 30: letters 488 and
519. Faille 1939, nr 595: Arles 1888
EDITORS' COMMENT The following paintings are
very closely related stylistically: F 595, F 597, F 748
and F 749. Since F 595 belonged to Gachet, we can
assume that it – and therefore the whole group – was
painted in Auvers.
COLLECTION Copenhagen, Ny Carlsberg
Glyptotek [acquired 1927; gift of Helge Jacobsen],
inv nr 1836, cat 1961, nr 946

F 597 [H 805] DOG-ROSES OR BRANCHES OF
WILD BRIAR

Canvas 23.5 × 32 [9¼ × 12½]
Saint Rémy-Auvers May 1890
LITERATURE Faille 1928, nr 597: Arles. Scherjon
and de Gruyter 1937, Saint Rémy nr 177. Faille
1939, nr 805: Saint Rémy May 1889; letter T 12
EDITORS' COMMENT See F 595. In his manuscript
for the present edition Faille cites letter T 12 in
connection with F 597 and F 748. In that letter,
however, Theo speaks only of drawings.
COLLECTION Amsterdam, Rijksmuseum Vincent
van Gogh [Vincent van Gogh Foundation, inv
nr F 597]

F 598 [H 600] STILL LIFE: VASE WITH
CARNATIONS AND STOCK-GILLIFLOWERS

Canvas 41 × 32 [16¼ × 12½]
Auvers June 1890
LITERATURE Faille 1928, nr 598: Arles. Scherjon
and de Gruyter 1937, Arles nr 191. Faille 1939,
nr 600: Arles 1889
EDITORS' COMMENT In his manuscript for the
present edition Faille dates F 598 Arles 1889. For
stylistic reasons the editors place it in Auvers.
COLLECTION New York, A. Peralta-Ramos

F 599 [H 804] STILL LIFE: VASE WITH
THISTLES

Canvas 41 × 34 [16¼ × 13½]
Auvers June 1890
LITERATURE Faille 1928, nr 599: Arles. Scherjon
and de Gruyter 1937, Arles nr 190. Faille 1939,
nr 804: Arles or Saint Rémy 1889
EDITORS' COMMENT In his manuscript for the
present edition Faille dates F 599 Saint Rémy 1889.
For stylistic reasons the editors place it in Auvers.
COLLECTION Canada, Private Collection

F 636 [H 755] FIELD WITH POPPIES IN
ALFALFA

Canvas 73 × 91.5 [28¾ × 36]
Auvers June 1890
LETTER 641 [14 June] '...now I am working on a
field of poppies in alfalfa.'
LITERATURE A.Plasschaert, Onze Kunst 1904,
part 2, p 152. Faille 1928, nr 636: Saint Rémy
October 1889; letters 607 and 608. Scherjon and
de Gruyter 1937, Auvers nr 128: letter 641. Faille
1939, nr 755: Auvers June 1890; letter 641
COLLECTION The Hague, Gemeentemuseum [on
loan since 1948 from the Dienst voor 's Rijks
verspreide Kunstvoorwerpen], inv nr 3-x-1948, cat
1962, nr 137

F 740 [HP 557] THE LITTLE STREAM

Canvas 25.5 × 34 [10 × 13½]
Auvers May 1890
LITERATURE Faille 1928, nr 740: Saint Rémy.

F 740

Scherjon and de Gruyter 1937, Saint Rémy nr 188 [not reproduced]. Faille 1939, p 557: Saint Rémy April 1890 [not reproduced]
EDITORS' COMMENT In his manuscript for the present edition Faille dates F 740 Saint Rémy 1890. For stylistic reasons the editors place it in May 1890, either at the end of the Saint Rémy period or early in Auvers.
COLLECTION New York, Heirs of C. V. Starr

F 748 [H 706] BUTTERFLIES AND POPPIES

Canvas 33.5 × 24.5 [13¼ × 9¾]
Saint Rémy-Auvers May 1890
LITERATURE Faille 1928, nr 748: Saint Rémy.
Scherjon and de Gruyter 1937, Saint Rémy nr 173.
Faille 1939, nr 706: Saint Rémy May 1889; letter
T 12
EDITORS' COMMENT See F 595 and F 597
COLLECTION Amsterdam, Rijksmuseum Vincent van Gogh [Vincent van Gogh Foundation, inv nr F 748]

F 749 [H 707] ROSES AND A BEETLE

Canvas 32.5 × 23.5 [12¾ × 9¼]
Saint Rémy-Auvers May 1890
LITERATURE Faille 1928, nr 749: Saint Rémy.
Scherjon and de Gruyter 1937, Saint Rémy nr 174.
Faille 1939, nr 707: Saint Rémy May 1889
EDITORS' COMMENT See F 595. In his manuscript for the present edition Faille dates F 749 May 1889. For stylistic reasons the editors place it in Auvers.
COLLECTION Amsterdam, Rijksmuseum Vincent van Gogh [Vincent van Gogh Foundation, inv nr F 749]

F 748

F 749

Catalogue Drawings

INSTRUCTIONS FOR USE OF THE
CATALOGUE

This edition in one volume follows a different
system than the 1928 edition, which consisted of
four volumes: two of text and two of plates [divided
into paintings and drawings]. Illustrations and text
are now in one volume, eliminating the need for
descriptions, and the illustrations of paintings and
drawings are also united in one volume.

NUMBERING

The numbers of the 1928 edition, preceded by the
letter F, are in general use in the van Gogh literature.
Van Gogh's paintings, though, have another
'Faille-number' in addition: their catalogue number
in the 1939 Hyperion edition. These are preceded
by an H. The drawings were not included in the 1939
edition, so that they have only F numbers. In
publications from 1939 on it was always necessary
to make it clear whether F or H numbers were being
used, and the reader had to refer to the concordance
in the 1939 edition to find the equivalent number in
the other edition.
The problem involved in the third edition, this time
including the drawings, is once again the numbering; since so many illustrations have been
rearranged in order to obtain a better chronological
order, the advantage of the numerical sequence was
on the verge of disappearing. The obvious solution
was to adopt a new numbering system, for the third
time, but it was thought advisable to avoid the
complications which this would lead to with respect
to the international study of van Gogh and the
process of drawing up new catalogues.
Dr J. B. de la Faille himself advocated a return to
the original numbering system of 1928, but a
method had to be found to deal with the
inconsistencies caused by the rearrangement of the
works.
The editors decided to meet with this problem by
means of a system of references, eliminating the
need for a concordance of F and H numbers. At the
top of each page, the period and number are
repeated, to facilitate finding specific works.
De la Faille's original system of having the
numbering of the drawings immediately follow that
of the paintings has been left unchanged.

LITERATURE

References are restricted to works or studies in
which the results were published of research having
to do with factual data or the problems of dating
and authenticity. Personal opinions and interpretations are not included, except in cases where
they have led to factual conclusions. Variations in
dating or repudiations of authenticity are
mentioned in an EDITORS' COMMENT or under the
heading LITERATURE, which also includes the
original source of the dating adopted by the editors
if it differs from that in de la Faille's manuscript.

PROVENANCE

These have been corrected and modified as
accurately as possible. The name of the last known
owner is to be found in the captions next to the
illustrations.
In order to save space in the catalogue the full
information has been moved to a separate section,
EXHIBITIONS AND PROVENANCE.

EXHIBITIONS

Exhibitions, sometimes extremely extensive, are
solely referred to in the section EXHIBITIONS AND
PROVENANCES

DISSENTING VIEWS

Works that are now dated to another period than in
the 1928 and 1939 editions are placed at the end of
their *new* period, under the heading REDATED.
In his manuscript for the present edition de la Faille
added many works which first came to his
attention since the appearance of the previous
editions. He inserted these works between the
existing catalogue numbers of the 1928 edition,
giving them an F number followed by the word
'bis.' Since he sometimes added more than one
work between two F numbers, the editors have
replaced the word 'bis' with a, b, c, d and so on.
Paintings and drawings which did not come to light
until after the death of de la Faille and which the
editors consider eligible to be included in the
catalogue, are treated in a supplement.
De la Faille left out of his manuscript for the
present edition a number of works for which he had
written certificates of authenticity in the past.
Unless the editors had positive evidence that a
particular piece was left out inadvertently, they
considered the manuscript as de la Faille's last
opinion.

ABBREVIATIONS

F precedes catalogue numbers of the 1928 edition
   and the present edition
H precedes catalogue numbers of the 1939 edition
Faille 1928: J. B. de la Faille, L'Oeuvre de Vincent
   van Gogh, Catalogue raisonné, Paris and Brussels
   1928 [4 volumes]
Faille 1939: J. B. de la Faille, Vincent van Gogh,
   Paris 1939
Vanbeselaere 1937: W. Vanbeselaere, De holland-
   sche periode in het werk van Vincent van Gogh,
   Antwerp 1937
Scherjon and de Gruyter 1937: W. Scherjon and
   Jos de Gruyter, Vincent van Gogh's great period,
   Amsterdam 1937
SP: Supplementary Paintings
SD: Supplementary Drawings
LETTERS: The complete letters of Vincent van
   Gogh, Greenwich, Connecticut [3 volumes]. All
   references to the correspondence of van Gogh are
   given in the translation of this edition, unless
   otherwise indicated.
B: letters to Bernard
R: letters to van Rappard
T: letters from Theo van Gogh to Vincent
W: letters to Wilhelmina, Vincent's sister
Chetham: Ch. Scott Chetham, The role of Vincent
   van Gogh's copies in the development of his art,
   Cambridge, Massachusetts 1960 [thesis]
Tralbaut Antwerp 1948: M. E. Tralbaut, Vincent
   van Gogh in zijn Antwerpsche Periode,
   Amsterdam 1948
Tralbaut Drenthe 1959: M. E. Tralbaut, Vincent
   van Gogh in Drenthe, Assen 1959
Measurements are given first in centimeters, then [in
   brackets] in inches.

F 827

F 828

F 825 VIEW OF HELVOIRT
See JUVENILIA

F 826 THE CHURCH OF THE AUSTIN FRIARS
See JUVENILIA

CUESMES-BRUSSELS PERIOD

F 827 COAL SHOVELER

Black lithographic chalk, pencil, pen, brush,
heightened and washed with white [water color
paper with an unidentifiable watermark] 49.5 × 27.5
[19½ × 10¾]
Cuesmes July-August 1879, possibly retouched in
The Hague period
LITERATURE Vanbeselaere 1937, pp 36, 41, 67,
192, 407. J. Leymarie, Van Gogh, 1951, p 138,
nr VII, 2 : Cuesmes July-August 1879; letter 132.
Cat van Gogh 1966, Rijksmuseum Kröller-Müller,
nr 5 : The Hague about December 1882, following
Miss Szymańska's suggestion that the drawing is
from The Hague period. A. Szymańska, Unbekannte Jugendzeichnungen Vincent van Goghs,
1967, p 32 : June 1883
COLLECTION Otterlo, Rijksmuseum Kröller-
Müller, inv nr 186-13, cat van Gogh 1970, nr 5

F 828 THE DIGGERS [after Millet]

Pencil 35 × 55 [13¾ × 21¾]
Annotated in lower right : Vincent
Compare painting F 648 and F 829
Brussels October 1880
LETTER 138 [1 November] '...I have drawn "The
Diggers" by Millet, from a Braun photograph...'
LITERATURE Vanbeselaere 1937, pp 36, 41, 407:
August 1880; letter 134. Chetham 1960, pp 10-1,
14: letter 138
COLLECTION The Hague, Heirs of H. P. Bremmer

F 829 THE DIGGERS [after Millet]

Pencil, stumped, and charcoal [ordinary gray paper,
wove] 37 × 62 [14½ × 24¼]
Annotated in lower right : Vincent; in lower left :
d'après J. F. Millet, Les Bêcheurs
Compare painting F 648 and F 828
Brussels October 1880
LETTER 138 [1 November] See F 828
LITERATURE Album Hidde Nijland Collection
1905, plate 24. Vanbeselaere 1937, pp 36, 41, 407:
letter 134; 20 August. Chetham 1960, p 14: letter
138
COLLECTION Otterlo, Rijksmuseum Kröller-
Müller, inv nr 958-28, cat van Gogh 1970, nr 7

F 830 THE SOWER [after Millet]
Etten period; see after F 905

F 831 MINERS

Pencil, lightly colored [ordinary wove paper]
44.5 × 56 [17½ × 22]
Compare sketch reproduced with letter 135
[similar motif]
Cuesmes September 1880
LETTER 135 [7 September] 'Yet I could not keep
from sketching in a rather large size the drawing of
the miners going to the shaft which I sent you a hasty
sketch of, though I changed the placement of the
figures a little.'
LITERATURE Album Hidde Nijland Collection
1905, plate 12. Vanbeselaere 1937, pp 36, 40, 407.
Chetham 1960, p 13. Cat van Gogh 1966, Rijks-
museum Kröller-Müller, nr 2 : September 1880.
A. Szymańska, Unbekannte Jugendzeichnungen
Vincent van Goghs, 1967, pp 30-2
COLLECTION Otterlo, Rijksmuseum Kröller-
Müller, inv nr 946-28, cat van Gogh 1970, nr 2

F 829

F 832 MINERS' WOMEN CARRYING SACKS
[THE BEARERS OF THE BURDEN]

Pen, pencil, brush [ordinary wove paper, pasted]
43×60 [17×23½]
Annotated in lower right: the bearers of the burden
Compare F 994 [similar motif]
Brussels April 1881 or shortly later
LETTERS 143 [12 April] '...I have sketched two
drawings at Rappard's,...and "The Bearers of the
Burden"...'
R 16 [September-October 1882] 'You may remember
that when I was there I did some drawings of it...'
LITERATURE H. J. Haverman, De Kroniek 3 March
1895, p 75. Album Hidde Nijland Collection 1905,
plate 65. Vanbeselaere 1937, pp 36-7, 40-1, 185, 192,
407. Chetham 1960, p 17
COLLECTION Otterlo, Rijksmuseum Kröller-
Müller, inv nr 996-28, cat van Gogh 1970, nr 3

F 833 THE DAUGHTER OF JACOB MEYER
[after Holbein]
Etten period; see after F 905

F 834 THE ANGELUS [after Millet]

Pencil, red chalk, heightened and washed with
white [Ingres paper with watermark: Ba St. Mars]
47×62 [18½×24½]
Annotated in lower right: Atel. Vincent; in lower
left: d'après J. F. Millet, l'Angélus du Soir
Brussels October 1880
LETTER 138 [1 November] 'I have drawn "The
Diggers" by Millet, from a Braun photograph...
together with that of "The Angelus." I sent both
these drawings to Dad...'
LITERATURE Album Hidde Nijland Collection
1905, plate 77. Vanbeselaere 1937, pp 37, 41, 407.
Chetham 1960, pp 12, 14
COLLECTION Otterlo, Rijksmuseum Kröller-
Müller, inv nr 1007-28, cat van Gogh 1970, nr 4

F 835 OLD BRETON WOMAN ASLEEP IN
CHURCH [after F. Rops]
See JUVENILIA

F 836 A COUNTRY LANE
See JUVENILIA

F 837 THE LANGE VIJVERBERG
See JUVENILIA

F 838 THE DITCH
See JUVENILIA

F 839 THE CANAL
See JUVENILIA

F 840 WOMAN STANDING: FACING LEFT
The Hague period; see after F 1093

F 841 WOMAN ON HER DEATHBED
The Hague period; see after F 1093

F 832

F 831

F 834

F 847

F 848

F 847 THE DAUGHTER OF JACOB MEYER
[after Holbein]

Charcoal, pencil 43 × 30.5 [17 × 12]
Annotated in lower margin: d'après Hans Holbein
La fille du bourgmestre Jacques Meyer
Compare F 833
Brussels October 1880
LETTERS 137 [15 October] '...*I am as far as the
portraits after Holbein in the third part of the Cours
de Dessin...*'
138 [1 November] '*Those Holbeins in The Models
from the Masters are splendid. Now that I am
drawing them, I feel it even more strongly than
before.*'
LITERATURE Faille 1928, nr 847: Etten July-
August 1881; letter 147. Vanbeselaere 1937, pp 52,
60, 407: Etten June-July 1881; letter 147. Chetham
1960, p 14: Brussels October 1880; letter 137;
precedes F 833
EDITORS' COMMENT F 833 and F 847 are copied
after plate nr 10 in Charles Bargues' Cours de
dessin exécuté avec le concours de J. L. Gérôme,
2me Partie: Modèles d'après les maîtres de toutes
les époques et de toutes les écoles [place and date of
publication unknown]. The Holbein drawing is in
the museum at Basle.
COLLECTION The Hague, Heirs of H. P. Bremmer

F 848 FIGURE OF A WOMAN [after Holbein]

Pencil 41 × 29 [16 × 11½]
Brussels October 1880
LETTERS 137 [15 October] and 138 [1 November]
See F 847
LITERATURE Faille 1928, nr 848: Etten July-August
1881; letter 147. Vanbeselaere 1937, pp 53, 60, 407:
Etten June-July 1881; letter 147. Chetham 1960,
p 14: Brussels October 1880; letter 137
EDITORS' COMMENT This drawing is copied after
plate nr 27, erroneously called A Woman of the
Court of Henri VIII, in the work of Bargues cited
under F 847.
COLLECTION The Hague, Heirs of H. P. Bremmer

F 874 recto [formerly F 874 verso] SKETCH OF A
LANDSCAPE WITH FACTORIES

Pencil, the roofs tinted red 19 × 28 [7½ × 11]
Cuesmes summer 1880
LITERATURE Not in Faille 1928 or Vanbeselaere
1937. A. Szymańska, Unbekannte Jugend-
zeichnungen Vincent van Goghs, 1967, pp 27, 29:
between winter 1879-80 and August 1880
EDITORS COMMENT Dated to the end of the
Cuesmes period on the basis of resemblance to the
sketch reproduced with letter 135
COLLECTION St Louis, City Art Museum

F 1105 TWO MEN ON A COUNTRY ROAD

Pencil, chalk and pen, washed 23 × 31 [9 × 12¼]
Brussels 1880-1
LITERATURE Faille 1928, nr 1105: Drenthe.
Vanbeselaere 1937, pp 38, 45, 410: Brussels
January-April 1881 [in the index 1880]
EDITORS' COMMENT Stylistically related to sketch
reproduced with letter 140.
COLLECTION New York, Private Collection

ETTEN PERIOD

F 842 SHACKS

Black chalk, pencil, pen and China ink and brown
ink, washed with white and gray 45.5 × 61 [18 × 24]
Etten May 1881
LETTER 145 [probably May] '*I make my studies on

F 874 recto

F 1105

a rather large scale... so I have done, among other things, a cottage in the heath, and also that barn with a thatched roof on the road to Roozendaal, which locally they call the Protestant barn.'
LITERATURE D. Hannema, Verslag van het Museum Boymans te Rotterdam over het jaar 1922, p 4 [with reproduction]. Vanbeselaere 1937, pp 46, 51, 59, 407
EDITORS' COMMENT Close in style to F 874 verso and F 875.
COLLECTION Rotterdam, Museum Boymans-van Beuningen [acquired 1922; gift of D. Hannema], inv nr VvG I, cat 1927, nr 790

F 843 WINDMILL BY A CANAL

Pencil, charcoal [old Dutch paper] 35.5 × 60 [14 × 23½]
Annotated in lower right: At. Vincent
Compare F 850 [nearby site]
Dordrecht [Etten period] August 1881
LETTER 149 [August] *'I stayed at The Hague until Thursday morning, then I went to Dordrecht because I had seen from the train a spot I wanted to draw – that row of mills.'*
LITERATURE Album Hidde Nijland Collection 1905, plate 98. Vanbeselaere 1937, pp 52, 59, 126-7, 407: May 1881
COLLECTION Otterlo, Rijksmuseum Kröller-Müller, inv nr 1030-28, cat van Gogh 1970, nr 9

F 844 THE WINDMILL

Pencil and water color 37 × 55.5 [14½ × 21¾]
Etten August 1881
LITERATURE Vanbeselaere 1937, pp 52, 59, 126, 407.
EDITORS' COMMENT Faille cites letter 145 in connection with this number. In this letter mention is made of 'the mill... on that meadow.' But in letter 146 van Gogh writes that he is studying Cassagnes's Traité d'aquarelle, 'which may come in useful some day, but as yet I have only been drawing with pencil.' If that is so, the mill referred to in the earlier letter 145 cannot be identical with F 844, which is a water color.
COLLECTION The Hague, Mrs M. A. R. van der Leeuw-Wentges [acquired 1930]

F 845 MARSH WITH WATER LILIES

Pencil, pen and reed pen 23.5 × 31 [9¼ × 12¼]
Signed in lower left: Vincent
Etten June 1881
LETTER 146 [June] *'... I made a drawing in pen and ink of another spot in the swamp, where a lot of water lilies grow...'*
LITERATURE Vanbeselaere 1937, pp 52, 59, 124, 126, 407. Chetham 1960, p 20
COLLECTION Oegstgeest, Netherlands, Heirs of Mrs A. T. Scholte-van Houten

F 846 MARSH

Pen and pencil 42.5 × 56.5 [16¾ × 22¼]
Etten June 1881
LITERATURE Vanbeselaere 1937, pp 52, 59, 124, 407
COLLECTION Zurich, Mrs M. Feilchenfeldt

F 847 THE DAUGHTER OF JACOB MEYER [after Holbein]
Cuesmes-Brussels period; see after F 841

F 848 FIGURE OF A WOMAN [after Holbein]
Cuesmes-Brussels period; see after F 841

F 842

F 843

F 844

F 845

F 846

F 854

F 855

F 849 PORTRAIT OF VINCENT'S SISTER, WILLEMINA VAN GOGH [after a photograph]

Pencil [old Dutch paper with watermark: v. H.]
35 × 24.5 [13¾ × 9¾] Oval
Etten June-July 1881
LETTER 147 [probably July] '*Remembering what you told me once, I have tried to draw a few portraits after photographs, and I think this is good practice.*'
LITERATURE Vanbeselaere 1937, pp 53, 60, 407. Chetham 1960, p 19. E. P. Engel, Anton Mauve, 1967, pp 82, 85: portrait of Ariette [Jet] Mauve-Carbentus. Engel's identification of the sitter is rejected by V. W. van Gogh
COLLECTION Otterlo, Rijksmuseum Kröller-Müller, inv nr 188-20, cat van Gogh 1970, nr 20

F 849a BUST OF A YOUNG GIRL [copy]

Pencil 31 × 24.5 [12¼ × 9½]
Etten July 1881
LITERATURE Not in Faille 1928 or Vanbeselaere 1937
EDITORS' COMMENT The title and the qualification 'copy' are taken from Faille's manuscript for this edition. To the editors the authenticity of this drawing, possibly a copy after an Italian painting, seems doubtful.
COLLECTION Formerly Hilversum, C. Bakker Present owner unknown

F 850 WINDMILLS ON THE WEESKINDEREN-DIJK AT DORDRECHT

Water color, pencil, black and green chalk, heightened with white [Ingres paper with watermark: E. D. & Cie–P. L. Bas] 26 × 60 [10¼ × 23½]
Signed in lower right: Vincent
Compare F 843 [nearby site]
Etten early autumn 1881
LETTER 149 [August] See F 843
LITERATURE Beeldende Kunst 1926, nr 13, plate 59. Vanbeselaere 1937, pp 53, 61, 407: August 1881. D. Cooper, Zeichnungen und Aquarelle von Vincent van Gogh, 1954, p 16
EDITORS' COMMENT F 850 is a copy after a sketch Vincent made on the spot in Dordrecht. The original drawing has disappeared.
COLLECTION Otterlo, Rijksmuseum Kröller-Müller, inv nr 218-20, cat van Gogh 1970, nr 42

F 851 YOUNG PEASANT WITH SICKLE

Black chalk and water color [Ingres paper with watermark: E. D. & Cie–P. L. Bas] 47 × 61 [18½ × 24]
Signed in lower left: Vincent
Compare sketch in letter 150, F 855 and F 859 [same model]
Etten October 1881
LETTER R 3 [2 November] '*Today I drew another digger. And also since your visit, a boy cutting grass with a sickle.*'
LITERATURE Cat Hidde Nijland Collection 1905, plate 44. H. van den Eerenbeemt, Opgang 1924, p 276 [reproduction]. J. E. Blanche, L'Art Vivant 1927, p 568 [with reproduction]. Vanbeselaere 1937, pp 55, 63-5, 67, 407
COLLECTION Otterlo, Rijksmuseum Kröller-Müller, inv nr 977-28, cat van Gogh 1970, nr 33

F 852 THE SOWER: FACING RIGHT
The Hague period; see after F 1093

F 853 TWO SOWERS
The Hague period; see after F 1093

F 854 PEASANT WOMAN PEELING POTATOES

Black chalk and water color [pasted paper] 59.5 × 47
[23½ × 18½]
Signed in lower left: Vincent
Etten September 1881
LETTER 150 [September] '*Then a woman in a white
cap, peeling potatoes...*'
LITERATURE Album Hidde Nijland Collection
1905, plate 94. Vanbeselaere 1937, pp 54, 407
COLLECTION Otterlo, Rijksmuseum Kröller-
Müller, inv nr 1026-28, cat van Gogh 1970, nr 40

F 855 YOUNG PEASANT DIGGING: FACING
RIGHT

Charcoal, washed, and water color, heightened
with white [Ingres paper] 52 × 31.5 [20½ × 12½]
Annotated in lower left: V v G
Compare sketch in letter 150, F 851 and F 859 [same
model]
Etten September 1881
LETTER 150 [September] '*I have drawn five times
over a man with a spade, in short "un bêcheur," in
different positions...*'
LITERATURE Album Hidde Nijland Collection
1905, plate 28. Vanbeselaere 1937, pp 55, 67, 407
COLLECTION Otterlo, Rijksmuseum Kröller-
Müller, inv nr 962-28, cat van Gogh 1970, nr 41

F 849

F 849a

F 851

F 850

F 856

F 860a

F 856 PEASANT SOWING: FACING RIGHT

Charcoal, black chalk, pencil [Ingres paper]
56.5 × 34 [22¾ × 13½]
Annotated in lower left: Port. Vincent
Compare F 858 [same model]
Etten autumn 1881
LITERATURE Album Hidde Nijland Collection
1905, plate 8. Vanbeselaere 1937, pp 54, 66-7, 126,
172-4
COLLECTION Otterlo, Rijksmuseum Kröller-
Müller, inv nr 942-28, cat van Gogh 1970, nr 14

F 857 THE SOWER: FULL FACE

Pen and brown ink, the apron and pouch slightly
heightened with blue 11.5 × 7 [4½ × 2¾]
Annotated in lower right: Zaayer [Sower]
Compare sketch in letter 150 and F 862
Etten September-October 1881
LITERATURE Vanbeselaere 1937, pp 54, 67, 172,
192, 407
EDITORS' COMMENT Probably a sketch sent to van
Rappard. See letter R 2 [15 October 1881].
COLLECTION The Hague, Heirs of H. P. Bremmer

F 858 THE SOWER: FACING RIGHT

Black chalk 58 × 31 [22¾ × 12¼]
Signed in lower right: Vincent
Compare F 856 [same model]
Etten autumn 1881
LITERATURE Vanbeselaere 1937, pp 54, 66-7,
172-4, 407
COLLECTION Heirs of F. A. C. Guépin

F 859 YOUNG PEASANT DIGGING: FACING
RIGHT

Black chalk, washed, water color [Ingres paper
with watermark: fragment of [E.D.] & Cie–
P. L. Bas] 44 × 34 [17¼ × 13½]
Compare sketch in letter 150, F 851 and F 855 [same
model]
Etten September 1881
LETTER 150 [September] See F 855
LITERATURE Album Hidde Nijland Collection
1905, plate 78. Vanbeselaere 1937, pp 53, 65-7, 407
COLLECTION Otterlo, Rijksmuseum Kröller-
Müller, inv nr 1008-28, cat van Gogh 1970, nr 32

F 860 PEASANT DIGGING: FACING LEFT

Black chalk 29.5 × 22 [11½ × 8¾]
Signed in lower right: Vincent
Etten September 1881
LETTER 150 [September] See F 855
LITERATURE Vanbeselaere 1937, pp 54, 67, 407
COLLECTION Amsterdam, P. and N. de Boer
Foundation

F 860a PEASANT DIGGING: FACING RIGHT

Black chalk, heightened with color [grayish-sand
colored paper] 61 × 46 [24 × 18]
Signed in lower left: Vincent
Etten September 1881
LETTER 150 [September] See F 855

Signed in lower left: Vincent
Etten September 1881
LETTER 150 [September] See F 855
LITERATURE Album Hidde Nijland Collection
1905, plate 59. Vanbeselaere 1937, pp 54, 67, 192, 407
COLLECTION Otterlo, Rijksmuseum Kröller-
Müller, inv nr 990-28, cat van Gogh 1970, nr 16

F 862 PEASANT SOWING

Black chalk and pencil, heightened with white,
lightly washed [Ingres paper with watermark:
E. M. Thiers] 61 × 45 [24 × 17¾]
Compare sketch in letter 150 and F 857
Etten September 1881
LETTER 150 [September] '...a sower twice...'
LITERATURE Album Hidde Nijland Collection
1905, plate 14. Vanbeselaere 1937, pp 54, 65, 67, 74,
172, 407
COLLECTION Otterlo, Rijksmuseum Kröller-
Müller, inv nr 948-28, cat van Gogh 1970, nr 15

F 861

F 857

F 858

F 859

F 860

F 862

F 863

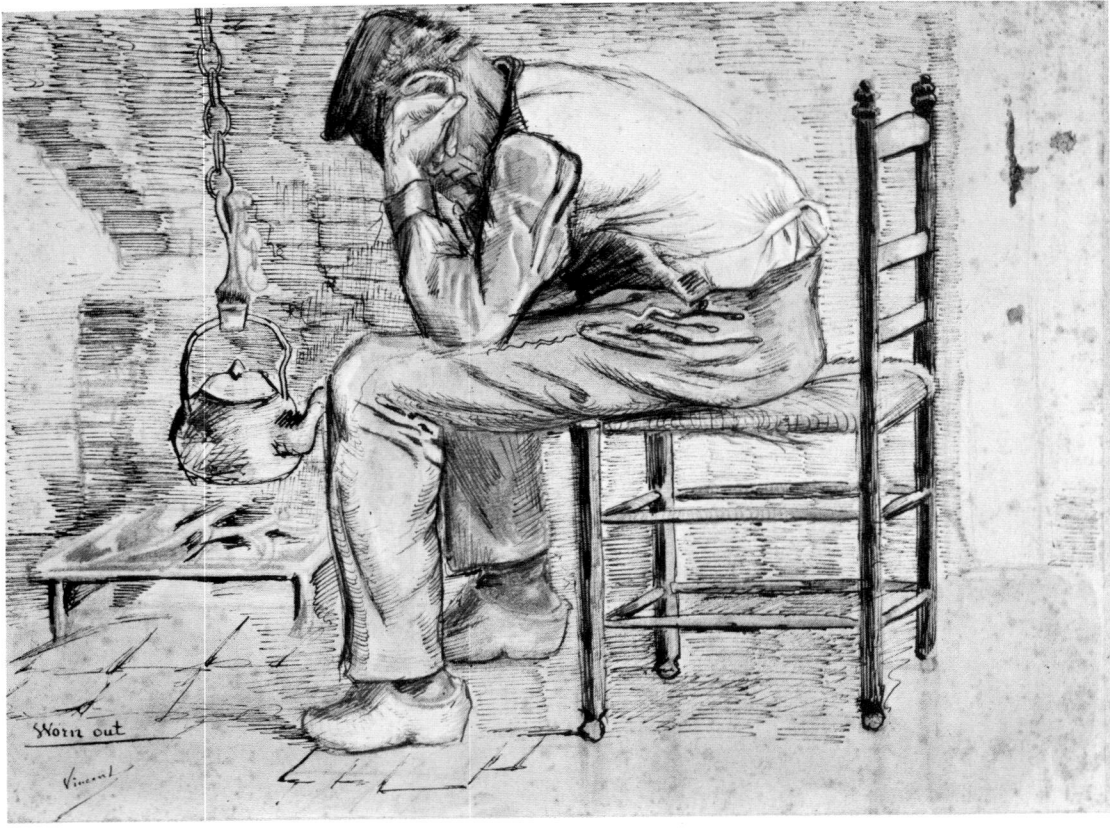

F 864

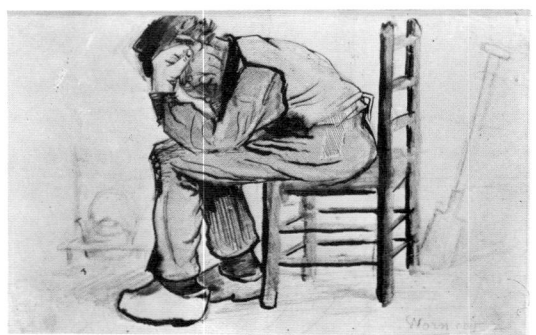

F 865

F 866a

F 867

F 863 WORN OUT

Pen and water color 23.5 × 31 [9¼ × 12¼]
Signed and annotated by Vincent in lower left:
Worn out. Vincent
Compare sketch in letter 150 and F 864, other treatments of the same composition. The same old man probably posed for F 864, F 868 and F 897. The tea kettle and the pile of kindling recur in F 868 and F 1216. For a study of the hearth with different objects, see F 888 verso
Etten September 1881
LETTERS 150 [September] '... and, finally, an old sick farmer sitting on a chair near the hearth, his head in his hands and his elbows on his knees.'
R 2 [15 October] 'And then I shall bring along a number of drawings, the large one, "Worn Out"...'
248 [24 November 1882] 'Today and yesterday I drew two figures of an old man sitting with his elbows on his knees and his head in his hands. Long ago Schuitemaker sat for me, and I kept the drawing because I wanted to make a better one someday.'
LITERATURE Vanbeselaere 1937, pp 54, 57, 407. Chetham 1960, p 21
EDITORS' COMMENT This is one of the earliest versions of WORN OUT. A later version is given in F 997, F 998 and painting F 702. A similar motif appears in F 1060 and F 1069.
COLLECTION Amsterdam, P. and N. de Boer Foundation

F 864 WORN OUT

Water color 13 × 21 [5 × 8¼]
Annotated by Vincent in lower right: Worn out
Compare sketch in letter 150, F 863, F 868 and F 897
Etten September 1881
LETTER 150 [September] See F 863
LITERATURE Vanbeselaere 1937, pp 54, 67, 407
EDITORS' COMMENT Folded, probably sent in a letter to van Rappard.
COLLECTION New York, Private Collection

F 865 MAN WITH BASKET, SOWING

Black chalk, washed, water color heightened with white [Ingres paper with watermark: E.D. & Cie – P.L. Bas] 62 × 47.5 [24½ × 18¾]
Compare sketch in letter 150 and SD 1675
Etten September 1881
LETTER 150 [September] 'The other sower has a basket.'
LITERATURE Album Hidde Nijland Collection 1905, plate 38. Vanbeselaere 1937, pp 54, 407
COLLECTION Otterlo, Rijksmuseum Kröller-Müller, inv nr 971-28, cat van Gogh 1970, nr 43

F 866 PEASANT DIGGING: FACING LEFT

Black and colored chalk [blue, brown and green], water color [Ingres paper with watermark: E.D. & Cie] 62.5 × 47 [24½ × 18½]
Signed in lower left: Vincent
Compare sketch in letter 151
Etten September 1881
LETTER 151 [September] 'Then I had a model again a few times, a digger...'
LITERATURE Vanbeselaere 1937, pp 55, 67, 407: shortly before 12 October; letter 151
COLLECTION Amsterdam, Rijksmuseum Vincent van Gogh [Vincent van Gogh Foundation, inv nr F 866]

F 866a THE SOWER

Black chalk, water color, the ground of brown wash 60 × 45 [23½ × 17¾]
Compare F 879 [same model]
Etten October 1881
LITERATURE Not in Faille 1928 or Vanbeselaere

F 866

1937. Expertised under the auspices of the
Expertise Instituut, Amsterdam [1954]
COLLECTION New York, Mr and Mrs L. M. Rogers and Mr A. E. Rogers, cat Rogers Collection
1958, nr 11

F 867 PEASANT WOMAN SEWING

Black chalk heightened with water color 49.5 × 31.5
[19½ × 12½]
Etten October-November 1881
LETTER 153 [3 November] *'Now that it is so cold I
draw almost exclusively from the figure indoors, a
seamstress, a basket weaver, etc.'*
LITERATURE Vanbeselaere 1937, pp 55, 74, 191,
407
COLLECTION New York, P. Rosenberg Art
Gallery

F 868 OLD PEASANT BY THE FIREPLACE

Charcoal, washed, heightened with white and red
[Ingres paper] 56 × 45 [22 × 17¾]
Annotated in lower right: Atelier Vincent
Compare sketch in letter 150, F 863, F 864 and F 897
Etten November 1881
LETTER 158 [18 November] *'Yesterday I made
another* [drawing]...*and another, of an old man
putting kindling wood on the hearth.'*
LITERATURE Album Hidde Nijland Collection
1905, plate 95. Vanbeselaere 1937, pp 57, 73-4, 126,
137, 192, 407: November-December 1881
EDITORS' COMMENT See F 863
COLLECTION Otterlo, Rijksmuseum Kröller-
Müller, inv nr 1027-28, cat van Gogh 1970, nr 28

F 868

F 869

F 870

F 869 YOUNG SCHEVENINGEN WOMAN,
SEATED: FACING LEFT

Water color 48 × 35 [19 × 13¾]
Signed in lower left: Vincent
Compare sketch in letter 163
The Hague [Etten period] December 1881
LETTER 163 [about 18 December] '...the water
colors are made after the model, a Scheveningen
girl.'
LITERATURE Vanbeselaere 1937, pp 57, 407
COLLECTION Amsterdam, P. and N. de Boer
Foundation

F 870 YOUNG SCHEVENINGEN WOMAN,
KNITTING: FACING RIGHT

Water color 51 × 35 [20 × 13¾]
With added touches by Anton Mauve
Signed in lower left: Vincent
Compare sketch in letter 163
The Hague [Etten period] December 1881
LETTERS 163 [about 18 December] '...the water
colors are made after the model, a Scheveningen
girl... Especially the one which Mauve has brushed a
little.'
214 [7 July 1882] 'Friday evening... This afternoon I
at once sent a drawing to the doctor who treated me –
not the superintendent – to show my gratitude. It was
a Scheveningen girl knitting, done at Mauve's studio,
and really the best water color I had, especially since
Mauve had put in some touches, and had watched me
do it and called some details to my attention.'
LITERATURE Vanbeselaere 1937, pp 57, 115, 407
EDITORS' COMMENT From letter 163 we judge
that Mauve worked up only one drawing of van
Gogh's – the present one. This is confirmed by the
drawing's provenance.
COLLECTION New York, Private Collection

F 871 YOUNG FISHERWOMAN FROM
SCHEVENINGEN, STANDING: FACING LEFT

Water color 23.5 × 9.5 [9¼ × 3¾]
Signed in lower left: Vincent
Compare sketch in letter 163
The Hague [Etten period] December 1881
LETTER 163 [about 18 December] See F 869
LITERATURE Vanbeselaere 1937, pp 57, 407
COLLECTION Amsterdam, Rijksmuseum Vincent
van Gogh [Vincent van Gogh Foundation, inv
nr F 871]

F 872 AN ADVENTURER SETTING OUT
The Hague period; see after F 1093

F 873 GIRL WITH BLACK CAP, ON
THE GROUND BY THE FIRE: FACING LEFT

Charcoal, black chalk, pen, water color, heightened
[Ingres paper with watermark: E. D. & Cie –
P. L. Bas] 44 × 57 [17¼ × 22½]
Annotated in lower left: Atelier Vincent
Compare F 896 [same model]
Etten December 1881
LETTER 165 [between 22 and 24 December] 'The
other day I made some drawings of children...'
LITERATURE Album Hidde Nijland Collection
1905, plate 31. Vanbeselaere 1937, pp 57, 407.
Chetham 1960, p 22
COLLECTION Otterlo, Rijksmuseum Kröller-
Müller, inv nr 965-28, cat van Gogh 1970, nr 31

F 874 recto [formerly F 874 verso] SKETCH OF
A LANDSCAPE WITH FACTORIES
Cuesmes-Brussels period; see after F 841

F 874 verso [formerly F 874 recto] LANDSCAPE

Pen and water color 19×28 [7½×11]
Etten early spring 1881
LITERATURE Faille 1928, nr 874: Etten. Van-
beselaere 1937, pp 37-8, 407: Brussels January
1881; probably letter 140. A. Szymańska,
Unbekannte Jugendzeichnungen Vincent van
Goghs, 1967, pp 27, 29: between winter 1879–80
and August 1880
EDITORS' COMMENT See F 842
COLLECTION St Louis, City Art Museum

F 875 THE THATCHED HUT

Black chalk 13.5×36 [5¼×14¼]
Signed in lower right: Vincent
Compare F 1235 [same site]
Etten May 1881
LETTER 145 [probably May] See F 842
LITERATURE Vanbeselaere 1937, pp 51, 59, 407
EDITORS' COMMENT See F 842
COLLECTION London, F. Wilson

F 876 THE ARTIST'S FATHER THEODORUS
VAN GOGH [after a photograph]

Pencil, black ink and wash, heightened with white
33×25 [13×9¾]
Etten July 1881
LETTER 147 [probably July] See F 849
LITERATURE Vanbeselaere 1937, pp 53, 60, 407.
Cnetham 1960, p 19
COLLECTION The Hague, Mrs A. R. W. Nieuwen-
huizen Segaar-Aarse

F 877 SHEPHERD WITH FLOCK NEAR A
CHURCH AT ZWEELOO
Drenthe period; see after F 1106

F 878 THE CARPENTER

Charcoal [Ingres paper with watermark: P. L. Bas–
E. D. & Cie] 57.5×40.5 [22¾×16]
Etten May 1881
LITERATURE H. P. Bremmer, Album Kröller-
Müller Collection 1919, plate 2. Vanbeselaere 1937,
pp 56, 67, 175, 192, 407: November-December 1881
COLLECTION Otterlo, Rijksmuseum Kröller-
Müller, inv nr 187-18, cat van Gogh 1970, nr 13

F 871

F 873

F 874 verso

F 875

F 878

F 876

F 879

F 880

F 879 A KNEELING MAN PLANTING

Charcoal, washed, black chalk, heightened with white [Ingres paper with watermark: fragment of [E.]D. & Cie–P. L.[Bas]] 38.5 × 41.5 [15¼ × 16¼]
Compare F 866a [same model]
Etten autumn 1881
LITERATURE Album Hidde Nijland 1905, plate 49. Vanbeselaere 1937, pp 55, 64, 67, 407
COLLECTION Otterlo, Rijksmuseum Kröller-Müller, inv nr 981-28, cat van Gogh 1970, nr 30

F 880 GIRL KNEELING IN FRONT OF BUCKET

Pencil and charcoal, heightened with white, the ground of red-brown wash 43 × 55 [17 × 21¾]
Compare F 881 [same model]
Etten December 1881
LETTER 165 [between 22 and 24 December] See F 873
LITERATURE Vanbeselaere 1937, pp 57, 67, 408
COLLECTION Chicago, Mr and Mrs Leigh B. Block

F 881 PEASANT GIRL GATHERING POTATOES

Black chalk, pencil, washed, heightened with white 47.5 × 61.5 [18¾ × 24¼]
Annotated in lower left: 43; in lower right: 120 Vincent v. Gogh
Compare F 880 [same model]
Etten December 1881
LETTER 165 [between 22 and 24 December] See F 873
LITERATURE Vanbeselaere 1937, pp 57, 64, 67, 408
COLLECTION The Hague, F. Bremmer

F 882 A MAN SOWING: FACING LEFT
The Hague period; see after F 1093

F 883 A WOMAN SOWING, WITH BASKET

Black chalk and water color 62 × 47 [24½ × 18½]
Etten September 1881
LETTER 150 [September] 'Above all, I should like to have a woman pose with a seed basket...'
LITERATURE Vanbeselaere 1937, pp 54, 408
COLLECTION Cologne, H. Abels Art Gallery, cat 1925 [?], pp 44-5, with reproduction

F 884 YOUNG GIRL GARDENING

Black chalk and water color 58 × 46 [22¾ × 18]
Etten December 1881
LETTER 165 [between 22 and 24 December] See F 873
LITERATURE Vanbeselaere 1937, pp 57-8, 67, 408
COLLECTION Utrecht, Museum van Baaren Foundation, inv nr 33

F 885 INTERIOR WITH WOMAN SEWING: FACING LEFT

Black chalk and water color, heightened with white [Ingres paper with watermark: E. D. & Cie–P. L. Bas] 59 × 45 [23¼ × 17¾]
Signed in lower left: Vincent
Etten October-November 1881
LETTER 153 [3 November] See F 867
LITERATURE Album Hidde Nijland Collection 1905, plate 69. W. Steenhoff, Elsevier's Geïllustreerd Maandschrift 1928, p 137 [with reproduction]. Vanbeselaere 1937, pp 56, 74, 408: November-December 1881
COLLECTION Otterlo, Rijksmuseum Kröller-Müller, inv nr 1000-28, cat van Gogh 1970, nr 24

F 886 WOMAN, SEWING BY THE WINDOW:
FACING RIGHT

Water color 59.5 × 44 [23½ × 17¼]
Etten October-November 1881
LETTER 153 [3 November] See F 867
LITERATURE Vanbeselaere 1937, pp 56, 74, 408:
November-December 1881
COLLECTION Corseaux, Switzerland, A. Stoll
[acquired 1951], cat 1961, nr 74

F 887 A YOUNG WOMAN SEWING, WITH
WHITE CAT

Black chalk, water color, heightened with white
[Ingres paper with watermark: scutcheon with
caduceus] 60 × 45.5 [23½ × 18]
Signed in lower left: Vincent
Etten October-November 1881
LETTER 153 [3 November] See F 867
LITERATURE Album Hidde Nijland Collection
1905, plate 60. Vanbeselaere 1937, pp 56, 74, 408:
November-December 1881
COLLECTION Otterlo, Rijksmuseum Kröller-
Müller, inv nr 991-28, cat van Gogh 1970, nr 25

F 881

F 883

F 884

F 887

F 885

F 886

F 888 recto

F 888 verso

F 889

F 890

F 891

F 888 recto WOMAN MENDING STOCKINGS

Black chalk, washed, and water color [Ingres paper]
52 × 32 [20½ × 12½]
Etten November-December 1881
LITERATURE Album Hidde Nijland Collection
1905, plate 64. Vanbeselaere 1937, pp 56, 74, 408
COLLECTION Otterlo, Rijksmuseum Kröller-
Müller, inv nr 995-28, cat van Gogh 1970, nr 34

F 888 verso PART OF AN INTERIOR WITH
FIREPLACE [unfinished sketch]

Black chalk
Etten 1881

F 889 WOMAN GRINDING COFFEE

Pen, pencil, water color, heightened with white
[wove water-color paper with watermark: An 1881–
B] 56 × 39 [22 × 15¼]
Annotated in lower right: Atelier Vincent
Etten October-November 1881
LETTER 153 [3 November] See F 867
LITERATURE Album Hidde Nijland Collection
1905, plate 27. Vanbeselaere 1937, pp 56, 74, 408:
November-December 1881. Cat van Gogh 1966,
Rijksmuseum Kröller-Müller, nr 26: about
September 1881
COLLECTION Otterlo, Rijksmuseum Kröller-
Müller, inv nr 961-28, cat van Gogh 1970, nr 26

F 890 MAN SWEEPING

Black chalk, washed, water color, heightened with
white [Ingres paper] 55 × 27.5 [21¾ × 10¾]
Etten October 1881
LITERATURE Album Hidde Nijland Collection
1905, plate 42. Vanbeselaere 1937, pp 56, 74, 408:
November-December 1881
COLLECTION Otterlo, Rijksmuseum Kröller-
Müller, inv nr 975-28, cat van Gogh 1970, nr 37

F 891 PEASANT SIEVING GRAIN

Pencil, black chalk, stumped, water color [Ingres
paper with watermark: P. L. Bas – E. D. & Cie]
62.5 × 47.5 [24½ × 18¾]
Compare sketch in letter 150
Etten September 1881
LITERATURE Album Hidde Nijland Collection
1905, plate 13. Vanbeselaere 1937, pp 56, 67, 408:
November-December 1881
COLLECTION Otterlo, Rijksmuseum Kröller-
Müller, inv nr 947-28, cat van Gogh 1970, nr 19

F 892 WOMAN CHURNING BUTTER

Black chalk, washed, water color, pen, pencil,
heightened with white [old Dutch paper, laid]
55 × 32 [21¼ × 12½]
Etten November 1881
LETTER 153 [3 November] See F 867
LITERATURE Album Hidde Nijland Collection
1905, plate 22. Vanbeselaere 1937, pp 56, 74, 408:
November-December 1881
COLLECTION Otterlo, Rijksmuseum Kröller-
Müller, inv nr 956-28, cat van Gogh 1970, nr 21

F 893 MAN WITH A STICK

Black chalk, stumped, [light brown paper]
54 × 38.5 [21¼ × 15¼]
Etten October 1881
LITERATURE Vanbeselaere 1937, pp 56, 67, 408:
November-December 1881
COLLECTION Netherlands, Private Collection

F 894 MAN CHOPPING WOOD

Pencil, black chalk 40 × 19.5 [15¾ × 7¾]
Etten October 1881
LITERATURE Vanbeselaere 1937, pp 56, 67, 408:
November-December 1881
COLLECTION Zaandam, Netherlands,
Mrs W. Takens-Bremmer

F 895 PEASANT WITH HATCHET

Black chalk 57.5 × 38 [22¾ × 15]
Etten October 1881
LITERATURE Vanbeselaere 1937, pp 57, 67, 408:
November-December 1881
COLLECTION Zeist, Netherlands, H. Bremmer

F 892

F 894

F 895

F 893

F 896

F 900

F 897

F 903

F 830

F 896 GIRL STANDING: FACING RIGHT

Black and red chalk, washed, heightened with light blue [Ingres paper] 40 × 20.5 [15¾ × 8]
Annotated in lower left: V v G
Compare F 873 [same model]
Etten December 1881
LETTER 165 [between 22 and 24 December] See F 873
LITERATURE Album Hidde Nijland Collection 1905, plate 83. Vanbeselaere 1937, pp 57-8, 67, 408
COLLECTION Otterlo, Rijksmuseum Kröller-Müller, inv nr 1014-28, cat van Gogh 1970, nr 35

F 897 PEASANT READING BY THE FIREPLACE

Charcoal, water color, heightened with white [Ingres paper with watermark: Michallet] 45 × 56 [17¾ × 22]
Signed in lower left: Vincent
Compare sketch in letter 150, F 863, F 864, F 868 [same model] and F 1216 [companion piece]
Etten late October 1881
LETTER R 3 [2 November] *'I drew...since you visited me...a man and a woman sitting by the fire...'*
LITERATURE Album Hidde Nijland Collection 1905, plate 71. J. B. J. Stokvis, Kunst und Künstler April 1927, p 250 [with reproduction]. Vanbeselaere 1937, pp 55, 74, 408
EDITORS' COMMENT See F 863
COLLECTION Otterlo, Rijksmuseum Kröller-Müller, inv nr 1002-28, cat van Gogh 1970, nr 27

F 898 SIEN WITH CIGAR, SITTING ON THE GROUND BY THE STOVE
The Hague period; see after F 1093

F 899 A STOOPING WOMAN
The Hague period; see after F 1093

F 900 THE HOUSE OF THE RAILWAY ATTENDANT

Charcoal a little heightened with white [Ingres paper] 44 × 59.5 [17¼ × 23½]
Annotated in lower right: Atelier Vincent
Compare sketch in letter R 1 [same road]
Etten after 12 October 1881
LETTER R 1 [12 October] *'Do you know what is so superb these days – the road to the railway station and to de Leur with those old pollard willows...'*
LITERATURE Album Hidde Nijland Collection 1905, plate 32. Idem 1907, plate 2. J. B. J. Stokvis, Kunst und Künstler April 1927, p 252 [with reproduction]. Vanbeselaere 1937, pp 55, 74, 126, 408. Chetham 1960, p 21
COLLECTION Otterlo, Rijksmuseum Kröller-Müller, inv nr 966-28, cat van Gogh 1970, nr 17

F 901 THE SAW MILL
The Hague period; see after F 1093

F 902 CORNER OF A GARDEN WITH AN ARBOR

Pencil, black chalk, pen and water color [Ingres paper with watermark: H.v.I. Climbing lion] 44.5 × 56.5 [17½ × 22¼]
Annotated in lower left: Atelier Vincent
Etten June 1881
LITERATURE Album Hidde Nijland Collection 1905, plate 46. Idem 1907, plate 3. H. P. Bremmer, Vincent van Gogh – Inleidende Beschouwingen, 1911, pp 74-86, plate 9. Vincent van Gogh, Lettres à Bernard, 1911, plate VI. H. van den Eerenbeemt, Opgang March 1924, p 272 [with reproduction]. Vanbeselaere 1937, pp 52, 59, 408. D. Cooper, Zeichnungen und Aquarelle von Vincent van Gogh, 1954, p 14

COLLECTION Otterlo, Rijksmuseum Kröller-Müller, inv nr 978-28, cat van Gogh 1970, nr 18

F 902a ORCHARD

Charcoal, pen and brown ink, heightened with white 25.5 × 32 [10 × 12½]
Etten June 1881
LITERATURE Not in Faille 1928 or Vanbeselaere 1937. A. Tellegen, Bulletin Museum Boymans-van Beuningen 1967, pp 2-7: Drenthe November 1883; letter 340; close in technique to three drawings of the Drenthe period [F 877, F 1248 and F 1347]; the dimensions of F 902a and F 877 are identical; the subject is the same depicted by M. Liebermann in his painting THE BLEACHING GREEN [Cologne, Wallraf-Richartz Museum, cat 1965, nr 2939]
EDITORS' COMMENT The house in this drawing is not identical with the farm at Zweelo depicted by Liebermann in his painting in Cologne [see LITERATURE]. Moreover, there are leaves on the trees, whereas van Gogh visited Zweelo on 20 November.
COLLECTION Rotterdam, Museum Boymans-van Beuningen [acquired 1965; bequest of Miss S. M. C. Kronenberg], inv nr MB 1965-T2

F 903 THE OUTSKIRTS OF A WOOD

Charcoal, stumped, heightened with white [laid paper with watermark: H.v.I. Climbing lion] 42 × 55 [16½ × 21¾]
Annotated in lower left: Atelier Vincent
Compare painting F 192 [same site]
Etten July 1881
LETTER 147 [probably July] 'I have made another drawing in the Liesbosch...'
LITERATURE Album Hidde Nijland Collection 1905, plate 15. Idem 1907, plate 16. Vanbeselaere 1937, pp 52, 60, 408. Chetham 1960, p 20
EDITORS' COMMENT See F 833
COLLECTION Otterlo, Rijksmuseum Kröller-Müller, inv nr 949-28, cat van Gogh 1970, nr 12

F 904 A SUBURBAN FIELD ENCLOSURE
The Hague period; see after F 1093

F 905 CHURCH WITH SPIRE SEEN BETWEEN TREES
See JUVENILIA

REDATED TO ETTEN

F 830 THE SOWER [after Millet]

Pen and wash, heightened with green and white [ordinary gray wove paper] 48 × 36.5 [18¾ × 14¼]
Compare paintings F 689 and F 690
Etten April 1881
LETTER 144 [1 May] 'Meanwhile, I have started on the Millets. "The Sower" is finished...'
LITERATURE Faille 1928, nr 830: Cuesmes-Brussels August 1880; letter 134. Vanbeselaere 1937, pp 36, 192, 407: Borinage-Brussels August 1880; letter 134. D. Cooper, Zeichnungen und Aquarelle von Vincent van Gogh, 1954, pp 11-13. Chetham 1960, pp 11-12, 18: Etten April 1881; letter 144
EDITORS' COMMENT Probably copied after Le Rat's etching of THE SOWER.
COLLECTION Amsterdam, Rijksmuseum Vincent van Gogh [Vincent van Gogh Foundation, inv nr F 830

F 902

F 902a

F 833

F 1070

F 833 THE DAUGHTER OF JACOB MEYER
[after Holbein]

Pen and pencil [old Dutch paper, laid, with water-
mark: H.v.I.] 42 × 30 [16½ × 11¾]
Compare F 847
Etten July 1881
LETTER 147 [probably July 1881] '...so I work at
home now, and I am copying the drawings by Holbein
from the Bargues.'
LITERATURE Faille 1928, nr 833: Brussels October
1880. Vanbeselaere 1937, pp 37, 407: Brussels
October 1880; letter 137. Chetham 1960, p 18
EDITORS' COMMENT See F 847. Vincent usually
drew on Ingres paper, but when the supply was
exhausted, as he reported in letter 147, he used old
Dutch paper with the watermark H.v.I. This
drawing and F 903 – also mentioned in letter 147 –
were done on this paper, confirming the dating of
F 833 to the Etten period rather than to Brussels.
COLLECTION Otterlo, Rijksmuseum Kröller-
Müller, inv nr 219-22, cat van Gogh 1970, nr 8

F 995 TRUNK OF A WILLOW

Black chalk and water color, heightened with white
58 × 44 [22¾ × 17¼]
Etten 1881; reworked in The Hague November
1882
LETTER 242 [5 November] 'Today I have been
working on old drawings from Etten, because in the
fields I saw the pollard willows in the same leafless
condition again, and it reminded me of what I saw last
year ... A row of pollard willows sometimes resembles
a procession of almshouse men.'
LITERATURE Vanbeselaere 1937, pp 47, 92, 180,
194, 407
COLLECTION New York, Mrs Julius Joelson
[acquired 1950]

F 1070 NURSING MOTHER AND A CHILD ON
THE FLOOR

Charcoal, black chalk, washed, and water color
[Ingres paper] 46 × 59.5 [18 × 23½]
Annotated in lower left: Atelier Vincent
Etten 1881
LITERATURE Album Hidde Nijland Collection
1905, plate 97. Faille 1928, nr 1070: The Hague.
Vanbeselaere 1937, pp 49, 106, 207, 410: The
Hague April 1883. Cat van Gogh 1959, Rijks-
museum Kröller-Müller, nr 23: Etten
COLLECTION Otterlo, Rijksmuseum Kröller-
Müller, inv nr 1029-28, cat van Gogh 1970, nr 23

F 1085 MAN WRITING: FACING LEFT

Pen, pencil and water color 31.5 × 22.5 [12½ × 8¾]
Perhaps Etten 1881
LITERATURE Faille 1928, nr 1085: The Hague.
Vanbeselaere 1937, pp 92-3, 173, 185, 410: The
Hague November 1882
EDITORS' COMMENT The style of this drawing and
of F 1086 shows no relation to The Hague period.
COLLECTION Formerly Delft, H. Tutein-
Nolthenius [until ca 1940]
Present owner unknown

F 1086 OLD MAN WARMING HIMSELF

Pencil and ink 32.5 × 24.5 [12¾ × 9½]
Signed in lower left: Vincent
Perhaps Etten 1881
LITERATURE Faille 1928, nr 1086: The Hague.
Vanbeselaere 1937, pp 92-3, 173, 185, 410:
The Hague November 1882
EDITORS' COMMENT See F 1085
COLLECTION Delft, Mrs K. de Kanter-Crommelin

F 1116a recto MAN SEATED BESIDE STOVE

Pencil, black chalk 21 × 35 [8¼ × 13¾]
Etten 1881
LITERATURE Not in Faille 1928 or Vanbeselaere
1937
EDITORS' COMMENT Dated November 1882 by
Faille in his manuscript.
COLLECTION New York, P. Rosenberg Art
Gallery

F 1209 PEASANT WOMAN PEELING
POTATOES: FACING LEFT

Black chalk, washed with ink, water color,
heightened with white [Ingres paper with water-
mark: fragment of P. L. Bas] 40.5 × 33 [16 × 13]
Signed in lower left: Vincent
Annotated in lower right: verz. Hidde Nijland
Compare sketch in letter 150 and F 1213
Etten September 1881
LETTER 150 [September] See F 854
LITERATURE Album Hidde Nijland Collection
1905, plate 40. Faille 1928, nr 1209: Nuenen March
1885; letter 396. Vanbeselaere 1937, pp 58, 279,
412: Etten December 1881
COLLECTION Otterlo, Rijksmuseum Kröller-
Müller, inv nr 973-28, cat van Gogh 1970, nr 39

F 1213 PEASANT WOMAN PEELING
POTATOES: FACING LEFT

Black and colored chalk, water color [Ingres paper
with watermark: fragment of E.D. & Cie] 30 × 22.5
[11¾ × 8¾]
Compare sketch in letter 150 and F 1209. The
landscape seen through the window is very similar
to a sketch in letter 151
Etten September 1881
LETTER 150 [September] See F 854
LITERATURE Faille 1928, nr 1213: Nuenen March
1885; letter 396. Vanbeselaere 1937, pp 58, 279,
412: Etten December 1881
COLLECTION Otterlo, Rijksmuseum Kröller-
Müller, inv nr 253-17, cat van Gogh 1970, nr 38

F 995

F 1085

F 1086

F 1209

F 1116a

F 1213

F 1221

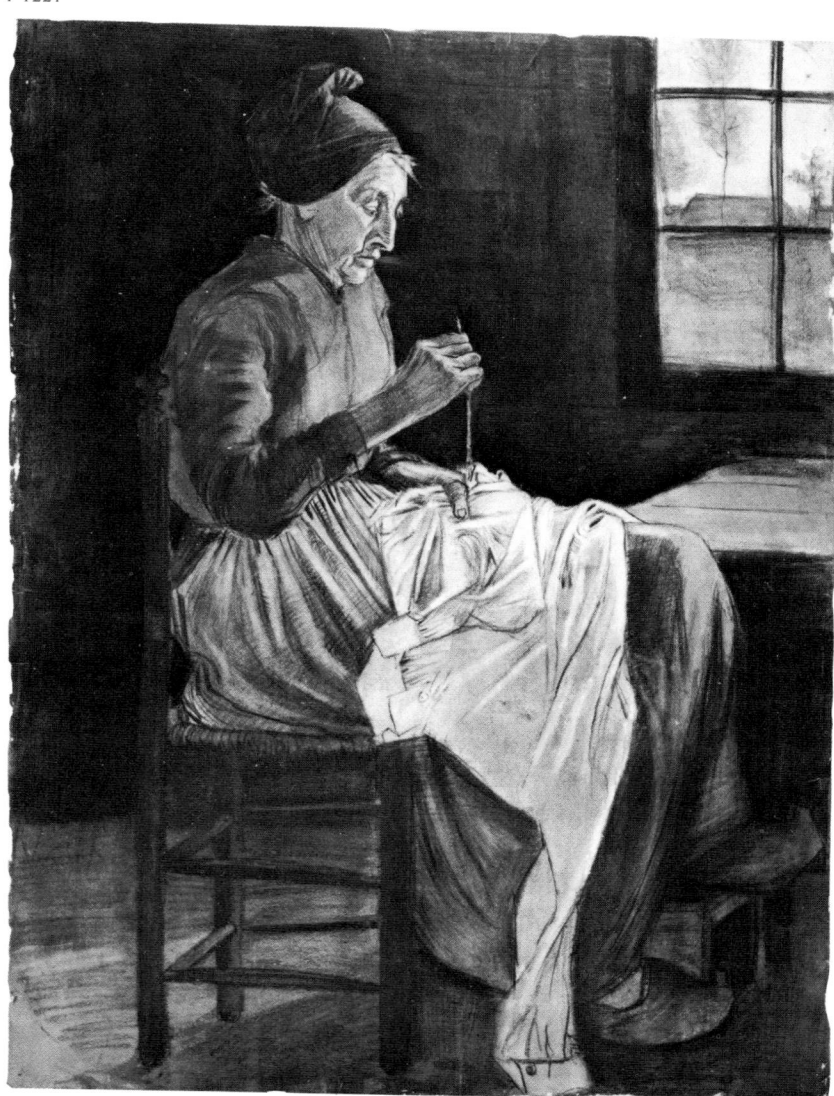

F 906

F 1216 WOMAN BY THE HEARTH

Black chalk, pencil, water color, heightened with white [Ingres paper with watermark: E.D. & Cie – P. L. Bas] 45 × 62.5 [17¾ × 24½]
Signed in lower right: Vincent
Compare sketch in letter 150, F 842, F 868 [same interior] and F 897 [companion piece]
Etten October 1881
LETTER R 3 [2 November] See F 897
LITERATURE Beeldende Kunst June 1921, plate 60. Faille 1928, nr 1216: Nuenen March 1885; letter 396. Vanbeselaere 1937, pp 58, 279, 412: Etten December 1881
COLLECTION Otterlo, Rijksmuseum Kröller-Müller, inv nr 255-20, cat van Gogh 1970, nr 29

F 1221 OLD PEASANT WOMAN, SEWING: FACING RIGHT

Charcoal, black chalk, water color, heightened with white [old Dutch paper, laid] 62.5 × 47.5 [24½ × 18¾]
Signed in lower left: Vincent
Etten November 1881
LITERATURE Faille 1928, nr 1221: Nuenen March 1885; letter 396. Vanbeselaere 1937, pp 58, 279, 412: Etten December 1881
COLLECTION Otterlo, Rijksmuseum Kröller-Müller, inv nr 254-20, cat van Gogh 1970, nr 22

F 1235 WINTER

Pencil, heightened with colors 20.5 × 38.5 [8 × 15¼]
Signed in lower right: Vincent
Compare F 875 [same site]
Etten end 1881
LITERATURE Faille 1928, nr 1235: Nuenen. Vanbeselaere 1937, pp 262, 412: Nuenen January 1885
COLLECTION The Hague, F. Bremmer

THE HAGUE PERIOD

F 906 MAN DIGGING: SEEN FROM THE BACK

Pencil [thick water-color paper] 50.5 × 31.5 [20 × 12½]
Compare F 907 and F 908 [similar motifs]
The Hague November 1882
LETTERS 243 [between 6 and 9 November] 'I have just finished drawing two more diggers.'
245 [between 16 and 18 November] 'I am now busy drawing diggers which I hope will lead to something.'
R 18 [end November] 'I drew the Digger in twelve different poses and am still trying to find something better. He is a marvelously fine model, a true veteran digger.'
LITERATURE Faille 1928, nr 906: letter 169. Vanbeselaere 1937, pp 78, 95-6, 185, 408: The Hague November 1882; letters 169, 243, 245, 246, 287, 315 and R 18
COLLECTION Amsterdam, Rijksmuseum Vincent van Gogh [Vincent van Gogh Foundation, inv nr F 906]

F 907 MAN DIGGING: SEEN FROM THE BACK

Pencil [thick water-color paper] 49.5 × 28.5 [19½ × 11¼]
Compare F 906, F 908 [similar motifs], F 1399 and F 1399a [partly the same motif]
The Hague November 1882
LETTERS 243 [between 6 and 9 November], 245 [between 16 and 18 November] and R 18 [end November] See F 906
LITERATURE Faille 1928, nr 907: letter 169. Vanbeselare 1937, pp 78, 96, 185, 208, 408: November 1882

F 907

COLLECTION Amsterdam, Rijksmuseum Vincent
van Gogh [Vincent van Gogh Foundation, inv
nr F 907]

F 908 MAN DIGGING: THREE QUARTERS TO
THE RIGHT

Pencil and ink [thick water-color paper] 47.5 × 29.5
[18¾ × 11½]
Compare F 906, F 907 [similar motifs], F 1399 and
F 1399a [partly the same motif]
The Hague November 1882
LETTERS 243 [between 6 and 9 November], 245
[between 16 and 18 November] and R 18 [end
November] See F 906
LITERATURE Faille 1928, nr 908: letter 169.
Vanbeselaere 1937, pp 78, 95-6, 185, 408:
November 1882
COLLECTION Amsterdam, Rijksmuseum Vincent
van Gogh [Vincent van Gogh Foundation, inv
nr F 908]

F 1216

F 1235

F 908

F 909

F 912

F 910

F 911 recto

F 911 verso

F 909 THIRD-CLASS WAITING ROOM

Water color 27 × 37.5 [10½ × 14¾]
The Hague January 1882
LETTERS 170 [between 15 and 20 January] '*I started at once a few small water colors and also a large one ... When I go out, I often make sketches in the communal kitchens or in the third-class waiting room, and such places.*'
178 [3 March] '*When I draw separate figures, it is always with a view to a composition of more figures, for instance, a third-class waiting room ...*'
LITERATURE Vanbeselaere 1937, pp 78, 408
COLLECTION New York, Mrs J. K. Thannhauser

F 910 THE SCHENKWEG, THE HAGUE

Water color 38 × 56 [15 × 22]
Compare sketch in letter 170
The Hague January 1882
LETTER 170 [between 15 and 20 January] '*This is a little sketch of the Schenkweg, the view from my window.*'
LITERATURE Vanbeselaere 1937, pp 78, 118, 145-6, 408. J. Hulsker, Bulletin Rijksmuseum Vincent van Gogh 1970, pp 2-13
COLLECTION London, Private Collection

F 910a WOMAN KNITTING NEAR A WINDOW

Water color 33 × 26 [13 × 10¼]
The Hague January 1882 or shortly later
LETTER 170 [between 15 and 20 January] '*I started at once a few smaller water colors and also a large one ...*'
LITERATURE Not in Faille 1928 or Vanbeselaere 1937. J. Hulsker, Bulletin Rijksmuseum Vincent van Gogh 1970, pp 2-13
COLLECTION Formerly The Hague, Mettes & Co Art Gallery
Present owner unknown

F 911 recto LITTLE CHILD: FACING LEFT

Pen 10 × 7 [4 × 2¾]
Reproduced with letter 258
Compare F 912 [same child]
The Hague 1883
LITERATURE Vanbeselaere 1937, pp 78, 103, 408: February 1882
COLLECTION Amsterdam, Rijksmuseum Vincent van Gogh [Vincent van Gogh Foundation, inv nr F 911]

F 911 verso STOOPING WOMAN, PICKING UP A NET

Reproduced with letter 258
The Hague 1883
LITERATURE Not in Vanbeselaere 1937

F 912 PORTRAIT OF LITTLE CHILD: FACING LEFT

Black lithographic chalk, washed 31 × 24 [12¼ × 9½]
Compare F 911 recto [same child]
The Hague 1883
LITERATURE Vanbeselaere 1937, pp 78, 103, 408: March 1883
COLLECTION Zeist, Netherlands, Mrs A. Cohen Tervaert-Henny

F 913 WOMAN WALKING WITH A STICK

Pencil, pen and brown ink, washed [ordinary paper, doubled] 57 × 32 [22½ × 12½]
Signed in lower left: Vincent
Compare sketch in letter 178 and F 914 [same figure]

The Hague March 1882
LETTER 178 [3 March] '*In this way I made a
drawing like the above of an old woman I saw on the
Geest, where the insane asylum is.*'
LITERATURE Vanbeselaere 1937, pp 79, 137, 408
COLLECTION Amsterdam, Rijksmuseum Vincent
van Gogh [Vincent van Gogh Foundation;
acquired 1967, inv nr F 913]

F 914 THE BAKERY IN THE GEEST, THE
HAGUE

Pencil with some pen strokes 20.5 × 33.5 [8 × 13¼]
Signed in lower left: Vincent
Compare sketch in letter 178 and F 913 [same
figure]
The Hague March 1882
LETTER 180 [10 March] '*...C.M. asks me to make
12 small pen drawings for him, views of The Hague,
apropos of some that were ready. (The Paddemoes,
The Geest and the Vleersteg were finished.)*'
LITERATURE Vanbeselaere 1937, pp 79, 80, 126,
408
EDITORS' COMMENT The twelve pen drawings
mentioned in letter 180, made for Vincent's uncle,
C. M. van Gogh, and sent to him around 24 March,
were numbers F 914, F 917, F 918, F 920, F 921, F 922,
F 922a, F 924, F 925, SD 1679 and two drawings – 'The
Vleersteg' and 'The Fishmarket' – that cannot be
identified.
COLLECTION The Hague, Heirs of H. P. Bremmer

F 910a

F 913

F 914

F 915

F 916

F 917

F 915 GROUP OF HOUSES

Pencil, heightened with chalk and sepia 40 × 69 [15¾ × 27¼]
The Hague 1882
LITERATURE Vanbeselaere 1937, pp 79, 80, 127-8, 408: March 1882
COLLECTION The Hague, Mrs A. R. W. Nieuwenhuizen Segaar-Aarse [acquired 1954]

F 916 VIEW OF THE HAGUE FROM THE NORTHEAST, WITH THE NEW CHURCH AND THE JACOBUSKERK

Water color, heightened with white 30 × 52.5 [11¾ × 20¾]
The Hague 1882
LITERATURE Vanbeselaere 1937, pp 79, 84, 147, 408: July 1882
COLLECTION Formerly Rotterdam, P. Verschure
Present owner unknown

F 917 STREET AND BRIDGE IN THE OUTSKIRTS OF THE HAGUE

Pencil 21.5 × 33.5 [8½ × 13¼]
Signed in lower left: Vincent
The Hague March 1882
LITERATURE Vanbeselaere 1937, pp 80, 128, 408
EDITORS' COMMENT See F 914
COLLECTION The Hague, F. Bremmer

F 918 JEWISH QUARTER OF THE HAGUE, THE PADDEMOES

Pen and ink, pencil [ordinary wove paper, pasted] 25 × 31 [9¾ × 12¼]
Signed in lower left: Vincent
The Hague February-March 1882
LETTERS 180 [10 March] See F 914
181 [11 March] '*He [C.M.] did not say anything until we came to a little drawing which I once sketched at twelve o'clock at night while strolling around with Breitner, the Paddemoes (that Jewish quarter near the New Church) as seen from the Peat Market. Next morning I had worked on it again with my pen.*'
LITERATURE Album Hidde Nijland Collection 1905, plate 9. J. Cohen-Gosschalk, Zeitschrift für Bildende Kunst 1908, p 225 [with reproduction]. Vincent van Gogh, Lettres à Bernard, 1911, plate IX. H. P. Bremmer, Vincent van Gogh–Inleidende Beschouwingen, 1911, pp 28-39. Vanbeselaere 1937, pp 79, 80, 128, 408. M. Op de Coul, Museumjournaal February 1969, pp 42-4 [with reproduction]
EDITORS' COMMENT See F 914
COLLECTION Otterlo, Rijksmuseum Kröller-Müller, inv nr 943-28, cat van Gogh 1970, nr 45

F 919 THE RAILWAY STATION RIJNSPOOR [NOW STAATSSPOOR], THE HAGUE

Pencil and pen 24 × 33.5 [9½ × 13¼]
Signed in lower left: Vincent
The Hague March 1882
LITERATURE Vanbeselaere 1937, pp 80, 128, 408
COLLECTION The Hague, F. Bremmer

F 920 HOUSE IN THE SCHEVENINGEN ROAD

Pencil and pen 20 × 33.5 [8 × 13¼]
Signed in lower left: Vincent
The Hague 1882
LETTER 182 [between 14 and 18 March] '*I have made two more little drawings for C.M., a part of the Scheveningen road and sand diggers in the dunes.*'
LITERATURE Vanbeselaere 1937, pp 80, 128, 408
EDITORS' COMMENT See F 914
COLLECTION The Hague, F. Bremmer

F 918

F 920

F 919

F 921

F 922a

F 923

F 921 THE STRAIGHT CANAL: SCHENKWEG

Pen, pencil, black chalk, charcoal heightened with
white [Ingres paper with watermark: scutcheon
with E. [?] D.R.] 18.5 × 34 [7¼ × 13½]
Signed in lower left: Vincent
Annotated on the back: Gronde nabij de Rijn-
spoor [Grounds near the Rijnspoor]
The Hague March 1882
LITERATURE Vanbeselaere 1937, pp 80, 128, 408.
J. Hulsker, Bulletin Rijksmuseum Vincent van
Gogh 1970, pp 2-13
EDITORS' COMMENT See F 914
COLLECTION Otterlo, Rijksmuseum Kröller-
Müller, inv nr 212-15, cat van Gogh 1970, nr 44

F 922 SAND DIGGERS IN THE DUNES

Pencil 27 × 20 [10½ × 8]
Signed in lower left: Vincent
The Hague March 1882
LETTER 182 [between 14 and 18 March] See F 920
LITERATURE Vanbeselaere 1937, pp 80, 408
EDITORS' COMMENT See F 914
COLLECTION The Hague, Heirs of H. P. Bremmer

F 922a CORNER IN THE VAN STOLK PARK

Black chalk, charcoal, pen, heightened with white
18 × 33.5 [7 × 13¼]
Signed in lower left: Vincent
The Hague March 1882
LITERATURE Not in Faille 1928 or Vanbeselaere
1937
EDITORS' COMMENT See F 914. H. J. Michaël has
identified this subject [erroneously called 'Vue sur
les petits jardins au Schenkweg' in the 1902 sale
catalogue] as the van Stolk Park in The Hague.
COLLECTION Zurich, Mrs M. Feilchenfeldt

F 923 FLORIST'S GARDEN ON THE
SCHENKWEG, THE HAGUE

Black chalk, pen, wash, China ink, slightly
heightened with white 23.5 × 33 [9¼ × 13]
Signed in lower left: Vincent
Compare F 930 [same site]
The Hague March 1882
LETTER 183 [24 March] '*Friday morning ... I am
busy drawing some figures and also a few landscapes,
for instance a nursery here on Schenkweg.*'
LITERATURE Vanbeselaere 1937, pp 79, 81, 128-9,
408: end April 1882
EDITORS' COMMENT In letter 184 Vincent writes:
'*C. M. has paid me and given a new order, but a very
difficult one – six special detailed views of the town.
However, I will try to make them, for if I understand
it correctly, I shall get as much for these six* [the
English translation erroneously says twelve] *as for
the first twelve.*'
On May 28th he sent a series of seven drawings to
his uncle. In letter R 8 of that date he writes: '*I have
just now put my drawings into the package for
Amsterdam. There are seven in all.*' He mentions
five subjects out of the seven: two 'Charity Courts'
[mistranslation for 'back yards'], 'Florist's
Garden,' 'Carpenter's Shed' and 'Fish Drying
Barn' seen from a height.
The whole series of seven consisted of numbers
F 923, F 930, F 938, F 939, F 941, F 942 and F 946a.
COLLECTION Amsterdam, Stedelijk Museum [on
loan from the Rijksmuseum, cat 1934, nr 2926d]

F 924 THE GAS TANKS OF THE HAGUE

Chalk and pencil 24 × 33.5 [9½ × 13¼]
Signed in lower left: Vincent
The Hague March 1882
LITERATURE Vanbeselaere 1937, pp 80, 128, 408
EDITORS' COMMENT See F 914
COLLECTION The Hague, R. Bremmer

F 925 A FACTORY IN THE HAGUE [according to
Faille the factory of Sterkman]

Pencil and pen 24 × 33 [9½ × 13]
Signed in lower left: Vincent
The Hague March 1882
LITERATURE Vanbeselaere 1937, pp 79, 80, 128,
408
EDITORS' COMMENT See F 914
COLLECTION Zurich, F. and P. Nathan

F 926 THE FACTORY OF ENTHOVEN ON THE
ZIEKEN, THE HAGUE

Water color 33.5 × 59.5 [13¼ × 23½]
The Hague July 1882
LETTER 220 [26 July] 'Wednesday morning…It is a
road which runs through the meadows of the Schenk-
weg to Enthoven's factory on the Zieke.'
LITERATURE Faille 1928, nr 926: March 1882;
letter 183. Vanbeselaere 1937, pp 79, 84-5, 146, 408
COLLECTION Formerly The Hague, Heirs of
H. P. Bremmer [until 1961]
Present owner unknown

F 927 WORK IN THE FIELDS

Water color 30 × 49 [11¾ × 19¼]
The Hague summer 1882
LITERATURE Faille 1928, nr 926: March 1882.
Vanbeselaere 1937, pp 79, 84-5, 408
COLLECTION Basle, Beyeler Art Gallery

F 924

F 925

F 926

F 922

F 927

F 929

F 929a

F 928 THE BENCH

Pencil, pen and brown ink 28 × 44 [11 × 17¼]
Signed in lower left: Vincent
The Hague September 1882
LITERATURE Vanbeselaere 1937, pp 79, 85, 126,
408
COLLECTION The Hague, G. J. Nieuwenhuizen
Segaar Art Gallery [acquired 1965]

F 929 SORROW

Pencil, washed 45.5 × 29.5 [18 × 11½] Restored
Signed in lower left: Vincent
Annotated by Vincent in lower right: Sorrow
Compare F 929a and lithograph F 1655
The Hague April 1882
LETTERS 186 [about 15 April] *Today I mailed you a
drawing…In my opinion* [it] *is the best figure I have
drawn yet…It is not the study from the model, and
yet it is directly after the model. You should know
that I had two underlayers beneath my paper. I had
been working hard to get the right contour; when I
took the drawing from the board, it had been
imprinted quite correctly on the two underlayers, and
I finished them immediately according to the first
study. So this one is even fresher than the first. I am
keeping the other two for myself.'*
219 [23 July] *'Sunday morning…My very best
drawing, "Sorrow" – at least, I think it's the best I've
done – well, she* [Sien] *posed for that.'*
LITERATURE Vanbeselaere 1937, pp 81, 135-6, 138,
394, 408
EDITORS' COMMENT According to letter 186,
there were originally *three* copies of SORROW: the
original drawing and two imprinted and retouched
ones. F 929 [which now shows no traces of imprint]
may be the original or one of the two imprinted
ones. Vincent must have given it to van Rappard,
probably in May 1882, when van Rappard visited
Vincent and received a drawing from him [letter
202]. The copy mailed to Theo, according to letter
186, must be F 929a, in which plant and tree motifs
have been added. The third copy is missing.
According to letters 180, 195, 196, 200 and 211,
Vincent also made a larger replica of SORROW.
This drawing is also missing.
COLLECTION The Hague, F. Bremmer

F 929a [formerly F 929bis] SORROW

Black chalk 44.5 × 27 [17½ × 10¾]
Signed in lower left: Vincent del.
Annotated by Vincent in lower right: Sorrow; in
lower margin: Comment se fait-il qu'il y ait sur la
terre une femme seule – délaissé. Michelet
Compare F 929 and lithograph F 1655
The Hague April 1882
LETTER 186 [about 15 April] See F 929
LITERATURE Vanbeselaere 1937, pp 81, 134, 136,
138, 408: Chetham 1960, p 26
EDITORS' COMMENT See F 929
COLLECTION London, Lady Epstein

F 930 FLORIST'S GARDEN ON THE
SCHENKWEG, THE HAGUE

Pencil, pen, China ink, black chalk, heightened
with white 29¼ × 58½ [11½ × 23]
Signed in lower left: Vincent
Compare F 923 [same site]
The Hague May 1882
LETTERS 183 [24 March] See F 923
195 [1 May] *'I have worked on the "Laan van
Meerdervoort" again.'*
R 8 [28 May] *'Then there is the "Florist's Garden";
this I changed the way you suggested, i.e. I studied*

the side of the ditch more carefully, as well as the water in the foreground, and only now it shows to its full advantage, I think, and expresses "Spring" and a gentle silence.'
LITERATURE Vanbeselaere 1937, pp 81-2, 128-9, 131, 408: letter 195. C. Virch, Bulletin Metropolitan Museum of Art June 1960, pp 316-7
EDITORS' COMMENT See F 923
COLLECTION New York, Walter C. Baker
[C. Virch, Master Drawings in the Collection of Walter C. Baker, 1962, p 63, nr 112]

F 930a THE ROAD WORKERS

Pencil, pen, heightened with white and colors
43 × 63 [17 × 24¾]
Signed in lower left: Vincent
Compare sketch in letter 190
The Hague April 1882
LETTER 189 [between 15 and 27 April] *'...I am doing a drawing of a street where they are digging to lay sewer or waterpipes, "Diggers in a Trench."'*
190 [between 15 and 27 April] *'Enclosed is a little sketch of diggers, I will tell you why I'm sending it ... Now, to come back to this sketch – it was done in the Geest, in the rain, in a street where I was standing in the mud, amid all the noise and confusion, and I send it to you to show that my sketchbook proves I try to catch things "in motion."'*
LITERATURE Not in Faille 1928 or Vanbeselaere 1937. Eckhardt, Van Gogh und Deutschland, 1956, p 58
COLLECTION East Berlin, Nationalgalerie [acquired 1929; gift of M. Flersheim], inv nr F III-1767

F 928

F 930a

F 930

F 931

F 932

F 933 verso

F 934

F 933 recto

F 931 SIEN IN WHITE BONNET: LEFT PROFILE

Pencil, black lithographic chalk, washed [water-color paper] 47.5 × 26 [18¾ × 10¼]
Signed in lower left: Vincent
The Hague December 1882
LETTER 255 [end December] '*I think I wrote you in my last letter that I am at present doing large heads…*'
LITERATURE Vincent van Gogh, Lettres à Bernard, 1911, plate XXXVII. Faille 1928, nr 931: April 1882. Vanbeselaere 1937, pp 49, 99, 408: December 1882
COLLECTION Amsterdam, Rijksmuseum Vincent van Gogh [Vincent van Gogh Foundation, inv nr F 931]

F 932 SIEN SEWING: WHOLE FIGURE IN RIGHT PROFILE

Pencil, black chalk, washed [Ingres paper with watermark: E.D. & Cie – P.L. Bas] 58 × 45.5 [22¾ × 18]
The Hague April-May 1882
LETTER 192 [between 3 and 9 May] '*I send you a few studies because you can see from them that she [Sien] helps me a great deal by posing…The large figure's chair is not finished because what I want there is an old oak chair.*'
LITERATURE Album Hidde Nijland Collection 1905, plate 48. H. van den Eerenbeemt, Opgang March 1924, nr 279. Vanbeselaere 1937, pp 49, 82, 136-7, 408
COLLECTION Otterlo, Rijksmuseum Kröller-Müller, inv nr 980-28, cat van Gogh 1970, nr 62

F 933 recto STUDY OF A TREE

Black and white chalk, black ink, pencil, water color, lightly washed [water-color paper with water-mark: Hallines 1877] 51 × 71 [20 × 28]
Annotated in lower right: Atelier Vincent
The Hague April 1882
LETTERS 195 [1 May] '*The other, "The Roots," shows some tree roots on sandy ground…But as they are rather large (a full page Ingres), I don't know if I can send them immediately…Though "The Roots" is only a pencil drawing, I have brushed it in with lead pencil and scraped it off again, as I would if I were painting.*'
196 [2 May; postcard, written in English] '*This day I have sent to you by bookpost 1 drawing "A Root in a dry ground."…With regard to this one I hammered it off in a single day, having studied the same spot and trees for "Les Racines." So it has been done "tout d'un trait" out of doors, and has not even been in my studio.*'
LITERATURE Album Hidde Nijland Collection 1905, plate 4. Idem 1907, plate 23. Vanbeselaere 1937, pp 82, 408. Chetham 1960, p 25. Cat van Gogh 1966, Rijksmuseum Kröller-Müller, nr 53: according to Miss Szymańska probably the second version of ROOTS, mentioned in letter 196
COLLECTION Otterlo, Rijksmuseum Kröller-Müller, inv nr 938-28, cat van Gogh 1970, nr 53

F 933 verso [formerly F 1076] BLIND MAN

Black chalk, washed, black ink, brushed, heightened with white
Annotated in lower left: Port Vincent Hidde Nijland
The Hague 1882 or 1883
LITERATURE Album Hidde Nijland Collection 1905, plate 45. Vanbeselaere 1937, pp 106, 207, 410: April 1883
EDITORS' COMMENT We cannot know with certainty when this drawing was made. On stylistic grounds 1883 seems possible. In that case the recto

F 936

of the sheet is much earlier and the drawing must be one of those Theo sent back to Vincent, at the latter's repeated request, in November 1882 [see letters 235, 238 and 241].
COLLECTION Otterlo, Rijksmuseum Kröller-Müller, inv nr 938-28, cat van Gogh 1970, nr 83

F 934 OLD WOMAN, STANDING: RIGHT PROFILE

Water color 66.5 × 37.5 [26¼ × 14¾]
Signed in lower left: Vincent
The Hague 1882
LITERATURE Vanbeselaere 1937, pp 87, 408: October 1882; letter 236
COLLECTION Basle, Beyeler Art Gallery

F 935 SIEN RESTING HEAD ON LEFT HAND, SEATED: RIGHT PROFILE

Pencil, pen and brush, sepia, washed [Ingres paper with watermark: E.D. & Cie – P.L. Bas] 58 × 42 [22¾ × 16½]
The Hague April 1882
LETTER 195 [1 May] 'In front of me is a drawing of a woman in a black merino dress ...'
LITERATURE Album Hidde Nijland Collection 1905, plate 54. Idem 1907, plate 4. J.B.J. Stokvis, Kunst und Künstler April 1927. Vanbeselaere 1937, pp 49, 82, 136-7, 408
COLLECTION Otterlo, Rijksmuseum Kröller-Müller, inv nr 986-28, cat van Gogh 1970, nr 75

F 936 SIEN'S MOTHER SITTING: RIGHT PROFILE

Pen, pencil and brush, sepia [Ingres paper with watermark: P.L. Bas] 61 × 37 [24 × 14½]
The Hague April 1882
LETTER 195 [1 May] See F 935
LITERATURE Album Hidde Nijland Collection 1905, plate 18. Idem 1907, plate 1. H.P. Bremmer, Vincent van Gogh – Inleidende Beschouwingen, 1911, pp 50-62, plate 7. Vanbeselaere 1937, pp 82, 136-7, 408
COLLECTION Otterlo, Rijksmuseum Kröller-Müller, inv nr 952-28, cat van Gogh 1970, nr 65

F 935

F 939

F 937 recto

F 937 verso

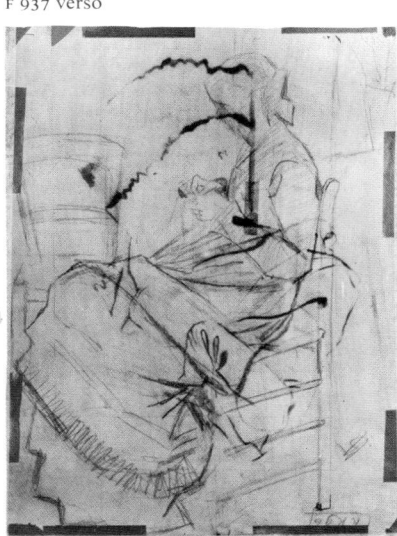

F 938

F 937 recto SIEN RESTING HER HEAD ON
HER LEFT HAND, SEATED: LEFT PROFILE

Pencil, pen and brush, sepia, washed [Ingres paper]
58 × 43 [22¾ × 17]
The Hague April 1882
LETTER 195 [1 May] See F 935
LITERATURE Album Hidde Nijland Collection
1905, plate 96. H. van den Eerenbeemt, Opgang
March 1924, p 273. Vanbeselaere 1937, pp 49, 82,
136-8, 194, 408. Chetham 1960, p 27
COLLECTION Otterlo, Rijksmuseum Kröller-
Müller, inv nr 1028-28, cat van Gogh 1970, nr 76

F 937 verso SIEN SEWING [unfinished sketch]

Pencil
The Hague April 1882

F 938 FISH DRYING BARN AT
SCHEVENINGEN

Pencil, pen and brush, heightened with white
[Ingres paper with an unidentifiable watermark]
28 × 44 [11 × 17¼]
Signed and annotated by Vincent in lower left:
Vincent del. Scharrendroogerij te Scheveningen
Compare F 940 and F 945 [same site]
The Hague May 1882
LETTER R 8 [28 May] '…and went to the dunes to
draw a fish-drying barn, also seen from a height like
the carpenter's shed…'
LITERATURE Album Hidde Nijland Collection
1905, plate 74. Vanbeselaere 1937, pp 83, 130,
144-5, 408. Chetham 1960, p 25
EDITORS' COMMENT See F 923
COLLECTION Otterlo, Rijksmuseum Kröller-
Müller, inv nr 1004-28, cat van Gogh 1970, nr 49

F 939 CARPENTER'S WORKSHOP, SEEN
FROM THE ARTIST'S STUDIO WINDOW

Pencil, ink, pen and brush, heightened with white
[old Dutch paper, laid], 28.5 × 47 [11¼ × 18½]
Signed in lower left [pen]: Vincent del; annotated
with pencil: 82

Compare sketches in letters 220 [reproduced in the
Dutch edition of the letters only] and 276, water
color F 943, drawing F 944, water color F 1022 and
drawing F 1023 [same site]
The Hague May 1882
LETTERS 202 [27 May] 'I wish you could see that
one too, as well as another of a carpenter's shop and
yard where little figures are busy.'
R 8 [28 May] 'Sunday evening…And then the
"Carpenter's Shed" – taken from the window of my
studio – by working on it with pen and ink I have
brought a new kind of black in it, and now "the sun is
shining," because the lights show up more strongly.'
LITERATURE Album Hidde Nijland Collection
1905, plate 66. Vanbeselaere 1937, pp 82-3, 131,
408: May 1882; letters 204 and R 8. D. Cooper,
Zeichnungen und Aquarelle von Vincent van Gogh,
1954, p 22. Chetham 1960, p 25. J. Hulsker, Bulletin
Rijksmuseum Vincent van Gogh 1970, pp 2-13
EDITORS' COMMENT See F 923
COLLECTION Otterlo, Rijksmuseum Kröller-
Müller, inv nr 940-28, cat van Gogh 1970, nr 46

F 939a BACK YARDS WITH TWO FIGURES

Charcoal 24 × 35 [9½ × 13¾]
The Hague 1882
LITERATURE Not in Faille 1928 or Vanbeselaere
1937
COLLECTION New York, The Galerie St Etienne
[acquired 1953]

F 940 FISH DRYING BARN NEAR THE DUNES
AT SCHEVENINGEN

Pencil and pen, heightened with white 28.5 × 45
[11¼ × 17¾]
Signed and annotated by Vincent in lower left:
Scharrendroogerij in de duinen Scheveningen
Vincent
Compare F 938 and F 945 [same site]
The Hague June 1882
LETTERS 204 [1 June] *'Did you receive the drawing,
"The Fish Drying Barn"? I am busy doing a few more
of them, so that you will have about three done in the
same way.'*
205 [3 June] *'Today, Saturday, I am sending you
those two drawings, "Fish Drying Barn" in the dunes
at Scheveningen, and "Carpenter's Workshop and a
Laundry" (seen from my studio window).'*
LITERATURE Vanbeselaere 1937, pp 83, 130-1, 144,
408: letter 204
COLLECTION Basle, Private Collection

F 941 HOUSES SEEN FROM THE BACK
WINDOW OF SIEN'S MOTHER'S HOUSE

Pencil, heightened with white 29 × 45 [11½ × 17¾]
Signed in lower left: Vincent
Compare F 942 [same site]
The Hague May 1882
LETTER 210 [2 July] *'Sunday afternoon…I am
writing you at Sien's mother's, near a window which
looks out on a courtyard. I have drawn it twice, once
in a large size and once small. C.M. has got these
two…'*
LITERATURE Vanbeselaere 1937, pp 78, 83, 130-1,
408
EDITORS' COMMENT See F 923
COLLECTION The Hague, F. Bremmer

F 942 BACK GARDEN OF SIEN'S MOTHER'S
HOUSE

Pencil, pen, heightened with white [brown wove
paper] 46 × 59.5 [18 × 23½]
Annotated in lower left: Vincent del.
Compare F 941 [same site]
The Hague May 1882
LETTERS 202 [27 May] *'Among other things he
[Rappard] saw the drawings I am doing for C.M., and
they seemed to please him, especially a large one of
the court or yard where Sien's mother lives.'*
R 8 [28 May] *'Sunday evening…The big one of the
two courtyards has become quite flat, because I pasted
it on Bristol board, and the lines have greatly gained
in quickness.'*
210 [2 July] See F 941
LITERATURE Vanbeselaere 1937, pp 78, 83, 130-1,
138, 408
EDITORS' COMMENT See F 923
COLLECTION New York, D. Daniels [acquired
1955]

F 939a

F 940

F 941

F 942

F 944

F 945

F 946 recto

F 943 ROOFS SEEN FROM THE ARTIST'S ATTIC WINDOW

Water color, heightened with white 39×55 [$15\frac{1}{4} \times 21\frac{3}{4}$]
Compare sketches in letters 220 [reproduced in the Dutch edition of the letters only] and 276, drawings F 939, F 944, water color F 1022 and drawing F 1023 [same site]
The Hague July 1882
LETTER 219 [23 July] '*Sunday morning…Just imagine me sitting at my attic window as early as four o'clock in the morning, studying, with my perspective frame, the meadows and the carpenter's workshop when they are lighting the fires to make coffee in the cottages and the first workman comes loitering in the yard. Over the red tiled roofs a flock of white pigeons comes soaring between the black smoky chimneys. Behind it all, wide stretch of soft, tender green, miles and miles of flat pasture…This view of the roof ridges and the gutters in which grass grows, and those first signs of life awakening, the bird that flies, the chimney that smokes, the little figure loitering far down below – this is the subject of my water color.*'
LITERATURE Vanbeselaere 1937, pp 84, 131, 143-8, 154, 159, 168, 204, 230, 408. J. Hulsker, Bulletin Rijksmuseum Vincent van Gogh 1970, pp 2-13
COLLECTION Paris, Private Collection

F 944 CARPENTER'S WORKSHOP SEEN FROM THE ARTIST'S STUDIO WINDOW

Black chalk, heightened with white 27×43.5 [$10\frac{1}{2} \times 17$]
Signed in lower left: Vincent
Compare sketches in letters 220 [reproduced in the Dutch edition of the letters only] and 276, F 939, water colors F 943, F 1022 and drawing F 1023 [same site]
The Hague April 1882
LITERATURE Faille 1928, nr 944, not reproduced. Vanbeselaere 1937, p 408. J. Hulsker, Bulletin Rijksmuseum Vincent van Gogh 1970, pp 2-13
COLLECTION New York, Mrs S. Kramarsky

F 945 THE FISH DRYING BARN AT SCHEVENINGEN

Water color 35.5×52 [$14 \times 20\frac{1}{2}$]
Compare drawings F 938 and F 940 [same site]
The Hague July 1882
LETTER 220 [26 July] '*Wednesday morning…I have now made three [watercolors] of Scheveningen, also the "Fish Drying Barns"…When I returned to that fish drying barn, a wonderfully bright fresh green of turnips or rapes had sprouted in those baskets full of sand in the foreground which serve to prevent the sand from drifting off the dunes. Two months ago everything was bare except the grass in the little garden, and now this rough, wild, luxuriant growth forms a pretty effect in contrast to the bareness of the rest. I hope you will like this drawing, the distant horizon, the view across the roofs of the village with the little church steeple, and the dunes – it was all so fine. I can't tell you what great pleasure I had making it.*'
LITERATURE Vanbeselaere 1937, pp 84, 143, 145, 148, 408
COLLECTION New York, Heirs of M. Frank

F 946 recto BLEACHERY IN SCHEVENINGEN

Water color, heightened with white [torchon paper] 32×52 [$12\frac{1}{2} \times 20\frac{1}{2}$]
Compare sketch in letter 220
The Hague July 1882
LETTER 220 [26 July] '*Wednesday morning…I also did a bleaching ground at Scheveningen right on the*

F 946 verso

*spot, washed in at one sitting, almost without
preparation, on a piece of very coarse Torchon.
Enclosed a few small sketches of it.'*
LITERATURE Vanbeselaere 1937, pp 84, 147-8, 408.
H. L. C. Jaffé, Museumjournaal September 1956,
pp 5-6
COLLECTION Schipluiden, Netherlands,
W. Brinkman

F 946 verso WOMAN FROM SCHEVENINGEN,
SEATED

Water color
The Hague 1882

F 943

F 946a

F 947

F 948

F 949

F 946a THE FISH DRYING SHED NEAR SCHEVENINGEN

Pencil, pen, China ink, heightened 27.5 × 46.5 [10¾ × 18¼]
Signed in lower left: Vincent
The Hague May-June 1882
LITERATURE Not in Faille 1928 or Vanbeselaere 1937
EDITORS' COMMENT See F 923
COLLECTION Groningen, Groninger Museum voor Stad en Lande, inv nr 1951/560

F 947 POLLARD WILLOW BY THE SIDE OF A ROAD

Water color 36 × 56.5 [14¼ × 22¼]
Compare sketch in letter 221
The Hague 1882
LETTERS 220 [26 July] '*I saw a dead willow trunk there, just the thing for Barye, for instance. It was hanging over a pool ... I am going to attack it tomorrow morning.*'
221 [31 July] '*This is approximately the effect of the pollard willow, only in the water color itself there is no black other than a broken tone,*'
LITERATURE Vanbeselaere 1937, pp 84, 147, 408: July 1882. J. Hulsker, Bulletin Rijksmuseum Vincent van Gogh 1970, pp 2-13
COLLECTION New York, Mr and Mrs L. M. Rogers

F 948 THREE WOOD CUTTERS

Water color 36 × 25 [14¼ × 9¾]
The Hague June 1883 or shortly later
LETTER 288 [3 June] '*... I should also like to do the tree felling in the wood ... Don't you think that a number of drawings of tree felling etc. might be done in the same style in which I just did "Peat Cutters" and "Sand Diggers" – and in that way would be interesting enough to serve as illustrations?*'
LITERATURE Vanbeselaere 1937, pp 85, 108, 212, 408: May 1883; letter 288
COLLECTION Cincinnati, The Cincinnati Art Museum [gift of Mr and Mrs John Emery], inv nr 1962-14

F 949 WOMAN IN A WOOD

Water color 34.5 × 24 [13½ × 9½]
The Hague September-October 1882
LITERATURE Vanbeselaere 1937, pp 85, 408
COLLECTION The Hague, H. M. Cramer Art Gallery

F 950 FOUR WOOD CUTTERS

Black chalk and water color [ordinary wove drawing paper] 35 × 45 [13¾ × 17¾]
The Hague June 1883 or shortly later
LETTER 288 [3 June] See F 948
LITERATURE Album Hidde Nijland Collection 1905, plate 63. Vanbeselaere 1937, pp 85, 108, 212, 408: May 1883
COLLECTION Otterlo, Rijksmuseum Kröller-Müller, inv nr 994-28, cat van Gogh 1970, nr 52

F 951 PEOPLE SEATED ON A BENCH IN BEZUIDENHOUT PARK [second version]

Water color 25 × 37 [9¾ × 14½]
Signed in lower left: Vincent
Compare sketches in letters 230 and R 12, drawing F 952 recto and water color F 1039
The Hague September 1882
LETTER R 12 [about 15 September] '*Herewith a very hasty sketch of a water color I am working on.*'
LITERATURE Faille 1928, nr 951: letter 221. Vanbeselaere 1937, pp 85, 162, 408
EDITORS' COMMENT See F 952 recto

F 950

COLLECTION Ellecom, Netherlands, Sanatorium
Dalsteyn

F 952 recto PEOPLE SEATED ON A BENCH IN
BEZUIDENHOUT PARK [first version]

Pen, pencil, lightly washed [water-color paper,
with rough surface] 20.5 × 19.5 [8 × 7¾]
Annotated by Vincent in lower left: Bezuidenhout
Compare sketches in letters 230 and R 12, water
colors F 951 and F 1039
The Hague September 1882
LETTER 230 [11 September] '*Enclosed again small
water colors... Well, I hope this little bench will show
you that I am not averse to choosing subjects that are
pleasant or attractive... I enclose with the little bench
another one as a pendant... I struck off the little
bench after a larger water color I am working on... I
do not know whether I shall succeed in finishing it
well.*'
LITERATURE Album Hidde Nijland Collection
1905, part 1, reproduction on cover. Vanbeselaere
1937, pp 85, 162, 408
EDITORS' COMMENT Drawing F 952 recto,
evidently done on the spot, probably preceded the
'larger water color' after which the small one
enclosed in letter 230 was sketched. Van Gogh does
not seem to have completed the larger water color.
Instead, in the same month of September, he made
a second version of the subject, changing the figures
to the left and adding a man with a broom to the
right of the small chestnut tree. This is water color
F 951. The pendant of the small water color
enclosed in letter 230 is probably water color F 1039.
COLLECTION Otterlo, Rijksmuseum Kröller-
Müller, inv nr 1038-28, cat van Gogh 1970, nr 48

F 952 verso ROAD WITH TWO CARTS,
HORSES, A BARREL ON THE LEFT, THREE
FIGURES

Pen, pencil
The Hague September 1882
LETTER 230 [11 September] '*Recently I have also
been very busy drawing horses in the street... I love
to make those sketches in the street...*'

F 951

F 952 recto

F 952 verso

F 954

F 954a

F 955

F 956

F 956a

F 959

F 957

F 953 ORPHAN MAN HOLDING A TOP HAT IN HIS LEFT HAND

Pencil [gray paper] 49 × 23.5 [19¼ × 9¼]
The Hague September-December 1882
LETTERS 235 [about 1 October] '*He wears a large old overcoat, which gives him a curiously broad figure; I think you would enjoy this collection of almshouse men in their Sunday and their everyday clothes. I also drew him sitting with a pipe. He has an amusing bald head, large and deaf ears and white sideburns.*'
236 [8 October] '*Sunday…I have made even more studies of the old men…*'
238 [about 10 October] '*This week I have drawn…a few old men from the almshouse.*'
R 14 [September-October] '*I am very busy working on drawings of an orphan-man, as these poor old fellows from the workhouse are popularly called here.*'
LITERATURE Vanbeselaere 1937, pp 86, 88-9, 170, 192, 408
COLLECTION New York, B. Sonnenberg [acquired 1962]

F 954 HEAD OF AN ORPHAN MAN WITH TOP HAT: RIGHT PROFILE

Pencil and brush 40 × 24.5 [15¾ × 9¾]
Compare F 954a and F 955 [same model]
The Hague December 1882
LETTER 254 [about 20 December] '*So I am now working on two large heads of an orphan man, with his white beard and his old-fashioned top hat. The old fellow has the kind of wrinkled, witty face that one should like to have near a cozy Christmas fire.*'
LITERATURE Vanbeselaere 1937, pp 88, 91, 99, 188-9, 408: December 1882; letter 254. Horst Vey, Worcester Art Museum Annual 1958, p 42
COLLECTION Worcester, Worcester Art Museum [gift of Mr Chapin Riley], inv nr 1957-153, cat 1958, nr 29

F 954a HEAD OF AN ORPHAN MAN WITH TOP HAT

Black chalk, charcoal, heightened with white 44 × 29 [17¼ × 11½]
Compare F 954 and F 955 [same model]
The Hague December 1882
LETTER 254 [about 20 December] See F 954
LITERATURE Not in Faille 1928 or Vanbeselaere 1937
COLLECTION Johannesburg, Kunsmuseum, cat new acquisitions 1948, nr 3

F 955 BALD-HEADED ORPHAN MAN FACING RIGHT

Pencil, washed with black [turpentine] 32 × 25 [12½ × 9¾]
False signature in lower right: Vincent
Compare F 954 and F 954a [same model]
The Hague winter 1882-3
LITERATURE Vanbeselaere 1937, pp 88, 91, 101, 188-9, 408: January 1883
COLLECTION The Hague, Heirs of H. P. Bremmer

F 956 ORPHAN MAN WITH TOP HAT EATING

Pencil [gray paper] 46.5 × 24.5 [18¼ × 9¾]
The Hague September-December 1882
LETTERS 235 [about 1 October], 236 [8 October], 238 [about 10 October] and R 14 [September-October] See F 953
LITERATURE Vanbeselaere 1937, pp 89, 170, 408: October 1882
COLLECTION Bergen, Netherlands, D. A. Hoogendijk [acquired 1959]

F 956a ORPHAN MAN WITH CAP, EATING

Pencil 51 × 27.5 [20 × 10¾]
The Hague September-December 1882
LETTERS 235 [about 1 October], 236 [8 October],
238 [about 10 October] and R 14 [September-
October] See F 953
LITERATURE Not in Faille 1928 or Vanbeselaere
1937
COLLECTION Geneva, Motte Art Gallery
[acquired 1956]

F 957 ORPHAN MAN HOLDING A CUP

Pencil 49 × 24.5 [19¼ × 9¾]
The Hague September-December 1882
LETTERS 235 [about 1 October], 236 [8 October],
238 [about 10 October] and R 14 [September-
October] See F 953
LITERATURE Vanbeselaere 1937, pp 89, 170, 173,
409
COLLECTION Worcester, Massachusetts, Mr and
Mrs Chapin Riley [acquired 1959]

F 958 ORPHAN MAN WITH WALKING STICK

Pencil 48.5 × 26 [19 × 10¼]
The Hague September-December 1882
LETTERS 235 [about 1 October], 236 [8 October],
238 [about 10 October] and R 14 [September-
October] See F 953
LITERATURE Vanbeselaere 1937, pp 88-9, 170, 176,
409
COLLECTION Schipluiden, Netherlands,
W. Brinkman [acquired 1955]

**F 959 ORPHAN MAN WITH GLASS AND
HANDKERCHIEF**

Pencil [gray Ingres paper] 49 × 25 [19¼ × 9¾]
Annotated in lower left: Port. Vincent
The Hague September-December 1882
LETTERS 235 [about 1 October], 236 [8 October],
238 [about 10 October] and R 14 [September-
October] See F 953
LITERATURE Vanbeselaere 1937, pp 88-9, 170,
409. Chetham 1960, p 29
COLLECTION Otterlo, Rijksmuseum Kröller-
Müller, inv nr 1035-28, cat van Gogh 1970, nr 87

**F 960 ORPHAN MAN WITH WALKING
STICK: SEEN FROM THE BACK**

Pencil [ordinary paper with mark: Lanson & Mon-
golfier Vidalon–Anno ? AY B] 47.5 × 26 [18¾ × 10¼]
The Hague September-December 1882
LETTERS 235 [about 1 October], 236 [8 October],
238 [about 10 October] and R 14 [September-
October] See F 953
LITERATURE Vanbeselaere 1937, pp 88-9, 170,
408. Chetham 1960, p 29
COLLECTION Amsterdam, Vincent van Gogh
Rijksmuseum [Vincent van Gogh Foundation, inv
nr F 960]

F 961 ORPHAN MAN WITH TOP HAT

Black chalk, pencil 45 × 24.3 [17¾ × 9¾]
Compare F 985 [same model]
The Hague October 1882
LETTER 238 [about 10 October] 'This week I have
drawn a few heads...'
LITERATURE Vanbeselaere 1937, pp 99, 188-9,
409: December 1882; letter 254. D. Hannema,
Kunst in Oude Sfeer, 1952, p 104. E. Schlumberger,
Connaissance des Arts April 1961, pp 68-78
COLLECTION Heino, Netherlands, Hannema-de
Stuers Foundation, cat 1967, nr 106

F 953

F 958

F 961

F 960

F 962

F 963

F 964

F 964a

F 964b

F 962 ORPHAN MAN WITH WALKING STICK

Pencil [thick water-color paper] 50 × 30.5
[19¾ × 12]
The Hague September-December 1882
LETTERS 235 [about 1 October], 236 [8 October],
238 [about 10 October] and R 14 [September-
October] See F 953
LITERATURE Vanbeselaere 1937, pp 88-9, 170,
173, 192, 409. Chetham 1960, p 29
COLLECTION Amsterdam, Rijksmuseum Vincent
van Gogh [Vincent van Gogh Foundation, inv
nr F 962]

**F 963 ORPHAN MAN WITH WALKING
STICK: FACING RIGHT**

Black chalk 48 × 24.5 [19 × 9¾]
The Hague September-October 1882
LETTERS 235 [about 1 October], 236 [8 October],
238 [about 10 October] and R 14 [September-
October] See F 953
LITERATURE Vanbeselaere 1937, pp 88-9, 170,
173-4, 192, 409
COLLECTION Utrecht, Museum van Baaren
Foundation, inv nr 63

**F 964 OLD MAN CARRYING A BASKET:
FACING RIGHT**

Pencil, wash 48 × 22.5 [19 × 9]
The Hague December 1882
LETTER 251 [between 4 and 9 December] *'Then one
of those little old fellows in a short jacket and big old
top hat, which one sometimes meets in the dunes. He
is carrying a basket full of peat.'*
LITERATURE Vanbeselaere 1937, pp 97, 170, 208,
409
COLLECTION Ubbergen, Netherlands, Mrs
A. W. Maclaine Pont-Stork

**F 964a [formerly F 964bis] MAN WITH A
SPADE, RESTING**

Black chalk, pencil 59.5 × 41.5 [23½ × 16¼]
The Hague 1882
LITERATURE Vanbeselaere 1937, pp 91, 170, 190,
409: November 1882
COLLECTION New York, F. A. P. Zimmermann

**F 964b MAN SEATED DRINKING A CUP OF
COFFEE**

Chalk, pencil, charcoal 32 × 25 [12½ × 9¾]
Signed in lower left: Vincent
The Hague towards the end of 1882
LITERATURE Not in Faille 1928 or Vanbeselaere
1937. Expertised under the auspices of the Expertise
Instituut, Amsterdam [1957]
COLLECTION New York, Van Diemen-Lilienfeld
Galleries

F 965 ORPHAN MAN SEEN FROM THE BACK

Pencil and black chalk 50 × 28 [19¾ × 11]
Signed in lower right: Vincent
The Hague September-December 1882
LETTERS 235 [about 1 October], 236 [8 October],
238 [about 10 October] and R 14 [September-
October] See F 953
LITERATURE Vincent van Gogh, Lettres à
Bernard, 1911, plate XXXIV. Vanbeselaere 1937,
pp 88-9, 170, 191, 409
COLLECTION East Germany, Private Collection

F 966 ORPHAN MAN READING: FACING RIGHT

Pencil and bistre wash [ordinary drawing paper]
48 × 28.5 [19 × 11¼]
The Hague September-December 1882
LETTERS 235 [about 1 October], 236 [8 October],
238 [about 10 October] and R 14 [September-
October] See F 953
LITERATURE Vanbeselaere 1937, pp 88, 90, 409
COLLECTION Amsterdam, Rijksmuseum Vincent
van Gogh [Vincent van Gogh Foundation, inv
nr F 966]

F 967 IN THE CHURCH

Water color, pen and pencil [ordinary wove paper
with pressmark: J.D.K.] 28 × 38 [11 × 15]
Compare sketch in letter 235 [the first row only]
The Hague October 1882
LETTER 235 [about 1 October] *I am also making
one of a church bench which I saw in a little church in
the Geest, where the people from the almshouse go
(here they call them very expressively orphan men
and orphan women) ... This is a fragment of those
benches; in the background there are still other heads
of men.'*
LITERATURE H. P. Bremmer, Album Kröller-
Müller Collection 1919, plate 3. J. Meier-Graefe,
Vincent, 1921, volume 2, plate 1. Vanbeselaere
1937, pp 86, 164, 409
COLLECTION Otterlo, Rijksmuseum Kröller-
Müller, inv nr 193-12, cat van Gogh 1970, nr 54

F 968 ORPHAN MAN WITH UMBRELLA:
SEEN FROM THE BACK

Pencil 48.5 × 27.5 [19 × 10¾]
Annotated on the reverse: no 183
Compare sketch in letter R 14
The Hague September-October 1882
LETTER R 14 [September-October] *Herewith
another rough sketch of an orphan-man.'*
LITERATURE Vanbeselaere 1937, pp 88-9, 170,
409: October 1882
COLLECTION Sale London [Sotheby], 7 July 1960,
nr 46
Present owner unknown

F 969 ORPHAN MAN CLEANING BOOTS

Pencil 48.5 × 28 [19 × 11]
The Hague September-December 1882
LETTERS 235 [about 1 October], 236 [8 October],
238 [about 10 October] and R 14 [September-
October] See F 953
LITERATURE Vanbeselaere 1937, pp 88, 91, 170,
190, 409: November 1882
COLLECTION Switzerland, Private Collection

F 967

F 965

F 966

F 968

F 969

F 972

F 971

F 970

F 973

F 974

F 970 THE STATE LOTTERY OFFICE

Water color [ordinary drawing paper] 38 × 57
[15 × 22½]
Compare sketch in letter 235
The Hague October 1882
LETTER 235 [about 1 October] '*You remember
perhaps Moorman's State Lottery office at the
beginning of Spuistraat? I passed there on a rainy
morning when a crowd of people stood waiting to get
their lottery tickets. For the most part they were old
women and the kind of people of whom one cannot
say what they are doing or how they live, but who
evidently have a great deal of drudgery and trouble
and care ... But that little group of people – their
expression of waiting – struck me, and while I
sketched it, it took on a larger, deeper significance
for me than at first ... However it may be, I am making
a large water color of it.*'
LITERATURE Vanbeselaere 1937, pp 86, 164, 409.
Chetham 1960, p 28. H. L. C. Jaffé, Miscellanea
Jozef Duverger, 1968, pp 383-7
COLLECTION Amsterdam, Rijksmuseum Vincent
van Gogh [Vincent van Gogh Foundation, inv
nr F 970]

F 971 ORPHAN MAN WITH A CHILD STANDING BETWEEN HIS KNEES

Pencil and chalk 48 × 25 [19 × 9¾]
The Hague September-December 1882
LETTERS 235 [about 1 October], 236 [8 October],
238 [about 10 October] and R 14 [September-
October] See F 953
LITERATURE Vanbeselaere 1937, pp 89, 91, 170-1,
409: November 1882
COLLECTION Knightdale, North Carolina,
Mary Enole Witt

F 972 ORPHAN MAN WITH AN UMBRELLA UNDER HIS ARM

Pencil, lightly washed [water-color paper with
watermark: A. M. Brécourt Frères] 48.5 × 24.5
[19 × 9¾]
The Hague September-December 1882
LETTERS 235 [about 1 October], 236 [8 October],
238 [about 10 October] and R 14 [September-
October] See F 953
LITERATURE Beeldende Kunst 12 October 1915,
nr 96. H. P. Bremmer, Album Kröller-Müller
Collection 1919, plate 14. Vanbeselaere 1937,
pp 88-9, 170, 173-4, 192, 409
COLLECTION Otterlo, Rijksmuseum Kröller-
Müller, inv nr 213-11, cat van Gogh 1970, nr 85

F 972a ORPHAN MAN WITH UMBRELLA: SEEN FROM BEHIND

Pencil 49 × 30 [19¼ × 11¾]
Compare sketch in letter 270 and F 978a
The Hague September-December 1882
LETTERS 235 [about 1 October], 236 [8 October],
238 [about 10 October] and R 14 [September-
October] See F 953
LITERATURE Not in Faille 1928 or Vanbeselaere
1937
EDITORS' COMMENT The sketch in letter 270,
dating from around 2 March 1883, was made after
a now lost water color.
COLLECTION Bern, M. Huggler

F 973 ORPHAN MAN STANDING, TOP HAT IN HIS RIGHT HAND: FULL FACE

Pencil, lightly washed [water-color paper with
watermark: A. M. Brécourt Frères] 47 × 22
[18½ × 8¾]
The Hague September-December 1882
LETTERS 235 [about 1 October], 236 [8 October],

238 [about 10 October] and R 14 [September-October] See F 953
LITERATURE H. P. Bremmer, Album Kröller-Müller Collection 1919, plate 11. Vanbeselaere 1937, pp 90, 170, 173, 175, 181, 390, 409
COLLECTION Otterlo, Rijksmuseum Kröller-Müller, inv nr 211-11, cat van Gogh 1970, nr 84

F 974 ORPHAN MAN WARMING HIMSELF: SEEN FROM THE BACK

Pencil, heightened with white [ordinary laid paper] 56 × 30 [22 × 11¾]
The Hague September-December 1882
LETTERS 235 [about 1 October], 236 [8 October], 238 [about 10 October] and R 14 [September-October] See F 953
LITERATURE H. P. Bremmer, Album Kröller-Müller Collection 1919, plate 12. Vanbeselaere 1937, pp 88, 90, 170, 409
COLLECTION Otterlo, Rijksmuseum Kröller-Müller, inv nr 206-11, cat van Gogh 1970, nr 88

F 975 ORPHAN MAN WITH TOP HAT AND CROSSED HANDS

Pencil [ordinary wove paper, toned] 49 × 25 [19¼ × 9¾]
Signed in lower left: Vincent
The Hague September-December 1882
LETTERS 235 [about 1 October], 236 [8 October], 238 [about 10 October] and R 14 [September-October] See F 953
LITERATURE H. P. Bremmer, Album Kröller-Müller Collection 1919, plate 10. Vanbeselaere 1937, pp 88, 90, 170, 176, 208, 409: October 1882
COLLECTION Otterlo, Rijksmuseum Kröller-Müller, inv nr 202-00, cat van Gogh 1970, nr 89

F 976 ORPHAN MAN DRINKING A CUP OF COFFEE

Pencil and black chalk, lightly washed [water-color paper with watermark: Hallines 1877] 49 × 29 [19¼ × 11½]
Compare F 996a, lithograph F 1657 and SD 1682 [same model]
The Hague November 1882
LETTERS 235 [about 1 October], 236 [8 October], 238 [about 10 October] and R 14 [September-October] See F 953
LITERATURE H. P. Bremmer, Album Kröller-Müller Collection 1919, plate 15. Vanbeselaere 1937, pp 88, 90, 170, 192, 409: October 1882. Chetham 1960, p 29. V. W. van Gogh, Museumjournaal 1968, part I, pp 42-5
COLLECTION Otterlo, Rijksmuseum Kröller-Müller, inv nr 199-11, cat van Gogh 1970, nr 82

F 976a MAN SEATED, DRINKING: FULL FACE

This number is identical with F 1082
LITERATURE Vanbeselaere 1937, p 88

F 977 ORPHAN MAN WITH TOP HAT AND WALKING STICK: FULL FACE

Pencil [ordinary drawing paper] 47 × 23.5 [18½ × 9¼]
The Hague September-December 1882
LETTERS 235 [about 1 October], 236 [8 October], 238 [about 10 October] and R 14 [September-October] See F 953
LITERATURE Vincent van Gogh, Lettres à Bernard, 1911, plate XXI. Vanbeselaere 1937, pp 88, 90, 170, 173, 192, 409
COLLECTION Amsterdam, Rijksmuseum Vincent van Gogh [Vincent van Gogh Foundation, inv nr F 977]

F 975

F 977

F 972a

F 976

F 978

F 978a

F 979

F 979a

F 980

F 978 ORPHAN MAN LOOKING AT HIS WATCH

Pencil [water-color paper with watermark: Hallines 1877] 48 × 28.5 [19 × 11¼]
The Hague September-December 1882
LETTERS 235 [about 1 October], 236 [8 October], 238 [about 10 October] and R 14 [September-October] See F 953
LITERATURE H. P. Bremmer, Album Kröller-Müller Collection 1919, plate 13. Vanbeselaere 1937, pp 88, 90, 170, 173, 192, 409
COLLECTION Otterlo, Rijksmuseum Kröller-Müller, inv nr 195-11, cat van Gogh 1970, nr 86

F 978a ORPHAN MAN

Pencil 12 × 7.5 [4¾ × 3]
Signed: Vincent
Compare sketch in letter 270 and F 972a
The Hague October 1882
LETTERS 235 [about 1 October], 236 [8 October], 238 [about 10 October] and R 14 [September-October] See F 953
LITERATURE Vincent van Gogh, Lettres à Bernard, 1911, plate XXXIII. Not in Faille 1928 or Vanbeselaere 1937
EDITORS' COMMENT See F 972a
COLLECTION Munich, Mrs Reichert

F 979 MAN WITH A RAKE: FACING RIGHT

Pencil 44 × 22 [17¼ × 8¾]
The Hague autumn 1882
LITERATURE Vanbeselaere 1937, pp 88, 91, 409: November 1882
COLLECTION Curaçao, H. J. Nolte [acquired 1965]

F 979a YOUNG MAN WITH A BROOM

Pencil 43 × 29.5 [17 × 11½]
The Hague autumn 1882
LITERATURE Not in Faille 1928 or Vanbeselaere 1937
COLLECTION The Hague, Gemeente Museum [on loan from the Wibbina Foundation]

F 980 FIGURES ON THE BEACH AT SCHEVENINGEN

Pencil [thin wove paper] 16 × 25.5 [6¼ × 10]
Signed in lower left: Vincent
Compare water color F 1038
The Hague September 1882
LETTER 231 [17 September] 'Recently I made a study of ladies and gentlemen on the beach, a bustling crowd of people.'
LITERATURE Vanbeselaere 1937, pp 86-7, 409: letter 304; preliminary study for water color F 1038
COLLECTION Otterlo, Rijksmuseum Kröller-Müller, inv nr 204-13, cat van Gogh 1970, nr 51

F 981 ORPHAN MAN HOLDING A CHILD

Pencil 36.5 × 25 [14½ × 9¾]
The Hague September-December 1882
LETTERS 235 [about 1 October], 236 [8 October], 238 [about 10 October] and R 14 [September-October] See F 953
LITERATURE Vanbeselaere 1937, pp 88, 91, 170-1, 190, 409: November 1882
EDITORS' COMMENT The baby may be Sien's youngest child.
COLLECTION Zaandam, Netherlands, Mrs W. Takens-Bremmer

F 982 THE BEACH AT SCHEVENINGEN

Water color 27 × 45 [10½ × 17¾]
Compare sketch in letter 237
The Hague October 1882
LETTER 237 [22 October] *'Sunday afternoon…and I also started another of the beach, of which this is the composition.'*
LITERATURE Vanbeselaere 1937, pp 86-7, 409
COLLECTION Haarlem, Netherlands, Private Collection

F 983 STANDING GIRL, KNITTING: FACING RIGHT

Pencil 52 × 25.5 [20½ × 10]
Compare F 984 [same model]
The Hague 1882
LITERATURE Vanbeselaere 1937, pp 86, 88, 176, 409
COLLECTION New York, A. Hailparn

F 984 SEATED GIRL, KNITTING: FACING LEFT

Pencil 43 × 26.5 [17 × 10½]
Compare F 983 [same model]
The Hague 1882
LITERATURE Vanbeselaere 1937, pp 86, 88, 176, 409
COLLECTION The Hague, Heirs of H. P. Bremmer

F 981

F 983

F 984

F 982

F 986

F 989

F 988

F 988a

F 985

F 985 ORPHAN MAN WITH TOP HAT: HALF FIGURE

Pencil, black lithographic chalk, washed, pen and brown ink [thick water-color paper] 60.5 × 36 [23¾ × 14¼]
Signed in lower left: Vincent
Compare F 961 [same model]
The Hague autumn or early winter 1882
LITERATURE Vanbeselaere 1937, pp 91, 99, 189, 409: December 1882
COLLECTION Amsterdam, Rijksmuseum Vincent van Gogh [Vincent van Gogh Foundation, inv nr F 985]

F 986 BOY WITH SPADE, SEATED ON A BARREL

Pencil, pen and ink, washed 50.5 × 31.5 [20 × 12½]
Signed in lower left: Vincent feci...
The Hague October 1882
LETTER 238 [about 10 October] 'I had a model for a few hours today, a boy with a spade, hod-carrier by trade, a very intriguing type – flat nose, thick lips and very coarse, straight hair...'
LITERATURE Vanbeselaere 1937, pp 86, 88, 409
COLLECTION Sale Stuttgart [Stuttgarter Kunst-kabinett] 7-9 November 1951, nr 1057
Present owner unknown

F 987 MAN WITH AN AXE ON HIS SHOULDER

Black chalk 45.5 × 21.5 [18 × 8½]
Signed in lower right: Vincent
The Hague October 1882
LITERATURE Vanbeselaere 1937, pp 91, 170, 192, 409: December 1882
COLLECTION Johannesburg, A. P. de Jong

F 988 TWO WOMEN STANDING TALKING

Black chalk and pencil, heightened with white 49 × 27.5 [19¼ × 10¾]
The Hague October 1882
LETTER 238 [about 10 October] 'I can even work with several people at the same time, for instance, two women standing talking...'
LITERATURE Vanbeselaere 1937, pp 91, 105, 190-1, 409: March-April 1883; pp 91, 105: March 1883
COLLECTION Formerly Amsterdam, Buffa Art Gallery
Present owner unknown

F 988a TWO WOMEN STROLLING, ONE OF THEM CARRYING A KETTLE

Pencil 45.5 × 26 [18 × 10¼]
Signed in lower right: Vincent
The Hague first half of 1882
LITERATURE Not in Faille 1928 or Vanbeselaere 1937. H. P. Bremmer, Het Volk 25 October 1941 [with reproduction]
EDITORS' COMMENT The woman to the right is Sien, during a pregnancy.
COLLECTION Netherlands, Private Collection

F 989 ORPHAN MAN CONVERSING WITH A WOMAN

Pencil and black chalk [laid paper with fragment of watermark in script-letters] 45.5 × 26 [18 × 10¼]
The Hague October-November 1882
LITERATURE H. P. Bremmer, Album Kröller-Müller Collection 1919, plate 15a. Vanbeselaere 1937, pp 91, 170-1, 190-3, 409: November 1882
COLLECTION Otterlo, Rijksmuseum Kröller-Müller, inv nr 189-19, cat van Gogh 1970, nr 78

F 990 PEOPLE UNDER UMBRELLAS

Water color 28.5 × 21 [11¼ × 8¼]
The Hague 1883
LITERATURE Vanbeselaere 1937, pp 107, 190-1,
409: April 1883
COLLECTION The Hague, Gemeente Museum [on
loan from Wibbina Foundation], inv nr T II-X-1957

F 991 OLD COUPLE: SEEN FROM THE BACK

Pencil [thick water-color paper] 50 × 31 [19¾ × 12¼]
The Hague October 1882
LETTER 238 [about 10 October] *'I can even work
with several people at the same time, for instance…a
man and a woman arm in arm, etc.'*
LITERATURE Vincent van Gogh, Lettres à
Bernard, 1911, plate XXXVI. Vanbeselaere 1937,
pp 91, 170, 190-1, 409
COLLECTION Amsterdam, Rijksmuseum Vincent
van Gogh [Vincent van Gogh Foundation, inv
nr F 991]

F 991

F 987

F 990

F 996

F 993

F 996a

F 994

F 992 COUPLE WALKING
Arles period; see after F 1521 verso

F 993 PORTRAIT [probably of the bookseller
Blok]

Pencil, pen and China ink and water color 38.5 × 26
[15¼ × 10¼]
The Hague November 1882
LETTER 241 [2 or 3 November] '*Do you know
whose portrait I drew this morning? Blok, the Jewish
book dealer – not David, but the little one who has his
stand on the Binnenhof.*'
LITERATURE Vanbeselaere 1937, pp 91, 179, 189,
409
COLLECTION Rotterdam, R. W. Wentges
[acquired 1944]

F 994 MINERS' WIVES CARRYING SACKS OF
COAL

Water color, heightened with white [water-color
paper with dull surface] 32 × 50 [12½ × 19¾]
Compare F 832 [same subject]
The Hague October-November 1882
LETTER 241 [2 or 3 November] '*I again worked on a
water color of miners' wives carrying bags of coal in
the snow.*'
R 16 [early November] '*Not without some trouble I
have at last discovered how the miners' wives in the
Borinage carry their sacks... Now I have made twelve
studies of the subject.*'
LITERATURE Album Hidde Nijland Collection
1905, plate 25. Idem 1907, plate 15. H. P. Bremmer,
Vincent van Gogh – Inleidende Beschouwingen,
1911, pp 63-73. Vanbeselaere 1937, pp 92, 180, 194,
409
COLLECTION Otterlo, Rijksmuseum Kröller-
Müller, inv nr 959-28, cat van Gogh 1970, nr 6

F 995 TRUNK OF A WILLOW
Etten period; see after F 905

F 996 ORPHAN MAN WITH A BROOM

Pencil, heightened with wash [gray paper] 50 × 21
[19¾ × 8¼]
The Hague October-November 1882
LETTERS 235 [about 1 October], 236 [8 October],
238 [about 10 October] and R 14 [September-
October] See F 953
LITERATURE Vanbeselaere 1937, pp 92, 185, 409
COLLECTION Geneva, Matthiesen Art Gallery

F 996a ORPHAN MAN WITH TOP HAT
DRINKING A CUP OF COFFEE

Black chalk, washed, heightened with white
49.5 × 30 [19½ × 11¾]
Compare F 976 [same model], lithograph F 1657
and SD 1682 [same motif]
The Hague November 1882
LETTER 246 [22 November] '*Wednesday morning...
Along with this letter you will receive the first proofs
of a lithograph, "A Digger" and a lithograph of a
"Man Drinking Coffee." ...The drawings were better.*'
LITERATURE Not in Faille 1928 or Vanbeselaere
1937. V. W. van Gogh, Museumjournaal 1968, part
I, pp 42-5
COLLECTION Basle, F. Hagemann [acquired 1946]

F 997 OLD MAN WITH HIS HEAD IN HIS
HANDS

Pencil [water-color paper] 50 × 31 [19¾ × 12¼]
Signed in lower left: Vincent
Compare painting F 702, drawing F 998 and
lithograph F 1662
The Hague November 1882
LETTER 247 [24 November] See F 863

LITERATURE Vanbeselaere 1937, pp 94, 96, 185, 192, 409. Chetham 1960, p 26
EDITORS' COMMENT Of the two figures of old men with head in hands mentioned in letter 247, F 863 depicts Schuitemaker. The model for F 997 is an 'orphan man.' In St Rémy Vincent took up this motif in painting F 702.
COLLECTION Amsterdam, Rijksmuseum Vincent van Gogh [Vincent van Gogh Foundation, inv nr F 997]

F 998 A MAN IN SORROW

Black lithographic chalk, pencil, washed, heightened with white [water-color paper, pasted] 45.5 × 47.5 [18 × 18¾] Severely damaged
Annotated in lower left: Atelier Vincent; on the reverse: Gekocht van de kunstkoper Oldenzeel te Rotterdam, Smart van Vincent van Gogh, Hidde Nijland, Dordrecht Dec. 1892
Compare painting F 702, drawing F 997 and lithograph F 1662
The Hague March-April 1883
LITERATURE H. J. Haverman, De Kroniek 3 March 1895, p 75. Album Hidde Nijland Collection 1905, plate 86. Idem 1907, nr 18. J. B. J. Stokvis, Kunst und Künstler April 1927, p 253 [with reproduction]. Vanbeselaere 1937, pp 96, 409: November 1882; letter 247. Chetham 1960, p 27
COLLECTION Otterlo, Rijksmuseum Kröller-Müller, inv nr 1017-28, cat van Gogh 1970, nr 81

F 998

F 997

F 999

F 1001

F 999 THE SOWER: FACING RIGHT

Pencil 49 × 28.5 [19¼ × 11¼]
Compare F 853
The Hague December 1882
LETTER possibly 251 [between 4 and 9 December]
'*In the first place a sower. A big old fellow, a dark silhouette against a dark ground...*'
LITERATURE Vanbeselaere 1937, pp 66, 98, 186-7, 409
COLLECTION Zurich, Mrs H. Glatt-Kisling

F 1000 THE SOWER: FRONT VIEW

Pencil 48 × 23.5 [19 × 9¼]
Signed in lower right: Vincent
The Hague December 1882
LETTER 251 [between 4 and 9 December] '*Then a second Sower...against a clear sky.*'
LITERATURE Vanbeselaere 1937, pp 66, 98, 186-7, 190, 192, 206, 233, 409
COLLECTION Sale London [Sotheby] 5 December 1968, nr 283
Present owner unknown

F 1001 MAN READING HIS BIBLE

Pencil [water-color paper with watermark: Hallines 1877] 47 × 30.5 [18½ × 12]
Compare F 1002 and SD 1683 [same model]
The Hague December 1882
LETTER 256 [31 December] '*...I made a drawing of an old man sitting reading, with the light falling on his bald head, on his hand and the book.*'
LITERATURE H. P. Bremmer, Album Kröller-Müller Collection 1919, plate 21. Vanbeselaere 1937, pp 98, 100, 188, 192, 196, 409. Chetham 1960, p 29. Cat van Gogh 1966, Rijksmuseum Kröller-Müller, nr 90: letter 256 does not refer to this drawing, for technical reasons
EDITORS' COMMENT This drawing is probably connected with the motif mentioned in letter 253 [see F 1002]. The drawing spoken of there is unknown.
COLLECTION Otterlo, Rijksmuseum Kröller-Müller, inv nr 194-11, cat van Gogh 1970, nr 90

F 1002 SAYING GRACE

Pencil, black chalk, ink, heightened with white 60 × 50 [23½ × 19¾]
Compare F 1001 [same model] and SD 1683 [same model and same bench]
The Hague December 1882
LETTER 253 [between 12 and 20 December] '*I have two new drawings now, one of a man reading his Bible, and the other of a man saying grace before dinner, which is on the table.*'
LITERATURE R. Jacobsen, Onze Kunst 1903, part I, pp 114-6. H. P. Bremmer, Moderne Kunstwerken 1903, nr 59. Faille 1928, nr 1002: letter 256. Vanbeselaere 1937, pp 98-9, 105, 188, 206, 409: March 1883
COLLECTION Switzerland, Doyer Family

F 1003 ORPHAN MAN WITH TOP HAT AND BANDAGE OVER HIS EYE

Pencil, lithographic chalk, washed, heightened with black and white 46.5 × 27.5 [18¼ × 10¾]
Signed in upper left: Vincent
Compare F 1004 [same model]
The Hague December 1882
LETTERS 256 [31 December] '*And the second one, the bandaged head of an injured man. The model who sat for this really had a head injury and a bandage over his left eye.*'
R 37 [May-June 1883] '*A fellow with a wheelbarrow, the same whose head you may remember I drew, but then in his Sunday clothes and with a Sunday-clean*'

bandage around his blind eye.'
LITERATURE Vanbeselaere 1937, pp 99, 189, 196-9, 409
COLLECTION Cambridge, Massachusetts, The Fogg Museum of Art [on loan since 1928; bequest Meta and Paul J. Sachs 1965], inv nr 1965.289, cat acquisitions 1965, p 31

F 1004 MAN WITH A BANDAGE OVER HIS EYE, SMOKING A GOUDA PIPE

Pencil, black lithographic chalk, washed, heightened with white [water-color paper with watermark: Hallines 1877] 45 × 27.5 [17¾ × 10¾]
Compare F 1003 [same model]
The Hague December 1882
LETTER 256 [31 December] See F 1003
LITERATURE H. P. Bremmer, Album Kröller-Müller Collection 1919, plate 6. Vanbeselaere 1937, pp 102, 199, 200, 203, 409
COLLECTION Otterlo, Rijksmuseum Kröller-Müller, inv nr 1004-11, cat van Gogh 1970, nr 93

F 1005 HEAD OF A WOMAN WITH A CAP: LEFT PROFILE

Pencil, black lithographic chalk, washed with white and black [water-color paper] 45 × 26.5 [17¾ × 10½]
The Hague January 1883
LITERATURE Vanbeselaere 1937, pp 100, 198-9, 409
COLLECTION Amsterdam, Rijksmuseum Vincent van Gogh [Vincent van Gogh Foundation, inv nr F 1005]

F 1006 BUST OF A WOMAN WITH A CAP: RIGHT PROFILE

Pencil, black lithographic chalk, washed with white [water-color paper] 50 × 28.5 [19¾ × 11¼]
Signed in lower left: Vincent
The Hague January 1883
LETTER 259 [about 11 January] *'I also did a woman's head this way, standing out against the light, so the whole is in tone, with high lights on the profile, etc.'*
LITERATURE Vincent van Gogh, Lettres à Bernard, 1911, plate XXIII. Vanbeselaere 1937, pp 99, 189, 409
COLLECTION Amsterdam, Rijksmuseum Vincent van Gogh [Vincent van Gogh Foundation, inv nr F 1006]

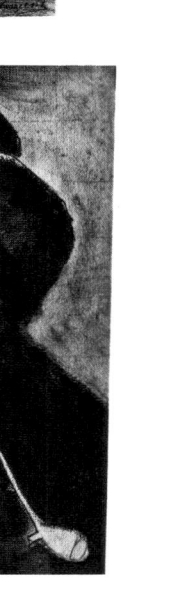

F 1007

F 1008

F 1007 SIEN'S DAUGHTER WITH SHAWL:
LEFT PROFILE

Black chalk, washed, pencil, heightened with white
[water-color paper with watermark: Brécourt
Frères] 43.5 × 25 [17¼ × 9¾]
Compare sketch in letter 276, F 1008, F 1024 and
SD 1685 [same model]
The Hague January 1883
LETTER 260 [between 12 and 20 January] 'And the
poor little girl, you see from the drawing that the old
deep misery has not been erased...'
LITERATURE H. P. Bremmer, Album Kröller-
Müller Collection 1919, plate 9. Vanbeselaere 1937,
pp 100, 197, 409
J. Hulsker, Maatstaf September 1958. Idem, Delta
Spring 1960: the model is probably Sien's little
sister
COLLECTION Otterlo, Rijksmuseum Kröller-
Müller, inv nr 200-11, cat van Gogh 1970, nr 71

F 1008 SIEN'S DAUGHTER SEATED: LEFT
PROFILE

Pencil, black lithographic chalk [water-color paper]
50.5 × 31 [20 × 12¼]
Signed in lower left in white: Vincent
Compare sketch in letter 278, F 1007, F 1024 and
SD 1685 [same model]
The Hague January 1883
LETTER 260 [between 12 and 20 January] See F 1007
LITERATURE Vanbeselaere 1937, pp 100, 409.
COLLECTION Amsterdam, Rijksmuseum Vincent
van Gogh [Vincent van Gogh Foundation, inv
nr F 1008]

F 1009 PORTRAIT HEAD OF A WOMAN: FULL
FACE

Pencil, black lithographic chalk, washed with black
[water-color paper] 39 × 24.5 [15¼ × 9¾]
Signed in lower left: Vincent
Compare F 1009a [same model]
The Hague January 1883
LITERATURE Vanbeselaere 1937, pp 100, 409
COLLECTION Amsterdam, Rijksmuseum Vincent
van Gogh [Vincent van Gogh Foundation, inv
nr F 1009]

F 1009a PORTRAIT HEAD OF A WOMAN WITH
A CAP: FULL FACE

Black and colored chalk, pencil 36 × 26 [14¼ × 10¼]
Compare F 1009 [same model]
The Hague January 1883
LITERATURE Not in Faille 1928 or Vanbeselaere
1937
COLLECTION The Hague, Gemeente Museum [on
loan since 1957 from Paul Citroen], inv nr
T 4-X-1957

F 1010 FISHERMAN WITH PIPE

Pen, pencil, black chalk, washed, heightened with
white [yellowish-brown wove paper] 46 × 26
[18 × 10¼]
Signed in lower left: Vincent
Compare F 1013
The Hague July 1883
LETTER 300 [13-14 July] 'Today the almshouse man
again posed for a thing that I suddenly felt I had to
make before I started anything else... Last evening I
received a present which pleased me enormously
(from those two land surveyors – for there has been a
second one since), namely a very picturesque
Scheveningen jacket with high turn-up collar,
picturesque, faded and patched.'
LITERATURE H. P. Bremmer, Album Kröller-
Müller Collection 1919, plate 23. Faille 1928,
nr 1010: letters 261 and 262. Vanbeselaere 1937,

pp 110, 218, 409: August 1883; letter 300
COLLECTION Otterlo, Rijksmuseum Kröller-Müller, inv nr 1351-18, cat van Gogh 1970, nr 79

F 1011 HEAD OF AN OLD FISHERMAN WITH
SOU'WESTER: FULL FACE

Black chalk, brush, heightened with black and
white, lightly washed [water-color paper with
watermark: Brécourt Frères] 43 × 25 [17 × 9¾]
Compare F 1014, F 1030 and F 1031 [same model]
The Hague January-February 1883 or shortly later
LETTERS 261 [about 21 January] '*Tomorrow I get a
sou'wester for the heads. Heads of fishermen, old and
young, that's what I have been thinking of for a long
time, and I have made one already, then afterwards
I couldn't get a sou'wester. Now I shall have one of
my own, an old one over which many storms and seas
have passed.*'
267 [between 12 and 17 February] '*Boy, I have been
drawing with such delight – fishermen's heads with
that sou'wester I told you about …*'
R 22 [February] '*What I have been working at
especially of late is heads – heads of the people –
fishermen's heads with sou'westers, among other
things.*'
LITERATURE H. P. Bremmer, Album Kröller-Müller Collection 1919, plate 5. Vanbeselaere 1937.
pp 101, 189, 409: January-February 1883
COLLECTION Otterlo, Rijksmuseum Kröller-Müller, inv nr 198-11, cat van Gogh 1970, nr 80

F 1009a

F 1011

F 1009

F 1010

F 1013

F 1012

F 1014

F 1015

F 1016

F 1012 HEAD OF A FISHERMAN: THREE QUARTERS TO THE RIGHT

Pencil, lithographic chalk 44 × 27.5 [17¼ × 10¾]
Compare F 1083 [same model]
The Hague January-February 1883
LETTERS 261 [about 21 January], 267 [between 12 and 17 February] and R 22 [February] See F 1011
LITERATURE Vanbeselaere 1937, pp 101, 200, 409
COLLECTION Fullerton, California, Norton Simon Foundation

F 1013 FISHERMAN SEATED

Pen and pencil 10.5 × 6.5 [4¼ × 2½]
Reproduced with letter 262 [erroneously; it belongs with letter 300]
Compare F 1010
The Hague July 1883
LETTER 300 [13-14 July] See F 1010
LITERATURE Vanbeselaere 1937, pp 19, 110, 217, 409: August 1883
COLLECTION Amsterdam, Rijksmuseum Vincent van Gogh [Vincent van Gogh Foundation, inv nr F 1013]

F 1014 HEAD OF A FISHERMAN: THREE QUARTERS TO THE LEFT

Pencil, black lithographic chalk, ink, heightened with black and white [water-color paper] 50.5 × 31.5 [20 × 12½]
Compare F 1011, F 1030 and F 1031 [same model]
The Hague January 1883 or shortly later
LETTERS 261 [about 21 January], 267 [between 12 and 17 February] and R 22 [February] See F 1011
LITERATURE Vanbeselaere 1937, pp 101, 199, 200, 409
COLLECTION Amsterdam, Rijksmuseum Vincent van Gogh [Vincent van Gogh Foundation, inv nr F 1014]

F 1015 HEAD OF AN OLD FISHERMAN WITH PIPE

Pencil, black lithographic chalk, washed [water-color paper] 41.5 × 26 [16¼ × 10¼]
The Hague January 1883
LETTERS 261 [about 21 January], 267 [between 12 and 17 February] and R 22 [February] See F 1011
LITERATURE Vanbeselaere 1937, pp 101, 199, 409
COLLECTION Amsterdam, Rijksmuseum Vincent van Gogh [Vincent van Gogh Foundation, inv nr F 1015]

F 1016 HEAD OF AN ORPHAN MAN WITH PIPE AND COAL PAN: FULL FACE

Pencil, black lithographic chalk, washed with black and white [water-color paper] 44 × 28 [17¼ × 11]
The Hague January 1883
LITERATURE Vanbeselaere 1937, pp 101, 199-200, 409
COLLECTION Amsterdam, Rijksmuseum Vincent van Gogh [Vincent van Gogh Foundation, inv nr F 1016]

F 1017 HEAD OF AN OLD FISHERMAN: FULL FACE

Pencil, black lithographic chalk, pen and ink, heightened with white [water-color paper] 47.5 × 29 [18¾ × 11½]
The Hague January 1883
LETTER 262 [end January] '*I am very glad to have my sou'wester...with a white fringe.*'
LITERATURE Vanbeselaere 1937, pp 101, 199-200, 409

F 1018

F 1018 ORPHAN MAN: BUST-LENGTH,
FACING LEFT

Pencil, heightened with black 34.5 × 27.5 [13½ × 10¾]
Compare F 966 [same model]
The Hague end 1882
LITERATURE Vanbeselaere 1937, pp 99, 187, 409:
December 1882
COLLECTION The Hague, Heirs of H. P. Bremmer

F 1019 STUDY OF OLD RETERING: FACING
FRONT

Pencil, black chalk, pen, washed 45 × 28 [17¾ × 11]
Signed in lower right: Vincent
The Hague October-November 1883
LITERATURE Vanbeselaere 1937, pp 106, 409:
Nuenen April 1883
EDITORS' COMMENT Research into the identity of
'old Retering,' as Faille names this model, has
failed to turn up any information. The same model
is depicted in F 962 and a number of other drawings
of orphan men.
COLLECTION Bern, H. R. Hahnloser

F 1017

F 1019

F 1020

F 1020a

F 1020 THE PUBLIC SOUP KITCHEN

Pen 10 × 10 [4 × 4]
Erroneously reproduced with letter 273
Compare sketches in letters 271 and 272, F 1020a
and water color F 1020b
The Hague March 1883
LITERATURE Vanbeselaere 1937, pp 102, 202, 409
EDITORS' COMMENT Faille connects letters 271
and 272 with this drawing. In these letters, however,
only the subject is mentioned, not this particular
drawing. For the passages concerned see F 1020a
and F 1020b. The same subject is however
mentioned in letter R 28.
COLLECTION Amsterdam, Rijksmuseum Vincent
van Gogh [Vincent van Gogh Foundation, inv
nr F 1020]

F 1020a THE PUBLIC SOUP KITCHEN

Black mountain chalk 57 × 44.5 [22½ × 17½]
Signed in lower left: Vincent
Compare sketches in letters 271 and 272, F 1020 and
F 1020b
The Hague March 1883
LETTERS 271 [about 3 March] 'I enclose a little
sketch which I made in the soup kitchen. They sell the
soup in a large passage where the light falls from
above, through a door to the right. Now I tried that
same effect in the studio ...'
R 30 [March] 'Do you know "black mountain
chalk"? ... Well, yesterday I made a drawing with it –
women and children at the serving window of the
public soup kitchen.'
LITERATURE Not in Faille 1928 or Vanbeselaere
1937
COLLECTION Arlesheim-Corseaux, Switzerland,
Arthur Stoll [acquired 1953], cat 1961, p 18

F 1020b THE PUBLIC SOUP KITCHEN

Pencil, black mountain chalk, water color 34 × 49
[13½ × 19¼]
Compare sketches in letters 271 and 272, F 1020 and
water color F 1020a
The Hague March 1883
LETTERS 271 [about 3 March] 'I enclose a little
sketch which I made in the soup kitchen ... I should
like to try this again in water color, for instance, and
work hard on it to develop it more.'
272 [about 4 March] 'This morning I began a water
color of a boy and a girl in such a soup kitchen, with
another figure of a woman in a corner. That water
color became too blurred, which was partly because
the paper was not suitable.'
LITERATURE Not in Faille 1928 or Vanbeselaere
1937. H. L. C. Jaffé, Miscellanea Jozef Duverger,
1968, pp 383-7
COLLECTION Enschede, Netherlands, A. Menko

F 1021 PEASANT WOMAN WITH
WHEELBARROW

Pencil and water color 67 × 45 [26½ × 17¾]
Compare F 1030 and F 1031
The Hague May-June 1883
LITERATURE Vanbeselaere 1937, pp 104, 208, 409:
The Hague 1883 [with erroneous dimensions and
technique]
COLLECTION Oberägeri, Switzerland, S. van
Deventer

F 1022 VIEW FROM THE WINDOW OF
VINCENT'S STUDIO IN WINTER

Water color 39 × 58.5 [15¼ × 23]
Compare sketches in letters 220 [reproduced in the
Dutch edition of the letters only] and 276, drawing
F 939, water color F 943, drawings F 944 and F 1023
[same site]

The Hague March 1883
LITERATURE Vanbeselaere 1937, pp 102-3, 204,
409. J. Hulsker, Bulletin Rijksmuseum Vincent van
Gogh 1970, pp 2-13
COLLECTION The Hague, F. Bremmer

F 1020b

F 1021

F 1022

F 1023

F 1024

F 1025

F 1026

F 1027

F 1023 VIEW FROM THE WINDOW OF VINCENT'S STUDIO IN THE SNOW

Pencil and pen 20.5 × 13.5 [8 × 5¼]
Compare sketches in letters 220 [reproduced in the Dutch edition of the letters only] and 276, F 939, water color F 943, drawing F 944 and water color F 1022 [same site]
The Hague March 1883
LETTERS 276 [end March] '...*this once I am giving you a peep through my window onto the snowy yard... I take this sketch from a water color I made, which, however, I do not think strong and animated enough.*'
R 31 [end March] '*You are no doubt having winter weather again in Utrecht. Herewith a little sketch from my window.*'
LITERATURE Vanbeselaere 1937, pp 103, 208, 409.
J. Hulsker, Bulletin Rijksmuseum Vincent van Gogh 1970, pp 2-13
EDITORS' COMMENT The water color mentioned in letter 276 could not be identified with any known piece.
COLLECTION Rotterdam, Mrs J. E. Greutert-de Kanter

F 1024 CHILD KNEELING IN FRONT OF THE CRADLE

Black chalk, pencil, heightened with white [ordinary wove paper, yellowish] 48 × 32 [19 × 12½]
Signed in lower left: Vincent
Compare sketch in letter 276, F 1007, F 1008 and SD 1685 [same model]
The Hague March 1883
LETTER 276 [end March] '*As I am making little sketches anyway, I'll add another very hastily done, of a drawing in mountain chalk – the little girl in front of the cradle...*'
LITERATURE Vanbeselaere 1937, pp 104, 204, 409
EDITORS' COMMENT The letter refers to the sketch enclosed with it, which is very similar to F 1024. The children are Sien's, Maria Wilhelmina and Willem.
COLLECTION Amsterdam, Rijksmuseum Vincent van Gogh [Vincent van Gogh Foundation, inv nr F 1024]

F 1025 THE SEAMSTRESS [second version]

Pencil and black mountain chalk 53 × 37.5 [20¾ × 14¾]
Signed in lower left: Vincent
Compare F 1026 [same model]
The Hague March 1883
LETTER 277 [1 April] '*I already wrote you that I made a drawing with that chalk – yesterday I began a second one with it, of a seamstress, especially for the chiaroscuro.*'
LITERATURE Vanbeselaere 1937, pp 104, 409
COLLECTION Rotterdam, Museum Boymans-van Beuningen [acquired 1949], inv nr MB 1949-T6

F 1026 THE SEAMSTRESS [first version]

Pencil, lightly washed [Ingres paper with watermark: E.D. & Cie – P.L. Bas] 54 × 38.5 [21¼ × 15¼]
Annotated in lower left: At. Vincent
Compare F 1025 [same model]
The Hague March 1883
LETTER 277 [1 April] See F 1026
LITERATURE Album Hidde Nijland Collection 1905, plate 52. Vanbeselaere 1937, pp 104, 109
COLLECTION Otterlo, Rijksmuseum Kröller-Müller, inv nr 984-28, cat van Gogh 1970, nr 61

F 1026a WOMAN ON HER DEATHBED [after an anonymous Dutch 17th-century painting in the museum at Brussels]

Pencil and black chalk 25 × 33 [9¾ × 13]
Probably The Hague 1883

LITERATURE Not in Faille 1928 or Vanbeselaere 1937. Cat van Gogh 1966, Rijksmuseum Kröller-Müller, nr 91: probably September 1880-April 1881
COLLECTION The Hague, Heirs of H. P. Bremmer

F 1027 ORPHAN MAN KNEELING IN PRAYER: FACING RIGHT

Pencil, black chalk with some touches of China ink
56×46 [22×18]
The Hague April 1883
LETTER 281 [30 April or 1 May] '*And a figure of a man kneeling.*'
LITERATURE Vanbeselaere 1937, pp 105, 409
COLLECTION Formerly Berlin-Grünewald, Franz von Mendelssohn-Bartholdy
Present owner unknown

F 1028 THE SAND PIT AT DEKKER'S DUNE

Pencil 10.5×21 [4¼×8¼]
Annotated in lower left: 1 mètre×½ mètre [this seems to refer to F 1029 and F 1030]
Reproduced with letter 287
Compare F 1029
The Hague May 1883
LETTERS 286 [about 21 May] '*However, I prefer to see diggers digging, and have found glory outside Paradise, where one thinks more of the severer: "Thou shalt eat thy bread in the sweat of thy brow."*'
287 [about 31 May] '*A few days ago I was with van der Weele in the dunes. There we found a spot where they were digging sand from the dunes, a splendid thing with diggers and wheelbarrows.*'
288 [3 June] '*I was with van der Weele in Dekker's Dune, where we saw that sand pit; and since then I have gone there regularly and had a model every day, and now the second drawing is also done. It represents men with wheelbarrows and men who are digging. I shall try to make a sketch of it too, but it is a complicated composition and can hardly be judged from a sketch, any more than the other one can.*'
289 [about 4 or 5 June] '*...my plan of making a series of drawings of the work in the dunes.*'
301 [22 July] '*As you see, the photos are: Sower, Potato Diggers, Peat Cutters. I've had some others made: Sand Pit...*'
LITERATURE Vanbeselaere 1937, pp 96, 107, 212, 409: May 1883; letter 288
COLLECTION Amsterdam, Rijksmuseum Vincent van Gogh [Vincent van Gogh Foundation, inv nr F 1028]

F 1029 WORKMEN IN THE SAND PIT AT DEKKER'S DUNE

Pencil 10×20.5 [4×8]
Compare F 1028
The Hague May 1883
LETTER 288 [3 June] See F 1028
LITERATURE Vanbeselaere 1937, pp 96, 107, 212, 409: May 1883; letters 287 and 288
COLLECTION Zurich, Private Collection

F 1026a

F 1028

F 1029

F 1030

F 1031

F 1032

F 1030 THE PEATERY

Pen and pencil 11.5 × 21 [4½ × 8¼]
Included with letter 287 and reproduced there in the letters
Compare F 1031 [same composition], F 1011, F 1014 and F 1021 [partly the same motif]
The Hague May 1883
LETTER 287 [about 31 May] 'These are "Peat Cutters" in the dunes – the original drawing is about one meter by half a meter.'
LITERATURE Vanbeselaere 1937, pp 96, 104, 107, 208, 409
COLLECTION Amsterdam, Rijksmuseum Vincent van Gogh [Vincent van Gogh Foundation, inv nr F 1030]

F 1031 THE PEATERY

Material and dimensions unknown
Compare F 1030 [same composition], F 1011, F 1014 and F 1021 [partly the same motif]
The Hague May 1883
LETTER 287 [about 31 May] See F 1030
LITERATURE Faille 1928, nr 1031 : April-May 1883; letter 288. Vanbeselaere 1937, pp 96, 104, 107, 208, 409 : May 1883; letter 287
COLLECTION Present owner unknown

F 1032 THE WHITE HORSE

Pencil, black chalk, washed 42 × 59 [16½ × 23¼]
The Hague June 1883
LETTER 289 [about 4 or 5 June] 'This drawing requires studies of horses, and I made two of them today, in the stables of the Rhine railway station; and probably I shall get an old horse at the refuse dump.'
LITERATURE Vanbeselaere 1937, pp 108, 214, 409
COLLECTION The Hague, Gemeente Museum [on loan from R. T. Steinmetz], inv nr T 17-X-1963

F 1033 WOMAN SEWING: FACING RIGHT

Pencil, water color, black chalk [Whatman paper with dull surface, watermark: J. Whatman 1881] 56.5 × 48 [22¼ × 19]
The Hague 1883
LITERATURE Vanbeselaere 1937, pp 108, 409: letter 292. D. Cooper, Zeichnungen und Aquarelle von Vincent van Gogh, 1954, p 32. Cat van Gogh 1966, Rijksmuseum Kröller-Müller, nr 68 : January-February 1882
COLLECTION Otterlo, Rijksmuseum Kröller-Müller, inv nr 197-16, cat van Gogh 1970, nr 68

F 1034 POTATO DIGGERS

Material and dimensions unknown
Compare sketch in letter 296 and painting F 9
The Hague June-July 1883
LETTERS 296 [between 22 and 27 June] 'Here follows a little sketch of potato diggers, but on the drawing they are sitting a little wider apart.'
R 38 [early July] 'I am working on the "Potato Diggers"...'
301 [22 July] See F 1028
LITERATURE Vanbeselaere 1937, pp 108, 216, 409
COLLECTION Present owner unknown

F 1035 THE SOWER

Material and dimensions unknown
The Hague June-July 1883
LETTERS 297 [about 2 July] 'Further I am doing a sower in a large field, with lumps of earth, which I think is better than the other sowers I tried before. I have at least six more of them, solely as studies of the figure, but now I have put him into surroundings more especially like a real composition, and I have carefully studied the earth and sky besides.'

301 [22 July] See F 1028
LITERATURE Vanbeselaere 1937, pp 109, 217, 409
COLLECTION Present owner unknown

F 1035a PEASANT BURNING WEEDS

Water color 20 × 36 [7¾ × 14¼]
Compare sketch in letter 299 and lithographs
F 1036 and F 1660
The Hague June 1883
LETTERS 297 [about 2 July] *'Then I have studies of
the burning of weeds, and of a man with a sack of
potatoes on his back, and one with a wheelbarrow.'*
299 [about 10 July] *'The topmost is the burning of
weeds; the other one, the return from the potato field.'*
LITERATURE Not in Faille 1928 or Vanbeselaere
1937
COLLECTION Rotterdam, Private Collection
[acquired 1950]

F 1034

F 1035

F 1033

F 1035a

F 1038

F 1039

F 1040

F 1036 PEASANT BURNING WEEDS
See lithograph F 1660

F 1037 POTATO FIELDS BEHIND THE DUNES

Brush and ink, heightened with white [toned laid paper with watermark: J V] 27.5 × 42 [10¾ × 16½]
Signed in lower right: Vincent
The Hague July 1883
LETTERS 298 [between 4 and 7 July] '...I have also done a few landscape studies this week, one yesterday at de Bock's, a potato field in the dunes...Together with de Bock, I found splendid potato fields in the dunes behind the lighthouse.'
299 [about 10 July] 'For a change, this week I have done a few water colors out-of-doors, a little wheatfield and a small potato field, and I have also drawn a few landscapes as studies for the surroundings of a few figure drawings I am planning.'
LITERATURE Album Hidde Nijland Collection 1905, plate 89. Vanbeselaere 1937, pp 85, 109, 217, 409: July 1883; letter 298
COLLECTION Otterlo, Rijksmuseum Kröller-Müller, inv nr 1021-28, cat van Gogh 1970, nr 47

F 1038 THE BEACH AT SCHEVENINGEN

Water color 34 × 49.5 [13½ × 19½]
Compare drawing F 980
The Hague October 1882
LETTER 236 [8 October] 'Sunday...I also started another one with many more figures, the last summer guests on the beach—an evening effect.'
LITERATURE Vanbeselaere 1937, pp 87, 165, 409
COLLECTION Baltimore, The Baltimore Museum of Art [The Cone bequest 1949], cat Cone Collection 1967, nr 25

F 1039 IN THE WOOD

Water color 12.5 × 21 [5 × 8¼]
The Hague September 1882
LITERATURE Vanbeselaere 1937, pp 85, 162, 409
EDITORS' COMMENT See F 952
COLLECTION The Hague, Mrs M. A. R. van der Leeuw-Wentges [acquired 1944]

F 1040 A FACTORY

Water color [ordinary wove paper, yellowish] 26 × 37.5 [10¼ × 14¾]
The Hague 1882
LITERATURE Vanbeselaere 1937, pp 80, 128, 409
COLLECTION Amsterdam, Rijksmuseum Vincent van Gogh [Vincent van Gogh Foundation, inv nr F 1040]

F 1041 BARNS AND HOUSES AT SCHEVENINGEN

Pencil, black chalk, water color and white chalk [ordinary wove paper, yellowish] 43.5 × 60 [17 × 23½]
The Hague 1882
LITERATURE Vanbeselaere 1937, pp 78, 410.
A. Bowness, exhib cat van Gogh London [Hayward Gallery] 1968-9, nr 9: The Hague July-August 1882 [?]
COLLECTION Amsterdam, Rijksmuseum Vincent van Gogh [Vincent van Gogh Foundation, inv nr F 1041]

F 1042 THE CARPENTER: SEEN FROM THE BACK

Pencil 47.5 × 23.5 [18¾ × 9¼]
The Hague November 1882
LITERATURE Faille 1928, nr 1042 [not reproduced].
Vanbeselaere 1937, p 410
COLLECTION England, H. J. Hyams

F 1042

F 1041

F 1037

F 1048

F 1043

F 1044

F 1043 THE CARPENTER: FULL FACE

Pencil 48.5 × 27 [19 × 10½]
The Hague November 1882
LITERATURE Vanbeselaere 1937, pp 92, 185, 410
COLLECTION The Hague, R. Bremmer

F 1044 THE BLACKSMITH: FACING RIGHT

Pencil [hand-made paper] 45 × 24 [17¾ × 9½]
The Hague November 1882
LITERATURE Vanbeselaere 1937, pp 92, 185, 410
COLLECTION Zug, Switzerland, Mayfair Kunst
Art Gallery

F 1045 GIRL CARRYING BREAD: FACING
RIGHT

Pencil 49 × 28 [19¼ × 11]
The Hague November 1882
LITERATURE Vanbeselaere 1937, pp 96, 410
COLLECTION New York, S. E. Neikrug [acquired
1959]

F 1046 OLD SEAMAN SEATED: FULL FACE

Pencil [gray paper] 47 × 26 [18½ × 10¼]
The Hague October 1882
LITERATURE Vanbeselaere 1937, pp 110, 410:
August 1883
COLLECTION Winnipeg, S. Kobrinsky

F 1047 PEASANT WOMAN SEATED: FACING
LEFT

Pencil and pink wash, the back of the seat brown
48 × 30 [18¾ × 11¾]
Signed in lower left: Vincent
The Hague 1882-3
LITERATURE Vanbeselaere 1937, pp 106, 410:
April 1883
COLLECTION Winnipeg, S. Sair

F 1048 WOMAN AND CHILD UNDER AN
UMBRELLA [probably Sien and her daughter]

Pencil, heightened with white 45 × 25.5 [17¾ × 10]
False signature in lower right: Vincent
The Hague 1883
LITERATURE Vanbeselaere 1937, pp 105, 190, 206,
410: April 1883
COLLECTION The Hague, Heirs of H. P. Bremmer

F 1049 THE FISHERMAN: FACING RIGHT

Pencil 48.5 × 22 [19 × 8¾]
False signature in lower right: Vincent
The Hague November 1882
LITERATURE Vanbeselaere 1937, pp 92, 410:
November 1882
COLLECTION London, Heirs of F. A. C. Guépin

F 1050 WOMAN IN A LONG CLOAK: FACING
LEFT

Pencil [wove paper] 32 × 15.5 [12½ × 6]
The Hague October 1882
LITERATURE H. P. Bremmer, Album Kröller-
Müller Collection 1919, plate 7. Vanbeselaere 1937,
pp 90, 176, 410: October 1882
COLLECTION Otterlo, Rijksmuseum Kröller-
Müller, inv nr 201-13, cat van Gogh 1970, nr 56

F 1051 WOMAN WITH A KETTLE

Pencil [ordinary wove paper] 46 × 23 [18 × 9]
The Hague October 1882
LITERATURE H. P. Bremmer, Album Kröller-
Müller Collection 1919, plate 8. Vanbeselaere 1937,
pp 90, 176, 410: October 1882

COLLECTION Otterlo, Rijksmuseum Kröller-
Müller, inv nr 196-08, cat van Gogh 1970, nr 66

F 1052 SIEN WITH AN UMBRELLA AND A
PRAYER BOOK UNDER HER ARM

Pencil and black chalk 45.5 × 22 [18 × 8¾]
False signature in lower left: Vincent
The Hague 1883
LITERATURE Vanbeselaere 1937, pp 105, 206, 410:
March 1883
COLLECTION The Hague, Heirs of H. P. Bremmer

F 1045

F 1046

F 1047

F 1050

F 1049

F 1051

F 1052

F 1053

F 1053a

F 1054

F 1056

F 1055

F 1053 WOMAN SAYING GRACE

Black chalk, pencil, brush, black ink, washed, heightened with white [water-color paper] 63 × 39.5 [24¾ × 15½]
The Hague March-April 1883
LITERATURE Vincent van Gogh, Lettres à Bernard, 1911, plate XXVIII. H. P. Bremmer, Album Kröller-Müller Collection 1919, plate 17. Vanbeselaere 1937, pp 105, 206, 410: March 1883. Cat van Gogh 1966, Rijksmuseum Kröller-Müller, nr 57: details concerning the use of thinned printer's ink
COLLECTION Otterlo, Rijksmuseum Kröller-Müller, inv nr 203-12, cat van Gogh 1970, nr 57

F 1053a WOMAN PEELING POTATOES

Black chalk [water-color paper] 60 × 37 [23½ × 14½]
The Hague March-April 1883
LITERATURE Not in Faille 1928 or Vanbeselaere 1937
COLLECTION The Hague, Gemeente Museum [on loan from Paul Citroen], inv nr T 3-X-1957

F 1054 BUST OF WOMAN WITH HAT: FACING RIGHT

Black chalk, brush, ink, washed 46.5 × 26 [18¼ × 10¼]
The Hague January 1883
LETTER 262 [end January] *I am still busy making heads this week, especially women's heads...*
LITERATURE Vanbeselaere 1937, pp 100, 199, 410
COLLECTION Bern, Berner Kunstmuseum [acquired 1946]

F 1055 SIEN WITH A WHITE BONNET: FACING RIGHT

Black chalk, pencil and ink [water-color paper] 43 × 27 [17 × 10½]
Signed in lower left: Vincent
The Hague January 1883
LETTER 262 [end January] See F 1054
LITERATURE Vanbeselaere 1937, pp 101, 199, 410
COLLECTION Amsterdam, Rijksmuseum Vincent van Gogh [Vincent van Gogh Foundation, inv nr F 1055]

F 1056 WOMAN SITTING ON BENCH: FACING LEFT

Charcoal, washed, pencil, brush, black ink, heightened with white oils [Whatman paper with watermark: Whatman...Mills] 56.5 × 44 [22¼ × 17¼]
Annotated in lower right: Port. Vincent
The Hague March-April 1883
LITERATURE Album Hidde Nijland Collection 1905, plate 1; Idem 1907, plate 17. H. P. Bremmer, Vincent van Gogh – Inleidende Beschouwingen, 1911, pp 50-62, plate 6. H. van den Eerenbeemt, Opgang March 1924, p 268 [with reproduction]. W. F. Douwes, Vincent van Gogh, [1930], plate 18. Vanbeselaere 1937, pp 49, 105, 206, 410: March 1883
COLLECTION Otterlo, Rijksmuseum Kröller-Müller, inv nr 935-28, cat van Gogh 1970, nr 58

F 1057 BUST OF A WOMAN: FULL FACE, AGAINST A DARK BACKGROUND

Lithographic chalk, pencil, water color, heightened with white 47.5 × 26 [18¾ × 10¼]
Signed in lower left: Vincent
Compare F 1057a [same model]
The Hague January 1883
LETTER 262 [end January] See F 1054
LITERATURE Vanbeselaere 1937, pp 100, 199, 410:

F 1058

January 1883; letter 262
COLLECTION Groningen, Groninger Museum voor
Stad en Lande [W. Moll bequest], inv nr 1962-201

F 1057a BUST OF A WOMAN: FULL FACE,
AGAINST A LIGHT BACKGROUND

Charcoal, heightened with white 44 × 23.5
[17¼ × 9¼]
Compare F 1057 [same model]
The Hague January 1883
LETTER 262 [end January] See F 1054
LITERATURE Not in Faille 1928 or Vanbeselaere
1937
COLLECTION Liège, Mrs L. Stiennon-de Neuville

F 1058 TWO WOMEN KNEELING IN PRAYER;
ONE WOMAN STANDING IN THE
BACKGROUND

Pencil, black chalk [laid paper with fragment of
watermark in script letters] 43 × 28.5 [17 × 11¼]
The Hague 1883
LITERATURE H. P. Bremmer, Album Kröller-
Müller Collection 1919, plate 16. Vanbeselaere
1937, pp 106, 190, 410: April 1883
COLLECTION Otterlo, Rijksmuseum Kröller-
Müller, inv nr 205-13, cat van Gogh 1970, nr 70

F 1057

F 1057a

F 1059

F 1061
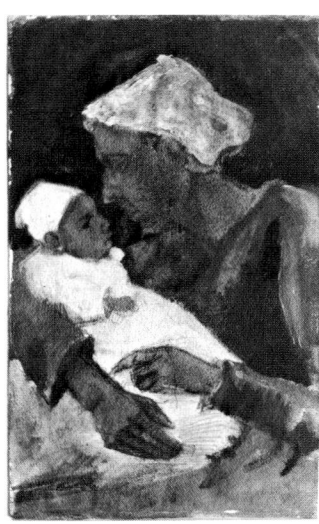

F 1062

F 1063

F 1060

F 1059 HEAD OF A WOMAN

Pencil 27.5 × 17 [10¾ × 6¾]
False signature in lower right: Vincent
The Hague 1883
LITERATURE Faille 1928, nr 1059: The Hague.
Vanbeselaere 1937, p 410: Antwerp. Tralbaut
Antwerp 1948, nr 12, pp 267-9, 281, 283: Antwerp
EDITORS' COMMENT Stylistically close to F 1067
COLLECTION The Hague, Heirs of H. P. Bremmer

**F 1060 WOMAN WITH HER HEAD IN HER
HANDS, SITTING ON AN OVERTURNED
BASKET**

Black chalk, washed and heightened with white
[water-color paper with watermark: Hallines: 1877]
47.5 × 29.5 [18¾ × 11½]
Compare F 1069 [same motif]
The Hague March-April 1883
LITERATURE H. P. Bremmer, Album Kröller-Mül-
ler Collection 1919, plate 20. Vanbeselaere 1937,
pp 105, 207, 410: April 1883. Chetham 1960, p 27
COLLECTION Otterlo, Rijksmuseum Kröller-
Müller, inv nr 210-11, cat van Gogh 1970, nr 63

**F 1061 SIEN WITH CHILD IN HER RIGHT
ARM, FACING LEFT**

Pencil, water color, heightened with white oils
[water-color paper with watermark: Brécourt
Frères] 40.5 × 24 [16 × 9½]
The Hague 1882-3
LITERATURE Vanbeselaere 1937, pp 49, 105, 190,
207, 410: April 1883
COLLECTION Otterlo, Rijksmuseum Kröller-
Müller, inv nr 217-20, cat van Gogh 1970, nr 73

F 1062 SIEN SUCKLING HER CHILD

Pencil [ordinary Dutch laid paper, pasted]
43.5 × 27 [17¼ × 10¾]
The Hague 1883
LITERATURE H. P. Bremmer, Album Kröller-
Müller Collection 1919, plate 19. Vanbeselaere
1937, pp 49, 106, 190, 193-4, 207, 410
COLLECTION Otterlo, Rijksmuseum Kröller-
Müller, inv nr 216-19, cat van Gogh 1970, nr 69

**F 1063 MOTHER IN ARMCHAIR WITH CHILD
ON HER LAP**

Pencil [wove paper] 49.5 × 27 [19½ × 10¾]
The Hague 1882-3
LITERATURE H. P. Bremmer, Album Kröller-
Müller Collection 1919, plate 20a. Vanbeselaere
1937, pp 106, 190, 193-4, 207, 390, 410
COLLECTION Otterlo, Rijksmuseum Kröller-
Müller, inv nr 214-18, cat van Gogh 1970, nr 72

F 1064 SIEN WITH HER CHILD: FACING LEFT

Pencil and black chalk 28 × 26 [11 × 10¼]
The Hague 1882-3
LITERATURE Vanbeselaere 1937, pp 49, 106, 190,
207, 410: April 1883
COLLECTION Sale New York [Parke-Bernet]
17 May 1945, nr 29
Present owner unknown

F 1065 SIEN WITH HER CHILD: FACING LEFT

Pencil, sepia, washed, China ink 36.5 × 24
[14½ × 9½]
The Hague 1882-3
LITERATURE Vanbeselaere 1937, pp 49, 106, 190,
207, 410: April 1883
COLLECTION Sale London [Sotheby] 10 July 1957,
nr 55
Present owner unknown

F 1066 WOMAN WITH CHILD ON HER LAP

Black chalk, washed and heightened with white
[Ingres paper with watermark: E.D. & Cie–P.L.
Bas] 41 × 27 [16¼ × 10¾]
The Hague 1883
LITERATURE H. P. Bremmer, Album Kröller-
Müller Collection 1919, plate 18. Vanbeselaere
1937, pp 106, 190, 207, 410: April 1883
COLLECTION Otterlo, Rijksmuseum Kröller-
Müller, inv nr 209-13, cat van Gogh 1970, nr 67

F 1067 SIEN WITH CHILD ON HER LAP

Charcoal, pencil, heightened with white and brown
[ordinary wove paper, yellowish]
53.5 × 35 [21 × 13¾]
Signed in lower left: Vincent
The Hague 1883
LITERATURE Vanbeselaere 1937, pp 106, 207, 410:
April 1883
COLLECTION Amsterdam, Rijksmuseum Vincent
van Gogh [Vincent van Gogh Foundation, inv
nr F 1067]

F 1066

F 1064

F 1065

F 1067

F 1068

F 1071

F 1069

F 1068 NURSING MOTHER

Water color and black chalk 47.5 × 30 [18¾ × 11¾]
Signed or annotated in lower right: Vincent
The Hague 1883
LITERATURE Vanbeselaere 1937, pp 106, 190, 207,
410: April 1883
COLLECTION USA, Private Collection

F 1069 WOMAN WITH HER HEAD IN HER
HANDS, SEATED ON A BASKET

Black chalk, heightened with white chalk 49 × 30.5
[19¼ × 12]
Compare F 1060 [same motif]
The Hague 1883
LITERATURE Vanbeselaere 1937, pp 105, 207, 410:
April 1883
COLLECTION Chicago, The Art Institute [gift of
Mr Tiffani and Margarete Blake], inv nr 47.23

F 1070 NURSING MOTHER
Etten period; see after F 905

F 1071 SIEN WITH CHILD ON HER LAP: LEFT
PROFILE

Pencil [Ingres paper, pasted, with watermark: E.D.
& Cie–P.L. Bas] 54 × 41.5 [21¼ × 16¼]
The Hague 1883
LITERATURE Album Hidde Nijland Collection
1905, plate 62. Vanbeselaere 1937, pp 49, 106, 190,
207, 410: April 1883
COLLECTION Otterlo, Rijksmuseum Kröller-
Müller, inv nr 993-28, cat van Gogh 1970, nr 60

F 1072 SIEN SEWING AND LITTLE GIRL

Pencil, ink and black mountain chalk [ordinary
wove paper, yellowish] 56.5 × 30 [22¼ × 11¾]
Signed or annotated with ink in lower left: Vincent
The Hague March 1883
LETTER 274 [about 11 March] 'As to what you write
about the sketch of those two figures, one above the
other, it is mostly an effect of perspective – and also
of great difference in size between the little child and
the woman on the basket.'
LITERATURE Vanbeselaere 1937, pp 103, 190, 207,
410: March 1883; letter 274
COLLECTION Amsterdam, Rijksmuseum Vincent
van Gogh [Vincent van Gogh Foundation, inv
nr F 1072]

F 1073 HEAD OF A WOMAN WITH A DARK
CAP
Drenthe period; see after F 1106

F 1074 WOMAN WITH BROOM: FACING
RIGHT

Pencil, pen and ink, heightened with water color
[water-color paper] 49.5 × 27.5 [19½ × 10¾]
The Hague October 1882
LITERATURE Vanbeselaere 1937, pp 90, 176, 410:
October 1882. A. Bowness, exhib cat van Gogh
London [Hayward Gallery] 1968-9, nr 8: The
Hague April-May 1882 [?]; the model may be
Sien's mother
COLLECTION Amsterdam, Rijksmuseum Vincent
van Gogh [Vincent van Gogh Foundation, inv
nr F 1074]

F 1075 WOMAN WITH BROOM: FULL FACE

Pencil and water color [water-color paper]
45.5 × 23 [18 × 9]
The Hague October 1882
LITERATURE Vanbeselaere 1937, pp 90, 176, 410:
October 1882
COLLECTION Amsterdam, Rijksmuseum Vincent

van Gogh [Vincent van Gogh Foundation, inv
nr F 1075]

F 1076 recto and verso STUDY OF A TREE;
BLIND PEASANT
Identical with F 933 recto and verso

F 1077 STUDY OF A MAN AND A BOY SEATED
IN A BARN

Black chalk and black China ink 24 × 34 [9½ × 13½]
The Hague 1883
LITERATURE Vanbeselaere 1937, pp 102, 202, 410:
January-February 1883
COLLECTION Formerly Blaricum, Netherlands,
S. B. Slijper Collection [until ca 1938]
Present owner unknown

F 1078 TWO MEN UNLOADING BRICKS
FROM A CART

Pencil [wove paper with watermark: S. & C.]
21 × 34 [8¼ × 13½]
The Hague 1883
LITERATURE H. P. Bremmer, Album Kröller-
Müller Collection 1919, plate 4. Vanbeselaere 1937,
pp 102, 202, 410: January-February 1883
COLLECTION Otterlo, Rijksmuseum Kröller-
Müller, inv nr 208-13, cat van Gogh 1970, nr 50

F 1078a THE DUSTMAN

Pencil 20.5 × 32 [8 × 12½]
Signed in lower left: Vincent
Annotated by Vincent in lower right: The dustman
The Hague 1883
LITERATURE Not in Faille 1928 or Vanbeselaere
1937
COLLECTION Formerly Leipzig, Museum der
bildenden Künste [the drawing has disappeared]

F 1078

F 1072

F 1074

F 1075

F 1077

F 1078a

F 1080

F 1084

F 1079 recto THE DONKEY CART [destroyed]

Pen and pencil 11.5 × 20 [4½ × 7¾]
The Hague 1883
LITERATURE Vanbeselaere 1937, pp 102, 202, 410:
January-February 1883
COLLECTION Formerly Rotterdam,
Mrs A.J. Kolff-Havelaar Collection [destroyed by
fire 14 May 1940]

F 1079 verso STUDY OF A HORSE [destroyed]
LITERATURE Not in Vanbeselaere 1937
Not reproduced

F 1080 PEASANT WOMAN FEEDING FOWLS

Pencil, black ink, heightened with white [wove
paper, with dull surface] 61 × 33.5 [24 × 13¼]
Annotated in lower left: Port. Vincent
The Hague 1883
LITERATURE Album Hidde Nijland Collection
1905, plate 39. Vanbeselaere 1937, pp 107, 410:
April 1883
COLLECTION Otterlo, Rijksmuseum Kröller-
Müller, inv nr 972-28, cat van Gogh 1970, nr 10

F 1081 MAN CARRYING A BUNDLE OF
BRANCHES
Nuenen period; see after F 1349 verso

F 1082 MAN SEATED, DRINKING: FULL FACE

Pencil, black chalk 32 × 25 [12½ × 9¾]
The Hague October 1882
LITERATURE Vanbeselaere 1937, pp 92, 185, 410:
November 1882
COLLECTION New York, M. Futter

F 1083 FISHERMAN WITH BASKET ON HIS
BACK

Pencil 46.5 × 24 [18¼ × 9½]
Compare F 1012 [same model]
The Hague January-February 1883
LITERATURE Vanbeselaere 1937, pp 92, 185, 410:
November 1882
COLLECTION Sale Amsterdam [F. Muller]
3 December 1918, nr 127
Present owner unknown

F 1084 THE FORGE

Pencil and pen, washed, heightened with white
[wove paper, pasted] 37 × 26 [14½ × 10¼]
The Hague 1882
LITERATURE Vincent van Gogh, Lettres à
Bernard, 1911, plate XXVII. Vanbeselaere 1937,
pp 80, 128, 410: The Hague March 1882. Cat van
Gogh 1949, Rijksmuseum Kröller-Müller, nr 151:
Nuenen. Idem 1953, nr 151: Etten June 1881; letter
146
EDITORS' COMMENT On stylistic grounds to be
dated in The Hague period, notwithstanding the
passage in letter 146 [Etten June 1881]: 'What I have
been doing lately demanded that way of working,
because the subjects required much drawing – drawing
in perspective, too, for instance, a few workshops in
the village here, a forge ...'
COLLECTION Otterlo, Rijksmuseum Kröller-
Müller, inv nr 215-20, cat van Gogh 1970, nr 151

F 1085 MAN WRITING
Possibly Etten period: see after F 905

F 1086 OLD MAN WARMING HIMSELF
Possibly Etten period; see after F 905

F 1087 THE LAUNDRESS

Water color 25.5 × 40 [10 × 15¾]
The Hague 1883
LITERATURE Vanbeselaere 1937, pp 103, 205, 410:
March 1883
COLLECTION Sale Bern [Kornfeld and Klipstein]
13 June 1968, nr 398
Present owner unknown

F 1088 A LANE

Water color 24 × 35 [9½ × 13¾]
The Hague possibly 1882
LITERATURE Vanbeselaere 1937, pp 85, 153, 410:
August 1882
COLLECTION Formerly Santpoort, Netherlands,
C. H. Guépin
Present owner unknown

F 1079 recto

F 1082

F 1087

F 1083

F 1088

F 1091

f 840

F 1089 ROAD AT LOOSDUINEN

Black chalk and pen, heightened with white [laid paper] 26 × 35.5 [10¼ × 14]
Signed in lower right: Vincent
The Hague early 1882
LITERATURE Vincent van Gogh, Lettres à Bernard, 1911, plate 11. Vanbeselaere 1937, pp 85, 148, 410: July 1882. A. Bowness, exhib cat van Gogh London [Hayward Gallery] 1968-9, nr 7: The Hague March 1882
COLLECTION Amsterdam, Rijksmuseum Vincent Van Gogh [Vincent van Gogh Foundation, inv nr F 1089]

F 1090 PEASANTS WORKING
Arles period; see after F 1521 verso

F 1091 POTATO MARKET

Water color 35 × 43.5 [13¾ × 17]
The Hague October 1882
LETTERS 229 [9 September] 'Look, for instance, at this little sketch of the potato market on the North Wall.'
239 [29 October] 'But you remember that not long ago I wrote you (when sending you a sketch in color of a potato market), "I must try to paint the bustle of the streets again." The result of this is about twelve water colors which I am doing right now...'
LITERATURE Vanbeselaere 1937, pp 87, 159, 410: October 1882; letters 229 and 239
COLLECTION New York, D. A. Bennahum

F 1092 WOMAN ON A COUNTRY LANE WITH WILLOWS: NEAR THE DUNES

Pencil, stumped, black chalk, washed [Ingres paper with watermark: E.D. & Cie – P.L. Bas] 35.5 × 60.5 [14 × 23¾]
Annotated in lower left: at. Vincent
The Hague 1883
LITERATURE Vanbeselaere 1937, pp 110, 227, 410: September 1883; letter 319. Cat van Gogh 1966, Rijksmuseum Kröller-Müller, nr 77: according to Miss Szymańska done in the Etten period and reworked in The Hague; letter 242
COLLECTION Otterlo, Rijksmuseum Kröller-Müller, inv nr 1034-28, cat van Gogh 1970, nr 77

F 1093 LANDSCAPE WITH FIGURES
Antwerp period; see after F 1361

REDATED TO THE HAGUE

F 840 HALF FIGURE OF STANDING WOMAN: FACING LEFT

Black chalk, pencil and water color 42 × 25.5 [16½ × 10]
Signed in lower left: Vincent
The Hague 1882-3
LITERATURE Faille 1928, nr 840: Cuesmes-Brussels. Vanbeselaere 1937, pp 38, 81, 124, 407: The Hague April 1882
COLLECTION Haarlem, Netherlands, Private Collection

F 1092

F 1089

F 852

F 853

F 841 WOMAN ON HER DEATHBED

Black chalk, pencil, washed, water color, heightened with white, partly oils [water-color paper, pasted] 35 × 62 [13¾ × 24½] Annotated in lower left: Atel. Vincent The Hague April 1883 LETTER 280 [about 21 April] '*This week I drew a few reclining figures; some time I shall need figures of corpses or of sick people, men as well as women.*' LITERATURE H. J. Haverman, De Kroniek 3 March 1895, p 75. Album Hidde Nijland Collection 1905, plate 55. Faille 1928, nr 840: Cuesmes-Brussels. Vanbeselaere 1937, pp 38, 47-9, 105, 205, 407: April 1883; letter 280. B. S. Meyers, Modern Art in the Making, 1950, p 237, plate 119 COLLECTION Otterlo, Rijksmuseum Kröller-Müller, inv nr 987-28, cat van Gogh 1970, nr 91

F 852 THE SOWER: FACING RIGHT

Pencil, brush and China ink 61 × 40 [24 × 15¾] The Hague December 1882 LETTER 251 [between 4 and 9 December] '*Then a second Sower, with a light brown fustian jacket and trousers, so this figure stands out light against the black field, bordered by a little row of pollard willows. This is quite a different type, with a clipped beard, broad shoulders, rather thick-set, somewhat like an ox, in that his whole frame has been shaped by his labor in the fields. Perhaps more of an Eskimo type, thick lips, broad nose.*' LITERATURE Faille 1928, nr 852: Etten September 1881; letter 150. Vanbeselaere 1937, pp 58, 66, 98, 186-7, 407: December 1882; letter 251 COLLECTION Amsterdam, P. and N. de Boer Foundation

F 853 TWO SOWERS

Pencil [water-color paper] 31.5 × 21 [12½ × 8¼] Signed in lower left: Vincent Compare F 999 The Hague December 1882 LETTER 251 [between 4 and 9 December] '*In the first place, a Sower. A big old fellow, a tall dark silhouette against a dark ground. Far away in the distance a little cottage with a moss-covered roof and a bit of sky with a lark. The man is a kind of cock type, a clean-shaven face, rather a sharp nose and chin, small eyes and sunken mouth. Long legs with boots.*' LITERATURE Vincent van Gogh, Lettres à Bernard, 1911, plate XXXV. Faille 1928, nr 853: Etten September 1881; letter 150. Vanbeselaere 1937, pp 58, 66, 98, 186-7: December 1882; letter 251 COLLECTION Amsterdam, Rijksmuseum Vincent van Gogh [Vincent van Gogh Foundation, inv nr F 853]

F 872 AN ADVENTURER SETTING OUT

Mountain chalk 7 × 9 [2¾ × 3½] Annotated by Vincent in lower left: aventurier en voyage The Hague March 1883 LETTER 273 [about 5 March] '*I wrote Rappard [R 30] about the mountain chalk yesterday, because I had to write him about various things concerning lithography; and as I wanted to send him a few sketches done with it, I used it for some drawings of our baby, in different positions, and I found it is very well suited to sketching, too.*' LITERATURE Faille 1928, nr 872: Etten December 1881; letter 165. Vanbeselaere 1937, pp 58, 103, 394, 407: March 1883 COLLECTION Bilthoven, Netherlands, Mrs H. Hupkes-de Kanter

F 872

F 882

F 882 A MAN SOWING: FACING LEFT

Black chalk, washed, pencil, black ink, heightened
with white [water-color paper with rough surface]
62.5 × 41.5 [24½ × 16¼]
The Hague March-April 1883
LITERATURE Album Hidde Nijland Collection
1905, plate 16. Faille 1928, nr 882: Etten. Vanbeselaere 1937, pp 54, 74, 172, 408: Etten September
1881
COLLECTION Otterlo, Rijksmuseum Kröller-
Müller, inv nr 950-28, cat van Gogh 1970, nr 11

F 841

F 899

F 901

F 904

F 1179

F 1294

F 898 SIEN WITH A CIGAR, SITTING ON THE GROUND BY THE STOVE

Pencil, black chalk, pen and brush, sepia, washed and heightened with white [Ingres paper with watermark: E.D. & Cie–P.L. Bas] 45.5 × 56 [18 × 22]
Annotated in lower left: Port. Vincent
The Hague April 1882
LITERATURE H. J. Haverman, De Kroniek 3 March 1895, p 75. Album Hidde Nijland Collection 1905, plate 85. H. J. Haverman, exhib cat Amsterdam 1924. Faille 1928, nr 898: Etten. Vanbeselaere 1937, pp 49, 58, 82, 138, 408: April 1882
COLLECTION Otterlo, Rijksmuseum Kröller-Müller, inv nr 1016-28, cat van Gogh 1970, nr 74

F 899 A STOOPING WOMAN

Pencil and pen 40 × 30 [15¾ × 11¾]
The Hague probably 1882
LITERATURE Faille 1928, nr 899: Etten. Vanbeselaere 1937, pp 58, 82, 138, 208, 408: April 1882
COLLECTION Formerly Zeist, Netherlands, H. A. Hidde Nijland
Present owner unknown

F 901 THE SAW MILL

Black chalk, heightened with white 31 × 37.5 [12¼ × 14¾]
Signed in lower left: Vincent
The Hague 1882
LITERATURE Faille 1928, nr 901: Etten. Vanbeselaere 1937, pp 58, 80, 128, 408: March 1882
COLLECTION Hoorn, Netherlands, J. E. de Visser

F 904 A SUBURBAN FIELD ENCLOSURE

Water color, charcoal and black chalk 45 × 60 [17¾ × 23¾]
The Hague probably 1882
LITERATURE Faille 1928, nr 904: Etten. Vanbeselaere 1937, pp 58, 84, 147, 408: July 1882
COLLECTION Formerly Rotterdam, A. W. Gelber
Present owner unknown

F 1179 SIEN WITH SHAWL, AT THE TABLE

Pencil, ink, brushed, water color [Ingres paper with watermark: L. Berville] 47 × 31 [18½ × 12¼]
The Hague March 1883
LITERATURE Faille 1928, nr 1179: Nuenen February-April 1885; letter 393-8. Vanbeselaere 1937, pp 104, 411: March 1883
COLLECTION Otterlo, Rijksmuseum Kröller-Müller, inv nr 256-20, cat van Gogh 1970, nr 59

F 1294 WOMAN SEWING, SITTING ON A BASKET: FACING RIGHT

Black chalk, washed, heightened with white [watercolor paper] 38.5 × 23 [15¼ × 9]
The Hague March 1883
LITERATURE Faille 1928, nr 1294: Nuenen. Vanbeselaere 1937, pp 275, 413: Nuenen summer 1885
COLLECTION Otterlo, Rijksmuseum Kröller-Müller, inv nr 192-00, cat van Gogh 1970, nr 64

DRENTHE PERIOD

F 1094 PEATERY [IN DRENTHE?]

Water color 41 × 54 [16¼ × 21¼]
Possibly Drenthe September 1883
LITERATURE Vanbeselaere 1937, pp 236, 410. Tralbaut Drenthe 1959, p 217: not by van Gogh
COLLECTION Amsterdam, Private Collection

F 1095 LANDSCAPE WITH BOG TRUNKS

Pen and pencil 31 × 37.5 [12¼ × 14¾]
Drenthe October 1883
LETTER 331 [9 October] '*Yesterday I drew some
decayed oak roots, so-called bog trunks…These
trunks were lying in a pool, in black mud.*'
LITERATURE Vanbeselaere 1937, pp 237, 244, 410.
Tralbaut Drenthe 1959, pp 211, 223
COLLECTION Boston, John Goelet

F 1095

F 1094

F 898

F 1096 recto

F 1096 verso

F 1097

F 1102

F 1098

F 1099

F 1096 recto PLOWMAN AND THREE WOMEN

Pencil [Dutch paper, laid, with watermark: pro patria–Eendracht maakt Macht] 21 × 34 [8¼ × 13½]
Compare sketch in letter 333
Drenthe October 1883
LETTER 333 [21 October] *'Today I have been walking behind the plowers who were plowing a potato field, with women trudging to pick up a few potatoes that were left. This was quite a different field from the one I sketched for you yesterday, but it is curious here–always exactly the same, and yet with just enough variation…'*
LITERATURE Album Hidde Nijland Collection 1905, plate 19. Idem 1907, plate 10. Vanbeselaere 1937, pp 237, 248, 410. Tralbaut Drenthe 1959, pp 93, 104, 212, 224
COLLECTION Otterlo, Rijksmuseum Kröller-Müller, inv nr 953-28, cat van Gogh 1970, nr 101

F 1096 verso FIGURE SKETCHES

Drenthe October 1883
LITERATURE Not in Faille 1928, Vanbeselaere 1937 or Tralbaut Drenthe 1959

F 1097 COTTAGE IN THE HEATH

Pen and ink [Ingres paper] 22.5 × 29 [8¾ × 11½]
Compare sketch in letter 335
Drenthe October-November 1883
LETTER 335 [31 October] *'…and I found this cottage on a muddy evening after the rain; seen on the spot, it is splendid.'*
LITERATURE Album Hidde Nijland Collection 1905, plate 2. Vincent van Gogh, Lettres à Bernard, 1911, plate III. H. van den Eerenbeemt, Opgang March 1924, p 269 [with reproduction]. Vanbeselaere 1937, pp 237, 248, 410. Tralbaut Drenthe 1959, pp 107, 212, 224
COLLECTION Otterlo, Rijksmuseum Kröller-Müller, inv nr 936-28, cat van Gogh 1970, nr 99

F 1098 THE DRAWBRIDGE AT NIEUW-AMSTERDAM

Water color 38.5 × 81 [15¼ × 32]
Drenthe November 1883
LETTER 342 [26 November] *'Did you receive my studies? Since then I have made a large painted one, and a large sketch of a drawbridge…'*
LITERATURE Vanbeselaere 1937, pp 237, 250, 410. Tralbaut Drenthe 1959, pp 213, 224
COLLECTION Groningen, Groninger Museum voor Stad en Lande, inv nr 1961/188

F 1099 LANDSCAPE TOWARDS EVENING

Water color 40 × 53 [15¾ × 20¾]
Drenthe September 1883
LETTER 326 [about 20 September] *'I have made a few studies of the heath which I shall send you when they are dry, and I have also started a few water colors.'*
LITERATURE Vanbeselaere 1937, pp 236, 410. Tralbaut Drenthe 1959, pp 214, 223
COLLECTION Wassenaar, Netherlands, Mrs C.E. van Beuningen-Fentener van Vlissingen

F 1100 THE HEATH: WITH A WHEELBARROW

Water color 24 × 35 [9½ × 13¾]
Drenthe September 1883
LETTER 326 [about 20 September] See F 1099
LITERATURE Vanbeselaere 1937, pp 236, 410. Tralbaut Drenthe 1959, pp 214, 223
COLLECTION Cleveland, Museum of Art [acquired 1958], inv nr 58.30

F 1100

F 1101 LANDSCAPE IN DRENTHE WITH A HUT

Water color 24 × 35.5 [9½ × 14]
Drenthe September 1883
LETTER 326 [about 20 September] See F 1099
LITERATURE Vanbeselaere 1937, pp 236, 410.
Tralbaut Drenthe 1959, pp 214, 223
COLLECTION New York, Private Collection

F 1102 A HUT IN DRENTHE

Water color 25 × 36.5 [9¾ × 14¼]
Drenthe September 1883
LETTER 326 [about 20 September] See F 1099
LITERATURE Vanbeselaere 1937, pp 236, 410.
Tralbaut Drenthe 1959, pp 214, 223
COLLECTION New York, Galerie St Etienne
[acquired 1969]

F 1101

F 1103

F 1104

F 1073

F 1347

F 1103 A GROUP OF PEASANT HOUSES IN
DRENTHE

Water color 25 × 36.5 [9¾ × 14¼]
Drenthe September 1883
LETTER 326 [about 20 September] See F 1099
LITERATURE Vanbeselaere 1937, pp 236, 410.
Tralbaut Drenthe 1959, pp 214, 223
COLLECTION Wuppertal, West Germany, Von der
Heydt-Museum der Stadt Wuppertal, inv nr KK
1965/27, cat Handzeichnungen, Pastelle und
Aquarelle 1965, nr 62

F 1104 LANDSCAPE IN DRENTHE WITH
CANAL AND SAILBOAT

Pen and pencil, washed 28 × 40 [11 × 15¾]
Drenthe November 1883
LITERATURE Vanbeselaere 1937, pp 237, 410.
Tralbaut Drenthe 1959, pp 215, 224
COLLECTION Sale London [Sotheby] 10 July 1957,
nr 54
Present owner unknown

F 1105 TWO MEN ON A COUNTRY ROAD
Cuesmes-Brussels period; see after F 841

F 1106 WINTER LANDSCAPE WITH WOMAN
AND WHEELBARROWS
Nuenen period; see after F 1349 verso

REDATED TO DRENTHE

F 877 SHEPHERD WITH FLOCK NEAR A
CHURCH AT ZWEELOO

Pen and pencil, heightened with white 25 × 31.5
[9¾ × 12½]
Annotated in ink by Vincent on reverse:
Kerkje te Zweeloo
Drenthe November 1883
LETTER 340 [November] 'I passed a little old church
exactly, exactly "L'Eglise de Greville" in Millet's
little picture in the Luxembourg; instead of the little
peasant with his spade in that picture, there was here
a shepherd with a flock of sheep walking along the
hedge.'
LITERATURE Faille 1928, nr 877: Etten. Van-
beselaere 1937, pp 51, 74, 407: Etten May 1881.
M. E. Tralbaut, 8 × van Gogh, 1962, pp 61-2:
Drenthe November 1883; letter 340
COLLECTION Rockanje, Netherlands, R. W. van
Hoey Smith

F 1073 HEAD OF A WOMAN WITH DARK CAP

Pen and ink, washed [ordinary drawing paper,
pasted] 21 × 13.5 [8¼ × 5¼]
Drenthe October-November 1883
LITERATURE Album Hidde Nijland Collection
1905, plate 88a. Faille 1928, nr 1073: The Hague.
Vanbeselaere 1937, pp 110, 238, 243, 410: Drenthe
October-November 1883; Tralbaut Drenthe 1959,
pp 215, 224: Drenthe November 1883
COLLECTION Otterlo, Rijksmuseum Kröller-
Müller, inv nr 1019-28, cat van Gogh 1970, nr 147

F 1248 COTTAGES IN THE HEATHER

Black chalk, heightened with white [Ingres paper]
46 × 60.5 [18 × 23¾]
Drenthe October 1883
LITERATURE Faille 1928, nr 1248: Nuenen.
Vanbeselaere 1937, pp 238, 412: Drenthe October-
November 1883. Tralbaut Drenthe 1959, pp 215-6,
224: Drenthe November 1883
COLLECTION Otterlo, Rijksmuseum Kröller-
Müller, inv nr 1033-28, cat van Gogh 1970, nr 100

F 1347 LANDSCAPE WITH A BRIDGE

Black chalk, washed and heightened with white
[Ingres paper with watermark: S.C. Mars] 30×44
[11¾ × 17¼]
Signed in lower right: Vincent
Drenthe October 1883
LITERATURE Faille 1928, nr 1347: Nuenen. Album
Hidde Nijland Collection 1905, plate 20. Van-
beselaere 1937, pp 238, 413: Drenthe October-
November 1883. Tralbaut Drenthe 1959, pp 216,
224: Drenthe November 1883. Cat van Gogh 1966,
Rijksmuseum Kröller-Müller, nr 55: The Hague
COLLECTION Otterlo, Rijksmuseum Kröller-
Müller, inv nr 954-28, cat van Gogh 1970, nr 55

F 877

F 1248

F 1107

F 1108

F 1110

F 1111

NUENEN PERIOD

F 1107 THE WEAVER: THE WHOLE LOOM, FACING LEFT

Water color [Dutch laid paper with watermark:
H.F.d.C. Scutcheon with fleur-de-lis]
Signed in lower left: Vincent
Compare painting F 29
Nuenen January 1884 or shortly later
LETTERS 351 [early January] '*So since I have been
here, for instance, I have been absorbed in the weavers.
Do you know many drawings of weavers? I know only
a very few. I began by making three water colors of
them.*'
351a [to Furnée; mid-January] '*Now the last few
weeks I have done four water colors of* weavers.'
LITERATURE Vanbeselaere 1937, pp 256, 317, 410
COLLECTION Amsterdam, Rijksmuseum Vincent
van Gogh [Vincent van Gogh Foundation, inv
nr F 1107]

F 1108 THE WEAVER: THE WHOLE LOOM, FACING RIGHT

Water color 32 × 47 [12½ × 18½]
Compare painting F 162 and drawing F 1121
Nuenen January 1884 or shortly later
LITERATURE Vanbeselaere 1937, pp 257, 317, 410:
May 1884
COLLECTION Zurich, Fritz and Peter Nathan Art
Gallery [acquired 1968]

F 1109 THE WEAVER: PART OF THE LOOM, FACING RIGHT

Pencil, black chalk, pen, brush and ink, heightened
with white [wove water-color paper] 24.5 × 33.5
[9¾ × 13¼]
Signed in lower left: Vincent
Nuenen February 1884 or shortly later
LITERATURE Album Hidde Nijland Collection
1905, plate 91. Vanbeselaere 1937, pp 256, 315, 410
COLLECTION Otterlo, Rijksmuseum Kröller-
Müller, inv nr 1023-28, cat van Gogh 1970, nr 103

F 1110 INTERIOR WITH A WEAVER FACING RIGHT

Pen and ink, black chalk, pencil and water color
[Dutch paper, laid, with watermark: Scutcheon
with fleur-de-lis] 24.5 × 29.5 [9¾ × 11½]
Annotated in lower left: Port. Vincent
Nuenen February 1884 or shortly later
LITERATURE Album Hidde Nijland Collection
1905, plate 11. Vanbeselaere 1937, pp 256, 315
COLLECTION Otterlo, Rijksmuseum Kröller-
Müller, inv nr 945-28, cat van Gogh 1970, nr 102

F 1111 FOUR FIGURES WORKING AT A LOOM

Pen and ink, washed [ordinary white paper]
10.2 × 13.5 [4 × 5¼]
Nuenen probably February 1884
LETTERS Perhaps to be connected with the letters
under F 1120
LITERATURE Album Hidde Nijland Collection
1905, part 8, reproduction on cover. Vanbeselaere
1937, pp 257, 317, 410
COLLECTION Otterlo, Rijksmuseum Kröller-
Müller, inv nr 1044-28, cat van Gogh 1970, nr 152

F 1112 recto STUDIES OF AN AUCTION NEAR NUENEN

Black chalk [Dutch laid paper with watermark:
v. d. L.] 35 × 21 [13¾ × 8¼]
Compare F 1112 verso, water color F 1230 and
drawings P 1231 recto and verso
Nuenen May 1885

LETTER 408 [after 8 May] *'These last days I have been working hard on drawings. They are busy pulling down the old tower in the fields. So there was an auction of lumber and slates and old iron, including the cross. I have finished a water color of it, in the style of the lumber auction...'*
LITERATURE Album Hidde Nijland Collection 1905, plate 82. Vanbeselaere 1937, pp 268, 410
COLLECTION Otterlo, Rijksmuseum Kröller-Müller, inv nr 1013-28, cat van Gogh 1970, nr 160a

F 1112 verso THE ENTRANCE OF THE OLD CHURCH TOWER AT NUENEN

Black chalk
Compare F 1112 recto, water color F 1230 and drawings F 1231 recto and verso
Nuenen May 1885
LITERATURE Not in Faille 1928 or Vanbeselaere 1937

F 1113 A LUMBER SALE

Water color [Dutch laid paper with illegible water-mark] 33.5 × 44.5 [13¼ × 17½]
Signed in lower left: Vincent
Nuenen January 1884
LETTER 351a [to Furnée; mid-January] *'Now the last few weeks I have done four water colors of weavers. And some others of a lumber auction...'*
LITERATURE Vanbeselaere 1937, pp 257, 411
COLLECTION Amsterdam, Rijksmuseum Vincent van Gogh [Vincent van Gogh Foundation, inv nr F 1113]

F 1109

F 1112 recto

F 1112 verso

F 1113

F 1114

F 1115

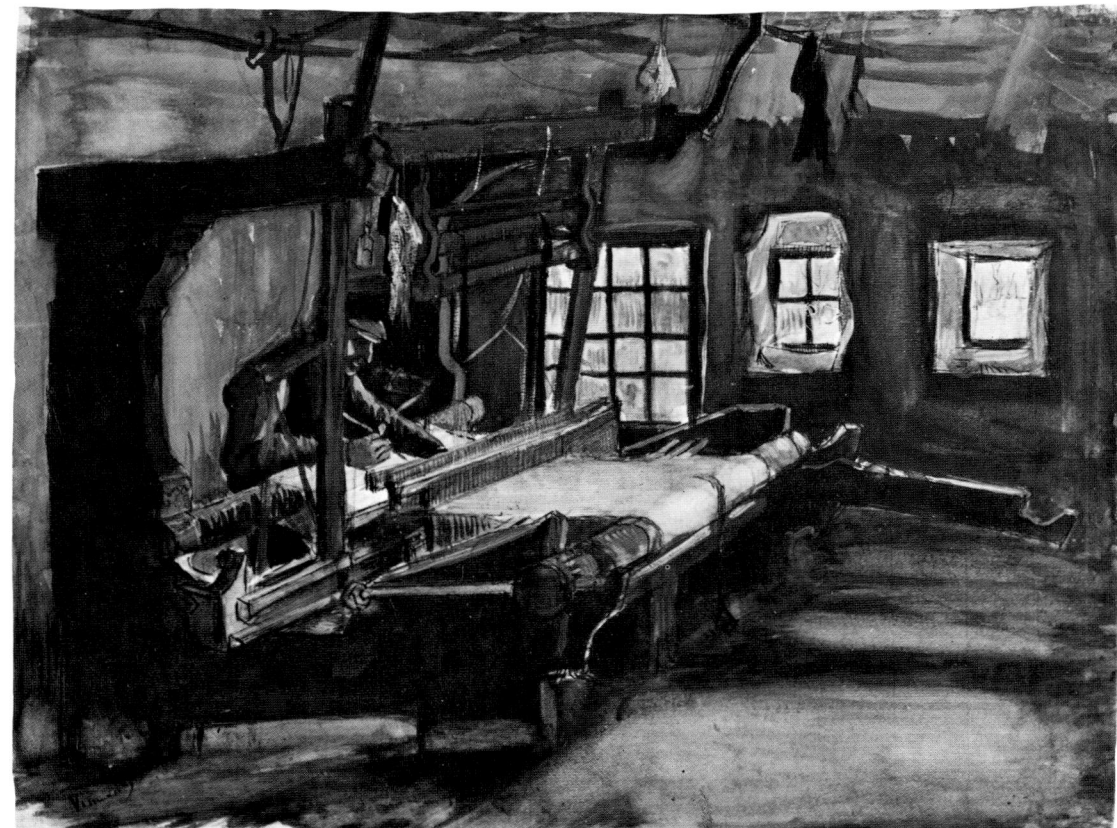

F 1114 THE WEAVER: THE WHOLE LOOM,
FACING LEFT

Pencil, water color [Dutch laid paper with water-
mark: H.F.d.C. Scutcheon with fleur-de-lis]
35 × 45 [13¾ × 17¾]
Signed in lower left: Vincent
Nuenen January 1884 or shortly later
LETTERS 351 [early January] and 351a [mid-
January] See F 1107
LITERATURE Vanbeselaere 1937, pp 257, 317, 411:
May 1884; letters 351, 353, 355-9, and 369
COLLECTION Amsterdam, Rijksmuseum Vincent
van Gogh [Vincent van Gogh Foundation, inv
nr F 1114]

F 1115 THE WEAVER, FACING RIGHT:
INTERIOR WITH THREE WINDOWS

Water color, pen and ink [Dutch laid paper]
33.5 × 45 [13¼ × 17¾]
Signed in lower left: Vincent
Compare painting F 37
Nuenen June 1884
LETTER 372 [about 1 July] See F 37
LITERATURE Vanbeselaere 1937, pp 257, 318, 411:
July 1884
COLLECTION Amsterdam, Rijksmuseum Vincent
van Gogh [Vincent van Gogh Foundation, inv
nr F 1115]

F 1116 THE WEAVER, SEEN FROM THE FRONT

Pencil, black and white chalk, pen and ink [Ingres
paper, yellowish] 21 × 35 [8¼ × 13¾]
Nuenen February 1884
LETTER 359 [between 20 and 24 February] 'One of
these days I am going to send you another pen-and-
ink drawing of a weaver – larger than the other five;
the loom seen from the front …'
LITERATURE Vanbeselaere 1937, pp 256, 315, 411:
January 1884
COLLECTION Amsterdam, Rijksmuseum Vincent
van Gogh [Vincent van Gogh Foundation, inv
nr F 1116]

F 1116a recto A MAN SEATED BESIDE THE
STOVE
Etten period; see after F 905

F 1116a verso THE WEAVER: PART OF THE
LOOM, THREE QUARTERS TO THE LEFT

Water color 44 × 35 [17¼ × 13¾]
Nuenen about April 1884
LITERATURE Not in Faille 1928 or Vanbeselaere
1937
EDITORS' COMMENT Probably the last of the
weavers.
COLLECTION New York, P. Rosenberg & Co Art
Gallery

F 1117 CHAPEL AT NUENEN BETWEEN
TREES WITH FIGURES

Pen and ink [machine paper] 16.5 × 13.5 [6½ × 5¼]
Compare sketch in letter 355 and painting F 25
Nuenen January 1884
LETTER 355 [about 24 January] See F 25
LITERATURE Vanbeselaere 1937, pp 258, 411
COLLECTION Otterlo, Rijksmuseum Kröller-
Müller, inv nr 1037-28, cat van Gogh 1970, nr 162

F 1118 INTERIOR OF A WEAVER'S
WORKSHOP WITH BABY CHAIR

Pencil, pen and brown ink [ordinary wove paper]
32 × 40 [12½ × 15¾] Damaged in lower right
Signed in lower right: Vincent
Compare painting F 24 [same interior] and water

color F 1119 [same composition]
Nuenen late January–early February 1884
LETTER 355 [about 24 January] See F 26
LITERATURE Vanbeselaere 1937, pp 256, 316, 411
COLLECTION Amsterdam, Rijksmuseum Vincent
Van Gogh [Vincent van Gogh Foundation, inv
nr F 1118]

F 1116

F 1117

F 1116a verso

F 1118

F 1119

F 1120

F 1124

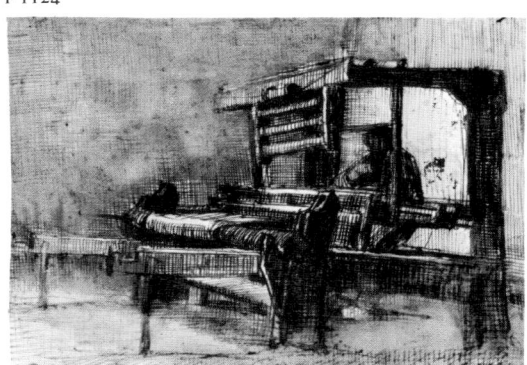

F 1121

F 1119 INTERIOR OF A WEAVER'S WORKSHOP WITH BABY CHAIR

Water color 30.5 × 43 [12 × 17]
Signed in lower right: Vincent
Compare painting F 24 [same interior] and drawing
F 1118 [same composition]
Nuenen January 1884
LETTER 355 [about 24 January] See F 26
LITERATURE Vanbeselaere 1937, pp 251, 315, 411
COLLECTION Sale London [Sotheby] 31 March
1965, nr 9
Present owner unknown

F 1120 THE WEAVER: THE WHOLE LOOM, FACING LEFT

Pen 12.5 × 19.5 [5 × 7¾]
Nuenen February 1884
LETTERS 357 [about 18 February] '*I can send you five such drawings of weavers, which I drew after my painted studies, and which are a little different – and I think more vigorous of technique, than the pen drawings of mine you have seen up to now. I am working at them early and late, for except the painted studies, and the pen-and-ink drawings, I have also some new water colors of them on the easel.*'
R 40 [25 February] '*Five pen drawings of weavers besides.*'
358 [between 25 February and about 9 March] '*Just listen – after having read your letter about the drawings, I at once sent you a new water color of a weaver, and five pen drawings.*'
R 43 [April] '*I was delighted to hear that you saw something in my drawings.*'
R 44 [April] '*Your letter about the drawings delighted me. As for the weaving loom, the study of that apparatus was indeed made on the spot from start to finish, and it was a hard job – on account of the fact that one must sit so close to it that it is difficult to make measurements; I did include the figure in the drawing after all. But what I wanted to express by it was just this: "When that monstrous black thing of grimed oak with all those sticks is seen in such sharp contrast to the grayish atmosphere in which it stands, then there in the center of it sits a black ape or goblin or spook that clatters with those sticks from early morning till late at night." And I indicated that spot by putting in some sort of apparition of a weaver, by means of a few scratches and blots, where I had seen it sitting. Consequently I hardly gave a thought to the proportions of the arms and the legs.*'
LITERATURE Vanbeselaere 1937, pp 257, 317, 411
COLLECTION Amsterdam, Rijksmuseum Vincent
van Gogh [Vincent van Gogh Foundation, inv
nr F 1120]

F 1121 THE WEAVER: THE WHOLE LOOM, FACING RIGHT, WITH OIL LAMP

Pencil, pen and brown ink [ordinary wove paper]
27 × 40 [10½ × 15¾]
Signed in lower right: Vincent
Compare painting F 162 and water color F 1108
Nuenen January 1884 or shortly later
LITERATURE Vincent van Gogh, Lettres à
Bernard, 1911, plate XIX. Vanbeselaere 1937, pp
257, 281, 317, 411: May 1884; letters 351, 353,
355-9, and 369
COLLECTION Amsterdam, Rijksmuseum Vincent
van Gogh [Vincent van Gogh Foundation, inv
nr F 1121]

F 1122 THE WEAVER: HALF LENGTH, FACING RIGHT

Ink, bistre wash, heightened with white [ordinary
wove paper] 26 × 21 [10¼ × 8¼]
Signed in lower left: Vincent
Compare painting F 26

Nuenen late January-early February 1884
LETTERS 357 [about 18 February], R 40 [25 February], 358 [between 25 February and about 9 March], R 43 [April] and R 44 [April] See F 1120
LITERATURE Vanbeselaere 1937, pp 256, 280, 316, 411 : January 1884
COLLECTION Amsterdam, Rijksmuseum Vincent van Gogh [Vincent van Gogh Foundation, inv nr F 1122]

F 1123 THE WEAVER: THE WHOLE LOOM, FACING LEFT, WITH OIL LAMP

Pen, heightened with white [ordinary wove paper]
30.5×40.5 [12×16]
Signed in lower left: Vincent
Nuenen February 1884
LETTERS 357 [about 18 February], R 40 [25 February], 358 [between 25 February and about 9 March], R 43 [April] and R 44 [April] See F 1120
LITERATURE Vanbeselaere 1937, pp 257, 317, 411
COLLECTION Amsterdam, Rijksmuseum Vincent van Gogh [Vincent van Gogh Foundation, inv nr F 1123]

F 1124 THE WEAVER: THE WHOLE LOOM, FACING LEFT

Pen, washed 9.5 × 13 [3¾ × 5]
Nuenen February 1884
LETTERS 357 [about 18 February], R 40 [25 February], 358 [between 25 February and about 9 March], R 43 [April] and R 44 [April] See F 1120
LITERATURE Vanbeselaere 1937, pp 257, 317, 411 : May 1884
COLLECTION The Hague, Heirs of H. P. Bremmer

F 1122

F 1123

F 1125

F 1126

F 1127

F 1127a

F 1125 THE WEAVER: THE WHOLE LOOM, FACING RIGHT

Pencil, water color [Dutch laid paper] 32 × 44
[12½ × 17¼]
Signed in lower left: Vincent
Nuenen January 1884 or shortly later
LETTERS 351 [early January] and 351a [mid-January] See F 1107
LITERATURE Vanbeselaere 1937, pp 257, 317, 411:
May 1884
COLLECTION Amsterdam, Rijksmuseum Vincent
van Gogh [Vincent van Gogh Foundation, inv
nr F 1125]

F 1126 WINTER LANDSCAPE WITH FIGURE BEARING WOOD

Black and colored chalk [Dutch laid paper?]
22.5 × 29 [8¾ × 11½]
Nuenen early 1885
LITERATURE Vanbeselaere 1937, pp 259, 322, 411:
March 1884
EDITORS' COMMENT Faille dates F 1126 March
1884 in the manuscript for this edition, but on
stylistic grounds it is dated by the editors to the
following year.
COLLECTION Amsterdam, Rijksmuseum Vincent
van Gogh [Vincent van Gogh Foundation, inv
nr F 1126]

F 1127 THE VICARAGE GARDEN WITH A VIEW ON THE OLD TOWER OF NUENEN IN WINTER

Pen [ordinary wove paper] 29 × 21 [11½ × 8¼]
Annotated in lower left: Mélancolie
Nuenen December 1883
LITERATURE Faille 1928: March 1884; letter 364.
Vanbeselaere 1937, pp 259, 322, 411: March 1884
EDITORS' COMMENT This drawing belongs to a
series of snow scenes [F 1131, F 1232, F 1233 recto,
F 1236 recto, F 1237, F 1238, SD 1686 and SD 1687]
that can be dated to December 1883. The style
indicates a date in the winter of 1883-4, and
meteorological evidence fixes December as the only
possible time the drawings could have been made:
the weather station in De Bilt reported no snow for
either November 1883 or January-February 1884.
See EDITORS' COMMENT to F 1237.
COLLECTION Amsterdam, Rijksmuseum Vincent
van Gogh [Vincent van Gogh Foundation, inv
nr F 1127]

F 1127a GARDEN IN WINTER

Pencil and pen 19 × 28 [7½ × 11]
Nuenen March-April 1884
LETTERS 364 [about 1 April] *'For this month I have
some pen-and-ink drawings for you, in the first place
those that are at Rappard's for the moment, about
which I had a letter from him, telling me that he liked
them all, and especially admired the sentiment in
"Behind the Hedges" and "The Kingfisher" and the
first three "Winter Gardens" which he also liked very
much.'*
R 44 [April] *'...and since then I have made another
one of the same subject, also with a little black spook
in it...I am sending you a few others too..."Winter
Garden."'*
LITERATURE Not in Faille 1928 or Vanbeselaere
1937. Expertised under the auspices of the
Expertise Instituut, Amsterdam [1956]
COLLECTION Stuttgart, Staatsgalerie [acquired
1963], inv nr C 63/1064

F 1128 THE VICARAGE GARDEN AT NUENEN
IN WINTER

Pencil and pen [ordinary wove paper] 39 × 53
[15¼ × 20¾]
Signed in lower left: Vincent
Compare sketch in letter 367 and F 1130 [same site]
Nuenen March 1884
LETTERS 364 [about 1 April] and R 44 [April] See
F 1127a
LITERATURE Vincent van Gogh, Lettres à Bernard,
1911, plate XVI. Vanbeselaere 1937, pp 259, 322,
411
COLLECTION Amsterdam, Rijksmuseum Vincent
van Gogh [Vincent van Gogh Foundation, inv
nr F 1128]

F 1129 ROAD WITH POLLARD WILLOWS
AND MAN WITH A WHEELBARROW

Pencil, pen and ink 40 × 53 [15¾ × 20¾]
Signed in lower left: Vincent
Compare painting F 44 [same trees]
Nuenen March 1884
LETTER R 44 [April] *'I am sending you a few others
too...pen-and-ink drawings, "Pollard Willows" –
"Poplar Avenue" – "Behind the Hedges" – the "Kingfisher" – "Winter Garden."'*
LITERATURE Vincent van Gogh, Lettres à Bernard,
1911, plate XV. Vanbeselaere 1937, pp 259, 322,
411: letters 364, 366 and R 44. Cat van Gogh 1959,
Rijksmuseum Kröller-Müller, nr 256: the same
trees as depicted in painting F 44
COLLECTION Amsterdam, Stedelijk Museum [on
loan since 1957 from the Rijksmuseum, Amsterdam;
acquired 1906, gift of Mrs Cohen Gosschalk; cat
1911, nr 2926b]

F 1130 THE VICARAGE GARDEN AT NUENEN
IN WINTER

Pen, heightened with white 51.5 × 38 [20¼ × 15]
Signed in lower left: Vincent
Compare sketch in letter 367 and F 1128 [same site]
Nuenen March 1884
LETTERS 364 [about 1 April] and R 44 [April] See
F 1127a
LITERATURE Vincent van Gogh, Lettres à Bernard,
1911, plate XXXII, S. Meller, Die graphische
Künste 1919 [with reproduction]. L. Éber, Ars Una
1923, p 23. E. M. Hajos, Der Kunstwanderer 1932,
p 219 [with reproduction]. S. Meller, Ungarische
Kunst 1935, p 143 [with reproduction]. Vanbese-
laere 1937, pp 259, 322, 411: letters 364, 366 and
R 44. E. Hoffmann, Europa 1943, p 154. D. Pataky,
Von Delacroix bis Picasso, Zeichnungen aus der
Sammlung des Museums... Budapest, 1958, p 28,
nr 85
COLLECTION Budapest, Museum of Fine Arts, inv
nr 1935-2791, cat 1956, nr 112

F 1131 THE VICARAGE GARDEN AT NUENEN
WITH THREE WOMEN IN WINTER

Pen [ordinary wove paper] 28 × 20.5 [11 × 8]
Annotated in lower left: Jardin d'hiver
Nuenen December 1883
LITERATURE Vanbeselaere 1937, pp 259, 322, 411:
March 1884
EDITORS' COMMENT See F 1127
COLLECTION Amsterdam, Rijksmuseum Vincent
van Gogh [Vincent van Gogh Foundation, inv
nr F 1131]

F 1128

F 1129

F 1130

F 1131

F 1132

F 1133

F 1134

F 1132 THE VICARAGE GARDEN AT NUENEN

Pencil and pen [ordinary wove paper] 20 × 23.5
[8 × 9¼]
Signed in lower left: Vincent
January 1884
LITERATURE Vincent van Gogh, Lettres à Bernard,
1911, plate XI. Vanbeselaere 1937, pp 263, 353, 411:
January 1885
COLLECTION Amsterdam, Rijksmuseum Vincent
van Gogh [Vincent van Gogh Foundation, inv
nr F 1132]

F 1133 LANDSCAPE WITH THE OLD TOWER OF NUENEN, WITH BLACK FIGURE

Pen 9 × 21 [3½ × 8¼]
Nuenen early spring 1884
LITERATURE Vanbeselaere 1937, pp 259, 282, 411
COLLECTION Sale Amsterdam [P. Brandt] 15-18
November 1954, nr 40
Present owner unknown

F 1134 THE WEAVER STANDING IN FRONT OF A LOOM: LEFT PROFILE

Pencil, pen and ink, heightened with white [thin
wove paper] 27 × 40 [10¾ × 15¾]
Signed in lower right: Vincent
Compare paintings F 32 and F 35
Nuenen April-May 1884
LETTER 367 [about 1 May] See F 32
LITERATURE Cat Kröller-Müller Collection 1917,
nr 125. H. P. Bremmer, Album Kröller-Müller
Collection 1919, plate 37. H. P. Bremmer, cat
Kröller-Müller Collection 1928, nr 209.
Vanbeselaere 1937, pp 257, 318, 411
COLLECTION Otterlo, Rijksmuseum Kröller-
Müller, inv nr 252-17, cat van Gogh 1970, nr 104

F 1135 THE POND IN THE VICARAGE GARDEN AT NUENEN, WITH A KINGFISHER

Pen, heightened with white 39 × 53 [15¼ × 20¾]
Signed in lower left: Vincent
Nuenen March-April 1884
LETTER R 44 [April] '...since then I have made
another one of the same subject, also with a little
black spook in it... I am sending you a few others
too...pen-and-ink drawings...the "Kingfisher"...'
LITERATURE Vincent van Gogh, Lettres à Bernard,
1911, plate X. Vanbeselaere 1937, pp 259, 322, 411
COLLECTION The Netherlands, Private Collection

F 1136 WOMAN WINDING BOBBINS

Pen and ink [thin wove paper, pasted] 14 × 20
[5½ × 7¾]
Signed in lower left: Vincent
Compare water color F 68 [same model]
Nuenen April 1884
LITERATURE Album Hidde Nijland Collection
1905, part 2, reproduction on cover. Vanbeselaere
1937, pp 260, 323, 351, 411: June 1884. Tralbaut
Drenthe 1959, pp 128-30, 216-7, 229: Drenthe
November 1883; letter 340. Cat van Gogh 1959,
Rijksmuseum Kröller-Müller, nr 127: letter R 43
[April 1884]
COLLECTION Otterlo, Rijksmuseum Kröller-
Müller, inv nr 1039-28, cat van Gogh 1970, nr 127

F 1137 WOMAN WINDING BOBBINS

Pen and ink [Dutch wove paper, pasted] 15 × 21
[6 × 8¼]
Compare gouache F 1139
Nuenen April 1884

LITERATURE Album Hidde Nijland Collection
1905, part 10, reproduction on cover. Vanbeselaere
1937, pp 260, 323, 351, 411. Cat van Gogh 1966,
Rijksmuseum Kröller-Müller, nr 126: April 1884.
Tralbaut Drenthe 1959, pp 126-30, 212-3, 216-7,
229: November 1883
COLLECTION Otterlo, Rijksmuseum Kröller-
Müller, inv nr 1046-28, cat van Gogh 1970, nr 126

F 1138 MAN REELING YARN

Pencil, black chalk, pen and ink [old Dutch paper,
laid] 22.5 × 23 [8¾ × 9]
Signed in lower right: Vincent
Compare sketch in letter 371 [same motif] and water
color F 1140 [similar composition]
Nuenen May-June 1884
LETTERS 370 [June] '*I hope to make another one, of
an old man at the spooling wheel, near a little window,
of which you perhaps remember a small study.*'
371 [June] '*I think I already told you in my last letter
that I also wanted to start a large man's figure besides
that woman spinning. Enclosed you will now find a
sketch of it. Perhaps you remember two studies of the
same nook, which I already had in the studio when
you were here.*'
LITERATURE Vanbeselaere 1937, pp 260, 323, 351,
411: letters 370, 371 and R 40
COLLECTION Otterlo, Rijksmuseum Kröller-
Müller, inv nr 1036-28, cat van Gogh 1970, nr 105

F 1139 WOMAN WINDING BOBBINS

Gouache 33 × 44 [13 × 17¼]
Signed in lower left: Vincent
Compare drawing F 1137
Nuenen April 1884
LITERATURE Vanbeselaere 1937, pp 260, 323, 351,
411. Cat van Gogh 1959, Rijksmuseum Kröller-
Müller, nr 126: very similar to F 1137
COLLECTION New York, Wildenstein Art Gallery

F 1135

F 1136

F 1137

F 1138

F 1139

F 1140

F 1141

F 1142

F 1143

F 1144

F 1144a

F 1140 MAN REELING YARN

Water color 44 × 34 [17¼ × 13½]
Compare sketch in letter 371 [same motif] and
drawing F 1138 [similar composition]
Nuenen May-June 1884
LETTERS 370 [June] and 371 [June] See F 1138
LITERATURE Vanbeselaere 1937, pp 260, 323, 351,
411. Cat van Gogh 1966, Rijksmuseum Kröller-
Müller, nr 105
COLLECTION Amersfoort, Netherlands,
G. J. Dekker

F 1141 POTATO DIGGERS

Pen and ink 5 × 13 [2 × 5]
Compare painting F 41
Nuenen August 1884
LETTERS 374 [August] and R 47 [August] See F 41
LITERATURE Vanbeselaere 1937, pp 260-1, 326,
411
EDITORS' COMMENT This and the three following
numbers are to be connected with the series of
paintings for Hermans, consisting of F 41, F 42,
F 43 and F 172.
COLLECTION Rockanje, Netherlands, R. W. van
Hoey Smith

F 1142 THE PLOW

Pen and ink 5.5 × 15 [2¼ × 6]
Compare painting F 172 and underpainting [visible
in x-ray] of SP 1669
Nuenen August 1884
LETTERS 374 [August] and R 47 [August] See F 41
LITERATURE Vanbeselaere 1937, pp 260-1, 326, 411
EDITORS' COMMENT See F 1141
COLLECTION Rockanje, Netherlands, R. W. van
Hoey Smith

F 1143 THE SOWER

Pen and ink 5.5 × 14 [2¼ × 5½]
Nuenen August 1884
LETTERS 374 [August] and R 47 [August] See F 41
LITERATURE Vanbeselaere 1937, pp 260-1, 326, 411
EDITORS' COMMENT See F 1141
COLLECTION Rockanje, Netherlands, R. W. van
Hoey Smith

F 1144 OX WAGON IN THE SNOW

Pen and ink 5 × 13.5 [2 × 5¼]
Compare painting F 39
Nuenen August 1884
LETTERS 374 [August] and R 47 [August] See F 41
LITERATURE Vanbeselaere 1937, pp 260-1, 326, 411
EDITORS' COMMENT See F 1141
COLLECTION Rockanje, Netherlands, R. W. van
Hoey Smith

F 1144a MILL AT GENNEP, NEAR NUENEN

Water color 30.5 × 47 [12 × 18½]
Compare paintings F 46, F 47 and F 125 [same mill]
Nuenen November 1884
LETTER 387 [before 20 November] 'I have also
started another water color of the water mill.'
LITERATURE Not in Faille 1928 or Vanbeselaere
1937. A. Tellegen, Museumjournaal 1968, pp
117-22: identifies motif as mill at Gennep; done
after painting F 125 was completed; letter 387 and
F 1144a should be dated December 1884. Idem,
Museumjournaal 1968, inside back cover: the
relevant passage in letter 387 mistranslated in the
official English translation of the letters, and should
read: 'Also I am working on a water color of the mill.'
COLLECTION Sale London [Sotheby] 3 July 1969,
nr 211
Present owner unknown

F 1145 HEAD OF A YOUNG PEASANT:
RIGHT PROFILE

Pencil [old Dutch paper, laid, with watermark:
Concordia res parvae crescunt] 35 × 21 [13¾ × 8¼]
Nuenen early 1885
LITERATURE Vanbeselaere 1937, pp 264, 340, 342,
411: March 1885
COLLECTION Amsterdam, Rijksmuseum Vincent
van Gogh [Vincent van Gogh Foundation, inv
nr F 1145]

F 1146 HEAD OF A YOUNG PEASANT:
RIGHT PROFILE

Pencil [Dutch laid paper with watermark: Pro
Patria – Concordia res parvae crescunt] 35 × 21.5
[13¾ × 8½]
Nuenen early 1885
LITERATURE Vanbeselaere 1937, pp 264, 340, 342,
411: March 1885
COLLECTION Amsterdam, Rijksmuseum Vincent
van Gogh [Vincent van Gogh Foundation, inv
nr F 1146]

F 1147 HEAD OF A YOUNG PEASANT: FULL
FACE, SMOKING A PIPE

Pen and black chalk [old Dutch paper, laid, with
watermark: v.d. L.] 32.5 × 21 [12¾ × 8¼]
Nuenen March 1885
LITERATURE Vanbeselaere 1937, pp 264, 340, 342,
411: March 1885
COLLECTION Amsterdam, Rijksmuseum Vincent
van Gogh [Vincent van Gogh Foundation, inv
nr F 1147]

F 1147

F 1146

F 1148

F 1149

F 1150 recto

F 1150 verso

F 1152 recto

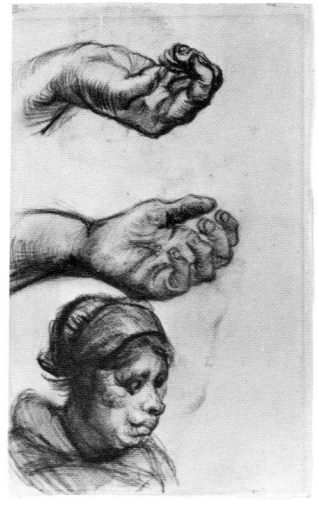

F 1152 verso

F 1151

F 1155

F 1148 HEAD OF A PEASANT WOMAN: FULL FACE

Black chalk, pen and wash 13 × 10 [5¼ × 4]
Compare painting F 146a, drawings F 1193 [same model] and F 1224 [perhaps the same model]
Nuenen December 1884 or shortly later
LETTERS 390 [mid-December] See F 80
394 [February 1885] and 395 [1 March] See F 69
LITERATURE Vanbeselaere 1937, pp 261, 340-1, 411
COLLECTION Formerly Amsterdam, C. M. van Gogh Art Gallery
Present owner unknown

F 1149 HEAD OF A PEASANT WOMAN WITH DARK CAP: FULL FACE

Pencil, pen and ink [Dutch laid paper] 10 × 9 [4 × 3½]
Compare paintings F 74, F 75, F 146 and drawing F 1193a [same model]
Nuenen December 1884
LETTER 391 [1 January 1885] '*In two or three days you will receive twelve little pen-and-ink drawings after studies of heads.*'
LITERATURE Vanbeselaere 1937, pp 261, 340-1, 411
EDITORS' COMMENT Little pen-and-ink drawings belonging to this series are F 1149, F 1150 recto, F 1171, F 1172, F 1173, F 1174, F 1176, F 1177, F 1198 and F 1200. There are some more small pen-and-ink drawings of this period, but they seem to be of a different type: F 1148 and F 1193 [black pencil with some ink] and F 1178 [completely different in style].
COLLECTION Amsterdam, Rijksmuseum Vincent van Gogh [Vincent van Gogh Foundation, inv nr F 1149]

F 1150 recto HEAD OF A PEASANT WOMAN: FACING LEFT

Pen and ink, background washed 12.5 × 8 [5 × 3¼]
Compare sketch in letter 392, painting F 132 and drawing F 1151 [same model]
Nuenen December 1884
LETTER 391 [1 January 1885] See F 1149
LITERATURE Vanbeselaere 1937, pp 261, 341, 411
EDITORS' COMMENT See F 1149
COLLECTION Amsterdam, Rijksmuseum Vincent van Gogh [Vincent van Gogh Foundation, inv nr F 1150]

F 1150 verso SKETCH OF TWO PERSONS

Pencil
Probably Nuenen
LITERATURE Not in Vanbeselaere 1937

F 1151 STUDIES OF THE HEADS OF TWO WOMEN; A PEASANT WALKING

Pen and ink, lightly washed [white laid paper] 16.5 × 10 [6½ × 4]
Compare sketch in letter 392, painting F 132 and drawing F 1150 recto [same model as head to the right]
Nuenen December 1884
LETTER 391 [1 January 1885] See F 1149
LITERATURE Vanbeselaere 1937, pp 261, 332, 341, 411
COLLECTION Otterlo, Rijksmuseum Kröller-Müller, inv nr 1042-28, cat van Gogh 1970, nr 148

F 1152 recto [formerly F 1152 verso] STUDY OF A RIGHT AND LEFT HAND; HEAD OF A PEASANT

Black chalk, stumped [Dutch laid paper with watermark: Pro Patria – Concordia res parvae

crescunt] 16.5 × 20 [6½ × 8]
Nuenen April 1885
LITERATURE Not in Vanbeselaere 1937
COLLECTION Amsterdam, Rijksmuseum Vincent
van Gogh [Vincent van Gogh Foundation, inv
nr F 1152]

F 1152 verso [formerly F 1152 recto]
THATCHED FARM IN THE EVENING

Black chalk
Nuenen November 1885
LITERATURE Vanbeselaere 1937, pp 277, 411:
October-November 1885
EDITORS' COMMENT The Stichting Historisch
Boerderij-Onderzoek in Arnhem has kindly
informed us that the type of farm depicted points
without any doubt to Brabant.

F 1153 recto STUDY OF HANDS

Black chalk [Dutch laid paper with watermark:
v.d.L.] 21 × 34.5 [8¼ × 13½]
Nuenen April 1885
LITERATURE Vanbeselaere 1937, pp 267, 411:
April 1885
COLLECTION Amsterdam, Rijksmuseum Vincent
van Gogh [Vincent van Gogh Foundation, inv
nr F 1153]

F 1153 verso STILL LIFE WITH HEARTH
KETTLE; COTTAGE WITH A PEASANT

Black chalk
Compare F 1349 verso [same kettle]
Nuenen April 1885
LITERATURE Not in Faille 1928 or Vanbeselaere
1937

F 1154 STUDY OF A RIGHT AND A LEFT HAND

Pencil [Dutch laid paper with watermark: Pro
Patria – Concordia res parvae crescent] 21 × 34.5
[8¼ × 13½]
Nuenen January-February 1885
LETTER 393 [about 24 January] '*I am working at
various heads and hands all the time – I have also
drawn them again…*'
LITERATURE Vanbeselaere 1937, pp 267, 411:
April-May 1885
COLLECTION Amsterdam, Rijksmuseum Vincent
van Gogh [Vincent van Gogh Foundation, inv
nr F 1154]

F 1155 STUDY OF HANDS AND ARMS

Black chalk [Dutch laid paper with watermark:
v.d.L.] 20 × 33 [8 × 13]
Nuenen April 1885
LITERATURE Vanbeselaere 1937, pp 266, 411:
April 1885
COLLECTION Amsterdam, Rijksmuseum Vincent
van Gogh [Vincent van Gogh Foundation, inv
nr F 1155]

F 1153 recto

F 1154

F 1153 verso

F 1156 recto

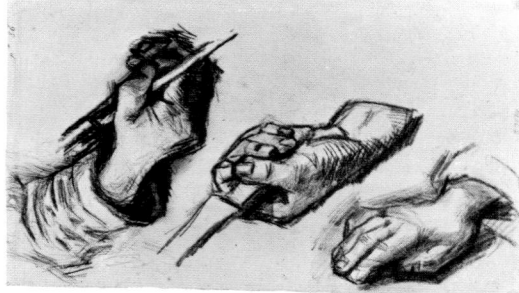

F 1156 verso

F 1158 recto

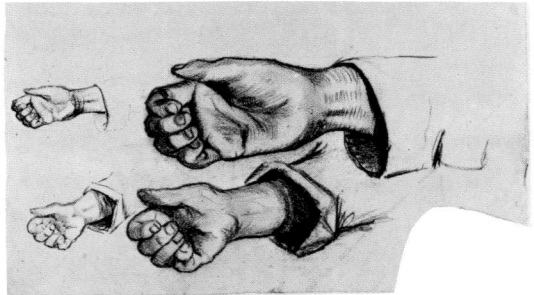

F 1158 verso

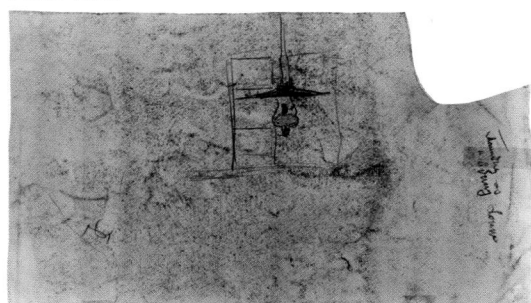

F 1159 recto

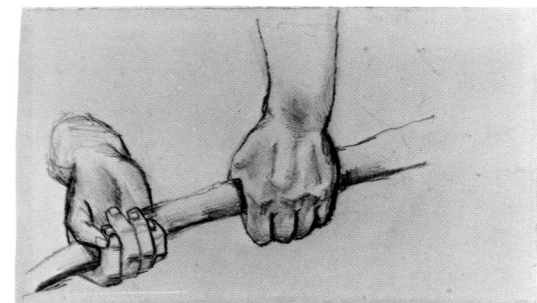

F 1159 verso

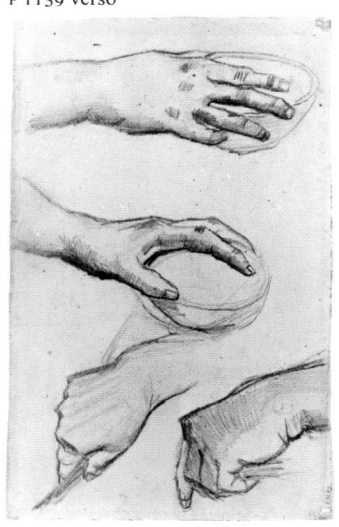

F 1161 recto

F 1161 verso

F 1157

F 1156 recto STUDY OF THREE HANDS, TWO OF THEM HOLDING A STICK

Black chalk [Dutch laid paper with watermark: Pro Patria–Concordia res parvae crescunt] 29.5 × 33 [11½ × 13]
Nuenen January-March 1885
LETTER 393 [about 24 January] See F 1154
LITERATURE Vanbeselaere 1937, pp 262, 340, 411: January 1885
COLLECTION Amsterdam, Rijksmuseum Vincent van Gogh [Vincent van Gogh Foundation, inv nr F 1156]

F 1156 verso HEAD OF A YOUNG PEASANT: FULL FACE

Black chalk
Nuenen January-March 1885
LITERATURE Vanbeselaere 1937, p 262

F 1157 STUDY OF A RIGHT HAND WITH A KETTLE, [for the final version of THE POTATO EATERS]

Black chalk [Dutch laid paper with watermark: v.d.L.] 21 × 34.5 [8¼ × 13½]
Compare F 82. See there for other comparisons
Nuenen April 1885, later than painting F 78
LITERATURE Vanbeselaere 1937, pp 266, 411: April 1885
COLLECTION Amsterdam, Rijksmuseum Vincent van Gogh [Vincent van Gogh Foundation, inv nr F 1157]

F 1158 recto STUDY OF FOUR RIGHT HANDS

Black chalk, pen and brown ink [Dutch laid paper with watermark: v.d.L.] 21 × 34.5 [8¼ × 13½]
Nuenen March 1885
LETTER 393 [about 24 January] See F 1154
LITERATURE Vanbeselaere 1937, pp 262, 340, 411: January 1885
COLLECTION Amsterdam, Rijksmuseum Vincent van Gogh [Vincent van Gogh Foundation, inv nr F 1158]

F 1158 verso SKETCH OF A LAMP HANGING BEFORE A WINDOW [sketch for THE POTATO EATERS]

Pencil
Annotated in black chalk: Maandag as…daag Louw
Compare F 82
Nuenen March 1885
LITERATURE Not in Faille 1928 or Vanbeselaere 1937

F 1159 recto STUDY OF TWO HANDS HOLDING A STICK

Pencil [Dutch laid paper with watermark: v.d.L.] 20 × 33 [8 × 13]
Nuenen January-March 1885
LETTER 393 [about 24 January] See F 1154
LITERATURE Vanbeselaere 1937, pp 267, 411: April-May 1885
COLLECTION Amsterdam, Rijksmuseum Vincent van Gogh [Vincent van Gogh Foundation, inv nr F 1159]

F 1159 verso STUDY OF FOUR HANDS, TWO OF THEM HOLDING A CUP

Pencil
Nuenen January-March 1885
LITERATURE Vanbeselaere 1937, p 267

F 1160 recto and verso STUDY OF A LEFT ARM; STUDY OF A RIGHT ARM
Probably Antwerp period; see after F 1361

F 1161 recto STUDY OF THREE HANDS, TWO OF THEM WITH A FORK [for the final version of THE POTATO EATERS]

Black chalk [Dutch laid paper with watermark: Pro Patria – Concordia res parvae crescunt] 20 × 33 [8 × 13]
Compare F 82. See there for other comparisons
Nuenen April 1885, later than F 78
LITERATURE Vanbeselaere 1937, pp 266, 411: April 1885
COLLECTION Amsterdam, Rijksmuseum Vincent van Gogh [Vincent van Gogh Foundation, inv nr F 1161]

F 1161 verso SKETCH OF AN INTERIOR [background of THE POTATO EATERS] AND COMPOSITION SKETCH OF THE POTATO EATERS

Compare F 77, F 78 and F 82. See F 82 for other comparisons
Nuenen April 1885
LITERATURE Vanbeselaere 1937, p 266

F 1162 STUDY OF HANDS

Pencil [Dutch laid paper with watermark: v.d.L.] 35 × 21 [13¾ × 8¼]
Nuenen January-March 1885
LETTER 393 [about 24 January] See F 1154
LITERATURE Vanbeselaere 1937, pp 267, 411: April-May 1885
COLLECTION Amsterdam, Rijksmuseum Vincent van Gogh [Vincent van Gogh Foundation, inv nr F 1162]

F 1163 STUDY OF THREE HANDS [not reproduced]

Black chalk 41.5 × 35 [16¼ × 13¾]
Nuenen January-March 1885
LETTER 393 [about 24 January] See F 1154
LITERATURE Faille 1928, 1163 [the drawing, reproduced under nr 1163 is in fact F 1167 verso]
EDITORS' COMMENT Drawing F 1163 is not known to the editors and could be traced in the files of the Vincent van Gogh Foundation
COLLECTION Amsterdam, Rijksmuseum Vincent van Gogh [Vincent van Gogh Foundation, inv nr F 1163]

F 1164 recto STUDY OF FOUR HANDS

Pencil [Dutch laid paper with watermark: v.d.L.] 21 × 35 [8¼ × 13¾]
Nuenen January-March 1885
LETTER 393 [about 24 January] See F 1154
LITERATURE Vanbeselaere 1937, pp 262, 340, 411: January 1885
COLLECTION Amsterdam, Rijksmuseum Vincent van Gogh [Vincent van Gogh Foundation, inv nr F 1164]

F 1164 verso STUDY OF THREE HANDS

Pencil, pen and brown ink 35 × 21 [13¾ × 8¼]
Nuenen January-March 1885
LITERATURE Vanbeselaere 1937, pp 262, 340

F 1165 TWO HANDS HOLDING A BOWL

Black chalk [Dutch laid paper with watermark: v.d.L] 20.5 × 34.5 [8 × 13½]
Nuenen January-March 1885
LETTER 393 [about 24 January] See F 1154
LITERATURE Vanbeselaere 1937, pp 267, 411: April-May 1885
COLLECTION Amsterdam, Rijksmuseum Vincent van Gogh [Vincent van Gogh Foundation, inv nr F 1165]

F 1162
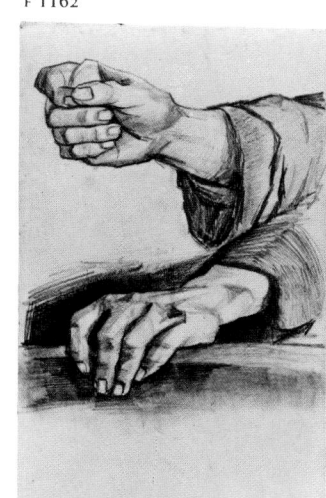

F 1164 recto
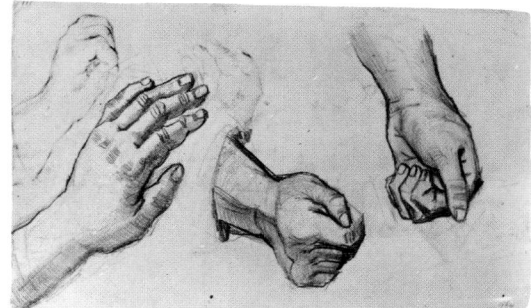

F 1164 verso
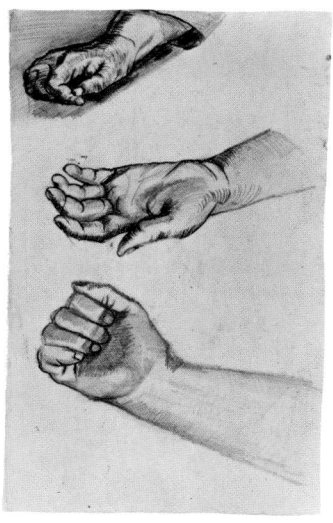

F 1165

F 1166

F 1167 recto

F 1167 verso

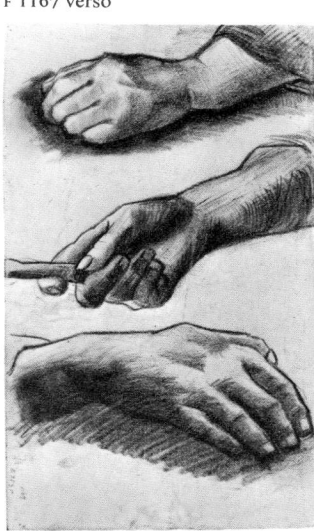

F 1169

F 1170

F 1166 STUDY OF HANDS HOLDING A
SHOVEL

Black chalk [Dutch laid paper with watermark:
v.d.L.] 21 × 34.5 [8¼ × 13½]
Nuenen April 1885 or shortly later
LITERATURE Vanbeselaere 1937, pp 267, 411:
April-May 1885
COLLECTION Amsterdam, Rijksmuseum Vincent
van Gogh [Vincent van Gogh Foundation, inv
nr F 1166]

F 1167 recto STUDY OF HANDS IN REPOSE

Black chalk [Dutch laid paper with watermark:
Pro Patria – Concordia res parvae crescunt] 21 × 34
[8¼ × 13½]
Compare painting F 126 [includes this motif]
Nuenen January-March 1885
LETTER 393 [about 24 January] See F 1154
LITERATURE Vanbeselaere 1937, pp 268, 411:
April-May 1885
COLLECTION Amsterdam, Rijksmuseum Vincent
van Gogh [Vincent van Gogh Foundation, inv
nr F 1167]

F 1167 verso STUDY OF THREE HANDS

Black chalk 34 × 21 [13½ × 8¼]
Nuenen January-March 1885
LITERATURE Not in Faille 1928 or Vanbeselaere
1937
EDITORS' COMMENT As far as can be made out
from the reproduction in Faille 1928, F 1167 verso
is reproduced as nr 1163

F 1168 recto STUDY OF A HAND CLASPING A
STICK; AN INTERIOR WITH FOUR PERSONS

Black chalk [old Dutch paper, laid, with watermark: Concordia res parvae crescunt and v.d.L.]
42 × 34.5 [16½ × 13½]
Nuenen April 1885 or shortly later
LITERATURE Vincent van Gogh, Lettres à Bernard,
1911, plate XXVI. Vanbeselaere 1937, pp 268, 390,
411: April-May 1885
COLLECTION Amsterdam, Rijksmuseum Vincent
van Gogh [Vincent van Gogh Foundation, inv
nr F 1168]

F 1168 verso THREE HANDS HOLDING A
STICK

Black chalk
Nuenen April 1885 or shortly later
LITERATURE Vanbeselaere 1937, pp 268, 390

F 1169 HEAD OF A PEASANT WOMAN: LEFT
PROFILE

Black chalk 26 × 21 [10¼ × 8¼]
Nuenen February-March 1885
LITERATURE Vanbeselaere 1937, pp 265, 411
COLLECTION Dallas, L. Pollock

F 1170 HEAD OF A PEASANT WOMAN:
FACING RIGHT, AGAINST A DARK
BACKGROUND

Black chalk 34.5 × 20.5 [13½ × 8]
Compare paintings F 134, F 135 and F 136 [same
model]
Nuenen December 1884 or shortly later
LETTERS 390 [mid-December] See F 80
394 [February 1885] and 395 [1 March] See F 69
LITERATURE Vanbeselaere 1937, pp 264, 411:
January-March 1885
COLLECTION Amsterdam, Rijksmuseum Vincent
van Gogh [Vincent van Gogh Foundation, inv
nr F 1170]

F 1171 HEAD OF A PEASANT WOMAN WITH
WHITE CAP: THREE QUARTERS TO THE LEFT

Pen and wash [vergé paper] 16 × 10 [6¼ × 4]
Signed in lower left: Vincent
Compare painting F 156 [same model]
Nuenen December 1884
LETTER 391 [1 January 1885] See F 1149
LITERATURE Vanbeselaere 1937, pp 261, 265, 341,
411: April-June 1885
EDITORS' COMMENT See F 1149
COLLECTION Amsterdam, Rijksmuseum Vincent
van Gogh [Vincent van Gogh Foundation, inv
nr F 1171]

F 1172 HEAD OF A PEASANT WOMAN

Pen 8 × 6.5 [3¼ × 2½]
Compare paintings F 137, F 138, drawings F 1173
and F 1175 [same model]
Nuenen December 1884
LETTER 391 [1 January 1885] See F 1149
LITERATURE Vanbeselaere 1937, pp 261, 265, 341,
411: April-June 1885
EDITORS' COMMENT See F 1149
COLLECTION Amsterdam, Rijksmuseum Vincent
van Gogh [Vincent van Gogh Foundation, inv
nr F 1172]

F 1168 recto

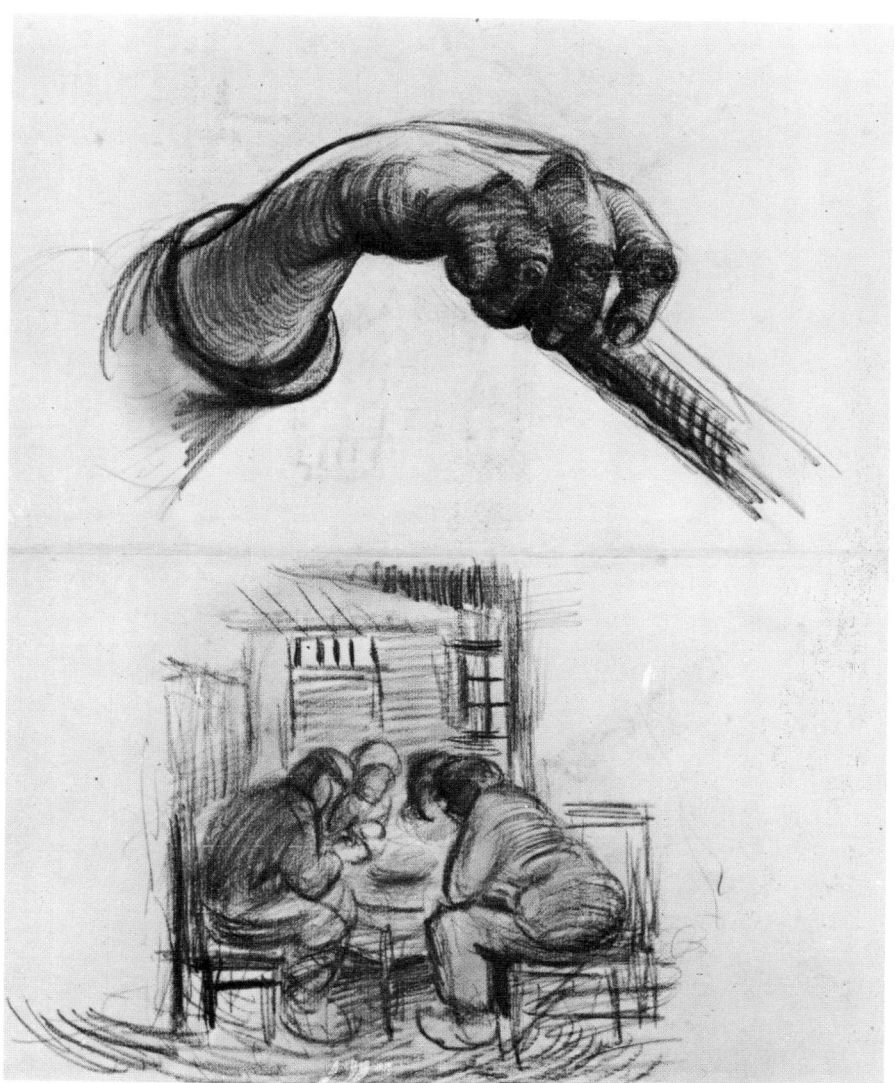

F 1171

F 1172

F 1168 verso

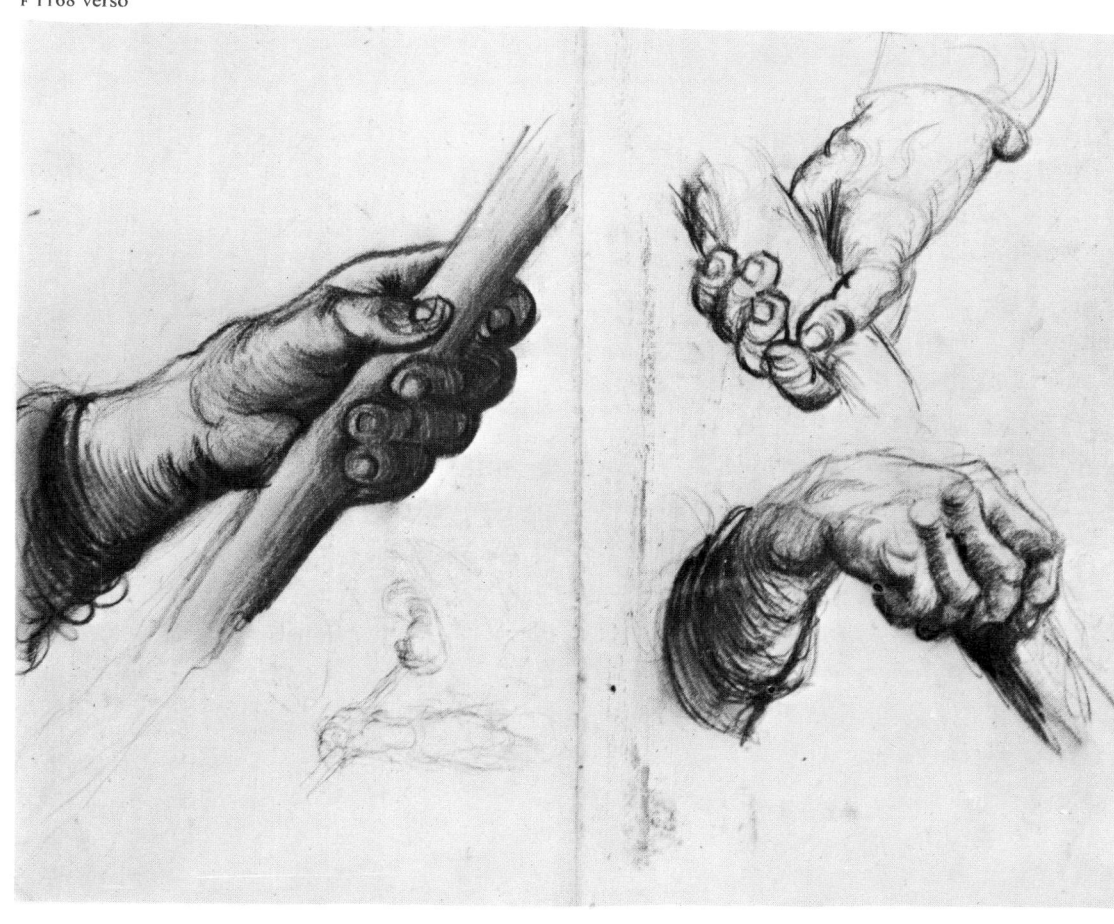

F 1173

F 1174

F 1175

F 1176

F 1177

F 1178

F 1180

F 1182

F 1173 HEAD OF A PEASANT WOMAN: THREE QUARTERS TO THE RIGHT

Pen [vergé paper] 14.5 × 10 [5¾ × 4]
Signed in lower left: Vincent
Compare paintings F 137, F 138, drawings F 1172
and F 1175 [same model]
Nuenen December 1884
LETTERS 389 [14 December] See F 136a
391 [1 January 1885] See F 1149
LITERATURE Vanbeselaere 1937, pp 261, 341, 411
EDITORS' COMMENT See F 1149
COLLECTION Amsterdam, Rijksmuseum Vincent
van Gogh [Vincent van Gogh Foundation, inv
nr F 1173]

**F 1174 HEAD OF A PEASANT WOMAN:
FACING RIGHT**

Pen 16 × 10.5 [6¼ × 4¼]
Compare painting F 144 [same model]
Nuenen December 1884
LETTER 391 [1 January 1885] See F 1149
LITERATURE Vanbeselaere 1937, pp 263, 342, 411:
January-March 1885
EDITORS' COMMENT See F 1149
COLLECTION Bentveld, Netherlands, P. D. San-
derse [acquired 1960]

**F 1175 HEAD OF A PEASANT WOMAN: FULL
FACE**

Pencil and black chalk 32 × 19 [12½ × 7½]
Compare paintings F 137, F 138, drawings F 1172
and F 1173 [same model]
Nuenen December 1884 or shortly later
LETTERS 390 [mid-December] See F 80
394 [February 1885] and 395 [1 March] See F 69
LITERATURE Vanbeselaere 1937, pp 264, 342, 411:
January-March 1885
COLLECTION New York, H. Levine [acquired
1955]

**F 1176 HEAD OF A PEASANT WOMAN WITH
DARK CAP**

Pen and pencil 12 × 9 [4¾ × 3½]
Reproduced with letter 389
Compare painting F 136a [same model]
Nuenen December 1884 or shortly later
LETTER 389 [14 December] See F 136a
LITERATURE Vanbeselaere 1937, pp 261, 341, 411:
December 1884
EDITORS' COMMENT See F 1149
COLLECTION Amsterdam, Rijksmuseum Vincent
van Gogh [Vincent van Gogh Foundation, inv
nr F 1176]

**F 1177 HEAD OF A PEASANT WOMAN:
FACING LEFT**

Pencil, pen and brown ink, washed [ordinary
drawing paper] 14 × 10.5 [5½ × 4¼]
Signed in lower left: Vincent
Compare painting F 154 [same model]
Nuenen December 1884 or shortly later
LETTERS 390 [mid-December] See F 80
394 [February 1885] and 395 [1 March] See F 69
LITERATURE Vanbeselaere 1937, pp 264, 341, 411:
April 1885. Cat van Gogh 1966, Rijksmuseum
Kröller-Müller, nr 171: after painting F 154
EDITORS' COMMENT See F 1149
COLLECTION Amsterdam, Rijksmuseum Vincent
van Gogh [Vincent van Gogh Foundation, inv
nr F 1177]

F 1178 HEAD OF A PEASANT WOMAN: RIGHT
PROFILE

Pen and ink, washed [ordinary drawing paper]
17.5 × 13.5 [7 × 5¼]
Compare paintings F 133, F 153 and drawing F 1185
[same model]
Nuenen December 1884 or shortly later
LETTERS 390 [mid-December] See F 80
394 [February 1885] and 395 [1 March] See F 69
LITERATURE Vanbeselaere 1937, pp 265, 268, 342,
411
COLLECTION Otterlo, Rijksmuseum Kröller-
Müller, inv nr 1045-28, cat van Gogh 1970, nr 142

F 1179 SIEN WITH SHAWL, AT THE TABLE
The Hague period; see after F 1093

F 1180 HEAD OF A PEASANT WOMAN WITH
WHITE CAP: FULL FACE

Black chalk 41.5 × 29 [16½ × 11½]
Signed in lower right: Vincent
Compare painting F 143, drawings F 1189 and
F 1192 [same model]
Nuenen December 1884 or shortly later
LETTERS 390 [mid-December] See F 80
394 [February 1885] and 395 [1 March] See F 69
LITERATURE Vincent van Gogh, Lettres à Bernard,
1911, plate XXIX. Vanbeselaere 1937, pp 263, 341,
411: October-December 1884
COLLECTION Formerly Paris, Georges Bernheim
Art Gallery
Present owner unknown

F 1181 HEAD OF A PEASANT WOMAN WITH
WHITE CAP: FACING RIGHT

Black chalk, pen and ink, washed 29.5 × 20
[11¾ × 8]
Compare painting F 144a and drawing F 1190 [same
model]
Nuenen February-April 1885
LITERATURE Vanbeselaere 1937, pp 264, 342, 411:
March 1885
COLLECTION Switzerland, D. Bührle

F 1182 HEAD OF A PEASANT WOMAN: RIGHT
PROFILE

Black chalk [ordinary wove paper] 40 × 33
[15¾ × 13]
Nuenen May-June 1885
LITERATURE Vanbeselaere 1937, pp 264, 342, 411:
March 1885
COLLECTION Amsterdam, Rijksmuseum Vincent
van Gogh [Vincent van Gogh Foundation, inv
nr F 1182]

F 1183 HEAD OF A PEASANT WOMAN:
FACING RIGHT

Black chalk 31 × 21 [12¼ × 8¼]
Compare F 1184 [same model]
Nuenen February-March 1885
LITERATURE Vanbeselaere 1937, pp 264, 342, 411:
March 1885
COLLECTION Dallas, L. Pollock

F 1184 HEAD OF A PEASANT WOMAN: THREE
QUARTERS TO THE RIGHT

Pencil [Dutch laid paper with watermark: Pro
Patria – Concordia res parvae crescunt] 33.5 × 21
[13¼ × 8¼]
Compare F 1183 [same model]
Nuenen February-March 1885
LITERATURE Vincent van Gogh, Lettres à Bernard,
1911, plate XVIII. Vanbeselaere 1937, pp 264, 342,
411: March 1885

COLLECTION Amsterdam, Rijksmuseum Vincent
van Gogh [Vincent van Gogh Foundation, inv
nr F 1184]

F 1185 HEAD OF A PEASANT WOMAN WITH
BONNET: FACING RIGHT

Black chalk [Ingres paper with watermark: v.d.L.]
34 × 20 [13½ × 8]
Compare paintings F 133, F 153 and drawing F 1178
[same model]
Nuenen February-April 1885
LITERATURE Faille 1928, nr 1185, not reproduced.
Vanbeselaere 1937, p 411
COLLECTION Amsterdam, Rijksmuseum Vincent
van Gogh [Vincent van Gogh Foundation, inv
nr F 1185]

F 1183

F 1184

F 1185

F 1181

F 1186

F 1187 recto

F 1187 verso

F 1188

F 1189

F 1186 HEAD OF A PEASANT WOMAN

Black chalk [old Dutch paper, laid, with water-mark: Concordia res parvae crescunt] 30 × 18
[11¾ × 7]
Nuenen May 1885
LITERATURE Faille 1928, nr 1186, not reproduced.
Vanbeselaere 1937, p 411
COLLECTION Amsterdam, Rijksmuseum Vincent
van Gogh [Vincent van Gogh Foundation, inv
nr F 1186]

F 1187 recto PEASANT WOMAN STANDING:
SEEN FROM THE BACK

Black chalk [Ingres paper] 35 × 21 [13¾ × 8¼]
Nuenen summer 1885
LITERATURE Vanbeselaere 1937, pp 271, 411:
May-June 1885
COLLECTION Amsterdam, Rijksmuseum Vincent
van Gogh [Vincent van Gogh Foundation, inv
nr F 1187]

F 1187 verso PEASANT WOMAN STANDING:
FACING RIGHT

Black chalk
Nuenen summer 1885
LITERATURE Not in Faille 1928 or Vanbeselaere
1937

F 1188 PEASANT WOMAN: FACING LEFT

Black chalk, stumped [Dutch laid paper with water-mark: Concordia res parvae crescunt] 30.5 × 19
[12 × 7½]
Nuenen May-June 1885
LITERATURE Vanbeselaere 1937, pp 271, 411:
May-June 1885
COLLECTION Amsterdam, Rijksmuseum Vincent
van Gogh [Vincent van Gogh Foundation, inv
nr F 1188]

F 1189 PEASANT WOMAN WITH WHITE CAP,
SEATED: SEEN FROM THE FRONT

Pencil, pen and brown ink [old Dutch paper, laid,
with watermark: Concordia res parvae crescunt]
32 × 20.5 [12½ × 8]
Compare painting F 143, drawings F 1180 and
F 1192 [same model]
Nuenen December 1884 or shortly later
LETTERS 390 [mid-December] See F 80
394 [February 1885] and 395 [1 March] See F 69
LITERATURE Vanbeselaere 1937, pp 264, 411:
January-March 1885
COLLECTION Amsterdam, Rijksmuseum Vincent
van Gogh [Vincent van Gogh Foundation, inv
nr F 1189]

F 1190 PEASANT WOMAN WITH WHITE CAP,
SEATED: FACING RIGHT

Pencil, pen and brown ink [Ingres paper with water-mark: v. d. L.] 35 × 21 [13¾ × 8¼]
Compare painting F 144a and drawing F 1181 [same
model]
Nuenen February-April 1885
LITERATURE Vanbeselaere 1937, pp 264, 411:
January-March 1885
COLLECTION Amsterdam, Rijksmuseum Vincent
van Gogh [Vincent van Gogh Foundation, inv
nr F 1190]

F 1191 PEASANT WOMAN WITH DARK CAP,
SEATED: SEEN FROM THE FRONT

Pencil [Ingres paper with watermark: v.d.L.] 35 × 21
[13¾ × 8¼]
Nuenen December 1884 or shortly later

LETTERS 390 [mid-December] See F 80
394 [February 1885] and 395 [1 March] See F 69
LITERATURE Vanbeselaere 1937, pp 263, 411:
October-December 1884
COLLECTION Amsterdam, Rijksmuseum Vincent
van Gogh [Vincent van Gogh Foundation, inv
nr F 1191]

F 1192 PEASANT WOMAN WITH WHITE CAP:
FULL FACE

Pencil, black chalk, washed [Ingres paper with
watermark: v.d.L] 34.5 × 21 [13¼ × 8¼]
Compare painting F 143, drawings F 1180 and
F 1189 [same model]
Nuenen December 1884 or shortly later
LETTERS 390 [mid-December] See F 80
394 [February 1885] and 395 [1 March] See F 69
LITERATURE Vanbeselaere 1937, pp 263, 341, 411:
October-December 1884
COLLECTION Amsterdam, Rijksmuseum Vincent
van Gogh [Vincent van Gogh Foundation, inv
nr F 1192]

F 1193 PEASANT WOMAN WITH A WHITE
CAP

Black chalk, pen and washed 11.5 × 8 [4½ × 3¼]
Compare painting F 146a, drawings F 1148 [same
model] and F 1224 [perhaps the same model]
Nuenen December 1884 or shortly later
LETTERS 390 [mid-December] See F 80
394 [February 1885] and 395 [1 March] See F 69
LITERATURE Vanbeselaere 1937, pp 261, 411
COLLECTION Amersfoort, Netherlands,
Miss R. Nieweg

F 1193a HEAD OF A PEASANT WOMAN

Pencil, pen and wash 12.5 × 9 [5 × 3½]
Compare paintings F 74, F 75, F 146 and drawing
F 1149 [same model]
Nuenen December 1884 or shortly later
LETTERS 390 [mid-December] See F 80
394 [February 1885] and 395 [1 March] See F 69
LITERATURE Not mentioned in Faille 1928 or
Vanbeselaere 1937
COLLECTION Southampton, New York, Mr and
Mrs Clifford Michel

F 1190

F 1191

F 1192

F 1193

F 1193a

F 1194

F 1194a

F 1195 recto

F 1195 verso

F 1196

F 1194 PEASANT WOMAN: FACING RIGHT

Water color 25 × 18 [9¾ × 7]
Nuenen April-May 1885
LETTER 400 [13 or 14 April] '*I have a great mind to do water colors and drawings again, and as soon as I live in my studio, I shall find time for it in the evening.*'
LITERATURE Vanbeselaere 1937, pp 263, 342, 411: October-December 1884
COLLECTION London, Jacques O'Hana Ltd Collection

F 1194a HEAD OF A PEASANT WOMAN [study for THE POTATO EATERS]

Black chalk 23 × 17 [9 × 6¾] Damaged
Compare painting F 82 [the figure on the right: same model]
Nuenen April 1885
LITERATURE Not in Faille 1928 or Vanbeselaere 1937. Expertised under the auspices of the Expertise Instituut, Amsterdam [1957]
COLLECTION Formerly Amsterdam, M. L. de Boer Art Gallery [until 1959]
Present owner unknown

F 1195 recto STUDY OF A WOMAN WITH A SHAWL

Black chalk [Dutch laid paper with watermark: Pro Patria – Concordia res parvae crescunt] 35 × 21 [13¾ × 8¼]
Nuenen September 1885
LITERATURE Album Hidde Nijland Collection 1905, plate 76. Vanbeselaere 1937, pp 276, 411: September-October 1885
COLLECTION Otterlo, Rijksmuseum Kröller-Müller, inv nr 1006-28, cat van Gogh 1970, nr 146

F 1195 verso WOMAN WITH SHAWL, BEARING A SACK: WALKING TO THE LEFT

Black chalk
Annotated in lower right: verz. H.N.
Nuenen September 1885
LITERATURE Not in Faille 1928 or Vanbeselaere 1937

F 1196 STUDY OF A WOMAN WITH SKIRT OVER HER HEAD

Charcoal [Dutch laid paper with watermark: v.d.L.] 35 × 21 [13¾ × 8¼]
Nuenen September 1885
LITERATURE Album Hidde Nijland Collection 1905, plate 73. Vanbeselaere 1937, pp 276, 411: September-October 1885
COLLECTION Otterlo, Rijksmuseum Kröller-Müller, inv nr 1003-28, cat van Gogh 1970, nr 135

F 1197 OLD WOMAN WITH A SHAWL

Black chalk, stumped [Dutch laid paper with indistinct watermark: probably Pro patria – Concordia res parvae crescunt] 34.5 × 20.5 [13½ × 8]
Nuenen September 1885
LITERATURE Faille 1928, nr 1197, not reproduced. Vanbeselaere 1937, p 411
COLLECTION Amsterdam, Rijksmuseum Vincent van Gogh [Vincent van Gogh Foundation, inv nr F 1197]

F 1198 HEAD OF A PEASANT [study for THE POTATO EATERS]

Pen, pencil, black chalk and brown ink, washed [old Dutch paper, laid] 14.5 × 10.5 [5¾ × 4¼]
Signed in lower left: Vincent
Compare paintings F 160a [same model], F 78 and F 82 [model for man in background]. See F 82 for

other comparisons
Nuenen April 1885
LITERATURE Vanbeselaere 1937, pp 264, 341, 344,
411: April 1885
EDITORS' COMMENT See F 1149
COLLECTION Amsterdam, Rijksmuseum Vincent
van Gogh [Vincent van Gogh Foundation, inv
nr F 1198]

F 1199 YOUNG PEASANT WITH A PIPE:
FACING LEFT

Pencil and wash [ordinary laid paper] 39 × 28.5
[15½ × 11¼]
Signed in lower right: Vincent
Nuenen January-March 1885
LITERATURE Vanbeselaere 1937, pp 264, 342, 412:
March 1885
COLLECTION Amsterdam, Rijksmuseum Vincent
van Gogh [Vincent van Gogh Foundation, inv
nr F 1199]

F 1200 HEAD OF A MAN WITH HAT: FACING
RIGHT

Pen and wash 14.5 × 8 [5¾ × 3¼]
Nuenen December 1884 or shortly later
LITERATURE Vanbeselaere 1937, pp 265, 412:
April 1885
EDITORS' COMMENT See F 1149
COLLECTION Amsterdam, Rijksmuseum Vincent
van Gogh [Vincent van Gogh Foundation, inv
nr F 1200]

F 1201 recto PEASANT SEATED: FULL FACE

Black chalk [Dutch laid paper with watermark:
Concordia res parvae crescunt] 33 × 19.5 [13 × 7¾]
Nuenen summer 1885
LITERATURE Vanbeselaere 1937, p 412: summer
1885
COLLECTION Rotterdam, R. W. Wentges

F 1201 verso PEASANT DIGGING: FACING
LEFT

Black chalk
Annotated in upper right: Port. Vincent. Hidde
Nijland
Nuenen summer 1885
LITERATURE Not in Faille 1928 or Vanbeselaere
1937

F 1197

F 1198

F 1200

F 1199

F 1201 recto

F 1201 verso

F 1202

F 1203

F 1205

F 1206

F 1207

F 1207a

F 1208

F 1210

F 1202 WINTER LANDSCAPE WITH FIGURES

Water color 7 × 11 [2¾ × 4¼]
Signed in lower left: Vincent
Sketch erroneously reproduced with letter 374
[Nuenen August 1884] in the American edition of
the letters
Formed a set or part of a set with F 1245
Nuenen probably winter 1884-5
LITERATURE Vanbeselaere 1937, pp 265, 353, 412
COLLECTION Amsterdam, Rijksmuseum Vincent
van Gogh [Vincent van Gogh Foundation, inv
nr F 1202]

F 1203 INTERIOR WITH A PEASANT WOMAN
SEWING: FACING LEFT

Black chalk [Ingres paper with watermark: E.D. &
Cie–P.L. Bas] 39 × 23.5 [15½ × 9¼]
Signed in lower left: Vincent
Nuenen March 1885
LETTER 396 [mid-March] *'I am brooding over a
couple of larger, more elaborate things... I have
studies of heads for it, against the light as well as
turned toward the light, and I have worked several
times already on the complete figure: spooling yarn,
sewing, or peeling potatoes.'*
LITERATURE Album Hidde Nijland Collection
1905, plate 35. Vanbeselaere 1937, pp 265, 393, 412:
summer 1885
COLLECTION Otterlo, Rijksmuseum Kröller-
Müller, inv nr 968-28, cat van Gogh 1970, nr 144

F 1204 INTERIOR WITH A PEASANT WOMAN
SEWING: FACING LEFT

Black chalk, heightened with white [Ingres paper]
24.5 × 28.5 [9¾ × 11¼]
Nuenen March 1885
LETTER 396 [mid-March] See F 1203
LITERATURE Vanbeselaere 1937, pp 265, 271, 412
EDITORS' COMMENT The literature and
provenance under this number in the 1928 edition
pertain to the present nr 1207a.
COLLECTION Amsterdam, Rijksmuseum Vincent
van Gogh [Vincent van Gogh Foundation, inv
nr F 1204]

F 1205 PEASANT WOMAN SEWING: FACING
LEFT

Black chalk [Ingres paper] 34.5 × 28 [13½ × 11]
Compare painting F 157
Nuenen May-June 1885
LETTER 396 [mid-March] See F 1203
LITERATURE Vanbeselaere 1937, pp 265, 271, 412:
May-June 1885
COLLECTION Amsterdam, Rijksmuseum Vincent
van Gogh [Vincent van Gogh Foundation, inv
nr F 1205]

F 1206 INTERIOR WITH A PEASANT WOMAN
SEWING: FACING RIGHT

Black chalk [Ingres paper with watermark: E.D. &
Cie–P.L. Bas] 29 × 26 [11½ × 10¼]
Signed in lower right: Vincent
Nuenen March 1885
LETTER 396 [mid-March] See F 1203
LITERATURE Album Hidde Nijland Collection
1905, plate 21. Vanbeselaere 1937, pp 271, 412:
May-June 1885
COLLECTION Otterlo, Rijksmuseum Kröller-
Müller, inv nr 955-28, cat van Gogh 1970, nr 157

F 1207 INTERIOR WITH A PEASANT WOMAN
KNITTING: SEEN FROM THE FRONT

Black chalk [Ingres paper, blue-gray color]
28.5 × 22 [11¼ × 8¾]

F 1204

Nuenen March 1885
Compare F 1207a
LETTER 396 [mid-March] see F 1203
LITERATURE Album Hidde Nijland Collection
1905, plate 41. Vanbeselaere 1937, pp 265, 412
COLLECTION Otterlo, Rijksmuseum Kröller-
Müller, inv nr 974-28, cat van Gogh 1970, nr 158

F 1207a INTERIOR WITH A PEASANT WOMAN
KNITTING: SEEN FROM THE FRONT

Black chalk [Ingres paper] 32.6 × 25.4 [12¾ × 10]
Annotated in lower right: dessin de Vincent van
Gogh
Compare F 1207
Nuenen March 1885
LETTER 396 [mid-March] See F 1203
LITERATURE Vincent van Gogh, Lettres à Bernard,
1911, plate XXXI. S. Meller, Die graphischen
Künste 1919, p 31 [with reproduction]. L. Éber, Ars
Una 1923, p 21 [with reproduction]. Not in Faille
1928. S. Meller, Ungarische Kunst 1935, p 145
[with reproduction]. Not in Vanbeselaere 1937.
E. Hoffmann, Europa 1923, p 154. D. Pataky, Von
Delacroix bis Picasso, Zeichnungen aus der
Sammlung des Museums ... Budapest, 1958, p 28,
nr 84
COLLECTION Budapest, Museum of Fine Arts,
inv nr Ltsz 1935-2793

F 1208 INTERIOR WITH A PEASANT WOMAN
PEELING POTATOES: SEEN FROM THE
FRONT

Black chalk [Ingres paper with unidentifiable
fragment of a watermark] 29 × 22.5 [11½ × 9]
Compare painting F 145
Nuenen March 1885
LITERATURE Vanbeselaere 1937, pp 265, 412
COLLECTION Amsterdam, Rijksmuseum Vincent
van Gogh [Vincent van Gogh Foundation, inv
nr F 1208]

F 1209 PEASANT WOMAN PEELING
POTATOES
Etten period; see after F 905

F 1210 INTERIOR WITH A PEASANT WOMAN
PEELING POTATOES: FACING LEFT

Black chalk [Ingres paper with watermark:
P.L. Bas] 30 × 22.5 [11¾ × 9]
Nuenen March 1885
LETTER 396 [mid-March] See F 1203
LITERATURE Vanbeselaere 1937, pp 265, 277,
392-3, 412: October-November 1885
COLLECTION Amsterdam, Rijksmuseum Vincent
van Gogh [Vincent van Gogh Foundation, inv
nr F 1210]

F 1211 PEASANT WOMAN BY THE FIRE
PEELING POTATOES [left: fragment of another
woman]

Charcoal and black chalk [Dutch wove paper]
57 × 78.5 [22½ × 31]
Compare paintings F 158, F 176, drawings F 1212,
F 1288, F 1291 [same model in same interior], F 1215,
F 1217 and F 1218 [same interior]
Nuenen March 1885
LETTER 396 [mid-March] See F 1203
LITERATURE Vincent van Gogh – 40 Photo-
collographies d'après ses Tableaux et Dessins,
[1904], nr 12. Vanbeselaere 1937, pp 265, 392, 412
COLLECTION Otterlo, Rijksmuseum Kröller-
Müller, inv nr 257-20, cat van Gogh 1970, nr 125

F 1211

F 1212

F 1215

F 1212 PEASANT WOMAN BY THE FIRE PEELING POTATOES

Black chalk, heightened with water color 27.5 × 25.5 [10¾ × 10]
False signature in lower right: Vincent
Compare paintings F 158, F 176, drawings F 1211, F 1288, F 1291 [same model in same interior], F 1215, F 1217 and F 1218 [same interior]
Nuenen March 1885
LETTER 396 [mid-March] See F 1203
LITERATURE Vanbeselaere 1937, pp 266, 412
COLLECTION Formerly Brussels. A. van Buuren Present owner unknown

F 1213 PEASANT WOMAN PEELING POTATOES
Etten period; see after F 905

F 1214 INTERIOR WITH A PEASANT WOMAN SHELLING PEAS: THREE QUARTERS TO THE RIGHT

Black chalk [ordinary wove paper] 42 × 26 [16½ × 10¼]
Signed in lower left: Vincent
Annotated: Ecosseuse de pois
Nuenen summer 1885
LETTER 422 [mid-August] 'As I told you, I added to this little package of drawings a few new ones, but I shall try to make several more this month, the size of that woman shelling peas, which was the last one I did.'
LITERATURE Vanbeselaere 1937, pp 278, 412: October-November 1885
COLLECTION Amsterdam, Rijksmuseum Vincent van Gogh [Vincent van Gogh Foundation, inv nr F 1214]

F 1215 INTERIOR WITH A PEASANT WOMAN MAKING PANCAKES

Black chalk, heightened with white [Ingres paper with watermark: E.D. & Cie] 29 × 35.5 [11½ × 14]
Compare paintings F 158, F 176, drawings F 1211, F 1212, F 1217, F 1218, F 1288 and F 1291 [same interior]
Nuenen second half of 1885
LITERATURE Vanbeselaere 1937, pp 278, 299, 392-3, 412: October-November 1885
COLLECTION Amsterdam, Rijksmuseum Vincent van Gogh [Vincent van Gogh Foundation, inv nr F 1215]

F 1216 WOMAN BY THE HEARTH
Etten period; see after F 905

F 1217 INTERIOR WITH A WOMAN BY THE FIREPLACE: FACING RIGHT

Black chalk [Ingres paper, blue-gray color, with fragment of watermark: E.D. & Cie–P.L. Bas] 22 × 29.5 [8¾ × 11½]
Compare paintings F 158, F 176, drawings F 1211, F 1212, F 1215, F 1218, F 1288 and F 1291 [same interior]
Nuenen second half of 1885
LITERATURE Album Hidde Nijland Collection 1905, plate 90. Vanbeselaere 1937, pp 278, 299, 392-3, 412: October-November 1885
COLLECTION Otterlo, Rijksmuseum Kröller-Müller, inv nr 1022-28, cat van Gogh 1970, nr 156

F 1218 INTERIOR WITH A WOMAN BY THE FIREPLACE: FACING RIGHT

Black chalk [wove paper with fragment of watermark: [(T.S.) R.Z.] 43.5 × 28.5 [17¼ × 11¼]
Signed in lower right: Vincent
Compare paintings F 158, F 176, drawings F 1211,

F 1212, F 1215, F 1217, F 1288 and F 1291 [same interior]
Nuenen second half of 1885
LITERATURE Album Hidde Nijland Collection 1905, plate 29. Vanbeselaere 1937, pp 278, 299, 392-3, 412: October-November 1885
COLLECTION Otterlo, Rijksmuseum Kröller-Müller, inv nr 963-28, cat van Gogh 1970, nr 155

F 1219 recto INTERIOR WITH A STANDING WOMAN SLICING BREAD: SEEN FROM THE BACK

Black chalk, pen and brown ink and wash [Ingres paper] 30 × 22 [11¾ × 8¾]
Nuenen March 1885
LETTER 396 [mid-March] See F 1203
LITERATURE Vanbeselaere 1937, pp 271, 412: May-June 1885
COLLECTION Amsterdam, Rijksmuseum Vincent van Gogh [Vincent van Gogh Foundation, inv nr F 1219]

F 1219 verso WOMAN SLICING BREAD

Black chalk
Nuenen March 1885
LITERATURE Not in Faille 1928 or Vanbeselaere 1937

F 1220 INTERIOR WITH PEASANT WOMAN SEWING: SEEN FROM THE FRONT

Black chalk [Ingres paper with watermark: E.D. & Cie (–P.L. Bas)] 44 × 30 [17¼ × 11¾]
Nuenen March 1885
LETTER 396 [mid-March] See F 1203
LITERATURE Album Hidde Nijland Collection 1905, plate 100. Idem 1907, plate 6. Vanbeselaere 1937, pp 278, 380, 392-3, 412: October-November 1885
COLLECTION Otterlo, Rijksmuseum Kröller-Müller, inv nr 1031-28, cat van Gogh 1970, nr 154

F 1221 OLD PEASANT WOMAN MENDING A MAN'S SHIRT
Etten period; see after F 905

F 1214

F 1217

F 1218

F 1219 verso

F 1219 recto

F 1220

F 1222

F 1225

F 1223

F 1226

F 1222 INTERIOR WITH A PEASANT WOMAN BY THE FIREPLACE

Water color [Ingres paper] 34.5 × 44.5 [13½ × 17½]
Signed in lower right: Vincent
Nuenen second half of 1885
LITERATURE Vanbeselaere 1937, pp 278, 393, 412:
October-November 1885
COLLECTION Amsterdam, Rijksmuseum Vincent
van Gogh [Vincent van Gogh Foundation, inv
nr F 1222]

F 1223 INTERIOR WITH A WOMAN AT THE LEFT BY THE FIREPLACE

Water color 32 × 43 [12½ × 17]
Nuenen second half of 1885
LITERATURE Vanbeselaere 1937, pp 278, 393, 412:
October-November 1885
COLLECTION Sale London [Christie] 19 June 1964,
nr 9
Present owner unknown

F 1224 PEASANT WOMAN WITH A WHITE CAP: FULL FACE

Pencil [old Dutch paper, laid, with watermark:
Concordia res parvae crescunt] 34.5 × 21.5
[13½ × 8½]
Compare painting F 146a, drawings F 1148 and
F 1193 [perhaps the same model]
Nuenen December 1884 or shortly later
LETTERS 390 [mid-December] See F 80
394 [February 1885] and 395 [1 March] See F 69
LITERATURE Vincent van Gogh, Lettres à Bernard,
1911, plate XX. Vanbeselaere 1937, pp 263, 341, 391,
412: October-December 1884
COLLECTION Amsterdam, Rijksmuseum Vincent
van Gogh [Vincent van Gogh Foundation, inv
nr F 1224]

F 1225 TWO PEASANTS PLANTING POTATOES

Pen 6.5 × 9 [2½ × 3½]
Sketch enclosed in letter 399
Compare sketch in postcard 399a and painting
F 129a [similar motifs]
Nuenen April 1885
LETTERS 399 [between 9 and 13 April] '*Enclosed
you will find two sketches of a few studies I made…*'
399a [to Kerssemakers; 9 April] '*I am making some
studies of the planting of potatoes here…*'
LITERATURE Vanbeselaere 1937, pp 266, 412
COLLECTION Amsterdam, Rijksmuseum Vincent
van Gogh [Vincent van Gogh Foundation, inv
nr F 1225]

F 1226 THE POTATO EATERS

Pen and lithographic chalk 11 × 18 [4¼ × 7]
Compare sketch in letter 399, paintings F 77 recto,
F 77a, F 78, F 82, drawing F 1594 and lithograph
F 1661
Nuenen April 1885
LETTER 400 [13 or 14 April] '*…and enclose a sketch
more exactly like my last study than the one before…
If you meet somebody from Le Chat noir, you can
show them this little sketch as a trial,* but I can make
a better one if they like, *for this was done in a hurry,
and only made to give you a better idea of the effect
and composition than the first one.*'
LITERATURE Vanbeselaere 1937, pp 266, 412
COLLECTION New York, J. K. Thannhauser Art
Gallery

F 1227 recto STUDY FOR THE POTATO
EATERS

Black chalk [Dutch laid paper, with watermark:
v.d.L.] 21 × 35 [8¼ × 13¾]
Study for painting F 77 recto. See other comparisons
under F 82
Nuenen March 1885
LITERATURE Vanbeselaere 1937, pp 266, 412
COLLECTION Amsterdam, Rijksmuseum Vincent
van Gogh [Vincent van Gogh Foundation, inv
nr F 1227]

F 1227 verso PEASANT WOMAN STANDING:
SEEN FROM THE FRONT

Black chalk
Nuenen March 1885
LITERATURE Not in Faille 1928 or Vanbeselaere
1937

F 1228 TWO PEASANT WOMEN, WORKING
IN THE FIELDS

Pen 6 × 8.5 [2¼ × 3¼]
Sketch enclosed in letter 399 and reproduced there
in the American edition of the letters [wrongly
reproduced with letter 402 in the Dutch edition]
Nuenen April 1885
LETTER 399 [between 9 and 13 April] See F 1225
LITERATURE Vanbeselaere 1937, pp 266, 412
COLLECTION Amsterdam, Rijksmuseum Vincent
van Gogh [Vincent van Gogh Foundation, inv
nr F 1228]

F 1229 recto STUDY OF A HAND HOLDING A
CUP; STUDY OF A CAT [for the final version of
THE POTATO EATERS]

Black chalk [Dutch paper, laid, with watermark:
v.d.L.] 20 × 33 [8 × 13]
Compare second figure from the right in painting
F 82. See other comparisons under F 82
Nuenen April 1885
LITERATURE Vanbeselaere 1937, pp 267, 412
COLLECTION Amsterdam, Rijksmuseum Vincent
van Gogh [Vincent van Gogh Foundation, inv
nr F 1229]

F 1229 verso MAN AND TWO WOMEN AROUND
A TABLE

Black chalk, stumped
Compare sketch in letter 405 [similar motif]
Nuenen May 1885
LETTER 405 [early May] 'When I went to the cottage
tonight, I found the people at supper in the light of the
small window instead of under the lamp – oh, it was
splendid! The color was extraordinary too; you
remember those heads painted against the window –
the effect was like that, but even darker. So the two
women and the interior were exactly the color of dark
soft soap. But the figure of the man to the left was just
lit up by light streaming through a door further on.
So the head and hands became the color of a 10-
centime piece, namely dull brass. And where the light
touched it, the blouse became of the most tender
faded blue.'
LITERATURE Vanbeselaere 1937, p 267

F 1224

F 1227 verso

F 1227 recto

F 1229 recto

F 1229 verso

F 1228

F 1230

F 1231 recto

F 1231 verso

F 1232

F 1230 PUBLIC SALE OF CROSSES OF THE
CEMETERY AT NUENEN

Water color [thick water-color paper] 37.5 × 55
[14¾ × 21¾]
Signed in lower left: Vincent
Compare drawings F 1112 recto and verso and
F 1231 recto and verso
Nuenen May 1885
LETTER 408 [after 8 May] See F 1112 recto
LITERATURE Vanbeselaere 1937, pp 269, 412
COLLECTION Amsterdam, Rijksmuseum Vincent
van Gogh [Vincent van Gogh Foundation, inv
nr F 1230]

F 1231 recto STUDY FOR THE PUBLIC SALE
OF CROSSES OF THE CEMETERY AT NUENEN

Black chalk [Dutch laid paper with watermark:
Pro Patria – Concordia res parvae crescunt]
21 × 34.5 [8¼ × 13½]
Compare F 1112 recto and verso, water color F 1230
and drawing F 1231 verso
Nuenen May 1885
LETTER 408 [after 8 May] See F 1112 recto
LITERATURE Vanbeselaere 1937, pp 268, 412
COLLECTION Amsterdam, Rijksmuseum Vincent
van Gogh [Vincent van Gogh Foundation, inv
nr F 1231]

F 1231 verso STUDY FOR THE PUBLIC SALE
OF CROSSES OF THE CEMETERY AT NUENEN

Black chalk, stumped
Compare F 1112 recto and verso, water color F 1230
and drawing F 1231 recto
Nuenen May 1885
LITERATURE Not in Faille 1928 or Vanbeselaere
1937

F 1232 WINTER LANDSCAPE

Pen and pencil [brown wrapping paper] 20.5 × 28.5
[8 × 11¼]
Compare F 1233 recto [same motif]
Nuenen December 1883
LITERATURE Album Hidde Nijland Collection
1905, plate 88b. H. van den Eerenbeemt, Opgang
March 1924, p 280. Vanbeselaere 1937, pp 262, 353,
412: January 1885
EDITORS' COMMENT See F 1127
COLLECTION Otterlo, Rijksmuseum Kröller-
Müller, inv nr 1020-28, cat van Gogh 1970, nr 161

F 1233 recto SNOW LANDSCAPE

Black chalk, stumped [ordinary paper] 16 × 25.5
[6¼ × 10]
Compare F 1232 [same motif]
Nuenen December 1883
LITERATURE Vanbeselaere 1937, pp 262, 353, 412:
January 1885
EDITORS' COMMENT See F 1127
COLLECTION Amsterdam, Rijksmuseum Vincent
van Gogh [Vincent van Gogh Foundation, inv
nr F 1233]

F 1233 verso SKETCH OF FIGURES IN A
LANDSCAPE
Upper right SKETCH OF A WOMAN WITH A
BASKET ON HER BACK

Black chalk
Nuenen December 1883
LITERATURE Not in Faille 1928 or Vanbeselaere
1937

F 1233 recto

F 1233 verso

F 1234 THE VICARAGE GARDEN WITH FIGURES

Water color 38 × 49 [15 × 19¼]
Compare painting F 124
Nuenen October-November 1885
LETTER 430 [4 November] '*I have made another autumn study of the pond in the garden at home.*'
LITERATURE Vanbeselaere 1937, pp 278, 412.
D. Cooper, Zeichnungen und Aquarelle von Vincent van Gogh, 1954, p 40
COLLECTION Wassenaar, Netherlands, B. Meijer
Colorplate, p 571

F 1235 WINTER
Etten period; see after F 905

F 1236 recto THE CHURCHYARD AND THE OLD TOWER AT NUENEN IN WINTER

Black chalk, pen and ink, brush [wove paper, yellowish] 18 × 28 [7 × 11]
Compare F 1237 [same motif]
Nuenen December 1883
LITERATURE Vanbeselaere 1937, pp 262, 412: January 1885
EDITORS' COMMENT See F 1127
COLLECTION Amsterdam, Rijksmuseum Vincent van Gogh [Vincent van Gogh Foundation, inv nr F 1236]

F 1236 verso SKETCH OF A CHURCH

Black chalk 10.5 × 10.3 [4¼ × 4]
December 1883
LITERATURE Not in Faille 1928 or Vanbeselaere 1937

F 1237 THE CHURCHYARD AND THE OLD TOWER AT NUENEN IN WINTER

Black chalk, pen and ink, brush [wove paper, yellowish] 16 × 25.5 [6¼ × 10]
Compare F 1236 recto [same motif]
Nuenen December 1883
LITERATURE Vanbeselaere 1937, pp 262, 412: January 1885
EDITORS' COMMENT On the reverse of this drawing is a Dutch postage stamp and Theo's address in Paris, along with the word 'imprimée.' The postmark is dated Nuenen 7 December 188. The last numeral is illegible. It might be a 3 or a 4, as Vincent was in Nuenen in December 1883 and December 1884. For stylistic reasons the editors place this drawing not in December 1884 but in December 1883, together with some other drawings of winter landscapes, mostly centered around the old tower and churchyard: F 1127, F 1131, F 1232, F 1233, F 1236 recto, F 1238 recto, SD 1686 and SD 1687. Vincent traveled from Hoogeveen [province of Drenthe] to Nuenen probably on 4 December [see letter 344, which tells us that there was snow on the day he traveled]. The first letters from Nuenen [344-50] don't mention any paintings or drawings; the first mention of drawing activity [water colors of weavers] in Vincent's letters dates from the first days of January 1884 [letter 351]. In a letter of Vincent's father to Theo of the first days of December 1883, however, quoted in the Preface to the Complete Letters, we find this passage: '*Do you not like the pen drawings of the tower that Vincent sent you?*' And again on 20 December, Vincent's father wrote: '*One thing is certain, he works hard and finds lots of subjects here; he has already made several drawings which we like very much.*' The above-mentioned drawings may belong to this series. See also the EDITORS' COMMENT to F 1127.
COLLECTION Amsterdam, Rijksmuseum Vincent van Gogh [Vincent van Gogh Foundation, inv nr F 1237]

F 1234

F 1236 recto

F 1236 verso

F 1237

F 1238

F 1240

F 1239

F 1241

F 1238 THE CHURCH AT TONGELRE IN WINTER

Pencil, pen and ink [wove paper, yellowish] 20.5 × 28.5 [8 × 11¼]
LITERATURE Vanbeselaere 1937, pp 262, 412: April 1885
Nuenen December 1883
EDITORS' COMMENT See F 1127. The site was identified by L. J. van der Klooster, head of the Topographic Division of the Netherlands Institute of Art History, The Hague
COLLECTION Amsterdam, Rijksmuseum Vincent van Gogh [Vincent van Gogh Foundation, inv nr F 1238]

F 1239 AVENUE OF POPLARS WITH FIGURE

Pen and ink [ordinary wove paper] 54 × 39 [21¼ × 15½]
Compare painting F 123 [same site]
Nuenen March 1884
LETTER R 44 [April] See F 1129
LITERATURE Vanbeselaere 1937, pp 259, 322, 412
COLLECTION Amsterdam, Rijksmuseum Vincent van Gogh [Vincent van Gogh Foundation, inv nr F 1239]

F 1240 ALLEY OF WILLOWS WITH SHEPHERD AND PEASANT WOMAN

Pencil and pen 39.5 × 54.5 [15½ × 21½]
Signed in lower left: Vincent
Nuenen early spring 1884
LITERATURE Vanbeselaere 1937, pp 263, 353, 412: February-March 1885
COLLECTION Amsterdam, Rijksmuseum Vincent van Gogh [Vincent van Gogh Foundation, inv nr F 1240]

F 1240a LANDSCAPE WITH WILLOWS AND SUN SHINING THROUGH THE CLOUDS

Pencil and pen 34 × 44 [13½ × 17¼]
Nuenen March 1884
LITERATURE Not in Faille 1928 or Vanbeselaere 1937
COLLECTION Chicago, The Art Institute [Robert Allerton Fund) inv nr 69.268

F 1241 AVENUE OF TREES IN WINTER

Pen 19 × 27 [7½ × 10½]
Nuenen early 1884
LITERATURE Vanbeselaere 1937, pp 263, 353, 412: February-March 1885
COLLECTION New York, Heirs of M. Frank

F 1242 HUTS WITH THATCHED ROOFS

Pencil, pen and ink, heightened with white 30 × 44 [11¾ × 17¼]
Compare sketch in letter R 42 [same site]
Nuenen March-April 1884
LETTER R 45 [April] 'A few days ago I sent you three more pen-and-ink drawings... "Thatched Roofs"...'
LITERATURE Vincent van Gogh, Lettres à Bernard, 1911, plate XVII. Vanbeselaere 1937, pp 259, 322, 412
COLLECTION London, Tate Gallery [acquired 1933; C. Frank Stoop bequest], inv nr 4715, cat 1959, p 274

F 1243 THE DITCH

Pencil, pen and ink, heightened with white [wove paper, yellowish] 39 × 33 [15½ × 13]
Nuenen April 1884
LETTER R 45 [April] 'A few days ago I sent you three more pen-and-ink drawings, "Little Ditch"...'

F 1240a

LITERATURE Vanbeselaere 1937, pp 260, 412
COLLECTION Amsterdam, Rijksmuseum Vincent
van Gogh [Vincent van Gogh Foundation, inv
nr F 1243]

F 1244 recto and verso STUDY OF FOUR
FLYING SWALLOWS; SKETCH OF ONE
SWALLOW
Paris period; see after F 1412

F 1244a recto and verso THE VIOLINIST
Paris period; see p 000

F 1244b recto and verso THE CLARINETTIST;
THE FLUTIST; PORTRAIT OF A WOMAN
SITTING
Paris period; see after F 1412

F 1244c recto and verso THE CONTRABASS
PLAYER; THE PIANIST
Paris period; see after F 1412

F 1244d recto and verso HEAD OF A MAN;
MAN WITH A TALL HAT
Paris period; see after F 1412

F 1245 THE ORCHARD

Water color 6 × 10.5 [2½ × 4¼]
Signed in lower left: Vincent
Erroneously reproduced as the sketch enclosed with
letter 374 [Nuenen August 1884] in the American
edition of the letters
Formed a set or part of a set with F 1202
Nuenen probably winter 1884-5
LITERATURE Vanbeselaere 1937, pp 107, 412: The
Hague April 1883
COLLECTION Amsterdam, Rijksmuseum Vincent
van Gogh [Vincent van Gogh Foundation, inv
nr F 1245]

F 1246 AVENUE OF TREES WITH FIGURES

Pencil, pen and ink, heightened with white 20.5 ×
12.5 [8 × 5]
Signed in lower right: Vincent
Compare painting F 123 [similar motif and style]
Nuenen autumn 1885
LITERATURE Faille 1928: October-November
1885. Vanbeselaere 1937, pp 261, 412: autumn
1884
EDITORS' COMMENT The date seems uncertain.
COLLECTION Amsterdam, S. Polak

F 1245

F 1243

F 1242

F 1246

F 1247

F 1250

F 1249

F 1252

F 1253

F 1247 WILLOWS

Black chalk, heightened with blue and red
47.5 × 30.5 [18¾ × 12]
Nuenen November 1885 [?]
LITERATURE Vanbeselaere 1937, pp 277, 393, 412:
October 1885
EDITORS' COMMENT The editors cannot connect
the style of this drawing with that of any of the
other drawings of trees by van Gogh.
COLLECTION Sale London [Christie] 27 November
1964, nr 100
Present owner unknown

F 1248 COTTAGES IN THE HEATHER
Drenthe period; see after F 1106

F 1249 PINE TREES IN THE FEN

Pen and ink [ordinary wove paper] 34.5 × 44
[13½ × 17¼]
Nuenen April 1884
LETTER R 45 [April] '*A few days ago I sent you three
more pen-and-ink drawings… "Pine Trees in the
Fen"…*'
LITERATURE Vincent van Gogh, Lettres à Bernard,
1911, plate VII. Vanbeselaere 1937, pp 260, 412
COLLECTION Amsterdam, Rijksmuseum Vincent
van Gogh [Vincent van Gogh Foundation, inv
nr F 1249]

F 1250 PEASANT WOMAN WITH A SPADE:
FACING RIGHT

Black chalk, stumped [ordinary wove paper]
53 × 42 [21 × 16½]
Compare F 1251 [same model]
Nuenen June-August 1885
LETTER 412 [June] '*I am very busy drawing figures,
but I shall have to make a hundred of them before I
paint them…*'
413 [June] '*As I already told you, recently I have been
very busy drawing figures: I will send them…*'
414 [June] '*Every day I work hard on drawing figures.
But I must have a hundred of them, even more, before
I am through.*'
422 [mid-August] '*By way of provisional answer to
what you wrote with regard to drawings of figures in
their surroundings, I sent you a few today. But I
doubt whether they are suitable for framing, and if,
being in the fields, I am fortunate enough to find
something better, I shall try and add a few others
shortly.*'
LITERATURE Vanbeselaere 1937, pp 271, 412:
June-July 1885
COLLECTION Amsterdam, Rijksmuseum Vincent
van Gogh [Vincent van Gogh Foundation, inv
nr F 1250]

F 1251 PEASANT WOMAN WITH A
PITCHFORK: FACING RIGHT

Black chalk, stumped [ordinary wove paper]
49.5 × 40 [19½ × 15¾]
Compare 1250 [same model]
Nuenen June-August 1885
LETTERS 414 [June] and 422 [mid-August]
See F 1250
LITERATURE Vanbeselaere 1937, pp 271, 412:
June-July 1885
COLLECTION Amsterdam, Rijksmuseum Vincent
van Gogh [Vincent van Gogh Foundation, inv
nr F 1251]

F 1252 PEASANT WOMAN DIGGING:
FACING RIGHT

Black chalk 47 × 31 [18½ × 12¼]
Signed in lower left: Vincent
Nuenen June-August 1885

LETTERS 414 [June] and 422 [mid-August]
See F 1250
LITERATURE Vanbeselaere 1937, pp 271, 396, 412:
June-July 1885
COLLECTION New York, Mr and Mrs
H. Lawrence Herring

F 1253 PEASANT WOMAN DIGGING:
FACING LEFT

Black chalk [Ingres paper, blue] 30 × 23 [11¾ × 9]
Nuenen June-August 1885
LETTERS 414 [June] and 422 [mid-August]
See F 1250
LITERATURE Album Hidde Nijland Collection
1905, plate 56. Vanbeselaere 1937, pp 277, 392, 412:
October-November 1885
COLLECTION Otterlo, Rijksmuseum Kröller-
Müller, inv nr 988-28, cat van Gogh 1970, nr 124

F 1254 PEASANT WOMAN DIGGING : SEEN
FROM THE FRONT

Black chalk [old Dutch paper, laid, with watermark:
Concordia res parvae crescunt] 35.5 × 21 [14 × 8¼]
Nuenen June-August 1885
LETTERS 414 [June] and 422 [mid-August]
See F 1250
LITERATURE Album Hidde Nijland Collection
1905, plate 50. Vanbeselaere 1937, pp 274, 390-1,
412: September-October 1885
COLLECTION Otterlo, Rijksmuseum Kröller-
Müller, inv nr 982-28, cat van Gogh 1970, nr 109

F 1255 PEASANT WOMAN DIGGING: SEEN
FROM BEHIND

Black chalk [ordinary wove paper] 55.5 × 40.5
[22 × 16]
Compare painting F 95 [similar motif]
Nuenen June-July 1885
LETTER 416 [6 July] See F 94
LITERATURE Vanbeselaere 1937, pp 272, 390, 412
COLLECTION Amsterdam, Rijksmuseum Vincent
van Gogh [Vincent van Gogh Foundation, inv
nr F 1255]

F 1251

F 1255

F 1254

F 1256

F 1258

F 1257 recto

F 1257 verso

F 1259

F 1260

F 1261

F 1262

F 1256 PEASANT WOMAN WITH A FORK:
SEEN FROM BEHIND, A WINDMILL IN THE
BACKGROUND

Black chalk, pen and ink [Ingres paper with
fragment of a watermark: P.L. Bas (?)] 28.5 × 22.5
[11¼ × 8¾]
Compare painting F 94 and F 1258 [similar motif]
Nuenen July 1885
LETTERS 414 [June] and 422 [mid-August]
See F 1250
LITERATURE Vanbeselaere 1937, pp 272, 412
COLLECTION Amsterdam, Rijksmuseum Vincent
van Gogh [Vincent van Gogh Foundation, inv
nr F 1256]

F 1257 recto PEASANT WOMAN DIGGING
POTATOES: SEEN FROM THE FRONT

Black chalk [Dutch laid paper with watermark:
Pro Patria – Concordia res parvae crescunt]
33 × 20 [13 × 8]
Nuenen June-August 1885
LETTERS 414 [June] and 422 [mid-August]
See F 1250
LITERATURE Vanbeselaere 1937, pp 272, 412: July
1885
COLLECTION Amsterdam, Rijksmuseum Vincent
van Gogh [Vincent van Gogh Foundation, inv
nr F 1257]

F 1257 verso PEASANT WOMAN: SEEN FROM
BEHIND

Black chalk
Nuenen June-August 1885
LETTERS 414 [June] and 422 [mid-August]
See F 1250
LITERATURE Not in Faille 1928 or Vanbeselaere
1937

F 1258 PEASANT WOMAN DIGGING: SEEN
FROM BEHIND

Black chalk, stumped, pen and brown ink [Ingres
paper with fragment of a watermark: E.D. & Cie]
29 × 22.5 [11½ × 8¾]
Compare painting F 94 and F 1256 [similar motif]
Nuenen July 1885
LETTERS 414 [June] and 422 [mid-August]
See F 1250
LITERATURE Vanbeselaere 1937, pp 272, 412
COLLECTION Amsterdam, Rijksmuseum Vincent
van Gogh [Vincent van Gogh Foundation, inv
nr F 1258]

F 1259 PEASANT WOMAN TOSSING HAY:
SEEN FROM BEHIND

Black chalk 54 × 41 [21¼ × 16¼]
Signed in lower right: Vincent
Nuenen June-August 1885
LETTERS 414 [June] and 422 [mid-August]
See F 1250
LITERATURE Vanbeselaere 1937, pp 272, 391, 412:
July 1885
COLLECTION Dordrecht, Dordrechts Museum
[acquired 1914; J. Hidde Nijland bequest], cat 1928,
nr 276

F 1260 PEASANT WOMAN TOSSING HAY:
SEEN FROM THE FRONT

Black chalk [wove paper with watermark: T.S. & Z.]
57 × 44.5 [22½ × 17½]
Nuenen June-August 1885
LETTERS 414 [June] and 422 [mid-August]
See F 1250
LITERATURE Album Hidde Nijland Collection
1905, plate 7. Vanbeselaere 1937, pp 272, 390, 412:

July 1885
COLLECTION Otterlo, Rijksmuseum Kröller-Müller, inv nr 941-28, cat van Gogh 1970, nr 117

F 1261 PEASANT WOMAN TOSSING HAY: FACING RIGHT

Black chalk [ordinary wove paper] 53 × 43 [20¾ × 17]
Signed in lower right: Vincent
Nuenen June-November 1885
LETTERS 414 [June] and 422 [mid-August] See F 1250
LITERATURE Album Hidde Nijland Collection 1905, plate 67. Vanbeselaere 1937, pp 272, 389-90, 412: July 1885
COLLECTION Otterlo, Rijksmuseum Kröller-Müller, inv nr 998-28, cat van Gogh 1970, nr 113

F 1262 PEASANT WOMAN BINDING SHEAVES: FACING RIGHT

Black chalk, lightly washed [Dutch laid paper with watermark: H.F.d.C. Scutcheon with fleur-de-lis] 44.5 × 58.5 [17½ × 23]
Signed in lower right: Vincent
Nuenen July-August 1885
LETTERS 416 [6 July] See F 94
419 [early August] *I am rather busy, as they are reaping the corn in the fields, for, as you know, this lasts only a few days, and it is one of the most beautiful things.'*
LITERATURE Album Hidde Nijland Collection 1905, plate 75. Vanbeselaere 1937, pp 272, 391, 412
COLLECTION Otterlo, Rijksmuseum Kröller-Müller, inv nr 1005-28, cat van Gogh 1970, nr 112

F 1262a [formerly F 1262bis] PEASANT WOMAN KNEELING: FACING LEFT

Black chalk, gray washed, heightened with white 52.5 × 42 [20¾ × 16½]
Signed in lower right: Vincent
Nuenen July-August 1885
LETTERS 416 [6 July] See F 94
419 [early August] See F 1262
LITERATURE Not in Vanbeselaere 1937
COLLECTION Sale London [Sotheby] 4 May 1960, nr 183
Present owner unknown

F 1262b PEASANT WOMAN KNEELING AND PULLING OUT CARROTS

Black chalk 37 × 46 [14½ × 18]
Signed in lower right: Vincent
Nuenen July-August 1885
LITERATURE Not in Faille 1928 or Vanbeselaere 1937
COLLECTION Beverly Hills, California, Charles Vidor

F 1263 PEASANT WOMAN BINDING WHEAT: FACING RIGHT

Black chalk [wove paper with watermark: T.S. & Z.] 55.5 × 43 [21¾ × 17]
Signed in lower left and right: Vincent
Nuenen August 1885
LETTERS 416 [6 July] See F 94
419 [early August] See F 1262
LITERATURE Album Hidde Nijland Collection 1905, plate 53. Vanbeselaere 1937, pp 272, 390-1, 412
COLLECTION Otterlo, Rijksmuseum Kröller-Müller, inv nr 985-28, cat van Gogh 1970, nr 120

F 1264 PEASANT WOMAN BINDING WHEAT: STOOPING, SEEN FROM THE FRONT

Black chalk, washed [wove paper with watermark: T.S. & Z.] 45 × 53 [17¾ × 20¾]
Nuenen August 1885
LETTERS 416 [6 July] See F 94
419 [early August] See F 1262
LITERATURE Album Hidde Nijland Collection 1905, plate 81. Vanbeselaere 1937, pp 272, 391, 412
COLLECTION Otterlo, Rijksmuseum Kröller-Müller, inv nr 1014-28, cat van Gogh 1970, nr 116

F 1265 PEASANT WOMAN GLEANING GRAIN: SEEN FROM THE FRONT

Black chalk, lightly washed [Dutch paper] 52 × 38 [20½ × 15]
Nuenen August 1885
LETTERS 416 [6 July] See F 94
419 [early August] See F 1262
LITERATURE Vanbeselaere 1937, pp 272, 391, 412
COLLECTION Otterlo, Rijksmuseum Kröller-Müller, inv nr 250-12, cat van Gogh 1970, nr 122

F 1265 a [formerly F 1265bis] PEASANT WOMAN GLEANING GRAIN: FACING LEFT

Black chalk 52 × 43 [20½ × 17]
Nuenen August 1885
LETTERS 416 [6 July] See F 94
419 [early August] See F 1262
LITERATURE Not in Vanbeselaere 1937
COLLECTION London, Charles Clore

F 1262a

F 1263

F 1262b

F 1264

F 1265

F 1265a

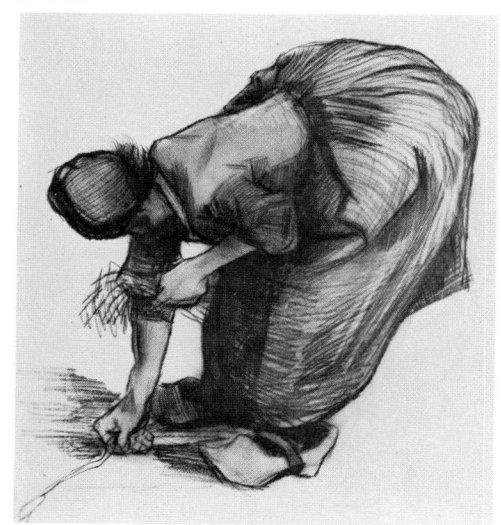

F 1266

F 1267

F 1268

F 1270

F 1272

F 1272a

F 1273

F 1275a

F 1266 PEASANT WOMAN PICKING UP A
SHEAF OF GRAIN: SEEN FROM THE FRONT

Black chalk, stumped [ordinary wove paper]
56.5 × 44.5 [22¼ × 17½]
Nuenen August 1885
LETTERS 416 [6 July] See F 94
419 [early August] See F 1262
LITERATURE Vanbeselaere 1937, pp 272, 412
COLLECTION Amsterdam, Rijksmuseum Vincent
van Gogh [Vincent van Gogh Foundation, inv
nr F 1266]

F 1267 PEASANT WOMAN CARRYING A
SHEAF OF GRAIN: SEEN FROM THE FRONT

Black chalk, stumped, and wash 57 × 42
[22½ × 16½]
Nuenen August 1885
LETTERS 416 [6 July] See F 94
419 [early August] See F 1262
LITERATURE Vanbeselaere 1937, pp 273, 391, 412
COLLECTION Oslo Nasjonal Galleriet [acquired
1919]

F 1268 PEASANT WOMAN CARRYING HAY:
FACING LEFT

Black chalk, washed [Dutch laid paper with
watermark: H.F.d.C. Scutcheon with fleur-de-lis]
58.5 × 38 [23 × 15]
Nuenen August 1885
LETTERS 416 [6 July] See F 94
419 [early August] See F 1262
LITERATURE Album Hidde Nijland Collection
1905, plate 5. H. van den Eerenbeemt, Opgang
March 1924, p 275 [with reproduction].
Vanbeselaere 1937, pp 273, 412
COLLECTION Otterlo, Rijksmuseum Kröller-
Müller, inv nr 939-28, cat van Gogh 1970, nr 150

F 1269 PEASANT WOMAN STOOPING: SEEN
FROM THE BACK AND THE SIDE
Upper right SKETCHES OF FIGURES
HARVESTING

Black chalk, washed [Dutch wove paper] 52.5 × 43.5
[20¾ × 17¼]
Nuenen August 1885
LETTERS 416 [6 July] See F 94
419 [early August] See F 1262
LITERATURE Vanbeselaere 1937, pp 273, 391, 412
COLLECTION Otterlo, Rijksmuseum Kröller-
Müller, inv nr 251-00, cat van Gogh 1970, nr 123

F 1270 PEASANT WOMAN PLANTING
BEETS

Black chalk [drawing paper, yellowish] 53.5 × 44
[21 × 17¼]
Annotated by Vincent in lower left: Planteuse de
betteraves (Juin)
Compare F 1272a and SD 1691 [same motif]
Nuenen June-July 1885
LITERATURE Vanbeselaere 1937, pp 271, 394-5,
412: June 1885
COLLECTION Rotterdam, Museum Boymans-van
Beuningen [acquired 1899; gift of J. Hidde Nijland],
inv nr V v G 2, cat 1928, nr 789

F 1271 PEASANT WOMAN PULLING OUT
BEETS

Left out by Faille in his manuscript for the present
edition
See REJECTED WORKS

F 1272 PEASANT WOMAN PLANTING
POTATOES: SEEN FROM THE FRONT

Black chalk, stumped 42 × 44.5 [16½ × 17½]
Signed in lower left: Vincent
Annotated in lower left: Planteuse de pommes de
terre
Nuenen 1885
LITERATURE Vanbeselaere 1937, pp 274, 412:
September-October 1885
COLLECTION Frankfurt, Städelsches Kunstinstitut

F 1272a PEASANT WOMAN PLANTING
BEETS

Black chalk 45 × 52 [17¾ × 20½]
Signed and annotated by Vincent in lower left:
planteuse de betteraves, Juin, Vincent
Compare F 1270 and SD 1691 [same motif]
Nuenen June 1885
LITERATURE Not in Faille 1928 or Vanbeselaere
1937
COLLECTION Easton, Pennsylvania, E. R. Schaible

F 1273 PEASANT WOMAN DIGGING UP
POTATOES

Black chalk [wove paper, yellowish] 40.5 × 46.5
[16 × 18¼]
Signed in lower right: Vincent
Annotated in lower left: arracheuse de pommes de
terre
Nuenen August-November 1885
LITERATURE Vincent van Gogh, Lettres à Bernard,
1911, plate XIII. Vanbeselaere 1937, pp 277, 412:
October-November 1885
COLLECTION Amsterdam, Rijksmuseum Vincent
van Gogh [Vincent van Gogh Foundation, inv
nr F 1273]

F 1274 PEASANT WOMAN WORKING

Black chalk 56 × 41 [22 × 16¼]
Nuenen June-November 1885
LITERATURE Faille 1928, nr 1274, not reproduced.
Vanbeselaere 1937, p 412
EDITORS' COMMENT Drawings F 1274 and F 1275
were not available for study during the preparation
of this edition, nor could they be photographed.
COLLECTION Amsterdam, Rijksmuseum Vincent
van Gogh [Vincent van Gogh Foundation, inv
nr F 1274]

F 1275 PEASANT WOMAN DIGGING UP
POTATOES

Black chalk 28.5 × 22.5 [11¼ × 8¾]
Nuenen
LITERATURE Faille 1928, nr 1275, not reproduced.
Vanbeselaere 1937, p 412. Not in Faille's manuscript
EDITORS' COMMENT See F 1274
COLLECTION Amsterdam, Rijksmuseum Vincent
van Gogh [Vincent van Gogh Foundation, inv
nr F 1275]

F 1275a PEASANT WOMAN GLEANING
GRAIN: FACING LEFT

Black chalk 30 × 46 [11¾ × 18]
Signed in lower left: Vincent
Nuenen August 1885
LETTERS 416 [6 July] See F 94
419 [early August] See F 1262
LITERATURE Not in Faille 1928 or Vanbeselaere
1937
COLLECTION The Hague, G. J. Nieuwenhuizen
Segaar Art Gallery

F 1276 recto WOMAN DIGGING: FULL FACE

Black chalk, lightly washed [wove paper with
watermark: T.S. & Z.] 45 × 56.5 [17¾ × 22¼]
Nuenen August-October 1885
LITERATURE Album Hidde Nijland Collection
1905, plate 30. Vanbeselaere 1937, pp 275, 412:
September-October 1885. Cat van Gogh 1966,
Rijksmuseum Kröller-Müller, nr 108a: summer
1885
COLLECTION Otterlo, Rijksmuseum Kröller-
Müller, inv nr 964-28, cat van Gogh 1970, nr 108

F 1276 verso PEASANT WOMAN STOOPING:
FACING LEFT

Black chalk, washed and heightened
Nuenen August-October 1885
LITERATURE Not in Faille 1928 or Vanbeselaere
1937

F 1276 recto

F 1276 verso

F 1269

F 1277

F 1278

F 1280

F 1281

F 1282

F 1284

F 1283 recto

F 1283 verso

F 1277 PEASANT WOMAN WORKING: FACING LEFT

Black chalk, stumped [Dutch wove paper] 54.5 × 37
[21½ × 14½]
Signed in lower right: Vincent
Compare painting F 139 [similar motif]
Nuenen August 1885
LETTERS 416 [6 July] See F 94
419 [early August] See F 1262
LITERATURE Album Hidde Nijland Collection
1905, plate 71. Vanbeselaere 1937, pp 273, 412
COLLECTION Otterlo, Rijksmuseum Kröller-
Müller, inv nr 951-28, cat van Gogh 1970, nr 129

F 1278 WOMAN WITH BROOM: FULL FACE

Black chalk, stumped [Dutch laid paper with
watermark: v.d.L.] 35 × 21 [13¾ × 8¼]
Nuenen September-October 1885
LITERATURE Album Hidde Nijland Collection
1905, plate 37. Vanbeselaere 1937, pp 275, 391, 412:
September-October 1885
COLLECTION Otterlo, Rijksmuseum Kröller-
Müller, inv nr 970-28, cat van Gogh 1970, nr 121

F 1279 PEASANT WOMAN GLEANING GRAIN: FACING LEFT

Black chalk 51.5 × 41.5 [20¼ × 16¼]
Nuenen August 1885
LETTERS 416 [6 July] See F 94
419 [early August] See F 1262
LITERATURE Vanbeselaere 1937, pp 273, 412
COLLECTION Essen, Folkwang Museum, cat 1929,
nr 439

F 1280 PEASANT WOMAN KNEELING: SEEN FROM THE BACK

Black chalk 43 × 52 [17 × 20½]
Nuenen August 1885
LETTERS 416 [6 July] See F 94
419 [early August] See F 1262
LITERATURE Vanbeselaere 1937, pp 274, 391, 412:
COLLECTION Oslo, Nasjonal Galleriet [acquired
1919]

F 1281 WOMAN WITH AN AX: FACING LEFT

Black chalk, stumped [ordinary wove paper, toned]
36 × 40 [14¼ × 15¾]
Signed in lower right: Vincent
Nuenen September-October 1885
LITERATURE Album Hidde Nijland Collection
1905, plate 29. Vanbeselaere 1937, pp 275, 412
COLLECTION Otterlo, Rijksmuseum Kröller-
Müller, inv nr 1024-28, cat van Gogh 1970, nr 128

F 1282 WOMAN SCOURING A CALDRON

Black chalk [thin wove paper with watermark:
T.S. & Z.] 54.5 × 43.5 [21½ × 17¼]
Signed in lower right: Vincent
Nuenen August-September 1885
LITERATURE Album Hidde Nijland Collection
1905, plate 51. H. van den Eerenbeemt, Opgang
March 1924, p 271, [with reproduction]. Van-
beselaere 1937, pp 274, 412. A. M. Hammacher,
The Scottish Art Review 1953, nr 4, p 23 [with
reproduction]
COLLECTION Otterlo, Rijksmuseum Kröller-
Müller, inv nr 983-28, cat van Gogh 1970, nr 134

F 1283 recto WOMAN WITH A WOODEN PAIL: FACING LEFT

Black chalk [Dutch laid paper with watermark:
v.d.L.] 33.5 × 20 [13¼ × 7¾]
Nuenen summer 1885

LITERATURE Album Hidde Nijland Collection 1905, plate 66. Vanbeselaere 1937, pp 274, 412: August-September 1885
COLLECTION Otterlo, Rijksmuseum Kröller-Müller, inv nr 997-28, cat van Gogh 1970, nr 136

F 1283 verso PEASANT WOMAN SWEEPING: FACING LEFT

Black chalk, stumped
Nuenen summer 1885
LITERATURE Not in Faille 1928 or Vanbeselaere 1937

F 1284 WOMAN BY THE WASH TUB, IN A GARDEN

Pen, pencil and black chalk 32 × 25.5 [12½ × 10]
Signed in lower right: Vincent
Nuenen September-October 1885
LITERATURE Vanbeselaere 1937, pp 275, 395, 412
COLLECTION Basle, Robert von Hirsch

F 1285 PEASANT WOMAN SCRUBBING AN IRON POT
Left out by Faille in his manuscript for the present edition
See REJECTED WORKS

F 1286 PEASANT WOMAN PEELING POTATOES
Left out by Faille in his manuscript for the present edition
See REJECTED WORKS

F 1287 SKETCH OF A WOMAN STOOPING BY THE FIREPLACE

Black chalk [laid paper, gray, with fragment of a watermark] 30 × 22.5 [11¾ × 8¾]
Nuenen spring 1885
LITERATURE Vanbeselaere 1937, pp 277, 392, 413: October-November 1885
COLLECTION Amsterdam, Rijksmuseum Vincent van Gogh [Vincent van Gogh Foundation, inv nr F 1287]

F 1288 PEASANT WOMAN SEATED BY THE FIREPLACE: FACING LEFT

Black chalk, washed [wove paper, yellowish] 43 × 35 [17 × 13¾]
Compare paintings F 158, F 176, drawings F 1211, F 1212, F 1291 [same model in same interior], F 1215, F 1217 and F 1218 [same interior]
Nuenen May 1885
LITERATURE Vanbeselaere 1937, pp 277, 392, 413: October-November 1885
COLLECTION Amsterdam, Rijksmuseum Vincent van Gogh [Vincent van Gogh Foundation, inv nr F 1288]

F 1289 recto PEASANT WOMAN: WALKING TO THE LEFT

Black chalk, stumped [Dutch laid paper with watermark: Pro Patria – Concordia res parvae crescunt] 34.5 × 21 [13½ × 8¼]
Nuenen May-June 1885
LITERATURE Album Hidde Nijland Collection 1905, plate 3. Vanbeselaere 1937, pp 275, 391, 413: September-October 1885
COLLECTION Otterlo, Rijksmuseum Kröller-Müller, inv nr 927-28, cat van Gogh 1970, nr 145

F 1279

F 1287

F 1288

F 1289 recto

F 1289 verso

F 1290

F 1290a

F 1291

F 1292

F 1293

F 1295

F 1296

F 1289 verso PEASANT WOMAN CARRYING SOMETHING IN HER APRON: SEEN FROM THE FRONT

Black chalk, stumped
Nuenen May-June 1885
LITERATURE Not in Faille 1928 or Vanbeselaere 1937

F 1290 PEASANT WOMAN AT THE SPINNING WHEEL: FACING LEFT

Black chalk [Ingres paper, reddish] 30 × 23 [11¾ × 9]
Nuenen March 1885
LITERATURE Vanbeselaere 1937, pp 277, 391, 413: October-November 1885
COLLECTION Amsterdam, Rijksmuseum Vincent van Gogh [Vincent van Gogh Foundation, inv nr F 1290]

F 1290a [formerly F 1290bis] THE SPINNER

Black chalk 28 × 36 [11 × 14¼]
Compare painting F 36 [same model]
Nuenen March 1885
LETTER 396 [mid-March] See F 1203
LITERATURE Not in Vanbeselaere 1937
COLLECTION Wassenaar, Netherlands, H. J. de Koster

F 1291 WOMAN ON A BENCH BY THE HEARTH: FACING LEFT

Pen and ink [ordinary drawing paper] 10 × 13.5 [4 × 5¼]
Compare paintings F 158, F 176, drawings F 1211, F 1212, F 1288 [same model in same interior], F 1215, F 1217 and F 1218 [same interior]
Nuenen May 1885
LITERATURE Album Hidde Nijland Collection 1905, part 4, reproduction on cover. Vanbeselaere 1937, pp 268, 392, 413
COLLECTION Otterlo, Rijksmuseum Kröller-Müller, inv nr 1040-28, cat van Gogh 1970, nr 143

F 1292 PEASANT WOMAN BY A POOL

Pen and ink, washed [ordinary white paper] 17.5 × 10.5 [7 × 4¼]
Nuenen spring 1885
LITERATURE Album Hidde Nijland Collection 1905, part 5, reproduction on cover. Vanbeselaere 1937, pp 268, 413: May 1885
COLLECTION Otterlo, Rijksmuseum Kröller-Müller, inv nr 1041-28, cat van Gogh 1970, nr 149

F 1293 PEASANT WOMAN WITH A KETTLE, STANDING NEAR A FIREPLACE

Water color 42.3 × 30.7 [16¾ × 12]
Signed in lower left: Vincent
Nuenen August 1885 or shortly later
LETTER 421 [August] 'I also made some studies of interiors.'
LITERATURE Vanbeselaere 1937, pp 278, 393, 413: October-November 1885
COLLECTION Stuttgart, Staatsgalerie [acquired 1967], inv nr C 67/1470

F 1294 WOMAN SEWING, SITTING ON A BASKET: FACING RIGHT
The Hague period; see after F 1093

F 1295 TWO WOMEN DIGGING

Black chalk, washed [Dutch laid paper with watermark: Pro Patria–Eendracht maakt macht] 20 × 32 [7¾ × 12½]
Annotated in lower left: Port. Vincent

Compare sketch in letter R 57 and painting F 97
[similar motifs]
Nuenen August 1885
LETTER R 57 [August] '*Herewith a third little sketch
of a study I did yesterday... From my little sketch you
will see that I take rather great pains to get action
into my little figures, to express their being at work,
their* doing *something.'*
LITERATURE Album Hidde Nijland Collection
1905, plate 84. Vanbeselaere 1937, pp 277, 396, 413:
October-November 1885
COLLECTION Otterlo, Rijksmuseum Kröller-
Müller, inv nr 1015-28, cat van Gogh 1970, nr 107

F 1296 TWO PEASANT WOMEN DIGGING

Water color 23 × 42 [9 × 16½]
Compare paintings F 96 and F 147
Nuenen August 1885
LETTERS 414 [June] and 422 [early August]
See F 1250
LITERATURE Vanbeselaere 1937, pp 277, 393, 413:
October-November 1885
COLLECTION Switzerland, Doyer Family

F 1297 recto SKETCH OF A MAN'S HEAD
[fragment: upper part]

Black chalk, stumped
Probably The Hague period

F 1297 verso STUDY OF TWO WOMEN;
STUDY OF A MAN CARRYING A BUNDLE OF
BRANCHES ON HIS BACK

Black chalk [wove paper] 27 × 45 [10¾ × 17¾]
Nuenen May 1885
LITERATURE Vanbeselaere 1937, pp 268, 392, 413
COLLECTION Amsterdam, Rijksmuseum Vincent
van Gogh [Vincent van Gogh Foundation, inv
nr F 1297]

F 1297a recto HEAD OF A PEASANT WOMAN

Black chalk, pen and ink [on an envelope] 12.5 × 7
[5 × 2¾]
Nuenen summer 1885
LITERATURE Not in Faille 1928 or Vanbeselaere
1937
COLLECTION Wassenaar, Netherlands, Paul
Citroen

F 1297a verso WOMAN SWEEPING: FACING
LEFT

Black chalk, pen and ink
Nuenen summer 1885

F 1298 recto THREE PEASANT WOMEN

Black chalk [Dutch laid paper with watermark:
v.d. L.] 21.5 × 35 [8½ × 13¾]
Nuenen early summer 1885
LITERATURE Vanbeselaere 1937, pp 275, 413:
September-October 1885
COLLECTION Amsterdam, Rijksmuseum Vincent
van Gogh [Vincent van Gogh Foundation, inv
nr F 1298]

F 1298 verso PEASANT WOMAN: FACING
LEFT

Black chalk
Nuenen early summer 1885
LITERATURE Not in Faille 1928 or Vanbeselaere
1937

F 1297 recto

F 1297 verso

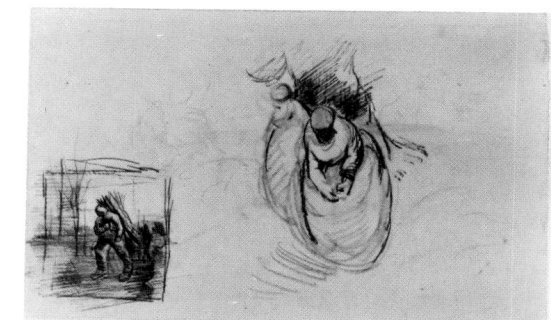

F 1297a recto

F 1297a verso

F 1298 recto

F 1298 verso

F 1299 PEASANT AND PEASANT WOMAN
DIGGING

Black chalk and water color [thin laid paper, pasted]
20 × 33 [7¾ × 13]
Nuenen August 1885
LETTERS 412 [June], 413 [June], 414 [June] and 422
[mid-August] See F 1250
LITERATURE Vanbeselaere 1937, pp 277, 396, 413:
October-November 1885
COLLECTION Otterlo, Rijksmuseum Kröller-
Müller, inv nr 259-20, cat van Gogh 1970, nr 106

F 1300 DIGGING UP POTATOES
Left out by Faille in his manuscript for the present
edition
See REJECTED WORKS

F 1299

F 1301 recto

F 1301 verso

F 1302

F 1303

F 1304

F 1301 recto HARVEST: PEASANT WOMAN STOOPING AND PEASANT REAPING WHEAT

Black chalk, heightened with white [ordinary wove paper] sheet 27 × 38.5 [10¾ × 15¼]; drawing field 24.5 × 34 [9¾ × 13½]
Signed in lower right: Vincent
Compare F 1321 recto [figure on the right: same motif]
Nuenen August 1885
LETTER 421 [August] '*Since you left, I have made another little picture of the harvest, the size of those carrot diggers in the snow – a reaper, a woman binding sheaves, and the mill, like those drawings you saw. An evening effect after sunset.*'
LITERATURE Album Hidde Nijland Collection 1905, plate 26. Idem 1907, plate 11. J.B.J. Stokvis, Kunst und Künstler April 1927, p 249 [with reproduction]. Vanbeselaere 1937, pp 273, 413. J. de Gruyter, Tekeningen van Vincent van Gogh, 1962, p 99, plate 24
COLLECTION Otterlo, Rijksmuseum Kröller-Müller, inv nr 960-28, cat van Gogh 1970, nr 115

F 1301 verso STUDY OF A PEASANT WORKING [the lower part of a drawing torn in half; the upper part is F 1321 verso]

Black chalk 24.5 × 34 [9¾ × 13½]
Annotated in lower left: eig. Hidde Nijland
Nuenen August 1885
LITERATURE Not in Faille 1928 or Vanbeselaere 1937

F 1302 PEASANT DIGGING: SEEN FROM THE BACK

Black chalk [wove paper] 54 × 41 [21¼ × 16¼]
Annotated in lower left: Bêcheur dans un champ de pommes de terre, février
Nuenen August 1885
LETTERS 414 [June] and 422 [mid-August]
See F 1250
LITERATURE Vanbeselaere 1937, pp 275, 413: September-October 1885
EDITORS' COMMENT There are no other indications that Vincent did any full-size figure studies in February, as the annotation on the drawing has it. On stylistic grounds the drawing can better be dated in August, particularly on account of its closeness to F 1305.
COLLECTION Amsterdam, Rijksmuseum Vincent van Gogh [Vincent van Gogh Foundation, inv nr F 1302]

F 1303 PEASANT DIGGING: SEEN FROM THE BACK

Black chalk [Ingres paper with watermark: E.D. & Cie – P.L. Bas] 53 × 41 [21 × 16¼]
Annotated in lower left: betterave
Nuenen June-August 1885
LETTERS 414 [June] and 422 [mid-August]
See F 1250
LITERATURE Vanbeselaere 1937, pp 275, 413: September-October 1885
COLLECTION Amsterdam, Rijksmuseum Vincent van Gogh [Vincent van Gogh Foundation, inv nr F 1303]

F 1304 PEASANT DIGGING UP POTATOES: SEEN FROM THE FRONT

Black chalk [gray paper] 28 × 22 [11 × 8¾]
Nuenen August 1885
LETTERS 414 [June] and 422 [mid-August]
See F 1250
LITERATURE Vanbeselaere 1937, pp 275, 413: September-October 1885
COLLECTION Sale London [Sotheby] 23 October

1963, nr 73
Present owner unknown

F 1305 PEASANT DIGGING: FACING LEFT

Black chalk [wove paper] 53 × 35.5 [21 × 14]
Nuenen August 1885
LETTERS 414 [June] and 422 [mid-August]
See F 1250
LITERATURE Faille 1928, nr 1305: text under
nr 1307. Vanbeselaere 1937, pp 275, 413:
September-October 1885
COLLECTION Amsterdam, Rijksmuseum Vincent
van Gogh [Vincent van Gogh Foundation, inv
nr F 1305]

F 1306 YOUNG PEASANT, DIGGING: FACING
RIGHT

Black chalk, stumped 52 × 39 [20½ × 15¼]
Nuenen June-August 1885
LETTERS 414 [June] and 422 [mid-August]
See F 1250
LITERATURE Vanbeselaere 1937, pp 275, 413:
September-October 1885
COLLECTION Oslo, Nasjonal Galleriet [acquired
1919]

F 1307 YOUNG PEASANT DIGGING: FACING
LEFT

Black chalk, pencil, brush and ink, heightened with
white [laid paper, reddish] 44 × 30 [17¼ × 11¾]
Nuenen June-August 1885
LETTERS 414 [June] and 422 [mid-August]
See F 1250
LITERATURE Faille 1928, nr 1307: text under
F 1305. Vanbeselaere 1937, pp 278, 413: October-
November 1885
COLLECTION Amsterdam, Rijksmuseum Vincent
van Gogh [Vincent van Gogh Foundation, inv
nr F 1307]

F 1308 PEASANT DIGGING: FACING RIGHT

Black chalk [laid paper, reddish] 29.5 × 22.5
[11½ × 8¾]
Nuenen August 1885
LETTERS 414 [June] and 422 [mid-August]
See F 1250
LITERATURE Vanbeselaere 1937, pp 275, 413:
September-October 1885
COLLECTION Amsterdam, Rijksmuseum Vincent
van Gogh [Vincent van Gogh Foundation, inv
nr F 1308]

F 1309 PEASANT DIGGING: SEEN FROM THE
FRONT

Black chalk [Ingres paper with watermark: E.D. &
Cie] 23 × 32.5 [9 × 12¾]
Nuenen August 1885
LETTERS 414 [June] and 422 [mid-August]
See F 1250
LITERATURE Vanbeselaere 1937, pp 275, 413:
September-October 1885
COLLECTION Amsterdam, Rijksmuseum Vincent
van Gogh [Vincent van Gogh Foundation, inv
nr F 1309]

F 1305

F 1306

F 1307

F 1308

F 1309

F 1310

F 1311

F 1313

F 1314

F 1317

F 1315

F 1318

F 1310 PEASANT DIGGING: FACING RIGHT

Black chalk [ordinary wove paper] 44 × 28
[17¼ × 11]
Nuenen June-August 1885
LETTERS 414 [June] and 422 [mid-August]
See F 1250
LITERATURE Faille 1928, nr 1310, not reproduced.
Vanbeselaere 1937, p 413
COLLECTION Amsterdam, Rijksmuseum Vincent
van Gogh [Vincent van Gogh Foundation, inv
nr F 1310]

F 1311 SKETCH OF A PEASANT WORKING:
FACING RIGHT

Black chalk [Dutch laid paper with watermark:
Pro patria – Concordia res parvae crescunt]
35 × 21 [13¾ × 8¼]
Compare painting F 166 [same model]
Nuenen August 1885
LETTERS 414 [June] and 422 [mid-August]
See F 1250
LITERATURE Album Hidde Nijland Collection
1905, plate 68. Vanbeselaere 1937, pp 276, 413:
September-October 1885
COLLECTION Otterlo, Rijksmuseum Kröller-
Müller, inv nr 999-28, cat van Gogh 1970, nr 131

F 1312 THE REAPER WITH HAT: SEEN FROM
THE BACK

Black chalk and ink [wove paper, yellowish]
44 × 28 [17¼ × 11]
Compare F 1313
Nuenen August 1885
LETTERS 419 [early August] See F 1262
R 57 [August] *'I want to tell you further that I have
drawn a number of heads since you were here, and
quite a lot of peasants besides: diggers, weeders,
harvesters.'*
LITERATURE Vanbeselaere 1937, pp 273, 391, 413:
August 1885
COLLECTION Amsterdam, Stedelijk Museum [on
loan from the Rijksmuseum]

F 1313 THE REAPER WITH HAT: SEEN FROM
THE BACK

Black chalk, heightened with white [wove paper
with watermark: T.S.& Z.] 56 × 38 [22 × 15]
Compare F 1312
Nuenen August 1885
LETTERS 419 [early August] See F 1262
R 57 [August] See F 1312
LITERATURE Album Hidde Nijland Collection
1905, plate 61. Idem 1907, plate 9. J.B.J. Stokvis,
Kunst und Künstler April 1927, p 255 [with
reproduction]. Vanbeselaere 1937, pp 273, 391, 413.
W. Weisbach, Vincent van Gogh – Kunst und
Schicksal, volume 1, 1949, p 192
COLLECTION Otterlo, Rijksmuseum Kröller-
Müller, inv nr 992-28, cat van Gogh 1970, nr 118

F 1314 THE REAPER WITH HAT: FACING
RIGHT

Black chalk [ordinary wove paper] 44.5 × 28.5
[17½ × 11¼]
Signed in lower right: Vincent
Nuenen August 1885
LETTERS 419 [early August] See F 1262
R 57 [August] See F 1312
LITERATURE Album Hidde Nijland Collection
1905, plate 36. Vanbeselaere 1937, pp 273, 391, 413
COLLECTION Otterlo, Rijksmuseum Kröller-
Müller, inv nr 969-28, cat van Gogh 1970, nr 111

F 1312

F 1316

F 1315 THE REAPER WITH HAT: SEEN FROM
THE BACK

Black chalk [wove paper with watermark: T.S. &
Z.] 44.5 × 57 [17½ × 22½]
Signed in lower right: Vincent
Nuenen August 1885
LETTERS 419 [early August] See F 1262
R 57 [August] See F 1312
LITERATURE Album Hidde Nijland Collection
1905, plate 70. Idem 1907, plate 5. H. van den
Eerenbeemt, Opgang March 1924, p 162.
J. E. Blanche, L'Art Vivant July 1927, p 68 [with
reproduction]. Vanbeselaere 1937, pp 273, 391, 413
COLLECTION Otterlo, Rijksmuseum Kröller-
Müller, inv nr 1001-28, cat van Gogh 1970, nr 114

F 1316 THE REAPER WITH HAT: FACING
RIGHT

Black chalk, stumped [wove paper, yellowish]
43.5 × 55.5 [17 × 21¾]
Nuenen August 1885
LETTERS 419 [early August] See F 1262
R 57 [August] See F 1312
LITERATURE Vanbeselaere 1937, pp 273, 391, 413
COLLECTION Amsterdam, Rijksmuseum Vincent
van Gogh [Vincent van Gogh Foundation, inv
nr F 1316]

F 1317 THE REAPER WITH CAP: MOVING TO
THE RIGHT

Black chalk, stumped [wove paper, yellowish]
43 × 55 [17 × 21¾]
Nuenen August 1885
LETTERS 419 [early August] See F 1262
R 57 [August] See F 1312
LITERATURE Vanbeselaere 1937, pp 273, 391, 413
COLLECTION Amsterdam, Rijksmuseum Vincent
van Gogh [Vincent van Gogh Foundation, inv
nr F 1317]

F 1318 THE REAPER WITH CAP: MOVING TO
THE RIGHT

Black chalk, stumped [wove paper, yellowish]
41 × 51 [16¼ × 20]
Nuenen August 1885
LETTER 419 [early August] See F 1262
R 57 [August] See F 1312
LITERATURE Vanbeselaere 1937, pp 273, 391, 413
COLLECTION Amsterdam, Rijksmuseum Vincent
van Gogh [Vincent van Gogh Foundation, inv
nr F 1318]

F 1322 recto

F 1322 verso

F 1319 recto

F 1320

F 1319 recto THE REAPER WITH CAP: SEEN
FROM THE FRONT

Black chalk, stumped [wove paper, yellowish]
56.5 × 44.5 [22¼ × 17½]
Nuenen August 1885
LETTERS 419 [early August] See F 1262
R 57 [August] See F 1312
LITERATURE Vanbeselaere 1937, pp 273, 391, 413
COLLECTION Amsterdam, Rijksmuseum Vincent
van Gogh [Vincent van Gogh Foundation, inv
nr F 1319]

F 1319 verso LANDSCAPE WITH SHEAVES OF
WHEAT AND A WINDMILL

Black chalk, stumped 44.5 × 56.5 [17½ × 22¼]
Compare F 1321 recto, F 1340, F 1341 and F 1342
[same site]
Nuenen August 1885
LITERATURE Not in Faille 1928 or Vanbeselaere
1937

F 1320 THE REAPER WITH HAT: MOVING TO
THE RIGHT

Black chalk 43 × 54 [17 × 21¼]
Nuenen August 1885
LETTERS 419 [early August] See F 1262
R 57 [August] See F 1312
LITERATURE Vincent van Gogh, Lettres à Bernard,
plate XXX. Vanbeselaere 1937, pp 274, 391, 413
COLLECTION Zurich, Mrs D. Hahnloser-Gassmann

F 1321 recto A REAPER AND A WOMAN
BINDING SHEAVES: A WINDMILL IN THE
BACKGROUND

Black chalk, stumped [wove paper, yellowish]
27 × 39.5 [10½ × 15½]
Compare F 1301 recto [in part the same motif],
F 1319 verso, F 1340, F 1341 and F 1342 [same site]
Nuenen August 1885
LETTER 421 [August] See F 1301 recto
LITERATURE Vanbeselaere 1937, pp 274, 391, 413
COLLECTION Amsterdam, Rijksmuseum Vincent
van Gogh [Vincent van Gogh Foundation, inv
nr F 1321]

F 1321 verso FIGURE OF A MAN WITH A HAT
[the upper part of a drawing torn in half; the
lower part is F 1301 verso]

Black chalk, stumped
Nuenen August 1885
LITERATURE Not in Faille 1928 or Vanbeselaere
1937

F 1322 recto PEASANT REAPING WHEAT IN
A LANDSCAPE WITH TREES AND A LITTLE
HOUSE

Black chalk [wove paper with watermark: T.S. &
Z.] 41.5 × 58 [16¼ × 22¾]
Signed in lower right: Vincent
Annotated in lower left: Port. Vincent
Nuenen August 1885
LETTERS 419 [early August] See F 1262
R 57 [August] See F 1312
LITERATURE Album Hidde Nijland Collection
1905, plate 80. Vanbeselaere 1937, pp 274, 391, 413
COLLECTION Otterlo, Rijksmuseum Kröller-
Müller, inv nr 1011-28, cat van Gogh 1970, nr 110

F 1322 verso THE REAPER WITH HAT: SEEN
FROM THE BACK

Black chalk
Annotated in lower left: Port. Vincent. Hidde
Nijland

F 1319 verso

Nuenen August 1885
LETTERS 419 [early August] See F 1262
R 57 [August] See F 1312
LITERATURE Not in Faille 1928 or Vanbeselaere
1937

F 1323 THE REAPER WITH HAT: SEEN FROM
THE BACK

Black chalk [wove paper with watermark: T.S. &
Z.] 52.5 × 37 [20¾ × 14½]
Signed in lower left and lower right: Vincent
Nuenen August 1885
LETTERS 419 [early August] See F 1262
R 57 [August] See F 1312
LITERATURE Album Hidde Nijland Collection
1905, plate 47. K. Pfister, Vincent van Gogh, 1929
[2d edition], p 9 [with reproduction]. Vanbeselaere
1937, pp 274, 391, 413: wrongly called F 1223
COLLECTION Otterlo, Rijksmuseum Kröller-
Müller, inv nr 979-28, cat van Gogh 1970, nr 119

F 1324 PEASANT REAPING WHEAT
Left out by Faille in his manuscript for the present
edition
See REJECTED WORKS

F 1321 verso

F 1321 recto

F 1323

F 1325

F 1328 recto

F 1328 verso

F 1329 recto

F 1329 verso

F 1325 PEASANT WORKING: FACING RIGHT, TWO COTTAGES IN THE BACKGROUND

Black chalk, stumped [thin wove paper] 44 × 33.5 [17¼ × 13¼]
Signed in lower right: Vincent
Compare F 1326 [similar motif]
Nuenen probably autumn 1885
LITERATURE Album Hidde Nijland Collection 1905, plate 43. Idem 1907, plate 21. W. Steenhoff, Elseviers Geïllustreerd Maandschrift 1928, nr 8, plate xxvii. W. F. Douwes, Vincent van Gogh, [1930], plate 29. Vanbeselaere 1937, pp 276, 413: September-October 1885
COLLECTION Otterlo, Rijksmuseum Kröller-Müller, inv nr 976-28, cat van Gogh 1970, nr 132

F 1326 A PEASANT WORKING: FACING RIGHT, TWO COTTAGES IN THE BACKGROUND

Black chalk, stumped [Dutch paper with watermark: T.S. & Z.] 43 × 32 [17 × 12½]
Signed in lower right: Vincent
Compare F 1325 [similar motif]
Nuenen probably autumn 1885
LITERATURE Vanbeselaere 1937, pp 276, 413
COLLECTION Otterlo, Rijksmuseum Kröller-Müller, inv nr 1032-28, cat van Gogh 1970, nr 130

F 1327 THE WOODCUTTER: FACING RIGHT

Black chalk, stumped [Dutch laid paper with watermark: H.F.d.C. Scutcheon with fleur-de-lis] 44 × 54.5 [17¼ × 21½]
Nuenen autumn 1885
LITERATURE Vincent van Gogh, Lettres à Bernard, 1911, plate XIV. Vanbeselaere 1937, p 413
COLLECTION Amsterdam, Rijksmuseum Vincent van Gogh [Vincent van Gogh Foundation, inv nr F 1327]

F 1328 recto PEASANT: FACING RIGHT

Black chalk [Dutch laid paper with watermark: v.d. L.] 34.8 × 21 [13¾ × 8¼]
Nuenen August 1885
LITERATURE Album Hidde Nijland Collection 1905, plate 58. Vanbeselaere 1937, pp 276, 392, 413
COLLECTION Otterlo, Rijksmuseum Kröller-Müller, inv nr 989-28, cat van Gogh 1970, nr 137

F 1328 verso THREE STUDIES OF A PEASANT; A HEAD: SEEN FROM THE BACK

Black chalk, stumped
Nuenen August 1885
LITERATURE Not in Faille 1928 or Vanbeselaere 1937

F 1329 recto PEASANT WALKING TO THE LEFT

Black chalk, stumped [Dutch laid paper with watermark: v.d. L.] 35 × 21 [13¾ × 8¼]
Nuenen August 1885
LITERATURE Album Hidde Nijland Collection 1905, plate 10. Vanbeselaere 1937, pp 64-5, 276, 392, 413
COLLECTION Otterlo, Rijksmuseum Kröller-Müller, inv nr 944-28, cat van Gogh 1970, nr 140

F 1329 verso STUDIES OF FOUR FIGURES

Black chalk, stumped
Annotated in lower left: Verz. Hidde Nijland
Nuenen August 1885
LITERATURE Not in Faille 1928 or Vanbeselaere 1937

F 1330 recto PEASANT WALKING: SEEN FROM THE FRONT

Black chalk, stumped [laid Dutch paper with watermark: Pro Patria – Concordia res parvae crescunt] 34 × 19 [13½ × 7½]
Nuenen May-June 1885
LITERATURE Album Hidde Nijland Collection 1905, plate 33. Vanbeselaere 1937, pp 276, 392, 413
EDITORS' COMMENT This drawing is clearly an example of a drawing style inspired by Delacroix, as Vincent mentioned it in two letters of April.
401 [April] *'Enclosed you will find some interesting pages about color, namely the great principles which Delacroix believed in.'*
402 [April] *'...that question of drawing the figure starting with the circle...'*
COLLECTION Otterlo, Rijksmuseum Kröller-Müller, inv nr 967-28, cat van Gogh 1970, nr 133

F 1330 verso STUDY FOR A PEASANT; THREE HANDS HOLDING A STICK

Black chalk, stumped
Annotated in lower left: Verz. Hidde Nijland
Nuenen May-June 1885
LITERATURE Not in Faille 1928 or Vanbeselaere 1937

F 1331 SHORT-LEGGED OLD MAN WITH A BALD HEAD: SEEN FROM THE FRONT

Black chalk, stumped [Dutch laid paper with watermark: v.d.L.] 34.5 × 21 [13½ × 8¼]
Compare F 1332 recto [same model]
Nuenen summer 1885
LITERATURE Vincent van Gogh, Lettres à Bernard, 1911, plate XXIV. Vanbeselaere 1937, pp 276, 392, 413
EDITORS' COMMENT Until now this drawing and F 1332 recto have been called, for unknown reasons, 'THE GRAVE DIGGER.' The title may have something to do with the mention in letter 418 [July 1885] of *'the mourning peasant.'*
COLLECTION Amsterdam, Rijksmuseum Vincent van Gogh [Vincent van Gogh Foundation, inv nr F 1331]

F 1327

F 1326

F 1330 recto

F 1331

F 1330 verso

F 1332 recto

F 1332 verso

F 1333 recto

F 1333 verso

F 1335

F 1336 verso

F 1337

F 1339

F 1332 recto SHORT-LEGGED OLD MAN WITH A BALD HEAD: SEEN FROM THE FRONT

Black chalk, stumped [Dutch laid paper] 34.5 × 21 [13½ × 8¼]
Compare F 1331 [same model]
Nuenen summer 1885
LITERATURE Vanbeselaere 1937, pp 276, 392, 413
EDITORS' COMMENT See F 1331
COLLECTION Amsterdam, Rijksmuseum Vincent van Gogh [Vincent van Gogh Foundation, inv nr F 1332]

F 1332 verso PEASANT AND PEASANT WOMAN WITH BABY

Black chalk
Nuenen May-June 1885
LITERATURE Not in Faille 1928 or Vanbeselaere 1937

F 1333 recto STUDY OF TWO PEASANTS

Black chalk, stumped [Dutch laid paper with watermark: Pro patria–Concordia res parvae crescunt] 35 × 21 [13¾ × 8¼]
Nuenen summer 1885
LITERATURE Album Hidde Nijland Collection 1905, plate 87. Vanbeselaere 1937, pp 276, 413
COLLECTION Otterlo, Rijksmuseum Kröller-Müller, inv nr 1018-28, cat van Gogh 1970, nr 141

F 1333 verso STUDY OF TWO PEASANTS

Black chalk, stumped 21 × 35 [8¼ × 13¾]
Annotated in lower right: Vincent. Verz. Hidde Nijland
Nuenen summer 1885
LITERATURE Not in Faille 1928 or Vanbeselaere 1937

F 1334 PEASANT RESTING IN A CHAIR

Left out by Faille in his manuscript for the present edition
See REJECTED WORKS

F 1335 MAN LOADING A CART

Pen and ink, washed [ordinary drawing paper] 10.5 × 17.5 [4¼ × 7]
Nuenen spring 1885
LITERATURE Album Hidde Nijland Collection 1905, part 7, reproduction on cover. Vanbeselaere 1937, pp 259, 413: March 1884
EDITORS' COMMENT On account of stylistic relation to F 1291 and F 1292, the editors date F 1335 to spring 1885.
COLLECTION Otterlo, Rijksmuseum Kröller-Müller, inv nr 1043-28, cat van Gogh 1970, nr 139

F 1336 recto THE OLD TOWER AT NUENEN; STUDIES OF FIGURES

Black chalk, stumped [Dutch laid paper with watermark: Pro Patria–Concordia res parvae crescunt] 34.5 × 20.5 [13½ × 8]
Nuenen May 1885
LETTER 408 [after 8 May] See F 1112 recto
LITERATURE Album Hidde Nijland Collection 1905, plate 93. Vanbeselaere 1937, pp 269, 413.
S. Leurs and M. E. Tralbaut, Brabantia February 1957, p 54
COLLECTION Otterlo, Rijksmuseum Kröller-Müller, inv nr 1035-28, cat van Gogh 1970, nr 138

F 1336 verso MAN WITH LADDER ON HIS
SHOULDER; A GROUP OF FIGURES
Below CEMETERY WITH WOODEN CROSSES

Black chalk
Annotated in lower left: V.v.G. verz. Hidde Nijland
Nuenen May 1885
LETTER 408 [after 8 May] See F 1112 recto
LITERATURE Not in Faille 1928 or Vanbeselaere
1937

F 1337 MANGLE WITH TWO WOMEN AND A
MAN

Pencil, pen and ink [ordinary wove paper] 23 × 29.5
[9 × 11½] Unfinished
Nuenen 1884 [?]
LITERATURE Album Hidde Nijland Collection
1905, plate 23. Vanbeselaere 1937, p 413: Paris
period
COLLECTION Otterlo, Rijksmuseum Kröller-
Müller, inv nr 957-28, cat van Gogh 1970, nr 153

F 1338 A COUPLE ON THE ROAD
Antwerp period; see after F 1361

F 1339 FIELD WITH A MAN BINDING
SHEAVES

Black chalk [Dutch laid paper with watermark:
v.d. L.] 20 × 33 [7¾ × 13]
Nuenen August 1885
LETTERS 416 [6 July] See F 94
419 [early August] See F 1262
LITERATURE Vanbeselaere 1937, pp 274, 391, 413
COLLECTION Amsterdam, Rijksmuseum Vincent
van Gogh [Vincent van Gogh Foundation, inv
nr F 1339]

F 1340 FIELD WITH SHEAVES: WINDMILL
IN THE LEFT BACKGROUND

Black chalk, stumped and slightly heightened with
white [laid paper] 22.5 × 29.5 [8¾ × 11½]
Compare F 1319 verso, F 1321 recto, F 1341 and
F 1342 [same site]
Nuenen August 1885
LETTER 416 [6 July] See F 94
419 [early August] See F 1262
LITERATURE Vanbeselaere 1937, pp 274, 391, 413
COLLECTION Amsterdam, Rijksmuseum Vincent
van Gogh [Vincent van Gogh Foundation, inv
nr F 1340]

F 1336 recto

F 1340

F 1341

F 1342

F 1343a

F 1344

F 1345

F 1346

F 1348

F 1341 FIELD WITH ONE SHEAF: WINDMILL
IN THE RIGHT BACKGROUND

Black chalk, stumped [Ingres paper with water-
mark: E.D. & Cie–P.L. Bas] 25 × 34 [9¾ × 13½]
Compare F 1319 verso, F 1321 recto, F 1340 and
F 1342 [same site]
Compare F 1319 verso, F 1340 and F 1342 [same site]
Nuenen August 1885
LETTERS 416 [6 July] See F 94
419 [early August] See F 1262
LITERATURE Vanbeselaere 1937, pp 274, 391, 413
COLLECTION Amsterdam, Rijksmuseum Vincent
van Gogh [Vincent van Gogh Foundation, inv
nr F 1341]

F 1342 SHEAVES: WINDMILL IN THE RIGHT
BACKGROUND

Black chalk, stumped [Ingres paper with water-
mark: E.D. & Cie–P.L. Bas] 25 × 34 [9¾ × 13½]
Compare F 1319 verso, F 1321 recto, F 1340 and
F 1341 [same site]
Nuenen August 1885
LETTERS 416 [6 July] See F 94
419 [early August] See F 1262
LITERATURE Vanbeselaere 1937, pp 274, 391, 413
COLLECTION Amsterdam, Rijksmuseum Vincent
van Gogh [Vincent van Gogh Foundation, inv
nr F 1342]

F 1343 THE VICARAGE AT NUENEN: SEEN
FROM THE BACK, WITH THE ARTIST'S
STUDIO ON THE RIGHT

Pen, black chalk, heightened with white 24 × 36
[9½ × 14¼]
Compare painting F 183 [same site]
Nuenen probably early 1884
LITERATURE Publisher's list De Bois, Haarlem
1928, reproduction nr 32. Vanbeselaere 1937,
pp 278, 413: October-November 1885
COLLECTION Canada, Private Collection

F 1343a THE VICARAGE AT NUENEN: SEEN
FROM THE FRONT

Pencil, pen and ink [wove paper] 7.5 × 10 [3 × 4]
Compare painting F 182 [same site]
Nuenen autumn 1885
LITERATURE Not in Faille 1928 or Vanbeselaere
1937
COLLECTION Oegstgeest, Netherlands,
Heirs of Mrs J. P. Scholte-van Houten

F 1344 THE FARM

Black chalk, stumped 10 × 13.5 [4 × 5¼]
Reproduced with letter 411
Nuenen probably June 1885
LITERATURE Vanbeselaere 1937, pp 217, 413
COLLECTION Amsterdam, Rijksmuseum Vincent
van Gogh [Vincent van Gogh Foundation, inv
nr F 1344]

F 1345 FARM WITH WINDMILL IN THE
BACKGROUND

Black chalk, stumped [laid paper] 22.5 × 30
[8¾ × 11¾]
Nuenen probably summer 1885
LITERATURE Faille 1928, nr 1345, not reproduced.
Vanbeselaere 1937, p 413
COLLECTION Amsterdam, Rijksmuseum Vincent
van Gogh [Vincent van Gogh Foundation, inv
nr F 1345]

F 1346 TWO ISOLATED TREES UNDER STORM
CLOUDS: A WINDMILL IN THE
BACKGROUND

Black chalk, stumped, heightened with white [laid
paper] 29 × 22.5 [11½ × 8¾]
Nuenen summer 1885
LITERATURE Faille 1928, nr 1346, not reproduced.
Vanbeselaere 1937, p 413
COLLECTION Amsterdam, Rijksmuseum Vincent
van Gogh [Vincent van Gogh Foundation, inv
nr F 1346]

F 1347 LANDSCAPE WITH A BRIDGE
Drenthe period; see after F 1106

F 1348 STREET IN RAINY WEATHER
[IN EINDHOVEN]

Water color [water-color paper] 21 × 29.5 [8¼ × 11½]
Annotated by Vincent and signed in lower left: Un
dimanche à Eindhoven, Vincent
Eindhoven [Nuenen period] autumn 1885 [?]
LITERATURE Vanbeselaere 1937, pp 258, 413:
January 1884
COLLECTION Amsterdam, Rijksmuseum Vincent
van Gogh [Vincent van Gogh Foundation, inv
nr F 1348]

F 1349 recto STUDIES OF A CLOCK, A SPOON
RACK AND A WOODEN SHOE [studies for
THE POTATO EATERS]

Black chalk [Ingres paper with watermark:
v.d. L.] 34.5 × 20.5 [13½ × 8]
Nuenen April 1885
LETTER 398 [early April] See F 82
LITERATURE Vanbeselaere 1937, pp 267, 413.
J. G. van Gelder, The Potato Eaters, 1949, p 11:

April 1885
COLLECTION Amsterdam, Rijksmuseum Vincent
van Gogh [Vincent van Gogh Foundation, inv
nr F 1349]

F 1349 verso STUDIES OF A PLATE, TWO
KNIVES AND A WATER KETTLE [studies for
THE POTATO EATERS]

Black chalk
Compare painting F 82 and F 1153 verso
Nuenen April 1885
LITERATURE J.G. van Gelder, The Potato Eaters,
1949, p 11: April 1885

F 1349 recto

F 1349 verso

F 1343

F 68

F 1081

F 1106

F 1350 recto

F 1350 verso

REDATED TO NUENEN

F 68 PEASANT WOMAN WINDING BOBBINS

Water color, heightened with white 33 × 41
[13 × 16¼]
Compare F 1136 [same model]
Nuenen April-July 1884
LETTER 370 [June] '*I should be very glad to receive the measures of your frames soon, then I should be able to get going. Perhaps if the measure fits, I shall make a small one of that woman spinning.*'
372 [between 1 and 7 July] '*... I intend to make a little woman spinning after the large study.*'
LITERATURE Faille 1928, nr 68: Nuenen February-March 1885; letter 396. Vanbeselaere 1937, pp 282, 351, 414. Faille 1939, nr 75. Cat van Gogh 1966, Rijksmuseum Kröller-Müller, nr 127
EDITORS' COMMENT The passages from the letters quoted by Faille all have to do with paintings.
COLLECTION New York, Wildenstein Art Gallery [acquired 1955]

F 1081 MAN CARRYING A BUNDLE OF BRANCHES

Water color 32.5 × 25 [12¾ × 9¾]
Nuenen August 1884
LITERATURE Faille 1928, nr 1081: The Hague. Vanbeselaere 1937, pp 110, 261, 410: Nuenen
COLLECTION Sale London [Sotheby] 10 July 1957, nr 52
Present owner unknown

F 1106 WINTER LANDSCAPE WITH WOMAN AND WHEELBARROW

Pen [ordinary paper] 21 × 13 [8¼ × 5]
Annotated on verso: port. Vincent – Hidde Nijland
Nuenen February 1884
LITERATURE Album Hidde Nijland Collection 1905, plate 79a. Faille 1928, nr 1106: Drenthe. Vanbeselaere 1937, pp 237, 410: Drenthe October 1883. Tralbaut Drenthe 1959, pp 215, 224: Drenthe October 1883. Cat van Gogh 1966, Rijksmuseum Kröller-Müller, nr 163: Nuenen
EDITORS' COMMENT Faille dates F 1106 to Nuenen February 1884 in the manuscript for this edition.
COLLECTION Otterlo, Rijksmuseum Kröller-Müller, inv nr 1009-28, cat van Gogh 1970, nr 163

ANTWERP PERIOD

F 1350 recto THE STEEN AT ANTWERP

Black and colored chalk [(dis)colored paper]
9.3 × 16.4 [3¾ × 6½]
Antwerp December 1885
LITERATURE Tralbaut Antwerp 1948, nr 18, pp 234-6, 283: December 1885; study for a lost painting described in letter 440; belongs to the same sketchbook as F 1350a and F 1350b
EDITORS' COMMENT F 1350 belonged to the same sketchbook of which F 1350a, F 1350b, F 1355, F 1358 and F 1359 also formed part.
COLLECTION Amsterdam, Rijksmuseum Vincent van Gogh [Vincent van Gogh Foundation, inv nr F 1350]

F 1350 verso TWO SKETCHES OF A WOMAN SEATED IN A BOX AT THE THEATER

Black and colored chalk
Antwerp early December 1885
LETTER 438 [first half of December] '*Yesterday I was at the Café-concert Scala, something like the Folies Bergères; I found it very dull, and of course insipid – but the public amused me. There were splendid women's heads, really extraordinarily fine, among the good middle-class folks on the back*

seats...'
LITERATURE Tralbaut Antwerp 1948, nr 7,
pp 241-3, 245-6, 283: early December 1885
EDITORS' COMMENT See F 1350 recto

F 1350a DANCING HALL

Black and colored chalk [thick wove sketchbook
paper] 9.3 × 16.4 [3¾ × 6½]
Antwerp early December 1885
LETTER 438 [first half of December] See F 1350
verso
LITERATURE Not in Faille 1928. Tralbaut Antwerp
1948, nr 8, reproduction XXVIII, pp 45-6, 246-8,
283: early December 1885; letter 438; belongs to
the same sketchbook as F 1350 and F 1350b
EDITORS' COMMENT See F 1350 recto
COLLECTION Amsterdam, Rijksmuseum Vincent
van Gogh [Vincent van Gogh Foundation, inv
nr F 1350a]

F 1350b WOMEN DANCING

Black and colored chalk [thick wove sketchbook
paper] 9.3 × 16.4 [3¾ × 6½]
Antwerp early December 1885
LETTER 438 [first half of December] See F 1350
verso
LITERATURE Not in Faille 1928. Tralbaut Antwerp
1948, nr 9, reproduction XXIX, pp 45-6, 249-51,
283: early December 1885; belongs to the same
sketchbook as F 1350 and F 1350a
EDITORS' COMMENT See F 1350 recto
COLLECTION Amsterdam, Rijksmuseum Vincent
van Gogh [Vincent van Gogh Foundation, inv
nr F 1350b]

F 1351 THE STEEN AT ANTWERP

Pencil and pen, heightened with colored chalk
[wove graph paper] 13.2 × 21 [5¼ × 8¼]
Reproduced with letter 440 in the American edition
of the letters
Antwerp December 1885
LITERATURE Tralbaut Antwerp 1948, nr 19,
pp 236-8, 284: December 1885; later than drawing
F 1350
COLLECTION Amsterdam, Rijksmuseum Vincent
van Gogh [Vincent van Gogh Foundation, inv
nr F 1351]

F 1352 THE GROTE MARKT IN ANTWERP

Black chalk, heightened with colors [blue Ingres
paper] 22.5 × 30 [8¾ × 11¾]
Antwerp 18 December 1885
LETTER 441 [19 December] *'So yesterday I made a
few drawings of a spot with a view of the Cathedral.'*
LITERATURE Tralbaut Antwerp 1948, nr 22,
pp 238-9, 284: 18 December 1885; letter 441
COLLECTION Amsterdam, Rijksmuseum Vincent
van Gogh [Vincent van Gogh Foundation, inv
nr F 1352]

F 1350a

F 1350b

F 1351

F 1352

F 1353

F 1354a recto

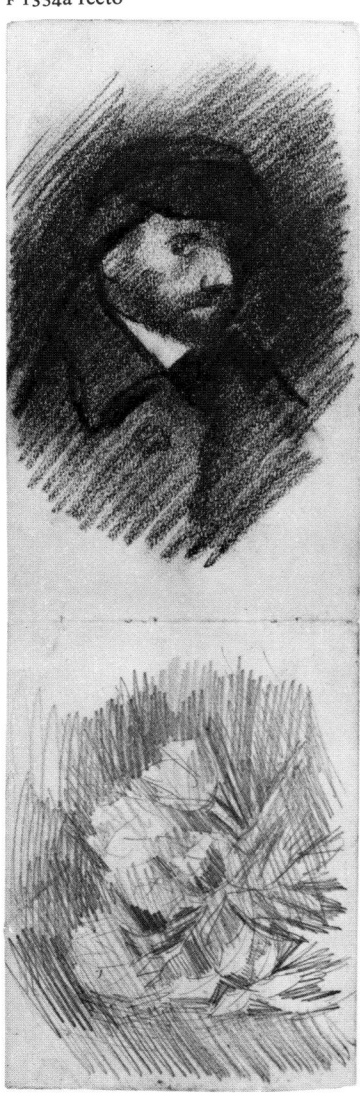

F 1354a verso

F 1353 NUDE WOMAN

Black chalk [wove paper] 19.5 × 11 [7¾ × 4¼]
Probably Antwerp winter 1885-6
LITERATURE Tralbaut Antwerp 1948, nr 39,
pp 253-5, 284: end January 1886; letter 447; belongs
to the same sketchbook as F 1354 and F 1354a
COLLECTION Amsterdam, Rijksmuseum Vincent
van Gogh [Vincent van Gogh Foundation, inv
nr F 1353]

F 1354 SQUARE IN ANTWERP

Pencil and black chalk [wove paper] 10.9 × 19.6
[4¼ × 7¾]
Antwerp probably December 1885
LITERATURE Tralbaut Antwerp 1948, pp 266-7, 272:
not Antwerp but Paris; belongs to the same sketchbook as F 1353 and F 1354a. A. M. Hammacher,
exhib cat van Gogh-Signac London 1962, nr 23:
Antwerp winter 1885-6
EDITORS' COMMENT Dated Paris 1886 by Faille in
his manuscript for the present edition.
COLLECTION Amsterdam, Rijksmuseum Vincent
van Gogh [Vincent van Gogh Foundation, inv
nr F 1354]

F 1354a recto SELF PORTRAIT
Adjoining page SKETCH OF A FLOWER

Black chalk [drawing paper] 19.7 × 10.9 [7¾ × 4¼];
adjoining page: pencil 15.1 × 10.9 [6 × 4¼]
Antwerp 1885
LITERATURE Not in Faille 1928. Tralbaut
Antwerp 1948, nr 42, reproduction XLIV, pp 272,
285: February 1886; belongs to the same sketchbook as F 1353 and F 1354. K. Bromig-Kolleritz,
Die Selbstbildnisse Vincent van Goghs, 1955,
pp 91-2: January-February 1886, based on
L. Piérard's report that Victor Hagemans identified
the clothes Vincent wears in this self portrait as
those he owned when he entered the painting class
in the Academy in late January 1886. F. Erpel, Die
Selbstbildnisse Vincent van Goghs, 1963, nr 4
COLLECTION Amsterdam, Rijksmuseum Vincent
van Gogh [Vincent van Gogh Foundation, inv
nr F 1354a]

F 1354a verso SELF PORTRAIT
Adjoining page FIGURE SKETCHES

Black chalk
Antwerp 1885
LITERATURE Not in Faille 1928. Tralbaut
Antwerp 1948, nr 43, reproduction XLV: February
1886; belongs to the same sketchbook as F 1353 and
F 1354

F 1355 TOWN VIEW IN ANTWERP

Black chalk [wove paper] 9.5 × 16.5 [3¾ × 6½]
Antwerp probably December 1885
LITERATURE Tralbaut Antwerp 1948, pp 266-7:
not Antwerp but Paris
EDITORS' COMMENT See F 1350 recto. Dated Paris
1886 by Faille in his manuscript for the present
edition.
COLLECTION Amsterdam, Rijksmuseum Vincent
van Gogh [Vincent van Gogh Foundation, inv
nr F 1355]

F 1356 SPIRE OF THE CHURCH OF OUR LADY
IN ANTWERP

Black chalk [pink Ingres paper] 30 × 22.5
[11¾ × 8¾]
Antwerp 18 December 1885
LETTER 441 [19 December] See F 1352
LITERATURE Tralbaut Antwerp 1948, nr 23,
pp 240, 284: identifies the motif as the spire of the

F 1356

Church of our Lady in Antwerp; 18 December 1885; letter 441
COLLECTION Amsterdam, Rijksmuseum Vincent van Gogh [Vincent van Gogh Foundation, inv nr F 1356]

F 1357 PORTRAIT OF A WOMAN

Charcoal and black and red chalk [water-color paper with watermark: J. Whatman 1884]
50.6 × 39.4 [20 × 15½]
Antwerp December 1885
LITERATURE Tralbaut Antwerp 1948, nr 6, pp 255-7, 283: early December 1885
COLLECTION Amsterdam, Rijksmuseum Vincent van Gogh [Vincent van Gogh Foundation, inv nr F 1357]

F 1354

F 1355

F 1357

F 1357a

F 1358

F 1359

F 1361

F 1093

F 1357a PORTRAIT OF A WOMAN WITH HAT

Pen, brush and pencil 13 × 9.5 [5 × 3¾]
Antwerp December 1885
LITERATURE Not in Faille 1928 or Tralbaut
Antwerp 1948. M. E. Tralbaut, exhib cat van Gogh
Essen 1957, nr 221 : Antwerp
COLLECTION Deurne, Netherlands, Heirs of
Dr J. Wiegersma

F 1358 HEAD OF A MAN

Black chalk [wove sketchbook paper] 16.5 × 9
[6½ × 3½]
Antwerp winter 1885-6
LITERATURE Tralbaut Antwerp 1948, nr 41,
pp 258, 284 : belongs to the same sketchbook as
F 1350, F 1350a, F 1350b and F 1359
EDITORS' COMMENT See F 1350 recto
COLLECTION Amsterdam, Rijksmuseum Vincent
van Gogh [Vincent van Gogh Foundation, inv
nr F 1358]

F 1359 HEAD OF A MAN WITH PIPE: LEFT PROFILE

Black chalk [wove sketchbook paper] 16.5 × 9
[6½ × 3½]
Antwerp winter 1885-6
LITERATURE Tralbaut Antwerp 1948, nr 10,
pp 257, 283 : belongs to the same sketchbook as
F 1350, F 1350a, F 1350b and F 1358
EDITORS' COMMENT See F 1350 recto
COLLECTION Amsterdam, Rijksmuseum Vincent
van Gogh [Vincent van Gogh Foundation, inv
nr F 1359]

F 1360 recto and verso STUDY OF SEVEN
HANDS; THREE STUDIES OF A DEAD
SPARROW
St Remy period; see after F 1622

F 1361 HANGING SKELETON

Pencil 10.5 × 6 [4¼ × 2¼]
Antwerp December 1885-January 1886
LITERATURE Tralbaut Antwerp 1948, nr 60,
pp 258-60, 285. M. E. Tralbaut, Aesculape
December 1957, p 23
COLLECTION Amsterdam, Rijksmuseum Vincent
van Gogh [Vincent van Gogh Foundation, inv
nr F 1361]

REDATED TO ANTWERP

F 1093 LANDSCAPE WITH FIGURES

Black chalk 13 × 21 [5 × 8¼]
Antwerp early 1886
LITERATURE Faille 1928, nr 1093 : The Hague.
Vanbeselaere 1937, pp 110, 237, 410. Tralbaut
Drenthe 1959, pp 213, 223 : September 1883
EDITORS' COMMENT Stylistically connected with
the Antwerp and early Paris periods. The type of
windmill seems to indicate a locale in the outskirts
of Antwerp.
COLLECTION Sale Bern [Kornfeld and Klipstein]
9-11 June 1966, nr 350
Present owner unknown

F 1160 recto STUDY OF A LEFT ARM

Black chalk [Dutch laid paper with watermark:
Pro Patria – Concordia res parvae crescunt]
19.5 × 33 [7¾ × 13]
Probably Antwerp winter 1885-6
LITERATURE Faille 1928, nr 1160 : Nuenen
January 1885; letter 393. Vanbeselaere 1937,
pp 268, 412 : Nuenen May 1885; letter 408
COLLECTION Amsterdam, Rijksmuseum Vincent

van Gogh [Vincent van Gogh Foundation, inv nr F 1160]

F 1160 verso STUDY OF A RIGHT ARM

Black chalk
Probably Antwerp 1885-6
LITERATURE Faille 1928, nr 1160 verso: Nuenen January 1885; letter 393. Vanbeselaere 1937, pp 261, 268, 390: Nuenen May 1885; letter 408

F 1338 A COUPLE ON THE ROAD

Pencil, contours of the figures in pen 7.3 × 12.5 [2¾ × 5]
Antwerp 1885
LITERATURE Faille 1928, nr 1338: Nuenen. Vanbeselaere 1937, p 413: Antwerp or Paris. Not in Tralbaut Antwerp 1948
COLLECTION Netherlands, Private Collection

F 1362 recto STUDY AFTER THE LIVING MODEL: STANDING MALE NUDE
Below **PEASANT DIGGING, SEEN FROM THE BACK**

Pen and pencil [wove paper] 21.5 × 13 [8½ × 5]
Antwerp winter 1885-6
LETTER 447 [about 28 January 1886] '*I have been tremendously busy this week, for besides the painting class, I go and draw in the evening too, and after that, from half past ten till half past eleven, I work from the model at a club. For I have become a member of not less than two of these clubs… Verlat…and… Vinck…strongly advise me* especially *to draw for at least a year,* if need be to draw nothing *but plaster casts and the nude…*'
LITERATURE Faille 1928, nr 1362: Paris. Not in Tralbaut Antwerp 1948. A. M. Hammacher, exhib cat van Gogh-Signac London 1962, nr 29: Antwerp winter 1885-6
EDITORS' COMMENT In his manuscript for the present edition Faille dates F 1362 recto to the Paris period, but the editors find the style too academic for Paris, while the figure of the peasant is still close to the Nuenen style.
COLLECTION Amsterdam, Rijksmuseum Vincent van Gogh [Vincent van Gogh Foundation, inv nr F 1362]

F 1363a recto STUDY AFTER LIVING MODELS: STANDING MALE AND SITTING FEMALE NUDES

Black chalk and charcoal [gray vergé with watermark: Michallet] sheet 47 × 30.5 [18½ × 12]; drawing field 30.5 × 21.5 [12 × 8½]
Antwerp winter 1885-6
LITERATURE Faille 1928, probably included under nr 1364 [not reproduced]: Paris. Not in Tralbaut Antwerp 1948. A. M. Hammacher, exhib cat van Gogh-Signac London 1962, nr 30: Antwerp winter 1885-6
EDITORS' COMMENT Although the verso belongs to the Paris period the style of the recto points to Antwerp.
COLLECTION Amsterdam, Rijksmuseum Vincent van Gogh [Vincent van Gogh Foundation, inv. nr F 1363a]

F 1160 recto

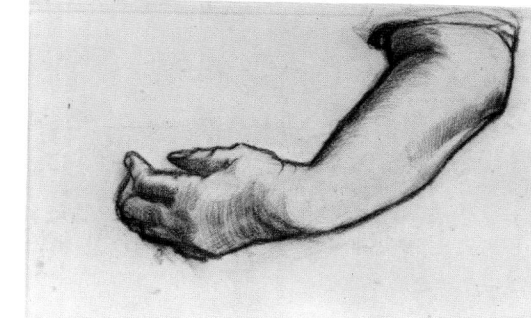

F 1160 verso

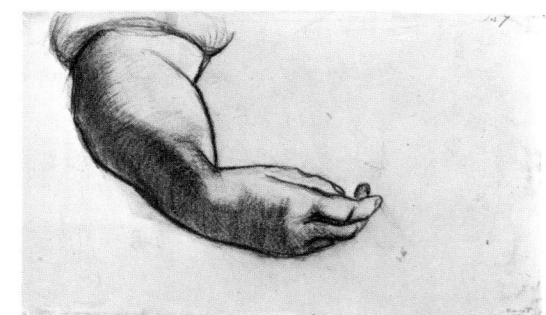

F 1338

F 1362 recto

F 1363a recto

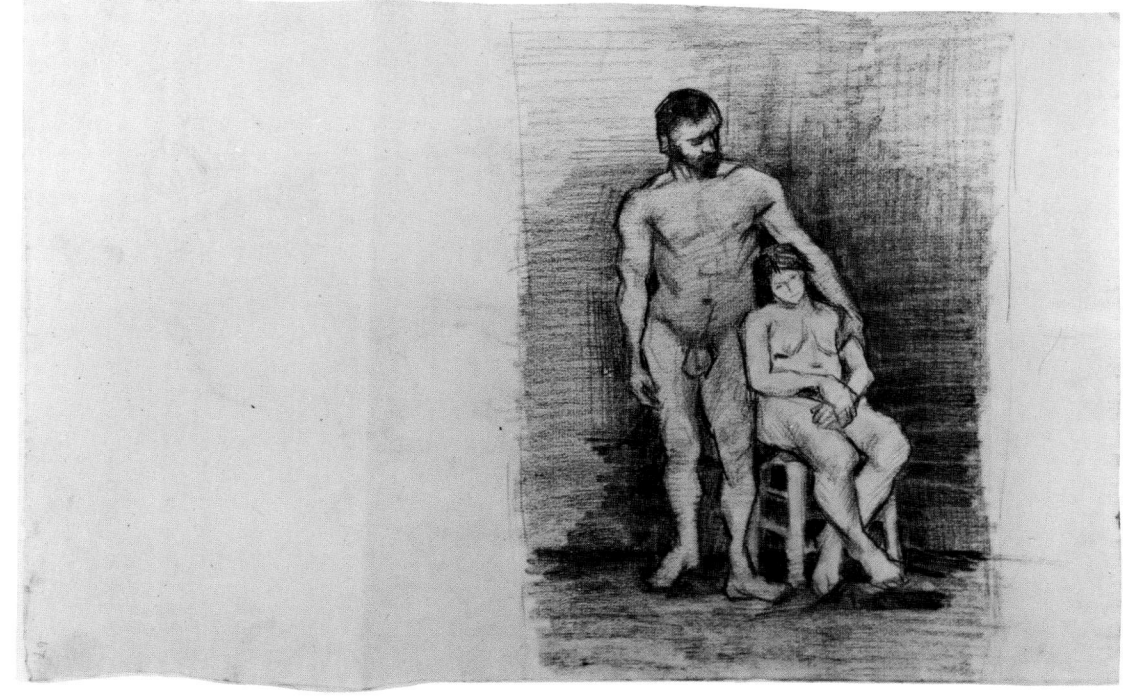

F 1364-1

F 1364-2

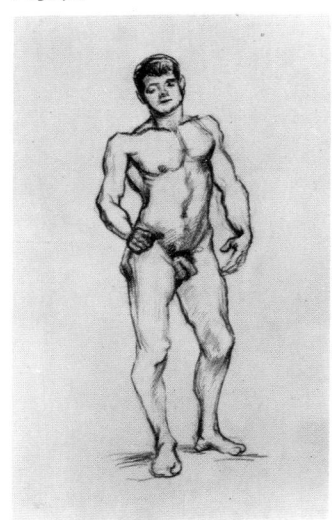

F 1372 recto

F 1372 verso

F 1368

F 1364–1 STUDY AFTER LIVING MODEL:
STANDING MALE NUDE

Black chalk [vergé paper, yellowed, with watermark: P. L. Bas] 47.4 × 31 [18¾ × 12¼]
Antwerp winter 1885-6
LITERATURE Faille 1928, nr 1364: Paris.
Not in Tralbaut Antwerp 1948
EDITORS' COMMENT Faille numbered both this
and the following drawing 1364. The editors have
distinguished between them by calling them 1364-1
and 1364-2.
COLLECTION Amsterdam, Rijksmuseum Vincent
van Gogh [Vincent van Gogh Foundation, inv
nr F 1364-1]

F 1364–2 STUDY AFTER LIVING MODEL:
STANDING MALE NUDE

Black chalk [vergé paper, pinkish, with watermark:
I.A.] 47.5 × 30.5 [18¾ × 12]
Antwerp winter 1885-6
LITERATURE Faille 1928, nr 1364: Paris. Not in
Tralbaut Antwerp 1948
EDITORS' COMMENT See F 1364-1
COLLECTION Amsterdam, Rijksmuseum Vincent
van Gogh [Vincent van Gogh Foundation, inv
nr F 1364-2]

F 1368 STUDY AFTER LIVING MODEL:
SEATED FEMALE NUDE

Charcoal [thick brownish paper] 73.5 × 59
[29 × 23¼] Outlines heavily overdrawn
Antwerp winter 1885-6
LITERATURE Vincent van Gogh, Lettres à Bernard,
1911, plate XXXIX. Faille 1928, nr 1368: Paris. Not
in Tralbaut Antwerp 1948
COLLECTION Amsterdam, Rijksmuseum Vincent
van Gogh [Vincent van Gogh Foundation, inv
nr F 1368]

F 1369 recto SEATED WORKER WITH A CAP:
SEEN FROM THE FRONT

Black chalk and charcoal [wove brownish paper]
74.5 × 58 [29¼ × 22¾]
Antwerp winter 1885-6
LITERATURE Vincent van Gogh, Lettres à Bernard,
1911, plate XXXVIII. Faille 1928, nr 1369: Paris.
Not in Tralbaut Antwerp 1948
COLLECTION Amsterdam, Rijksmuseum Vincent
van Gogh [Vincent van Gogh Foundation, inv
nr F 1369]

F 1369 verso SEATED WORKER, WITH BEARD

Black chalk, charcoal
Antwerp winter 1885-6
LITERATURE Faille 1928, nr 1369 verso: Paris. Not
in Tralbaut Antwerp 1948

F 1372 recto HEAD OF A MAN WITH HAT
AND PIPE

Black chalk 19.5 × 11 [7¾ × 4¼]
Antwerp 1885
LITERATURE Faille 1928, nr 1372 recto: Paris.
Tralbaut Antwerp 1948, pp 282, 285, nr 45:
Antwerp; a leaf from the same sketchbook to which
F 1354a recto and verso and F 1353 also belonged
EDITORS' COMMENT The date seems uncertain.
COLLECTION Amsterdam, Rijksmuseum Vincent
van Gogh [Vincent van Gogh Foundation, inv
nr F 1372]

F 1372 verso HEAD OF A MAN: FULL FACE

Black chalk
Antwerp 1885
LITERATURE Faille 1928, nr 1372 verso: Paris.
Tralbaut Antwerp 1948, nr 46: a leaf from the same
sketchbook to which F 1354a recto and verso and
F 1353 also belonged

F 1369 recto

F 1369 verso

F 1363a verso

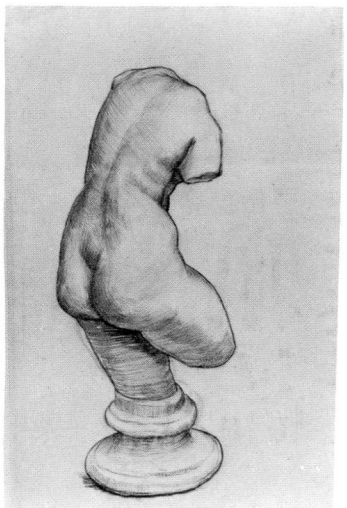

F 1363b

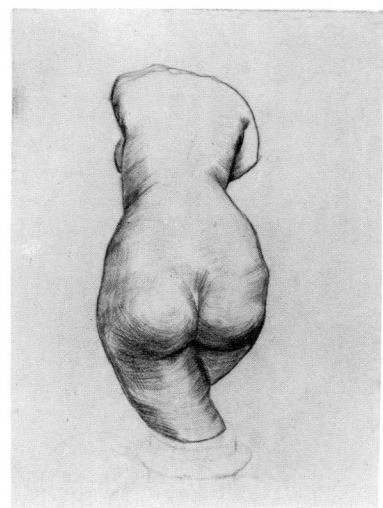

F 1363c recto

F 1363c verso

F 1363d

F 1363e

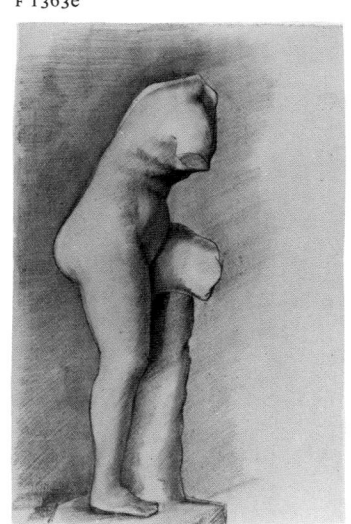

F 1363f recto

F 1363f verso

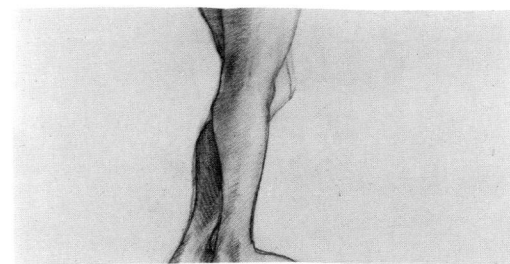

PARIS PERIOD

F 1362 recto STUDY AFTER LIVING MODEL:
STANDING MALE NUDE
Below WORKING PEASANT, SEEN FROM
THE BACK
Antwerp period; see after F 1361

F 1362 verso
Drawing of heads not by van Gogh

F 1363 STUDIES AFTER PLASTER
STATUETTES

LITERATURE Faille 1928, nr 1363: 'Quinze feuilles
d'études d'après des statuettes en plâtre dans la
collection V. W. van Gogh, Laren.'
EDITORS' COMMENT Of the fifteen drawings
mentioned by Faille in the 1928 edition only one is
reproduced. This drawing, however, is part of a
large sheet with various drawings [F 1366]: it is the
study on the right side of F 1366 verso. Among the
material Faille set aside for the present edition are
eight photographs of drawings marked F 1363a,
F 1363b, F 1363c, F 1363d, F 1363e, F 1363f, F 1363g
and F 1363h. The remaining seven could not be
identified by the editors. They are probably to be
found among the numbers treated as supplementary
drawings in the present work.

F 1363a recto STUDY AFTER LIVING MODEL:
STANDING MAN WITH SITTING WOMAN
Antwerp period; see after F 1361

F 1363a verso STUDY AFTER PLASTER
STATUETTE: FEMALE TORSO ON ROUND
PEDESTAL, SEEN FROM THE BACK

Black chalk 47×30.5 [$18\frac{1}{2} \times 12$]
Compare F 1363b, F 1371 recto, SD 1707, SD 1708
recto and verso, SD 1709 recto, SD 1711 recto and
verso, SD 1712 recto and verso and SD 1713 recto
[same statuette]
COLLECTION Amsterdam, Rijksmuseum Vincent
van Gogh [Vincent van Gogh Foundation, inv
nr F 1363a]

F 1363b STUDY AFTER PLASTER STATUETTE:
FEMALE TORSO ON ROUND PEDESTAL,
SEEN FROM THE BACK

Black chalk [vergé paper] 43×31 [$17 \times 12\frac{1}{4}$]
Compare numbers noted under F 1363a verso
[same statuette]
Paris 1887
COLLECTION Amsterdam, Rijksmuseum Vincent
van Gogh [Vincent van Gogh Foundation, inv
nr F 1363b]

F 1363c recto STUDY AFTER PLASTER
STATUETTE: FEMALE TORSO WITH ONE
THIGH

Black chalk and charcoal [vergé paper] 30×24.5
[$11\frac{3}{4} \times 9\frac{3}{4}$]
Compare paintings F 216d, F 216i and F 360 [same
statuette]
Paris 1886-7
COLLECTION Amsterdam, Rijksmuseum Vincent
van Gogh [Vincent van Gogh Foundation, inv
nr F 1363c]

F 1363c verso STUDIES AFTER PLASTER
STATUETTE: TWO STUDIES OF THE SAME
MALE NUDE ON A PEDESTAL, LEFT HAND
BEFORE THE EYES

Black chalk
Paris 1886

F 1364a

F 1363d STUDY AFTER PLASTER STATUETTE: MAN KNEELING

Pencil, pen and black ink [vergé paper] 32.5 × 24.5 [12¾ × 9¾] Upper right-hand corner missing
Compare painting F 216f [same statuette]
Paris 1886
COLLECTION Amsterdam, Rijksmuseum Vincent van Gogh [Vincent van Gogh Foundation, inv nr F 1363d]

F 1363e STUDY AFTER PLASTER STATUETTE: FEMALE TORSO WITH ONE LEG, SEEN FROM THE RIGHT

Black chalk [yellowish vergé paper] 48 × 31 [19 × 12¼]
Compare F 1363f recto, F 1363g, F 1366 recto and verso, SD 1709 verso and SD 1710 verso [same statuette]
Paris 1886
COLLECTION Amsterdam, Rijksmuseum Vincent van Gogh [Vincent van Gogh Foundation, inv nr F 1363e]

F 1363f recto STUDY AFTER PLASTER STATUETTE: FEMALE TORSO WITH ONE LEG AND TOP HAT

Black chalk [gray vergé paper] 38 × 19.5 [15 × 7¾]
Compare numbers noted under F 1363e [same statuette]
Paris 1886
LITERATURE A. M. Hammacher, exhib cat van Gogh-Signac London 1962, nr 32: Paris March 1886-20 February 1888
COLLECTION Amsterdam, Rijksmuseum Vincent van Gogh [Vincent van Gogh Foundation, inv nr F 1363f]

F 1363f verso STUDY OF BARE LEGS

Black chalk 19.5 × 38 [7¾ × 15]
Compare SD 1710 recto [upper part of same model]
Paris 1886

F 1363g STUDY AFTER PLASTER STATUETTE: FEMALE TORSO WITH ONE LEG, SEEN FROM THE BACK

Black chalk and charcoal [gray paper with watermark: J. Whatman 1884] 50.7 × 39.3 [20 × 15½]
Compare numbers noted under F 1363e [same statuette]
Paris 1886
COLLECTION Amsterdam, Rijksmuseum Vincent van Gogh [Vincent van Gogh Foundation, inv nr F 1363g]

F 1364 STUDIES AFTER LIVING MODELS, STUDIES OF FEET, ETC

LITERATURE Faille 1928, nr 1364: 'Quinze feuilles d'études d'après des modèles vivants, études de pieds, etc, dans la collection V. W. van Gogh, Laren.'
EDITORS' COMMENT Of the fifteen drawings mentioned by Faille in the 1928 edition only three were reproduced: F 1364a, F 1364b and F 1364c. Among the material Faille set aside for the present edition are five photographs of other drawings marked F 1364d, F 1364e, F 1364f, F 1364g and F 1364h. The remaining seven could not be identified by the editors. They are probably to be found among the numbers treated as supplementary drawings in the present work.

F 1364-1 STUDY AFTER LIVING MODEL: STANDING MALE NUDE
Antwerp period; see after F 1361

F 1364-2 STUDY AFTER LIVING MODEL: MALE NUDE
Antwerp period; see after F 1361

F 1364a STUDY AFTER LIVING MODEL: STANDING NUDE BOY, SEEN FROM THE BACK

Black chalk [vergé paper, pinkish, with watermark: Michallet] 47.5 × 30.5 [18¾ × 12]
Compare F 1364b recto and verso, F 1364d recto and verso and SD 1710 verso [same model]
Paris 1886
COLLECTION Amsterdam, Rijksmuseum Vincent van Gogh [Vincent van Gogh Foundation, inv nr F 1364a]

F 1364b recto STUDY AFTER LIVING MODEL: STANDING NUDE BOY

Black chalk [pinkish vergé paper] 47.5 × 31 [18¾ × 12¼]
Compare numbers noted under F 1364a [same model]
Paris 1886
COLLECTION Amsterdam, Rijksmuseum Vincent van Gogh [Vincent van Gogh Foundation, inv nr F 1364b]

F 1364b verso STUDY AFTER LIVING MODEL: NUDE BOY, SEEN FROM THE BACK

Black chalk
Compare numbers noted under F 1364a [same model]
Paris 1886

F 1364c STUDY AFTER LIVING MODEL: MALE NUDE WITH RAISED RIGHT ARM, IN RIGHT PROFILE

Pencil and charcoal, brushed [yellowish vergé paper] 48.5 × 31.3 [19 × 12¼]
Compare SD 1703 recto [same feet]
Paris 1886
LITERATURE Faille 1928: reproduced under F 1364
COLLECTION Amsterdam, Rijksmuseum Vincent van Gogh [Vincent van Gogh Foundation, inv nr F 1364c]

F 1364b recto

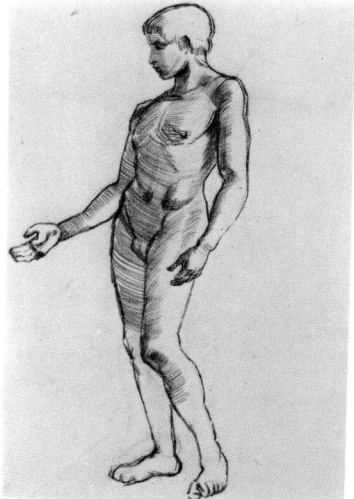

F 1364b verso

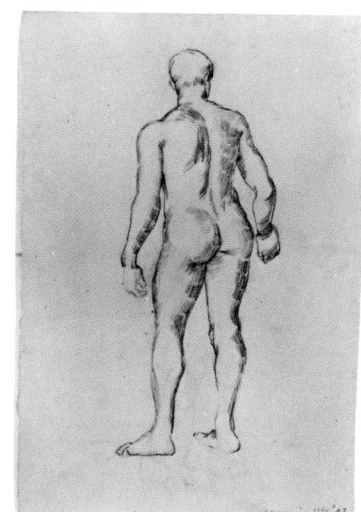

F 1363g

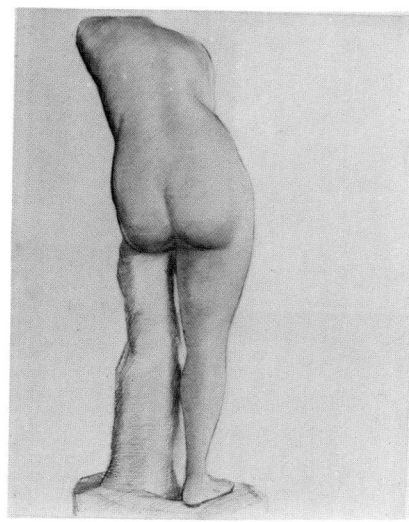

F 1364c

F629[H623] PORTRAIT OF TRABU, AN
ATTENDENT OF SAINT PAUL'S HOSPITAL
Saint Rémy between 4 and 10 September 1889

F 1364d recto

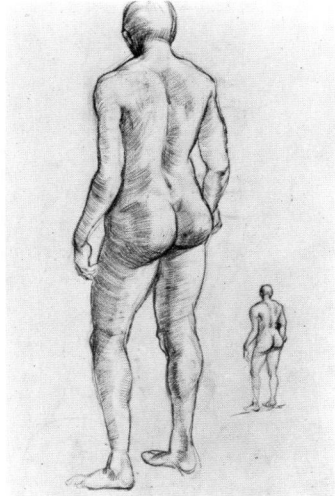

F 1364d verso

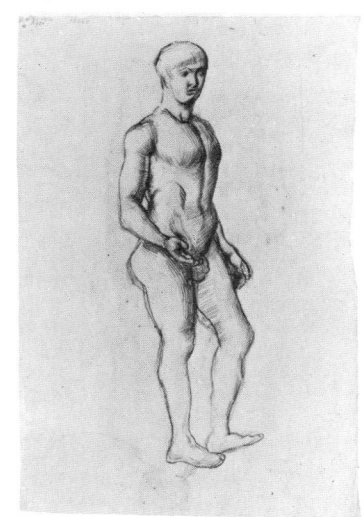

F 1364e

F 1365

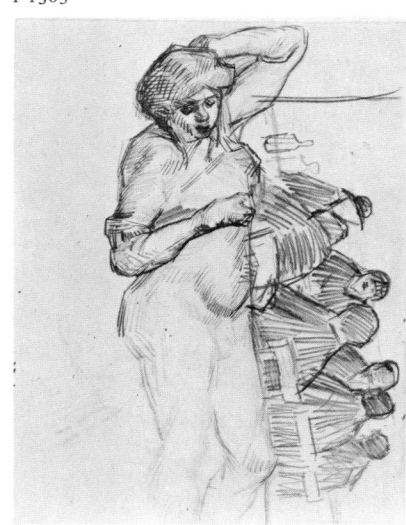

F 1366 recto

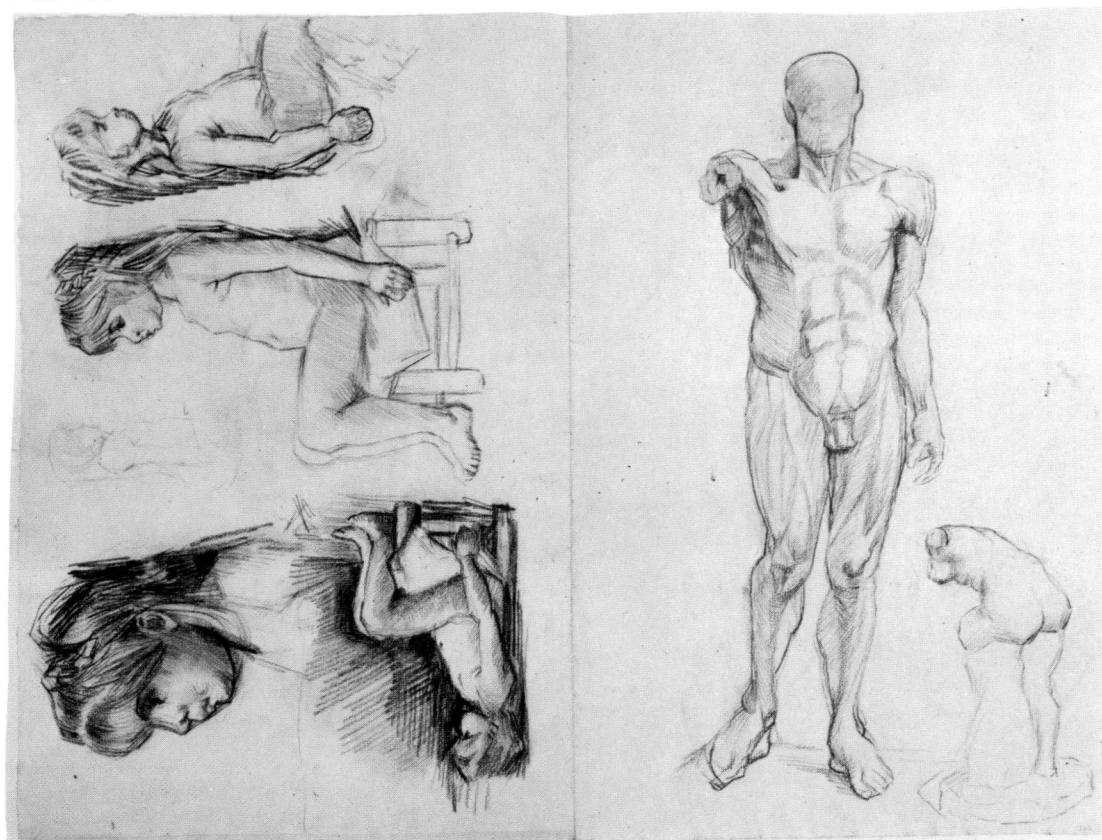

F 1364d recto STUDY AFTER LIVING MODEL:
TWO VIEWS OF A NUDE BOY, SEEN FROM
THE BACK

Black chalk [vergé paper with watermark:
Michallet] 45 × 29 [17¾ × 11½]
Compare numbers noted under F 1364a [same
model]
Paris 1886
COLLECTION Amsterdam, Rijksmuseum Vincent
van Gogh [Vincent van Gogh Foundation, inv
nr F 1364d]

F 1364d verso STUDY AFTER LIVING MODEL:
STANDING NUDE BOY, SEEN FROM THE
FRONT

Black chalk
Compare numbers noted under F 1364a [same
model]
Paris 1886

F 1364e STUDY AFTER PLASTER STATUETTE:
THE DISCUS THROWER, SEEN FROM THE
BACK

Black chalk [laid paper with watermark: TS & Z]
56 × 44 [22 × 17¼]
Paris 1886
LITERATURE Faille 1928, probably included under
nr 1363: 15 sheets of studies after plaster statuettes
COLLECTION Amsterdam, Rijksmuseum Vincent
van Gogh [Vincent van Gogh Foundation, inv
nr F 1364e]

F 1365 STUDY AFTER LIVING MODEL:
STANDING FEMALE NUDE
To the right SEVEN FIGURES SEATED AT A
TABLE

Pen, dark blue ink and pencil [left half] Pencil and
blue chalk [right half] [wove paper] 35 × 25.5
[13¾ × 10]
Paris 1886
EDITORS' COMMENT The seven figures seated at a
table are of the same period as the series of
musicians [F 1244a etc] of summer 1886 or shortly
later; the standing nude must be earlier, though it
too dates from Paris 1886.
COLLECTION Amsterdam, Rijksmuseum Vincent
van Gogh [Vincent van Gogh Foundation, inv
nr F 1365]

F 1366 recto Left half FIVE SKETCHES OF A
SITTING NUDE GIRL
Right half STUDIES AFTER PLASTER
STATUETTES: STANDING MAN WITH ONE
ARM, SEEN FROM THE FRONT
Below FEMALE TORSO WITH ONE LEG,
SEEN FROM THE BACK

Black chalk [vergé paper with watermark:
Michallet] 47.5 × 61.5 [18¾ × 24¼]
Compare painting F 215, F 1366 verso, F 1367
[NUDE GIRL: same model], SD 1702 recto and verso
[STANDING MAN: same statuette] and the numbers
noted under F 1363e [FEMALE TORSO: same
statuette]
Paris early 1886
EDITORS' COMMENT The nude girl was a model in
Cormon's studio. See LITERATURE under F 1367
for the remark of A. Bowness.
COLLECTION Amsterdam, Rijksmuseum Vincent
van Gogh [Vincent van Gogh Foundation, inv
nr F 1366]

F630[625] PIÉTA [after Delacroix]
Saint Rémy September 1889

F 1364d recto 1364d verso 1364e 1365 1366 recto 1366 verso 1367 1368
1369 recto and verso 1370 1371 recto 1371 verso 1372 recto and verso

F 1366 verso Left half TWO STUDIES AFTER
PLASTER STATUETTES: FEMALE TORSO
WITH ONE LEG, SEEN FROM THE BACK
Below MAN BOXING, SEEN FROM THE BACK
Right half NUDE GIRL SITTING, SEEN FROM
THE LEFT

Black chalk [right half], black chalk and charcoal
[FEMALE TORSO] and pencil [MAN BOXING]
Compare painting F 215, F 1366 recto, F 1367
[NUDE GIRL: same model] and the numbers noted
under F 1363e [FEMALE TORSO: same statuette]
Paris early 1886
EDITORS' COMMENT The nude girl was a model in
Cormon's studio. See LITERATURE under F 1367
for the remark of A. Bowness. The left half of
F 1366 verso was reproduced in previous editions
under nr 1363.

F 1367 NUDE GIRL SITTING

Black chalk [pinkish brown vergé paper] 30.5 × 23.5
[12 × 9¼]
Compare painting F 215 and F 1366 recto and verso
[same model]
Paris early 1886
LITERATURE A. Bowness, exhib cat van Gogh
London [Hayward Gallery] 1968-9, nr 61: painted
in the studio of Cormon; such naked children can
be seen in Cormon's own paintings
COLLECTION Amsterdam, Rijksmuseum Vincent
van Gogh [Vincent van Gogh Foundation, inv
nr F 1367]

F 1368 NUDE YOUNG WOMAN
Antwerp period; see after F 1361

F 1369 recto and verso SEATED WORKER
WITH A CAP, SEEN FROM THE FRONT;
SEATED WORKER, WITH BEARD
Antwerp period; see after F 1361

F 1370 MAN SEATED, FACING LEFT

Chalk [wove paper with watermark: J. Whatman
1884] 51 × 39.5 [20 × 15½]
Paris 1886
COLLECTION Amsterdam, Rijksmuseum Vincent
van Gogh [Vincent van Gogh Foundation, inv
nr F 1370]

F 1371 recto STUDY AFTER PLASTER
STATUETTE: FEMALE TORSO ON PEDESTAL,
THREE QUARTERS TO THE RIGHT

Black chalk [vergé paper with watermark:
Michallet] 48 × 31.5 [19 × 12½]
Compare numbers noted under F 1363a verso [same
statuette]
Paris 1886
COLLECTION Amsterdam, Rijksmuseum Vincent
van Gogh [Vincent van Gogh Foundation, inv
nr F 1371]

F 1371 verso VENUS DE MILO [first sketch for
a study]

Crayon
Paris 1886

F 1372 recto and verso HEAD OF A MAN WITH
HAT AND PIPE: LEFT PROFILE; HEAD OF A
MAN: FULL FACE
Antwerp period; see after F 1361

F 1367
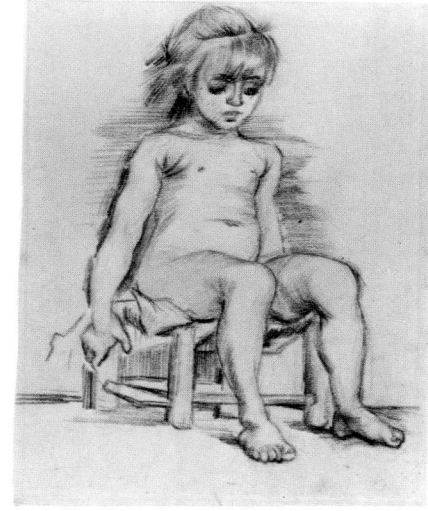

F 1370

F 1371 recto

F 1371 verso
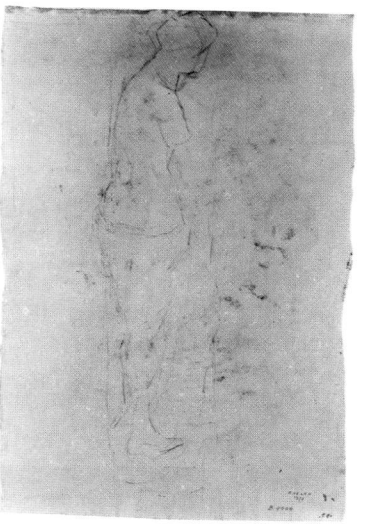

F 1366 verso
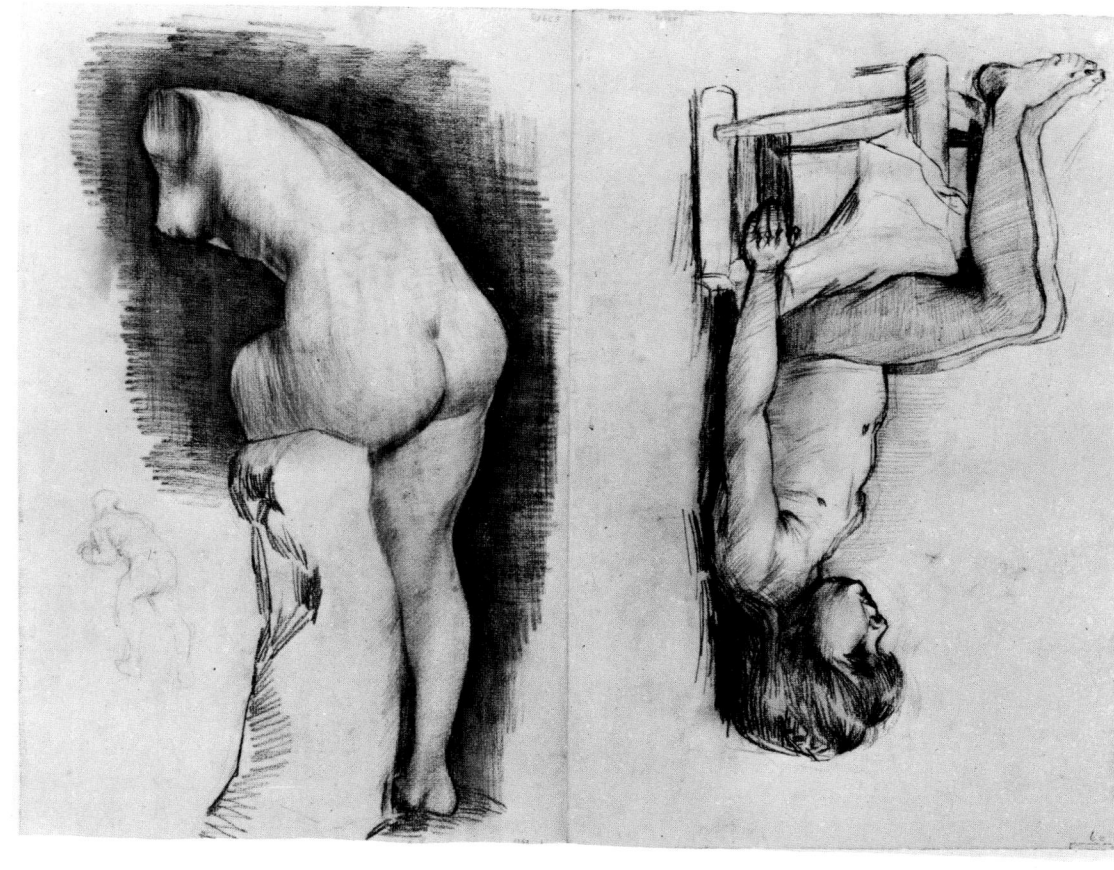

F 1373 recto

F 1373 verso

F 1374

F 1376 recto

F 1377

F 1373 recto OWL SEEN IN PROFILE

Pencil and pen, blue ink [pasteboard] 35.5 × 26
[14 × 10¼]
Paris 1886
COLLECTION Amsterdam, Rijksmuseum Vincent
van Gogh [Vincent van Gogh Foundation, inv
nr F 1373]

F 1373 verso OWL SEEN FROM THE FRONT

Pencil and pen, blue ink
Paris 1886

F 1374 STUDY OF HOUSES

Pencil 29 × 23 [11½ × 9]
Annotated by Vincent with color notes
Paris summer 1887
COLLECTION Amsterdam, Rijksmuseum Vincent
van Gogh [Vincent van Gogh Foundation, inv
nr F 1374]

F 1375 STUDIES: FIGURE; THE ENCLOSURE
WALL OF SAINT PAUL'S HOSPITAL; AND
OTHERS
Saint Rémy period; see after F 1622

F 1376 NUDE WOMAN SQUATTING

Pencil [wove paper] 21 × 13.5 [8¼ × 5¼] Sketched on
the back of the menu of the Grand Bouillon
Restaurant du Chalet at 43 Avenue de Clichy, Paris
Paris 1887
LITERATURE Faille 1928, nr 1376: Paris. L. Anfray,
Arts Documents 1953, nr 29, p 10-1: not by van
Gogh but by E. Bernard. A. M. Hammacher, exhib
cat van Gogh-Signac London 1962, nr 33: the old
attribution to van Gogh is correct
EDITORS' COMMENT In his manuscript for the
present edition Faille accepts the attribution to
Bernard. The editors do not agree.
COLLECTION Amsterdam, Rijksmuseum Vincent
van Gogh [Vincent van Gogh Foundation, inv
nr F 1376]

F 1377 PEOPLE WALKING IN A WOOD

Pencil and pen, violet and black ink [wove paper]
11.2 × 23.3 [4½ × 9¼] Drawing field 3.2 × 23.3
[1¼ × 9¼] Sketched on the border of a menu dated
8 April 1886
Paris first half of 1886
LITERATURE Faille 1928, nr 1377: Paris.
A. M. Hammacher, exhib cat van Gogh-Signac
London 1962, nr 45: Paris; subject reminiscent of
painting F 223
EDITORS' COMMENT Left out by Faille in his
manuscript for the present edition because he
ascribed it to E. Bernard. The editors do not agree.
COLLECTION Amsterdam, Rijksmuseum Vincent
van Gogh [Vincent van Gogh Foundation, inv
nr F 1377]

F 1378 recto TWO SELF PORTRAITS;
FRAGMENTS OF A THIRD

Pen, pencil, ink [drawing paper with watermark:
Ganson & Montgolfier–Vidalon–1...] 31.6 × 24.1
[12½ × 9½] Upper left corner cut out
Compare painting F 380
Paris summer 1887
LITERATURE K. Bromig-Kolleritz, Die Selbstbild-
nisse Vincent van Goghs, 1955, p 101: preliminary
study for painting F 345. F. Erpel, Die Selbst-
bildnisse Vincent van Goghs, 1963, nr 21.
A. Bowness, exhib cat van Gogh London [Hayward
Gallery] 1968-9, nr 92: Paris September-December
1887
COLLECTION Amsterdam, Rijksmuseum Vincent

F 1378 recto

van Gogh [Vincent van Gogh Foundation, inv
nr F 1378]

F 1378 verso SKETCH OF A SITTING WOMAN

Pencil
Paris first half of 1886

F 1379 SELF PORTRAIT

Pencil [laid paper] 19.3 × 21 [7½ × 8¼]
Paris summer 1887
LITERATURE K. Bromig-Kolleritz, Die Selbstbildnisse Vincent van Goghs, 1955, p 101 : preparatory
study for painting F 345. A. M. Hammacher, exhib
cat van Gogh-Signac London 1962, nr 44: Paris
summer 1886; sent with letter 460. F. Erpel, Die
Selbstbildnisse Vincent van Goghs, 1963, nr 20:
compare F 1378 recto. A. Bowness, exhib cat van
Gogh London [Hayward Gallery] 1968-9, nr 91 :
September-December 1887
COLLECTION Amsterdam, Rijksmuseum Vincent
van Gogh [Vincent van Gogh Foundation, inv
nr F 1379]

F 1380 recto THE STREET

Black crayon and black chalk, washed [drawing
paper] 10 × 16.8 [4 × 6½]
Paris early 1886
LITERATURE A. M. Hammacher, exhib cat van
Gogh-Signac London 1962, nr 41 : Paris March
1886
COLLECTION Amsterdam, Rijksmuseum Vincent
van Gogh [Vincent van Gogh Foundation, inv
nr F 1380]

F 1380 verso MAN ON A BENCH ; SKETCH
OF A HORSE

Pencil and ink
Paris early 1886

F 1378 verso

F 1379

F 1380 recto

F 1380 verso

F 1381 recto

F 1381 verso

F 1382 recto

F 1382 verso

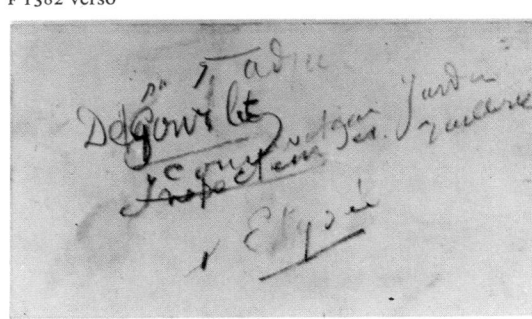

F 1383

F 1385

F 1381 recto A RAINY DAY

Pencil [drawing paper] 10.2 × 13.6 [4 × 5¼]
Paris early 1886
COLLECTION Amsterdam, Rijksmuseum Vincent
van Gogh [Vincent van Gogh Foundation, inv
nr F 1381]

F 1381 verso SKETCH OF A FEMALE FIGURE

Pencil
Paris early 1886

F 1382 THE FOREST BROOK

Black crayon [Bristol paper] 6 × 10.5 [2¼ × 4¼]
Annotated on the verso by Vincent:
    ...adju
    De Gourlet
    Conservateur Jardin
    et
    Inspecteur Tuileries
    Elysée
Compare SD 1703 verso [same motif]
Paris early 1886
COLLECTION Amsterdam, Rijksmuseum Vincent
van Gogh [Vincent van Gogh Foundation, inv
nr F 1382]

F 1383 THE TERRACE OF THE TUILERIES

Pencil [vergé paper with fragment of watermark]
9.8 × 15.8 [3¾ × 6¼]
Compare painting F 223 [same site]
Paris early 1886
LITERATURE W. J. de Gruyter, Tekeningen van
Vincent van Gogh, 1962, p 103, nr 35: 1886
COLLECTION Amsterdam, Rijksmuseum Vincent
van Gogh [Vincent van Gogh Foundation, inv
nr F 1383]

F 1384 THE GARDEN OF THE TUILERIES

Pencil [drawing paper] 11 × 20 [4¼ × 8]
Paris early 1886
COLLECTION Amsterdam, Rijksmuseum Vincent
van Gogh [Vincent van Gogh Foundation, inv
nr F 1384]

F 1385 THE BANKS OF THE SEINE AT PARIS

Pencil [drawing paper] 10.9 × 19.7 [4¼ × 7¾]
Paris early 1886
COLLECTION Amsterdam, Rijksmuseum Vincent
van Gogh [Vincent van Gogh Foundation, inv
nr F 1385]

F 1386 PARK IN PARIS

Pencil [drawing paper] 10 × 16.7 [4 × 6½]
Paris early 1886
COLLECTION Amsterdam, Rijksmuseum Vincent
van Gogh [Vincent van Gogh Foundation, inv
nr F 1386]

F 1387 VIEW OF PARIS ROOFTOPS, WITH THE PANTHEON

Red, black and white chalk [vergé paper with
indecipherable fragment of a watermark]
22.5 × 30 [8¾ × 11¾]
Compare painting F 261
Paris summer or autumn 1886
LITERATURE A. Bowness, exhib cat van Gogh
London [Hayward Gallery] 1968-9, nr 64: late
June-July 1886; view across Paris from Vincent's
room, with the Dôme des Invalides
EDITORS' COMMENT F 1387, F 1388, F 1389 and
F 1390, all of the same period, are of approximately
the same dimensions – those of a common type of

F 1387

sketchbook.
COLLECTION Amsterdam, Rijksmuseum Vincent van Gogh [Vincent van Gogh Foundation, inv nr F 1387]

F 1388 VIEW OF PARIS FROM THE HILL OF MONTMARTRE

Brownish-black crayon heightened with red [white vergé paper] 24.5 × 31.5 [9¾ × 12½]
Paris summer or autumn 1886
EDITORS' COMMENT See F 1387
COLLECTION Amsterdam, Rijksmuseum Vincent van Gogh [Vincent van Gogh Foundation, inv nr F 1388]

F 1389 VIEW OF PARIS WITH NOTRE DAME AND TOUR SAINT JACQUES

Charcoal, black crayon, red and white chalk
24 × 31.5 [9½ × 12½]
Paris summer or autumn 1886
EDITORS' COMMENT See F 1387
COLLECTION Formerly London, R. Rienaecker
Present owner unknown

F 1389

F 1384

F 1386

F 1388

F 1390

F 1391

F 1394

F 1395

F 1390 VIEW OF PARIS WITH THE OPERA

Black, white and brownish-red chalk [vergé paper
with indecipherable watermark] 22.5 × 30
[8¾ × 11¾]
Paris summer or autumn 1886
LITERATURE A. Bowness, exhib cat van Gogh
London [Hayward Gallery] 1968-9, nr 65: Paris late
June-July 1886; view across Paris from Vincent's
room, with the back of the Opera
EDITORS' COMMENT See F 1387
COLLECTION Amsterdam, Rijksmuseum Vincent
van Gogh [Vincent van Gogh Foundation, inv
nr F 1390]

F 1391 VIEW FROM VINCENT'S ROOM IN THE RUE LEPIC

Pencil and pen, washed [yellow-brown vergé paper]
39.5 × 53.5 [15½ × 21]
Compare paintings F 341 and F 341a
Paris February-March 1887
LITERATURE A. M. Hammacher, exhib cat van
Gogh-Signac London 1962, nr 49: view from Theo's
apartment in the Rue Lepic; Paris 1887
EDITORS' COMMENT F 1391, F 1392, F 1393 and
F 1396, all from the same period, are of
approximately the same dimensions – those of a
common type of sketchbook.
COLLECTION Amsterdam, Rijksmuseum Vincent
van Gogh [Vincent van Gogh Foundation, inv
nr F 1391]

F 1392 THE WINDOW AT THE RESTAURANT CHEZ BATAILLE

Pen and blue chalk, pink, yellow and white crayon
[gray vergé paper] 54 × 40 [21¼ × 15½]
Signed and annotated by Vincent in lower right:
La fenêtre chez Bataille. Vincent 87
Paris February-March 1887
LITERATURE D. Cooper, Zeichnungen und
Aquarelle von Vincent van Gogh, 1954, nr 16:
spring 1887. A. Bowness, exhib cat van Gogh
London [Hayward Gallery] 1968-9, nr 75: Paris
January-February 1887; close in style to Lautrec;
Chez Bataille was a restaurant in the Rue des
Abbesses
EDITORS' COMMENT See F 1391
COLLECTION Amsterdam, Rijksmuseum Vincent
van Gogh [Vincent van Gogh Foundation, inv
nr F 1392]

F 1393 THE BOULEVARD DE CLICHY

Pen, blue, pink and white crayon [yellowish-brown
vergé paper] 39.8 × 54 [15¾ × 21¼]
Compare painting F 292
Paris February-March 1887
LITERATURE D. Cooper, Zeichnungen und
Aquarelle von Vincent van Gogh, 1954, nr 19:
winter 1886-7; presumably a study for painting
F 292. A. Bowness, exhib cat van Gogh London
[Hayward Gallery] 1968-9, nr 69: Paris December
1886
EDITORS' COMMENT See F 1391
COLLECTION Amsterdam, Rijksmuseum Vincent
van Gogh [Vincent van Gogh Foundation, inv
nr F 1393]

F 1394 A VIEW OF THE HILL OF MONTMARTRE

Pen, heightened with colored crayons [drawing
paper] 10.1 × 16.7 [4 × 6½]
Compare painting F 266 and F 1398 [same site]
Paris autumn 1886
COLLECTION Amsterdam, Rijksmuseum Vincent
van Gogh [Vincent van Gogh Foundation, inv
nr F 1394]

F 1392

F 1395 THE MOULIN DE LA GALETTE

Pencil [drawing paper] 11 × 20 [4¼ × 7¾]
Compare painting F 271, F 1396a and the painting
by A. H. Koning in exhib cat Theo van Gogh
Amsterdam-Otterlo 1960, nr 70 [same site]
Paris winter 1886-7
COLLECTION Amsterdam, Rijksmuseum Vincent
van Gogh [Vincent van Gogh Foundation, inv
nr F 1395]

F 1396 THE MOULIN DE LA GALETTE

Pencil, blue crayon and pink and green pastels
[yellow vergé paper] 39.8 × 54 [15¾ × 21¼]
Compare paintings F 272, F 274, F 346, F 348 and
F 348a [same site]
Paris early 1887
LITERATURE A. M. Hammacher, exhib cat van
Gogh-Signac London 1962, nr 50: the mill 'Le
Radet,' previously called 'Le Moulin de la Galette'
EDITORS' COMMENT See F 1391
COLLECTION Amsterdam, Rijksmuseum Vincent
van Gogh [Vincent van Gogh Foundation, inv
nr F 1396]

F 1396a THE MOULIN DE LA GALETTE

Pen and black crayon 53 × 39 [20¾ × 15¼]
Compare painting F 271, F 1395 and the painting by
A. H. Koning in exhib cat Theo van Gogh
Amsterdam-Otterlo 1960, nr 70 [same site]
Paris winter 1886-7
LITERATURE Not in Faille 1928
COLLECTION Syracuse, New York, Miss
E. Hudson [acquired 1934]

F 1396

F 1396a

F 1393

F 1397

F 1398

F 1399

F 1400

F 1397 THE MOULIN DE LA GALETTE

Black crayon and water color [rough torchon pasted onto panel] 31 × 24.7 [12¼ × 9¾]
Paris autumn 1886
LITERATURE Faille 1928, nr 1397 [not reproduced]
COLLECTION Amsterdam, P. and N. de Boer Foundation

F 1398 VIEW FROM MONTMARTRE

Charcoal and black crayon [yellowish vergé paper, with watermark: P.L. Bas] 30.8 × 47.5 [12 × 18¾]
Compare painting F 266 and F 1394 [same site]
Paris autumn 1886
COLLECTION Amsterdam, Rijksmuseum Vincent van Gogh [Vincent van Gogh Foundation, inv nr F 1398]

F 1399 THE GRAVEYARD

Pencil, pen and ink 23 × 37 [9 × 14½]
Compare F 907, F 908 [figures of diggers] and F 1399a
Paris 1886
LITERATURE Vincent van Gogh, Lettres à Bernard, 1911, plate XL. F. Novotny, Albertina-Studien 1963, pp 15-20
COLLECTION Vienna, Albertina [acquired 1937], inv nr 27.791

F 1399a THE GRAVEYARD

Ink, pen and brush, colored chalk, heightened with white [Ingres paper, toned] 36.5 × 48 [14¼ × 19]
Compare F 907, F 908 [figures of diggers] and F 1399
Paris 1886
LITERATURE Not in Faille 1928. J. H. de Bois Art Gallery Bulletin 1941, p 4. Cat van Gogh 1966, Rijksmuseum Kröller-Müller, nr 193: in the opinion of A. Szymańska The Hague November 1882: letter 236
COLLECTION Otterlo, Rijksmuseum Kröller-Müller, inv nr 1121-42, cat van Gogh 1970, nr 193

F 1400 SUBURB OF PARIS [LA BARRIÈRE]

Water color, heightened with white [yellowish vergé paper] 39.5 × 53.5 [15½ × 21]
Compare F 1401 and drawing SD 1719 recto [same site]
Paris summer 1887
COLLECTION Amsterdam, Rijksmuseum Vincent van Gogh [Vincent van Gogh Foundation, inv nr F 1400]

F 1401 LA BARRIÈRE WITH HORSE-TRAMWAY

Water color, pen and pencil [water-color paper] 24 × 31.5 [9½ × 12½]
Compare F 1400 and drawing SD 1719 recto [same site]
Paris summer 1887
LITERATURE D. Cooper, Zeichnungen und Aquarelle von Vincent van Gogh, 1954, nr 18: summer 1887. A. Bowness, exhib cat van Gogh London [Hayward Gallery] 1968-9, nr 85: July-August 1887
COLLECTION Amsterdam, Rijksmuseum Vincent van Gogh [Vincent van Gogh Foundation, inv nr F 1401]

F 1402 THE RAMPARTS OF PARIS

Water color, heightened with colors [light brown paper] 39.5 × 54 [15½ × 21¼]
Paris summer 1887
LITERATURE Art News Annual 1948, p 161
COLLECTION London, Private collection

F 1403 THE RAMPARTS OF PARIS WITH HOUSES

Water color 39.5 × 53.5 [15½ × 21]
Compare SD 1719 verso
Paris summer 1887
COLLECTION Manchester, The Whitworth Institute, Whitworth Art Gallery [acquired 1928; gift of Sir Thomas Barlow]

F 1404 NUDE WOMAN RECLINING

Pencil [heavy drawing paper] 23.7 × 31.5 [9¼ × 12½]
Compare paintings F 330 [same composition] and F 357 [probably the same model]
Paris first half of 1887
LITERATURE J. Leymarie, Van Gogh, 1951, p 99: sketch for painting F 330
COLLECTION Amsterdam, Rijksmuseum Vincent van Gogh [Vincent van Gogh Foundation, inv nr F 1404]

F 1405 THE BOULEVARD DE CLICHY [?] IN PARIS

Water color [water-color paper] Sheet 34.2 × 51.2 [13½ × 20¼] Drawing field 31 × 48 [12¼ × 19]
Paris late 1886
LITERATURE A. M. Hammacher, exhib cat van Gogh-Signac London 1962, nr 46: Paris 1886
EDITORS' COMMENT Not the same site as depicted in F 1393. Title doubtful.
COLLECTION Amsterdam, Rijksmuseum Vincent van Gogh [Vincent van Gogh Foundation, inv nr F 1405]

F 1401

F 1402

F 1399a

F 1403

F 1404
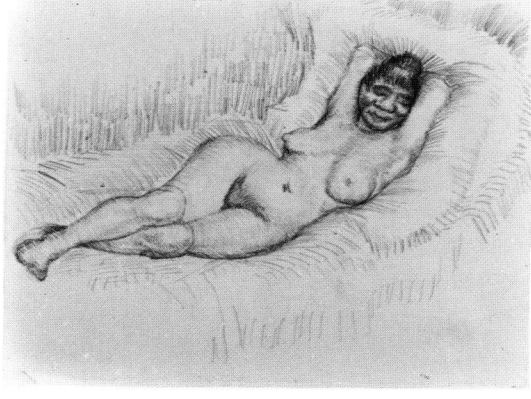

F 1405

F 1406

F 1407

F 1406 GARDEN ENTRANCE ON A SUNNY DAY

Black chalk and water color [water-color paper with watermark: Vidalon les annonay ♡ Anc^{ne} Manuf^{re} Ganson] 31.5 × 24 [12½ × 9½]
Paris summer 1887
LITERATURE A. Bowness, exhib cat van Gogh London [Hayward Gallery] 1968-9, nr 84: Paris July 1887; sometimes called QUATORZE JUILLET because the flag is out; the date suits the foliage of that time of the year and Vincent's style of July 1887
EDITORS' COMMENT The old title QUATORZE JUILLET is not justified. The direction of the stripes seems to indicate a Dutch flag, not a French one.
COLLECTION Amsterdam, Rijksmuseum Vincent van Gogh [Vincent van Gogh Foundation, inv nr F 1406]

F 1407 LA GUINGUETTE

Pen and pencil, heightened with white [gray Ingres paper] 37.9 × 52.3 [15 × 20½]
Compare painting F 238 [same site]
Paris October 1886
LITERATURE W. J. de Gruyter, Tekeningen van Vincent van Gogh, 1962: March 1886. A. Bowness, exhib cat van Gogh London [Hayward Gallery] 1968-9, nr 59: terrace of café La Guinguette in winter; Paris March 1886
COLLECTION Amsterdam, Rijksmuseum Vincent van Gogh [Vincent van Gogh Foundation, inv nr F 1407]

F 1408 THE RESTAURANT DE LA SIRÈNE AT ASNIÈRES

Pencil and green crayon [vergé paper] 40 × 54.5 [15¾ × 21½]
Compare paintings F 312 and F 313 [same site]
Paris spring-summer 1887
LITERATURE P. Leprohon, Rectifications et précisions sur les paysages de l'époque de Paris [typescript]: Restaurant de la Sirène at Asnières, near the Pont d'Asnières. A. M. Hammacher, exhib cat van Gogh-Signac London 1962, nr 47: Restaurant de la Sirène at Suresnes; elaborate drawing for painting F 312; late Paris style
COLLECTION Amsterdam, Rijksmuseum Vincent van Gogh [Vincent van Gogh Foundation, inv nr F 1408]

F 1409 SAILING BOAT AT ASNIÈRES

Pencil [vergé paper] 53.5 × 39.5 [21 × 15½]
Annotated by Vincent with color notes
Paris summer 1887
LITERATURE Vincent van Gogh, Lettres à Bernard, 1911, plate XLI. W. J. de Gruyter, Tekeningen van Vincent van Gogh, 1962, nr 36: summer 1887. A. Bowness, exhib cat van Gogh London [Hayward Gallery] 1968-9, nr 81: Paris May-July 1887; the color notes indicate that Vincent thought of making an oil painting of the subject, but no such painting is known
COLLECTION Amsterdam, Rijksmuseum Vincent van Gogh [Vincent van Gogh Foundation, inv nr F 1409]

F 1410 OUTSKIRTS OF PARIS NEAR MONTMARTRE

Water color, heightened with white [vergé paper] 39.5 × 53.5 [15½ × 21]
Paris summer 1887
LITERATURE D. Cooper, Zeichnungen und Aquarelle von Vincent van Gogh, 1954, nr 17: spring 1887; presumably Asnières. J. G. van Gelder, Openbaar Kunstbezit 1958. W. J. de Gruyter, Tekeningen van Vincent van Gogh, 1962, p 90:

summer 1887
COLLECTION Amsterdam, Stedelijk Museum
[acquired 1912; gift of Vereniging van Hedendaagse
Kunst]

F 1411 SHELTER ON THE HILL OF
MONTMARTRE, WITH SUNFLOWERS

Pencil, pen and blue and green water color [heavy
drawing paper] 30.5 × 23.9 [12 × 9½]
Compare painting F 264a [same site]
Paris late summer 1887
LITERATURE D. Cooper, Zeichnungen und
Aquarelle von Vincent van Gogh, 1954, nr 19:
summer 1887; possibly near Asnières. A. Bowness,
exhib cat van Gogh London [Hayward Gallery]
1968-9, nr 86: July-August 1887; compositionally
nearly a pendant of F 1406; compare painting F 264a
EDITORS' COMMENT Same motif as oil sketch
F 264a of 1886. On stylistic grounds the water color
is to be dated one year later.
COLLECTION Amsterdam, Rijksmuseum Vincent
van Gogh [Vincent van Gogh Foundation, inv
nr F 1411]

F 1408

F 1410

F 1409

F 1411

F 1412

F 1508 recto

F 1244 recto

F 1244 verso

F 1244a recto

F 1244a verso

F 1244b recto

F 1244b verso

F 1412 LE PÈRE TANGUY

Pencil [wove paper] 21.5 × 13.5 [8½ × 5¼] Drawn on
the back of the menu of the Grand Bouillon
Restaurant du Chalet, 43 Avenue de Clichy, Paris
Compare paintings F 263 [for which F 1412 is a
study], F 363 and F 364 [same model]
Paris late 1887
COLLECTION Amsterdam, Rijksmuseum Vincent
van Gogh [Vincent van Gogh Foundation, inv
nr F 1412]

REDATED TO PARIS

F 1244 recto STUDY OF FOUR FLYING
SWALLOWS; LANDSCAPE SKETCHES

Ink, washed [SWALLOWS], pencil [LANDSCAPE]
[wove cardboard] 26.5 × 35 [10½ × 13¾]
Paris 1887
LITERATURE Faille 1928, nr 1244: Nuenen.
Vanbeselaere 1937, pp 279, 412: Paris
COLLECTION Amsterdam, Rijksmuseum Vincent
van Gogh [Vincent van Gogh Foundation, inv
nr F 1244]

F 1244 verso STUDY OF FLYING SWALLOW

Pencil
Paris 1886

F 1244a recto THE VIOLINIST

Blue and green crayon [drawing paper] 35 × 26
[13¾ × 10¼]
Paris summer 1886 or later
LITERATURE Not in Faille 1928. M. E. Tralbaut,
Vincent van Gogh in het caf'conc' of het raakpunt
met Raffaëlli, 1955, reproduction nr 14: a sheet
from a Paris sketchbook of which F 1244b,
F 1244c and F 1244d also formed a part;
reproductions 5, 7, 12, 15, 16, 19, 21 and 24; the
drawings were made after 1 August 1886 under the
influence of Raffaëlli's illustrations for an article on
Les Cafés-Concerts in nr 50 of Paris Illustré,
1 August 1886. A. Bowness, exhib cat van Gogh
London [Hayward Gallery] 1968-9, nr 63: Paris
March-June 1886
COLLECTION Amsterdam, Rijksmuseum Vincent
van Gogh [Vincent van Gogh Foundation, inv
nr F 1244a]

F 1244a verso THE VIOLINIST

Blue crayon
Paris summer 1886 or later
LITERATURE M. E. Tralbaut, 1955: See under
F 1244a recto

F 1244b recto THE CLARINETTIST AND
FLUTIST

Blue crayon [drawing paper] 26 × 35 [10¼ × 13¾]
Paris Summer 1886 or later
LITERATURE Not in Faille 1928. M. E. Tralbaut,
1955: See under F 1244a recto. A. Bowness, exhib
cat van Gogh London [Hayward Gallery] 1968-9,
nr 62: Paris March-June 1886
COLLECTION Amsterdam, Rijksmuseum Vincent
van Gogh [Vincent van Gogh Foundation, inv
nr F 1244b]

F 1244b verso PORTRAIT OF A SITTING
WOMAN; SKETCH OF SAILBOATS

Pencil
Paris summer 1886 or later
LITERATURE M. E. Tralbaut, 1955: See under
F 1244a recto

F 1244c recto

F 1244c verso

EDITORS' COMMENT The pose of the sitter reminds one of the sitter in painting F 369, but the identification of the person portrayed remains uncertain.

F 1244c recto THE PIANIST

Green crayon [drawing paper] 25.5 × 34.3 [10 × 13½]
Paris summer 1886 or later
LITERATURE Not in Faille 1928. M. E. Tralbaut, 1955: See under F 1244a recto
COLLECTION Amsterdam, Rijksmuseum Vincent van Gogh [Vincent van Gogh Foundation, inv nr F 1244c]

F 1244c verso THE CONTRABASS PLAYER

Green crayon
Paris summer 1886 or later
LITERATURE M. E. Tralbaut, 1955: See under F 1244a recto

F 1244d recto A MAN SEEN IN LEFT PROFILE

Charcoal and colored crayon [drawing paper]
35 × 26 [13¾ × 10¼]
Paris summer 1886 or later
LITERATURE Not in Faille 1928. M. E. Tralbaut, 1955: See under F 1244a recto
COLLECTION Amsterdam, Rijksmuseum Vincent van Gogh [Vincent van Gogh Foundation, inv nr F 1244d]

F 1244d verso MAN WITH TOP HAT

Blue and green crayon
Paris summer 1886 or later
LITERATURE M. E. Tralbaut, 1955: See under F 1244a recto

F 1508 recto [formerly F 1508 verso] STANDING MALE NUDE [drawn over a sitting figure]

Pencil 43.5 × 26 [17 × 10¼]
Paris early 1886
COLLECTION Amsterdam, Rijksmuseum Vincent van Gogh [Vincent van Gogh Foundation, inv nr F 1508]

ARLES PERIOD

F 1413 VINCENT'S HOUSE AT ARLES

Chalk, pen, brown ink and water color, heightened with white [Ingres paper with watermark: Glaslam] 25.5 × 31.5 [10 × 12½]
Compare painting F 464, F 1453 [same composition] and F 1513 [same house]
Arles September-October 1888
LITERATURE D. Cooper, Zeichnungen und Aquarelle von Vincent van Gogh, 1954, nr 23: July-September 1888. A. Bowness, exhib cat van Gogh London [Hayward Gallery] 1968-9, nr 127: June-July 1888
EDITORS' COMMENT F 1413 is probably the drawing Vincent had in mind when he sent Theo a small sketch of his house at Arles with letter 543 [probably 28 September] and wrote: 'later on I shall send you a better drawing than this rough improvised sketch I made from memory.'
COLLECTION Amsterdam, Rijksmuseum Vincent van Gogh [Vincent van Gogh Foundation, inv nr F 1413]
Colorplate, p 572

F 1244d recto

F 1244d verso

F 1413

F 1414

F 1415

F 1416 recto

F 1416 verso

F 1414 ORCHARD IN THE PROVENCE

Reed pen, heightened with white [Ingres paper, yellowish, no watermark] 39.5 × 54 [15½ × 21¼]
Signed and annotated by Vincent in lower left: Verger de Provence Vincent
Compare sketch in letter 477 and painting F 403
Arles April 1888
LETTER 486 [probably 10 May] 'Next the series of orchards. I think that the white orchard which I'm sending you a pen drawing of ...'
COLLECTION Amsterdam, Rijksmuseum Vincent van Gogh [Vincent van Gogh Foundation, inv nr F 1414]

F 1415 THE FARMHOUSE IN THE WHEATFIELD

Pencil, pen and reed pen, brown ink [ordinary wove paper] 25.5 × 34.5 [10 × 13½]
Compare sketches in letters 487 and B 6 and painting F 408
Arles early May 1888
LETTER 487 [about 12 May] '...you have a drawing of one of them already, a farm by the high road among wheatfields.'
LITERATURE A. Bowness, exhib cat van Gogh London [Hayward Gallery] 1968-9, nr 109: April 1888
COLLECTION Amsterdam, Rijksmuseum Vincent van Gogh [Vincent van Gogh Foundation, inv nr F 1415]

F 1416 recto VIEW OF ARLES WITH IRISES IN THE FOREGROUND

Reed pen and ink 43.5 × 55.5 [17 × 21¾]
Signed and annotated by Vincent in lower left: Vue d'Arles Vincent
Compare sketch in letter 487 and painting F 409
Arles May 1888
LETTER 487 [about 12 May] 'A meadow full of very yellow buttercups, a ditch with irises, green leaves and purple flowers, the town in the background, some gray willows, and a strip of blue sky.'
COLLECTION Providence, Rhode Island, Museum of Art, Rhode Island School of Design, inv nr 42.212

F 1416 verso DRAWBRIDGE IN ARLES

Crayon
Arles May 1888
LITERATURE Not in Faille 1928. Heinrich Schwarz, Museum Notes, Museum of Art, Rhode Island School of Design, April 1946: Arles May 1888

F 1417 THE RUINS OF MONTMAJOUR

Chalk or pencil, reed pen, lilac ink [yellowed Ingres paper with watermark: P.L. Bas] 31 × 47.5 [12¼ × 18¾]
Annotated by Vincent in lower left: Ruine de Montmajour
Compare sketch in letter 492, F 1423 and F 1446 [same site]
Arles May 1888
LETTERS 490 [26 May] 'Today I sent you some more drawings, and I am adding another two. They are views taken from a rocky hill from which you see the country toward La Crau ...the town of Arles and the country toward Fontvieilles ...The two drawings that I am now adding will give you an idea of the ruin that crowns the rocks.' [F 1417 and F 1423]
492 [probably 29 May] 'You know what you must do with these drawings – make sketchbooks with 6 or 10 or 12 like those books of original Japanese drawings.'
[In the sketch with which Vincent illustrates his idea, F 1423 and perhaps F 1415 and F 1418 can be

recognized]

495 [9 June] *'If the roll is not too big to be accepted by the post office, you will receive a big drawing, again with pen, which I should like the Pissarros to see when they come on Sunday.'* [F 1452]

498a [to A. H. Koning; 9 June] *'I made a drawing recently, even larger than the first two, of a cluster of straight pines on a rock, seen from the top of a hill. Behind this foreground a perspective of meadows, a road with poplars, and in the far distance the town. The trees very dark against the sunlit meadow; perhaps you will still be there to see this drawing. I did it with very thick reeds on thin Whatman paper, and in the background I worked with a quill for the finer strokes.'* [F 1452]

505 [about 15 July] *'They made trouble at the post office, saying that the drawings which I was sending you were too big to be forwarded that way. I have two big ones. When there are six of them I will send them in a roll by rail.'*

506 [about 16 July] *'I have just come back from a day in Mont Majour ... I brought back another big drawing, but not of the garden. That makes three drawings. When I have half a dozen I shall send them along.'*

B 10 [mid-July] *'I have done some large pen-and-ink drawings. Two: an immense sketch of flat country – a bird's eye view seen from the top of a hill – vineyards and fields of newly reaped wheat. All this multiplied in endless repetition, stretching away toward the horizon like the surface of a sea, bordered by the little hills of La Crau* [F 1420]. *It does not have a Japanese look and yet it is really the most Japanese thing I have done; a microscopic figure of a laborer* [F 1420 and F 1424], *a little train running across the wheat fields* [F 1424] – *that is the only sign of life there is in it.'* [F 1424]

509 [about 18 July] *'I have sent off to you by post a roll containing five big pen drawings* [F 1420, F 1424, F 1446, F 1447; the 5th is unknown]. *You have a sixth of that series from Mont Majour – a group of very dark pines and the town of Arles in the background* [F 1452]. *Afterwards I want to add a view of the whole of the ruins (you have a hurried scribble of it* [F 1417] *among the small drawings) ... In my opinion the two views of La Crau* [F 1420] *and of the country on the side of the banks of the Rhône* [F 1424] *are the best things I have done in pen and ink. If Thomas should happen to want them, he cannot have them for less than 100 fr. each.'*

LITERATURE A. Tellegen, Bulletin Museum Boymans-van Beuningen 1967, pp 16-33: in May 1888 Vincent made plein-air sketches on the Mont Majour, a steep hill in the plain of La Crau, which he immediately sent to Theo [letters 490 and 492]; they are F 1417, F 1418, F 1419, F 1423, F 1448, F 1475 and F 1493, all done on half sheets of drawing paper; these were followed by a series of finished drawings of the same site done on a whole sheet, F 1452, early in June [letters 495 and 498a], while F 1420, F 1424, F 1446 and F 1447 were done in July [letters 505, 506, B 10 and 509]; F 1420 and F 1424 are companion pieces
COLLECTION Amsterdam, Rijksmuseum Vincent van Gogh [Vincent van Gogh Foundation, inv nr F 1417]

F 1418 VIEW OF LA CRAU WITH TREE IN THE FOREGROUND [unfinished]

Chalk, reed pen and ink 31 × 48 [12¼ × 19]
Signed in lower left: Vincent
Arles May 1888
LETTERS See under F 1417, especially 490
LITERATURE A. Tellegen, Bulletin Museum Boymans-van Beuningen 1967: May 1888; see under F 1417
COLLECTION San Francisco, Nicol Smith

F 1419 VIEW OF LA CRAU

Pen, reed pen and black chalk 29 × 47 [11½ × 18½]
Annotated by Vincent in lower left: Vue de la Crau
Arles May 1888
LETTERS See under F 1417, especially 490
LITERATURE M. E. Tralbaut, cat Documentary exhibition Amsterdam 1958, nr 245: photograph of the site with view on the Montagne de Corde.
A. Tellegen, Bulletin Museum Boymans-van Beuningen 1967: May 1888; see under F 1417
COLLECTION Essen, Folkwang Museum, cat 1929, nr 436

F 1420 LA CRAU SEEN FROM MONTMAJOUR-

Black chalk, pen, reed pen, brown and black ink [water-color paper with watermark: J. Whatman Turkey Mill 1879] 49 × 61 [19¼ × 24]
Signed and annotated in lower left: Vincent, La Crau, vue prise à Montmajour
Companion piece of F 1424
Arles mid-July 1888
LETTERS See F 1417, especially B 10 and 509
LITERATURE Christian Carroy, Bulletin van het Rijksmuseum 1962, pp 139-42: right half of panoramic landscape, the other half being F 1446. A. Tellegen, Bulletin van het Rijksmuseum 1964, pp 57-61: July 1888; letters B 10 and 509; rejects Carroy's hypothesis; F 1420 is a companion piece of F 1424. A. Tellegen, Bulletin Museum Boymans-van Beuningen 1967: see under F 1417
COLLECTION Amsterdam, Rijksmuseum Vincent van Gogh [Vincent van Gogh Foundation, inv nr F 1420]

F 1417

F 1418

F 1419

F 1420

F 1421

F 1422

F 1424

F 1421 THE PARK OPPOSITE THE YELLOW HOUSE

Pencil, reed pen and brown ink [ordinary wove paper] 25.5 × 34.5 [10 × 13½]
Compare sketches in letters 508 and 553b [in the English edition of the letters only], paintings F 428, F 468, drawings F 1449, F 1450, F 1451 and F 1465 [same site]
Arles July 1888
LITERATURE A. Bowness, exhib cat van Gogh London [Hayward Gallery] 1968-9, nr 128: July 1888
COLLECTION Amsterdam, Rijksmuseum Vincent van Gogh [Vincent van Gogh Foundation, inv nr F 1421]

F 1422 BRETON WOMEN IN THE PLAIN OF PONT-AVEN [after Emile Bernard]

Water color 47.5 × 62 [18¾ × 24½]
Signed in lower right: Vincent
Annotated by Vincent in lower left: D'après un tableau d'E. Bernard
Arles October-December 1888
LETTER W 16 [Saint Rémy after 8 December 1889]
'*Ask Theo to show you the water color that I made after this picture.*'
LITERATURE Vincent van Gogh, Lettres à Bernard, 1911, plate XCIV. J. Rewald, Post-Impressionism, 1956, p 251. M. Chesneau, Art-Documents 1959, p 17. Françoise Cachin, Gauguin, 1968, pp 111, 131
EDITORS' COMMENT The painting by Emile Bernard is dated 1888 [see J. Rewald, 1956, p 251]
COLLECTION Milan, Civica Galleria d'Arte Moderna di Milano [Grassi Collection]

F 1423 THE RUINS OF MONTMAJOUR

Pencil or chalk, reed pen and lilac ink [yellowed Ingres paper with watermark: P.L. Bas] 47.5 × 31 [18¾ × 12¼]
Annotated by Vincent in lower left: Montmajour
Compare sketch in letter 492, F 1417 and F 1446 [same site]
Arles May 1888
LETTERS See F 1417, especially 490 and 492
LITERATURE M. E. Tralbaut, cat Documentary exhibition Amsterdam 1958, nr 251: photograph of the site. W. J. de Gruyter, Tekeningen van Vincent van Gogh, 1962, p 105, nr 38. A. Tellegen, Bulletin Museum Boymans-van Beuningen 1967: May 1888; see under F 1417
COLLECTION Amsterdam, Rijksmuseum Vincent van Gogh [Vincent van Gogh Foundation, inv nr F 1423]

F 1424 LANDSCAPE NEAR MONTMAJOUR, WITH THE LITTLE TRAIN FROM ARLES TO ORGON

Pen, reed pen and black chalk 49 × 61 [19¼ × 24]
Signed in lower left: Vincent
Annotated by Vincent in lower right: La campagne du côté des bords du Rhône, vue de Montmajour
Companion piece of F 1420
Arles mid-July 1888
LETTERS See F 1417, especially B 10 and 509
LITERATURE A. Tellegen, Bulletin van het Rijksmuseum 1964: see under F 1420. A. Tellegen, Bulletin Museum Boymans-van Beuningen 1967: mid-July; see under F 1417. P. H. Hulton, The César Mange de Hauke Bequest, 1968, cat nr 14
COLLECTION London, The British Museum [The César Mange de Hauke bequest], inv nr 1968-2-10-20
Colorplate, p 589

F 1425 HAYRICKS

Pen and wash 50 × 62 [19¾ × 24½]
Compare painting F 425
Arles June 1888
LETTER 498 [about 16 June] See F 425
EDITORS' COMMENT F 1425, F 1426 and F 1427,
are all related to painting F 425. F 1425 is taken
from another spot than F 1426 and F 1427, which
are closer to the picture. Since the same woman
appears in both drawings, one of them must be a
copy after the other. Stylistically, the editors deem
F 1427 the copy. F 1426 was probably the study used
for painting F 425. F 1425 is probably the third of
the series.
COLLECTION Berlin, M. Meirowsky [acquired
1913]

F 1426 HAYRICKS

Pen, reed pen and ink 24 × 31.5 [9½ × 12½]
Compare painting F 425
Arles June 1888
LETTER 498 [about 16 June] See F 425
LITERATURE Vincent van Gogh, Lettres à
Bernard, 1911, plate LIX. Ars Una October 1923,
p 25
EDITORS' COMMENT See F 1425
COLLECTION Budapest, Museum of Fine Arts,
inv nr Ltsz 1935-2792

F 1425

F 1423

F 1426

F 1427

F 1428

F 1429

F 1430

F 1427 HAYRICKS

Pen and ink 24 × 31 [9½ × 12½]
Signed in lower left: Vincent
Compare painting F 425
Arles June 1888
LETTERS 498 [about 16 June] See F 425
517 [3 August] 'I have sent Russell 12 drawings after
painted studies, and so I had an opportunity to speak
to him about it again.'
LITERATURE H. Thannhauser, Burlington
Magazine 1938, part I, pp 94-104. Bulletin of the
Philadelphia Museum of Art, 1963, p 262
EDITORS' COMMENT See F 425. Twelve drawings
formerly in the possession of John Russell that
seem to fit the description in letter 517 are F 1427,
F 1430a, F 1433, F 1449, F 1454, F 1458, F 1482a,
F 1486, F 1489, F 1490, F 1502a and F 1503.
COLLECTION Philadelphia, Philadelphia Museum
of Art, inv nr 62-229-1

F 1428 BOATS ON THE BEACH AT SAINTES-MARIES

Reed pen 39.5 × 53.5 [15½ × 21]
Signed in lower left: Vincent
Annotated by Vincent in upper left: Souvenir de
St. Maries Méditerranée. On the boats are color
annotations and the name AMITIÉ
Compare sketch in letter B 6, painting F 413, and
water color F 1429
Saintes-Maries [Arles period] June 1888
LETTERS 499 [probably 22 June] 'I brought three
canvases and have covered them—two marines, a view
of the village, and then some drawings which I will
send you by post when I return to Arles tomorrow...
Besides half-page drawings I have a big drawing
[F 1439], the pendant of the last one.'
500 [probably 23 June] 'I am sending you by the same
post the drawings of Saintes-Maries. I made the
sketch of the boats just as I was going to start in the
morning...'
B 6 [about 24 June] 'I spent a week at Saintes-
Maries, and to get there I drove in a diligence across
the Camargue with its vineyards, moors and flat
fields like Holland... On the perfectly flat, sandy
beach little green, red, blue boats, so pretty in shape
and color that they made one think of flowers.'
LITERATURE Elseviers Geïllustreerd Maandschrift
1905, p 229. Onze Kunst 1905, part I, p 60
COLLECTION Heirs of H. von Tschudi

F 1429 BOATS ON THE BEACH AT SAINTES-MARIES

Water color 39 × 54 [15¼ × 21¼]
Compare sketch in letter B 6, painting F 413, and
drawing F 1428
Saintes-Maries [Arles period] June 1888
LETTERS 499 [probably 22 June], 500 [about 23
June] and B 6 [about 24 June] See F 1428
LITERATURE J. Meier-Graefe, Entwicklungs-
geschichte der modernen Kunst, volume 3, plate
510
COLLECTION Berlin, Bernhard Köhler [acquired
1937]

F 1430 SAILING BOATS COMING ASHORE

Reed pen and ink 24 × 32 [9½ × 12½]
Compare sketch in letter B 6, painting F 417,
F 1430a and F 1430b
Saintes-Maries [Arles period] June 1888
LETTER 499 [probably 22 June] See F 1428
LITERATURE Paul Gauguin, Kunst und Künstler
1910, pp 579-86 [with reproduction]. Paul Fierens,
Bulletin Koninklijke Musea voor Schone Kunsten
1956 [Brussels], pp 40-7
COLLECTION East Berlin, National Galerie
[acquired 1906], inv nr F 923, cat 2

F 1430a SAILING BOATS COMING ASHORE

Reed pen 24.5 × 32 [9½ × 12½]
Compare sketch in letter B 6, painting F 417, F 1430
and F 1430b
Saintes-Maries [Arles period] June 1888
LETTERS 499 [probably 22 June] See F 1428
517 [3 August] See F 1427
LITERATURE H. Thannhauser, Burlington
Magazine 1938, part I, pp 94-104
EDITORS' COMMENT See F 1427. Faille mentions
letter 500, which pertains, however, to F 1428 rather
than to F 1430a.
COLLECTION New York, Guggenheim Museum
[on loan since 1963 from J. K. Thannhauser], cat
The Thannhauser Foundation 1965, nr 14

F 1430b SAILING BOATS COMING ASHORE

Reed pen 24 × 31.5 [9½ × 12½]
Signed in lower right: Vincent
Compare sketch in letter B 6, painting F 417, F 1430
and F 1430a
Saintes-Maries [Arles period] June 1888
LETTER 499 [probably 22 June] See F 1428
LITERATURE Paul Fierens, Bulletin Koninklijke
Musea voor Schone Kunsten 1956 [Brussels],
pp 40-7
COLLECTION Brussels, Musée d'Art Moderne
[acquired 1955], inv nr 6743

F 1431 SEA WITH SAILING BOATS

Reed pen 24 × 32 [9½ × 12½]
Compare painting F 415 and F 1433
Saintes-Maries [Arles period] June 1888
LETTER 499 [probably 22 June] See F 1428
LITERATURE Vincent van Gogh, Lettres à
Bernard, 1911, plate XLIX
COLLECTION Cologne-Marienburg, Werner
Vowinckel

F 1432 DUNES, BEACH AND SEA WITH SAILING BOATS

Pen, reed pen and pencil 30.5 × 47.5 [12 × 18¾]
Saintes-Maries [Arles period] June 1888
LETTER 499 [probably 22 June] See F 1428
COLLECTION Amsterdam, Rijksmuseum Vincent
van Gogh [Vincent van Gogh Foundation, inv
nr F 1432]

F 1430a

F 1430b

F 1431

F 1432

F 1433

F 1434

F 1435

F 1436

F 1433 SEA WITH SAILING BOATS NEAR SAINTES-MARIES

Reed pen and ink 24 × 31.5 [9½ × 12½]
Compare painting F 415 and F 1431
Saintes-Maries [Arles period] June 1888
LETTERS 499 [probably 22 June] See F 1428
517 [3 August] See F 1427
LITERATURE H. Thannhauser, Burlington
Magazine 1938, part I, pp 94-104
EDITORS' COMMENT See F 1427
COLLECTION Saint Louis, Joseph Pulitzer jr

F 1434 STREET AT SAINTES-MARIES

Reed pen and ink 30.5 × 47 [12 × 18½]
Compare sketch in letter B 6, painting F 420 and
F 1435
Saintes-Maries [Arles period] June 1888
LETTERS 499 [probably 22 June] 'And the houses –
like the ones on our heaths and peat bogs in Drenthe;
you will see some specimens of them in the drawings.'
500 [about 23 June] 'I have three more drawings of
cottages which I still need, and which will follow
these: they are rather harsh, but I have some more
carefully drawn ones.'
LITERATURE Vincent van Gogh, Lettres à
Bernard, 1911, plate LXXIV
COLLECTION Basle, Robert von Hirsch

F 1435 STREET AT SAINTES-MARIES

Reed pen 24 × 31 [9½ × 12¼]
Signed in lower left: Vincent
Compare sketch in letter B 6, painting F 420 and
F 1434
Saintes-Maries [Arles period] June 1888
LETTERS 499 [probably 22 June] and 500 [about
23 June] See F 1434
COLLECTION New York, Museum of Modern Art
[Abby Aldrich Rockefeller bequest], inv nr 243.48

F 1436 ROAD AT SAINTES-MARIES

Reed pen 29 × 49 [11½ × 19¼]
Saintes Maries [Arles period] June 1888
LETTER 499 [probably 22 June] See F 1434
COLLECTION Paris, Heinz Berggruen Art Gallery

F 1437 ROAD AT SAINTES-MARIES IN SUNSHINE

Reed pen and ink 30.5 × 47 [12 × 18½]
Saintes-Maries [Arles period] June 1888
LETTERS 499 [probably 22 June] and 500 [about
23 June] See F 1434
COLLECTION Amsterdam, Rijksmuseum Vincent
van Gogh [Vincent van Gogh Foundation, inv
nr F 1437]

F 1438 THREE HUTS AT SAINTES-MARIES

Pencil, reed pen, brown ink [Ingres paper with
watermark: A.L.] 30 × 47 [11¾ × 18½]
Compare painting F 419 [same composition] and
F 1440 [same site]
Saintes-Maries [Arles period] June 1888
LETTERS 499 [probably 22 June] and 500 [about
23 June] See F 1434
LITERATURE Vincent van Gogh, Lettres à
Bernard, 1911, plate LXIX
COLLECTION Amsterdam, Rijksmuseum Vincent
van Gogh [Vincent van Gogh Foundation, inv
nr F 1438]

F 1439 VIEW ON SAINTES-MARIES WITH CHURCH AND RAMPARTS

Pen and ink 43 × 60 [17 × 23½]
Compare painting F 416
Saintes-Maries [Arles period] June 1888
LETTER 499 [probably 22 June] See F 1428
LITERATURE Vincent van Gogh, Lettres à
Bernard, 1911, plate LI
EDITORS' COMMENT F 1439 being the only known
large drawing from Saintes-Maries, it is probably
the drawing Vincent referred to in letter 499.
COLLECTION Winterthur, Switzerland,
Oscar Reinhart

F 1440 TWO HUTS AT SAINTES-MARIES

Pencil, pen and reed pen 29 × 46 [11½ × 18]
Saintes-Maries [Arles period] June 1888
Compare painting F 419 and F 1438 [same site]
LETTERS 499 [probably 22 June] and 500 [about
23 June] See F 1434
COLLECTION Scarsdale, New York, Ritter
Foundation Inc

**F 1441 THE SOWER IN A WHEATFIELD WITH
THE SETTING SUN**

Reed pen 24.5 × 32 [9½ × 12½]
Compare sketches in letters 501a and B 7, painting
F 422 and F 1442
Arles June 1888
LETTERS 501a [about 27 June] and B 7 [about
28 June] See F 422
501 [about 29 June] *'I have had a week's hard, close
work among the wheatfields in the full sun. The result
is some studies of wheatfields, landscapes, and a
sketch of a sower.'*
COLLECTION Amsterdam, Rijksmuseum Vincent
van Gogh [Vincent van Gogh Foundation, inv
nr F 1441]

F 1441

F 1437

F 1438

F 1439

F 1440

F 1442

F 1443

F 1444

F 1445

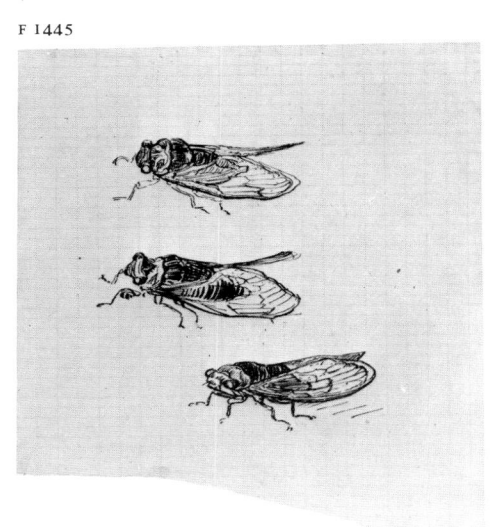

F 1446

F 1442 THE SOWER IN A WHEATFIELD WITH THE SETTING SUN

Reed pen 25 × 31 [9¾ × 12¼]
Signed in lower right: Vincent
Compare sketches in letters 501a and B 7, painting
F 422 and F 1441
Arles June 1888
LETTERS 501a [about 27 June] and B 7 [about
28 June] See F 422
501 [about 29 June] See F 1441
LITERATURE H. Thannhauser, Burlington
Magazine 1938, part I, pp 94-104
COLLECTION Formerly Berlin, Thannhauser Art
Gallery
Present owner unknown

F 1443 THE ZOUAVE SEATED: FULL FACE

Reed pen 52 × 66 [20½ × 26]
Signed in lower left: Vincent
Compare paintings F 423, F 424, water color F 1482
and drawing F 1482a [same model]
Arles June 1888
LETTERS 501 [about 29 June], 502 [about 30 June]
and B 8 [about 1 July] See F 423
COLLECTION Providence, Rhode Island, John
Nicholas Brown

F 1444 THE CANAL LA ROUBINE DU ROI WITH WASHERWOMEN

Pen and ink 31.5 × 24 [12½ × 9½]
Compare painting F 427 and F 1473 [same site]
Arles June 1888
LETTER 504 [about 7 July] See F 427
LITERATURE Vincent van Gogh, Lettres à
Bernard, 1911, plate LVIII
EDITORS' COMMENT This drawing was probably
executed after painting F 427.
COLLECTION Otterlo, Rijksmuseum Kröller-
Müller, inv nr 306-20, cat van Gogh 1970, nr 231

F 1445 STUDY OF THREE CICADAS

Pen and ink [graph paper] 20.5 × 18 [8 × 7]
Compare sketch in letter 506
Arles July 1888
LETTER 506 [about 16 July] '*The grasshoppers – not
like ours at home, but like those you see in Japanese
sketchbooks, and Spanish flies, gold and green in
swarms on the olives. The grasshoppers (I think they
are called cicadas) sing as loud as a frog.*'
COLLECTION Amsterdam, Rijksmuseum Vincent
van Gogh [Vincent van Gogh Foundation, inv
nr F 1445]

F 1446 MONTMAJOUR

Pen and ink 47.5 × 59 [18¾ × 23¼]
Signed in lower right: Vincent
Compare sketch in letter 492, F 1417 and F 1423
[same site]
Arles July 1888
LETTERS See F 1417, especially 505, 506 and 509
LITERATURE K. G. Boon, Vereeniging Rembrandt
Verslag over 1962, pp 15-6. Christian Carroy,
Bulletin van het Rijksmuseum 1962: see under
F 1420. A. Tellegen, Bulletin van het Rijksmuseum
1964: see under F 1420. A. Tellegen, Bulletin
Museum Boymans-van Beuningen 1967: see under
F 1417
COLLECTION Amsterdam, Rijksmuseum [acquired
1962], inv nr 1962: 65

F 1447 THE ROCK: MONTMAJOUR

Pencil, pen, reed pen, brush and black ink [water-
color paper with watermark: Whatman Turkey
Mill 1879] 49 × 60 [19¼ × 23¾]

Arles July 1888
LETTERS See F 1417, especially letters 505, 506 and 509
LITERATURE M. E. Tralbaut, cat Documentary exhibition Amsterdam 1958, nr 253: photograph of the same rock taken on the Montmajour.
A. Tellegen, Bulletin Museum Boymans-van Beuningen 1967, p 27: July; see under F 1417
COLLECTION Amsterdam, Rijksmuseum Vincent van Gogh [Vincent van Gogh Foundation, inv nr F 1447]

F 1448 THE PLAIN OF LA CRAU

Reed pen and ink 30 × 46.5 [11¾ × 18¼]
Signed in lower left: Vincent
Annotated by Vincent in lower right: vue prise à ...[illegible]
Arles May 1888
LETTERS See under F 1417
LITERATURE A. Tellegen, Bulletin Museum Boymans-van Beuningen 1967, May 1888; see under F 1417
COLLECTION Sale Bern [Kornfeld and Klipstein] 24 December 1955, nr 11
Present owner unknown

F 1449 VIEW IN THE PARK

Pen and ink 31.5 × 24.5 [12½ × 9¾]
Signed in lower left: Vincent
Compare sketches in letters 508 and 553b [in the English edition of the letters only], paintings F 428, F 468, drawings F 1421, F 1450, F 1451 and F 1465 [same site]
Arles September 1888
LETTERS See under F 468
LITERATURE H. Thannhauser, Burlington Magazine 1928, part 1, p 73
EDITORS' COMMENT See F 468 and F 1427
COLLECTION Sale New York [Parke-Bernet] 22 November 1949, nr 28
Present owner unknown

F 1450 A PARK IN ARLES

Pen and ink 22.5 × 31 [9 × 12¼]
Signed in lower left: Vincent
Compare sketches in letters 508 and 553b [in the English edition of the letters only], paintings F 428, F 468, drawings F 1421, F 1449, F 1465 [same site] and F 1451 [same composition]
Arles September 1888
LETTERS See under F 468
COLLECTION Toronto, M. F. Feheley

F 1447

F 1448

F 1449

F 1450

F 1451

F 1453

F 1452

F 1455

F 1451 A PARK IN ARLES

Pen and ink 24×31.5 [$9\frac{1}{2} \times 12\frac{1}{2}$]
Compare sketches in letters 508 and 553b [in the English edition of the letters only], paintings F 428, F 468, drawings F 1421, F 1449, F 1465 [same site] and F 1450 [same composition]
Arles September 1888
LETTERS See under F 468
EDITORS' COMMENT See F 468
COLLECTION USA, Private Collection

F 1452 VIEW OF ARLES FROM MONTMAJOUR

Pen and ink 48×59 [$19 \times 23\frac{1}{4}$]
Signed in lower left: Vincent
Arles early June 1888
LETTERS See F 1417, especially 495, 498a and 509
LITERATURE A. Tellegen, Bulletin Museum Boymans-van Beuningen 1967, pp 16-33: early June; see under F 1417
COLLECTION Oslo, Nasjonal Galleriet [acquired 1893]

F 1453 VINCENT'S HOUSE AT ARLES

Pen and ink 13×20.5 [$5\frac{1}{4} \times 8$]
Included in letter 543
Compare painting F 464, F 1413 [same composition] and F 1513 [same house]
Arles September 1888
LETTER 543 [probably 28 September] '*Also a sketch of a size 30 canvas representing the house and its surroundings in sulphur-colored sunshine, under a sky of pure cobalt...later on I shall send you a better drawing than this rough improvised sketch I made out of my head.*'
LITERATURE Vincent van Gogh, Lettres à Bernard, 1911, plate XLV. P. Gauguin, Kunst und Künstler 1910, reproduced on p 581
EDITORS' COMMENT The editors believe F 1453 to be one of the sketches Vincent inserted in a letter. The text of letter 543, not mentioned by Faille, makes it seem likely that F 1453 belongs to it. Letter B 18 mentions only the painting, not the drawing. On the basis of the date of letter 543, the editors have redated F 1453 from July to September. This date is confirmed by Vincent's annotation on the back of the drawing, in which he mentions the portrait he made of Milliet [F 473].
COLLECTION Brienz, Switzerland, N. Dreher [acquired 1918]

F 1454 A GARDEN

Pen and ink 24×31.5 [$9\frac{1}{2} \times 12\frac{1}{2}$]
Signed in lower left: Vincent
Compare sketch in letter 512, paintings F 430, F 1455 [same site] and painting F 429 [same composition]
Arles July 1888
LETTERS 512 [about 24 July] '*I have a new drawing of a garden full of flowers, and two painted studies as well.*'
516 [about 1 August] '*I am working hard for Russell, I thought that I would do him a series of drawings after my painted studies...*'
517 [3 August] See F 1427
LITERATURE H. Thannhauser, Burlington Magazine 1928, part 1, p 73
EDITORS' COMMENT See F 1427. Letter 516 makes it clear that F 1454 was made after painting F 429, for which F 1455 was a preliminary sketch.
COLLECTION Formerly Lausanne, A. Strölin Art Gallery
Present owner unknown

F 1455 A GARDEN

Pen and ink 49 × 61 [19¼ × 24]
Signed in lower middle: Vincent
Compare sketch in letter 512, paintings F 429, F 430
and drawing F 1454 [same site]
Arles July 1888
LETTERS 512 [about 24 July] '*I have a new drawing
of a garden full of flowers, and two painted studies as
well...You will see from this sketch the subject of the
new studies. There is one vertical and another
horizontal of the same subject, size 30 canvases.*'
519 [8 August] '*The little cottage garden done
vertically is, I think, the best of the three big ones.
The one with the sunflowers is a little garden of a
bathing establishment, the third garden, horizontal, is
the one from which I made some painted studies as
well ...If the drawings I send you are too hard, it is
because I have done them in such a way as to be able
later on, if they're still around, to use them as guides
for painting.*'
521 [about 12 August] '*...I have a supply of paints
and canvas, because I already have my eye on half a
dozen subjects, especially that little cottage garden I
sent you the drawing of yesterday.*'
EDITORS' COMMENT See F 1454. The drawings
mentioned by Vincent in letter 519 are F 1455,
F 1456 and F 1457.
COLLECTION Winterthur, Switzerland, Oscar
Reinhart

F 1456 A GARDEN

Reed pen and ink 61 × 49 [24 × 19¼]
Signed in lower left: Vincent
Compare painting F 578
Arles August 1888
LETTERS 519 [8 August] and 521 [about 12 August]
See F 1455
EDITORS' COMMENT See F 1455
COLLECTION Zurich, Fritz Nathan

F 1457 FLOWERBED WITH SUNFLOWERS

Pencil, reed pen and brown ink [Ingres paper with
watermark: J. Whatman, Turkey Mill, 1879]
60 × 48.5 [23¾ × 19]
Signed in lower right [on bucket]: Vincent
Arles August 1888
LETTERS 519 [8 August] and 521 [about 12 August]
See F 1455
EDITORS' COMMENT See F 1455
COLLECTION Amsterdam, Rijksmuseum Vincent
van Gogh [Vincent van Gogh Foundation, inv
nr F 1457]

F 1456

F 1457

F 1454

F 1458

F 1459

F 1460

F 1461

F 1464

F 1458 THE POSTMAN ROULIN

Pen and ink 31.5 × 24 [12½ × 9½]
Compare paintings F 433, F 434, F 435, F 436, F 439
[same composition], F 432, drawings F 1459 and
SD 1723 [same model]
Arles August 1888
LETTERS 517 [3 August] See F 432 and F 1427
520 [11 August] '*Today I am sending you the drawing
I made after this painting as well as the drawing after
the portrait of the postman Roulin.*'
LITERATURE H. Thannhauser, Burlington
Magazine 1938, part I, pp 94-104
EDITORS' COMMENT See F 1427
COLLECTION Bern, H. R. Hahnloser

**F 1459 THE POSTMAN ROULIN: HALF-
LENGTH, SITTING AT A TABLE**

Pen and ink 59 × 44.5 [23¼ × 17½]
Compare painting F 432, SD 1723 [same
composition], paintings F 433, F 434, F 435, F 436,
F 439 and drawing F 1458 [same model]
Arles August 1888
LETTERS 517 [3 August] and 520 [11 August]
See F 432 and F 1458
LITERATURE K. Pfister, Van Gogh, 1923, p 37. Art
News September 1946, p 32. Cat Work by Vincent
van Gogh 1948, Cleveland Museum of Art, p 26.
R. Shodman and C. E. Slatkin, Six Centuries of
French Master Drawings in America, 1950, plate 123
COLLECTION Los Angeles, County Museum [De
Sylva Collection], inv nr M 49.17.1, cat The George
Gard de Sylva Collection 1950, p 55

F 1460 PORTRAIT OF PATIENCE ESCALIER

Pencil, pen, reed pen and brown ink 49.5 × 38
[19½ × 15]
Signed in lower left: Vincent
Compare paintings F 443, F 444 and drawing F 1461
[same model]
Arles August 1888
LETTERS 520 [11 August] '*You are shortly to make
the acquaintance of Master Patience Escalier, a sort
of "man with a hoe," formerly cowherd of the
Camargue, now gardener at a house in the Crau.
Today I am sending you the drawing I made after this
painting ...*'
522 [about 13 August] '*Have you got the drawings of
the gardens, and the two figure drawings?*'
LITERATURE A. Aurier, Mercure de France 1893,
p 313. C. Nordenfalk, Konsthistorisk Tidskrift
1946, p 89-96. F. Novotny, Art Bulletin 1953, p 40.
J. G. van Gelder, Great Drawings of all Time,
volume 2, 1962, nr 626
COLLECTIONS Cambridge, Massachusetts, Fogg
Art Museum [Grenville L. Winthrop bequest], inv
nr 1943-515, cat 1969, nr 125

F 1461 PORTRAIT OF PATIENCE ESCALIER

Reed pen and ink 14 × 13 [5½ × 5]
Compare paintings F 443, F 444 and drawing F 1460
[same model]
Arles August 1888
LETTERS 520 [11 August] See F 1460
B 15 [about 18 August] '*...I have another figure ...I
wanted to send you a very large and very careful
drawing. Very well! It turned out quite different,
though it is correct.*'
COLLECTION Switzerland, Private Collection

F 1462 RIVER WITH TWO BOATS

Pen, reed pen and ink 48 × 62.5 [19 × 24½]
Compare sketch in letter 524 and painting F 449
Arles August 1888
LETTERS 524 [14 or 15 August] and 525 [15 August]
See F 449

526 [about 21 August] See F 437
LITERATURE C. Nordenfalk, Konsthistorisk
Tidskrift 1946, p 94
COLLECTION New York, Miss Edith Wetmore

F 1463 INTERIOR OF THE NIGHT CAFÉ IN
ARLES

Water color 42 × 61.5 [16½ × 24¼]
Compare painting F 463
Arles early September 1888
LETTERS 533 [8 September] *'The room is blood red
and dark yellow with a green billiard table in the
middle; there are four citron-yellow lamps with a
glow of orange and green…I am making a drawing of
it with the tones in water color to send to you
tomorrow to give you some idea of it.'*
534 [9 September] See F 463
LITERATURE A. Plasschaert, Onze Kunst 1904,
part 2, p 152. D. Cooper, Zeichnungen und
Aquarelle von Vincent van Gogh, 1954, nr 24
COLLECTION Bern, H. R. Hahnloser

F 1464 THE MILL

Pen and water color 30 × 50 [11¾ × 19¾]
Arles September 1888
COLLECTION West Germany, Private Collection

F 1465 A PARK IN ARLES

Pen and ink 13.5 × 17 [5¼ × 6¾]
Compare sketches in letters 508 and 553b [in the
English edition of the letters only], F 1421, F 1449,
F 1450 and F 1451 [same site]
Arles September 1888
LETTERS See under F 468, especially 541
LITERATURE Vincent van Gogh, Lettres à
Bernard, 1911, plate LIII
EDITORS' COMMENT See F 468. The picture
mentioned in letter 541 is unknown.
COLLECTION Sale London [Sotheby] 3 December
1958, nr 47
Present owner unknown

F 1466 THISTLES ALONG THE ROADSIDE

Pencil, pen and brown ink [ordinary wove paper]
24.5 × 32 [9¾ × 12½]
Arles autumn 1888
EDITORS' COMMENT From the Arles period there
are two paintings of thistles: F 447 and F 447a,
neither of which has any relation to this drawing.
COLLECTION Amsterdam, Rijksmuseum Vincent
van Gogh [Vincent van Gogh Foundation, inv
nr F 1466]

F 1462

F 1463

F 1465

F 1466

F 1467

F 1468

F 1470

F 1471

F 1467 THE COURTYARD OF THE HOSPITAL IN ARLES

Pencil, reed pen and brown ink [Ingres paper,
pasted] 45.5 × 59 [18 × 23¼]
Signed on the watering can: Vincent
Compare painting F 519 [same site]
Arles April-May 1889
LETTER 595 [Saint Rémy 18 June] *'I am sending you
a roll of drawings … The drawings – "Hospital at
Arles" … are a continuation of those old ones of
Montmajour, the others are hasty studies made in
the garden.'*
COLLECTION Amsterdam, Rijksmuseum Vincent
van Gogh [Vincent van Gogh Foundation, inv
nr F 1467]

F 1468 VIEW IN THE PARK IN ARLES

Chalk, pen, reed pen and ink [wove white paper
with watermark: J. Whatman Manufacturer 1888]
49 × 61.5 [19¼ × 24¼]
Arles September 1888
LETTERS See under F 468
LITERATURE J. G. van Gelder, Great Drawings of
all Time, volume 2, 1962, nr 629
EDITORS' COMMENT See F 468. Faille dates this
drawing May 1889 in connection with letter 595.
Since however it belongs to the series of THE
POET'S GARDEN [see F 468] it must be dated
September 1888.
COLLECTION Chicago, The Art Institute [gift of
Tiffany and Margaret Blake], inv nr 45.31

F 1469 THE FLOWERING TREE

Charcoal and water color [water-color paper with
watermark: J. Whatman] 45.5 × 30.5 [18 × 12]
Compare sketch in letter 477, paintings F 394 and
F 404
Arles March 1888
LITERATURE A. Bowness, exhib cat van Gogh
London [Hayward Gallery] 1968-9, nr 103: March
1888; the water color may precede painting F 394
COLLECTION Amsterdam, Rijksmuseum Vincent
van Gogh [Vincent van Gogh Foundation, inv
nr F 1469]

F 1470 THE LANGLOIS BRIDGE SEEN FROM THE ROAD

Pen, reed pen and ink 35.5 × 47 [14 × 18½]
Compare paintings F 397, F 400, F 570, F 571,
drawing F 1471 and water color F 1480 [same site]
Arles March 1888
LITERATURE E. H. du Quesne-van Gogh, Kunst
und Künstler 1911, reproduced on p 225. J. Meier-
Graefe, Vincent van Gogh der Zeichner, 1928,
plate 24
COLLECTION Stuttgart, Graphische Sammlung,
inv nr C 67/1491

F 1471 THE LANGLOIS BRIDGE WITH A WOMAN CARRYING AN UMBRELLA

Pen and ink 23.5 × 31 [9¼ × 12¼]
Compare paintings F 397, F 400, F 571, drawing
F 1470 and water color F 1480 [same site] and
painting F 570 [same composition]
Arles March 1888
EDITORS' COMMENT Faille dated this drawing
May 1888. But there is no reason not to date it in
March, together with the group of other drawings
and paintings of the same site.
COLLECTION Los Angeles, County Museum
[George Gard de Sylva Collection], inv nr M 49.17.2,
cat George de Sylva Collection 1950, nr 21

F 1472 THE RHÔNE

Pen and ink 22.5 × 34.5 [8¾ × 13½]
Compare sketch in letter 553b [in the English
edition of the letters only], F 474 and drawing F 1515
[same site]
Arles summer 1888
LITERATURE M. E. Tralbaut, exhib cat van Gogh
Essen 1957, nr 288: summer 1888
COLLECTION Munich, Staatliche Graphische
Sammlung, inv nr 44329

F 1472a THE RHÔNE SEEN FROM THE
TRINQUETAILLE BRIDGE

Reed pen, lilac ink 38.5 × 60.5 [15¼ × 23¾]
Signed and annotated in lower left: Bords du
Rhône. Vincent
Arles August 1888
COLLECTION Rotterdam, Museum Boymans-van
Beuningen [acquired 1929; gift of Mr H. van Beek
and Mr H. Nygh], inv nr VvG 3

F 1473 THE BANK OF THE CANAL LA
ROUBINE DU ROI

Pen and ink 22.5 × 34.5 [8¾ × 13½]
Compare painting F 427 and F 1444 [same site]
Arles summer 1888
LETTER 504 [about 7 July] See F 427
COLLECTION Munich, Staatliche Graphische
Sammlung, inv nr 44330

F 1474 MEADOW WITH FLOWERS

Pencil, pen and brown ink [ordinary wove paper]
25.5 × 34.5 [10 × 13½]
Compare painting F 576
Arles September 1888
LITERATURE Vincent van Gogh, Lettres à
Bernard, 1911, plate LXVI
COLLECTION Amsterdam, Rijksmuseum Vincent
van Gogh [Vincent van Gogh Foundation, inv
nr F 1474]

F 1475 VIEW OF ARLES SEEN FROM A HILL

Pencil, reed pen and ink [Ingres paper with water-
mark: AL] 47.5 × 30.5 [18¾ × 12]
Annotated by Vincent in lower left: Vue d'Arles
[barely legible]
Arles May 1888
LETTERS See under F 1417, especially 490
LITERATURE Faille 1928, nr 1475: not reproduced.
A. Tellegen, Bulletin Museum Boymans-van
Beuningen 1967: May 1888; see under F 1417
COLLECTION Rotterdam, Museum Boymans-van
Beuningen, inv nr F II, 198

F 1469

F 1472

F 1472a

F 1473

F 1474

F 1475

F 1476

F 1477

F 1478

F 1480a

F 1476 PARK IN ARLES WITH A CORNER OF THE YELLOW HOUSE

Pen, reed pen and ink 35 × 26 [13¾ × 10¼]
Arles 19 September 1888 or shortly thereafter
LETTERS See under F 468, especially letter 539
EDITORS' COMMENT See F 468
COLLECTION Amsterdam, Rijksmuseum Vincent van Gogh [Vincent van Gogh Foundation, inv nr F 1476]

F 1477 PARK ALONG THE FENCE

Pencil, pen and brown ink [ordinary wove paper] 32 × 24.5 [12½ × 9¾]
Arles 19 September 1888 or shortly thereafter
LETTERS See under F 468, especially letter 539
EDITORS' COMMENT See F 468
COLLECTION Amsterdam, Rijksmuseum Vincent van Gogh [Vincent van Gogh Foundation, inv nr F 1477]

F 1478 MAS IN THE PROVENCE

Pencil, reed pen and brown ink [Ingres paper, doubled] 39 × 53.5 [15½ × 21]
Signed and annotated by Vincent in lower right: Un Mas de Provence. Vincent
Compare paintings F 425 and F 565 [same composition]
Arles June 1888
LITERATURE A. Aurier, Mercure de France August 1893, reproduced on p 307. Vincent van Gogh, Lettres à Bernard, 1911, plate LX. A. Plasschaert, XIXe Eeuwse Hollandsche Schilderkunst, nd, reproduced on p 77. A. M. Hammacher, Les grands maîtres du dessin, 1953, reproduction nr 22
COLLECTION Amsterdam, Stedelijk Museum [on loan from Rijksmuseum]

F 1478a DWELLING AND GARDEN BEHIND A WALL

Reed pen 23 × 32 [9 × 12½]
Arles summer 1888
LITERATURE Not in Faille 1928. Carl Zigrosser, Philadelphia Museum of Art Bulletin 1956-7, pp 23-7
COLLECTION Bradford, Pennsylvania, Mr and Mrs T. Edward Hanley

F 1479 FIELD WITH THE CEMETERY OF SAINTES-MARIES IN THE BACKGROUND

Pen, reed pen and ink 29.5 × 47.5 [11½ × 18¾]
Annotated by Vincent in upper left: Cimetière de Stes Maries
Saintes-Maries [Arles period] June 1888
LITERATURE Vincent van Gogh, Lettres à Bernard, 1911, plate LXXV
COLLECTION Switzerland, Private Collection

F 1480 THE LANGLOIS BRIDGE

Water color 30 × 30 [11¾ × 11¾]
Signed in lower left: Vincent
Annotated by Vincent in lower left: Le pont de l'Anglais Arles
Compare paintings F 397, F 571 [same composition], F 400, F 570, drawings F 1470 and F 1471 [same site]
Arles March 1888
LITERATURE Paul Fechter, Kunst und Künstler 1910, reproduced on p 358
COLLECTION Private Collection

F 1480

F1480a VIEW OF ROOFS WITH THE TOWER OF SAINT JULIEN AT ARLES

Pencil, reed pen and ink 25.5 × 34.5 [10 × 13½]
Arles early spring 1888
LITERATURE Not in Faille 1928. M.E. Tralbaut, exhib cat van Gogh Essen 1957, nr 264: February 1889
EDITORS' COMMENT According to the oral communication of Mr Latour, the late curator of the Réattu Museum in Arles, this drawing may have been made from the top floor of the Restaurant Carrel.
COLLECTION Paris, Heinz Berggruen Art Gallery

F1481 WHEATFIELD WITH THE ALPILLES IN THE BACKGROUND

Pen, reed pen and ink 24 × 31.5 [9½ × 12½]
Compare painting F 411
Arles July 1888
LITERATURE A. Aurier, Mercure de France 1893, reproduced on p 112. Vincent van Gogh, Lettres à Bernard, 1911, plate LXXVI
COLLECTION New York, Mrs Max J. H. Rossbach

F 1478a

F 1479

F 1481

F 1482

F 1482a

F 1483

F 1484

F 1482 THE ZOUAVE: HALF LENGTH

Black chalk, pen and water color 30 × 23 [11¾ × 9]
Signed and annotated by Vincent in upper right:
A mon cher copain Emile Bernard. Vincent
Compare painting F 423, drawing F 1482a [same
composition], painting F 424 and drawing F 1443
[same model]
Arles June 1888
LETTER 501 [about 29 June] See F 423
LITERATURE Vincent van Gogh, Lettres à
Bernard, 1911, plate LXXXI. The Metropolitan
Museum of Art Bulletin October 1963, p 63
COLLECTION New York, The Metropolitan
Museum of Art [acquired 1962; gift of Emanie
Philips], inv nr 62.151

F 1482a THE ZOUAVE: HEAD AND SHOULDERS

Pen and reed pen 32 × 24.5 [12½ × 9¾]
Signed in lower left: Vincent
Compare painting F 423, water color F 1482a [same
composition], painting F 424 and drawing F 1443
[same model]
Arles June 1888
LITERATURE Not in Faille 1928. H. Thannhauser,
Burlington Magazine 1938, part I, pp 94-104.
F. Elgar, Van Gogh, 1958, p 154
EDITORS' COMMENT See F 1427
COLLECTION New York, Guggenheim Museum
[on loan since 1963 from J. K. Thannhauser], cat
The Thannhauser Foundation 1965, nr 17

F 1483 HARVEST IN THE PROVENCE, AT THE LEFT MONTMAJOUR

Pen and ink, washed with water color 48 × 60
[19 × 23¾]
Signed in lower right: Vincent
Annotated on the left: La moisson en Provence
Compare painting F 412, F 1484, F 1485 and F 1486
Arles June 1888
LETTER 496 [12 June] See F 412
LITERATURE F. Fels, Vincent van Gogh, 1928,
p 148. Mark Roskill, Oud-Holland 1966, pp 3-19:
see under F 412
EDITORS' COMMENT Emil Rudolph Weiss made a
colored lithograph after this drawing for an edition
of Zola's Germinal issued in 1899 by J. Meier-Graefe
COLLECTION London, Mrs J. B. A. Kessler

F 1484 HARVEST IN THE PROVENCE, AT THE LEFT MONTMAJOUR

Pen, brush and water color 39.5 × 52.5 [15½ × 20½]
Compare painting F 412, F 1483, F 1485 and F 1486
Arles June 1888
LETTER 496 [12 June] See F 412
LITERATURE J. Meier-Graefe, Vincent van Gogh
der Zeichner, 1928, plate 20. Mark Roskill, Oud-
Holland 1966, pp 3-19: see under F 412
COLLECTION Cambridge, Massachusetts, Fogg
Art Museum [Winthrop bequest], inv nr 1943.279

F 1485 HARVEST IN THE PROVENCE, AT THE LEFT MONTMAJOUR

Pen and ink 24 × 32 [9½ × 12½]
Compare painting F 412, F 1483, F 1484 and F 1486
Arles June 1888
LETTERS 496 [12 June] See F 412
498 [about 16 June] 'Today I am sending you 3
drawings by post ... The "Harvest" is rather more
serious.'
519 [8 August] 'I have just sent off three big drawings,
as well as some smaller ones ... Now the Harvest, the
Garden, the Sower, and the two marines are sketches
after painted studies.'
LITERATURE M. Roskill, Oud-Holland 1966,

pp 3-19: see under F 412
EDITORS' COMMENT The other drawings
mentioned in letter 498 are F 1426 and F 1427.
COLLECTION East Berlin, National Galerie,
[acquired 1906], inv nr F 923, cat 1

F 1486 HARVEST IN THE PROVENCE, AT THE
LEFT MONTMAJOUR

Pen and ink 24 × 32 [9½ × 12½]
Signed in lower left: Vincent
Compare painting F 412, water colors F 1483, F 1484
and drawing F 1485
Arles June 1888
LETTER 517 [3 August] See F 1427
LITERATURE Mark Roskill, Oud-Holland 1966,
pp 3-19: see under F 412
EDITORS' COMMENT See F 1427. Faille reports
that F 1486 is annotated 'La moisson en Provence,'
but this cannot be seen on the photograph.
COLLECTION Upperville, Virginia, Mr and Mrs
Paul Mellon

F 1487 THE PARK

Reed pen and ink 26 × 35 [10¼ × 13¾]
Arles September 1888
COLLECTION Paris, Heinz Berggruen Art Gallery

F 1488 SHEAVES

Pen and ink 24.5 × 32 [9¾ × 12½]
Signed in lower right: Vincent
Compare painting F 561 and F 1489
Arles summer 1888
LITERATURE Kunst und Künstler 1909-10, p 580
[with reproduction]
EDITORS' COMMENT This drawing must have been
executed on the spot.
COLLECTION East Berlin, National Galerie
[acquired 1906], inv nr F 923, cat 3

F 1489 SHEAVES

Pen and ink 24 × 32 [9½ × 12½]
Signed in lower left: Vincent
Compare painting F 561 and F 1488
Arles summer 1888
LETTER 517 [3 August] See F 1427
EDITORS' COMMENT See F 1427. F 1489 is the more
elaborated version done after the picture.
COLLECTION Bern, H. R. Hahnloser

F 1485

F 1486

F 1487

F 1488

F 1489

F 1490

F 1491

F 1492

F 1493

F 1496

F 1490 ARLES: VIEW FROM THE WHEATFIELDS

Pen and ink 31.5 × 23.5 [12½ × 9¼]
Signed in lower left: Vincent
Compare painting F 545, F 1491 and F 1492 [same site]
Arles June 1888
LETTER 517 [3 August] See F 1427
LITERATURE H. Thannhauser, Burlington Magazine 1938, part 1, pp 95-104
EDITORS' COMMENT See F 1427
COLLECTION Chicago, Mr and Mrs Leigh B. Block

F 1491 ARLES: VIEW FROM THE WHEATFIELDS

Pen and ink 32 × 24 [12½ × 9½]
Compare painting F 545, F 1490 and F 1492
Arles summer 1888
LITERATURE H. Thannhauser, Burlington Magazine 1938, part 1, pp 95-104
EDITORS' COMMENT The drawing must have been executed on the spot.
COLLECTION Formerly Paris, Henri Matisse Present owner unknown

F 1492 ARLES: VIEW FROM THE WHEAT-FIELDS

Pen and ink 31.5 × 24 [12½ × 9½]
Signed in lower right: Vincent
Compare painting F 545, F 1490 and F 1491
Arles summer 1888
LETTER 519 [8 August] See F 1485
EDITORS' COMMENT Close in style to F 1490, which apparently preceded it. The other drawings mentioned in letter 519 include F 1455, F 1456, F 1457 and F 1485.
COLLECTION Basle, Robert von Hirsch

F 1493 SLOPE OF A HILL WITH BUSHES

Chalk, reed pen and violet ink [Ingres paper, yellowish discolored, with watermark: P.L. Bas] 31 × 47.5 [12¼ × 18¾]
Annotated by Vincent in the lower center: Bruyère
Arles May 1888
LETTERS See F 1417, especially 490
LITERATURE A. Tellegen, Bulletin Museum Boymans-van Beuningen 1967: May 1888; see under F 1417
COLLECTION Amsterdam, Rijksmuseum Vincent van Gogh [Vincent van Gogh Foundation, inv nr F 1493]

F 1494 FIELD WITH POPPIES
Saint Rémy period; see after F 1622 verso

F 1495 ROAD WITH TELEGRAPH-POLE AND CRANE

Pencil, pen and ink [ordinary thick paper] 24 × 32 [9½ × 12½]
Signed in lower left: Vincent
Arles summer 1888
LITERATURE J. Meier-Graefe, Vincent van Gogh der Zeichner, 1928, plate 34. A. Bowness, exhib cat van Gogh London [Hayward Gallery] 1968-9, nr 131: related to F 446
COLLECTION Amsterdam, Rijksmuseum Vincent van Gogh [Vincent van Gogh Foundation, inv nr F 1495]

F 1496 LANDSCAPE WITH THE WINDMILL OF ALPHONSE DAUDET [FONTVIEILLE]

Pencil, reed pen and brown ink [ordinary wove paper] 25.5 × 34.5 [10 × 13½]
Arles summer 1888

LITERATURE A. Bowness, exhib cat van Gogh
London [Hayward Gallery] 1968-9, nr 111 : April
1888
COLLECTION Amsterdam, Rijksmuseum Vincent
van Gogh [Vincent van Gogh Foundation, inv
nr F 1496]

F 1497 CORNER OF THE GARDEN OF SAINT
PAUL'S HOSPITAL
Saint Rémy period; see after F 1622 verso

F 1498 recto FIELD WITH GUARDIAN'S HUT,
CAMARGUE

Pencil, pen, reed pen and brown ink [ordinary wove
paper] 34.5 × 25.5 [13½ × 10]
Arles June 1888
COLLECTION Amsterdam, Rijksmuseum Vincent
van Gogh [Vincent van Gogh Foundation, inv
nr F 1498]

F 1498 verso AVENUE IN THE PARK IN ARLES

Blue chalk, pen and blue ink
Arles September 1888

F 1499 PATH THROUGH A FIELD WITH
WILLOWS

Pencil, pen and brown ink [ordinary wove paper]
25.5 × 35 [10 × 13¾]
Annotated by Vincent in lower middle: Arles Mars
'88
Compare painting F 407
Arles March 1888
LETTER 484 [7 May] See F 407
LITERATURE A. Bowness, exhib cat van Gogh
London [Hayward Gallery] 1968-9, nr 102 : letter
484
COLLECTION Amsterdam, Rijksmuseum Vincent
van Gogh [Vincent van Gogh Foundation, inv
nr F 1499]

F 1495

F 1498 recto

F 1498 verso

F 1499

F 1500

F 1502

F 1504

F 1506

F 1500 THE FACTORY

Pencil, chalk, pen and ink 25.5 × 35 [10 × 13¾]
Arles early spring 1888
LITERATURE Vincent van Gogh, Lettres à
Bernard, 1911, plate LXVIII
COLLECTION London, The Courtauld Institute
Galleries, cat 1954, nr 155

F 1501 LANDSCAPE WITH TREES
Saint Rémy period; see after F 1622 verso

**F 1502 THE ROAD TO TARASCON WITH
FIGURE**

Pencil, pen, reed pen and ink 25 × 34 [9¾ × 13½]
Compare painting F 448, drawings F 1502a and
F 1518 [same site]
Arles August 1888
LITERATURE J. Meier-Graefe, Vincent van Gogh
der Zeichner, 1928, plate 33
COLLECTION Zurich, Kunsthaus

**F 1502a THE ROAD TO TARASCON: SKY WITH
SUN**

Pen and reed pen 24.5 × 32 [9¾ × 12½]
Compare painting F 448, F 1502 and F 1518 [same
site]
Arles August 1888
LETTER 517 [3 August] See F 1427
LITERATURE Not in Faille 1928. H. Thannhauser,
Burlington Magazine 1938, part I, p 104
EDITORS' COMMENT See F 1427
COLLECTION New York, Guggenheim Museum
[on loan since 1963 from J. K. Thannhauser], cat
The Thannhauser Foundation 1965, nr 18

F 1503 PORTRAIT OF LA MOUSMÉ: BUST

Pen and reed pen 31.5 × 24 [12½ × 9½]
Signed in lower left: Vincent
Compare painting F 431, F 1504 and SD 1722 [same
model]
Arles July 1888
LETTER 517 [3 August] See F 1427
EDITORS' COMMENT See F 1427
COLLECTION New York, Paul M. Hirschland

**F 1504 LA MOUSMÉ SITTING IN AN ARM-
CHAIR**

Pencil, pen and reed pen [brownish paper]
32.5 × 24.5 [12¾ × 9¾]
Annotated by Vincent in the margin with color
notes
Compare painting F 431, SD 1722 [same
composition] and F 1503 [same model]
Arles July 1888
LITERATURE F. Fels, Vincent van Gogh, 1928,
p 130
EDITORS' COMMENT The notes on color seem to
indicate that drawing F 1504 was executed after
painting F 431.
COLLECTION Moscow, Pushkin Museum

**F 1505 CORNER OF THE GARDEN OF
SAINT PAUL'S HOSPITAL**
Saint Rémy period; see after F 1622 verso

**F 1506 FIELD WITH HOUSES AND SKY WITH
SUN**

Pencil, pen, reed pen and brown ink [ordinary wove
paper] 24.5 × 35.5 [9¾ × 14]
Arles summer 1888
LITERATURE J. Meier-Graefe, Vincent van Gogh
der Zeichner, 1928, plate 26. A. Bowness, exhib cat
van Gogh London [Hayward Gallery] 1968-9,
nr 112: Arles April-May 1888; letters 480 and 483

COLLECTION Amsterdam, Rijksmuseum Vincent van Gogh [Vincent van Gogh Foundation, inv nr F 1506]

F 1507 THE BRIDGE AT TRINQUETAILLE

Pen and ink 24 × 31 [9½ × 12¼]
Compare painting F 426
Arles June-July 1888
LITERATURE A. Aurier, Mercure de France 1893, pp 211-17. Vincent van Gogh, Lettres à Bernard, 1911, plate LVI
COLLECTION New York, Estate of Robert Lehman [bequeathed to the Metropolitan Museum, 1969]

F 1507a HEAD OF A GIRL [THE MUDLARK]

Reed pen [checked letter paper] 15 × 12.5 [6 × 5]
Sketch enclosed with letter 501a
Compare painting F 535 [same model]
Arles June 1888
LETTER 501a [to John Russell; about 27 June]
'Well, instead of continuing the letter I began to draw on the very paper the head of the dirty little girl I saw this afternoon whilst I was painting a view of the river with a greenish yellow sky. This dirty "mudlark" I thought yet had a vague Florentine sort of figure like the heads in the Monticelli pictures, and reasoning and drawing this wise I worked on the letter I was writing to you.'
LITERATURE Not in Faille 1928. H. Thannhauser, Burlington Magazine 1938, part I, p 104
COLLECTION New York, Guggenheim Museum [on loan since 1963 from J. K. Thannhauser], cat The Thannhauser Foundation 1965, nr 15

F 1508 recto [formerly F 1508 verso] STANDING MALE NUDE [drawn over a standing figure]
Paris period; see after F 1412

F 1502a

F 1503

F 1507

F 1507a

F 1508 verso

F 1510

F 1509

F 1511

F 1512 recto

F 1508 verso [formerly F 1508] THE INTERIOR OF A RESTAURANT

Pencil [laid paper with watermark : Hallines]
26 × 43.5 [10¼ × 17¼]
Arles autumn 1888
EDITORS' COMMENT In the lower middle are sketched faint traces of Vincent's bedroom [F 482].
COLLECTION Amsterdam, Rijksmuseum Vincent van Gogh [Vincent van Gogh Foundation, inv nr F 1508]

F 1509 A TRUNK OF A TREE

Pencil, reed pen and ink 25 × 34 [9¾ × 13½]
Arles summer 1888
LITERATURE A. Aurier, Mercure de France January 1894, p 31 [with reproduction]. Vincent van Gogh, Lettres à Bernard, 1911, plate LXXIII. C. S. Chetham, The role of Vincent van Gogh's copies in the development of his art, 1960, p 41, reproduction nr 122: summer 1888
COLLECTION New York, Mrs George F. Baker

F 1510 CHAIR AT THE LEFT SIDE OF A FIREPLACE

Pencil, chalk [ordinary thin paper] 32.5 × 25 [12¾ × 9¾]
Compare F 1511
Arles December 1888
LITERATURE A. Bowness, exhib cat van Gogh London [Hayward Gallery] 1968-9, nr 151: Saint Rémy probably May 1889
EDITORS' COMMENT This subject interested Vincent in connection with paintings F 498 and F 499.
COLLECTION Amsterdam, Rijksmuseum Vincent van Gogh [Vincent van Gogh Foundation, inv nr F 1510]

F 1511 CHAIR ON THE RIGHT SIDE OF A FIREPLACE

Pencil, chalk [ordinary thin paper] 32.5 × 25 [12¾ × 9¾]
Compare F 1510
Arles December 1888
EDITORS' COMMENT See F 1510
COLLECTION Amsterdam, Rijksmuseum Vincent van Gogh [Vincent van Gogh Foundation, inv nr F 1511]

F 1512 recto THE CANE-BOTTOMED CHAIR [sketched over an erased landscape]

Pencil [ordinary drawing paper] 33 × 24.5 [13 × 9¾]
Arles December 1888
EDITORS' COMMENT See F 1510
COLLECTION Amsterdam, Rijksmuseum Vincent van Gogh [Vincent van Gogh Foundation, inv nr F 1512]

F 1512 verso SKETCHES OF PLOWING HORSES
Saint Rémy period; see after F 1622 verso

F 1513 THE POND IN THE PARK, THE YELLOW HOUSE IN THE BACKGROUND

Pencil, reed pen and brown ink [ordinary wove paper] 31.5 × 49.5 [12½ × 19½] Corners restored
Annotated by Vincent on the back probably previous to the drawing: 'als je morgenochtend om 5 uur wakker mocht zijn roep mij dan even s.v.p.' [should you be awake tomorrow morning at 5 o'clock, please wake me up]
Compare painting F 464, F 1413 and F 1453 [same house]
Arles September 1888

F 1513

LITERATURE A. Bowness, exhib cat van Gogh London [Hayward Gallery] 1968-9, nr 134: Arles September 1888; letter 541
COLLECTION Amsterdam, Rijksmuseum Vincent van Gogh [Vincent van Gogh Foundation, inv nr F 1513]

F 1514 ARLES SEEN FROM THE FIELDS: SUMMER EVENING

Pen and reed pen 24 × 31.5 [9½ × 12½]
Compare sketch in letter B 7 and painting F 465
Arles June 1888
LETTER B 7 [about 28 June] See F 465
LITERATURE A. Aurier, Mercure de France September 1892, p 71. Vincent van Gogh, Lettres à Bernard, 1911, plate LXXI. Ars Una October 1923, p 24. Gotthard Jedlicka, Hauptwerke des Kunstmuseums Winterthur, 1949, plate XVII
COLLECTION Winterthur, Switzerland, Kunstmuseum [acquired 1928; gift of E. Hahnloser]

F 1515 RHÔNE BANK, STARRY NIGHT

Pen and ink [measurements unknown]
Compare sketch in letter 553b [in the English edition of the letters only], painting F 474 [same composition] and F 1472 [same site]
Arles September 1888
LETTERS 543 [probably 28 September] and 553b [4 October] See F 474
LITERATURE A. Aurier, Mercure de France February 1895, p 213. Vincent van Gogh, Lettres à Bernard, 1911, plate LXXII
COLLECTION Present owner unknown

F 1516 AN ORCHARD WITH THE TOWERS OF ARLES IN THE BACKGROUND

Pencil, pen and black and lilac ink 53.5 × 39.5 [21 × 15½]
Compare paintings F 515 [same site] and F 552 [same composition]
Arles March 1888
COLLECTION Glens Falls, New York, The Hyde Collection [acquired 1952]

F 1517 LANDSCAPE WITH FARM AND TWO TREES

Pencil, reed pen and ink 25 × 34 [9¾ × 13½]
Arles early spring 1888
COLLECTION Upperville, Virginia, Mr and Mrs Paul Mellon

F 1514

F 1515

F 1516

F 1517

F 1518a

F 992

F 1549 recto

F 1554

F 1641

F 1518 THREE TREES, ROUTE DE TARASCON

Reed pen and ink 25.5 × 35 [10 × 13¾]
Compare painting F 448, F 1502 and F 1502a [same site]
Arles summer 1888
LITERATURE Faille 1928, nr 1518 [not reproduced]
COLLECTION Sale New York [Parke-Bernet]
6 June 1949, nr 29
Present owner unknown

F 1518a ROAD WITH TREES NEAR A HOUSE

Pencil, reed pen and brown ink 24 × 34 [9½ × 13½]
Compare sketch in letter B 6 and painting F 567 [same site]
Arles second half of June 1888
LITERATURE Not in Faille 1928. J. H. de Bois Art Gallery Bulletin 1935, cat nr 15. F. Novotny, Albertina Studien 1963, pp 15-20
COLLECTION Vienna, Albertina [acquired 1936], inv nr 26.871

F 1519 CAFÉ IN ARLES: PLACE DU FORUM

Reed pen 62 × 47 [24½ × 18½]
Compare painting F 467
Arles September 1888
LITERATURE E. H. du Quesne-van Gogh, Persönliche Erinnerungen, 1911, reproduced opposite p 64. Vincent van Gogh, Lettres à Bernard, 1911, plate LII. Kurt Pfister, Van Gogh, 1922, p 35. J. Meier-Graefe, Vincent van Gogh der Zeichner, 1928, plate 31
EDITORS' COMMENT Some details in the drawing are different from painting F 467. There are no stars and no branches of trees in the drawing. The editors are inclined to date the drawing slightly earlier than the painting.
COLLECTION Roquebrune, France, Emery Reves

F 1520 recto and verso MASK OF AN
EGYPTIAN MUMMY; SKETCH OF A HEAD
Saint Rémy period; see after F 1622 verso

F 1521 recto and verso MASK OF AN
EGYPTIAN MUMMY
Saint Rémy period; see after F 1622 verso

REDATED TO ARLES

F 992 COUPLE WALKING

Pencil [ordinary drawing paper] 11 × 9.5 [4¼ × 3¾]
Arles 1888
LITERATURE Faille 1928, nr 992: The Hague October 1882. Vanbeselaere 1937, pp 91, 110, 190, 191, 409: Paris
COLLECTION Amsterdam, Rijksmuseum Vincent van Gogh [Vincent van Gogh Foundation, inv nr F 992]

F 1090 PEASANTS WORKING

Reed pen, ink 26 × 34.5 [10¼ × 13½]
Arles June 1888
LITERATURE Faille 1928, nr 1090: The Hague. Vanbeselaere 1937, pp 110, 410: Arles. W. Gaunt, Art News Annual 1950, p 62: Auvers
COLLECTION Amsterdam, Rijksmuseum Vincent van Gogh [Vincent van Gogh Foundation, inv nr F 1090]

F 1549 recto [formerly F 1549 verso] STUDY OF A CHAIR AND A LEFT HAND

Black chalk [ordinary wove paper] 31 × 23.5
[12½ × 9¼]
Compare F 1510 [same type of chair], F 1511 and
F 1512

Arles December 1888
LITERATURE Faille 1928, nr 1549 verso: Saint
Rémy
EDITORS' COMMENT See F 1510. The study of the
hand was probably added later on in Saint Rémy.
COLLECTION Amsterdam, Rijksmuseum Vincent
van Gogh [Vincent van Gogh Foundation, inv
nr F 1549]

F 1554 ROCKY GROUND: MONTMAJOUR

Pen, reed pen and ink 24 × 31 [9½ × 12¼]
Compare painting F 466
Arles summer 1888
LITERATURE Faille 1928, nr 1554: Saint Rémy
COLLECTION Madrid, Mrs M. L. Caturla

F 1641 SHEAVES

Black chalk, brush and thin black ink [Ingres paper
with watermark, twice: MBM] 47.5 × 62.5
[18¾ × 24½]
Arles summer 1888
LITERATURE Faille 1928, nr 1641: Auvers
EDITORS' COMMENT The form of the sheaves is
usual for southern France [compare painting F 560]
but different from those which van Gogh painted at
Auvers [compare painting F 771].
COLLECTION Amsterdam, Rijksmuseum Vincent
van Gogh [Vincent van Gogh Foundation, inv
nr F 1641]

F 1651 recto STUDIES OF FIGURES AND
WOODEN SHOES

Black chalk 23 × 31 [9 × 12¼]
Arles end 1888
LITERATURE Faille 1928, nr 1651 verso: Auvers
[not reproduced]
EDITORS' COMMENT A careful analysis of the
complicated sketch reveals that the face of one of
the models could be related to the portrait formerly
called THE ACTOR, F 533. The woman seen in
profile near a window is certainly Mme Roulin
[see F 503]. The style and some models of the
drawing belong to the Arles period. Vincent painted
wooden shoes in F 607, also an Arles theme. The
sower and figures around a table were added at
Saint Rémy in the period January-April 1890 [see
EDITORS' COMMENT under F 1585 recto]
COLLECTION New York, Private Collection

F 1518

F 1651 recto

F 1519

F 1090

F 1522
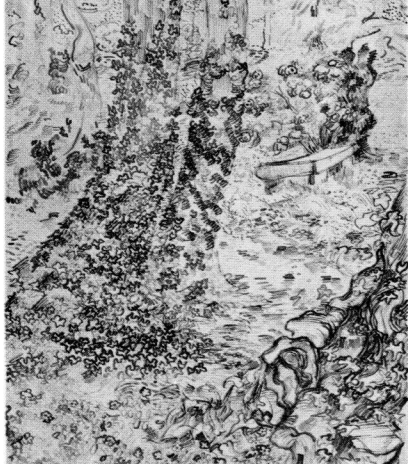

F 1523
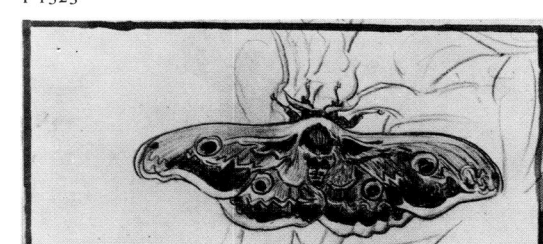

F 1524

F 1525

F 1526

SAINT RÉMY PERIOD

F 1522 TREE WITH IVY AND A STONE BENCH IN THE GARDEN OF SAINT PAUL'S HOSPITAL

Pencil, reed pen and brown ink [wove paper with dry mark: Latune et Cie Blacons] 62 × 47 [24½ × 18½]
Compare sketch in letter 592 and painting F 609
Saint Rémy May 1889
COLLECTION Amsterdam, Rijksmuseum Vincent van Gogh [Vincent van Gogh Foundation, inv nr F 1522]

F 1523 DEATH'S-HEAD MOTH

Black chalk, pen and brown ink, washed [Ingres paper with watermark: P.L. Bas] 16 × 26 [6¼ × 10¼]
Compare sketch in letter 592 and painting F 610 [same moth]
Saint Rémy May 1889
LETTER 592 [22 May] See F 610
LITERATURE A. Bowness, exhib cat van Gogh London [Hayward Gallery] 1968-9, nr 153: clearly the emperor moth and not the death's-head, as Vincent calls it
EDITORS' COMMENT See F 610
COLLECTION Amsterdam, Rijksmuseum Vincent van Gogh [Vincent van Gogh Foundation, inv nr F 1523]

F 1524 CYPRESSES

Pen, reed pen and ink 62.5 × 46.5 [24½ × 18¼]
Compare paintings F 620, F 621 and drawing F 1525a
Saint Rémy June 1889
LETTER 596 [25 June] '*I think that of the two canvases of cypresses, the one I am making this sketch of will be the best. The trees in it are very big and massive. The foreground, very low with brambles and brushwood. Behind some violet hills, a green and pink sky with a crescent moon. The foreground especially is painted very thick, clumps of brambles with touches of yellow, violet and green. I will send you the drawings of it with two other drawings that I have done too.*'
LITERATURE C. Nordenfalk, Konsthistorisk Tidskrift December 1946, pp 89-96
EDITORS' COMMENT Which of the four drawings of cypresses Vincent enclosed in letter 596 is uncertain. He included a sketch of painting F 613 in letter 596. F 1525 seems to be copied after this painting. F 1525a and F 1539 recto were probably executed on the spot and the more abstract F 1524 and F 1525 in the studio.
COLLECTION Chicago, The Art Institute of Chicago [R. Allerton bequest], inv nr 27.543

F 1525 CYPRESSES

Pen, reed pen and ink [colored paper] 62.5 × 47 [24½ × 18½]
Compare sketch in letter 596 and painting F 613
Saint Rémy June 1889
LETTER 596 [25 June] See F 1524
LITERATURE E. H. du Quesne-van Gogh, Persönliche Erinnerungen, 1911, p 72. K. Pfister, Vincent van Gogh, 1922, p 41
EDITORS' COMMENT See F 1524
COLLECTION Brooklyn, The Brooklyn Museum [acquired 1938], inv nr 38.123.19, cat 1967, p 402

F 1525a CYPRESSES, WITH TWO WOMEN IN THE FOREGROUND

Black chalk, reed pen and ink [colored or discolored paper] 31 × 23 [12¼ × 9]
Compare paintings F 620, F 621 and drawing F 1524

Saint Rémy June 1889
LETTER 596 [25 June] See F 621 and F 1524
LITERATURE Not in Faille 1928
EDITORS' COMMENT See F 1524
COLLECTION Otterlo, Rijksmuseum Kröller-Müller, inv nr 1110-42, cat van Gogh 1970, nr 252

F 1526 OLEANDERS IN THE HOSPITAL GARDEN AT SAINT RÉMY

Water color [probably same technique as in F 1527 and F 1533] 61 × 47 [24 × 18½]
Compare painting F 580 [same subject]
Saint Rémy May-June 1889
COLLECTION Formerly Paris, Sacha Guitry
Present owner unknown

F 1527 FLOWERS IN THE GARDEN OF THE HOSPITAL AT SAINT RÉMY

Water color [ordinary toned paper] 62 × 47 [24½ × 18½]
Annotated on the back [not by Mrs van Gogh-Bonger]: geteekend door Vincent van Gogh 1890. Wed. Th. van Gogh-Bonger
Saint Rémy May-June 1889
LITERATURE H. P. Bremmer, cat van Gogh 1919, Kröller-Müller Collection, plate 61. D. Cooper, Zeichnungen und Aquarelle von Vincent van Gogh, 1954, pp 79-80, nr 26
COLLECTION Otterlo, Rijksmuseum Kröller-Müller, inv nr 281-15, cat van Gogh 1970, nr 229

F 1528 WINDOW OF VINCENT'S STUDIO AT SAINT PAUL'S HOSPITAL

Black chalk, gouache [Ingres paper with watermark: A L (in oval)] 61.5 × 47 [24¼ × 18½]
Saint Rémy May-early June 1889
LITERATURE D. Cooper, Zeichnungen und Aquarelle von Vincent van Gogh, 1954, p 84. A. Bowness, exhib cat van Gogh London [Hayward Gallery] 1968-9, nr 154
COLLECTION Amsterdam, Rijksmuseum Vincent van Gogh [Vincent van Gogh Foundation, inv nr F 1528]

F 1529 A PASSAGE AT SAINT PAUL'S HOSPITAL

Black chalk, gouache 65 × 49 [25½ × 19¼]
Saint Rémy May-early June 1889
LITERATURE D. Cooper, Zeichnungen und Aquarelle von Vincent van Gogh, 1954, p 84
COLLECTION New York, Museum of Modern Art [acquired 1948; Mrs Abby Aldrich D. Rockefeller bequest], inv nr 242-48
Colorplate, p 590

F 1530 THE VESTIBULE OF SAINT PAUL'S HOSPITAL

Black chalk, gouache [Ingres paper, toned pink, with watermark: A L (in oval)] 61.5 × 47 [24¼ × 18½]
Saint Rémy May-early June 1889
LITERATURE D. Cooper, Zeichnungen und Aquarelle von Vincent van Gogh, 1954, p 84. A. Bowness, exhib cat van Gogh London [Hayward Gallery] 1968-9, nr 155: May-early June 1889
COLLECTION Amsterdam, Rijksmuseum Vincent van Gogh [Vincent van Gogh Foundation, inv nr F 1530]

F 1525a

F 1527

F 1528

F 1529

F 1530

F 1531

F 1532

F 1533

F 1534

F1531 THE FOUNTAIN IN THE GARDEN OF SAINT PAUL'S HOSPITAL

Black chalk, pen, reed pen and brown ink
[ordinary wove paper] 49.5 × 46 [19½ × 18]
Saint Rémy May-early June 1889
LITERATURE Vincent van Gogh, Lettres à
Bernard, 1911, plate LXXVIII. A. Bowness, exhib
cat van Gogh London [Hayward Gallery] 1968-9,
nr 148: May 1889
COLLECTION Amsterdam, Rijksmuseum Vincent
van Gogh [Vincent van Gogh Foundation, inv
nr F 1531]

F1532 TREE WITH IVY IN THE GARDEN OF SAINT PAUL'S HOSPITAL

Pencil, reed pen, brush and brown ink [Ingres paper
with watermark: P.L. Bas] 60.5 × 47 [23¾ × 18½]
Saint Rémy July 1889
LITERATURE A. Bowness, exhib cat van Gogh
London [Hayward Gallery] 1968-9, nr 147: May
1889
COLLECTION Amsterdam, Rijksmuseum Vincent
van Gogh [Vincent van Gogh Foundation, inv
nr F 1532]

F1533 A TREE IN THE GARDEN OF SAINT PAUL'S HOSPITAL, WITH A FIGURE IN THE BACKGROUND

Black chalk, pencil, pen, brush with brown ink and
water color [ordinary wove paper] 47 × 62
[18½ × 24½]
Compare F 1534 [same site]
Saint Rémy May-early June 1889
LITERATURE D. Cooper, Zeichnungen und
Aquarelle von Vincent van Gogh, 1954, p 82.
A. Bowness, exhib cat van Gogh London [Hayward
Gallery] 1968-9, nr 157: May-early June 1889
COLLECTION Amsterdam, Rijksmuseum Vincent
van Gogh [Vincent van Gogh Foundation, inv
nr F 1533]
Colorplate, p 607

F1534 A TREE IN THE GARDEN OF SAINT PAUL'S HOSPITAL

Black chalk, pencil, pen, brush with brown ink and
water color 47.5 × 61.5 [18¾ × 24¼]
Compare F 1533 [same site]
Saint Rémy May-June 1889
COLLECTION Formerly Thannhauser Art Gallery,
Berlin
Present owner unknown

F1535 THE GARDEN OF SAINT PAUL'S HOSPITAL WITH THE STONE STEPS

Black chalk, pencil, brush with brown ink and
water color [white cardboard] 63 × 45 [24¾ × 17¾]
Compare paintings F 640 and F 731 [same site]
Saint Rémy July 1889
LITERATURE D. Cooper, Zeichnungen und
Aquarelle von Vincent van Gogh, 1954, p 86:
autumn 1889. A. Bowness, exhib cat van Gogh
London [Hayward Gallery] 1968-9, nr 156: May-
early June 1889
COLLECTION Amsterdam, Rijksmuseum Vincent
van Gogh [Vincent van Gogh Foundation, inv
nr F 1535]

F1536 THE GARDEN OF SAINT PAUL'S HOSPITAL IN SUMMER

Water color 46.5 × 61.5 [18¼ × 24¼]
Saint Rémy summer 1889
EDITORS' COMMENT In his manuscript for the
present edition Faille dates F 1536 April 1890. On
the basis of resemblance to water color F 1533 and

F 1536

other works of early summer, the editors prefer an earlier dating.
COLLECTION Berlin, Mrs Paret

F 1537 STONE BENCH IN THE GARDEN OF SAINT PAUL'S HOSPITAL

Black chalk, brush, water color and gouache [Ingres paper with watermark: P. L. Bas] 37 × 61 [14½ × 24] Paper partly eaten away at the top
Saint Rémy autumn 1889
COLLECTION Amsterdam, Rijksmuseum Vincent van Gogh [Vincent van Gogh Foundation, inv nr F 1537]

F 1538 WHEATFIELDS AND CYPRESSES

Black chalk, pen, reed pen and brown ink [ordinary wove paper, highly yellowed, with dry mark: Blacons] 47 × 62 [18½ × 24½]
Compare paintings F 615, F 717 and F 743
Saint Rémy June-July 1889
LITERATURE A. Bowness, exhib cat van Gogh London [Hayward Gallery] 1968-9, nr 160: late June-early July 1889
EDITORS' COMMENT F 1538 seems to be done after painting F 717, dated to October 1889 by Faille. The editors are more inclined to connect the drawing with paintings F 615 and F 743 and accordingly to date it June or early July 1889.
COLLECTION Amsterdam, Rijksmuseum Vincent van Gogh [Vincent van Gogh Foundation, inv nr F 1538]

F 1535

F 1537

F 1538

F 1539 recto

F 1539 verso

F 1540

F 1541 recto

F 1541 verso

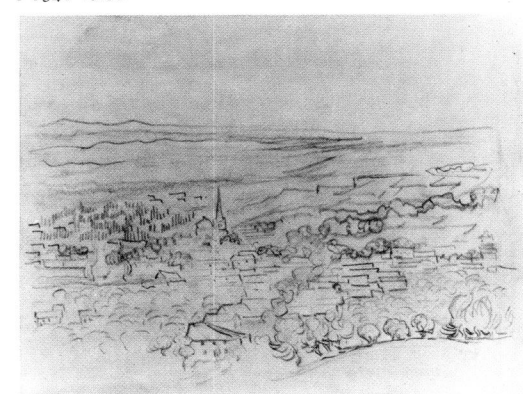

F 1539 recto LANDSCAPE WITH CYPRESSES AND FOUR FIGURES

Black chalk 32 × 23.5 [12½ × 9¼]
Saint Rémy summer 1889
EDITORS' COMMENT See F 1524
COLLECTION Essen, Folkwang Museum, cat 1929, nr 438

F 1539 verso SIX SKETCHES OF FIGURES, AMONG OTHERS A MAN SOWING WHEAT

Black chalk 23.5 × 31 [9¼ × 12½]
Saint Rémy February-April 1890

F 1540 CYPRESSES IN STARRY NIGHT [lost]

Pen and ink 47 × 62.5 [18½ × 24½]
Compare painting F 612 [same composition] and
F 1541 verso [same church]
Saint Rémy June 1889
LETTER 595 [18 June] See F 612
COLLECTION Bremen, Kunsthalle [acquired 1918]
The drawing disappeared during Second World War.

F 1541 recto LANDSCAPE WITH CYPRESSES

Pencil [ordinary drawing paper] Sheet 24 × 63.5
[9½ × 25] Drawing F 1541 recto 24 × 32 [9½ × 12½]
Saint Rémy June 1889
EDITORS' COMMENT F 1541 recto and verso and
F 1611 recto and verso are drawn on a single sheet.
In the present edition Faille's numbers are
maintained, however, and the different drawings on
the sheet are reproduced separately.
COLLECTION Amsterdam, Rijksmuseum Vincent
van Gogh [Vincent van Gogh Foundation, inv
nr F 1541]

F 1541 verso VIEW OF A TOWN WITH A SPIRE

Pencil, pen and wash 16.5 × 30.1 [6½ × 11¾]
Compare painting F 612 and F 1540 [same church]
Saint Rémy summer 1889
EDITORS' COMMENT See F 1541 recto

F 1542 WILD VEGETATION IN THE HILLS

Reed pen and brown ink [wove paper with dry
mark: Latune et Cie Blacons] 47 × 62 [18½ × 24½]
Saint Rémy July 1889
LITERATURE A. Bowness, exhib cat van Gogh
London [Hayward Gallery] 1968-9, nr 161: late
June-early July 1889
COLLECTION Amsterdam, Rijksmuseum Vincent
van Gogh [Vincent van Gogh Foundation, inv
nr F 1542]

F 1543 OLIVE TREES IN THE MOUNTAINS

Black chalk, brush and brown ink [ordinary
drawing paper, damaged in upper right corner]
50 × 65 [19¾ × 25½]
Saint Rémy September-October 1889
COLLECTION Amsterdam, Rijksmuseum Vincent
van Gogh [Vincent van Gogh Foundation, inv
nr F 1543]

**F 1544 OLIVE TREES IN LANDSCAPE WITH
MOUNT GAUSSIER AND THE ROCK WITH
TWO HOLES**

Pencil, pen, reed pen and ink 47 × 62.5 [18½ × 24½]
Compare painting F 712
Saint Rémy July-September 1889
LETTER 607 [19 September] See F 712
EDITORS' COMMENT Presumably done after
painting F 712.
COLLECTION East Berlin, National Galerie
[acquired 1935], inv nr F IV 721, cat nr 6

F 1545 THE PARK OF SAINT PAUL'S
HOSPITAL

Black chalk, pen, reed pen and ink 47 × 61
[18½ × 24]
Compare paintings F 659 and F 660
Saint Rémy October 1889
EDITORS' COMMENT See F 660
COLLECTION Fullerton, California, Norton Simon
Foundation

F 1546 REAPER IN A WHEATFIELD WITH
RISING SUN

Pen, reed pen and ink 45 × 58.5 [17¾ × 23]
Compare paintings F 617, F 618 and F 619
Saint Rémy June-July 1889
LETTER 597 [between 30 June and 4 July] *'In order
that you have some idea of what I am doing, I am
sending you a dozen drawings today, all from
canvases I am working on. The latest one I've started
is the ''Wheat-Field,'' in which there is a little reaper
and a big sun.'*
LITERATURE Cat van Gogh 1970, Rijksmuseum
Kröller-Müller, nr 244
EDITORS' COMMENT Vincent describes his view of
the field enclosure in letter 592 [22 May] *'Through
the ironbarred window I see a square field of wheat in
an enclosure, a perspective like Van Goyen, above
which I see the morning sun rising in all its glory.'*
COLLECTION East Berlin, National Galerie
[acquired 1928], inv nr F III 1693, cat nr 4

F 1547 WHEATFIELD BEHIND SAINT PAUL'S
HOSPITAL

Pen, reed pen and brown ink [wove paper, yellowed,
with dry mark: Latune et Cie Blacons] 47 × 62
[18½ × 24½]
Compare paintings F 611 and F 722
Saint Rémy June 1889
EDITORS' COMMENT See F 1546
COLLECTION Amsterdam, Rijksmuseum Vincent
van Gogh [Vincent van Gogh Foundation, inv
nr F 1547]

F 1542

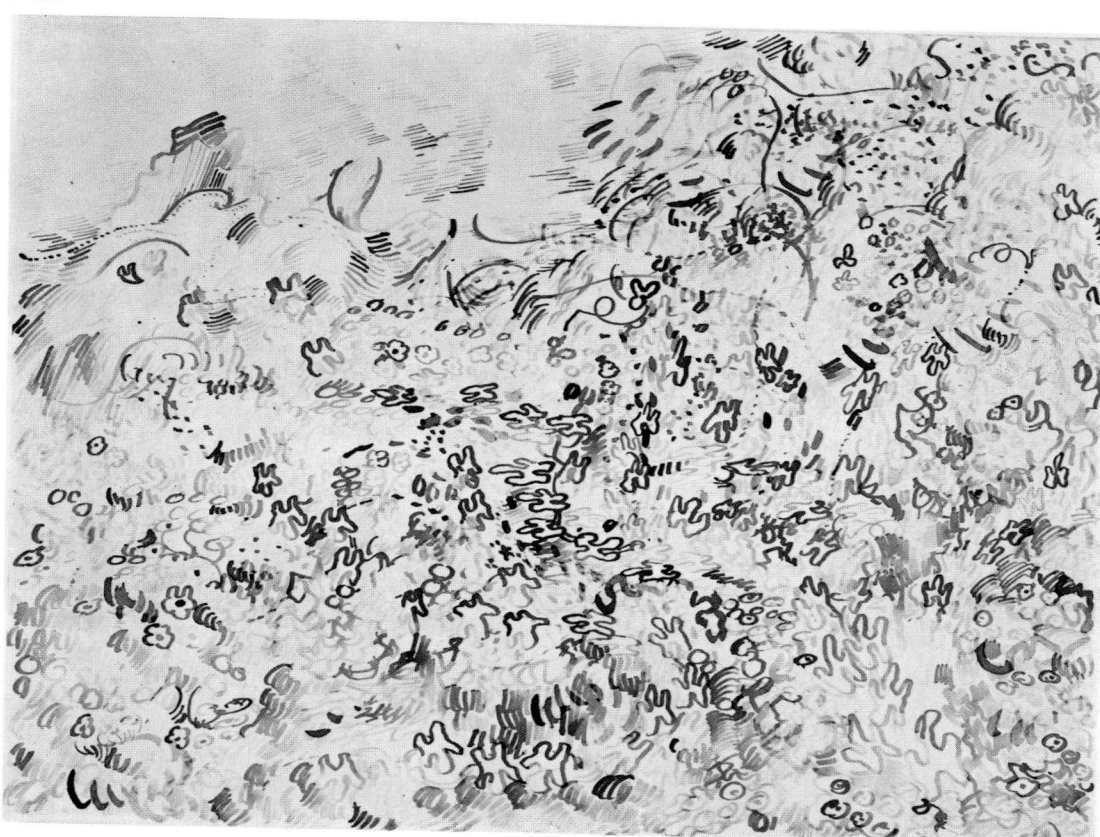

F 1543

F 1545

F 1546

F 1544

F 1547

F 782 [H 759] THE PLAIN WITH FARM NEAR
AUVERS
Auvers July 1890

F 1548

F 1550

F 1552

F 1555

F 1548 WHEATFIELD WITH CYPRESS

Pen and ink 46 × 61 [18 × 24]
Compare painting F 719
Saint Rémy June 1889
COLLECTION Formerly New York, J. K. Thann-
hauser Art Gallery
Present owner unknown

F 1549 recto [formerly F 1549 verso] STUDY OF
A CHAIR AND A LEFT HAND
Arles period; see after F 1521 verso

F 1549 verso [formerly F 1549] FIELD BEHIND
SAINT PAUL'S HOSPITAL

Black chalk [ordinary drawing paper] 31 × 23.5
[12¼ × 9¼]
Color annotations by Vincent
Compare painting F 723
Saint Rémy June 1889
COLLECTION Amsterdam, Rijksmuseum Vincent
van Gogh [Vincent van Gogh Foundation, inv
nr F 1549]

F 1550 SOWER IN THE RAIN

Pencil and chalk 23.5 × 31.5 [9¼ × 12½]
Compare painting F 650 [landscape in the rain] and
F 1551 [same motif]
Saint Rémy January-April 1890
COLLECTION Essen, Folkwang Museum, cat 1929,
nr 437

F 1551 recto SOWER IN THE RAIN

Black chalk [ordinary wove paper, irregularly cut]
24 × 27.5 [9½ × 10¾]
Compare painting F 650 [landscape in the rain] and
F 1550 [same motif]
Saint Rémy January-April 1890
LITERATURE Faille 1928, nr 1551: Auvers.
A. Bowness, exhib cat van Gogh London [Hayward
Gallery] 1968-9, nr 179: late April 1890
COLLECTION Amsterdam, Rijksmuseum Vincent
van Gogh [Vincent van Gogh Foundation, inv
nr F 1551]

F 1551 verso PEASANT WORKING

Black chalk
Saint Rémy January-April 1890

F 1552 ENCLOSURE BEHIND SAINT PAUL'S
HOSPITAL: RISING SUN

Black chalk, reed pen and ink [toned paper] 47 × 62
[18½ × 24½]
Compare paintings F 650, F 720, F 737 and drawing
SD 1728 [same site]
Saint Rémy November 1889
EDITORS' COMMENT See F 1546
COLLECTION Munich, Staatliche Graphische
Sammlung, inv nr 44336

F 1553 LANDSCAPE WITH SUN AND TWO
PEASANTS

Pen, reed pen, brush 63 × 48 [24¾ × 19]
Saint Rémy summer 1889
COLLECTION Formerly Berlin, G. Schweitzer
Present owner unknown

F 1554 ROCKY GROUND: MONTMAJOUR
Arles period; see after F 1521 verso

F 1555 OLIVE TREES

Reed pen, brown ink [ordinary wove paper with
illegible letter dry mark and the year 1889]

Annotated on the back : Douane Paris Centrale
Compare painting F 714
Saint Rémy September-November 1889
COLLECTION Amsterdam, Rijksmuseum Vincent
van Gogh [Vincent van Gogh Foundation, inv
nr F 1555]

F 1556 CORNER OF THE ENCLOSURE
BEHIND SAINT PAUL'S HOSPITAL

Pencil [thin wove paper] 25.5 × 32.5 [10 × 12¾]
Saint Rémy May-June 1889
EDITORS' COMMENT See F 1546
COLLECTION Amsterdam, Rijksmuseum Vincent
van Gogh [Vincent van Gogh Foundation, inv
nr F 1556]

F 1557 CORNER OF THE ENCLOSURE
BEHIND SAINT PAUL'S HOSPITAL

Pencil, black chalk [thin wove paper] 25 × 32.5
[9¾ × 12¾]
Saint Rémy May-June 1889
EDITORS' COMMENT See F 1546
COLLECTION Amsterdam, Rijksmuseum Vincent
van Gogh [Vincent van Gogh Foundation, inv
nr F 1557]

F 1558 CORNER OF THE ENCLOSURE
BEHIND SAINT PAUL'S HOSPITAL

Pencil, black chalk [thin wove paper] 25 × 32.5
[9¾ × 12¾]
Saint Rémy May-June 1889
EDITORS' COMMENT See F 1546
COLLECTION Amsterdam, Rijksmuseum Vincent
van Gogh [Vincent van Gogh Foundation, inv
nr F 1558]

F 1559 CORNER OF THE ENCLOSURE
BEHIND SAINT PAUL'S HOSPITAL

Pencil 25 × 33 [9¾ × 13]
Saint Rémy June 1889
EDITORS' COMMENT See F 1546
COLLECTION Amsterdam, Rijksmuseum Vincent
van Gogh [Vincent van Gogh Foundation, inv
nr F 1559]

F 1549 verso

F 1553

F 1551 recto

F 1551 verso

F 1556

F 1557

F 1558

F 1559

F 1560

F 1561

F 1562

F 1564

F 1563

F 1565

F 1566

F1560 CORNER OF THE ENCLOSURE
BEHIND SAINT PAUL'S HOSPITAL

Pencil 25 × 33 [9¾ × 13]
Saint Rémy June 1890
EDITORS' COMMENT See F 1546
COLLECTION Amsterdam, Rijksmuseum Vincent
van Gogh [Vincent van Gogh Foundation, inv
nr F 1560]

F1561 CORNER OF THE ENCLOSURE
BEHIND SAINT PAUL'S HOSPITAL

Pencil [thin wove paper, highly yellowed and
damaged] 25 × 32.5 [9¾ × 12¾]
Saint Rémy June 1889
EDITORS' COMMENT See F 1546
COLLECTION Amsterdam, Rijksmuseum Vincent
van Gogh [Vincent van Gogh Foundation, inv
nr F 1561]

F1562 TREE IN THE ENCLOSURE BEHIND
SAINT PAUL'S HOSPITAL

Pencil [thin wove paper] 23.5 × 32.5 [9¼ × 12¾]
Compare painting F 641 [same tree]
Saint Rémy winter 1889-90
COLLECTION Amsterdam, Rijksmuseum Vincent
van Gogh [Vincent van Gogh Foundation, inv
nr F 1562]

F1563 ENCLOSURE WITH PINE TREES

Pencil [ordinary wove paper] 20.5 × 30 [8 × 11¾]
Saint Rémy May-autumn 1889
EDITORS' COMMENT In letter 592 [22 May]
Vincent gave a general description of the
surroundings: 'Since I have been here, the deserted
garden, planted with large pines beneath which the
grass grows tall and unkempt and mixed with various
weeds, has sufficed for my work ...' Most of the
drawings of pine trees that follow are close in style
to the autumn gardens in paintings F 642, F 643,
F 730, F 732 and F 742.
COLLECTION Amsterdam, Rijksmuseum Vincent
van Gogh [Vincent van Gogh Foundation, inv
nr F 1563]

F1564 SIX PINES NEAR THE ENCLOSURE
WALL

Pencil 25 × 32.5 [9¾ × 12¾]
Saint Rémy May-autumn 1889
EDITORS' COMMENT See F 1563
COLLECTION Bergen, Netherlands, D. de Wolff
Peereboom [acquired 1943]

F1565 PINE TREES IN THE GARDEN OF
SAINT PAUL'S HOSPITAL

Pencil [ordinary wove paper; irregularly cut]
21 × 30 [8¼ × 11¾]
Saint Rémy May-autumn 1889
EDITORS' COMMENT See F 1563
COLLECTION Amsterdam, Rijksmuseum Vincent
van Gogh [Vincent van Gogh Foundation, inv
nr F 1565]

F1566 THREE PINE TREES IN THE
ENCLOSURE

Pencil 25 × 32.5 [9¾ × 12¾]
Saint Rémy May-autumn 1889
EDITORS' COMMENT See F 1563
COLLECTION Amsterdam, Private Collection

F1567 A CLUSTER OF PINE TREES

Pencil [thin wove paper] 25.5 × 32.5 [10 × 12¾]
Saint Rémy May-autumn 1889

EDITORS' COMMENT See F 1563
COLLECTION Amsterdam, Rijksmuseum Vincent
van Gogh [Vincent van Gogh Foundation, inv
nr F 1567]

F 1568 PINE TREES NEAR THE ENCLOSURE

Pencil [thin wove paper] 33 × 25 [13 × 9¾]
Saint Rémy May-autumn 1889
EDITORS' COMMENT See F 1563
COLLECTION Amsterdam, Rijksmuseum Vincent
van Gogh [Vincent van Gogh Foundation, inv
nr F 1568]

F 1569 ROAD WITH PINE TREES

Black chalk, stumped [thin wove paper] 25 × 32.5
[9¾ × 12¾]
Saint Rémy May-autumn 1889
EDITORS' COMMENT See F 1563
COLLECTION Amsterdam, Rijksmuseum Vincent
van Gogh [Vincent van Gogh Foundation, inv
nr F 1569]

F 1570 PINE TREES IN THE GARDEN OF
SAINT PAUL'S HOSPITAL

Pencil and black chalk [thin wove paper] 25 × 32
[9¾ × 12½]
Saint Rémy May-autumn 1889
LITERATURE A. Bowness, exhib cat van Gogh
London [Hayward Gallery] 1968-9, nr 149: May
1889
EDITORS' COMMENT See F 1563
COLLECTION Amsterdam, Rijksmuseum Vincent
van Gogh [Vincent van Gogh Foundation, inv
nr F 1570]

F 1571 CORNER OF THE ENCLOSURE WITH
PINE TREES

Pencil [ordinary wove paper] 30 × 20.5 [11¼ × 8]
Saint Rémy May-autumn 1889
EDITORS' COMMENT See F 1563
COLLECTION Amsterdam, Rijksmuseum Vincent
van Gogh [Vincent van Gogh Foundation inv.
nr F 1571]

F 1567

F 1568

F 1569

F 1570

F 1571

F 1572 recto

F 1572 verso

F 1573

F 1575

F 1574

F 1572 recto FOUR PINE TREES WITH WALL
OF THE ENCLOSURE

Pencil [ordinary wove paper] 29×18.5 [$11\frac{1}{2} \times 7\frac{1}{4}$]
Saint Rémy May-autumn 1889
EDITORS' COMMENT See F 1563
COLLECTION Amsterdam, Rijksmuseum Vincent
van Gogh [Vincent van Gogh Foundation, inv
nr F 1572]

F 1572 verso STONE BENCH IN THE GARDEN
OF SAINT PAUL'S HOSPITAL

Pencil, black chalk, stumped 18.5×29 [$7\frac{1}{4} \times 11\frac{1}{2}$]
Saint Rémy May-autumn 1889
EDITORS' COMMENT See F 1563

F 1573 GROUP OF PINES

Black chalk, stumped [thin wove paper] 25×32.5
[$9\frac{3}{4} \times 12\frac{3}{4}$]
Saint Rémy May-autumn 1889
EDITORS' COMMENT See F 1563
COLLECTION Amsterdam, Rijksmuseum Vincent
van Gogh [Vincent van Gogh Foundation, inv
nr F 1573]

F 1574 THE GARDEN OF SAINT PAUL'S
HOSPITAL

Pencil 33×25.5 [13×10]
Color annotations by Vincent
Saint Rémy autumn 1889
EDITORS' COMMENT See F 1563. The color
annotations point to autumn. No painting is known
of this composition.
COLLECTION Amsterdam, H. M. Wezelaar
[acquired about 1944]

F 1575 A STORM-BROKEN PINE TREE

Pencil 33×25 [$13 \times 9\frac{3}{4}$]
Saint Rémy spring-summer 1889
EDITORS' COMMENT See F 1563
COLLECTION Amsterdam, Rijksmuseum Vincent
van Gogh [Vincent van Gogh Foundation, inv
nr F 1575]

F 1576 recto DEAD TREE IN THE GARDEN OF
SAINT PAUL'S HOSPITAL

Pencil [ordinary wove paper] 30×16.5 [$11\frac{3}{4} \times 6\frac{1}{2}$]
Saint Rémy May-autumn 1889
EDITORS' COMMENT See F 1563
COLLECTION Amsterdam, Rijksmuseum Vincent
van Gogh [Vincent van Gogh Foundation, inv
nr F 1576]

F 1576 verso ENCLOSURE WITH TREES

Pencil
Saint Rémy May-autumn 1889
EDITORS' COMMENT See F 1563

F 1577 GARDEN WITH STONE BENCH AND
SAINT PAUL'S HOSPITAL IN THE
BACKGROUND

Pencil [ordinary wove paper] 19.5×29 [$7\frac{3}{4} \times 11\frac{1}{2}$]
Saint Rémy May-autumn 1889
EDITORS' COMMENT See F 1563
COLLECTION Amsterdam, Rijksmuseum Vincent
van Gogh [Vincent van Gogh Foundation, inv
nr F 1577]

F 1578 ENCLOSURE WITH PINE TREES

Black chalk, stumped [Ingres paper, toned pink,
with watermark: A L (in oval)] 23.5×30.5
[$9\frac{1}{4} \times 12$]

Saint Rémy May-autumn 1889
EDITORS' COMMENT See F 1563
COLLECTION Amsterdam, Rijksmuseum Vincent
van Gogh [Vincent van Gogh Foundation, inv
nr F 1578]

F 1578a TWO TREES

Black chalk 39 × 50 [15¼ × 19¾]
Saint Rémy 1889-90
LITERATURE Not in Faille 1928
EDITORS' COMMENT None of the editors has seen
the original drawing.
COLLECTION Sale New York [Parke-Bernet]
26 May 1949, nr 87
Present owner unknown

F 1579 TRUNKS OF TWO PINE TREES

Pencil [ordinary wove paper] 30 × 20.5 [11¾ × 8]
Saint Rémy May-autumn 1889
EDITORS' COMMENT See F 1563
COLLECTION Amsterdam, Rijksmuseum Vincent
van Gogh [Vincent van Gogh Foundation, inv
nr F 1579]

F 1580 A TREE WITH A BRICK WALL IN THE
BACKGROUND

Pencil [ordinary wove paper] 30 × 20.5 [11¾ × 8]
Saint Rémy May-autumn 1889
COLLECTION Amsterdam, Rijksmuseum Vincent
van Gogh [Vincent van Gogh Foundation, inv
nr F 1580]

F 1581 PINE TREES IN THE GARDEN OF
SAINT PAUL'S HOSPITAL

Pencil, stumped [ordinary wove paper] 30 × 20
[11¾ × 7¾]
Saint Rémy May-autumn 1889
EDITORS' COMMENT See F 1563
COLLECTION Amsterdam, Rijksmuseum Vincent
van Gogh [Vincent van Gogh Foundation, inv
nr F 1581]

F 1582 PATH IN THE PINES

Black chalk, stumped [ordinary wove paper]
20.5 × 30 [8 × 11¾]
Saint Rémy May-autumn 1889
EDITORS' COMMENT See F 1563
COLLECTION Amsterdam, Rijksmuseum Vincent
van Gogh [Vincent van Gogh Foundation, inv
nr F 1582]

F 1576 recto

F 1576 verso

F 1577

F 1578

F 1578a

F 1579

F 1580

F 1581

F 1582

F 1583

F 1584

F 1585 recto

F 1585 verso

F 1586 recto

F 1586 verso

F 1587 recto

F 1587 verso

F1583 SKETCH OF A FIELD WITH THE
TRUNK OF A PINE TREE

Pencil, black chalk [thin wove paper] 25 × 32.5
[9¾ × 12¾]
Color annotations by Vincent
Saint Rémy autumn 1889
LITERATURE A. Bowness, exhib cat van Gogh
London [Hayward Gallery] 1968-9, nr 162: late
June-early July 1889
EDITORS' COMMENT Although the color
annotations indicate that Vincent intended to make
paintings of this and the following drawing, no
such paintings are known. The colors point to
autumn.
COLLECTION Amsterdam, Rijksmuseum Vincent
van Gogh [Vincent van Gogh Foundation, inv
nr F 1583]

F1584 STUDY OF CLOUDS

Pencil [thin wove paper] 25 × 32.5 [9¾ × 12¾]
Color annotations by Vincent
Saint Rémy autumn 1889
EDITORS' COMMENT See F 1583
COLLECTION Amsterdam, Rijksmuseum Vincent
van Gogh [Vincent van Gogh Foundation, inv
nr F 1584]

F1585 recto COUPLE ARM IN ARM IN
WINTER

Pencil [ordinary wove paper] 24.5 × 32 [9¾ × 12½]
Saint Rémy January-April 1890
EDITORS' COMMENT According to A. Bowness, in
exhib cat van Gogh London [Hayward Gallery]
1968-9, nr 100 [F 1585 verso], F 1585 recto is a
Memory of the North. The editors, however, see it
as a member of a series in which impressions both
from the North and Vincent's surroundings at that
moment are mixed up. The whole series consists of
the following drawings: F 1585 recto and verso,
F 1587 verso, F 1588, F 1589 recto and verso, F 1591
recto and verso, F 1592 recto, F 1593 recto, F 1594
verso, F 1595 verso, F 1596 recto and verso, F 1597
verso, F 1600 verso, F 1601 recto and verso, F 1620
recto, F 1648 recto and verso, F 1649 verso and
F 1651 recto.
COLLECTION Amsterdam, Rijksmuseum Vincent
van Gogh [Vincent van Gogh Foundation, inv
nr F 1585]

F1585 verso INTERIOR OF A FARMHOUSE
WITH TWO PEASANTS AT THE TABLE

Pencil
Compare F 1588, F 1589 verso, F 1594 verso, F 1595
verso and F 1596 verso [similar motifs]
Saint Rémy January-April 1890
LITERATURE A. Bowness, exhib cat van Gogh
London [Hayward Gallery] 1968-9, nr 180: late
April 1890
EDITORS' COMMENT See F 1585 recto

F1586 recto TWO MEN ON A ROAD WITH
PINE TREES

Black chalk [pink Ingres paper with fragment of
watermark: P. L. Bas] 23.5 × 28 [9¼ × 11]
Saint Rémy winter-spring 1890
COLLECTION Amsterdam, Rijksmuseum Vincent
van Gogh [Vincent van Gogh Foundation, inv
nr F 1586]

F1586 verso STOOPING PEASANT WOMEN

Black chalk
Compare painting F 695 [similar motif]
Saint Rémy March-April 1890
EDITORS' COMMENT See F 695

F 1587 recto THE CARRIAGE AND TWO
FIGURES ON THE ROAD

Black chalk [pink Ingres paper with watermark:
P. L. Bas] 28.5 × 23.5 [11¼ × 9¼]
Compare sketch in letter 643, painting F 760, F 1610
recto [motif of horse and carriage] and painting
F 683 [similar motif]
Saint Rémy May 1890
COLLECTION Amsterdam, Rijksmuseum Vincent
van Gogh [Vincent van Gogh Foundation, inv
nr F 1587]

F 1587 verso PEASANT SHOVELING

Black chalk
Saint Rémy spring 1890
EDITORS' COMMENT See F 1585 recto

F 1588 PEASANTS AT A MEAL

Black chalk [ordinary wove paper] 34 × 50
[13½ × 19¾]
Compare F 1585 verso, F 1589 verso, F 1594 verso,
F 1595 verso and F 1596 verso [similar motifs]
Saint Rémy April 1890
LITERATURE A. Bowness, exhib cat van Gogh
London [Hayward Gallery] 1968-9, nr 181: late
April 1890
EDITORS' COMMENT See F 1585 recto
COLLECTION Amsterdam, Rijksmuseum Vincent
van Gogh [Vincent van Gogh Foundation, inv
nr F 1588]

F 1589 recto FAMILY: THREE FIGURES ON A
ROAD

Pencil 25 × 24.5 [9¾ × 9½]
Saint Rémy April 1890
EDITORS' COMMENT See F 1585 recto
COLLECTION Amsterdam, Rijksmuseum Vincent
van Gogh [Vincent van Gogh Foundation, inv
nr F 1589]

F 1589 verso PEASANT INTERIOR WITH
THREE FIGURES

Black chalk
Compare F 1585 verso, F 1588, F 1594 verso, F 1595
verso and F 1596 verso [similar motifs]
Saint Rémy April 1890
EDITORS' COMMENT See F 1585 recto

F 1589a PATH BETWEEN GARDEN WALLS
Auvers period; see after F 1654 verso

F 1590 recto [formerly F 1590 verso] SKETCH
OF TWO TREES

Black chalk, stumped [thin wove paper] 24.2 × 32.5
[9½ × 12¾]
Saint Rémy May-autumn 1889
COLLECTION Amsterdam, Rijksmuseum Vincent
van Gogh [Vincent van Gogh Foundation, inv
nr F 1590]

F 1590 verso [formerly F 1590 recto] FOUR MEN
ON THE ROAD

Pencil
Saint Rémy spring 1890

F 1588

F 1589 recto

F 1589 verso

F 1590 recto

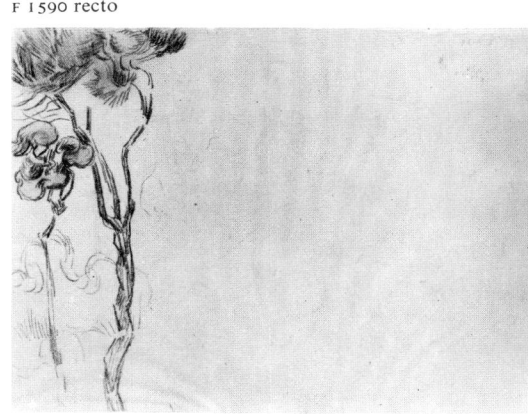

F 1590 verso

F 1591 recto

F 1591 verso

F 1592 recto

F 1592 verso

F 1593 recto

F 1593 verso

F 1594 recto

F 1594 verso

F 1591 recto WINTER LANDSCAPE WITH PEOPLE ON THE ROAD

Pencil [ordinary wove paper] 24 × 32 [9½ × 12½]
Saint Rémy January-April 1890
LITERATURE A. Bowness, exhib cat van Gogh London [Hayward Gallery] 1968-9, nr 183: late April 1890
EDITORS' COMMENT See F 1585 recto
COLLECTION Amsterdam, Rijksmuseum Vincent van Gogh [Vincent van Gogh Foundation, inv nr F 1591]

F 1591 verso LANDSCAPE WITH FARMS AND PEASANTS

Pencil
Compare paintings F 673 and F 674 [similar motif]
Saint Rémy January-April 1890
EDITORS' COMMENT See F 1585 recto

F 1592 recto WINTER LANDSCAPE WITH MANY FIGURES

Pencil [ordinary wove paper] 24 × 32 [9½ × 12½]
Saint Rémy January-April 1890
EDITORS' COMMENT See F 1585 recto
COLLECTION Amsterdam, Rijksmuseum Vincent van Gogh [Vincent van Gogh Foundation, inv nr F 1592]

F 1592 verso A MAN SOWING

Pencil
Saint Rémy January-April 1890
LITERATURE Faille 1928, nr 1592 verso [not reproduced]

F 1593 recto HUT WITH CYPRESSES IN WINTER: THREE PEASANTS WORKING

Pencil [ordinary wove paper] 31.5 × 23.5 [12½ × 9¼]
Saint Rémy January-April 1890
EDITORS' COMMENT See F 1585 recto
COLLECTION Amsterdam, Rijksmuseum Vincent van Gogh [Vincent van Gogh Foundation, inv nr F 1593]

F 1593 verso SKETCHES OF PEASANT AND HOUSES

Pencil 23.5 × 31.5 [9¼ × 12½]
Saint Rémy April 1890
LITERATURE Not in Faille 1928

F 1594 recto FARMS WITH DIGGING PEASANTS

Pencil [ordinary wove paper] 23.5 × 32 [9¼ × 12½]
Compare F 1595 recto
Saint Rémy March-April 1890
LITERATURE A. Bowness, exhib cat van Gogh London [Hayward Gallery] 1968-9, nr 182: the landscape is close to that of paintings F 673, F 674 and F 675
EDITORS' COMMENT The editors agree with the suggestions of Bowness.
COLLECTION Amsterdam, Rijksmuseum Vincent van Gogh [Vincent van Gogh Foundation, inv nr F 1594]

F 1594 verso FAMILY AROUND THE TABLE

Pencil and black chalk
Compare F 1585 verso, F 1588, F 1589 verso, F 1595 verso and F 1596 verso [similar motifs]
Saint Rémy April 1890
LETTER 629 [29 April] '*I am thinking of doing the picture of the "Peasants at Dinner" with the lamp-light effect again. That canvas must be quite black*

now, perhaps I could do it again altogether from memory.'
LITERATURE A. Bowness, exhib cat van Gogh London [Hayward Gallery] 1968-9, nr 182: late April 1890
EDITORS' COMMENT See F 1585 recto. This is more particularly a memory of THE POTATO EATERS.

F 1595 recto STREET LINED WITH FARM-HOUSES

Pencil 24 × 32 [9½ × 12½]
Compare F 1594 recto
Saint Rémy April 1890
COLLECTION Formerly New York, Sidney Janis Art Gallery
Present owner unknown

F 1595 verso PEASANTS AT TABLE; BUSTS OF TWO PEASANTS

Pencil
Compare F 1585 verso, F 1588, F 1589 verso, F 1594 verso and F 1596 verso [PEASANTS AT TABLE: similar motifs]
Saint Rémy April 1890
EDITORS' COMMENT See F 1585 recto

F 1596 recto ON THE ROAD

Pencil [ordinary drawing paper] 24.5 × 25 [9½ × 9¾]
Saint Rémy January-April 1890
EDITORS' COMMENT See F 1585 recto
COLLECTION Amsterdam, Rijksmuseum Vincent van Gogh [Vincent van Gogh Foundation, inv nr F 1596]

F 1596 verso PEASANTS AT TABLE

Pencil
Compare F 1585 verso, F 1588, F 1589 verso, F 1594 verso and F 1595 verso [similar motifs]
Saint Rémy January-April 1890
EDITORS' COMMENT See F 1585 verso

F 1596a recto MASK OF AN EGYPTIAN MUMMY; SKETCH OF A GIRL STANDING

Blue chalk [bluish-gray Ingres paper with water-mark: M B M] 31.5 × 23.5 [12½ × 9¼]
Compare F 1520 recto and verso, F 1521 recto and verso and F 1635 recto [same mask]
Saint Rémy June 1889 or later
LITERATURE Not in Faille 1928
EDITORS' COMMENT See F 1520 recto
COLLECTION Amsterdam, Rijksmuseum Vincent van Gogh [Vincent van Gogh Foundation, inv nr F 1596a]

F 1596a verso A PEASANT STOOPING

Black chalk
Saint Rémy January-April 1890
LITERATURE Not in Faille 1928

F 1595 recto

F 1595 verso

F 1596 recto

F 1596 verso

F 1596a recto

F 1596a verso

F 1597 recto

F 1597 verso

F 1598 recto

F 1598 verso

F 1599 verso

F1597 recto RETURN OF THE FIELD-
WORKERS IN THE RAIN

Pencil [ordinary wove paper] 32 × 23.5 [12½ × 9¼]
Saint Rémy January-April 1890
COLLECTION Amsterdam, Rijksmuseum Vincent
van Gogh [Vincent van Gogh Foundation, inv
nr F 1597]

F 1597 verso LANDSCAPE WITH HUT AND
TWO PEASANTS WITH WHEELBARROW

Pencil 23.5 × 32 [9¼ × 12½]
Saint Rémy January-April 1890
EDITORS' COMMENT See F 1585 recto

F 1598 recto LANDSCAPE WITH FOUR
FIGURES AND WHEELBARROWS

Pencil [ordinary wove paper] 23.5 × 32 [9¼ × 12½]
Saint Rémy January-April 1890
COLLECTION Amsterdam, Rijksmuseum Vincent
van Gogh [Vincent van Gogh Foundation, inv
nr F 1598]

F 1598 verso STUDIES OF PEASANTS AT
WORK

Pencil, stumped
Saint Rémy January-April 1890
LITERATURE A. Bowness, exhib cat van Gogh
London [Hayward Gallery] 1968-9, nr 185: late
April 1890

F 1599 recto STUDIES OF PEASANTS; MAN
WITH A WHEELBARROW; WOMAN WITH A
WHEELBARROW

Pencil [ordinary wove paper] 24 × 31.5 [9½ × 12½]
Saint Rémy January-April 1890
COLLECTION Amsterdam, Rijksmuseum Vincent
van Gogh [Vincent van Gogh Foundation, inv
nr F 1599]

F 1599 verso A MAN SEATED AT TABLE;
STUDIES OF PEASANTS WORKING

Pencil, black chalk
Saint Rémy January-April 1890

F 1600 recto SKETCHES OF MEN DIGGING

Black chalk [ordinary wove paper] 23.5 × 32
[9¼ × 12½]
Saint Rémy January-April 1890
COLLECTION Amsterdam, Rijksmuseum Vincent
van Gogh [Vincent van Gogh Foundation, inv
nr F 1600]

F 1600 verso SKETCHES OF DIGGING
PEASANTS AND HOUSES

Pencil and black chalk
Saint Rémy January-April 1890
LITERATURE Faille 1928, nr 1600 verso [not
reproduced]
EDITORS' COMMENT See F 1585 recto

F 1601 recto SKETCHES OF A FIGURE SITTING
AT A TABLE

Pencil [ordinary wove paper] 32 × 23.5 [12½ × 9¼]
Saint Rémy January-April 1890
EDITORS' COMMENT See F 1585 recto
COLLECTION Amsterdam, Rijksmuseum Vincent
van Gogh [Vincent van Gogh Foundation, inv
nr F 1601]

F 1601 verso STUDIES OF SEATED FIGURES

Pencil
Saint Rémy January-April 1890
EDITORS' COMMENT See F 1585 recto

F 1602 recto THE ENCLOSURE BEHIND
SAINT PAUL'S HOSPITAL

Black chalk [ordinary wove paper] 23.5 × 32
[9½ × 12½]
Saint Rémy autumn 1889
COLLECTION Amsterdam, Rijksmuseum Vincent
van Gogh [Vincent van Gogh Foundation, inv
nr F 1602]

F 1602 verso SIX SKETCHES OF PEASANTS
DIGGING

Black chalk
Saint Rémy January-April 1890

F 1599 recto

F 1602 recto

F 1600 recto

F 1600 verso

F 1602 verso

F 1601 recto

F 1601 verso

F 1603 recto

F 1603 verso

F 1604 recto

F 1604 recto

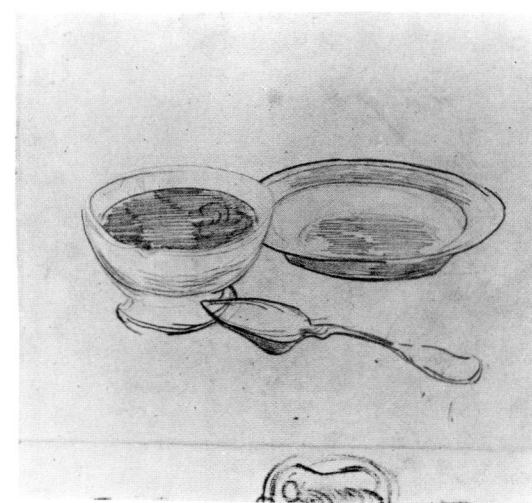

F 1604 verso

F 1605 recto

F 1605 verso

F 1603 recto TWO STUDIES OF A SOWER AND SIX STUDIES OF RIGHT HANDS SOWING

Pencil, black chalk [ordinary wove paper] 23.5 × 32 [9¼ × 12½]
Saint Rémy April-May 1890
LITERATURE A. Bowness, exhib cat van Gogh London [Hayward Gallery] 1968-9, nr 187: late April-early May 1890
COLLECTION Amsterdam, Rijksmuseum Vincent van Gogh [Vincent van Gogh Foundation, inv nr F 1603]

F 1603 verso STUDIES OF PEASANTS AND HANDS

Pencil, black chalk
Compare F 1608 [woman with child on her lap: similar motif]
Saint Rémy January-April 1890

F 1604 recto FIGURES IN A LANDSCAPE

Pencil, black chalk [pink Ingres paper with watermark: A L] Sheet 28 × 47.5 [11 × 18¾] Drawing F 1604 recto 24 × 28 [9½ × 11]
Saint Rémy January-April 1890
EDITORS' COMMENT On the other half of the sheet is a study of kitchen utensils.
COLLECTION Amsterdam, Rijksmuseum Vincent van Gogh [Vincent van Gogh Foundation, inv nr F 1604]

F 1604 verso A GROUP OF FIGURES ON THE BEACH

Pencil, black chalk 28 × 47.5 [11 × 18¾]
Saint Rémy January-April 1890
LITERATURE Faille 1928, nr 1604 verso [not reproduced]

F 1605 recto PEASANTS WORKING OUT-DOORS

Black chalk 24 × 32 [9½ × 12½]
Saint Rémy January-April 1890
COLLECTION Amsterdam, Rijksmuseum Vincent van Gogh [Vincent van Gogh Foundation, inv nr F 1605]

F 1605 verso TWO WINDOWS WITH IRON BARS IN SAINT PAUL'S HOSPITAL

Black chalk
Saint Rémy January-April 1890
LITERATURE Faille 1928, nr 1605 verso [not reproduced]

F 1606 recto STUDIES OF A WOMAN AT THE TABLE AND A WOMAN STANDING

Pencil [ordinary drawing paper, irregularly cut] 23.5 × 7 [9¼ × 2¾]
Saint Rémy May 1890
COLLECTION Amsterdam, Rijksmuseum Vincent van Gogh [Vincent van Gogh Foundation, inv nr F 1606]

F 1606 verso A MAN AT WORK; A DOG

Pencil
Saint Rémy May 1890

F 1607 recto STUDIES OF A WOMAN ON THE ROAD AND A MAN ON THE ROAD

Pencil [ordinary drawing paper, irregularly cut] 23.5 × 7.5 [9¼ × 3]
Saint Rémy May 1890
COLLECTION Amsterdam, Rijksmuseum Vincent

van Gogh [Vincent van Gogh Foundation, inv nr F 1607]

F 1607 verso TWO WOMEN BLEACHING LAUNDRY

Pencil
Saint Rémy May 1890
LITERATURE Faille 1928, nr 1607 verso [not reproduced]

F 1608 recto PEASANT FAMILY NEAR THE FIREPLACE

Black chalk [ordinary wove paper] 23.5 × 32 [9¼ × 12½]
Compare F 1603 verso [woman with child on her lap : similar motif]
Saint Rémy May 1890
COLLECTION Amsterdam, Rijksmuseum Vincent van Gogh [Vincent van Gogh Foundation, inv nr F 1608]

F 1608 verso SKETCHES OF HANDS; A PEASANT DIGGING

Black chalk
Saint Rémy winter-spring 1890
LITERATURE Faille 1928, nr 1608 verso [not reproduced]

F 1609 recto and verso HORSE AND CARRIAGE; SEATED NUDE [after Bargue]
Auvers period; see after F 1654

F 1610 recto and verso HORSE AND CARRIAGE; SKETCH OF TWO WOMEN WORKING
Auvers period; see after F 1654

F 1611 recto and verso LEAF AND POD OF A CHESTNUT TREE; SKETCHES OF A PERSPECTIVE FRAME
Auvers period; see after F 1654

F 1612 BRANCHES OF FEATHER HYACINTH [MUSCARI COMMOSUM]
Auvers period; see after F 1654

F 1608 recto

F 1608 verso

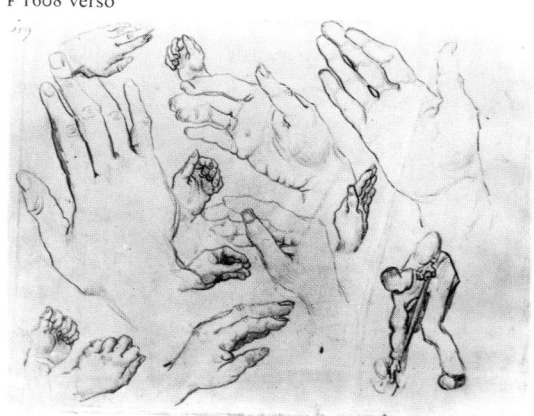

F 1606 recto

F 1607 recto

F 1606 verso

F 1607 verso

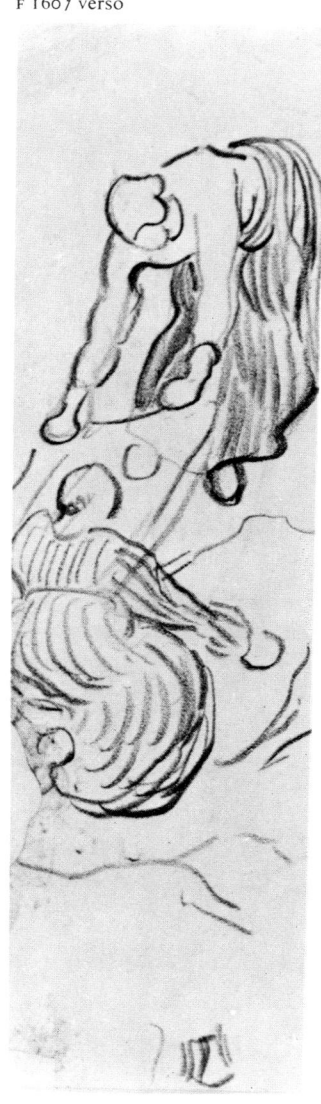

F 1618

F 1620 verso

F 1375

F 1494

F 1620 recto

F 1360 recto

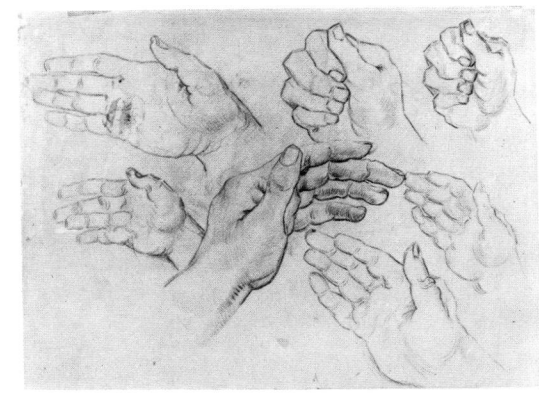

F 1360 verso

F 1497

F1613 STUDY OF ARUM
Auvers period; see after F 1654

F1614 BRANCHES OF PERIWINKLE
Auvers period; see after F 1654

F1615 recto and verso HARVESTING HAY;
HILLY LANDSCAPE WITH HARVESTERS
Auvers period; see after F 1654

F1616 WOMAN, MAN AND CHILD WALKING
TO THE RIGHT
Auvers period; see after F 1654

F1617 SITTING WOMAN WITH CHILD:
FACING RIGHT
Auvers period; see after F 1654

F1618 THE SOWERS

Black chalk 28.5 × 22 [11¼ × 8¾]
Saint Rémy January-April 1890
LITERATURE Faille 1928, nr 1618 [not reproduced]
COLLECTION Mr and Mrs Joram Piatagorski

F1619 recto and verso STUDY OF TWO
WOMEN; STUDY OF A WOMAN STANDING,
TWO HEADS AND ANOTHER FIGURE
Auvers period; see after F 1654

F1620 recto WORK IN THE FIELDS

Pencil and black chalk 23 × 31 [9 × 12¼]
Saint Rémy January-April 1890
LITERATURE Faille 1928, nr 1620 [not reproduced]
EDITORS' COMMENT See F 1585 recto
COLLECTION Bradford, Pennsylvania,
T. E. Hanley

F1620 verso A MAN DIGGING, TWO SEATED
CHILDREN AND OTHER SKETCHES

Pencil and black chalk
Saint Rémy January-April 1890
LITERATURE Faille 1928, nr 1620 verso [not
reproduced]

F1621 recto STUDY [not reproduced]

Pencil [pink Ingres paper] 20.5 × 23.5 [8 × 9¼]
Annotated by Vincent: violet
Saint Rémy 1889-90
LITERATURE Faille 1928, nr 1621 [not reproduced]
EDITORS' COMMENT The sort of paper seems to
indicate Auvers [compare F 1623].
COLLECTION Formerly Auvers, P. Gachet
Present owner unknown

F1621 verso SKETCH OF A LANDSCAPE WITH
TREES

Pencil
Saint Rémy 1889-90
LITERATURE Faille 1928, nr 1621 verso [not
reproduced]

F1622 recto THE HIND LEGS OF A HORSE
Auvers period; see after F 1654

F 1613 1614 1615 recto and verso 1616 1617 1618 1619 recto and verso 1620 recto
1620 verso 1621 recto 1621 verso 1622 recto 1622 verso 1360 recto 1360 verso 1375 1494
1497 1501 1505

F 1501

F 1622 verso HEAD OF A YOUNG MAN WITH
HAT: FULL FACE
Auvers period; see after F 1654

REDATED TO SAINT RÉMY

F 1360 recto STUDY OF SEVEN HANDS

Black crayon [brownish paper] 24 × 32 [9½ × 12½]
Saint Rémy April-May 1890
LITERATURE Faille 1928, nr 1360: Antwerp.
Tralbaut Antwerp 1948, pp 260-2, 285, nr 61:
possibly Paris, but more probably February 1886,
late in the Antwerp period
EDITORS' COMMENT In his manuscript for the
present edition Faille again dated F 1360 recto and
verso Antwerp February 1886. The editors,
however, comparing F 1603 recto and verso and
F 1608 verso, redated them to Saint-Rémy April-
May 1890.
COLLECTION Amsterdam, Rijksmuseum Vincent
van Gogh [Vincent van Gogh Foundation, inv
nr F 1360]

F 1360 verso THREE STUDIES OF A DEAD
SPARROW

Black crayon
Saint Rémy April-May 1890
LITERATURE Faille 1928, nr 1360 verso: Antwerp.
Tralbaut Antwerp 1948, pp 265, 285, nr 64: end of
Antwerp period
EDITORS' COMMENT See F 1360 recto

F 1375 STUDIES: FIGURE; THE ENCLOSURE
WALL OF SAINT PAUL'S HOSPITAL; AND
OTHERS

Pencil 23 × 29 [9 × 11½]
Saint Rémy 1889
LITERATURE Faille 1928, nr 1375: Paris
EDITORS' COMMENT In his manuscript for the
present edition Faille dated F 1375 Paris 1886
COLLECTION Amsterdam, Rijksmuseum Vincent
van Gogh [Vincent van Gogh Foundation, inv
nr F 1375]

F 1494 FIELD WITH POPPIES

Reed pen 48 × 64 [19 × 25¼]
Compare painting F 581
Saint Rémy April 1890
LITERATURE Faille 1928, nr 1494: Arles
COLLECTION Saint Louis, Mrs Mark C. Steinberg

F 1497 CORNER OF THE GARDEN OF
SAINT PAUL'S HOSPITAL

Reed pen 63.5 × 48 [25 × 19]
Saint Rémy June 1889
LITERATURE Faille 1928, nr 1497: Arles
COLLECTION London, Tate Gallery [acquired
1933; gift of Frank C. Stoop], inv nr 4716

F 1501 LANDSCAPE WITH TREES

Pencil, reed pen and ink [pink Ingres paper with
watermark: P. L. Bas] 47 × 60 [18½ × 23¾]
Saint Rémy autumn 1889
LITERATURE Faille 1928, nr 1501: Arles
COLLECTION Amsterdam, Rijksmuseum Vincent
van Gogh [Vincent van Gogh Foundation, inv
nr F 1501]

F 1505 CORNER OF THE GARDEN OF
SAINT PAUL'S HOSPITAL

Charcoal, brush, pen and brown ink 45.5 × 60.5
[18 × 23¾]
Saint Rémy July 1889

F 1505

LITERATURE H. P. Bremmer, cat van Gogh 1919,
Kröller-Müller Collection, nr 67. Faille 1928,
nr 1505: Arles. D. Cooper, Zeichnungen und
Aquarelle von Vincent van Gogh, 1954, p 76: May
1889
EDITORS' COMMENT Stylistically close to F 1535
and F 1536.
COLLECTION Otterlo, Rijksmuseum Kröller-
Müller, inv nr 297-17, cat van Gogh 1970, nr 230

F 1512 verso

F 1520 recto

F 1521 recto

F 1520 verso

F 1521 verso

F 1635 recto

F 1645 recto

F 1645 verso

F 1512 verso SKETCHES OF PLOWING HORSES

Pencil [ordinary drawing paper] 33 × 24.5 [13 × 9¾]
Compare sketch in letter 602 and the painting F 625
Saint Rémy early September 1889
LITERATURE Not in Faille 1928
EDITORS' COMMENT Though the sketches of
horses are done quickly and in a loose way, the
horse at the top is recognizable as the outline of the
horse of the picture F 625 dated Saint Rémy early
September.
COLLECTION Amsterdam, Rijksmuseum Vincent
van Gogh [Vincent van Gogh Foundation, inv
nr F 1512]

F 1520 recto MASK OF AN EGYPTIAN MUMMY;
SKETCH OF A HEAD

Black chalk [Ingres paper with watermark: M B M]
35.5 × 31 [14 × 12¼]
Compare F 1520 verso, F 1521 recto and verso,
F 1596a verso and F 1635 recto [same mask]
Saint Rémy June 1889 or later
LETTER 594 [9 June] *'Now what makes Egyptian art,
for instance, extraordinary – isn't it that these serene,
calm kings, wise and gentle, patient and kind, look as
though they could never be other than what they are,
eternal tillers of the soil, worshipers of the sun?'*
LITERATURE Faille 1928, nr 1520: Arles
EDITORS' COMMENT The passage in letter 594 was
written with reference to the World's Fair in Paris.
The model for drawings F 1520 recto and verso,
F 1521 recto and verso, F 1596a verso and F 1635
recto has not become known to the editors.
COLLECTION Amsterdam, Rijksmuseum Vincent
van Gogh [Vincent van Gogh Foundation, inv
nr F 1520]

F 1520 verso MASK OF AN EGYPTIAN MUMMY

Black chalk
Compare F 1520 recto, F 1521 recto and verso,
F 1596a verso and F 1635 recto [same mask]
Saint Rémy June 1889 or later
LETTER 594 [9 June] See F 1520 recto
EDITORS' COMMENT See F 1520 recto

F 1521 recto MASK OF AN EGYPTIAN MUMMY

Black chalk [Ingres paper] 31 × 23.5 [12¼ × 9¼]
Compare F 1520 recto and verso, F 1521 verso,
F 1596a verso and F 1635 recto [same mask]
Saint Rémy June 1889 or later
LETTER 594 [9 June] See F 1520 recto
LITERATURE Faille 1928, nr 1521: Arles
EDITORS' COMMENT See F 1520 recto
COLLECTION Amsterdam, Rijksmuseum Vincent
van Gogh [Vincent van Gogh Foundation, inv
nr F 1521]

F 1521 verso MASK OF AN EGYPTIAN MUMMY

Blue chalk
Compare F 1520 recto and verso, F 1521 recto,
F 1596a verso and F 1635 recto [same mask]
Saint Rémy June 1889 or later
LETTER 594 [9 June] See F 1520 recto
EDITORS' COMMENT See F 1520 recto

F 1635 recto MASK OF AN EGYPTIAN MUMMY

Blue and black chalk [bluish-gray Ingres paper]
31 × 23.5 [12¼ × 9¼]
Compare F 1520 recto and verso, F 1521 recto and
verso and F 1596a verso
Saint Rémy June 1889 or later
LETTER 594 [9 June] See F 1520 recto
LITERATURE Faille 1928, nr 1635 verso [not
reproduced]: Auvers

F 816 [H 801] TREES, ROOTS AND BRANCHES
Auvers July 1890

F 1512 verso 1520 recto 1520 verso 1521 recto 1521 verso 1635 recto 1645 recto
1645 verso 1647 recto 1647 verso 1648 recto 1648 verso 1649 recto 1649 verso
1651 verso

EDITORS' COMMENT See F 1520 recto
COLLECTION Amsterdam, Rijksmuseum Vincent
van Gogh [Vincent van Gogh Foundation, inv
nr F 1635]

F 1645 recto STUDY OF A SOWER AND A MAN
WITH A SPADE

Black chalk 31 × 25 [12¼ × 9¾]
Saint Rémy January-April 1890
LITERATURE Faille 1928, nr 1645 [not
reproduced]: Auvers
EDITORS' COMMENT Stylistically close to F 1618
COLLECTION Paris, Jacques Dubourg

F 1645 verso STUDY OF TWO SOWERS

Pencil
Saint Rémy January-April 1890
LITERATURE Faille 1928, nr 1645 verso [not
reproduced]: Auvers

F 1647 recto LANDSCAPE WITH TWO
FIGURES

Pencil and black chalk 29.5 × 20.5 [11½ × 8]
Saint Rémy January-April 1890
LITERATURE Faille 1928, nr 1647 [not
reproduced]: Auvers
EDITORS' COMMENT In his manuscript for the
present edition Faille dated F 1647 recto Saint
Rémy April 1890.
COLLECTION Saint Louis, Mr and Mrs Sydney
M. Schoenberg

F 1647 verso FIGURES ON A ROAD

Pencil and black chalk
Saint Rémy January-April 1890
LITERATURE Faille 1928, nr 1647 verso [not
reproduced]: Auvers

F 1648 recto SNOW LANDSCAPE

Pencil 23.5 × 31 [9¼ × 12¼]
Saint Rémy January-April 1890
LITERATURE Faille 1928, nr 1648 [not
reproduced]: Saint Rémy
EDITORS' COMMENT See F 1585 recto
COLLECTION Caracas, Venezuela, Ernesto Blohm

F 1648 verso PEASANT COTTAGES SEEN
FROM THE FIELDS

Pencil, stumped 31 × 23.5 [12¼ × 9¼]
Saint Rémy January-April 1890
LITERATURE Faille 1928, nr 1648 verso [not
reproduced]: Auvers
EDITORS' COMMENT See F 1585 recto

F 1649 recto STUDIES OF PEASANTS
WORKING: SOWERS AND DIGGERS

Pencil 23 × 30.5 [9 × 12]
Compare painting F 694 [two of the figures]
Saint Rémy January-April 1890
LITERATURE Faille 1928, nr 1649 [not
reproduced]: Auvers
COLLECTION Formerly Zurich, W. Feilchenfeldt
Present owner unknown

F 1649 verso A MAN IN FRONT OF A
FARMSTEAD; OTHER SKETCHES

Black chalk
Saint Rémy spring 1890
LITERATURE Faille 1928, nr 1649 verso: Auvers
EDITORS' COMMENT See F 1585 recto

F 1651 verso SKETCHES OF FIGURES AND
HANDS

Black chalk 23 × 31 [9 × 12¼]
Saint Rémy April-May 1890
LITERATURE Faille 1928, nr 1651 [not
reproduced]: Auvers
COLLECTION New York, Private Collection

F 1647 recto

F 1647 verso

F 1648 recto

F 1648 verso

F 1649 recto

F 1649 verso

F 1651 verso

F 1623 recto

F 1623 verso

F 1624

F 1625

F 1627

AUVERS PERIOD

F 1623 recto MISS GACHET AT THE PIANO

Black chalk [pink Ingres paper with watermark:
P. L. Bas] Sheet 31.6 × 23.8 [12½ × 9½] Drawing field
30 × 19.3 [11¾ × 7½]
Compare sketches in letter 645 [reproduced in the
Dutch edition of the letters only] and painting F 772
Auvers June 1890
LETTER 645 [27, 28 or 29 June] See F 772
LITERATURE P. Gachet, Van Gogh à Auvers, 1953.
A. Bowness, exhib cat van Gogh London [Hayward
Gallery] 1968-9, nr 199: the idea and the
composition were probably suggested by Toulouse-
Lautrec's painting MLLE DIHAU AT THE PIANO,
exhibited at the Salon in spring 1890; letter 649
COLLECTION Amsterdam, Rijksmuseum Vincent
van Gogh [Vincent van Gogh Foundation, inv
nr F 1623]

F 1623 verso STUDY OF A FRUIT TREE AND
OF TWO PEOPLE AT WORK

Black chalk. Drawing field 27.2 × 23.8 [10¾ × 9½]
Auvers June 1890

F 1624 OLD VINEYARD WITH PEASANT
WOMAN

Pencil, brush, washed with blue, red and white
gouache 43.5 × 54 [17¼ × 21¼]
Auvers end May 1890
LETTER 648 [about 23 May] 'You will see a drawing
of an old vineyard with the figure of a peasant woman.'
LITERATURE D. Cooper, Zeichnungen und
Aquarelle von Vincent van Gogh, 1954, p 90, nr 31
COLLECTION Amsterdam, Rijksmuseum Vincent
van Gogh [Vincent van Gogh Foundation, inv
nr F 1624]
Colorplate, p 608

F 1625 LANDSCAPE

Water color 33 × 42 [13 × 16½]
Signed in lower right: Vincent. N.B. See EDITORS'
COMMENT
Auvers 1890. N.B. See EDITORS' COMMENT
EDITORS' COMMENT Authenticity doubtful.
COLLECTION New York, Metropolitan Museum
of Art [acquired 1924; Rogers Fund], inv nr 24.196

F 1626 recto PEASANT WOMAN IN A
WHEATFIELD

Black chalk [pink Ingres paper with fragment of
unidentifiable watermark] 30.5 × 23.5 [12 × 9¼]
Auvers June-July 1890
COLLECTION Amsterdam, Rijksmuseum Vincent
van Gogh [Vincent van Gogh Foundation, inv
nr F 1626]

F 1626 verso TWO PEASANT WOMEN
BINDING SHEAVES

Black chalk 23.5 × 30.5 [9¼ × 12]
Auvers June-July 1890

F 1627 WOODED SHORE OF THE OISE

Pencil and black chalk [Ingres paper with fragment
of watermark: P. L. Bas] 23.5 × 30.5 [9¼ × 12]
Compare F 1629 [similar subject]
Auvers June-July 1890
COLLECTION Amsterdam, Rijksmuseum Vincent
van Gogh [Vincent van Gogh Foundation, inv
nr F 1627]

F 1628 PATH IN THE FIELDS

Pencil and black chalk [pink Ingres paper with
fragment of watermark: P. L. Bas] 23.5 × 30.5
[9¼ × 12]
Auvers June-July 1890
COLLECTION Amsterdam, Rijksmuseum Vincent
van Gogh [Vincent van Gogh Foundation, inv
nr F 1628]

F 1629 WOODED SHORE OF THE OISE

Pencil and black chalk [Ingres paper] 23.5 × 30.5
[9¼ × 12]
Compare F 1627 [similar subject]
Auvers June-July 1890
COLLECTION Amsterdam, Rijksmuseum Vincent
van Gogh [Vincent van Gogh Foundation, inv
nr F 1629]

F 1630 recto THE TOWN HALL OF AUVERS

Black chalk [Ingres paper] Sheet 48 × 31 [19 × 12¼]
Drawing F 1630 recto 23.5 × 31 [9½ × 12¼]
Compare painting F 790 [same site]
Auvers July 1890
EDITORS' COMMENT F 1630 recto and verso and
F 1637 recto and verso are drawn on a single sheet.
In the present edition Faille's numbers are
maintained, however, and the different drawings
are reproduced separately.
COLLECTION Amsterdam, Rijksmuseum Vincent
van Gogh [Vincent van Gogh Foundation, inv
nr F 1630]

F 1630 verso A HUT; OTHER SKETCHES

Blue chalk
Auvers July 1890
EDITORS' COMMENT See F 1630 recto

F 1631 recto SKETCH OF A MULE

Black chalk [pink Ingres paper with watermark:
P. L. Bas] Sheet 21.5 × 47 [8½ × 18½] Drawing F 1631
recto 21.5 × 23.5 [8½ × 9¼]
Auvers June-July 1890
EDITORS' COMMENT Formerly part of a larger
sheet, on which F 1610 recto, F 1631 verso and
F 1633 were drawn on one side, and F 1610 verso
F 1631 and F 1632 on the other. The sheet was torn
in half, leaving F 1610 recto and verso and F 1633 on
one sheet and F 1631 recto and verso and F 1632 on
the other.
COLLECTION Amsterdam, Rijksmuseum Vincent
van Gogh [Vincent van Gogh Foundation, inv
nr F 1631]

F 1631 verso SKETCH OF FIVE LAUNDRESSES

Pencil and black chalk
Auvers June-July 1890
EDITORS' COMMENT See F 1631 recto

F 1626 recto

F 1626 verso

F 1628

F 1629

F 1630 recto

F 1630 verso

F 1631 recto

F 1631 verso

F 1632

F 1633

F 1634 recto

F 1634 verso

F 1635 verso

F 1636

F 1637 recto

F 1637 verso

F 1632 SKETCH OF THREE COWS AND TWO
CHILDREN

Pencil [pink Ingres paper] 23.5 × 20 [9¼ × 8]
Color annotations by Vincent
Auvers June-July 1890
EDITORS' COMMENT See F 1631 recto
COLLECTION Amsterdam, Rijksmuseum Vincent
van Gogh [Vincent van Gogh Foundation, inv
nr F 1632]

F 1633 SKETCH OF A CHILD IN A
PERAMBULATOR

Black chalk [pink Ingres paper] 21.5 × 23.5 [8½ × 9¼]
Auvers June-July 1890
EDITORS' COMMENT See F 1631 recto. The child is
presumably referred to in letter 646 [about 1 July]:
*'The people at the inn here used to live in Paris, where
they were constantly unwell, parents and children;
here they never have anything wrong with them at all,
especially the youngest one, who came when he was
two months old...'*
COLLECTION Amsterdam, Rijksmuseum Vincent
van Gogh [Vincent van Gogh Foundation, inv
nr F 1633]

F 1634 recto STUDIES OF A STANDING
WOMAN AND A PEASANT WOMAN WITH A
RAKE

Black chalk, pen and lilac ink [Ingres paper]
23.5 × 30 [9¼ × 11¾]
Color annotations by Vincent
Auvers July 1890
COLLECTION Amsterdam, Rijksmuseum Vincent
van Gogh [Vincent van Gogh Foundation, inv
nr F 1634]

F 1634 verso SKETCH OF ROOFS

Blue chalk
Auvers July 1890
LITERATURE Faille 1928, nr 1634 verso [not
reproduced]

F 1635 recto SKETCH OF AN EGYPTIAN HEAD;
SKETCH OF A WOMAN
Saint Rémy period; see after F 1622 verso

F 1635 verso [formerly F 1635] MAN WITH A
SCYTHE

Blue chalk [bluish-gray Ingres paper] 31 × 23.5
[12¼ × 9¼]
Auvers July 1890
COLLECTION Amsterdam, Rijksmuseum Vincent
van Gogh [Vincent van Gogh Foundation, inv
nr F 1635]

F 1636 HOUSES AT AUVERS WITH PEASANT
WOMAN IN THE FOREGROUND

Pencil and black chalk [laid paper with watermark:
Hallines] 44.5 × 27 [17½ × 10½]
Auvers June-July 1890
LITERATURE A. Bowness, exhib cat van Gogh
London [Hayward Gallery] 1968-9, nr 198: June
1890
COLLECTION Amsterdam, Rijksmuseum Vincent
van Gogh [Vincent van Gogh Foundation, inv
nr F 1636]

F 1637 recto MONTCEL: HOUSES BEHIND
TREES

Black and blue chalk, pen and lilac ink [Ingres
paper] Sheet 48 × 31 [19 × 12¼] Drawing F 1637
recto 24 × 31 [9½ × 12¼]
Compare painting F 792 [similar houses and trees]

F 1638 recto

F 1638 verso

Auvers July 1890
EDITORS' COMMENT See F 1630 recto
COLLECTION Amsterdam, Rijksmuseum Vincent
van Gogh [Vincent van Gogh Foundation, inv
nr F 1630]

F 1637 verso SKETCH OF A MAN'S HEAD;
SKETCH OF A PERSPECTIVE FRAME

Blue chalk
Compare F 1611 verso [same motif]
Auvers 1890
LITERATURE Faille 1928, nr 1637 verso [not
reproduced]
EDITORS' COMMENT See F 1630 recto

F 1638 recto STREET IN AUVERS: THE HOUSE
OF PÈRE PILON

Pencil, pen and brown ink [laid paper with watermark: Hallines Dambricourt Frères, irregularly cut]
44.5 × 55 [17½ × 21¾]
Color annotations by Vincent
Compare painting F 791 [same site]
Auvers May-early June 1890
COLLECTION Amsterdam, Rijksmuseum Vincent
van Gogh [Vincent van Gogh Foundation, inv
nr F 1638]

F 1638 verso SKETCH OF A VILLAGE STREET
WITH HOUSES

Black chalk 55 × 44.5 [21¾ × 17½]
Auvers June-July 1890
LITERATURE Not in Faille 1928

F 1639 VIEW ACROSS THE OISE TOWARDS
MÉRY AND THE PARIS ROAD

Pencil and water color and gouache [pink Ingres
paper] 47.5 × 63 [18¾ × 24¾]
Auvers May-June 1890
LITERATURE D. Cooper, Zeichnungen and
Aquarelle von Vincent van Gogh, 1954, p 88:
May-June
COLLECTION London, Tate Gallery [acquired
1933; Frank C. Stoop bequest], inv nr 4714

F 1640 recto WOODED LANDSCAPE WITH
HOUSES

Pencil, brush and blue water color 45 × 54.5
[17¾ × 21½]
Compare painting F 750 [similar motif]
Auvers July 1890
LITERATURE D. Cooper, Zeichnungen und
Aquarelle von Vincent van Gogh, 1954, p 92
COLLECTION Amsterdam, Rijksmuseum Vincent
van Gogh [Vincent van Gogh Foundation, inv
nr F 1640]

F 1640 verso HOUSE AND CHESTNUT TREES

Black chalk
Compare painting F 751 [same house]
Auvers May 1890
LITERATURE Not in Faille 1928

F 1639

F 1640 recto

F 1640 verso

F 1640a

F 1652 verso

F 1642

F 1643

F1640a VIEW OF A VILLAGE WITH TWO WOMEN IN THE FOREGROUND

Black chalk 44 × 56.5 [17¼ × 22¼]
Auvers May-June 1890
LITERATURE Not in Faille 1928
COLLECTION Sale New York [Parke-Bernet]
26 May 1949, nr 86
Present owner unknown

F1641 SHEAVES
Arles period; see after F 1521

F1642 LANDSCAPE WITH HOUSES AND A WOMAN WORKING IN THE FIELD

Charcoal, reed pen, India ink and pastel 47 × 62.5
[18½ × 24½]
Auvers May-June 1890
COLLECTION Chicago, The Art Institute
[acquired 1949; Kate L. Brewster bequest], inv
nr 49.382

F1643 HAYRICKS

Brown water color, brushed, with slight traces of an
underlying pencil sketch [wove paper] 46.5 × 60.7
[18¼ × 24]
Auvers June 1890
COLLECTION Manchester, Whitworth Institute
[acquired 1926]

F1644 recto PEASANT WOMAN WALKING TO THE RIGHT

Pencil [yellowed blue graph paper] 13.5 × 8.5
[5¼ × 3¼]
Auvers June 1890
LITERATURE Faille 1928, nr 1644 [not reproduced]
EDITORS' COMMENT The measurements indicate
that this drawing belonged to the sketchbook of
which F 1616, F 1617 and F 1622 also formed part.
COLLECTION Paris, Musée National du Louvre,
inv nr RF 29.883

F1644 verso WOMAN WITH HAT IN CHECKED COAT

Black chalk
Auvers June 1890
LITERATURE Faille 1928, nr 1644 verso [not
reproduced]
EDITORS' COMMENT See F 1644 recto. The woman
is not dressed like a French woman and may be one
of the Americans Vincent mentioned in letter 640
[10 June] '*A whole colony of Americans has just
established itself next door to the house where I am;
they are painting, but I have yet seen what they are
doing.*'

F1645 recto and verso STUDY OF A SOWER AND A MAN WITH A SPADE; STUDY OF TWO SOWERS
Saint Rémy period; see after F 1622 verso

F1646 recto THREE STUDIES [not reproduced]

Pencil 43.5 × 26.5 [17 × 10½]
Auvers 1890
LITERATURE Faille 1928, nr 1646 [not reproduced]
COLLECTION Formerly Auvers, P. Gachet
Present owner unknown

F 1640a 1641 1642 1643 1644 recto 1644 verso 1645 recto and verso 1646 recto
1646 verso 1647 recto and verso 1648 recto and verso 1649 recto and verso 1650 recto
1650 verso 1651 recto 1651 verso 1652 recto 1652 verso

F 1644 recto

F 1644 verso

F1646 verso A STEAMER WITH SEVERAL
PEOPLE [not reproduced]

Pencil
Auvers 1890
Color annotations by Vincent
LITERATURE Faille 1928, nr 1646 verso [not
reproduced]

F1647 recto and verso LANDSCAPE WITH
TWO FIGURES; A MAN AND A WOMAN SEEN
FROM BEHIND AND OTHER PERSONS
Saint Rémy period; see after F 1622 verso

F1648 recto and verso SNOW-LANDSCAPE;
TREES AND GRASSES IN THE FOREGROUND
AND HOUSES BEHIND
Saint Rémy period; see after F 1622 verso

F1649 recto and verso STUDIES OF
PEASANTS WORKING: SOWERS AND
DIGGERS; A MAN IN FRONT OF A
FARMSTEAD AND OTHER SKETCHES
Saint Rémy period; see after F 1622 verso

F1650 recto STILL LIFE: CAN, BOOKS,
WINEGLASS, BREAD AND ARUM; SKETCH
OF TWO WOMEN AND A GIRL

Pencil 44 × 27 [17¼ × 10½]
Color annotations by Vincent
Compare painting F 610 and F 1613 [arum]
Auvers May-June 1890
EDITORS' COMMENT The two women and a girl
were probably added at some time after the still life
had been completed.
COLLECTION Sale London [Sotheby] 22 June 1966,
nr 4
Present owner unknown

F1650 verso A MAN AND A WOMAN;
OUTLINES OF LANDSCAPE WITH FIGURES

Pencil and chalk
Auvers June-July 1890
LITERATURE Faille 1928, nr 1650 verso [not
reproduced]

F1651 recto STUDIES OF FIGURES AND
WOODEN SHOES
Arles period; see after F 1521

F1651 verso SKETCHES OF FIGURES AND
HANDS
Saint Rémy period; see after F 1622 verso

F1652 recto FIGURE SKETCHES

Black chalk 43.5 × 27 [17 × 10½]
Auvers July 1890
LITERATURE Faille 1928, nr 1652 [not reproduced]
COLLECTION New York, Mr and Mrs Harry
M. Goldblatt

F1652 verso SKETCH OF A YOUNG WOMAN
AND OTHER SKETCHES

Pencil, black chalk
Auvers July 1890
LITERATURE Faille 1928, nr 1652 verso [not
reproduced]

F 1650 recto

F 1650 verso

F 1652 recto

F 1653

F 1654 recto

F 1654 verso

F 1609 recto

F 1609 verso

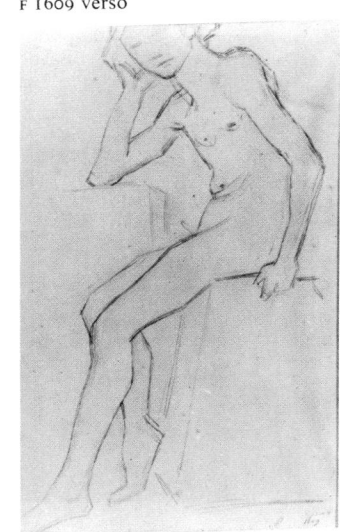

F 1653 THE FARM OF PÈRE ELOI, IN THE FOREGROUND A WOMAN WORKING

Pencil, pen and ink [Ingres paper] 47 × 61.5 [18½ × 24¼]
Auvers June 1890
COLLECTION Paris, Musée National du Louvre [acquired 1954; gift of P. Gachet], inv nr R F 30.271, L. Suppl. 1886a

F 1654 recto COUNTER AT RAVOUX' INN

Pencil 8 × 13.3 [3¼ × 5¼]
Auvers June-July 1890
LITERATURE Faille 1928, nr 1654 [not reproduced]. M. de Sablonière, Het Cahier-De Nevelvlek 1955, pp 46-7 [with reproduction]. M. E. Tralbaut, Vincent le mal aimé, 1969, p 308
EDITORS' COMMENT A sketch from Vincent's last sketchbook.
COLLECTION Richmond, Virginia, E. Buckman [gift of P. Gachet]

F 1654 verso COCK; HEN

Pencil 13.3 × 8 [5¼ × 3¼]
Auvers June-July 1890
LITERATURE Not in Faille 1928. M. de Sablonière, Het Cahier-De Nevelvlek 1955, pp 46-7 [with reproduction]. M. E. Tralbaut, Vincent le mal aimé, 1969, p 317

REDATED TO AUVERS

F 1589a PATH BETWEEN GARDEN WALLS

Charcoal, washed and heightened with white 30 × 40 [11¾ × 15¾]
Auvers May-June 1890
LITERATURE Not in Faille 1928
EDITORS' COMMENT In his manuscript for the present edition Faille dated F 1589a Saint Rémy 1889-90.
COLLECTION Burlingame, California, Mr and Mrs Philip N. Lilienthal

F 1609 recto HORSE AND CARRIAGE

Pencil [Ingres paper with watermark: Dambricourt Frères] 27 × 43.5 [10½ × 17¼] Irregularly cut
Compare painting F 760, F 1587 recto and F 1610 recto [similar motif]
Auvers June 1890
LITERATURE Faille 1928, nr 1609: Saint Rémy
EDITORS' COMMENT Either Saint Rémy or Auvers.
COLLECTION Amsterdam, Rijksmuseum Vincent van Gogh [Vincent van Gogh Foundation, inv nr F 1609]

F 1609 verso SEATED NUDE [after Bargues]

Pencil
Auvers June 1890
LITERATURE Not in Faille 1928; Chetham 1960, p 46, plate 49: Auvers; connects F 1609 verso with letters 636 and 638 from Auvers, in which Vincent asks Theo to send him a copy of Bargues when he gets a chance
EDITORS' COMMENT The style of this drawing does not point specifically either to the Saint Rémy or Auvers period.

F 1610 recto HORSE AND CARRIAGE

Pencil and black chalk [pink Ingres paper with watermark: P. L. Bas] Sheet 21.5 × 47 [8½ × 18½]
Drawing F 1610 recto 20 × 23.5 [8 × 9¼]
Compare painting F 760, F 1587 recto and F 1609 recto [similar motif]

Auvers June 1890
LITERATURE Faille 1928, nr 1610: Saint Rémy
EDITORS' COMMENT See F 1631 recto
COLLECTION Amsterdam, Rijksmuseum Vincent
van Gogh [Vincent van Gogh Foundation, inv
nr F 1610]

F 1610 verso SKETCH OF TWO WOMEN
WORKING

Black chalk
Auvers June 1890
LITERATURE Faille 1928, nr 1610 verso: Saint
Rémy
EDITORS' COMMENT See F 1610 recto

F 1611 recto CHESTNUT LEAF AND HUSK

Black chalk [ordinary drawing paper] Sheet
24 × 63.5 [9½ × 25] Drawing F 1611 recto 24 × 31.5
[9½ × 12½]
Compare painting F 820 [similar motif]
Auvers May 1890
LITERATURE Faille 1928, nr 1611; Saint Rémy
1889
EDITORS' COMMENT See F 1541 recto
COLLECTION Amsterdam, Rijksmuseum Vincent
van Gogh [Vincent van Gogh Foundation, inv
nr F 1541]

F 1611 verso SKETCHES OF A PERSPECTIVE
FRAME

Pencil. Sheet 24 × 63.5 [9½ × 25] Drawing F 1611
verso 12.5 × 8.7 [5 × 3½]
Compare F 1637 verso
Auvers 1890
EDITORS' COMMENT See F 1541 recto

F 1589a

F 1610 recto

F 1610 verso

F 1611 recto

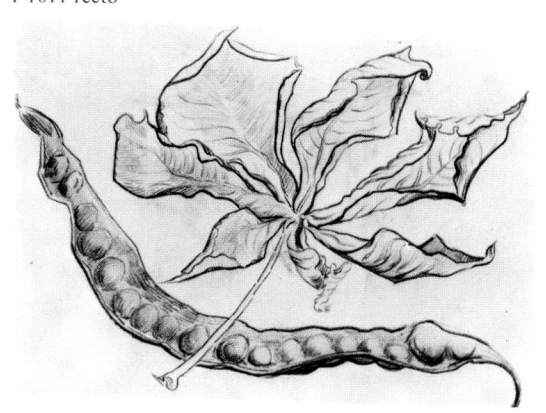

F 1611 verso

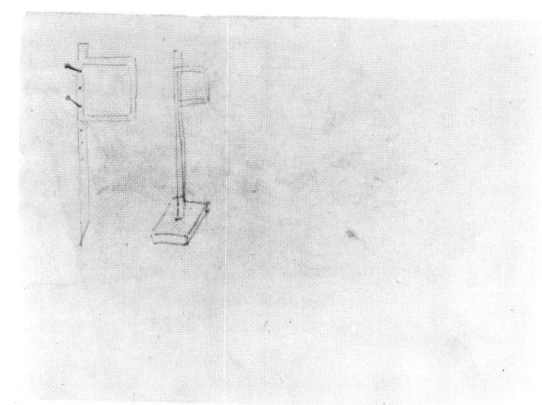

F 1612

F 1614
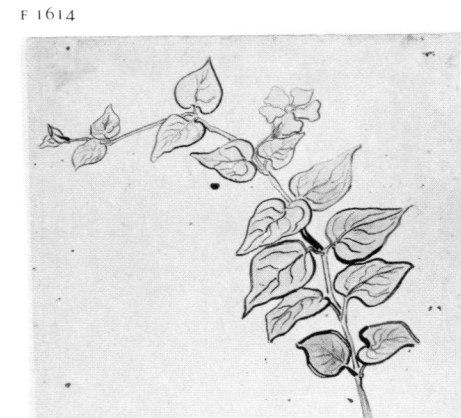

F 1613

F 1615 recto

F 1615 verso

F1612 BRANCHES OF FEATHER HYACINTH
[MUSCARI COMMOSUM]

Pencil, reed pen and brown ink [ordinary wove paper] 41 × 31 [16¼ × 12¼]
Auvers May-June 1890
LITERATURE Faille 1928, nr 1612: Saint Rémy.
A. Bowness, exhib cat van Gogh London [Hayward Gallery] 1968-9, nr 188: Saint Rémy late April-early May 1890
COLLECTION Amsterdam, Rijksmuseum Vincent van Gogh [Vincent van Gogh Foundation, inv nr F 1612]

F1613 STUDY OF ARUM

Pen, reed pen and brown ink [ordinary wove paper] 31 × 41 [12¼ × 16¼]
Compare painting F 610 and F 1650 recto [orchids]
Auvers May-June 1890
LITERATURE Vincent van Gogh, Lettres à Bernard, 1911, plate LXV. Faille 1928, nr 1613: Saint Rémy. A. Bowness, exhib cat van Gogh London [Hayward Gallery] 1968-9, nr 189: Saint Rémy late April-early May 1890
COLLECTION Amsterdam, Rijksmuseum Vincent van Gogh [Vincent van Gogh Foundation, inv nr F 1613]

F1614 BRANCHES OF PERIWINKLE

Black chalk, brush and ink [Ingres paper with watermark: AL (in oval)] 47.5 × 40 [18¾ × 15¾]
Auvers May-June 1890
LITERATURE Faille 1928, nr 1614: Saint Rémy
COLLECTION Amsterdam, Rijksmuseum Vincent van Gogh [Vincent van Gogh Foundation, inv nr F 1614]

F1615 recto HARVESTING HAY

Black and blue chalk [Ingres paper with watermark: MBM] 23.5 × 31 [9¼ × 12¼]
Auvers June-July 1890
LITERATURE Faille 1928, nr 1615 [not reproduced]: Saint Rémy
COLLECTION Amsterdam, Rijksmuseum Vincent van Gogh [Vincent van Gogh Foundation, inv nr F 1615]

F1615 verso HILLY LANDSCAPE WITH HARVESTERS

Black and blue chalk
Color annotation by Vincent
Auvers June-July 1890
LITERATURE Faille 1928, nr 1615 verso [not reproduced]: Saint Rémy

F1616 WOMAN, MAN AND CHILD WALKING TO THE RIGHT

Black chalk [yellowed blue graph paper] 13.5 × 8.5 [5¼ × 3¼]
Auvers June 1890
LITERATURE Faille 1928, nr 1617 [not reproduced]: Saint Rémy
EDITORS' COMMENT See F 1644 recto
COLLECTION Paris, Musée National du Louvre, inv nr RF 29.886

F1617 SITTING WOMAN WITH CHILD: FACING RIGHT

Black chalk, faded [yellowed blue graph paper] 13.5 × 8.5 [5¼ × 3¼]
Auvers June 1890
LITERATURE Faille 1928, nr 1617 [not reproduced]: Saint Rémy
EDITORS' COMMENT See F 1644 recto

F 1619 recto STUDY OF TWO WOMEN

Pencil [pink Ingres paper] 22 × 18.5 [8¾ × 7¼]
Annotated by Vincent: rouge gris et noir cravate
rose, chapeau pourpre et noir
Auvers June-July 1890
LITERATURE Faille 1928, nr 1619 [not reproduced]:
Saint Rémy
COLLECTION Poughkeepsie, New York, Vassar
College Art Gallery [acquired 1959; gift of Alastair
B. Martin], inv nr 59.10, cat 1967, p 47

F 1619 verso STUDY OF A WOMAN
STANDING; TWO HEADS; ANOTHER
FIGURE

Pencil 18.5 × 22
Annotated by Vincent: ocre jaune, bleu, cobalt
Auvers June-July 1890
LITERATURE Faille 1928, nr 1619 verso [not
reproduced]: Saint Rémy

F 1622 recto THE HIND LEGS OF A HORSE

Black chalk [yellowed blue graph paper] 13.5 × 8.5
[5¼ × 3¼]
Compare SD 1730
Auvers June 1890
LITERATURE Faille 1928, nr 1622 [not
reproduced]: Saint Rémy
EDITORS' COMMENT See F 1644 recto
COLLECTION Paris, Musée National du Louvre,
inv nr RF 29.884

F 1622 verso HEAD OF A YOUNG MAN WITH
HAT: FULL FACE

Black chalk
Auvers June 1890
LITERATURE Faille 1928, nr 1622 verso [not
reproduced]: Saint Rémy
EDITORS' COMMENT See F 1644 recto
COLLECTION Paris, Musée National du Louvre,
inv nr RF 29.885

LITHOGRAPHS AND ONE ETCHING

Nine lithographs by van Gogh are known: F 1655
[SORROW], F 1656 [MAN DIGGING], F 1657 [OLD
MAN DRINKING COFFEE], F 1658 [ORPHAN MAN
STANDING], F 1659 [MAN DIGGING IN AN
ORCHARD], F 1660 [MAN BURNING WEEDS AND
WOMAN SITTING ON A WHEELBARROW], F 1661
[THE POTATO EATERS], F 1662 [WORN OUT] and
F 1663 [MAN SITTING ON A BASKET CUTTING
BREAD]. They were made in the following order:
F 1658 [6-9 November 1882]; F 1655 [9-11 November
1882]; F 1656 and F 1657 [shortly before 25 Novem-
ber 1882]; F 1662 [26 November 1882]; F 1663
[around 1 December 1882]; F 1659 and F 1660
[probably July 1883]; F 1661 [mid-April 1885].
Having heard from Theo of the technique of
transferring a drawing onto a lithographic stone
with the aid of a special paper Vincent started
experiments with this method in November 1882
[see letters 241 and those following it]. Details
concerning the technique are to be found in letter
R 29 [March 1883]. In the summer of 1883 Vincent
must have resumed these experiments, as two
lithographs are made after drawings of that period,
though no mention of lithography is made in his
letters of those months. Finally, when working on
his painting THE POTATO EATERS in April 1885,
Vincent made another isolated experiment with
lithography. This time he drew directly on the
stone, so that the print is in reverse to the drawing.
In all the other lithographs he had drawn on
transfer paper, which results in a reverse image on
the stone and a positive one on the print.

F 1616
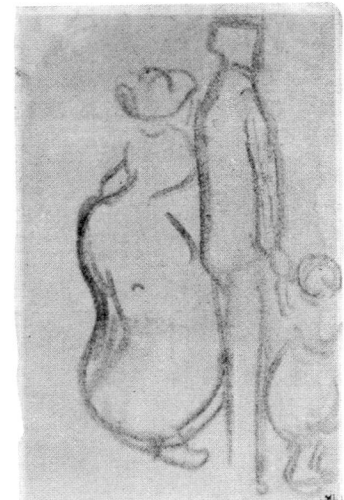

F 1617

F 1619 recto

F 1619 verso

F 1622 recto
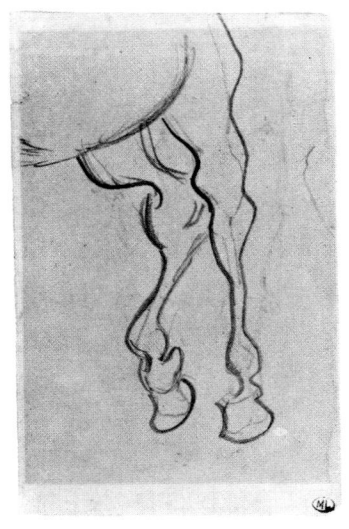

F 1622 verso

F 1656

F 1657

F 1655 SORROW

Lithograph. Printed surface 38.5 × 29 [15¼ × 11½]
Imprinted in lower left: Vincent
Imprinted in lower right: Sorrow
Three impressions are known to the editors
Impression I is reproduced
I Annotated by Vincent: épreuve d'essai
II Annotated by Vincent: épreuve d'essai
III Annotated by Vincent: 1re épreuve
Compare drawings F 929 and F 929a
The Hague November 1882
LETTERS 244 [14 November] '*On what was left of
the printing paper, I made another trial last week
with the little figure "Sorrow."*'
245 [between 16 and 18 November] '*...by the same
mail you will receive the* very first *print of "Sorrow."
I added another one with a larger margin for
Heyerdahl, and another one for Buhot, but as they
are larger, I do not know if the post office will accept
them. You can of course take the one you like best
and get as many copies as you like, but I marked the
very first one: 1re épreuve.*'
246 [22 November] '*Wednesday morning... I hope
you received the roll with lithographs containing
"Sorrow" and the letter which accompanied it. I
mention it again to make sure, not because I had
already expected an answer.*'
LITERATURE Vanbeselaere 1937, pp 136, 180
COLLECTIONS I Amsterdam, Rijksmuseum
Vincent van Gogh [Vincent van Gogh Foundation,
inv nr F 1655/I]
II New York, The Museum of Modern Art
III Amsterdam, Rijksmuseum Vincent van Gogh
[Vincent van Gogh Foundation, inv nr F 1655/III]

F 1656 THE DIGGER

Lithograph 52 × 37 [20½ × 14½] Impression II:
52 × 38.5 [20½ × 15¼]
Imprinted in lower left: Vincent
Two impressions are known to the editors
Impression II is reproduced
I Annotated by Vincent in lower left: 1re épreuve
II Worked up by Vincent
The Hague November 1882
LETTERS 246 [22 November] '*Wednesday morning.
Along with this letter you will receive the first proofs
of a lithograph, "A Digger"...*'
R 18 [end November] *First I want to tell you that I
am working on my fourth stone, and am sending you
herewith the impressions of the three you don't have.
I shall have to retouch two of them, namely the
"Digger" and the "Coffee Drinker." The latter was
much more striking as a drawing; in the lithograph I
have used autographic ink, which did not transfer
very well, and the "quickness" of the drawing has to
a great extent gone out of it. There was also more
animation in the black parts, as the hatching
expressed the direction and form of the folds much
more strongly. Well, the same is true of the "Digger,"
but this sheet has in general acquired a certain vigor
and ruggedness which corresponds with the character
of the figure, though I should have liked a greater
diversity of tone. I am now trying to find a way to
combine the new method (transferring the drawing on
paper) with the old (working directly on the stone).'
LITERATURE Vanbeselaere 1937, pp 95, 96, 169,
180, 185, 208. Bulletin J. H. de Bois 15 March
1914, nr 17: concerning impression II. Jahrbuch der
Staatlichen Kunstsammlungen in Baden-
Württemberg 1967, p 190: concerning impression II
EDITORS' COMMENT The drawing on which this
lithograph is based has not yet been found.
COLLECTIONS I Amsterdam, Rijksmuseum
Vincent van Gogh [Vincent van Gogh Foundation,
inv nr F 1656/I]
II Stuttgart, Staatsgalerie [acquired 1966], inv
nr A 66/4444

F 1657 OLD MAN DRINKING COFFEE

Lithograph 57 × 37.5 [22½ × 14¾]
Imprinted in lower left: Vincent
Three impressions are known to the editors
Impression I is reproduced
I Annotated by Vincent: 1re épreuve
Compare drawings F 976, F 996a [same motif] and
SD 1682 [same model]
The Hague November 1882
LETTERS 246 [22 November] '*Wednesday morning…
Along with this letter you will receive the first proofs
of a lithograph…"Man Drinking Coffee."*'
R 18 [end November] See F 1656
LITERATURE Vanbeselaere 1937, pp 95, 180, 193.
V. W. van Gogh, Museumjournaal 1968, pp 42-5
COLLECTIONS I Amsterdam, Rijksmuseum
Vincent van Gogh [Vincent van Gogh Foundation,
inv nr F 1657/I]
II Amerongen, Netherlands, Mrs d'Audretsch-
Krop
III Switzerland, Private Collection

F 1658 ORPHAN MAN, STANDING

Lithograph 61 × 39.5 [24 × 15½]
Imprinted in lower left: Vincent
Four impressions are known to the editors
Impression III is reproduced
I Marginless impression annotated by Vincent in
lower left: épreuve d'essai
II Annotated by Vincent in lower left: épreuve
d'essai
III Annotated by Vincent: 1re épreuve
Compare drawing F 962
The Hague November 1882
LETTERS 243 [between 6 and 9 November] '*While
waiting for more information on the process, I have,
with the help of Smulders's printer, made a lithograph
of which I have the pleasure of sending you the very
first print.*'
245 [about 16 November] '*Smulders's workmen at
the other store on the Laan saw the stone of the old
man from the almshouse, and asked the printer if they
could have a copy to hang on the wall… Well, this
very first lithograph doesn't count yet, but certainly I
hope it will lead to something more serious.*'
LITERATURE Vanbeselaere 1937, pp 93, 94, 169,
180
COLLECTIONS I Amsterdam, Rijksmuseum
Vincent van Gogh [Vincent van Gogh Foundation,
inv nr F 1658/I]
II Jenkintown, Pennsylvania, Lessing J. Rosenwald
III Amsterdam, Rijksmuseum Vincent van Gogh
[Vincent van Gogh Foundation, inv nr F 1658/III]
IV Formerly Amsterdam, Houthakker Art Gallery

F 1659 MAN DIGGING IN THE ORCHARD

Lithograph, pen and autographic ink. Printed
surface 25 × 32.5 [9¾ × 12¾]
Imprinted in lower left: Vincent
Four impressions are known to the editors
Impression I is reproduced
I Annotated on the back: Imprimé contient 2
f[euilles?] estampes imprimés. Monsieur Theo van
Gogh, 25 Rue de Laval, Paris
III Worked up by Vincent
Compare sketch in letter 300
The Hague after 13 or 14 July 1883
LETTERS 291 [5 or 6 June] '*From the window* [of the
old people's home] *I sketched an old gardener near a
twisted apple tree…*'
300 [13 or 14 July] '*Today the almshouse man again
posed for a thing that I suddenly felt I had to make
before I started anything else. I must tell you that I
went to the almshouse again on a visiting day after
all. Then I saw the little old gardener, and have drawn
him from the window. Well, I could not let that go,
and I have got as much of it fixed on paper as I can*

remember.'
LITERATURE Vanbeselaere 1937, pp 109, 110, 137:
August 1883
COLLECTIONS I Amsterdam, Rijksmuseum
Vincent van Gogh [Vincent van Gogh Foundation,
inv nr F 1659/I]
II Amerongen, Mrs d'Audretsch-Krop
III Stuttgart, Staatsgalerie [acquired 1954], inv
nr GVL 32 [A 54/1529]
IV Formerly Auvers, Paul Gachet [according to
Vanbeselaere 1937]
Present owner unknown

F 1660 MAN BURNING WEEDS AND A WOMAN SITTING ON A WHEELBARROW

Lithograph with pen and autographic ink
15.5 × 26 [6 × 10¼]
Imprinted in lower right: Vincent
Three impressions are known to the editors
Impression III is reproduced
II Worked up by Vincent
III Formerly F 1036. Worked up by Vincent in pen
and ink. Annotated on the back: Hidde Nijland
Compare sketch in letter 299 and water color
F 1035a
The Hague after 2 July 1883
LETTERS R 38 [early July] '*…and then a series of
rough studies done during the potato harvest – a man
burning weeds…*'
297 [about 2 July] '*Then I have studies of the
burning of weeds…*'
299 [about 10 July] '*For a change, this week I have
done a few water colors out-of-doors… and I have
also drawn a few landscapes as studies for the
surroundings of a few figure drawings I am planning.
These are very hasty sketches of those figure
drawings. The topmost is the burning of weeds…*'
LITERATURE Faille 1928, nr 1660: Nuenen 1885;
impression III erroneously identified as a drawing,
and given nr 1036. Vanbeselaere 1937, pp 109, 110.
Idem, pp 85, 109, 217, 218, plate 79b: concerning
impression III
EDITORS' COMMENT The passage from letter 299
concerns only the general subject, not this
particular lithograph. Sien seems to have posed for
the woman on the wheelbarrow, as becomes plain
from this passage in letter 300 [13 or 14 July]: '*As
soon as I have looked around in Scheveningen a little,
I shall take the woman with me occasionally, to pose
or at least to indicate the place and the size of the
figures.*'
COLLECTIONS I Amsterdam, Rijksmuseum
Vincent van Gogh [Vincent van Gogh Foundation,
inv nr F 1660/I]
II Sale Bern [Gutekunst und Klipstein] 20 June
1938, nr 271
Present owner unknown
III Otterlo, Rijksmuseum Kröller-Müller, inv nr
1010-28, cat van Gogh 1970, nr 159

F 1655

F 1658

F 1659

F 1660

F 1662

At Eternity's gate

F 1663

F 1661 POTATO EATERS

Lithograph 26.5 × 30.5 [10½ × 12]
Imprinted in lower left in mirror writing: Vincent
Seven impressions are known to the editors
Impression I is reproduced
Compare painting F 78
Nuenen mid–April 1885
LETTERS 400 [13 or 14 April] *'Today I went to
Eindhoven to order a small lithographic stone ... You
need not tell the people of* Le Chat Noir *that I myself
intend to make a lithograph of this subject.'*
401 [between 13 and 17 April] *'By the same mail you
will receive a few copies of a lithograph ...If I make a
picture of the sketch* [F 78], *I shall make at the same
time a new lithograph of it, and in such a way that the
figures, which, I am sorry to say, are now turned the
wrong way, come right again.'*
402 [end April] *'By the same mail you will receive a
number of copies of the lithograph. Please give
Mr Portier as many as he wants.'*
405 [early May] *'What you say about the lithograph,
that the effect is woolly, I think too, and it is not my
own fault in that the lithographer insisted that, as I
had left hardly any white on the stone, it would not
print well. At this suggestion I had the light spots
corroded; if I had simply printed it as the drawing
was, the general effect would have been darker, but
not crude, and there would have been atmosphere
between the planes.'*
R 51a [to Vincent; Utrecht 24 May] *'In connection
with what you sent me this time, I want to refer to
your last letter ... You can agree with me that such
work is not meant seriously. Fortunately you can do
better than that, but why then did you see and treat
everything so superficially? Why didn't you study the
movements? Now they are only posing.'*
R 52 [June] *'In the first place, even if your remarks
about the lithograph were right, even if I were unable
to contradict them, you still had no right to condemn
my whole work in the insulting way you did.'*
R 53 [second half of June] *'Here is my explanation of
the lithograph. I did it entirely from memory and in a
single day; I thought a certain composition somewhat
forced, and was using an altogether different process
in an attempt to find a new idea to put it together.
Besides, it was only an experiment and nothing more,
and I used corrosives on the stone later on.'*
R 57 [August] See F 78
LITERATURE J. Havelaar, Vincent van Gogh, 1915,
plate 6b. Oude Kunst April 1917, reproduced on
p 201. J. Meier-Graefe, Vincent van Gogh der Zeichner, 1928, plate 10. Vanbeselaere 1937, pp 296, 364,
365. J. G. van Gelder, Beeldende Kunst 1942
[English translation 1947, p 10, plate 6]. W. Weis-
bach, Vincent van Gogh, 1949, p 183. Tralbaut
Bildbiographie 1958, reproduced on p 55. L. Anfray,
Les Cahiers de van Gogh 1958, pp 11-20. Cat van
Gogh 1959, Rijksmuseum Kröller-Müller, nr 167a
COLLECTIONS I Amsterdam, Rijksmuseum
Vincent van Gogh [Vincent van Gogh Foundation,
inv nr F 1661/I]
II Amsterdam, Rijksmuseum Vincent van Gogh
[Vincent van Gogh Foundation, inv nr F 1661/II]
III Jenkintown, Pennsylvania, Lessing J. Rosenwald
IV Otterlo, Rijksmuseum Kröller-Müller, inv
nr A 17-kl. 1-00, cat van Gogh 1970, nr 167a
V Rockanje, Netherlands, R. van Hoey Smith
VI Formerly The Hague, d'Audretsch Art Gallery
Present owner unknown
VII Sale Stuttgart [Stuttgarter Kunstkabinett]
7-9 November 1951, nr 1058
Present owner unknown

F 1662 WORN OUT: AT ETERNITY'S GATE

Lithograph. Printed surface 55.5 × 36.5 [22 × 14½]
Imprinted in lower left: Vincent
Seven impressions are known to the editors
Impression III is reproduced

IV Annotated on upper margin: il faut que ces feuilles se vendent à 15 cts.
Compare painting F 702, drawings F 863, F 997, F 998
The Hague end November 1882
LETTERS 248 [26 and 27 November] '*Sunday... As to lithography, tomorrow I hope to get the proof of a little old man ...Monday ...This morning I had to go to the printing office with my little old man ... Enclosed you will find the first print, not counting one spoiled proof ...the infinitely touching expression of such a little old man, which he himself is perhaps unconscious of, when he is sitting quietly in his corner by the fire.*'
R 18 [end November] '*You may remember the drawing "Worn out" ...For the present I have one which will be the subject of the fifth stone ...*'
250 [about 2 December] '*...other old man ...these [the hands and head] are the best parts.*'
LITERATURE Vanbeselaere 1937, pp 94, 95, 96. J. Rewald, Post-Impressionism, 1956, p 355. Cat van Gogh 1959, Rijksmuseum Kröller-Müller, nrs 81, 25
COLLECTIONS I Amsterdam, Rijksmuseum Vincent van Gogh [Vincent van Gogh Foundation, inv nr F 1662/I]
II Amsterdam, Rijksmuseum Vincent van Gogh [Vincent van Gogh Foundation, inv nr F 1662/II]
III Private Collection
IV Sale The Hague [Pulchri] 5-6 October 1937, nr 49
Present owner unknown
V Arlesheim, Arthur Stoll, cat 1961, nr 73
VI Amsterdam, Houthakker Art Gallery
VII Sale Paris [Drouot] 31 March 1920, nr 71: Le vieil ouvrier pleurant. Lithographie. Fort rare
Present owner unknown

F 1663 MAN SITTING ON A BASKET CUTTING HIS BREAD

Lithograph 45 × 29 [17¾ × 11½]
Imprinted in lower left: Vincent
Four impressions are known to the editors
Impression III is reproduced
The Hague November-December 1882
LETTERS 250 [about 2 December] '*You will have received a copy of a lithograph by now. ...But look, for instance, at that left leg with the muddy shoe.*'
R 20 [early February 1883] '*As for my lithographs – the one of the fellow sitting on a basket cutting his bread is a failure.*'
LITERATURE Vanbeselaere 1937, pp 97, 180. Bulletin J. H. de Bois 15 March 1914, cat nr 17; idem December 1920, cat nr 13: concerning impression III
COLLECTIONS I Amsterdam, Rijksmuseum Vincent van Gogh [Vincent van Gogh Foundation, inv nr F 1663/I]
II Amsterdam, Rijksmuseum Vincent van Gogh [Vincent van Gogh Foundation, inv nr F 1663/II]
III Formerly Haarlem, J. H. de Bois Art Gallery
Present owner unknown
III Haarlem, J. H. de Bois Art Gallery
IV Formerly Delft, Ph. de Kanter
Present owner unknown

F 1664 PORTRAIT OF DR GACHET: L'HOMME À LA PIPE

Etching 18 × 15 [7 × 6]
Imprinted in upper right: 25 Mai 90
Sixteen impressions are known to the editors.
Impression XVI is reproduced
II Annotated on the back: l'Homme à la pipe. Portrait de mon père, le docteur Gachet. Eau-forte de Vincent van Gogh. Auvers-sur-Oise Mai 1890. Epreuve ancienne tirée par le docteur Gachet. Nr 22
Auvers 25 May 1890
LETTER T 38 [23 June] '*And now I must tell you something about your etching.*'
LITERATURE Beeldende Kunst September 1918 [reproduced on cover]. P. Gachet, Souvenirs de Cézanne et de van Gogh – Auvers 1873-1890, 1953.

L. Anfray, Art-Documents December 1953, p 5.
Idem, Art-Documents March 1954, pp 1, 8-9, 11.
Idem, Art-Documents April 1954, p 4. Idem, Art-Documents June 1954, pp 8-9. P. Gachet, Paul van Rijssel, le docteur Gachet graveur, 1954, p 37.
J. Rewald, Post-Impressionism, 1956, pp 397, 399, 432: quotes an unpublished letter from Gauguin to van Gogh [Le Pouldu end June 1890] '*...I found your letter as well as the proof of your etching...*'
Margrit de Sablonière, Museumjournaal June 1957, p 42. J. B. de la Faille, Les Cahiers de Vincent van Gogh 1958, pp 4-7. L. Anfray, Les Cahiers de Vincent van Gogh 1958, pp 8-11. Cat van Gogh 1959, Rijksmuseum Kröller-Müller, nr 255
EDITORS' COMMENT The editors refer the reader to cat van Gogh 1970, Rijksmuseum Kröller-Müller, nr 255, for the history of this etching.
COLLECTIONS I Amsterdam, Rijksmuseum Vincent van Gogh [Vincent van Gogh Foundation, inv nr F 1664/I]
II Otterlo, Rijksmuseum Kröller-Müller, inv nr C 23-kl. 1-00, cat van Gogh 1970, nr 255
III Amsterdam, Rijksprentenkabinet
IV Cincinnati, Ohio, Cincinnati Museum of Art, inv nr 1960.699

F 1664

V Heemstede, Netherlands, Heirs of J. B. de la Faille
VI Formerly Düsseldorf, A. Flechtheim
Present owner unknown
VII Heirs of Paul Gachet
VIII The Hague, Gemeentemuseum, inv nr 1/1926
IX Hamburg, Kunsthalle
X Munich, Staatliche Graphische Sammlung
XI New York, Museum of Modern Art
XII Rotterdam, Museum Boymans-van Beuningen
XIII W. G. Russell Allen
XIV New York, Galerie St Etienne
XV Toledo, Ohio, Toledo Museum, inv nr 1940.98
XVI Washington, Phillips Gallery
Impressions that may or may not be identical with the preceding 16 are mentioned in the following catalogues:
Exhib cat Paris 1925, nr 56
Exhib cat New York etc 1935-6, nr 127 [Private Collection, New York]
Sale Bern [Kornfeld and Klipstein] 9 May 1963, nr 373
Cat Prints and Drawings 1966, William H. Schab Gallery, New York, nr 161 [ex-P. Gachet Collection]
Sale Bern [Kornfeld and Klipstein] 9 June 1966, nr 352 [ex P. Gachet Collection]

F 1661

SP 1665

SP 1666

SP 1667

SP 1669

SP 1668

SUPPLEMENTARY PAINTINGS

SP1665 TWO WOMEN IN THE WOODS

Paper on panel 31 × 24.5 [12¼ × 9¾]
The Hague probably August 1882
LITERATURE M. E. Tralbaut, Van Gogh le mal
aimé, 1969, p 103 [with color illustration]
COLLECTION Paris, Private Collection

SP1666 THREE FIGURES WALKING ALONG
A CANAL

Material and dimensions unknown
The Hague August 1883[?]
LETTER 309 [early August] '*The last painted studies
seem firmer to me, and more solid in color. So for
instance a few I made recently in the rain – of a man
on a wet, muddy road – express the atmosphere better,
I think ... Most of them are impressions of landscape ...
and a tow path with windmills ... Those two studies,
for instance, which I made while it was raining ...*'
LITERATURE N. H. Wolf, Wereldkroniek
November 1903, p 533 [described as 'Winter' and
reproduced]
EDITORS' COMMENT The painting is known only
from the reproduction in the Wereldkroniek in
1903. H. P. Bremmer visited the exhibition of 1903
and saw the painting there; he dated it tentatively
The Hague August 1883, referring to letter 309.
COLLECTION Present owner unknown

SP1667 HEAD OF A PEASANT WOMAN:
THREE-QUARTERS TO THE LEFT

Canvas on panel 41 × 31 [16¼ × 12¼]
Compare sketch in letter 392 [reproduced with
letter 393] and F 65 [same model]
Nuenen January 1885
LETTERS 392 [about 20 January] and 393 [about
24 January] See F 65
EDITORS' COMMENT Seen by the editors in 1962.
COLLECTION Scheveningen, Netherlands,
Mrs E. de Ridder-Pierson

SP1668 HEAD OF A PEASANT WOMAN WITH
WHITE CAP: FULL FACE

Canvas on panel 41 × 32.5 [16¼ × 12¾]
Compare sketches in letters 397 and 409, paintings
F 81, F 85, F 85a, F 130, F 140 and F 141 [same model]
Nuenen April 1885
EDITORS' COMMENT Seen by the editors in 1964.
COLLECTION Zurich, Mrs A. M. Pierson

SP1669 PEASANT HUT WITH BARNS

Canvas 62 × 113 [24½ × 44½]
Signed in lower left: Vincent
Nuenen May-July 1885
LITERATURE A. Bowness, Burlington Magazine
1969, part 1, pp 299-300: May-July 1885; cf the
other paintings of cottages F 83, F 89, F 90, F 91,
F 92 etc; the hut is painted over another picture of a
plowman with ox [with color reproduction of the
painting of the hut and x-ray of the plowman]
EDITORS' COMMENT See F 41. Seen by the editors
in 1969. The study of the plowman underneath is to
be connected to the series executed for Hermans the
goldsmith in Eindhoven [see drawing F 1142].
COLLECTION London, Luigi Grosso

SP 1670 STILL LIFE: MEAT, CELERY AND
POTS

Canvas 33.5 × 41 [13¼ × 16¼]
Paris early 1886
EDITORS' COMMENT Seen by A. M. Hammacher in
1962.
COLLECTION Hastings-on-Hudson, New York,
Jacques Lipchitz

SP 1671 STILL LIFE: TWO HERRINGS,
TOWEL AND GLASS

Canvas 32.5 × 46 [12¾ × 18]
Signed in lower right: Vincent
Paris spring 1886
EDITORS' COMMENT Seen by the editors in 1969
In poor condition.
COLLECTION USA, Mr and Mrs Scharenguival

SP 1672 TWILIGHT, BEFORE THE STORM:
MONTMARTRE

Pasteboard 14.8 × 10 [5¾ × 4]
Annotated on the back by Vincent: 8 heures soir.
27 Juillet pour le crepuscule ... orage
Paris 27 July 1886
EDITORS' COMMENT Seen by the editors in 1969.
COLLECTION Paris, G. Darrieutort

SP 1672a SELF PORTRAIT

Canvas 46 × 38 [18 × 15]
Paris 1887[?]
LITERATURE Fritz Novotny, Alte und Moderne
Kunst September-October 1962, pp 2-4 [with
reproduction]: genuine, Paris 1886-7. Die Welt-
kunst 1 May 1965, p 343 [with reproduction].
N. Oberhammer, cat 1966, Gemäldegalerie, Vienna:
Paris 1886
EDITORS' COMMENT Faille noted on the back of
his photograph of the picture: false van Gogh. All
of the editors who have seen the painting disagree
with this judgment. The dating is uncertain.
COLLECTION Vienna, Gemäldegalerie des Kunsthistorischen Museums, Vienna [acquired 1964], inv
nr MG 319, cat Neuerworben 1955 bis 1966, 1966,
nr 12 [illustration p 24]

SP 1670

SP 1671

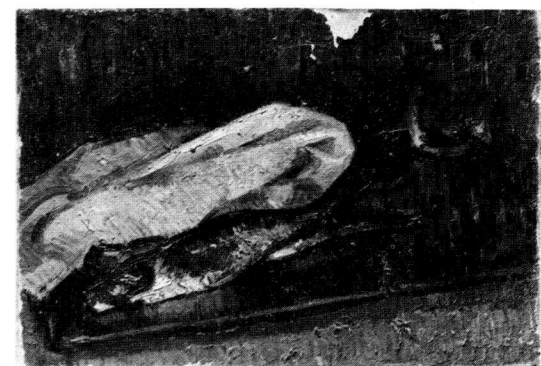

SP 1672

SP 1672a

SD 1673

SD 1674

SD 1675

SD 1677

SD 1676

SUPPLEMENTARY DRAWINGS

SD 1673 FRENCH PEASANT WOMAN [after Dalou]

Pencil, pen [thick wove paper] 48.2 × 26.2 [19 × 10¼]
Annotated in lower left: Paysanne française d'après la terre-cuite de Dalou
Etten winter 1880-1
LITERATURE Chetham 1960, p 15
EDITORS' COMMENT After a facsimile of a drawing by A. Gilbert after THE TERRA COTTA by J. Dalou, reproduced in l'Art II, Paris 1876, p 38
COLLECTION Amsterdam, Rijksmuseum Vincent van Gogh [Vincent van Gogh Foundation, inv nr SD 1673]

SD 1674 A MOWER [after Millet]

Pencil, washed with sepia [brown paper] 55.5 × 30.5 [22 × 12]
Compare painting F 687
Etten late summer 1881
LETTERS 144 [1 May] '...I...have to do "Les Travaux des Champs."'
149 [August] '...he [Tersteeg]...attaches some value to my making them, also to my occasionally copying a figure by Millet...'
LITERATURE Expertised in 1960 under the auspices of the Expertise Instituut, Amsterdam. L. Gans, Museumjournaal July 1961, p 33: Etten October-November 1881
EDITORS' COMMENT Copied from a wood-engraving by J. A. Lavieille after Millet's series LES TRAVAUX DES CHAMPS. Vincent already copied Millet during his stay in Brussels [compare F 828 and F 829]; he repeated the same motif in Saint Rémy [F 687].
COLLECTION Amsterdam, Rijksmuseum Vincent van Gogh [Vincent van Gogh Foundation, inv nr SD 1674]

SD 1675 MAN WITH BASKET, SOWING

Charcoal, black chalk, washed with brown-red in sleeves [vergé] 30.5 × 23 [12 × 9]
Signed in lower left: Vincent
Compare sketch reproduced with letter 150 [in the Dutch edition of the letters with letter 149] and F 865
Etten late summer 1881
LETTER 150 [September] See F 865
EDITORS' COMMENT Shown by Mrs van Velthuysen at the Rijksbureau voor Kunsthistorische Documentatie, The Hague, in 1964.
COLLECTION The Hague, Heirs of Mrs van Velthuysen

SD 1676 FIELD OF STUBBLE WITH A THUNDERSTORM OVERHEAD

Pencil, black chalk, washed and heightened with white 46 × 49 [18 × 19¼]
Compare sketch in letter 150
Etten September 1881
LETTER 150 [September] 'This is a field of stubble, where they are plowing and sowing. I made a rather large sketch of it, with a thunderstorm overhead.'
LITERATURE Maasbode 30 December 1948. Rotterdamsch Nieuwsblad 3 January 1949. Nieuwe Courant 8 January 1949. De Nieuwe Gids 1 February 1949
COLLECTION Netherlands, Private Collection

SD 1677 DONKEY CART

Charcoal, black chalk, washed and heightened with white [Ingres paper with watermark: P. L. Bas–E.D. & Cie] 42 × 59.5 [16½ × 23½]
Etten autumn 1881

SD 1678

LETTER 151 [September] '*I am also trying to get a horse and a donkey.*'
LITERATURE Expertised in 1960 under the auspices of the Expertise Instituut, Amsterdam. L. Gans, Museumjournaal July 1961, pp 33-4. The Connoisseur March 1968, p 200
COLLECTION Amsterdam, Rijksmuseum Vincent van Gogh [Vincent van Gogh Foundation, inv nr SD 1677]

SD 1678 THE STATIONSSTRAAT AT ETTEN

Pencil and washed [Dutch laid paper] 39.5 × 60.5 [15½ × 23¾]
Etten October 1881
LITERATURE L. Aalders, Stemmen des Tijds 1937, pp 250-8 [with reproduction]. Helmondse Courant 10 December 1949. M. E. Tralbaut, Vincent le mal aimé, 1969, p 81 [with reproduction]
COLLECTION New York, Estate of Robert Lehman [bequeathed to the Metropolitan Museum, 1969]

SD 1679 CORNER OF HERENGRACHT AND PRINSESSEGRACHT IN THE HAGUE

Pencil, washed with China ink, heightened with white [vergé with unidentifiable watermark] 24 × 33.5 [9½ × 13¼]
Signed in lower left: Vincent
Annotated on the back: Hoek Heerengracht en Prinsengracht en Boschbrug [inaccurate description of the locale]
The Hague March 1882
LETTER 180 [10 March] See F 914
LITERATURE M. Op de Coul, Museumjournaal 1969, pp 42ff: March 1882; very probably belongs to the first series of twelve drawings commissioned by C. M. van Gogh
EDITORS' COMMENT See F 914
COLLECTION Amsterdam, Rijksmuseum Vincent van Gogh [Vincent van Gogh Foundation, inv nr SD 1679]

SD 1680 VIEW IN THE HAGUE

Water color, pen and ink 24.5 × 35.5 [9¾ × 14]
Signed in lower left: Vincent
Compare painting F 204 [nearby site]
The Hague March 1882
LITERATURE Ch. W[entinck], Elseviers Weekblad 9 July 1960: a view in The Hague, with the New Church left and the Enthoven factory right
COLLECTION The Netherlands, Private Collection

SD 1681 BOY WITH WOODEN SHOES, STANDING: FULL FACE

Pencil [ordinary paper] 31 × 16 [12¼ × 6¼]
Signed in lower right: Vincent
The Hague October 1882
LITERATURE A. Bowness, exhib cat van Gogh London [Hayward Gallery] 1968-9, nr 26: possibly The Hague October 1882
COLLECTION Amsterdam, Rijksmuseum Vincent van Gogh [Vincent van Gogh Foundation, inv nr SD 1681]

SD 1679

SD 1680

SD 1681

SD 1682

SD 1683

SD 1684

SD 1685

SD 1686

SD 1682 ORPHAN MAN DRINKING COFFEE

Black lithographic chalk [water-color paper]
49.5 × 28.5 [19½ × 11¼]
Signed in lower left: Vincent del
Compare F 976 [same model], F 996a, and
lithograph F 1657 [same composition]
The Hague November 1882
LETTER 246 [22 November] '*Wednesday morning.
Along with this letter you will receive the first proofs
of a lithograph…"Man Drinking Coffee."*'
LITERATURE Museumjournaal 1968, pp 42-5.
A. Bowness, exhib cat van Gogh London [Hayward
Gallery] 1968-9, nr 16: November 1882
EDITORS' COMMENT The editors believe SD 1682
to have been executed previously to F 996a.
COLLECTION Amsterdam, Rijksmuseum Vincent
van Gogh [Vincent van Gogh Foundation, inv
nr SD 1682]

SD 1683 MAN STANDING, READING A BOOK

Black chalk, brushed, pen and ink, washed.
Dimensions unknown
Compare F 1001 [same model] and F 1002 [same
model and same bench]
The Hague December 1882
LETTER 253 [between 12 and 20 December] '*I have
two new drawings now, one of a man reading his
Bible … In one there is a view of the snowy fields
through the window.*'
LITERATURE De Week 14 November 1903 [with
reproduction]
EDITORS' COMMENT The window in the drawing
mentioned in letter 253 may have been brushed over
with dark wash.
COLLECTION Present owner unknown

SD 1684 SIEN: FACING LEFT

Pencil and black mountain chalk [water-color
paper] 28.5 × 18 [11¼ × 7]
The Hague 1883
EDITORS' COMMENT Same technique and
pedigree as F 1062.
COLLECTION Bergen, Norway, H. Claussen

SD 1685 YOUNG GIRL: HALF FIGURE, RIGHT PROFILE

Pencil, lithographic chalk, pen, brush and ink,
heightened with white [torchon] 48.3 × 25.4 [19 × 10]
Compare sketch in letter 276, F 1007, F 1008 and
F 1024 [probably the same model]
The Hague 1883
COLLECTION New York-Amsterdam, John Streep
Art Gallery [acquired 1969]

SD 1686 FUNERAL AT NUENEN IN WINTER

Black chalk, pen and brown ink, washed 16 × 25
[6¼ × 9¾]
Nuenen December 1883
EDITORS' COMMENT See F 1127
COLLECTION Munich, Mrs F. von Werz

SD 1687 WINTER LANDSCAPE WITH THE OLD TOWER OF NUENEN IN THE BACKGROUND

Pencil and pen [wove paper, yellowish] 20.5 × 28.6
[8 × 11¼]
Nuenen December 1883
EDITORS' COMMENT See F 1127. The editors saw
the drawing in 1968 at the Rijksbureau voor
Kunsthistorische Documentatie in The Hague.
COLLECTION Stockholm, A. M. Obermayer

SD 1688 THE WEAVER STANDING IN FRONT OF A LOOM

Water color [dimensions unknown]
Compare paintings F 32, F 35 and drawing F 1134
Nuenen May 1884
LETTER 367 [about 1 May] See F 32
EDITORS' COMMENT Included here only on the basis of an old and unsatisfactory photograph.
COLLECTION Present owner unknown

SD 1689 WOMAN WITH A BUNDLE OF BRANCHES, STUDIES OF HANDS

Pencil [wove paper, yellowish] 22.5 × 35.5 [8¾ × 14]
Compare painting F 43 [partly the same motif]
Nuenen second half of 1884; the hands first months of 1885
EDITORS' COMMENT To be connected with F 43, a study for the dining-room decorations for Hermans in Eindhoven.
COLLECTION Amsterdam, Rijksmuseum Vincent van Gogh [Vincent van Gogh Foundation, inv nr SD 1689]

SD 1690 PEASANT WOMAN DIGGING UP CARROTS

Black chalk [ordinary wove paper] 52 × 41.5 [20½ × 16¼]
Annotated in lower right: arracheuse de carottes [hiver]
Nuenen June-July 1885
LETTERS 414 [June] and 422 [mid-August]
See F 1250
416 [6 July] See F 94
EDITORS' COMMENT A photo of this drawing was shown at the Rijksbureau voor Kunsthistorische Documentatie, The Hague, in 1965 by Mrs Edinburg of the USA.
COLLECTION Formerly Paris, Hébrard [acquired 1906]
Present owner unknown

SD 1691 PEASANT WOMAN DIGGING UP CARROTS

Black chalk 53 × 44 [21 × 17¼]
Annotated in lower left: arracheuse de carottes [Hiver]
Compare F 1270 and F 1272a [similar motif]
Nuenen June-July 1885
LETTERS 414 [June] and 422 [mid-August]
See F 1250
416 [6 July] See F 94
COLLECTION Bucharest, Colectia de Arte Comparata

SD 1687

SD 1688

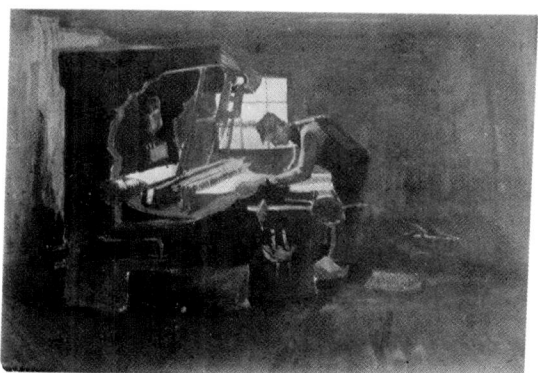

SD 1689

SD 1690

SD 1691

SD 1692

SD 1693a

SD 1693b

SD 1693c

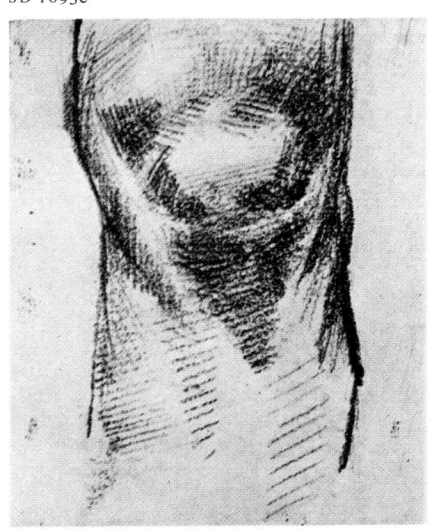

SD 1693d

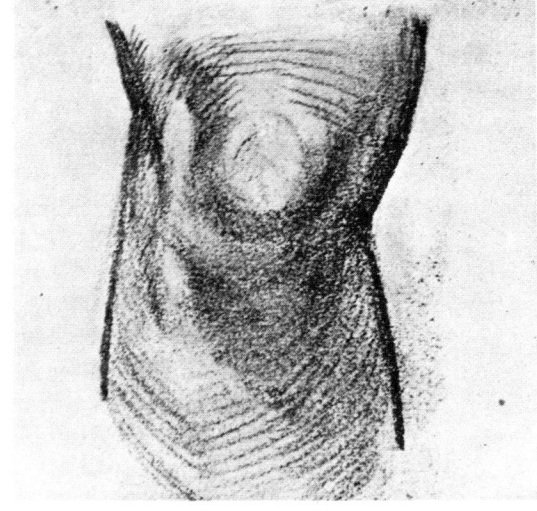

SD 1693e

SD 1693f

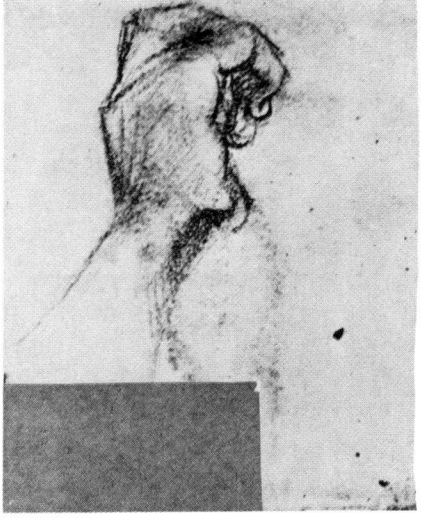

SD 1693g

SD 1692 THE ANTWERP MARKET AT NIGHT

Pencil, blue chalk [thin yellowish-brown paper]
20.7 × 29.8 [8¼ × 11¾]
Antwerp winter 1885-6
LITERATURE Not in Tralbaut Antwerp 1948.
A. M. Hammacher, exhib cat van Gogh-Signac
London 1962, nr 24 [with reproduction]: Antwerp
winter 1885-6
COLLECTION Amsterdam, Rijksmuseum Vincent
van Gogh [Vincent van Gogh Foundation, inv
nr SD 1692]

SD 1693a FIELD WITH WAGON AND RABBITS

Black chalk 9 × 11.5 [3½ × 4½]
Antwerp winter 1885-6
LITERATURE Tralbaut Antwerp 1948, pp 278, 285,
nr 15, reproduction LII
EDITORS' COMMENT The ten drawings listed under
SD 1693a-j all belong to the same sketchbook which
was used by Vincent during his stay in Antwerp.
COLLECTION Amsterdam, Rijksmuseum Vincent
van Gogh [Vincent van Gogh Foundation, inv
nr SD 1693a]

SD 1693b WOMEN ON THE BEACH

Black chalk 9 × 11.5 [3½ × 4½]
Antwerp winter 1885-6
LITERATURE Tralbaut Antwerp 1948, pp 277, 285,
nr 14, reproduction LI
EDITORS' COMMENT See SD 1693a.
COLLECTION Amsterdam, Rijksmuseum Vincent
van Gogh [Vincent van Gogh Foundation, inv
nr SD 1693b]

SD 1693c STUDY OF A KNEE

Black chalk 11.5 × 9 [4½ × 3½]
Antwerp winter 1885-6
LITERATURE Tralbaut Antwerp 1948, pp 276-7,
285, nr 52, reproduction XLIX
EDITORS' COMMENT See SD 1693a.
COLLECTION Amsterdam, Rijksmuseum Vincent
van Gogh [Vincent van Gogh Foundation, inv
nr SD 1693c]

SD 1693d STUDY OF A KNEE

Black chalk 11.5 × 9.5 [4½ × 3¾]
Antwerp winter 1885-6
LITERATURE Tralbaut Antwerp 1948, pp 276-7,
285, nr 53, reproduction L
EDITORS' COMMENT See SD 1693a.
COLLECTION Amsterdam, Rijksmuseum Vincent
van Gogh [Vincent van Gogh Foundation, inv
nr SD 1693d]

SD 1693e HEAD OF A WOMAN: RIGHT PROFILE

Pencil and black chalk 9 × 11.5 [3½ × 4½]
Antwerp winter 1885-6
LITERATURE Tralbaut Antwerp 1948, pp 280-1,
284, nr 32, reproduction LIV
EDITORS' COMMENT See SD 1693a.
COLLECTION Amsterdam, Rijksmuseum Vincent
van Gogh [Vincent van Gogh Foundation, inv
nr SD 1693e]

SD 1693f STUDY OF A RIGHT HAND

Black chalk 11.5 × 9 [4½ × 3½]
Antwerp winter 1885-6
LITERATURE Tralbaut Antwerp 1948, pp 275, 285,
nr 50, reproduction XLVII
EDITORS' COMMENT See SD 1693a.
COLLECTION Amsterdam, Rijksmuseum Vincent

van Gogh [Vincent van Gogh Foundation, inv nr SD 1693f]

SD 1693g STUDY OF A LEFT HAND

Black chalk 11.5 × 9 [4½ × 3½]
Annotated in upper right [according to Tralbaut]:
Place de Meir/Florens [?] Louizenstrotje [?]
Antwerp winter 1885-6
LITERATURE Tralbaut Antwerp 1948, pp 274, 285, nr 49, reproduction XLVI
EDITORS' COMMENT See SD 1693a.
COLLECTION Amsterdam, Rijksmuseum Vincent van Gogh [Vincent van Gogh Foundation, inv nr SD 1693g]

SD 1693h STUDY AFTER PLASTER STATUETTE: FEMALE TORSO SEEN FROM THE FRONT

Pencil 11.5 × 9 [4½ × 3½]
Compare SD 1693i [same statuette]
Antwerp January 1886
LITERATURE Tralbaut Antwerp 1948, pp 269-70, 285, nr 56, reproduction XLII. M.E. Tralbaut, Vincent le mal aimé, 1969, p 189: February 1886
EDITORS' COMMENT See SD 1693a.
COLLECTION Amsterdam, Rijksmuseum Vincent van Gogh [Vincent van Gogh Foundation, inv nr SD 1693h]

SD 1693i STUDY AFTER PLASTER STATUETTE: FEMALE TORSO, SEEN FROM THE SIDE

Pencil 11.5 × 9 [4½ × 3½]
Compare SD 1693h [same statuette]
Antwerp January 1886
LITERATURE Tralbaut Antwerp 1948, pp 271, 285, nr 57, reproduction XLIII
EDITORS' COMMENT See SD 1693a.
COLLECTION Amsterdam, Rijksmuseum Vincent van Gogh [Vincent van Gogh Foundation, inv nr SD 1693i]

SD 1693j STUDY OF A FOREARM

Black chalk 11.5 × 9 [4½ × 3½]
Antwerp winter 1885-6
LITERATURE Tralbaut Antwerp 1948, pp 276, 280, nr 51, reproduction XLVIII
EDITORS' COMMENT See SD 1693a. Stylistically close to F 1160.
COLLECTION Amsterdam, Rijksmuseum Vincent van Gogh [Vincent van Gogh Foundation, inv nr SD 1693j]

SD 1694 HEAD OF A MAN: LEFT PROFILE

Black chalk 13.5 × 10 [5¼ × 4]
Antwerp winter 1885-6
LITERATURE Tralbaut Antwerp 1948, pp 281, 285, nr 44, reproduction LV
COLLECTION Amsterdam, Rijksmuseum Vincent van Gogh [Vincent van Gogh Foundation, inv nr SD 1694]

SD 1695 HEAD OF A WOMAN: FACING RIGHT

Pencil 8 × 9 [3¼ × 3½]
Antwerp winter 1885-6
LITERATURE Tralbaut Antwerp 1948, pp 279, 285, nr 58, reproduction LIII: Antwerp sketchbook
EDITORS' COMMENT The size is different from the sheets of the only known Antwerp sketchbook [see SD 1693a].
COLLECTION Amsterdam, Rijksmuseum Vincent van Gogh [Vincent van Gogh Foundation, inv nr SD 1695]

SD 1696 STUDY AFTER LIVING MODEL: FEMALE NUDE WITH RAISED ARMS

Black, blue and red crayon [paper with watermark: J. Whatman 1884] 50.3 × 39.1 [19¾ × 15½]
Antwerp winter 1885-6
LITERATURE Not in Tralbaut Antwerp 1948
COLLECTION Amsterdam, Rijksmuseum Vincent van Gogh [Vincent van Gogh Foundation, inv nr SD 1696]

SD 1693h
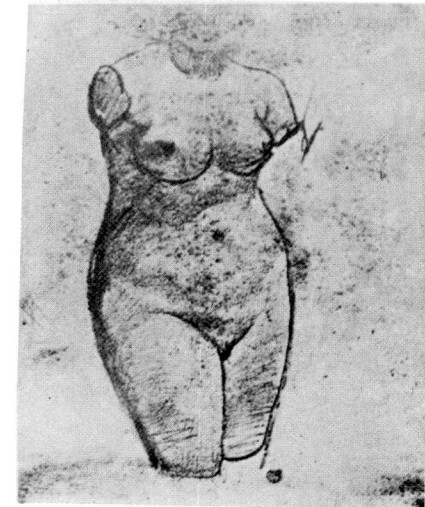

SD 1693i

SD 1693j
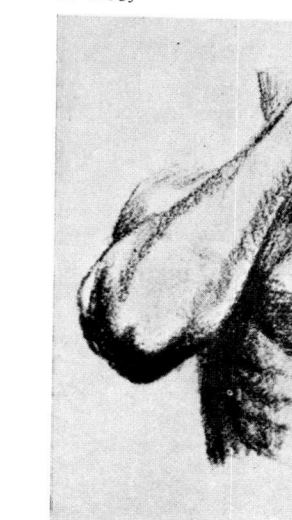

SD 1694

SD 1695

SD 1696

SD 1697 recto

SD 1697 verso

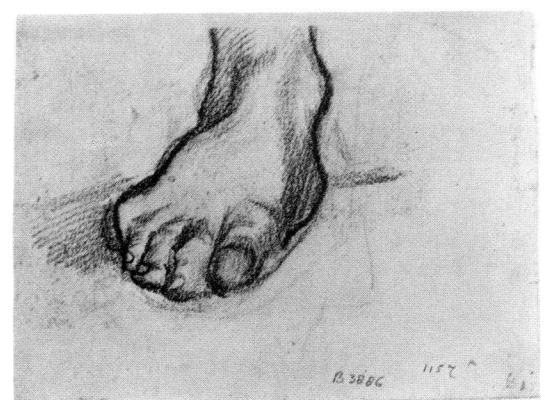

SD 1698

SD 1699

SD 1700

SD 1701 recto

SD 1702 recto

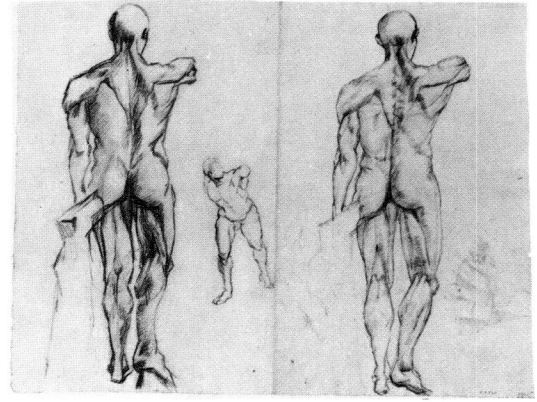

SD 1701 verso

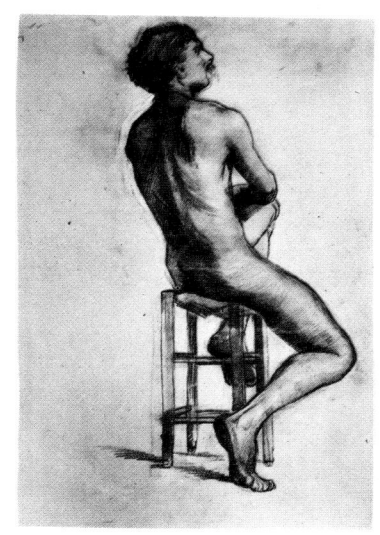

SD 1697 recto FOUR STUDIES OF FEET

Black chalk [smooth paper, yellowish] 10 × 13.5
[4 × 5¼]
Annotated by Vincent in red: L'tiaple n'egsisde
boind [Le diable n'existe point]
Antwerp winter 1885-6
LITERATURE Not in Tralbaut Antwerp 1948. Cat
van Gogh 1953, Stedelijk Museum, Amsterdam,
nr 1: Nuenen January 1885
COLLECTION Amsterdam, Rijksmuseum Vincent
van Gogh [Vincent van Gogh Foundation, inv
nr SD 1697]

SD 1697 verso STUDY OF A FOOT

Black chalk
Antwerp 1886
LITERATURE Not in Tralbaut Antwerp 1948

**SD 1698 STUDY AFTER LIVING MODEL:
STANDING FEMALE NUDE, FACING RIGHT**

Carpenter's pencil [paper with watermark:
J. Whatman 1884] 51 × 39.5 [20 × 15½]
Antwerp winter 1885-6
LITERATURE Not in Tralbaut Antwerp 1948
COLLECTION Amsterdam, Rijksmuseum Vincent
van Gogh [Vincent van Gogh Foundation, inv
nr SD 1698]

**SD 1699 STUDY AFTER LIVING MODEL:
STANDING FEMALE NUDE IN LEFT
PROFILE**

Carpenter's pencil [paper with watermark:
J. Whatman 1884] 50 × 39.5 [19¾ × 15½]
Antwerp winter 1885-6
LITERATURE Not in Tralbaut Antwerp 1948.
A. M. Hammacher, exhib cat van Gogh-Signac
London 1962, nr 31: Antwerp February 1886
COLLECTION Amsterdam, Rijksmuseum Vincent
van Gogh [Vincent van Gogh Foundation, inv
nr SD 1699]

**SD 1700 STUDY AFTER LIVING MODEL:
SITTING FEMALE NUDE, THREE QUARTERS
TO THE RIGHT; TRACES OF A MALE NUDE**

Pencil [vergé with watermark: Michallet] 47.5 × 31
[18¾ × 12¼]
Antwerp winter 1885-6
LITERATURE Not in Tralbaut Antwerp 1948
COLLECTION Amsterdam, Rijksmuseum Vincent
van Gogh [Vincent van Gogh Foundation, inv
nr SD 1700]

**SD 1701 recto STUDY AFTER PLASTER: BUST
BY ANTONIO DEL POLLAIUOLO IN THE
BARGELLO IN FLORENCE**

Charcoal and black chalk [brownish vergé]
61.5 × 47.5 [24¼ × 18¾]
Paris early 1886
COLLECTION Amsterdam, Rijksmuseum Vincent
van Gogh [Vincent van Gogh Foundation, inv
nr SD 1701]

**SD 1701 verso STUDY AFTER LIVING MODEL:
NUDE MAN SITTING ON A STOOL, SEEN
FROM THE BACK**

Black chalk
Paris early 1886

SD 1702 recto STUDIES AFTER PLASTER
STATUETTES
Left STANDING MALE WITH ONE ARM,
SEEN FROM THE BACK; STRIDING MALE
WITHOUT ARMS, SEEN FROM THE FRONT
Right STANDING MALE WITH ONE ARM,
SEEN FROM THE BACK

Black chalk [vergé paper with watermark:
Michallet] 47.5 × 63 [18¾ × 24¾]
Compare F 1366 recto and SD 1702 verso
[STANDING MALE: same statuette]
Paris early 1886
COLLECTION Amsterdam, Rijksmuseum Vincent
van Gogh [Vincent van Gogh Foundation, inv
nr SD 1702]

SD 1702 verso STUDY AFTER PLASTER
STATUETTE: STANDING MALE WITH ONE
ARM SEEN FROM THE BACK

Black chalk
Compare F 1366 recto and SD 1702 recto [same
statuette]
Paris early 1886

SD 1703 recto THREE STUDIES OF FEET

Black chalk [vergé paper with watermark:
Lalanne] 31.7 × 46 [12½ × 18]
Compare F 1364c
Paris early 1886
COLLECTION Amsterdam, Rijksmuseum Vincent
van Gogh [Vincent van Gogh Foundation, inv
nr SD 1703]

SD 1703 verso PART OF A CANAL BORDERED
BY TREES

Blue chalk
Compare F 1382 [same motif]
Paris early 1886

SD 1704 WOMAN AND DOG: IN THE BACK-
GROUND THE ENTRANCE OF THE BAL
BOULE NOIR

Pen and ink and colored crayon [drawing paper]
16.6 × 10 [6½ × 4]
Annotated by Vincent in the lower right: De son
métier elle ne faisait rien. Le soir elle baladait son
chien. La Villette
Paris first half of 1886
COLLECTION Amsterdam, Rijksmuseum Vincent
van Gogh [Vincent van Gogh Foundation, inv
nr SD 1704]

SD 1705 recto TWO LOVERS

Pencil and black crayon [drawing paper] 11 × 7.9
[4¼ × 3]
Paris first half of 1886
LITERATURE A. M. Hammacher, exhib cat van
Gogh-Signac London 1962, nr 40 [with
reproduction]: Paris March 1886
COLLECTION Amsterdam, Rijksmuseum Vincent
van Gogh [Vincent van Gogh Foundation, inv
nr SD 1705]

SD 1705 verso SKETCH OF A HOUSE; TWO
LOVERS

Black crayon
Paris first half of 1886

SD 1706 STUDY AFTER LIVING MODEL: A
MAN SEEN FROM THE BACK WITH HIS
RIGHT ARM RAISED

Pencil, black chalk, lightly erased [smooth paper
with watermark: J. Whatman 1884] 50.4 × 39.4
[20 × 15½]
Paris early 1886
COLLECTION Amsterdam, Rijksmuseum Vincent
van Gogh [Vincent van Gogh Foundation, inv
nr SD 1706]

SD 1702 verso

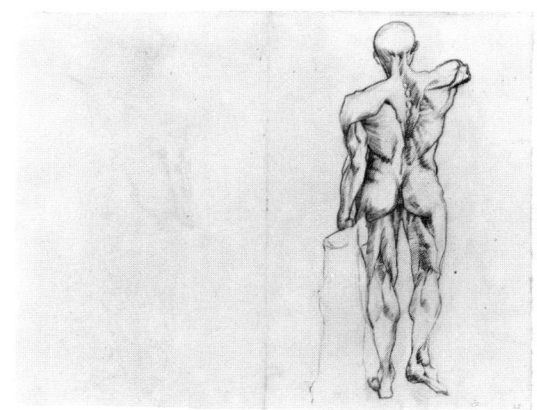

SD 1703 recto

SD 1703 verso

SD 1704

SD 1705 recto

SD 1706

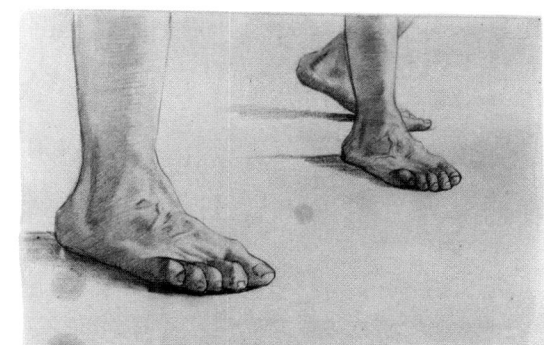

SD 1705 verso

SD 1707

SD 1708 recto

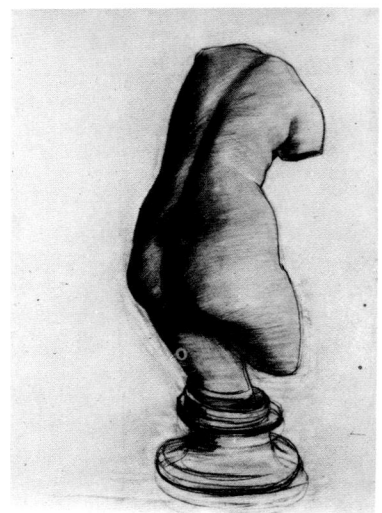

SD 1708 verso

SD 1709 recto

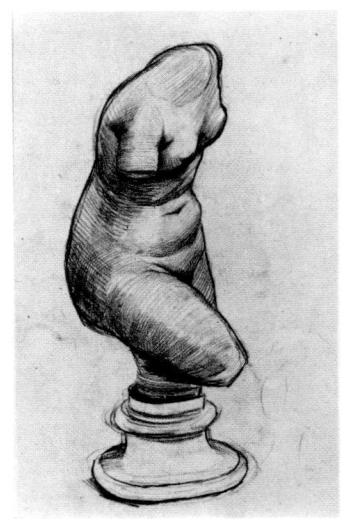

SD 1709 verso

SD 1710 recto

SD 1710 verso

SD 1711 recto

SD 1707 STUDY AFTER PLASTER
STATUETTE: FEMALE TORSO ON PEDESTAL,
FACING RIGHT

Pencil [vergé paper with watermark: L. Berville]
49.2 × 31.5 [19½ × 12¼]
Compare numbers noted under F 1363a verso [same
statuette]
Paris early 1886
COLLECTION Amsterdam, Rijksmuseum Vincent
van Gogh [Vincent van Gogh Foundation, inv
nr SD 1707]

SD 1708 recto STUDY AFTER PLASTER
STATUETTE: FEMALE TORSO ON ROUND
PEDESTAL, SEEN FROM THE BACK

Charcoal [brownish vergé paper] 61 × 45 [24 × 17¾]
Compare numbers noted under F 1363a verso [same
statuette]
Paris early 1886
COLLECTION Amsterdam, Rijksmuseum Vincent
van Gogh [Vincent van Gogh Foundation, inv
nr SD 1708]

SD 1708 verso STUDY AFTER PLASTER
STATUETTE: FEMALE TORSO ON ROUND
PEDESTAL, FACING RIGHT

Charcoal
Compare numbers noted under F 1363a verso [same
statuette]
Paris early 1886

SD 1709 recto STUDY AFTER PLASTER
STATUETTE: FEMALE TORSO ON ROUND
PEDESTAL, FACING RIGHT

Black chalk [vergé paper] 47.5 × 31 [18¾ × 12¼]
Compare numbers noted under F 1363a verso [same
statuette]
Paris early 1886
COLLECTION Amsterdam, Rijksmuseum Vincent
van Gogh [Vincent van Gogh Foundation, inv
nr SD 1709]

SD 1709 verso STUDY AFTER PLASTER
STATUETTE: FEMALE TORSO WITH ONE
LEG, RIGHT PROFILE

Pencil
Compare numbers noted under F 1363e [same
statuette]
Paris 1886

SD 1710 recto STUDY AFTER LIVING MODEL:
STANDING FEMALE NUDE, FROM THE
THIGHS UP

Black chalk [vergé paper with watermark:
Michallet] 35.2 × 46 [13¾ × 18]
Compare F 1363f verso [lower part of the same
model]
Paris 1886
COLLECTION Amsterdam, Rijksmuseum Vincent
van Gogh [Vincent van Gogh Foundation, inv
nr SD 1710]

SD 1710 verso STUDY AFTER THE LIVING
MODEL: STANDING NUDE BOY, SEEN
FROM THE BACK; THREE STUDIES AFTER A
PLASTER STATUETTE: FEMALE TORSO,
WITH ONE LEG, FACING RIGHT

Black chalk
Compare numbers noted under F 1364a [NUDE
BOY: same model] and under F 1363e [FEMALE
TORSO: same statuette]
Paris 1886

SD 1711 recto STUDY AFTER PLASTER
STATUETTE: FEMALE TORSO ON ROUND
PEDESTAL, SEEN FROM THE FRONT

Black chalk [vergé paper with watermark:
L. Berville] 31.5 × 24.5 [12½ × 9¾]
Compare numbers noted under F 1363a verso [same
statuette]
Paris late 1886
COLLECTION Amsterdam, Rijksmuseum Vincent
van Gogh [Vincent van Gogh Foundation, inv
nr SD 1711]

SD 1711 verso STUDY AFTER PLASTER
STATUETTE: FEMALE TORSO, FACING LEFT

Black chalk
Compare numbers noted under F 1363a verso [same
statuette]
Paris late 1886

SD 1712 recto STUDY AFTER PLASTER
STATUETTE: FEMALE TORSO, FACING
RIGHT

Black chalk [vergé paper] 32 × 24.5 [12½ × 9¾]
Compare numbers noted under F 1363a verso
[same statuette]
Paris late 1886
COLLECTION Amsterdam, Rijksmuseum Vincent
van Gogh [Vincent van Gogh Foundation, inv
nr SD 1712]

SD 1712 verso STUDY AFTER PLASTER
STATUETTE: FEMALE TORSO SEEN FROM
ABOVE AND TO THE RIGHT
Lower left LANDSCAPE

Torso in black chalk, the landscape in pen and
India ink
Compare other numbers noted under F 1363a verso
[same statuette]
Paris late 1886
EDITORS' COMMENT The sketch of the landscape
represents the hill with one of the mills in Mont-
martre. The composition is not known otherwise.

SD 1713 recto STUDY AFTER PLASTER
STATUETTE: FEMALE TORSO, SEEN FROM
THE FRONT

Black chalk [vergé paper] 32 × 24.5 [12½ × 9¾]
Compare numbers noted under F 1363a verso [same
statuette]
Paris late 1886
COLLECTION Amsterdam, Rijksmuseum Vincent
van Gogh [Vincent van Gogh Foundation, inv
nr SD 1713]

SD 1713 verso STUDY AFTER PLASTER
STATUETTE: MALE TORSO, SEEN FROM THE
FRONT; SITTING WOMAN

Black chalk
Compare painting F 216e [MALE TORSO: same
statuette]
Paris late 1886

SD 1714 SKETCH OF A VIOLINIST AND A
LADY PIANIST

Pencil [wove paper] 13.7 × 20.8 [5½ × 8¼] Drawn on
the back of a menu of the Grand Bouillon
Restaurant du Chalet, 43 Avenue de Clichy
Paris summer 1886 or later
LITERATURE M. E. Tralbaut, Vincent van Gogh in
het caf'conc' of het raakpunt met Raffaëlli, 1955,
p 38-9, reproduction 22: other sketches in the café
concert are F 1244a-d
COLLECTION Amsterdam, Rijksmuseum Vincent

van Gogh [Vincent van Gogh Foundation, inv
nr SD 1714]

SD 1715 SKETCH OF A MAN'S HEAD

Black chalk [dimensions unknown]
Signed in lower right: Vincent
Paris 1887
LITERATURE Vincent van Gogh, Lettres à
Bernard, 1911, plate XLIII
EDITORS' COMMENT This sketch is known only
from the reproduction in Lettres à Bernard.
COLLECTION Present owner unknown

SD 1711 verso

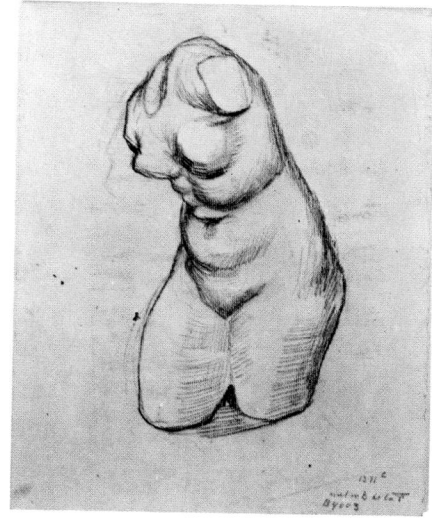

SD 1712 recto

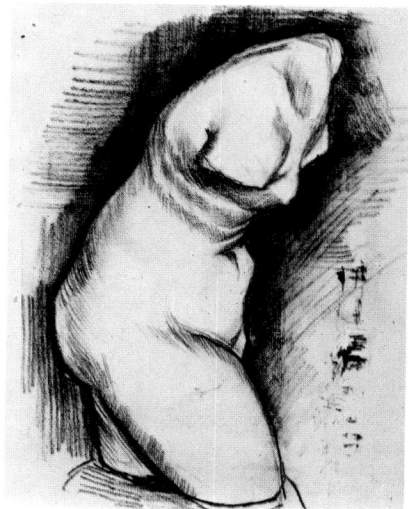

SD 1712 verso

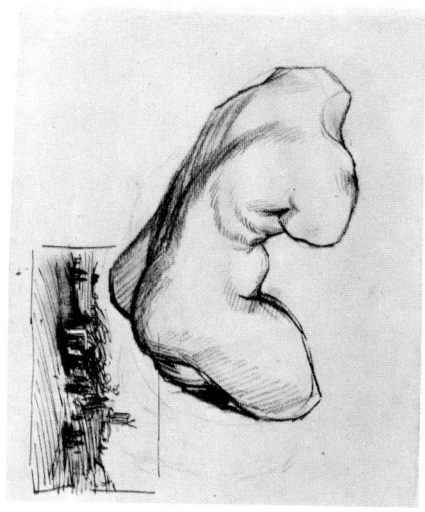

SD 1713 recto

SD 1713 verso

SD 1714

SD 1715

SD 1716 recto

SD 1716 verso

SD 1717

SD 1718

SD 1719 recto

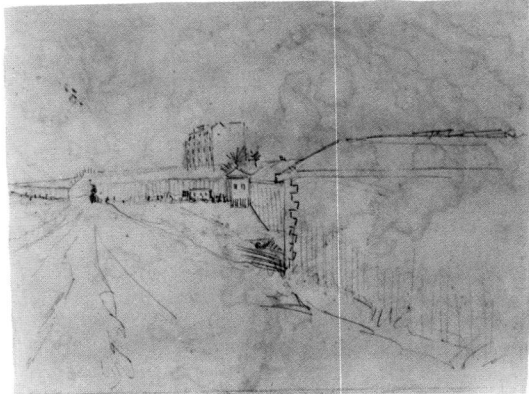

SD 1719 verso

SD 1719 recto

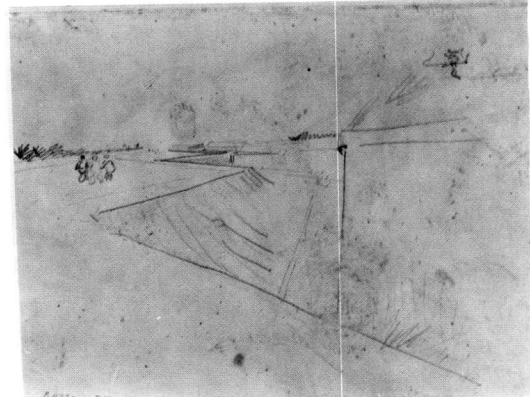

SD 1720

SD 1716 recto STUDY AFTER PLASTER STATUETTE: FEMALE TORSO WITH ONE LEG

Blue and black crayon and pencil [drawing paper] 20.5 × 13 [8 × 5¼]
Annotated in the margin by Vincent with arithmetical calculations and some words that look like '74 Rochechouart' and 'Rue Taitbout'
Paris 1887
EDITORS' COMMENT At the boulevard Rochechouart is the café Quat'Z'Arts, frequently visited by Vincent.
COLLECTION Amsterdam, Rijksmuseum Vincent van Gogh [Vincent van Gogh Foundation, inv nr SD 1716]

SD 1716 verso STUDY AFTER PLASTER STATUETTE: FEMALE TORSO WITH ONE LEG
Lower left RIVER LANDSCAPE

Pencil and black crayon
Paris 1887
LITERATURE A. M. Hammacher, exhib cat van Gogh-Signac London 1962, nr 34 [with reproduction]: Paris summer 1887

SD 1717 SKETCH OF A SITTING FEMALE NUDE

Pencil [vergé paper with watermarks: Pro Patria– Eendracht maakt macht around a standing lion and v. d. L.] 31 × 19.7 [12¼ × 7¾]
Paris 1887
COLLECTION Amsterdam, Rijksmuseum Vincent van Gogh [Vincent van Gogh Foundation, inv nr SD 1717]

SD 1718 SKETCH OF A SEATED WOMAN DRESSING

Pencil [drawing paper with drymark: Annonay… Canson & Montgolfier] 30.3 × 24.8 [12 × 9¾]
Paris summer 1887
COLLECTION Amsterdam, Rijksmuseum Vincent van Gogh [Vincent van Gogh Foundation, inv nr SD 1718]

SD 1719 recto Above SKETCH OF A ROAD WITH BUILDINGS
Below RAMPARTS WITH THREE FIGURES

Pencil [wove paper] 45.8 × 28.8 [18 × 11¼]
Compare water colors F 1400 and F 1401 [same site]
Paris summer 1887
COLLECTION Amsterdam, Rijksmuseum Vincent van Gogh [Vincent van Gogh Foundation, inv nr SD 1719]

SD 1719 verso SKETCH OF A BUILDING

Pencil
Compare F 1403
Paris summer 1887

SD 1720 COUPLE STROLLING UNDER SUNFLOWERS ON A HILL OVERLOOKING THE CITY

Pencil [wove paper] 13.5 × 21 [5¼ × 8¼] Drawn on the back of a menu of the Grand Bouillon Restaurant du Chalet at 43 Avenue de Clichy
Paris summer 1887
COLLECTION Amsterdam, Rijksmuseum Vincent van Gogh [Vincent van Gogh Foundation, inv nr SD 1720]

SD 1721 GYPSIES AT SAINTES-MARIES

Pen and ink [dimensions unknown]
Signed in upper right: V.

Annotated by Vincent in upper left: Stes Maries
Compare painting F 445 [same motif]
Saintes-Maries [Arles period] June 1888
LITERATURE T. Duret, Vincent van Gogh, 1916,
plate X
COLLECTION Present owner unknown

SD 1722 LA MOUSMÉ

Pen and ink [checked letter paper] 14.8 × 12.7
[5¾ × 5] Pasted into Gauguin's manuscript Noa Noa
Annotated in upper right: du regretté Vincent van
Gogh –
Compare painting F 431, F 1503 [same composition]
and F 1504 [same model]
Arles July 1888
LITERATURE J. Rewald, Post Impressionism, 1956,
p 227 [with reproduction]
EDITORS' COMMENT A mousmé is an attendant
in a Japanese teahouse.
COLLECTION Paris, Musée National du Louvre

SD 1723 THE POSTMAN ROULIN

Pen 32 × 24 [12½ × 9½]
Color annotations on the bottom
Compare F 432, F 1459 [same composition], F 433,
F 434, F 435, F 436, F 439 and F 1458 [same model]
Arles August 1888
COLLECTION Sale Paris [Drouot] 27 February
1919, nr 144 [with reproduction]
Present owner unknown

SD 1724 recto STUDY OF TWO LEFT FEET

Pencil, black chalk [smooth paper, yellowish]
33 × 25 [13 × 9¾]
Saint Rémy April-May 1890
COLLECTION Amsterdam, Rijksmuseum Vincent
van Gogh [Vincent van Gogh Foundation, inv
nr SD 1724]

SD 1724 verso SKETCHES OF PEASANT
PLOWING WITH HORSES

Brown chalk 25 × 33 [9¾ × 13]
Auvers June 1890
EDITORS' COMMENT Close in style to F 1632 and
the sketch of a plower in an unpublished sketchbook in the Rijksmuseum Vincent van Gogh.

SD 1725 STUDY OF SIX HANDS

Black chalk [brownish paper] 23.5 × 32 [9¼ × 12½]
Saint Rémy April-May 1890
LITERATURE Tralbaut Antwerp 1948, pp 263, 285,
nr 63, reproduction XXXVII: end of Antwerp period
COLLECTION Amsterdam, Rijksmuseum Vincent
van Gogh [Vincent van Gogh Foundation, inv
nr SD 1725]

SD 1726 STUDY OF EIGHT HANDS

Pencil and black chalk 24 × 32 [9½ × 12½]
Saint Rémy April-May 1890
LITERATURE Tralbaut Antwerp 1948, pp 262-4,
285, nr 62, reproduction XXVI. M.E. Tralbaut, Van
Gogh le mal aimé, 1969, p 187: Antwerp period
COLLECTION Amsterdam, Rijksmuseum Vincent
van Gogh [Vincent van Gogh Foundation, inv
nr SD 1726]

SD 1727 STUDY OF A LEFT HAND

Pencil and black chalk [wove paper with watermark: Michallet] 24 × 31 [9½ × 12¼]
Saint Rémy April-May 1890
COLLECTION Amsterdam, Rijksmuseum Vincent
van Gogh [Vincent van Gogh Foundation, inv
nr SD 1727]

SD 1721

SD 1722

SD 1723

SD 1724 recto
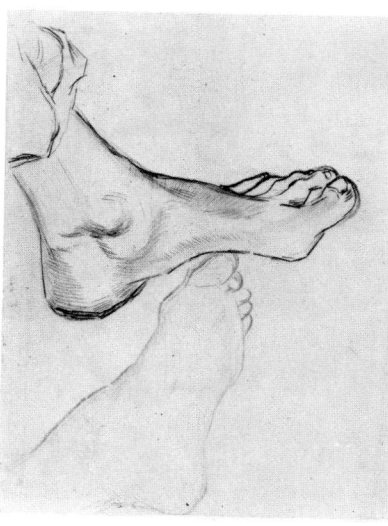

SD 1724 verso

SD 1725
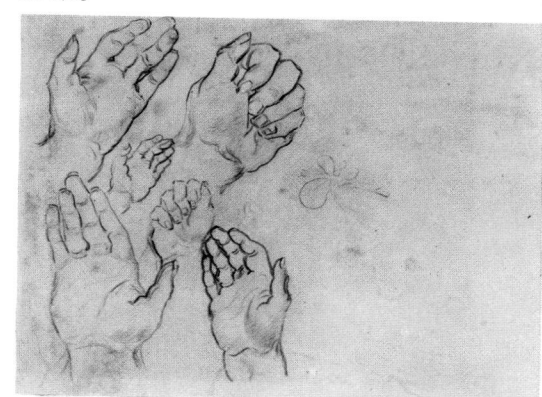

SD 1726
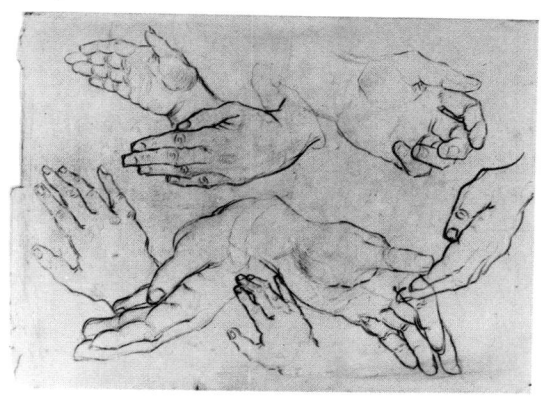

SD 1727
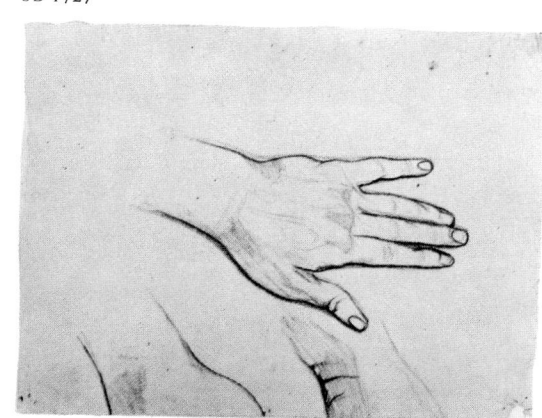

SD 1728

SD 1729

SD 1730

SD 1731

SD 1732

SD 1728 WHEATFIELD SEEN FROM THE WINDOW OF VINCENT'S ROOM IN SAINT PAUL'S HOSPITAL

Black chalk, pen and brown ink, heightened with white and black chalk [Ingres paper] 47.5 × 56 [18¾ × 22]
Compare paintings F 650, F 720, F 737 and drawing F 1552 [same motif]
Saint Rémy autumn 1889
COLLECTION Otterlo, Rijksmuseum Kröller-Müller [acquired 1970], inv nr 1517-70

SD 1729 LES OLIVEUSES

Black chalk [graph paper] 8.3 × 13.3 [3¼ × 5¼]
Compare paintings F 654, F 655 and F 656
Saint Rémy November 1889
LITERATURE M. E. Tralbaut, De Tafelronde 1955, 8-9, pp 6-9
COLLECTION Amsterdam, Rijksmuseum Vincent van Gogh [Vincent van Gogh Foundation, inv nr SD 1729]

SD 1730 HORSE AND CART

Black chalk and pencil 13.3 × 8.3 [5¼ × 3¼]
Compare recto F 1622
Auvers June 1890
LITERATURE Het Cahier De Nevelvlek 1955, p 10 [with reproduction]. M. E. Tralbaut, Van Gogh le mal aimé, 1969, p 317
COLLECTION Amsterdam, Rijksmuseum Vincent van Gogh [Vincent van Gogh Foundation, inv nr SD 1730]

SD 1731 HEN

Pencil, black chalk [blue graph paper] 8.3 × 13.3 [3¼ × 5¼]
Auvers June 1890
LITERATURE Margrit de Sablonière, Het Cahier De Nevelvlek 1955, pp 46-7 [reproduced on p 31]. Idem, Museumjournaal 1955, part 1, pp 68-9 [with reproduction]. M. E. Tralbaut, Vincent le mal aimé, 1969, p 317
COLLECTION Amsterdam, Rijksmuseum Vincent van Gogh [Vincent van Gogh Foundation, inv nr SD 1731]

SD 1732 STOOPING WOMAN ON ROAD WITH TREES

Black chalk 13.3 × 8.3 [5¼ × 3¼]
Auvers June 1890
LITERATURE Het Cahier De Nevelvlek 1955, p 10 [with reproduction]
COLLECTION Amsterdam, Rijksmuseum Vincent van Gogh [Vincent van Gogh Foundation, inv nr SD 1732]

In addition to the three sketchbooks from van Gogh's youth, which were acquired later than the original legacy, the Rijksmuseum Vincent van Gogh in Amsterdam also possesses sketchbooks from the Brabant and Paris periods and from Saint-Rémy and Auvers. Mark Edo Tralbaut has published a number of drawings from these sketchbooks [they are described and reproduced in this catalogue under nrs SD 1693, SD 1694 and SD 1695]. The particularly interesting sketchbooks are no longer complete, so that, for example, four leaves from Auvers [with six studies] reached the Cabinet des dessins, Musée du Louvre, in 1969. As the Rijksmuseum Vincent van Gogh hopes to reproduce the sketchbooks in their entirety in a special publication, it was not possible to include this material in the present edition of this catalogue.

Rejected Works

F 23

F 284

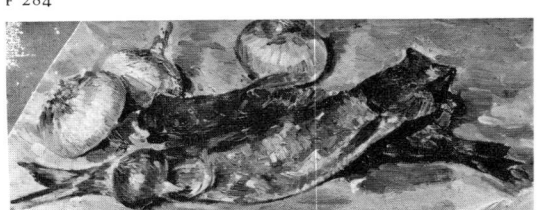

F 385

F 401

F 173

F 325

F 387

F 414

F 1424 LANDSCAPE NEAR MONTMAJOUR, WITH THE LITTLE TRAIN FROM ARLES TO ORGON
Arles mid-July 1888

The editors thought it useful to list separately the works regarded as not by van Gogh. Literature, exhibitions and provenances are given, just as in the case of the accepted works, and all the rejected works are illustrated. For the code used in the listing of the exhibitions, see the LIST OF EXHIBITIONS.

A. WORKS REJECTED BY FAILLE IN HIS MANUSCRIPT FOR THE PRESENT EDITION

PAINTINGS

F 23 [H 27] WOMAN WITH STALKS OF WHEAT

Canvas on pasteboard 33.5 × 31 [13¼ × 12¼]
False signature in lower right: Vincent
LITERATURE Faille 1928, nr 23: Drenthe. Van-beselaere 1937, pp 112, 239: The Hague August-September 1883. Faille 1939, nr 27: Drenthe or The Hague. Not in Tralbaut Drenthe 1959. Expertised under the auspices of the Expertise Instituut, Amsterdam, 1958: false
EXHIBITION 1956 Amsterdam, 12
PROVENANCE De Vries Art Gallery, Arnhem; P. H. J. J. Ras, Arnhem; Heemstede, Mrs A. M. Ras-Lundbye

F 173 THE MIDWIFE

Canvas 105 × 73 [41½ × 28¾]
LITERATURE Faille 1928, nr 173: Nuenen. Van-beselaere 1937, p 416: Antwerp. Faille 1939, p 586: false. Not in Tralbaut Antwerp 1948. M. M. van Dantzig, Vincent?, 1952, pp 137-47, plate 14: accepts it as a genuine piece from The Hague period
EDITORS' COMMENT Faille noted on the back of his photograph: Probably painted by J. V. Zürcher.
PROVENANCE Oldenzeel Art Gallery, Rotterdam [on the back of the painting is a label of Oldenzeel's dated 3 September 1909]; J. de Vries, Heemstede [1928]; Joseph Bergman, Paris; New York, J. Weissberg [1952]

F 284 [H 310] STILL LIFE: HERRINGS AND ONIONS

Oil on paper pasted on canvas 15.5 × 40 [6 × 15¾]
LITERATURE Faille 1928, nr 284: Paris. Faille 1939, nr 310: Paris
EXHIBITIONS 1917 Geneva; 1924 Basle, 15; 1947 Basle, 48
PROVENANCE Bernheim jeune Art Gallery, Paris; Paul Vallotton Art Gallery, Lausanne; Geneva, Musée d'art et d'histoire [acquired 1917; gift of the Société auxiliaire du Musée], inv nr 1917-26

F 325 STILL LIFE: VASE WITH DAISIES AND POPPIES

Canvas 41 × 33.5 [16¼ × 13¼]
LITERATURE Faille 1928, nr 325: Paris; corrigenda [on insert]: false. Faille Faux 1930, p 21, nr 86, plate XXV: false; p 13: Meier-Graefe declares that all the Wacker paintings are authentic though weak in execution. C. Veth, Schoon Schip!, 1932 [German translation: Falsche Expertisen? Falsche Experten!!, pp 67-9]: reproduced as one of the 33 paintings that Wacker introduced on the art market as Vincent van Gogh; they are Faille nrs 325, 385, 387, 418, 418a, 421, 442, 521, 523, 527a, 539, 539a, 577, 590, 614, 616, 625a, 639, 681a [erroneously reproduced as 748bis], 685, 691, 705, 710a, 713, 715a, 729, 736, 741, 741a, 812, 813, 823 and 824. Faille 1939, p 586: false.
EXHIBITIONS 1923 Manchester, 20; 1926 London 2, p 7
PROVENANCE Otto Wacker Art Gallery, Berlin; Eisenloeffel Art Gallery, Amsterdam; Rainer Art

Gallery, London; The French Gallery, London; James Murray, London; Sale London [Christie] 29 April 1927, nr 44 [with reproduction]; Present owner unknown

F 385 SELF PORTRAIT

Canvas 41 × 32.5 [16 × 12¾]
LITERATURE Faille 1928, nr 385: Paris. Faille Faux 1930, p 5, nr 1, plate I: false. H. P. Bremmer in handwritten list of accepted and rejected works from the Wacker Collection dated 21 August 1930 [the list is reproduced in C. Veth, Schoon Schip! [1932] p 37]: genuine. W. Scherjon, Catalogue des Tableaux de Vincent van Gogh décrits dans ses lettres, 1932, nr 30: authentic; Saint Rémy. Scherjon and de Gruyter 1937, Saint Rémy nr 30: letters 604, 608, 612, 618: little study for mother and sister. Faille 1939, nr 812: authentic; Saint Rémy; letters 608 and 612. W. Weisbach, Vincent van Gogh, volume 2, 1951, p 174. K. Bromig-Kolleritz, Die Selbstbildnisse Vincent van Goghs, 1954, pp 81-2, 107-8: in spite of all objections the authenticity cannot be doubted as stylistically this portrait is very close to F 522. F. Erpel, Die Selbst-bildnisse Vincent van Goghs, 1963, nr 32: with the exception of M. van Dantzig most writers including Scherjon and de Gruyter, and Weisbach accept the authenticity. See also under F 325
EXHIBITION 1929 Berlin 2 [no cat]
COLLECTIONS Otto Wacker Art Gallery, Berlin; Matthiesen Art Gallery, Berlin; M. Silberberg Art Gallery, Breslau; De Steeg, S. van Deventer [1970]

F 387 STILL LIFE WITH BREADROLLS

Canvas 46 × 57 [18 × 22½]
False signature in lower right: Vincent
LITERATURE Faille 1928, nr 387: Paris; corrigenda [on insert]: false. L. Justi, Vossische Zeitung 27 January 1929 [cited in Faille Faux 1930, p 14]: false. H. P. Bremmer, in handwritten list of accepted and rejected works from the Wacker Collection dated 21 August 1930 [the list is reproduced in C. Veth, Schoon Schip! [1932], pp 37-8]: false, as are F 387, F 421, F 616, F 685, F 691, F 705, F 713 and F 813. Faille Faux 1930, p 5, nr 5, plate II. Faille 1939, p 587: false. See also under F 325
EXHIBITION 1929 Berlin 2 [no cat]
PROVENANCE Otto Wacker Art Gallery, Berlin; Thannhauser Art Gallery, Munich [1928]; Berlin, Hugo Perls Art Gallery

F 401 THE LANGLOIS BRIDGE

Canvas 60 × 73 [23½ × 28¾]
False signature in lower left: Vincent
LITERATURE Faille 1928, nr 410: Arles. Not in Scherjon and de Gruyter 1937. Faille 1939, p 587: false. See also under F 325
EDITORS' COMMENT None of the editors has seen this painting. There was no photograph of it among Faille's papers. To judge by the reproduction in Faille 1928 it would seem to be a copy [by van Gogh?] of F 400.
PROVENANCE Paris, Private Collection [1928]; Present owner unknown

F 414 BOATS AT SAINTES-MARIES

Canvas 65 × 81 [25½ × 32]
LITERATURE Faille 1928, nr 414: Saintes-Maries [Arles period]; letter 499. Not in Scherjon and de Gruyter 1937. Faille 1939, p 587: false
PROVENANCE Paris, Private Collection [1928]; Present owner unknown

F 418 [H 814] THE SEA AT SAINTES-MARIES

Canvas 44.5 × 57 [17½ × 22½]
LITERATURE Faille 1928, nr 418: Saintes-Maries [Arles period] June 1888; letter 499. L. Justi, Vossische Zeitung 27 January 1929 [cited in Faille Faux 1930, p 14]: false. Faille Faux 1930, p 5, nr 7, plate II: false; copy after drawing F 1413, probably in the same hand as F 418a. H. P. Bremmer, in handwritten list of accepted and rejected works from the Wacker Collection dated 21 August 1930 [the list is reproduced in C. Veth, Schoon Schip! [1932], pp 37-8]: authentic. Scherjon and de Gruyter 1937, Arles nr 180: authentic. Faille 1939, nr 814: Arles June 1888. M. M. van Dantzig, Vincent? 1955: false. Cat van Gogh 1959, Rijks-museum Kröller-Müller: regarded as authentic by H. P. Bremmer. See also under F 325
EDITORS' COMMENT Mrs Kröller-Müller bought the painting as an authentic van Gogh. It has not been exhibited in the Rijksmuseum Kröller-Müller since 1947.
EXHIBITIONS 1927 Paris; 1929 Berlin 2 [no cat]; Hamburg, 85; 1930 Amsterdam, 223; 1949 Gouda
PROVENANCE Otto Wacker Art Gallery, Berlin; d'Audretsch Art Gallery, The Hague [from 1928 until 1929]; Otterlo, Rijksmuseum Kröller-Müller, inv nr 934-29, cat van Gogh 1970, nr 210

F 418a [formerly F 418bis] BOATS AT SAINTES-MARIES

Canvas 46 × 57 [18 × 22½]
LITERATURE Faille 1928, nr 418bis, supplement p 233: Saintes-Maries [Arles period]; letter 499; corrigenda [on insert]: false. Faille Faux 1930, pp 11-2, nr 55, plate XVI: false; copy after drawing F 1430, probably in the same hand as F 418. Not in Scherjon and de Gruyter 1937. Faille 1939, p 587: false. See also under F 325
EDITORS' COMMENT According to C. Veth, Schoon Schip! [1932], p 13, Dr Feilchenfeldt refused to exhibit some of the paintings, all owned by Wacker, mentioned in the catalogue of Cassirer's van Gogh exhibition. It seems likely that the catalogue nrs concerned were 42, 53, 57, 62, 73 and 79, Faille nrs 418a, 527a, 539, 625a, 691 and 741.
EXHIBITION 1928 Berlin, 42
PROVENANCE Otto Wacker Art Gallery, Berlin; Private Collection, Switzerland [1928]

F 421 MAS AT SAINTES-MARIES

Canvas 49 × 60 [19¼ × 23½]
LITERATURE Faille 1928, nr 421: Saintes-Maries [Arles period] June 1888; corrigenda [on insert]: false. L. Justi, Vossische Zeitung 27 January 1929 [cited in Faille Faux 1930, p 14]: false. Faille Faux 1930, p 6, nr 9, plate III: copy after drawing F 1435; same subject as F 421. H. P. Bremmer, 1930: see under F 387. Not in Scherjon and de Gruyter 1937. Not in Faille 1939. See also under F 325
PROVENANCE Otto Wacker Art Gallery, Berlin; Hugo Perls Art Gallery, Berlin; Fritz Roeder, Berlin; Hamburg, M. Gildemeister [1928]

F 442 THE SMALL GARDEN

Canvas 45 × 36 [17¾ × 14¼]
LITERATURE Faille 1928, nr 442: Arles August 1888; letter 519; corrigenda [on insert]: false. Faille Faux 1930, p 28, nr 117, plate XXXIII: false; considered authentic by Emile Bernard. Faille 1939, p 587: false. See also under F 325
EDITORS' COMMENT The mention of a certificate by Emile Bernard in Faille Faux 1930 might be due to a printer's error. Bernard wrote the certificate concerned for a Paris still life with apples, Faille Faux 1930, p 20, nr 83, plate XXIV.
EXHIBITION 1925 Elberfeld

F 418

F 418a

F 421

F 442

PROVENANCE Otto Wacker Art Gallery, Berlin; E. Blot Art Gallery, Paris [1912]; Elberfeld, Mrs Julius Schmits [1925]

F 509

F 512

F 521

F 523

F 527a

F 530

F 539

F 539a

F 509 LA BERCEUSE

Canvas 92 × 73 [36¼ × 28¾]
LITERATURE Faille 1928: Arles January-February
1889; letters 573, 578 and 592, with sketch. Not in
Scherjon and de Gruyter 1937. Faille 1939, p 587:
false
PROVENANCE Paris, Private Collection [1928]

F 512 OLIVE ORCHARD

Canvas 72 × 92 [28¼ × 36¼]
LITERATURE Faille 1928, nr 512: Arles April 1888.
Not in Scherjon and de Gruyter 1937. Faille 1939,
p 587: false
PROVENANCE Paris, Private Collection [1928]

F 521 SELF PORTRAIT

Canvas 61 × 51 [24 × 20]
False signature and date in lower right: Vincent 88
LITERATURE Faille 1928, nr 521: Arles; corrigenda
[on insert]: false. Faille Faux 1930, p 6, nr 12, plate
III: false. Faille 1939, p 588: false. See also under
F 325
EXHIBITION 1927 Berlin 3, 118
PROVENANCE Otto Wacker Art Gallery, Berlin;
Hugo Perls Art Gallery, Berlin; R. Abdy, Paris;
Munich, Thannhauser Art Gallery [1927]

**F 523 [H 813] SELF PORTRAIT BEFORE HIS
EASEL**

Canvas 59 × 49 [23¼ × 19¼]
LITERATURE Faille 1928, nr 523: Arles; corrigenda
[on insert]: false. W. Scherjon, Art News 13 April
1929, pp 1-2. Faille Faux 1930, p 6, nr 14, plate IV:
false; varied copy after F 626. W. Scherjon, Art
News 12 July 1930, pp 14-15: cites proof of
genuineness. H. P. Bremmer in handwritten list of
accepted and rejected works from the Wacker
Collection dated 21 August 1930 [the list is
reproduced in C. Veth, Schoon Schip! [1932],
pp 37-8]: authentic. W. Scherjon, Catalogue des
Tableaux par Vincent van Gogh décrits dans ses
Lettres, 1932, Saint Rémy nr 29. Scherjon and de
Gruyter 1937, Saint Rémy nr 29: letters 603, 604
and 607. Faille 1939, nr 813: Saint Rémy September
1889; letters 604 and 607. See also under F 325
EXHIBITION 1929 Utrecht
PROVENANCE Otto Wacker Art Gallery, Berlin;
Chester Dale, New York; Washington, National
Gallery of Art, inv nr 1814, cat Chester Dale
collection 1965, p 128

**F 527a [formerly F 527bis] SELF PORTRAIT
WITH BANDAGED EAR**

Canvas 43 × 33 [17 × 13]
LITERATURE Faille 1928, nr 527bis, supplement
p 233: Arles; corrigenda [on insert]: false. Faille
Faux 1930, p 12, nr 52, plate XV: this falsification
must have been executed after reproductions of
F 527 and F 529. Not in Scherjon and de Gruyter
1937. Faille 1939, p 588: false. See also under F 325
EDITORS' COMMENT See F 418a
EXHIBITION 1928 Berlin, 53
PROVENANCE Otto Wacker Art Gallery, Berlin;
Switzerland, Private Collection

F 530 [H 508] SELF PORTRAIT

Canvas 62 × 51 [24½ × 20]
LITERATURE Faille 1928, nr 530: Arles. Not in
Scherjon and de Gruyter 1937. Judith Gérard,
Comoedia 10 December 1931: F 530 is a copy made
by her of F 476, which she had signed: d'après
Vincent, Judith. Faille 1939, nr 508: Arles, 'soi
disant painted by Judith Gérard'
PROVENANCE Amédée Schuffenecker, Clamart;

J. Keller, Paris; E. Druet Art Gallery, Paris
[acquired 1911]; Berlin, Paul von Mendelssohn-
Bartholdy [acquired 1911] [1928 and 1939]

F 539 THE ZOUAVE

Canvas 65 × 54 [25½ × 21¼]
LITERATURE Faille 1928, nr 539: Arles; corrigenda
[on insert]: false. Justi, Vossische Zeitung
27 January 1929 [cited in Faille Faux 1930, p 14]:
false. Faille Faux 1930, p 6, nr 16, plate v: false;
compare F 424. Not in Scherjon and de Gruyter
1937. Faille 1939, p 588: false. See also under F 325
EDITORS' COMMENT See F 418a
EXHIBITIONS 1927 Berlin 1, 27 [repr]; 1928
Berlin, 57
PROVENANCE Otto Wacker Art Gallery, Berlin;
Hugo Perls Art Gallery, Berlin; Holzdorf, O. Krebs
[1928]; Present owner unknown

F 539a [formerly F 539bis] THE ZOUAVE

Canvas 62 × 52 [24½ × 20½]
LITERATURE Faille 1928, nr 539bis, supplement
p 233: Arles; corrigenda [on insert]: false. Faille
Faux 1930, p 6, nr 17, plate v: false; compare F 424.
Not in Scherjon and de Gruyter 1937. Faille 1939,
p 588: false. See also under F 325
PROVENANCE Otto Wacker Art Gallery, Berlin;
Mr Ozmella, Mannheim; Switzerland, Private
Collection [1928]

F 546 PORTRAIT OF PAUL GAUGUIN [?]

Canvas 37.5 × 33 [14¾ × 13]
LITERATURE Faille 1928, nr 546: Arles. Scherjon
and de Gruyter 1937, Arles nr 178 and p 28 [note 3]:
doubt about the authenticity. Faille 1939, p 588:
false. Åke Meyerson, Konsthistorisk Tidskrift
1946, pp 135-49: according to Carl Nordenfalk it is
questionable whether the portrait was actually
painted by van Gogh. J. Stellingwerff, Werkelijkheid en grondmotief bij Vincent Willem van Gogh,
1959, reproduction nr 18
EDITORS' COMMENT As the painting was in
Theo's possession there cannot be any doubt that it
was painted before 1890, though it remains
uncertain whether it is by van Gogh or some artist
from the group around Gauguin. It is not a
falsification, but a problem of attribution.
EXHIBITION 1960 Amsterdam, Otterlo, 101: author
unknown
PROVENANCE Mrs J. van Gogh-Bonger, Amsterdam; V. W. van Gogh, Laren; Amsterdam, Rijksmuseum Vincent van Gogh [Vincent van Gogh
Foundation, inv nr F 546]

F 577 THE GARDEN

Canvas 43 × 33.5 [17 × 13¼]
LITERATURE Faille 1928, nr 577: Arles. Faille
Faux 1930, p 7, nr 19, plate v: false; copied after
drawing F 1456. Not in Scherjon and de Gruyter
1937. Faille 1939, p 588: false. See also under F 325
PROVENANCE Berlin, Otto Wacker Art Gallery
[1928]; Present owner unknown

F 590 STILL LIFE: ASTERS

Canvas 50.5 × 42.5 [20 × 16¾]
False signature in lower right: Vincent
LITERATURE Faille 1928, nr 590: Arles; signed in
lower right: Vincent; corrigenda [on insert]: false.
Faille Faux 1930, p 21, nr 88, plate XXVI: false. Not
in Scherjon and de Gruyter 1937. Faille 1939, p 588:
false. See also under F 325
PROVENANCE Blot Art Gallery, Paris; A. von der
Heydt, Elberfeld; E. Baron von der Heydt, Zand-
voort [on loan to the Gemeentemuseum, The
Hague]; Wuppertal, Von der Heydt Museum der

Stadt Wuppertal, cat 1964, p 26

F 614 [H 816] THE CYPRESSES

Canvas 90 × 69.5 [35½ × 27¼]
LITERATURE Faille 1928, nr 614: Saint Rémy;
letter 596. L. Justi, Vossische Zeitung 27 January
1929 [cited in Faille Faux 1930, p 14]: false. Faille
Faux 1930, p 7, nr 21, plate VI: false; copy after
drawing F 1525. H. P. Bremmer, in handwritten list
of accepted and rejected works from the Wacker
Collection dated 21 August 1930 [the list is
reproduced in C. Veth, Schoon Schip! [1932],
pp 37-8]: authentic. W. Scherjon, Catalogue des
Tableaux par Vincent van Gogh décrits dans ses
Lettres, 1932, nr 122: Auvers. Scherjon and de
Gruyter 1937, Auvers nr 122: 4 June 1890; letter
638. Faille 1939, nr 816: negative judgment
withdrawn; Auvers May 1890. M. M. van Dantzig,
Vincent? 1952, plate 5: false. See also under F 325
EXHIBITION 1929 Berlin 2 [no cat]
PROVENANCE Otto Wacker Art Gallery, Berlin;
Thannhauser Art Gallery, Berlin; S. van Deventer,
De Steeg [1939]; D. G. van Beuningen, Vier-
houten, cat van Beuningen Collection 1949, nr 143;
Vierhouten, Mrs A. E. van Beuningen-Charlouis

F 616 THE CYPRESSES

Canvas 70 × 56 [27½ × 22]
LITERATURE Faille 1928, nr 616: Saint Rémy June
1889; letter 596. L. Justi, Vossische Zeitung
27 January 1929 [cited in Faille Faux 1930, p 14]:
false. Faille Faux 1930, p 7, nr 24, plate VII: false.
H. P. Bremmer, 1930: see under F 387. Not in
Scherjon and de Gruyter 1937. Faille 1939, p 588:
false. See also under F 325
EXHIBITION 1929 Berlin 2 [no cat]
PROVENANCE Otto Wacker Art Gallery, Berlin;
Hugo Perls Art Gallery, Berlin; E. Wolff Art
Gallery, Hamburg [1928]; Miss Hartung; Present
owner unknown

F 546

F 577

F 590

F 614

F 616

F 625a

F 628

F 679

F 681a

F 685

F 691

F 705

F 710a

F 625a [formerly F 625bis; H 630] RISING MOON

Canvas 61 × 77.5 [24 × 30½]
LITERATURE Faille 1928, nr 625bis, supplement p 234: Saint Rémy August 1889; letter 603; corrigenda [on insert]: false. Faille Faux 1930, p 10, nr 42, plate XII: false; copy after F 735. H. P. Bremmer in handwritten list of accepted and rejected works from the Wacker Collection dated 21 August 1930 [the list is reproduced in C. Veth, Schoon Schip! [1932], pp 37-8]: authentic. W. Scherjon, Catalogue des Tableaux par Vincent van Gogh décrits dans ses Lettres, 1932, nr 18: Saint Rémy. Scherjon and de Gruyter 1937, Saint Rémy 18, p 28, note 3: doubts about authenticity. Faille 1939, nr 630: Saint Rémy September 1889; letters 603 and 604. See also under F 325
EDITORS' COMMENT See F 418a
EXHIBITION 1928 Berlin 62
PROVENANCE Bernard Wacker, Paris; The Hague, H. P. Bremmer [1930]

F 628 THE HARVEST

Canvas 34 × 42 [13½ × 16½]
LITERATURE Faille 1928, nr 628: Saint Rémy September 1889; letters 604 and B 21. Faille Faux 1930, nr 66, pp 13-14, plate XIX: authentic. Not in Scherjon and de Gruyter 1937. Faille 1939, p 588: false
EXHIBITION 1927 Paris
PROVENANCE Bernheim jeune Art Gallery, Paris; Berlin, Nationalgalerie [acquired 1929]; Confiscated by the Nazis in 1937; it has not turned up since then

F 679 BOUQUET OF IRISES

Canvas 92 × 73 [36¼ × 28¾]
LITERATURE Faille 1928, nr 679: Saint Rémy May 1890; letter 633. Not in Scherjon and de Gruyter 1937. Faille 1939, p 588: false
PROVENANCE Paris, Private Collection [1928]

F 681a [formerly F 681bis] STILL LIFE: ROSES

Canvas 88.5 × 68.5 [34¾ × 27]
LITERATURE Faille 1928, nr 681bis [erroneously reproduced as F 748bis], supplement p 234: Saint Rémy; corrigenda [on insert]: false. Faille Faux 1930, p 12, nr 57, plate XVI: copy after F 681 and F 682. Not in Faille 1939. See also under F 325
PROVENANCE Otto Wacker Art Gallery, Berlin; Switzerland, Private Collection [1928]

F 685 PEASANT WITH HAYFORK [after Millet; detail from F 684]

Canvas 57 × 47.5 [22½ × 18¾]
LITERATURE Faille 1928, nr 685: Saint Rémy; corrigenda [on insert]: false. L. Justi, Vossische Zeitung 27 January 1929 [cited in Faille Faux 1930, p 14]: false. Faille Faux 1930, p 9, nr 28, plate IX: detail of F 684. H. P. Bremmer, 1930: false; see under F 387. Not in Scherjon and de Gruyter 1937. Faille 1939, p 588: false. See also under F 325
EDITORS' COMMENT See F 699a
EXHIBITION 1929 Berlin 2 [no cat]
PROVENANCE Berlin, Otto Wacker Art Gallery [1928]

F 691 THE SOWER

Canvas 74.5 × 59 [29¼ × 23¼]
LITERATURE Faille 1928, nr 691: Saint Rémy; corrigenda [on insert]: false. Faille Faux 1930, p 9, nr 30, plate IX: copy after F 689. H. P. Bremmer, 1930: false; see under F 387. Not in Scherjon and de Gruyter 1937. Faille 1939, p 588: false. See also under F 325

EDITORS' COMMENT See F 418a
EXHIBITION 1928 Berlin, 73
PROVENANCE K. Osthaus, Hagen; Private
Collection, Switzerland; Otto Wacker Art Gallery,
Berlin; Berlin, Matthiesen Art Gallery [1928]

F 705 THE SOWER

Canvas 48 × 62 [19 × 24½]
LITERATURE Faille 1928, nr 705: Saint Rémy;
corrigenda [on insert]: false. L. Justi, Vossische
Zeitung 27 January 1929 [cited in Faille Faux 1930,
p 14]: false. Faille Faux 1930, p 9, nr 32, plate IX:
false; copy after drawing F 1441. H. P. Bremmer,
1930: false; see under F 387. Not in Scherjon and de
Gruyter 1937. Faille 1939, p 589: false. See also
under F 325
EXHIBITION 1929 Berlin 2 [no cat]
PROVENANCE Otto Wacker Art Gallery, Berlin;
Berlin, Hugo Perls Art Gallery

F 710a [formerly F 710bis] OLIVE TREES

Canvas 72 × 91 [28¼ × 35¾]
LITERATURE Faille 1928, nr 710bis, supplement
p 234: Saint Rémy; corrigenda [on insert]: false.
L. Justi, Vossische Zeitung 27 January 1929 [cited
in Faille Faux 1930, p 14]: false. Faille Faux 1930,
p 9, nr 35, plate X: false. Not in Scherjon and de
Gruyter 1937. Faille 1939, p 589: false. See also
under F 325
EXHIBITION 1929 Berlin 2 [no cat]
PROVENANCE Otto Wacker Art Gallery, Berlin;
Goldschmidt Art Gallery, Berlin; Mrs F., Zurich
[1928]; New York, Private Collection [1964]; Sale
New York [Parke-Bernet] 8 April 1964 [retired
before the sale]; Present owner unknown

F 713 OLIVE TREES

Canvas 55 × 65 [21¾ × 25½]
LITERATURE Faille 1928, nr 713: Saint Rémy;
corrigenda [on insert]: false. L. Justi, Vossische
Zeitung 27 January 1929 [cited in Faille Faux 1930,
p 14]: false. Faille Faux 1930, p 9, nr 34, plate X:
falsification inspired by F 710. H. P. Bremmer, 1930:
false; see under F 387. Not in Scherjon and de
Gruyter 1937. Faille 1939, p 589: false. See also
under F 325
EXHIBITION 1929 Berlin 2 [no cat]
PROVENANCE Otto Wacker Art Gallery, Berlin;
Hugo Perls Art Gallery; Commeter Art Gallery,
Hamburg; Hamburg, M. Gildemeister [1928]

F 715a [formerly F 715bis] OLIVE TREES

Canvas 72 × 91 [28¼ × 35¾]
LITERATURE Faille 1928, nr 715bis, supplement
p 234: Saint Rémy; corrigenda [on insert]: false.
Faille Faux 1930, p 9, nr 37, plate X: falsification
inspired by F 710. Not in Scherjon and de Gruyter
1937. Faille 1939, p 589: false. See also under F 325
PROVENANCE Otto Wacker Art Gallery, Berlin;
Switzerland, Private Collection [1928]

F 729 LANDSCAPE

Canvas 63 × 53 [24¾ × 20¾]
LITERATURE Faille 1928, nr 729: Saint Rémy;
corrigenda [on insert]: false. L. Justi, Vossische
Zeitung 27 January 1929 [cited in Faille Faux 1930,
p 14]: false. Faille Faux 1930, p 10, nr 38, plate XI:
false. Not in Scherjon and de Gruyter 1937. Faille
1939, p 589: false. See also under F 325
EXHIBITION 1929 Berlin 2 [no cat]
PROVENANCE Kuenze Art Gallery, Berlin; Otto
Wacker Art Gallery, Berlin; Berlin, Matthiesen Art
Gallery [1928]

F 736 [H 815] HAYCOCKS: RISING MOON

Canvas 56 × 87 [22 × 34¼]
LITERATURE Faille 1928, nr 736: Saint Rémy;
corrigenda [on insert]: false. Faille Faux 1930, p 10,
nr 41, plate XII: false; copy after F 735. H. P. Bremmer, in handwritten list of accepted and rejected
works from the Wacker Collection dated 21 August
1930 [the list is reproduced in C. Veth, Schoon
Schip! [1932], pp 37-8]: authentic. Scherjon and de
Gruyter 1937, Saint Rémy nr 162, p 28, note 3:
slight doubt about authenticity. Faille 1939, nr 815:
negative judgment withdrawn; Saint Rémy
September 1889. See also under F 325
PROVENANCE Otto Wacker Art Gallery, Berlin;
Switzerland, Private Collection [1928 and 1939]

F 713

F 715

F 729

F 736

F 738

F 741

F 741a

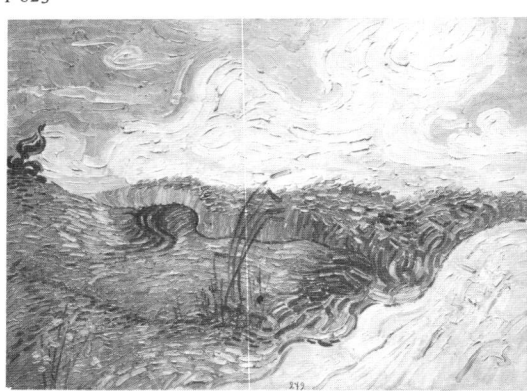

F 813

F 823

F 824

F 1271

F 1285

F 738 [H 740] SUNSET

Canvas 33 × 41 [13 × 16¼]
LITERATURE Faille 1928, nr 738: Saint Rémy. Not in Scherjon and de Gruyter 1937. Faille 1939, nr 740: Saint Rémy 1889
EDITORS' COMMENT In the archives of the Rijks-bureau voor Kunsthistorische Documentatie, The Hague, is a photograph of a photograph of F 738 on which Emile Bernard had written: Tableau authentique de Vincent van Gogh Arles 1887 Emile Bernard
PROVENANCE Amédée Schuffenecker, Paris; G. Schweitzer, Berlin; Sale Berlin [Cassirer] 20 October 1932, 128; Present owner unknown

F 741 THE CYPRESSES

Canvas 80 × 60 [31½ × 23½]
LITERATURE Faille 1928, nr 741: Saint Rémy; corrigenda [on insert]: false. L. Justi, Vossische Zeitung 27 January 1929 [cited in Faille Faux 1930, p 14]: false. Faille Faux 1930, p 10, nr 44, plate XIII: false. Not in Scherjon and de Gruyter 1937. Faille 1939, p 589: false. See also under F 325
EDITORS' COMMENT See F 418a
EXHIBITIONS 1927 Berlin 1, 30; 1928 Berlin, 79
PROVENANCE Otto Wacker Art Gallery, Berlin; Berlin, Hugo Perls Art Gallery [1928]

F 741a [formerly F 741bis] THE CYPRESSES

Canvas 74 × 58 [29 × 22¾]
LITERATURE Faille 1928, nr 741bis, supplement p 235: Saint Rémy; corrigenda [on insert]: false. Faille Faux 1930, p 12, nr 60, plate XIII: false; inspired by F 620 and drawing F 1524. Not in Scherjon and de Gruyter 1937. Faille 1939, p 589: false. See also under F 325
PROVENANCE O. Wacker Art Gallery, Berlin; Switzerland, Private Collection [1928]

F 813 THE FIELDS

Canvas 70 × 53 [27½ × 20¾]
LITERATURE Faille 1928, nr 813: Auvers; corrigenda [on insert]: false. L. Justi, Vossische Zeitung 27 January 1929 [cited in Faille Faux 1930, p 14]: false. Faille Faux 1930, p 10, nr 47, plate XIII: inspired by F 781. H. P. Bremmer, 1930: false; see under F 387. Not in Scherjon and de Gruyter 1937. Faille 1939, p 589: false. See also under F 325
EXHIBITION 1927 Berlin 1, 28; 1929 Berlin 2 [no cat]
PROVENANCE Otto Wacker Art Gallery, Berlin; Berlin, Hugo Perls Art Gallery [1928]

F 823 THE WHEATFIELD

Canvas 57 × 76 [22½ × 30]
LITERATURE Faille 1928, nr 823: Auvers; corrigenda [on insert]: false. L. Justi, Vossische Zeitung 27 January 1929 [cited in Faille Faux 1930, p 14]: false. Faille Faux 1930, p 11, nr 49, plate XIV: false; copy after F 807. Not in Scherjon and de Gruyter 1937. Faille 1939, p 589: false. See also under F 325
EXHIBITIONS 1927 Berlin 1, 29; 1929 Berlin [no cat]
PROVENANCE Otto Wacker Art Gallery, Berlin; Hugo Perls Art Gallery, Berlin; Holzdorf, Otto Krebs [1928]

F 824 LANDSCAPE

Canvas 51 × 79 [20 × 31]
LITERATURE Faille 1928, nr 824: Auvers; corrigenda [on insert]: false; Faille Faux 1930, p 11, nr 51, plate XIV: false; chaotic composition not to be linked with any known work by Vincent

F 1286

van Gogh. H. P. Bremmer, in handwritten list of accepted and rejected works from the Wacker Collection dated 21 August 1930 [the list is reproduced in C. Veth, Schoon Schip! [1932], pp 37-8]: authentic. Not in Scherjon and de Gruyter 1937. Faille 1939, p 589: false. See also under F 325
EXHIBITIONS 1927 Berlin 1, 31; 1928 Amsterdam, 35
PROVENANCE Otto Wacker Art Gallery, Berlin; Berlin, Hugo Perls Art Gallery [1928]

DRAWINGS

F 1271 PEASANT WOMAN PULLING OUT BEETS

Charcoal and black chalk 52 × 36 [20½ × 14¼]
False signature and annotation in lower left:
Récolte de betteraves en campagne. Vincent
LITERATURE Faille 1928, nr 1271: Nuenen.
Vanbeselaere 1937, pp 278, 394, 395, 412: false?
EDITORS' COMMENT Drawings F 1271, F 1285, F 1286, F 1300 and F 1334 obviously go back to the same source.
EXHIBITIONS 1927-8 Berlin etc, 100; 1961 Munich, 47
PROVENANCE A. Hahnloser, Winterthur; Bern, H. R. Hahnloser

F 1285 PEASANT WOMAN SCRUBBING AN IRON POT

Black chalk 61 × 46 [24 × 18]
False signature and annotation in lower left:
Femme nettoyant son chaudron. Vincent
Annotated in lower right: Ton grisâtre
LITERATURE Faille 1928, nr 1285: Nuenen.
Vanbeselaere 1937, pp 279, 394, 395, 413: false?
Albright Art Gallery Notes [Buffalo] June 1947, pp 22-3 [with reproduction]: authentic
EDITORS' COMMENT See F 1271
PROVENANCE Miedema Art Gallery, Rotterdam; A. W. Gelber, Rotterdam [1928]; H. Scheffer, New York; Buffalo, Albright-Knox Art Gallery [acquired 1946 from Clifton and Tracy Funds], nr 46:6, Check list of drawings, nr 53

F 1286 PEASANT WOMAN PEELING POTATOES

Charcoal and black chalk 46 × 35.5 [18 × 14]
False signature and annotation in lower left:
Paysanne épluchant des pommes de terre. Vincent
LITERATURE Faille 1928, nr 1286: Nuenen.
Vanbeselaere 1937, pp 279, 394, 413: false?
EDITORS' COMMENT See F 1271
EXHIBITION 1912 Haarlem, 25
PROVENANCE Oldenzeel Art Gallery, Rotterdam; F. J. G. Bosman, Scheveningen/The Hague; Sale Bosman, The Hague [Biesing] 6-7 May 1908, nr 35; De Vries Art Gallery, Arnhem; Erich Schall, Baden-Baden; Cologne, Heinrich Stinnes [acquired 1912]

F 1300 DIGGING UP POTATOES

Charcoal 46 × 58 [18 × 22¾]
False signature and annotation in lower left:
Récolte de pommes de terre. Vincent; à peindre vers le soir
LITERATURE Faille 1928, nr 1300: Nuenen.
Vanbeselaere 1937, pp 279, 394, 413: false?
EDITORS' COMMENT See F 1271
PROVENANCE L. Maier, Rotterdam [1928]

F 1324 PEASANT REAPING WHEAT

Black chalk 60 × 52 [23¾ × 20½]
LITERATURE Faille 1928, nr 1324: Nuenen.

Vanbeselaere 1937, pp 274, 413: Nuenen August 1885. Albright Art Gallery Notes [Buffalo] May 1943, pp 3, 4, 17: authentic
EXHIBITIONS 1943 New York 2, 69; 1944 Montreal, 114
PROVENANCE J. W. I. W. Plooster van de Roest, Bussum; Sale Amsterdam [F. Muller] 12 May 1908, 141a; Independent Gallery, London [1928]; Buffalo, Albright-Knox Art Gallery [gift of A. Conger Goodyear], nr 43:7, Check list of drawings, nr 54

F 1334 PEASANT RESTING IN A CHAIR

Charcoal 50 × 39 [19¾ × 15¼]
False signature and annotation in lower left:
Paysan au repos. Vincent
LITERATURE Faille 1928, nr 1334: Nuenen.
Vanbeselaere 1937, pp 279, 394, 395, 413: false?
EDITORS' COMMENT See F 1271
EXHIBITION 1947 San Francisco, 129
PROVENANCE L. Maier [1928]; Cambridge, Massachusetts, Arthur K. Solomon [1947]

B. WORKS REJECTED BY FAILLE AND ACCEPTED BY THE EDITORS

F 562, F 812, F 821, F 822, F 1376, F 1377

C. WORKS ACCEPTED BY FAILLE BUT REJECTED BY THE EDITORS

F 77a, F 185a, F 203a, F 215a, F 215c, F 215d, F 221a, F 235a, F 246a, F 257, F 326, F 476a, F 560, F 639, F 699a, F 849a, F 1625

F 1300

F 1324

F 1334

Juvenilia

by Jan G. van Gelder

VAN GOGH'S EARLY DRAWINGS

The question of whether Vincent van Gogh had done any drawing before reaching the age of twenty-seven did not receive any attention until 1955, a good hundred years after Vincent's birth. It is true that his early talent for drawing had been known since the publication of the letters in 1914/15 by Mrs J. van Gogh-Bonger. Research into the early drawings was, in fact, put to the side by J. B. de la Faille at that time. For the re-issue, however, he did include in his manuscript the drawings which had been recorded by J. G. van Gelder, initially in an article in 'De Tafelronde' [Antwerp, 1955, ii, 8-9, p. 23-28] and after re-working in the English edition of the Van Gogh catalogue of the State Museum Kröller-Müller [1957, 1959]. After 1955 the number of pre-1879/80 drawings could be considerably expanded, not least thanks to Anna Szymańska, who discovered three tattered sketchbooks of May 1873 and July 1874 [letter 19] and published their contents in her *Unbekannte Jugendzeichnungen Vincent van Goghs* [Berlin, 1967]. Vincent's enthusiasm and gift for drawing come as no surprise. Like everybody else he was quite young when he learned to draw, i.e., to copy. And his ability to perceive sharply and with originality is evident right from his earliest letters. This ability doesn't falter for a moment. Without too much trouble you can find even in his letters countless passages that could be immediately translated into drawings. Eduard Plüss calls these descriptive passages 'Ungemalte Bilder' in his contribution to the 'Festschrift Kurt Badt zum siebzigsten Geburtstage,' [Berlin, 1961, p. 231-259].[1] The string of quotations can easily be extended, and there are also countless passages in which Vincent mentions the fact that he does draw. It is quite plain that prominence in Vincent's written notes is repeatedly given to his awareness of color [particularly of blue] and further to subjects which were to recur constantly in his later work, such as his preference for parks, flower beds, long [and frequently wide] avenues, distant prospects and, most especially, views from a window that makes a kind of frame for the subject. In this Vincent is following a typical 19th century fashion [C. D. Friedrich, K.Spitzweg, A. Menzel, etc. etc.]. Later, unlike his contemporaries, Van Gogh was continually to feel the need of and use a perspective frame in setting up a view or prospect of this kind. Although we do not know Vincent's Thames-side views of London [the drawings have apparently perished] we do know that many years later he regretted not having had at that time any knowledge of perspective [letter 332, II, p. 163].[2] It can be concluded, however, that his London drawings, too, were of river banks, bridges and squares. Only a few drawings have remained, including the view from his window in Ramsgate [21 April, letter 62 and 31 May 1876, letter 67]. Here we can recognize without any doubt the beginnings of an individual handwriting, and those same typical properties are visible also in the composition with its disappearing lines that are planned to convey the perspective, its empty foreground, the street-lanterns and the 'field of grass shut off by an iron gate and surrounded by lilac bushes' [letter 62]. The views that Vincent drew in Etten, probably in the beginning of April 1876, just before he left for London [letter 59] are stylistically similar to these London drawings. Other occasional drawings date from 1876, but offer little that is new [letter 82, November 1876: Petersham and Turnham Green]. The period immediately previous to this, on the other hand, from 1873 to 1875, gives much more information, thanks to the three sketchbooks of 1873 and 1874 already mentioned. There are also the four larger drawings of The Hague and surroundings [F 836, 837, 838, 839] which Szymańska, using the rediscovered leaves of the sketchbook made by Vincent for Betsy Tersteeg [the five or six-year-old daughter of the art dealer for whom Vincent worked] for a comparison, is probably right in placing in the first months of 1873. The sketchbooks contain for the most part animals and people drawn from memory, and obviously drawn for a child. The third sketchbook, however, definitely datable June/July 1874 [Szymańska, p. 70, 71], contains several drawings in black crayon; a landscape with trees, a prospect of Helvoirt and a little portrait drawing, all taken from nature and life. The sketches, particularly those of the trees, can be related to some extent to F 874 [circa 1880] but even more to the drawing of the bridge represented in letter 121 [1878]. The copies of an etching after Corot [letter 25, London, April 1875] and a painting of the Italian Giuseppe De Nittis [letter 32, Paris, July 1875], the first of a pond, the second of London with the Westminster Bridge, confirm quite clearly that the way in which he drew during these three to five years remained more or less constant. In both conception and style there are already distinct characteristics.

The same can not be said of the surviving drawings bearing the name V. W. van Gogh and dates varying from 3 January 1862 till 8 February 1864. With a few exceptions they are all copies. The exceptions are: heads in profile on the back of the drawing with a bridge [11 January 1862], the drawing of a milkjug [5 September 1862] and the 'Barn and Farmhouse at Zundert' [8 February 1864] drawn from nature and which was intended for Vincent's father on his birthday. People have raised doubts as to whether all these drawings [12] could have been made by the nine to eleven-year-old Vincent.[3] They certainly could have been, considering the then current learning methods. We know of early drawings that are even more skilful [those of Toulouse-Lautrec, for example, in the E.E.Wolf Collection, New York]. It is of course possible that some of the drawings were corrected by the drawing master or Vincent's own mother, who drew quite passable bunches of flowers. But no matter how the pros are weighed against the cons, the precise dates and usually very reliable origins speak convincingly for Vincent Willem as the author. The fact however remains that there hardly seems to be any connection between these first drawings and those of 1873 and later. At present we have nothing dating from the period between these two groups, a good eight years. We do however know that even at a later stage Vincent expended enormous concentration on the making of most splendid copies of drawings. Three or more times [1881] he copied the drawing examples [Exercises] of Bargue, he copied photographs, reproductions after Millet, Holbein, Fél. Rops, M.Maris, Corot. The free 'translations' of yet again Millet, G. Doré, Delacroix and Rembrandt come much later, in St. Rémy. We also know from remarks made by Vincent's father and mother and from written notes of other people who knew Vincent [e.g. the statement of J. Franken, the son of the Rev. T. van Gogh's carpenter] that he drew prolifically and proficiently, and that his visual gifts more or less earmarked him for the trade of art dealer, a profession already practised most successfully by different members of the family. When after six years Vincent finally failes in this business [his career began in 1869 in The Hague and ended on 1 April 1876 in Paris] there was talk of his becoming a painter even at this late date [see the introduction of Mrs J. van Gogh-Bonger, p XXIV], which was Theo's wish, or of his choosing some position in a museum, which was his father's idea. Even an art business of his own was considered.

In the years before Vincent became 27 [30 March 1880] there are periods of several months in which he did no drawing at all, periods filled with his activities as preacher or spent in the depths of his great personal sorrows. But, just as conditions which Vincent couldn't take threatened in 1879 yet once more to take the upper hand, his urge to draw returned, never more to be restrained. On 5 August 1879 [letter 131] he wrote to Theo from Cuesmes in the Borinage: 'Could show you a few more drawings, the kind of people you find here...' and further on in a post-script: 'Reverend Pietersen, who paints rather like Schelfhout or Hoppenbrouwer and has some understanding of art... asked for one of my sketches, one of a miner type[4] [cf. F 827]. Often sit drawing till the small hours of the night, trying to give permanence to memories and body to the thoughts that involuntarily arise on seeing all these things.' This one sentence reveals Van Gogh's attitude, which wasn't to change essentially thereafter. The same letter tells us that he had received a box of paints from Tersteeg and that his sketchbook was 'already half-full'. He also wrote: 'Bought another big sketchbook with old Dutch paper in Brussels...' Not a year earlier [letter 126, 15 November 1878] he had sent Theo a drawing, 'Au Charbonnage', which showed 'a small bar attached to the big coal shed, where the workers in their dinner-break gather to eat their bread and drink their glass of beer.' This drawing is rather clumsily executed, more like the drawings from Etten and England in 1876. Of the many drawings which must have been in the possession of the Delsaut family in Cuesmes two have turned up which till April 1970 belonged to a member of the family, Mr S. Delsaut. Dr V.W. van Gogh published these, crayon drawings of houses in Cuesmes [autumn or winter 1879] in the Museumjournaal [October 1959, v, no. 4, p. 80, 81]. Louis Piérard [*La vie tragique de Vincent van Gogh*, Paris, 1939] quotes the words which G. Delsaut had sent him [see letters I, p. 228]: 'Il [Vincent] mangeait toujours seul ou s'arrangeait à ne pas manger en société. En mangeant dessinait sur les genoux ou lisait. Tout son temps était employé à dessiner. Se rendai souvent au bois de Ghlin, au cimetière de Mons, et souvent à la campagne. Dessinait surtout beaucoup de paysages, château, berger avec son troupeau, vaches dans les pâturages. Le tableau le plus frappant et qui est resté dans la mémoire de ma belle-soeur, chez qui il logeait, est le dessin représentant la famille en train de faire la récolte des pommes de terre; les uns bêchant, les autres [les femmes] ramassant les pommes de terre.'

Only the two studies of houses have remained from 1879 in Cuesmes; almost everything–including the work of earlier years–has been lost. One cannot but reach this final conclusion. And yet, the few relics of 1862 to 1880, along with the written sources of the same 18 years, are enough to indicate that most of his themes had already been found and experienced during this time. We may here perhaps repeat the conclusion written in 1955: 'Vincent's

1. His examples are to be found in letters 1, 60, 67, 72, 84, 85, 91, 97, 100, 101, 104, 110, 115, 127-131 etc.
2. 1883, N. Amsterdam, Drenthe... 'In London how often I stood drawing on the Thames Embankment, on my way home from Southampton Street in the evening, and it came to nothing. If there had been somebody then to tell me what perspective was, how much misery I should have been spared...'
3. M. E. Tralbaut, Van Gogh, *Début et évolution*, Amsterdam/Antwerpen, 1957; Anna Szymańska, o.c, 1967, p. 7.
4. On the basis of this remark F 827 is dated by de la Faille and Vanbeselaere July-August 1879. Anna Szymańska pointed out that the figure was not exactly a minder, but probably a coal heaver which was one of the subjects sketched by Van Gogh in The Hague in 1882 or 1883. It may be, however, that the drawing was made in Belgium and reworked in The Hague.
5. See for the English period: Vincent van Gogh on England compiled from his letters by his nephew Dr. V. W. van Gogh. M. E. [Amsterdam, 1968]. Neither Vincent's drawings nor his draughtsmanship itself are analysed but the book is important because of the 22 reproductions of wood engravings once in the possession of Vincent himself and now in Amsterdam, Rijksmuseum Vincent van Gogh [Vincent van Gogh Foundation].

real career as a draughtsman dates from 1862, and
perhaps even earlier. Once he had started again [in
1879] he made up for lost time within a few years by
his terrific exertion, by an almost superhuman *tour
de force* which cost him his health and the
abandonment of the tender, too diffident pursuit of
the visible world that marked his first years at
The Hague.'[5]

I SKETCHES OF A DOG HEAD, COW HEAD AND THREE MEN'S HEADS

Black chalk [old Dutch paper with watermark:
De Erven D.B. ... 22 × 17.5 [8¾ × 7]
Signed and annotated in lower right: V. W. van
Gogh 3 Januarij 1862
Zundert January 1862
LITERATURE Not in Faille 1928 or Vanbeselaere
1937
EDITORS' COMMENT Probably drawn after
sketches in a model book. H. Kokkeel accepted
three drawings as payment from Mr Cloos [father
of Mr A. M. Cloos, Amsterdam], who received the
drawing from the Aalbersberg family, relatives of a
servant in the van Gogh household.
PROVENANCE Fam. Aalbersberg; Fam. Cloos,
Amsterdam; H. Kokkeel, Utrecht; V.W. van Gogh,
Laren; Amsterdam, Rijksmuseum Vincent van
Gogh [Vincent van Gogh Foundation]

II recto THE BRIDGE [after drawing-copies by V. Adam]

Pencil 12 × 36.5 [4¾ × 14¼]
Signed and annotated in lower left: V. W. van Gogh
11 Januarij 1862
Zundert 11 January 1862
LITERATURE J. G. van Gelder, Vincent's Begin,
De Tafelronde [Antwerp], 2, 8-9, 1955, p 27.
J.G. van Gelder, The Beginnings of Vincent's Art,
cat van Gogh, Rijksmuseum Kröller-Müller,
Otterlo 1959, pp XVIII, XIX, XXI. Joost
A. M. Meerloo, Vincent van Gogh's Quest for
identity, Nederlands Kunsthistorisch Jaarboek 14,
1963, p 189
EXHIBITIONS 1958 Tokyo, Kyoto, 1; 1952 London
1,1
PROVENANCE J.G. van Gelder, Utrecht; Otterlo,
Rijksmuseum Kröller-Müller, inv nr 1148-47, cat
van Gogh 1970, 1a

II verso SKETCHES OF HEADS IN PROFILE

Pencil [old Dutch paper, laid] 12 × 36.5 [4¾ × 13¼]
Zundert January 1862
LITERATURE Not in Faille 1928 or Vanbeselaere
1937

III MILK JUG

Pencil, lightly washed 27.8 × 22 [11 × 8¾]
Signed and annotated in lower right: V. W. van
Gogh 5 September 1862
Zundert 5 September 1862
LITERATURE J. G. van Gelder, Vincent's Begin,
De Tafelronde [Antwerp], 2, 8-9, 1955, p 27.
J. G. van Gelder, The Beginnings of Vincent's Art,
cat van Gogh, Rijksmuseum Kröller-Müller,
Otterlo 1959, pp XVIII, XXI
EXHIBITIONS 1956 Munich, 1; 1958 Vienna, 2;
1962 Warsaw, 2; 1963 Tel Aviv, Haifa, 2
PROVENANCE A. Declemy, The Hague [1953];
Otterlo, Rijksmuseum Kröller-Müller, inv
nr 1302-53, cat van Gogh 1970, 1d

IV SAW-MILL

Black chalk [old Dutch paper] 18.5 × 14 [7¼ × 5½]
Signed and annotated in lower right: V.W. van
Gogh 2 October 1862

Zundert 2 October 1862
LITERATURE Not in Faille 1928 or Vanbeselaere
1937
EDITORS' COMMENT After a sketch in a model
book
PROVENANCE Fam. Aalbersberg; Fam. Cloos,
Amsterdam; H. Kokkeel, Utrecht; V. W. van
Gogh, Laren; Amsterdam, Rijksmuseum Vincent
van Gogh [Vincent van Gogh Foundation]

V THE GOAT-HERD

Black chalk 13.5 × 18.5 [5¼ × 7¼]
Signed and annotated in lower right: V. W. van
Gogh 9 October 1862
Zundert 9 October 1862
LITERATURE J. G. van Gelder, The Beginnings of
Vincent's Art, cat van Gogh, Rijksmuseum Kröller-
Müller, Otterlo 1959, pp XVIII, XXI
PROVENANCE Present owner unknown

II verso

III

IV

V

I

II recto

VI

VII

VIII

IX

X

XI

XII

XIII verso

VI A DOG [after drawing-copies by V. Adam]

Pencil 18 × 28.5 [7 × 11¾]
Signed and annotated in lower right: V. W. van
Gogh 28 December 1862 in lower left: V. Adam
Zundert 28 December 1862
LITERATURE J. G. van Gelder, Vincent's Begin,
De Tafelronde [Antwerp], 2, 8-9, 1955, p 27.
J. G. van Gelder, The Beginnings of Vincent's Art,
cat van Gogh, Rijksmuseum Kröller-Müller,
Otterlo 1959, pp XVIII, XXI Chetham 1960, p 9
EXHIBITIONS 1950 's-Hertogenbosch, Breda; 1958
Vienna, 1; Tokyo, Kyoto, 2; 1962 Warsaw, 1; 1963
Tel Aviv, Haifa, 1
PROVENANCE J. G. van Gelder, Utrecht; Otterlo,
Rijksmuseum Kröller-Müller, inv nr 1149-47, cat
van Gogh 1970, 1b

VII BARN

Black chalk [old Dutch paper with watermark:
E. D. ...] 22 × 14 [8½ × 5½]
Signed and annotated in lower right: V. W. van
Gogh 25 Januarij 1863
Zundert 25 January 1863
LITERATURE Not in Faille 1928 or Vanbeselaere
1937
EDITORS' COMMENT After a sketch in a model
book
PROVENANCE Fam. Aalbersberg; Fam. Cloos,
Amsterdam; H. Kokkeel, Utrecht; V. W. van Gogh,
Laren; Amsterdam, Rijksmuseum Vincent van
Gogh [Vincent van Gogh Foundation]

VIII CORINTHIAN CAPITAL

Pencil 30 × 20.5 [11¾ × 8]
Signed and annotated in lower right: V. W. van
Gogh 22 Augustus 1863
Zundert 22 August 1863
LITERATURE J. G. van Gelder, Vincent's Begin,
De Tafelronde [Antwerp], 2, 8-9, 1955, p 27.
J. G. van Gelder, The Beginnings of Vincent's Art,
cat van Gogh, Rijksmuseum Kröller-Müller,
Otterlo 1959, pp XVIII, XXI
EXHIBITION 1956 Munich, 2
EDITORS' COMMENT Very probably made after a
sketch in a model book
PROVENANCE A. Declemy, The Hague [1953];
Otterlo, Rijksmuseum Kröller-Müller, inv
nr 1303-53, cat van Gogh 1970, 1c

IX THISTLE

Black chalk 18 × 14 [7 × 5½]
Signed and annotated in lower right: V. W. van
Gogh 6 October 1863
Zundert 6 October 1863
LITERATURE The Complete Letters of Vincent van
Gogh, London 1958, LVI. J. G. van Gelder,
Vincent's Begin, De Tafelronde [Antwerp], 2, 8-9,
1955, pp 26, 27. J. G. van Gelder, The Beginnings of
Vincent's Art, cat van Gogh, Rijksmuseum Kröller-
Müller, Otterlo 1959, pp XVIII, XX, XXI. Chetham
1960, p 9
PROVENANCE Miss J. van Erkelens, Helvoirt;
Mrs Rijnders-Coolen, Laren; W. Hoffman, Vught;
Sale London [Sotheby] 30 June 1966, 139 [not sold];
V. W. van Gogh, Laren [1966]; Amsterdam, Rijks-
museum Vincent van Gogh [Vincent van Gogh
Foundation]

X A BOUQUET

Watercolour 15.5 × 13.5 [6 × 5¼]
Signed and annotated in lower right: V. van
Gogh jr ft
Zundert 1863
LITERATURE The Complete Letters of Vincent van
Gogh, London 1958, LV. J. G. van Gelder, Vincent's

Begin, De Tafelronde [Antwerp], 2, 8-9, 1955, pp 26-27. J. G. van Gelder, The Beginnings of Vincent's Art, cat van Gogh, Rijksmuseum Kröller-Müller, Otterlo 1959, pp XVIII, XX, XXI. Chetham 1960, p 9
EDITORS' COMMENT Chetham believes that IX and X are both copies after drawings by Vincent's mother
PROVENANCE Miss J. van Erkelens, Helvoirt; Mrs Rijnders-Coolen, Laren; Sale London [Sotheby] 30 June 1966, 138 [not sold]; V.W. van Gogh, Laren [1966]; Amsterdam, Rijksmuseum Vincent van Gogh [Vincent van Gogh Foundation]

XI THE SURROUNDINGS OF CROY CASTLE NEAR AARLE [?]

Black chalk, water-colour 10 × 16 [4 × 6¼]
Signed and annotated in lower right: V.W. ... Gogh 1863
Zundert 1863 [?]
LITERATURE J. G. van Gelder, The Beginnings of Vincent's Art, cat van Gogh, Rijksmuseum Kröller-Müller, Otterlo 1959, pp XVIII, XX, XXI. Chetham 1960, p 9. Probably a copy after Breton or Daubigny
PROVENANCE Mrs Rijnders-Coolen, Laren; Amsterdam, Mrs E. Rijnders-Rehbock

XII BARN AND FARMHOUSE

Pencil 20 × 27 [7¾ × 10¾]
Annotated on verso: 8 Februari 1864 Vincent [handwriting of Rev T. van Gogh]
Zundert 8 February 1864 [Drawn for the birthday of his father]
LITERATURE J. G. van Gelder, The Beginnings of Vincent's Art, cat van Gogh, Rijksmuseum Kröller-Müller, Otterlo 1959, pp XVIII, XIX, XXI
EXHIBITION 1957 Essen, 69
PROVENANCE J.E. Scholte, Lochem; Mrs J.P. Scholte-van Houten, Lochem; Scholte-van Houten collection [1970]

XIII [F 836 recto] A COUNTRY LANE [verso] SKETCH OF A BUILDING AND NOTES [probably not by Van Gogh]

Pen and brown ink, pencil [ordinary drawing-paper] 18.5 × 22.5 [7¼ × 8¾]
The Hague Early 1873
LITERATURE Faille 1928, nr 836: Cuesmes-Brussels. Vanbeselaere 1937, pp 38, 46, 52, 59, 124, 126-7, 407: Early Etten period May 1881. J.G. van Gelder, The Beginnings of Vincent's Art, cat van Gogh, Rijksmuseum Kröller-Müller, Otterlo 1959, pp XVII, XX, XXI: The Hague 1869-73. A. Szymańska 1967, pp 19, 21: The Hague, Spring 1873
EXHIBITIONS 1914-5 Amsterdam, 2; 1945 Amsterdam, no cat nr; 1946 Stockholm etc, 1; 1954-5 Bern, 74; 1964 Zundert, 1
PROVENANCE Mrs J. van Gogh-Bonger, Amsterdam; V.W. van Gogh, Laren; Amsterdam, Rijksmuseum Vincent van Gogh [Vincent van Gogh Foundation, inv nr F 836]

XIV [F 837] THE 'LANGE VIJVERBERG'

Pen and brown ink, pencil [water-colour paper] 22 × 17 [8½ × 6¾]
The Hague Spring 1873
LITERATURE Faille 1928, nr 837: Cuesmes-Brussels. Vanbeselaere 1937, pp 38, 407: Brussels January-April 1881. J. G. van Gelder, The Beginnings of Vincent's Art, cat van Gogh, Rijksmuseum Kröller-Müller, Otterlo 1959, pp XVII, XX, XXI: The Hague 1869-73. A.Szymańska 1967, p 19: The Hague Spring 1873
EXHIBITIONS 1914-5 Amsterdam, 3; 1945 Amsterdam, no cat nr; 1946 Stockholm etc, 2

PROVENANCE Mrs J. van Gogh-Bonger, Amsterdam; V.W. van Gogh, Laren; Amsterdam, Rijksmuseum Vincent van Gogh [Vincent van Gogh Foundation, inv nr F 837]

XV [F 838] THE DITCH

Pen and brown ink, pencil [ordinary drawing-paper with watermark: fragment of J. Whatman] 24.5 × 18.5 [9½ × 7¼]
The Hague [?] Spring 1873
LITERATURE Faille 1928, nr 838: Cuesmes-Brussels. Vanbeselaere 1937, pp 46, 52, 59, 124, 126, 407: Etten May 1881. J.G. van Gelder, The Beginnings of Vincent's Art, cat van Gogh, Rijksmuseum Kröller-Müller, Otterlo 1959, pp XVII, XX, XXI: The Hague 1869-73. A.Szymańska 1967, p 19: Helvoirt May 1873
EXHIBITION 1958-9 San Francisco etc, 87
PROVENANCE Mrs J. van Gogh-Bonger, Amsterdam; V.W. van Gogh, Laren; Amsterdam, Rijksmuseum Vincent van Gogh [Vincent van Gogh Foundation, inv nr F 838]

XIV

XV

XIII recto

XVI

sketchbook I

sketchbook II

sketchbook III

XVII

sketchbook I

sketchbook II

sketchbook III

XVI [F 839] THE CANAL

Pen and brown ink, pencil [ordinary thick drawing-paper] 25 × 25.5 [9¾ × 10]
The Hague [?] Spring 1873
LITERATURE Faille 1928, nr 839: Cuesmes-Brussels. Vanbeselaere 1937, pp 38, 46-7, 52, 59, 60, 124, 126-7, 407: Etten May 1881. J.G. van Gelder, The Beginnings of Vincent's Art, cat van Gogh, Rijksmuseum Kröller-Müller, Otterlo 1959, pp XVII, XX, XXI: The Hague 1869-73; A. Szymańska 1967, p 19: Helvoirt May 1873
EXHIBITIONS 1927-8 Berlin, 2 [repr]; 1928 Vienna, 2; 1954-5 Bern, 75; 1957 Stockholm, 5; 1964 Zundert, 2
PROVENANCE Mrs J. van Gogh-Bonger, Amsterdam; V.W. van Gogh, Laren; Amsterdam, Rijksmuseum Vincent van Gogh [Vincent van Gogh Foundation, inv nr F 839]

XVII [F 835] OLD BRETON WOMAN, ASLEEP IN CHURCH [after F. Rops' 'En attendant la Confession' in the periodical 'Uylenspieghel' March 29, 1857]

Pencil heightened with white chalk [ordinary weave paper] 26.5 × 19.5 [10 × 7½]
Annotated in lower right: d'après F. Rops
Compare sketches in letters 140 and 141
Probably before 1873-4
LITERATURE Vanbeselaere 1937, pp 37, 45, 407: January 1881. Chetham 1960, p 15
EDITORS' COMMENT Charles S. Chetham pointed out that this drawing was made after an illustration by F. Rops in the periodical 'Uylenspieghel'. The date is based on a passage in letter 239 [29 October 1882]: 'I am awfully sorry that I don't have those De Grouxs and Ropses any more. I gave them away in England ...'
PROVENANCE Mrs J. van Gogh-Bonger, Amsterdam; V.W. van Gogh, Laren; Amsterdam, Rijksmuseum Vincent van Gogh [Vincent van Gogh Foundation, inv nr F 835]

ILLUSTRATIONS FROM VINCENT'S SKETCHBOOKS

Sketchbook I, 25 drawings
original size 16.3 × 10.3 [6⁷/₁₆ × 4¹/₁₆]
Sketchbook II, 15 drawings
original size 17.9 × 10 [7¹/₁₆ × 3¹⁵/₁₆]
Sketchbook III, 5 drawings
original size 15.2 × 10 [6 × 3¹⁵/₁₆]
COLLECTION Amsterdam, Rijksmuseum Vincent van Gogh [Vincent van Gogh Foundation]

XVIII [F 905] THE CHURCH OF HELVOIRT

Black chalk 21 × 32 [8¼ × 12½]
Helvoirt June-October 1874
LITERATURE Faille 1928, nr 905: Etten. Vanbeselaere 1937, pp 58, 277, 408: Nuenen October-November 1885
EXHIBITION 1939 Paris
PROVENANCE Miss W. van Gogh, Nuenen; Mrs J. van Gogh-Bonger, Amsterdam; V.W. van Gogh, Amsterdam; A. Alexandre, Paris; O. Wacker Art Gallery, Berlin; J.K. Thannhauser, New York; Sale New York [Parke-Bernet] 12 April 1954, 86; New York, Mr and Mrs Howard Cullman

XIX [F 825] VIEW OF HELVOIRT

Pencil 11 × 19 [4¼ × 7½]
Helvoirt July 1874
LITERATURE Not in Vanbeselaere 1937
PROVENANCE Miss W. van Gogh, Dieren; Present owner unknown

XX 'VILLE D'AVRAY': L'ÉTANG AU
BATELIER [after Corot]

Pencil 4 × 10 [1½ × 4]
Sketch in letter 25
London April 1875
EDITORS' COMMENT Drawing after Corot's
etching 'Ville d'Avray: l'étang au batelier' [Robaut,
nr 3125, Delteil, nr 3]
PROVENANCE Mrs J. van Gogh-Bonger, Amster-
dam; V.W. van Gogh, Laren; Amsterdam, Rijks-
museum Vincent van Gogh [Vincent van Gogh
Foundation]

XXI VICARAGE AND CHURCH AT ETTEN

Pencil 9 × 17.5 [3½ × 7]
Compare XXII
Etten April 1876
LITERATURE Not in Faille 1928 or Vanbeselaere
1937. J.G. van Gelder, The Beginnings of Vincent's
Art, cat van Gogh, Rijksmuseum Kröller-Müller,
Otterlo 1959, pp XV, XXI. A. Szymańska, pp 23, 24,
52: Spring 1878
EXHIBITIONS 1957 Essen, 120; 1962 London, 3
PROVENANCE Mrs S.M. de Jong-van Houten,
Bloemendaal; V.W. van Gogh, Laren; Amsterdam,
Rijksmuseum Vincent van Gogh [Vincent van
Gogh Foundation]

XXII VICARAGE AT ETTEN

Pencil, pen and brown ink 6 × 12 [2¼ × 4¾]
Compare XXI
Etten April 1876
LITERATURE Not in Faille 1928 or Vanbeselaere
1937
EXHIBITION 1957 Essen, 121
PROVENANCE Miss W. van Gogh, Dieren; Mrs
A.C. van Houten-van Gogh, Dieren; Mrs S.M. de
Jong-van Houten, Bloemendaal; Sale Amsterdam
[Brandt] 30 November 1959, 38 [not sold]; Present
owner unknown

XXIII SKETCH OF WESTMINSTER BRIDGE
AND THE HOUSES OF PARLIAMENT [after
De Nittis]

Pen
Sketch in letter 32
Paris 24 July 1875
LETTER 32 [Paris 24 July] 'A few days ago we
received a picture by De Nittis, a view of London on a
rainy day, including Westminster Bridge and the
Houses of Parliament. I used to pass Westminster
Bridge every morning and every evening, and I know
how it looks when the sun sets behind Westminster
Abbey and the Houses of Parliament, and how it
looks early in the morning, and in winter in snow
and fog.'
EDITORS' COMMENT The painting of Giuseppe de
Nittis, The Victoria Embankment, London [panel
7½ × 12½ inches, signed and dated '75] was sold at
Sotheby's 15th April 1970, nr 10 [with color
reproduction] and bought by Acquavella Galleries,
New York
PROVENANCE Mrs J. van Gogh-Bonger, Amster-
dam; V.W. van Gogh, Laren; Amsterdam, Rijksmuseum Vincent van Gogh [Vincent van Gogh
Foundation]

sketchbook III

XVIII

XIX

XX

XXI

XXII

XXIII

XXIV

XXV

XXVI

XXVII

XXVIII

XXIX

XXX

XXXI

XXIV HOUSES AT ISLEWORTH

Pencil 14 × 14.5 [5½ × 5¾]
Sent with letter 70 [not reproduced in the English edition of the letters]
Isleworth July 1876
LETTER 70 [Isleworth 5 July] *'Last week I was at Hampton Court to see the beautiful gardens and long avenues of chestnut and lime trees, where many crows and rooks have their nests,...'*
EXHIBITION 1962 London I, VI
PROVENANCE Mrs J. van Gogh-Bonger, Amsterdam; V. W. van Gogh, Laren; Amsterdam, Rijksmuseum Vincent van Gogh [Vincent van Gogh Foundation]

XXV [F 826] THE CHURCH, AUSTIN FRIARS

Pen 10 × 17 [4 × 6¾]
Annotated by the artist below [translated]: *'This little church is a remarkable remnant of an old Austin Friars foundation dating at least from the year 1354 if not 100 years earlier. Since as long ago as 1550, as a result of a voluntary gift of Edward VI, the Dutch Reformed Parish has held its gatherings here.'*
England April-December 1876
LITERATURE Not in Vanbeselaere 1937. J. G. van Gelder, The Beginnings of Vincent's Art, cat van Gogh, Rijksmuseum Kröller-Müller, Otterlo 1959, p XIX, note I
EXHIBITIONS 1914-5 Amsterdam, 4; 1945 Amsterdam, no cat nr; 1946 Stockholm etc, I
PROVENANCE Mrs J. van Gogh-Bonger, Amsterdam; Mrs A. C. van Houten-van Gogh, Dieren; J. Nieweg, Amersfoort [acquired 1914]; Amersfoort Miss R. Nieweg [1970]

XXVI SQUARE AT RAMSGATE [View from the window of the boarding school]

Pen and pencil 6.5 × 10.5 [2½ × 4¼]
Sent with letter 62
Compare sketch in letter 67
Ramsgate April 1876
LETTER 62 [21 April] *'The house stands in a square ... In the middle of the square is a large lawn, shut off by iron railings and surrounded by lilac bushes; the boys play there during the recreation hour. The house where I stay is in the same square.'*
LITERATURE J.G. van Gelder, De Tafelronde 2, 1955, 8-9, pp 23-24. J. G. van Gelder, The Beginnings of Vincent's Art, in cat van Gogh, Rijksmuseum Kröller-Müller, Otterlo 1959, pp XV-XXI; Vincent van Gogh on England, Amsterdam 1968, p 32, repr actual size
EXHIBITION 1962 London I, IV
PROVENANCE Mrs J. van Gogh-Bonger, Amsterdam; V. W. van Gogh, Laren; Amsterdam, Rijksmuseum Vincent van Gogh [Vincent van Gogh Foundation]

XXVII SQUARE AT RAMSGATE [View from the window of the boarding school]

Pen and pencil 5.5 × 5.5 [2¼ × 2¼]
Sent with letter 67
Compare sketch in letter 62
Ramsgate 31 May 1876
LETTER 67 [Ramsgate 31 May] *'Enclosed is a little drawing of the view from the school window ...'*
LITERATURE Vincent van Gogh on England, Amsterdam 1968, p 32, repr actual size; Tralbaut 1969, pp 48, 49 [with a photograph of the present situation]
EXHIBITIONS 1957 Essen, 86; 1962 London I, V
PROVENANCE Mrs J. van Gogh-Bonger, Amsterdam; V.W. van Gogh, Laren; Amsterdam, Rijksmuseum Vincent van Gogh [Vincent van Gogh Foundation]

XXVIII CHURCHES AT PETERSHAM AND TURNHAM GREEN

Pen, pencil 4 × 10 [1½ × 4]
Sketch in letter 82
Isleworth November 1876
LETTER 82 [Isleworth 25 November] '*Last Sunday... I had been... in Turnham Green, and... then to Petersham... there was a beautiful little wooden church...*'
LITERATURE Vincent van Gogh on England, Amsterdam 1968, p 25, repr; Tralbaut 1969, p 55
EXHIBITION 1962 London I, VII
PROVENANCE Mrs J. van Gogh-Bonger, Amsterdam; V.W. van Gogh, Laren; Amsterdam, Rijksmuseum Vincent van Gogh [Vincent van Gogh Foundation]

XXIX MILLS IN THE NEIGHBOURHOOD OF DORDRECHT

Black chalk
Sent with letter 92
Dordrecht April 1877
LETTER 92 [Dordrecht 16 April] '*This afternoon I took a long walk... along the dike where the mills are that one can see in the distance when one walks near the station.*'
EDITORS' COMMENT The date of the drawing is problematic
PROVENANCE Mrs J. van Gogh-Bonger, Amsterdam; V.W. van Gogh, Laren; Amsterdam, Rijksmuseum Vincent van Gogh [Vincent van Gogh Foundation]

XXX LANDSCAPE WITH BRIDGE

Sketch in letter 121
Amsterdam April 1878
LITERATURE J.G. van Gelder, Tafelronde 2, 1955, 8-9, pp 27-28: before 1880
PROVENANCE Mrs J. van Gogh-Bonger, Amsterdam; V.W. van Gogh, Laren; Amsterdam, Rijksmuseum Vincent van Gogh [Vincent van Gogh Foundation]

XXXI CAFÉ 'AU CHARBONNAGE' ['AT THE COAL MINE'] AT LAEKEN

Pencil, pen 14 × 14 [5½ × 5½]
Annotated on the house: Au charbonnage Charbons Cokes
Sent with letter 126
Laeken November 1878
LETTER 126 [Laeken 15 November] '*I enclose that hasty little sketch, "Au Charbonnage". '... The little drawing "Au Charbonnage" is not particularly remarkable, but I made it because one sees here so many people who work in the coal mines, and they are a distinctive type. This little house stands not far from the road; it is a small inn which adjoins the big coal shed,...*'
LITERATURE M.E. Tralbaut 1969, p 71
EXHIBITION 1962 London I, VIII
PROVENANCE Mrs J. van Gogh-Bonger, Amsterdam; V.W. van Gogh, Laren; Amsterdam, Rijksmuseum Vincent van Gogh [Vincent van Gogh Foundation]

XXXII 'LA MAISON MAGROS'

Charcoal 23 × 29.5 [9 × 11½]
Annotated in lower left: VG
Annotated in lower right: Mon Magros
Cuesmes 1879
LITERATURE V.W. van Gogh, Museumjournaal 5, nr 4, 1959, p 80. M.E. Tralbaut 1969, p 62
EXHIBITIONS 1960 Cuesmes, 9; Paris, 199
PROVENANCE M.G. Delsaut, Cuesmes; S. and C. Delsaut, Cuesmes [1960]; Sale London

XXXII

XXXIII

[Christie's] 14 April 1970, nr 41; Los Angeles, A. Hammer

XXXIII 'LA MAISON DE ZANDMENNIK'

Charcoal 23 × 29.5 [9 × 11½]
Annotated in lower right: V.G.
Cuesmes 1879
LITERATURE V.W. van Gogh, Museumjournaal 5, nr 4, 1959, p 80. M.E. Tralbaut 1969, p 63
EXHIBITIONS 1960 Cuesmes, 8; Paris, 200
PROVENANCE M.G. Delsaut, Cuesmes; S. and C. Delsaut, Cuesmes [1960]; Sale London [Christie's] 14 April 1970, nr 42; Los Angeles, A. Hammer

XXXIV [F 827] A COAL HEAVER
See catalogue F 827 and Juvenilia, note 4

Additional Data

Exhibitions and Provenances

The exhibitions are listed in abbreviated form:
year [this is not repeated when two or more exhibitions from the same years follow one another],
city [followed by 'etc' in the case of traveling exhibitions], and, when more than one exhibition was held in one year in a given city, a numeral to indicate which exhibition is intended. Full references are to be found in the LIST OF EXHIBITIONS. In the PROVENANCES, an R before a date stands for 'reference,' indicating that the work concerned is recorded as having been in the collection mentioned in that year.

ETTEN PERIOD

F 1 [H 2] STILL LIFE WITH CABBAGE
EXHIBITIONS 1903 Rotterdam 1, 11; 1967 Wolfsburg, 1; 1968-9 London, 5
PROVENANCE Oldenzeel Art Gallery, Rotterdam [1903]; J. Willebeek le Mair, Rotterdam [1903]; H. E. d'Audretsch, Amerongen; Amsterdam, Rijksmuseum Vincent van Gogh [Vincent van Gogh Foundation, inv nr F 1]

F 1a [formerly F 1bis, H 1] STILL LIFE WITH BEER MUG AND FRUIT
EXHIBITION 1947 Basle, 1
PROVENANCE D. A. Hoogendijk Art Gallery, Amsterdam; H. Abels Art Gallery, Cologne; Baron E. von der Heydt, Ascona [1947]; Wuppertal, Von der Heydt-Museum der Stadt Wuppertal [bequest Baron Von der Heydt, 1964]

THE HAGUE PERIOD

F 1b LYING COW
EXHIBITIONS 1960 Paris, 2; 1963 Hamburg, 69
PROVENANCE Oldenzeel Art Gallery, Rotterdam; Sale Rotterdam, 30 April 1912, 41; The Hague, A. Brandsma [1963]

F 1c LYING COW
PROVENANCE Ed. van Biema, The Hague [according to him formerly in the collection of C. Mouwen jr, Breda and M. Janssen, Breda]; F. P. Hirschel, Amsterdam; Franz Heinz, Lochham near Munich; Private collection, New York; Sale New York [Parke-Bernet] 11 November 1959, 41; Present owner unknown

F 2 [H 7] BEACH AT SCHEVENINGEN IN CALM WEATHER
EXHIBITIONS 1903 Rotterdam 1, 17; 1905 Amsterdam 1
PROVENANCE C. Mouwen jr, Breda; Oldenzeel Art Gallery, Rotterdam; H. van Kempen, Amsterdam [1903-1929]; Aalst, Netherlands, Mrs H. van Ogtrop-van Kempen [1929, 1965]

F 2a [formerly F 2bis, H 5] THE DUNE
EXHIBITION 1904 Rotterdam, 40
PROVENANCE Oldenzeel Art Gallery, Rotterdam [1904]; H.A. Burgerhout, The Hague [1964]; Sale Amsterdam [Mak van Waay] 27 February 1968, 135; Amsterdam, Private collection

F 3 [H 4] DUNES, WITH FIGURES
EXHIBITIONS 1924 Zurich, 1; 1940 Lucerne, 48
PROVENANCE A. Hahnloser, Winterthur [bought before 1914 from an unknown Dutch miller]; Bern, H. R. Hahnloser [1970]

F 4 [H 8] BEACH AT SCHEVENINGEN IN STORMY WEATHER
EXHIBITIONS 1903 Rotterdam 1, 18; 1904 Rotterdam, 1; 1905 Amsterdam, 1a; 1932 Amsterdam 2, 1; 1953 The Hague, 12; Otterlo, Amsterdam, 6; 1954 Zurich, 1; 1954-55 Bern, 1; 1955 Antwerp 1, 22; 1955-6 Liverpool etc, 1; 1956 Munich, 40; 1957 Essen, 145; 1960 Paris, 1; 1963 Tel Aviv, Haifa, 15
PROVENANCE Oldenzeel Art Gallery, Rotterdam [1903]; J. Ribbius Peletier, Utrecht [1903]; Scheveningen, Miss E. Ribbius Peletier [on loan to Stedelijk Museum, Amsterdam]

F 5 [H 6] FISHERMAN ON THE BEACH
EXHIBITIONS 1903 Rotterdam 1; 1927 Basle etc, 5; 1928 Düsseldorf, 70; Karlsruhe, 5; 1929 Berlin 1, 9; 1930 Amsterdam, 158; 1949-50 New York, Chicago, 1; 1953-4 St Louis etc, 7; 1955 Antwerp 3, 11; 1956 Eindhoven, 14; 1958 Vienna, 36; Tokyo, Kyoto, 34; 1962 Warsaw, 28; 1963 Tel Aviv, Haifa, 28; 1966 Belgrade, 43
PROVENANCE Oldenzeel Art Gallery, Rotterdam [1903]; Sale Rotterdam [Oldenzeel] 10 December 1918, 43; H. P. Bremmer, The Hague [until 1920]; Otterlo, Rijksmuseum Kröller-Müller, inv nr 190-20, cat van Gogh 1970, 98

F 6 [H 3] FISHERMAN'S WIFE ON THE BEACH
EXHIBITIONS 1903 Rotterdam 1; 1927 Basle etc, 6; 1928 Düsseldorf, 72; Karlsruhe, 7; 1929 Berlin 1, 10; Hamburg, 2; 1930 Amsterdam, 156; 1935-6 New York etc, 1; 1952 Milan, 29; 1956 Munich, 42; 1960-1 Montreal etc, 2
PROVENANCE Oldenzeel Art Gallery, Rotterdam [1903]; Sale Rotterdam [Oldenzeel] 10 December 1918, 44; H. P. Bremmer, The Hague [until 1920]; Otterlo, Rijksmuseum Kröller-Müller, inv nr 191-20, cat van Gogh 1970, 97

F 7 [H 11] MENDING THE NETS
EXHIBITION 1957 Essen, 142
PROVENANCE C. Mouwen jr, Breda; Oldenzeel Art Gallery, Rotterdam; G. Ribbius Peletier, Utrecht; Doorn, Mrs L. Schokking-Ribbius Peletier [on loan to Gemeente Museum, The Hague, inv nr 5-x-1961, cat 1962, 131]

F 8 [H 10] GIRL IN WHITE IN THE WOODS
EXHIBITIONS 1927 Basle etc, 36; 1928 Düsseldorf, 101; Karlsruhe, 36; 1929 Berlin 1, 13; Hamburg, 3; 1930 Amsterdam, 157; 1947 Basle, 2; 1947-8 London etc, 1; 1952 Milan, 28; 1953 The Hague, 13; Otterlo, Amsterdam, 4; 1953-4 St Louis etc, 8; 1956 Eindhoven, 10; Munich, 41; 1958 Vienna, 34; Tokyo, Kyoto, 33; 1960-1 Montreal etc, 1; 1962 Warsaw, 27; 1963 Hamburg, 70; Tel Aviv, Haifa, 27; 1966 Belgrade, 42
PROVENANCE L. C. Enthoven, Voorburg; Sale Enthoven, Amsterdam [F. Muller] 18 May 1920, 200; Otterlo, Rijksmuseum Kröller-Müller, inv nr 220-20, cat van Gogh 1970, 96

F 8a [formerly F 8bis, H 12] GIRL IN THE WOODS
PROVENANCE C. Mouwen jr, Breda; Sale Mouwen, Amsterdam [F. Muller] 3 May 1904, 11 [not sold]; Oldenzeel Art Gallery, Rotterdam; Netherlands, Private collection [1967]

F 9 [H 9] POTATO DIGGING
EXHIBITION 1903 Rotterdam 3, 52 [or F 41]
PROVENANCE J. Hidde Nijland, The Hague; Sale Hidde Nijland, The Hague [Pulchri Studio] 5-6 October 1937, 309; Nieuwenhuizen Segaar Art Gallery, The Hague; Miss T. B. van Baaren, Utrecht; Van Wisselingh Art Gallery, Amsterdam; New York, Mr and Mrs Julian J. Raskin [1964]

F 10 [H 16] A WIND-BEATEN TREE
EXHIBITION 1903 Rotterdam 3, 4
PROVENANCE Oldenzeel Art Gallery, Rotterdam; L. C. Enthoven, Voorburg; Sale Enthoven, Amsterdam [F. Muller] 18 May 1920, 201; Buffa Art Gallery, Amsterdam; J. de Vos jr, Bussum; Sale Amsterdam [F. Muller] 26 January 1944, 281; Neupert Art Gallery, Zurich [before 1964]; Present owner unknown

F 11 [H 14] THE SOWER [sketch]
PROVENANCE L. C. Enthoven, Voorburg, Netherlands; Sale Enthoven, Amsterdam [F. Muller] 18 May 1920, 202; J. E. Goldschmidt, Amsterdam; Sale Amsterdam [Mak van Waay] 1 May 1923, 99; E. Alexander, Paris [1923]; Present owner unknown

F 12 [H 13] MAN AT WORK
EXHIBITIONS 1955 New York 2, 1; 1956 Munich, 44 [Drente]; 1965 London, 40 [Drente]
PROVENANCE Oldenzeel Art Gallery, Rotterdam, nr 227 Incomplete reference from Faille ms. that could not be checked; F.W. R. Wentges, Rotterdam [1909-44]; Heirs of F. W. R. Wentges [1944-7]; W. Brinkman, Schipluiden [1947-56]; Mainz en Legat Art Gallery, The Hague; Van Wisselingh Art Gallery, Amsterdam; W. Weinberg, Scarsdale, USA [1955]; Sale Weinberg, London [Sotheby] 10 July 1957, 49; Mr. Wrightsman, Paris; Sale Paris [Rheims] 12 December 1960, addenda H; P. M. Bloch, Paris; Sale P. M. Bloch, Paris [Ader, Galliéra] 12 March 1964, 48; I. Hollick, Fenny Compton, Warwicks, England [1964]; England, Private collection [R 1970]

F 13 [H 18] A COACH STAND
EXHIBITIONS 1924 Zurich, 3; Basle, 7; 1940 Lucerne, 49; 1953 The Hague, 14; Otterlo, Amsterdam, 5
PROVENANCE A. Hahnloser, Winterthur [bought before 1914 from an unknown Dutch miller]; Winterthur, Mrs L. Jäggli-Hahnloser [R 1970]

F 14 [H 19] THE GREEN PARROT
EXHIBITIONS 1904 Rotterdam, 6; 1905 Amsterdam, 1b [as Hague period]; 1905 Amsterdam, 40; 1927-8 Rotterdam, 29; 1956 Amsterdam, 6 [as Hague period]
PROVENANCE Oldenzeel Art Gallery, Rotterdam [R 1904]; Miss G. P. van Stolk, Rotterdam [1904-1956]; Mrs J. van Hoey Smith-van Stolk, Rockanje; Rockanje, J. W. van Hoey Smith [R 1968]

F 15a [formerly F 15bis, H 17] IN THE DUNES
EXHIBITIONS 1904 Rotterdam, 5; 1960 Paris, 4
PROVENANCE Oldenzeel Art Gallery, Rotterdam [1904]; H. Sijthoff, Wassenaar; Mrs A. M. Sijthoff-Burgerhout, Wassenaar [1960]; Sale The Hague [Van Marle en Bignell] 21 May 1963, 32; Private collection, Netherlands; Sale London [Sotheby] 4 December 1968, 18; Brook Street Galleries, London; New York, Hirschl & Adler Galleries Inc [R 1970]

DRENTE PERIOD

F 16 [H 21] OLD FARMS IN LOOSDUINEN AT TWILIGHT
EXHIBITIONS 1904 Rotterdam, 8; 1956 Amsterdam, 9; 1966 Gouda, 13
PROVENANCE H. P. Bremmer, The Hague; Nieuwenhuizen Segaar Art Gallery, The Hague [1955]; L. H. van Baaren,

Utrecht; Utrecht, Museum van Baaren [acquired 1956], inv nr 37

F 17 [H 25] FARM HOUSES
EXHIBITIONS 1905 Amsterdam, 2; 1955 Antwerp 1, 40; 1967 Wolfsburg, 2; 1968-9 London, 18
PROVENANCE Mrs J. van Gogh-Bonger, Amsterdam; V. W. van Gogh, Laren; Amsterdam, Rijksmuseum Vincent van Gogh [Vincent van Gogh Foundation, inv nr F 17]

F 18 [H 22] THE FARM
EXHIBITIONS 1924 Basle, 4; Zurich, 4; 1947 Basle, 3
PROVENANCE C. Mouwen jr, Breda; Sale Mouwen, Amsterdam [F. Muller] 3 May 1904, 3 [not sold]; Oldenzeel Art Gallery, Rotterdam; Mr Neter, Brussels; Zurich, F. Meyer-Fierz [1924, 1947]

F 19 [H 23] TWO WOMEN DIGGING AND A WHEELBARROW
EXHIBITIONS 1903 Rotterdam 1, 13; 1953 The Hague, 15; Otterlo, Amsterdam, 15; 1953-4 St Louis etc, 24; 1955 Antwerp 1, 41; 1965-6 Stockholm, Göteborg, 1
PROVENANCE Mrs J. van Gogh-Bonger, Amsterdam; V. W. van Gogh, Laren; Amsterdam, Rijksmuseum Vincent van Gogh [Vincent van Gogh Foundation, inv nr F 19]

F 20 [H 24] PEASANT BURNING WEEDS
EXHIBITIONS 1905 Amsterdam, 4; 1956 Amsterdam, 10
PROVENANCE C. Mouwen jr, Breda; Sale Mouwen, Amsterdam [F. Muller] 3 May 1904, 12; Herman Gorter, Bussum [1905]; d'Audretsch Art Gallery, The Hague; D. G. van Beuningen, Vierhouten; Goudstikker Art Gallery, Amsterdam; H. E. d'Audretsch, Amerongen [1941]; Almelo, Tj. Bendien [acquired 1941]

F 21 [H 26] THE PEAT BOAT
EXHIBITIONS 1904 Rotterdam, 4; Groningen; 1914 Berlin, 14; 1927-8 Rotterdam, 19; 1956 Amsterdam, 11; 1960 Paris, 5
PROVENANCE Oldenzeel Art Gallery, Rotterdam; J. van Hoey Smith, Rotterdam; Mrs. J. van Hoey Smith-van Stolk, Rockanje [1965]; Rockanje, R. W. van Hoey Smith [1968]

F 22 [H 28] THE HUT
EXHIBITIONS 1905 Amsterdam, 3; 1955 Antwerp 1, 42; 1957 Los Angeles, 7; Marseilles, 5; Stockholm, 99; 1959-60 Utrecht, 1
PROVENANCE Mrs J. van Gogh-Bonger, Amsterdam; V. W. van Gogh, Laren; Amsterdam, Rijksmuseum Vincent van Gogh [Vincent van Gogh Foundation, inv nr F 22]

F 23 [H 27] WOMAN WITH STALKS OF WHEAT
Left out by Faille in his manuscript for the present edition. See REJECTED WORKS

NUENEN PERIOD

F 24 [H 31] WEAVER WITH A VIEW OF THE NUENEN TOWER THROUGH A WINDOW: PART OF THE LOOM, FACING RIGHT
EXHIBITIONS 1904 Rotterdam, 43; 1956 Munich, 76
PROVENANCE Oldenzeel Art Gallery, Rotterdam [1904]; M. Gieseler, The Hague; Sale Gieseler, Amsterdam [Mak van Waay] 27 October 1925, 30 [repr]; Huinck Art Gallery, Utrecht; Th. Snellen, Utrecht; Huinck en Scherjon Art Gallery, Amsterdam; F. Möller Art Gallery, Berlin; Berlin, Theodor Werner [1956]

F 25 [H 29] COMING OUT OF CHURCH IN NUENEN
EXHIBITIONS 1905 Amsterdam, 29; 1957 Essen, 164; 1959-60 Utrecht, 2; 1961-2 Baltimore etc, 1; 1963 Sheffield, 1; Humlebaek, 1; 1964 Washington, New York, 1; 1965 Nuenen, without cat nr; 1967 Wolfsburg, 3; 1968-9 London, 19
PROVENANCE Mrs A. C. van Gogh-Carbentus, Leiden; Mrs A. C. van Houten-van Gogh, Dieren; B. de Jong-van Houten, Haarlem; Mrs S. M. de Jong-van Houten, Haarlem [1957]; V. W. van Gogh, Laren; Amsterdam, Rijksmuseum Vincent van Gogh [Vincent van Gogh Foundation, inv nr F 25]

F 26 [H 30] WEAVER: FIGURE APART
EXHIBITIONS 1924 Basle, 5; Zurich, 5; 1940 Lucerne, 50; 1956 Munich, 76
PROVENANCE L. C. Enthoven, Voorburg, Netherlands; Sale Enthoven, Amsterdam [F. Muller] 18 May 1920, 216; A. Hahnloser, Winterthur; Bern, H. R. Hahnloser

F 27 [H 32] WEAVER: FACING FRONT
EXHIBITIONS 1904 Rotterdam, 32; 1927-8 Rotterdam, 26; 1952 Antwerp, 35
PROVENANCE Oldenzeel Art Gallery, Rotterdam; W. Smith, Rotterdam; A. P. van Hoey Smith, Rotterdam [1927-8]; Rotterdam, Museum Boymans-van Beuningen [acquired 1930; A. P. van Hoey Smith bequest], inv nr 1237, cat 1963, p 48

F 28 [H 39] THE KINGFISHER
EXHIBITIONS 1905 Amsterdam, 35 [as Paris period]; 1954-5 Bern, 2; 1955 Antwerp 1, 53; 1957 Stockholm, 106
PROVENANCE Mrs J. van Gogh-Bonger, Amsterdam; V. W. van Gogh, Laren; Amsterdam, Rijksmuseum Vincent van Gogh [Vincent van Gogh Foundation, inv nr F 28]

F 29 [H 34] WEAVER WITH LOOM AND SPINNING WHEEL
EXHIBITION Probably 1903 Rotterdam 3 [description by A. Plasschaert, Onze Kunst 1903, II, p 174, refers to either F 29 or F 162]
PROVENANCE Mrs C. Dekker-Fortanier, The Hague; Miss Nelly Dekker, The Hague; Mrs C. Dekker-Weinberg, Wassenaar; Unknown Art Gallery, Amsterdam; Boston, Museum of Fine Arts [acquired 1958; Arthur Gordon Tompkins Residuary Fund], acc nr 58.356

F 30 [H 33] THE WEAVER: THE WHOLE LOOM, FACING FRONT
EXHIBITIONS 1903 Rotterdam 3, 56; 1904 Rotterdam, 29; 1927 Basle etc, 64; 1928 Düsseldorf, 130; Karlsruhe, 65; 1929 Berlin 1, 41; Hamburg, 31; 1930 Amsterdam, 178; 1947 Basle, 5; 1947-8 London etc, 2; 1949-50 New York, Chicago, 2; 1953-4 St Louis etc, 26; 1956 Munich, 74; 1958-9 San Francisco etc, 8; 1959 Sao Paulo, 1; 1960-1 Montreal etc, 3; 1962 Warsaw, 43; 1963 Tel Aviv, Haifa, 43; 1966 Belgrade, 44; 1967 Montreal, 44
PROVENANCE Oldenzeel Art Gallery, Rotterdam; L. C. Enthoven, Voorburg, Netherlands; Sale Enthoven, Amsterdam [F. Muller] 18 May 1920, 217; Otterlo, Rijksmuseum Kröller-Müller, inv nr 247-20, cat van Gogh 1970, 166

F 31 [H 38] POLLARD BIRCHES
EXHIBITIONS 1903 Rotterdam 3, 47; 1927-8 Rotterdam, 21
PROVENANCE Oldenzeel Art Gallery, Rotterdam [1903]; J. A. Fruin, Rotterdam [1927-8]; W. Moll, The Hague; W. Brinkman, Schipluiden, Netherlands; Paris, Private collection

F 32 [H 36] WEAVER FACING LEFT STANDING
EXHIBITIONS 1953 Berlin, 2; 1956 Munich, 75
PROVENANCE Mrs G. W. van Dijk-Buysman, Nuenen; Sale Amsterdam [Mak van Waay] 8 January 1952, 196; W. Brinkman, Schipluiden, Netherlands [1953]; Munich, Karin Hielscher Art Gallery [1956, 1970]

F 33 [H 35] WEAVER STANDING: SEEN FROM THE BACK
EXHIBITIONS 1904 Rotterdam, 16; 1927-8 Rotterdam, 27; 1943 New York 2, 1; 1944 Montreal, 113; 1948 New York 2, 64; 1955 New York 2, 2; 1957 Los Angeles, 1; 1965 New York 2, 40
PROVENANCE Oldenzeel Art Gallery, Rotterdam; C. A. P. van Stolk, Rotterdam [1927-8]; Huinck en Scherjon Art Gallery, Amsterdam; M. Kapferer, Paris; Wildenstein Art Gallery, New York; London, Wildenstein Art Gallery [1964]

F 34 [H 37] THE OLD TOWER IN THE CEMETERY AT NUENEN, WITH A PLOWMAN
EXHIBITIONS 1927 Basle etc, 37; 1928 Düsseldorf, 102; Karlsruhe, 37; 1929 Berlin 1, 38; Hamburg, 4; 1930 Amsterdam, 177; 1947 Basle, 4; 1950 's Hertogenbosch, Breda; 1952 Milan, 62; 1956 Munich, 73; 1962 Warsaw, 52; 1963 Tel Aviv, Haifa, 53
PROVENANCE Miss Margot Begemann, Nuenen [who received it from Vincent van Gogh himself]; Mrs Begemann-Elbing, Nuenen; Otterlo, Rijksmuseum Kröller-Müller, inv nr 221-00, cat van Gogh 1970, 192

F 35 [H 40] WEAVER FACING LEFT: WHOLE FIGURE
EXHIBITIONS 1903 Rotterdam 3, 57; 1904 Rotterdam, 39; 1912 Cologne, 4; 1913 The Hague, 8; 1914 Antwerp, 1; 1928 Basle etc, 44; Düsseldorf, 110; Karlsruhe, 45; 1929 Berlin 1, 40; Hamburg, 11; 1930 Amsterdam, 136; 1952 Milan, 47; 1955 Antwerp 3, 13; 1957 Geneva, 348; 1958 Vienna, 56; Tokyo, Kyoto, 70; 1962 Warsaw, 42; 1963 Tel Aviv, Haifa, 42; Hamburg, 71
PROVENANCE Oldenzeel Art Gallery, Rotterdam [1903-4]; Prince of Wagram, Paris [1908]; Druet Art Gallery, Paris [1912]; Otterlo, Rijksmuseum Kröller-Müller, inv nr 228-12, cat van Gogh 1970, 165

F 36 [H 42] THE SPINNER
EXHIBITION 1965 Nuenen, without cat nr
PROVENANCE Mrs J. van Gogh-Bonger, Amsterdam; V. W. van Gogh, Laren; Amsterdam, Rijksmuseum Vincent van Gogh [Vincent van Gogh Foundation, inv nr F 36]

F 37 [H 41] THE WEAVER: INTERIOR WITH THREE WINDOWS
EXHIBITIONS 1903 Rotterdam 1, 24; 1904 Rotterdam, 24; 1927 Basle etc, 50; 1928 Düsseldorf, 116; Karlsruhe, 51; 1929 Berlin 1, 42; Hamburg, 17; 1930 Amsterdam, 185; 1935-6 New York etc, 2; 1945 The Hague, 28; 1946-7 Liège etc, 20; 1947 Paris 1, 20; Geneva, 20; 1950 's Hertogenbosch, Breda; 1953 The Hague, 29; Otterlo, Amsterdam, 16; 1956 Eindhoven, 20; 1958 Vienna, 57; Tokyo, Kyoto, 68; 1960 Brussels, 75
PROVENANCE Oldenzeel Art Gallery, Rotterdam; L. C. Enthoven, Voorburg, Netherlands; Sale Enthoven, Amsterdam [F. Muller] 18 May 1920, 218 [repr]; Otterlo, Rijksmuseum Kröller-Müller, inv nr 234-20, cat van Gogh 1970, nr 164

F 38 [H 44] THE OX CART: RED AND WHITE OX
EXHIBITIONS 1910-1 Rotterdam, 24 [or 25]; 1927 Basle etc, 45; 1928 Düsseldorf, 111; Karlsruhe, 46; 1929 Berlin 1, 46; Hamburg, 12; 1930 Amsterdam, 167; 1935-6 New York etc, 3 [wrongly repr is F 39]; 1946-7 Liège etc, 19; 1947 Paris 1, 19; Basle, 8; Geneva, 19; 1949 Gouda; 1950 's Hertogenbosch, Breda; 1956 Eindhoven, 23; Munich, 77; 1958 Vienna, 58; Tokyo, Kyoto, 69; 1959 Sao Paulo, 2; 1960-1 Montreal etc, 4; 1966 Belgrade, 45
PROVENANCE W. Scherjon, Utrecht [1910?, 1918]; Otterlo, Rijksmuseum Kröller-Müller, inv nr 229-18, cat van Gogh 1970, 182

F 39 [H 43] THE OX CART: SPOTTED BLACK OX
EXHIBITIONS 1903 Rotterdam 1, 3; 1904 Rotterdam, 46; 1910-1 Rotterdam, 24 [or 25]; 1949 Amsterdam 2, 13
PROVENANCE Oldenzeel Art Gallery, Rotterdam [1903-4]; L. C. Enthoven, Voorburg, Netherlands; Sale Enthoven, Amsterdam [F. Muller] 18 May 1920, 219; S. van Deventer, De Steeg, Netherlands; Van Wisselingh Art Gallery, Amsterdam; Katz Art Gallery, Dieren [1950]; USA, F. Julius Fohs [1950]

F 40 [H 47] THE OLD TOWER IN THE FIELDS
EXHIBITIONS 1903 Rotterdam 2; 1905 Rotterdam
PROVENANCE Oldenzeel Art Gallery, Rotterdam [1903-5]; Jan Smit, Alblasserdam, Netherlands [acquired about 1905]; Sale Smit, Amsterdam [Mak van Waay] 10 February 1919, 35; M. Rutgers, The Hague; Sale London [Sotheby] 9 July 1958, 181; W. J. Holliday, Indianapolis; Sale London [Sotheby] 10 December 1969, 34; London, Brook Street Gallery

F 41 [H 46] POTATO PLANTING
EXHIBITIONS 1903 Rotterdam 3, 52 [or F 9]; 1927 Basle etc, 49; 1928 Düsseldorf, 115; Karlsruhe, 50; 1929 Berlin 1, 47; Hamburg, 16; 1930 Amsterdam, 169; 1935-6 New York etc, 4; 1947 Basle, 9; 1949-50 New York, Chicago, 3; 1950-1 Leiden etc, 9; 1952 Milan, 27; 1956 Munich, 78; 1958 Vienna, 59; 1962 Warsaw, 26; 1963 Tel Aviv, Haifa, 44
PROVENANCE Oldenzeel Art Gallery, Rotterdam [1903]; L. C. Enthoven, Voorburg, Netherlands; Sale Enthoven, Amsterdam [F. Muller] 18 May 1920, 204 [repr]; Otterlo, Rijksmuseum Kröller-Müller, inv nr 233-20, cat van Gogh 1970, 94

F 42 [H 48] SHEPHERD: STORM EFFECT
EXHIBITIONS 1903 Rotterdam 3, 45; 1956 Munich, 79; Amsterdam, 15
PROVENANCE C. Mouwen jr, Breda; Sale Mouwen, Amsterdam [F. Muller] 3 May 1904, 4 [repr] [not sold]; Oldenzeel Art Gallery, Rotterdam; G. Ribbius Peletier, Utrecht; Mrs D. van Wely-Ribbius Peletier, The Hague [1955]; Van Wisselingh Art Gallery, Amsterdam [1956]; Sam Salz, New York [1962, loan to Metropolitan Museum, New York]; Martin J. and Sidney A. Zimet collection; Sale Henry Zimet Foundation, London [Sotheby] 23 October 1963, 5 [the cat mentions erroneously an exhib in Amsterdam in 1906]; E. Speelman, London; Sale London [Sotheby] 24 April 1968, 77; Present owner unknown

F 43 [H 45] WOOD GATHERERS IN THE SNOW
EXHIBITIONS 1905 Amsterdam, 4a; 1932 Amsterdam 2, 10; 1938-9 Amsterdam, without cat nr
PROVENANCE C. Mouwen jr, Breda; Sale Mouwen, Amsterdam [F. Muller] 3 May 1904, 7 [repr] [not sold]; Oldenzeel Art Gallery, Rotterdam; G. Ribbius Peletier, Utrecht [1905]; Mrs A. L. Ubbens-Ribbius Peletier, Haren; Doorn, Mrs L. Schokking-Ribbius Peletier [1969]

F 44 [H 49] AUTUMN LANDSCAPE WITH FOUR TREES
EXHIBITIONS 1937 Paris, 27; 1938 Venice, 15; 1953 The Hague, 43; Otterlo, Amsterdam, 30; 1955 Antwerp 1, 46; Amsterdam 1, 19; 1956 Munich, 93; 1957 Essen, 209; 1958 Vienna, 66; Tokyo, Kyoto, 82; 1960-1 Montreal etc, 11; 1963 Tel Aviv, Haifa, 54
PROVENANCE Anton Kerssemakers, Eindhoven [acquired 1885]; H. P. Bremmer, The Hague [since 1917 on loan to Rijksmuseum, Amsterdam, cat 1920 and 1934, nr 984 K]; Otterlo, Rijksmuseum Kröller-Müller, inv nr 1334-56, cat van Gogh 1970, nr 256

F 45 [H 50] LANE OF POPLARS NEAR NUENEN
EXHIBITIONS 1929 London 1, 449; 1935 Budapest; 1937 Paris, 26; 1946-7 Liège etc, 34; 1947 Basle, 10; Paris 1, 34; Geneva, 34; 1949-50 New York, Chicago, 4; 1956 Munich, 80; 1957 Essen, 176; 1962 Warsaw, 90
PROVENANCE Mrs J. van Gogh-Bonger, Amsterdam [until 1903]; Rotterdam, Museum Boymans-van Beuningen [acquired 1903; gift of Friends of the Museum], cat 1963, nr 1239

F 46 [H 53] WATER MILL AT GENNEP: STUDY OF THE WHEELS
EXHIBITIONS 1903 Rotterdam 3, 43; 1904 Rotterdam, 30; 1953 The Hague, 30; Otterlo, Amsterdam, 17
PROVENANCE C. Mouwen jr, Breda; Oldenzeel Art Gallery, Rotterdam; G. Ribbius Peletier, Utrecht; Mrs A. Ubbens-Ribbius Peletier, Haren [1953]; Scheveningen, Miss E. Ribbius Peletier [on loan to Stedelijk Museum, Amsterdam]

F 47 [H 54] WATER MILL AT GENNEP
EXHIBITIONS 1914 Berlin, 16 [repr]; 1935-6 New York etc, 5; 1943 New York 2, 2; 1948 Cleveland, 1
PROVENANCE Théodore Duret, Paris; Paul Cassirer Art Gallery, Berlin; H. Thannhauser Art Gallery, Munich; Otto Nyquist, Oslo; New York, Private collection [R 1970]

F 48 [H 52] WATER MILL AT OPWETTEN
EXHIBITIONS 1904 Rotterdam, 48; 1956 Amsterdam, 16; 1962 Amsterdam, 25
PROVENANCE Oldenzeel Art Gallery, Rotterdam; Tabingh Suermondt, Velp, Netherlands; Mrs J. J. E. IJssel de Schepper-Tabingh Suermondt, Aerdenhout, Netherlands; Sale London [Sotheby] 30 March 1966, 40; London, A. T. Smith

F 48a [formerly F 48bis, H 51] WATER MILL AT KOL, NEAR NUENEN
EXHIBITION 1903 Rotterdam 1, 2
PROVENANCE C. Mouwen jr, Breda; Sale Mouwen, Amsterdam [F. Muller] 3 May 1904, 2 [not sold]; Oldenzeel Art Gallery, Rotterdam; Unger en Van Mens Art Gallery, Rotterdam; Private collection, Netherlands; Sale Amsterdam [Mak van Waay] 25 April 1966, 41; Sale New York [Parke-Bernet] 6 April 1967, 18; New York, Mr and Mrs S. J. Lefrak

F 49 [H 57] STILL LIFE WITH THREE BEER-MUGS
EXHIBITIONS 1905 Amsterdam, 446; 1954-5 Bern, 4; 1955 Antwerp 1, 54
PROVENANCE Mrs. J. van Gogh-Bonger, Amsterdam; V. W. van Gogh, Laren; Amsterdam, Rijksmuseum Vincent van Gogh [Vincent van Gogh Foundation, inv nr F 49]

F 50 [H 58] STILL LIFE WITH FIVE BOTTLES AND CUP
EXHIBITIONS 1927 Basle etc, 48; 1928 Düsseldorf, 114; Karlsruhe, 49; 1929 Berlin 1, 51; Hamburg, 15; 1930 Amsterdam, 166; 1946-7 Liège etc, 22; 1947 Paris 1, 22; Geneva, 22; 1958 Tokyo, Kyoto, 76; 1962 Warsaw, 50; 1963 Tel Aviv, Haifa, 51; 1966 Belgrade, 51
PROVENANCE L. C. Enthoven, Voorburg, Netherlands; Sale Enthoven, Amsterdam [F. Muller] 18 May 1920, 220; Otterlo, Rijksmuseum Kröller-Müller, inv nr 232-20, cat van Gogh 1970, nr 188

F 51 [H 55] STILL LIFE WITH BRASS BOWL
EXHIBITIONS 1905 Amsterdam, 19; Utrecht, 8; 1906 Rotterdam, 7; 1924 Amsterdam, 3; 1928 Berlin, 2; Frankfort, 1; Vienna, 1; 1932 Manchester, 4; 1945 Amsterdam, without cat nr; 1954-5 Bern, 3; 1955 Antwerp 1, 57; 1957 Marseilles, 11; 1959-60 Utrecht, 7; 1961-2 Baltimore etc, 9; 1964 Washington, New York, 6; 1967 Wolfsburg, 14; 1968-9 London, 28
PROVENANCE Mrs J. van Gogh-Bonger, Amsterdam; V. W. van Gogh, Laren; Amsterdam, Rijksmuseum Vincent van Gogh [Vincent van Gogh Foundation, inv nr F 51]

F 52 [H 56] STILL LIFE WITH COFFEE MILL, PIPE CASE AND JUG
EXHIBITIONS 1903 Rotterdam 3, 42; 1927 Basle etc, 55; 1928 Düsseldorf, 121; Karlsruhe, 56; 1929 Berlin 1, 48; Hamburg, 22; 1930 Amsterdam, 164; 1958 Tokyo, Kyoto, 79
PROVENANCE L. C. Enthoven, Voorburg, Netherlands; Sale Enthoven, Amsterdam [F. Muller] 18 May 1920, 221; Otterlo, Rijksmuseum Kröller-Müller, inv nr 239-20, cat van Gogh 1970, nr 187

F 53 [H 65] STILL LIFE WITH CUPS, BOWLS AND THREE BOTTLES
EXHIBITIONS 1905 Amsterdam, 23; 1932 Manchester, 7; 1937 Paris, 51; 1945 Amsterdam, without cat nr; 1946 Stockholm etc, 10; 1951 Lyons etc, 1; 1955 Antwerp 1, 55; Palm Beach etc, 4; 1958-9 San Francisco etc, 1; 1961-2 Baltimore etc, 7; 1963 Humlebaek, 6; 1965 Nuenen without cat nr; Charleroi, Ghent, 4; 1965-6 Stockholm, Göteborg, 2; 1967 Wolfsburg, 11; 1968-9 London, 27
PROVENANCE Mrs J. van Gogh-Bonger, Amsterdam; V. W. van Gogh, Laren; Amsterdam, Rijksmuseum Vincent van Gogh [Vincent van Gogh Foundation, inv nr F 53]

F 54 [H 60] STILL LIFE WITH CLOGS AND POTS
EXHIBITIONS 1903 Rotterdam 3; 1904 Rotterdam, 17; 1956 New York, 15; Amsterdam, 17; 1966 Gouda, 16
PROVENANCE C. Mouwen jr, Breda; Sale Mouwen, Amsterdam [F. Muller] 3 May 1904, 17 [not sold]; Oldenzeel Art Gallery, Rotterdam; H. P. Bremmer, The Hague; Nieuwenhuizen Segaar Art Gallery, The Hague [1955]; Van Wisselingh Art Gallery, Amsterdam [1956]; L. H. van Baaren, Utrecht; Utrecht, Museum van Baaren [acquired 1956], inv nr 63a

F 55 [H 59] STILL LIFE WITH A BOTTLE AND TWO BAGS
EXHIBITIONS 1903 Rotterdam 2; 1903 Rotterdam 3, 27; 1950 The Hague, 33; 1955 Antwerp 3, 7; 1957 Essen, 188; 1960 Paris, 9
PROVENANCE C. Mouwen jr, Breda; Oldenzeel Art Gallery, Rotterdam; H. P. Bremmer, The Hague [until 1956]; The Hague, Heirs of H. P. Bremmer [R 1970]

F 56 [H 61] STILL LIFE WITH FIVE BOTTLES
EXHIBITIONS 1932 Amsterdam 2, 13; 1933 Amsterdam 2, 112; 1950 The Hague, 31; 1953 Berlin, 3; 1954 Dordrecht, 49; 1955 Antwerp 3, 8; 1960 Paris, 8; 1968 The Hague, without cat nr
PROVENANCE H. P. Bremmer, The Hague [until 1956]; The Hague, Heirs of H. P. Bremmer [R 1970]

F 57 [H 62] STILL LIFE WITH POTTERY AND TWO BOTTLES
EXHIBITIONS 1956 Amsterdam, 18; 1957 Milwaukee, 77
PROVENANCE J. J. Biesing Art Gallery, The Hague; H. P. Bremmer, The Hague [about 1910-1956]; Van Wisselingh Art Gallery, Amsterdam; Laing Galleries, Toronto [1957]; London, Arnold Hofland [R 1963]

F 58 [H 63] STILL LIFE WITH POTTERY, BEER GLASS AND BOTTLES
EXHIBITIONS 1903 Rotterdam 1, 8; 1909 Rotterdam, 30; 1932 Amsterdam 2, 12; 1933 Amsterdam 2, 113; 1950 The Hague, 30
PROVENANCE C. Mouwen jr, Breda; H. P. Bremmer, The Hague [1909]; Heirs of H. P. Bremmer, The Hague; D. A. Hoogendijk, Amsterdam [acquired 1957]; USA, Private collection

F 59 [H 68] STILL LIFE WITH TWO JARS AND TWO PUMPKINS
EXHIBITIONS 1903 Rotterdam 3, 23; 1912 Cologne, 3; 1955 New York 2, 3; 1958 Zurich, 234
PROVENANCE Oldenzeel Art Gallery, Rotterdam; H. Tutein Nolthenius, Delft [1912]; d'Audretsch Art Gallery, The Hague [until 1947]; M. Frank, The Hague-New York [1947-1952]; Samuel A. Berger, New York; Walter P. Chrysler jr, New York [1956]; Zurich, Sammlung E. G. Bührle [acquired 1956], cat 1958, nr 234; Private collection [R 1970]

F 60 [H 69] STILL LIFE WITH PAINTBRUSHES IN A POT
EXHIBITIONS 1904 Rotterdam, 28; 1956 Amsterdam, 19
PROVENANCE Oldenzeel Art Gallery, Rotterdam; J. R. Tutein Nolthenius, Amersfoort; H. E. Jaeger, Delft [1956]; Van Wisselingh Art Gallery, Amsterdam; H. J. Vermeulen [1956]; F. A. C. Guépin, London [until 1966]; Present owner unknown

F 61 recto [H 66] STILL LIFE WITH BOX AND OTHER OBJECTS
EXHIBITIONS 1905 Amsterdam, 24; 1924 Amsterdam, 8; 1932 Manchester, 1
PROVENANCE Mrs J. van Gogh-Bonger, Amsterdam; V. W. van Gogh, Laren; Amsterdam, Rijksmuseum Vincent van Gogh [Vincent van Gogh Foundation, inv nr F 61]

F 61 verso [H 410] SELF PORTRAIT WITH STRAW HAT
EXHIBITIONS 1953 The Hague, 60; Otterlo, Amsterdam, 52; 1955 Antwerp 1, 199; 1960 London 4, 9
PROVENANCE Mrs J. van Gogh-Bonger, Amsterdam; V. W. van Gogh, Laren; Amsterdam, Rijksmuseum Vincent van Gogh [Vincent van Gogh Foundation, inv nr F 61]

F 62 [H 70] STILL LIFE WITH STRAW HAT AND PIPE
EXHIBITIONS 1903 Rotterdam 1, 12; 1927 Basle etc, 52; 1928 Düsseldorf, 118; Karlsruhe, 53; 1929 Berlin 1, 50; Hamburg, 19; 1930 Amsterdam, 188; 1935-6 New York etc, 6; 1947 Basle, 62; 1949-50 New York, Chicago, 5; 1952 Milan, 58; 1953 The Hague, 32; Otterlo, Amsterdam, 29; 1953-4 St Louis etc, 32
PROVENANCE L. C. Enthoven, Voorburg, Netherlands; Sale Enthoven, Amsterdam [F. Muller] 18 May 1920, 222 [repr]; Otterlo, Rijksmuseum Kröller-Müller, inv nr 236-20, cat van Gogh 1970, nr 189

F 63 [H 64] STILL LIFE WITH BOTTLE, CLOGS AND POT WITH BRUSHES
EXHIBITIONS 1903 Rotterdam 3, 9; 1913 The Hague, 23; 1914 Antwerp, 4; 1927 Basle etc, 38; 1928 Düsseldorf, 104; Karlsruhe, 39; 1929 Berlin 1, 49; Hamburg, 5; 1930 Amsterdam, 189; 1946-7 Liège etc, 23; 1947 Paris 1, 23; Basle, 12; Geneva, 23; 1947-8 London etc, 4; 1952 Milan, 56; 1956 Eindhoven, 24
PROVENANCE C. Mensink, The Hague; Sale Amsterdam [F. Muller] 12 November 1912, 59; Otterlo, Rijksmuseum Kröller-Müller, inv nr 222-12, cat van Gogh 1970, nr 186

F 64 [H 67] STILL LIFE WITH MANTELPIECE ORNAMENT, COWRIE SHELL, INK BOTTLES AND SMOKING SET
EXHIBITIONS 1904 Rotterdam, 11; 1965 The Hague, 11
PROVENANCE H. P. Bremmer, The Hague; F. Bremmer, The Hague [on loan to the Centraal Museum, Utrecht]; R. van de Maele, Bellegem, Belgium [1966-7]; R. Bouve, Westende, Belgium [1967]; Sale London [Sotheby] 3 July 1968, 47; Present owner unknown

F 65 [H 71] PEASANT WOMAN WITH WHITE CAP: HEAD, THREE QUARTERS LEFT
PROVENANCE E. Blot Art Gallery, Paris; M. Zetlin, Paris [1928 or earlier]; Present owner unknown

F 66 [H 72] STUDY OF HANDS
PROVENANCE H. P. Bremmer, The Hague [until 1956]; The Hague, F. Bremmer [R 1970]

F 67 [H 73] THE GARDEN OF THE VICARAGE AT NUENEN
EXHIBITIONS 1904 Rotterdam, 31; 1953 The Hague, 31; Otterlo, Amsterdam, 18; 1955 Dordrecht, 52; 1960 Paris, 11
PROVENANCE Oldenzeel Art Gallery, Rotterdam; Jan Smit, Kinderdijk, Netherlands [acquired about 1905]; Sale Smit, Amsterdam [Mak van Waay] 10 February 1919, 30 [repr]; L. J. Smit, Kinderdijk; L. C. Smit, Kinderdijk [acquired 1952]; Sale New York [Parke-Bernet] 20 November 1968, 37; Present owner unknown

F 67a THE STATION AT EINDHOVEN
EXHIBITIONS 1957 Essen 183; 1960 Paris, 10
PROVENANCE Anton Kerssemakers, Eindhoven; H. Kerssemakers, Helmond; M. H. Korting, Gilze [1960]; Driel, Netherlands, Mrs I. Hendrikx-Korting [loan since 1964 to Rijksmuseum Kröller-Müller, Otterlo]

F 68 [H 75] PEASANT WOMAN WINDING BOBBINS
EXHIBITIONS 1928 Berlin, 3; 1955 New York 2, 5; 1957 Los Angeles, 2
PROVENANCE G. and L. Bollag Art Gallery, Zurich; Sale Zurich [Bollag] 3 April 1925, 116 [repr]; H. Stahl, Berlin [R 1928]; New York, Wildenstein Art Gallery [acquired 1955; R 1966]

F 69 [H 74] HEAD OF A PEASANT WOMAN: FULL FACE
EXHIBITIONS 1905 Amsterdam, 10; Utrecht, 3; 1906 Rotterdam, 3
PROVENANCE Mrs J. van Gogh-Bonger, Amsterdam; V. W. van Gogh, Laren; Amsterdam, Rijksmuseum Vincent van Gogh [Vincent van Gogh Foundation, inv nr F 69]

F 70 [H 76] HEAD OF A PEASANT WOMAN: RIGHT PROFILE AGAINST A WINDOW
EXHIBITION 1905 Amsterdam, 8
PROVENANCE Mrs J. van Gogh-Bonger, Amsterdam; V. W. van Gogh, Laren; Bergen, D. de Wolff Peereboom [acquired 1943]

F 70a [formerly F 70bis, H 77] STUDY OF A PEASANT WOMAN: FULL FACE, HALF LENGTH AGAINST A WINDOW
EXHIBITION 1965 Nuenen, without cat nr
PROVENANCE Mrs J. van Gogh-Bonger, Amsterdam; V. W. van Gogh, Laren; Amsterdam, Rijksmuseum Vincent van Gogh [Vincent van Gogh Foundation, inv nr F 70a]

F 71 [H 78] PEASANT WOMAN SEWING
EXHIBITIONS 1945 Amsterdam, without cat nr; 1951 Lyons etc, 5; 1954-5 Bern, 5; 1955 Antwerp 1, 49; 1957 Stockholm, 100; 1958-9 San Francisco etc, 6; 1961-2 Baltimore etc, 11; 1965-6 Stockholm, Göteborg, 3; 1967 Wolfsburg, 7; 1968-9 London, 35
PROVENANCE Mrs J. van Gogh-Bonger, Amsterdam; V. W. van Gogh, Laren; Amsterdam, Rijksmuseum Vincent van Gogh [Vincent van Gogh Foundation, inv nr F 71]

F 72 [H 80] PEASANT WOMAN TAKING HER MEAL
EXHIBITIONS 1927 Basle etc, 59; 1928 Düsseldorf, 125; Karlsruhe, 60; 1929 Berlin 1, 53; Hamburg, 26; 1930 Amsterdam, 186; 1949 Gouda; 1950 's Hertogenbosch, Breda; 1956 Munich, 84; 1958 Vienna, 61; Tokyo, Kyoto, 74
PROVENANCE L. C. Enthoven, Voorburg, Netherlands; Sale Enthoven, Amsterdam [F. Muller] 18 May 1920, 228; Otterlo, Rijksmuseum Kröller-Müller, inv nr 242-20, cat van Gogh 1970, nr 177

F 73 [H 79] WOMAN SEATED BEFORE AN OPEN DOOR, PEELING POTATOES
EXHIBITIONS 1904 Rotterdam, 22; 1947 Basle, 16
PROVENANCE C. Mouwen jr, Breda; Sale Amsterdam [F. Muller] 3 May 1904, 18 [not sold]; Oldenzeel Art Gallery, Rotterdam [1905]; H. Doyer, Chailly-Lausanne; Switzerland, Family Doyer [R 1968]

F 74 [H 83] HEAD OF AN OLD PEASANT WOMAN: FULL FACE, WITH DARK CAP
EXHIBITIONS 1927 Basle etc, 47; 1928 Düsseldorf, 113; Karlsruhe, 48; 1929 Berlin 1, 70; Hamburg, 14; 1930 Amsterdam, 159; 1950 's Hertogenbosch, Breda; 1956 Munich, 88; 1959 Aix-en-Provence, 1; 1962 Warsaw, 44; 1963 Tel Aviv, Haifa, 45; 1966 Belgrade, 47
PROVENANCE L. C. Enthoven, Voorburg, Netherlands; Sale Enthoven, Amsterdam [F. Muller] 18 May 1920, 214; Otterlo, Rijksmuseum Kröller-Müller, inv nr 231-20, cat van Gogh 1970, nr 170

F 75 [H 82] HEAD OF AN OLD PEASANT WOMAN: FULL FACE, WITH WHITE CAP
EXHIBITIONS 1928 Berlin, 4; 1947 Basle, 15
PROVENANCE L. C. Enthoven, Voorburg, Netherlands; Sale Enthoven, Amsterdam [F. Muller] 18 May 1920, 224; J. Hageraats Art Gallery, The Hague; E. Baron von der Heydt, Ascona [on loan to Gemeente Museum, The Hague]; Wuppertal, Von der Heydt-Museum der Stadt Wuppertal [bequest of E. Baron von der Heydt, 1964]

F 76 [H 81] STILL LIFE: SATIN FLOWERS AND A BOWL WITH LEAVES AND FLOWERS
EXHIBITIONS 1905 Amsterdam, 17; 1924 Amsterdam, 9; 1926 Dresden, 216; 1954 Zurich, 8; 1955 Antwerp 1, 56; Palm Beach etc, 3; 1955-6 Liverpool etc, 2; 1967 Wolfsburg, 12; 1968-9 London, 36
PROVENANCE Mrs J. van Gogh-Bonger, Amsterdam; V. W. van Gogh, Laren; Amsterdam, Rijksmuseum Vincent van Gogh [Vincent van Gogh Foundation, inv nr F 76]

F 77 recto [H 91] INTERIOR OF A PEASANT'S HOUSE WITH FOUR PERSONS [First study for THE POTATO EATERS]
EXHIBITIONS 1905 Amsterdam, 445; 1945 Amsterdam, without cat nr; 1957 Stockholm, 101; 1962 Recklinghausen, 22C; 1965 Nuenen, without cat nr
PROVENANCE Mrs J. van Gogh-Bonger, Amsterdam; V. W. van Gogh, Laren; Amsterdam, Rijksmuseum Vincent van Gogh [Vincent van Gogh Foundation, inv nr F 77]

F 77 verso [H VI] SELFPORTRAIT: FRONTVIEW
EXHIBITIONS 1937 Paris, 4; 1953 The Hague, 61; Otterlo, Amsterdam, 53; 1954-5 Bern, 32; 1955 Antwerp 1, 197; 1960 London 4, 5
PROVENANCE Mrs J. van Gogh-Bonger, Amsterdam; V. W. van Gogh, Laren; Amsterdam, Rijksmuseum Vincent van Gogh [Vincent van Gogh Foundation, inv nr F 77]

F 77a THE POTATO EATERS
PROVENANCE Unknown art gallery in Paris [1944]; Louis Anfray, Cherbourg [acquired 1944]; Sale Versailles [Blache] 7 June 1966, 26; France, Private collection

F 78 [H 92] THE POTATO EATERS
EXHIBITIONS 1904 Rotterdam, 26; 1912 Cologne, 1; 1913 The Hague, 6; 1925 Potsdam, 37 [repr]; 1927-8 Rotterdam, 28; 1930 Amsterdam, not in cat; 1946-7 Liège etc, 24; 1947 Paris 1, 24; Geneva, 24; Basle, 18
PROVENANCE C. Mouwen jr, Breda; Oldenzeel Art Gallery, Rotterdam [1905]; H. Tutein Nolthenius, Delft [1912, 1927-8]; d'Audretsch Art Gallery, The Hague [1946]; Otterlo, Rijksmuseum Kröller-Müller, inv nr 1145-46, cat van Gogh 1970, nr 167

F 79 [H 90] SUNSET
PROVENANCE Chr. Tetzen-Lund, Copenhagen; Paul Guillaume Art Gallery, Paris; H. Graber, Morcote [on loan to Kunsthaus, Zurich, until 1937]; Rüschlikon, Switzerland, R. Graber [1963]

F 80 [H 86] HEAD OF A PEASANT WOMAN WITH WHITE CAP: FACING RIGHT
EXHIBITIONS 1925 Potsdam, 36; 1943 Zurich, 710; 1947 Basle, 17; 1954 Zurich, not in cat; 1958 Zurich, 235
PROVENANCE Oldenzeel Art Gallery, Rotterdam; W. G. H. van Houweninge, Rotterdam; Sale Rotterdam [Van Marle and De Sille] 21-22 April 1925, 254 [repr]; d'Audretsch Art Gallery, The Hague [1925]; G. Schweitzer, Berlin; Sale Berlin [Cassirer] 20 October 1932, 125; Private collection, France [until 1942]; Zurich, Sammlung E. G. Bührle [acquired 1942], cat 1958, nr 235

F 80a [formerly F 80bis, H 84] HEAD OF A PEASANT WOMAN WITH WHITE CAP: FACING RIGHT
EXHIBITIONS 1955 Antwerp 3, 15; 1957 Stockholm, 102; 1965 Nuenen, without cat nr
PROVENANCE Mrs J. van Gogh-Bonger, Amsterdam; V. W. van Gogh, Laren; Amsterdam, Rijksmuseum Vincent van Gogh [Vincent van Gogh Foundation, inv nr F 80a]

F 81 [H 85] HEAD OF A PEASANT WOMAN WITH A WHITE CAP: FULL FACE
EXHIBITION 1956 Raleigh
PROVENANCE Oldenzeel Art Gallery, Rotterdam; F. W. R. Wentges, The Hague [acquired 1909]; R. W. Wentges, Rotterdam [acquired 1944]; Sale Amsterdam [F. Muller] 14 December 1948, 185; New York, J. K. Thannhauser – Courtesy of Thannhauser Foundation [on loan to Guggenheim Museum, New York]

F 82 [H 1] THE POTATO EATERS
EXHIBITIONS 1892 Amsterdam, 1; 1905 Amsterdam, 26; Utrecht, 12; 1914 Berlin, 9 [repr]; 1915 Amsterdam, 1; 1924 Amsterdam, 2 [repr]; 1930 Amsterdam, 1; 1935-6 New York etc, 9; 1937 Paris, 24; 1938 Amsterdam 2, 16; 1945 Amsterdam, without cat nr; 1946 Stockholm etc, 12; 1946-7 Liège etc, 25; 1947 Geneva, 25; London etc, 6; Paris 1, 25; 1948 Bergen, Oslo, 2; 1949-50 New York, Chicago, 82; 1951 Lyons etc, 9; 1953 The Hague, 34; Otterlo, Amsterdam, 22; 1954 Zurich, 2; 1955 Antwerp 1, 52; Palm Beach etc, 5; 1955-6 Liverpool etc, 4; 1957 Marseilles, 10; 1959-60

Utrecht, 3; 1960-1 Montreal etc, 12; 1961-2 Baltimore etc, 6; 1962 Recklinghausen, 22; 1963 Humlebaek, 3; 1964 Washington, New York, 3; 1965 Charleroi, Ghent, 2; Nuenen, without cat nr; 1965-6 Stockholm, Göteborg, 6; 1967 Wolfsburg, 10; 1968-9 London, 38
PROVENANCE Mrs J. van Gogh-Bonger, Amsterdam; V. W. van Gogh, Laren; Amsterdam, Rijksmuseum Vincent van Gogh [Vincent van Gogh Foundation, inv nr F 82]

F 83 [H 93] COTTAGE AT NIGHTFALL
EXHIBITIONS 1905 Amsterdam, 16; 1924 Amsterdam, 6 [repr]; 1928 Berlin, 5; Frankfurt, 2; Vienna, 2; 1945 Amsterdam, without cat nr; 1946-7 Liège etc, 29; 1947 Paris 1, 29; Geneva, 29; 1954-5 Bern, 6; 1955 Antwerp 1, 43; 1957 Marseilles, 6; 1958-9 San Francisco etc, 9; 1959-60 Utrecht, 5; 1960-1 Montreal etc, 13; 1961-2 Baltimore etc, 2; 1963 Humlebaek, 2; 1964 Washington, New York, 2; 1965 Charleroi-Ghent, 1; Nuenen, without cat nr; 1965-6 Stockholm, Göteborg, 7; 1967 Wolfsburg, 4
PROVENANCE Mrs J. van Gogh-Bonger, Amsterdam; V. W. van Gogh, Laren; Amsterdam, Rijksmuseum Vincent van Gogh [Vincent van Gogh Foundation, inv nr F 83]

F 84 [H 94] THE OLD TOWER
EXHIBITIONS 1905 Amsterdam, 25; Utrecht, 11; 1906 Rotterdam, 10; 1923 Amsterdam 2, 118; 1924 Amsterdam, 5; 1925 The Hague, 43; 1926 Munich, 2074; 1946 Stockholm etc, 13; 1946-7 Liège etc, 28; 1947 Paris 1, 28; Geneva, 28; 1947-8 London etc, 7; 1948 Bergen, Oslo, 3; 1949-50 New York, Chicago, 8; 1951 Lyons etc, 3; 1953-4 St Louis etc, 27; 1954-5 Bern, 7; 1955 Antwerp 1, 44; 1958-9 San Francisco etc, 10; 1960-1 Montreal etc, 14; 1963 Humlebaek 5; 1964 Washington, New York, 5; 1965 Nuenen, without cat nr; 1968-9 London, 41
PROVENANCE Mrs J. van Gogh-Bonger, Amsterdam; V. W. van Gogh, Laren; Amsterdam, Rijksmuseum Vincent van Gogh [Vincent van Gogh Foundation, inv nr F 84]

F 85 [H 100] HEAD OF A PEASANT WOMAN WITH WHITE CAP: FULL FACE
EXHIBITIONS 1927 Basle etc, 42; 1928 Düsseldorf, 108; Karlsruhe, 43; 1929 Berlin 1, 56; Hamburg, 9; 1930 Amsterdam, 182; 1935-6 New York etc, 7; 1945 The Hague, 26; 1952 Milan, 48; 1953-4 St Louis etc, 28; 1956 Eindhoven, 21; Munich, 85; 1957 Essen, 189; 1958 Vienna, 62; Tokyo, Kyoto, 72; 1959 São Paulo, 3
PROVENANCE Albert Aurier, Paris and Châteauroux; Mr Williame, Notary at Châteauroux [1914]; H. P. Bremmer, The Hague [1914-1917]; Otterlo, Rijksmuseum Kröller-Müller, inv nr 226-17, cat van Gogh 1970, nr 168

F 85a HEAD OF A PEASANT WOMAN WITH WHITE CAP: FULL FACE
PROVENANCE Oldenzeel Art Gallery, Rotterdam; H. J. Nieboer, Rotterdam [1905]; Mrs S. de Voogd-Nieboer, Rijswijk; Sale New York [Parke-Bernet] 14 March 1956, 89; Hammer Galleries, New York; Sale London [Sotheby] 6 December 1961, 61; Boston, USA, R. M. Light [1963]

F 86 [H 95] HEAD OF A PEASANT WOMAN: LEFT PROFILE
EXHIBITIONS 1927 Basle etc, 62; 1928 Düsseldorf, 128; Karlsruhe, 63; 1929 Berlin 1, 55; Hamburg, 29; 1930 Amsterdam, 165; 1935-6 New York etc, 8; 1952 Milan, 50; 1956 Munich, 87
PROVENANCE L. C. Enthoven, Voorburg, Netherlands; Sale Enthoven [F. Muller] 18 May 1920, 229; Otterlo, Rijksmuseum Kröller-Müller, inv nr 245-20, cat van Gogh 1970, nr 174

F 87 [H 96] THE COUNTRY CHURCHYARD AT NUENEN IN THE SNOW
EXHIBITIONS 1945 Basle, 1; 1957-8 New York etc, 22; 1958 London 2, 23
PROVENANCE Mrs E. H. du Quesne-van Gogh, Baarn; d'Audretsch Art Gallery, The Hague; Mr Haas, Rotterdam; Sale Amsterdam [F. Muller] 5 April 1921, 32; d'Audretsch Art Gallery, The Hague; Unger and Van Mens Art Gallery, Rotterdam; A. van Hoboken, Ascona; Sale D.W. a.o., Paris [Charpentier] 12 December 1953, 1; Athens, Stavros S. Niarchos, exhib cat 1957, nr 22

F 88 [H 97] THE OLD CHURCH TOWER AT NUENEN
EXHIBITIONS 1947 Basle, 6; 1950 Zurich, p 28; 1957 Essen, 163; 1958 Zurich, 233; 1961 Edinburgh, London, 54
PROVENANCE Oldenzeel Art Gallery, Rotterdam; J. A. Maas Geesteranus, Utrecht; Paul Cassirer Art Gallery, Amsterdam; Fritz Nathan Art Gallery, Zurich; Zurich, Sammlung E. G. Bührle [acquired 1945], cat 1958, nr 233

F 89 [H 103] COTTAGE WITH PEASANT WOMAN DIGGING
EXHIBITIONS 1953 Toronto; 1954 Ottawa, 14
PROVENANCE C. Mouwen jr, Breda; Scholtens Art Gallery, Groningen; F. F. Beukema, Groningen; W. J. Beukema, Groningen; Van Wisselingh Art Gallery, Amsterdam; Winnipeg, John A. MacAulay [R 1963]

F 90 [H 102] COTTAGE AND FIGURE WITH GOAT
EXHIBITION 1931 Frankfurt, 67
PROVENANCE C. Mouwen jr, Breda; Sale Mouwen, Amsterdam [F. Muller] 3 May 1904, 1 [repr] [not sold]; Oldenzeel Art Gallery, Rotterdam; Druet Art Gallery, Paris [since 1906]; Frankfurt, Städelsches Kunstinstitut [acquired 1908, property of the Städelsche Museumverein] inv nr 1436, cat 1924, p 83

F 91 [H 101] THE COTTAGE
EXHIBITIONS 1955 New York 2, 6; 1966 New York 2, 66
PROVENANCE Oldenzeel Art Gallery, Rotterdam; S. van Dantzig, Rotterdam; G. van den Bergh, Amsterdam; H. Tannenbaum Art Gallery, New York; Alfred Schwabacher, New York [1955]; Harrison, New York, Johny Natanson [R 1966]

F 92 [H 98] THE COTTAGE
EXHIBITION 1927 The Hague, 11 [repr]
PROVENANCE Margot Begemann, Nuenen; J. van der Linden sr, Amsterdam [1908]; J. van der Linden, Amsterdam; Sale Amsterdam [F. Muller] 15 December 1925, 270; N. Eisenloeffel Art Gallery, Amsterdam; L. Bignou, Paris; Alex Reid and Lefevre Art Gallery, London; Sir Matthew Smith; Mrs Mary Keene; Sale London [Sotheby] 28 June 1961, 28; Present owner unknown

F 92a THE COTTAGE
EXHIBITION 1953 Berlin, 5
PROVENANCE Miss A. Loudon, The Hague; Sale Amsterdam [Mak van Waay] 23 June 1953, 190; F. de Bry Art Gallery, Rotterdam and W. Brinkman, Schipluiden Netherlands [1953, sold before 1965]; Present owner unknown

F 93 [H 99] THE FARM
EXHIBITIONS 1904 Rotterdam, 9; 1913 Rotterdam, 27; 1956 Amsterdam, 20
PROVENANCE Oldenzeel Art Gallery, Rotterdam; Mr and Mrs A. Plate-Engelbrecht, Rotterdam; Mr and Mrs A. Plate-s'Jacob; Oegstgeest, Mr and Mrs Th. Plate [1967]

F 94 [H 104] PEASANT WOMAN DIGGING: SEEN FROM THE BACK
PROVENANCE Miss M. Haan, Groningen; Mrs E. Brugmans-Beukema, Groningen [until 1944]; Miss R. Smit, Utrecht; W. Neseker Art Gallery, Amsterdam; Stockholm, Private collection [1968]

F 95 [H 105] PEASANT WOMAN DIGGING
EXHIBITIONS 1932 Amsterdam 2, 11; 1956 Amsterdam, 21
PROVENANCE C. Mouwen jr, Breda; Utrecht, G. Ribbius Peletier [until 1969]; Utrecht, Heirs of G. Ribbius Peletier

F 95a PEASANT WOMAN DIGGING
EXHIBITIONS 1957 London, 86; 1959 London, 77
PROVENANCE Mrs J. van Gogh-Bonger, Amsterdam; Oldenzeel Art Gallery, Rotterdam; d'Audretsch Art Gallery, The Hague; H. E. van Gelder, The Hague; Private collection, Germany; Marlborough Fine Art Ltd, London [1957]; Birmingham, Barber Institute [acquired 1961]

F 96 [H 106] TWO PEASANT WOMEN DIGGING, FACING EACH OTHER
PROVENANCE Oldenzeel Art Gallery, Rotterdam [1903]; S. J. R. de Monchy, Rotterdam; Present owner unknown

F 97 [H 108] TWO PEASANT WOMEN DIGGING POTATOES, FACING RIGHT
EXHIBITIONS 1903 Rotterdam 3 [repr in Wereldkroniek November 1903]; 1905 Rotterdam; 1927 Basle etc, 77 [repr]; 1928 Düsseldorf, 103; Karlsruhe, 38; 1929 Berlin 1, 71; Hamburg, 35; 1930 Amsterdam, 173; 1946-7 Liège etc, 32; 1947 Paris 1, 32; Geneva, 32; Basle, 20; 1952 Milan, 52; 1953 The Hague, 37; Otterlo, Amsterdam, 23; 1956 Munich, 89; 1960-1 Montreal etc, 7
PROVENANCE Oldenzeel Art Gallery, Rotterdam; J. Smit, Kinderdijk, Netherlands [1905-1919]; Sale Smit, Amsterdam [Mak van Waay] 10 February 1919, 32 [repr]; Otterlo, Rijksmuseum Kröller-Müller, inv nr 260-19, cat van Gogh 1970, nr 179

F 98 [H 107] PEASANT WOMAN DIGGING POTATOES: LEFT PROFILE
EXHIBITIONS 1903 Rotterdam 1, [30 ?]; 1955 Antwerp 3, 17
PROVENANCE Oldenzeel Art Gallery, Rotterdam; J. Willebeek le Mair, Rotterdam; H. P. van Tuyll van Serooskerken, The Hague; Sale Amsterdam [Mak van Waay] 16 October 1951, 144; R. Leten, Ghent [1955]; Mr le Brun, Brussels; Sale Brussels [Palais des Beaux-Arts] 9-10 December 1958, 174; Antwerp, Koninklijk Museum voor Schone Kunsten, inv nr 2889

F 99 [H 112] STILL LIFE: BASKET WITH APPLES
EXHIBITIONS 1905 Amsterdam, 21; Utrecht, 10; 1906 Rotterdam, 9; 1924 Amsterdam, 7; 1955 Antwerp 3, 19
PROVENANCE Mrs J. van Gogh-Bonger, Amsterdam; V. W. van Gogh, Laren; Amsterdam, Rijksmuseum Vincent van Gogh [Vincent van Gogh Foundation, inv nr F 99]

F 100 [H 110] STILL LIFE: BASKET WITH POTATOES
EXHIBITIONS 1905 Amsterdam, 22; 1954 Zurich, 7; 1954-5 Bern, 8; 1955 Antwerp 1, 58; 1958-9 San Francisco etc, 3; 1960-1 Montreal etc, 16; 1965 Nuenen, without cat nr; 1965-6 Stockholm, Göteborg, 8
PROVENANCE Mrs J. van Gogh-Bonger, Amsterdam; V. W. van Gogh, Laren; Amsterdam, Rijksmuseum Vincent van Gogh [Vincent van Gogh Foundation, inv nr F 100]

F 101 [H 113] STILL LIFE: BASKET WITH APPLES
EXHIBITIONS 1957 Stockholm, 103; 1958-9 San Francisco etc, 2; 1968-9 London, 50
PROVENANCE Mrs J. van Gogh-Bonger, Amsterdam; V. W. van Gogh, Laren; Amsterdam, Rijksmuseum Vincent van Gogh [Vincent van Gogh Foundation, inv nr F 101]

F 102 [H 114] STILL LIFE: CABBAGES, POTATOES AND LEAVES
EXHIBITIONS 1924 Zurich, 6; 1945 Basle, 2; 1953 Brussels, 68; 1954 Eindhoven, 18
PROVENANCE L. C. Enthoven, Voorburg, Netherlands; Sale Enthoven, Amsterdam [F. Muller] 18 May 1920, 232; E. Hahnloser, Zurich [1924]; M. Moos, Geneva; Liège, F. C. Graindorge [R 1954]

F 103 [H 111] STILL LIFE: VEGETABLES AND FRUIT
PROVENANCE Mrs J. van Gogh-Bonger, Amsterdam; V. W. van Gogh, Laren; Amsterdam, Rijksmuseum Vincent van Gogh [Vincent van Gogh Foundation, inv nr F 103]

F 104 [H 109] STILL LIFE: GINGER POT AND APPLES
EXHIBITIONS 1904 Rotterdam, 44; 1956 Amsterdam, 22
PROVENANCE Oldenzeel Art Gallery, Rotterdam; Mrs A. C. Kapteyn-van Heyst, Utrecht; S. Crena de Jongh, Dordrecht [until 1956]; Van Wisselingh Art Gallery, Amsterdam; Laing Galleries, Toronto, Canada [1956]; Toronto, Canada, Private collection [R 1970]

F 104a STILL LIFE: GINGER POT AND ONIONS
EXHIBITION 1958 London 3, 73
PROVENANCE Mrs G. W. van Dyk-Buysman, Nuenen; Mrs T. Kramer-Gardenier, Nuenen; Paris, Private collection; Private collection

F 105 [H 115] STILL LIFE: BOWL WITH PEARS
EXHIBITIONS 1905 Amsterdam, 15; Utrecht, 7; 1932 Amsterdam 2, 15; 1956 Amsterdam, 23; 1966 Gouda, 15
PROVENANCE Mrs J. van Gogh-Bonger, Amsterdam; A. W. den Beer Poortugael, Amersfoort; Huinck en Scherjon Art Gallery, Amsterdam [1955]; L. H. van Baaren, Utrecht; Utrecht, Museum van Baaren, inv nr 35

F 106 [H 116] STILL LIFE: APPLES AND TWO PUMPKINS
EXHIBITIONS 1927 Basle etc, 57; 1928 Düsseldorf, 123; Karlsruhe, 58; 1929 Berlin 1, 73; Hamburg, 24; 1930 Amsterdam, 161; 1935-6 New York etc, 10; 1950 's Hertogenbosch, Breda; 1952 Milan, 57; 1956 Munich, 91; 1958 Vienna, 64; Tokyo, Kyoto, 78; 1962 Warsaw, 49; 1963 Tel Aviv, Haifa, 50; 1966 Belgrade, 46
PROVENANCE L. C. Enthoven, Voorburg, Netherlands; Sale Enthoven, Amsterdam [F. Muller] 18 May 1920, 230; Otterlo, Rijksmuseum Kröller-Müller, inv nr 240-20, cat van Gogh 1970, nr 185

F 107 [H 122] STILL LIFE: TWO BASKETS WITH POTATOES
EXHIBITIONS 1924 Amsterdam, 4; 1937 Paris, 25; 1946-7 Liège etc, 30; 1947 Geneva, 30; Paris 1, 30; 1949-50 New York, Chicago, 9; 1953 The Hague, 39; Otterlo, Amsterdam, 28; 1960 Cuesmes, 4
PROVENANCE Mrs J. van Gogh-Bonger, Amsterdam; V. W. van Gogh, Laren; Amsterdam, Rijksmuseum Vincent van Gogh [Vincent van Gogh Foundation, inv nr F 107]

F 108 [H 124] THREE BIRDS' NESTS
EXHIBITIONS 1927 Basle etc, 66; 1928 Düsseldorf, 132; Karlsruhe, 67; 1929 Berlin 1, 75; Hamburg, 33; 1930 Amsterdam, 160
PROVENANCE L. C. Enthoven, Voorburg, Netherlands; Sale Enthoven, Amsterdam [F. Muller] 18 May 1920, 231; Otterlo, Rijksmuseum Kröller-Müller, inv nr 249-20, cat van Gogh 1970, nr 184

F 109 recto [H 125] TWO BIRDS' NESTS
EXHIBITIONS 1905 Amsterdam, 18; 1906 Rotterdam, 6
PROVENANCE Mrs J. van Gogh-Bonger, Amsterdam; V. W. van Gogh, Laren; Amsterdam, Rijksmuseum Vincent van Gogh [Vincent van Gogh Foundation, inv nr F 109]

F 109 verso [H 411] SELFPORTRAIT: FULL FACE
EXHIBITIONS 1905 Amsterdam, 18; 1937 Paris, 3; 1945 Amsterdam, without cat nr; 1953 The Hague, 62; Otterlo, Amsterdam, 54; 1954 Zurich, 25; 1955 Antwerp 1, 200; 1960 London 4, 10
PROVENANCE Mrs J. van Gogh-Bonger, Amsterdam; V. W. van Gogh, Laren; Amsterdam, Rijksmuseum Vincent van Gogh [Vincent van Gogh Foundation, inv nr F 109]

F 110 [H 128] THREE BIRDS' NESTS WITH TREE TRUNK AND LEAVES
EXHIBITIONS 1903 Rotterdam 3, 38; 1904 Rotterdam, 35; 1913 Rotterdam, 26; 1925 Potsdam, 35; 1947 Basle, 21; 1956 Amsterdam, 26; 1957 Essen, 110; 1960 Paris, 18
PROVENANCE C. Mouwen jr, Breda; Sale Mouwen,

Amsterdam [F. Muller] 3 May 1904, 16 [not sold]; Oldenzeel Art Gallery, Rotterdam; M. Gieseler, The Hague; Sale Gieseler, Amsterdam [Mak van Waay] 27 October 1925, 31 [repr]; Goudstikker Art Gallery, Amsterdam; J. M. P. Glerum, Amsterdam; J. E. van der Meulen, Wapenveld, Netherlands; The Hague, Wibbina Foundation [loan to Gemeente Museum, The Hague, inv nr 69-x-1947, cat 1962, nr 133]

F 111 [H 127] FOUR BIRDS' NESTS AGAINST A LIGHT BACKGROUND
EXHIBITIONS 1920 New York, 67; 1924 Amsterdam, 10; 1926 Munich, 2088; 1954 Zurich, 4; 1954-5 Bern, 10; 1955 Antwerp 1, 59; 1955-6 Liverpool etc, 7; 1961-2 Baltimore etc, 10; 1965 Nuenen, without cat nr; 1968-9 London, 51
PROVENANCE Mrs J. van Gogh-Bonger, Amsterdam; V. W. van Gogh, Laren; Amsterdam, Rijksmuseum Vincent van Gogh [Vincent van Gogh Foundation, inv nr F 111]

F 112 [H 126] THREE BIRDS' NESTS
EXHIBITIONS 1927 Basle etc, 65; 1928 Düsseldorf, 131; Karlsruhe, 66; 1929 Berlin 1, 74; Hamburg, 32; 1930 Amsterdam, 162; 1935-6 New York etc, 11; 1949 Gouda; 1950 's Hertogenbosch, Breda; 1952 Milan, 55; 1953 The Hague, 38; Otterlo, Amsterdam, 27; 1956 Munich, 90; 1958 Tokyo, Kyoto, 77; 1960 Montreal etc, 8; 1962 Warsaw, 48; 1963 Tel Aviv, Haifa, 49
PROVENANCE Otterlo, Rijksmuseum Kröller-Müller, inv nr 248-00, cat van Gogh 1970, nr 183

F 113 [H 117] VIEW IN AMSTERDAM FROM CENTRAL STATION
EXHIBITIONS 1904 Rotterdam, 12 [Central Station]; 1905 Amsterdam, 13; Utrecht, 5; 1906 Rotterdam, 1; 1966 Laren, 87
PROVENANCE Mrs J. van Gogh-Bonger, Amsterdam; V. W. van Gogh, Laren; W. J. R. Dreesmann, Amsterdam, cat 1951, vol 3, pp 677, 762; Sale Amsterdam [F. Muller] 22 March 1960, 75; P. de Boer, Amsterdam, P. and N. de Boer Foundation

F 114 [H 129] LANDING STAGE AT AMSTERDAM
EXHIBITIONS 1904 Rotterdam, 12; 1924 Zurich, 11; 1938 Paris 1, 121a; 1940 Lucerne, 52
PROVENANCE A. Hahnloser, Winterthur [bought before 1914]; Bern, H. R. Hahnloser [R 1970]

F 115 [H 123] STILL LIFE: BASKET WITH APPLES
EXHIBITIONS 1947 Basle, 22; 1960 Paris, 17
PROVENANCE C. M. van Gogh Art Gallery, Amsterdam; D. Komter Art Gallery, Amsterdam; H. P. Bremmer, The Hague; The Hague, Heirs of H. P. Bremmer [loan since 1929 originally from H. P. Bremmer, after his death from his heirs to the Gemeente Museum, The Hague, inv nr 55-x-1956, cat 1962, nr 134]

F 116 [H 119] STILL LIFE: BASKET WITH POTATOES
EXHIBITIONS 1905 Amsterdam, 20; Utrecht, 9; 1906 Rotterdam, 8; 1914 Berlin, 5; 1932 Manchester, 5; 1943 New York 2, 3; 1944 Montreal, 115; 1955 Antwerp 3, 18
PROVENANCE Mrs J. van Gogh-Bonger, Amsterdam; V. W. van Gogh, Laren; Amsterdam, Rijksmuseum Vincent van Gogh [Vincent van Gogh Foundation, inv nr F 116]

F 117 [H 121] STILL LIFE WITH OPEN BIBLE, EXTINGUISHED CANDLE AND ZOLA'S JOIE DE VIVRE
EXHIBITIONS 1905 Amsterdam, 14; Utrecht, 6; 1920 New York, 36 [repr]; 1924 Basle, 2; Zurich, 10; Stuttgart, 3; 1925 Paris 1, 9; 1926 London 3, 35; The Hague, 18; 1928 Munich, 1; Berlin, 6; Frankfort, 3; Vienna, 3; 1946 Stockholm etc, 17; 1946-7 Liège etc, 31; 1947 Paris 1, 31; Geneva, 31; 1947-8 London etc, 9; 1948 Bergen, Oslo, 4; 1949-50 New York, Chicago, 10; 1951 Lyons etc, 4; 1953 The Hague, 40; Otterlo, Amsterdam, 26; 1953-4 St Louis etc, 33; 1954 Zurich, 3; 1954-5 Bern, 9; 1955 New York 2, 7; 1955-6 Liverpool etc, 6; 1960-1 Montreal etc, 17; 1963 Humlebaek, 8; 1964 Washington, New York, 3; 1965 Charleroi, Ghent, 5; 1965-6 Stockholm, Göteborg, 9; 1967 Wolfsburg, 13; 1968-9 London, 53
PROVENANCE Mrs J. van Gogh-Bonger, Amsterdam; V. W. van Gogh, Laren; Amsterdam, Rijksmuseum Vincent van Gogh [Vincent van Gogh Foundation; inv nr F 117]

F 118 [H 120] STILL LIFE: EARTHEN BOWL WITH POTATOES
EXHIBITIONS 1902 Paris; 1956 Amsterdam, 25
PROVENANCE Mrs J. van Gogh-Bonger, Amsterdam [1902]; Miss A. Haan, Groningen [about 1910]; Groningen, Mrs E. Brugmans-Beukema [R 1970]

F 119 [H 118] AUTUMN LANDSCAPE
EXHIBITIONS 1904 Rotterdam, 3; 1956 Amsterdam, 24; 1962 Amsterdam, 26
PROVENANCE Tabingh Suermondt, Velp, Netherlands; Van Wisselingh Art Gallery, Amsterdam; Mrs J. J. E. Yssel de Schepper-Tabingh Suermondt, Aerdenhout, Netherlands; Sale London [Sotheby] 30 March 1966, 41; England, Garman-Ryan collection [R 1970]

F 120 [H 134] LANE IN AUTUMN
EXHIBITIONS 1924 Basle, 6; Zurich, 7; 1940 Lucerne, 51
PROVENANCE A. Hahnloser, Winterthur [bought before 1914]; Winterthur, Mrs L. Jäggli-Hahnloser [R 1970]

F 121 [H 130] THE CLOSE OF DAY IN AUTUMN
EXHIBITION 1904 Groningen
PROVENANCE C. Mouwen jr, Breda; Sale Mouwen, Amsterdam [F. Muller] 3 May 1904, 14 [repr] [not sold]; Oldenzeel Art Gallery, Rotterdam; G. Ribbius Peletier, Utrecht; Mrs A. L. Ubbens-Ribbius Peletier, Groningen; Utrecht, Centraal Museum [acquired 1963; gift of the heirs of Mrs A. L. Ubbens-Ribbius Peletier]

F 122 [H 132] AUTUMN
EXHIBITIONS 1904 Rotterdam, 21; 1927-8 Rotterdam, 23 [repr]; 1952 Milan, 59; 1953 The Hague, 41; 1956 Munich, 92; Amsterdam, 27; 1960 Paris, 19; 1961 Wolfsburg, 70
PROVENANCE Oldenzeel Art Gallery, Rotterdam; J. G. L. Nolst Trénité, Rotterdam [acquired 1904, 1927-8]; W. Nolst Trénité, Rotterdam [1952, 1960]; Rotterdam, Heirs of W. Nolst Trénité [R 1970]

F 123 [H 133] AUTUMN LANE AT SUNSET
EXHIBITIONS 1927 Basle etc, 63; 1928 Düsseldorf, 129; Karlsruhe, 64; 1929 Berlin 1, 76; Hamburg 30; 1930 Amsterdam, 181; 1950 's Hertogenbosch, Breda; 1952 Milan, 61; 1956 Eindhoven, 25; 1958 Tokyo, Kyoto, 81; Vienna, 65; 1960-1 Montreal etc, 10; 1962 Warsaw, 51; 1963 Tel Aviv, Haifa, 52; 1966 Belgrade, 52
PROVENANCE L. C. Enthoven, Voorburg, Netherlands; Sale Enthoven, Amsterdam [F. Muller] 18 May 1920, 211; Otterlo, Rijksmuseum Kröller-Müller, inv nr 246-20, cat van Gogh 1970, 191

F 124 [H 131] THE POND IN THE VICARAGE GARDEN AT NUENEN
EXHIBITION 1927-8 Rotterdam, 24
PROVENANCE Mrs C. Smith-van Stolk, Rotterdam; Rotterdam, A. P. van Hoey Smith [the painting was destroyed in the battle of Arnhem, 1944]

F 125 [H 135] WATER MILL AT GENNEP
EXHIBITIONS 1903 Rotterdam 3, 48; 1904 Rotterdam, 45; 1927-8 Rotterdam, 18
PROVENANCE C. Mouwen jr, Breda; Sale Mouwen, Amsterdam [F. Muller] 3 May 1904, 5 [repr] [not sold]; Oldenzeel Art Gallery, Rotterdam; Rotterdam, Museum Boymans [loan from 'Mr x' since December 1904, cat 1905, nr 367]; Sale Rotterdam [Oldenzeel] 10 December 1918, 42 [repr]; F. J. P. van der Eerden Art Gallery, Rotterdam; C. Staib, Rotterdam [1927-8]; Regnault jr, Laren; E. Regnault, Laren [until 1947]; Van Wisselingh Art Gallery, Amsterdam; Private collection [acquired 1947]

F 126 [H 150] PEASANT WOMAN SEATED
PROVENANCE E. Blot Art Gallery, Paris; A. Loewy, Paris [1928]; Present owner unknown

F 126a [formerly F 126bis, H 149] PEASANT WOMAN SEWING
EXHIBITION 1961 Wolfsburg, 69
PROVENANCE Charpentier Art Gallery, Paris; Hans Bammann Art Gallery, Düsseldorf; Thannhauser Art Gallery, Berlin; W. Grosshennig Art Gallery, Düsseldorf [1953]; Schweinfurt, Germany, Georg Schäfer [R 1970]
EDITORS' COMMENT The unknown Russian collector mentioned as first owner in earlier editions acted in fact for the Galery Charpentier, so that Faille changed the provenance accordingly

F 127 [H 144] PEASANT WOMAN: HALF FIGURE
EXHIBITIONS 1921 Berlin; 1928 Berlin, 7
PROVENANCE Bernheim jeune Art Gallery, Paris; Paul Cassirer Art Gallery, Berlin; H. Freudenberg, Berlin-Nikolassee [1928]; Eugène Bottenwieser, London; Roland, Browse and Delbanco Art Gallery, London; London, Leonard Slotover

F 128 [H 148] PEASANT WOMAN STANDING INDOORS
EXHIBITION 1904 Rotterdam, 27
PROVENANCE Oldenzeel Art Gallery, Rotterdam [1905]; H. Doyer, Chailly-Lausanne; d'Audretsch Art Gallery, The Hague; Prince Paul, Belgrade; Belgrade, Narodni Muzej

F 129 TWO PEASANT WOMEN DIGGING POTATOES, FACING RIGHT
This is the same painting as F 97

F 129a [formerly F 129bis, H 192] POTATO PLANTING: A MAN AND A WOMAN
EXHIBITIONS 1943 Zurich, 719; 1947 Basle, 19; 1950 Zurich, p 28
PROVENANCE Charpentier Art Gallery, Paris; Hans Bamman Art Gallery, Düsseldorf; J. K. Thannhauser Art Gallery, Berlin; Zurich, Kunsthaus [acquired 1927], inv nr 1860
EDITORS' COMMENT see under F 126a

F 130 [H 137] HEAD OF A PEASANT WOMAN WITH WHITE CAP: FRONT VIEW
EXHIBITIONS 1928 Berlin, 8; Frankfurt, 4; Vienna, 4; 1932 Manchester, 3; 1948 Bergen, Oslo, 6; 1955 Antwerp 3, 16; 1961-2 Baltimore etc, 4; 1963 Sheffield, 2; Humlebaek, 4; 1964 Washington, New York, 4; 1965 Charleroi, Ghent, 5; Nuenen, without cat nr; 1965-6 Stockholm, Göteborg, 5; 1967 Wolfsburg, 9; 1968-9 London, 30
PROVENANCE Mrs J. van Gogh-Bonger, Amsterdam; V. W. van Gogh, Laren; Amsterdam, Rijksmuseum Vincent van Gogh [Vincent van Gogh Foundation, inv nr F 130]

F 131 [H 162] HEAD OF A PEASANT WOMAN: LEFT PROFILE
PROVENANCE C. Mouwen jr, Breda; Oldenzeel Art Gallery, Rotterdam; S. R. Steinmetz, Amsterdam; The Hague, R. Th. Steinmetz [since 1963 on loan to Gemeente Museum, The Hague, inv nr 53-x-1963]

F 132 [H 136] HEAD OF A PEASANT WOMAN: LEFT PROFILE
EXHIBITIONS 1908 Rotterdam, 68; 1956 Amsterdam, 28
PROVENANCE Oldenzeel Art Gallery, Rotterdam; H. Tutein Nolthenius, Delft; Mrs Müller, The Hague; Walrecht Art Gallery, The Hague; E. M. Brändlin, Naarden [until 1961]; B. de Bruin; Sale London [Christie] 6-10 December 1968, 52; Present owner unknown

F 133 [H 160] HEAD OF A PEASANT WOMAN: RIGHT PROFILE
EXHIBITIONS 1903 Rotterdam 3, [14 ?]; 1904 Rotterdam, 7; 1927-8 Rotterdam, 25
PROVENANCE Oldenzeel Art Gallery, Rotterdam; Miss G. P. van Stolk, Rotterdam [1927-8]; The Hague, Nieuwenhuizen Segaar Art Gallery [acquired 1946, R 1970]

F 134 [H 143] HEAD OF A PEASANT WOMAN: HALF PROFILE TO THE LEFT
EXHIBITION 1904 Rotterdam, 25
PROVENANCE Oldenzeel Art Gallery, Rotterdam; F. W. R. Wentges, The Hague [acquired 1909]; Sale Amsterdam [F. Muller] 14 December 1948, 184; J. K. Thannhauser Art Gallery, New York; Paris, Musée National du Louvre, inv nr RF 1954-20, cat Impressionistes 1959, nr 142

F 135 [H 142] HEAD OF A PEASANT WOMAN: RIGHT PROFILE
EXHIBITION 1957 Milwaukee, 75
PROVENANCE Oldenzeel Art Gallery, Rotterdam; F. W. R. Wentges, The Hague [acquired 1909]; W. Brinkman, Schipluiden, Netherlands; Mr and Mrs John J. Emery, Cincinnati, USA [1957]; Cincinnati, The Cincinnati Art Museum [gift of Mr and Mrs John J. Emery], inv nr 1962-15

F 136 [H 141] HEAD OF A PEASANT WOMAN: RIGHT PROFILE
PROVENANCE Oldenzeel Art Gallery, Rotterdam; F. W. R. Wentges, The Hague [1909-after 1945]; Paris, Dufresne Art Gallery

F 136a [formerly F 136bis, H 170] HEAD OF A PEASANT WOMAN WITH DARK CAP: FULL FACE
EXHIBITION 1904 Rotterdam, 15
PROVENANCE C. Mouwen jr, Breda; Oldenzeel Art Gallery, Rotterdam; T. G. M. van Hettinga Tromp, The Hague; Mrs H. T. Feldmann-van Hettinga Tromp, Epse [acquired 1962]; Amsterdam, Private collection

F 137 [H 157] BUST-LENGTH STUDY OF A PEASANT WOMAN: FULL FACE, LIGHT BACKGROUND
EXHIBITION 1946 Stockholm etc, 11
PROVENANCE Mrs E. A. Redelé-van der Hoeven, Laren; F. de Jonge; Sale Amsterdam [Mak van Waay] 11 May 1926, 43; d'Audretsch Art Gallery, The Hague; Valentin Art Gallery, Munich; Stockholm, Mrs H. Nordin [1941]

F 138 [H 158] HEAD OF A PEASANT WOMAN: FULL FACE, LIGHT BACKGROUND
EXHIBITION 1943 New York 2, 4
PROVENANCE L. C. Enthoven, Voorburg, Netherlands; Sale Amsterdam [F. Muller] 18 May 1920, 215; Huinck Art Gallery, Utrecht; Thannhauser Art Gallery, Berlin; P. Schmolka, Prague, New York [1943]; New York, Koetser Art Gallery [R 1947]

F 139 [H 172] PEASANT WOMAN RAKING
EXHIBITION 1930 Amsterdam, 2
PROVENANCE L. C. Enthoven, Voorburg, Netherlands; Sale Amsterdam [F. Muller] 18 May 1920, 209; Huinck Art Gallery, Utrecht; H. Cleyndert Azn, The Hague [1930]; Private collection, France; Sale New York [Parke-Bernet] 9 March 1955, 90; Private collection, Westchester; Sale R. Coe and other owners, New York [Parke-Bernet] 14 January 1959, 72; Schoneman Galleries, New York; New York, Mr and Mrs P. Schweitzer [1963]

F 140 [H 138] PEASANT WOMAN WITH A WHITE CAP: LEFT THREE-QUARTER VIEW
EXHIBITIONS 1905 Amsterdam, 7; Utrecht, 2; 1906

Rotterdam, 2; 1908 Paris 1, 2; 1923 London, 15; 1954 Edinburgh
PROVENANCE Mrs J. van Gogh-Bonger, Amsterdam [until 1923]; Mrs Flemming, London [1923-1951]; Alex Reid and Lefevre Art Gallery, London [1951]; Mr and Mrs A. Maitland, Scotland [acquired 1951]; Edinburgh, National Gallery of Scotland [Maitland gift 1961], reg nr 2216

F 141 [H 139] HEAD OF A PEASANT WOMAN WITH A WHITE CAP: LEFT THREE-QUARTER VIEW
PROVENANCE H. P. Bremmer, The Hague [Amsterdam, Rijksmuseum, on loan since 1917, cat 1920 and 1934, nr 984h]; Heirs of H. P. Bremmer, The Hague; Van Wisselingh Art Gallery, Amsterdam [acquired February 1959]; Winnipeg, Canada, John A. MacAulay [1964]

F 142 [H 190] PEASANT WOMAN DIGGING IN FRONT OF HER COTTAGE
PROVENANCE C. Mouwen jr, Breda; Sale Amsterdam [F. Muller] 3 May 1904, 13 [repr]; Miss Cosman, The Hague [1935]; Van Wisselingh Art Gallery, Amsterdam; S. H. Southam, Ottawa [1935]; E. and A. Silberman Art Gallery, New York; John J. Ireland, Chicago [1964]; Chicago, The Art Institute of Chicago [acquired 1968; bequest of John J. Ireland], inv nr 1968.92

F 143 [H 151] PEASANT WOMAN SEATED WITH ARMS CROSSED
PROVENANCE Mr Bernard, Paris; Druet Art Gallery, Paris [1906]; H. Fenz, Bern [1912]; P. Linder, Basle [1928 or earlier]; Basle, Max Wirth

F 144 [H 154] HEAD OF A PEASANT WOMAN: RIGHT PROFILE
EXHIBITIONS 1904 Rotterdam, 18; 1960 Montreal, 153
PROVENANCE C. Mouwen jr, Breda; Oldenzeel Art Gallery, Rotterdam; G. Ribbius Peletier, Utrecht; Mrs L. Schokking-Ribbius Peletier, Doorn; Van Wisselingh Art Gallery, Amsterdam; Montreal, Miss Olive Hosmer [R 1960; until 1962]

F 144a [formerly F 144bis, H 153] PEASANT WOMAN SEATED: RIGHT PROFILE
EXHIBITION 1904 Rotterdam, 14
PROVENANCE C. Mouwen jr, Breda; Sale Amsterdam [F. Muller] 3 May 1904, 15 [not sold]; Oldenzeel Art Gallery, Rotterdam; W. C. H. Bolleurs, Rotterdam; H. Nijgh, Rotterdam [before 1933; not in the cat of this collection, Rotterdam 1933]; E. van den Bosch, Antwerp; Sale E. van den Bosch, Antwerp [Breckpot] 21 December 1936, 165; C. van den Bosch, Antwerp; The Hague, Dienst voor 's Rijks Verspreide Kunstvoorwerpen

F 145 [H 155] PEASANT WOMAN PEELING POTATOES
PROVENANCE Oldenzeel Art Gallery, Rotterdam; J. van Hoey Smith, Rotterdam [1955]; Van Wisselingh Art Gallery, Amsterdam; A. S. Cooper, Winnipeg, Canada [1955]; Mrs E. S. Cooper, Winnipeg; Sale London [Christie] 9 July 1965, 39; Objets d'art international établissement, Vaduz, Lichtenstein; London, Jacques O'Hana Ltd Collection [R 1970]

F 146 [H 145] HEAD OF AN OLD PEASANT WOMAN WITH WHITE CAP: FULL FACE
EXHIBITION 1903 Rotterdam 1, [?]
PROVENANCE C. Mouwen jr, Breda; Oldenzeel Art Gallery, Rotterdam; H. van Kempen, Amsterdam; Aalst, Netherlands, Mrs H. van Ogtrop-van Kempen [acquired 1929, R 1966]

F 146a [formerly F 146bis, H 146] HEAD OF A PEASANT WOMAN WITH WHITE CAP: FULL FACE
PROVENANCE Charpentier Art Gallery, Paris; Hans Bammann Art Gallery, Düsseldorf; J. K. Thannhauser Art Gallery, Berlin; Thannhauser Art Gallery, New York; Prague – New York, Paul Schmolka
EDITORS' COMMENT see under F 126a

F 147 [H 171] PEASANT WOMAN DIGGING POTATOES
EXHIBITION 1904, Rotterdam, 23
PROVENANCE Oldenzeel Art Gallery, Rotterdam; Jan Smit, Alblasserdam, Netherlands; Sale Amsterdam [Mak van Waay] 10 February 1919, 33; John Enthoven, Voorburg, Netherlands; J. Enthoven, Woubrugge, Netherlands; W. Brinkman, Schipluiden, Netherlands [1952]; The Netherlands, Private collection [R 1969]

F 148 [H 191] PEASANT WOMAN LAUNDERING
EXHIBITIONS 1937 Paris, 20; 1951 Newcastle upon Tyne, 13
PROVENANCE L. C. Enthoven, Voorburg, Netherlands; Sale Enthoven, Amsterdam [F. Muller] 18 May 1920, 208; B. M. A. Carp, Bloemendaal, Netherlands; Frans Buffa Art Gallery, Amsterdam [1937]; Hexam, Northumberland, England, Clive Cookson [R 1951]

F 149 [H 156] MOTHER WITH A BOY ON HER LAP
EXHIBITIONS 1950 The Hague, 29; 1958 Vevey, 22
PROVENANCE Mrs J. van Gogh-Bonger, Amsterdam; H. P. Bremmer, The Hague; W. Brinkman, Schipluiden, Netherlands [acquired 1954]; M. L. de Boer Art Gallery, Amsterdam; Abels Art Gallery, Cologne [acquired 1956]; J. Rosensaft, New York [R 1958]; London, Jacques O'Hana Ltd Collection [R 1970]

F 150 [H 166] HEAD OF A PEASANT WOMAN: LEFT HALF PROFILE, LIGHT BACKGROUND
EXHIBITIONS 1927 Basle etc, 58; 1928 Düsseldorf, 124; Karlsruhe, 59; 1929 Berlin 1, 52; Hamburg, 25; 1930 Amsterdam, 174
PROVENANCE L. C. Enthoven, Voorburg, Netherlands; Sale Enthoven, Amsterdam [F. Muller] 18 May 1920, 227; Otterlo, Rijksmuseum Kröller-Müller, inv nr 241-20, cat van Gogh 1970, nr 172

F 151 [H 152] HEAD OF A PEASANT WOMAN: LEFT THREE-QUARTER VIEW
EXHIBITIONS 1927 Basle etc, 53; 1928 Düsseldorf, 119; Karlsruhe, 54; 1929 Berlin 1, 43; Hamburg, 20; 1930 Amsterdam, 163
PROVENANCE L. C. Enthoven, Voorburg, Netherlands; Sale Enthoven, Amsterdam [F. Muller] 18 May 1920, 212; Otterlo, Rijksmuseum Kröller-Müller, inv nr 237-20, cat van Gogh 1970, nr 169

F 152 [H 176] PEASANT WOMAN SWEEPING
EXHIBITIONS 1904 Rotterdam, 20; 1913 The Hague, 24; 1914 Antwerp, 3; 1927 Basle etc, 43; 1928 Düsseldorf, 109 [repr]; Karlsruhe, 44; 1929 Berlin 1, 78; Hamburg, 10; 1930 Amsterdam, 170; 1952 Milan, 53; 1956 Munich, 83; 1958 Tokyo, Kyoto, 75
PROVENANCE Blot Art Gallery, Paris [1913]; Otterlo, Rijksmuseum Kröller-Müller, inv nr 227-13, cat van Gogh 1970, nr 180

F 153 [H 165] HEAD OF A PEASANT WOMAN: RIGHT PROFILE, LIGHT BACKGROUND
EXHIBITIONS 1914 Antwerp, 2; 1927 Basle etc, 40; 1928 Düsseldorf, 106; Karlsruhe, 41; 1929 Berlin 1, 60; Hamburg, 7; 1930 Amsterdam, 176; 1949 Gouda; 1955 Antwerp 3, 14
PROVENANCE W. H. C. Bolleurs, Rotterdam; Sale Amsterdam [F. Muller] 25 November 1913, 119; Otterlo, Rijksmuseum Kröller-Müller, inv nr 224-13, cat van Gogh 1970, nr 173

F 153a [formerly F 153bis, H 161] HEAD OF A PEASANT WOMAN: LEFT PROFILE, LIGHT BACKGROUND
EXHIBITIONS 1903 Rotterdam 3, [14 ?]; 1953 Berlin, 4; 1962 London, 23
PROVENANCE Oldenzeel Art Gallery, Rotterdam; D. Klinkhamer, Amsterdam; Sale Amsterdam [Mak van Waay] 4 November 1930, 76; F. Buffa Art Gallery, Amsterdam; F. Logeman, Bremen; Th. Werner, Berlin; Sale Stuttgart [Stuttgarter Kunstkabinett] 25-27 April 1951, 1344; Th. Werner, Berlin; Paul Roemer Art Gallery, Berlin; Günther Franke Art Gallery, Munich; Sale Stuttgart [Stuttgarter Kunstkabinett] 3-4 May 1962, 128; New York, Mr and Mrs Donald B. Stralem

F 154 [H 167] HEAD OF A PEASANT WOMAN: LEFT THREE-QUARTER VIEW
EXHIBITIONS 1927 Basle etc, 41; 1928 Düsseldorf, 107 [repr]; Karlsruhe, 42; 1929 Berlin 1, 58; Hamburg, 8; 1930 Amsterdam, 187; 1952 Milan, 49; 1956 Munich, 86; 1958 Vienna, 63; Tokyo, Kyoto, 73; 1966 Belgrade, 48
PROVENANCE Mr Williame, Châteauroux, France; H. P. Bremmer, The Hague; Otterlo, Rijksmuseum Kröller-Müller, inv nr 225-17, cat van Gogh 1970, nr 171

F 155 [H 163] PEASANT WOMAN IN A MOSS-GREEN SHAWL
EXHIBITIONS 1925 Paris 1, 2; 1926 Paris, 2957b; 1951 Lyons, 7; 1960 Paris, 13
PROVENANCE L. C. Enthoven, Voorburg, Netherlands; Sale Enthoven, Amsterdam [F. Muller] 18 May 1920, 213; Le Fauconnier, Paris [1920-1937]; Lyons, Musée de Lyon, inv nr 1937-34, cat VII La Peinture du XIXe et XXe siècle 1956, nr 196, pp 248-50

F 156 [H 140] PEASANT WOMAN IN A WHITE CAP: BUST, LEFT THREE-QUARTER VIEW
EXHIBITIONS 1905 Amsterdam, 6; Utrecht, 1; 1906 Rotterdam, 4; 1955 Antwerp 1, 50; 1960-1 Montreal etc, 15; 1967 Wolfsburg, 8; 1968-9 London, 29
PROVENANCE Mrs J. van Gogh-Bonger, Amsterdam; V. W. van Gogh, Laren; Amsterdam, Rijksmuseum Vincent van Gogh [Vincent van Gogh Foundation, inv nr F 156]

F 157 [H 169] PEASANT WOMAN DARNING STOCKINGS
PROVENANCE C. Mouwen jr, Breda; H. P. Bremmer, The Hague [until 1956]; Heirs of H. P. Bremmer, The Hague; Present owner unknown

F 158 [H 175] PEASANT WOMAN BY THE FIREPLACE
EXHIBITION 1960 Paris, 14
PROVENANCE C. Mouwen jr, Breda; Oldenzeel Art Gallery Rotterdam; H. P. Bremmer, The Hague; Sale Paris [Charpentier] 15 June 1954, 80bis; G. Renand, Paris [until 1968]; Paris, Private collection [R 1970]

F 159 [H 168] SKETCH OF THE HEAD OF A PEASANT WOMAN: FULL FACE, LIGHT BACKGROUND
PROVENANCE H. P. Bremmer, The Hague; Heirs of H. P. Bremmer, The Hague; Van Wisselingh Art Gallery, Amsterdam [acquired March 1960]; Amsterdam, H. A. D. Thomas [1962]

F 160 [H 159] PEASANT WOMAN IN A RED BONNET
EXHIBITIONS 1905 Amsterdam, 9; 1914 Berlin, 2; 1926 Munich, 2081; 1946-7 Liège etc, 26; 1947 Paris 1, 26; Geneva, 26; London etc, 5; 1948 Bergen, Oslo, 1; 1949-50 New York, Chicago, 6; 1951 Lyons etc, 6; 1953 The Hague, 33; Otterlo, Amsterdam, 19; 1955 Antwerp 1, 47; 1955-6 Liverpool etc, 3; 1958-9 San Francisco etc, 4; 1963 Humlebaek, 7; 1964 Washington, New York, 7; 1965 Nuenen, no cat nr; 1967 Wolfsburg, 5; 1968-9 London, 37
PROVENANCE Mrs J. van Gogh-Bonger, Amsterdam; V. W. van Gogh, Laren; Amsterdam, Rijksmuseum Vincent van Gogh [Vincent van Gogh Foundation, inv nr F 160]

F 160a PORTRAIT OF A PEASANT
PROVENANCE G. A. Aurier, Châteauroux, France; Mrs S. Williame-Aurier, Châteauroux; Aix-en-Provence, Mrs E. Mahé-Williame

F 161 [H 164] HOODED PEASANT WOMAN: HALF LENGTH
EXHIBITIONS 1905 Amsterdam, 11; Utrecht, 4; 1906 Rotterdam, 5
PROVENANCE Mrs J. van Gogh-Bonger, Amsterdam; V. W. van Gogh, Laren; Amsterdam, Rijksmuseum Vincent van Gogh [Vincent van Gogh Foundation, inv nr F 161]

F 162 [H 180] THE WEAVER: THE WHOLE LOOM, FACING RIGHT
EXHIBITIONS Probably 1903 Rotterdam 3 [description by A. Plasschaert, Onze Kunst 1903, 2, p 174 refers to either F 29 or F 162]; 1947 Basle, 7; 1952 Antwerp, 36; 1960 Paris, 6
PROVENANCE C. Mouwen jr, Breda; Oldenzeel Art Gallery, Rotterdam; H. P. Bremmer, The Hague; The Hague, Heirs of H. P. Bremmer [on loan to Gemeente Museum, The Hague, inv nr 56-x-1956, cat 1962, nr 132]

F 163 [H 183] HEAD OF A PEASANT
EXHIBITIONS 1905 Amsterdam, 434; 1924 Berlin, 1; Basle, 1; Zurich, 9; Stuttgart, 2; 1925 Paris 1, 3; The Hague, 24; 1957 Essen, 178; 1959-60 Utrecht, 4; 1960 Paris, 7
PROVENANCE Mrs J. van Gogh-Bonger, Amsterdam; V. W. van Gogh, Laren; Brussels, Koninklijk Museum voor Schone Kunsten [acquired 1931]

F 164 [H 184] HEAD OF A YOUNG PEASANT WITH A PIPE
EXHIBITIONS 1905 Amsterdam, 5; 1951 Lyons etc, 8; 1953 The Hague, 35; Otterlo, Amsterdam, 21; 1953-4 St Louis etc, 29; 1954 Zurich, 6; 1955 Antwerp 1, 48; Palm Beach etc, 2; 1957 Marseilles, 8; 1961-2 Baltimore etc, 3; 1965-6 Stockholm, Göteborg, 4; 1967 Wolfsburg, 6; 1968-9 London, 34
PROVENANCE Mrs J. van Gogh-Bonger, Amsterdam; V. W. van Gogh, Laren; Amsterdam, Rijksmuseum Vincent van Gogh [Vincent van Gogh Foundation, inv nr F 164]

F 165 [H 185] PORTRAIT OF A PEASANT
EXHIBITIONS 1948 Cleveland, 2; 1954 Detroit, 120
PROVENANCE Mrs A. Müller-Abeken, Scheveningen; Sale Müller-Abeken a.o., Amsterdam [F. Muller] 19 May 1920, 87; Huinck Art Gallery, Utrecht; Miss E. Snellen, Utrecht; Sale Amsterdam [F. Muller] 10 November 1935, 103; Bernheim jeune Art Gallery, Paris; Theodore Schempp, Los Angeles; Kansas City, Nelson Gallery – Atkins Museum [acquired 1937], inv nr 37.1

F 166 [H 173] PEASANT DIGGING
EXHIBITIONS 1927 Basle etc, 61; 1928 Düsseldorf, 127; Karlsruhe, 62; 1929 Berlin 1, 57; Hamburg, 28; 1930 Amsterdam, 168; 1940 New York 3, 1; 1942 Baltimore, Worcester, 1; 1943-4 Indianapolis etc, 1; 1947 Basle, 14; 1952 Milan, 54; 1958 Vienna, 67; 1962 Warsaw, 47; 1963 Tel Aviv, Haifa, 48
PROVENANCE L. C. Enthoven, Voorburg, Netherlands; Sale Enthoven, Amsterdam [F. Muller] 18 May 1920, 226; Otterlo, Rijksmuseum Kröller-Müller, inv nr 244-20, cat van Gogh 1970, nr 181

F 167 [H 179] PEASANT SEATED AT TABLE
EXHIBITIONS 1927 Basle etc, 60; 1928 Düsseldorf, 126; Karlsruhe, 61; 1929 Berlin 1, 54; Hamburg, 27; 1930 Amsterdam, 184; 1947 Basle, 24; 1949 Gouda; 1950 's Hertogenbosch, Breda; 1952 Milan, 51; 1960-1 Montreal etc, 5; 1966 Belgrade, 50
PROVENANCE L. C. Enthoven, Voorburg, Netherlands; Sale Enthoven, Amsterdam [F. Muller] 18 May 1920, 225; Otterlo, Rijksmuseum Kröller-Müller, inv nr 243-20, cat van Gogh 1970, nr 178

F 168 [H 189] HEAD OF A PEASANT: RIGHT PROFILE
EXHIBITIONS 1927 Basle etc, 54; 1928 Düsseldorf, 120; Karlsruhe, 55; 1929 Berlin 1, 44; Hamburg, 21; 1930 Amsterdam, 175; 1962 Warsaw, 45; 1963 Tel Aviv, Haifa, 46; 1966 Belgrade, 49
PROVENANCE L. C. Enthoven, Voorburg, Netherlands;

Sale Enthoven, Amsterdam [F. Muller] 18 May 1920, 210; Otterlo, Rijksmuseum Kröller-Müller, inv nr 238-20, cat van Gogh 1970, nr 175

F 169 [H 182] HEAD OF A PEASANT WITH A PIPE: RIGHT PROFILE
EXHIBITIONS 1927 Basle etc, 51; 1928 Düsseldorf, 117; Karlsruhe, 52; 1929 Berlin 1, 63; Hamburg, 18; 1930 Amsterdam, 172; 1949 Gouda; 1950 's Hertogenbosch, Breda; 1956 Eindhoven, 22; Munich, 81; 1957 Essen, 177; 1958 Vienna, 60; Tokyo, Kyoto, 71; 1962 Warsaw, 46; 1963 Tel Aviv, Haifa, 47
PROVENANCE L. C. Enthoven, Voorburg, Netherlands; Sale Enthoven, Amsterdam [F. Muller] 18 May 1920, 206; Otterlo, Rijksmuseum Kröller-Müller, inv nr 235-20, cat van Gogh 1970, nr 176

F 169a HEAD OF A PEASANT
PROVENANCE A. Kerssemakers, the friend of Van Gogh, Eindhoven; G. van Steenwegen, Antwerp; Sale Paris [Charpentier] 6 April 1954, 47; Athens, Stavros S. Niarchos

F 170 [H 204] COTTAGE WITH PEASANT GOING HOME
EXHIBITIONS 1932 Amsterdam 2, 14; 1950 The Hague, 32; 1952 London 3, 27; 1959-60 Plymouth, Bristol, 28
PROVENANCE J. J. Biesing Art Gallery, The Hague; H. P. Bremmer, The Hague; Huinck and Scherjon Art Gallery, Amsterdam; A. Reid and Lefevre Art Gallery, London; W. Hallsborough Art Gallery, London; Lefevre Art Gallery, London [1952]; London, Mrs M. Q. Morris [R 1959]

F 171 [H 178] THE BASKET MAKER
EXHIBITIONS 1925 Paris 1, 4; 1926 Paris, 2950bis; 1945 Basle, 3; 1947 Basle, 23
PROVENANCE A. Schuffenecker, Paris; A. Vollard Art Gallery, Paris; E. Blot Art Gallery, Paris; Antoine Villard, Paris [1925, 1926]; Matthiesen Art Gallery, London; Switzerland, Private collection [1947]

F 171a [formerly F 171b, H 810] THE BASKET MAKER
PROVENANCE E. Blot Art Gallery, Paris [1916]; A. Bernheim, Aix-en-Provence; Present owner unknown

F 172 [H 177] THE PLOWER
EXHIBITIONS 1905 Amsterdam, 28 [repr in 'Op de Hoogte', II, August 1905, p 478]; 1928 Berlin, 1; 1947 Basle, 11
PROVENANCE Paul Mulder, Nieuwer-Amstel, Netherlands [1905]; Sale Amsterdam [F. Muller] 29 April 1914, 280 [repr]; E. V. F. Ahn, The Hague; Sale Amsterdam [Mak van Waay] 16 September 1919, 632 [repr]; J. S. Sala Art Gallery, The Hague; E. Baron von der Heydt, Ascona; Wuppertal, Von der Heydt Museum der Stadt Wuppertal [acquired 1952; gift Baron von der Heydt]

F 173 THE MIDWIFE
Left out by Faille in his manuscript for the present edition. See REJECTED WORKS

F 174 [H 147] THE MIDWIFE: HEAD WITH WHITE BONNET
EXHIBITIONS 1928 Berlin, 9; Frankfort, 5; Vienna, 5; 1955 Antwerp 1, 124; 1958-9 San Francisco etc, 14; 1967 Wolfsburg, 16; 1968-9 London, 56
PROVENANCE Mrs J. van Gogh-Bonger, Amsterdam; V. W. van Gogh, Laren; Amsterdam, Rijksmuseum Vincent van Gogh [Vincent van Gogh Foundation, inv nr F 174]

F 175 [H 181] THE SPINNING WHEEL
PROVENANCE Mrs J. van Gogh-Bonger, Amsterdam; V. W. van Gogh, Laren; Amsterdam, Rijksmuseum Vincent van Gogh [Vincent van Gogh Foundation, inv nr F 175]

F 176 [H 174] PEASANT WOMAN BY THE FIREPLACE
EXHIBITIONS 1901 Paris, 44; 1905 Paris, 41; 1943 New York 2, 5; 1955 New York 2, 8; 1957 Los Angeles, 3
PROVENANCE A. Schuffenecker, Clamart [1901, 1905]; A. Pellerin, Paris; E. Blot Art Gallery, Paris; Sale Blot, Paris [Drouot] 2 June 1933, 49; Sale Blot, Paris [Drouot] 23 April 1937, 69; M. Levy-Hermanos, Paris [1943]; Norwalk, Connecticut, Mr and Mrs Mortimer Hays [1955]

F 177 [H 205] TWO RATS
EXHIBITIONS 1904 Rotterdam, 34; 1910-1 Rotterdam, 23
PROVENANCE Oldenzeel Art Gallery, Rotterdam; M. Gieseler, The Hague [1910-1]; Sale Gieseler, Amsterdam [Mak van Waay] 27 October 1925, 29 [repr]; W. van Beuningen, Utrecht; Wassenaar, Mrs Ch. E. van Beuningen-Fentener van Vlissingen [R 1969]

F 177a STUFFED KALONG
EXHIBITION 1904 Rotterdam, 36
PROVENANCE Oldenzeel Art Gallery, Rotterdam; A. F. Philips, Eindhoven [acquired at the Oldenzeel Art Gallery]; Eindhoven, Mrs A. H. E. M. Philips-de Jongh [R 1967]

F 178 recto [formerly F 178 verso, H 217] STILL LIFE WITH POTTERY, BEERGLASS AND BOTTLES
PROVENANCE Mrs E. H. du Quesne-van Gogh, Baarn; d'Audretsch Art Gallery, The Hague; The Hague, Gemeente Museum [acquired 1918], inv nr 3-1918, cat 1962, nr 135

F 178 verso [formerly F 178, H 187] SELF PORTRAIT
EXHIBITIONS 1922 Copenhagen, 175; 1946-7 Liège etc, 73; 1947 Paris 1, 74; Geneva, 74; 1953 The Hague, 63; Berlin, 6; 1958 Tokyo, Kyoto, 93; 1962 Warsaw, 91; 1963 Tel Aviv, Haifa, 6; Schaffhausen, 51
PROVENANCE Mrs E. H. du Quesne-van Gogh, Baarn; d'Audretsch Art Gallery, The Hague; The Hague, Gemeentemuseum, inv nr 3-1918, cat 1953, nr 159; cat 1962, nr 135

F 179 recto [formerly F 179 verso, not in Faille 1939] PORTRAIT OF A FARMER
PROVENANCE Mrs J. van Gogh-Bonger, Amsterdam; V. W. van Gogh, Laren; Amsterdam, Rijksmuseum Vincent van Gogh [Vincent van Gogh Foundation, inv nr F 179]

F 179 verso [formerly F 179, H 229] SELF PORTRAIT
EXHIBITIONS 1905 Amsterdam, 439; 1924 Amsterdam, 1 [repr]; 1953 The Hague, 64; Otterlo, Amsterdam, 55; 1960 London 4, 4
PROVENANCE Mrs J. van Gogh-Bonger, Amsterdam; V. W. van Gogh, Laren; Amsterdam, Rijksmuseum Vincent van Gogh [Vincent van Gogh Foundation, inv nr F 179]

F 180 [H 188] SELF PORTRAIT
EXHIBITIONS 1930 Amsterdam, 3; 1945 Amsterdam, without cat nr; 1946 Stockholm etc, 18; 1946-7 Liège etc, 38; 1947 Paris, 38; Geneva, 39; 1947-8 London etc, 11; 1948 Bergen, Oslo, 7; 1949-50 New York, Chicago, 12; 1951 Lyons etc, 10; 1953 The Hague, 49; Otterlo, Amsterdam, 46; 1953-4 St Louis etc, 56; 1954 Zurich, 10; 1955 Palm Beach etc, 6; 1955 Antwerp 1, 121; 1955-6 Liverpool etc, 11; 1957 Marseilles, 19; 1958-9 San Francisco etc, 13; 1959-60 Utrecht, 11; 1960 London 4, 2; 1961-2 Baltimore etc, 13; 1963 Humlebaek, 18; 1964 Washington, New York, 10; 1965 Nuenen, without cat nr; 1968-9 London, 49
PROVENANCE Mrs J. van Gogh-Bonger, Amsterdam; V. W. van Gogh, Laren; Amsterdam, Rijksmuseum Vincent van Gogh [Vincent van Gogh Foundation, inv nr F 180]

F 181 [H 186] SELFPORTRAIT IN FRONT OF THE EASEL
EXHIBITION 1960 London 4, 1
PROVENANCE Mrs J. van Gogh-Bonger, Amsterdam; V. W. van Gogh, Laren; Amsterdam, Rijksmuseum Vincent van Gogh [Vincent van Gogh Foundation, inv nr F 181]

F 182 [H 199] THE VICARAGE AT NUENEN: THE HOUSE OF VINCENT'S PARENTS, FRONTVIEW
EXHIBITIONS 1937 Paris, 101; 1945 Amsterdam, without cat nr; 1946 Stockholm etc, 8; 1946-7 Liège etc, 33; 1947 Geneva, 33; London etc, 10; Paris, 33; 1948 Bergen, Oslo, 5; 1951 Lyons etc, 2; 1953 The Hague, 42; Otterlo, Amsterdam, 24; 1953-4 St Louis etc, 31; 1954 Zurich, 9; 1955 Antwerp 1, 45; Palm Beach etc, 1; 1955-6 Liverpool etc, 8; 1957 Marseilles, 7; 1959-60 Utrecht, 8; 1965 Nuenen, without cat nr; 1968-9 London, 20
PROVENANCE Mrs J. van Gogh-Bonger, Amsterdam; V. W. van Gogh, Laren; Amsterdam, Rijksmuseum Vincent van Gogh [Vincent van Gogh Foundation, inv nr F 182]

F 183 [H 195] THE VICARAGE AT NUENEN BY MOONLIGHT: VIEW FROM THE GARDEN
PROVENANCE L. C. Enthoven, Voorburg, Netherlands; Sale Enthoven, Amsterdam [F. Muller] 18 May 1920, 205; F. J. P. van der Eerden, Rotterdam; F. W. R. Wentges, The Hague; R. W. Wentges, Rotterdam; Sale London [Sotheby] 1 July 1959, 73; L. Cohen Ltd, London; Cannes, France, Stoliar Galeries [1968]

F 184 [H 194] THE OLD TOWER AT NUENEN
EXHIBITIONS 1903 Rotterdam 1, 26; 1953 The Hague, 28; Otterlo, Amsterdam, 25; 1956 Amsterdam, 29
PROVENANCE Oldenzeel Art Gallery, Rotterdam [1902]; Mrs van Panhuys, The Hague; Mrs A. W. Mees-Moll, Utrecht; H. E. d'Audretsch, Amerongen; Amerongen, Mrs d'Audretsch-Krop

F 185 [H 197] THE VICARAGE GARDEN AT NUENEN
EXHIBITION 1927-8 Rotterdam, 22
PROVENANCE Oldenzeel Art Gallery, Rotterdam; J. A. Fruin, Rotterdam [1927-8]; W. Moll, The Hague; Groningen, Groninger Museum voor Stad en Ommelanden [acquired 1962], inv nr 1962-200

F 185a [formerly F 185bis, H 198] LANDSCAPE WITH CHURCH
PROVENANCE J. S. H. Kever, Laren; Huinck en Scherjon Art Gallery, Amsterdam; W. A. van Emden, Amsterdam; Mrs E. Dukkers van Emden-Schmid, Amsterdam [1965]; Sale Amsterdam [Brandt] 23 April 1968, 562; Sale London [Christie] 6-10 December 1968, 67; Present owner unknown

F 186 [H 20] BULBFIELDS
EXHIBITIONS 1904 Rotterdam, 2; 1905 Rotterdam, 2; 1960 New Haven, 68; 1966 Washington, 129
PROVENANCE Oldenzeel Art Gallery, Rotterdam; Jan Smit, Alblasserdam, Netherlands [since 1905]; Sale Smit, Amsterdam [Mak van Waay] 10 February 1919, 31 [repr]; John Enthoven, Voorburg, Netherlands; J. Enthoven, Woubrugge, Netherlands; W. Brinkman, Schipluiden, Netherlands [R 1956]; Frank Perls, Beverley Hills, USA; Upperville, Virginia, Mr and Mrs Paul Mellon [R 1966]

F 187 [H 193] COTTAGE UNDER THE TREES, WITH A PEASANT WOMAN
EXHIBITIONS 1904 Groningen; 1957 New York, 3
PROVENANCE Oldenzeel Art Gallery, Rotterdam; F. W. R. Wentges, The Hague [since 1909]; W. Brinkman, Schipluiden, Netherlands [after 1945]; René Gas, Paris; Irving H. Vogel, Philadelphia, USA; Sale New York [Parke-Bernet] 22 April 1954, 82; Mrs William Woodward jr, New York; Knoedler Galleries, New York [since January 1956]; Richard L. Feigen Gallery, Chicago – New York [since July 1957]; A. G. Modernart; Sale London [Sotheby] 6 July 1960 119; A. G. Modernart [R 1968]

F 188 [H 207] LANDSCAPE WITH A CHURCH AT TWILIGHT
EXHIBITIONS 1903 Rotterdam 1, [?]; 1905 Rotterdam; 1953 Berlin, 1
PROVENANCE Oldenzeel Art Gallery, Rotterdam; Jan Smit, Alblasserdam, Netherlands [since about 1905]; Sale Smit, Amsterdam [Mak van Waay] 10 February 1919, 34; J. L. Smit, Kinderdijk, Netherlands; G. K. Smit, Kinderdijk; Sale Dordrecht [Mak] 9 June 1953, 5; W. Brinkman Art dealer, Schipluiden, Netherlands [R 1953]; Rotterdam, Private collection [R 1970]

F 189 [H 206] FOOTBRIDGE ACROSS A DITCH
EXHIBITION 1904 Rotterdam, 13
PROVENANCE C. Mouwen jr, Breda; Sale Mouwen, Amsterdam [F. Muller] 3 May 1904, 8; Oldenzeel Art Gallery, Rotterdam; H. J. Nieboer, Rotterdam [R 1905]; Mrs S. de Voogd-Nieboer, Rijswijk, Netherlands; Nassau Galleries, Andover, Massachusetts; Sale London [Sotheby] 27 March 1957, 145; Sale Paris [Charpentier] 18 June 1957. 180; C. G. Stiebel Art Gallery, Paris [R 1957]; Sale New York [Parke-Bernet] 15 April 1959, 73; Chagrin Falls, Ohio, Mrs Gordon Stouffer

F 190 [H 208] VILLAGE AT SUNSET
EXHIBITIONS 1903 Rotterdam 1; 1904 Rotterdam, 19
PROVENANCE Oldenzeel Art Gallery, Rotterdam; M. Gieseler, The Hague; Sale Gieseler, Amsterdam [Mak van Waay] 27 October 1925, 32 [repr]; Sale Amsterdam [Mak van Waay] 11 May 1926, 44; d'Audretsch Art Gallery, The Hague; Unger and Van Mens Art Gallery, Rotterdam; Amsterdam, Rijksmuseum [gift of Mr and Mrs D. A. J. Kessler-Hülsmann, nr 22] Inv nr A 3307, annual report 1940, pp 14 and 18

F 191 [H 201] LANDSCAPE WITH DITCH
EXHIBITION 1905 Amsterdam, 12
PROVENANCE Mrs J. van Gogh-Bonger, Amsterdam [1905]; W. P. Ingenegeren, Utrecht; Sale Ingenegeren a.o., Amsterdam [F. Muller] 18 May 1920, 64; Mrs J. C. Böhtlingk, The Hague; Unknown owner; Sale London [Sotheby] 22 June 1966, 37; Castagnola, Switzerland, Collection Thyssen Bornemisza [R 1970]

F 191a [formerly F 191bis, H 202] COUNTRY LANE WITH TWO FIGURES
PROVENANCE C. Bakker, Hilversum; B. Houthakker Art Gallery, Amsterdam; Present owner unknown

F 192 [H 200] EDGE OF A WOOD
EXHIBITIONS 1912 Cologne, 2; 1913 The Hague, 9; 1927 Basle etc, 39; 1928 Düsseldorf, 105 [repr]; Karlsruhe, 40; 1929 Berlin 1, 62; Hamburg, 6; 1930 Amsterdam, 179; 1955 Antwerp 3, 192; 1958 Vienna, 35
PROVENANCE C. Mouwen jr, Breda, Sale Mouwen, Amsterdam [F. Muller] 3 May 1904, 10 [not sold]; Oldenzeel Art Gallery, Rotterdam; Sale The Hague [Biesing] 1909; Otterlo, Rijksmuseum Kröller-Müller, inv nr 223-09, cat van Gogh 1970, nr 95

F 193 [H 203] SHEAVES OF WHEAT
EXHIBITIONS 1927 Basle etc, 46; 1928 Düsseldorf, 112; Karlsruhe, 147; 1929 Berlin 1, 59; Hamburg, 13; 1930 Amsterdam, 180; 1950 's Hertogenbosch, Breda; 1958 Tokyo, Kyoto, 80; 1960-1 Montreal etc, 6
PROVENANCE L. C. Enthoven, Voorburg, Netherlands; Sale Enthoven, Amsterdam [F. Muller] 18 May 1920, 207; Otterlo, Rijksmuseum Kröller-Müller, inv nr 230-20, cat van Gogh 1970, nr 190

F 194 [H 209] THE VICARAGE GARDEN UNDER SNOW
EXHIBITIONS 1904 Rotterdam, 37; 1905 Amsterdam, 27; 1946-7 Liège etc, 21; 1947 Paris 1, 21; Geneva, 21; 1952 Antwerp, 37; 1956 Munich, 82; 1960 Paris, 10b; 1963 Amsterdam, 12; 1966 London, 15
PROVENANCE C. Mouwen jr, Breda; Sale Mouwen, Amsterdam [F. Muller] 3 May 1904, 6 [not sold]; Oldenzeel Art Gallery, Rotterdam; H. P. Bremmer, The Hague [1905]; Centraal Museum, Utrecht, suppl cat 1934, nr 15 [loan

H. P. Bremmer since 1923]; Heirs of H. P. Bremmer, The Hague [1967]; Fullerton, California, Norton Simon Foundation [R 1970]

F 195 [H 196] THE WILLOW
EXHIBITIONS 1903 Rotterdam 3; 1927-8 Rotterdam, 20; 1955 Dordrecht, 53; 1956 Amsterdam, 30; 1965 Amsterdam, 11
PROVENANCE Oldenzeel Art Gallery, Rotterdam; A. P. van Hoey Smith, Rotterdam [acquired 1903]; Van Wisselingh Art Gallery, Amsterdam [1965]; Ottawa, Haso Ltd [R 1970]

F 196 [H 211] A ROW OF TREES
EXHIBITION 1904 Rotterdam, 10
PROVENANCE C. Mouwen jr, Breda; Sale Mouwen, Amsterdam [F. Muller] 3 May 1904, 9 [not sold]; Oldenzeel Art Gallery, Rotterdam; E. van Biema, The Hague; F. Hirschel, Amsterdam; P. Verschure, Rotterdam; Present owner unknown

F 197 [H 210] STILL LIFE: BOUQUET OF FLOWERS
EXHIBITIONS 1903 Rotterdam 1, 9; 1906 Rotterdam; 1909 Rotterdam, 29; 1927-8 Rotterdam, 31; 1956 Amsterdam, 31; 1960 London 5, 13
PROVENANCE Oldenzeel Art Gallery, Rotterdam; J. G. L. Nolst Trénité, Rotterdam [acquired 1903]; Van Wisselingh Art Gallery, Amsterdam; Sale London [Sotheby] 3 December 1958, 154; E. L. Catz, Curaçao [1960]; Lefevre Art Gallery, London [R 1963]; Wildenstein Art Gallery, London [R 1966]; St David's [Penns.], Mr and Mrs William Coxe Wright [R 1970]

F 198 [H 219] STILL LIFE: GINGER POT FILLED WITH CHRYSANTHEMUMS
EXHIBITIONS 1904 Rotterdam, 41; 1953 Berlin, 7
PROVENANCE Oldenzeel Art Gallery, Rotterdam; H. Tutein Nolthenius, Delft; d'Audretsch Art Gallery, The Hague; A. Goekoop, The Hague; W. Brinkman, Schipluiden, Netherlands [1953]; J. Duquet, Basle; Nassau Galleries, Andover, Mass., USA; Mrs Kaars Sijpesteijn, Blaricum; Sale New York [Parke-Bernet] 14 March 1956, 87; Hammer Galleries, New York; Sale Paris [Charpentier] 10-11 June 1958, 265bis; Sale New York [Parke-Bernet] 6 April 1967, 23; New York, Howard I. Lepow Collection [1967]

F 199 [H 212] STILL LIFE: HELLEBORES
EXHIBITIONS Year unknown, Rotterdam Academy; 1904 Rotterdam, 38; 1955 Amsterdam 2, 15
PROVENANCE F. J. G. Bosman, Scheveningen; Sale Bosman, The Hague [Biesing] 6-7 May 1908, 33; A. B. Henny, Blaricum; Van Wisselingh Art Gallery, Amsterdam; Miss H. T. Reiger, Utrecht [1956]; Sale London [Sotheby] 6 July 1960, 101; Greenfield; Sale London [Sotheby] 5 July 1961, 168; M. R. Schweitzer; Sale Geneva [Motte] 9-10 June 1967, 54; Present owner unknown

F 200 [H 215] STILL LIFE: DEAD LEAVES
EXHIBITIONS 1904 Rotterdam, 47; 1960 Paris, 15
PROVENANCE J. W. Moll, Groningen [acquired about 1900]; W. Moll, The Hague; Private collection [R 1970]

F 201 [H 218] STILL LIFE: GERANIUM IN A POT
EXHIBITIONS 1952 Milan, 60; 1956 Munich, 231; Amsterdam, 33; 1957 Essen, 231; 1960 Paris, 24; 1962 Warsaw, 93; 1963 Tel Aviv, Haifa, 58
PROVENANCE Mrs A. C. van Gogh-Carbentus, Leiden; Mrs A. C. van Houten-van Gogh, Dieren; Mrs A. T. Scholte-van Houten, Lochem [until 1969]; Oegstgeest, Heirs of Mrs Scholte-van Houten [on loan to Rijksmuseum Kröller-Müller, Otterlo]

F 202 [H 216] STILL LIFE: COPPER COFFEE-POT AND TWO WHITE BOWLS [study for THE POTATO EATERS]
PROVENANCE Utrecht, J. E. van der Meulen

F 203 [H 214] STILL LIFE: HERRINGS
EXHIBITIONS 1935-6 Rotterdam, 58; 1947 Basle, 25; 1956 Eindhoven, 26; 1966 Belgrade, 53
PROVENANCE C. Hoogendijk, The Hague; Sale coll C. Hoogendijk, Amsterdam [F. Muller] 21 May 1912, 27 [repr]; Otterlo, Rijksmuseum Kröller-Müller, inv nr 258-12, cat van Gogh 1970, nr 195

F 203a [formerly F 203bis, H 213] STILL LIFE: LEMONS
EXHIBITIONS 1943 New York 2, 6; 1944 Montreal, 116; 1955 New York 2, 9
PROVENANCE W. P. Ingeneregen, Utrecht; H. L. Timmers Verhoeven, Brussels; F. H. Hirschland, Harrison, USA [1963]; Berkeley Heights, New Jersey, H. E. Hirschland

ANTWERP PERIOD

F 204 [H 228] CLUSTER OF OLD HOUSES WITH THE NEW CHURCH AT THE HAGUE
EXHIBITIONS 1903 Rotterdam 2; 1904 Rotterdam, not in the cat; 1905 Rotterdam; 1955 Antwerp 1, 116; 1960 Paris, 20
PROVENANCE Oldenzeel Art Gallery, Rotterdam; Jan Smit, Kinderdijk, Netherlands [acquired 1905]; Sale

Amsterdam [Mak van Waay] 10 February 1919, 36; L. J. Smit, Kinderdijk; L. C. Smit, Kinderdijk; Sale New York [Parke-Bernet] 20 November 1968, 59; Present owner unknown

F 205 [H 225] HEAD OF AN OLD MAN: LEFT PROFILE
EXHIBITIONS 1955 Antwerp 1, 119; 1960-1 Montreal etc, 18; 1968-9 London, 57
PROVENANCE Mrs J. van Gogh-Bonger, Amsterdam; V. W. van Gogh, Laren; Amsterdam, Rijksmuseum Vincent van Gogh [Vincent van Gogh Foundation, inv nr F 205]

F 206 [H 222] HEAD OF A WOMAN: NEARLY FULL FACE
EXHIBITIONS 1905 Amsterdam, 74; Utrecht, 21; 1906 Rotterdam, 21; 1948 Bergen, Oslo, 8; 1953 The Hague, 47; Otterlo, Amsterdam, 49; 1953-4 St Louis etc, 55; 1954 Zurich, 11; 1954-5 Bern, 12; 1955 Antwerp 1, 118; 1955-6 Liverpool etc, 10; 1957 Stockholm, 104
PROVENANCE Mrs J. van Gogh-Bonger, Amsterdam; V. W. van Gogh, Laren; Amsterdam, Rijksmuseum Vincent van Gogh [Vincent van Gogh Foundation, inv nr F 206]

F 207 [H 223] PORTRAIT OF A WOMAN: BUST, LEFT PROFILE
EXHIBITIONS 1939 Paris; 1955 Antwerp 1, 122
PROVENANCE Emile Bernard, Paris [who acquired it from the painter himself]; Vollard Art Gallery, Paris; A. Bauchy, Livry; J. K. Thannhauser Art Gallery, New York; Sale J. K. Thannhauser, New York [Parke-Bernet] 12 April 1945, 104; New York, Alfred Wyler [1955]

F 207a PORTRAIT OF A WOMAN IN BLUE: RIGHT THREE-QUARTER PROFILE
EXHIBITIONS 1951 Lyons, 11; 1960-1 Montreal etc, 19; 1961-2 Baltimore etc, 11; 1963 Humlebaek, 11; 1964 Washington, New York, 11; 1965 Charleroi, Ghent, 7; Stockholm, 11
PROVENANCE Mrs J. van Gogh-Bonger, Amsterdam; V. W. van Gogh, Laren; Amsterdam, Rijksmuseum Vincent van Gogh [Vincent van Gogh Foundation, inv nr F 207a]

F 208 [H 224] SELF PORTRAIT WITH PIPE: RIGHT THREE-QUARTER VIEW
EXHIBITIONS 1905 Amsterdam, 69; 1953 The Hague, 48; Otterlo, Amsterdam, 47; 1955 Antwerp 1, 120; 1960 London 4, 3
PROVENANCE Mrs J. van Gogh-Bonger, Amsterdam; V. W. van Gogh, Laren; Amsterdam, Rijksmuseum Vincent van Gogh [Vincent van Gogh Foundation, inv nr F 208]

F 208a SELF PORTRAIT WITH FELT HAT
EXHIBITIONS 1960 London 4, 18 [as Paris 1887]; 1968-9 London, 95
PROVENANCE Mrs J. van Gogh-Bonger, Amsterdam; V. W. van Gogh, Laren; Amsterdam, Rijksmuseum Vincent van Gogh [Vincent van Gogh Foundation, inv nr F 208a]

F 209 [H 220] HEAD OF A MAN: LEFT THREE-QUARTER VIEW
EXHIBITION 1939 Adelaide etc, 135
PROVENANCE Abels Art Gallery, Cologne; Sale Amsterdam [F. Muller] 13 June 1933, 17; G. Stein Art Gallery, Paris [R 1937]; V. A. Cazalet, London [1939]; Melbourne, National Gallery of Victoria [acquired 1939] cat 1948, nr 57 [Felton bequest]

F 210 [H 227] VIEW OF AN UNKNOWN TOWN WITH DRAWBRIDGE
EXHIBITIONS 1904 Rotterdam, 33; 1956 Amsterdam, 32; Munich, 94; 1960 Paris, 12
PROVENANCE Oldenzeel Art Gallery, Rotterdam; Mrs E. A. E. M. Klüssener-d'Hamecourt, Rotterdam; W. C. A. Arbeiter, The Hague; Mrs E. A. E. M. van Meeteren-van Diemen Arbeiter [R 1960]

F 211 [H 226] THE ANTWERP QUAY
EXHIBITIONS 1945 Amsterdam, without cat nr; 1946 Stockholm etc, 20; 1953 The Hague, 46; Otterlo, Amsterdam, 48; 1953-4 St Louis etc, 52; 1955 Antwerp 1, 117; 1957 Marseilles, 18; 1959-60 Utrecht, 10
PROVENANCE Mrs J. van Gogh-Bonger, Amsterdam; V. W. van Gogh, Laren; Amsterdam, Rijksmuseum Vincent van Gogh [Vincent van Gogh Foundation, inv nr F 211]

F 212 [H 221] SKULL WITH A BURNING CIGARETTE
EXHIBITIONS 1910 Berlin 1, 3; 1953-4 St Louis etc, 53; 1955 Antwerp 1, 125; 1967 Wolfsburg, 17; 1968-9 London, 58
PROVENANCE Mrs J. van Gogh-Bonger, Amsterdam; V. W. van Gogh, Laren; Amsterdam, Rijksmuseum Vincent van Gogh [Vincent van Gogh Foundation, inv nr F 212]

F 212a STILL LIFE: VEGETABLES
PROVENANCE W. P. Ingeneregen, Utrecht; H. L. Timmers Verhoeven, Brussels; S. van der Graaf, Netherlands; Private collection, Switzerland; Paul Vogel-Brunner Art Gallery, Lucerne; Private collection, Germany; Private collection, New York [R 1959]; Sale New York [Parke-Bernet] 11 November 1959, 49; Landsberg/Lech, Anneliese Brand [R 1970]

PARIS PERIOD

F 213 [H 298] STILL LIFE: FRITILLARIES IN A COPPER VASE
EXHIBITION 1961-2 Tokyo, 174
PROVENANCE Eugène Mürer, Auvers-sur-Oise; E. Blot Art Gallery, Paris; E. Druet Art Gallery, Paris; Isaac de Camondo, Paris [1907-11], cat collection Is de Camondo, Paris, Louvre [without year] nr 208 [repr]; Paris, Musée National du Louvre [acquired 1908; bequest of Is. de Camondo], inv nr RF 1989, cat 1959, nr 143

F 214 [H 297] STILL LIFE WITH FRITILLARIES
PROVENANCE Th. Duret, Paris; Present owner unknown

F 215 [H 247] NUDE STUDY: LITTLE GIRL SEATED
EXHIBITIONS 1905 Amsterdam, 52; 1928 Berlin, 10; Frankfort, 8; Vienna, 9; 1945 Amsterdam, without cat nr; 1946-7 Liège etc, 39; 1947 Geneva, 40; London etc, 12; Paris 1, 39; 1948 Bergen, Oslo, 9; 1953 The Hague, 65; Otterlo, Amsterdam, 71; 1953-4 St Louis etc, 51; 1955 Antwerp 1, 191
PROVENANCE Mrs J. van Gogh-Bonger, Amsterdam; V. W. van Gogh, Laren; Amsterdam, Rijksmuseum Vincent van Gogh [Vincent van Gogh Foundation, inv nr F 215]

F 215a STUDY OF A YOUNG WOMAN: HALF-LENGTH, LEFT PROFILE
PROVENANCE Unknown art dealer near Porte Louise, Brussels; Albert Nepper, Profondeville [1927–about 1947-8]; Pierre O'Connell, Paris [acquired about 1947-8]; Sale London [Sotheby] 26 April 1967, 5; London, Brook Street Gallery [R 1970]

F 215b PORTRAIT OF A WOMAN: FACING RIGHT
PROVENANCE Mrs J. van Gogh-Bonger, Amsterdam; V. W. van Gogh, Laren; Amsterdam, Rijksmuseum Vincent van Gogh [Vincent van Gogh Foundation, inv nr F 215b]

F 215c PORTRAIT OF A WOMAN WITH HAT
PROVENANCE Mrs J. van Gogh-Bonger, Amsterdam; V. W. van Gogh, Laren; Amsterdam, Rijksmuseum Vincent van Gogh [Vincent van Gogh Foundation, inv nr F 215c]

F 215d PORTRAIT OF A WOMAN SEATED
PROVENANCE Mrs J. van Gogh-Bonger; V. W. van Gogh, Laren; Amsterdam, Rijksmuseum Vincent van Gogh [Vincent van Gogh Foundation, inv nr F 215d]

F 216 [H 241] PLASTER STATUETTE: FEMALE TORSO, SEEN FROM THE FRONT
EXHIBITIONS 1914 Berlin, 43; 1927 Berlin, 117; 1928 Berlin, 11; 1954 Rotterdam, 115; 1956 Munich, 107; 1959 Paris, 66; 1960-1 Paris, 195; 1963 Hamburg, 77; 1964 New York 2
PROVENANCE Mrs J. van Gogh-Bonger, Amsterdam; Paul Cassirer Art Gallery, Berlin; J. Guthmann, Mittel-Schreiberhau; Leo Lewin, Breslau; S. Chweitzer, Berlin; Sale G. Schweitzer a.o., Berlin [Cassirer] 20 October 1932, 126; Private collection, Paris; Mrs W. Feilchenfeldt, Zurich [1956, 1963]; Richard Feigen Gallery, New York [1963, 1964]; New York, H. Spiro [R 1970]

F 216a [H 240] PLASTER STATUETTE: FEMALE TORSO, SEEN FROM THE BACK
EXHIBITION 1965-6 Stockholm, Göteborg, 14
PROVENANCE Mrs J. van Gogh-Bonger, Amsterdam; V. W. van Gogh, Laren; Amsterdam, Rijksmuseum Vincent van Gogh [Vincent van Gogh Foundation, inv nr F 216a]

F 216b [H 238] PLASTER STATUETTE: FEMALE TORSO ON PEDESTAL, SEEN FROM THE FRONT
EXHIBITIONS 1955 Antwerp 1, 186; 1957 Stockholm, 107; 1958-9 San Francisco etc, 20; 1961-2 Baltimore etc, 15
PROVENANCE Mrs J. van Gogh-Bonger, Amsterdam; V. W. van Gogh, Laren; Amsterdam, Rijksmuseum Vincent van Gogh [Vincent van Gogh Foundation, inv nr F 216b]

F 216c [H 245] PLASTER STATUETTE: HORSE
PROVENANCE Mrs J. van Gogh-Bonger, Amsterdam; V. W. van Gogh, Laren; Amsterdam, Rijksmuseum Vincent van Gogh [Vincent van Gogh Foundation, inv nr F 216c]

F 216d [H p 557] PLASTER STATUETTE: FEMALE TORSO. WITH ONE LEG, SEEN FROM THE FRONT
PROVENANCE Mrs J. van Gogh-Bonger, Amsterdam; V. W. van Gogh, Laren; Amsterdam, Rijksmuseum Vincent van Gogh [Vincent van Gogh Foundation, inv nr F 216d]

F 216e [H 242] PLASTER STATUETTE: MALE TORSO, SEEN FROM THE FRONT, THREE QUARTERS TO THE RIGHT
PROVENANCE Mrs J. van Gogh-Bonger, Amsterdam; V. W. van Gogh, Laren; Amsterdam, Rijksmuseum Vincent van Gogh [Vincent van Gogh Foundation, inv nr F 216e]

F 216f [H 243] PLASTER STATUETTE: MAN KNEELING
PROVENANCE Mrs. J. van Gogh-Bonger, Amsterdam; V. W. van Gogh, Laren; Amsterdam, Rijksmuseum Vincent van Gogh [Vincent van Gogh Foundation, inv nr F 216f]

F 216g [H p 557] PLASTER STATUETTE: FEMALE TORSO ON PEDESTAL, SEEN FROM THE BACK
EXHIBITION 1965-6 Stockholm, Göteborg, 15
PROVENANCE Mrs J. van Gogh-Bonger, Amsterdam; V.W. van Gogh, Laren; Amsterdam, Rijksmuseum Vincent van Gogh [Vincent van Gogh Foundation, inv nr F 216g]

F 216h [H 239] PLASTER STATUETTE: FEMALE TORSO ON PEDESTAL, SEEN FROM THE FRONT
EXHIBITIONS 1955 Antwerp 1, 16; 1967 Wolfsburg, 18; 1968-9 London, 60
PROVENANCE Mrs J. van Gogh-Bonger, Amsterdam; V.W. van Gogh, Laren; Amsterdam, Rijksmuseum Vincent van Gogh [Vincent van Gogh Foundation, inv nr F 216h]

F 216i [H 244] PLASTER STATUETTE: FEMALE TORSO WITH ONE LEG, SEEN FROM THE SIDE
PROVENANCE Mrs J. van Gogh-Bonger, Amsterdam; V.W. van Gogh, Laren; Amsterdam, Rijksmuseum Vincent van Gogh [Vincent van Gogh Foundation, inv nr F 216i]

F 216j [H p 557] PLASTER STATUETTE: FEMALE TORSO ON PEDESTAL, SEEN FROM THE FRONT
PROVENANCE Mrs J. van Gogh-Bonger, Amsterdam; V.W. van Gogh, Laren; Amsterdam, Rijksmuseum Vincent van Gogh [Vincent van Gogh Foundation, inv nr F 216j]

F 217 [H p 557] STILL LIFE: BOWL WITH CHRYSANTHEMUMS
EXHIBITIONS 1955 Paris 1, 128; Paris 1960, 26
PROVENANCE P.F. Gachet, Auvers-sur-Oise [1890-1909]; Paul Gachet, Auvers-sur-Oise; Wildenstein Art Gallery, New York; Present owner unknown

F 218 [H 344] STILL LIFE: VASE WITH ROSES
EXHIBITION 1926 Dresden, 215
PROVENANCE Mrs J. van Gogh-Bonger, Amsterdam; V.W. van Gogh, Laren; Amsterdam, Rijksmuseum Vincent van Gogh [Vincent van Gogh Foundation, inv nr F 218]

F 219 [H 311] STILL LIFE: BASKET WITH APPLES, MEAT AND A BREAD ROLL
EXHIBITIONS 1912 Cologne, 8; 1913 The Hague, 70; 1914 Antwerp, 15; 1927 Basle etc, 90; 1928 Düsseldorf, 153; Karlsruhe, 88; 1929 Berlin 1, 79; Hamburg, 47; 1930 Amsterdam, 194; 1935-6 Rotterdam, 63; 1958 Vienna, 69; 1960-1 Montreal etc, 21; 1962 Warsaw, 54; 1963 Tel Aviv-Haifa, 57
PROVENANCE Amédée Schuffenecker, Meudon [1912]; Otterlo, Rijksmuseum Kröller-Müller, inv nr 270-12, cat van Gogh 1970, nr 194

F 220 [H 340] STILL LIFE: VASE WITH CARNATIONS
EXHIBITION 1908 Paris 1, 4 [as Dutch period]
PROVENANCE Mrs Ferd. Bing, Paris; Sale G. Bing, Paris [Drouot] 9 June 1927, 74 [reproduced]; The Leicester Galleries, London; Sale Zurich [Bollag] 21 April 1934, 56; J.D. Klaassen, Rotterdam; W. van der Vorm, Rotterdam [until 1956]; Rotterdam, Willem van der Vorm Foundation, cat 1962, nr 30

F 221 [H 389] THE PONT DU CARROUSEL AND THE LOUVRE
EXHIBITIONS 1928 Berlin, 12; 1955 New York 2, 22
PROVENANCE Julien Tanguy Art Gallery, Paris; A. Bauchy, Livry; A. Vollard Art Gallery, Paris; Zborowski Art Gallery, Paris; F. Hermann, Berlin; Los Angeles, F. Herman [R 1955]

F 221a [formerly F 221b; H 395] THE TRAMP
EXHIBITIONS 1904 Paris; 1943 New York 2, 20
PROVENANCE Arthur Fontaine, Paris; Sale Paris [Drouot] 13 April 1932, nr 72; Huinck and Scherjon Art Gallery, Amsterdam; Charles Boise, Paris [1943]; London, Private collection [R 1970]

F 222 [H 387] THE FOURTEENTH OF JULY CELEBRATION IN PARIS
EXHIBITIONS 1901 Paris, 22; 1924 Basle, 12; Zurich, 14; 1940 Lucerne, 53; 1947 Basle, 29; 1953 The Hague, 66; Otterlo, Amsterdam, 82
PROVENANCE Jos Hessel, Paris [1901]; Aghion, Paris; Sale Aghion, Paris [Drouot] 29 March 1918, 16 [repr]; Paul Vallotton Art Gallery, Lausanne; Bernheim jeune Art Gallery, Paris; A. Hahnloser, Winterthur; Heirs of A. Hahnloser, Bern; Winterthur, Mrs L. Jäggli-Hahnloser [R 1963]

F 223 [H 388] THE TERRACE AT THE TUILERIES
EXHIBITIONS 1905 Amsterdam, 447; 1908 Zurich, 19; 1939 New York, 5
PROVENANCE Mrs J. van Gogh-Bonger, Amsterdam; G. Tanner Art Gallery, Zurich; N. Eisenloeffel Art Gallery, Amsterdam; Leicester Art Galleries, London; Unknown collector, presumably in USA [1939]

F 224 [H 390] IN THE BOIS DE BOULOGNE
EXHIBITIONS 1924 Basle, 11; 1943 Zurich, 712; 1947 Basle, 27
PROVENANCE L.C. Enthoven, Voorburg, Netherlands; Sale Enthoven, Amsterdam [F. Muller] 18 May 1920, nr 238; E. Hahnloser, Zurich; Zurich, Mrs Dora Hahnloser-Gassmann [R 1963]

F 225 [H 254] A PUBLIC GARDEN IN PARIS
EXHIBITION 1947 Basle, 28
PROVENANCE Miss W. van Gogh, Dieren, Netherlands; Mrs J.H. le Cosquino de Bussy, Amsterdam [on loan to Museum Boymans, Rotterdam, about 1936-8, cat 1937, nr 730]; A. Kruysse, The Hague; Private collection, USA

F 226 [H 270] THE MILL LE RADET, RUE LEPIC
EXHIBITIONS 1917 Zurich, 112a; 1924 Basle, 10; 1938 Paris 1, 122
PROVENANCE M. Tabarant, Paris; E. Druet Art Gallery, Paris [1914]; Denys Cochin, Paris [1915]; H. Aubry, Paris; E. Druet Art Gallery, Paris; Sidney W. Brown, Baden [acquired 1917]; Baden, Switzerland, Collection Brown [R 1970]

F 227 [H 267] THE MILL LE RADET, RUE LEPIC
EXHIBITIONS 1901 Paris, 45; 1912 Cologne, 12; 1913 The Hague, 75; 1914 Antwerp, 18; 1927 Basle etc, 89; 1928 Düsseldorf, 152 [reproduced]; Karlsruhe, 87; 1929 Berlin 1, 85; Hamburg, 46; 1930 Amsterdam, 192; 1946-7 Liège etc, 50; 1947 Paris 1, 51; Geneva, 52; Basle, 26; 1947-8 London etc, 13; 1952 Milan, 69; 1956 Eindhoven, 27; Munich, 97; 1958 Tokyo, Kyoto, 87; 1960-1 Montreal etc, 20; 1963 Hamburg, 72
PROVENANCE A. Schuffenecker, Meudon [1901, 1912]; Otterlo, Rijksmuseum Kröller-Müller, inv nr 268-12, cat van Gogh 1970, nr 199

F 228 [H 268] THE MILL LE RADET, RUE LEPIC
EXHIBITIONS 1915 San Francisco, 4031; 1953 Berlin, 8; 1957 Essen, 234; 1960 Paris, 30; 1963 Hamburg, 73
PROVENANCE A. Vollard Art Gallery, Paris; Bernheim jeune Art Gallery, Paris; Orosdi, Paris; L. Nardus, Suresnes; M.H. Souget, Bussum; Sale Amsterdam [F. Muller] 19 June 1917, 38 [reproduced]; A.P. Nielsen, Amsterdam; A. Gold Art Gallery, Berlin; Berlin, Nationalgalerie [acquired 1929], inv nr NG 1616, cat 1968, p 83

F 229 [H 261] MONTMARTRE: QUARRY, GENERAL VIEW
EXHIBITIONS 1920 New York, 51; 1949-50 New York, Chicago, 45
PROVENANCE Mrs J. van Gogh-Bonger, Amsterdam; V.W. van Gogh, Laren; Amsterdam, Rijksmuseum Vincent van Gogh [Vincent van Gogh Foundation, inv nr F 229]

F 230 [H 262] MONTMARTRE: QUARRY, THE MILLS
EXHIBITIONS 1905 Amsterdam, 59; Utrecht, 18; 1906 Rotterdam, 18; 1923 Amsterdam 2, 119; 1928 Berlin, 13; Frankfort, 10; Vienna, 10; Munich, 2; 1955 Antwerp 1, 179; 1957 Marseilles, 28; 1959-60 Utrecht, 18; 1960 Cuesmes 5; 1961 Paris 1, 117; 1961-2 Baltimore etc, 20; 1963 Humlebaek, 16; 1964 Washington, New York, 16; 1967 Wolfsburg, 25; 1968-9 London, 68
PROVENANCE Mrs J. van Gogh-Bonger, Amsterdam; V.W. van Gogh, Laren; Amsterdam, Rijksmuseum Vincent van Gogh [Vincent van Gogh Foundation, inv nr F 230]

F 231 [H 252] VIEW OF ROOFTOPS IN PARIS
EXHIBITIONS 1905 Amsterdam, 49; 1928 Berlin, 14; Frankfort, 6; Vienna, 6; 1961 Paris 1, 118
PROVENANCE Mrs J. van Gogh-Bonger, Amsterdam; V.W. van Gogh, Laren; Amsterdam, Rijksmuseum Vincent van Gogh [Vincent van Gogh Foundation, inv nr F 231]

F 232 [H 356] MONTMARTRE
EXHIBITION 1905 Amsterdam, 55
PROVENANCE Mrs J. van Gogh-Bonger, Amsterdam; V.W. van Gogh, Laren; Amsterdam, Rijksmuseum Vincent van Gogh [Vincent van Gogh Foundation inv nr F 232]

F 233 [H 253] MONTMARTRE: QUARRY
EXHIBITION 1932 Manchester, 11
PROVENANCE Mrs J. van Gogh-Bonger, Amsterdam; V.W. van Gogh, Laren; Amsterdam, Rijksmuseum Vincent van Gogh [Vincent van Gogh Foundation, inv nr F 233]

F 234 [H 300] STILL LIFE: ONE-EARED VASE WITH ASTERS AND PHLOX
EXHIBITIONS 1905 Amsterdam, 64; 1926 Munich, 2069; 1928 Munich, 3; 1932 Manchester, 6; 1939 San Francisco, 170; 1940 New York 3, 13; 1942 Baltimore, Worcester, 6; 1943 New York 2, 8; 1943-4 Indianapolis etc, 2; 1953-4 St Louis etc, 65; 1954 Zurich, 15; 1954-5 Bern, 26; 1955 Antwerp 1, 164; 1955-6 Liverpool etc, 12; 1967 Wolfsburg, 19; 1968-9 London, 66
PROVENANCE Mrs J. van Gogh-Bonger, Amsterdam; V.W. van Gogh, Laren; Amsterdam, Rijksmuseum Vincent van Gogh [Vincent van Gogh Foundation, inv nr F 234]

F 235 [H 334] STILL LIFE: ONE-EARED VASE WITH HOLLYHOCKS
EXHIBITIONS 1905 Paris, 4; 1912 Cologne, 69; 1928 Berlin, 15; 1933-4 Rotterdam, 36; 1934 Bern, 60; 1938 Paris 1, 123; 1943 Zurich, 720; 1947 Basle, 31; 1950 Zurich, p 28; 1954 Rotterdam, 116; 1956 Munich, 99; 1957 Essen, 230; 1960 Paris, 25
PROVENANCE E. Blot, Paris; Sale Blot, Paris [Drouot] 9 May 1900, 162; E. Blot, Paris; Sale Blot, Paris [Drouot] 10 May 1906, 81 [repr]; Druet Art Gallery, Paris; Bernheim jeune Art Gallery, Paris; Rothermundt, Dresden-Blasewitz [about 1909]; Caspari Art Gallery, Munich; Mrs L. Katzenellenbogen, Berlin; Zurich, Kunsthaus, inv nr 2414, cat 1958, p 27

F 235a [H 327] STILL LIFE: BOUQUET OF FLOWERS
EXHIBITIONS 1943 Zurich, 714; 1947 Basle, 35; 1958 Zurich, 239; 1961 Edinburgh, London, 55
PROVENANCE Paul Gallimard, Paris; Paul Cassirer Art Gallery, Berlin; Knoedler Art Gallery, New York; F. Nathan Art Gallery, Zurich [R 1938]; Zurich, Sammlung E.G. Bührle [acquired 1938], cat 1958, nr 239

F 236 [H 301] STILL LIFE: ONE-EARED VASE WITH DIANTHUS
EXHIBITIONS 1924 Paris, 13; 1929 New York, 93; 1935-6 New York etc, 14; 1943 New York 2, 9
PROVENANCE Matthew L. Justice, Dundee; Bernheim jeune Art Gallery, Paris; Knoedler Art Gallery, New York; Scott and Fowles Art Gallery, New York [R 1927]; James W. Barney, New York; Sale New York [Parke-Bernet] 26 October 1944, 84; Sessler, Philadelphia [R 1944]; Chas. Chaplin, Haverford, Penns.; Sale New York [Parke-Bernet] 9 November 1955, 82; A. Ball Art Gallery, New York; Present owner unknown

F 237 [H 302] STILL LIFE: ONE-EARED VASE WITH PHYSOSTEGIA, GLADIOLUS AND LYCHNIS
EXHIBITIONS 1936 Amsterdam, 16; 1938-9 Rotterdam, 11; 1960 Paris, 27
PROVENANCE L.C. Enthoven, Voorburg, Netherlands; Sale Enthoven, Amsterdam [F. Muller] 18 May 1920, 235 [repr]; B.M.A. Carp, Bloemendaal, Netherlands; D.G. van Beuningen, Vierhouten, Netherlands, cat 1949, 140; Rotterdam, Museum Boymans-van Beuningen [acquired 1958], inv nr 2607, cat 1963, p 50

F 238 [H 393] LA GUINGUETTE
EXHIBITIONS 1925 Paris 1, 8; 1955 Marseilles, 12
PROVENANCE Bernheim jeune Art Gallery, Paris [1908]; Druet Art Gallery, Paris [1909]; P. Goujon, Paris [1909-1914]; Paris, Musée de Luxembourg [bequest of P. Goujon, 1914]; Paris, Musée National du Louvre [acquired 1929], inv nr RF 2243, cat 1959, nr 144

F 239 [H 385] THE VIADUCT
EXHIBITION 1955 New York 2, 21
PROVENANCE Charpentier Art Gallery, Paris; Hans Bammann Art Gallery, Düsseldorf; Thannhauser Art Gallery, Berlin; J.K. Thannhauser Art Gallery, New York; New York, J.K. Thannhauser – Courtesy of Thannhauser Foundation [ou loan to Guggenheim Museum, New York]
EDITORS' COMMENT For altered pedigree see F 126a

F 240 [H 386] THE BRIDGE ACROSS THE SEINE AT ASNIÈRES [PONT ROUTE]
EXHIBITIONS 1928 Berlin, 16; Frankfort, 9; 1942 Baltimore, Worcester, 9; 1943 New York 2, 18; 1952 London 4, 93; 1954 Geneva, 92; 1960 Houston; 1964 New York, without cat nr
PROVENANCE Mrs E.H. du Quesne-van Gogh, Baarn; Siegbert Stern, Berlin-Neubabelsberg; Jacob M. Goldschmidt Art Gallery, Paris; J.K. Thannhauser Art Gallery, New York [1943]; Max Moos, Geneva [1954]; Mr and Mrs Marc Mizne, Rio de Janeiro; Sale London [Sotheby] 25 November 1959, 81; Bryanston-Jones; Mr and Mrs John de Menil, New York, Houston; Sale New York [Parke-Bernet] 19 May 1966, nr 22 [not sold]; New York, Houston, Mr and Mrs John de Menil

F 241 [H 294] STILL LIFE: VASE WITH ZINNIAS AND GERANIUMS
EXHIBITIONS 1929 London 1, 448; 1930 Amsterdam, 4; 1932 Manchester, 2; 1933 Amsterdam 2, 120; 1945 Amsterdam, without cat nr
PROVENANCE C.M. van Gogh Art Gallery, Amsterdam; J. Hidde Nijland, The Hague; W.J.R. Dreesmann, Amsterdam [1929]; Van Wisselingh Art Gallery, Amsterdam; Ottawa, National Gallery of Canada [acquired 1950], inv nr 5045, cat paintings and sculpture 1959, vol. II, p 29

F 242 [H 335] STILL LIFE: VASE WITH ONOETHERA AND ALSTROEMERIA
EXHIBITIONS 1925 Paris 1, 12; 1927 Berlin 2, not in cat; 1928 Berlin, 17
PROVENANCE Mrs J. van Gogh-Bonger, Amsterdam; G. Camentron, Paris [R 1911]; Paul Cassirer Art Gallery, Berlin [R 1912]; H. Eissler, Vienna [R 1925]; Paul Cassirer Art Gallery, Berlin; Thannhauser Art Gallery, Munich [before 1928]; Haber, Berlin [before 1938]; Riggisberg, Switzerland, Abegg-Stiftung [R 1970]

F 243 [H 317] STILL LIFE: VASE WITH CARNATIONS
EXHIBITIONS 1954 New York, 26; 1955 New York 2, 14
PROVENANCE Mrs H. Ullmann, Frankfort; W. Goetz, New

York; Wildenstein Art Gallery, New York; New York, Mrs Charles B. Murphy [1954]

F 243a [formerly F 243bis, H 337] STILL LIFE: VASE WITH MYOSOTIS AND PEONIES
EXHIBITIONS 1957 Stockholm, 105; 1960 Cuesmes, 6
PROVENANCE Mrs J. van Gogh-Bonger, Amsterdam; H. C. Bonger, Amsterdam; Miss E. H. Bonger, Amsterdam; V. W. van Gogh, Laren; Amsterdam, Rijksmuseum Vincent van Gogh [Vincent van Gogh Foundation, inv nr F 243a]

F 244 [H 286] STILL LIFE: BOWL WITH PANSIES
EXHIBITIONS 1905 Amsterdam, 51; 1906 Rotterdam, 15; 1910 Berlin 1, 6; 1954-5 Bern, 24; 1955 Antwerp 1, 165
PROVENANCE Mrs J. van Gogh-Bonger, Amsterdam; V.W. van Gogh, Laren; Amsterdam, Rijksmuseum Vincent van Gogh [Vincent van Gogh Foundation, inv nr F 244]

F 245 [H 338] STILL LIFE: VASE WITH CARNATIONS
EXHIBITIONS 1930 Amsterdam, 5; 1937 Paris, 19; 1951 Lyons etc, 15; 1954 Dordrecht, 51; 1955 Dordrecht, 55; 1962 Warsaw, 92; 1963 Tel Aviv, Haifa, 60
PROVENANCE F. J. Michelsen, Amsterdam; Sale Michelsen, Amsterdam [F. Muller] 3 December 1918, 304 [repr]; Vereniging tot het vormen van een openbare verzameling van hedendaagse kunst, Amsterdam [bought November 1918]; Amsterdam, Stedelijk Museum, inv nr A 2235

F 246 [H 312] STILL LIFE: ONE-EARED VASE WITH CARNATIONS AND ROSES AND A BOTTLE
EXHIBITIONS 1913 The Hague, 71; 1914 Antwerp, 17; 1927 Basle etc, 86; 1928 Düsseldorf, 149; Karlsruhe, 84; 1929 Berlin 1, 84; Hamburg, 43; 1930 Amsterdam, 195; 1935-6 Rotterdam, 62; 1947 Basle, 30; 1956 Eindhoven, 26
PROVENANCE E. Blot Art Gallery, Paris [1913]; Otterlo, Rijksmuseum Kröller-Müller, inv nr 266-13, cat van Gogh 1970, nr 196

F 246a STILL LIFE: FLOWERS
PROVENANCE H. Oelze, Amsterdam; Private collection, Paris; Private collection [R 1969]

F 247 [H V] STILL LIFE: VASE WITH GLADIOLI
EXHIBITIONS 1905 Amsterdam, 80; Utrecht, 24; 1906 Rotterdam, 24; 1934 Amsterdam 1, 55; 1935 Amsterdam 3, 17; 1937 Paris, 53; 1943 New York 2, 11
PROVENANCE Mrs J. van Gogh-Bonger, Amsterdam [1905]; V. W. van Gogh, Laren; Independent Gallery, London; Mrs Käte Perls, Paris; Hugo Perls Art Gallery, New York [1943]; Short Hills, N Y, Albert W. Blum

F 248 [H 343] STILL LIFE: VASE WITH RED GLADIOLI
PROVENANCE Bernheim jeune Art Gallery, Paris; Alden Brooks, Paris [before 1928]; Present owner unknown

F 248a STILL LIFE: VASE WITH GLADIOLI
EXHIBITIONS 1906 Rotterdam, 24; 1954 Zurich, 32; 1955 Antwerp 1, 166; Amsterdam 1, 80; 1955-6 Liverpool etc, 13; 1958-9 San Francisco etc, 32; 1961-2 Baltimore etc, 17; 1967 Wolfsburg, 20; 1968-9 London, 67
PROVENANCE Mrs J. van Gogh-Bonger, Amsterdam; V. W. van Gogh, Laren; Amsterdam, Rijksmuseum Vincent van Gogh [Vincent van Gogh Foundation, inv nr F 248a]

F 248b STILL LIFE: ONE-EARED VASE WITH RED GLADIOLI
PROVENANCE E. Blot Art Gallery, Paris; Mr Alexandre Sr, Paris; Mr Alexandre Jr and sister, Paris; Beyeler Art Gallery, Basle; Morges, Switzerland – Paris, J. Planque [acquired 1956]

F 249 [H 288] STILL LIFE: BOWL WITH PEONIES AND ROSES
EXHIBITIONS 1912 Cologne, 5; 1913 The Hague, 77; 1914 Antwerp, 16; 1927 Basle etc, 84; 1928 Düsseldorf, 147; Karlsruhe, 82; 1929 Berlin 1, 83; Hamburg, 41; 1930 Amsterdam, 193; 1935-6 Rotterdam, 61; 1946-7 Liège etc, 55; 1947 Paris 1, 53; Geneva, 54; Basle, 32; 1947-8 London etc, 15; 1952 Milan, 64; 1956 Eindhoven, 28; Munich, 100; 1958 Vienna, 70; Tokyo, Kyoto, 85; 1959 São Paulo, 4; 1962 Warsaw, 55; 1963 Tel Aviv, Haifa, 61; Hamburg, 74; 1966 Belgrade, 58
PROVENANCE Sale Amsterdam [F. Muller] 1909; A. G. Kröller, Wassenaar [1941]; Otterlo, Rijksmuseum Kröller-Müller, inv nr 1106-41, cat van Gogh 1970, nr 197

F 250 [H 289] STILL LIFE: BOWL WITH SUNFLOWERS AND OTHER FLOWERS
EXHIBITIONS 1905 Paris, 2; 1914 Berlin, 31; 1937 Paris, 29
PROVENANCE E. Blot, Paris [1905]; Second sale Blot, Paris [Drouot] 10 May 1906, 82; E. Druet Art Gallery, Paris; Paul Cassirer Art Gallery, Berlin; Mannheim, Städtische Kunsthalle [acquired 1911], cat 1957, nr 59

F 251 [H 295] STILL LIFE: BOWL WITH SUMMERFLOWERS [HELIOPSIS AND GYPSOPHILA?]
EXHIBITIONS 1892 [?] Amsterdam; 1945 Amsterdam, without cat nr; 1946-7 Liège etc, 54; 1947 Basle, 34; Paris 1, 55; Geneva, 56
PROVENANCE Miss Oldenboom, Amsterdam [1946]; Alex Reid and Lefevre Art Gallery, London; Ottawa, National Gallery of Canada [acquired 1951], inv nr 5808, cat Paintings and sculpture 1959, vol 11, p 30

F 252 [H 293] STILL LIFE: BOWL WITH ZINNIAS
EXHIBITIONS 1914 Berlin, 25; 1955 New York 2, 13; 1965 New York 2, 50
PROVENANCE Paul Cassirer Art Gallery, Berlin; J. Hessel Art Gallery, Paris; Mr and Mrs H. P. Newman, Hamburg [1914]; Wildenstein Art Gallery, New York; Myrtil Frank, New York; Mr and Mrs Grover A. Magnin, San Francisco [R 1955, 1965]; Sale New York [Parke-Bernet] 15 October 1969, 4; Present owner unknown

F 253 [H 308] STILL LIFE: A BOTTLE, TWO GLASSES AND A PLATE OF BREAD
EXHIBITIONS 1928 Berlin, 18; Frankfort, 7; Vienna, 7; 1951 Lyons etc, 13; 1953-4 St Louis etc, 66; 1954-5 Bern, 27; 1955 Antwerp 1, 163
PROVENANCE Mrs J. van Gogh-Bonger, Amsterdam; V. W. van Gogh, Laren; Amsterdam, Rijksmuseum Vincent van Gogh [Vincent van Gogh Foundation, inv nr F 253]

F 253a [formerly F 253bis, H 284] STILL LIFE: PLATE WITH ROLLS
EXHIBITIONS 1932 Manchester, 13; 1953-4 St Louis etc, 67; 1958-9 San Francisco etc, 15; 1961-2 Baltimore etc, 26
PROVENANCE Mrs J. van Gogh-Bonger, Amsterdam; V. W. van Gogh, Laren; Amsterdam, Rijksmuseum Vincent van Gogh [Vincent van Gogh Foundation, inv nr F 253a]

F 254 [H 281] STILL LIFE: APPLES
EXHIBITIONS 1905 Amsterdam, 56; Utrecht, 17; 1906 Rotterdam, 17; 1914 Berlin, 19; 1954 Zurich, 16; 1954-5 Bern, 23; 1955 Antwerp 1, 174; 1955-6 Liverpool etc, 20; 1958-9 San Francisco etc, 19; 1968-9 London, 89
PROVENANCE Mrs J. van Gogh-Bonger, Amsterdam; V. W. van Gogh, Laren; Amsterdam, Rijksmuseum Vincent van Gogh [Vincent van Gogh Foundation, inv nr F 254]

F 255 [H 248] A PAIR OF SHOES
EXHIBITIONS 1920 New York, 41; 1923 London, 14; 1924 Basle, 3; Zurich, 8; Stuttgart, 1; 1925 Paris 1, 6; The Hague, 12; 1928 Munich, 4; 1930 Amsterdam, 6; 1945-6 Amsterdam, 14; 1946-7 Liège etc, 77; 1947 Geneva, 75; London etc, 14; Paris 1, 75; 1948 Bergen, Oslo, 10; 1951 Lyons etc, 14; 1954-5 Bern, 17; 1955 Antwerp 1, 167; 1955-6 Liverpool etc, 15; 1957 Marseilles, 23; 1958-9 San Francisco etc, 18; 1959-60 Utrecht, 14; 1960-1 Montreal etc, 26; 1961-2 Baltimore etc, 16; 1963 Sheffield, 3; Humlebaek, 12; 1964 Washington, New York, 12; 1965 Charleroi, Ghent, 8; 1965-6 Stockholm, Göteborg, 12; 1967 Wolfsburg, 21; 1968-9 London, 52
PROVENANCE Mrs J. van Gogh-Bonger, Amsterdam; V. W. van Gogh, Laren; Amsterdam, Rijksmuseum Vincent van Gogh [Vincent van Gogh Foundation, inv nr F 255]

F 256 [H 287] MUSSELS AND SHRIMPS
EXHIBITIONS 1905 Amsterdam, 88; 1906 Rotterdam, 29; 1927 Paris; 1930 Amsterdam, 7; 1932 Manchester, 9; 1954-5 Bern, 25; 1955 Antwerp 1, 175; 1963 Utica, New York, 432
PROVENANCE Mrs J. van Gogh-Bonger, Amsterdam; V. W. van Gogh, Laren; Amsterdam, Rijksmuseum Vincent van Gogh [Vincent van Gogh Foundation, inv nr F 256]

F 257 [H 341] STILL LIFE: PLATE, VASE AND FLOWERS
EXHIBITION 1912 Cologne, 13
PROVENANCE Baron Blanquet de Fulde, Paris; Sale Heirs of Baron Blanquet de Fulde, Paris [Drouot] 24 May 1907, nr 45; Orosdi, Paris; G. F. Reber, Barmen [R 1912]; Knoedler Art Gallery, New York [about 1948-50]; São Paulo, Museu de Arte [gift of Ricardo Fasanello], cat 1963, nr 111

F 258 [H 330] STILL LIFE: WHITE VASE WITH ROSES AND OTHER FLOWERS
PROVENANCE B. Goudchaux, Paris; Paul Vallotton Art Gallery, Lausanne; Huinck Art Gallery, Utrecht; Otterlo, Rijksmuseum Kröller-Müller, cat Auping [1942], nr 177 [on loan, not in cat 1956]; Private collection, Berlin; Present owner unknown

F 259 [H 331] STILL LIFE: VASE WITH CARNATIONS AND ZINNIAS
EXHIBITIONS 1958 Amsterdam 2, 15; 1959 London, 78; 1960 Paris, 21
PROVENANCE d'Audretsch Art Gallery, The Hague; H. P. Bremmer, The Hague [on loan to the Rijksmuseum, Amsterdam, since 1917, cat 1920 and 1934, nr 984i]; Heirs H. P. Bremmer, The Hague [1956-1960]; M. Frank, New York [acquired 1960]; Present owner unknown

F 260 [H 260] HOUSES IN ANTWERP
EXHIBITIONS 1905 Amsterdam, 46; 1945 Amsterdam, without cat nr; 1951 Lyons etc, 12; 1953 The Hague, 45; Otterlo, Amsterdam, 50; 1953-4 Saint Louis etc, 54; 1954 Zurich, 12; 1954-5 Bern, 13; 1955 Antwerp 1, 115; 1955-6 Liverpool etc, 9; 1957 Marseilles, 17; 1958-9 San Francisco etc, 12; 1959-60 Utrecht, 9; 1961-2 Baltimore etc, 12; 1963 Humlebaek, 9; 1964 Washington, New York, 9; 1965 Charleroi, Ghent, 6; 1965-6 Stockholm, Göteborg, 10; 1967 Wolfsburg, 15; 1968-9 London, 54
PROVENANCE Mrs J. van Gogh-Bonger, Amsterdam; V. W. van Gogh, Laren; Amsterdam, Rijksmuseum Vincent van Gogh [Vincent van Gogh Foundation, inv nr F 260]

F 261 [H 259] VIEW OF PARIS
EXHIBITIONS 1905 Amsterdam, 77; Utrecht, 23; 1906 Rotterdam, 23; 1928 Berlin, 19; Frankfort 11; Vienna, 11; Munich, 5; 1945 Amsterdam, without cat nr; 1946 Stockholm etc, 22; 1953-4 St Louis etc, 73; 1954-5, Bern, 18; 1955 Antwerp 1, 177; 1955-6 Liverpool etc, 14; 1957 Marseiles, 26; 1958-9 San Francisco etc, 21; 1959-60 Utrecht, 15; 1961 Paris, 119
PROVENANCE Mrs J. van Gogh-Bonger, Amsterdam; V. W. van Gogh, Laren; Amsterdam, Rijksmuseum Vincent van Gogh [Vincent van Gogh Foundation, inv nr F 261]

F 262 [H 258] VIEW FROM MONTMARTRE
EXHIBITIONS 1905 Paris, 45; Berlin, 11; 1912 Cologne, 14; 1922 Rotterdam; 1927-8 Rotterdam, 32; 1952 Milan, 66
PROVENANCE Georges Viau, Paris [1905]; Second Sale Viau, Paris [Durand-Ruel] 21-22 March 1907, nr 83; Bernheim jeune Art Gallery, Paris; H. Tutein Nolthenius, Delft [1927-1928]; d'Audretsch Art Gallery, The Hague; Basle, Öffentliche Kunstsammlung [acquired 1946], inv nr 1982, cat 1946, p 148, cat 1961, p 12
EDITORS' COMMENT It is uncertain which of the views from Montmartre was on the Berlin exhibition;

F 263 [H 416] PORTRAIT OF PÈRE TANGUY
EXHIBITIONS 1901 Paris, 13; 1912 Paris, 207; 1945 Copenhagen, 110; 1957-8 Copenhagen, 60
PROVENANCE Julien Tanguy, Paris; A. Vollard Art Gallery, Paris [1901]; J. Keller, Paris; Druet Art Gallery, Paris [1910]; Bernheim jeune Art Gallery, Paris [1911]; Octave Mirbeau, Paris; Sale Mirbeau, Paris [Durand-Ruel] 24 February 1919, nr 19 [reproduced]; Wilh. Hansen, Charlottenlund-Copenhagen; Copenhagen, Ny Carlsberg Glyptotek [acquired 1923; Ny Carlsbergfondet], inv nr 1908, cat 1961, nr 944

F 263a [formerly F 263bis, H 414] SELFPORTRAIT WITH PIPE AND GLASS
EXHIBITIONS 1905 Amsterdam, 69; 1914 Berlin, 38; 1927 Paris; 1930 Amsterdam, 8; 1932 Manchester, 10; 1937 Paris 28; 1945 Amsterdam, without cat nr; 1951 Lyons etc, 16; 1953 The Hague, 67; Otterlo, Amsterdam, 56; 1953-4 Saint Louis etc, 59; 1954-5 Bern, 34; 1955 Antwerp 1, 196; 1955-6 Liverpool etc, 26; 1960 London 4, 12
PROVENANCE Mrs J. van Gogh-Bonger, Amsterdam; V. W. van Gogh, Laren; Amsterdam, Rijksmuseum Vincent van Gogh [Vincent van Gogh Foundation, inv nr F 263a]

F 264 [H 256] THE OUTSKIRTS OF PARIS
EXHIBITIONS 1905 Amsterdam, 30; 1906 Rotterdam, 11; 1926 Munich, 2086; London 3, 6 [repr]; 1930 Amsterdam, 9; 1947-8 London etc, 13a; 1957 Los Angeles, 5
PROVENANCE Mrs J. van Gogh-Bonger, Amsterdam; V. W. van Gogh, Laren; Earl of Sandwich, Huntingdon [1930, 1947]; Wildenstein Art Gallery, New York; Norman B. Woolworth, Monmouth, Maine; Sale Woolworth, New York [Parke-Bernet] 31 October 1962, 21; Mrs Norman B. Woolworth, New York; Sale London [Christie] 1 December 1967, 42; Present owner unknown

F 264a [formerly F 264bis, H 394] SHELTER ON THE HILL OF MONTMARTRE
EXHIBITIONS 1952 London 1, 8; 1965 San Francisco, 146
PROVENANCE Mrs J. van Gogh-Bonger, Amsterdam; V. W. van Gogh, Laren; D. C. Roëll, Amsterdam; H. A. Roëll, Mexico City; Frederick J. Hellman, San Francisco; San Francisco, California Palace of the Legion of Honor, the Mr and Mrs Frederick J. Hellman collection

F 265 [H 257] VIEW OF PARIS IN THE NEIGHBORHOOD OF MONTMARTRE
PROVENANCE L. C. Enthoven, Voorburg, Netherlands; Sale Enthoven, Amsterdam [F. Muller] 18 May 1920, nr 234 [reproduced]; Huinck Art Gallery, Utrecht; W. Scherjon, Utrecht; Mr Pagenstecher, Wiesbaden; Western Germany, Private collection [R 1963]

F 266 [H 271] THE HILL OF MONTMARTRE
EXHIBITIONS 1913 The Hague, 74; 1927 Basle etc, 81 [repr]; 1928 Düsseldorf, 145 [repr]; Karlsruhe, 80 [repr]; 1929 Berlin 1, 81; Hamburg, 38; 1930 Amsterdam, 198; 1935-6 New York etc, 12; 1946-7 Liège etc, 51; 1947 Paris 1, 52; Geneva, 52; 1957 Essen, 235; 1958 Vienna, 71; 1959 Aix-en-Provence, 2; 1962 Warsaw, 56; 1963 Tel Aviv, Haifa, 64; 1966 Belgrade, 55
PROVENANCE E. Blot Art Gallery, Paris [1912]; Otterlo, Rijksmuseum Kröller-Müller, inv nr 262-12, cat van Gogh 1970, nr 200

F 266a [formerly F 266bis, H 255] FACTORIES SEEN FROM A HILLSIDE IN MOONLIGHT
EXHIBITIONS 1905 Amsterdam, 70; 1952 Milan, 76
PROVENANCE A. Bonger, Amsterdam [1905]; Mrs

F. Bonger-van der Borch van Verwolde, Almen, Netherlands [until 1970]; Amsterdam, Rijksmuseum Vincent van Gogh [Vincent van Gogh Foundation, inv nr F 266a]

F 267 [H 418] SELFPORTRAIT: THREE QUARTERS TO THE LEFT
EXHIBITIONS 1949-50 New York, Chicago, 47; 1953 The Hague, 68; Otterlo, Amsterdam, 57; 1955 Antwerp 1, 202; 1955-6 Liverpool etc, 28; 1960 London 4, 13; 1961-2 Baltimore etc, 29; 1963 Sheffield, 6; 1965-6 Stockholm, Göteborg, 25
PROVENANCE Mrs J. van Gogh-Bonger, Amsterdam; V. W. van Gogh, Laren; Amsterdam, Rijksmuseum Vincent van Gogh [Vincent van Gogh Foundation, inv nr F 267]

F 268 [H 417] SELFPORTRAIT: THREE QUARTERS TO THE RIGHT
EXHIBITIONS 1901 Paris, 1; 1921 New York, 119 [repr]; 1963 Utica, New York, 582
PROVENANCE A. Vollard Art Gallery, Paris [1901]; Alphonse Kann, Saint Germain-en-Laye; John Quinn, New York [1921]; Mrs J. S. Goodwin, New York [1927-1939]; Philip L. Goodwin, New York; Hartford, Connecticut Wadsworth Atheneum [acquired 1954; gift Philip L. Goodwin], acc nr 1954.189, handbook 1958, nr 134

F 269 recto [formerly F 269 verso; H 88] STUDY OF A PEASANT WOMAN
PROVENANCE Mrs J. van Gogh-Bonger, Amsterdam; V. W. van Gogh, Laren; Amsterdam, Rijksmuseum Vincent van Gogh [Vincent van Gogh Foundation, inv nr F 269]

F 269 verso [formerly F 269, H 419] SELF PORTRAIT: FULL FACE
EXHIBITIONS 1937 Paris, 2; 1945 Amsterdam, without cat number; 1953 The Hague, 69; Otterlo, Amsterdam, 58; 1953-4 Saint Louis etc, 61; 1955 Antwerp 1, 203; 1957 Stockholm, 108; 1960 London 4, 14
PROVENANCE Mrs J. van Gogh-Bonger, Amsterdam; V. W. van Gogh, Laren; Amsterdam, Rijksmuseum Vincent van Gogh [Vincent van Gogh Foundation, inv nr F 269]

F 270 [H 404] PORTRAIT OF ALEXANDER REID
EXHIBITIONS 1914 Berlin, 35; 1928 Munich, 6; 1955 New York 2, 24
PROVENANCE Mrs J. van Gogh-Bonger, Amsterdam; V. W. van Gogh, Laren; Wildenstein Art Gallery, New York; M. Frank, New York [about 1956-7]; David B. Findlay Galleries, New York; Oklahoma City, A. M. Weitzenhoffer [R 1970]

F 270a [formerly F 270bis, H 359] THE CHESTNUT TREE IN FLOWER
EXHIBITIONS 1905 Amsterdam, 61; Utrecht, 19; 1906 Rotterdam, 19; 1908 Paris 1, 10; 1924 Basle, 19; Zurich, 16; Stuttgart, 4; 1925 The Hague, 22; Paris 1, 7; 1928 Berlin, 20; Frankfort, 12; Vienna, 12; 1932 Manchester, 43; 1955 Antwerp 1, 188; Dordrecht, 54
PROVENANCE Mrs J. van Gogh-Bonger, Amsterdam; V. W. van Gogh, Laren; Amsterdam, Rijksmuseum Vincent van Gogh [Vincent van Gogh Foundation, inv nr F 270a]

F 271 [H 376] WINDMILL ON MONTMARTRE [destroyed]
EXHIBITIONS 1938 New York 1, 1; London 2, 39
PROVENANCE Mrs J. van Gogh-Bonger, Amsterdam; J. H. de Bois Art Gallery, Haarlem [1914, 1916]; Sale Amsterdam [F. Muller] 26 October 1920, nr 140 [reproduced]; E. Blot Art Gallery, Paris; G. Urion; Sale Urion, Paris [Petit] 30-31 May 1927, nr 35 [reproduced]; R. Sauerbach, Paris; Sale Sauerbach, Paris [Drouot] 11 March 1931, 34; M. Lindon, Paris; Bignou Art Gallery, Paris; Reid and Lefevre Art Gallery, London [1938]; Private collection, Scotland; Sale W. A. Cargill, London [Sotheby] 11 June 1963, 49; Picture destroyed by fire [1967]

F 272 [H 370] MONTMARTRE NEAR THE UPPER MILL
EXHIBITIONS 1905 Amsterdam, 40; 1923 London, 18; 1924 Paris, 15; 1933 Chicago, 380; 1934 Chicago, 313; 1943 New York 2, 16; 1948 Cleveland, 5; 1949-50 New York, Chicago, 46; 1951 Houston, 3
PROVENANCE Mrs J. van Gogh-Bonger, Amsterdam; Mrs Carstairs, London [acquired 1923]; M. Knoedler Art Gallery, Paris; Mr Viaud, Paris; Helen Birch Bartlett, New York; Chicago, The Art Institute of Chicago [acquired 1926; Helen Birch Bartlett Memorial collection], inv nr 26.202, cat 1961, p 181

F 273 [H 263] WINDMILLS ON MONTMARTRE
EXHIBITIONS 1928 Berlin, 21; 1955 New York 4, 30
PROVENANCE J. D. C. Titsingh, Arnhem; Sale Titsingh, The Hague [Pulchri] 12-13 March 1901, 60; L. C. Enthoven, Voorburg, Netherlands; Sale Enthoven, Amsterdam [F. Muller] 18 May 1920, 233 [repr]; Paul Kempner, Berlin; E. and A. Silberman Galleries, New York; Milch Galleries; New York, J. S. Lasdon [R 1955]

F 274 [H 272] MOULIN DE LA GALETTE
EXHIBITIONS 1943 Glasgow, 53; 1962 London 5, 238
PROVENANCE Bernheim jeune Art Gallery, Paris; Alex Reid and Lefevre Art Gallery, Glasgow; William McInnes, Glasgow; Glasgow, Glasgow Art Gallery [acquired 1944; McInnes bequest], inv nr 2425, cat French Paintings 1953, p 52; cat 1967, pp 15 and 63

F 275 [H 354] VIEW IN VOYER-D'ARGENSON PARK AT ASNIÈRES
EXHIBITION 1905 Amsterdam, 33
PROVENANCE Mrs J. van Gogh-Bonger, Amsterdam; V. W. van Gogh, Laren; Amsterdam, Rijksmuseum Vincent van Gogh [Vincent van Gogh Foundation, inv nr F 275]

F 276 [H 353] CORNER IN VOYER-D'ARGENSON PARK AT ASNIÈRES
EXHIBITIONS 1905 Amsterdam, 65; 1914 Berlin, 61; 1951 Aberdeen, 145; 1956 New Haven, 98; 1968 New York, 118
PROVENANCE Mrs J. van Gogh-Bonger, Amsterdam [1905]; V. W. van Gogh, Laren; L. Sutro, London; Sale London [Sotheby] 10 November 1943, nr 103; Private collection, England [1951]; Mr and Mrs Henry R. Luce, New York [1956]; New Haven, Yale University Art Gallery [gift of H. R. Luce], inv nr 1958.59, cat 1968, p 11

F 277 [H 352] THE AVENUE IN VOYER-D'ARGENSON PARK AT ASNIÈRES
EXHIBITIONS 1938 London 1, 27; 1943 New York 2, 14; 1955 New York 2, 17
PROVENANCE F. Kranenburg, Amsterdam [on loan to Rijksmuseum, Amsterdam since 1909, cat 1911, nr 984h]; Sale Amsterdam [F. Muller] 21 May 1912, nr 30 [property F. Kranenburg]; A. M. Baron van Tuyll van Serooskerken, Amsterdam; Marcel Kapferer, Paris [1938]; Wildenstein Art Gallery, New York; Charles Gilman, New York; New York, Mrs Charles Gilman [1955]

F 278 [H 329] STILL LIFE: VASE WITH DAISIES AND DAHLIAS
PROVENANCE L. C. Enthoven, Voorburg, Netherlands; Sale Enthoven, Amsterdam [F. Muller] 18 May 1920, nr 236 [and reproduced]; M. Lam jr, Amsterdam; Sale Lam a o, Amsterdam [F. Muller] 2 April 1935, nr 11; A. F. Philips, Eindhoven; Eindhoven, Mrs A. H. Philips-de Jongh [R 1967]

F 279 [H 342] STILL LIFE: RED POPPIES
PROVENANCE A. Vollard Art Gallery, Paris; Paul Rosenberg Art Gallery, Paris; L. Nardus, Paris; M. H. Souget, Bussum; Sale Amsterdam [F. Muller] 19 June 1917, nr 37; L. Nardus, Paris; Mrs Demotte, Paris; Mrs Anne Parrish Titzell, Georgetown, Conn.; North Hartford, Connecticut, Wadsworth Atheneum [gift of Mr and Mrs Audrey G. Carey], inv nr 1957.617

F 280 [H 325] STILL LIFE: DAISIES AND POPPIES
EXHIBITIONS 1929 New York, 92; 1935-6 New York etc, 15
PROVENANCE Paul Cassirer Art Gallery, Berlin; Mrs A. Albert, Munich [R 1918]; Caspari Art Gallery, Munich; Knoedler Art Gallery, London; A. Conger Goodyear, New York [R 1935]; Buffalo, USA, George F. Goodyear

F 281 [H 324] STILL LIFE: COLEUS PLANT IN A FLOWER POT
EXHIBITIONS 1905 Amsterdam, 87; 1932 Manchester, 31
PROVENANCE Mrs J. van Gogh-Bonger, Amsterdam; V. W. van Gogh, Laren; Amsterdam, Rijksmuseum Vincent van Gogh [Vincent van Gogh Foundation, inv nr F 281]

F 282 [H 345] STILL LIFE: CINERARIA IN A FLOWERPOT
EXHIBITIONS 1921 Berlin; 1927 Berlin 2, 106 or 111; 1928 Berlin, 22; 1939 Amsterdam 2, 14; 1939-40 Rotterdam, 21; 1960 Paris, 28
PROVENANCE C. Hoogendijk, The Hague; Sale Hoogendijk, Amsterdam [F. Muller] 21 May 1912, nr 28 [reproduced]; Paul Cassirer Art Gallery, Berlin; Hans Wenuland, Berlin; Thannhauser Art Gallery, Munich; Oskar Skaller, Berlin [acquired 1917]; Sale Berlin [Graupe] 13 November 1930, nr 8; B. Houthakker, Amsterdam [1939]; H. van Beek, Rotterdam [1939]; Rotterdam, Museum Boymans-Van Beuningen [acquired 1951; gift of Mrs E. Y. van Beek-van Hoorn Janssen and children], inv nr St. 92, cat 1963, p 50

F 283 [H 313] STILL LIFE: RED HERRINGS
EXHIBITIONS 1924 Basle, 14; 1934 Bern, 58; 1945 Basle, 6; 1947 Basle, 49; 1964 Paris 1, 31
PROVENANCE Bernheim jeune Art Gallery, Paris; Basle, R. Staechelin Foundation [acquired 1931]

F 283a STILL LIFE: TWO HERRINGS
PROVENANCE Jean Krebs, Brussels; Sale Paris [Charpentier] 15 December 1958, 161; France, Francis Junker

F 283b STILL LIFE: HERRINGS WITH A GARLIC
PROVENANCE Tokyo, Shojiro Ishibashi, Bridgestone Museum of Art, cat 1959, nr 61

F 284 [H 310] STILL LIFE: HERRINGS AND ONIONS
Left out by Faille in his manuscript for the present edition; See REJECTED WORKS

F 285 [H 314] STILL LIFE: HERRINGS, LEMONS AND TOMATOES
EXHIBITIONS 1924 Basle, 13; Zurich, 15; 1955 Winterthur 2, 71
PROVENANCE A. Tavernier, Paris; Sale Tavernier, Paris [Petit] 6 March 1900, 82; Octave Mirbeau, Paris; Sale Mirbeau, Paris [Durand-Ruel] 24 February 1919, 20 [repr]; Paul Rosenberg Art Gallery, Paris; Winterthur, Oskar Reinhart

F 286 [H 323] STILL LIFE: VASE WITH DELPHINIUM, ASTER, SALVIA AND SPIRAEA
EXHIBITIONS 1937 Paris, 52; 1947 Basle, 33; 1952 Milan, 73; 1953 The Hague, 70; Otterlo, Amsterdam, 69; 1957 Essen, 228; 1958 Tokyo, Kyoto, 94; 1960 Paris, 22; 1962 Warsaw, 94; 1963 Tel Aviv, Haifa, 59
PROVENANCE Mrs E. H. du Quesne-van Gogh, Baarn; N. Eisenloeffel Art Gallery, Amsterdam; The Hague, Gemeentemuseum [acquired 1920], inv nr 2-1920, cat 1962, nr 136

F 286a STILL LIFE: VASE WITH GLADIOLI AND LILACS
EXHIBITIONS 1955 Antwerp 2, 174 A; 1957 Essen, 229; 1960 Paris, 23
PROVENANCE E. Blot Art Gallery, Paris; Schneider Art Gallery, Frankfort; Ritter von Kahler, Vienna [acquired 1911]; Private collection, Switzerland; H. Tannenbaum Art Gallery, Amsterdam; D. Wolf, Wassenaar; A. Nystad Art Gallery, The Hague [R 1955]; J. H. Loudon, Aerdenhout, Netherlands [until 1964]; E. V. Thaw and Co, New York; Saint Louis, Mr and Mrs Edwin McClellan Johnston

F 286b [formerly F 286bis, H 296] STILL LIFE: LILAC
EXHIBITIONS 1945 Basle, 5; 1947 Basle, 36
PROVENANCE Huinck and Scherjon Art Gallery, Amsterdam; Switzerland, Private collection; Zurich, Fritz and Peter Nathan [R 1969]

F 287 [H 316] STILL LIFE: VASE WITH FLOWERS, COFFEEPOT AND SOME FRUIT
PROVENANCE M. Goldschmidt Art Gallery, Frankfort; Aug. Baron von der Heydt, Elberfeld; E. Baron von der Heydt, Ascona [on loan to Gemeentemuseum, The Hague]; Wuppertal, Von der Heydt-Museum der Stadt Wuppertal [acquired 1952; gift of E. Baron von der Heydt], cat 1964, p 26

F 288 [H 413] PORTRAIT OF A MAN
PROVENANCE Marcel Noréro, Paris; Sale Noréro, Paris [Drouot] 14 February 1927, nr 106 [repr]; Allard Art Gallery, Paris; Present owner unknown

F 289 [H 415] MAN IN A SKULL CAP
EXHIBITIONS 1905 Amsterdam, 60; 1920 New York, 61 [repr]; 1924 Basle, 21; Zurich, 19; Stuttgart, 7; 1925 The Hague, 21; 1926 Munich, 2087; 1954 Zurich, 19; 1954-5 Bern, 35; 1955 Antwerp 1, 192; 1958-9 San Francisco etc, 33
PROVENANCE Mrs J. van Gogh-Bonger, Amsterdam; V. W. van Gogh, Laren; Amsterdam, Rijksmuseum Vincent van Gogh [Vincent van Gogh Foundation, inv nr F 289]

F 290 [H 371] LANDSCAPE WITH SNOW
EXHIBITION 1956 Raleigh [N.C.], without cat nr
PROVENANCE Charpentier Art Gallery, Paris; Hans Bammann Art Gallery, Düsseldorf [cat Galerie Bammann, Düsseldorf, autumn 1927, with repr.]; J. K. Thannhauser Art Gallery, Berlin; New York, J. K. Thannhauser
EDITORS' COMMENT see under F 126a

F 291 [H 372] TREES IN A FIELD ON A SUNNY DAY
EXHIBITIONS 1940 Amsterdam, 17; 1952 London 2, 15; 1966 Laren, 91
PROVENANCE Mrs E.H. du Quesne-van Gogh, Baarn; M. P. Voûte, Amsterdam; Van Wisselingh Art Gallery, Amsterdam; P. de Boer Art Gallery, Amsterdam [acquired 1940]; P. de Boer, Amsterdam [acquired 1952]; Amsterdam, P. and N. de Boer Foundation

F 292 [H 374] BOULEVARD DE CLICHY
EXHIBITIONS 1905 Amsterdam, 54; 1945 Amsterdam, without cat nr; 1946 Stockhom etc, 35; 1946-7 Liège etc, 53; 1947 Geneva, 55; Paris 1, 54; 1953 The Hague, 71; Otterlo, Amsterdam, 81; 1955 Antwerp 1, 183; 1957 Marseilles, 30; 1959-60 Utrecht, 20; 1967 Wolfsburg, 27; 1968-9 London, 70
PROVENANCE Mrs J. van Gogh-Bonger, Amsterdam; V. W. van Gogh, Laren; Amsterdam, Rijksmuseum Vincent van Gogh [Vincent van Gogh Foundation, inv nr F 292]

F 293 [H 379] THE BANKS OF THE SEINE
EXHIBITIONS 1905 Amsterdam, 68; 1920 Venice, 31; 1930 Amsterdam, 10; 1932 Manchester, 14
PROVENANCE Mrs J. van Gogh-Bonger, Amsterdam; V. W. van Gogh, Laren; Amsterdam, Rijksmuseum Vincent van Gogh [Vincent van Gogh Foundation, inv nr F 293]

F 294 [H 420] SELF PORTRAIT WITH STRAW HAT: THREE QUARTERS TO THE LEFT
EXHIBITIONS 1949-50 New York, Chicago, 56; 1953 The Hague, 72; Otterlo, Amsterdam, 59; 1955 Antwerp 1, 204;

1955-6 Liverpool etc, 29; 1960 London 4, 15; 1961-2 Baltimore etc, 27; 1963 Sheffield, 6; 1965-6 Stockholm, Göteborg, 23
PROVENANCE Mrs J. van Gogh-Bonger, Amsterdam; V.W. van Gogh, Laren; Amsterdam, Rijksmuseum Vincent van Gogh [Vincent van Gogh Foundation, inv nr F 294]

F 295 [H 422] SELF PORTRAIT WITH GRAY FELT HAT: BUST, FULL FACE
EXHIBITIONS 1905 Amsterdam, 31; 1907 Rotterdam, 13; 1912 Cologne, 10; 1923 Haarlem, 19 [according to De la Faille; no other reference of this exhibition available]; 1947 Basle, 47; 1952 Milan, 74; 1953 The Hague, 73; Otterlo, Amsterdam, 60; 1954-5 Bern, 72; 1955 Antwerp 1, 207; 1955-6 Liverpool etc, 29 A; 1956 Munich, 101; 1957 Essen, 25; 1960 Paris, 32
PROVENANCE A. Bonger, Amsterdam [bought before 1905]; Mrs F. Bonger- van der Borch van Verwolde, Almen Amsterdam, Rijksmuseum [acquired 1936; gift of Mrs Bonger; on loan to Stedelijk Museum, Amsterdam since 1950, inv nr B 855]

F 296 [H 421] SELF PORTRAIT WITH GRAY FELT HAT: FULL FACE
EXHIBITIONS 1901 Paris, 11; 1935-6 New York etc, 16; 1949-50 New York, Chicago, 57; 1953 The Hague, 74; Otterlo, Amsterdam, 61; 1955 Antwerp 1, 205; 1955-6 Liverpool etc, 30; 1960 London 4, 16; 1961-2 Baltimore etc, 28; 1963 Sheffield, 6; 1965-6 Stockholm, Göteborg, 24
PROVENANCE Mrs J. van Gogh-Bonger, Amsterdam; V.W. van Gogh, Laren; Amsterdam, Rijksmuseum Vincen van Gogh [Vincent van Gogh Foundation, inv nr F 296]

F 297 [H 402] THE SKULL
PROVENANCE Mrs J. van Gogh-Bonger, Amsterdam; V.W. van Gogh, Laren; Amsterdam, Rijksmuseum Vincent van Gogh [Vincent van Gogh Foundation, inv nr F 297]

F 297a [formerly F 297bis, H 403] THE SKULL
PROVENANCE Mrs. J. van Gogh-Bonger, Amsterdam; V.W. van Gogh, Laren; Amsterdam, Rijksmuseum Vincent van Gogh [Vincent van Gogh Foundation, inv nr F 297a]

F 298 THE SEINE
PROVENANCE E. Bernard, Paris; A. Vollard Art Gallery, Paris; P. Mortier, Paris [acquired 1894]; Jos. Hessel Art Gallery, Paris; Sale Paris [Charpentier] 26 June 1934, nr 15; Paris, Private collection [acquired 1934, R 1970]

F 299 [H 383] RIVERSIDE WALK NEAR ASNIÈRES
EXHIBITIONS 1905 Amsterdam, 41; 1914 Berlin, 32; 1920 Venice; 1925 The Hague, 56; 1927 Paris; 1928 Munich, 7; 1930 Amsterdam, 11; 1953 The Hague, 75; Otterlo, Amsterdam, 77; 1955 Antwerp 1, 185; 1967 Wolfsburg, 32; 1968-9 London, 80
PROVENANCE Mrs J. van Gogh-Bonger, Amsterdam; V.W. van Gogh, Laren; Amsterdam, Rijksmuseum Vincent van Gogh [Vincent van Gogh Foundation, inv nr F 299]

F 300 [H 384] MOORED WHERRIES
EXHIBITION 1929 London 1, 468
PROVENANCE Bernheim Art Gallery, Paris; J. Tattersall, Dundee [until about 1935]; Aberdeen, Mr Middleton

F 301 [H 380] THE BRIDGES AT ASNIÈRES
EXHIBITIONS 1910-1 London, 68; 1930 Amsterdam, 12; 1954 Zurich, not in cat; 1957 Essen, 245; 1958 Zurich, 237; 1960 Paris, 33; 1961 Edinburgh, London, 57
PROVENANCE Prince of Wagram, Paris; E. Druet Art Gallery, Paris [R 1908]; Pierre Goujon, Paris [R 1911]; Bernheim jeune Art Gallery, Paris; Mrs L. Reinach-Goujon, Paris [R 1930]; Sale Paris [Charpentier] 23 May 1951, nr 16; Marlborough Fine Art Gallery, London; Zurich, Sammlung E. G. Bührle [acquired 1951], cat 1958, nr 237

F 302 [H 381] PONT DE CLICHY
EXHIBITIONS 1928 Vienna, 44 [repr]; 1945 Basle, 7; 1955 New York 2, 20; 1957-8 New York etc, 24; 1958 London 2, 25
PROVENANCE J. H. de Bois Art Gallery, Haarlem; Unger and Van Mens Art Gallery, Rotterdam; A. van Hoboken, Vienna; Athens, Stavros S. Niarchos, exhib cat 1957, nr 24

F 303 [H 373] PONT DE CLICHY
EXHIBITIONS 1901 Paris, 15; 1905 Amsterdam, 85; Utrecht, 26; 1906 Rotterdam, 28; 1935-6 New York etc, 17; 1943 New York 2, 17; New York 1, 27; 1944 Montreal, 131; 1955 New York 2, 19
PROVENANCE Mrs J. van Gogh-Bonger, Amsterdam [R 1905]; Caspari Art Gallery, Munich; Harrison, New York, F. H. Hirschland [R 1935, 1965]

F 304 [H 382] BRIDGE ACROSS THE SEINE
EXHIBITIONS 1905 Amsterdam, 38; 1928 Munich, 8; 1932 Manchester, 17; 1957 Stockholm, 109
PROVENANCE Mrs J. van Gogh-Bonger, Amsterdam; V.W. van Gogh, Laren; Amsterdam, Rijksmuseum Vincent van Gogh [Vincent van Gogh Foundation, inv nr F 304]

F 305 [H 351] ENTRANCE OF VOYER-D'ARGENSON PARK AT ASNIÈRES
EXHIBITIONS 1938 London 1, 28; 1942 Baltimore, Worcester, 5; 1943 New York 2, 13; 1955 New York 2, 16
PROVENANCE C. Hoogendijk, The Hague [on loan to Rijksmuseum, Amsterdam since 1907, cat 1911, nr 984c]; Sale Amsterdam [F. Muller] 21 May 1912, nr 29; A. M. Baron van Tuyll van Serooskerken, Amsterdam; Marcel Kapferer, Paris; Wildenstein Art Gallery, New York [R 1942]; Charles Gilman, New York; New York, Mrs Charles Gilman [R 1955]

F 306 [H 346] UNDERGROWTH
EXHIBITIONS 1932 Amsterdam 2, 17; 1933 Rotterdam 2, 25; 1935 Amsterdam 1, 13; 1956 Amsterdam, 34; 1966 Gouda, 17
PROVENANCE A. Schuffenecker, Clamart; E. Blot Art Gallery, Paris; Charles Vincent, Paris; Huinck and Scherjon Art Gallery, Amsterdam [R 1932, 1935]; L. H. van Baaren, Utrecht; Utrecht, Museum van Baaren, inv nr 56

F 307 [H 349] UNDERGROWTH
EXHIBITIONS 1905 Amsterdam, 58; 1927 Paris; 1928 Berlin, 23; Frankfort, 13; Vienna, 13; Munich, 9
PROVENANCE Mrs J. van Gogh-Bonger, Amsterdam; V.W. van Gogh, Laren; Amsterdam, Rijksmuseum Vincent van Gogh [Vincent van Gogh Foundation, inv nr F 307]

F 308 [H 350] UNDERGROWTH
EXHIBITIONS 1905 Amsterdam, 44; 1906 Rotterdam, 12
PROVENANCE Mrs J. van Gogh-Bonger, Amsterdam; V.W. van Gogh, Laren; Amsterdam, Rijksmuseum Vincent van Gogh [Vincent van Gogh Foundation, inv nr F 308]

F 309 [H 348] A PATH IN THE WOODS
EXHIBITIONS 1905 Amsterdam, 39; 1938 London 1, 25; 1955 Antwerp 1, 186
PROVENANCE Mrs J. van Gogh-Bonger, Amsterdam; V.W. van Gogh, Laren; Amsterdam, Rijksmuseum Vincent van Gogh [Vincent van Gogh Foundation, inv nr F 309]

F 309a [formerly F 309bis, H 347] UNDERGROWTH
EXHIBITIONS 1905 Amsterdam, 48; 1955 Antwerp 1, 187; 1955-6 Liverpool etc, 24; 1958-9 San Francisco etc, 35; 1965-6 Stockholm, Göteborg, 20; 1967 Wolfsburg, 29; 1968-9 London, 82
PROVENANCE Mrs J. van Gogh-Bonger, Amsterdam; H. C. Bonger, Amsterdam; Miss E. H. Bonger, Amsterdam; V.W. van Gogh, Laren; Amsterdam, Rijksmuseum Vincent van Gogh [Vincent van Gogh Foundation, inv nr F 309a]

F 310 [H 360] A WHEAT FIELD WITH A LARK
EXHIBITIONS 1905 Amsterdam, 62; 1923 Amsterdam 2, 122; 1930 Amsterdam, 13; 1935 Amsterdam 2, 16; 1935-6 New York etc, 18; 1939 San Francisco, 171; 1940 New York 3, 5; 1942 Baltimore, Worcester, 8; 1943 New York 2, 15; 1943-4 Indianapolis etc, 4; 1944 Montreal, 118; 1946-7 Liège etc, 56; 1947 Paris 1, 57; Geneva, 58; 1947-8 London etc, 16; 1948 Bergen, Oslo, 11; 1949-50 New York, Chicago, 53; 1951 Lyons etc, 22; 1955 Antwerp 1, 189; 1955-6 Liverpool etc, 25; 1957 Marseilles, 32; 1958-9 San Francisco etc, 34; 1959-60 Utrecht, 23; 1961-2 Baltimore etc, 23; 1963 Sheffield, 5; Humlebaek, 18; 1964 Washington, New York, 18; 1965-6 Stockholm, Göteborg, 21; 1967 Wolfsburg, 30; 1968-9 London, 83
PROVENANCE Mrs J. van Gogh-Bonger, Amsterdam; V.W. van Gogh, Laren; Amsterdam, Rijksmuseum Vincent van Gogh [Vincent van Gogh Foundation, inv nr F 310]

F 310a [formerly F 310bis, H 355] EDGE OF A WHEATFIELD
EXHIBITION 1905 Amsterdam, 34
PROVENANCE W. van Gogh, Haarlem; Mrs J. van Gogh-Bonger, Amsterdam; W. P. Ingenegeren, Utrecht; Sale Amsterdam [F. Muller] 9-10 April 1918, nr 117; d'Audretsch Art Gallery, The Hague; N. Eisenloeffel Art Gallery, Amsterdam; Mr Herman, Boston [R 1928]; Boston, Mrs William Herman [R 1966]

F 311 [H 378] BATHING PLACE ON THE SEINE AT ASNIÈRES
EXHIBITIONS 1912 Cologne, 21; 1914 Berlin, 29; 1928 Berlin, 24; Frankfort, 14; 1933 Amsterdam 3, 48; 1935 Amsterdam 2, 18; 1956 New Haven, 100; 1966 Washington, 130
PROVENANCE Mrs Tilla Durieux-Cassirer, Berlin [R 1912]; Mrs Paret, Berlin; Alfred Tietz, Cologne; Mr and Mrs Edward Patterson, Glen Head, Long Island [R 1956]; Upperville, Virginia, Mr and Mrs Paul Mellon [R 1966]

F 312 [H 377] RESTAURANT DE LA SIRÈNE AT ASNIÈRES
EXHIBITION 1901 Paris, 54
PROVENANCE M. Aghion, Paris [R 1901]; Sale Aghion, Paris [Drouot] 29 March 1918, nr 14 [repr]; Chr. Tetzen-Lund, Copenhagen [R 1921]; Paul Guillaume Art Gallery, Paris; Tanner Art Gallery, Zurich; Otto Wacker Art Gallery, Berlin; G. Matthiesen Art Gallery, Berlin; Mrs Paret, Berlin [R 1928 or later]; Present owner unknown

F 313 [H 375] RESTAURANT DE LA SIRÈNE AT ASNIÈRES
EXHIBITIONS 1896 Rotterdam, 14; 1904 Groningen; 1905 Amsterdam, 57; 1908 Munich 2, 10; 1925 Paris 1, 9; Vienna, 79
PROVENANCE Mrs J. van Gogh-Bonger, Amsterdam [R 1905]; Amédée Schuffenecker, Clamart; Joseph Reinach, Paris; Musée du Luxembourg [bequest of Reinach 1921], Paris; Paris, Musée National du Louvre [acquired 1929], inv nr RF 2325, cat Impressionistes 1959, nr 145

F 314 [H 368] VOYER-D'ARGENSON PARK AT ASNIÈRES
EXHIBITIONS 1905 Amsterdam, 78; 1923 London, 20; 1924 Basle, 20; Zurich, 17; Stuttgart, 5; 1925 Paris 1, 16; The Hague, 16; 1926 Munich, 2094; 1927 Paris; 1930 Amsterdam, 14; 1936 Rotterdam, 15; 1945 Amsterdam, without cat nr; 1946 Stockholm etc, 39; 1946-7 Liège etc, 57; 1947 Geneva, 59; Paris 1, 58; 1947-8 London etc, 17; 1948 Bergen, Oslo, 12; 1951 Lyons etc, 23; 1953 The Hague, 76; Otterlo, Amsterdam, 79; 1953-4 Saint Louis etc, 70; 1954 Zurich, 17; 1954-5 Bern, 31; 1955 Antwerp 1, 184; 1957 Marseilles, 31; 1958-9 San Francisco etc, 26; 1959-60 Utrecht, 21; 1960-1 Montreal etc, 29; 1961-2 Baltimore etc, 24; 1963 Humlebaek, 19; 1964 Washington, New York, 19; 1967 Wolfsburg, 31; 1968-9 London, 79
PROVENANCE Mrs J. van Gogh-Bonger, Amsterdam; V.W. van Gogh, Laren; Amsterdam, Rijksmuseum Vincent van Gogh [Vincent van Gogh Foundation, inv nr F 314]

F 315 [H 361] CORNER OF VOYER-D'ARGENSON PARK AT ASNIÈRES
PROVENANCE Arthur Rümann, Berlin; Paul Cassirer Art Gallery, Berlin; Thannhauser Art Gallery, Munich; Chr. Tetzen-Lund, Copenhagen [R 1928]; Present owner unknown

F 316 [H 364] VIEW FROM MONTMARTRE
EXHIBITIONS 1888 Paris, 660; 1905 Amsterdam, 66; Utrecht, 16; 1906 Rotterdam, 16; 1926 Venice, 26; 1927 Paris; 1929 London 1, 460; 1930 Amsterdam, 15; 1932 Manchester, 29; 1945 Amsterdam, without cat nr; 1946 Stockholm etc, 33; 1946-7 Liège etc, 58; 1947 Paris 1, 59; Geneva, 60; 1947-8 London etc, 20; 1948 Bergen, Oslo, 14; 1951 Lyons etc, 24; 1954 Zurich, 31; 1954-5 Bern, 29; 1955 Antwerp 1, 178; 1955-6 Liverpool etc, 21; 1957 Marseilles, 27; 1958-9 San Francisco etc, 36; 1959-60 Utrecht, 17; 1960-1 Montreal etc, 28; 1961-2 Baltimore etc, 19; 1963 Humlebaek, 14; 1964 Washington, New York, 14; 1967 Wolfsburg, 24; 1968-9 London, 87
PROVENANCE Mrs J. van Gogh-Bonger, Amsterdam; V.W. van Gogh, Laren; Amsterdam, Rijksmuseum Vincent van Gogh [Vincent van Gogh Foundation, inv nr F 316]

F 317 [H 397] FACTORIES AT ASNIÈRES, SEEN FROM THE QUAI DE CLICHY
EXHIBITIONS 1901 Paris, 27; 1910-1 London, 69; 1914 Berlin, 24; 1930 Amsterdam, 16; 1955 New York 2, 23; 1956 Munich, 104; 1962 Warsaw, 97
PROVENANCE Père Tanguy Art Gallery, Paris; Sale Tanguy, Paris [Petit] 2 June 1894, nr 61; E. Blot Art Gallery, Paris; Maurice Fabre, Paris [R 1901]; Bernheim jeune Art Gallery, Paris [R 1910-1]; Paul M. Robinow; Mrs E. Robinow, Hamburg; Sale Berlin [Cassirer] 30 October 1928, nr 58 [repr]; W. Weinberg, Scarsdale [R 1956]; Sale Weinberg, London [Sotheby] 10 July 1957, nr 47; M. Knoedler Art Gallery, New York; Mrs M. Steinberg, St Louis; Saint Louis, City Art Museum

F 318 [H 396] THE FACTORY AT ASNIÈRES
PROVENANCE Bernheim jeune Art Gallery, Paris [R 1913]; A. Barnes, Merion; Merion, Pennsylvania, The Barnes Foundation [acquired 1922]

F 319 [H 399] SELF PORTRAIT WITH A JAPANESE PRINT
EXHIBITIONS 1905 Paris, 10; 1925 Paris 1, 19; 1926 Paris, 2955; 1930 Amsterdam, 17
PROVENANCE Christian Cherfils, Paris [R 1905]; A. Vollard Art Gallery, Paris [R 1905]; Druet Art Gallery, Paris [R 1906]; Maurice Denis, Saint Germain-en-Laye [R 1906, 1930]; Sale Paris [Drouot] 9 March 1935, nr 38; Basle, Emile Dreyfus

F 320 [H 400] SELF PORTRAIT: THREE QUARTERS TO THE LEFT
EXHIBITIONS 1923 London, 13 [repr]; 1924 London 1; 1931 Paris, 40; 1947 Paris 1, 45; Geneva, 46; 1960 Paris, 31
PROVENANCE Mrs J. van Gogh-Bonger, Amsterdam; Paul Rosenberg Art Gallery, Paris; H. J. Laroche, Paris [R 1960]; Paris, Musée National du Louvre [acquired 1947; gift of H. J. Laroche], inv nr RF 1947-28, cat Impressionistes 1959, p 247

F 321 [H 365] RESTAURANT AT ASNIÈRES
EXHIBITIONS 1905 Amsterdam, 37; 1930 Amsterdam, 18; 1937 Paris, 141; 1945 Amsterdam, without cat nr; 1946-7 Liège etc, 59; 1947 Paris 1, 62; Geneva, 63; 1947-8 London etc, 18; 1948 Bergen, Oslo, 13; 1949-50 New York, Chicago, 50; 1958-9 San Francisco etc, 16; 1959-60 Utrecht, 22; 1963 Humlebaek, 20; 1964 Washington, New York, 20; 1965 Charleroi, Ghent, 11
PROVENANCE Mrs J. van Gogh-Bonger, Amsterdam; V.W. van Gogh, Laren; Amsterdam, Rijksmuseum Vincent van Gogh [Vincent van Gogh Foundation, inv nr F 321]

F 322 [H 333] STILL LIFE: VASE WITH LILACS, DAISIES AND ANEMONES
EXHIBITIONS 1929 London 1, 451; 1930 Amsterdam, 19; 1933 Amsterdam 2, 119; 1933 Rotterdam 1, 37; 1936 Rotterdam, 18; 1954 Rotterdam, 117; 1967 Paris, 102
PROVENANCE Mrs E. H. du Quesne-van Gogh, Baarn; d'Audretsch Art Gallery, The Hague; D. G. van Beuningen, Vierhouten, Netherlands, cat collection Van Beuningen 1949, nr 141; Beyeler Art Gallery, Basle; Switzerland, Private collection [R 1969]

F 323 [H 328] STILL LIFE: VASE WITH DAISIES AND ANEMONES
EXHIBITIONS 1927 Basle etc, 82; 1928 Düsseldorf, 143; Karlsruhe, 78; 1929 Berlin 1, 80; Hamburg, 39; 1930 Amsterdam, 201; 1935-6 Rotterdam, 60; 1945 The Hague, 29; 1946-7 Liège etc, 61; 1947 Paris 1, 56; Geneva, 57; Basle, 37; 1947-8 London etc, 22; 1952 Milan, 71; 1953-4 Saint Louis etc, 79; 1956 Eindhoven, 31; 1959 São Pãulo,5; 1962 Warsaw, 58; 1963 Tel Aviv, Haifa, 67; Hamburg, 75; 1966 Belgrade, 56
PROVENANCE Mr Williame, Châteauroux [R 1914]; Otterlo, Rijksmuseum Kröller-Müller, inv nr 263-14, cat van Gogh 1970, nr 204

F 324 [H 332] STILL LIFE: CORNFLOWERS AND POPPIES
EXHIBITIONS 1914 Berlin, 22; 1921 Berlin; 1928 Berlin, 25
PROVENANCE P. Gachet, Auvers; Camentron Art Gallery, Paris; Paul Cassirer Art Gallery, Berlin; C. Harries, Kiel [R 1914]; Mrs H. Harries-von Siemens, Berlin-Grunewald [R 1928 or earlier]; Present owner unknown

F 324a [formerly F 324bis, H 336] STILL LIFE: VASE WITH VISCARIA
PROVENANCE Tedesco Art Gallery, Paris; Bernheim Jeune Art Gallery, Paris; Mohammed Mahmoud Bey Khalil, Giza, Egypt; Republic of Egypt [acquired 1960; bequest of the widow of Mohammed Mahmoud Bey Khalil]

F 325 STILL LIFE: VASE WITH DAISIES AND POPPIES
Left out by Faille in his manuscript for the present edition; See REJECTED WORKS

F 326 [H 339] STILL LIFE: CORNFLOWERS
EXHIBITIONS 1927 Berlin 3, 119; 1955 New York 2, 15
PROVENANCE N. Eisenloeffel Art Gallery Amsterdam; M. P. Voûte jr, Amsterdam [R 1922]; N. Eisenloeffel Art Gallery, Amsterdam; Matthiesen Art Gallery, Berlin; Mamaroneck, New York, Mrs George S. Hirschland [R 1965]

F 327 [H 290] ONE-EARED VASE WITH CARNATIONS
EXHIBITIONS 1927 Basle etc, 94; 1928 Düsseldorf, 157; Karlsruhe, 92; 1929 Berlin 1, 88; Hamburg, 51; 1930 Amsterdam, 190
PROVENANCE L. C. Enthoven, Voorburg, Netherlands; Sale Enthoven, Amsterdam [F. Muller] 18 May 1920, nr 237 [and repr]; Otterlo, Rijksmuseum Kröller-Müller, inv nr 273-20, cat van Gogh 1970, nr 201

F 328 [H 236] NUDE WOMAN RECLINING: SEEN FROM THE BACK
EXHIBITIONS 1925 Paris 1; 1953 Paris, 199; 1956 Munich 109; 1960 Paris, 29
PROVENANCE Prince of Wagram, Paris; Druet Art Gallery, Paris [acquired 1908]; Mrs L. Reinach-Goujon, Paris [acquired 1909]; Paris, Private collection [R 1970]
EDITORS' COMMENT not in exhib cat 1925, Art Gallery Bernheim, Paris

F 329 [H 111] NUDE WOMAN RECLINING
EXHIBITIONS 1935-6 New York etc, 13; 1937 Paris, 54; 1938 Amsterdam 3, 33; 1952 Milan, 75; 1953 The Hague,77; Otterlo, Amsterdam, 72
PROVENANCE Bernheim jeune Art Gallery, Paris; Paul Cassirer Art Gallery, Berlin; E. Druet Art Gallery, Paris; Pierre Goujon, Paris [R 1911]; Komter Art Gallery, Amsterdam; S. van Deventer, De Steeg, Netherlands [R 1935, 1970]

F 330 [H 235] NUDE WOMAN ON A BED
PROVENANCE A. Vollard Art Gallery, Paris; Paul Cassirer Art Gallery, Berlin; C. Sternheim, La Hulpe-lez-Bruxelles; Paul Cassirer Art Gallery, Berlin; Thannhauser Art Gallery, Lucerne; Chr. Tetzen-Lund, Copenhagen; Merion, Pennsylvania, The Barnes Foundation

F 331 [H 249] A PAIR OF SHOES
EXHIBITIONS 1905 Amsterdam, 72; Utrecht, 20; 1906 Rotterdam, 20; 1914 Berlin, 40; 1932 Manchester, 8; 1953 The Hague, 78; Otterlo, Amsterdam, 68; 1953-4 St Louis etc, 69; 1954 Zurich, 13; 1955 Antwerp 1, 169; 1955 Palm Beach etc, 7; 1955-6 Liverpool etc, 23
PROVENANCE Mrs J. van Gogh-Bonger, Amsterdam; V. W. van Gogh, Laren; Amsterdam, Rijksmuseum Vincent van Gogh [Vincent van Gogh Foundation, inv nr F 331]

F 332 [H 250] THREE PAIRS OF SHOES
EXHIBITIONS 1925 Paris 1, 5; 1926 Paris, 2954; 1927 Paris; 1930 Amsterdam, 20; 1937 Paris, 132; 1943 New York 2, 7; 1946 Cambridge, USA; 1948 New York 2, 65; 1960 Raleigh, USA, p 16; 1962 Houston, 5
PROVENANCE Sale Paris [Drouot] 31 March 1920, nr 62; J. Hessel Art Gallery, Paris; Mrs M. Kapferer, Paris [R 1925]; Wildenstein Art Gallery, New York; M. Wertheim, New York; Cambridge, USA, Fogg Art Museum [acquired 1951; bequest of Maurice Wertheim], inv nr 1951.66

F 332a A PAIR OF SHOES
EXHIBITIONS 1946-7 Liège etc, 34bis [as Dutch period]; 1947 Paris 1, 34bis; Geneva, 35
PROVENANCE G. A. Aurier, Châteauroux; Mrs S. Williame-Aurier, Châteauroux; J. Williame, Châteauroux; Private collection, Antwerp [R 1946]; Europe Art Gallery, Brussels [R 1960]; E. Schumacher, Brussels [R 1967]

F 333 [H 251] A PAIR OF SHOES
EXHIBITIONS 1901 Paris, 9; 1905 Paris, 3; 1924 Basle, 16; 1942 Baltimore, Worcester, 2; 1956 Milwaukee, Cincinnati, 54
PROVENANCE J.Tanguy, Paris; Sale Tanguy, Paris [Petit] 2 June 1894, 64; A. Vollard Art Gallery, Paris; E. Blot Art Gallery, Paris; Sale Blot, Paris [Drouot] 9 May 1900, 163; J. Hessel Art Gallery, Paris; Paul Cassirer Art Gallery, Berlin; E. Blot, Paris [R 1901, 1905]: Second sale Blot, Paris [Drouot] 10 May 1906, 83; Edwards, Paris; Paul Vallottou Art Gallery, Lausanne; Marquis de Biron, Geneva; Paul Vallotton Art Gallery, Lausanne; Miss E. Cone, Baltimore [R 1942]; Baltimore, The Baltimore Museum of Art [acquired 1949 with the Cone collection], cat The Cone Collection 1955, 121; revised ed 1967, nr 26

F 334 [H 277] STILL LIFE: A BASKET OF CROCUSES
EXHIBITIONS 1905 Amsterdam, 67; 1928 Munich, 10; 1932 Manchester, 12; 1955 Antwerp 1, 172
PROVENANCE Mrs J. van Gogh-Bonger, Amsterdam; V. W. van Gogh, Laren; Amsterdam, Rijksmuseum Vincent van Gogh [Vincent van Gogh Foundation, inv nr F 334]

F 335 [H 246] STILL LIFE: THREE BOOKS [Emile Zola, Au Bonheur des Dames; Jean Richepin, Braves Gens; J. et Ed. de Goncourt, Fille Elisa]
EXHIBITIONS 1905 Amsterdam, 73; 1954-5 Bern, 16; 1955 Antwerp 1, 168
PROVENANCE Mrs J. van Gogh-Bonger, Amsterdam; V. W. van Gogh, Laren; Amsterdam, Rijksmuseum Vincent van Gogh [Vincent van Gogh Foundation, inv nr F 335]

F 336 [H 276] STILL LIFE: BASKET OF BULBS
EXHIBITIONS 1905 Amsterdam, 86; 1926 Munich, 2082; 1930 Amsterdam, 21; 1954 Zurich, 14; 1954-5 Bern, 22; 1958-9 San Francisco etc, 17; 1965-6 Stockholm, Göteborg, 13
PROVENANCE Mrs J. van Gogh-Bonger, Amsterdam; V. W. van Gogh, Laren; Amsterdam, Rijksmuseum Vincent van Gogh [Vincent van Gogh Foundation inv nr F 336]

F 337 [H 315] STILL LIFE: POT WITH CHIVE
EXHIBITIONS 1905 Amsterdam, 36; 1949-50 New York, Chicago, 54; 1953 The Hague, 79; Otterlo, Amsterdam, 70; 1958-9 San Francisco etc, 31
PROVENANCE Mrs J. van Gogh-Bonger, Amsterdam; V. W. van Gogh, Laren; Amsterdam, Rijksmuseum Vincent van Gogh [Vincent van Gogh Foundation, inv nr F 337]

F 338 [H 309] STILL LIFE: LEMONS ON A PLATE
EXHIBITIONS 1905 Amsterdam, 32; 1957 Stockholm, 110
PROVENANCE Mrs J. van Gogh-Bonger, Amsterdam; V. W. van Gogh, Laren; Amsterdam, Rijksmuseum Vincent van Gogh [Vincent van Gogh Foundation, inv nr F 338]

F 339 [H 306] STILL LIFE: ABSINTHE
EXHIBITIONS 1905 Amsterdam, 92; 1926 Dresden, 214; 1928 Berlin, 26; Frankfurt, 15; Munich, 11; Vienna, 14; 1954 Rotterdam, 118; 1955 Antwerp 1, 170; 1957 Marseilles, 24; 1959-60 Utrecht, 16; 1967 Wolfsburg, 22; 1968-9 London, 76
PROVENANCE Mrs J. van Gogh-Bonger, Amsterdam; V. W. van Gogh, Laren; Amsterdam, Rijksmuseum Vincent van Gogh [Vincent van Gogh Foundation, inv nr F 339]

F 340 [H 307] STILL LIFE: DECANTER AND LEMONS ON A PLATE
EXHIBITIONS 1905 Amsterdam, 43; 1906 Rotterdam, 13; 1920 New York, 62 [repr]; 1921 New York, 120; 1923 London, 19; 1924 Basle, 17; Zurich, 20; Stuttgart, 8; 1925 Paris 1, 14; The Hague, 4; Potsdam, 39; 1926 Munich, 2083; 1927 Paris; 1932 Manchester, 18; 1947-8 London etc, 24; 1948 Bergen, Oslo, 16; 1953 The Hague, 80; Otterlo, Amsterdam, 76; 1954 Zurich, 30; 1955 Antwerp 1, 171; Palm Beach etc, 8; 1955-6 Liverpool etc, 18; 1958-9 San Francisco etc, 30; 1961-2 Baltimore etc, 18; 1963 Sheffield, 4; Humlebaek, 13; 1964 Washington, New York, 13; 1965 Charleroi, Ghent, 9; 1965-6 Stockholm, Göteborg, 18; 1967 Wolfsburg, 23; 1968-9 London, 97
PROVENANCE Mrs J. van Gogh-Bonger, Amsterdam; V. W. van Gogh, Laren; Amsterdam, Rijksmuseum Vincent van Gogh [Vincent van Gogh Foundation, inv nr F 340]

F 341 [H 392] VIEW FROM VINCENT'S ROOM IN THE RUE LEPIC
EXHIBITIONS 1928 Berlin, 27; Frankfort, 16; Munich, 12; Vienna, 15; 1930 Amsterdam, 23; 1932 Manchester, 33; 1936 Rotterdam, 14; 1945 Amsterdam, without cat nr; 1946 Stockholm etc, 40; 1951 Lyons etc, 17; 1953 The Hague, 81; Otterlo, Amsterdam, 78; 1953-4 Saint Louis etc, 76; 1955 Antwerp 1, 190; 1965-6 Stockholm, Göteborg, 17; 1967 Wolfsburg, 28; 1968-9 London, 72
PROVENANCE Mrs J. van Gogh-Bonger, Amsterdam; V. W. van Gogh, Laren; Amsterdam, Rijksmuseum Vincent van Gogh [Vincent van Gogh Foundation, inv nr F 341]

F 341a [formerly F 341bis, H 398] VIEW FROM VINCENT'S ROOM IN THE RUE LEPIC
EXHIBITION 1951 Houston, 4
PROVENANCE Henri de Toulouse Lautrec, Paris; Countess A. de Toulouse Lautrec, mother of the painter, Paris; Comte Sère de Rivières, Paris [until 1934]: Miss E. Hudson, Syracuse, USA [acquired 1934]; Mrs Huddleston Rogers, New York; New York, Miss Millicent Rogers [R 1951]

F 342 [H 369] INTERIOR OF A RESTAURANT
EXHIBITIONS 1892 Rotterdam [?], 43; 1905 Amsterdam, 50; 1908 Paris 1, 20; Amsterdam, 14; 1911 Amsterdam, 21; 1913 The Hague, 82; 1927 Basle etc, 91; 1928 Düsseldorf, 154; Karlsruhe, 89; 1929 Berlin 1, 86; Hamburg, 48; 1930 Amsterdam, 207; 1935-6 New York etc, 19; 1946-7 Liège etc, 60; 1947 Paris 1, 63; Geneva, 64; Basle, 40; 1947-8 London etc, 19; 1952 Milan, 72; 1953 The Hague, 64; Otterlo, Amsterdam, 83; 1953-4 Saint Louis etc, 71; 1956 Eindhoven, 32; Munich, 103; 1957 Essen, 244; 1958 Vienna, 73; Tokyo, Kyoto, 90; 1960-1 Montreal etc, 24; 1962 Warsaw, 59; 1963 Tel Aviv, Haifa, 68
PROVENANCE Mrs J. van Gogh-Bonger, Amsterdam; Artz and de Bois Art Gallery, The Hague [1912]; Otterlo, Rijksmuseum Kröller-Müller, inv nr 271-12, cat van Gogh 1970, nr 205

F 343 [H 401] PORTRAIT OF ALEXANDER REID
EXHIBITIONS 1914 Berlin, 36; 1930 London 3, 14; Glasgow 20; 1932 Manchester, 16; 1934 Edinburgh, 352; 1939-40 Adelaide etc, 133; 1947 London, 46; 1947-8 London etc, 26; 1951 London, 36; 1963 London 2, 70; 1965 Guildford, 19
PROVENANCE Mrs. J. van Gogh-Bonger, Amsterdam; V. W. van Gogh, Laren; A. J. MacNeill Reid, London [R 1930, 1951]; Graham H. Reid [on loan to Glasgow Art Gallery and Museum, May 1963-April 1964; on loan to National Galleries of Scotland, Edinburgh 1969]

F 344 [H VII] SELF PORTRAIT IN A GRAY FELT HAT: THREE QUARTERS TO THE LEFT
EXHIBITIONS 1928 Berlin, 28; Frankfurt, 17; Munich, 13; 1930 Amsterdam, 24; 1932 Manchester, 45; 1937 Paris, 6; 1939 San Francisco, 172; 1939-40 San Francisco, 122; 1940 New York 3, 11; 1942 Baltimore, Worcester, 7; 1943 New York 2, 21; 1943-4 Indianapolis etc, 3; 1944 Montreal, 119; 1946-7 Liège etc, 69; 1947 Paris 1, 70; Geneva, 71; 1947-8 London etc, 28; 1948 Bergen, Oslo, 20; 1951 Lyons etc, 21; 1953 The Hague, 83; Otterlo, Amsterdam, 62; 1953-4 St. Louis etc, 62; 1954 Zurich, 26; 1955 Antwerp 1, 206; 1955 Palm Beach etc, 9; 1955-6 Liverpool etc, 31; 1958-9 San Francisco etc, 28; 1959 Aix-en-Provence, 3; 1959-60 Utrecht, 25; 1960-1 Montreal etc. 31; 1961-2 Baltimore etc, 30; 1963 Humlebaek, 21; 1964 Washington, New York, 21; 1965 Charleroi, Ghent, 13; 1965-6 Stockholm, Göteborg, 25; 1967 Wolfsburg, 35; Glasgow, 42; 1968-9 London, 96
PROVENANCE Mrs J. van Gogh-Bonger, Amsterdam; V. W. van Gogh, Laren; Amsterdam, Rijksmuseum Vincent van Gogh [Vincent van Gogh Foundation, inv nr F 344]

F 345 [H 406] SELF PORTRAIT: THREE QUARTERS TO THE LEFT
EXHIBITIONS 1912 Cologne, 11; 1914 Berlin, 28; 1928 Berlin, 29; Frankfurt, 18; 1930 Amsterdam, 25; 1933 Amsterdam, 13; Amsterdam 3, 32; 1935-6 New York etc, 20; 1938 New York 2, 45; 1939 Boston, 53; 1941 New York, 64 A; 1943 New York 2, 22; 1948 Cleveland, 4; 1955 Chicago, 20
PROVENANCE Mrs. J. van Gogh-Bonger, Amsterdam; L. Tietz, Cologne [R 1912]; A. Tietz, Cologne [R 1930]; Van Wisselingh Art Gallery, Amsterdam; Bignou Art Gallery, Paris [R 1933]; Mr and Mrs Joseph Winterbotham, Burlington, Vermont; Chicago, The Art Institute of Chicago [acquired 1954; bequest J. Winterbotham], inv nr 54.326, cat 1961, pp 181-2

F 346 [H 265] VIEW OF KITCHEN GARDENS ON MONTMARTRE
EXHIBITIONS 1905 Amsterdam, 82; 1906 Rotterdam, 27; 1928 Berlin, 30; Frankfort, 19; Munich, 14; Vienna, 17; 1946 Stockhom etc, 25; 1947-8 London etc, 21; 1948 Bergen, Oslo, 15; 1949-50 New York, Chicago, 49; 1951 Lyons etc, 18; 1953 The Hague, 84; Otterlo, Amsterdam, 80; 1953-4 Saint Louis etc, 68; 1954-5 Bern, 20; 1955 Antwerp 1, 182; 1955-6 Liverpool etc, 22; 1958-9 San Francisco etc, 23; 1967 Wolfsburg, 26; 1968-9 London, 74
PROVENANCE Mrs J. van Gogh-Bonger, Amsterdam; V. W. van Gogh, Laren; Amsterdam, Rijksmuseum Vincent

van Gogh [Vincent van Gogh Foundation, inv nr F 346]

F 347 [H 264] A CORNER OF MONTMARTRE
EXHIBITIONS 1905 Amsterdam, 75; 1906 Rotterdam, 25; 1930 Amsterdam, 26; 1932 Manchester, 15; 1945 Amsterdam, without cat nr; 1946 Stockholm etc, 24; 1946-7 Liège etc, 52; 1947 Paris 1, 61; Geneva, 62; 1949-50 New York, Chicago, 48; 1954 Zurich, 23; 1954-5 Bern, 19; 1955 Antwerp 1, 181; 1957 Marseilles, 29; 1958-9 San Francisco etc, 22; 1959-60 Utrecht, 19; 1960-1 Montreal etc, 27; 1961-2 Baltimore etc, 21; 1963 Humlebaek, 15; 1964 Washington, New York, 15; 1965 Charleroi, Ghent, 10; 1965-6 Stockholm, Göteborg, 16; 1968-9 London, 73
PROVENANCE Mrs J. van Gogh--Bonger, Amsterdam; V.W. van Gogh, Laren; Amsterdam, Rijksmuseum Vincent van Gogh [Vincent van Gogh Foundation, inv nr F 347]

F 348 [H 266] THE MOULIN DE LA GALETTE
EXHIBITIONS 1927 Rotterdam, 8; 1957 Los Angeles, 4
PROVENANCE Mrs J. van Gogh-Bonger, Amsterdam; J.H. de Bois Art Gallery, Haarlem, stock cat [Augustus 1924], nr 9 [and reproduced]; d'Audretsch Art Gallery, The Hague; A. van Hoboken, Vienna; Unger and Van Mens Art Gallery, Rotterdam [R 1927]; Thannhauser Art Gallery, Berlin; Buenos Aires, Museo nacional de bellas artes

F 348a [formerly F 348bis, H 269] THE MOULIN DE LA GALETTE
EXHIBITION 1955 New York 2, 10
PROVENANCE A. Bonger, Amsterdam [until 1936]; C.L. Huguenot van der Linden, Amsterdam; Georges Bigar, New York; Mr and Mrs Raymond Bigar, New York [R 1955]; Wildenstein Art Gallery, New York; Pittsburgh, USA, Carnegie Institute [gift of the Sarah Mellon Scaife family]

F 349 [H 273] THE MOULIN DE LA GALETTE
EXHIBITIONS 1905 Amsterdam, 84; 1906 Rotterdam, 22; 1910 Frankfort; 1921 Paris, 162; 1924 The Hague, 3; 1932 Amsterdam 1, 20; 1934 Ottawa, possibly cat nr 62; 1947 Basle, 38; 1965 New York 2, 48
PROVENANCE Mrs J. van Gogh-Bonger, Amsterdam [R 1905]; Isaac Israëls, The Hague [R 1921; 1924]; d'Audretsch Art Gallery, The Hague; T. Bendien, The Hague; A. Bendien, Almelo [R 1945]; Myrtil Frank, New York [R 1959]; Newark, USA, Mr and Mrs Charles W. Engelhard [R 1965]

F 350 [H IV] KITCHEN GARDENS ON MONTMARTRE
EXHIBITIONS 1888 Paris, 659; 1930 Amsterdam, 30; 1937 Paris, 30; 1941 New York, 64; Chicago, 76; 1946-7 Liège etc, 62; 1947 Geneva, 65; Basle, 39; Paris, 64; 1949-50 New York, Chicago, 58; 1952 Milan, 67; 1953 The Hague, 85; Otterlo, Amsterdam, 73; 1953-4 Saint Louis etc, 74; 1955 Antwerp 1, 180; 1956 Munich, 106; 1957 Essen, 236; 1960 Paris, 35; 1961 Paris 1, 121; 1962 Warsaw, 96; 1963 Tel Aviv, Haifa, 66; Hamburg, 76
PROVENANCE Mrs J. van Gogh-Bonger, Amsterdam; Amsterdam, Stedelijk Museum [acquired 1913], cat 1914, nr 126 [repr]

F 351 [H 362] IN THE OUTSKIRTS OF PARIS
EXHIBITIONS 1948 Cleveland, 3; 1955 New York 2, 18; 1957 Los Angeles, 6; 1966 New York 1, 11
PROVENANCE Mrs Cornelia van Gogh-Carbentus, Princenhage; Sale Mrs Cornelia van Gogh-Carbentus a.o, Amsterdam [F. Muller] 25 November 1913, nr 26 [and reproduced]; M.Emden, Hamburg; Sale Emden, Berlin [Ball-Graupe] 9 June 1931, nr 40; Thannhauser Art Gallery, New York; Scarsdale, New York, Mrs Salman Schocken [R 1965]

F 352 [H 363] THE RIVERSIDE IN SPRING: PONT DE CLICHY
EXHIBITIONS 1926 Paris, 2956; 1927 Paris; 1960 Paris, 36; 1965 New York 2, 51
PROVENANCE Mrs Olivier Sainsère, Paris [acquired 1900]; Texas, Private collection [R 1965]

F 353 [H 366] BOAT MOORED TO THE BANK
EXHIBITIONS 1913 Berlin 1; 1930 Amsterdam, 28; 1938 Venice, 16; 1950 London, 23
PROVENANCE C. Hoogendijk, The Hague [on loan to Rijksmuseum, Amsterdam since 1907, cat 1911, nr 984b]; Mrs van Blaaderen-Hoogendijk, Amsterdam [R 1930]; Alex. Reid and Lefevre Art Gallery, London; H. Wilcox, London; Private collection, Glasgow; Sam. Salz Art Gallery, New York; A. Kirkeby, New York; Sale Kirkeby, New York [Parke-Bernet] 19 November 1958, nr 19; New York, Farkas Foundation [R 1970]

F 354 [H 367] FISHING IN SPRING, PROBABLY NEAR THE PONT LEVALLOIS
EXHIBITIONS 1930 Amsterdam, 29; 1937 Paris, 31; 1938 Venice, 14; 1949-50 New York, Chicago, 51
PROVENANCE C. Hoogendijk, The Hague; Mrs van Blaaderen-Hoogendijk, Amsterdam [R 1930; 1937]; Van Wisselingh Art Gallery, Amsterdam; Katz Art Gallery, The Hague; Chicago, Mr Chauncey Mc Cormick [R 1949]; Chicago, The Art Institute of Chicago [acquired 1965; gift of Charles Deering McCormick, Brooks McCormick and Roger McCormick]

F 355 [H 391] RESTAURANT RISPAL AT ASNIÈRES
EXHIBITIONS 1905 Amsterdam, 78; 1920 New York, 58 [repr]; 1924 Basle, 18; Zurich, 18; Stuttgart, 6; 1925 Paris 1, 15; The Hague, 20; 1926 Munich, 2067; London 3, 13; 1930 London 1, 18; 1943 New York 2, 19; 1948 Cleveland, 6; 1955 New York 2, 26
PROVENANCE Mrs J. van Gogh-Bonger, Amsterdam; V.W. van Gogh, Laren; N.Ch. Beechman, London; Paris, Georges Bernheim Art Gallery; Hugo Moser, Heemstede before 1939, later on New York [still in 1955]; New York, Mrs Hugo L. Moser [R 1970]
EDITORS' COMMENT De la Faille identified this painting with exhib cat Amsterdam 1905, nr 79. This cat number is mentioned as View from Asnières and in a letter [March 1909] from Paul Cassirer to Mrs van Gogh-Bonger as View from Asnières with bridge. In the cat 1905 nr 78 is called: View of Asnières with chestnut trees in blossom and this must be F 355 [H 391]

F 356 [H 412] SELF PORTRAIT: THREE QUARTERS TO THE RIGHT
EXHIBITIONS 1905 Amsterdam, 45; 1909 Munich; 1920 New York, 64 [repr]; 1926 Munich, 2084; London 3, 5; 1928 Berlin, 31; Frankfort, 20 [repr]; Vienna, [?] [repr]; Munich, 15; 1930 Amsterdam, 30; 1945 Amsterdam, without cat nr; 1946 Stockholm etc, 29; 1953 The Hague, 86; Otterlo, Amsterdam, 63; 1953-4 Saint Louis etc, 60; 1954 Zurich, 24; 1954-5 Bern, 33; 1955 Antwerp 1, 201; 1957 Marseilles, 35; 1958-9 San Francisco etc, 27; 1959-60 Utrecht, 26; 1960 London 4, 11; 1967 Wolfsburg, 37; 1968-9 London, 94
PROVENANCE Mrs J. van Gogh-Bonger, Amsterdam; V.W. van Gogh, Laren; Amsterdam, Rijksmuseum Vincent van Gogh [Vincent van Gogh Foundation, inv nr F 356]

F 357 [H 232] HEAD OF A WOMAN [MRS TANGUY?]
EXHIBITIONS 1924 Basle, 22; 1934 Bern, 59; 1945 Basle, 4; 1964 Paris 1, 30
PROVENANCE Thannhauser Art Gallery, Munich; R. Staechelin, Basle; Basle, Öffentliche Kunstsammlung Basel, Depositum 'Sammlung Rudolf Staechelin' 1947, cat 1961, p 12

F 358 [H 230] STILL LIFE: ROMANS PARISIENS
EXHIBITIONS 1923 London, 17; 1924 Basle, 23; Zurich, 44; Stuttgart, 19; 1925 Paris 1, 20; The Hague, 9; 1926 Munich, 2092; 1927 Paris; 1930 Paris, 31; 1933 Amsterdam 2, 114; 1945 Amsterdam, without cat nr; 1946 Stockholm etc, 28; 1946-7 Liège etc, 63; 1947 Geneva, 61; Paris 1, 60; 1947-8 London etc, 32; 1948 Bergen, Oslo, 17; 1951 Lyons etc, 25; 1954 Zurich, 33; 1955 Antwerp 1, 176; Palm Beach etc, 12; 1955-6 Liverpool etc, 34; 1957 Marseilles, 25; 1960-1 Montreal etc, 34; 1961 Amsterdam, 48; 1961-2 Baltimore etc, 34; 1963 Humlebaek, 25; 1964 Washington, New York, 25; 1965 Charleroi, Ghent, 15; 1965-6 Stockholm, Göteborg, 22; 1967 Wolfsburg, 41; 1968-9 London, 98
PROVENANCE Mrs J. van Gogh-Bonger, Amsterdam; V.W. van Gogh, Laren; Amsterdam, Rijksmuseum Vincent van Gogh [Vincent van Gogh Foundation, inv nr F 358]

F 359 [H 231] STILL LIFE: ROMANS PARISIENS WITH A ROSE
EXHIBITIONS 1888 Paris, 658; 1909 Berlin, 65 [repr]; 1914 Berlin, 98 [repr]; 1924 Basle, 23; Zurich, 22; 1927 Berlin 3, 124; 1938 Paris 1, 125; 1947 Basle, 43; 1959 Paris, 65; 1964 Lausanne, 112; 1967 Paris, 101
PROVENANCE Paul Vallotton Art Gallery, Lausanne; G. Boner, Zurich [R 1938; 1947]; Baden, Switzerland, Private collection [R 1967]
EDITORS' COMMENT It cannot be stated with certainty which of the two versions has been exhibited in 1888 at the 'Indépendants'

F 360 [H 237] STILL LIFE: PLASTER STATUETTE AND BOOKS [G. de Maupassant, Bel-Ami; J. et Ed. de Goncourt, Germinie Lacerteux]
EXHIBITIONS 1910 Berlin 1, 29; 1912 Cologne, 23; 1913 The Hague, 107; 1914 Antwerp, 49; 1927 Basle etc, 85; 1928 Düsseldorf, 148; Karlsruhe, 83; 1929 Berlin 1, 91; Hamburg, 42; 1930 Amsterdam, 203; 1945 The Hague, 66; 1946-7 Liège etc, 64; 1947 Paris 1, 65; Geneva, 66; Basle, 42; 1947-8 London etc, 23; 1953 The Hague, 88; Otterlo, Amsterdam, 75; 1953-4 St. Louis etc, 72; 1956 Munich, 108; 1958 Vienna, 74; Tokyo, Kyoto, 89; 1960-1 Montreal etc, 22; 1966 Belgrade, 57
PROVENANCE Mrs. J. van Gogh-Bonger, Amsterdam; Otterlo, Rijksmuseum Kröller-Müller, inv nr 265-12, cat Van Gogh 1970, nr 203

F 361 [H 357] OUTSKIRTS OF PARIS: ROAD WITH PEASANT SHOULDERING A SPADE
EXHIBITIONS 1905 Amsterdam, 83; 1906 Rotterdam, 26; 1930 Amsterdam, 32; 1962 Fort Worth; 1964 New York 3, 17; New York 2, without cat nr
PROVENANCE Mrs J. van Gogh-Bonger, Amsterdam [R 1905]; Thannhauser Art Gallery, Munich; Mrs C. Jordan, Wetter an der Ruhr [R 1930]; Knoedler Art Gallery, New York; Mrs J. Lee Johnson, Fort Worth [R 1956]; Fort Worth, Texas, Miss Karen Carter Johnson [R 1964]

F 362 [H 358] A PARK IN SPRING
EXHIBITIONS 1919 Haarlem, 16; 1955 Rotterdam, 188; 1957 Cologne, 71
PROVENANCE Mrs E.H. du Quesne-van Gogh, Baarn; J.H. de Bois Art Gallery, Haarlem [acquired 1917]; F. Muller and Co, Haarlem; Chr. Tetzen-Lund, Juleback near Helleback; Sale Amsterdam [F. Muller] 20 November 1923, nr 1 [and reproduced]; Aug. Volz, The Hague; P.F. Volz, Laren [acquired 1941]; Laren, R.F. Volz [R 1957, R 1970]

F 363 [H 304] PORTRAIT OF PÈRE TANGUY
EXHIBITIONS 1901 Paris, 7; 1905 Paris, 33; 1930 Amsterdam, 33; 1931 Paris, 39; 1935 Brussels, 94; 1936 London 4, 103; 1937 Paris, 32; 1947 Paris 1, 71; 1960 Paris, not in cat
PROVENANCE Daughter of Julien Tanguy, Paris; Auguste Rodin, Paris [R 1901; 1916]; Paris, Musée Rodin, cat 1938, nr 386

F 364 [H 305] PORTRAIT OF PÈRE TANGUY
EXHIBITIONS 1896 Rotterdam, 39; 1905 Amsterdam, 63; 1908 Paris 2, 18; 1912 Cologne, 106 [repr]; 1913 Frankfurt 27]repr]; 1928 Berlin, 32 [repr]; Frankfurt, 21 [repr]; 1933 Los Angeles, 50; Cincinnati, 4; 1934 San Francisco, 163; 1935-6 New York etc, 21; 1937 Hartford, 40; 1938 New York 2, 48; 1943 New York 2, 10; 1953 Washington, 14; 1956-7 Los Angeles, San Francisco, 25; 1958 London 2, 24; 1957-8 New York etc, 23; 1960 Paris, 34; 1961 Paris 1, 120
PROVENANCE Mrs J. van Gogh-Bonger, Amsterdam [1905]; Bernheim jeune Art Gallery, Paris; Druet Art Gallery, Paris [1907]; J. Keller, Paris [1908]; M. Goldschmidt Art Gallery, Frankfort; A. Hagelstange, Cologne; R.R. Bauer, Frankfurt [acquired 1912]; Wildenstein Art Gallery, New York/Paris [about 1934-about 1938]; E.G. Robinson, Beverley Hills [about 1943-about 1957]; Atheus, Stavros S. Niarchos, exhib cat 1957, nr 23

F 365 recto [formerly F 365 verso; H 87] PEASANT WOMAN SEATED
PROVENANCE Charpentier Art Gallery, Paris; Hans Bammann Art Gallery, Düsseldorf [Cat Galerie Hans Bammann, Düsseldorf, Autumn 1927, with reproduction]; J.K. Thannhauser Art Gallery, Berlin; J.K. Thannhauser Art Gallery, New York; Miss Adelaide Milton de Groot, New York [before 1936]; New York, The Metropolitan Museum of Art [on loan since 1936 from Miss Adelaide Milton de Groot; acquired 1967 with Ad. Milton de Groot bequest], inv nr 67.187.70a
EDITORS' COMMENT see under F 126a

F 365 verso [formerly F 365 recto, H 409] SELF PORTRAIT WITH STRAW HAT
EXHIBITION 1949-50 New York, Chicago, 49 A
PROVENANCE New York, The Metropolitan Museum of Art, inv nr 67.187.70a

F 366 [H 405] SELF PORTRAIT: NEARLY FULL FACE
EXHIBITIONS 1912 Paris, 206; 1925 Paris 1, 13; Vienna, 93; 1930 Amsterdam, 34; 1933-4 Rotterdam, 37; 1947 Basle, 46; 1950 Zurich, 28; 1958 Zurich, 238; 1960 London 4, 6; 1961 Edinburgh, London, 56
PROVENANCE A. Vollard Art Gallery, Paris; Louis Bernard, Paris [R 1912]; Barbazanges Art Gallery, Paris; E. Eissler, Vienna [R 1925]; A. Gold Art Gallery, Berlin; A. Lewin, Guben [R 1930]; Gräfin H. Bopp von Oberstadt; Zurich, Sammlung E.G. Bührle [acquired 1945], cat 1958, nr 238

F 367 [H 292] WOMAN SEATED IN THE GRASS
EXHIBITIONS 1901 Paris, 40; 1947 Basle, 41; 1965 New York 2, 37
PROVENANCE A. Schuffenecker, Clamart [R 1901]; A. Vollard Art Gallery, Paris; Sale Amsterdam [Mak van Waay] 11 May 1926, 42 [and reproduced]; Mrs C.A. Polak, Zandvoort; J. Hegnauer, Lausanne-Ouchy [R 1947]; New York, Private collection [R 1965]

F 368 [H 291] A WOMAN WALKING IN A GARDEN
PROVENANCE Emile Bernard, Paris; A. Vollard Art Gallery, Paris; C. Hoogendijk, The Hague; Sale Hoogendijk, Amsterdam [F. Muller] 21 May 1912, nr 6 [in the catalogue erroneously described as a work by G. Caillebotte]; A. Vollard Art Gallery, Paris; Sale Amsterdam [Mak van Waay] 11 May 1926, nr 41 [repr]; E. Buffa Art Gallery, Amsterdam; C.W. Kraushaar Art Gallery, New York [R 1927]; Mrs E. Slater Kerrigan, New York [R 1942]; USA, E.J. Bowes

F 369 [H 318] WOMAN WITH CRADLE
EXHIBITIONS 1905 Amsterdam, 76; 1914 Berlin, 33; 1925 The Hague, 45; Potsdam, 38; 1927 Paris; 1930 Amsterdam, 35; 1936 Rotterdam, 16; 1945 Amsterdam, without cat nr; 1946 Stockholm etc, 37; 1946-7 Liège etc, 65; 1947 Geneva, 67; Paris 1, 66; 1947-8 London etc, 25; 1948 Bergen, Oslo, 18; 1953 The Hague, 89; Otterlo, Amsterdam, 84; 1953-4 Saint Louis etc, 77; 1954 Zurich, 18; 1954-5 Bern,

28; 1955 Antwerp 1, 193; 1955-6 Liverpool etc, 16; 1957 Marseilles, 33; 1958-9 San Francisco etc, 24; 1959-60 Utrecht, 24; 1960-1 Montreal etc, 30; 1961-2 Baltimore etc, 25; 1967 Wolfsburg, 33; 1968-9 London, 71
PROVENANCE Mrs J. van Gogh-Bonger, Amsterdam; V.W. van Gogh, Laren; Amsterdam, Rijksmuseum Vincent van Gogh [Vincent van Gogh Foundation, inv nr F 369]

F 370 [H 299] WOMAN SITTING IN THE CAFÉ DU TAMBOURIN [Avenue de Clichy, Paris]
EXHIBITIONS 1914 Berlin, 50; 1928 Berlin, 33; Frankfort, 22; Vienna, 20; Munich, 16; 1932 Manchester, 20; 1945 Amsterdam, without cat nr; 1946 Stockholm etc, 32; 1946-7 Liège etc, 66; 1947 Geneva, 68; Paris 1, 67; 1947-8 London etc, 27; 1948 Bergen, Oslo, 19; 1949-50 New York, Chicago, 59; 1951 Lyons etc, 19; 1953 The Hague, 90; Otterlo, Amsterdam, 85; 1953-4 Saint Louis etc, 78; 1954 Zurich, 20; 1955 Antwerp 1, 194; 1955-6 Liverpool etc, 17; 1958-9 San Francisco etc, 25; 1959-60 Utrecht, 28; 1960-1 Montreal etc, 33; 1961-2 Baltimore etc, 32; 1963 Sheffield, 7; Humlebaek, 23; 1964 Washington, New York, 23; 1965 Charleroi, Ghent, 14; 1965-6 Stockholm, Göteborg, 19; 1967 Wolfsburg, 39; 1968-9 London, 77
PROVENANCE Mrs J. van Gogh-Bonger, Amsterdam; V.W. van Gogh, Laren; Amsterdam, Rijksmuseum Vincen van Gogh [Vincent van Gogh Foundation, inv nr F 370]

F 371 [H II] JAPONAISERIE: THE FLOWERING PLUMTREE [after Hiroshige]
EXHIBITIONS 1905 Amsterdam, 94; 1926 Munich, 2075; 1927 Paris; 1928 Berlin, 34; Frankfort, 23; Vienna, 21; 1932 Manchester, 30; 1937 Paris, 151; 1945 Amsterdam, without cat nr; 1946-7 Liège etc, 68; 1947 Paris 1, 69; Geneva, 70; 1953-4 Saint Louis etc, 81; 1955 Antwerp 1, 209
PROVENANCE Mrs J. van Gogh-Bonger, Amsterdam; V.W. van Gogh, Laren; Amsterdam, Rijksmuseum Vincent van Gogh [Vincent van Gogh Foundation, inv nr F 371]

F 372 [H 233] JAPONAISERIE: THE BRIDGE IN THE RAIN [after Hiroshige]
EXHIBITIONS 1905 Amsterdam, 93; 1927 Paris; 1930 Amsterdam, 36; 1945 Amsterdam, without cat nr; 1946-7
EXHIBITIONS AND PROVENANCE 84
Liège etc, 67; 1947 Geneva, 69; Paris 1, 68; 1947-8 London etc, 29; 1948 Bergen, Oslo, 21; 1949-50 New York, Chicago, 52; 1951 Lyons etc, 20; 1953 The Hague, 91; Otterlo, Amsterdam, 86; 1953-4 Saint Louis etc, 82; 1954 Zurich, 22; 1954-5 Bern, 14; 1955 Antwerp 1, 209; 1955-6 Liverpool etc, 32; 1958-9 San Francisco etc, 37; 1959-60 Utrecht, 29; 1960-1 Montreal etc, 32; 1963 Humlebaek, 24; 1964 Washington, New York, 24
PROVENANCE Mrs J. van Gogh-Bonger, Amsterdam; V.W. van Gogh, Laren; Amsterdam, Rijksmuseum Vincent van Gogh [Vincent van Gogh Foundation, inv nr F 372]

F 373 [H 234] JAPONAISERIE OIRAN [after Kesaï Yeisen]
EXHIBITIONS 1905 Amsterdam, 71; 1920 New York, 38 [and reproduced]; 1928 Berlin, 35; Munich, 17; Frankfort, 24; Vienna, 22; 1953 The Hague, 92; Otterlo, Amsterdam 87; 1953-4 Saint Louis etc, 83; 1954 Zurich, 21; 1954-5 Bern, 15; 1955 Antwerp 1, 211; 1957 Marseilles, 37; 1960 Paris, 38; 1961-2 Baltimore etc, 33; 1967 Wolfsburg, 40; 1968-9 London, 78
PROVENANCE Mrs J. van Gogh-Bonger, Amsterdam; V.W. van Gogh, Laren; Amsterdam, Rijksmuseum Vincent van Gogh [Vincent van Gogh Foundation, inv nr F 373]

F 374 [H 274] STILL LIFE: RED CABBAGES AND ONIONS
EXHIBITION 1928 Berlin, 36; Frankfort, 25; Munich, 18; Vienna, 23; 1930 Amsterdam, 37; 1951 Lyons etc, 36; 1954-5 Bern, 21; 1955 New York 2, 11; Antwerp 1, 173; 1955-6 Liverpool etc, 19; 1961-2 Baltimore etc, 35; 1967 Wolfsburg, 24; 1968-9 London, 90
PROVENANCE Mrs J. van Gogh-Bonger, Amsterdam; V.W. van Gogh, Laren; Amsterdam, Rijksmuseum Vincent van Gogh [Vincent van Gogh Foundation, inv nr F 374]

F 375 [H 278] STILL LIFE: SUNFLOWERS
EXHIBITIONS 1917 Zurich, 109; 1922 Winterthur 1, 52; 1944 Montreal, 120; 1949-50 New York, Chicago, 60; 1951 Houston, 5; 1955 New York 2, 12
PROVENANCE C. Hoogendijk, The Hague; Sale Amsterdam [F. Muller] 21 May 1912, nr 31; Alphonse Kann, Paris [R 1917]; Richard Bühler, Winterthur; Thannhauser Art Gallery, Munich [R about 1928]; Thannhauser Art Gallery, New York [R 1944]; New York, The Metropolitan Museum of Art [acquired 1944; Purchase, Rogers Fund], inv nr 49.41 cat French paintings, 1967, vol 3, p 182

F 376 [H 279] STILL LIFE: SUNFLOWERS
EXHIBITIONS 1922 Winterthur 1, 51; 1924 Basle, 33; Zurich, 21; 1938 Paris 1, 126; 1940 Lucerne, 54; 1953 Bern, 40; 1960 Paris, 37
PROVENANCE P. Gauguin, Paris [R 1887]; A. Vollard Art Gallery, Paris; E. Degas, Paris; Sale Degas, Paris [Petit] 26 March 1918, nr 93; Paul Rosenberg Art Gallery, Paris; A. Hahnloser, Winterthur [R 1938]; Bern, H.R. Hahnloser [R 1967]

F 377 [H 275] STILL LIFE: SUNFLOWER
PROVENANCE Mrs J. van Gogh-Bonger, Amsterdam; V.W. van Gogh, Laren; Amsterdam, Rijksmuseum Vincent van Gogh [Vincent van Gogh Foundation, inv nr F 377]

F 378 [H 319] STILL LIFE: BASKET OF APPLES
EXHIBITIONS 1908 Paris 2, 1; 1912 Cologne, 18; 1913 The Hague, 132; 1914 Antwerp, 34; 1927 Basle etc, 79; 1928 Düsseldorf, 144 [repr]; Karlsruhe, 79; 1929 Berlin 1, 90; Hamburg, 36; 1930 Amsterdam, 206; 1935-6 Rotterdam, 59; 1946-7 Liège etc, 71; 1947 Paris 1, 72; Geneva, 72; 1956 Munich, 112; 1958 Vienna, 75; Tokyo, Kyoto, 91; 1959 São Paulo, p 241, 7; 1960-1 Montreal etc, 25; 1966 Belgrade, 65
PROVENANCE Lucien Pissarro, Paris [R 1887]; M. Aubry, Paris [R 1908]; Druet Art Gallery, Paris [R 1912]; Otterlo, Rijksmuseum Kröller-Müller, inv nr 261-12, cat van Gogh 1970, nr 217

F 379 [H 322] STILL LIFE: BASKET OF APPLES
EXHIBITIONS 1905 Paris, 44; 1925 Paris 1, 17; 1935 Kansas City, 62; 1937 Chicago, 24; 1938 Hartford, 15; Washington, 21; 1939 Adelaide etc, 132; 1941 Los Angeles, 54; 1943 New York 2, 12; 1944 New York 3; 1947 Albuquerque
PROVENANCE Alexander Reid, Glasgow [1888]; Jos Hessel Art Gallery, Paris; Félix Vallotton, Paris [about 1905-1925]; Paul Vallotton Art Gallery, Lausanne [acquired 1925]; Wildenstein Art Gallery, New York [about 1935–about 1943]; Mrs Millicent Rogers, New York; Mrs Charles S. Payson, New York [R 1954]; Knoedler Art Gallery, New York; St Louis, Mr and Mrs Sydney M. Shoenberg

F 380 [H 407] SELF PORTRAIT: THREE QUARTERS TO THE LEFT
EXHIBITIONS 1912 Cologne; 1927 Basle etc, 95 [repr]; 1928 Düsseldorf, 158 [repr]; Karlsruhe, 93 [repr]; 1929 Berlin 1, 98; Hamburg, 52; 1930 Amsterdam, 196; 1946-7 Liège etc, 74; 1947 Paris 1, 76; Geneva, 76; Basle, 45; 1952 Milan, 68; 1953 The Hague, 93; Otterlo, Amsterdam, 67; 1956 Eindhoven, 29; Munich, 102; 1958 Vienna, 72; Tokyo, Kyoto, 86; 1960 London 4, 7; 1962 Warsaw, 95; 1963 Tel Aviv, Haifa, 63; 1966 Belgrade, 54
PROVENANCE Mrs J. van Gogh-Bonger, Amsterdam; Mrs Thea Sternheim, La Hulpe-lez-Bruxelles; Sale Sternheim, Amsterdam [F. Muller] 11 February 1919, nr 5 [repr]; Otterlo, Rijksmuseum Kröller-Müller, inv nr 274-19, cat van Gogh 1970, nr 198

F 381 [H 285] THE ITALIAN WOMAN WITH CARNATIONS [LA SÉGATORI?]
EXHIBITIONS 1920 New York, 53 [repr]; 1923 London, 32; 1924 Basle, 34; Zurich, 23; Stuttgart, 9; 1925 Paris 1, 18; The Hague, 17
PROVENANCE Mrs J. van Gogh-Bonger, Amsterdam; Paul Rosenberg Art Gallery, New York; Mr and Mrs N. Gourgaud, Paris; Paris, Musée National du Louvre [acquired 1965]

F 382 [H 321] STILL LIFE: FRUIT
EXHIBITIONS 1929 Cambridge, USA, 94; New York, 94; 1949-50 New York, Chicago, 55
PROVENANCE H.G.E. Degas, Paris; Sale Degas, Paris [Petit] 26 March 1918, 92; Paul Rosenberg Art Gallery, Paris; H.J. Laroche, Paris; Walter S. Brewster, Chicago; Chicago, The Art Institute of Chicago [acquired 1949; gift of Kate L. Brewster], inv nr 49.215, cat 1961, p 182

F 383 [H 320] STILL LIFE: LEMONS, PEARS AND GRAPES
EXHIBITIONS 1905 Amsterdam, 53; 1914 Berlin, 34; 1925 The Hague, 48; 1961-2 Baltimore etc, 22; 1963 Humlebaek, 17; 1964 Washington, New York, 17; 1968-9 London, 88
PROVENANCE Mrs J. van Gogh-Bonger, Amsterdam; V.W. van Gogh, Laren; Amsterdam, Rijksmuseum Vincent van Gogh [Vincent van Gogh Foundation, inv nr F 383]

F 384 [H 598] STILL LIFE: LEMONS
EXHIBITIONS 1904 Rotterdam, 74; 1909 Rotterdam, 32; 1910 Rotterdam, 28; 1912 Cologne, 19; 1935-6 New York etc, 22; 1947 Basle, 56; Paris 1, 73; 1952 Milan, 78; 1953 The Hague, 123; Otterlo, Amsterdam, 101; 1953-4 Saint Louis etc, 96; 1956 Eindhoven, 35; Munich, 123
PROVENANCE M.M. van Valkenburg, Laren [R 1904]; Reckers Art Gallery, Rotterdam [R 1909]; Otterlo, Rijksmuseum Kröller-Müller, inv nr 268-09, cat van Gogh 1970, nr 216

F 385 [H 812] SELF PORTRAIT
Left out by Faille in his manuscript for the present edition; See REJECTED WORKS

F 386 [H 283] STILL LIFE: POTATOES
EXHIBITIONS 1912 Cologne, 31; 1947 Basle, 51; 1958 Vienna, 79; 1962 Warsaw, 64; 1963 Tel Aviv, Haifa, 74; 1966 Belgrade, 63
PROVENANCE A. Flechtheim Art Gallery, Düsseldorf [R 1912]; Bernheim Jeune, Paris; Huinck Art Gallery, Utrecht [R 1917]; Otterlo, Rijksmuseum Kröller-Müller, inv nr 272-17, cat van Gogh 1970, nr 215

F 387 STILL LIFE WITH BREADROLLS
Left out by Faille in his manuscript for the present edition; See REJECTED WORKS

F 388 recto [formerly F 388 verso, H 89] HEAD OF A PEASANT WOMAN
EXHIBITIONS 1945 Amsterdam, without cat nr; 1946-7 Liège etc, 27; 1947 Paris 1, 27; Geneva, 4; 1949-50 New York, Chicago, 11; 1953 The Hague, 36; Otterlo, Amsterdam, 20; 1954 Zurich, 5; 1954-5 Bern, 11; 1955 Antwerp 1, 51; 1955-6 Liverpool etc, 5; 1957 Marseilles, 9; 1958-9 San Francisco etc, 5; 1959-60 Utrecht, 6; 1960 Cuesmes, 3
PROVENANCE Mrs J. van Gogh-Bonger, Amsterdam; V.W. van Gogh, Laren; Amsterdam, Rijksmuseum Vincent van Gogh [Vincent van Gogh Foundation, inv nr F 388]

F 388 verso [formerly F 388, H 282] GARDEN WITH SUNFLOWERS
EXHIBITIONS 1905 Amsterdam, 435;1961-2Baltimore etc, 5
PROVENANCE Mrs J. van Gogh-Bonger, Amsterdam; V.W. van Gogh, Laren; Amsterdam, Rijksmuseum Vincent van Gogh [Vincent van Gogh Foundation, inv nr F 388]

ARLES PERIOD

F 389 [H 428] A PORK-BUTCHER'S SHOP
EXHIBITIONS 1905 Amsterdam, 448; 1945 Amsterdam, without cat nr; 1951 Lyons etc, 47; 1955 Antwerp 1, 241; 1957 Stockholm, 111; 1961-2 Baltimore etc, 37
PROVENANCE Mrs J. van Gogh-Bonger, Amsterdam; V.W. van Gogh, Laren; Amsterdam, Rijksmuseum Vincent van Gogh [Vincent van Gogh Foundation, inv nr F 389]

F 390 [H 429] AN OLD ARLESIAN WOMAN
EXHIBITIONS 1955 Antwerp 1, 258; 1960 Paris, 39; 1968-9 London, 100
PROVENANCE Mrs J. van Gogh-Bonger, Amsterdam; V.W. van Gogh, Laren; Amsterdam, Rijksmuseum Vincent van Gogh [Vincent van Gogh Foundation, inv nr F 390]

F 391 [H 430] SNOWY LANDSCAPE WITH ARLES IN THE BACKGROUND
EXHIBITIONS 1908 Paris 2, 31; 1912 Düsseldorf, 120
PROVENANCE Druet Art Gallery, Paris [R 1908]; A. Schuffenecker, Paris; E. Blot Art Gallery, Paris; Marczell de Nemes Art Gallery, Budapest; Sale Nemes, Paris [Drouot] 21 November 1918, nr 43; Antonio Santa-Marina, Buenos Aires [R 1941]; Durand-Matthiesen Art Gallery, Geneva; Mr and Mrs Diego Lezica-Alvear [about 1954 exhibited for 3 months at the Tate Gallery, London]; Matthiesen Art Gallery, London; Private collection, London [R 1965]; Basle, Private collection [R 1968]

F 392 [H 427] STILL LIFE: BLOSSOMING ALMOND BRANCH IN A GLASS
EXHIBITIONS 1930 Amsterdam, 38; 1937 Paris, 150; 1939 San Francisco, 173; 1940 New York 3, 14; 1942 Baltimore, Worcester, 10; 1943 New York 2, 23; 1943-4 Indianapolis etc, 5; 1944 Montreal, 121; 1946-7 Liège etc, 124; 1947 Geneva, 124; Paris 1, 124; 1947-8 London etc, 33; 1948 Bergen, Oslo, 23; 1949-50 New York, Chicago, 66; 1951 Lyons etc, 30; 1955 Antwerp 1, 264; 1955-6 Liverpool etc, 35; 1958-9 San Francisco etc, 42; 1959 Aix-en-Provence, 4; 1961-2 Baltimore etc, 36; 1963 Humlebaek, 26; 1964 Washington, New York, 26; 1965 Charleroi, Ghent, 16; 1965-6 Stockholm, Göteborg, 28
PROVENANCE Mrs J. van Gogh-Bonger, Amsterdam; V.W. van Gogh, Laren; Amsterdam, Rijksmuseum Vincent van Gogh [Vincent van Gogh Foundation, inv nr F 392]

F 393 [H 426] STILL LIFE: BOOK AND BLOSSOMING ALMOND BRANCH IN A GLASS
EXHIBITIONS 1912 Cologne, 25; 1924 Basle, 27; Zurich, 25
PROVENANCE C.M. van Gogh Art Gallery, Amsterdam [R 1909]; Richard Kisling, Zurich [R 1912]; Mrs. H. Glatt-Kisling, Zurich; Switzerland, Private collection

F 394 [H 431] PINK PEACH-TREE IN BLOSSOM ['SOUVENIR DE MAUVE']
EXHIBITIONS 1896 Rotterdam, 50; 1927 Basle etc, 123; 1928 Düsseldorf, 191; Karlsruhe, 126; 1929 Berlin 1, 94; Hamburg, 78; 1930 Amsterdam, 233; 1946-7 Liège etc, 96; 1947 Paris 1, 99; Geneva, 99; Basle, 54; 1947-8 London etc, 39; 1952 Milan, 77; 1953 The Hague, 122; Otterlo, Amsterdam, 100; 1953-4 Saint Louis etc, 95; 1956 Munich, 122; 1958 Vienna, 78; Tokyo, Kyoto, 97; 1959 Aix-en-Provence, 6; 1963 Tel Aviv, Haifa, 69
PROVENANCE Mrs H. Mauve-Carbentus; Mrs H. van den Broek-Mauve, Scheveningen [1918]; Otterlo, Rijksmuseum Kröller-Müller, inv nr 302-18, cat van Gogh 1970, nr 206

F 395 [H 433] BASKET WITH SIX ORANGES
EXHIBITIONS 1905 Amsterdam, 81; 1933 Amsterdam 2, 118; 1935-6 New York etc, 24; 1937 Paris, 55; 1937-8 Amsterdam; 1949 Amsterdam 2, 12; 1953 Berlin, 9; 1962 New York, 33
PROVENANCE Mrs J. van Gogh-Bonger, Amsterdam; L.C. Enthoven, Voorburg, Netherlands; Sale Enthoven, Amsterdam [F. Muller] 18 May 1920, nr 241 [and repr]; S. van Deventer, De Steeg [from about 1935 until about 1955]; Wildenstein Art Gallery, New York; New York, Mr and Mrs Basil P. Goulandris

F 396 [H 438] THE GLEIZE BRIDGE OVER THE VIGUEYRET CANAL, NEAR ARLES
EXHIBITIONS 1914 Antwerp; 1921 Paris, 168
PROVENANCE Mrs J. van Gogh-Bonger, Amsterdam; L. C. Enthoven, Voorburg [Netherlands]; Sale Enthoven, Amsterdam [F. Muller] 18 May 1920, nr 240 [repr]; E. Heldring, Amsterdam [R 1921]; H. Stokvis, Brussels; Sale Amsterdam [F. Muller] 17 April 1923, nr 146 [repr]; Wildenstein Art Gallery, New York; Private collection [R 1970]

F 397 [H 435] THE LANGLOIS BRIDGE WITH WOMEN WASHING
EXHIBITIONS 1905 Amsterdam, 129; Utrecht, 39; 1906 Rotterdam, 37; 1913 Brussels; The Hague, 112; 1914 Antwerp, 45; 1927 Basle etc, 111; 1928 Düsseldorf, 179; Karlsruhe, 114; 1929 Berlin 1, 95; Hamburg, 67; 1930 Amsterdam, 227; 1935-6 New York etc, 23; 1945 The Hague, 32; 1946-7 Liège etc, 106; 1947 Paris 1, 109; Geneva, 109; Basle, 52; 1947-8 London etc, 35; 1952 Milan, 88; 1953 The Hague, 120; Otterlo, Amsterdam, 98; 1953-4 Saint Louis etc, 93; 1956 Eindhoven; Munich, 120; 1957 Essen, 267; 1958 Vienna, 77; Tokyo, Kyoto, 96; 1959 Aix-en-Provence, 5; 1966 Belgrade, 59
PROVENANCE Mrs J. van Gogh-Bonger, Amsterdam; C. Hoogendijk, The Hague; Sale Hoogendijk, Amsterdam [F. Muller] 21 May 1912, nr 24 [repr]; Otterlo, Rijksmuseum Kröller-Müller, inv nr 290-12, cat van Gogh 1970, nr 208

F 398 [H 439] AVENUE OF PLANE TREES NEAR THE STATION
EXHIBITIONS 1905 Paris, 34; 1936 Paris 1, 1057; 1955-6 Paris, 89
PROVENANCE Auguste Rodin, Meudon [R 1905]; Paris, Musée Rodin, cat 1938, nr 388

F 399 [H 437] APRICOT TREES IN BLOSSOM
EXHIBITIONS 1905 Amsterdam, 158; Utrecht, 30; 1921 Berlin; 1928 Berlin, 37
PROVENANCE Anna van Gogh-Carbentus, Leiden [R 1905]; Mrs Vincent van Gogh-Carbentus, Princenhage, Netherlands; Sale van Gogh-Carbentus a.o., Amsterdam [F. Muller] 25 November 1913, nr 27 [and reproduced] [not sold]; Bruno Cassirer, Berlin; Hugo Cassirer, Berlin; Mrs L. Fürstenberg-Cassirer, Johannesburg [on loan to Gemeentemuseum, The Hague 1933-1939, inv nr 38-33, cat 1935, p 77; on loan to Johannesburg, Kunsmuseum [from 1939 until sometime after 1963]

F 400 [H 436] THE LANGLOIS BRIDGE WITH ROAD ALONGSIDE THE CANAL
EXHIBITIONS 1905 Amsterdam, 139; 1914 Berlin, 77; 1921 Paris, 165; 1923 Amsterdam 2, 117; London, 31; 1924 Basle, 26; Zurich, 29; Stuttgart, 13; 1925 Paris 1, 21; The Hague, 38; Potsdam, 40; 1928 Munich, 19; Berlin, 38; Frankfurt, 26; Vienna, 24 [repr]; 1929 New York, 81; 1930 Amsterdam, 39; 1945 Amsterdam, without cat nr; 1946 Stockholm etc, 42; 1946-7 Liège etc, 102; 1947 Geneva, 103; Paris 1, 103; 1947-8 London etc, 34; 1948 Bergen, Oslo, 28; 1949-50 New York, Chicago, 67; 1951 Lyons, 35; 1954 Zurich, 38; 1955 Antwerp 1, 242; Palm Beach etc, 22; 1955-6 Liverpool etc, 36; 1957 Marseilles, 42; 1958-9 San Francisco etc, 43; 1959-60 Utrecht, 30; 1961-2 Baltimore etc, 38; 1963 Sheffield, 8; Humlebaek, 27; 1964 Washington, New York, 27; 1965 Charleroi, Ghent, 17; 1965-6 Stockholm, Göteborg, 29; 1967 Wolfsburg, 42; 1968-9 London, 101
PROVENANCE Mrs J. van Gogh-Bonger, Amsterdam; V. W. van Gogh, Laren; Amsterdam, Rijksmuseum Vincent van Gogh [Vincent van Gogh Foundation, inv nr F 400]

F 401 THE LANGLOIS BRIDGE
Left out by Faille in his manuscript for the present edition
See REJECTED WORKS

F 402 [H 705] TWO WHITE BUTTERFLIES
EXHIBITIONS 1928 Berlin, 39; Frankfort, 27; Vienna, 25; Munich, 20; 1954 Zurich, 41; 1954-5 Bern, 64; 1955 Antwerp 1, 268; 1960 Paris, 50; 1968-9 London, 190a
PROVENANCE Mrs J. van Gogh-Bonger, Amsterdam; V. W. van Gogh, Laren; Amsterdam, Rijksmuseum Vincent van Gogh [Vincent van Gogh Foundation, inv nr F 402]

F 403 [H 432] THE WHITE ORCHARD
EXHIBITIONS 1905 Amsterdam, 95; Utrecht, 28; 1914 Berlin, 62; 1925 The Hague, 46; 1930 Amsterdam, 40; 1945 Amsterdam, without cat nr; 1946-7 Liège etc, 97; 1947 Geneva, 97; Paris 1, 97; 1947-8 London etc, 36; 1948 Bergen, Oslo, 24; 1949-50 New York, Chicago, 68; 1951 Lyons etc, 27; 1953-4 Saint Louis etc, 94; 1954 Zurich, 35; 1954-5 Bern, 39; 1955 Antwerp 1, 245; 1955-6 Liverpool etc, 37; 1957 Marseilles, 45; 1958-9 San Francisco etc, 40; 1959-60 Utrecht, 34; 1961-2 Baltimore etc, 41; 1963 Humlebaek, 30; 1964 Washington, New York, 30; 1965-6 Stockholm, Göteborg, 31; 1967 Wolfsburg, 45; 1968-9 London, 106
PROVENANCE Mrs J. van Gogh-Bonger, Amsterdam; V. W. van Gogh, Laren; Amsterdam, Rijksmuseum Vincent van Gogh [Vincent van Gogh Foundation, inv nr F 403]

F 404 [H VIII] ORCHARD IN BLOOM
EXHIBITIONS 1905 Amsterdam, 101; 1914 Berlin, 63; 1924 Basle, 29; Zurich, 26; 1925 Paris 1, 32; 1930 Amsterdam, 41; 1945 Amsterdam, without cat nr; 1946 Stockholm etc, 43; 1946-7 Liège etc, 99; 1947 Paris 1, 101; Geneva, 101; 1947-8 London etc, 37; 1948 Bergen, Oslo, 25; 1949-50 New York, Chicago, 70; 1951 Lyons etc, 29; 1954 Zurich, 36; 1954-5 Bern, 40; 1955 Antwerp 1, 244; 1955-6 Liverpool etc, 38; 1957 Los Angeles, 8; Marseilles, 44; 1958-9 San Francisco etc, 39; 1959-60 Utrecht, 33; 1960-1 Montreal etc, 48; 1961-2 Baltimore etc, 40; 1963 Humlebaek, 29; 1964 Washington, New York, 29; 1965 Charleroi, Ghent, 18; 1965-6 Stockholm, Göteborg, 30; 1967 Wolfsburg, 44; 1968-9 London, 104
PROVENANCE Mrs J. van Gogh-Bonger, Amsterdam; V. W. van Gogh, Laren; Amsterdam, Rijksmuseum Vincent van Gogh [Vincent van Gogh Foundation, inv nr F 404]

F 405 [H 434] PEAR TREE IN BLOSSOM
EXHIBITIONS 1905 Amsterdam, 100; 1912 Cologne, 26 [repr]; 1928 Berlin, 40; Frankfurt, 28; Vienna, 26; Munich, 21; 1930 Amsterdam, 42; 1932 Manchester, 28; 1945 Amsterdam, without cat nr; 1946 Stockholm etc, 45; 1948 Bergen, Oslo, 26; 1949-50 New York, Chicago, 71; 1951 Lyons etc, 31; 1953 The Hague, 121; Otterlo, Amsterdam, 99; 1955 Antwerp 1, 246; Palm Beach etc, 14; 1955-6 Liverpool etc, 40; 1957 Marseilles, 46; 1958-9 San Francisco etc, 41; 1959-60 Utrecht, 31; 1961-2 Baltimore etc, 42; 1963 Sheffield, 9; Humlebaek, 31; 1964 Washington, New York, 31; 1965-6 Stockholm, Göteborg, 32; 1965 Charleroi, Ghent, 19; 1967 Wolfsburg, 46; 1968-9 London, 108
PROVENANCE Mrs J. van Gogh-Bonger, Amsterdam; V. W. van Gogh, Laren; Amsterdam, Rijksmuseum Vincent van Gogh [Vincent van Gogh Foundation, inv nr F 405]

F 406 [H 440] ORCHARD IN BLOSSOM
EXHIBITION 1905 Amsterdam, 97
PROVENANCE Mrs J. van Gogh-Bonger, Amsterdam; J. H. de Bois Art Gallery, Haarlem; Albert Stern, Amsterdam; Manchester, Mrs E. Friedlaender [1954-5 on loan to Tate Gallery, London]

F 407 [H 443] A MEADOW WITH A ROAD
EXHIBITIONS 1908 Zurich, 28 or 29; 1938 Paris 1, 127; 1946 Bern, 23 PROVENANCE Glarus, Mrs I. Schuler-Ganzoni [acquired 1908, bought at Van Gogh exhibition 'Züricher Kunstgesellschaft', Zurich]; Present owner unknown

F 408 [H 441] THE FARMHOUSE IN THE WHEATFIELD
EXHIBITIONS 1905 Amsterdam, 164; 1920 Venice; 1928 Berlin, 41; Frankfurt, 29; Munich, 22; Vienna, 28; 1955 Antwerp 1, 248; Palm Beach etc, 19
PROVENANCE Mrs J. van Gogh-Bonger, Amsterdam; V. W. van Gogh, Laren; Amsterdam, Rijksmuseum Vincent van Gogh [Vincent van Gogh Foundation, inv nr F 408]

F 409 [H 442] VIEW OF ARLES WITH IRISES IN THE FOREGROUND
EXHIBITIONS 1905 Amsterdam, 127; 1914 Berlin, 76; 1923 Amsterdam 2, 120; 1926 London 3, 16; 1928 Munich, 23; 1930 Amsterdam, 43; 1932 Manchester, 409; 1945 Amsterdam, without cat nr; 1946 Stockholm etc, 50; 1946-7 Liège etc, 103; 1947 Geneva, 104; 1947-8 London etc, 41; 1948 Bergen, Oslo, 29; 1949-50 New York, Chicago, 72; 1951 Lyons etc, 34; 1954 Zurich, 39; 1954-5 Bern, 41; 1955 Antwerp 1, 249; 1955-6 Liverpool etc, 41; 1957 Marseilles, 47; 1958-9 San Francisco etc, 44; 1959 Aix-en-Provence, 8; 1959-60 Utrecht, 35; 1968-9 London, 114
PROVENANCE Mrs J. van Gogh-Bonger, Amsterdam; V. W. van Gogh, Laren; Amsterdam, Rijksmuseum Vincent van Gogh [Vincent van Gogh Foundation, inv nr F 409]

F 410 [H IX] STILL LIFE: BLUE ENAMEL COFFEEPOT, SOME EARTHENWARE AND FRUIT
EXHIBITIONS 1898 The Hague, 34 [repr]; 1905 Amsterdam, 130; Utrecht, 41; 1906 Rotterdam, 38; 1910 Berlin 1, 38; 1912 Cologne, 27; 1914 Berlin, 85; 1922 Winterthur 1, 56; 1924 Basle, 25; Zurich, 28; 1930 Amsterdam, 44; 1931 Paris, 41; 1934 New York 1, 22; 1936 London 4, 104
PROVENANCE Mrs J. van Gogh-Bonger, Amsterdam [R 1905]; Carl Sternheim, Munich [acquired 1909]; Sale Sternheim, Amsterdam [F. Muller] 11 February 1919, nr 6 [repr]; Karl Sternheim, Reichenberg [Bezirk Dresden] [R 1924]; Mrs Thea Sternheim, Paris [R 1931]; Paul Guillaume Art Gallery, Paris; Paul Rosenberg Art Gallery, New York; France, Marquise de Chabannes [R 1934]

F 411 [H 444] THE WHEATFIELD
EXHIBITIONS 1905 Amsterdam, 114; 1929 London 1, 465; 1930 Amsterdam, 45; 1932 Manchester, 23; 1945 Amsterdam, without cat nr; 1946 Stockholm etc, 57; 1951 Lyons etc, 37; 1953 The Hague, 127; Otterlo, Amsterdam, 106; 1954 Zurich, 42; 1954-5 Bern, 44; 1955 Antwerp 1, 257; 1955-6 Liverpool etc, 51; 1958-9 San Francisco etc, 47; 1967 Wolfsburg, 52; 1968-9 London, 124
PROVENANCE Mrs J. van Gogh-Bonger, Amsterdam [on loan to Rijksmuseum, Amsterdam, since 1909; cat 1911 and 1920, nr 984e]; V. W. van Gogh, Laren; Amsterdam, Rijksmuseum Vincent van Gogh [Vincent van Gogh Foundation, inv nr F 411]

F 412 [H X] HARVEST AT LA CRAU
EXHIBITIONS 1905 Amsterdam, 102; Utrecht, 32; 1923 Amsterdam 2, 123; 1925 The Hague, 39; 1930 Amsterdam, 46; 1935 Amsterdam 2, 14; 1935-6 New York etc, 25; 1937 Paris, 34; 1945 Amsterdam, without cat nr; 1946 Stockholm etc, 52; 1946-7 Liège etc, 108; 1947 Geneva, 108; Paris 1, 108; 1947-8 London etc, 46; 1948 Bergen, Oslo, 30; 1949-50 New York, Chicago, 76; 1951 Lyons etc, 38; 1953 The Hague, 126; Otterlo, Amsterdam, 104; 1953-4 Saint Louis etc, 101; 1954 Zurich, 44; 1954-5 Bern, 42; 1955 Antwerp 1, 250; 1955-6 Liverpool etc, 45; 1957 Marseilles, 48; 1958-9 San Francisco etc, 49; 1959 Aix-en-Provence, 9; 1959-60 Utrecht, 37; 1960-1 Montreal etc, 50; 1961-2 Baltimore etc, 44; 1963 Humlebaek, 32; 1965 Charleroi, Ghent, 20; 1965-6 Stockholm, Göteborg, 33; 1967 Wolfsburg, 48; Montreal, 88; 1968-9 London, 118
PROVENANCE Mrs J. van Gogh-Bonger, Amsterdam; V. W. van Gogh, Laren; Amsterdam, Rijksmuseum Vincent van Gogh [Vincent van Gogh Foundation, inv nr F 412]

F 413 [H 451] BOATS ON THE BEACH AT SAINTES-MARIES
EXHIBITIONS 1898 The Hague, 30 [repr]; 1905 Amsterdam, 151; 1912 Cologne, 48 [repr]; 1914 Berlin, 45; 1915 Amsterdam, 6; 1924 Basle, 28; Zurich, 30; Stuttgart, 14; 1925 Paris 1, 22; The Hague, 29; 1926 Venice, 27; 1927 Paris; 1928 Munich, 24; 1930 Amsterdam, 47; 1935-6 New York etc, 26; 1937 Paris, 225; 1945 Amsterdam, without cat nr; 1946 Stockholm etc, 53; 1946-7 Liège etc, 111; 1947 Paris 1, 112; Geneva, 112; 1947-8 London etc, 43; 1948 Bergen, Oslo, 31; 1949-50 New York, Chicago, 73; 1951 Lyons etc, 39; 1953 The Hague, 125; Otterlo, Amsterdam, 102; 1953-4 Saint Louis etc, 97; 1954 Zurich, 40; 1955 Antwerp 1, 252; Palm Beach etc, 21; 1955-6 Liverpool etc, 43; 1957 Marseilles, 49; 1958-9 San Francisco etc, 45; 1959 Aix-en-Provence, 13; 1959-60 Utrecht, 38; 1961-2 Baltimore etc, 45; 1963 Sheffield, 10; Humlebaek, 33; 1964 Washington, New York, 33; 1965 Charleroi, Ghent, 21; 1965-6 Stockholm, Göteborg, 34; 1967 Wolfsburg, 49; 1968-9 London, 122
PROVENANCE Mrs J. van Gogh-Bonger, Amsterdam; V. W. van Gogh, Laren; Amsterdam, Rijksmuseum Vincent van Gogh [Vincent van Gogh Foundation, inv nr F 413]

F 414 BOATS AT SAINTES-MARIES
Left out by Faille in his manuscript for the present edition; See REJECTED WORKS

F 415 [H 454] SEASCAPE
EXHIBITIONS 1905 Amsterdam, 152; 1915 Amsterdam, 7; 1921 Paris, 167; 1925 The Hague, 52; 1930 Amsterdam, 48; London 2; 1939 San Francisco, 174; 1940 New York 3, 7; 1942 Baltimore, Worcester, 11; 1943 New York 2, 25; 1943-4 Indianapolis etc, 6; 1944 Montreal, 124; 1951 Lyons etc, 40; 1953-4 Saint Louis etc, 98; 1955 Antwerp 1, 251; Palm Beach etc, 20; 1955-6 Liverpool etc, 42; 1958-9 San Francisco etc, 46; 1959-60 Utrecht, 39; 1960-1 Montreal etc, 52; 1968-9 London, 119
PROVENANCE Mrs J. van Gogh-Bonger, Amsterdam; V. W. van Gogh, Laren; Amsterdam, Rijksmuseum Vincent van Gogh [Vincent van Gogh Foundation, inv nr F 415]

F 416 [H 456] VIEW OF SAINTES-MARIES
EXHIBITIONS 1913 Brussels; The Hague, 114; 1914 Antwerp, 29; 1927 Basle etc, 108; 1928 Düsseldorf, 176 [repr]; Karlsruhe, 111 [repr]; 1929 Berlin 1, 98; Hamburg, 64; 1930 Amsterdam, 214; 1946-7 Liège etc, 107; 1947 Paris 1, 107; Geneva, 107; Basle, 59; 1947-8 London etc, 42; 1949-50 New York, Chicago, 75; 1952 Milan, 79; 1953 The Hague, 124; Otterlo, Amsterdam, 103; 1953-4 Saint Louis etc, 99; 1957 Essen, 281; 1958 Vienna, 80; Tokyo, Kyoto, 98; 1959 Aix-en-Provence, 12; 1960-1 Montreal etc, 38; 1962 Warsaw, 61; 1963 Tel Aviv, Haifa, 71; 1966 Belgrade, 60
PROVENANCE C. Hoogendijk, The Hague; Sale Hoogendijk, Amsterdam [F. Muller] 21 May 1912, nr 25 [repr]; Otterlo, Rijksmuseum Kröller-Müller, inv nr 287-12, cat van Gogh 1970, nr 209

F 417 [H 455] SEASCAPE
EXHIBITION 1926 Moscow, 3
PROVENANCE I. A. Morosov, Moscow; Moscow, Museum of Modern Western Art; Moscow, Pushkin Museum [acquired 1948, from the Museum of Modern Western Art], inv nr 3438, cat 1961, p 53

F 418 [H 814] THE SEA AT SAINTES-MARIES
Left out by Faille in his manuscript for the present edition; See REJECTED WORKS

F 418a [formerly F 418bis] BOATS AT SAINTES-MARIES
Left out by Faille in his manuscript for the present edition; See REJECTED WORKS

F 419 [H 445] WHITE MAS AT SAINTES MARIES
EXHIBITIONS 1901 Paris, 36; 1908 Paris 2, 8; 1934 San Francisco, 161; 1936 San Diego, 154; 1940 San Francisco 2, 10; 1943 New York 2, 23; 1948 Cleveland, 7; 1960 San Francisco, without cat nr
PROVENANCE Julien Leclercq, Paris [R 1901]; M. Fabre, Paris [R 1908]; E. Druet Art Gallery, Paris [R 1908]; G. Fayet, Igny [from 1909 until about 1925]; Wildenstein

Art Gallery, New York; Mr and Mrs W. H. Crocker, San Francisco [R 1934]; W. H. Crocker Estate, Burlingame, California [R 1950]; San Francisco, Henry P. Russell [R 1960]

F 420 [H 446] MAS AT SAINTES-MARIES
EXHIBITIONS 1905 Amsterdam, 150; 1912 Cologne, 49; 1913 Düsseldorf, without cat nr [repr]; 1914 Berlin, 57
PROVENANCE Mrs J. van Gogh-Bonger, Amsterdam [R 1905]; Carl Sternheim, Reichenberg near Dresden, later on Munich [acquired 1909]; Paul Cassirer Art Gallery, Berlin; Ernst Goldschmidt, Copenhagen; Present owner unknown

F 421 MAS AT SAINTES MARIES
Left out by Faille in his manuscript for the present edition; See REJECTED WORKS

F 422 [H 448] THE SOWER
EXHIBITIONS 1905 Amsterdam, 110; 1927 Basle etc, 124; 1928 Düsseldorf, 192 [repr]; Karlsruhe, 127; 1929 Berlin I, 100; Hamburg, 79; 1930 Amsterdam, 232; 1958 Vienna, 81; 1960-1 Montreal etc, 39; 1962 Brussels, Otterlo, 47; Warsaw, 63; 1963 Tel Aviv, Haifa, 73
PROVENANCE Mrs J. van Gogh-Bonger, Amsterdam; F. J. Michelsen, Amsterdam; Sale Michelsen, Amsterdam [F. Muller] 3 December 1918, nr 303 [repr]; Otterlo, Rijksmuseum Kröller-Müller, inv nr 303-18, cat van Gogh 1970, nr 214

F 423 [H 449] A BUGLER OF THE ZOUAVE REGIMENT
EXHIBITIONS 1912 Cologne, 57; 1914 Berlin, 48; 1920 New York, 57 [repr]; 1923 London, 40; 1924 Basle, 32; Zurich, 31; Stuttgart, 15; 1925 Paris I, 23; The Hague, 6; 1926 Munich, 2095; 1927 Paris; 1928 Berlin, 43 [repr]; Frankfurt, 30 [repr]; Vienna [repr]; 1930 Amsterdam, 49; 1945 Amsterdam, without cat nr; 1946 Stockholm etc, 56; 1946-7 Liège etc, 105; 1947 Paris I, 106; Geneva, 106; 1947-8 London etc, 44; 1948 Bergen, Oslo, 32; 1949-50 New York, Chicago, 74; 1951 Lyons etc, 48; Zurich 1954, 50; 1955 Antwerp I, 259; Palm Beach etc, 18; 1955-6 Liverpool etc, 44; 1957 Marseilles, 52; 1958-9 San Francisco etc, 52; 1959 Aix-en-Provence, 11; 1959-60 Utrecht, 40; 1961-2 Baltimore etc, 49; 1963 Sheffield, 11; Humlebaek, 36; 1964 Washington, New York, 36; 1965 Charleroi, Ghent, 24; 1965-6 Stockholm, Göteborg, 35; 1967 Wolfsburg, 53; 1968-9 London, 125
PROVENANCE Mrs J. van Gogh-Bonger, Amsterdam; V. W. van Gogh, Laren; Amsterdam, Rijksmuseum Vincent van Gogh [Vincent van Gogh Foundation, inv nr F 423]

F 424 [H 450] THE ZOUAVE
EXHIBITIONS 1905 Amsterdam, 436; 1945 Basle, 8; 1947 Basle, 61; 1955 New York 2, 29; 1957 Los Angeles, 9; 1959 Washington, p 51; New York 2, 53
PROVENANCE Mrs J. van Gogh-Bonger, Amsterdam; Prince of Wagram, Paris [acquired 1906]; Druet Art Gallery Paris [acquired November 1908]; Flechtheim Art Gallery, Berlin [acquired October 1912]; Sale Flechtheim, Berlin [Cassirer] 5 June 1917, nr 140 [repr]; Goltz [on loan to National Galerie, Kronprinzenpalais, Berlin about 1929]; Tanner Art Gallery, Zurich; Paul Vallotton Art Gallery, Lausanne; Eisenloeffel Art Gallery, Amsterdam; Unger and Van Mens Art Gallery, Rotterdam; A. van Hoboken, Lausanne, Ascona [R 1947]; New York, Mrs A. D. Lasker [R 1970]

F 425 [H 447] HAYSTACKS IN PROVENCE
EXHIBITIONS 1927 Basle etc, 126; 1928 Düsseldorf, 194; Karlsruhe, 129; 1929 Berlin I, 97; Hamburg, 81; 1930 Amsterdam, 231; 1935-6 New York etc, 27; 1946-7 Liège etc, 104; 1947 Paris I, 105; Geneva, 105; Basle, 58; 1947-8 London etc, 45; 1952 Milan, 80; 1953-4 Saint Louis etc, 100; 1959 Aix-en-Provence, 10; 1960-1 Montreal etc, 37
PROVENANCE L. C. Enthoven, Voorburg, Netherlands; Sale Enthoven, Amsterdam [F. Muller] 18 May 1920, nr 242 [repr]; Otterlo, Rijksmuseum Kröller-Müller, inv nr 305-20, cat van Gogh 1970, nr 226

F 426 [H 452] THE BRIDGE AT TRINQUETAILLE
EXHIBITIONS 1904 Groningen; 1905 Amsterdam, 109; 1923 Paris; 1924 London 2; 1928 New York 2, 30 [repr]; 1934 San Francisco, 156; 1948 New York I, 2; 1962 Washington, 26
PROVENANCE Mrs J. van Gogh-Bonger, Amsterdam; A. Vollard Art Gallery, Paris; Mrs Redlich, Vienna; Hodebert Art Gallery, Paris; Etienne Bignou Art Gallery, Paris; Mrs R. A. Workman, London; Alex Reid and Lefevre Art Gallery, London; Knoedler Art Gallery, New York; Mrs W. A. Clark, New York [R 1934]; New York, André Meyer [R 1962]

F 427 [H 453] THE CANAL LA ROUBINE DU ROI WITH WASHERWOMEN
EXHIBITIONS 1892 The Hague, 6; 1905 Amsterdam, 147; 1914 Berlin, 105; 1928 Berlin, 44 [repr]; 1944 Montreal, 125; 1955 New York 2, 28
PROVENANCE Mrs J. van Gogh-Bonger, Amsterdam; Gustav Schiefler, Mellingstedt [R 1914]; Kunsthalle, Hamburg [on loan]; Martin Gerson, Berlin; Knoedler Art Gallery, New York; French Art Gallery, New York; New York, Private collection [acquired 1943]

F 428 [H 457] SUNNY LAWN, PUBLIC PARK
EXHIBITIONS 1905 Amsterdam, 141; 1913 Düsseldorf, without cat nr [repr]; 1914 Berlin, 86; 1930 Amsterdam, 50; 1943 New York 2, 26; 1947 Basle, 60
PROVENANCE Mrs J. van Gogh-Bonger, Amsterdam; Mrs Thea Sternheim, Uttwil; Sale Sternheim, Amsterdam [F. Muller] 11 February 1919, nr. 7 [repr]; Zurich, B. Mayer [deposited in Kunsthaus Zurich]

F 429 [H 458] FLOWERING GARDEN WITH PATH
EXHIBITIONS 1905 Amsterdam, 148; 1930 Amsterdam, 51; 1953 The Hague, 128; Otterlo, Amsterdam, 105; 1955 Rotterdam, 189
PROVENANCE Mrs J. van Gogh-Bonger, Amsterdam; J. W. Moll, Groningen [acquired 1905]; W. Moll, The Hague [until 1962]; The Netherlands Government [acquired 1962; on loan to Gemeente Museum, The Hague]

F 430 [H 459] FLOWERING GARDEN
EXHIBITIONS 1905 Amsterdam, 107; 1914 Berlin, 140; 1952 Milan, 81; 1955 Winterthur I, 100; 1960 Paris, 199; 1964 Lausanne, 115
PROVENANCE Mrs J. van Gogh-Bonger, Amsterdam; Gustav Schiefler, Mellingstedt [1914]; Max Emden, Hamburg; Herman Lütjens, Zurich-Küssnacht; Zurich, Private collection [R 1964]

F 431 [H 460] LA MOUSMÉ
EXHIBITIONS 1905 Amsterdam, 121; 1906 Rotterdam, 35; 1907 Rotterdam, 12; 1917 Zurich I, 108; 1929 London 2, 3a; New York, 75; 1933 Chicago, 382; 1946 Washington, p 76
PROVENANCE Mrs J. van Gogh-Bonger, Amsterdam; Bernheim jeune Art Gallery, Paris; C. M. van Gogh Art Gallery, Amsterdam; Carl Sternheim, La Hulpe-lez-Bruxelles; J. Hessel Art Gallery, Paris; Paul Rosenberg Art Gallery, Paris; Georges Bernheim Art Gallery, Paris; Alphonse Kann, Saint-Germain-en-Laye [R 1917]; J. B. Stang, Oslo [acquired 1918]; Alex Reid and Lefevre Art Gallery, London; Chester Dale, New York [R 1929]; Washington, National Gallery of Art, inv nr 1815, cat Chester Dale collection 1965, p 125

F 432 [H 461] THE POSTMAN JOSEPH ROULIN: HALF LENGTH, SITTING AT A TABLE
EXHIBITIONS 1914 Berlin, 117 [repr]; 1922 Winterthur I, 54; 1924 Zurich, 33; Basle, 35; 1928 New York 2, 32 [repr]; 1929 Cambridge, USA, 93; New York, 76; 1930 Providence, 42; 1933 Chicago, 384; 1935-6 New York etc, 28; 1949-50 New York, Chicago, 77
PROVENANCE C. Hoogendijk, The Hague; Sale Amsterdam [F. Muller] 21 May 1912, nr 26; Bernheim jeune Art Gallery, Paris; Paul Cassirer Art Gallery, Berlin; Thea Sternheim, Uttwil; Sale Sternheim, Amsterdam [F. Muller] 11 February 1919, nr 8 [repr]; Karl Sternheim, Reichenberg [1924]; Alfred Flechtheim Art Gallery, Berlin; Reid and Lefevre Art Gallery, London; Knoedler Art Gallery, New York; Robert Treat Paine 2nd, Boston [1929; 1935]; Boston Museum of Fine Arts [Robert Treat Paine II bequest], inv nr 35.1982, cat 1955, p 29

F 433 [H 466] HEAD OF THE POSTMAN ROULIN
EXHIBITIONS 1921 Berlin; 1926 Dresden, 211; 1928 Berlin, 45 [repr]; 1929 London I, 461
PROVENANCE Mrs J. van Gogh-Bonger, Amsterdam; Paul Cassirer Art Gallery, Berlin; J. Freudenberg, Berlin [R 1926; 1929]; Arnold Seligmann Art Gallery, New York; Museum of Fine Arts, Boston; Wildenstein Art Gallery, New York; Edsel B. Ford, Detroit; Private collection [R 1970]

F 434 [H 463] ROULIN THE POSTMAN
EXHIBITIONS 1905 Paris, 13; 1908 Paris 2, 32; 1947 Basle, 62; 1957 Essen, 295; 1961 Wolfsburg, 73
PROVENANCE M. Fabre, Gasparets [R 1905]; Druet Art Gallerie, Paris [acquired 1907]; Mr Keller, Paris; Druet Art Gallery, Paris; Georg Reinhart, Winterthur [acquired May 1915]; Winterthur, Kunstmuseum [acquired 1955; gift Heirs of G. Reinhart], inv nr 868, cat 1958, nr 178

F 435 [H 462] THE POSTMAN ROULIN: FLOWERY BACKGROUND
EXHIBITION 1908 Paris 2, 17
PROVENANCE M. Fabre, Gasparets; Druet Art Gallery, Paris; J. Keller, Paris [acquired 1907]; Druet Art Gallery, Paris [acquired 1910]; Merion, Pennsylvania, Barnes Foundation [acquired 1912]

F 436 [H 464] THE POSTMAN ROULIN
EXHIBITIONS 1905 Amsterdam, 443; 1920 New York, 63 [repr]; 1921 New York, 22; 1923 London, 21 [repr]; 1930 Amsterdam, 52; 1943 New York 2, 27; 1947 Basle, 80; 1963 Schaffhausen, 55
PROVENANCE Mrs J. van Gogh-Bonger, Amsterdam; Thannhauser Art Gallery, Lucerne [acquired 1923]; National Gallery, London; Thannhauser Art Gallery, Munich; B. Mayer, Zurich; Zurich/Ascona, Private collection [R 1966]

F 437 [H 483] THE STEVEDORES
EXHIBITIONS 1901 Paris, 17; 1922 Paris; 1931 New York, 26; 1941 Chicago, 77; 1942 Baltimore, Worcester, 14; 1943 New York 2, 30; 1959 Washington, p 52
PROVENANCE Bernheim jeune Art Gallery, Paris; Ackermann, Paris; Knoedler Art Gallery, New York and Salz Art Gallery, New York [R 1941]; J. K. Thannhauser Art Gallery, New York; Annapolis, DC, Mr and Mrs Carleton Mitchell jr [R 1959]

F 438 [H 484] THE STEVEDORES
EXHIBITIONS 1901 Paris, 21; 1905 Amsterdam, 112; Utrecht, 40; 1906 Rotterdam, 33; 1928 Berlin, 46; 1933-4 Rotterdam, 38; 1948 Cleveland, 10; New York I, 3; 1961 London 2, 48; 1967 Paris, 104
PROVENANCE Mrs J. van Gogh-Bonger, Amsterdam [R 1905]; Bernheim jeune Art Gallery, Paris; Paul Cassirer Art Gallery, Berlin; F. Kallmann, Berlin; Paul Rosenberg Art Gallery, New York; William H. Taylor, Westchester, Penna., [R 1948]; Mrs Charles Hopkins, Topeka, Kansas; Sale London [Sotheby] 25 November 1959, nr 86; Patch; Sale London [Sotheby] 12 June 1963, nr 72 [not sold]; Sale New York [Parke-Bernet] 14 April 1965, nr 76; Castagnola Switzerland, Sammlung Thyssen-Bornemisza [R 1969]

F 439 [H 465] THE POSTMAN ROULIN
EXHIBITIONS 1905 Paris, 40; 1910 Berlin I; 1913 The Hague, 130; 1914 Antwerp, 31; 1927 Basle etc, 107; 1928 Düsseldorf, 174 [repr]; Karlsruhe, 109 [repr]; 1929 Berlin I, 102; Hamburg, 63; 1930 Amsterdam, 229; 1935 Brussels, 98; 1946-7 Liège etc, 109; 1947 Paris I, 111; Geneva, 111; Basle, 81; 1947-8 London etc, 66; 1948 Amsterdam; 1952 Milan, 91; 1953 The Hague, 139; Otterlo, Amsterdam, 117; 1953-4 Saint Louis etc, 113; 1956 Munich, 136; 1958 Vienna, 88; Tokyo, Kyoto, 107; 1959 Aix-en-Provence 20; 1960-1 Montreal etc, 46; 1962 Warsaw, 65; 1963 Tel Aviv, Haifa, 75; 1966 Belgrade, 66
PROVENANCE Amédée Schuffenecker, Clamart; Mr Leonard, Paris; Otterlo, Rijksmuseum Kröller-Müller, inv nr 286-12, cat van Gogh 1970, nr 218

F 440 [H 475] THE BABY [MARCELLE ROULIN]
EXHIBITION 1950 Paris 2, 49 [or F 441a]
PROVENANCE Mrs Jules Armand, Arles; A. Mak Art Gallery, Amsterdam; E. Bignou Art Gallery, Paris; Alex Reid and Lefevre Art Gallery, London; Chester Dale, New York; Washington, National Gallery of Art, inv nr 1695, cat collection Chester Dale 1965, p 126

F 441 [H 476] THE BABY [MARCELLE ROULIN]
EXHIBITIONS 1905 Amsterdam, 116; 1914 Berlin, 52; 1924 Basle, 37; Zurich, 43; Stuttgart, 18; 1925 Paris I, 30; The Hague, 37; 1926 London, 3; 1927 Paris; 1930 Amsterdam, 53; 1945 Amsterdam, without cat nr; 1947-8 London etc, 59; 1948 Bergen, Oslo, 36; 1951 Lyons etc, 46; 1953 The Hague, 134; Otterlo, Amsterdam, 112; 1953-4 Saint Louis etc, 109; 1954 Zurich, 48; 1954-5 Bern, 45; 1955 Antwerp I, 260; 1955-6 Liverpool etc, 53; 1957 Stockholm, 112; 1960-1 Montreal etc, 53; 1961-2 Baltimore etc, 50
PROVENANCE Mrs J. van Gogh-Bonger, Amsterdam; V. W. van Gogh, Laren; Amsterdam, Rijksmuseum Vincent van Gogh [Vincent van Gogh Foundation, inv nr F 441]

F 441a [formerly F 441bis, H 477] THE BABY [MARCELLE ROULIN]
EXHIBITIONS 1925 Paris I, 29; 1938 Amsterdam I, 13; 1939 London I, 15; 1950 Paris 2, 49 [or F 440]; 1955 Antwerp 2, 171
PROVENANCE Joseph Roulin, Marseilles; A. Schuffenecker, Paris; A. Vollard Art Gallery, Paris [R about 1895]; A. Bauchy, Livry; A. Pellerin, Paris [R 1905]; Louis Bernard, Paris; M. Clerc, Paris [R 1925]; Huinck and Scherjon Art Gallery, Amsterdam; H. E. ten Cate, Almelo [R 1939]; Van Wisselingh Art Gallery, Amsterdam; Bernheim jeune Art Gallery, Paris [R 1939]; Alex Reid and Lefevre Art Gallery, London; Bignou Galleries, New York [R 1947]; Gstaad, Louis Franck [R 1970]
EDITORS' COMMENT See F 441a in cat

F 442 THE LITTLE GARDEN
Left out by Faille in his manuscript for the present edition; See REJECTED WORKS

F 443 [H 478] PORTRAIT OF PATIENCE ESCALIER [SHEPHERD IN THE PROVENCE]
EXHIBITIONS 1898 The Hague, 36 [?] [repr]; 1904 Rotterdam, 66; 1905 Amsterdam, 153; 1912 Cologne, 62 [repr]; 1922 Copenhagen, 176 [repr]; 1936 Cleveland, 320; 1938 New York 2, 46; 1940 New York 2, 361; 1943 New York 2, 29; 1953 New York 2, 15; 1955 New York 2, 30
PROVENANCE Mrs J. van Gogh-Bonger, Amsterdam; H. P. Bremmer, The Hague [R 1904; on loan since 1924 to Gemeente Museum The Hague, inv nr 39-24, cat 1935, p 77] Mrs E. L. Jonas, New York [R 1938; R 1940]; New York, Mrs H. Harris Jonas [R 1943; R 1955]

F 444 [H 479] PORTRAIT OF PATIENCE ESCALIER [SHEPHERD IN THE PROVENCE]
EXHIBITIONS 1896 Rotterdam, 44; 1917 Zurich 2, 112 [repr]; 1927 Paris; 1934 London, 20; 1939 London 2, 20
PROVENANCE Bernheim Jeune Art Gallery, Paris

[R 1917]; A. Bauchy, Livry [R 1934]; Alex Reid and Lefevre Art Gallery, London; A. Chester Beatty, London; London, Heirs of A. Chester Beatty

F 445 [H 487] ENCAMPMENT OF GYPSIES WITH CARAVANS
EXHIBITIONS 1901 Paris, 29; 1905 Paris, 11; 1908 Paris 2, 6; 1914 London, 87; Paris, Rétrospective, Champs de Mars; 1923 Prague, 187; 1927 Paris; 1941 Albi; 1945 Paris, 119
PROVENANCE M. Fabre, Gasparets [R 1901; R 1908]; Druet Art Gallery, Paris [R 1909]; Paul Rosenberg Art Gallery, Paris; Raymond Koechlin, Paris [R 1909-1931]; Paris, Musée National du Louvre [acquired 1931; Koechlin Bequest], inv nr RF 3670, cat Impressionistes 1959, nr 146

F 446 [H 486] RAILWAY CARRIAGES
EXHIBITIONS 1925 Paris 3, 163; 1927 Paris; 1960 Paris, 43
PROVENANCE Prince of Wagram, Paris; Druet Art Gallery, Paris [aquired 1908]; Paul Rosenberg, Paris [acquired 1909]; Jacques Doucet, Paris [R 1925]; Present owner unknown

F 447 [H 482] THE THISTLES
EXHIBITIONS 1905 Paris, 17; 1916 Paris; 1918 Oslo; 1942 Paris, 182; 1945 Paris, 99; 1948 Paris, 40; 1949 Lyons, 124 [as being signed in lower right but not traceable]; 1951 Paris 2, 68; 1955 New York 2, 31; 1957-8 New York etc, 25; 1958 London 2, 26; 1960 Paris, 42
PROVENANCE G. Fayet, Paris [R 1905]; Druet Art Gallery, Paris [acquired 1912]; Denys Cochin, Paris [acquired 1913]; Druet Art Gallery, Paris [acquired 1917]; Gösta Olson Art Gallery, Stockholm; M. C. Pineus, Göteborg [acquired 1918]; Axel Jacobsen, Stockholm; Gold Art Gallery, Paris; Gabriel Cognacq, Paris; Sale Cognacq, Paris [Charpentier] 14 May 1952, 62; Athens, Stavros S. Niarchos, exhib cat 1957, nr 25

F 447a TWO THISTLES
PROVENANCE Eugène Murer, Auvers-sur-Oise; A. Vollard Art Gallery, Paris; Léon Marseille Art Gallery, Paris; Ernest Girard, Paris; Private collection, Paris; Raymonde Cazenave, Paris; Sale London [Christie] 28 June 1968, nr 76; Present owner unknown

F 448 [H 474] THE PAINTER ON THE ROAD TO TARASCON [destroyed]
EXHIBITIONS 1896 Rotterdam, 26 [description in Nieuwe Rotterdamsche Courant 22 March 1896]; 1905 Amsterdam, 162; 1912 Cologne, 61 [repr]
PROVENANCE Mrs J. van Gogh-Bonger, Amsterdam; J. H. de Bois Art Gallery, Haarlem; Alfred Flechtheim Art Gallery, Düsseldorf [R 1910]; Formerly Magdeburg, Kaiser Friedrich Museum [acquired 1912], inv nr GK 558
The painting was destroyed by fire in May 1945 together with the whole collection of the museum

F 449 [H 485] BOATS WITH MEN UNLOADING SAND
EXHIBITIONS 1905 Paris, 9; 1930 Amsterdam, 54; 1951 Paris 1, 44; 1953 Berlin, 10; 1953-4 Saint Louis etc, 105; 1955 Winterthur 1, 97; 1956 Munich, 127; 1957 Essen, 297; 1961 Wolfsburg, 72
PROVENANCE Christian Cherfils, Paris [R 1905]; Prince of Wagram, Paris; Druet Art Gallery, Paris [R 1908]; Mr Langlois, France; Denys Cochin, Paris; Druet Art Gallery, Paris [R 1912]; Essen, Museum Folkwang [acquired 1912], inv nr G 61, cat 1961, nr 60

F 450 [H 481] THE SOWER
EXHIBITIONS 1891 Brussels, 1; 1905 Amsterdam, 112a; 1921 Berlin; 1954 Zurich, not in the cat; 1958 Zurich, 241; 1958-9 Munich, 72; 1961 Edinburgh, London, 59; 1964 Lausanne, 114
PROVENANCE Mrs J. van Gogh-Bonger, presented the painting to Frederik van Eeden, Bussum [R 1891; R 1905]; Mrs Frederik van Eeden-van Vloten, Laren; d'Audretsch Art Gallery, The Hague; Paul Cassirer Art Gallery, Berlin; Franz von Mendelssohn-Bartholdy, Grunewald; Heirs of F. von Mendelssohn-Bartholdy, Zurich; Fritz Nathan, Zurich; Emil Bührle, Zurich [acquired 1951]; Zurich, E. G. Bührle, cat 1958, nr 241

F 451 [H 480] THE SOWER
EXHIBITIONS 1905 Amsterdam, 113; Utrecht, 37; 1906 Rotterdam, 34; 1914 Berlin, 51; 1920 New York, 47; 1923 Amsterdam 2, 127; 1925 The Hague, 53; 1926 Dresden 213; 1928 Munich, 25; 1930 Amsterdam, 55; 1945 Amsterdam, without cat nr; 1947-8 London etc, 56; 1948 Bergen, Oslo, 35; 1949-50 New York, Chicago, 85; 1951 Lyons etc, 43; 1954 Zurich, 46; 1955 Antwerp 1, 255; Palm Beach etc, 17; 1955-6 Liverpool etc, 50; 1957 Marseilles, 51; 1958-9 San Francisco etc, 54; 1959 Aix-en-Provence, 19; 1959-60 Utrecht, 43; 1961-2 Baltimore etc, 47; 1963 Humlebaek, 35; 1964 Washington, New York, 35; 1965 Charleroi, Ghent, 23; 1965-6 Stockholm, Göteborg, 39; 1967 Wolfsburg, 51; 1968-9 London, 140
PROVENANCE Mrs J. van Gogh-Bonger, Amsterdam; V. W. van Gogh, Laren; Amsterdam, Rijksmuseum Vincent van Gogh [Vincent van Gogh Foundation, inv nr F 451]

F 452 [H 280] STILL LIFE: SUNFLOWERS
EXHIBITIONS 1896 Rotterdam, 28; 1904 Groningen; 1905 Amsterdam, 47; Utrecht, 14; 1906 Rotterdam, 14; 1908 Paris 1, 26; 1910 Rotterdam, 26; 1912 Cologne, 29; 1913 The Hague, 133; 1914 Antwerp, 26; 1927 Basle etc, 100 [repr]; 1928 Düsseldorf, 167 [repr]; Karlsruhe, 102 [repr]; 1929 Berlin 1, 101; Hamburg, 57; 1930 Amsterdam, 209; 1935-6 New York etc, 30; 1946-7 Liège etc, 76; 1947 Paris 1, 78; Geneva, 78; Basle, 44; 1947-8 London etc, 30; 1952 Milan, 70; 1953 The Hague, 94; Otterlo, Amsterdam, 74; 1953-4 Saint Louis etc, 80; 1956 Eindhoven, 30; Munich, 110; 1958 Vienna, 76; Tokyo, Kyoto, 88; 1960-1 Montreal etc, 23; 1962 Warsaw, 57; Brussels, Otterlo, 45; 1963 Tel Aviv, Haifa, 65; Amsterdam, 100
PROVENANCE Mrs J. van Gogh-Bonger, Amsterdam; C. M. van Gogh Art Gallery, Amsterdam [R 1908]; Otterlo, Rijksmuseum Kröller-Müller, inv nr 279-08, cat van Gogh 1970, nr 202

F 453 [H 473] STILL LIFE: VASE WITH THREE SUNFLOWERS
EXHIBITIONS 1901 Paris, 4; 1927 Paris; 1948 Cleveland, 9
PROVENANCE Maison [Julien] Tanguy, Paris [in commission from Theo van Gogh]; Octave Mirbeau, Paris [R 1892 and 1901]; Jacques Doucet, Paris [R before 1928]; USA, Private collection

F 454 [H 467] STILL LIFE: VASE WITH FOURTEEN SUNFLOWERS
EXHIBITIONS 1889 Probably Brussels [Vingtistes]; 1905 Amsterdam, 103; 1915 Amsterdam, 10; 1921 Paris, 164; 1923 Amsterdam 2, 125; London, 26 [repr]; 1947-8 London etc, 48; 1948 London 1, 30; 1955 Paris 3, 63; 1968-9 London, 132
PROVENANCE Mrs J. van Gogh-Bonger, Amsterdam; Isaac Israëls, The Hague [on loan from 1917 until 1920]; Leicester Galleries, London [R about 1923]; London, Tate Gallery [acquired 1924; Courtauld Fund], cat TG nr 3863; cat Courtauld coll. London 1954, nr 83; since 1961 on loan to London, National Gallery

F 455 [H 469] STILL LIFE: VASE WITH TWELVE SUNFLOWERS
EXHIBITIONS 1901 Paris, 6; 1905 Paris, 8; 1935-6 New York etc, 31; 1943 New York 2, 28; 1954 New York, 27; 1963 Philadelphia, without cat nr
PROVENANCE Maison [Julien] Tanguy, Paris [in commission from Theo van Gogh]; Count A. de la Rochefoucauld, Paris [R 1901 and 1905]; Paul Rosenberg Art Gallery, Paris; Carroll S. Tyson jr, Chestnut Hill, Pa [R 1935 and 1943]; Philadelphia, The Philadelphia Museum of Art [acquired 1963; Mrs C. S. Tyson bequest], inv nr 63-116-19, check list of paintings 1 January 1965, p 28

F 456 [H 468] STILL LIFE: VASE WITH TWELVE SUNFLOWERS
EXHIBITIONS 1889 Probably Brussels [Vingtistes]; 1947 Munich, 60a; 1949 Hanover, 28; 1951 Paris 1, 43; 1953 The Hague, 129; 1956 Munich, 128
PROVENANCE Hugo von Tschudi, Munich; Munich, Bayerische Staatsgemäldesammlungen [acquired 1912; gift of a collector in memory of H. von Tschudi], inv nr 8672, cat 1955, p 61; cat 1966, p 43

F 457 [H 470] STILL LIFE: SUNFLOWERS
EXHIBITIONS 1901 Paris, 5; 1908 Paris 2, 35; 1910-1 London, 72; 1914 Berlin, 44
PROVENANCE Emile Schuffenecker, Paris [R 1901]; A. Schuffenecker Art Gallery, Paris; E. Druet Art Gallery, Paris [from 1907 until 1910]; Paul von Mendelssohn-Bartholdy, Berlin [acquired 1910; R 1911]; Alfred Chester Beatty, London; London, Miss Edith Beatty [on temporary loan to National Gallery, London, before 1966]

F 458 [H 471] STILL LIFE: VASE WITH FOURTEEN SUNFLOWERS
EXHIBITIONS 1905 Amsterdam, 104; 1912 Cologne, 28; 1915 Amsterdam, 9; 1924 Basle, 40; Zurich, 35; Stuttgart, 16; 1925 Paris 1, 26; The Hague, 28; 1930 Amsterdam, 56; 1935-6 New York etc, 32; 1937 Paris, 38; 1945 Amsterdam, without cat nr; 1946 Stockholm etc, 65; 1946-7 Liège etc, 110; 1947 Geneva, 113; Paris 1, 113; 1947-8 London etc, 47; 1948 Bergen, Oslo, 33; 1949-50 New York, Chicago, 78; 1951 Lyons etc, 41; 1953 The Hague, 130; Otterlo, Amsterdam, 107; 1953-4 Saint Louis etc, 102; 1954 Zurich, 45; 1954-5 Bern, 43; 1955 Antwerp 1, 265; 1955-6 Liverpool etc, 47; 1957 Marseilles, 54; 1958-9 San Francisco etc, 55; 1959 Aix-en-Provence, 24; 1959-60 Utrecht, 41; 1960-1 Montreal etc, 54; 1961-2 Baltimore etc, 52; 1963 Humlebaek, 38; 1964 Washington, New York, 38; 1965 Charleroi, Ghent, 26; Stockholm, 36; 1967 Wolfsburg, 56; 1968-9 London, 133
PROVENANCE Mrs J. van Gogh-Bonger, Amsterdam [R 1905]; V. W. van Gogh, Laren; Amsterdam, Rijksmuseum Vincent van Gogh [Vincent van Gogh Foundation, inv nr F 458]

F 459 [H 472] STILL LIFE: VASE WITH FIVE SUNFLOWERS [destroyed]
EXHIBITIONS 1905 Amsterdam, 105; Utrecht, 34; 1906 Rotterdam, 32; 1921 Tokyo
PROVENANCE Mrs J. van Gogh-Bonger, Amsterdam [R 1905]; Probably Bernheim jeune Art Gallery, Paris; F. Meyer-Fierz, Zurich; Paul Vallotton Art Gallery, Lausanne; Koyata Yamamoto, Yokohama [?] [acquired 1920 in Paris, burnt in war damage 1946]

F 460 [H 703] CORNER OF A GARDEN WITH BUTTERFLIES
EXHIBITION 1960 Paris, 55
PROVENANCE Druet Art Gallery, Paris; Jos Reinach, Paris; Mrs L. Reinach-Goujon, Paris; Paris, Private collection [R 1970]

F 461 [H 488] STILL LIFE: SHOES
EXHIBITIONS 1905 Amsterdam, 136; 1912 Cologne, 17; 1927 Basle, 130; Bern, 130; 1928 Düsseldorf, 175; 1929 Hamburg, 84; Berlin 1, 103; 1935-6 New York etc, 29; 1955 New York 2, 32; 1958 New York, 66; 1960 New York 2, 50
PROVENANCE Mrs J. van Gogh-Bonger, Amsterdam [R 1905]; A. G. Kröller, Harskamp [acquired December 1910]; Mrs G. Kröller-Jesse, Otterlo; Rijksmuseum Kröller-Müller [Loan of Mrs G. Kröller-Jesse, Otterlo], cat van Gogh 1942, p 127; Katz Art Gallery, Dieren; Van Wisselingh Art Gallery, Amsterdam; Siegfried Kramarsky, New York [R 1953; R 1960]: Heirs of Kramarsky, USA; S. Kramarsky Trust Fund [R 1970]

F 462 [H 490] PORTRAIT OF EUGÈNE BOCH, A BELGIAN PAINTER
EXHIBITIONS 1908 Paris 2, 2; 1947 Paris 3, 74; 1947-8 London etc, 53
PROVENANCE Mrs J. van Gogh-Bonger, Amsterdam; Eugène Boch, La Louvière, Belgium [R 1908]; Paris, Musée National du Louvre [acquired 1941; Eugène Boch bequest], inv nr RF 1944-9, cat Impressionistes 1959, nr 147

F 463 [H 491] THE NIGHT-CAFÉ [now Café de l'Alcazar, Place Lamartine]
EXHIBITIONS 1905 Amsterdam, 133; Utrecht, 43; 1906 Rotterdam, 39; 1908 Moscow; 1928 Moscow, 81; 1934 Chicago, 312; 1934-5 New York, 17; 1935-6 New York etc, 34; 1940 Chicago, 32; New York 1, 10; New York 2, 360; 1942 New York, 1; 1943 New York 2, 32; 1948 New York 1, 6; Cleveland, 11; 1949-50 New York, Chicago, 80A; 1955 New York 3, 45; 1958 New York, 65; 1959 New York 2, 51; 1960 New York 2, 47; New Haven, 70
PROVENANCE Mrs J. van Gogh-Bonger, Amsterdam [R 1905]; I. A. Morosov, Moscow [acquired at the exhib of the Golden Fleece, Moscow 1908]; Moscow, Museum of Modern Art [R 1925]; Knoedler Art Gallery, New York; Stephen Clark, New York [R 1935; R 1943]; New Haven, Yale University Art Gallery [acquired 1961; Stephen Carlton Clark bequest], inv nr 1961.18.34

F 464 [H 489] VINCENT'S HOUSE IN ARLES [Place Lamartine]
EXHIBITIONS 1910 Berlin 1, 40; 1912 Cologne, 88; 1914 Berlin, 49; 1915 Amsterdam, 19; 1920 New York, 59; 1923 London, 27 [repr]; 1925 The Hague, 50; Potsdam, 42; 1927 Paris; 1928 Berlin, 47 [repr]; Vienna, 31 [repr]; Frankfort, 31 [repr]; 1929 New York, 80; 1930 Amsterdam, 57; 1932 Manchester, 32; 1935 Amsterdam 2, 15; 1935-6 New York etc, 33; 1939 San Francisco, 175; 1939-40 San Francisco, 123; 1940 New York 3, 4; 1942 Baltimore, Worcester, 12; 1943-4 Indianapolis etc, 7; 1943 New York 2, 31; 1944 Montreal, 126; 1946-7 Liège etc, 113; 1947 Paris 1, 115; Geneva, 115; 1947-8 London etc, 54; 1948 Bergen, Oslo, 34; 1949-50 New York, Chicago, 80; 1951 Lyons etc, 42; 1953 The Hague, 131; Otterlo, Amsterdam, 110; Paris, 131; 1953-4 Saint Louis etc, 103; 1954 Zurich, 43; 1955 Antwerp 1, 253; Palm Beach etc, 24; 1955-6 Liverpool etc, 48; 1957 Marseilles, 50; 1958-9 San Francisco etc, 53; 1959 Aix-en-Provence, 16; 1959-60 Utrecht, 42; 1960-1 Montreal etc, 55; 1961-2 Baltimore etc, 46; 1963 Humlebaek, 34; 1964 Washington, New York, 34; 1965 Charleroi, Ghent, 22; 1965-6 Stockholm, Göteborg, 37; 1967 Wolfsburg, 50; 1968-9 London, 136
PROVENANCE Mrs J. van Gogh-Bonger, Amsterdam; Isaac Israëls, The Hague [loan from Mrs J. van Gogh-Bonger 1917-1920]; V. W. van Gogh, Laren; Amsterdam, Rijksmuseum Vincent van Gogh [Vincent van Gogh Foundation, inv nr F 464]

F 465 [H 492] SUMMER EVENING
EXHIBITIONS 1922 Winterthur 1, 50; 1924 Basle, 59; Zurich, 32; 1938 Paris 1, 128; 1947 Basle, 64; 1950 Paris 2, 52; 1956 Munich, 124
PROVENANCE L. C. Enthoven, Voorburg, Netherlands; Sale Enthoven, Amsterdam [F. Muller] 18 May 1920, nr 239 [and reproduced]; Emil Hahnloser, Zurich; Winterthur, Kunstmuseum [acquired 1922; gift of Emil Hahnloser], inv nr 469, cat 1958, nr 179

F 466 [H 494] THE ROCKS
EXHIBITIONS 1912 Cologne, 44; 1914 Berlin, 92; 1921 Berlin; 1928 Berlin, 48; 1936 London 2, 20; 1962 London 3, 4
PROVENANCE Mrs J. van Gogh-Bonger, Amsterdam; Paul Cassirer Art Gallery, Berlin; Mrs Margarete Mauthner, Berlin [R 1912; R 1914]; Joseph Stransky, New York;

Wildenstein Art Gallery, New York [R 1938]; A. Chester Beatty, London; Miss Edith Beatty, London [loan to National Gallery, London until 1962]; A. Tooth Art Gallery, London [R 1962]; Houston, Texas, John A. Beck [R 1966]

F 467 [H 493] THE CAFÉ TERRACE AT NIGHT [PLACE DU FORUM, ARLES]
EXHIBITIONS 1927 Basle etc, 110; 1928 Düsseldorf, 178; Karlsruhe, 113; 1929 Berlin 1, 115; Hamburg, 66; 1930 Amsterdam, 222; 1935-6 New York etc, 35; 1945 The Hague, 33; 1946-7 Liège etc, 114; 1947 Paris 1, 110; Geneva, 110; Basle, 65; 1947-8 London etc, 51; 1949-50 New York, Chicago, 82; 1952 Milan, 84; 1953 The Hague, 132; Otterlo, Amsterdam, 109; 1953-4 Saint Louis etc, 104; 1956 Eindhoven, 36; Munich, 130; 1957 Essen, 302; 1958 Vienna, 83; Tokyo, Kyoto, 101; 1959 Aix-en-Provence, 14; 1960-1 Montreal etc, 40
PROVENANCE Albert Aurier, Châteauroux [R 1890-92]; Heirs of A. Aurier; Otterlo, Rijksmuseum Kröller-Müller [acquired before 1917 from Heirs of A. Aurier], inv nr 289-00, cat van Gogh 1970, nr 212

F 468 [H 497] SUNSHINE IN THE PARK [THE POET'S GARDEN]
EXHIBITIONS 1904 Rotterdam, 72; 1930 New York 1, 105; 1932 Chicago, 13; 1934 Chicago, 315; 1948 Cleveland, 12
PROVENANCE M. Gieseler, The Hague; Sale coll Gieseler, Amsterdam [Mak van Waay] 27 October 1925, 33 [repr]; H. d'Audretsch Art Gallery, The Hague; Unger and van Mens Art Gallery, Rotterdam; Howard Young Art Gallery, New York; Lewis Coburn, Chicago; Chicago, The Art Institute of Chicago [acquired 1933; Mr and Mrs Lewis L. Coburn Memorial Collection], inv nr 33.433, cat 1961, p 182

F 469 [H 408] SELF PORTRAIT WITH STRAW HAT
EXHIBITIONS 1905 Amsterdam, 167; Utrecht, 45; 1906 Rotterdam, 41; 1914 Berlin, 37; 1920 Venice; 1925 The Hague, 51; 1930 Amsterdam, 58; 1932 Manchester, 39; 1935 Brussels, 103 [?]; 1938 London 1, 26; 1945 Amsterdam, without cat number; 1953 The Hague, 95; Otterlo, Amsterdam, 64; 1953-4 Saint Louis etc, 63; 1954 Zurich, 28; 1955 Palm Beach etc, 13; Antwerp 1, 198; 1955-6 Liverpool etc, 27; 1960 London 4, 8; 1967 Wolfsburg, 36; 1968-9 London, 93
PROVENANCE Mrs J. van Gogh-Bonger, Amsterdam; V. W. van Gogh, Laren; Amsterdam, Rijksmuseum Vincent van Gogh [Vincent van Gogh Foundation, inv nr F 469]

F 470 [H 498] THE CEDAR WALK
EXHIBITIONS 1927 Basle etc, 120; 1928 Düsseldorf, 188; Karlsruhe 123; 1929 Berlin 1, 114; Hamburg, 75; 1930 Amsterdam, 217; 1946-7 Liège etc, 115; 1947 Paris 1, 116; Geneva, 116; Basle, 66; 1947-8 London etc, 50; 1952 Milan, 83; 1956 Munich, 129; 1957 Cologne, 72; 1958 Tokyo, Kyoto, 100; 1959 Aix-en-Provence, 15; 1962 Warsaw, 62; 1963 Tel Aviv, Haifa, 72; 1966 Belgrade, 62
PROVENANCE L. C. Enthoven, Voorburg; Sale coll Enthoven, Amsterdam [F. Muller] 18 May 1920, nr 244 [repr]; Otterlo, Rijksmuseum Kröller-Müller, inv nr 299-20, cat van Gogh 1970, nr 211

F 471 [H 496] THE PARK WITH THE ENTRANCE SEEN THROUGH THE TREES
EXHIBITIONS 1905 Amsterdam, 108; Utrecht, 36; 1906 Rotterdam, 30; 1928 Berlin, 49
PROVENANCE Mrs J. van Gogh-Bonger, Amsterdam [R 1905]; Julius Stern, Berlin; Sale Julius Stern, Berlin [Cassirer] 22 May 1916, 26 [repr]; Berlin, Eduard Arnhold [according to M. Frank the painting was destroyed in the second world war]

F 472 [H 495] THE PUBLIC PARK
EXHIBITIONS 1905 Amsterdam, 126; 1921 Berlin; 1930 Amsterdam, 58bis
PROVENANCE Mrs J. van Gogh-Bonger, Amsterdam [R 1905]; Cassirer Art Gallery, Berlin; Paul von Mendelssohn-Bartholdy, Berlin; Mrs Kesselstadt; Rosenberg & Stiebel Art Gallery, New York [sold 1967]; USA, Unknown private collection

F 473 [H 499] PORTRAIT OF MILLIET
EXHIBITIONS 1908 Paris 1, 51; Amsterdam, 45; 1910 Berlin 1, 52; 1912 Cologne, 56; 1913 The Hague, 129; 1914 Antwerp, 46; 1927 Basle etc, 101; 1928 Düsseldorf, 168; Karlsruhe, 103; 1929 Berlin 1, 108; Hamburg, 58; 1930 Amsterdam, 230; 1935-6 New York etc, 58; 1946-7 Liège etc, 116; 1947 Paris 1, 117; Geneva, 117; Basle, 67; 1947-8 London etc, 52; 1949-50 New York, Chicago, 81; 1952 Milan, 85; 1953 The Hague, 133; Otterlo, Amsterdam, 108; 1953-4 Saint Louis etc, 106; 1956 Eindhoven, 37; 1957 Essen, 304; 1958-9 San Francisco etc, 48; 1962 Warsaw, 66; 1963 Tel Aviv, Haifa, 76; 1966 Belgrade, 67
PROVENANCE Mrs J. van Gogh-Bonger, Amsterdam; Cassirer Art Gallery, Berlin; Otterlo, Rijksmuseum Kröller-Müller, inv nr 280-12, cat van Gogh 1970, nr 221

F 474 [H 500] THE STARRY NIGHT
EXHIBITIONS 1889 Paris, 272; 1892 The Hague, 15; Antwerp, 4; 1894 Nijmegen, 51; 1896 Rotterdam, 49; 1901 Paris, 65; 1905 Amsterdam, 156; 1927 Paris; 1931 Paris, 43; 1934 Paris, 148; 1936 Paris 1, 1058; 1937 Paris, 37; 1960 Paris, 44
PROVENANCE Mrs J. van Gogh-Bonger, Amsterdam; Bas Veth, Bussum [R 1905]; Sale Bas Veth a.o., Amsterdam [F. Muller] 20 June 1922, nr 3 [repr]; Buffa Art Gallery, Amsterdam; F. Moch, Paris [R 1931; R 1937]; Present owner unknown

F 475 [H 501] THE GREEN VINEYARD
EXHIBITIONS 1892 The Hague, 14; 1905 Amsterdam, 120; 1927 Basle etc, 121; 1928 Düsseldorf, 189; Karlsruhe, 124; 1929 Berlin 1, 107; Hamburg, 76; 1930 Amsterdam, 221; 1946-7 Liège etc, 118; 1947 Paris 1, 119; Geneva, 119; Basle, 68; 1947-8 London etc, 55; 1949-50 New York, Chicago, 83; 1952 Milan, 86; 1953-4 Saint Louis etc, 107; 1956 Munich, 131; 1958 Vienna, 84; Tokyo, Kyoto, 103; 1959 Aix-en-Provence, 18; 1960-1 Montreal etc, 41
PROVENANCE Mrs J. van Gogh-Bonger, Amsterdam; L. C. Enthoven, Voorburg; Sale Enthoven, Amsterdam [F. Muller] 18 May 1920, 245 [repr]; Otterlo, Rijksmuseum Kröller-Müller, inv nr 300-20, cat van Gogh 1970, nr 225

F 476 [H 505] PORTRAIT OF THE ARTIST [Dedicated to Paul Gauguin]
EXHIBITIONS 1924 Stuttgart, 40; 1948 New York 2, 66; 1949 New York 1, 1; 1949-50 New York, Chicago, 78A; 1960 Raleigh, p 18; 1962 Houston, cat p 16
PROVENANCE Paul Gauguin, Paris; A. Vollard Art Gallery, Paris; Paul Cassirer Art Gallery, Berlin; Neue Staatsgalerie, Munich [acquired 1919]; Sale Lucerne [Galerie Fischer] 30 June 1939, nr 45; Maurice Wertheim, New York [R 1949-50]; Cambridge, Massachussets, Fogg Art Museum [acquired 1951; bequest of Maurice Wertheim], inv nr 1951.65

F 476a STUDY BY CANDLELIGHT
EXHIBITIONS 1949 Beverly Hills; 1959 San Francisco, 57
PROVENANCE Mr Salles, Arles [R 1893]; Louis Carré Art Gallery, Paris; Associated American Artists Galleries, New York [before 1947]; Los Angeles, California, Mr and Mrs William Goetz [acquired 1948, R 1970]

F 477 [H 502] PORTRAIT OF THE ARTIST'S MOTHER [after a photograph]
EXHIBITIONS 1901 Paris, 20; 1914 Berlin, 73; 1925 Vienna, 74; 1926 Dresden, 212; 1943 New York 2, 33; 1960 Philadelphia
PROVENANCE Jos. Hessel Art Gallery, Paris [R 1901]; A. Vollard Art Gallery, Paris; A. Rosenberg, Paris; Paul Cassirer Art Gallery, Berlin; Carl Moll, Vienna [R 1906; R 1925-6]; Paul Rosenberg Art Gallery, Paris; Theodore Pitcairn, Bryn Athyn, USA [R 1943; R 1963]; Sale London [Christie] 28 June 1968, 112; Stephen Hahn Art Gallery, New York, Fullerton, California, Norton Simon Inc Museum of Art [R 1970]

F 478 [H 509] THE BROTHEL
PROVENANCE Prince of Wagram, Paris; Druet Art Gallery, Paris [R 1910]; Tripier, France; R. Candinelli, Lyons [acquired 1913]; Paul Guillaume Art Gallery, Paris; Merion, Pennsylvania, The Barnes Foundation

F 478a [H 811] THE TARASCON COACHES
EXHIBITIONS 1935 Montevideo, 68 [repr]; 1951 Pittsburg, 114; 1953-4 New York, 7; 1955 New York 3, 47; New York 2, 37; 1959 New York 1; 1961 New York 2, 44; 1965 New York 2, 68; 1966 New York 2, 67
PROVENANCE Maison [Julien] Tanguy Art Gallery, Paris [in commission from Theo van Gogh]; Medardo Rosso, Paris [until 1895]; Milo Beretta, Montevideo [about 1935]; 'La Passe' Art Gallery, Buenos Aires; Collection De Königsberg, Buenos Aires [R 1948]; New York, Mr. and Mrs. Henry Pearlman [acquired 1950]

F 479 [H 504] PARK [The Poet's Garden]
EXHIBITIONS 1908 Paris 2, 10; 1936 London 4, 106; 1940 New York, 15; 1941 New York, 65; 1942 New York, 2; 1943 New York 2, 34; 1948 New York 1,7;1949 New York 3,8
PROVENANCE Prince of Wagram, Paris [R 1907]; Druet Art Gallery, Paris [R 1907]; G. Fayet, Igny [R 1908], Beziers [R 1918 and 1925]; Jacob Goldschmidt, New York; Sale London [Sotheby] 15 October 1958, nr 4; Rosenberg and Stiebel Art Gallery, New York; Present owner unknown [R 1970]

F 480 [H 507] THE RAILWAY BRIDGE [Avenue Montmajour]
EXHIBITIONS 1905 Amsterdam, 132; 1909 Bremen, 88 [repr]; 1910 Berlin 2, not in cat; 1912 Cologne, 90 [repr]; 1914 Berlin, 69; 1926 Dresden, 208; 1927 Berlin 2, 110; 1934 Bern, 62; 1942 New York, 3; 1943 New York 3, 14; 1948 Cleveland, 15;New York 1, 4
PROVENANCE Mrs J. van Gogh-Bonger, Amsterdam [R 1905]; Paul Cassirer Art Gallery, Berlin; Tilla Durieux-Cassirer, Berlin [R 1912; R 1926]; Erich Maria Remarque, New York [R 1942; R 1964]; Zurich, Kunsthaus [on loan since 1958], inv nr 1958/21

F 481 [H 506] THE IRON BRIDGE OF TRINQUETAILLE
EXHIBITIONS 1905 Amsterdam, 146; 1928 Berlin, 50 [reproduced]; 1933-4 Rotterdam, 39; 1935 Brussels, 97; 1942 Baltimore, Worcester, 16; New York, 4; 1943 New York 2, 35; 1944 Montreal, 127; 1948 New York 1, 5; 1955 New York 2, 35; 1958 New York, 69; 1960 New York 2, 53
PROVENANCE Mrs J. van Gogh-Bonger, Amsterdam; Jos Hessel Art Gallery, Paris; A. W. von Heymel, Munich; Paul Cassirer Art Gallery, Berlin; H. von Tschudi, Munich; Neue Staatsgalerie, Munich [loan H. von Tschudi]; Max Silberberg, Breslau; Sale Silberberg a.o., Paris [Petit] 9 June 1932, 21; Paul Cassirer Art Gallery, Berlin; Siegfried Kramarsky, New York [R 1943; on loan to New York, Metropolitan Museum after 1948]; Brooklyn, NY, Mrs S. Binkhorst-Kramarsky

F 482 [H 627] VAN GOGH'S BEDROOM AT ARLES
EXHIBITIONS 1904 Rotterdam, 73; 1905 Amsterdam, 144; 1912 Cologne, 89; 1914 Berlin, 46; 1915 Amsterdam, 12; 1923 Amsterdam 2, 124; London, 25; 1925 The Hague, 49; Potsdam, 41; 1926 Munich, 2091; 1927 Paris; 1929 London 1, 457; 1930 Amsterdam, 59; 1935-6 New York etc, 36; 1945 Amsterdam, without cat nr; 1946 Stockholm etc, 71; 1946-7 Liège etc, 151; 1947 Paris 1, 152; London etc, 71; Geneva, 152; 1948 Bergen, Oslo, 44; 1949-50 NewYork, Chicago, 117; 1951 Lyons etc, 52; 1953 The Hague, 156; Otterlo, Amsterdam, 143; 1953-4 Saint Louis etc, 135; 1954 Zurich, 53; 1955 Palm Beach etc, 23; Antwerp 1, 308; 1955-6 Liverpool etc, 67; 1957 Marseilles, 69; 1958-9 San Francisco etc, 59; 1959 Aix-en-Provence, 44; 1959-60 Utrecht, 50; 1960-1 Montreal etc, 69; 1961-2 Baltimore etc, 62; 1963 Sheffield, 12; Humlebaek, 47; 1964 Washington, New York, 47; 1965 Stockholm, 38; Charleroi, Ghent, 33; 1967 Wolfsburg, 66; 1968-9 London, 164
PROVENANCE Mrs J. van Gogh-Bonger, Amsterdam; V. W. van Gogh, Laren; Amsterdam, Rijksmuseum Vincent van Gogh [Vincent van Gogh Foundation, inv nr F 482]

F 483 [H 628] VAN GOGH'S BEDROOM IN ARLES
EXHIBITIONS 1901 Paris, 19; 1913 Barmen; 1923 Prague, 190
PROVENANCE J. Hessel Art Gallery, Paris [R 1901]; Werner Dücker, Düsseldorf; P. Rosenberg Art Gallery, Paris; Prince Matsugata, Kobe, Japan [R 1923]; Paris, Musée National du Louvre [acquired 1952], inv nr RF 1959-2, cat Impressionistes 1959, nr 153

F 484 [H 510] VINCENT'S BEDROOM
EXHIBITIONS 1914 Berlin, 53; 1929 New York, 79; 1933 Chicago, 376; 1934 Chicago, 310; Toledo, 24
PROVENANCE Miss W. van Gogh, Leiden; P. Rosenberg Art Gallery, Paris; Bernheim Art Gallery, Paris; Carl Reininghaus, Vienna [R 1914]; H. Birch Bartlett, New York; Chicago, The Art Institute [acquired 1926; Helen B. Bartlett Coll], inv nr 26.417, cat 1961, p 198

F 485 [H 503] THE LOVERS [Fourth painting of the Poet's Garden]
EXHIBITIONS 1912 Cologne, 87; 1914 Berlin, 84; 1922 Winterthur 1, 55; 1924 Basle, 58; Zurich, 36
PROVENANCE J. Meier Graefe, Berlin [R 1893]; Paul Cassirer Art Gallery, Berlin [R 1905]; Prince of Wagram, Paris; Bernheim jeune Art Gallery, Paris; Carl and Thea Sternheim, Uttwil [acquired 1912]; Sale Sternheim, Amsterdam [F. Muller] 11 February 1919, nr 9 [repr]; Karl Sternheim, Reichenberg [Bezirk Dresden] [R 1924]; Berlin, National Galerie [confiscated in 1937]; Present owner unknown

F 486 [H 513] LES ALYSCAMPS
EXHIBITIONS 1901 Paris, 24; 1908 Paris 2; 1912 Cologne, 37; 1913 The Hague, 140; 1927 Basle etc, 98; 1928 Düsseldorf, 163; Karlsruhe, 98; 1929 Berlin 1, 119; Hamburg, 55; 1930 Amsterdam, 215; 1935-6 New York etc, 37; 1946-7 Liège etc, 119; 1947 Paris 1, 120; Geneva, 120; Basle, 71; 1947-8 London etc, 57; 1949-50 New York, Chicago, 86; 1952 Milan, 87; 1953 The Hague, 135; Otterlo, Amsterdam, 113; 1953-4 Saint Louis etc, 108; 1954 Arles, 41; 1956 Eindhoven, 39; Munich, 132; 1957 Essen, 306; 1958 Vienna, 85; Tokyo,Kyoto, 109; 1959 Aix-en-Provence, 21; 1962 Warsaw, 67; 1963 Tel Aviv, Haifa, 77; 1966 Belgrade, 69
PROVENANCE Maurice Fabre, Paris [R 1901]; Denys Cochin, Paris [before 1911]; Druet Art Gallery, Paris [R 1911]; Amédée Schuffenecker, Meudon [R 1912]; Otterlo, Rijksmuseum Kröller-Müller, inv nr 277-12, cat van Gogh 1970, nr 224

F 487 [H 514] LES ALYSCAMPS
EXHIBITIONS 1905 Amsterdam, 153a; 1928 Berlin, 51; Frankfort, 32; 1957-8 New York etc, 26; 1958 London 2, 27; 1959 Washington, 53; 1960 Paris, 45
PROVENANCE Mrs J. van Gogh-Bonger, Amsterdam; R. N. Roland Holst, Laren [R 1905]; Jos Hessel Art Gallery, Paris; Adolf Bensinger, Mannheim; Arthur Stoll, Arlesheim; Athens, Stavros S. Niarchos, exhib cat 1957, nr 26

F 488 [H 515] L'ARLESIENNE [Madame Ginoux] WITH BOOKS
EXHIBITIONS 1892 Paris, 13; 1901 Paris, 50; 1908 Paris 2, 29; 1912 Berlin, 81 [repr]; 1914 Berlin, 80 [repr]; 1924 Basle, 43 [repr]; Zurich, 41; 1925 Berlin, 22; 1927

New York, 24 [repr]; 1929 New York, 73; Cambridge, 92; 1931 New York, 2; 1932 New York; 1934-5 New York, 16; 1935-6 New York etc, 39; 1936 Cleveland, 318; 1938 New York 2, 47; 1939 New York, 62; 1940 New York 1, 11; New York 2, 358; 1943 New York 2, 36; 1949-50 New York, Chicago, 87; 1951 New York, 37; 1955 Paris 2, 33
PROVENANCE E. Schuffenecker, Paris [R 1901 and 1908]; Paul Cassirer Art Gallery, Berlin; Bernt Grönvoldt, Berlin [R 1912 and 1914]; Private collection, Basle [R 1924]; Fritz Schön, Grunewald/Berlin [until 1926]; S. Bourgeois Art Gallery, New York [R 1926]; Wildenstein Art Gallery, New York; Adolf Lewisohn, New York [until 1938]; Samuel A. Lewisohn, New York [acquired 1938]; New York, The Metropolitan Musem [acquired 1951; Samuel A. Lewisohn bequest], inv nr 51.112.3, cat European Paintings 1954, p 43

F 489 [H XI] L'ARLESIENNE [Madame Ginoux] WITH GLOVES AND UMBRELLA
EXHIBITIONS 1910 Berlin 1, 31; 1912 Cologne, 82 [repr]; 1914 Berlin, 82; 1921 Berlin; 1936 Paris 2, 28; London 4, 105; 1937 Paris, 35; 1942 New York, 5; 1947 Paris 2, 152; 1963 Schaffhausen, 54; 1967-8 Paris, 440
PROVENANCE Mrs J. van Gogh-Bonger, Amsterdam, sold 1907 to Bernheim [according to information from Ir. V. W. van Gogh]; J. K. Thannhauser Art Gallery, Munich [about 1909. according to information from J. K. Thannhauser: bought directly from Mrs J. van Gogh-Bonger]; Carl and Thea Sternheim, La Hulpe/Brussels; Mrs Friedländer-Fuld, Berlin [acquired 1915]; Mrs von Goldschmidt-de Rothschild, Berlin-New York [about July 1941 on loan to the Metropolitan Museum, New York]; Paris, Musée National du Louvre [gift of Mrs R. von Goldschmidt-de Rothschild, held in usufruct], inv nr RF 1952.6

F 490 [H 520] MOTHER ROULIN WITH HER BABY
EXHIBITIONS 1905 Paris, 38; 1908 Paris 2, 28; 1909 Vienna 3 [reproduced]; 1924 Basle, 36; Zurich, 42; 1927 Berlin 2; 1940 Detroit, 49; 1941 Worcester, 16; 1943 New York 2, 37; 1948 New York 1, 8
PROVENANCE E. Bernard, Paris; A. Vollard Art Gallery, Paris; A. Schuffenecker, Clamart [R 1908]; F. Meyer-Fierz, Zurich [R 1924]; Sale Meyer, Amsterdam [F. Muller] 13 July 1926, x [repr]; Thannhauser Art Gallery, Munich; Reid and Lefevre Art Gallery, London; Knoedler Art Gallery, New York [R 1943]; William M. Elkins, Philadelphia; Philadelphia, The Philadelphia Museum of Art [acquired 1950; bequest Lisa Norris Elkins], inv nr 50-92-22, [cat] check list of paintings 1 January 1965, p 28

F 491 [H 519] MOTHER ROULIN [IN PROFILE] WITH HER BABY
EXHIBITIONS 1949-50 New York, Chicago, 87a; 1951 Houston, 7; 1955 New York 2, 39; 1957 Paris, 81; 1959 Cincinnati, 189
PROVENANCE E. Blot Art Gallery, Paris; Paul von Mendelssohn-Barthold y, Berlin; W. Feilchenfeldt Art Gallery Zurich; New York, The collection of Robert Lehman [1956 on loan to the Metropolitan Museum, New York]; New York, Estate of Robert Lehman [bequeathed to New York, Metropolitan Museum 1969]

F 492 [H XIII] PORTRAIT OF ARMAND ROULIN
EXHIBITIONS 1937 Paris, 39; 1951 Paris 1, 42; 1956 Munich, 133; 1957 Essen, 305; 1960 Paris, 48; 1963 Hamburg, without cat nr
PROVENANCE Joseph Roulin, Marseilles; A. Vollard Art Gallery, Paris [about 1895]; Karl Osthaus, Hagen; Hagen, Museum Folkwang [acquired about 1904]; Essen, Museum Folkwang, inv nr G 63, cat 1961, nr 61
EDITORS' COMMENT See F 441a in cat

F 493 [H 518] PORTRAIT OF ARMAND ROULIN: FACING LEFT
EXHIBITIONS 1905 Amsterdam, 137; 1939-40 Rotterdam, 22; 1946-7 Liège etc, 120; 1947 Paris 1, 121; Geneva, 121; Basle, 72; 1947-8 London etc, 58; 1949-50 New York, Chicago, 88; 1955 Rotterdam, 190
PROVENANCE Mrs J. van Gogh-Bonger, Amsterdam; Paul Cassirer Art Gallery, Berlin; Bernheim jeune Art Gallery, Paris; M. Goldschmidt Art Gallery, Frankfort; Cologne, Wallraf-Richartz Museum [R 1910-1938], cat 1927, nr 1198; D. G. van Beuningen, Vierhouten [R 1938-1958], cat coll. Van Beuningen 1949, nr 142; Rotterdam, Museum Boymans-Van Beuningen, inv nr 2608, cat 1963, p 51

F 494 [H 511] THE SOWER
EXHIBITIONS 1938 Paris 1, 129; 1953 Bern, 41; 1955 Winterthur 1, 98
PROVENANCE L. C. Enthoven, Voorburg; Sale Enthoven, Amsterdam [F. Muller] 18 May 1920, 246 [repr]; E. Hahnloser, Zurich; H. R. Hahnloser, Bern [R 1955]; Winterthur, Mrs L. Jäggli-Hahnloser [R 1963; R 1969]

F 495 [H 512] THE RED VINEYARD: MONTMAJOUR
EXHIBITIONS 1890 Brussels, 6; 1904 Brussels; 1909 Paris
PROVENANCE Miss Anna Boch, Brussels; Prince of Wagram, Paris; Druet Art Gallery, Paris; I. A. Morosov, Moscow [acquired 1909]; Moscow, Museum of Modern Western Art [until 1948]; Moscow, Museum Pushkin [acquired 1948], inv nr 3372, cat 1961, p 53

F 496 [H 516] MEMORY OF THE GARDEN AT ETTEN [partly inspired by Gauguin]
EXHIBITIONS 1908 Paris 2, 30; 1926 Moscow; 1956 Moscow, Leningrad, p 11; 1960 Paris, 49
PROVENANCE Amédée Schuffenecker, Clamart [R 1908]; S. I. Stschukin, Moscow, cat 1913, nr 35; Moscow, Museum of Modern Western Art [acquired 1918], cat 1928, nr 79; Leningrad, Hermitage [acquired 1948], inv nr 9116, cat 1958, p 291, cat 1967, nrs 65-66

F 497 [H 517] THE NOVELREADER
EXHIBITIONS 1951 Houston, 6; 1955 New York 2, 38; 1956 London, 47; 1957 Paris 1, 103; 1963 London 3, 39
PROVENANCE C. Hoogendijk, The Hague; Sale Hoogendijk, Amsterdam [F. Muller] 21 May 1912, 22; P. Rosenberg Art Gallery, Paris; Chr. Tetzen-Lund, Copenhagen; Sale Chr. Tetzen-Lund, Copenhagen [Munch-Petersen] 18-19 May 1925, 78 [reproduced]; Sale Chr. Tetzen-Lund, Copenhagen [Winkel & Magnussen] 28 May 1934, 5; Sale Chr. Tetzen-Lund, Copenhagen [Winkel & Magnussen] 10 June 1936, 3; Winkel & Magnussen, Copenhagen; Mrs Karen Krogh, Denmark [R 1936-1947]; John Hay Whitney, New York [R 1947-1951]; Houston, Museum of Arts, gift of Mr and Mrs John Hay Whitney, 1951; Marlborough Fine Art Ltd., London; Gstaad, Switzerland, Mr and Mrs Louis Franck [R 1963; R 1969]

F 498 [H 521] VINCENTS'S CHAIR WITH HIS PIPE
EXHIBITIONS 1905 Amsterdam, 135; 1910 Berlin 1, 24; 1920 New York, 40 [reproduced]; 1921 New York, 121; 1923 London, 28; 1932 Manchester, 22; 1947-8 London etc, 60; 1948 London 1, 31; 1955 Paris 3, 64; 1968-9 London, 142
PROVENANCE Mrs J. van Gogh-Bonger, Amsterdam [R 1905; R 1921]; The Leicester Galleries, London; London, Tate Gallery [Courtauld Fund 1924], cat The Courtauld collection 1954, nr 84

F 499 [H 522] GAUGUIN'S ARMCHAIR, CANDLE AND BOOKS [HIS EMPTY CHAIR]
EXHIBITIONS 1914 Berlin, 47; 1928 Berlin, 52 [repr]; Frankfort, 33 [repr]; Vienna, 32; 1932 Manchester, 35; 1945 Amsterdam, without cat nr; 1946 Stockholm etc, 72; 1946-7 Liège etc, 121; 1947 Geneva, 122; Paris 1, 122; 1947-8 London etc, 61; 1948 Bergen, Oslo, 37; 1949-50 New York, Chicago, 89; 1951 Lyons etc, 49; 1953 The Hague, 136; Otterlo, Amsterdam, 114; 1954 Zurich, 52; 1954-5 Bern, 46; 1955 New York 2, 41; Antwerp 1, 266; 1955-6 Liverpool etc, 54; 1957 Marseilles, 55; 1958-9 San Francisco etc, 57; 1959 Aix-en-Provence, 22; 1959-60 Utrecht, 45; 1960-1 Montreal etc, 56; 1961-2 Baltimore etc, 53; 1963 Humlebaek, 40; 1964 Washington, New York, 40; 1965-6 Stockholm, Göteborg, 40; 1965 Charleroi, Ghent, 27; 1967 Wolfsburg, 57; 1968-9 London, 141
PROVENANCE Mrs J. van Gogh-Bonger, Amsterdam; V. W. van Gogh, Laren; Amsterdam, Rijksmuseum Vincent van Gogh [Vincent van Gogh Foundation, inv nr F 499]

F 500 [H 526] PORTRAIT OF DOCTOR FÉLIX REY
EXHIBITIONS 1956 Moscow, Leningrad; 1960 Paris, 49a; 1965 Bordeaux, 64 [with bibliography]; 1965-6 Paris, 61
PROVENANCE Félix Rey, Arles; Charles Camoin, Paris [R 1900]; A. Vollard Art Gallery, Paris; Paul Cassirer Art Gallery, Berlin; E. Druet Art Gallery, Paris [R 1908]; S. I. Stschukin, Moscow [R 1909-1918]; Moscow, Museum of Modern Western Art [R 1918-1948]; Moscow, Pushkin Museum [acquired 1948], inv nr 3272, cat 1961, p 53

F 501 [H 523] SELF PORTRAIT
EXHIBITIONS 1927 Paris; 1929 New York, 72a; 1959 Cincinnati, 190
PROVENANCE Ch. Laval, Pont-Aven; Bernheim jeune Art Gallery, Paris [R 1916; R 1929]; Gaston Bernheim de Villiers, Paris; New York, The collection of Robert Lehman [1957 on loan to the Metropolitan Museum of Art, New York]; New York, Estate of Robert Lehman [bequeathed to Metropolitan Museum, New York 1969]

F 502 [H 525] STILL LIFE WITH ORANGES, LEMONS AND BLUE GLOVES
EXHIBITIONS 1929 London 1, 464; 1930 Amsterdam, 60; 1932 Manchester, 27; 1945 Amstterdam, without cat nr; 1947 Basle, 76; 1947-8 London etc, 65; 1948 Amsterdam, 15; 1951 Houston, 8; 1955 London, 79; 1966 Washington, 134
PROVENANCE C. Hoogendijk, The Hague; Amsterdam, Rijksmuseum [loan C. Hoogendijk since 1907], cat 1911, nr 984d; not in cat 1918; Mrs van Blaaderen-Hoogendijk, Amsterdam [R 1929; R 1930]; T. van Blaaderen; Mrs H. F. Warren-van Geuns, Loenen aan de Vecht; Marlborough Fine Art Ltd., London; Alexander Korda, London; Sale Korda, London [Sotheby] 14 June 1962, 22; Charles Willis; Upperville, Virginia, Mr and Mrs Paul Mellon [R 1966]

F 503 [H 524] MADAME AUGUSTINE ROULIN
EXHIBITIONS 1901 Paris, 55; 1947 Basle, 73; 1955 Winterthur 2, 72
PROVENANCE A. Vollard Art Gallery, Paris; Th. Duret, Paris [R 1901]; Winterthur, Oskar Reinhart

F 504 [H 528] LA BERCEUSE MADAME AUGUSTINE ROULIN
EXHIBITIONS 1910-11 London, 76 [?]; 1912 Cologne, 58 [repr]; 1913 The Hague, 142; 1914 Antwerp, 35; 1927 Basle etc, 114; 1928 Düsseldorf, 182 [repr]; Karlsruhe, 117 [repr]; 1929 Berlin 1, 118; Hamburg, 70; 1930 Amsterdam, 220; 1935 Brussels, 99; 1935-6 New York etc, 40; 1945 The Hague, 34; 1946-7 Liège etc, 122; 1947 Paris 1, 125; Geneva, 125; Basle, 78; 1947-8 London etc, 67; 1949-50 New York, Chicago, 112; 1956 Eindhoven, 40; Munich, 134; 1957 Essen, 308; 1958 Vienna, 86; Tokyo, Kyoto, 106; 1960-1 Montreal etc, 45
PROVENANCE Bernheim jeune Art Gallery, Paris [R 1912]; Otterlo, Rijksmuseum Kröller-Müller, inv nr 293-12, cat van Gogh 1970, nr 222

F 505 [H XIV] LA BERCEUSE MADAME AUGUSTINE ROULIN
EXHIBITIONS 1905 Paris, 39; 1924 Basle, 38; 1934 Bern, 61; 1937 Paris, 36; 1945 Basle, 13; 1964 Paris 1, 32; 1969 London
PROVENANCE Joseph Roulin, Marseilles; A. Vollard Art Gallery, Paris [R about 1895]; A. Schuffenecker, Saint-Maur [R 1905]; Léon Marseille Art Gallery, Paris; Tanner Art Gallery, Zurich; R. Staechelin, Basle [R 1924; R 1937]; Basle, Öffentliche Kunstsammlung, Depositum 'Sammlung Rudolf Staechelin' 1947, cat 1961, p 12; Wildenstein Art Gallery, New York; London, Walter H. Annenberg [R 1970]
EDITORS' COMMENT See F 441a in cat

F 506 [H 530] LA BERCEUSE MADAME AUGUSTINE ROULIN
EXHIBITIONS 1933 Chicago, 377; 1934 Chicago, 311; 1955 New York 2, 45
PROVENANCE Paul Gauguin, Paris; Mr Pellerin, Paris; E. Blot Art Gallery, Paris; Amédée Schuffenecker, Saint-Maur; Marcel Bernheim Art Gallery, Paris; H. Birch Bartlett, New York; Chicago, The Art Institute of Chicago [acquired 1926; Helen Birch Bartlett Memorial collection], inv nr 26.200, cat 1961, p 198

F 507 [H 527] LA BERCEUSE MADAME AUGUSTINE ROULIN
EXHIBITIONS 1905 Amsterdam, 149; 1912 Cologne, 59; 1915 Amsterdam, 11; 1923 London, 24: 1924 Basle, 39; Zurich, 45; Stuttgart, 20; 1925 The Hague, 44; Paris 1, 28; 1926 Munich, 2080; 1927 Paris; 1930 Amsterdam, 61; 1932 Manchester, 26; 1945 Amsterdam, without cat nr; 1946 Stockholm etc, 73; 1947 Basle, 77; 1948 Bergen, Oslo, 39; 1949-50 New York, Chicago, 94; 1951 Lyons etc, 44; 1953 The Hague, 138; Otterlo, Amsterdam, 116; 1955 Antwerp 1, 262; 1955-6 Liverpool etc, 55; 1957 Marseilles, 53; 1958-9 San Francisco etc, 51; 1959-60 Utrecht, 44; 1961 Wolfsburg, 74; 1961-2 Balti more etc, 51; 1963 Humlebaek, 37; 1964 Washington, New York, 37; 1965 Charleroi, Ghent, 25; 1965-6 Stockholm, Göteborg, 41; 1967 Wolfsburg, 55; 1968-9 London, 144
PROVENANCE Mrs J. van Gogh-Bonger, Amsterdam; V. W. van Gogh, Laren; Amsterdam, Stedelijk Museum [gift V. W. van Gogh 1945], inv nr A 965

F 508 [H 529] LA BERCEUSE MADAME AUGUSTINE ROULIN
EXHIBITIONS 1905 Paris, 7; 1929 Cambridge, 89; 1931 Boston; 1935-6 New York etc, 40a [not mentioned in cat, only exhib in Boston February-March 1936]; 1939 Boston, 54; 1947 Basle, 78; 1949 Cambridge; 1950 Springfield; 1951 Houston, 9; 1955 New York, 44; 1957 Los Angeles, 12
PROVENANCE Maison [Julien] Tanguy [in commission from Theo van Gogh], Paris; Count A. de la Rochefoucauld, Paris [R 1905]; Paul Rosenberg Art Gallery, Paris; J. T. Spaulding, Boston [Massachusets] [R 1929 and 1939]; Boston, Museum of Fine Arts [acquired 1948; bequest J. T. Spaulding], inv nr 48.548, cat 1955, p 29

F 509 LA BERCEUSE
Left out by Faille in his manuscript for the present edition; See REJECTED WORKS

F 510 [H 532] BLOATERS ON A PIECE OF YELLOW PAPER
EXHIBITIONS 1905 Paris, 43; 1960 Paris, 52
PROVENANCE Paul Signac, Paris [who received it from Vincent himself on a visit to Arles in March 1889]; Paris, Mrs G. Signac [R 1960]

F 511 [H 709] ORCHARD IN BLOSSOM
EXHIBITIONS 1914 Berlin, 74; 1924 Basle, 30; Zurich, 27; Stuttgart, 12; 1925 The Hague, 32; 1926 Munich, 2073; 1927 Paris; 1929 London 1, 455; 1930 Amsterdam, 62; 1945 Amsterdam, without cat nr; 1946-7 Liège etc, 148; 1947 Paris 1, 147; Geneva, 147; 1951 Lyons etc, 51; 1954-5 Bern, 58; 1955 Antwerp 1, 298; 1958-9 San Francisco etc, 60; 1959-60 Utrecht, 51; 1964 Washington, New York, 28; 1968-9 London, 145
PROVENANCE Mrs J. van Gogh-Bonger, Amsterdam; V. W. van Gogh, Laren; Amsterdam, Rijksmuseum Vincent van Gogh [Vincent van Gogh Foundation, inv nr F 411]

F 512 ORCHARD IN BLOSSOM
Left out by Faille in his manuscript for the present edition; See REJECTED WORKS

F 513 [H 535] ORCHARD SURROUNDED BY CYPRESSES
EXHIBITIONS 1927 Basle etc, 119; 1928 Düsseldorf, 187 [repr]; Karlsruhe, 122 [repr]; 1929 Berlin 1, 116; Hamburg, 74; 1930 Amsterdam, 224; 1947 Basle, 55; 1956 Eindhoven, 34; 1957 Essen, 271; 1959 Aix-en-Provence, 7; 1962 Warsaw 60; 1963 Tel Aviv, Haifa, 70; 1966 Belgrade, 61
PROVENANCE L. Nardus, Suresnes near Paris; M. H. Souget, Bussum; Sale Amsterdam [F. Muller] 19 June 1917, 36 [repr]; Otterlo, Rijksmuseum Kröller-Müller, inv nr 298-17, cat van Gogh 1970, 207

F 514 [H 531] THE PLAIN OF LA CRAU WITH ORCHARD OF PEACH TREES
EXHIBITIONS 1929 London 1, 454; 1948 London 1, 33; 1955 Paris 3, 66
PROVENANCE Bernheim jeune Art Galley, Paris; Percy Moore Turner, London; S. Courtauld, London [R 1927; R 1929]; London, Courtauld Institute Galleries [acquired 1932; The Home House Trustees], cat 1962, nr 33

F 515 [H 533] THE ORCHARD WITH VIEW OF ARLES
EXHIBITIONS 1905 Amsterdam, 138; 1912 Cologne, 39; 1945 Amsterdam, without cat nr; 1946 Stockholm etc, 74; 1955 Antwerp 1, 256; Palm Beach etc, 15; 1958-9 San Francisco etc, 56; 1959-60 Utrecht, 36; 1961-2 Baltimore etc, 48
PROVENANCE Mrs J. van Gogh-Bonger, Amsterdam; V. W. van Gogh, Laren; Amsterdam, Rijksmuseum Vincent van Gogh [Vincent van Gogh Foundation, inv nr F 515]

F 516 [H 534] A VIEW OF ARLES
EXHIBITIONS 1890 Brussels, 4; 1903 Munich, 232; 1924 Stuttgart, 42; 1926 Paris, 2950; 1927 Hamburg 1, 242; 1947 Winterthur, 131; Munich, 60b; 1951 Paris 1, 46; 1956 Munich, 137; 1957 Essen, 274
PROVENANCE Maison [Julien] Tanguy, Paris [since 1889 loan from Theo van Gogh; since 1891 loan from Mrs J. van Gogh-Bonger]; Munich, Bayerische Staatsgemäldesammlungen [acquired 1912; gift of Miss Amy Roth, Zurich in memory of H. von Tschudi], inv nr 8671, cat 1966, p 43

F 517 [H 537] RED CHESTNUTS IN THE PUBLIC GARDEN AT ARLES
EXHIBITIONS 1896 Rotterdam, 37; 1902-3 Vienna; 1905 Amsterdam, 156A; 1930 Amsterdam, 63
PROVENANCE Bas Veth, Bussum [R 1905]; Sale Bas Veth a.o., Amsterdam [F. Muller] 20 June 1922, 1 [repr]; A. R. van Linge, Maarssen; USA, Private collection

F 518 [H 539] PORTRAIT OF A YOUNG GIRL, PINK BACKGROUND
EXHIBITIONS 1908 Amsterdam, 60; 1912 Cologne, 55; 1913 The Hague, 103; 1914 Antwerp, 28; 1927 Basle etc, 117; 1928 Düsseldorf, 185; Karlsruhe, 120; 1929 Berlin 1, 121; Hamburg, 73; 1930 Amsterdam, 208; 1946-7 Liège etc, 101; 1947 Paris 1, 100; Geneva, 100; Basle, 63; 1947-8 London etc, 49; 1952 Milan, 82; 1955-6 Liverpool etc, 46; 1958 Vienna, 82; Tokyo, Kyoto, 108; 1959 São Paulo, 8; 1960-1 Montreal etc, 42; 1966 Belgrade, 64
PROVENANCE Mrs J. van Gogh-Bonger, Amsterdam; V. W. van Gogh, Laren; Otterlo, Rijksmuseum Kröller-Müller, inv nr 296-10, cat van Gogh 1970, nr 220

F 519 [H 536] THE COURTYARD OF THE HOSPITAL AT ARLES
EXHIBITIONS 1908 Berlin, 64 [repr]; 1909 Vienna, 4 [repr]; 1914 Berlin, 89 [repr]; 1924 Basle, 53; Zurich, 47; 1955 Winterthur 2, 73
PROVENANCE A. Vollard Art Gallery, Paris; Barbazanges Art Gallery, Paris; Jos Hessel Art Gallery, Paris; Paul Cassirer Art Gallery, Berlin [before 1906]; Carl Moll, Vienna; O. Miethke Art Gallery, Vienna; Th. Behrens, Hamburg [R 1914]; Winterthur, Oskar Reinhart [R 1924; 1955]

F 520 [H 538] THE OLD WILLOWS
EXHIBITIONS 1905 Amsterdam, 168; 1914 Berlin, 141; 1930 London 2, 17; 1936 London 1, 46; 1938 London 2, 40; New York 1, 2; 1956-7 Los Angeles, San Francisco, 26; 1957-8 New York etc, 27; 1958 London 2, 28; 1960 Paris, 53
PROVENANCE Mrs J. van Gogh-Bonger, Amsterdam; Paul Cassirer Art Gallery, Berlin; Bernheim jeune Art Gallery, Paris; Curt Glaser, Berlin; Paul Cassirer Art Gallery, Berlin; Mrs Eva Cassirer, Berlin; Hodebert-Barbazanges Art Gallery, Paris; S. W. Sykes, London [R 1930]; Reid and Lefevre Art Gallery, London [R 1938]; Etienne Bignou Art Gallery, New York; Edward G. Robinson, Beverley Hills, Cal. [R 1939; 1957]; Athens, Stavros S. Niarchos [exhib cat 1957, nr 27]

F 521 SELF PORTRAIT
Left out by Faille in his manuscript for the present edition; See REJECTED WORKS

F 522 [H 425] SELF PORTRAIT BEFORE HIS EASEL
EXHIBITIONS 1905 Amsterdam, 89; Utrecht, 27; 1907 Rotterdam, 11; 1914 Berlin, 39; Antwerp; 1921 Paris, 163; 1926 Venice, 23; 1930 Amsterdam, 64; 1935-6 New York etc, 38; 1937 Paris, 5; 1945 Amsterdam, without cat nr; 1946 Stockholm etc, 41; 1946-7 Liège etc, 75; 1947 Geneva, 77; Paris 1, 77; 1947-8 London etc, 31; 1948 Bergen, Oslo, 22; 1949-50 New York, Chicago, 61; 1951 Lyons etc, 26; 1953 The Hague, 96; Otterlo, Amsterdam, 65; 1953-4 Saint Louis etc, 64; 1954 Zurich, 27; 1954-5 Bern, 37; 1955 New York 2, 25; Antwerp 1, 208; 1955-6 Liverpool etc, 33; 1957 Marseilles, 36; 1958-9 San Francisco etc, 29; 1959-60 Utrecht, 27; 1960-1 Montreal etc, 35; 1961-2 Baltimore etc, 31; 1963 Humlebaek, 22; 1964 Washington, New York, 22; 1965 Charleroi, Ghent, 12; Stockholm, 27; 1967 Wolfsburg, 38; 1968-9 London, 99
PROVENANCE Mrs J. van Gogh-Bonger, Amsterdam [Amsterdam, Rijksmuseum on loan, since 1909, cat 1911 and 1920, nr 984g]; V. W. van Gogh, Laren; Amsterdam, Rijksmuseum Vincent van Gogh [Vincent van Gogh Foundation, inv nr F 522]

F 523 SELF PORTRAIT BEFORE HIS EASEL
Left out by Faille in his manuscript for the present edition; See REJECTED WORKS

F 524 [H 423] SELF PORTRAIT WITH PIPE AND STRAW HAT
EXHIBITIONS 1926 Munich, 2085; 1927 Paris; 1930 Amsterdam, 65; 1945 Amsterdam, without cat nr; 1951 Lyons etc, 62; 1953 The Hague, 97; Otterlo, Amsterdam, 66; 1954 Zurich, 29; 1954-5 Bern, 36; 1955 Antwerp 1, 326; 1960 London 4, 17
PROVENANCE Mrs J. van Gogh-Bonger, Amsterdam; V. W. van Gogh, Laren; Amsterdam, Rijksmuseum Vincent van Gogh [Vincent van Gogh Foundation, inv nr F 524]

F 525 [H 545] SELF PORTRAIT WITHOUT BEARD
EXHIBITIONS 1906 Rotterdam, 46; 1950 Zurich, p 28; 1955 Winterthur 1, 99; 1959 Paris, 67; 1963 Hamburg, 78
PROVENANCE Mrs J. van Gogh-Bonger, Amsterdam [R 1905-6]; Paul Cassirer Art Gallery, Berlin; Oskar Reichel, Vienna; Thannhauser Art Gallery, Paris; W. Feilchenfeldt, Zurich; Herman Lütjens, Zurich, Küsnacht; Bolligen, Switzerland, J. Körfer [R 1963]

F 526 [H 424] SELF PORTRAIT WITH STRAW HAT
EXHIBITIONS 1929 New York, 72; 1934 Chicago, 314; 1940 Detroit, 48; 1948 Cleveland, 16; 1954 Detroit, 122
PROVENANCE Emile Bernard, Paris; Bernard Goudchaux, Paris; Dikran Khan Kelekian, Paris; Sale Kelekian, New York [American Art Association] 30-31 January 1922, nr 100 [repr]; Detroit, The Detroit Institute of Arts [acquired 1922; City appropriation], acc nr 22.13, cat 1944, nr 87

F 527 [H 547] SELF PORTRAIT WITH BANDAGED EAR
EXHIBITIONS 1901 Paris, 2; 1905 Paris, 6; 1929 London 1, 453; 1930 Amsterdam, 66; 1942 Baltimore, Worcester, 4; 1947-8 London etc, 64; 1948 London 1, 32; 1955 Paris, 65
PROVENANCE Maison [Julien] Tanguy Art Gallery, Paris [in commission from Theo van Gogh]; Count A. de la Rochefoucauld, Paris [1901; 1905]; Paul Rosenberg Art Gallery, Paris; S. Courtauld, London [1928; 1930]; London, The Courtauld Institute, cat The Courtauld collection, London 1954, nr 85

F 527a [formerly F 527bis] SELF PORTRAIT WITH BANDAGED EAR
Left out by Faille in his manuscript for the present edition; See REJECTED WORKS

F 528 [H 546] SELF PORTRAIT
EXHIBITIONS 1960 Paris, 51; 1965 Delft, 54
PROVENANCE A. Vollard Art Gallery, Paris; Pellerin, Paris; E. Blot Art Gallery, Paris; Oslo, Nasjonal Galleriet, inv nr 943

F 529 [H XII] SELF PORTRAIT WITH BANDAGED EAR AND PIPE
EXHIBITIONS 1901 Paris, 3; Berlin, 64 [repr]; 1905 Paris, 15; 1908 Paris 2, 13; 1925 Paris 3, 81 [reproduced]; 1934 New York 1, 23; 1936 Paris 2, 30; 1937 Paris, 33; 1949-50 New York, Chicago, 93; 1967 Washington, Los Angeles, 19
PROVENANCE A. Schuffenecker, Paris [R 1901]; G. Fayet, Igny [acquired 1902; 1925]; Wildenstein Art Gallery, New York; Paul Rosenberg Art Gallery, New York [R 1937]; Albert D. Lasker, New York; Chicago, Mr and Mrs Leigh B. Block [R 1949; 1967]

F 530 [H 507] SELF PORTRAIT
Left out by Faille in his manuscript for the present edition; See REJECTED WORKS

F 531 [H 778] THE PEASANT
EXHIBITIONS 1908 Paris 2, 33; 1952 Milan, 104
PROVENANCE M. Aubry, Paris; E. Druet Art Gallery, Paris [R 1908]; P. Rosenberg Art Gallery, Paris; E. Sforni, Florence [R 1939, 1952]; Milan, Civica Galleria d'Arte Moderna di Milano [Raccolta Grassi] [R 1969]

F 532 [H 559] THE ONE-EYED MAN
EXHIBITIONS 1905 Amsterdam, 166; 1920 Venice; 1928 Berlin, 54; Frankfort, 34; Vienna, 33; 1930 Amsterdam, 67; 1949-50 New York, Chicago, 109; 1951 Lyons etc, 56; 1953-4 Saint Louis etc, 115; 1954 Zurich, 59; 1954-5 Bern, 49; 1955 Antwerp 1, 263; New York 2, 46; 1955-6 Liverpool etc, 58; 1958-9 San Francisco etc, 58; 1968-9 London, 173
PROVENANCE Mrs J. van Gogh-Bonger, Amsterdam; V. W. van Gogh, Laren; Amsterdam, Rijksmuseum Vincent van Gogh [Vincent van Gogh Foundation, inv nr F 532]

F 533 [H 558] PORTRAIT OF A MAN
EXHIBITIONS 1908 Paris 2, 34; 1912 Cologne, 53 [repr]; 1913 The Hague, 90; 1914 Antwerp, 33; 1927 Basle etc, 87 [repr]; 1928 Düsseldorf, 150 [repr]; Karlsruhe, 85; 1929 Berlin 1, 109; Hamburg, 44; 1930 Amsterdam, 205; 1935-6 New York etc, 41; 1945 The Hague, 35; 1946-7 Liège etc, 100; 1947 Paris 1, 102; Geneva, 102; Basle, 75; 1947-8 London etc, 62; 1952 Milan, 88; 1953 The Hague, 140; Otterlo, Amsterdam, 111; 1953-4 Saint Louis etc, 114; 1956 Eindhoven, 45; Munich, 151; 1958 Vienna, 101; Tokyo, Kyoto, 117; 1959 Aix-en-Provence, 48; 1960-1 Montreal etc, 57
PROVENANCE Bernheim jeune Art Gallery, Paris; Druet Art Gallery, Paris [R 1908]; M. Senn [R 1909]; Druet Art Gallery, Paris [R 1912]; Otterlo, Rijksmuseum Kröller-Müller [acquired 1912], inv nr 267-12, cat van Gogh 1970, nr 219

F 534 [H 549] THE SMOKER
PROVENANCE Mrs J. van Gogh-Bonger, Amsterdam; Paul Cassirer Art Gallery, Berlin; Prince of Wagram, Paris [acquired September 1906; until 1908]; Druet Art Gallery, Paris [1908]; H. Aubry, Paris [acquired 1908]; Druet Art Gallery, Paris [1912]; Merion, Pennsylvania, The Barnes Foundation [acquired 1912]

F 535 [H 560] THE GIRL WITH THE RUFFLED HAIR
EXHIBITIONS 1912 Cologne, 64; 1914 Berlin, 71; 1945 Basle, 9; 1947 Basle, 57
PROVENANCE Mrs Tilla Durieux-Cassirer, Berlin [R 1912]; Paul Cassirer Art Gallery, Berlin; Kurt Oppenheim, Blonay; Rosengart Art Gallery, Lucerne; Switzerland, Private collection [R 1945]

F 536 [H 557] YOUNG MAN IN A CAP
EXHIBITIONS 1901 Paris, 12; 1912-13 Barmen etc, 81; 1914 Berlin, 99; 1927 Berlin 2, 109 [repr]; 1947 Basle, 74; 1950 Paris 2, 54; 1955 Winterthur 1, 101; 1956 Munich, 138; 1957 Essen, 296; 1960 Paris, 46; 1963 Hamburg, 79; 1967 Paris, 103
PROVENANCE A. Vollard Art Gallery, Paris [R 1901]; Druet Art Gallery, Paris; G. F. Reber, Barmen [R 1912; 1918]; Thannhauser Art Gallery, Lucerne [R 1923]; K. Neumann, Barmen; W. Feilchenfeldt Art Gallery, Zurich; Zurich, Fritz Nathan [R 1956; 1970]

F 537 [H 544] PORTRAIT OF CAMILLE ROULIN
EXHIBITIONS 1901 Paris, 41; 1912 Cologne, 60; 1921 New York, 123; 1928 Berlin, 55; 1935-6 New York etc, 42; 1936 London 2, 21; 1955 New York 2, 40
PROVENANCE Joseph Roulin, Marseille; Vollard Art Gallery, Paris; Amédée Schuffenecker, Paris; J. Meier Graefe, Berlin; Paul Cassirer Art Gallery, Berlin; Georg Caspari Art Gallery, Munich; Thannhauser Art Gallery, Lucerne; A. Lewisohn, New York; Marius de Zayas, New York [R 1921]; Sale M. de Zayas, New York [Anderson Gallery] 23-24 March 1923, 85 [repr]; J. K. Thannhauser Art Gallery, New York; Joseph Stransky, New York [R 1934]; Wildenstein Art Gallery, New York; Devon, Pennsylvania, Mr and Mrs Rodolphe Meyer de Schauensee [R 1950; 1970]
EDITORS' COMMENT See F 441a in cat

F 538 [H 543] PORTRAIT OF CAMILLE ROULIN
EXHIBITIONS 1905 Amsterdam, probably cat nr 442; 1928 Berlin, 56; Vienna, 34; Frankfort, 35; Munich, 26; 1945 Amsterdam, without cat nr; 1946-7 Liège etc, 125; 1947 Geneva, 123; Paris 1, 123; 1949 Lyons, 125; 1951 Lyons etc, 45; 1954 Zurich, 47; 1955 Antwerp 1, 261; Palm Beach etc, 16; 1955-6 Liverpool etc, 52; 1958-9 San Francisco etc, 50; 1964 Washington, New York, 57; 1967 Wolfsburg, 54; 1968-9 London, 139
PROVENANCE Mrs J. van Gogh-Bonger, Amsterdam; V. W. van Gogh, Laren; Amsterdam, Rijksmuseum Vincent van Gogh [Vincent van Gogh Foundation, inv nr F 538]
EDITORS' COMMENT According to Faille, F 538 was exhibited in Amsterdam 1905, under nr 137. The description of that number in the exhib cat, however, definitely pertains to F 493 rather than F 538. Exhib cat nr 442, on the other hand, described as THE HEAD OF A BOY, may very well be identical with F 538. Faille identified nr 442 of that exhibition as F 537, which, however, was in Paris at the time.

F 539 THE ZOUAVE
Left out by Faille in his manuscript for the present edition; See REJECTED WORKS

F 539a [formerly F 539bis] THE ZOUAVE
Left out by Faille in his manuscript for the present edition; See REJECTED WORKS

F 540 [H 712] L'ARLESIENNE, MADAME GINOUX [after a drawing by Paul Gauguin]
EXHIBITIONS 1905 Amsterdam, 115; 1908 Rotterdam; 1912 Cologne, 85; 1922 Copenhagen, 177; 1937 Paris, 163; 1951 Lyons etc, 50; 1954 Zurich, 51; 1954-5 Bern, 66; 1955 Antwerp 1, 323; 1957 Los Angeles, 20; 1960 Basle, 7; 1961 The Hague, 46
PROVENANCE Mrs J. van Gogh-Bonger, Amsterdam [R 1905]; Druet Art Gallery, Paris; H. P. Bremmer, The Hague [R 1912 and 1937] [on loan to Rijksmuseum, Amsterdam since 1916, Cat 1920 and 1934, nr 984l]; Myrtil Frank Art Gallery, New York; Wildenstein Art Gallery, New York; Mr and Mrs Harold Hecht, Los Angeles [R 1957]; G. D. Thompson, Pittsburgh [R 1960 and 1961]; Marlborough Fine Art, London; Roma, Galleria Nazionale d'Arte Moderna [acquired 1962]

F 541 [H 710] L'ARLESIENNE, MADAME GINOUX [after a drawing by Paul Gauguin]
EXHIBITIONS 1947 Basle, 96; Paris 1, 161; 1952 Milan 116; 1953 The Hague, 169; Otterlo, Amsterdam, 162; 1953-4 St. Louis etc, 144; 1956 Munich, 150; 1958 Vienna, 102; Tokyo, Kyoto, 125; 1959 Aix-en-Provence, 47; 1963 Tel Aviv, 90
PROVENANCE Mr Williame, Châteauroux [acquired 1914]; Otterlo, Rijksmuseum Kröller-Müller, inv nr 292-14, cat van Gogh 1970, nr 245

F 542 [H 713] L'ARLESIENNE, MADAME GINOUX [after a drawing by Paul Gauguin]
EXHIBITIONS 1901 Paris, 14; 1912 Cologne, 84; 1914 Berlin, 81; 1940 Detroit, 50; San Francisco, 271; 1953-4 Paris, 61; 1954 Utrecht, 52; 1955 New York 2, 66; 1962 Warsaw, 80
PROVENANCE Mrs J. van Gogh-Bonger, Amsterdam; A. Vollard Art Gallery, Paris [R 1901]; Mr Baudy, Paris; Mrs T. Durieux-Cassirer, Berlin [R 1912 and 1918]; Neue Galerie, Vienna; Oscar Federer, Moravska-Ostrava; St. Etienne Art Gallery, New York; Knoedler Art Gallery, New York; São Paulo, Museu de Arte, Cat 1963, nr 114

F 543 [H 711] L'ARLESIENNE, MADAME GINOUX [after a drawing by Paul Gauguin]
EXHIBITIONS 1912 Cologne, 83; 1927 Berlin 2, 116 [repr]; 1929 New York, 74; 1935-6 New York etc, 44; 1943 New York 2, 59; 1944 New York 2, 28; Montreal, 135; 1948 Cleveland, 29; 1951 Houston, 15; 1952 London 4, 92; 1954 Detroit, 121; 1955 New York 2, 65; 1957 Los Angeles, 19; 1965 New York 2, 61
PROVENANCE Private collection, Munich; Thannhauser Art Gallery, Berlin [R 1927]; New York, Mr and Mrs H. Bakwin [R 1929, 1965]

F 544 [H 548] A PAIR OF LOVERS [fragment]
PROVENANCE Henry Bernstein, Paris; Sale Bernstein, Paris [Drouot] 8 June 1911, 29; Bernheim jeune Art Gallery, Paris; Jos Hessel Art Gallery, Paris; Vildrac Art Gallery, Paris; Hermann Lie, Oslo; Lysaker near Oslo, J. E. Werenskiold [R 1968]

F 545 [H 562] THE MOWERS, ARLES IN THE BACKGROUND
EXHIBITION 1905 Paris, 35
PROVENANCE Miss Tanguy [daughter of Julien Tanguy], Paris; Auguste Rodin, Paris [R 1905]; Paris, Musée Rodin, cat 1938, nr 387

F 546 PORTRAIT OF PAUL GAUGUIN
Left out by Faille in his manuscript for the present edition; See REJECTED WORKS

F 547 [H 555] THE DANCE HALL
EXHIBITIONS 1908 Paris 2, 22; 1914 Berlin, 121a; 1925 Paris 1, 35; 1926 Paris, 2952; 1927 Paris; 1962 Washington, 24
PROVENANCE Mrs Michelot, Paris [R 1908; 1912]; Mrs E. Druet, Paris [R 1925, 1926]; André Meyer, New York; Paris, Musée National du Louvre, inv nr RF 1950-9, cat Impressionistes 1959, p 248

F 548 [H 556] A VIEW OF THE ARENA IN ARLES
EXHIBITIONS 1926 Moscow, 2; 1956 Moscow, Leningrad, p 11; 1960 Paris, 47; 1965 Bordeaux, 63; 1965-66 Paris, 60
PROVENANCE S. I. Stschukin, Moscow, cat 1913, nr 34; Moscow, Museum of Modern Western Art [1918-1931], cat 1928, nr 78; Leningrad, Hermitage [acquired 1931], inv nr 6529, cat 1958 p 291; cat 1967, nr 64

F 549 [H 554] INTERIOR OF A RESTAURANT IN ARLES
EXHIBITIONS 1909 London; 1923 London, 37; 1926 London 2, p 7; 1929 London 1, 463; 1930 Amsterdam, 68; 1932 Manchester; 1935 New York, 5; 1935-6 New York etc, 45; 1939 Boston, 55; 1943 New York 2, 39; 1963 Hartford, 17
PROVENANCE A. Vollard Art Gallery, Paris; Mrs Esther S. Sutro, London [R 1896]; A. Sutro, London [R 1929, 1930]; Mrs van Gruisen [until 1935]; Alex Reid and Lefevre Art Gallery, London [R 1935]; Marcel Gieuré; Carroll Carstairs Art Gallery, New York; Mrs Murray S. Danforth, Providence [R 1935]; Providence Rhode Island, Murray S. Danforth jr [R 1963]

F 549a INTERIOR OF A RESTAURANT IN ARLES
PROVENANCE A. Lucas, Paris; Zurich, V. Margutti, Neuchâtel, H. Vaucher and Zurich, Harry Stern; Coproperty Vittorio Margutti–Henri Vaucher [R 1970]

F 550 [H 561] THE OLD MILL [RUE MIREILLE, ARLES]
EXHIBITIONS 1905 Amsterdam, 161; 1929 Cambridge [Mass.], 91; New York, 83; 1933 Chicago, 379; 1935-6 New York etc, 46; 1943 New York 2, 40; 1948 Cleveland, 14; 1955 New York 2, 34; 1960 New Haven, 69
PROVENANCE Ernest Ponthier de Chamaillard, Paris [R 1888]; Bernheim jeune Art Gallery, Paris; A. Conger Goodyear, New York [R 1929]; Buffalo, Albright-Knox Art Gallery [gift of A. Conger Goodyear 1964]

F 551 [H 575] ORCHARD IN BLOSSOM WITH YELLOW ENCLOSURE
EXHIBITIONS 1905 Amsterdam, 169; 1912 Cologne, 22; 1923 Haarlem, 29; 1928 New York 1, 22; 1948 New York 1, 1; 1951 Houston, 11; 1955 New York 2, 27
PROVENANCE André Bonger, Amsterdam [R 1905, 1912]; d'Audretsch Art Gallery, The Hague; Jack Niekerk Art Gallery, The Hague; Howard Young Art Gallery, New York [R 1928]; N. H. Holston, New York; J. K. Newman, New York; Sale coll. Newman, New York [Am. Art Ass. Anderson Gall.] 6 December 1935, 39; Carroll Carstairs Art Gallery, New York; New York, Private collection [R 1944, R 1970]

F 552 [H 577] THE ORCHARD: WHITE BLOSSOMS AND VIOLET BRANCHES
EXHIBITIONS 1904 Rotterdam, 65; 1912 Cologne, 20; 1950 The Hague, 35; 1952 Milan, 94; 1955 Amsterdam 2, 14
PROVENANCE Oldenzeel Art Gallery, Rotterdam; H. P. Bremmer, The Hague [R 1904, 1955]; Gemeentemuseum, The Hague [loan H. P. Bremmer since 1924], inv nr 40-24, cat 1935, p 77; Henry Ittleson, New York [acquired 1955]: New York, Metropolitan Museum of Art [acquired 1956; Mr and Mrs Henry Ittleson jr. Purchase Fund]

F 553 [H 576] A CORNER OF THE ORCHARD
PROVENANCE Theo van Gogh, Paris; Private collection, England; William Boyd, Dundee; Alexander Maitland, Edinburgh [acquired 1937]; Edinburgh, National Gallery of Scotland [acquired 1960; The Maitland Gift], inv nr 2217, cat The Maitland Gift 1963, p 36

F 554 [H 581] THE ORCHARD IN FLOWER
EXHIBITIONS 1912 Cologne, 33; 1932 Amsterdam 2, 18; 1950 The Hague, 36; 1955 Rotterdam, 191; 1958 New York, 70; 1962 New York, 34; 1963 New York 2, 23; 1966 New York 2, 64
PROVENANCE C. M. van Gogh Art Gallery, Amsterdam; H. P. Bremmer, The Hague [R 1909, 1956]; Heirs H. P. Bremmer, The Hague [R 1957]; Myrtil Frank, New York [R 1957]; Wildenstein Art Gallery, New York [R 1957]; Mrs Arthur Lehman [acquired 1957] [on loan to The Metropolitan Museum of Art, New York 1957]; New York, Mrs Richard J. Bernhard [acquired 1965]

F 555 [H 578] THE PINK ORCHARD
EXHIBITIONS 1891 Paris 1, 1203; 1905 Amsterdam, 96; Utrecht, 29; 1914 Berlin, 75; 1925 The Hague, 47; 1930 Amsterdam, 69; 1945 Amsterdam, without cat nr; 1946 Stockholm etc, 44; 1946-7 Liège etc, 98; 1947 Paris 1, 98; Geneva, 98; London etc, 38; 1948 Bergen, Oslo, 27; 1949-50 New York, Chicago, 68; 1951 Lyons etc, 28; 1954 Zurich, 37; 1954-5 Bern, 38; 1955 Antwerp 1, 243; 1955-6 Liverpool etc, 39; 1957 Marseilles, 43; 1958-9 San Francisco etc, 38; 1959-60 Utrecht, 32; 1960-1 Montreal etc, 49; 1961-2 Baltimore etc, 39; 1963 Humlebaek, 28; 1967 Wolfsburg, 43; 1968-9 London, 105
PROVENANCE Mrs J. van Gogh-Bonger, Amsterdam; V. W. van Gogh, Laren; Amsterdam, Rijksmuseum Vincent van Gogh [Vincent van Gogh Foundation, inv nr F 555]

F 556 [H 579] APRICOT TREES IN BLOSSOM
EXHIBITIONS 1928 Vienna, 27 [repr]; 1943 Zurich, 715; 1945 Basle, 10; 1947 Basle, 53; 1950 Zurich, p 28; 1958 Zurich, 240; 1961 Edinburgh, London, 58
PROVENANCE Paul Dahlmann, Le Raincy; N. Eisenloeffel Art Gallery, Amsterdam; Unger and Van Mens Art Gallery Rotterdam [R about 1922]; A. van Hoboken, Vienna; Oscar Federer, Moravska Ostrava; W. Feilchenfeldt Art Gallery, Zurich; Georges Renand, Paris; Private collection, Switzerland; Sammlung E. G. Bührle [acquired 1940], cat 1958, p 240; Private collection [R 1970]
EDITORS' COMMENT The catalogue of the Bührle collection of 1958 mentions an exhibition in 1914 at Cassirer's in Berlin. As we could find no mention of the work in this catalogue, we have striked out the exhibition

F 557 [H 580] ALMOND TREE IN BLOSSOM
EXHIBITIONS 1905 Amsterdam, 98; Utrecht, 31; 1945 Amsterdam, without cat nr; 1946 Stockholm etc, 46; 1949 Lyons, 126; 1955 Antwerp 1, 247
PROVENANCE Mrs J. van Gogh-Bonger, Amsterdam; V. W. van Gogh, Laren; Amsterdam, Rijksmuseum Vincent van Gogh [Vincent van Gogh Foundation, inv nr F 557]

F 558 [H 563] HARVEST IN PROVENCE
EXHIBITIONS 1905 Amsterdam, 119; 1914 Berlin, 87; 1918 Chemnitz, 86 [repr]; 1966 London, no cat [Exhib Donation Hanadiv Group to the Israel Museum]
PROVENANCE Mrs J. van Gogh-Bonger, Amsterdam; Bernheim jeune Art Gallery, Paris; Paul Cassirer Art Gallery, Berlin [before 1914]; Herbert Esche, Chemnitz [R 1914]; W. Feilchenfeldt Art Gallery, Zurich; Private collection, USA; Private collection, Switzerland; Jerusalem, The Israel Museum [acquired 1966; gift of the 'Hanadiv' Rothschild Foundation], inv nr IM 504/135

F 559 [H 564] THE WHEAT STACKS WITH REAPER
EXHIBITIONS 1905 Amsterdam, 106; Utrecht, 35; 1906 Rotterdam, 31; 1908 Paris 2, 11; 1933 Los Angeles, 51; 1934 Toledo, Ohio, 26; Chicago, 316; 1940 Detroit, 51; 1942 New York, 6; 1943 New York 2, 41; 1948 Cleveland, 8
PROVENANCE Mrs J. van Gogh-Bonger, Amsterdam [R 1905]; J. Leclerq, Paris; Gustave Fayet, Igny [R 1908; 1925]; Mrs Alban d'Andoque de Sériège, Béziers; Wildenstein Art Gallery, Paris-New York [R 1934]; Edward Drummond Libbey, Toledo, Ohio; Toledo, Ohio, Toledo Museum of Art [acquired 1935; gift Edward Drummond Libbey], cat 1939, p 250

F 560 [H 565] THE WHEAT STACKS WITH REAPER AND PEASANT WOMAN
EXHIBITIONS 1946 Stockholm etc, 58
PROVENANCE P. Rosenberg Art Gallery, Paris [R 1912]; Stockholm, National Museum [acquired 1914], inv nr 1802, cat 1958, p 80

F 561 [H 566] THE FIELD OF WHEAT
EXHIBITIONS 1912 Cologne, 43; 1914 Berlin, 132; 1921 Berlin; 1928 Berlin, 58; 1930 Amsterdam, 70; 1934 Toledo, Ohio, 26; 1935 London, 4; 1937 Chicago, 25; 1939-40 San Francisco, 124; 1943 New York 2, 42; 1951 Houston, 10; 1955 New York 2, 42; 1957 Los Angeles, 10; 1965 New York 2, 53; 1966 Bordeaux, 65
PROVENANCE Mrs Margaretha Mauthner, Berlin [R 1912]; Wildenstein Art Gallery, Paris [R 1930]; Mrs Tony Lessing, Berlin [R 1937]; Wildenstein Art Gallery, New York [R 1943]; Honolulu, Academy of Arts [acquired 1946; gift Mrs Richard A. Cooke]

F 562 [H 567] GREEN EARS OF WHEAT
EXHIBITIONS 1952 London 2, 16; 1956 Munich, 148
PROVENANCE Thannhauser Art Gallery, Munich; P. von Mendelssohn-Bartholdy, Berlin; Private collection, Switzerland; Jeruzalem, The Israel Museum [acquired 1966; gift of the 'Hanadiv' Rothschild Foundation]

F 563 [H 550] LANDSCAPE WITH A STRAW-HEAP
EXHIBITIONS 1927 Basle etc, 122; 1928 Düsseldorf, 190 [reproduced]; Karlsruhe, 125; 1929 Berlin 1, 106; Hamburg, 77; 1930 Amsterdam, 216; 1946-7 Liège etc, 112; 1947 Paris 1, 114; Geneva, 114; 1953 Amsterdam 2; 1956 Munich, 125; 1958 Tokyo, Kyoto, 102; 1960-1 Montreal etc, 58; 1966 Belgrade, 68
PROVENANCE Otterlo, Rijksmuseum Kröller-Müller [acquired before 1919], inv nr 301-00, cat Van Gogh 1970, nr 227

F 564 [H 541] THE WHEATFIELD
EXHIBITIONS 1905 Amsterdam, 123; 1955 Rotterdam, 192; 1956 Munich, 126; 1964 Laren, 27; 1966 Laren, 93
PROVENANCE Mrs J. van Gogh-Bonger, Amsterdam [R 1905]; A. Bonger, Amsterdam [until 1941]; Van Wisselingh Art Gallery, Amsterdam; Mrs P. de Boer, Amsterdam [R 1956]; Amsterdam, P. and N. de Boer Foundation [R 1966]

F 565 [H 542] THE FARM GATE
EXHIBITIONS 1905 Amsterdam, 111; 1927 Paris; 1934 London, 21; 1961 San Francisco, 65; 1966 Washington, 131
PROVENANCE Mrs J. van Gogh-Bonger, Amsterdam [R 1905]; Bernheim jeune Art Gallery, Paris; Alex Reid and Lefevre Art Gallery, London; M. Ackermann, Paris [R 1934]; Edward Molyneux, Paris; New York, Estate of Mrs Ailsa Mellon Bruce [R 1952; 1969]

F 566 [H 553] THE ENTRANCE OF THE PUBLIC GARDEN
EXHIBITIONS 1912 Cologne, 92 [repr]; 1914 Berlin, 83; 1922 Winterthur 1, 53; 1924 Basle, 57; Zurich, 37; 1929 New York, 82; 1933 Chicago, 383; 1934-5 Baltimore, 37; 1940 New York 2, 362; 1943 New York 2, 38; 1948 Cleveland, 13; 1949-50 New York, Chicago, 79; 1950-1 Philadelphia, 91; 1955 New York 2, 33
PROVENANCE Prince of Wagram, Paris; Druet Art Gallery, Paris [R 1908]; Bernheim jeune Art Gallery, Paris; Thea Sternheim Uttwil [acquired 1909]; Sale Thea Sternheim, Amsterdam [F. Muller] 11 February 1919, nr 10 [repr]; Karl Sternheim, Reichenberg [R 1924]; Paul Rosenberg Art Gallery, Paris; Wildenstein Art Gallery, New York; A. Sachs, New York [R 1929]; Washington, DC, The Phillips Collection, cat 1952, p 42

F 567 [H 571] A WALK NEAR ARLES
EXHIBITIONS 1907 Mannheim; 1912 Cologne, 50

PROVENANCE A. Schuffenecker, Paris; Thannhauser Art Gallery, Munich; Stettin, Museum [acquired 1910]; Western Germany, The City of Coburg [1970]

F 568 [H 551] THE ALLEY OF LES ALYSCAMPS
EXHIBITIONS 1925 Paris 3, 80; 1927 Paris; 1955 New York 3, 46; New York 2, 36; 1957 Los Angeles, 11; 1959 New York 2, 56; 1961 New York 2, 45
PROVENANCE Bernheim jeune Art Gallery, Paris [R 1925]; Private collection, London; Alfred Daber Art Gallery, Paris; New York, Mr and Mrs Edwin C. Vogel [R 1953; 1970]

F 569 [H 552] THE ALLEY OF LES ALYSCAMPS
EXHIBITIONS 1924 Zurich, 40; 1930 Amsterdam, 71; 1947 Basle, 70; 1955 Winterthur 1, 102; 1963 Schaffhausen, 52
PROVENANCE Mr Aghion, Paris; Sale Aghion, Paris [Drout] 29 March 1918, nr 13 [repr]; Paul Vallotton Art Gallery, Lausanne; H. Mettler, Sankt Gallen [R 1930]; Zollikon, Switzerland, Mrs A. Mettler-Weber [R 1955]

F 570 [H 588] THE LANGLOIS BRIDGE
EXHIBITIONS 1951 Paris 1, 45; 1953 Berlin, 11; 1956 Munich, 121; 1957 Essen, 268; 1963 Hamburg, 80
PROVENANCE Bernheim jeune Art Gallery, Paris; Flechtheim Art Gallery, Düsseldorf; Paul Cassirer Art Gallery, Berlin; Cologne, Museum Wallraf-Richartz [acquired 1911], inv nr WRM 1197, cat 1964, p 45

F 571 [H 587] THE LANGLOIS BRIDGE
EXHIBITIONS 1914 Dresden, 51; 1926 Dresden, 207; 1928 Berlin, 59 [repr]; 1946 Paris, 90
PROVENANCE Mrs J. van Gogh-Bonger, Amsterdam; Paul Cassirer Art Gallery, Berlin; Oscar Schmitz, Dresden [acquired 1905], cat collection Schmitz, Dresden 1936, nr 60; Wildenstein Art Gallery, Paris; Private collection, Paris; Private collection of Hermann Goering, Germany [from 1940 until 1946]; Paris, Private collection [R 1946]

F 572 [H 540] WILLOWS AT SUNSET
EXHIBITIONS 1892 The Hague, 7; 1905 Amsterdam, 128; 1908 Paris 1, 50; Amsterdam, 50; 1910 Rotterdam, 29; 1912 Cologne, 34; 1913 The Hague, 85; 1914 Antwerp, 27; 1927 Basle etc, 112; 1928 Düsseldorf, 180 [repr]; Karlsruhe, 115; 1929 Berlin 1, 120; Hamburg, 68; 1930 Amsterdam, 213; 1946 Amsterdam; 1947 Basle, 69; 1949-50 New York, Chicago, 84; 1952 Milan, 92; 1958 Tokyo, Kyoto, 104; 1959 Aix-en-Provence, 17; 1960-1 Montreal etc, 43; 1961 Recklinghausen, 104; 1962 Warsaw, 66; 1963 Tel Aviv, Haifa, 78; 1966 Belgrade, 71
PROVENANCE Mrs J. van Gogh-Bonger, Amsterdam [R 1905]; C. M. van Gogh Art Gallery, Amsterdam [R 1910]; Mrs H. Kröller-Müller, The Hague [R 1910]; Otterlo, Rijksmuseum Kröller-Müller, inv nr 291-10, cat van Gogh 1970, nr 228

F 573 [H 570] TRUNK OF AN OLD YEW TREE
EXHIBITIONS 1896 Rotterdam, 32; 1905 Amsterdam, 131; 1957 Dublin, 90; 1959 Washington, p 54; 1966 Washington, 133
PROVENANCE Mrs J. van Gogh-Bonger, Amsterdam; Amédée Schuffenecker, Clamart; Paul Rosenberg Art Gallery, Paris; Paul von Mendelssohn-Bartholdy, Berlin; P. de Boer Art Gallery, Amsterdam; Sir Chester Beatty, Dublin [until 1958]; Private collection, Paris; Upperville, Virginia, Mr and Mrs Paul Mellon [R 1959; 1966]

F 574 [H 568] PLOUGHED FIELDS [THE FURROWS]
EXHIBITIONS 1905 Amsterdam, 118; Utrecht, 38; 1906 Rotterdam, 36; 1920 New York, 50; 1923 London, 23; 1924 Basle, 66; Zurich, 38; Stuttgart, 17; 1925 Paris 1, 27; The Hague, 2; 1926 Munich, 2078; 1930 Amsterdam, 72; 1945 Amsterdam, without cat nr; 1946 Stockholm etc, 66; 1946-7 Liège etc, 117; 1947 Geneva, 118; Paris 1, 118; 1948 Bergen, Oslo, 34a; 1951 Lyons etc, 53; 1955 Antwerp 1, 254; 1955-6 Liverpool etc, 49; 1963 Humlebaek, 39; 1964 Washington, New York, 39; 1968-9 London, 137
PROVENANCE Mrs J. van Gogh-Bonger, Amsterdam; V. W. van Gogh, Laren; Amsterdam, Rijksmuseum Vincent van Gogh [Vincent van Gogh Foundation, inv nr F 574]

F 575 [H 585] LANDSCAPE UNDER A STORMY SKY
EXHIBITIONS 1928 Paris; 1934 Ottawa, 61; 1938 New York 1, 3; London 2, 41; 1939 London 1, 16; 1955 Antwerp 2, 172
PROVENANCE Marczell de Nemes, Budapest; Sale M. de Nemes, Paris [Drouot] 21 November 1918, nr 45 [repr]; M. P. Voûte Jr, Amsterdam; N. Eisenloeffel Art Gallery, Amsterdam; H. S. Southam, Ottawa [R 1934]; Alex Reid and Lefevre Art Gallery, London; Max Moos, Geneva; Gstaad, Louis Franck [R 1955; 1970]

F 575a THE SOWER: OUTSKIRTS OF ARLES IN THE BACKGROUND
EXHIBITIONS 1920 New York, 46; 1960 Philadelphia
PROVENANCE Mrs J. van Gogh-Bonger, Amsterdam; Montross Art Gallery, New York [R 1920]; Theodore Pitcairn, Bryn Athyn, Pennsylvania [acquired 1920]; Sale London [Christie] 2 May 1969, nr 58; Los Angeles, California, A. Hammer [R 1970]

F 576 [H 569] LANDSCAPE NEAR ARLES
EXHIBITIONS 1947 Paris 2, 154; 1951 Lyons etc, 32; 1957 Stockholm, 113; 1960 Cuesmes, 7; 1961-2 Baltimore etc, 43; 1967 Wolfsburg, 47; 1968-9 London, 126
PROVENANCE Mrs J. van Gogh-Bonger, Amsterdam; H. C. Bonger, Amsterdam; Miss E. H. Bonger, Amsterdam; V. W. van Gogh, Laren; Amsterdam, Rijksmuseum Vincent van Gogh [Vincent van Gogh Foundation, inv nr F 576]

F 577 THE GARDEN
Left out by Faille in his manuscript for the present edition; See REJECTED WORKS

F 578 [H 572] GARDEN BEHIND A HOUSE
EXHIBITIONS 1905 Amsterdam, 160; Utrecht, 44; 1927 Paris; 1961 Paris 2, 81
PROVENANCE Mrs J. van Gogh-Bonger, Amsterdam [R 1905]; Bernheim jeune Art Gallery, Paris; F. Moch, Paris [acquired 1917]; Paris, Private collection [R 1961]

F 579 [H 582] BUSHES
EXHIBITIONS 1901 Paris, 59; 1926 Moscow; 1956 Moscow, Leningrad, p 11; 1960 Paris, 41
PROVENANCE Mrs Julien Leclercq, Paris; S. I. Stschukin, Moscow, cat 1913, 36; Moscow, Museum of Modern Western Art [acquired 1918], cat 1928, nr 77; Leningrad, Hermitage [acquired 1930], inv nr 6511, cat 1958, p 291; cat 1967, nrs 67, 68

F 580 [H 592] ROSEBUSHES IN FLOWER
EXHIBITIONS 1923 Prague, 191; 1960 Tokyo, 198
PROVENANCE P. F. Gachet, Auvers-sur-Oise [from 1890 until 1909]; Paul Gachet, Auvers-sur-Oise; Paul Rosenberg Art Gallery, Paris; Kojiro Matsukata, Kobe; Tokyo, National Museum of Western Art [acquired 1959; gift of the French government], inv nr P-299, cat 1961

F 581 [H 696] POPPIES IN THE FIELD
EXHIBITIONS 1901 Paris, 34; 1905 Amsterdam, 229; 1910 Berlin 1, 18; 1951 Paris 1, 47; 1953 Berlin, 12; 1956 Munich, 154; 1959 Recklinghausen, 110; 1960 Paris, 62; 1963 Hamburg, 82
PROVENANCE Julien Leclercq, Paris [R 1901]; Mrs J. van Gogh-Bonger, Amsterdam [R 1905]; Prince of Wagram, Paris; Barbazanges Art Gallery, Paris; Paul Cassirer Art Gallery, Berlin; Bremen, Kunsthalle [acquired 1911], cat 1935, p 37

F 582 [H 586] A GRASSY NOOK
EXHIBITION 1924 Basle, 51
PROVENANCE Mrs J. van Gogh-Bonger, Amsterdam; Werner von der Schulenburg, Ascona [acquired 1923]; Present owner unknown

F 583 [H 584] A CORNER IN THE MEADOW
EXHIBITIONS 1927 Basle etc, 83; 1928 Düsseldorf, 159; Karlsruhe, 94; 1929 Berlin 1, 110; Hamburg, 40; 1930 Amsterdam, 200; 1935-6 New York etc, 43; 1946 Amsterdam; 1947 Basle, 50; 1956 Munich, 111; 1958 Tokyo, Kyoto, 92
PROVENANCE G. Albert Aurier, Châteauroux [1914]; Mr Williame, Châteauroux [1914]; Otterlo, Rijksmuseum Kröller-Müller, inv nr 264-14, cat van Gogh 1970, nr 213

F 584 [H 583] A FIELD OF YELLOW FLOWERS
EXHIBITIONS 1905 Amsterdam, 163; 1914 Berlin, 137; 1945 Basle, 11
PROVENANCE Mrs J. van Gogh-Bonger, Amsterdam; Paul Cassirer Art Gallery, Berlin; Thannhauser Art Gallery, Munich; Otto Nyquist, Oslo; Oscar Federer, Moravska-Ostrava; Neue Galerie, Vienna; A. van Hoboken, Ascona [from about 1930 until 1966]; Sale London [Sotheby] 3 December 1958, nr 122 [not sold]; F. and P. Nathan Art Gallery, Zurich [R 1966]; Present owner unknown

F 585 [H 708] OLIVE YARD
EXHIBITIONS 1912 Cologne, 98; 1913 The Hague, 143; 1927 Basle etc, 104; 1928 Düsseldorf, 171 [repr]; Karlsruhe 106 [repr]; 1929 Berlin 1, 111; Hamburg, 60; 1930 Amsterdam, 243; 1935 Brussels, 101; 1947 Paris 1, 148; Geneva, 148; Basle, 87; 1947-8 London etc, 74; 1948 Amsterdam; 1949-50 New York, Chicago, 120; 1952 Milan, 108; 1953 The Hague, 160; Otterlo, Amsterdam, 148; 1953-4 Saint Louis etc, 137; 1956 Eindhoven, 41; Munich, 144; 1957 Essen, 334; 1958 Vienna, 95; Tokyo-Kyoto, 115; 1960 Paris, 204; 1963 Amsterdam, 108
PROVENANCE Amédée Schuffenecker, Clamart; Prince of Wagram, Paris; Druet Art Gallery, Paris [R 1912]; Barbazanges Art Gallery, Paris; Otterlo, Rijksmuseum Kröller-Müller, inv nr 283-12, cat van Gogh 1970, nr 234

F 586 [H 651] OLIVE YARD
EXHIBITION 1946 Stockholm etc, 84
PROVENANCE Bernheim jeune Art Gallery, Paris; Göteborg, Konstmuseum [acquired 1917], cat 1945, p 106

F 587 [H 650] OLIVE PICKING
EXHIBITIONS 1904 Brussels; 1905 Paris, 12; 1912 Cologne, 97; 1913 The Hague, 144; 1914 Antwerp, 137; 1927 Basle etc, 106 [repr]; 1928 Düsseldorf, 173; Karlsruhe, 108; 1929 Berlin 1, 113; Hamburg, 62; 1930 Amsterdam, 241; 1947 Paris 1, 151; 1953 Amsterdam 2; 1958 Vienna, 98; 1959 Aix-en-Provence, 45; 1960-1 Montreal etc, 61; 1966 Belgrade, 74
PROVENANCE M. Fabre, Gasparets [R 1904, 1905]; M. Aubry, Paris; Amédée Schuffenecker, Meudon [R 1912]; E. Druet Art Gallery, Paris [R 1912]; Otterlo, Rijksmuseum Kröller-Müller, inv nr 285-12, cat van Gogh 1970, nr 236

F 588 [H 602] STILL LIFE: WILD FLOWERS IN A VASE
EXHIBITIONS 1927 Paris; 1930 Amsterdam, 73; 1934 San Francisco, 158; 1935 Kansas City, 63; 1935-6 New York etc, 47; 1943 New York 2, 43; 1955 New York 2, 43; 1956 Washington, 38
PROVENANCE Jules Andorko, Paris; Druet Art Gallery, Paris; Mr and Mrs Charles Vildrac Art Gallery, Paris [R 1930]; Marie Harriman Gallery, New York [R 1934; 1935]; New York, Mr and Mrs Averell Harriman [R 1943; 1956]

F 589 [H 601] STILL LIFE: FLOWERS IN A VASE
PROVENANCE Ambroise Vollard Art Gallery, Paris [until 1908]; Association 'La Peau de l'Ours', Paris [acquired 1908]; Sale Association 'Peau de l'Ours', Paris [Drouot] 2 March 1914, 29 [repr]; E. Druet Art Gallery, Paris; Denys Cochin, Paris [acquired 1914]; Alex Reid and Lefèvre Art Gallery, London; New York, Paul Rosenberg & Co [R 1969]; Present owner unknown

F 590 STILL LIFE: ASTERS
Left out by Faille in his manuscript for the present edition; See REJECTED WORKS

F 591 [H 593] STILL LIFE: BASKET WITH DAISIES
EXHIBITIONS 1904 Rotterdam, 64; 1912 Cologne, 16; 1932 Amsterdam 2, 19; 1950 The Hague, 34; 1952 Milan, 93; 1954 Dordrecht, 50; 1955 Rotterdam, 193; 1962 London 4, 1962; 1966 Washington, 132
PROVENANCE Mrs J. van Gogh-Bonger, Amsterdam; H. P. Bremmer, The Hague [R 1904; until 1956]; Heirs of H. P. Bremmer, The Hague [from 1956 until 1962]; Van Wisselingh Art Gallery, Amsterdam [R March 1962]; Alex Reid and Lefevre Art Gallery, London [R 1962]; Upperville, Virginia, Mrs and Mrs Paul Mellon [R 1966]

F 592 [H 604] STILL LIFE: ONE-EARED VASE WITH ZINNIAS
EXHIBITIONS 1930 London 3, 16; 1948 New York 1, 10; 1957 Los Angeles, 11½
PROVENANCE Mrs E. H. du Quesne-van Gogh, Baarn; N. Eisenloeffel Art Gallery, Amsterdam; Alex Reid and Lefevre Art Gallery, London; D. Cargill, Glasgow; S. T. Kilpatrick, London; Stephan C. Clark, New York; Ralph Booth, Detroit; E. and A. Silberman Art Gallery, New York; H. S. Southam, Ottawa; Mrs Charles S. Payson, New York; Knoedler Art Gallery, New York; California, Private collection [R 1965]

F 593 [H 594] STILL LIFE: ONE-EARED VASE WITH OLEANDERS AND BOOKS
EXHIBITIONS 1924 London 2; 1925 Paris 1, 25; 1926 London 2, p 7; 1928 New York 2, 31 [repr]; 1934 San Francisco, 157; 1948 New York 1, 9; 1949-50 New York, Chicago, 90
PROVENANCE Joseph Roulin, Marseilles; A. Vollard Art Gallery, Paris [R 1895]; Mrs Redlich, Vienna; Barbazanges Art Gallery, Paris; M. E. Sadler, Oxford [R 1925]; Mrs R. A. Workman, London [R 1927]; Mrs W. A. Clark, New York [R 1934]; Alex Reid and Lefevre Art Gallery, London; Knoedler Art Gallery, New York; Mrs Charles Suydam-Cutting, New York [R 1935; 1950]; New York, The Metropolitan Museum of Art [Metropolitan Museum and Mr and Mrs John L. Loeb], inv nr 62.24
EDITORS' COMMENT In earlier editions Faille mentioned that this painting has been shown in the van Gogh exhibition if 1905 under nr 122. This number, however, was lent by Mrs van Gogh-Bonger and therefore cannot be F 593. It might have been F 594. See moreover F 441a in cat

F 594 [H 605] STILL LIFE: VASE WITH OLEANDERS
EXHIBITIONS 1896 Rotterdam, 47; 1905 Amsterdam, 122; 1927 Paris; 1932 New York, 16; 1933 Amsterdam 2, 117
PROVENANCE Mrs J. van Gogh-Bonger, Amsterdam; Bernheim jeune Art Gallery, Paris; Jean Dauberville, La Bachellerie, France; Present owner unknown [painting probably stolen in 1944]
EDITORS' COMMENT See F 593

F 595 [H 595] STILL LIFE: ROSES
EXHIBITION 1918 Copenhagen, 123
PROVENANCE Paul Ferd. Gachet, Auvers [1890-1909]; Paul Gachet, Auvers; Collection Reber, Munich; J. Hessel Art Gallery, Paris; Paul Rosenberg Art Gallery, Paris [R 1918]; Helge Jacobsen, Copenhagen [R 1918, 1927]; Copenhagen, Ny Carlsberg Glyptotek [acquired 1927; gift of Helge Jacobsen], inv nr I N 1836, cat 1961, p 60, nr 946

F 596 [H 303] VASE WITH FLOWERS: KENTRANTHUS, LYCHNIS, DIANTHUS
EXHIBITIONS 1905 Paris, 27; 1960 London 3, 17

PROVENANCE Camentron Art Gallery, Paris; F. Jourdain, Paris [R 1905]; Private collection, Switzerland; Marlborough Fine Art Gallery, London [R 1960]; Washington DC, Mr and Mrs D. L. Kreeger [acquired 1960]

F 597 [H 805] DOG-ROSES OR BRANCHES OF WILD-BRIAR
EXHIBITIONS 1905 Amsterdam, 157; 1930 Amsterdam, 74; 1955 Antwerp 1, 295
PROVENANCE Mrs J. van Gogh-Bonger, Amsterdam; V. W. van Gogh, Laren; Amsterdam, Rijksmuseum Vincent van Gogh [Vincent van Gogh Foundation, inv nr F 597]

F 598 [H 600] STILL LIFE: VASE WITH CARNATIONS
EXHIBITIONS 1917 Zurich 1, 573; 1927 Paris; 1948 Cleveland, 17
PROVENANCE Mrs J. van Gogh-Bonger, Amsterdam; Paul Cassirer Art Gallery, Berlin; Georg Schwarz, Berlin; Barbazanges Art Gallery, Paris; Alphonse Kann, St. Germain en Laye; Paul Rosenberg Art Gallery, New York [R 1948]; New York, Arturo Peralta-Ramos [R 1957]

F 599 [H 804] STILL LIFE: VASE WITH THISTLES
EXHIBITIONS 1917 Zurich 1, 106; 1927 Paris; 1953 London 2, 5
PROVENANCE Alphonse Kann, St. Germain-en-Laye; A. Tooth & Son, London; Canada, Private collection [R 1964]

F 600 [H 603] STILL LIFE: ONE-EARED VASE WITH WILD FLOWERS
PROVENANCE Bernheim jeune Art Gallery, Paris; Private collection, Paris; Merion, Pennsylvania, The Barnes Foundation [R 1964]

F 601 [H 591] STILL LIFE: THE IRIS
EXHIBITIONS 1947 Basle, 82; 1952 London 1; 1953 Toronto
PROVENANCE Miss Wilhelmina van Gogh, Dieren; Mrs J. H. Le Cosquino de Bussy, Amsterdam; Rotterdam, Boymans Museum [loan about 1936-1938], cat 1937, nr 729; Van Wisselingh Art Gallery, Amsterdam; C. Kruysse, Amersfoort [R 1952]; Ottawa, National Gallery of Canada [acquired 1955], inv nr 6294, cat Paintings and Sculpture 1959, volume 2, p 30

F 602 [H 599] STILL LIFE: QUINCE PEARS
EXHIBITIONS 1905 Amsterdam, 42 [as Paris]; 1955 Moscow; 1960 Paris, 40; 1965 Berlin-East, p 48
PROVENANCE Mrs J. van Gogh-Bonger, Amsterdam [R 1905]; Paul Cassirer Art Gallery, Berlin; Ernst Arnold Art Gallery, Dresden; Meyer-Dietl, Dresden; K. Haberstock Art Gallery, Berlin; Dresden, Staatliche Gemäldegalerie [acquired 1920], inv nr 2593, cat 1966, p 56

F 603 [H 326] STILL LIFE: GRAPES
EXHIBITIONS 1905 Amsterdam, 91 [as Paris period]; 1920 New York, 56
PROVENANCE Mrs J. van Gogh-Bonger, Amsterdam; V. W. van Gogh, Laren; Amsterdam, Rijksmuseum Vincent van Gogh [Vincent van Gogh Foundation, inv nr F 603]

F 604 [H 596] STILL LIFE: DRAWING BOARD WITH ONIONS ETC
EXHIBITIONS 1912 Düsseldorf, 121; 1913 The Hague, 139; 1914 Antwerp, 48; 1927 Basle etc, 109; 1928 Düsseldorf, 177; Karlsruhe, 112; 1929 Berlin 1, 105; Hamburg, 65; 1930 Amsterdam, 211; 1946-7 Liège etc, 123; 1947 Paris 1, 126; Geneva, 126; Basle, 79; 1947-8 London etc, 63; 1949-50 New York, Chicago, 91; 1952 Milan, 90; 1953 The Hague, 137; Otterlo, Amsterdam, 115; 1953-4 Saint Louis etc, 111; 1954 Rotterdam, 119; 1956 Munich, 135; 1958 Vienna, 87; Tokyo, Kyoto, 105; 1959 Aix-en-Provence, 23; 1960-1 Montreal etc, 44
PROVENANCE Marczell de Nemes, Budapest; Sale Paris [Manzi-Joyant] 18 June 1913, nr 106 [repr]; Otterlo, Rijksmuseum Kröller-Müller, inv nr 288-13, cat van Gogh 1970, nr 223

F 605 [H 589] A CRAB UPSIDE DOWN
EXHIBITIONS 1893 Copenhagen, 179; 1896 Rotterdam, 10; 1905 Amsterdam, 90; 1909 Munich; 1920 New York, 65; 1923 London, 16; 1924 Basle, 31; Zurich, 24; Stuttgart, 10; 1925 Paris 1, 11; The Hague, 15; 1930 Amsterdam, 75; 1946-7 Liège etc, 126; 1947 Geneva, 127; Paris 1, 127; 1948 Bergen, Oslo, 38; 1949-50 New York, Chicago, 92; 1954 Zurich, 34; 1954-5 Bern, 47; 1955 Antwerp 1, 267; 1955-6 Liverpool etc, 56; 1960-1 Montreal etc, 36
PROVENANCE Mrs J. van Gogh-Bonger, Amsterdam; V. W. van Gogh, Laren; Amsterdam, Rijksmuseum Vincent van Gogh [Vincent van Gogh Foundation, inv nr F 605]

F 606 [H 590] TWO CRABS [PROBABLY ONE CRAB, SEEN FROM ABOVE AND BELOW]
EXHIBITIONS 1892 The Hague, 2; 1925 Paris 1, 10; 1960 Paris, 49b
PROVENANCE Mrs J. van Gogh-Bonger, Amsterdam; W. C. Robinson, Bournemouth; Sale W. C. Robinson, Amsterdam [F. Muller] 13 November 1906, nr 33; Bernheim jeune Art Gallery, Paris; Marquis de Ganay, Paris [R 1925]; Present owner unknown

F 607 [H 597] A PAIR OF WOODEN SHOES
EXHIBITIONS 1928 Berlin, 60; Vienna, 35 [repr]; Frankfort, 37; 1933 Amsterdam 2, 115; Rotterdam 1, 35; 1946-7 Liège etc, 127; 1947 Geneva, 128; Paris 1, 128; 1951 Lyons etc, 33; 1954 Zurich, 49; 1954-5 Bern, 48; 1955 Antwerp 1, 269; 1955-6 Liverpool etc, 57; 1960-1 Montreal etc, 44; 1963 Utica, New York, 431; 1968-9 London, 143
PROVENANCE Mrs J. van Gogh-Bonger, Amsterdam; V. W. van Gogh, Laren; Amsterdam, Rijksmuseum Vincent van Gogh [Vincent van Gogh Foundation, inv nr F 607]

SAINT REMY PERIOD

F 608 [H 606] IRISES
EXHIBITIONS 1889 Paris, 273; 1901 Paris, 31; 1905 Paris, 32; 1925 Paris 3, 79; 1927 Paris; 1929 New York, 95; 1931 Paris, 44; 1935 Brussels, 95; 1937 Paris, 41; 1940 Detroit, 47; 1942 Baltimore, Worcester, 19; 1943 New York 2, 44; 1948 New York 1, 11; 1949 New York 1, 5; 1955 New York 3, 48; 1956 New Haven, 97
PROVENANCE Maison [Julien] Tanguy Art Gallery, Paris [in commission of Theo van Gogh]; Octave Mirbeau, Paris [acquired 1892; 1905]; Mr Pellerin, Paris; Bernheim jeune Art Gallery, Paris; Mrs Jacques Doucet, Neuilly-sur-Seine [1925; 1937]; Jacques Seligmann Art Gallery, New York [1943]; New York, Private collection [R 1970]

F 609 [H 607] A CORNER IN THE GARDEN OF SAINT PAUL'S HOSPITAL: IVY
EXHIBITIONS 1890 Brussels, Van Gogh nr 3; 1893 Copenhagen, 192; 1914 Berlin, 116
PROVENANCE Mrs J. van Gogh-Bonger, Amsterdam; F. Bendix, Copenhagen [1893]; Paul Cassirer Art Gallery, Berlin [before 1914]; Mrs F. Oppenheim, Berlin; Kurt Oppenheim, Blonay; Baron de Rothschild, Paris; Present owner unknown

F 610 [H 608] DEATH'S-HEAD MOTH
EXHIBITIONS 1905 Amsterdam, 198; 1930 Amsterdam, 76; 1937 Paris, 56; 1948 Bergen, Oslo, 41; 1951 Lyons etc, 57; 1953-4 Saint Louis etc, 134; 1954 Zurich, 54; 1954-5 Bern, 52; 1955 Antwerp 1, 307; 1955-6 Liverpool etc, 60; 1957 Marseilles, 68; 1958-9 San Francisco etc, 61; 1959-60 Utrecht, 48; 1967 Wolfsburg, 58; 1968-9 London, 153
PROVENANCE Mrs J. van Gogh-Bonger, Amsterdam; V. W. van Gogh, Laren; Amsterdam, Rijksmuseum Vincent van Gogh [Vincent van Gogh Foundation, inv nr F 610]

F 611 [H 609] MOUNTAINOUS LANDSCAPE BEHIND SAINT PAUL'S HOSPITAL
EXHIBITIONS 1892 The Hague, cat nr 24, 42 or 43; 1893 Copenhagen, 191
PROVENANCE Mrs J. van Gogh-Bonger, Amsterdam; J. Rohde, Copenhagen [acquired 1892]; H. C. Christensen, Copenhagen [1893]; Copenhagen, Statens Museum for Konst [acquired 1905; since 1915 on loan to Ny Carlsberg Glyptotek, Copenhagen, cat 1961, nr 945]

F 612 [H 612] THE STARRY NIGHT
EXHIBITIONS 1905 Amsterdam, 199; 1906 Rotterdam, 47; 1927-8 Rotterdam, 33; 1944 New York 2, 29; 1948 Cleveland, 19; 1949-50 New York, Chicago, 111A; 1950-1 Philadelphia, 90; 1952-3 New York, 4; 1954 Chicago, p 54; 1955 Paris 2, 34
PROVENANCE Mrs J. van Gogh-Bonger, Amsterdam [1905]; Miss G. P. van Stolk, Rotterdam [1906; 1928; on loan to Museum Boymans, Rotterdam until May 1924]; Paul Rosenberg Art Gallery, Paris; Miss L. P. Bliss, New York; New York, Museum of Modern Art [acquired 1941 through the L. P. Bliss bequest], inv nr 472.41, cat 1948, nr 280

F 613 [H 616] THE CYPRESSES
EXHIBITIONS 1908 Paris 2, 4; 1912 Cologne, 108 [reproduced]; 1924 Basle, 60 [reproduced]; 1927 Berlin 2, 119 [reproduced]; Paris; 1929 New York, 85; 1948 Cleveland, 18; 1949-50 New York, Chicago, 112
PROVENANCE M. Fabre, Paris [1908]; Druet Art Gallery, Paris; Sale Paris [Drouot] 16 May 1908, nr 25 [repr]; F. Meyer-Fierz, Zurich [acquired May 1908; 1924]; Thannhauser Art Gallery, New York [1929]; New York, Metropolitan Museum of Art [acquired 1949; Rogers Fund], inv nr 49.30, cat European paintings 1954, p 53

F 614 [H 816] THE CYPRESSES
Left out by Faille in his manuscript for the present edition; See REJECTED WORKS

F 615 [H 611] WHEATFIELD WITH CYPRESSES
EXHIBITIONS 1901 Paris, 32; 1926 London 2, p 7; 1947-8 London etc, 72; 1948 London 1, 34; 1955 Paris 3, 67
PROVENANCE Octave Mirbeau, Paris [R 1901]; Paul Rosenberg Art Gallery, Paris; Bernheim jeune Art Gallery, Paris; G. Jebsen, Oslo; Paul Rosenberg Art Gallery, Paris; Percy Moore Turner, London; London, The Tate Gallery [acquired 1923; Courtauld Fund], cat The Courtauld collection 1954, nr 87; cat Tate Gallery 1959, nr 3861

F 616 THE CYPRESSES
Left out by Faille in his manuscript for the present edition; See REJECTED WORKS

F 617 [H 614] THE CORNFIELD BEHIND SAINT PAUL'S HOSPITAL WITH A REAPER
EXHIBITIONS 1892 The Hague, 32 or 41 [?]; 1901 Paris, 48; 1905 Paris, 42; 1912 Cologne, 46; 1913 The Hague, 127; 1914 Antwerp, 40; 1927 Basle etc, 132; 1928 Düsseldorf, 197; Karlsruhe, 132; 1929 Berlin 1, 123; Hamburg, 87; 1930 Amsterdam, 240; 1935-6 New York etc, 48; 1946-7 Liège etc, 142; 1947 Paris 1, 143; Geneva, 143; Basle, 84; 1952 Milan, 115; 1956 Eindhoven, 42; Munich, 143; 1958 Vienna, 96; Tokyo, Kyoto, 116; 1960-1 Montreal etc, 60; 1962 Warsaw, 79; 1963 Tel Aviv, Haifa, 89
PROVENANCE Amédée Schuffenecker, Meudon [1905; 1912]; Otterlo, Rijksmuseum Kröller-Müller, inv nr 308-12, cat van Gogh 1970, nr 244

F 618 [H 613] THE WHEATFIELD BEHIND SAINT PAUL'S HOSPITAL AT THE FALL OF THE DAY WITH A REAPER
EXHIBITIONS 1926 Venice, 25; 1930 Amsterdam, 77; 1932 Manchester, 38; 1945 Amsterdam, without cat nr; 1946 Stockholm etc, 79; 1947-8 London etc, 70; 1948 Bergen, Oslo, 43; 1951 Lyons etc, 67; 1953 The Hague, 155; Otterlo, Amsterdam, 142; 1953-4 Saint Louis etc, 133; 1954 Zurich, 73; 1955 Antwerp 1, 296; Palm Beach etc, 29; 1955-6 Liverpool etc, 61; 1957 Marseilles, 63; 1958-9 San Francisco etc, 77; 1959 Aix-en-Provence, 38; 1959-60 Utrecht, 49; 1961-2 Baltimore etc, 54; 1963 Humlebaek, 41; 1964 Washington, New York, 41; 1965 Charleroi, Ghent, 28; 1965-6 Stockholm, Göteborg, 42; 1967 Wolfsburg, 60; 1968-9 London, 158
PROVENANCE Mrs J. van Gogh-Bonger, Amsterdam [on loan to Rijksmuseum, Amsterdam since 1909, cat 1911, 1920, nr 984f]; V. W. van Gogh, Laren; Amsterdam, Rijksmuseum Vincent van Gogh [Vincent van Gogh Foundation, inv nr F 618]

F 619 [H 632] THE WHEATFIELD BEHIND SAINT PAUL'S HOSPITAL WITH A REAPER
EXHIBITIONS 1957 Essen, 338; 1960 Paris, 59
PROVENANCE Karl Osthaus, Hagen [before 1904]; Hagen, Museum Folkwang; Essen, Museum Folkwang [acquired 1922], inv nr G 62, cat 1961, nr 62
EDITORS' COMMENT See F 619 in cat

F 620 [H 617] THE CYPRESSES
EXHIBITIONS 1927 Basle etc, 131; 1928 Düsseldorf, 196 [repr]; Karlsruhe, 131; 1929 Berlin 1, 122; Hamburg, 86; 1930 Amsterdam, 237; 1935-6 New York etc, 49; 1946-7 Liège etc, 143; 1947 Paris 1, 144; Geneva, 144; Basle, 85; 1947-8 London etc, 69; 1949-50 New York, Chicago, 113; 1953 The Hague, 154; Otterlo, Amsterdam, 159; 1953-4 Saint Louis etc, 132; 1956 Munich, 142; 1957 Essen, 356; 1958 Vienna, 94; Tokyo, Kyoto, 119; 1959 Aix-en-Provence, 39; 1963 Amsterdam, 107
PROVENANCE Albert Aurier, Paris; Heirs of A. Aurier, Châteauroux [sold 1914]; Otterlo, Rijksmuseum Kröller-Müller, inv nr 307-00, cat van Gogh 1970, nr 233

F 621 [H 618] THE CYPRESSES
EXHIBITIONS 1905 Amsterdam, 209; Utrecht, 54; 1906 Rotterdam, 52; 1925 The Hague, 41; 1926 London 3, 8 [repr]; 1930 Amsterdam, 78; 1935-6 New York etc, 50; 1939 San Francisco, 176; 1939-40 San Francisco, 125; 1940 New York 3, 12; 1942 Baltimore, Worcester, 22; 1943 New York 2, 45; 1943-4 Indianapolis etc, 9; 1944 Montreal, 130; 1948 Bergen, Oslo, 42; 1949-50 New York, Chicago, 113; 1951 Lyons etc, 64; 1955 New York 2, 47; Antwerp 1, 297; 1955-6 Liverpool etc, 62; 1958-9 San Francisco etc, 76; 1961-2 Baltimore etc, 55; 1963 Humlebaek, 42; 1964 Washington, New York, 42; 1965 Charleroi, Ghent, 29; 1965-6 Stockholm, Göteborg, 43; 1967 Wolfsburg, 61; 1968-9 London, 169
PROVENANCE Mrs J. van Gogh-Bonger, Amsterdam; V. W. van Gogh, Laren; Amsterdam, Rijksmuseum Vincent van Gogh [Vincent van Gogh Foundation, inv nr F 621]

F 622 [H 619] THE ALPILLES WITH DARK HUT
EXHIBITIONS 1908 Paris 2, 3; 1924 Prague; 1927 Berlin 2, 117 [repr]; 1940 San Francisco 2, 272; 1942 Baltimore, Worcester, 18; 1948 Cleveland, 20; 1963 Utica, New York, 424
PROVENANCE E. Boch, Monthyon, France [acquired in exchange with Vincent and still owned in 1908]; Druet Art Gallery, Paris; W. Halvorsen, Paris [acquired 1918]; New York, J.K. Thannhauser, courtesy of Thannhauser Foundation [R 1970; ok loan to Guggenheim Museum, New York]

F 623 [H 620] WOODEN SHEDS
EXHIBITIONS 1921 New York, 125 [repr]; 1925 Paris 1, 40; 1926 Paris, 2951
PROVENANCE E. Boch, La Louvière, Belgium; Marius de Zayas, New York; Sale Marius de Zayas, New York [Anderson] 23-24 March 1923, nr 84; Georges Bernheim Art Gallery, Paris [R 1926]; Georges Renand, Paris; Present owner unknown

F 624 [H 621] HALF FIGURE OF AN ANGEL
EXHIBITIONS 1904 Rotterdam, 69; 1912 Cologne, 81 [reproduced]; 1930 Amsterdam, 79; 1955 New York 2, 59; 1956 Munich, 147

PROVENANCE Oldenzeel Art Gallery, Rotterdam; J. J. Isaäcson, The Hague; H. Tutein Nolthenius, Delft [R 1904; 1930]; J. Tutein Nolthenius, Center Moriches; W. Weinberg, Scarsdale [R 1955]; Sale Weinberg, London [Sotheby] 10 July 1957, nr 48; Knoedler Art Gallery, London; Present owner unknown

F 625 [H 622] LANDSCAPE WITH PLOWMAN
EXHIBITIONS 1924 Basle, 56; Zurich, 50; 1928 Berlin, 61 [repr]; 1934 San Francisco, 162; 1940 San Francisco 1, 12
PROVENANCE F. Meyer-Fierz, Zurich; Sale Meyer, Amsterdam [F. Muller] 13 July 1926, XII [repr]; Huinck Art Gallery, Utrecht; Georges Bernheim Art Gallery, Paris; Feilchenfeldt Art Gallery, Zurich; Knoedler Art Gallery, Paris; Burlingame, California, W. W. Crocker [1934; on loan 1967-69 to San Francisco Museum]; Sale New York [Parke-Bernet] 25 February 1970, nr 13; Present owner unknown

F 625a [H 630] RISING MOON: HAYCOCKS
Left out by Faille in his manuscript for the present edition; See REJECTED WORKS

F 626 [H 624] SELF PORTRAIT
EXHIBITIONS 1904 Rotterdam, 70; 1906 Rotterdam, 46; 1912 Cologne, 86 [repr]; 1927-8 Rotterdam, 34 [repr]; 1929 London 1, 466; 1930 Amsterdam, 80; 1945 Basle, 12; 1948 New York 1, 14; 1949-50 New York, Chicago, 119; 1955 New York 3, 49; 1960-1 London, 32
PROVENANCE J. J. Isaacson, The Hague; H. Tutein Nolthenius, Delft [R 1904, 1930]; Private collection, Basle [from 1945 until 1946]; Knoedler Art Gallery, New York; New York, John Hay Whitney [R 1950, 1961]
EDITORS' COMMENT According to Faille, F 626 was exhibited in Amsterdam 1905, under nr 195. The owner of that painting, however, is identified in the exhib cat as Mrs J. van Gogh-Bonger, whereas F 626 was already in the Tutein Nolthenius Collection by 1904, precluding the possibility that F 626 is exhib cat nr 195

F 627 [H 748] SELF PORTRAIT
EXHIBITIONS 1905 Paris, 20; 1925 Paris 1, 50; 1937 Paris, 42; 1953 The Hague, 178; Otterlo, Amsterdam, 140; 1954-5 Paris, 42
PROVENANCE Paul Ferd. Gachet, Auvers-sur-Oise [1890 until 1909]; Paul Gachet, Auvers; Paris, Musée national du Louvre [acquired 1949; gift of Paul and Marguérite Gachet], inv nr RF 1949-17, cat Impressionistes 1959, nr 156

F 628 HARVEST
Left out by Faille in his manuscript for the present edition; See REJECTED WORKS

F 629 [H 623] PORTRAIT OF TRABU, AN ATTENDANT OF SAINT PAUL'S HOSPITAL
EXHIBITIONS 1892 The Hague, 34; 1893 Copenhagen, 176; 1896 Rotterdam, 15; 1905 Amsterdam, 192; Utrecht, 49; 1906 Rotterdam, 44; 1907 Rotterdam, 14; 1908 Paris 2, 15; 1912 Cologne, 101 [repr]; 1924 Basle, 55; Zurich, 52; 1930 Amsterdam, 82; 1936 London 4, 107; 1947 Basle, 89; 1953 The Hague, 157; Otterlo, Amsterdam, 144; 1955 Winterthur 1, 103; 1960 Paris, 57
PROVENANCE Mrs J. van Gogh-Bonger [R 1905, 1906]; Bernheim jeune Art Gallery, Paris [R 1907]; E. Druet Art Gallery, Paris; O. Miethke Art Gallery, Vienna; W. von Heymel, Munich [1908]; Solothurn, Mrs G. Dübi-Müller [acquired April 1908 and R 1960]

F 630 [H 625] PIETÀ [after Delacroix]
EXHIBITIONS 1905 Amsterdam, 172; Utrecht, 46; 1907 Berlin, 67; 1910-1 London, 74; 1912 Cologne, 79; 1920 Venice; 1924 Zurich, 59; Basle, 64; Stuttgart, 29; 1925 Paris 1, 48; The Hague, 35; Potsdam, 43; 1926 London 3, 15 [repr]; 1927 Paris; 1928 Munich, 27; 1929 New York, 78; 1930 Amsterdam, 83; 1937 Paris, 7; 1945 Amsterdam, without cat nr; 1946 Stockholm etc, 83; 1946-7 Liège etc, 146; 1947 Paris 1, 149; Geneva, 149; 1947-8 London etc, 90; 1948 Bergen, Oslo, 46; 1949-50 New York, Chicago, 118; 1951 Lyons etc, 65; 1953 The Hague, 187; Otterlo, Amsterdam, 151; 1953-4 Saint Louis etc, 172; 1954 Zurich, 65; 1954-5 Bern, 56; 1955 Antwerp 1, 313; 1955-6 Liverpool etc, 79; 1957 Marseilles, 72; 1958-9 San Francisco etc, 69; 1959 Aix-en-Provence, 43; 1960-1 Montreal etc, 71; 1961-2 Baltimore etc, 63; 1963 Humlebaek, 48; 1964 Washington, New York, 48; 1965 Stockholm, Göteborg, 47; 1967 Wolfsburg, 67; 1968-9 London, 165
PROVENANCE Mrs J. van Gogh-Bonger, Amsterdam; V. W. van Gogh, Laren; Amsterdam, Rijksmuseum Vincent van Gogh [Vincent van Gogh Foundation, inv nr F 630]

F 631 [H 637] PORTRAIT OF THE WIFE OF THE ATTENDANT TRABU
EXHIBITIONS 1926 Munich, 2068; London 3, 18; 1927 Berlin 2, 113 [repr]; 1928 Berlin, 63; Frankfort, 39
PROVENANCE Mrs J. van Gogh-Bonger, Amsterdam; V. W. van Gogh, Laren; Thannhauser Art Gallery, Berlin; Otto Krebs, Holzdorf [R 1928]; Present owner unknown

F 632 [H 686] THE PLOUGH AND THE HARROW [after Millet]
EXHIBITIONS 1905 Amsterdam, 178; 1912 Cologne, 71; 1920 New York, 60; 1921 New York, 124 [repr]; 1923 London, 29; 1924 Basle, 63; Zurich, 62; Stuttgart, 32; 1925 Paris 1, 44; The Hague, 13; 1926 Munich, 2077; 1928 Berlin, 64; Frankfort, 40; Vienna, 37; 1930 Amsterdam, 84; 1946 Stockholm etc, 88; 1948 Bergen, Oslo, 57; 1949-50 New York, Chicago, 128; 1951 Lyons etc, 70; 1953 The Hague, 166; Otterlo, Amsterdam, 161; 1953-4 Saint Louis etc, 140; 1954 Zurich, 63; 1954-5 Bern, 65; 1955 Antwerp 1, 324; 1955-6 Liverpool etc, 73; 1958-9 San Francisco etc, 73; 1963 Humlebaek, 51; 1964 Washington, New York, 51; 1967 Wolfsburg, 72; 1968-9 London, 177
PROVENANCE Mrs J. van Gogh-Bonger, Amsterdam; V. W. van Gogh, Laren; Amsterdam, Rijksmuseum Vincent van Gogh [Vincent van Gogh Foundation, inv nr F 632]

F 633 [H 698] THE GOOD SAMARITAN [after Delacroix]
EXHIBITIONS 1901 Paris, 51; 1913 The Hague, 145; 1914 Antwerp, 42; 1927 Basle etc, 135; 1928 Düsseldorf, 200 [repr]; Karlsruhe, 135; 1929 Berlin 1, 133; Hamburg, 90; 1930 Amsterdam, 239; 1935-6 New York etc, 54; 1945 The Hague, 38; 1946-7 Liège etc, 162; 1947 Paris 1, 163; Geneva, 163; Basle, 101; 1947-8 London etc, 85; 1950-1 Paris, 20; 1952 Milan, 119; 1953 The Hague, 174; Otterlo, Amsterdam, 166; 1953-4 Saint Louis etc, 149; 1956 Munich, 155; 1957 Essen, 361; 1958 Vienna, 105; Tokyo, Kyoto, 126; 1959 São Paulo, p 241, 11; 1962 Warsaw, 84; 1963 Tel Aviv, Haifa, 94; 1966 Belgrade, 81
PROVENANCE Emile Schuffenecker, Paris [R 1901]; Prince of Wagram, Paris; Druet Art Gallery, Paris; Barbazanges Art Gallery, Paris; Mr Leonard, Paris [R 1912]; Otterlo, Rijksmuseum Kröller-Müller, inv nr 311-12, cat van Gogh 1970, nr 250

F 634 [H 646] SHEEP SHEARERS [after Millet]
EXHIBITIONS 1905 Amsterdam, 182; 1920 Venice; 1925 The Hague, 55; 1928 Munich, 28 [repr]; 1930 Amsterdam, 85; 1945 Amsterdam, without cat nr; 1946-7 Liège etc, 153; 1947 Geneva, 153; Paris 1, 153; 1948 Bergen, Oslo, 50; 1949-50 New York, Chicago, 115; 1954 Zurich, 70; 1954-5 Bern, 53; 1955 Antwerp 1, 315; 1955-6 Liverpool etc, 64; 1957 Marseilles, 73; 1958-9 San Francisco etc, 71; 1959-60 Utrecht, 55; 1961-2 Baltimore etc, 65
PROVENANCE Mrs J. van Gogh-Bonger, Amsterdam; V. W. van Gogh, Laren; Amsterdam, Rijksmuseum Vincent van Gogh [Vincent van Gogh Foundation, inv nr F 634]

F 635 [H 644] QUARRY NEAR SAINT RÉMY
EXHIBITIONS 1914 Berlin, 104; 1925 Vienna, 88; 1926 Paris, 2953; 1943 New York 2, 50; 1955 New York 2, 55
PROVENANCE Collection Rothermundt, Dresden; Thannhauser Art Gallery, Munich; Paul Cassirer Art Gallery, Berlin; Alfred Cassirer, Berlin [R 1914]; A. Gold Art Gallery Paris; Barbazanges-Hodebert Art Gallery, Paris [R 1925, 1926]; Max Kaganowitsch, Switzerland; Knoedler Art Gallery, New York; New York, Mrs Morton M. Palmer and George A. Forman [R 1955]

F 636 [H 755] FIELD WITH POPPIES
EXHIBITIONS 1898 The Hague, 10 [?] [repr]; 1904 Rotterdam, 71; 1905 Amsterdam, 232; 1910 Rotterdam, 24; 1935-6 New York etc, 53; 1939 Amsterdam 1, 14; 1947 Basle, 103; 1948 Venice; 1952 Milan, 121; 1953 The Hague, 188; Otterlo, Amsterdam, 184; 1958 Tokyo, Kyoto, 118; 1960 Paris, 68; 1962 Warsaw, 100; 1963 Tel Aviv, Haifa, 99
PROVENANCE Mrs J. van Gogh-Bonger, Amsterdam; Paul Cassirer Art Gallery, Berlin; Prince of Wagram, Paris; E. Druet Art Gallery, Paris [R 1909]; Barbazanges Art Gallery, Paris; B. Kröller, The Hague; Gemeentemuseum [on loan]; Durand-Ruel Art Gallery, New York; Edward Drummond, Toledo, USA; The Hague, Dienst 's Rijks verspreide Kunstvoorwerpen [acquired 1948; on loan to Gemeentemuseum, inv nr 3-X-1948, cat 1962, nr 137]
Provenance as given by cat Gemeentemuseum, The Hague 1962, nr 137
EXHIBITIONS 1892 The Hague, 39; 1904 Brussels
PROVENANCE Mrs Fortanier, Utrecht [R 1904; 1910]; Prince of Wagram, Paris; E. Druet Art Gallery, Paris; Barbazanges Art Gallery, Paris; Kröller-Müller Foundation, The Hague [from 1935 until 1937]; B. Kröller, The Hague; Huinck and Scherjon Art Gallery, Amsterdam; The Hague, Dienst voor 's Rijks verspreide kunstvoorwerpen [acquired 1948; on loan to the Gemeentemuseum, The Hague, inv nr 3-X-1948, cat 1962, nr 137]
EDITORS' COMMENT It is not possible to take a decision in the question of the differences in provenance as given by Faille and The Hague Museum. It seems likely that Faille has mixed up the provenance of F 636 with that of F 581

F 637 [H 640] THE MULBERRY TREE
EXHIBITIONS 1890 Paris, 837; 1901 Paris, 46; 1927 Paris
PROVENANCE Mrs C. Pissarro, Paris [R 1901]; A. Vollard Art Gallery, Paris; Alphonse Kann, Saint Germain-en-Laye; Los Angeles, California, Mr and Mrs Norton Simon [R 1970]
EDITORS' COMMENT Faille mentions this painting as having figured under nr 570 at the exhibition in Zurich in 1917. He refers to nr 570 likewise for F 637, Mulberry tree. The catalogue of the Zurich exhibition includes however not more than 362 items, of which catalogue nrs 105-112a are works of Vincent. F 768 nor F 637 can be identified

F 638 [H 643] TWO POPLARS ON A ROAD THROUGH THE HILLS
EXHIBITIONS 1905 Amsterdam, 117; 1912 Cologne, 40; 1914 Berlin, 119; 1927 Berlin 2, 108 [repr]; 1928 Berlin, 65; 1930 Amsterdam, 86; 1942 Baltimore, Worcester, 24; 1948 Cleveland, 24; 1955 New York 2, 54
PROVENANCE Mrs J. van Gogh-Bonger, Amsterdam; Flechtheim Art Gallery, Düsseldorf [R 1912]; Max Siller, Barmen [R 1914]; Paul Cassirer Art Gallery, Berlin; Thannhauser Art Gallery, Munich; J. W. Böhler, Lucerne [R 1930]; Harry G. Sperling, New York [R 1942]; Sam Salz, New York; Leonard C. Hanna Jr, Cleveland [R 1948]; Cleveland, The Cleveland Museum of Art [acquired 1958; Leonard C. Hanna Bequest], inv nr 58.32, cat 1958 In memoriam L. C. Hanna Jr, nr 15

F 639 [H 817] TWO POPLARS ON A ROAD THROUGH THE HILLS
EXHIBITIONS 1927 Berlin 2, 115; Paris; 1932 Amsterdam 2, 22
PROVENANCE Otto Wacker Art Gallery, Berlin; Huinck and Scherjon Art Gallery, Amsterdam; Kurashiki, Japan, Museum of Fine Arts of Ohara

F 640 [H 642] THE PARK OF ST PAUL'S HOSPITAL
EXHIBITIONS 1905 Amsterdam, 207; 1920 New York, 66; 1924 Basle, 65; Zurich, 57; Stuttgart, 28; 1925 Paris 1, 36; The Hague, 26; 1926 Munich, 2071; 1927 Berlin 2, not in cat; 1929 Cleveland; 1936 Cleveland, not in cat; 1943 New York 2, 49; 1948 Cleveland, 23; 1950 Columbus, Ohio, 37; 1955 Yew York 2, 52; 1956 New Haven, 99; 1957 Los Angeles, 17; 1963 London 2, 71; 1967 Paris, 105
PROVENANCE Mrs J. van Gogh-Bonger, Amsterdam; V. W. van Gogh, Laren; Thannhauser Art Gallery, Paris; Ralph M. Coe, Cleveland [R 1943]; Sale R. M. Coe a o, New York [Parke-Bernet] 14 January 1959, nr 82; Private collection, New York; Wildenstein Art Gallery, New York [R 1961 and 1963]; Geneva, Private collection [acquired 1963]

F 641 [H 649] WHEAT FIELD WITH PEASANT BEARING A SHEAF
EXHIBITIONS 1921 Berlin; 1927 Berlin 2, 112 [repr]; 1940 New York 2, 363a; 1942 Baltimore, Worcester, 23; New York, 7; 1943 New York 2, 51
PROVENANCE Mrs J. van Gogh-Bonger, Amsterdam; Paul Cassirer Art Gallery, Berlin; Mrs Giuletta von Mendelssohn-Bartholdy, Grunewald/Berlin; Francesco and Eleonora von Mendelssohn, New York [R 1940 and 1943]; Thannhauser Art Gallery, New York; Indianapolis, Indianapolis Museum of Art [gift in memory of Daniel W. and Elizabeth C. Marmon], cat The Marmon Memorial collection 1948, pp 32-5

F 642 [H 647] THE GARDEN OF ST PAUL'S HOSPITAL
EXHIBITIONS 1924 Basle, 54; Zurich, 46; 1930 Amsterdam, 87
PROVENANCE A. Schuffenecker, Meudon; Josef Müller, Solothurn [R 1924 and 1930]; E. Bignou Art Gallery, New York; Thannhauser Art Gallery, New York; Ralph M. Coe, Cleveland; Alfred Wyler, New York [acquired 1952]; Switzerland, Private collection [R 1969]

F 643 [H 648] ST PAUL'S HOSPITAL
EXHIBITIONS 1908 Paris 2, 16; 1914 Berlin, 65; 1930 Amsterdam, 88; 1931 Frankfurt, 69
PROVENANCE A. Schuffenecker, Paris; E. Druet Art Gallery, Paris [R 1907]; J. Keller, Paris [R 1908 and 1910]; E. Druet Art Gallery, Paris [R 1910]; P. von Mendelssohn-Bartholdy, Berlin [acquired 1911]; P. Rosenberg Art Gallery New York; Los Angeles, California, Mr and Mrs Norton Simon [R 1964]

F 644 [H 654] THE MAN IS AT SEA [after Virginie Demont-Breton]
EXHIBITION 1905 Paris, 22
PROVENANCE P. F. Gachet, Auvers-sur-Oise [from 1890 until 1909]; Paul Gachet, Auvers-sur-Oise [R 1905]; Errol Flynn, Hollywood [R 1940?; 1964]; Sale London [Sotheby] 29 April 1964, nr 52 [not sold]; Present owner unknown

F 645 [H 727] LES PEIROULETS
EXHIBITIONS 1905 Amsterdam, 204; 1955 Antwerp 1, 303; 1957 Stockholm, 118; 1959 Aix-en-Provence, 40
PROVENANCE Mrs J. van Gogh-Bonger, Amsterdam; V. W. van Gogh, Laren; Amsterdam, Rijksmuseum Vincent van Gogh [Vincent van Gogh Foundation, inv nr F 645]

F 646 [H 645] THE HOSPITAL IN ARLES
EXHIBITIONS 1905 Amsterdam, 134; 1910 Berlin 1, 47; 1917 Zurich 2, 107 [repr]; 1923 Prague, 188 [repr]; 1924 London 2; 1925 Paris 1, 24; Vienna, 76 [repr]; 1951 Lyons etc, 73; 1955 Winterthur 2, 74
PROVENANCE Mrs J. van Gogh, Amsterdam [R 1905]; Paul Cassirer Art Gallery, Berlin; Prince of Wagram, Paris; Alphonse Kann, Saint Germain-en-Laye [R 1917]; Winkel and Magnussen Art Gallery, Copenhagen; Barbazanges-Hodebert Art Gallery, Paris [R 1923 and 1925]; Winterthur,

Oscar Reinhart [R 1955]
EDITORS' COMMENT See F 646 in cat

F 647 [H 655] NIGHT: THE WATCH [after Millet]
EXHIBITIONS 1905 Amsterdam, 176; Utrecht, 47; 1914 Berlin, 111; 1925 The Hague, 1; 1930 Amsterdam, 89; 1932 Manchester, 41; 1937 Paris, 10; 1939 San Francisco, 177; 1940 New York 3, 6; 1942 Baltimore, Worcester, 26; 1943 New York 2, 52; 1943-4 Indianapolis etc, 10; 1944 Montreal 134; 1947-8 London etc, 76; 1948 Bergen, Oslo, 54; 1951 Lyons etc, 69; 1953 The Hague, 165; Otterlo, Amsterdam, 152; 1953-4 Saint Louis etc, 138; 1954-5 Bern, 62; 1955 Antwerp 1, 322; 1955-6 Liverpool etc, 71; 1957 Marseilles, 75; 1960-1 Montreal etc, 72; 1961-2 Baltimore etc, 72; 1963 Humlebaek, 52; 1964 Washington, New York, 52; 1965 Charleroi, Ghent, 36; 1965-6 Stockholm, Göteborg, 50; 1967 Wolfsburg, 71; 1968-9 London, 174
PROVENANCE Mrs J. van Gogh-Bonger, Amsterdam; V.W. van Gogh, Laren; Amsterdam, Rijksmuseum Vincent van Gogh [Vincent van Gogh Foundation, inv nr F 647]

F 648 [H 658] TWO PEASANTS DIGGING [after a reproduction of a Millet etching: Delteil nr 13]
EXHIBITIONS 1905 Amsterdam, 179; 1914 Berlin, 108; 1915 Amsterdam, 13; 1920 New York, 55; 1923 London, 30; 1924 Basle, 61; Zurich, 60; Stuttgart, 30; 1925 Paris 1, 45; The Hague, 14; 1926 Munich, 2090; 1930 Amsterdam, 90; 1948 Bergen, Oslo, 53; 1954 Zurich, 67; 1954-5 Bern, 63; 1955 Antwerp 1, 321; 1961-2 Baltimore etc, 71
PROVENANCE Mrs J. van Gogh-Bonger, Amsterdam; V.W. van Gogh, Laren; Amsterdam, Stedelijk Museum [acquired 21 January 1927], inv nr A 411

F 649 [H 659] EVENING: THE END OF THE DAY [after Millet]
EXHIBITIONS 1914 Berlin, 118; 1942 Baltimore, Worcester 25; 1943 New York 2, 53; 1951 Houston, 17; 1955 New York 2, 61; 1960 Dayton; 1962 Provincetown, Ottawa, without cat nr
PROVENANCE Mrs J. van Gogh-Bonger, Amsterdam [R 1912]; Bernheim jeune Art Gallery, Paris; P. Vallotton Art Gallery, Lausanne; P. Cassirer Art Gallery, Berlin; Chr. Tetzen-Lund, Juleback; Barbazanges Art Gallery, Paris [R 1924]; Huinck Art Gallery, Utrecht; Mrs Ch. E. van Beuningen-Fentener van Vlissingen, Utrecht [R 1935; on loan to Centraal Museum, Utrecht]; Van Wisselingh Art Gallery, Amsterdam; Bernheim jeune Art Gallery, Paris [R 1935]; P. Matisse Art Gallery, New York [from 1949 until 1955]; New York, Walter P. Chrysler Jr [R 1955 and 1962]

F 650 [H 656] RAIN EFFECT: BEHIND THE HOSPITAL
EXHIBITIONS 1903 Munich, 231; 1905 Amsterdam, 209a; 1932 Paris, 55; 1935 Brussels, 102; 1935-6 New York etc, 52; 1937 Paris, 43; 1939 Belgrade, 61; 1939-40 Buenos Aires etc, 70; 1941 Chicago, 78; 1942 New York, 8; 1948 Cleveland, 28; 1949 Philadelphia; 1950 Philadelphia, 99; 1962 San Francisco, 24
PROVENANCE Mrs J. van Gogh-Bonger, Amsterdam [until 1903]; H. von Tschudi, Berlin-Munich [from 1903 until 1911]; Mrs H. von Tschudi, Munich [on loan to the Neue Staatsgalerie, Munich]; Wildenstein Art Gallery, Paris; P. Rosenberg Art Gallery, Paris [R 1935 and 1948]; Philadelphia, Henry P. McIlhenny [R 1950 and 1962]

F 651 [H 657] THE WALK: FALLING LEAVES
EXHIBITIONS 1920 New York, 42 [repr]; 1924 Basle, 47; Zurich, 56; Stuttgart, 27; 1925 Paris 1, 37; The Hague, 8; 1926 Munich, 2066; 1930 Amsterdam, 91; 1945 Amsterdam, without cat nr; 1946 Stockholm etc, 86; 1948 Bergen, Oslo, 55; 1951 Lyons etc, 59; 1953 The Hague, 162; Otterlo, Amsterdam, 156; 1954 Zurich, 58; 1955 Antwerp 1, 305; Palm Beach etc, 27; 1955-6 Liverpool etc, 72; 1957 Marseilles, 66; 1958-9 San Francisco etc, 67; 1959-60 Utrecht, 54; 1961-2 Baltimore etc, 59; 1967 Wolfsburg, 64; 1968-9 London, 175
PROVENANCE Mrs J. van Gogh-Bonger, Amsterdam; V.W. van Gogh, Laren; Amsterdam, Rijksmuseum Vincent van Gogh [Vincent van Gogh Foundation, inv nr F 651]

F 652 [H 573] FIR WOODS AT THE FALL OF DAY
EXHIBITIONS 1910 Berlin 1; 1912 Cologne, 36; 1913 The Hague, 136; 1914 Antwerp, 39; 1927 Basle etc, 97; 1928 Düsseldorf, 162 [repr]; Karlsruhe, 97; 1929 Berlin 1, 127; Hamburg, 54; 1930 Amsterdam, 219; 1935-6 New York etc, 51; 1946-7 Liège etc, 157; 1947 Paris 1, 158; Geneva, 158; 1949-50 New York, Chicago, 122; 1952 Milan 111; 1956 Eindhoven, 43; Munich, 148; 1958 Vienna, 99; Tokyo, Kyoto, 120; 1959 Aix-en-Provence, 46
PROVENANCE Amédée Schuffenecker, Meudon; Otterlo, Rijksmuseum Kröller-Müller, inv nr 276-12, cat van Gogh 1970, nr 240

F 653 [H 666] SAINT PAUL'S HOSPITAL
EXHIBITIONS 1914 Berlin, 58; 1928 Berlin, 66; 1937 Paris, 44; 1950 Paris 2, 50; 1956 Munich, 148a
PROVENANCE Joseph Peyron, Saint Rémy; Mrs Marie Gasquet [R 1891; given by the son of Dr Joseph Peyron to Miss Marie Girard, later on Marie Gasquet]; Bernheim jeune Art Gallery, Paris; P. Cassirer Art Gallery, Berlin; F. Kallmann, Berlin; E. Bignou Art Gallery, Paris; Alex Reid and Lefevre Art Gallery, London; Switzerland, Private collection [R 1937; until 1966 loan to the Kunstmuseum, Bern]

F 654 [H 664] OLIVE PICKING
EXHIBITIONS 1905 Amsterdam, 203; Utrecht, 52; 1906 Rotterdam, 49; 1912 Cologne, 95; 1924 Stuttgart, 39; 1926 Munich, 2093
PROVENANCE Mrs J. van Gogh-Bonger, Amsterdam [R 1905]; A. Vollard Art Gallery, Paris; Alfred Wolff, Munich [R 1912 and 1924]; New York, Metropolitan Museum of Art [acquired 1956; with funds provided by Mr and Mrs Richard J. Bernhard, New York], Bulletin April 1956, pp 198-204

F 655 [H 665] OLIVE PICKING
EXHIBITIONS 1948 Cleveland, 27; New York 2, 68; 1955 New York 2, 60; 1966 New York 1, 12
PROVENANCE Bernard Goudchaux, Paris; Dikran Khan Kelekian, Paris; Sale D.K.K., New York [American Art Association] 30-1 January 1922, nr 157 [reproduced]; Wildenstein Art Gallery, New York [R 1948]; Mr and Mrs Ira Haupt, New York [R 1955]; USA, Enid A. Haupt [R 1966]

F 656 [H 661] OLIVE PICKING
EXHIBITIONS 1912 Cologne, 96; 1914 Dresden, 52 [repr]; 1930 Paris, 30; New York 2, 8; 1931 Wilmington, Delaware, without cat nr; 1934 New York 2, 57; 1946 Washington, p 78;
PROVENANCE Mrs J. van Gogh-Bonger, Amsterdam; Julius Stern, Berlin [R 1912]; Sale J. Stern, Berlin [Cassirer] 22 May 1916, nr 27 [repr]; Fritz A. Moll, Brieg near Breslau [acquired 1916]; Alex Reid and Lefevre Art Gallery, London; Knoedler Art Gallery, New York [R 1930]; Chester Dale, New York; Washington, National Gallery of Art, inv nr 1816, cat Chester Dale collection 1965, p 127

F 657 [H 667] THE ROAD MENDERS AT BOULEVARD VICTOR HUGO IN SAINT RÉMY
EXHIBITIONS 1901 Paris, 63; 1908 Paris 2, 12; 1929 Cambridge, USA, 96; New York, 86; 1936 London 4, 108; 1948 Cleveland, 25; 1949-50 New York, Chicago, 123; 1958 Cleveland, 53
PROVENANCE J. Leclercq, Paris; G. Fayet, Igny [R 1908 and 1925]; P. Rosenberg Art Gallery, Paris; Gilbert E. Fuller, Boston [R 1929]; Cleveland, The Cleveland Museum of Art [acquired 1947; gift of Hanna Fund], inv nr 47.209, cat In memoriam L.C. Hanna 1958, nr 53

F 658 [H 668] THE ROAD MENDERS
EXHIBITIONS 1896 Rotterdam, 21; 1905 Berlin, 27; Amsterdam, 190; 1933 Chicago, 381; 1942 Baltimore, Worcester, 28; 1943 New York 2, 54; 1948 Cleveland, 26; New York 1, 13
PROVENANCE Mrs J. van Gogh-Bonger, Amsterdam; P. Cassirer Art Gallery, Berlin [R 1905]; H. von Tschudi, Munich [R 1918; on loan to the Neue Staatsgalerie, Munich] Wildenstein Art Gallery, Paris; Miss Dorothy Sturges, Providence; Mrs Elisabeth Hudson, Syracuse, USA [R 1942 and 1943]; Washington, The Phillips collection, cat 1952, p 43

F 659 [H p 557] THE GARDEN OF ST PAUL'S HOSPITAL IN AUTUMN
PROVENANCE Paul Ferd. Gachet, Auvers [1890-1909]; P. Gachet, Auvers; V.W. van Gogh, Laren [gift of P. Gachet, 1954]; Amsterdam, Rijksmuseum Vincent van Gogh [Vincent van Gogh Foundation, inv nr F 659]

F 660 [H 669] THE GARDEN OF ST PAUL'S HOSPITAL
EXHIBITIONS 1905 Amsterdam, 191; 1912 Cologne, 91; 1914 Berlin, 91; 1930 Amsterdam, 92; 1931 Frankfurt, 70; 1957 Essen, 341
PROVENANCE Mrs J. van Gogh-Bonger, Amsterdam; Karl Osthaus, Hagen [R 1912]; Hagen, Folkwang Museum [from 1905 until 1922]; Essen, Folkwang Museum [acquired 1922], inv nr G 64, cat 1961, nr 63

F 661 [H 670] LES PEIROULETS: THE RAVIN
EXHIBITIONS 1901 Paris, 37; 1904 Brussels; 1905 Paris, 37; 1908 Paris 2, 24; 1912 Cologne, 93; 1913 The Hague, 146; 1914 Antwerp, 32; 1927 Basle etc, 140 [repr]; 1928 Düsseldorf, 203; Karlsruhe, 138; 1929 Berlin 1, 128; Hamburg, 95; 1930 Amsterdam, 242; 1935-6 New York etc, 55; 1945 The Hague, 30; 1946-7 Liège etc, 158; 1947 Paris 1, 159; Geneva, 159; Basle, 94; 1947-8 London etc, 79; 1949-50 New York, Chicago, 125; 1952 Milan, 110; 1953 The Hague, 163; Otterlo, Amsterdam, 154; 1953-4 Saint Louis etc, 141; 1956 Eindhoven, 44; Munich, 149; 1957 Essen, 354; 1958 Vienna, 100; Tokyo, Kyoto, 113; 1960 Paris, 60; 1960-1 Montreal etc, 64; 1962 Warsaw, 75; 1963 Tel Aviv, Haifa, 85; 1966 Belgrade, 77
PROVENANCE A. Schuffenecker, Paris [R 1901 and 1908]; Barbazanges Art Gallery, Paris; Barnes, Merion [not in the Barnes Foundation but probably privately]; Prince of Wagram, Paris; Barbazanges Art Gallery, Paris; A. Schuffenecker, Paris; Count Kessler, Berlin; Druet Art Gallery, Paris [R 1912]; Otterlo, Rijksmuseum Kröller-Müller, inv nr 314-12, cat van Gogh 1970, nr 239

F 662 [H 671] LES PEIROULETS: THE RAVIN
EXHIBITIONS 1901 Paris, 58 [lent anonymously, probably Mrs J. van Gogh-Bonger]; 1926 London 3, 24; 1929 New York, 84; 1935-6 New York etc, addenda 55a [not in cat, only exhib in Boston]; 1939 Boston, 56; 1943 New York 2, 55
PROVENANCE Probably Mrs J. van Gogh-Bonger, Amsterdam; Prince of Wagram, Paris [before 1908]; Barbazanges Art Gallery, Paris; J.B. Stang, Oslo [R 1918]; Leicester Galleries, London [acquired 1926]; Thannhauser Art Gallery, New York; Keith McLeod, Boston [R 1929; 1943]; Boston, Museum of Fine Arts [acquired 1952; bequest of Keith McLeod], inv nr 52.1524, cat 1955, p 29

F 663 [H 672] LANDSCAPE WITH OLIVE AND MOUNTAINS IN THE BACKGROUND
PROVENANCE Joseph Roulin, Marseilles; A. Vollard Art Gallery, Paris; P. Pompidor, France [acquired 1901]; Present owner unknown
EDITORS' COMMENT Neither this nor the following number are included in the list of works Roulin's daughter Marcelle identified to John Rewald as belonging to her parents. See also comment under F 441a

F 664 [H 673] THE WHITE MAS AMONG THE OLIVE TREES
EXHIBITION 1901 Paris, 25
PROVENANCE Joseph Roulin, Marseilles; Maurice Fabre, Paris [R 1901]; Moline Art Gallery, Paris; P. Pompidor, France [acquired 1903]; Present owner unknown
EDITORS' COMMENT See under F 663

F 665 [H 678] THE SCHOOLBOY
EXHIBITIONS 1928 Berlin, 67 [repr]; 1933-4 Rotterdam, 40; 1953-4 Paris, 62; 1954 Utrecht, 53; 1955 New York 2, 64
PROVENANCE H. Thannhauser Art Gallery, Munich; H. Güttler, Reichenstein; H. Thannhauser Art Gallery, Munich; Meirowsky, Berlin [R 1928]; Wildenstein Art Gallery, New York; São Paulo, Museu de Arte, cat 1963, nr 112

F 666 [H 652] STILL LIFE: FLOWERS SCABIOSA AND RANUNCULUS
EXHIBITION 1967-8 Stuttgart, p 48
PROVENANCE Mr Salles, Arles [before 1928]; J. Vacher, Paris; Jean Dufresne Jr, Paris [R 1950]; Mr Geer Vis, Brussels; W. Brinkman, Schipluiden, Netherlands; J. Duquet, Basle; Mrs Kaars Sypesteyn, Castricum; Private collection, Netherlands [R 1963]; Stuttgart, Galerie Valentien [R 1970]
EDITORS' COMMENT See F 666 in cat

F 666a STILL LIFE: PEONIES
EXHIBITIONS 1928 Basle; 1938 Paris 2, 85; 1943 Paris
PROVENANCE G. Fayet, Igny; A. Vollard Art Gallery, Paris [R 1907]; A. Desjardins, Paris [R 1938]; Maxime Blum, Paris [R 1953]; O'Hana Gallery, London; Teltsch, London [acquired 1955 or 1956; 1966]; A.S. Teltsch, London [R 1966], in commission at A. Tooth Art Gallery, London [R 1966]; Sale Late E. Teltsch, London [Sotheby] 28 June 1967, nr 48; Present owner unknown

F 667 [H 687] THE TOPERS [after Daumier]
EXHIBITIONS 1901 Paris, 52; 1905 Paris, 1; 1909 Vienna, 10; 1914 Berlin, 113; 1925 Vienna, 89 [repr]; 1935-6 New York etc, 56
PROVENANCE Mr Aghion, Paris [R 1901; 1905]; Carl Reininghaus, Vienna [R 1914; 1925]; Mr and Mrs Joseph Winterbotham, Burlington, Vermont [R 1935-6]; Chicago, The Art Institute of Chicago [acquired 1953; bequest of Joseph Winterbotham], inv nr 53.178, cat 1961, p 199

F 668 [H 685] THE FIRST STEPS [after Millet]
EXHIBITIONS 1896 Rotterdam, 19; 1905 Amsterdam, 173; 1924 Zurich, 63; 1929 New York, 88; 1933 Chicago, 378; 1940 San Francisco 1, 9; 1949-50 New York, Chicago, 127
PROVENANCE Mrs J. van Gogh-Bonger, Amsterdam; Thannhauser Art Gallery, Munich; Karl Osthaus, Hagen [on loan to the Folkwang Museum, Essen 1910]; Alfred Flechtheim Art Gallery, Berlin; W. Russ-Young, Serrières; Paul Vallotton Art Gallery, Lausanne [from 1924 until 1926]; Julius Oppenheimer, New York [from 1926 until 1935]; Frank Oppenheimer, San Francisco [R about 1945]; Dalzell Hatfield Art Gallery, Los Angeles; Mr and Mrs George N. Richard, New York [from 1955 until 1964]: New York, Metropolitan Museum of Art [gift of Mr George N. Richard and Helen M. Richard], inv nr 64.165.2, cat French paintings vol III, 1967, pp 190-1

F 669 [H 690] THE PRISON COURT-YARD [after Gustave Doré]
EXHIBITIONS 1901 Paris, 26; 1905 Paris, 14; 1908 Munich, 7; 1909 Paris; 1937 Paris, 12; 1960 Paris, 61
PROVENANCE Mrs J. van Gogh-Bonger, Amsterdam; Mrs M. Slavona, Paris; M. Fabre, Paris [R 1901; 1905]; Druet Art Gallery, Paris [R 1906]; Prince of Wagram, Paris [R 1909]; Druet Art Gallery, Paris; I. A. Morosov, Moscow [acquired 1909]; Moscow, Museum of Modern Western Art [until 1948]; Moscow, Pushkin Museum [acquired 1948], inv nr 3373, cat 1961, p 53

F 670 [H 689] THE WOOD-CUTTER [after Millet]
EXHIBITIONS 1905 Amsterdam, 185; 1928 Berlin, 68; Frankfurt, 42; Munich, 29; Vienna, 39; 1932 Manchester, 40; 1945 Amsterdam, without cat nr; 1946-7 Liège etc, 154; 1947 Geneva, 155; Paris 1, 155; 1948 Bergen, Oslo, 52; 1949-50 New York, Chicago, 114; 1955 Antwerp 1, 319; 1961-2 Baltimore etc, 70
PROVENANCE Mrs J. van Gogh-Bonger, Amsterdam; V.W. van Gogh, Laren; Amsterdam, Rijksmuseum Vincent van Gogh [Vincent van Gogh Foundation, inv nr F 670]

F 671 [H 688] BRANCH OF AN ALMOND TREE IN BLOSSOM
EXHIBITIONS 1892 The Hague, 45; 1905 Amsterdam, 99; 1914 Berlin, 125; Antwerp; 1915 Amsterdam, 15; 1930 Amsterdam, 93; 1945 Amsterdam, without cat nr; 1953 The Hague, 168; Otterlo, Amsterdam, 160; 1953-4 Saint Louis etc, 143; 1955 Antwerp 1, 309; 1958-9 San Francisco etc, 64; 1960-1 Montreal etc, 70; 1961-2 Baltimore etc, 60; 1963 Humlebaek, 45; 1964 Washington, New York, 45; 1965 Charleroi, Ghent, 32; 1965-6 Stockholm, Göteborg, 51; 1967 Wolfsburg, 65; 1968-9 London, 178
PROVENANCE Mrs J. van Gogh-Bonger, Amsterdam; V.W. van Gogh, Laren; Amsterdam, Rijksmuseum Vincent van Gogh [Vincent van Gogh Foundation, inv nr F 671]

F 672 [H 694] THE MEADOW WITH BUTTERFLIES
EXHIBITIONS 1905 Amsterdam, 170; 1912 Cologne, 47; 1924 Basle, 50; Zurich, 49; Stuttgart, 22; 1925 Paris 1, 31; The Hague, 19; 1926 London 1, 18; 1947-8 London etc, 88; 1948 London 1, 35; 1955 Paris 3, 68
PROVENANCE Mrs J. van Gogh-Bonger, Amsterdam; Paul Rosenberg Art Gallery, Paris; French Gallery, London; S. Courtauld, London; London, Tate Gallery [Courtauld Fund 1926], cat of the modern foreign school 1926, 1928 and 1934, nr 4169, cat of the Courtauld collection, London 1954, nr 88; Loan to London, National Gallery since 1961

F 673 [H 691] HUTS: REMINISCENCE OF THE NORTH
EXHIBITIONS 1912 Cologne, 104; 1914 Berlin, 130
PROVENANCE Theo van Gogh, Paris [R 1890]; Mrs Chevalier [gift of Theo; from 1890 until 1904]; Moline Art Gallery, Paris; Hugo von Tschudi, Munich; Carl and Thea Sternheim, La Hulpe-Brussels [R 1914]; Sale Sternheim, Amsterdam [F. Muller] 11 February 1919, nr 11; G. Ribbius Peletier, Utrecht; Mrs D. van Wely-Ribbius Peletier, The Hague; H. van Wely [R 1955]; Van Wisseling Art Gallery, Amsterdam; Knoedler Art Gallery, New York [acquired March 1956], inv nr A 6311; Switzerland, Private collection [acquired April 1956]

F 674 [H 692] THATCHED HUTS IN THE SUNSHINE: REMINISCENCE OF THE NORTH
PROVENANCE P. F. Gachet, Auvers [from 1890 until 1909]; Paul Gachet, Auvers; Merion, Pennsylvania, The Barnes Foundation [acquired 1922]

F 675 [H 693] WINTER LANDSCAPE: REMINISCENCE OF THE NORTH
EXHIBITIONS 1905 Amsterdam, 171; 1906 Rotterdam, 53; 1925 The Hague, 42; 1940 New York 3, 2; 1942 Baltimore, Worcester, 31; 1943-4 Indianapolis etc, 12; 1945 Amsterdam, without cat nr; 1946 Stockholm etc, 92; 1948 Bergen, Oslo, 58; 1949-50 New York, Chicago, 129; 1951 Lyons etc, 68; 1953 The Hague, 170; Otterlo, Amsterdam, 163; 1954 Zurich, 72; 1954-5 Bern, 67; 1955 Antwerp 1, 306; 1955-6 Liverpool etc, 74; 1957 Marseilles, 67; 1959-60 Utrecht, 58; 1961-2 Baltimore etc, 61; 1963 Humlebaek, 46; 1964 Washington, New York, 46; 1965-6 Stockholm, Göteborg, 52
PROVENANCE Mrs J. van Gogh-Bonger, Amsterdam; V.W. van Gogh, Laren; Amsterdam, Rijksmuseum Vincent van Gogh [Vincent van Gogh Foundation, inv nr F 675]

F 676 [H 697] TREE TRUNKS
EXHIBITIONS 1927 Basle etc, 96; 1928 Düsseldorf, 160; Karlsruhe, 95; 1929 Berlin 1, 141; Hamburg, 53; 1930 Amsterdam, 250; 1946-7 Liège etc, 166; 1947 Geneva, 167; Paris 1, 167; Basle, 100; 1947-8 London etc, 82; 1949-50 New York, Chicago, 133; 1952 Milan, 113; 1953 The Hague, 172; Otterlo, Amsterdam, 164; 1953-4 Saint Louis etc, 147; 1956 Munich, 156; Eindhoven, 47; 1957 Essen, 360; 1958 Tokyo, Kyoto, 123; Paris, 48; 1960-1 Montreal etc, 59; 1962 Warsaw, 76; 1963 Tel Aviv, Haifa, 86; 1966 Belgrade, 78
PROVENANCE Bas Veth, Bussum; Sale Bas Veth a o, Amsterdam [F. Muller] 20 June 1922, nr 2 [repr]; Otterlo, Rijksmuseum Kröller-Müller, inv nr 275-22, cat van Gogh 1970, nr 241

F 677 [H 699] THE RAISING OF LAZARUS [after Rembrandt]
EXHIBITIONS 1891 Paris, 1202; 1905 Amsterdam, 194; Utrecht, 51; 1908 Rotterdam, 31; 1910-1 London, 75; 1912 Cologne, 80; 1914 Berlin, 112; 1915 Amsterdam, 17; 1923 Amsterdam 2, 121; 1924 Basle, 65; Zurich, 64; Stuttgart, 33; 1925 Paris 1, 47; The Hague, 34; 1928 Berlin, 69; Munich, 30; Frankfurt, 43; Vienna, 40; 1930 Amsterdam, 94; 1932 Manchester, 36; 1937 Paris, 8; 1945 Amsterdam, without cat nr; 1946 Stockholm etc, 96; 1947-8 London etc, 86; 1948 Bergen, Oslo, 59; 1949-50 New York, Chicago, 134; 1951 Lyons etc, 66; 1953 The Hague, 173; Otterlo, Amsterdam, 165; 1953-4 Saint Louis etc, 148; 1954 Zurich, 64; 1955 Antwerp 1, 325; Palm Beach etc, 28; 1955-6 Liverpool etc, 75; 1957 Marseilles, 76; 1958-9 San Francisco etc, 74; 1959-60 Utrecht, 59; 1960-1 Montreal etc, 73; 1961-2 Baltimore etc, 73; 1963 Sheffield, 13; Humlebaek, 53; 1964 Washington, New York, 53; 1965-6 Stockholm, Göteborg, 54; 1965 Charleroi, Ghent, 37; 1967 Wolfsburg, 73; 1968-9 London, 190
PROVENANCE Mrs J. van Gogh-Bonger, Amsterdam; V.W. van Gogh, Laren; Amsterdam, Rijksmuseum Vincent van Gogh [Vincent van Gogh Foundation, inv nr F 677]

F 678 [H 700] STILL LIFE: IRISES AGAINST A YELLOW BACKGROUND
EXHIBITIONS 1905 Amsterdam, 159; 1912 Cologne, 30 [repr]; 1914 Berlin, 107; 1923 Amsterdam 2, 129; 1924 Basle, 41; Zurich, 65; Stuttgart, 34; 1925 Paris 1, 34; The Hague, 30; 1926 London 3, 7 [repr]; 1927 Paris; 1929 London 1, 452; 1930 Amsterdam, 95; 1932 Manchester, 24; 1933 Rotterdam 1, 36; Amsterdam 2, 116; 1945 Amsterdam, without cat nr; 1946 Stockholm etc, 97; 1946-7 Liège etc, 152; 1947 Paris 1, 154; Geneva, 154; 1947-8 London etc, 87; 1948 Bergen, Oslo, 60; 1949-50 New York, Chicago, 132; 1951 Lyons etc, 54; 1853 The Hague, 175; Otterlo, Amsterdam, 167; 1953-4 Saint Louis etc, 150; 1954 Zurich, 56; 1955 Antwerp 1, 310; Palm Beach etc, 25; 1955-6 Liverpool etc, 76; 1957 Marseilles, 70; 1958-9 San Francisco etc, 63; 1959-60 Utrecht, 46; 1960-1 Montreal etc, 76; 1961-2 Baltimore etc, 58; 1963 Humlebaek, 44; 1964 Washington, New York, 44; 1965 Charleroi, Ghent, 31; 1965-6 Stockholm, Göteborg, 53
PROVENANCE Mrs J. van Gogh-Bonger, Amsterdam; V.W. van Gogh, Laren; Amsterdam, Rijksmuseum Vincent van Gogh [Vincent van Gogh Foundation, inv nr F 678]

F 679 STILL LIFE: BOUQUET OF IRISES
Left out by Faille in his manuscript for the present edition; See REJECTED WORKS

F 680 [H 701] STILL LIFE: VASE WITH IRISES AGAINST A PINK BACKGROUND
EXHIBITIONS 1921 Berlin; 1927 Paris; Berlin 3, 120 [repr]; Berlin 2, 114 [repr]; 1928 Berlin, 70; 1931 Frankfurt, 73; 1943 New York 2, 57; 1955 New York 2, 68; 1958 New York, 71; 1959 New York 2, 55
PROVENANCE Mrs J. van Gogh-Bonger, Amsterdam; Paul Cassirer Art Gallery, Berlin; Giulietta von Mendelssohn-Bartholdy, Grunewald-Berlin; Mr and Mrs David M. Levy, New York [R 1943]; New York, The Metropolitan Museum of Art [acquired 1958; gift of Adele R. Levy], inv nr 58.187, cat French paintings, vol III, 1967, pp 191-2

F 681 [H 702] STILL LIFE: ROSES IN A TERRACOTTA POT
EXHIBITIONS 1908 Paris 2, 76; 1917 Zurich 2, 111; 1925 Paris 2, 8; 1926 Paris, 2957; 1927 Paris; 1929 London 2; Lucerne, 24; 1932 New York, 17; 1933 Chicago, 386; 1935-6 New York etc, 58; 1940 New York 2, 363; 1942 Baltimore, Worcester, 27; 1943 New York 2, 58; 1953 New York 2, 13; 1954 New York, 28; 1955 New York 2, 69; 1959 Washington, 55; 1961 Washington, 17; 1963 Philadelphia, without cat nr
PROVENANCE Mr Gallimard, Paris [R 1905]; Bernheim jeune, Paris [R 1917; 1926]; Reid and Lefevre Art Gallery, London; Marie Harriman Art Gallery, New York; New York, Mr and Mrs William Averell Harriman [bought 1930]

F 681a [formerly F 681bis] STILL LIFE: ROSES
Left out by Faille in his manuscript for the present edition; See REJECTED WORKS

F 682 [H 703] STILL LIFE: ROSES IN GREEN POT
EXHIBITIONS 1914 Berlin, 134; 1928 Berlin, 71 [repr]; 1952 Paris 1, 102; 1959 New York 2, 54; 1965 New York 2, 60
PROVENANCE Mrs J. van Gogh-Bonger, Amsterdam; Paul Cassirer Art Gallery, Berlin; A. Rothermund, Dresden; Paul Cassirer Art Gallery, Berlin [R 1907]; Mrs Margaretha Reichenheim-Eissler, Berlin; Mrs F. Oppenheim-Eissler, Berlin [R 1914]; Mrs Franz von Mendelssohn-Bartholdy, Grunewald; G. Hirschland, Essen; M. Frank Art Gallery, New York; Wildenstein Art Gallery, New York; New York, Mrs Albert D. Lasker [R 1951 and 1970]

F 683 [H 695] ROAD WITH CYPRESS AND STAR
EXHIBITIONS 1901 Paris, 38; 1905 Paris, 36; 1910 Berlin 1; 1913 The Hague, 126; 1914 Antwerp, 43; 1927 Basle etc, 136; 1928 Düsseldorf, 201; Karlsruhe, 136; 1929 Berlin 1, 138; Hamburg, 91; 1930 Amsterdam, 236; 1935 Brussels, 100; 1935-6 New York etc, 59; 1945 The Hague, 37; 1946-7 Liège etc, 161; 1947 Paris 1, 162; Geneva, 162; Basle, 99; 1947-8 London etc, 83; 1949-50 New York, Chicago, 131; 1952 Milan, 114; 1953 The Hague, 176; Otterlo, Amsterdam 155; 1953-4 Saint Louis etc, 151; 1956 Eindhoven, 48; Munich, 158; 1958 Vienna, 104; Tokyo, Kyoto, 124; 1959 Aix-en-Provence, 51; 1960-1 Montreal etc, 68; 1962 Warsaw 78; 1963 Tel Aviv, Haifa, 88
PROVENANCE Amédée Schuffenecker, Clamart [R 1901 and 1905]; Mr Leonard, Paris [R 1912]; Otterlo, Rijksmuseum Kröller-Müller, inv nr 312-12, cat van Gogh 1970, nr 243

F 684 [H 676] MORNING: GOING OUT TO WORK [after Millet]
EXHIBITIONS 1905 Amsterdam, 175; 1928 Frankfurt, 41 [repr]
PROVENANCE Mrs J. van Gogh-Bonger, Amsterdam; Karl Osthaus, Hagen; Folkwang Museum, Essen [R 1910]; D. Komter Art Gallery, Amsterdam; Sale Amsterdam [Mak] 27 October 1925, nr 123 [repr]; Paul Cassirer Art Gallery, Berlin; J. S. Goldschmidt Art Gallery, Frankfurt; Otto Krebs, Holzdorf; Present owner unknown

F 685 PEASANT WITH HAY-FORK [after Millet; detail from the composition F 684]
Left out by Faille in his manuscript for the present edition; See REJECTED WORKS

F 686 [H 677] NOON: REST FROM WORK [after Millet]
EXHIBITIONS 1905 Amsterdam, 174; Hamburg; 1925 Paris 1, 43; 1927 Paris; 1935 Brussels, 96; 1967-8 Paris, 441
PROVENANCE Mrs J. van Gogh-Bonger, Amsterdam; Paul Cassirer Art Gallery, Berlin [R 1905]; Unknown collection, Dresden [R 1905]; Bernheim jeune Art Gallery, Paris; Druet Art Gallery, Paris [R 1909]; M. Aubry, Paris; Druet Art Gallery, Paris [R 1912]; Ch. Pacquement, Paris [R 1924]; Sale coll Pacquement, Paris [Petit] 12 December 1932, nr 32; Bignou Art Gallery, Paris; Mrs Fernand Halphen, Paris; Paris, Musée National du Louvre [acquired 1952; gift of Mrs F. Halphen], inv nr RF 1952-17, cat Impressionistes 1959, p 247

F 687 [H 674] THE REAPER [after Millet]
EXHIBITIONS 1905 Amsterdam, 180; 1912 Cologne, 76; 1924 Basle, 62; Stuttgart, 31; Zurich, 61; 1925 Paris 1, 46; The Hague, 33; 1928 Berlin, 72; Frankfurt, 44; Vienna, 41; Munich, 31 [repr]; 1930 Amsterdam, 96; 1935-6 New York etc, 57; 1939 San Francisco, 178; 1940 New York 3, 8; 1942 Baltimore, Worcester, 17; 1943 New York 2, 56; 1943-4 Indianapolis etc, 8; 1944 Montreal, 133; 1946-7 Liège etc, 144; 1947 Geneva, 145; Paris 1, 145; 1951 Lyons etc, 71; 1953 The Hague, 158; Otterlo, Amsterdam, 150; 1953-4 Saint Louis etc, 136; 1954 Zurich, 69; 1955 Antwerp 1, 316; Palm Beach etc, 30; 1955-6 Liverpool etc, 65; 1957 Marseilles, 74; 1958-9 San Francisco etc, 72; 1959-60 Utrecht, 56; 1961-2 Baltimore etc, 66; 1967 Wolfsburg, 69; 1968-9 London, 166
PROVENANCE Mrs J. van Gogh-Bonger, Amsterdam; V.W. van Gogh, Laren; Amsterdam, Rijksmuseum Vincent van Gogh [Vincent van Gogh Foundation, inv nr F 687]

F 688 [H 684] THE MOWER [after Millet]
EXHIBITION 1955 New York 2, 62
PROVENANCE Mrs J. van Gogh-Bonger, Amsterdam; Paul Cassirer Art Gallery, Berlin; Mr Rothermundt, Dresden; Paul Cassirer Art Gallery, Berlin; Mamaroneck, N.Y., Georg Hirschland [R 1955 and 1965]; Property of Trustees under the Will of the late Georg S. Hirschland [R 1970]

F 689 [H 660] THE SOWER [after Lerat's etching of Millet's Sower]
EXHIBITIONS 1904 Rotterdam, 75; 1908 Paris 2, 67; 1910 Rotterdam, 27; 1912 Cologne, 72; 1913 The Hague, 106; 1914 Antwerp, 24; 1927 Basle etc, 133; 1928 Düsseldorf, 198; Karlsruhe, 133; 1929 Berlin 1, 124; Hamburg, 88; 1930 Amsterdam, 251; 1953 The Hague, 167; Otterlo, Amsterdam, 153; 1956 Munich, 146; 1959 Recklinghausen, 689; São Paulo, 9; 1962 Brussels, Otterlo, 46; Warsaw, 83; 1963 Tel Aviv, Haifa, 93; 1966 Belgrade, 76
PROVENANCE M. M. van Valkenburg, Laren [R 1904]; Reckers Art Gallery, Rotterdam [R 1909]; Otterlo, Rijksmuseum Kröller-Müller, inv nr 309-09, cat van Gogh 1970, nr 249

F 690 [H 675] THE SOWER [after Millet]
EXHIBITIONS 1891 Brussels; 1905 Amsterdam, 177; 1912 Cologne, 73; 1953 New York 3, 23; 1955 New York 2, 63; 1957 Los Angeles, 18; 1960 New York 2, 48; 1962 New York; 1963 Miami, 54
PROVENANCE Mrs J. van Gogh-Bonger, Amsterdam [R 1905]; W. Peters, Berlin; W. Feilchenfeldt Art Gallery, Zurich; Fine Arts Associates, New York; Mr and Mrs Morris W. Haft, New York [R 1953]; Sale coll Haft, Palm Beach [Trosby Galleries] 9 February 1965, nr 12; Athens, Stavros S. Niarchos

F 691 THE SOWER
Left out by Faille in his manuscript for the present edition; See REJECTED WORKS

F 692 [H 683] THE THRESHER [after Millet]
EXHIBITIONS 1905 Amsterdam, 183; 1912 Cologne, 75; 1914 Berlin, 110; 1920 Venice; 1925 The Hague, 54; 1927 Paris; 1929 London 1, 456; 1930 Amsterdam, 97; 1945 Amsterdam, without cat nr; 1955 Antwerp 1, 318; 1957 Stockholm, 116; 1961-2 Baltimore etc, 68
PROVENANCE Mrs J. van Gogh-Bonger, Amsterdam; V.W. van Gogh, Laren; Amsterdam, Rijksmuseum Vincent van Gogh [Vincent van Gogh Foundation, inv nr F 692]

F 693 [H 681] THE SHEAF-BINDER [after Millet]
EXHIBITIONS 1905 Amsterdam, 181; 1927 Paris; 1929

London I, 459; 1930 Amsterdam, 98; 1932 Manchester, 37; 1937 Paris, 9; 1945 Amsterdam, without cat nr; 1946-7 Liège etc, 145; 1947 Paris I, 146; Geneva, 145; 1949-50 New York, Chicago, 116; 1951 Lyons etc, 72; 1953 The Hague, 159; Otterlo, Amsterdam, 149; 1954 Zurich, 68; 1954-5 Bern, 54; 1955 Antwerp I, 317; 1960 Paris, 59; 1960-1 Montreal etc, 74; 1961-2 Baltimore etc, 67; 1963 Humlebaek, 50; 1964 Washington, New York, 50; 1965 Charleroi, Ghent, 35; 1965-6 Stockholm, Göteborg, 49; 1967 Wolfsburg, 70; 1968-9 London, 168
PROVENANCE Mrs J. van Gogh-Bonger, Amsterdam; V. W. van Gogh, Laren; Amsterdam, Rijksmuseum Vincent van Gogh [Vincent van Gogh Foundation, inv nr F 693]

F 694 [H 717] PEASANTS DIGGING POTATOES [after Millet]
EXHIBITIONS 1905 Amsterdam, 188; 1912 Cologne, 52; 1914 Berlin, 120; 1928 Berlin, 74
PROVENANCE Mrs J. van Gogh-Bonger, Amsterdam [R 1905]; Paul Cassirer Art Gallery, Berlin; Mrs Tilla Durieux-Cassirer, Berlin [R 1912]; Mrs S. Paret, Berlin; Sale S. Paret a.o., Berlin [Cassirer] 17 May 1927, 39 [repr]; P. Schulenberg, Gera; New York, J. K. Thannhauser, Courtesy J. K. Thannhauser Foundation [onloan to Guggenheim Museum, New York]

F 695 [H 718] WOMEN DIGGING IN FIELD WITH SNOW
EXHIBITIONS 1905 Amsterdam, 188; 1912 Cologne, 41; 1921 Berlin; 1928 Berlin, 75; 1937 Paris, 11; 1950 Zurich, p 28; 1952 Milan, 112; 1958 Zurich, 245
PROVENANCE Mrs J. van Gogh-Bonger, Amsterdam [R 1905]; Bernheim jeune Art Gallery, Paris; Bernard Koehler, Berlin [R 1912 and 1937]; Emil Bührle, Zurich [acquired 1949]; Zurich, Sammlung E. G. Bührle, cat 1958, nr 245

F 696 [H 716] THE SPINNER [after Millet]
EXHIBITION 1928 Vienna, 38 [repr]
PROVENANCE Mrs A. C. van Houten-van Gogh, Dieren; d'Audretsch Art Gallery, The Hague; A. van Hoboken, Vienna; Alexander Lewin, Guben; French Art Galleries, New York; Julius Loeb, New York; Sale New York [Parke-Bernet] 6 February 1947, 64; Mrs L. Wolf

F 697 [H 680] PEASANT WOMAN CUTTING STRAW [after Millet]
EXHIBITIONS 1905 Amsterdam, 184; 1912 Cologne, 77; 1955 Antwerp I, 320; 1961-2 Baltimore etc, 69
PROVENANCE Mrs J. van Gogh-Bonger, Amsterdam; V. W. van Gogh, Laren; Amsterdam, Rijksmuseum Vincent van Gogh [Vincent van Gogh Foundation, inv nr F 697]

F 698 [H 679] PEASANT WOMAN MOWING [after Millet]
EXHIBITIONS 1912 Cologne, 78; 1956 Munich, 145
PROVENANCE Mrs G. H. Müller-Abeken, The Hague [R 1912]; H. Kröller-Müller, Otterlo, cat 1942, p 127; Georges Renand, Paris [R 1956]; Unknown owner; Sale Geneva [Galerie Motte] 9 June 1967, 55; Present owner unknown

F 699 [H 714] THE SHEPHERDESS [after Millet]
EXHIBITIONS 1896 Rotterdam, 17; 1905 Utrecht, 48; Amsterdam, 187; 1906 Rotterdam, 43; 1912 Cologne, 74; 1914 Berlin, 115; 1945 Basle, 15; 1947 Basle, 86
PROVENANCE Mrs J. van Gogh-Bonger, Amsterdam [R 1905]; R. von Hirsch, Frankfurt [R 1912], Basel [R 1970]

F 699a [formerly F 699bis, H 715] PEASANT WOMAN WALKING IN THE FIELDS
PROVENANCE Louis Rémy Matifas, Paris [R 1896]; Miss Matifas, Darmstadt; Wilhelm Horst, Darmstadt; F. L. M. Dony, The Hague; F. van Reigersberg Versluys; Sale New York [Parke-Bernet] 24 October 1951, nr 92; Herbert Tannenbaum Art Gallery, New York; G. Wurzweiler, New York; Lazarus Phillips, Neil F. Phillips and Ivan E. Phillips, Montreal; Sale London [Sotheby] 1 July 1964, nr 79; Present owner unknown

F 700 [H 682] PEASANT WOMAN BINDING WHEAT IN SHEAVES [after Millet]
EXHIBITIONS 1905 Amsterdam, 186; 1909 Munich; 1945 Amsterdam, without cat nr; 1951 Lyons etc, 74; 1954 Zurich, 71; 1954-5 Bern, 55; 1955 Antwerp I, 314; 1955-6 Liverpool etc, 63; 1958-9 San Francisco etc, 70; 1959 Aix-en-Provence, 42; 1959-60 Utrecht, 57; 1961-2 Baltimore etc, 64; 1963 Humlebaek, 49; 1964 Washington, New York, 49; 1965 Charleroi, Ghent, 34; 1965-6 Stockholm, Göteborg, 48; 1967 Wolfsburg, 68; 1968-9 London, 167
PROVENANCE Mrs J. van Gogh-Bonger, Amsterdam; H. C. Bonger, Amsterdam; Miss E. H. Bonger, Amsterdam; V. W. van Gogh, Laren; Amsterdam, Rijksmuseum Vincent van Gogh [Vincent van Gogh Foundation, inv nr F 700]

F 701 [H 721] THE DIGGERS
EXHIBITIONS 1905 Amsterdam, 438; 1912 Cologne, 51; 1913 Frankfurt, 28 [repr]; 1930 Amsterdam, 99
PROVENANCE Mrs J. van Gogh-Bonger, Amsterdam [R 1905]; Frankfurter Kunstverein, Frankfurt [R 1909]; Hugo Nathan [R 1912 and 1913]; Mrs Marthe Nathan, Frankfurt [R 1930]; Wildenstein Art Gallery, New York; J. K. Thannhauser Art Gallery, New York; Robert H. Tannahill, Detroit; Detroit, Detroit Institute of Arts [bequest Robert H. Tannahill]

F 702 [H 719] WORN OUT—AT ETERNITY'S GATE
EXHIBITIONS 1905 Amsterdam, 230; Utrecht, 58; 1906 Rotterdam, 57; 1909 Bremen, 89 [repr]; 1912 Cologne, 68 [repr]; 1913 The Hague, 138; 1914 Antwerp, 47; 1927 Basle etc, 137; 1928 Düsseldorf, 202; Karlsruhe, 137; 1929 Berlin I, 139; Hamburg, 92; 1930 Amsterdam, 252; 1946-7 Liège etc, 163; 1947 Paris I, 164; Geneva, 164; Basle, 98; 1947-8 London etc, 81; 1949-50 New York, Chicago, 130; 1952 Milan, 120; 1953 The Hague, 171; Otterlo, Amsterdam, 145; 1953-4 Saint Louis etc, 145; 1956 Eindhoven, 49; Munich, 157; 1958 Tokyo, Kyoto, 127; 1959 São Paulo, 12; 1960-1 Montreal etc, 65; 1962 Warsaw, 85; 1963 Tel Aviv, Haifa, 95; 1966 Belgrade, 82
PROVENANCE Mrs J. van Gogh-Bonger, Amsterdam [R 1905]; A. W. von Heymel, Bremen [R 1909]; Otterlo, Rijksmuseum Kröller-Müller, inv nr 313-12, cat van Gogh 1970, nr 251

F 703 [H 653] HEAD OF A PATIENT OF THE HOSPITAL AT SAINT RÉMY
PROVENANCE Mrs J. van Gogh-Bonger, Amsterdam; V. W. van Gogh, Laren; Amsterdam, Rijksmuseum Vincent van Gogh [Vincent van Gogh Foundation, inv nr F 703]

F 704 [H 720] THE EVENING WALK
EXHIBITIONS 1953-4 Paris, 63; 1954 Utrecht, 54; 1955 New York 2, 56
PROVENANCE Mrs J. van Gogh-Bonger, Amsterdam; A. G. Kröller, The Hague [R 1910]; P. R. Brückmann, The Hague [R 1910]; H. E. d'Audretsch Art Gallery, The Hague; M. Frank Art Gallery, New York; Wildenstein Art Gallery, New York; São Paulo, Museu de Arte, cat 1963, nr 113

F 705 THE SOWER
Left out by Faille in his manuscript for the present edition; See REJECTED WORKS

F 706 [H 722] LANDSCAPE AT FONTVIEILLE WITH PLOWMAN AND MILLS IN THE BACKGROUND
EXHIBITION 1926 Norwich, 61
PROVENANCE Bernheim jeune Art Gallery, Paris; W. Boyd, West Jerry near Dundee; A. Tooth Art Gallery, London; Cambridge, Massachusetts, W. A. Coolidge [acquired about 1936, R 1965]

F 707 [H 639] THE OLIVE TREES: PINK SKY
EXHIBITIONS 1905 Amsterdam, 201; 1920 New York, 49; 1923 London, 34; 1924 Basle, 44; Zurich, 54; Stuttgart, 25; 1925 Paris I, 33; The Hague, 7; 1926 Munich, 2079; 1927 Paris; 1930 Amsterdam, 100; 1945-6 Amsterdam, 13; 1947-8 London etc, 73; 1948 Bergen, Oslo, 47; 1951 Lyons etc, 63; 1954 Zurich, 61; 1954-5 Bern, 59; 1955 Antwerp I, 301; 1955-6 Liverpool etc, 69; 1965-6 Stockholm, Göteborg, 46; 1967 Ostende, 401; 1968-9 London, 176
PROVENANCE Mrs J. van Gogh-Bonger, Amsterdam; V. W. van Gogh, Laren; Amsterdam, Rijksmuseum Vincent van Gogh [Vincent van Gogh Foundation, inv nr F 707]

F 708 [H 723] OLIVE TREES: PALE BLUE SKY
EXHIBITIONS 1905 Amsterdam, 202; 1906 Rotterdam, 48; 1920 New York, 54; 1934 Montreal, 16; 1957 Los Angeles, 16
PROVENANCE Mrs J. van Gogh-Bonger, Amsterdam [R 1905, 1906]; Paul Rosenberg Art Gallery, Paris; Victor Schuster, London; Sale London [Sotheby] 26 July 1939, nr 76; Wildenstein Art Gallery, Paris; W. Feilchenfeldt Art Gallery, Zurich; Private collection, Zurich; Reid and Lefevre Art Gallery, London; S. Salz Art Gallery, New York; London, Mr and Mrs W. H. Annenberg [R 1970]

F 709 [H 725] OLIVE TREES: BRIGHT BLUE SKY
EXHIBITIONS 1912 Cologne, 99; 1920 New York, 54; 1924 Basle, 52; Zurich, 53; Stuttgart, 24; 1925 Paris I, 38; The Hague, 7; 1930 Amsterdam, 101; 1932 Manchester, 34; 1948 Bergen, Oslo, 56; 1951 Lyons etc, 55; 1954 Zurich, 60; 1955 Antwerp I, 300; 1955-6 Liverpool etc, 68; 1958-9 San Francisco etc, 65; 1961-2 Baltimore etc, 57; 1965-6 Stockholm, Göteborg, 45; 1968-9 London, 170
PROVENANCE Mrs J. van Gogh-Bonger, Amsterdam; V. W. van Gogh, Laren; Amsterdam, Rijksmuseum Vincent van Gogh [Vincent van Gogh Foundation, inv nr F 709]
EDITORS' COMMENT Faille mentions this painting and F 708 as having figured under cat nr 54 in the New York Van Gogh exhibition 1920. It cannot be determined which of the two works really was shown at that occasion

F 710 [H 638] OLIVE TREES: YELLOW SKY WITH SUN
EXHIBITIONS 1913 Düsseldorf, without cat nr [repr]; 1914 Munich, without cat nr [repr]; 1921 Berlin; 1926 Dresden, 209; 1934 Ottawa, 60; 1941 Worcester, 15; 1943 New York 2, 46; 1948 Cleveland, 21; 1955 New York 2, 50; 1957 Milwaukee, 78
PROVENANCE Schuffenecker, Paris; Prince of Wagram, Paris; Barbazanges Art Gallery, Paris; S. Falk, Mannheim; Paul Cassirer Art Gallery, Berlin; Mrs Tony Lessing, Berlin; Mrs Margarete Mauthner, Berlin; Otto Wacker Art Gallery, Berlin; Paul Rosenberg Art Gallery, Paris; A. and E. Silberman Art Gallery, New York; Wildenstein Art Gallery, New York; H. S. Southam, Ottawa [R 1934, 1943]; Fine Arts Associates, New York [R 1948]; Mr Ralph and Mrs Mary Booth, Detroit; Minneapolis, The Minneapolis Institute of Arts [acquired 1951; Dunwoody Fund], Bull. of the Minn. Inst. of Arts 1951, pp 113-20

F 710a [formerly F 710bis] OLIVE TREES
Left out by Faille in his manuscript for the present edition; See REJECTED WORKS

F 711 [H 724] THE OLIVE PLANTATION
EXHIBITIONS 1913 Haarlem, 2 [repr]; 1921 Paris, 161; 1924 The Hague, 12; 1932 Amsterdam I, 19; 1943 Zurich, 716; 1945 Basle, 16; 1946 Bern, 22; 1947 Basle, 88; 1950 Zurich, p 28; 1952 Zurich, without cat nr; 1958 Zurich, 242
PROVENANCE Mrs J. van Gogh-Bonger, Amsterdam; Isaac Israëls, The Hague [R from 1921 and 1924]; Sale I. Israëls, Amsterdam [F. Muller] 2 April 1935, I; Thannhauser Art Gallery, Paris; Nieuwenhuizen Segaar Art Gallery, The Hague [R from 1936]; Rosengart Art Gallery, Lucerne; Zurich, E. G. Bührle [acquired 1937], cat 1958, nr 242; Private collection [R 1970]

F 712 [H 635] OLIVE TREES: BLUE SKY WITH LARGE WHITE CLOUD
EXHIBITIONS 1905 Amsterdam, 206; 1909-10 Munich, Frankfurt; 1935-6 New York etc, 60; 1937 Paris, 45; 1938 Amsterdam 3, 32; 1939 Amsterdam I, 32; 1945 Basle, 14; 1948 New York I, 12; 1950 New Haven, 21; 1955 New York 2, 49; New York 3, 50; 1960-1 London, 31
PROVENANCE Mrs J. van Gogh-Bonger, Amsterdam [R 1905]; Karl Osthaus, Hagen [loan Museum Folkwang, Hagen, cat Moderne Kunst, Band I, 1912]; D. Komter Art Gallery, Amsterdam; S. van Deventer, Wassenaar [R 1937], Switzerland [R 1945]; Knoedler Art Gallery, New York; New York, Mr and Mrs John Hay Whitney [R 1961]

F 713 OLIVE TREES
Left out by Faille in his manuscript for the present edition; See REJECTED WORKS

F 714 [H 726] OLIVE TREES: BRIGHT BLUE SKY
EXHIBITIONS 1905 Amsterdam, 200; 1923 London, 38; 1947-8 London etc, 75
PROVENANCE Mrs J. van Gogh-Bonger, Amsterdam [R 1905]; M. E. Sadler, Oxford [from 1923 until 1934]; The Leicester Galleries, London [R 1934]; Edinburgh, National Gallery of Scotland [acquired 1934], inv nr 1803, cat 1957, p 108

F 715 [H 641] OLIVE TREES
EXHIBITIONS 1935 Kansas City, 64; 1943 New York 2, 48; 1944 Montreal, 129; 1948 New York 2, 67; Cleveland, 22; 1955 Yew York 2, 51; 1957 Milwaukee, 79; Los Angeles, 14
PROVENANCE Barbazanges Art Gallery, Paris; Paul Cassirer Art Gallery, Berlin; O. Miethke Art Gallery, Vienna; Adolf von Kohner, Budapest; Durand-Ruel Galleries, New York; Kansas City, Nelson Gallery-Atkins Museum [acquired 1932], inv nr 32.2, Handbook 1959, p 125

F 715a [formerly F 715bis] OLIVE TREES
Left out by Faille in his manuscript for the present edition; See REJECTED WORKS

F 716 [H 728] OLIVE TREES AGAINST A SLOPE OF A HILL
EXHIBITIONS 1945 Amsterdam, without cat nr; 1953 The Hague, 179; Otterlo, Amsterdam, 147; 1954 Zurich, 62; 1954-5 Bern, 60; 1955 Antwerp I, 302; 1957 Stockholm, 117; 1967 Wolfsburg, 74; 1968-9 London, 171
PROVENANCE Mrs J. van Gogh-Bonger, Amsterdam; V. W. van Gogh, Laren; Amsterdam, Rijksmuseum Vincent van Gogh [Vincent van Gogh Foundation, inv nr F 716]

F 717 [H 633] WHEATFIELD WITH CYPRESS AT THE HAUTE GALLINE, NEAR EYGALIÈRES
EXHIBITIONS 1921 Berlin; 1952 Milan, 107; 1954 Zurich, without cat nr; 1958 Zurich, 243; Berlin, 47; 1958-9 Munich 74; 1959 Paris, 68
PROVENANCE Prince of Wagram, Paris; Barbazanges Art Gallery, Paris; F. von Mendelssohn-Bartholdy, Grunewald [before 1921]; Fritz Nathan Art Gallery, Zurich; E. G. Bührle, Zurich [acquired 1951], cat 1958, nr 243; Private collection [R 1970]

F 718 [H 615] THE GREEN WHEATFIELD BEHIND THE HOSPITAL
EXHIBITIONS 1913 Berlin 2, 22 [repr]; 1914 Berlin, 131 [repr]; 1921 Berlin; 1926 Dresden, 210; 1936 Cleveland, 319; 1937 New York, 19
PROVENANCE Mrs J. van Gogh-Bonger, Amsterdam; Bruno Cassirer, Berlin; Paul Cassirer Art Gallery, Berlin; Mrs Margarethe Mauthner, Berlin [R 1914]; Hugo Moser, Berlin; Jacques Seligmann Art Gallery, New York [R 1936 and 1937]; Hugo Moser [R about 1940]; Present owner unknown

F 719 [H 610] GREEN WHEAT
EXHIBITIONS 1910 Berlin I, 28; 1937 Paris, 40; 1960 Paris,

54; 1965 Budapest, 13; Berlin, 48
PROVENANCE E. Thiel Art Gallery, Stockholm [R about 1910]; Paul Rosenberg Art Gallery, Paris [R 1923]; W. Halvorsen, Paris; Prague, Národní Galerie [acquired 1923], inv nr 0-3208, cat Sbírka francouzského umění 1962, nr 59

F 720 [H 662] THE FIELD ENCLOSURE
EXHIBITIONS 1905 Amsterdam, 205; 1906 Rotterdam, 50; Cologne 1912, 105; 1913 The Hague, 115; 1914 Antwerp, 41; 1927 Basle etc, 34; 1928 Düsseldorf, 172; Karlsruhe, 107; 1929 Berlin 1, 132; Hamburg, 61; 1930 Amsterdam, 247; 1946-7 Liège etc, 156; 1947 Paris 1, 157; Geneva, 157; Basle, 92; 1947-8 London etc, 77; 1949-50 New York, Chicago, 124; 1952 Milan, 109; 1953-4 Saint Louis etc, 139; 1956 Munich, 153; 1957 Essen, 359; 1958 Tokyo, Kyoto, 122; 1959 Aix-en-Provence, 50; 1960-1 Montreal etc, 66; 1962 Warsaw, 73; 1963 Tel Aviv, Haifa, 83; 1966 Belgrade, 73
PROVENANCE Mrs J. van Gogh-Bonger, Amsterdam [R 1905, 1906]; Amédée Schuffenecker, Clamart; Bernard Koehler, Berlin [R 1912]; Amédée Schuffenecker, Meudon [R 1912]; Otterlo, Rijksmuseum Kröller-Müller, inv nr 284-12, cat van Gogh 1970, nr 235

F 721 [H 730] A MEADOW IN THE MOUNTAINS: LE MAS DE ST PAUL, CALLED MAS DE GEORGE
EXHIBITIONS 1912 Cologne, 94; 1913 The Hague, 104; 1914 Antwerp, 38; 1927 Basle etc, 103; 1928 Düsseldorf, 170; Karlsruhe, 105; 1929 Berlin 1, 130; Hamburg, 59; 1930 Amsterdam, 244; 1946-7 Liège etc, 159; 1947 Paris 1, 160; Geneva, 160; Basle, 95; 1949-50 New York, Chicago, 126; 1952 Milan, 117; 1953 The Hague, 164; Otterlo, Amsterdam, 157; 1953-4 Saint Louis etc, 142; 1966 Belgrade, 80
PROVENANCE Prince of Wagram, Paris; Barbazanges Art Gallery, Paris; Amédée Schuffenecker, Meudon [R 1912]; Otterlo, Rijksmuseum Kröller-Müller, inv nr 282-12, cat van Gogh 1970, nr 247

F 722 [H 729] THE MEADOW BEHIND SAINT PAUL'S HOSPITAL
EXHIBITIONS 1912 Cologne, 32; 1932 Amsterdam 2, 20; 1950 The Hague, 37; 1958 Amsterdam 2, 14; 1960 Paris, 56
PROVENANCE Wilhelmina van Gogh, Dieren; C. M. van Gogh Art Gallery, Amsterdam; H. P. Bremmer, The Hague [acquired 1909]; Heirs of H. P. Bremmer, The Hague [R 1965]; Present owner unknown

F 723 [H 731] AT THE FOOT OF THE MOUNTAINS
EXHIBITIONS 1945 Amsterdam, without cat nr; 1946 Stockholm etc, 81
PROVENANCE C. M. van Gogh Art Gallery, Amsterdam; G. Ribbius Peletier, Utrecht; Scheveningen, Netherlands, Miss E. Ribbius Peletier

F 724 [H 732] ON THE BORDER OF THE ALPILLES
EXHIBITIONS 1892 The Hague, 43 [?]; 1912 Cologne, 45; 1913 The Hague, 123; 1914 Antwerp, 44; 1927 Basle etc, 99; 1928 Düsseldorf, 164; Karlsruhe, 99; 1929 Berlin 1, 129; Hamburg, 56; 1930 Amsterdam, 246; 1946-7 Liège etc, 164; 1947 Paris 1, 165; Geneva, 165; Basle, 97; 1947-8 London etc, 84; 1952 Milan, 118; 1953 The Hague, 177; Otterlo, Amsterdam, 158; 1956 Eindhoven, 46; Munich, 152; 1957 Essen, 357; 1958 Vienna, 103; Tokyo, Kyoto, 121; 1959 Aix-en-Provence, 49; 1960-1 Montreal etc, 67; 1962 Warsaw 82; 1963 Tel Aviv, Haifa, 92
PROVENANCE Amédée Schuffenecker, Clamart; Mr Leonard, Paris [R 1912]; Otterlo, Rijksmuseum Kröller-Müller, inv nr 278-12, cat van Gogh 1970, nr 248

F 725 [H 734] LE MONT GAUSSIER WITH THE MAS DE ST PAUL
EXHIBITIONS 1928 Berlin, 76; 1939 Adelaide etc, 124; 1953 London 1, 29
PROVENANCE Eugène Blot Art Gallery, Paris; Antoine Villard, Paris; Matthiesen Art Gallery, Berlin; Goldschmidt Art Gallery, Frankfurt; G. Schweitzer, Berlin; Sale G. Schweitzer a.o., Berlin [Cassirer] 20 October 1932, nr 127; London, Private collection

F 726 [H 733] LANDSCAPE IN THE NEIGHBORHOOD OF SAINT RÉMY
EXHIBITIONS 1951 Houston, 18; 1952-3 New York etc, 5; 1955 New York 2, 57
PROVENANCE P. F. Gachet, Auvers-sur-Oise [from 1890 until 1909]; Paul Gachet, Auvers; Private collection, Paris; A. Mak Art Gallery, Amsterdam; F. Buffa Art Gallery, Amsterdam; A. Conger Goodyear, New York; New York, Museum of Modern Art [gift of A. Conger Goodyear]

F 727 [H p 557] A SPOT OF GREENERY: VALLEY WITH PLOWMAN SEEN FROM ABOVE
PROVENANCE P. F. Gachet, Auvers-sur-Oise [from 1890 until 1909]; Paul Gachet, Auvers; W. Feilchenfeldt Art Gallery, Zurich; Caspari Art Gallery, Munich; Otto Krebs, Holzdorf; Present owner unknown

F 728 [H 735] A ROAD AT SAINT RÉMY WITH FIGURE
EXHIBITIONS 1955 New York 2, 70; 1957 Los Angeles, 21; 1967 Paris, 106
PROVENANCE P. F. Gachet, Auvers-sur-Oise [from 1890 until 1909]; Paul Gachet, Auvers; Paul Rosenberg Art Gallery, Paris; Thannhauser Art Gallery, Munich [R 1923]; Thannhauser Art Gallery, New York; Georges Bigar, New York; Mr and Mrs Guy A. Weill, Scarsdale, USA [R 1955]; Lausanne, Private collection [R 1967]

F 729 LANDSCAPE AT SUNRISE
Left out by Faille in his manuscript for the present edition; See REJECTED WORKS

F 730 [H 736] THE GARDEN OF ST PAUL'S HOSPITAL
EXHIBITIONS 1914 Berlin, 95; 1921 Berlin; 1928 Berlin, 77; 1933-4 Rotterdam, 41; 1934 Bern, 64; 1945 Amsterdam, without cat nr; 1947 Basle, 90; 1950 Paris 2, 51; Zurich, not in cat; 1952 Milan, 106; 1954 Zurich, not in cat; 1958 Zurich, 244; Berlin, 46; 1958-9 Munich, 75; 1961 Edinburgh London, 60; 1963 Hamburg, 81; 1966 Basle, 41
PROVENANCE Mrs J. van Gogh-Bonger, Amsterdam; Paul Cassirer Art Gallery, Berlin; Mrs H. Harries- von Siemens, Berlin Grunewald; W. Feilchenfeldt Art Gallery, Zurich; F. Nathan, Zurich; E. G. Bührle, Zurich [acquired 1948], cat 1958, nr 244; Private collection [R 1970]

F 731 [H 738] TREES IN THE GARDEN OF ST PAUL'S HOSPITAL
EXHIBITIONS 1924 Zurich, 58; Basle, 48; 1964 Lausanne, 116
PROVENANCE F. Meyer-Fierz, Zurich [R 1924]; Sale coll Meyer, Amsterdam [F. Muller] 13 July 1926, nr XIII; Wildenstein Art Gallery, Paris; Mr and Mrs Anderson, London [R 1936 and 1959]; Lausanne, Private collection [R 1964 and 1970]

F 732 [H 737] THE STONE BENCH IN THE GARDEN OF ST PAUL'S HOSPITAL
EXHIBITIONS 1896 Rotterdam, 11; 1905 Amsterdam, 193; Utrecht, 50; 1906 Rotterdam, 45; 1955 New York 2, 58
PROVENANCE Mrs J. van Gogh-Bonger, Amsterdam [R 1905]; Mrs van Hoey Smith-van Stolk, Rotterdam [acquired 1910]; Wildenstein Art Gallery, New York; São Paulo, Museu de Arte, cat 1963, nr 115

F 733 [H 663] THE GARDEN OF ST PAUL'S HOSPITAL WITH FIGURE
EXHIBITIONS 1927 Basle etc, 141; 1928 Düsseldorf, 204; Karlsruhe, 139; 1929 Berlin 1, 140; Hamburg, 96; 1930 Amsterdam, 249; 1947 Basle, 93; 1947-8 London etc, 78; 1959 Aix-en-Provence [Exhib instead of cat nr 46]; 1960-1 Montreal etc, 63; 1966 Belgrade, 75
PROVENANCE Mrs J. van Gogh-Bonger, Amsterdam; W. Steenhoff, Amsterdam [R 1917]; Otterlo, Rijksmuseum Kröller-Müller, inv nr 315-17, cat van Gogh 1970, nr 238

F 734 [H 741] THE GARDEN OF ST PAUL'S HOSPITAL
EXHIBITIONS 1927 Basle etc, 125; 1928 Düsseldorf, 193; Karlsruhe, 128; 1929 Berlin 1, 137; Hamburg, 80; 1930 Amsterdam, 238; 1945 The Hague, 36; 1946-7 Liège etc, 141; 1947 Paris 1, 142; Geneva, 142; Basle, 83; 1947-8 London etc, 68; 1949-50 New York, Chicago, 111; 1953 The Hague, 153; Otterlo, Amsterdam, 141; 1956 Munich, 141; 1958 Vienna, 93; Tokyo, Kyoto, 114; 1959 Aix-en-Provence, 37; 1960-1 Montreal etc, 59; 1962 Warsaw, 72; 1963 Tel Aviv, Haifa, 82; 1966 Belgrade, 70
PROVENANCE L. C. Enthoven, Voorburg; Sale coll Enthoven, Amsterdam [F. Muller] 18 May 1920, 247 [repr]; Otterlo, Rijksmuseum Kröller-Müller, inv nr 304-20, cat van Gogh 1970, nr 232

F 735 [H 631] RISING MOON: HAYCOCKS
EXHIBITIONS 1911 Paris; 1912 Cologne, 100; 1913 The Hague, 122; 1914 Antwerp, 36; 1927 Basle etc, 134 [repr]; 1928 Düsseldorf, 199; Karlsruhe, 134; 1929 Berlin 1, 125; Hamburg, 89; 1930 Amsterdam, 248; 1946 Amsterdam [no cat]; 1946-7 Liège etc, 147; 1947 Paris 1, 150; Geneva, 150; 1948 Venice, 94; 1958 Vienna, 97; 1958-9 San Francisco etc, 68; 1959 Bordeaux; São Paulo, 10; 1961 Wolfsburg, 75; Recklinghausen, 102; Amsterdam, 49; 1962 Warsaw, 81; 1963 Tel Aviv, Haifa, 91; 1966 Belgrade, 79
PROVENANCE Bernheim jeune Art Gallery, Paris [R 1912]; Otterlo, Rijksmuseum Kröller-Müller, inv nr 310-12, cat van Gogh 1970, nr 256

F 736 [H 815] RISING MOON: HAYCOCKS
Left out by Faille in his manuscript for the present edition; See REJECTED WORKS

F 737 [H 739] LANDSCAPE WITH RISING SUN
EXHIBITIONS 1890 Brussels, 5; 1912 Cologne, 35; 1914 Berlin, 70; 1929 New York, 87; 1933 Chicago, 385; 1934-5 New York, 19; 1940 San Francisco 1, 11; 1942 Baltimore, Worcester, 21; 1949-50 New York, Chicago, 110; 1957 Los Angeles, 15; 1958 New York, 72
PROVENANCE Paul Cassirer Art Gallery, Berlin; Mrs Tilla Durieux-Cassirer, Berlin [R 1912]; A. van Hoboken, Vienna; Julius Oppenheimer, New York [R 1929]; J. Robert Oppenheimer, New York [R 1934-5, 1942]; San Francisco [R 1950]/ Princeton [R 1957], J. R. Oppenheimer

F 738 [H 740] LANDSCAPE AT SUNSET
Left out by Faille in his manuscript for the present edition; See REJECTED WORKS

F 739 [H 742] LANDSCAPE WITH RABBITS
EXHIBITIONS 1905 Amsterdam, 143; 1926 Munich, 2076; 1927 Paris; 1928 Berlin, 78; Frankfurt, 47; Vienna, 42; 1939 San Francisco, 179; 1940 New York 3, 9; 1942 Baltimore, Worcester, 20; 1943 New York 2, 60; 1943-4 Indianapolis etc, 9; 1944 Montreal, 128; 1948 Bergen, Oslo, 51; 1949 Lyons, 127; 1951 Lyons etc, 61; 1958-9 San Francisco etc, 66; 1961-2 Baltimore etc, 74
PROVENANCE Mrs J. van Gogh-Bonger, Amsterdam; V. W. van Gogh, Laren; Amsterdam, Rijksmuseum Vincent van Gogh [Vincent van Gogh Foundation, inv nr F 739]

F 740 [H p 557] THE LITTLE STREAM
PROVENANCE Paul Ferd. Gachet, Auvers [from 1890 until 1909]; Paul Gachet, Auvers; Wildenstein Art Gallery, New York; C. V. Starr, New York; New York, Heirs of C. V. Starr

F 741 THE CYPRESSES
Left out by Faille in his manuscript for the present edition; See REJECTED WORKS

F 741a THE CYPRESSES
Left out by Faille in his manuscript for the present edition; See REJECTED WORKS

F 742 [H 744] A CLUMP OF TREES IN THE GARDEN OF ST PAUL'S HOSPITAL
EXHIBITIONS 1927 Basle etc, 142; 1928 Düsseldorf, 205 [repr]; Karlsruhe, 140; 1929 Berlin 1, 134; Hamburg, 97; 1930 Amsterdam, 245; 1947 Basle, 91; 1949-50 New York, Chicago, 127; 1954 Recklinghausen, 128; 1955 Antwerp, 173; 1960-1 Montreal etc, 62; 1962 Warsaw, 74; 1963 Tel Aviv, Haifa, 84; 1966 Belgrade, 72
PROVENANCE Otterlo, Rijksmuseum Kröller-Müller, inv nr 316-00, cat van Gogh 1970, nr 237

F 743 [H 634] THE CYPRESS AND THE FLOWERING TREE
EXHIBITIONS 1901 Paris, 49; 1934 San Francisco, 159; 1940 San Francisco 1, 8; 1943 Yew York 2, 46; 1955 New York 2, 48; 1956 New Haven, 101; 1957 Los Angeles, 13; 1960 San Francisco, without cat nr
PROVENANCE E. Schuffenecker, Paris [R 1901]; Bernheim jeune Art Gallery, Paris; G. Fayet, Igny [acquired 1908; R 1928]; Wildenstein Art Gallery, New York; Mr and Mrs W. W. Crocker, Burlingame, California [R 1934] [1967 on loan to San Francisco Museum]; Sale New York [Parke-Bernet] 25 February 1970, nr 10; Present owner unknown

F 744 [H 636] THE QUARRY
EXHIBITIONS 1920 New York, 39; 1923 London, 33; 1924 Basle, 45; Zurich, 55; Stuttgart, 26; 1925 Paris 1, 42; The Hague, 11; 1926 Munich, 2096; 1927 Paris; 1928 Berlin, 80; Frankfurt, 48; Vienna, 43; Munich, 32; 1945 Amsterdam, without cat nr; 1948 Bergen, Oslo, 49; 1951 Lyons etc, 60; 1953 The Hague, 161; Otterlo, Amsterdam, 146; 1954 Zurich, 57; 1954-5 Bern, 61; 1955 Antwerp 1, 304; 1955-6 Liverpool etc, 70; 1957 Marseilles, 65; 1959-60 Utrecht, 53; 1968-9 London, 172
PROVENANCE Mrs J. van Gogh-Bonger, Amsterdam; V. W. van Gogh, Laren; Amsterdam, Rijksmuseum Vincent van Gogh [Vincent van Gogh Foundation, inv nr F 744]

F 745 [H 745] UNDERGROWTH
EXHIBITIONS 1905 Amsterdam, 140; 1928 Berlin, 81; Frankfurt, 49; Vienna, 45
PROVENANCE Mrs J. van Gogh-Bonger, Amsterdam [R 1905]; V. W. van Gogh, Laren; Amsterdam, Rijksmuseum Vincent van Gogh [Vincent van Gogh Foundation, inv nr F 745]

F 746 [H 629] UNDERGROWTH
EXHIBITIONS 1890 Paris, 838; 1905 Amsterdam, 208; Utrecht, 53; 1906 Rotterdam, 51; 1914 Berlin, 109; 1923 Amsterdam 2, 126; 1924 Basle, 49; Zurich, 48; Stuttgart, 21; 1925 Paris 1, 41; The Hague, 31; Potsdam, 44; 1926 Venice, 24; 1927 Paris; 1930 Amsterdam, 102; 1932 Manchester, 44; 1946 Stockholm etc, 82; 1946-7 Liège etc, 155; 1947 Paris 1, 156; Geneva 156; 1948 Bergen, Oslo, 45; 1951 Lyons etc, 76; 1954 Zurich, 66; 1954-5 Bern, 57; 1955 Antwerp 1, 299; 1955-6 Liverpool etc, 66; 1957 Marseilles, 64; 1958-9 San Francisco etc, 78; 1959 Aix-en-Provence, 41; 1959-60 Utrecht, 52; 1960-1 Montreal etc, 75; 1961-2 Baltimore etc, 56; 1963 Humlebaek, 43; 1964 Washington, New York, 43; 1965 Charleroi, Ghent, 30; 1965-6 Stockholm, Göteborg, 44; 1967 Wolfsburg, 62; 1968-9 London, 163
PROVENANCE Mrs J. van Gogh-Bonger, Amsterdam [R 1905]; V. W. van Gogh, Laren; Amsterdam Rijksmuseum Vincent van Gogh [Vincent van Gogh Foundation, inv nr F 746]

F 747 [H 743] UNDERGROWTH
EXHIBITIONS 1905 Amsterdam, 124; 1912 Cologne, 38; 1913 The Hague, 81; 1927 Basle etc, 116; 1928 Düsseldorf, 184; Karlsruhe, 119; 1929 Berlin 1, 136; Hamburg, 72;

1930 Amsterdam, 225; 1935-6 New York etc, 61; 1949 Gouda; 1955 Antwerp 2, 174; 1962 Warsaw, 77; 1963 Tel Aviv, Haifa, 87
PROVENANCE Mrs J. van Gogh-Bonger, Amsterdam [R 1905]; C. M. van Gogh Art Gallery, Amsterdam [R 1910]; Otterlo, Rijksmuseum Kröller-Müller, inv nr 295-10, cat van Gogh 1970, nr 242

F 748 [H 706] BUTTERFLIES AND POPPIES
EXHIBITIONS 1905 Amsterdam, 197; 1930 Amsterdam, 103; 1947 Paris 2, 156; 1954-5 Bern, 50; 1955 Antwerp 1, 311; 1957 Stockholm, 114; 1967 Wolfsburg, 59; 1968-9 London, 152
PROVENANCE Mrs J. van Gogh-Bonger, Amsterdam; V. W. van Gogh, Laren; Amsterdam, Rijksmuseum Vincent van Gogh [Vincent van Gogh Foundation, inv nr F 748]

F 749 [H 707] ROSES AND A BEETLE
EXHIBITIONS 1905 Amsterdam, 197; 1930 Amsterdam, 104; 1937 Paris, 57; 1948 Bergen, Oslo, 40; 1951 Lyons etc, 58; 1953-4 St Louis etc, 146; 1954 Zurich, 55; 1954-5 Bern, 51; 1955 Antwerp 1, 312; 1955-6 Liverpool etc, 59; 1957 Marseilles, 71; Stockholm, 115; 1958-9 San Francisco etc, 62; 1959-60 Utrecht, 47
PROVENANCE Mrs J. van Gogh-Bonger, Amsterdam; V. W. van Gogh, Laren; Amsterdam, Rijksmuseum Vincent van Gogh [Vincent van Gogh Foundation, inv nr F 749]

AUVERS PERIOD

F 750 [H 746] COTTAGES WITH THATCHED ROOFS
EXHIBITIONS 1926 Moscow; 1939 Moscow; 1956 Moscow, Leningrad, 12; 1960 Paris, 65; 1965 Bordeaux, 65; 1965-6 Paris, 62
PROVENANCE Sale Paris [Drouot] 16 May 1908, 26; I. A. Morosov, Moscow; Museum of Modern Western Art, Moscow [acquired 1918], cat 1928, nr 84; Leningrad, Hermitage [acquired 1930 from Museum of Modern Western Art, Morosov Collection], inv nr 9117, cat 1967, nr 69

F 751 [H 749] CHESTNUT TREES IN FLOWER: PINK AND WHITE BLOSSOMS
EXHIBITIONS 1905 Amsterdam, 226; 1914 Berlin, 96; 1921 Berlin; 1928 Berlin, 82; 1933-4 Rotterdam, 42; 1934 Bern, 66; 1937 Paris, 46; 1938 London 1, 29; 1943 Yew York 2, 61; 1949-50 New York, Chicago, 148; 1955 New York 2, 71; 1961 New York 2, 43
PROVENANCE Mrs J. van Gogh-Bonger, Amsterdam [R 1905]; A. Schuffenecker, Paris; E. Druet Art Gallery, Paris; S. Fischer, Berlin [acquired 1909; R 1914]; W. Feilchenfeldt, Art Gallery, Zurich; Mrs Marcel Kapferer, Paris [R 1937]; Wildenstein Art Gallery, New York; Mr and Mrs George Gard de Sylva, Los Angeles [on loan to the County Museum, Los Angeles, inv nr L.2164.46-2, cat 1950, nr 20]; Buddy de Sylva, Hollywood; New York, Mrs H. Harris-Jonas [R 1955, 1965]

F 752 [H 574] CHESTNUT TREE IN FLOWER: WHITE BLOSSOMS
EXHIBITIONS 1912 Cologne, 107; 1947 Basle, 102; 1952 Milan, 123; 1956 Munich, 159; Eindhoven, 50; 1958 Vienna 109; 1962 Warsaw, 87; 1963 Tel-Aviv, Haifa, 98; 1966 Belgrade, 83
PROVENANCE Carl Sternheim, La Hulpe near Brussels [acquired 1909]; Alfred Flechtheim Art Gallery, Düsseldorf [acquired 1910]; C. M. van Gogh Art Gallery, Amsterdam [acquired 1910]; A. G. Kröller, Argentina; Otterlo, Rijksmuseum Kröller-Müller, inv nr 294-10, cat van Gogh 1970, nr 253

F 753 [H 752] PORTRAIT OF DOCTOR GACHET
EXHIBITIONS 1893 Copenhagen, 177; 1896 Rotterdam, 8; 1908 Paris 2, 21; 1910-11 London, 73; 1931 Frankfurt, 76; 1941 New York, 67; 1942 Baltimore, Worcester, 29; New York, 9; 1943 New York 2, 62; 1944 Montreal, 140; 1948 Cleveland, 30; New York 2, 70; 1949-50 New York, Chicago, 149A; 1951 Houston, 20; 1955 New York 2, 72; New York 3, 51; 1957 Los Angeles, 22; 1958 New York, 67; 1960 New York 2, 51; 1965 New York 2, 62; 1967 Montreal, 28
PROVENANCE Mrs J. van Gogh-Bonger, Amsterdam; Mr Mogens Ballin, Copenhagen; Paul Cassirer Art Gallery, Berlin [R 1904]; Mr H. Kessler, Berlin [R 1908]; J. Keller, Paris; E. Druet Art Gallery, Paris [acquired 1910]; Frankfurt, Städtische Galerie [acquired 1911; gift from Viktor Mössinger], inv nr 219, cat 1924, p 83; Mr and Mrs Siegfried Kramarsky, New York [R 1942]; New York, S. Kramarsky Trust Fund [R 1970]

F 754 [H 753] PORTRAIT OF DOCTOR GACHET
EXHIBITIONS 1905 Paris, 19; Amsterdam, 229a; 1925 Paris 1, 49; 1937 Paris, 48; 1954-5 Paris, 46
PROVENANCE Paul Ferd. Gachet, Auvers [1890-1909]; Paul Gachet, Auvers [1909-49]; Paris, Musée National du Louvre [acquired 1949; gift from P. Gachet and Marguérite Gachet], inv nr RF 1949-16, cat Impressionistes 1959, nr 155

F 755 [H p 557] DR GACHET'S GARDEN
EXHIBITION 1954-5 Paris, 43 [repr]
PROVENANCE Paul Ferd. Gachet, Auvers [1890-1909]; Paul Gachet, Auvers [1909-54]; Paris, Musée National du Louvre [acquired 1954; gift from Paul Gachet], inv nr RF 1954-15, cat Impressionistes 1959, nr 148

F 756 [H p 557] MARGUERITE GACHET IN THE GARDEN
EXHIBITION 1954-5 Paris, 44 [repr]
PROVENANCE Paul Ferd. Gachet, Auvers [1890-1909]; Paul Gachet, Auvers [1908-54]; Paris, Musée National du Louvre [acquired 1954; gift of Paul Gachet], inv nr RF 1954-13, cat Impressionistes 1959, nr 149

F 757 [H 626] PIETÀ [after Delacroix]
EXHIBITION 1966 Basle, 42
PROVENANCE Bernheim Jeune Art Gallery, Paris; G. Fayet Igny; Mrs Alban d'Andoque de Sériège, Béziers; Sale London [Sotheby] 1 December 1965, nr 61; Gallery Beyeler, Basel; Los Angeles, Private Collection

F 758 [H p 557] THE THATCH-ROOFED COTTAGES OF JORGUS
EXHIBITIONS 1955 New York 2, 74; 1957 Los Angeles, 24; 1963 New York 1, p 34
PROVENANCE Paul Ferd. Gachet, Auvers [1890-1909]; Paul Gachet, Auvers [acquired 1909]; Wildenstein Art Gallery, New York; New York, Reader's Digest Collection [R 1970]

F 759 [H 754] HOUSES AT AUVERS
EXHIBITIONS 1905 Amsterdam, 209b; 1934 New York 1, 24; Toledo, 25; 1935-6 New York etc, 65a; 1943 New York 2, 63; 1944 Montreal, 132; 1948 Cleveland, 31; 1954 Detroit, 123; 1955 New York 2, 73
PROVENANCE A. Bonger, Amsterdam [R 1905]; Toledo, Ohio, The Toledo Museum of Art [acquired 1935; gift of Edw. Drummond Libbey], cat 1939, p 252

F 760 [H 756] LANDSCAPE WITH CARRIAGE AND TRAIN
EXHIBITIONS 1905 Amsterdam, 227; 1960 Paris, 67
PROVENANCE Mrs J. van Gogh-Bonger, Amsterdam [acquired 1905]; Paul Cassirer Art Gallery, Berlin [acquired 1907]; Prince de Wagram, Paris; Bernheim Jeune Art Gallery, Paris; E. Druet Art Gallery, Paris [acquired 1909]; I. A. Morosov, Moscow [acquired 1909]; Museum of Modern Art, Moscow; Moscow, Museum Pushkin [acquired 1948], inv nr 3374, cat 1961, p 53

F 761 THE FIELDS
EXHIBITIONS 1921 Berlin; 1928 Berlin, 83; 1933-4 Rotterdam, 43; 1952 Milan, 125; 1956 Munich, 162; 1963 Hamburg, 83; 1967 Paris, 107
PROVENANCE Mrs J. van Gogh-Bonger, Amsterdam; Paul Cassirer Art Gallery, Berlin; H. Freudenberg, Nikolassee [acquired 25 January 1907]; Alexander Lewin, Guben; W. Feilchenfeldt Art Gallery, Zurich; A. Hausammann, Zurich; Zurich, Private collection [R 1967]

F 762 [H 751] VINEYARDS AT AUVERS
EXHIBITIONS 1930 Providence, 43; 1955 Chicago, 21
PROVENANCE Mrs J. van Gogh-Bonger, Amsterdam; Paul Cassirer Art Gallery, Berlin; Mrs Hugo von Tschudi, Munich [on loan Neue Staatsgalerie, Munich]; Paul Rosenberg Art Gallery, Paris; Molyneux, Paris; Paul Rosenberg Art Gallery, New York [R 1930]; Mrs Mark C. Steinberg, St. Louis; St. Louis, City Art Museum [gift of Mrs Mark C. Steinberg]

F 763 [H XV] STILL LIFE: VASE WITH FIELD FLOWERS AND THISTLES
EXHIBITIONS 1937 Paris, 50; 1954 Rotterdam, 120; 1954-5 Paris, 48; 1962 Washington, 25
PROVENANCE Paul Ferd. Gachet, Auvers [1890-1909]; Paul Gachet, Auvers; Paul Rosenberg Art Gallery, Paris; H. J. Laroche, Paris [R 1954, 1937]; New York, A. Meyer [R 1970]

F 764 [H p 557] STILL LIFE: JAPANESE VASE WITH ROSES AND ANEMONES
EXHIBITION 1954-5 Paris, 50 [repr]
PROVENANCE Paul Ferd. Gachet, Auvers [1890-1909]; Paul Gachet, Auvers [1909-1954]; Paris, Musée National du Louvre [acquired 1954; gift from Paul Gachet], inv nr RF 1954-12, cat Impressionistes 1959, nr 151

F 764a STILL LIFE: VASE WITH ROSE-MALLOWS
EXHIBITIONS 1951 Lyons etc, 75; 1953 The Hague, 198; Otterlo, Amsterdam, 190; 1953-54 St. Louis etc, 152; 1954 Zurich, 75; 1955-6 Liverpool etc, 77; 1958-9 San Francisco etc, 81; 1961-2 Baltimore etc, 77; 1963 Humlebaek, 56; 1964 New York, 56; 1965-6 Stockholm, Göteborg, 57; 1967 Wolfsburg, 77; 1968-9 London, 193
PROVENANCE Mrs J. van Gogh-Bonger, Amsterdam; V. W. van Gogh, Laren; Amsterdam, Rijksmuseum Vincent van Gogh [Vincent van Gogh Foundation, inv nr F 764a]

F 765 [H 760] CORNER IN THE GARDEN OF DAUBIGNY
EXHIBITIONS 1896 Rotterdam, 7; 1905 Amsterdam, 213; Utrecht, 57; 1910-11 London, 50; 1914 Berlin, 126; 1920 New York, 48; 1924 Basel, 74; Zurich, 68; Stuttgart, 35; 1925 Paris 1, 54; The Hague, 36; 1926 London 3, 4; 1930 Amsterdam, 313; 1939 San Francisco, 182; 1943 New York 2, 64; 1944 Montreal, 136; 1947-48 London etc, 91; 1948 Bergen, Oslo, 62; 1951 Lyons etc, 79; 1953 The Hague, 189; Otterlo, Amsterdam, 183; 1953-4 St. Louis etc, 165; 1961-2 Baltimore etc, 78; 1967 Wolfsburg, 78; 1968-9 London, 194
PROVENANCE Mrs J. van Gogh-Bonger, Amsterdam; V. W. van Gogh, Laren; Amsterdam, Rijksmuseum Vincent van Gogh [Vincent van Gogh Foundation, inv nr F 765]

F 766 [H 763] THE WHITE HOUSE AT NIGHT
EXHIBITIONS 1924 Basel, 77; Zurich, 39; 1928 Frankfurt, 45
PROVENANCE F. Meyer-Fierz, Zurich [R 1924]; Sale collection Meyer-Fierz, Amsterdam [Fred. Muller], 13 July 1926, XI [repr, named by mistake: 'La maison de santé à St. Rémy']; Paul Cassirer Art Gallery, Berlin; J. K. Thannhauser Art Gallery, Berlin; J. S. Goldschmidt Art Gallery, Berlin [after 1926]; Otto Krebs, Holzdorf [R 1928]; Present owner unknown

F 767 [H 761] EARS OF WHEAT
EXHIBITIONS 1905 Amsterdam, 221; 1914 Berlin, 106; 1920 New York, 43; 1924 Basel, 71; Zurich, 69; Stuttgart, 36; 1925 Paris 1, 39; The Hague, 25; 1927 Paris; 1928 Berlin, 84; Frankfurt, 53; Munich, 33; Vienna, 46; 1945 Amsterdam, without cat nr; 1946 Stockholm etc, 102; 1947-48 London etc, 89; 1948 Bergen, Oslo, 61; 1951 Lyons etc, 80; 1953 The Hague, 191; Otterlo, Amsterdam, 182; 1953-4 St. Louis etc, 166; 1954 Zurich, 74; 1955 Palm Beach etc, 31; Antwerp 1, 361; 1955-6 Liverpool etc, 78; 1957 Marseilles, 83; 1958-9 San Francisco etc, 79; 1961-2 Baltimore etc, 75; 1963 Humlebaek, 54; 1964 Washington, New York, 54; 1965-6 Stockholm, Göteborg, 55; 1967 Wolfsburg, 75; 1968-9 London, 196
PROVENANCE Mrs. J van Gogh-Bonger, Amsterdam; V. W. van Gogh, Laren; Amsterdam, Rijksmuseum Vincent van Gogh [Vincent van Gogh Foundation, inv nr F 767]

F 768 [H 767] PORTRAIT OF ADELINE RAVOUX: THE INN-KEEPER'S DAUGHTER
EXHIBITIONS 1926 London 1, 19; 1935-6 New York etc, 62; 1940 San Francisco 1, 13; 1942 Baltimore, Worcester, 37; 1955 New York 2, 76;
PROVENANCE Adeline Ravoux, Auvers [1890-about 1905]; Harry Harrison and 3 unknown persons, Meulan [about 1905]; Paul Rosenberg Art Gallery, Paris; Alphonse Kann, Saint-Germain-en-Laye; Georges Bernheim Art Gallery, Paris [R 1923]; Paul Rosenberg Art Gallery, Paris; J. R. Oppenheimer, San Francisco [R 1935-6]; San Francisco, Museum of Art [on loan since 1947, San Francisco Museum, of Art, Ed. 1947, p XXVI-XXVIII]; Switzerland, Private collection [R 1970]
EDITORS' COMMENT See F 637

F 769 [H 768] PORTRAIT OF ADELINE RAVOUX: THE INN-KEEPER'S DAUGHTER
EXHIBITIONS 1912 Cologne, 65; 1914 Berlin, 122; 1920 New York, 52; 1940 New York 2, 359; 1955 New York 2, 77; 1960 Philadelphia
PROVENANCE Mrs J. van Gogh-Bonger, Amsterdam; Montross Gallery, New York; Theodore Pitcairn, Bryn Athyn, Pa. [acquired 1921;] The Lord's New Church, Bryn Athyn, Pa.; Sale London [Christie] 24 June 1966, 49; Present owner unknown

F 770 [H 762] THE CHÂTEAU D'AUVERS
EXHIBITIONS 1905 Amsterdam, 215; 1914 Berlin, 129; 1925 The Hague, 40; 1926 Munich, 2065; 1927 Paris; 1930 Amsterdam, 105; 1946-7 Liège etc, 170; 1947-8 London etc, 92; 1948 Bergen, Oslo, 63; 1951 Lyons etc, 78; 1953-4 St. Louis etc, 167; 1954 Zurich, 76; 1954-5 Bern, 69; 1955 Antwerp 1, 362; 1955-6 Liverpool etc, 80; 1958-9 San Francisco etc, 83; 1959-60 Utrecht, 63; 1960-1 Montreal etc, 77; 1961-2 Baltimore etc, 79; 1963 Humlebaek, 58; 1964 Washington, New York, 58; 1967 Wolfsburg, 79; 1968-9 London, 195
PROVENANCE Mrs J. van Gogh-Bonger, Amsterdam; V. W. van Gogh, Laren; Amsterdam, Rijksmuseum Vincent van Gogh [Vincent van Gogh Foundation, inv nr F 770]

F 771 [H 757] SHEAVES OF WHEAT
EXHIBITIONS 1891 Paris 1, 1199; 1892 The Hague, 36; 1905 Amsterdam, 228; 1906 Rotterdam, 54; 1912 Cologne, 67; 1920 New York, 45; 1926 Munich, 2089; 1947 Paris 1, 171; Geneva, 171
PROVENANCE Mrs J. van Gogh-Bonger, Amsterdam; V. W. van Gogh, Laren; A. Chester Beatty, Dublin; [1954-57 on loan to National Gallery of Ireland from Chester Beatty]; London, Mrs Charles Beatty

F 772 [H 769] MARGUERITE GACHET AT THE PIANO
EXHIBITIONS 1947-8 London etc, 95; 1950 Paris 2, 53; 1951 Albi, 330; 1953 The Hague, 190; Otterlo, Amsterdam, 180
PROVENANCE Paul Ferd. Gachet, Auvers [1890-1909]; Paul Gachet, Auvers; Basle, Öffentliche Kunstsammlung [acquired 1934], inv nr 1635, cat 1961, p 13

F 773 [H 764] UNDERGROWTH WITH TWO FIGURES
EXHIBITIONS 1905 Amsterdam, 231; 1910 Berlin 1, 51; 1912 Cologne, 66; 1920 New York, 44; 1923 London, 36; 1924 Basle, 75; Zurich, 72; Stuttgart, 37; 1925 Paris 1, 52;

The Hague, 10; 1926 Munich, 2072; London 3, 11; 1929 Cambridge USA, 90; 1935-6 New York etc, Addenda nr 4; 1939 Boston, 57; 1948 Cleveland, 34; 1949-50 New York, Chicago, 149; 1956 Cincinnati, 11; 1957 Milwaukee, 76; 1963 Utica, New York, 429
PROVENANCE Mrs J. van Gogh Bonger, Amsterdam; V.W. van Gogh, Laren [until 1923]; Unknown French Art Gallery [acquired 1923]; Wildenstein Art Gallery, New York; Gilbert Fuller, Boston [R 1929 and 1939]; J. Seligmann, New York; Miss Mary E. Johnston, Glendale, Ohio [R 1949, 1956]; Cincinnati, Mary Johnston Collection [on loan to Cincinnati Museum, R 1970]

F 774 [H 766] PEASANT WOMAN AGAINST A BACKGROUND OF WHEAT
EXHIBITIONS 1912 Cologne, 54; 1922 Winterthur 1, 49; 1924 Basle, 73; Zurich, 70; 1938 Paris 1, 130; 1940 Winterthur, Luzern, 57; 1953 The Hague, 193; Bern, 42; 1960 Paris, 66; 1964 Lausanne, 117
PROVENANCE J. H. de Bois Art Gallery, Haarlem; Mr and Mrs G. Müller-Abeken, Scheveningen [1910-1920]; Sale coll. Müller-Abeken, Amsterdam [F. Muller] 19 May 1920, 86 [repr]; A. Hahnloser, Winterthur [until 1938]; Bern, H. R. Hahnloser [R 1970]

F 775 [H 808] THE PLAIN OF AUVERS
EXHIBITIONS 1902-3 Vienna; 1904 Vienna; 1924 Stuttgart, 41; 1925 Vienna, 77; 1953 The Hague, 192; 1954-5 Paris, 54; 1956-7 Vienna, 25; 1958 Vienna, 111; 1960 Paris, 70; 1961 Wolfsburg, 76; 1966 Zurich, 52
PROVENANCE C. M. van Gogh Art Gallery, Amsterdam; Vienna, Oesterreichische Staatsgalerie [Gift of the Society of the Artists of the Austrian Secession] [acquired 1903], inv nr MG 301, cat 1966, nr 52

F 776 [H 758] THE GARDEN OF DAUBIGNY
EXHIBITIONS 1901 Paris, 18; 1905 Paris, 16; 1930 Amsterdam, 106; 1934 Berlin, shown with F 777; 1944 Montreal, 138; 1948 Cleveland, 36; New York 2, 71; 1955 New York 2, 75; 1958 New York, 68; 1960 New York 2, 52; 1963 Hamburg, 84
PROVENANCE Sale collection d'un amateur, Paris [Drouot] 24 March 1900, nr 22 [repr]; Bernheim jeune Art Gallery, Paris [R 1901]; A. Schuffenecker, Paris; G. Fayet, Igny [acquired 1903, R 1905]; Paul Rosenberg Art Gallery, Paris [R 1928]; Berlin, National Galerie [R 1929, 1934]; Siegfried Kramarsky, New York [R 1944, 1960]; Mrs S. Kramarsky-Binkhorst, New York [R 1963]; New York, S. Kramarsky Trust Fund [R 1970]

F 777 [H 765] THE GARDEN OF DAUBIGNY WITH THE BLACK CAT
EXHIBITIONS 1906 Basle, 7; 1908 Paris 2, 25; 1910 Berlin 1, 20; 1924 Basle, 78; 1934 Berlin, shown with F 776; Bern, 67; 1945 Basle, 17; 1964 Paris 1, 33
PROVENANCE Julien Tanguy Art Gallery, Paris; A. Schuffenecker Art Gallery, Clamart [R 1908]; Paul Rosenberg Art Gallery, Paris [R 1908]; Eugène Blot Art Gallery, Paris; Louis Bernard, Paris; Bernheim jeune Art Gallery, Paris; P. Vallotton Art Gallery, Lausanne; R. Staechelin, Basle [R 1917]; Basle, Öffentliche Kunstsammlung [on loan since 1947 from 'Sammlung Rudolf Staechelin'], cat 1961, p 13

F 778 [H 806] FIELD UNDER THUNDERCLOUDS
EXHIBITIONS 1905 Amsterdam, 233; 1908 Paris 1, 98; 1920 Venice; 1928 Munich, 34; 1929 New York, 89; 1930 Amsterdam, 108; 1932 Manchester, 42; 1935 Brussels, 104; 1937 Paris, 49; 1939 San Francisco, 181; 1939-40 San Francisco, 127; 1940 New York 3, 10; 1942 Baltimore, Worcester, 34; 1943 New York 2, 67; 1943-4 Indianapolis etc, 14; 1944 Montreal, 141; 1946-7 Liège etc, 169; 1947 Paris 1, 170; Geneva, 170; 1947-8 London etc, 98; 1948 Bergen, Oslo, 66; 1949-50 New York, Chicago, 152; 1951 Lyons etc, 82; 1953 The Hague, 196; Otterlo, Amsterdam, 188; 1953-4 St. Louis etc, 173; 1954-5 Paris, 58; 1955 Antwerp 1, 362; 1955-6 Liverpool etc, 82; 1957 Marseilles, 84; 1958-9 San Francisco etc, 82; 1959-60 Utrecht, 62; 1960-1 Montreal etc, 78; 1961-2 Baltimore etc, 80; 1963 Sheffield, 14; Humlebaek, 59; 1964 Washington, New York, 59; 1965 Charleroi, Ghent, 40; 1965-6 Stockholm, Göteborg, 59; 1967 Wolfsburg, 80; 1968-9 London, 202
PROVENANCE Mrs J. van Gogh-Bonger, Amsterdam; V.W. van Gogh, Laren; Amsterdam, Rijksmuseum Vincent van Gogh [Vincent van Gogh Foundation, inv nr F 778]

F 779 [H 809] CROWS IN THE WHEATFIELDS
EXHIBITIONS 1905 Amsterdam, 234; Utrecht, 59; 1908 Paris 1, 100; Munich; 1910-1 London, 71; 1914 Berlin, 145; 1915 Amsterdam, 20; 1923 Amsterdam 2, 128; London, 39; 1924 Basle, 79 [repr]; Zurich, 76; Stuttgart, 38; 1925 Paris 1, 55; The Hague, 5; 1927 Paris; 1928 Munich, 35; 1930 Amsterdam, 108; 1935-6 New York etc, 66; 1945 Amsterdam, without cat nr; 1946 Stockholm etc, 104; 1946-7 Liège etc, 171; 1947 Geneva, 172; Paris 1, 172; 1947-8 London etc, 99; 1948 Bergen, Oslo, 67; 1949-50 New York, Chicago, 153; 1951 Lyons etc, 83; 1953 The Hague, 197; Otterlo, Amsterdam, 189; 1954 Zurich, 77; 1955 Palm Beach etc, 32; Antwerp 1, 364; 1955-6 Liverpool etc, 83; 1957 Marseilles, 87; 1958-9 San Francisco etc, 84; 1959-60 Utrecht, 64; 1960-1 Montreal etc, 79; 1961-2 Baltimore etc, 81; 1963 Humlebaek, 60; 1964 Washington, New York, 60; 1965 Charleroi, Ghent, 41; 1965-6 Stockholm, Göteborg, 60; 1967 Wolfsburg, 81; 1968-9 London, 201
PROVENANCE Mrs J. van Gogh-Bonger, Amsterdam; V.W. van Gogh, Laren; Amsterdam, Rijksmuseum Vincent van Gogh [Vincent van Gogh Foundation, inv nr F 779]

F 780 [H 770] THATCHED SANDSTONE COTTAGES AT CHAPONVAL
EXHIBITIONS 1924 Basle, 69; Zurich, 75; 1938 Paris 1, 131; 1943 Zurich, 718; 1947 Basle, 107; 1950 Zurich, p 28
PROVENANCE H. Schuler, Zurich; Zurich, Kunsthaus [acquired 1920; bequest of H. Schuler], inv nr 1398

F 781 [H 807] THE PLAIN OF AUVERS
EXHIBITIONS 1901 Berlin, 68; 1905 Amsterdam, 219; Berlin, 26; 1908 Paris 2, 20; 1914 Berlin, 90; 1925 Vienna, 90; 1928 Berlin, 85 [reproduced]; 1929 London 1, 462; 1941 New York, 66; 1942 Baltimore, Worcester, 35; New York, 10; 1943 New York 2, 68; 1948 Cleveland, 37; 1955 New York 2, 78; 1957 Los Angeles, 26; 1961 New York 1, 45; 1964 New York 1, 3; 1966 New York 1, 13; New York 2, 65
PROVENANCE Mrs J. van Gogh-Bonger, Amsterdam; Mrs Maria Slavona, Paris; Paul Cassirer Art Gallery, Berlin [R 1905]; H. von Kessler, Berlin [R 1908, 1929]; Reid and Lefevre Art Gallery, London; E. Bignou Art Gallery, New York; Mr and Mrs Marshall Field, New York [R 1941, 1968]; Pittsburgh, Carnegie Institute [donated by the family of Sarah Mellon Scaife]

F 782 [H 759] THE PLAIN WITH FARM NEAR AUVERS
EXHIBITIONS 1947 Winterthur, 132; Munich, 60c; 1949 Hanover, 29; 1952 Milan, 126; 1956 Munich, 165; 1957 Essen, 368
PROVENANCE Mrs J. van Gogh-Bonger, Amsterdam; Paul Cassirer Art Gallery, Berlin; Mrs Hugo von Tschudi, Munich; Wildenstein Art Gallery, Paris; Munich, Bayerische Staatsgemäldesammlungen [acquired 1929], inv nr 9584, cat 1966, p 44

F 783 [H 773] TWO CHILDREN
EXHIBITIONS 1905 Paris, 18; 1954-5 Paris, 51
PROVENANCE Paul Ferd. Gachet, Auvers [1890-1909]; Paul Gachet, Auvers [1909-54]; Paris, Musée National du Louvre [acquired 1954; gift of Paul Gachet], inv nr RF 1954-16, cat Impressionistes 1959, nr 152

F 784 [H 774] TWO CHILDREN
EXHIBITIONS 1907 Zurich; 1912 Cologne, 63 [repr]; 1924 Basle, 42; Zurich, 67; 1947 Basle, 104; 1966 Basle, 43
PROVENANCE C. M. van Gogh Art Gallery, Amsterdam; Richard Kisling, Zurich [R 1912, 1947]; Mrs H. Glatt-Kisling, Zurich; Private collection, Switzerland; France, Private collection [R 1970]

F 785 [H 777] LEVERT'S DAUGHTER WITH ORANGE
EXHIBITIONS 1891 Brussels; 1896 Rotterdam, 6; 1905 Amsterdam, 218; 1924 Basle, 70; Zurich, 66; 1938 Paris 1, 132; 1940 Lucerne, 56; 1947 Basle, 105; 1956 Munich, 163; 1963 Schaffhausen, 53
PROVENANCE Mrs J. van Gogh-Bonger, Amsterdam [R 1905]; F. Meyer-Fierz, Zurich; A. Hahnloser, Winterthur [R 1924, 1938]; Winterthur, Switzerland, Mrs L. Jäggli-Hahnloser [R 1964]

F 786 [H 776] PORTRAIT OF MISS ADELINE RAVOUX, THE INNKEEPER'S DAUGHTER
EXHIBITIONS 1912 Cologne, 65; 1913 New York etc, 1047; 1929 New York, 77; 1935-6 New York etc, 63; 1948 Cleveland, 35; 1963 Utica, New York, 1047
PROVENANCE Bernheim Jeune Art Gallery, Paris; Katherine S. Dreier, New York [R 1912-39]; Mrs Cornelius J. Sullivan, New York [R 1935]; Sale Sullivan, New York [Parke-Bernet] 6 December 1939, 56; Leonard C. Hanna jr., Cleveland [R 1948]; Cleveland, The Cleveland Museum of Art [acquired 1958; bequest of L. C. Hanna], inv nr 58.31, cat in memoriam L. C. Hanna, Cleveland 1958, nr 16

F 787 [H 772] YOUNG MAN WITH CORNFLOWER
EXHIBITIONS 1905 Amsterdam, 222; 1910-1 London, 67
PROVENANCE Mrs J. van Gogh-Bonger, Amsterdam [R 1905]; Bernheim jeune Art Gallery, Paris [R 1910-1]; Paul Cassirer Art Gallery, Berlin; Paul von Mendelssohn-Bartholdy, Berlin; Present owner unknown

F 788 [H 775] YOUNG GIRL STANDING AGAINST BACKGROUND OF WHEAT
EXHIBITIONS 1905 Amsterdam, 223; 1908 Zurich, 40; 1924 Basle, 72; Zurich, 71
PROVENANCE Mrs J. van Gogh-Bonger, Amsterdam; G. and L. Bollag Art Gallery, Zurich; Richard Kisling, Zurich; Mrs H. Glatt-Kisling, Zurich; Mr Chester Dale, New York [R 1952]; Washington, National Gallery of Art, inv nr 1694, cat Chester Dale collection 1965, p 129

F 789 [H p 557] THE CHURCH AT AUVERS
EXHIBITIONS 1953 Otterlo, Amsterdam, 187; The Hague, 195; 1954-5 Paris, 45; 1967-8 Paris, 442
PROVENANCE Paul Ferd. Gachet, Auvers [1890-1909]; Paul Gachet, Auvers [1909-51]; Paris, Musée National du Louvre [acquired 1951 from P. Gachet], inv nr RF 1951-42, cat Impressionistes 1959, nr 150

F 790 [H XVI] THE TOWN HALL IN AUVERS ON THE 14TH OF JULY
EXHIBITIONS 1914 Berlin, 46 [repr]; 1921 Berlin; 1930 Amsterdam, 109; 1931 Frankfurt, 75; 1942 Baltimore, Worcester, 38; New York, 11; 1944 Montreal, 142; 1948 New York 2, 69; 1949-50 New York, Chicago, 151; 1955 Paris 2, 35; 1967 Los Angeles, 20
PROVENANCE Gustave Ravoux, Auvers [R 1890]; Amédée Schuffenecker, Paris; Druet Art Gallery, Paris; Paul Rosenberg Art Gallery, Paris; Walter Bondy, Berlin; Paul Cassirer Art Gallery, Berlin; Bernheim jeune, Paris; Alfred Hagelstange, Cologne; Paul Cassirer Art Gallery, Berlin; Paul von Mendelssohn-Bartholdy, Berlin [R 1914, 1930]; Chicago, Mr and Mrs Leigh B. Block [acquired 1944]

F 791 [H 771] THE HOUSE OF PÈRE PILON
EXHIBITIONS 1912 Cologne, 102; 1954-5 Paris, 53; 1957-8 New York etc, 28; 1958 London 2, 29; 1960 Paris, 64
PROVENANCE Mrs J. van Gogh-Bonger, Amsterdam; Alexander von Jawlensky, Wiesbaden [R 1912]; K. Neumann, Barmen; Mrs M. Feilchenfeldt Art Gallery, Zurich [R 1954-5]; Athens, Stavros S. Niarchos, exhib cat 1957, 28

F 792 [H 779] THATCH-ROOFED COTTAGES AT CORDEVILLE
EXHIBITIONS 1905 Paris, 21; Amsterdam, 229b; 1947-8 London etc, 92; 1954-5 Paris, 47
PROVENANCE Paul Ferd. Gachet, Auvers [1890-1909]; Paul Gachet, Auvers [1909-54]; Paris, Musée National du Louvre [acquired 1954; gift of P. Gachet], inv nr RF 1954-14, cat Impressionistes 1959, nr 154

F 793 [H 781] FARMS NEAR AUVERS
EXHIBITIONS 1905 Amsterdam, 220; 1929 London 1, 467; 1930 Amsterdam, 110; 1947-8 London etc, 97
PROVENANCE Mrs J. van Gogh-Bonger, Amsterdam [R 1905]; A. W. von Heymel, Bremen; Paul Cassirer Art Gallery, Berlin; Frank Stoop, London [acquired about 1912]; London, Tate Gallery [acquired 1933; bequest of F. Stoop], inv nr 4713, cat 1959, p 273

F 794 [H 780] THE HOUSE OF PÈRE ÉLOI
EXHIBITIONS 1912 Cologne, 103; 1914 Berlin, 139; 1921 Berlin; 1928 Berlin, 86 [repr]
PROVENANCE Bernheim jeune Art Gallery, Paris; Paul Cassirer Art Gallery, Berlin; C. Herrmann, Berlin [R 1912, 1928]; J. K. Thannhauser Art Gallery, Berlin; F. H. Herrmann, London; Present owner unknown

F 795 [H 783] THE AUVERS STAIRS WITH FIVE FIGURES
EXHIBITIONS 1896 Rotterdam, 4; 1914 Berlin, 133; London, 88; 1923 Manchester, 19; 1926 London 2, p 7; 1942 Baltimore, Worcester, 32; 1944 Montreal, 137; 1948 Cleveland, 32; 1949-50 New York, Chicago, 150; 1954-5 Paris, 55; 1957 Los Angeles, 23; Milwaukee, 81; 1965 New York 2, 58
PROVENANCE Mrs J. van Gogh-Bonger, Amsterdam 1869; Paul Cassirer Art Gallery, Berlin; Bernheim jeune Art Gallery, Paris; Herbert Coleman [H. Kuhlmann], Manchester [R 1914 and 1926]; Sale Herbert Kullmann, Paris [Drouot] 16 May 1914, 6 [repr] not sold; St. Louis, City Art Museum [acquired 1935], Handbook 1953, p 144

F 796 [H 782] THE AUVERS STAIRS WITH TWO FIGURES
PROVENANCE Chr. Tetzen-Lund, Copenhagen; Sale Chr. Tetzen-Lund, Copenhagen [Munch-Petersen] 18 May 1925, 79; Sale Tetzen-Lund, Copenhagen [Winkel and Magnussen] 28 May 1934, 4; Tiegenhof, East-Germany, Mr Loebb

F 797 [H 784] THE VESSENOTS AT AUVERS
EXHIBITIONS 1922 Winterthur 1, 57; 1924 Basle, 68; 1938 Paris 1, 133; 1943 Zurich, 717; 1947 Basle, 108; 1954-5 Paris, 56
PROVENANCE Paul Ferd. Gachet, Auvers [1890-1909]; Paul Gachet, Auvers [1909-19]; Paul Rosenberg Art Gallery Paris [R 1919]; Emil Hahnloser, Zurich; Zurich, Mrs Dora Hahnloser-Gassmann

F 798 [H 785] THE BANK OF THE RIVER LA GRENOUILLÈRE
EXHIBITIONS 1905 Amsterdam, 145; 1914 Berlin, 143; 1927 Berlin 2, not in cat; 1933 Chicago, 375; 1940 Detroit, 52
PROVENANCE Mrs J. van Gogh-Bonger, Amsterdam [R 1905]; Paul Cassirer Art Gallery, Berlin; Carl Reininghaus, Vienna; Paul Cassirer Art Gallery, Berlin; Mrs F. Oppenheim, Berlin [R 1914]; Thannhauser Art Gallery, Berlin [R 1928]; Knoedler Art Gallery, New York [R 1935]; Detroit, USA, The Detroit Institute of Arts [on loan late 1930's-May 1940]; Private collection

F 799 [H 787] VIEW AT AUVERS
EXHIBITIONS 1905 Amsterdam, 224; 1914 Berlin, 124; 1928 Berlin, 87; Frankfurt, 54; Vienna, 47; 1945 Amsterdam, without cat nr; 1946 Stockholm etc, 103; 1946-7 Liège etc, 168; 1947 Paris 1, 169; Geneva, 169; 1947-8 London etc, 96;

1948 Bergen, Oslo, 65; 1951 Lyons etc, 77; 1953 The Hague, 194; Otterlo, Amsterdam, 185; 1953-4 St. Louis etc, 168; 1954 Zurich, 78; 1954-5 Bern, 71; 1955 Antwerp 1, 366; 1959-60 Utrecht, 65; 1963 Humlebaek, 57; 1965-6 Stockholm, Göteborg, 58
PROVENANCE Mrs J. van Gogh-Bonger, Amsterdam; V. W. van Gogh, Laren; Amsterdam, Rijksmuseum Vincent van Gogh [Vincent van Gogh Foundation, inv nr F 799]

F 800 [H 788] VIEW OF AUVERS WITH CHURCH
EXHIBITIONS 1914 Berlin, 54; 1928 Frankfurt, 52 [repr]; 1930 Providence, 45; 1948 Cleveland, 33
PROVENANCE A. Vollard Art Gallery, Paris; Sale Paris [Drouot] 16 May 1908, 24; Carl Moll, Vienna [R 1909, 1914]; M. Goldschmidt Art Gallery, Frankfurt; Thannhauser Art Gallery, Paris [R 1928]; Reid and Lefevre Art Gallery, London; Miss Dorothy Sturges [R 1930]; Mrs Elizabeth Hudson, Syracuse, USA; Providence, Rhode Island, Museum of Art, Rhode Island School of Design [acquired 1948; donated in memory of Miss Dorothy Sturges]

F 801 [H 786] WHEATFIELDS WITH AUVERS IN THE BACKGROUND
EXHIBITIONS 1905 Amsterdam, 225; 1914 Berlin, 124; 1939 Adelaide etc, 136
PROVENANCE Mrs J. van Gogh-Bonger, Amsterdam [R 1914]; Isaac Israëls, The Hague; Victor Cazalet, London [R 1939]; The Estate of Aline Barnsdall, Santa Barbara, California [until March 1952]; M. Knoedler Art Gallery, New York [acquired March 1952]; Mrs E. F. Hutton, Westbury, Long Island [acquired January 1953]; Sale coll. Mrs E. Hutton, London [Sotheby] 1 July 1964, 31; Galerie Beyeler, Basle; Switzerland, Private collection [R 1970]

F 802 [H 790] ROAD AT AUVERS
EXHIBITIONS 1891 Paris, 1204; 1954-5 Paris, 52; 1956 Munich, 161
PROVENANCE Mrs J. van Gogh-Bonger, Amsterdam; Mrs Julien Leclercq, Paris; Coll. Antell [nr 183]; Helsinki, Konstsammlingarna I Atheneum [acquired 1903], Cat 1962, p 40

F 803 [H 791] VIEW OF THE CHURCH OF LABBEVILLE NEAR AUVERS
EXHIBITIONS 1905 Amsterdam, 211; 1914 Berlin, 114; 1921 Berlin; 1928 Berlin, 88; 1949 Buenos Aires
PROVENANCE Mrs J. van Gogh-Bonger, Amsterdam; Paul Cassirer Art Gallery, Berlin; Mrs Margarete Mauthner, Berlin [R 1914]; Alfred Wolf, Stuttgart/South America; Sale A. Wolf, London [Sotheby] 24 April 1963, 6; Elizabeth Taylor

F 804 [H 793] HOUSE AT AUVERS
EXHIBITIONS 1930 Providence, 44; 1942 Baltimore, Worcester, 30; 1951 Houston, 21
PROVENANCE Mrs J. van Gogh-Bonger, Amsterdam; Paul Cassirer Art Gallery, Berlin; Mrs A. Albert, Munich; Caspari Art Gallery, Munich; M. Knoedler Art Gallery, London; A. Seligmann Art Gallery, New York; Miss Dorothy Sturges, Providence, USA [R 1930]; Mrs Elizabeth Hudson, Syracuse, N.Y. [R 1944 and 1951]; Washington, DC, The Phillips collection, not in cat 1952

F 805 [H 789] HOUSES AT AUVERS WITH ONE FIGURE
EXHIBITIONS 1905 Amsterdam, 210; 1929 New York, 90; Cambridge, 95; 1935-6 New York etc, 64; 1939 Boston, 58; 1956 Raleigh, USA, without cat nr
PROVENANCE Mrs J. van Gogh-Bonger, Amsterdam [R 1905]; Mrs Tilla Durieux-Cassirer, Berlin; Paul Cassirer Art Gallery, Berlin; Thannhauser Art Gallery, Lucerne; John T. Spaulding, Boston, USA [R 1929, 1935]; Boston, Museum of Fine Arts [acquired 1948; bequest of John T. Spaulding], inv nr 48.549, cat 1955, p 29

F 806 [H 792] FARM NEAR AUVERS WITH TWO FIGURES
EXHIBITIONS 1905 Amsterdam, 217; 1906 Rotterdam, 55; 1930 Amsterdam, 314; 1935 Amsterdam 2, 17; 1939 San Francisco, 180; 1939-40 San Francisco, 126; 1940 New York 3, 3; 1942 Baltimore, Worcester, 33; 1943 New York 2, 65; 1943-4 Indianapolis etc, 13; 1944 Montreal, 139; 1946-7 Liège etc, 167; 1947 Geneva, 168; Paris 1, 168; 1947-8 London etc, 93; 1948 Bergen, Oslo, 64; 1951 Lyons etc, 81; 1953 The Hague, 185; Otterlo, Amsterdam, 181; 1953-4 St Louis etc, 169; 1954 Zurich, 79; 1954-55 Bern, 70; 1955 Antwerp 1, 365; 1955-56 Liverpool etc, 81; 1957 Marseilles, 86; Stockholm, 119; 1958-59 San Francisco etc, 80; 1959-60 Utrecht, 61; 1961-62 Baltimore etc, 76; 1963 Humlebaek, 55; 1964 Washington, New York, 55; 1965 Charleroi, Ghent, 38; 1965-66 Stockholm, Göteborg, 56; 1967 Wolfsburg, 76; 1968-9 London, 197
PROVENANCE Mrs J. van Gogh-Bonger, Amsterdam; V. W. van Gogh, Laren; Amsterdam, Rijksmuseum Vincent van Gogh [Vincent van Gogh Foundation, inv nr F 806]

F 807 [H 794] FIELD OF GREEN WHEAT
EXHIBITIONS 1912 Cologne, 42; 1914 Berlin, 138; 1921 Berlin; 1928 Berlin, 89; 1966 Washington, 135
PROVENANCE Mrs J. van Gogh-Bonger, Amsterdam; Paul Cassirer Art Gallery, Berlin; Curt Herrmann, Berlin, Charlottenburg [R 1912, 1928]; F. H. Herrmann, London; Upperville, Virg., Mr and Mrs Paul Mellon [R 1966]

F 808 [H 796] WHEATFIELD WITH CORNFLOWERS
EXHIBITIONS 1914 Berlin, 128; 1921 Berlin; 1928 Berlin, 90; 1933-34 Rotterdam, 44; 1934 Bern, 65; 1942 Baltimore, Worcester, 36; 1943 New York 2, 66; 1964 Paris 2, 14
PROVENANCE Mrs J. van Gogh-Bonger, Amsterdam; Max Liebermann, Berlin [R 1914]; Mrs Käthe Riezler, Berlin [R 1928]; Mr and Mrs Kurt Riezler, New York [R 1943]; Private collection [R 1964]

F 809 [H 795] WHEAT STACKS
EXHIBITIONS 1905 Amsterdam, 214; 1906 Rotterdam, 56; 1924 Basle, 67; Zurich, 74; 1938 Paris 1, 134; 1940 Lucerne, 58; 1956 Munich, 164; 1960 Paris, 69
PROVENANCE Mrs J. van Gogh-Bonger, Amsterdam [R 1905]; Paul Vallotton Art Gallery, Lausanne; Bernheim Jeune Art Gallery, Paris; A. Hahnloser, Winterthur [R 1924, 1938]; Bern, H. R. Hahnloser [R 1970]

F 810 [H 799] HOUSES WITH SUNFLOWERS
EXHIBITIONS 1928 Frankfurt, 46; 1930 Amsterdam, 111; 1945 Basle, 18
PROVENANCE Thannhauser Art Gallery, Munich; Mrs A. Bonn-Schuster, Frankfurt [acquired 1916]; Emil Bührle, Zurich [R 1945]; Paris, Mrs A. Caroline M. Baronesse de Rothschild

F 811 [H 798] LANDSCAPE AT AUVERS IN THE RAIN
EXHIBITIONS 1905 Amsterdam, 212; 1914 Berlin, 121
PROVENANCE Mrs J. van Gogh-Bonger, Amsterdam [R 1905]; Bernheim Jeune Art Gallery, Paris [after 1914]; Miss G. E. Davies, Gregynog [Wales] [1920-1952] [through Hugh Blaker, 1920]; Cardiff, National Museum of Wales [acquired 1952; bequest of G. E. Davies], Cat Gwendoline E. Davies Bequest 1952, nr 102. Cat The Davies coll of French art 1967, pp 87-8

F 812 THE FIELDS
PROVENANCE Otto Wacker Art Galery, Berlin; Lutz Art Gallery, Berlin; Hodebert Gallery, Paris [R 1928]; Washington, The Phillips collection. not in cat 1952

F 813 THE FIELDS
Left out by Faille in his manuscript for the present edition; See REJECTED WORKS

F 814 [H 797] GARDEN AT AUVERS
EXHIBITIONS 1914 Berlin, 79; 1916 Munich, without cat nr; 1928 Berlin, 91; 1933-34 Rotterdam, 45; 1945 Amsterdam, without cat nr
PROVENANCE Amédée Schuffenecker, Clamart; Curt Glaser, Berlin; Caspari Art Gallery, Munich; Leo Lewin, Breslau [R 1914]; Caspari Art Gallery, Munich; A. Lewin, Guben [R 1928]; Rotterdam, Museum Boymans-Van Beuningen [on loan through P. Cassirer, Amsterdam, 1933-1945]; Mrs Alice Kurtz, Hastings on Hudson, USA; Wildenstein Art Gallery, New York; Paris, Jacques Walter

F 815 [H 800] THREE TREES
EXHIBITIONS 1911 Budapest; 1947 Basle, 106; Paris 1, 166; 1952 Milan, 124; 1953 The Hague, 186; Otterlo, Amsterdam, 186; 1953-54 St Louis etc, 170; 1954-55 Paris, 57; 1956 Munich, 160; Eindhoven, 51; 1958 Vienna, 110
PROVENANCE Marczell de Nemes, Budapest; Sale Paris [Manzi Joyant] 18 June 1913, 107 [repr]; Otterlo, Rijksmuseum Kröller-Müller, inv nr 317-13, cat van Gogh 1970, nr 254

F 816 [H 801] TREES, ROOTS AND BRANCHES
EXHIBITIONS 1905 Amsterdam, 216; 1953-54 St Louis etc, 171
PROVENANCE Mrs J. van Gogh-Bonger, Amsterdam; V. W. van Gogh, Laren; Amsterdam, Rijksmuseum Vincent van Gogh [Vincent van Gogh Foundation, inv nr F 816]

F 817 [H 803] THE GROVE
EXHIBITIONS 1925 Paris 1, 51; 1927 Berlin 2, 107; 1959 New York 2, 52; 1960 New York 2, 49; 1961 New York 2, 42; 1966-67 Jerusalem etc, 41
PROVENANCE Bernheim Jeune Art Gallery, Paris; Paul Vallotton Art Gallery, Paris; Paul Vallotton Art Gallery, Lausanne; W. Russ-Young, Serrières near Neuchâtel [R 1916]; Paul Vallotton Art Gallery, Lausanne; Wm. Boyd, West Jerry, near Dundee; J. K. Thannhauser Art Gallery, New York; New York, Mr and Mrs Joseph H. Hazen [R 1959, 1970]

F 818 [H 802] LANDSCAPE WITH FIGURES
EXHIBITIONS 1920 New York, 37; 1924 Zurich, 73; Stuttgart, 37; Basle, 76; 1925 The Hague, 27; Paris 1, 53; 1926 Munich, 2070; London 3, 9; 1927 Berlin 2
PROVENANCE Mrs J. van Gogh-Bonger, Amsterdam [R 1910]; V. W. van Gogh, Laren; Thannhauser Art Gallery, Munich [R 1956]; Thannhauser Art Gallery, Paris; Miss Etta M. Cone, Baltimore; Baltimore, The Baltimore Museum of Art, cat Cone collection 1955, nr 122 [revised ed 1967, nr 27]

F 819 [H 750] WOMEN WALKING ALONG THE FIELDS
EXHIBITIONS 1914 Berlin, 123; 1933 Chicago, 387; 1957 Los Angeles, 25
PROVENANCE Mrs J. van Gogh-Bonger, Amsterdam [R 1914]; V. W. van Gogh, Laren; Chester H. Johnson Galleries, Chicago [R 1933]; Wildenstein Art Gallery, New York; Mr Hunt Henderson, USA; San Antonio, Texas, Marion Koogler McNay Art Institute, inv nr 1950.49

F 820 [H 747] BLOSSOMING CHESTNUT BRANCHES
EXHIBITIONS 1914 Berlin, 135; 1921 Berlin; 1927 Berlin 3, 122; 1928 Berlin, 92; 1955 Winterthur 1, 104; 1958 Zurich, 246; Berlin, 48; 1958-9 Munich, 77; 1959 Paris, 69; 1961 Edinburgh, London, 61
PROVENANCE Paul Ferd. Gachet, Auvers [1890-1909]; Paul Gachet, Auvers; Bernheim jeune Art Gallery, Paris; F. von Mendelssohn-Bartholdy, Grunewald [R 1914, 1928]; Heirs of F. von Mendelssohn-Bartholdy [R 1961]; F. Nathan, St. Gallen [R 1964]; Emil Bührle, Zurich [acquired 1951]; Zurich, E. Bührle, cat 1958, nr 246

F 821 [H p 557] BRANCHES OF A WHITE FLOWERING ACACIA TREE
PROVENANCE Paul Ferd. Gachet, Auvers [1890-1909]; Paul Gachet, Auvers; Victor Doiteau [acquired 1941]; Mrs Yvonne Doiteau, Péronne, Somme [R 1960-6]; Sale London [Sotheby] 22 June 1966, 26; Stockholm, Nationalmuseum [acquired 1966], inv nr NM 5939

F 822 [H p 557] THE COWS
EXHIBITIONS 1954-5 Paris, 49; 1959 Recklinghausen, 111; 1960 Paris, 63
PROVENANCE Paul Ferd. Gachet, Auvers [1890-1909]; Paul Gachet, Auvers; Lille, Musée Palais des Beaux-Arts [acquired 1950; gift of P. Gachet]

F 823 THE WHEATFIELD
Left out by Faille in his manuscript for the present edition; See REJECTED WORKS

F 824 LANDSCAPE
Left out by Faille in his manuscript for the present edition; See REJECTED WORKS

DRAWINGS

F 825 VIEW OF HELVOIRT
See JUVENILIA

F 826 THE CHURCH OF THE AUSTIN FRIARS
See JUVENILIA

CUESMES–BRUSSELS PERIOD

F 827 COAL SHOVELER
EXHIBITIONS 1927 Basle etc, 2; 1928 Düsseldorf, 68; Karlsruhe, 3; 1929 Berlin 1, 1; Hamburg, 1; 1930 Amsterdam, 5; 1935-6 New York etc, 69; 1946-7 Liège etc, 1; 1947 Paris 1, 1; Geneva, 1; 1955 Paris 4, 158; 1956 Eindhoven, 1; Nuremberg, 1; 1957 Essen, 116; 1958 Tokyo, Kyoto, 5; 1960 Cuesmes, 1; 1962 Warsaw, 3; 1963 Tel Aviv, Haifa, 3
PROVENANCE M. de Zwart, Voorburg, Netherlands; H. P. baron van Tuyll van Serooskerken, Amsterdam; Sale Amsterdam [F. Muller] 25-26 November 1913, 133; Otterlo, Rijksmuseum Kröller-Müller, inv nr 186-13, cat van Gogh 1970, nr 5

F 828 THE DIGGERS [after Millet]
EXHIBITIONS 1960 Cuesmes, 2; Paris, 71; 1963 London 4, 37
PROVENANCE H. P. Bremmer, The Hague; Heirs of H. P. Bremmer, The Hague [R 1960]; Van Wisselingh Art Gallery, Amsterdam; Present owner unknown [R 1970]

F 829 THE DIGGERS [after Millet]
EXHIBITIONS 1918 The Hague; 1924 Amsterdam, 16; 1928 The Hague; 1929 Hamburg, 61; 1930 Amsterdam, 4; 1956 Munich, 3; 1960 Cuesmes; 1962 Warsaw, 5; 1963 Tel Aviv, Haifa, 4; 1966 Belgrade, 3
PROVENANCE J. Hidde Nijland, The Hague [1895-1928]; Dordrechts Museum, Dordrecht [loan Hidde Nijland 1904-1910]; Otterlo, Rijksmuseum Kröller-Müller, inv nr 958-28, cat van Gogh 1970, nr 7

F 830 THE SOWER [after Millet]
EXHIBITIONS 1914-5 Amsterdam, 148; 1927-8 Berlin etc, 1 [repr]; 1937 Paris, 109; 1954-5 Bern, 73; 1955 Antwerp 1, 17; 1957 Marseilles, 1; Stockholm, 1; 1958-9 San Francisco etc, 85; 1959-60 Utrecht, 66; 1960 Enschede, 1; 1961-2 Baltimore etc, 82; 1963 Humlebaek, 61; 1964 Washington, New York, 61; 1965 Charleroi, Ghent, 42; 1966 Paris, Albi, 1; 1967 Lille, Zurich, 1; 1967-8 Dallas etc, 1; 1968 Liège, 1; 1968-9 London, 2; 1969 Humlebaek, 1
PROVENANCE Mrs J. van Gogh-Bonger, Amsterdam; V. W. van Gogh, Laren; Amsterdam, Rijksmuseum Vincent van Gogh [Vincent van Gogh Foundation, inv nr F 830]

F 831 MINERS
EXHIBITIONS 1918 The Hague; 1924 Amsterdam, 14; 1928 The Hague; 1929 Hamburg, 49; 1930 Amsterdam, 1; 1935-6

New York etc, 70; 1946-7 Liège etc, 2; 1947 Paris 1, 2;
Geneva, 2; Basle, 109; 1947-8 London etc, 100; 1952 Paris
3, 333; 1953-4 St Louis etc, 1; 1956 Nuremberg, 1; 1958
Tokyo, Kyoto, 3; 1961 Munich, 1; 1962 London 1, 1
PROVENANCE J. Hidde Nijland, The Hague [1895-1928];
Dordrechts Museum, Dordrecht [loan Hidde Nijland
1904-1910]; Otterlo, Rijksmuseum Kröller-Müller, inv
nr 946-28, cat van Gogh 1970, nr 2

F832 MINERS' WOMEN CARRYING SACKS [THE
BEARERS OF THE BURDEN]
EXHIBITIONS 1895 The Hague; 1918 The Hague; 1924
Amsterdam, 13; 1928 The Hague; 1929 Hamburg, 91; 1930
Amsterdam, 2; 1946-7 Liège etc, 2; 1947 Paris 1, 3; Geneva,
3; Basle, 110; 1947-8 London etc, 101; 1949-50 New York,
Chicago, 13; 1952 Milan, 1; 1953 The Hague, 1; Otterlo,
Amsterdam, 1; 1956 Munich, 4; 1958 Vienna, 3; 1961
Munich, 3
PROVENANCE J. Hidde Nijland, The Hague [1895-1928];
Dordrechts Museum, Dordrecht [loan Hidde Nijland
1904-1910]; Otterlo, Rijksmuseum Kröller-Müller, inv
nr 996-28, cat van Gogh 1970, nr 3

F833 THE DAUGHTER OF JACOB MEYER [after Holbein]
EXHIBITIONS 1927 Basle etc, 35; 1928 Düsseldorf, 208;
1929 Berlin 1, 2; Hamburg, 29; 1930 Amsterdam, 6; Basle,
111; 1952 Milan, 3; 1956 Munich, 5; 1958 Vienna, 5;
1960-1 Montreal etc, 83; 1962 Warsaw, 6; 1963 Tel Aviv,
Haifa, 5
PROVENANCE L.C. Enthoven, Voorburg, Netherlands;
Sale Enthoven, Amsterdam [F. Muller] 18 May 1920, 249;
F. Muller, Amsterdam; Sale Amsterdam [F. Muller] 20 June
1922, 42; Otterlo, Rijksmuseum Kröller-Müller, inv
nr 219-22, cat van Gogh 1970, nr 8

F834 THE ANGELUS [after Millet]
EXHIBITIONS 1918 The Hague; 1924 Amsterdam, 15; 1928
The Hague; 1929 Hamburg, 100; 1930 Amsterdam, 3; 1956
Nuremberg, 2; 1958 Vienna, 4; Tokyo, Kyoto, 4; 1961
Munich, 2; 1966 Belgrade, 1
PROVENANCE J. Hidde Nijland, The Hague [1895-1928];
Dordrechts Museum, Dordrecht [loan Hidde Nijland
1904-1910]; Otterlo, Rijksmuseum Kröller-Müller, inv
nr 1007-28, cat van Gogh 1970, nr 4

F835 OLD BRETON WOMAN ASLEEP IN CHURCH
[after F. Rops]
See JUVENILIA

F836 A COUNTRY LANE
See JUVENILIA

F837 THE LANGE VIJVERBERG
See JUVENILIA

F838 THE DITCH
See JUVENILIA

F839 THE CANAL
See JUVENILIA

F840 WOMAN STANDING: FACING LEFT
EXHIBITIONS 1924 Amsterdam, 119
PROVENANCE J. Hidde Nijland, The Hague [van Marle]
Hague [van Marle] 9 November 1943, 29; Huinck and
Scherjon Art Gallery, Amsterdam; Haarlem, Private
collection

F841 WOMAN ON HER DEATHBED
EXHIBITIONS 1895 The Hague; 1918 The Hague; 1924
Amsterdam, 132 [repr]; 1928 The Hague; 1929 Hamburg,
149; 1930 Amsterdam, 142; 1935-6 New York etc, 71;
1946-7 Liège etc, 12; 1947 Paris 1, 12; Geneva, 12; Basle,
129; 1947-8 London, 12; 1949 Gouda; 1952 Milan, 23
PROVENANCE J. Hidde Nijland, The Hague [1895-1928];
Dordrechts Museum, Dordrecht [loan Hidde Nijland
1904-1910]; Otterlo, Rijksmuseum Kröller-Müller, inv
nr 987-28, cat van Gogh 1970, nr 91

ETTEN PERIOD

F842 SHACKS
EXHIBITION 1961 Munich, 4
PROVENANCE Mrs J. van Gogh-Bonger, Amsterdam;
A. van Veen, Rotterdam; M.M. van Valkenburg, Rotter-
dam; Rotterdam, Museum Boymans-Van Beuningen [gift of
D. Hannema 1922], inv nr VvG nr 1; cat 1927, nr 790

F843 WIND MILL BY A CANAL
EXHIBITIONS 1918 The Hague; 1924 Amsterdam, 12; 1928
The Hague; 1929 Hamburg, 118; 1930 Amsterdam, 4; 1958
Vienna, 6; Tokyo, Kyoto, 5; 1962 Warsaw, 7; 1963 Tel
Aviv, Haifa, 6; 1966 Belgrade, 4
PROVENANCE J. Hidde Nijland, The Hague [1895-1928];
Dordrechts Museum, Dordrecht [loan Hidde Nijland
1904-1910]; Otterlo, Rijksmuseum Kröller-Müller, inv
nr 1030-28, cat van Gogh 1970, nr 9

F844 THE WIND MILL
EXHIBITION 1961 Amsterdam 1, 1

PROVENANCE Oldenzeel Art Gallery, Rotterdam;
F.W.R. Wentges, The Hague [acquired 1909]; The Hague,
Mrs M.A.R. van der Leeuw-Wentges [acquired 1930;
R 1970]

F845 MARSH WITH WATER LILIES
EXHIBITIONS 1947 Basle, 112; 1956 Munich, 6; 1957
Essen, 128; 1960 Paris, 73; 1962 Warsaw, 89; 1963 Tel Aviv,
Haifa, 7
PROVENANCE Miss W. van Gogh, Dieren, Netherlands;
J.P. Scholte, Barchem, Netherlands; Lochem, Netherlands,
Mrs A.T. Scholte-van Houten; Scholte-van Houten
collection [R 1970]

F846 MARSH
EXHIBITIONS 1903 Rotterdam 3, 81; 1904 Rotterdam, 52;
1955 New York 2, 79; 1967 Lille, Zurich, 93; 1969 London
2, 35; 1969-70 Paris, 37
PROVENANCE Oldenzeel Art Gallery, Rotterdam;
H. Tutein Nolthenius, Delft; d'Audretsch Art Gallery, The
Hague; M. Frank, New York; Mrs Martin Nachmann,
New York; M. Frank, New York [acquired 1948]; Mrs
M. Feilchenfeldt, Zurich [1967]; Ottawa, National Gallery
of Canada [acquired 1968]

F847 THE DAUGHTER OF JACOB MEYER [after Holbein]
EXHIBITIONS 1937 Paris, 110; 1960 Paris, 74
PROVENANCE H.P. Bremmer, The Hague; Heirs of
H.P. Bremmer, The Hague [1960; 1961]; The Hague,
F. Bremmer [R 1970]

F848 FIGURE OF A WOMAN [after Holbein]
EXHIBITIONS 1960 Paris, 75; 1963 London, 38
PROVENANCE H.P. Bremmer, The Hague; Heirs of
H.P. Bremmer, The Hague [R 1960]; Van Wisselingh Art
Gallery, Amsterdam; Zurich, Mrs M. Feilchenfeldt
[R 1970]

F849 PORTRAIT OF VINCENT'S SISTER, WILLEMINA
VAN GOGH [after a photograph]
EXHIBITIONS 1927 Basle etc, 3; 1928 Düsseldorf, 69;
Karlsruhe, 4; 1929 Berlin 1, 4; Hamburg, 3; 1930 Amster-
dam, 25
PROVENANCE L.C. Enthoven, Voorburg, Netherlands;
Sale Enthoven, Amsterdam [F. Muller] 18 May 1920, 252;
Otterlo, Rijksmuseum Kröller-Müller, inv nr 188-20, cat
van Gogh 1970, nr 20

F849a BUST OF A YOUNG GIRL [copy]
PROVENANCE C. Bakker, Hilversum; Present owner
unknown

F850 WIND MILLS AT DORDRECHT [Weeskinderendijk]
EXHIBITIONS 1927 Basle etc, 34; 1928 Düsseldorf, 100;
Karlsruhe, 35; 1929 Berlin 1, 5; Hamburg, 139; 1930
Amsterdam, 155; 1935-6 New York etc, 73; 1956 Nurem-
berg, 12; Munich, 9; 1957 Essen, 130; 1958 Vienna, 8;
Tokyo, Kyoto, 16; 1960-1 Montreal etc, 80; 1962 Warsaw,
13; 1963 Tel Aviv, Haifa, 12; 1966 Belgrade, 10
PROVENANCE L.C. Enthoven, Voorburg, Netherlands;
Sale Enthoven, Amsterdam [F. Muller] 18 May 1920, 256;
Otterlo, Rijksmuseum Kröller-Müller, inv nr 218-20, cat
van Gogh 1970, nr 42

F851 YOUNG PEASANT WITH SICKLE
EXHIBITIONS 1918 The Hague; 1924 Amsterdam, 96
[repr]; 1928 The Hague; 1929 Hamburg, 80; 1930 Amster-
dam, 15; 1946-7 Liège etc, 4; 1947 Paris 1, 4; Geneva, 4;
Basle, 113; 1947-8 London etc, 102; 1949-50 New York,
Chicago, 14; 1952 Milan, 8; 1953 The Hague, 3; Otterlo,
Amsterdam, 3; 1953-4 St Louis etc, 6; 1956 Nuremberg, 10;
Munich, 12; 1957 Essen, 131; 1958 Tokyo, Kyoto, 14; 1961
Munich, 8
PROVENANCE J. Hidde Nijland, The Hague [1895-1928];
Dordrechts Museum, Dordrecht [loan Hidde Nijland
1904-1910]; Otterlo, Rijksmuseum Kröller-Müller, inv
nr 977-28, cat van Gogh 1970, nr 33

F852 THE SOWER: FACING RIGHT
EXHIBITIONS 1903 Rotterdam; 1964 Laren, without cat
nr; 1966 Laren, 89
PROVENANCE C. Mouwen jr, Breda; Sale Mouwen,
Amsterdam [F. Muller] 3 May 1904, 36 [not sold]; Oldenzeel
Art Gallery, Rotterdam; H. Tutein Nolthenius, Delft;
Ph. Gelb, New York; Sale London [Sotheby] 22 March
1961, 108; Ch. Sussmann, Paris; Sale Paris [Palais Galliéra]
16 June 1964, 24; Amsterdam, P. and N. de Boer
Foundation

F853 TWO SOWERS
EXHIBITIONS 1905 Amsterdam, 450; 1914-5 Amsterdam, 1
PROVENANCE Mrs J. van Gogh-Bonger, Amsterdam;
V.W. van Gogh, Laren; Amsterdam, Rijksmuseum Vincent
van Gogh [Vincent van Gogh Foundation, inv nr F853]

F854 PEASANT WOMAN PEELING POTATOES
EXHIBITIONS 1918 The Hague; 1924 Amsterdam, 39; 1928
The Hague; 1929 Hamburg, 157; 1930 Amsterdam, 33
PROVENANCE J. Hidde Nijland, The Hague [1895-1928];
Dordrechts Museum, Dordrecht [loan Hidde Nijland

1904-1910]; Otterlo, Rijksmuseum Kröller-Müller, inv
nr 1026-28, cat van Gogh 1970, nr 40

F855 YOUNG PEASANT DIGGING: FACING RIGHT
EXHIBITIONS 1918 The Hague; 1924 Amsterdam, 91; 1928
The Hague; 1929 Hamburg, 63; 1930 Amsterdam, 16; 1956
Eindhoven, 5; Nuremberg, 5
PROVENANCE J. Hidde Nijland, The Hague [1895-1928];
Dordrechts Museum, Dordrecht [loan Hidde Nijland
1904-1910]; Otterlo, Rijksmuseum Kröller-Müller, inv
nr 962-28, cat van Gogh 1970, nr 41

F856 PEASANT SOWING: FACING RIGHT
EXHIBITIONS 1918 The Hague; 1924 Amsterdam, 84; 1928
The Hague; 1929 Hamburg, 45; 1930 Amsterdam, 13
PROVENANCE J. Hidde Nijland, The Hague [1895-1928];
Dordrechts Museum, Dordrecht [loan Hidde Nijland
1904-1910]; Otterlo, Rijksmuseum Kröller-Müller, inv
nr 942-28, cat van Gogh 1970, nr 14

F857 THE SOWER: FULL FACE
EXHIBITION 1961 Amsterdam 1, 2
PROVENANCE A.G.A. van Rappard, Utrecht; Mrs van
Rappard-del Campo, Santpoort, Netherlands [R 1892];
P. de Kanter, Delft; H.P. Bremmer, The Hague; The Hague,
Heirs of H.P. Bremmer [R 1970]

F858 THE SOWER: FACING RIGHT
PROVENANCE H.P. Bremmer, The Hague; Heirs of
H.P. Bremmer, The Hague; Van Wisselingh Art Gallery,
Amsterdam; F.A.C. Guépin, Stanmore, Middlesex
[1960-1966]; Heirs of F.A.C. Guépin [R 1966]

F859 YOUNG PEASANT DIGGING: FACING RIGHT
EXHIBITIONS 1918 The Hague; 1924 Amsterdam, 51; 1928
The Hague; 1929 Hamburg, 101; 1930 Amsterdam, 18; 1956
Nuremberg, 9; Munich, 10; 1958 Tokyo, Kyoto, 13; 1966
Belgrade, 9
PROVENANCE J. Hidde Nijland, The Hague [1895-1928];
Dordrechts Museum, Dordrecht [loan Hidde Nijland
1904-1910]; Otterlo, Rijksmuseum Kröller-Müller, inv
nr 1008-28, cat van Gogh 1970, nr 32

F860 PEASANT DIGGING: FACING LEFT
PROVENANCE C.M. van Gogh Art Gallery, Amsterdam;
Van Wisselingh Art Gallery, London; G.H. Slot, London;
Sale Slot, London 1913; F. Wilson, London; Amsterdam,
P. and N. de Boer Foundation [R 1970]

F860a PEASANT DIGGING: FACING RIGHT
PROVENANCE E. van Biema, Rouen; Mrs Valin-van Biema
Rouen; Sale P. Lehmann, Paris; Sale London [Sotheby]
1 July 1959, 71; Packer; Sale London [Sotheby] 12 June
1963, 94; London, Jacques O'Hana Ltd Collection [R 1970];
Canada, Private Collection [R 1970]

F861 THE GARDENER LEANING ON A SPADE: LEFT
THREE-QUARTER VIEW
EXHIBITIONS 1918 The Hague; 1924 Amsterdam, 43; 1928
The Hague; 1929 Hamburg, 88; 1930 Amsterdam, 17; 1956
Munich, 11
PROVENANCE J. Hidde Nijland, The Hague [1895-1928];
Dordrechts Museum, Dordrecht [loan Hidde Nijland
1904-1910]; Otterlo, Rijksmuseum Kröller-Müller, inv
nr 990-28, cat van Gogh 1970, nr 16

F862 PEASANT SOWING
EXHIBITIONS 1918 The Hague; 1924 Amsterdam, 93; 1928
The Hague; 1929 Hamburg, 51; 1930 Amsterdam, 14
PROVENANCE J. Hidde Nijland, The Hague [1895-1928];
Dordrechts Museum, Dordrecht [loan Hidde Nijland
1904-1910]; Otterlo, Rijksmuseum Kröller-Müller, inv
nr 948-28, cat van Gogh 1970, nr 14

F863 WORN OUT
EXHIBITIONS 1958-9 Washington etc, 142; 1966 Laren, 90
PROVENANCE A.G.A. van Rappard, Utrecht; Mrs van
Rappard-del Campo, Santpoort [R 1892]; P. de Kanter,
Delft; H.E. d'Audretsch, Amerongen; M. Frank, New
York; P. de Boer Art Gallery, Amsterdam; Amsterdam,
P. and N. de Boer Foundation [R 1970]

F864 WORN OUT
PROVENANCE A.G.A. van Rappard, Utrecht; Mrs van
Rappard-del Campo, Santpoort [R 1892]; P. de Kanter,
Delft; H.E. d'Audretsch, Amerongen; M. Frank, New
York; New York, Private collection [R 1970]

F865 MAN WITH BASKET, SOWING
EXHIBITIONS 1918 The Hague; 1924 Amsterdam, 116;
1928 The Hague; 1929 Hamburg, 72; 1930 Amsterdam,
154; 1952 Milan, 9
PROVENANCE J. Hidde Nijland, The Hague [1895-1928];
Dordrechts Museum, Dordrecht [loan Hidde Nijland
1904-1910]; Otterlo, Rijksmuseum Kröller-Müller, inv
nr 971-28, cat van Gogh 1970, nr 43

F866 PEASANT DIGGING: FACING LEFT
EXHIBITIONS 1905 Amsterdam, 264; 1914-5 Amsterdam,
26; 1927-8 Berlin etc, 3; 1954-5 Bern, 76; 1955 Antwerp 1,

21; 1957 Stockholm, 2; 1968-9 London, 3
PROVENANCE Mrs J. van Gogh-Bonger, Amsterdam;
V. W. van Gogh, Laren; Amsterdam, Rijksmuseum Vincent
van Gogh [Vincent van Gogh Foundation, inv nr F 866]

F 866a THE SOWER
EXHIBITION 1957 Los Angeles, 27
PROVENANCE A. J. van der Goot, Breda; A. Nystad Art
Gallery, The Hague; John Streep Art Gallery, New York;
New York, Mr and Mrs L. M. Rogers and Mr A. E. Rogers,
cat Rogers Collection 1958, nr 11

F 867 PEASANT WOMAN SEWING
PROVENANCE Oldenzeel Art Gallery, Rotterdam;
H. A. Burgerhout, Wassenaar; Sale Laren [Huize de
Leeuwerik] 16 December 1942, 311; H. A. Burgerhout,
Wassenaar; New York, P. Rosenberg Art Gallery [R 1960]

F 868 OLD PEASANT BY THE FIREPLACE
EXHIBITIONS 1918 The Hague; 1924 Amsterdam, 68; 1928
The Hague; 1929 Hamburg, 158; 1930 Amsterdam, 135;
1956 Nuremberg, 7; Munich, 15; 1957 Essen, 132; 1960-1
Montreal etc, 82; 1966 Belgrade, 8
PROVENANCE J. Hidde Nijland, The Hague [1895-1928];
Dordrechts Museum, Dordrecht [loan Hidde Nijland
1904-1910]; Otterlo, Rijksmuseum Kröller-Müller, inv
nr 1027-28, cat van Gogh 1970, nr 28

F 869 YOUNG SCHEVENINGEN WOMAN, SEATED:
FACING LEFT
EXHIBITIONS 1964 Laren, 28; 1966 Laren, 88
PROVENANCE Miss Margot Begemann, Nuenen; H. D. van
Stipriaan Luïscius, The Hague; J. F. D. Scheltema, The
Hague; Sale Amsterdam [Brandt] 18 November 1963, 103;
Amsterdam, P. and N. de Boer Foundation [R 1970]

F 870 YOUNG SCHEVENINGEN WOMAN, KNITTING:
FACING RIGHT
EXHIBITION 1937 Paris, 111
PROVENANCE G. A. Molenaar, The Hague [gift from the
artist, 1882]; Miss G. P. Molenaar, Nunspeet [R 1960]; New
York, Private collection

F 871 YOUNG FISHERWOMAN FROM SCHEVENINGEN,
STANDING: FACING LEFT
PROVENANCE Mrs J. van Gogh-Bonger, Amsterdam;
V. W. van Gogh, Laren; Amsterdam, Rijksmuseum Vincent
van Gogh [Vincent van Gogh Foundation, inv nr F 871]

F 872 AN ADVENTURER SETTING OUT
PROVENANCE A. G. A. van Rappard, Utrecht; P. de
Kanter, Delft [acquired 1903]; Bilthoven, Mrs H. Hupkes-de
Kanter [R 1970]

F 873 GIRL WITH BLACK CAP, ON THE GROUND BY THE
FIRE: FACING LEFT
EXHIBITIONS 1918 The Hague; 1924 Amsterdam, 98; 1928
The Hague; 1929 Hamburg, 66; 1930 Amsterdam, 152; 1956
Nuremberg, 8; 1962 Warsaw, 12; 1963 Tel Aviv, Haifa, 11
PROVENANCE J. Hidde Nijland, The Hague [1895-1928];
Dordrechts Museum, Dordrecht [loan Hidde Nijland
1904-1910]; Otterlo, Rijksmuseum Kröller-Müller, inv
nr 965-28, cat van Gogh 1970, nr 31

F 874 recto [formerly F 874 verso] SKETCH OF A
LANDSCAPE WITH FACTORIES
PROVENANCE E. Schall, Baden-Baden; H. Stinnes,
Cologne-Lindenthal [acquired 1912]; Sale Stuttgart
[Stuttgarter Kunstkabinett] 28 May 1952, 1264; Knoedler
Art Gallery, New York; Fine Arts Associates, New York;
St Louis, City Art Museum [acquired 1954]

F 874 verso [formerly F 874 recto] LANDSCAPE
EXHIBITION 1962 Ann Arbor, 79
PROVENANCE See F 874 recto

F 875 THE THATCHED HUT
EXHIBITION 1926 London 2, p 10
PROVENANCE C. M. van Gogh Art Gallery, Amsterdam;
Van Wisselingh Art Gallery, London; G. H. Slot, London;
Sale Slot, London 1913; London, F. Wilson [R 1926]

F 876 THE ARTIST'S FATHER THEODORUS VAN GOGH
[after a photograph]
EXHIBITIONS 1903 Rotterdam 3, 85; 1960 Paris, not in cat
PROVENANCE Oldenzeel Art Gallery, Rotterdam;
H. Tutein Nolthenius, Delft [R 1904]; G. J. Nieuwenhuizen
Segaar Art Gallery, The Hague; The Hague, Mrs B. Nieu-
wenhuizen Segaar-Aarse [R 1970]

F 877 SHEPHERD WITH FLOCK NEAR A CHURCH AT
ZWEELOO
PROVENANCE Oldenzeel Art Gallery, Rotterdam [Dec.
1903]; Miss G. P. van Stolk, Rotterdam; Mr and Mrs J. van
Hoey Smith-van Stolk, Rockanje; Rockanje, R. W. van
Hoey Smith

F 878 THE CARPENTER
EXHIBITIONS 1927 Basle etc, 1; 1928 Düsseldorf, 66;
Karlsruhe, 1; 1929 Berlin 1, 2; Hamburg, 2; 1930 Amster-

dam, 12; 1935-6 New York etc, 72; 1958 Vienna, 10
PROVENANCE Jac. de Vries Art Gallery, Arnhem; Sale
Amsterdam [F. Muller] 3 December 1918, 126; Otterlo,
Rijksmuseum Kröller-Müller, inv nr 187-18, cat van Gogh
1970, nr 13

F 879 A KNEELING MAN PLANTING
EXHIBITIONS 1918 The Hague; 1924 Amsterdam, 101;
1928 The Hague; 1929 Hamburg, 148; 1930 Amsterdam,
19; 1958 Vienna, 14
PROVENANCE J. Hidde Nijland, The Hague [1895-1928];
Dordrechts Museum, Dordrecht [loan Hidde Nijland
1904-1910]; Otterlo, Rijksmuseum Kröller-Müller, inv
nr 981-28, cat van Gogh 1970, nr 30

F 880 GIRL KNEELING IN FRONT OF BUCKET
EXHIBITIONS 1961 Amsterdam 1, 3; 1967 Washington, Los
Angeles, 75
PROVENANCE d'Audretsch Art Gallery, The Hague;
Oldenzeel Art Gallery, Rotterdam; J. van der Hoop jr,
Rotterdam; V. M. L. Dumoulin, Vught; d'Audretsch Art
Gallery, The Hague; John Streep, London [R 1961]; Paul
Rosenberg Art Gallery, New York [R 1962]; Chicago, Mr
and Mrs Leigh B. Block [R 1967]

F 881 PEASANT GIRL GATHERING POTATOES
PROVENANCE H. P. Bremmer, The Hague; The Hague,
F. Bremmer [R 1970]

F 882 A MAN SOWING: FACING LEFT
EXHIBITION 1924 Amsterdam, 54
PROVENANCE J. Hidde Nijland, The Hague; Otterlo,
Rijksmuseum Kröller-Müller, inv nr 950-28, cat van Gogh
1970, nr 11

F 883 A WOMAN SOWING, WITH BASKET
PROVENANCE J. Dona, The Hague; D. A. Hoogendijk Art
Gallery, Amsterdam; H. Abels Art Gallery, Cologne, cat
1925 [?], pp 44-5 [repr]; Present owner unknown

F 884 YOUNG GIRL GARDENING
EXHIBITIONS 1952 Amsterdam, 10; 1956 Amsterdam, 1;
1961 Amsterdam 1, 4; 1966 Gouda, 12
PROVENANCE J. Hageraats Art Gallery, The Hague; De
Zonnebloem Art Gallery, The Hague; Mrs H. E. Hannema-
de Stuers, The Hague [acquired about 1920]; H. Hannema,
The Hague; Huinck and Scherjon Art Gallery, Amsterdam
[about 1952]; L. H. van Baaren, Utrecht; Utrecht, Museum
van Baaren, inv nr 33

F 885 INTERIOR WITH WOMAN SEWING: FACING LEFT
EXHIBITIONS 1918 The Hague; 1924 Amsterdam, 46; 1928
The Hague; 1929 Hamburg, 153; 1930 Amsterdam, 144;
1947 Basle, 114; Paris 1, 6; 1947-8 London etc, 103; 1960-1
Montreal etc, 84
PROVENANCE J. Hidde Nijland, The Hague [1895-1928];
Dordrechts Museum, Dordrecht [loan Hidde Nijland
1904-1910]; Otterlo, Rijksmuseum Kröller-Müller, inv
nr 1000-28, cat van Gogh 1970, nr 24

F 886 WOMAN, SEWING BY THE WINDOW: FACING
RIGHT
EXHIBITIONS 1904 Rotterdam, 61; 1927 Rotterdam, 34;
1945 Basle, 19
PROVENANCE Unger and Van Mens Art Gallery, Rotter-
dam; A. van Hoboken, Ascona [1945]; Arlesheim near
Basle/Corseaux, A. Stoll Collection [acquired 1951], cat
1961, nr 74

F 887 A YOUNG WOMAN SEWING, WITH WHITE CAT
EXHIBITIONS 1918 The Hague; 1924 Amsterdam, 37; 1928
Amsterdam; 1929 Hamburg, 141; 1930 Amsterdam, 149;
1947 Paris 1, 5; 1950 's Hertogenbosch, Breda; 1962
Warsaw, 11; 1963 Tel Aviv, Haifa, 10
PROVENANCE J. Hidde Nijland, The Hague [1895-1928];
Dordrechts Museum, Dordrecht [loan Hidde Nijland
1904-1910]; Otterlo, Rijksmuseum Kröller-Müller, inv
nr 991-28, cat van Gogh 1970, nr 25

F 888 recto WOMAN MENDING STOCKINGS
EXHIBITIONS 1918 The Hague; 1924 Amsterdam, 115;
1928 The Hague; 1929 Hamburg, 152; 1930 Amsterdam, 151
PROVENANCE J. Hidde Nijland, The Hague [1895-1928];
Dordrechts Museum, Dordrecht [loan Hidde Nijland
1904-1910]; Otterlo, Rijksmuseum Kröller-Müller, inv
nr 995-28, cat van Gogh 1970, nr 34

F 888 verso PART OF AN INTERIOR WITH FIREPLACE
[unfinished sketch]
PROVENANCE See F 888 recto

F 889 WOMAN GRINDING COFFEE
EXHIBITIONS 1895 The Hague; 1918 The Hague; 1924
Amsterdam, 38; 1928 The Hague; 1929 Hamburg, 146; 1930
Amsterdam, 137; 1956 Nuremberg, 6; Munich, 16; 1958
Tokyo, Kyoto, 10
PROVENANCE J. Hidde Nijland, The Hague [1895-1928];
Dordrechts Museum, Dordrecht [loan Hidde Nijland
1904-1910]; Otterlo, Rijksmuseum Kröller-Müller, inv
nr 961-28, cat van Gogh 1970, nr 26

F 890 MAN SWEEPING
EXHIBITIONS 1918 The Hague; 1924 Amsterdam, 65; 1928
The Hague; 1929 Hamburg, 147; 1930 Amsterdam, 146;
1958 Vienna, 15
PROVENANCE J. Hidde Nijland, The Hague [1895-1928];
Dordrechts Museum, Dordrecht [loan Hidde Nijland
1904-1910]; Otterlo, Rijksmuseum Kröller-Müller, inv
nr 975-28, cat van Gogh 1970, nr 37

F 891 PEASANT SIEVING GRAIN
EXHIBITIONS 1918 The Hague; 1924 Amsterdam, 85; 1928
The Hague; 1929 Hamburg, 50; 1930 Amsterdam, 24; 1962
Warsaw, 9; 1963 Tel Aviv, Haifa, 21a
PROVENANCE J. Hidde Nijland, The Hague [1895-1928];
Dordrechts Museum, Dordrecht [loan Hidde Nijland
1904-1910]; Otterlo, Rijksmuseum Kröller-Müller, inv
nr 947-28, cat van Gogh 1970, nr 19

F 892 WOMAN CHURNING BUTTER
EXHIBITIONS 1918 The Hague; 1924 Amsterdam, 94; 1928
The Hague; 1929 Hamburg, 59; 1930 Amsterdam, 147;
1935-6 New York etc, 74; 1950 's Hertogenbosch, Breda;
1956 Eindhoven, 2; Nuremberg, 2; 1966 Belgrade, 7
PROVENANCE J. Hidde Nijland, The Hague [1895-1928];
Dordrechts Museum, Dordrecht [loan Hidde Nijland
1904-1910]; Otterlo, Rijksmuseum Kröller-Müller, inv
nr 956-28, cat van Gogh 1970, nr 21

F 893 MAN WITH A STICK
EXHIBITION 1960 Paris, 72
PROVENANCE H. P. Bremmer, The Hague; Netherlands,
Private collection [R 1969]

F 894 MAN CHOPPING WOOD
EXHIBITIONS 1961 Amsterdam 1, 5; 1964 Amsterdam
PROVENANCE H. P. Bremmer, The Hague; Zaandam, Mrs
W. Takens-Bremmer [R 1967]

F 895 PEASANT WITH HATCHET
EXHIBITION 1960 Eindhoven, Schiedam, 143
PROVENANCE J. Hageraats Art Gallery, The Hague;
H. P. Bremmer, The Hague; H. Bremmer, Zeist [until about
1965]; Present owner unknown

F 896 GIRL STANDING: FACING RIGHT
EXHIBITIONS 1918 The Hague; 1924 Amsterdam, 106;
1928 The Hague; 1929 Hamburg, 155; 1930 Amsterdam,
153; 1956 Nuremberg, 11; Munich, 17; 1958 Tokyo, Kyoto,
15
PROVENANCE J. Hidde Nijland, The Hague [1895-1928];
Dordrechts Museum, Dordrecht [loan Hidde Nijland
1904-1910]; Otterlo, Rijksmuseum Kröller-Müller, inv
nr 1014-28, cat van Gogh 1970, nr 35

F 897 PEASANT READING BY THE FIREPLACE
EXHIBITIONS 1918 The Hague; 1924 Amsterdam, 97; 1928
The Hague; 1929 Hamburg, 154; 1930 Amsterdam, 141;
1935-6 New York etc, 75; 1950 's Hertogenbosch, Breda;
1952 Milan, 7; 1953-4 St Louis etc, 4; 1956 Eindhoven, 3;
Munich, 13; 1957 Essen, 126; 1958 Vienna, 13; Tokyo,
Kyoto, 12
PROVENANCE J. Hidde Nijland, The Hague [1895-1928];
Dordrechts Museum, Dordrecht [loan Hidde Nijland
1904-1910]; Otterlo, Rijksmuseum Kröller-Müller, inv
nr 1002-28, cat van Gogh 1970, nr 27

F 898 SIEN WITH CIGAR, SITTING ON THE GROUND BY
THE STOVE
EXHIBITIONS 1895 The Hague, 49; 1918 The Hague; 1924
Amsterdam, 49; 1928 The Hague; 1929 Hamburg, 108;
1930 Amsterdam, 64; 1952 Milan, 19; 1953-4 St Louis etc,
19; 1956 Nuremberg, 23; Munich, 14; 1957 Essen, 127;
Tokyo, Kyoto, 25; 1961 Munich, 16; 1962 London 1, 3
PROVENANCE J. Hidde Nijland, The Hague [until 1928];
Dordrechts Museum, Dordrecht [loan Hidde Nijland
1904-1910]; Otterlo, Rijksmuseum Kröller-Müller, inv
nr 1016-28, cat van Gogh 1970, nr 74

F 899 A STOOPING WOMAN
PROVENANCE J. Hidde Nijland, The Hague; H. A. Hidde
Nijland, Zeist; Present owner unknown

F 900 THE HOUSE OF THE RAILWAY ATTENDANT
EXHIBITIONS 1918 The Hague; 1924 Amsterdam, 83; 1928
The Hague; 1929 Hamburg, 67; 1930 Amsterdam, 20;
1935-6 New York etc, 76; 1952 Milan, 4; 1953-4 St Louis
etc, 3; 1956 Nuremberg, 3; Munich, 14; 1957 Essen, 127;
1958 Vienna, 11; Tokyo, Kyoto, 17; 1961 Munich, 9; 1962
Warsaw, 8; 1963 Tel Aviv, Haifa, 8; 1966 Belgrade, 6
PROVENANCE J. Hidde Nijland, The Hague [1895-1928];
Dordrechts Museum, Dordrecht [loan Hidde Nijland
1904-1910]; Otterlo, Rijksmuseum Kröller-Müller, inv
nr 966-28, cat van Gogh 1970, nr 17

F 901 THE SAW MILL
EXHIBITIONS 1961 Amsterdam 1, 6; 1966 Amsterdam, 12
PROVENANCE Art Gallery de Vries, Arnhem; C. W. de
Visser, Bloemendaal [acquired 1907]; Hoorn, J. E. de Visser

F 902 CORNER OF A GARDEN WITH AN ARBOR
EXHIBITIONS 1918 The Hague; 1924 Amsterdam, 23
[repr]; 1928 The Hague; 1929 Hamburg, 77; 1930
Amsterdam, 22; 1947 Basle, 115; 1950 's Hertogenbosch,
Breda; 1952 Milan, 5; 1953 The Hague, 2; Otterlo,
Amsterdam, 2; 1953-4 St Louis etc, 5; 1956 Nuremberg, 4;
Munich, 8; 1958 Vienna, 12; Tokyo, Kyoto, 7; 1961
Munich, 7; 1962 London 1,2
PROVENANCE Oldenzeel Art Gallery, Rotterdam [1892];
J. Hidde Nijland, The Hague [1892-1928]; Dordrechts
Museum, Dordrecht [loan Hidde Nijland 1904-1910];
Otterlo, Rijksmuseum Kröller-Müller, inv nr 978-28, cat
van Gogh 1970 ,nr 18

F 902a ORCHARD
PROVENANCE C. Mouwen jr, Breda; Sale Amsterdam
[F. Muller] 3 May 1904, 41; J. C. Meyers, The Hague;
H. J. W. van den Boogaard, Rotterdam; Sale Dordrecht
[A. Mak] 3 December 1912, 24; C. Vriesendorp, Dordrecht;
Sale Dordrecht [A. Mak] 11 May 1937, 581; d'Audretsch
Art Gallery, The Hague; Miss S. M. C. Kronenberg,
Utrecht; Rotterdam, Museum Boymans-van Beuningen
[acquired 1965; bequest Miss S. M. C. Kronenberg], inv
nr MB 1965/T2

F 903 THE OUTSKIRTS OF A WOOD
EXHIBITIONS 1918 The Hague; 1924 Amsterdam, 90; 1928
The Hague; 1929 Hamburg, 52; 1930 Amsterdam, 11; 1955
Antwerp 3, 20; 1961 Munich, 5
PROVENANCE J. Hidde Nijland, The Hague [1895-1928];
Dordrechts Museum, Dordrecht [loan Hidde Nijland
1904-1910]; Otterlo, Rijksmuseum Kröller-Müller, inv
nr 949-28, cat van Gogh 1970, nr 12

F 904 A SUBURBAN FIELD ENCLOSURE
PROVENANCE W. C. H. Bolleurs, The Hague; W. G. H. van
Houweninge, Rotterdam; Sale Rotterdam [van Marle and
de Sille] 21-22 April 1925, 255; A. W. Gelber, Rotterdam;
Present owner unknown

F 905 CHURCH WITH SPIRE SEEN BETWEEN TREES
See JUVENILIA

THE HAGUE PERIOD

F 906 MAN DIGGING: SEEN FROM THE BACK
EXHIBITIONS 1905 Amsterdam, 255; 1954-5 Bern, 77; 1955
Antwerp 1, 31; 1957 Stockholm, 13; 1958-9 San Francisco
etc, 88; 1960 Enschede, 4; 1961-2 Baltimore etc, 84; 1965
Stockholm, Göteborg, 62; 1967 Wolfsburg, 83
PROVENANCE Mrs J. van Gogh-Bonger, Amsterdam;
V. W. van Gogh, Laren; Amsterdam, Rijksmuseum Vincent
van Gogh [Vincent van Gogh Foundation, inv nr F 906]

F 907 MAN DIGGING: SEEN FROM THE BACK
PROVENANCE Mrs J. van Gogh-Bonger, Amsterdam;
V. W. van Gogh, Laren; Amsterdam, Rijksmuseum Vincent
van Gogh [Vincent van Gogh Foundation, inv nr F 907]

F 908 MAN DIGGING: RIGHT THREE-QUARTER VIEW
EXHIBITIONS 1905 Amsterdam, 238; 1914-5 Amsterdam,
5; 1957 Stockholm, 14; 1958-9 San Francisco etc, 89; 1960
Enschede, 5; 1966 Paris, Albi, 3; 1967 Lille, Zurich, 4;
1967-8 Dallas etc, 4; 1968 Liège, 4
PROVENANCE Mrs J. van Gogh-Bonger, Amsterdam;
V. W. van Gogh, Laren; Amsterdam, Rijksmuseum Vincent
van Gogh [Vincent van Gogh Foundation, inv nr F 908]

F 909 THIRD-CLASS WAITING ROOM
PROVENANCE Oldenzeel Art Gallery, Rotterdam;
F. W. R. Wentges, The Hague [acquired 1909]; Sale
Amsterdam [F. Muller] 14 December 1948, 183; New York,
Mrs J. K. Thannhauser [R 1970]

F 910 THE SCHENKWEG, THE HAGUE
EXHIBITIONS 1953 Amsterdam 1, 11; 1955 New York 2, 80;
1956 Munich, 19
PROVENANCE F. J. Michelsen, Amsterdam; Sale Amster-
dam [F. Muller] 3 December 1918, 305; D. Komter Art
Gallery, Amsterdam; Sale Amsterdam [F. Muller] 19 May
1920, 136; H. P. Bremmer, The Hague; Huinck and
Scherjon Art Gallery, Amsterdam [1952]; W. Weinberg,
Scarsdale; Sale London [Sotheby] 10 July 1957, 50; Cecil
Lewis, Bolney, England; London, Private collection [R 1970]

F 910a WOMAN KNITTING NEAR A WINDOW
PROVENANCE H. G. Tersteeg, The Hague; Sale Tersteeg,
The Hague [Boussod] 19-20 May 1914, nr 95 [repr]; Mettes
and Co Art Gallery, The Hague; Present owner unknown

F 911 recto LITTLE CHILD: FACING LEFT
verso STOOPING WOMAN, PICKING UP A NET
PROVENANCE Mrs J. van Gogh-Bonger, Amsterdam;
V. W. van Gogh, Laren; Amsterdam, Rijksmuseum Vincent
van Gogh [Vincent van Gogh Foundation, inv nr F 911]

F 912 PORTRAIT OF A LITTLE CHILD: FACING LEFT
EXHIBITION 1964 Zeist, 24
PROVENANCE A. Henny, The Hague [acquired about 1918];
Zeist, Mrs A. Cohen Tervaert-Henny [R 1970]

F 913 WOMAN WALKING WITH A STICK
EXHIBITIONS 1904 Rotterdam, 59; 1968-9 London, 6
PROVENANCE Oldenzeel Art Gallery, Rotterdam;
D. A. Daamen, The Hague [before 1914-about 1943];
L. Daamen-Drost, The Hague [about 1943-1960]; Heirs of
Daamen, The Hague [acquired 1960]; Amsterdam, Rijks-
museum Vincent van Gogh [Vincent van Gogh Foundation,
acquired 1967, inv nr F 913]

F 914 THE BAKERY IN DE GEEST, THE HAGUE
EXHIBITION 1961 Munich, 12
PROVENANCE C. M. van Gogh Art Gallery, Amsterdam;
Sale The Hague [R. W. P. de Vries] 13-15 May 1902, 440;
H. P. Bremmer, The Hague [before 1908]; The Hague, Heirs
of H. P. Bremmer

F 915 GROUP OF HOUSES
PROVENANCE Oldenzeel Art Gallery, Rotterdam; Mrs
J. E. Crommelin-Tutein Nolthenius, Delft; C. A. Cromme-
lin, Leiden; The Hague, Mrs B. Nieuwenhuizen Segaar-
Aarse [acquired 1954]

F 916 VIEW OF THE HAGUE FROM THE NORTHEAST,
WITH THE NEW CHURCH AND THE JACOBUSKERK
EXHIBITION 1903 Rotterdam 3, 76
PROVENANCE C. Mouwen jr, Breda; Sale Mouwen,
Amsterdam [F. Muller] 3 May 1904, 22 [repr]; E. van Biema,
The Hague; F. Hirschel, Amsterdam; P. Verschure,
Rotterdam; Present owner unknown

F 917 STREET AND BRIDGE IN THE OUTSKIRTS OF
THE HAGUE
EXHIBITIONS 1950 The Hague, 38; 1961 Amsterdam 1, 7
PROVENANCE D. Franken, Le Vésinet; H. P. Bremmer,
The Hague; The Hague, F. Bremmer [R 1970]

F 918 JEWISH QUARTER OF THE HAGUE, THE
PADDEMOES
EXHIBITIONS 1895 The Hague; 1918 The Hague; 1924
Amsterdam, 22; 1928 The Hague; 1929 Hamburg, 46; 1930
Amsterdam, 61; 1947 Basle, 116; 1949-50 New York,
Chicago, 16; 1952 Milan, 11; 1953 The Hague, 5; Otterlo,
Amsterdam, 8; 1953-4 St Louis etc, 9; 1956 Nuremberg, 21;
Munich, 21; 1958 Tokyo, Kyoto, 18; 1961 Munich, 13; 1962
London 1, 11; 1966 Belgrade, 11
PROVENANCE J. Hidde Nijland, The Hague [1895-1928];
Dordrechts Museum, Dordrecht [loan Hidde Nijland
1904-1910]; Otterlo, Rijksmuseum Kröller-Müller, inv
nr 943-28, cat van Gogh 1970, nr 45

F 919 THE RAILWAYSTATION RIJNSPOOR [NOW
STAATSSPOOR], THE HAGUE
EXHIBITIONS 1953 The Hague, 6; Otterlo, Amsterdam, 9;
1961 Munich, 14
PROVENANCE H. P. Bremmer, The Hague; The Hague,
F. Bremmer [R 1970]

F 920 HOUSE IN THE SCHEVENINGEN ROAD
EXHIBITION 1961 Amsterdam 1, 8
PROVENANCE Sale The Hague [R. W. P. de Vries] 13-15
May 1902, 433; D. Franken, Le Vésinet; H. P. Bremmer,
The Hague; The Hague, F. Bremmer [R 1970]

F 921 THE STRAIGHT CANAL: SCHENK WEG
EXHIBITIONS 1927 Basle etc, 27; 1928 Düsseldorf, 93;
Karlsruhe, 28; 1929 Berlin 1, 6; Hamburg, 23; 1930
Amsterdam, 26; 1935-6 New York etc, 77; 1952 Milan, 10;
1958 Tokyo, Kyoto, 17; 1959 São Paulo, p 242, 4; 1960-1
Montreal etc, 85; 1962 Warsaw, 14; 1963 Tel Aviv, Haifa,
13
PROVENANCE Sale The Hague [R. W. P. de Vries] 13-15
May 1902, 441; Sale Amsterdam [R. W. P. de Vries] 1913;
J. H. de Bois Art Gallery, Haarlem; H. P. Bremmer, The
Hague; Otterlo, Rijksmuseum Kröller-Müller, inv
nr 212-15, cat van Gogh 1970, nr 44

F 922 SAND DIGGERS IN THE DUNES
PROVENANCE C. M. van Gogh Art Gallery, Amsterdam;
Sale The Hague [R. W. P. de Vries] 13-15 May 1902, 443;
D. Franken, Le Vésinet; H. P. Bremmer, The Hague; The
Hague, Heirs of H. P. Bremmer [R 1970]

F 922a CORNER IN THE VAN STOLKPARK
EXHIBITIONS 1953 Zurich, without cat nr; 1956 Munich,
20; 1961 Munich, 11; 1963 Hamburg, 86; 1967 Lille,
Zurich, 92
PROVENANCE Sale The Hague [R. W. P. de Vries] 13-15
May 1902, 442; A. J. Verbeek van der Sande, Arnhem;
P. Cassirer Art Gallery, Amsterdam [R 1941]; W. Feilchen-
feldt, Zurich; Zurich, Mrs M. Feilchenfeldt [R 1970]

F 923 FLORIST'S GARDEN ON THE SCHENKWEG,
THE HAGUE
EXHIBITIONS 1957 Essen, 135; 1960 Paris, 78
PROVENANCE Sale The Hague [R. W. P. de Vries] 13-15
May 1902, 438; Mr and Mrs
J. C. J. Drucker-Fraser [on loan to Rijksmuseum, Amster-
dam since 1919, cat 1934, nr 2926d]; Amsterdam, Rijks-
museum [on loan to Stedelijk Museum, Amsterdam]

F 924 THE GAS TANKS OF THE HAGUE
EXHIBITIONS 1960 Paris, 80; 1961 Amsterdam 1, 9
PROVENANCE Sale The Hague [R. W. P. de Vries] 13-15
May 1902, 439; D. Franken, Le Vésinet; H. P. Bremmer,
The Hague; The Hague, R. Bremmer [R 1970]

F 925 A FACTORY IN THE HAGUE [according to
Faille the factory of Sterkman]
EXHIBITIONS 1961 Amsterdam 1, 10; 1967 Lille, Zurich, 94
PROVENANCE Sale The Hague [R. W. P. de Vries] 13-15
May 1902, 435; D. Franken, Le Vésinet; H. P. Bremmer,
The Hague; Heirs of H. P. Bremmer, The Hague; M. Frank,
New York [R 1964]; Zurich, F. and P. Nathan [R 1970]

F 926 THE FACTORY OF ENTHOVEN ON THE ZIEKEN,
THE HAGUE
EXHIBITIONS 1904 Rotterdam, 55; 1957 Essen, 134; 1960
Paris, 76
PROVENANCE H. P. Bremmer, The Hague; Heirs of
H. P. Bremmer, The Hague [until 1961]; Schweinfurt,
Collection Georg Schäfer [R 1970]

F 927 WORK IN THE FIELDS
EXHIBITIONS 1953 Berlin, 13; 1955 New York 2, 81; 1963
London 1, 179; 1966 Basle, 40
PROVENANCE H. P. Bremmer, The Hague; W. Brinkman,
Schipluiden, Netherlands [1953]; W. Weinberg, Scarsdale
[1955]; Sale London [Sotheby] 10 July 1957, 53; Mr Fisch-
bein, London; Mrs Gaby Schreiber; Sale London
[Christie] 27 November 1964, addenda 55 A; Galerie
Beyeler, Basle [R 1966]; Present owner unknown

F 928 THE BENCH
EXHIBITIONS 1950 The Hague, 39; 1960 Paris, 79
PROVENANCE H. P. Bremmer, The Hague [until 1956];
H. Bremmer, Eindhoven; The Hague, G. J. Nieuwenhuizen
Segaar Art Gallery [acquired 1965; R 1970]

F 929 SORROW
EXHIBITIONS 1932 Amsterdam 2, 6; 1950 The Hague, 40;
1952 Milan, 24; 1956 Munich, 23; 1960 Paris, 81; 1961
Amsterdam 1, 11; Munich, 17
PROVENANCE A. G. A. van Rappard, Utrecht; Ph. de
Kanter, Delft; H. P. Bremmer, The Hague [R 1952]; The
Hague, F. Bremmer [R 1970]

F 929a SORROW
EXHIBITIONS 1905 Amsterdam, 262; 1914-5 Amsterdam,
12; 1915 Amsterdam, 21; 1920 New York, 8 [erroneously as
litho]; 1960 Philadelphia
PROVENANCE Mrs J. van Gogh-Bonger, Amsterdam;
Montross Gallery, New York; Th. Pitcairn, Bryn Athyn,
USA; Sale London [Christie] 24 June 1966, 48; England,
Garman-Ryan collection [R 1970]

F 930 FLORIST'S GARDEN ON THE SCHENKWEG,
THE HAGUE
EXHIBITIONS 1953 New York 1, 79; 1955 Paris 2, 77; 1960
New York 1; 1962 New York
PROVENANCE J. H. de Bois Art Gallery, Haarlem; J. Cock,
Alkmaar; d'Audretsch Art Gallery, The Hague; M. Frank,
New York; New York, W. C. Baker [R 1955, 1970]

F 930a THE ROAD WORKERS
PROVENANCE M. Flersheim, Frankfurt [R 1904]; East
Berlin, Nationalgalerie [acquired 1929; gift of M. Flers-
heim], inv nr F 111-1767

F 931 SIEN IN WHITE BONNET: LEFT PROFILE
EXHIBITIONS 1905 Amsterdam, 245; 1914-5 Amsterdam,
10; 1923 Utrecht; Rotterdam, 64; 1945 Amsterdam,
without cat nr; 1954-5 Bern, 78; 1955 Antwerp 1, 32; 1957
Stockholm, 15
PROVENANCE Mrs J. van Gogh-Bonger, Amsterdam;
V. W. van Gogh, Laren; Amsterdam, Rijksmuseum Vincent
van Gogh [Vincent van Gogh Foundation, inv nr F 931]

F 932 SIEN SEWING: WHOLE FIGURE IN RIGHT PROFILE
EXHIBITIONS 1918 The Hague; 1924 Amsterdam, 27
[repr]; 1928 The Hague; 1929 Hamburg, 79; 1930 Amsterdam, 33; 1952 Antwerp, 37a; 1960-1 Montreal etc, 86
PROVENANCE J. Hidde Nijland, The Hague [1895-1928];
Dordrechts Museum, Dordrecht [loan Hidde Nijland
1904-1910]; Otterlo, Rijksmuseum Kröller-Müller, inv
nr 980-28, cat van Gogh 1970, nr 62

F 933 recto STUDY OF A TREE
verso [formerly F 1076] BLIND MAN
EXHIBITIONS 1918 The Hague; 1924 Amsterdam, 131;
1928 The Hague; 1929 Hamburg, 42; 1930 Amsterdam, 58;
1935-6 New York etc, 78; 1946-7 Liège etc, 7; 1947 Paris 1,
7; Geneva, 7; 1949-50 New York, Chicago, 15; 1952 Milan,
15; 1956 Nuremberg, 17; 1957 Essen, 136, 157 [verso]; 1958
Tokyo, Kyoto, 21; Vienna, 49 [verso]; 1962 London 1, 13
PROVENANCE J. Hidde Nijland, The Hague [1895-1928];
Dordrechts Museum, Dordrecht [loan Hidde Nijland
1904-1910]; Otterlo, Rijksmuseum Kröller-Müller, inv
nr 938-28, cat van Gogh 1970, nr 53, 83 [verso]

F 934 OLD WOMAN, STANDING: RIGHT PROFILE
EXHIBITIONS 1940 Amsterdam, 19; 1969 Basle, 67
PROVENANCE Mrs J. van Gogh-Bonger, Amsterdam; N.H. Wolf, Amsterdam; A. van Santen, Amsterdam [1968]; Basle, Galerie Beyeler [R 1969]

F 935 SIEN RESTING HEAD ON LEFT HAND, SEATED: RIGHT PROFILE
EXHIBITIONS 1918 The Hague; 1924 Amsterdam, 26; 1928 The Hague; 1929 Hamburg, 85; 1930 Amsterdam, 35; 1935-6 New York etc, 80; 1962 Warsaw, 21; London 1, 5; 1963 Tel Aviv, Haifa, 22
PROVENANCE J. Hidde Nijland, The Hague [1895-1928]; Dordrechts Museum, Dordrecht [loan Hidde Nijland 1904-1910]; Otterlo, Rijksmuseum Kröller-Müller, inv nr 986-28, cat van Gogh 1970, nr 75

F 936 SIEN'S MOTHER SITTING: RIGHT PROFILE
EXHIBITIONS 1918 The Hague; 1924 Amsterdam, 11 [repr]; 1928 The Hague; 1929 Hamburg, 55; 1930 Amsterdam, 41; 1958 Vienna, 17; 1961 Munich, 15; 1962 London 1, 6
PROVENANCE J. Hidde Nijland, The Hague [1895-1928]; Dordrechts Museum, Dordrecht [loan Hidde Nijland 1904-1910]; Otterlo, Rijksmuseum Kröller-Müller, inv nr 952-28, cat van Gogh 1970, nr 65

F 937 recto SIEN RESTING HER HEAD ON HER LEFT HAND, SEATED: LEFT PROFILE
verso SIEN SEWING [unfinished sketch]
EXHIBITIONS 1918 The Hague; 1924 Amsterdam, 28 [repr]; 1928 The Hague; 1929 Hamburg, 117; 1930 Amsterdam, 39; 1949-50 New York, Chicago, 15; 1957 Essen, 137 [recto and verso]
PROVENANCE J. Hidde Nijland, The Hague [1895-1928]; Dordrechts Museum, Dordrecht [loan Hidde Nijland 1904-1910]; Otterlo, Rijksmuseum Kröller-Müller, inv nr 1028-28, cat van Gogh 1970, nr 76a, 76b [verso]

F 938 FISH DRYING BARN AT SCHEVENINGEN
EXHIBITIONS 1918 The Hague; 1924 Amsterdam, 24; 1928 The Hague; 1929 Hamburg, 97; 1930 Amsterdam, 59; 1949-50 New York, Chicago, 18; 1952 Milan, 13; 1953-4 St Louis etc, 12; 1956 Munich, 25; 1957 Essen, 139; 1958 Vienna, 19; 1958-9 Schiedam [no cat]; 1960-1 Montreal etc, 87; 1962 Warsaw, 15; 1963 Tel Aviv, Haifa, 14; 1966 Belgrade, 13
PROVENANCE J. Hidde Nijland, The Hague [1895-1928]; Dordrechts Museum, Dordrecht [loan Hidde Nijland 1904-1910]; Otterlo, Rijksmuseum Kröller-Müller, inv nr 1004-28, cat van Gogh 1970, nr 49

F 939 CARPENTER'S WORKSHOP, SEEN FROM THE ARTIST'S STUDIO WINDOW
EXHIBITIONS 1918 The Hague; 1924 Amsterdam, 25; 1928 The Hague; 1929 Hamburg, 144; 1930 Amsterdam, 79; 1935-6 New York etc, 79; 1946-7 Liège etc, 8; 1947 Paris 1, 8; Geneva, 8; Basle, 117; 1947-8 London etc, 104; 1949-50 New York, Chicago, 19; 1953 The Hague, 7; Otterlo, Amsterdam, 10; 1953-4 St Louis etc, 10; 1956 Nuremberg, 14; Munich, 24; 1958 Vienna, 18; Tokyo, Kyoto, 19; 1961 Munich, 18; 1962 London 1, 12; 1964 Kassel, 1
PROVENANCE J. Hidde Nijland, The Hague [1895-1928]; Dordrechts Museum, Dordrecht [loan Hidde Nijland 1904-1910]; Otterlo, Rijksmuseum Kröller-Müller, inv nr 940-28, cat van Gogh 1970, nr 46

F 939a BACK YARDS WITH TWO FIGURES
EXHIBITIONS 1936 Haarlem, 15; 1955 New York 1, p 7; New York 2, 82
PROVENANCE C. M. van Gogh Art Gallery, The Hague; J. H. de Bois Art Gallery, Haarlem [1936]; Mrs L. Jaray-Bondi, Vienna [until 1938], London; New York, Private collection [courtesy The Galerie St Etienne 1969; acquired 1953]

F 940 FISH DRYING BARN NEAR THE DUNES AT SCHEVENINGEN
EXHIBITIONS 1943 Basle, 161; 1945 Basle, 20; 1947 Basle, 118
PROVENANCE Mrs C. E. de Boer-Gijsberti Hodenpijl, The Hague; Sale Amsterdam [R. W. P. de Vries] 16-17 July 1930, 63; Huinck and Scherjon Art Gallery, Amsterdam; S. Salz, Paris; Basle, Private collection [R 1947]

F 941 HOUSES SEEN FROM THE BACK WINDOW OF SIEN'S MOTHER'S HOUSE
EXHIBITIONS 1932 Amsterdam 2, 5; 1950 The Hague, 42; 1961 Amsterdam 1, 12; Munich, 19
PROVENANCE C. M. van Gogh Art Gallery, Amsterdam; H. P. Bremmer, The Hague; The Hague, F. Bremmer [R 1970]

F 942 BACK GARDEN OF SIEN'S MOTHER'S HOUSE
EXHIBITIONS 1932 Amsterdam 2, 8; 1950 The Hague, 41; 1960 Minneapolis, 60; 1961 Newark, 54; 1962 Minneapolis, New York, 118; 1968 Minneapolis etc, 61
PROVENANCE C. M. van Gogh Art Gallery, Amsterdam; Mr Roëll, Utrecht; W. C. A. Huinck Art Gallery, Utrecht; H. P. Bremmer, The Hague; John Streep art dealer, New York [acquired 1955]; New York, D. Daniels [acquired 1955; R 1969]

F 943 ROOFS SEEN FROM THE ARTIST'S ATTIC WINDOW
EXHIBITIONS 1903 Rotterdam 1 and 3; 1904 Rotterdam, 54; 1934 Bern, 57; 1935 Basle, 239; 1937 Paris, 62; 1947 Basle, 119; 1956 Munich, 26; 1960 Paris, 82; 1961 Munich, 20
PROVENANCE C. Mouwen jr, Breda; Sale Amsterdam [F. Muller] 3 May 1904, 21 [repr]; Oldenzeel Art Gallery, Rotterdam; M. Gieseler, The Hague; Sale Amsterdam [Mak] 27 October 1925, 27 [repr]; Paul Cassirer Art Gallery, Berlin; G. Renand, Paris [R 1935]; Paris, Private collection [R 1970]

F 944 CARPENTER'S WORKSHOP SEEN FROM THE ARTIST'S STUDIO WINDOW
EXHIBITION 1955 New York 2, 83
PROVENANCE L. C. Enthoven, Voorburg, Netherlands; Sale Amsterdam [F. Muller] 18 May 1920, 253; H. R. Weise, Warmond, Netherlands; A. Mak Art Gallery, Amsterdam; Huinck and Scherjon Art Gallery, Amsterdam; Mrs Verloop-Witteveen, Bilthoven; Huinck and Scherjon Art Gallery, Amsterdam; Mrs. S. Kramarsky, New York [R 1955]; New York, S. Kramarsky Trust Fund [R 1970]

F 945 THE FISH DRYING BARN AT SCHEVENINGEN
EXHIBITIONS 1932 Amsterdam 2, 2; 1950 The Hague, 43; 1955 Antwerp 3, 10; 1956 Amsterdam, 4; 1957 Essen, 138; 1960 Paris, 83; 1961 Amsterdam, 13; Munich, 21
PROVENANCE H. P. Bremmer, The Hague; Heirs of H. P. Bremmer, The Hague [R 1956]; F. Bremmer, The Hague [R 1961]; M. Frank, New York [R 1967]; Chicago, B. E. Bensinger [R 1970]

F 946 recto BLEACHERY IN SCHEVENINGEN
verso WOMAN FROM SCHEVENINGEN, SEATED
EXHIBITIONS 1953 Vlaardingen, 19; 1957 Essen, 141; 1960 Paris, 84
PROVENANCE Gift from Vincent to Miss Margot Begemann, Nuenen; Miss C. M. C. Begemann, Amstelveen; Stedelijk Museum, Amsterdam [on loan 1956]; A. Buysman, Noordwijk [R 1957]; Schipluiden, Netherlands, W. Brinkman

F 946a THE FISH DRYING SHED NEAR SCHEVENINGEN
PROVENANCE C. M. van Gogh Art Gallery, Amsterdam; Pictura Art Society, Groningen [R 1905]; Groningen, Groninger Museum voor Stad en Lande, inv nr 1951/560

F 947 POLLARD WILLOW BY THE SIDE OF A ROAD
EXHIBITIONS 1955 New York 2, 84; 1957 Los Angeles, 28
PROVENANCE Oldenzeel Art Gallery, Rotterdam; F. W. R. Wentges, The Hague [?]; C. Staib, Rotterdam; H. S. Nienhuis Art Gallery, Amsterdam; Hugo Perls Art Gallery, New York; New York, Mr and Mrs Leo M. Rogers [R 1955, R 1968]

F 948 THREE WOODCUTTERS
EXHIBITION 1903 Rotterdam 3, 68
PROVENANCE Oldenzeel Art Gallery, Rotterdam; F. W. R. Wentges, The Hague [acquired 1909]; Mr and Mrs John J. Emery, Cincinnati; Cincinnati, The Cincinnati Art Museum [gift of Mr and Mrs John Emery], inv nr 1962-14

F 949 WOMAN IN A WOOD
EXHIBITIONS 1903 Rotterdam 3, 95; 1961 Amsterdam 1, 14
PROVENANCE Oldenzeel, Apeldoorn; Sale Amsterdam [F. Muller] 12 May 1908, 141; Oldenzeel Art Gallery, Rotterdam; F. W. R. Wentges, The Hague [acquired 1909]; Mrs M. A. R. van der Leeuw-Wentges, The Hague [acquired 1944]; New York, Eugene V. Thaw Gallery [R 1970]

F 950 FOUR WOODCUTTERS
EXHIBITIONS 1918 The Hague; 1924 Amsterdam, 73; 1928 The Hague; 1929 Hamburg, 151; 1930 Amsterdam, 132; 1952 Milan, 14; 1959 São Paulo, 6; 1960-1 Montreal etc, 89; 1962 Warsaw, 16; 1963 Tel Aviv, Haifa, 16
PROVENANCE J. Hidde Nijland, The Hague [1895-1928]; Dordrechts Museum, Dordrecht [loan Hidde Nijland 1904-1910]; Otterlo, Rijksmuseum Kröller-Müller, inv nr 994-28, cat van Gogh 1970, nr 52

F 951 PEOPLE SEATED ON A BENCH IN BEZUIDENHOUT PARK [second version]
EXHIBITIONS 1903 Rotterdam 3, 70; 1904 Rotterdam, 49; 1956 Amsterdam, 5; 1961 Amsterdam 1, 15
PROVENANCE C. Mouwen jr, Breda; Sale Amsterdam [F. Muller] 3 May 1904, 25; S. R. Steinmetz, Amsterdam; R. Th. Steinmetz, Ellecom, Netherlands; The Hague, R. Steinmetz [R 1969]

F 952 recto PEOPLE SEATED ON A BENCH IN BEZUIDENHOUT PARK [first verson]
verso ROAD WITH TWO CARTS, HORSES, A BARREL ON THE LEFT, THREE FIGURES
EXHIBITIONS 1918 The Hague; 1924 Amsterdam, 20; 1928 The Hague; 1929 Hamburg, 126; 1930 Amsterdam, 62; 1949-50 New York, Chicago, 20; 1956 Nuremberg, 16; 1958 Vienna, 20; Tokyo, Kyoto, 20; 1960-1 Montreal etc, 88; 1966 Belgrade, 12
PROVENANCE J. Hidde Nijland, The Hague [1895-1928]; Dordrechts Museum, Dordrecht [loan Hidde Nijland 1904-1910]; Otterlo, Rijksmuseum Kröller-Müller, inv nr 1038-28, cat van Gogh 1970, nr 48a, 48b [verso]

F 953 ORPHAN MAN HOLDING A TOP HAT IN HIS LEFT HAND
EXHIBITIONS 1950 The Hague, 44; 1961 Amsterdam 1, 16
PROVENANCE H. P. Bremmer, The Hague [until 1956]; Heirs of H. P. Bremmer, The Hague; John Streep art dealer, New York; H. A. D. Thomas, Amsterdam [R 1961-2]; New York, B. Sonnenberg [acquired 1962]

F 954 HEAD OF AN ORPHAN MAN WITH TOP HAT: RIGHT PROFILE
EXHIBITION 1950 The Hague, 46
PROVENANCE H. P. Bremmer, The Hague; Van Wisselingh Art Gallery, Amsterdam; Chapin Riley, Worcester, Mass. [1957]; Worcester, Worcester Art Museum [gift of Chapin Riley], inv nr 1957-153, cat 1958, nr 29

F 954a HEAD OF AN ORPHAN MAN WITH TOP HAT
PROVENANCE J. F. van Royen, The Hague; C. Bakker, Hilversum; B. Houthakker Art Gallery, Amsterdam; Johannesburg, Kunsmuseum, cat new acquisitions 1948, nr 3

F 955 BALD HEADED ORPHAN MAN: FACING RIGHT
EXHIBITIONS 1950 The Hague, 45; 1955 New York 2, 85; 1960 Paris, 85; 1961 Amsterdam 1, 17
PROVENANCE H. P. Bremmer, The Hague [until 1957]; Heirs of H. P. Bremmer, The Hague [1960]; Van Wisselingh Art Gallery, Amsterdam; Summit, New Jersey, Mr and Mrs Dimitry Jodidio [R 1970]

F 956 ORPHAN MAN WITH TOP HAT EATING
PROVENANCE H. P. Bremmer, The Hague [until 1957]; Heirs of H. P. Bremmer, The Hague; Bergen, Netherlands, D. A. Hoogendijk [acquired 1959]

F 956a ORPHAN MAN WITH CAP EATING
EXHIBITION 1956 Amsterdam, 2
PROVENANCE C. M. van Gogh Art Gallery, Amsterdam [R 1902]; Mrs E. Kley-Funke, The Hague; Van Wisselingh Art Gallery, Amsterdam; P. Arntzenius [R 1956]; Geneva, Motte Art Gallery [acquired 1956]

F 957 ORPHAN MAN HOLDING A CUP
PROVENANCE C. Mouwen jr, Breda; C. M. van Gogh Art Gallery, Amsterdam; Sale Amsterdam [F. Muller] 18 May 1909, 153; H. P. Bremmer, The Hague [until 1957]; Heirs of H. P. Bremmer, The Hague; Van Wisselingh Art Gallery, Amsterdam [acquired 1959]; Worcester, Mass., Mr and Mrs Chapin Riley [R 1959]

F 958 ORPHAN MAN WITH WALKING STICK
EXHIBITION 1960 Paris, 86
PROVENANCE C. Mouwen jr, Breda; H. P. Bremmer, The Hague; Schipluiden, Netherlands, W. Brinkman [acquired 1955]

F 959 ORPHAN MAN WITH GLASS AND HANDKERCHIEF
EXHIBITIONS 1918 The Hague; 1924 Amsterdam, 21; 1928 The Hague; 1929 Hamburg, 123; 1930 Amsterdam, 53
PROVENANCE J. Hidde Nijland, The Hague [1895-1928]; Otterlo, Rijksmuseum Kröller-Müller, inv nr 1035-28, cat van Gogh 1970, nr 87

F 960 ORPHAN MAN WITH WALKING STICK: SEEN FROM THE BACK
EXHIBITIONS 1905 Amsterdam, 457; 1914-5 Amsterdam, 35; 1949-50 New York, Chicago, 23; 1954-5 Bern, 79; 1955 Antwerp 1, 30; 1957 Stockholm, 9; 1958-9 San Francisco etc, 90; 1960 Enschede, 6; 1961-2 Baltimore etc, 85; 1966 Paris, Albi, 4; 1967 Lille, Zurich, 5
PROVENANCE Mrs J. van Gogh-Bonger, Amsterdam; V. W. van Gogh, Laren; Amsterdam, Rijksmuseum Vincent van Gogh [Vincent van Gogh Foundation, inv nr F 960]

F 961 ORPHAN MAN WITH TOP HAT
EXHIBITIONS 1923 Rotterdam; 1953 Berlin, 18; 1954 Berlin, 18; 1956 Almelo, 48; 1961 Amsterdam 1, 18
PROVENANCE C. M. van Gogh Art Gallery, Amsterdam [R 1902]; Mrs H. E. Hannema-de Stuers, The Hague; D. Hannema, Heino, Netherlands; Heino, Hannema-de Stuers Foundation, cat 1967, nr 106

F 962 ORPHAN MAN WITH WALKING STICK
EXHIBITIONS 1905 Amsterdam, 249; 1914-5 Amsterdam, 22; 1923 Utrecht; Rotterdam, 76; 1947-8 London etc, 107; 1948 Bergen, Oslo, 68; 1953 The Hague, 10; Otterlo, Amsterdam, 13; 1953-4 St Louis etc, 21; 1954-5 Bern, 80; 1955 Antwerp 1, 28; 1957 Stockholm, 10; 1958-9 San Francisco etc, 91; 1960 Enschede, 7; 1961-2 Baltimore etc, 86; 1963 Sheffield, 15; 1964 Zundert, 3; 1965-6 Stockholm, Göteborg, 63; 1967 Wolfsburg, 84; 1967-8 Dallas etc, 5; 1968 Liège, 5; 1968-9 London, 11
PROVENANCE Mrs J. van Gogh-Bonger, Amsterdam; V. W. van Gogh, Laren; Rijksmuseum Vincent van Gogh [Vincent van Gogh Foundation, inv nr F 962]

F 963 ORPHAN MAN WITH WALKING STICK: FACING RIGHT
EXHIBITIONS 1952 Amsterdam, 9; 1956 Amsterdam, 3; 1966 Gouda, 14
PROVENANCE Mrs C. E. de Boer-Gijsberti Hodenpijl, The Hague; Sale Amsterdam [R. W. P. de Vries] 16-17 July 1930, 64; Huinck and Scherjon Art Gallery, Amsterdam; Miss J. F. van Baaren, Utrecht; Utrecht, Museum van Baaren, inv nr 63

F 964 OLD MAN CARRYING A BASKET: FACING RIGHT
PROVENANCE J. Dona, The Hague; H. C. Stork, Vienna; W. P. Maclaine Pont, Bilthoven [R 1913]; Zwolle, Mrs A. W. Maclaine Pont-Stork [R 1970]

F 964a [formerly F 964bis] MAN WITH A SPADE, RESTING
EXHIBITION 1955 New York 2, 86
PROVENANCE R. A. Kröller, Hoenderlo [on loan to Rijksmuseum Kröller-Müller, Otterlo, cat 1949, nr 92]; Huinck and Scherjon Art Gallery, Amsterdam; R. A. Kröller, Amsterdam; E. Weye Art Gallery, New York; New York, F. A. P. Zimmermann [R 1955]

F 964b MAN SEATED DRINKING A CUP OF COFFEE
PROVENANCE M. de Zwart, Voorburg, Netherlands; H. P. Baron van Tuyll van Serooskerken, Amsterdam; Sale Amsterdam [F. Muller] 25 November 1913, 126; Sale Amsterdam [F. Muller] 3 December 1918, 122; Mrs H. Kröller-Müller, The Hague [1920]; Mrs G. Kröller-Jesse, Ede; Mrs de Bondt, The Hague [1956]; Sale Bern [Klipstein and Kornfeld] 9 May 1963, 372; New York, Van Diemen-Lilienfeld Galleries [R 1964]

F 965 ORPHAN MAN SEEN FROM THE BACK
PROVENANCE A. Vollard Art Gallery, Paris; Paul Cassirer Art Gallery, Berlin; J. G. Licht, Berlin; Sale Leipzig [C. G. Boerner] 13 November 1924, 188 [repr]; C. Sachs, Breslau; Sale Leipzig [C. G. Boerner] 6 November 1931, 103; East Germany, Private collection

F 966 ORPHAN MAN READING: FACING RIGHT
EXHIBITIONS 1905 Amsterdam, 243; 1914-5 Amsterdam, 30; 1927-8 Berlin etc, 9
PROVENANCE Mrs J. van Gogh-Bonger, Amsterdam; V. W. van Gogh, Laren; Amsterdam, Rijksmuseum Vincent van Gogh [Vincent van Gogh Foundation, inv nr F 966]

F 967 IN THE CHURCH
EXHIBITIONS 1913 The Hague, 36; 1927 Basle etc, 8; 1928 Düsseldorf, 74; Karlsruhe, 9; 1929 Berlin 1, 191; Hamburg, 136; 1930 Amsterdam, 133; 1935-6 New York etc, 87; 1947 Basle, 120; 1947-8 London etc, 105; 1956 Eindhoven, 6; 1958 Vienna, 21; Tokyo, Kyoto, 22; 1959 São Paulo, 5; 1960-1 Montreal etc, 90; 1962 Warsaw, 17; 1963 Tel Aviv, Haifa, 17
PROVENANCE C. Mensink, The Hague; Sale Amsterdam [F. Muller] 12 November 1912, 60; Huinck and Scherjon Art Gallery, Amsterdam [1912]; Otterlo, Rijksmuseum Kröller-Müller, inv nr 193-12, cat van Gogh 1970, nr 54

F 968 ORPHAN MAN WITH UMBRELLA: SEEN FROM THE BACK
EXHIBITIONS 1955 New York 2, 87; 1957 Los Angeles, 29; 1958 New York
PROVENANCE C. M. van Gogh Art Gallery, Amsterdam; H. P. Bremmer, The Hague; M. Frank, New York; J. Rewald, New York [acquired 1955]; Sale London [Sotheby] 7 July 1960, 46; Present owner unknown

F 969 ORPHAN MAN CLEANING BOOTS
EXHIBITION 1961 Amsterdam 1, 19
PROVENANCE H. P. Bremmer, The Hague [until 1957]; Heirs of H. P. Bremmer, The Hague; Van Wisselingh Art Gallery, Amsterdam; Private collection, Switzerland [R 1966]; Sale Houston [Christies] 6 April 1970, 61; Los Angeles, A. Hammer [R 1970]

F 970 THE STATE LOTTERY OFFICE
EXHIBITIONS 1905 Amsterdam, 257; 1906 Rotterdam, 58; Middelburg; 1914-5 Amsterdam, 31; 1924 Amsterdam, 17 [repr]; 1926 Munich, 2110; 1927-8 Berlin etc, 10; 1949-50 New York, Chicago, 22; 1953 The Hague, 9; Otterlo, Amsterdam, 12; 1953-4 St Louis etc, 15; 1954-5 Bern, 81; 1955 Antwerp 1, 39; 1957 Stockholm, 8; 1963 Humlebaek, 64; 1964 Washington, New York, 64; 1966 Paris, Albi, 5; 1967 Lille, Zurich, 6; 1967-8 Dallas etc, 6; 1968 Liège, 6; 1968-9 London, 10; 1969 Humlebaek, 2
PROVENANCE Mrs J. van Gogh-Bonger, Amsterdam, V. W. van Gogh, Laren; Amsterdam, Rijksmuseum Vincent van Gogh [Vincent van Gogh Foundation, inv nr F 970]

F 971 ORPHAN MAN WITH A CHILD STANDING BETWEEN HIS KNEES
EXHIBITIONS 1954 Bern; 1960 Syracuse N.Y.; 1967 Raleigh [North Carolina], 270
PROVENANCE M. de Zwart, Voorburg, Netherlands [with whom van Gogh lodged]; H. P. Baron van Tuyll van Serooskerken, Amsterdam; Sale Amsterdam [F. Muller] 25-6 November 1913, 121 [repr]; Paul Cassirer Art Gallery, Amsterdam; Leo Klein-Diephold, Noordwijk; Franz von Mendelssohn-Bartholdy, Berlin; Mrs E. Witt-von Mendelssohn, St Georgenhof, Germany; Knightdale, North Carolina, Mrs M. E. Witt [R 1970]

F 972 ORPHAN MAN WITH AN UMBRELLA UNDER HIS ARM
EXHIBITIONS 1912 Cologne, 116; 1913 The Hague, 62; 1927 Basle etc, 28; 1928 Düsseldorf, 94; Karlsruhe, 29; 1929 Berlin 1, 15; Hamburg, 24; 1930 Amsterdam, 51; 1949-50 New York, Chicago, 21; 1952 Milan, 22; 1953-4 St Louis etc, 22; 1956 Nuremberg, 25; Munich, 28; 1958 Tokyo, Kyoto, 26; 1959 São Paulo, 9; 1961 Munich, 22; 1962 Warsaw, 23; 1963 Tel Aviv, Haifa, 24; 1966 Belgrade, 20
PROVENANCE C. M. van Gogh Art Gallery, Amsterdam [1911]; Otterlo, Rijksmuseum Kröller-Müller, inv nr 213-11, cat van Gogh 1970, nr 85

F 972a ORPHAN MAN WITH UMBRELLA: SEEN FROM BEHIND
PROVENANCE A. Vollard Art Gallery, Paris [R 1912]; Paul Cassirer Art Gallery, Berlin; Bern, M. Huggler [R 1970]

F 973 ORPHAN MAN STANDING, TOP HAT IN HIS RIGHT HAND: FULL FACE
EXHIBITIONS 1912 Cologne, 117; 1913 The Hague, 61; 1927 Basle etc, 26; 1928 Düsseldorf, 92; Karlsruhe, 27; 1929 Berlin 1, 16; Hamburg, 22; 1930 Amsterdam, 50; 1946-7 Liège etc, 9; 1947 Paris 1, 9; Geneva, 9; Basle, 9; 1947-8 London etc, 106; 1949 Gouda; 1956 Nuremberg, 24; Munich, 27; 1957 Essen, 15; 1958 Vienna, 24; 1962 London 1, 14
PROVENANCE C. M. van Gogh Art Gallery, Amsterdam [1911]; Otterlo, Rijksmuseum Kröller-Müller, inv nr 211-11, cat van Gogh 1970, nr 84

F 974 ORPHAN MAN WARMING HIMSELF: SEEN FROM THE BACK
EXHIBITIONS 1912 Cologne, 118; 1913 The Hague, 44; 1927 Basle etc, 21; 1928 Düsseldorf, 76; Karlsruhe, 11; 1929 Berlin 1, 31; Hamburg, 17; 1930 Amsterdam, 56; 1935-6 New York etc, 88; 1958-9 Schiedam, no cat; 1960-1 Montreal etc, 92; 1962 Warsaw, 24; 1963 Tel Aviv, Haifa, 25
PROVENANCE C. M. van Gogh Art Gallery, Amsterdam [R 1911]; Otterlo, Rijksmuseum Kröller-Müller, inv nr 206-11, cat van Gogh 1970, nr 88

F 975 ORPHAN MAN WITH TOP HAT AND CROSSED HANDS
EXHIBITIONS 1912 Cologne, 114; 1913 The Hague, 60; 1927 Basle etc, 17; 1928 Düsseldorf, 84; Karlsruhe, 19; 1929 Berlin 1, 7; Hamburg, 13; 1930 Amsterdam, 54; 1960-1 Montreal etc, 91
PROVENANCE Otterlo, Rijksmuseum Kröller-Müller, inv nr 202-00, cat van Gogh 1970, nr 89

F 976 ORPHAN MAN DRINKING A CUP OF COFFEE
EXHIBITIONS 1912 Cologne, 119; 1913 The Hague, 57; 1927 Basle etc, 14; 1928 Düsseldorf, 81; Karlsruhe, 16; 1929 Berlin 1, 22; Hamburg, 10; 1930 Amsterdam, 49; 1935-6 New York etc, 89; 1962 Warsaw, 22; 1963 Tel Aviv, Haifa, 23; 1966 Belgrade, 19
PROVENANCE C. M. van Gogh Art Gallery, Amsterdam [1911]; Otterlo, Rijksmuseum Kröller-Müller, inv nr 199-11, cat van Gogh 1970, nr 82

F 976a MAN SEATED, DRINKING: FULL FACE
This number is identical with F 1082

F 977 ORPHAN MAN WITH TOP HAT AND WALKING STICK: FULL FACE
EXHIBITIONS 1905 Amsterdam, 250; 1914-5 Amsterdam, 24; 1923 Utrecht, Rotterdam, 85; 1924 Basle, 80; Zurich, 80; Stuttgart, 5; 1925 The Hague, 57; 1932 Manchester, 54; 1955 Antwerp 1, 27; 1965 Stockholm, Göteborg, 64; 1967] Wolfsburg, 85
PROVENANCE Mrs J. van Gogh-Bonger, Amsterdam; V. W. van Gogh, Laren; Amsterdam, Rijksmuseum Vincent van Gogh [Vincent van Gogh Foundation, inv nr F 977]

F 978 ORPHAN MAN LOOKING AT HIS WATCH
EXHIBITIONS 1912 Cologne, 115; 1913 The Hague, 56; 1927 Basle etc, 10; 1928 Düsseldorf, 77; Karlsruhe, 12; 1929 Berlin 1, 20; Hamburg, 7; 1930 Amsterdam, 52; 1956 Nuremberg, 26; Munich, 29; 1958 Vienna, 23; Tokyo, Kyoto, 27
PROVENANCE C. M. van Gogh Art Gallery, Amsterdam [1911]; Otterlo, Rijksmuseum Kröller-Müller, inv nr 195-11, cat van Gogh 1970, nr 86

F 978a ORPHAN MAN
PROVENANCE E. Bernard, France; Munich, Mrs Reichert

F 979 MAN WITH A RAKE: FACING RIGHT
EXHIBITION 1961 Amsterdam 1, 20
PROVENANCE H. P. Bremmer, The Hague; Heirs of H. P. Bremmer, The Hague; Raffled by the Prins Bernhard Fonds, Amsterdam; Curaçao, H. J. Nolte [acquired 1965]

F 979a YOUNG MAN WITH A BROOM
EXHIBITION 1890-1 Rotterdam
PROVENANCE Miss H. M. Willink, Laren; Sale Amsterdam [A. Mak] 4 November 1930, 77; J. E. van der Meulen, Wapenveld, Netherlands [on loan since 1960 to Gemeente Museum, The Hague]; The Hague, Wibbina Foundation [still on loan to the Gemeente Museum]

F 980 FIGURES ON THE BEACH AT SCHEVENINGEN
EXHIBITIONS 1927 Basle etc, 19; 1928 Düsseldorf, 86; Karlsruhe, 21; 1929 Berlin 1, 27; Hamburg, 5; 1930 Amsterdam, 28; 1961 Munich, 23
PROVENANCE M. de Zwart, Voorburg, Netherlands; H. P. Baron van Tuyll van Serooskerken, Amsterdam; Sale Amsterdam [F. Muller] 25-6 November 1913, 138; Otterlo, Rijksmuseum Kröller-Müller, inv nr 204-13, cat van Gogh 1970, nr 51

F 981 ORPHAN MAN HOLDING A CHILD
EXHIBITION 1961 Amsterdam 1, 21
PROVENANCE H. P. Bremmer, The Hague; Zaandam, Mrs W. Takens-Bremmer [R 1966]

F 982 THE BEACH AT SCHEVENINGEN
EXHIBITIONS 1903 Rotterdam 3, 83; 1961 Amsterdam 1, 22
PROVENANCE C. Mouwen jr, Breda; Sale Amsterdam [F. Muller] 3 May 1904, 23; C. H. Guépin, Amsterdam; Haarlem, Private collection [R 1970]

F 983 STANDING GIRL, KNITTING: FACING RIGHT
PROVENANCE H. P. Bremmer, The Hague; John Streep art dealer, New York [acquired 1955]; New York, Mr A. Hailparn [R 1968]

F 984 SEATED GIRL, KNITTING: FACING LEFT
EXHIBITIONS 1912 Cologne, 122; 1960 Paris, 89; 1961 Munich, 24
PROVENANCE H. P. Bremmer, The Hague [R 1912]; Heirs of H. P. Bremmer, The Hague; J. W. Nieuwenhuizen Segaar, The Hague [R 1967]; Present owner unknown [R 1970]

F 985 ORPHAN MAN WITH TOP HAT: HALF FIGURE
EXHIBITIONS 1905 Amsterdam, 258; 1914-5 Amsterdam, 25; 1927-8 Berlin etc, 9a; 1954-5 Curaçao; 1955 Palm Beach etc, 33; Antwerp 1, 29; 1955-6 Liverpool etc, 87; 1956 Haarlem; 1957 Stockholm, 16; Breda, 22; Marseilles, 4; 1958-9 San Francisco etc, 92; 1959-60 Utrecht, 69; 1960 Enschede, 8; 1961-2 Baltimore etc, 87; 1963 Humlebaek, 68; 1964 Washington, New York, 68; 1965 Charleroi, Ghent, 44; 1966 Paris, Albi, 6; Lille, Zurich, 7; 1967-8 Dallas etc, 7; 1968 Liège, 7; 1968-9 London, 12; 1969 Humlebaek, 3
PROVENANCE Mrs J. van Gogh-Bonger, Amsterdam [R 1905]; V. W. van Gogh, Laren; Amsterdam, Rijksmuseum Vincent van Gogh [Vincent van Gogh Foundation, inv nr F 985]

F 986 BOY WITH SPADE, SEATED ON A BARREL
PROVENANCE M. de Zwart, Voorburg, Netherlands; H. P. Baron van Tuyll van Serooskerken, Katwijk, Netherlands; Sale Amsterdam [F. Muller] 25-26 November 1913, 132; Fetter Art Gallery, Amsterdam; Neue Kunsthandlung, Berlin; M. Perls Art Gallery, Berlin; H. Stinnes, Cologne; Sale Stuttgart [Stuttgarter Kunstkabinett] 7-9 November 1951, 1057; Present owner unknown

F 987 MAN WITH AN AXE ON HIS SHOULDER
EXHIBITION 1905 Amsterdam, 276
PROVENANCE Mrs J. van Gogh-Bonger, Amsterdam; L. C. Enthoven, Voorburg, Netherlands; Sale Amsterdam [F. Muller] 18 May 1920, 252a; M. L. de Jong, Amsterdam; Johannesburg, A. P. de Jong

F 988 TWO WOMEN STANDING TALKING
PROVENANCE H. P. Baron van Tuyll van Serooskerken, Katwijk, Netherlands; A. J. Kiewiet de Jonge, Hilversum; Sale Amsterdam [A. Mak] 11 March 1930, 77; Buffa Art Gallery, Amsterdam; Present owner unknown

F 988a TWO WOMEN STROLLING, ONE OF THEM CARRYING A KETTLE
PROVENANCE d'Audretsch Art Gallery, The Hague; Netherlands, Private collection [R 1970]

F 989 ORPHAN MAN CONVERSING WITH A WOMAN
EXHIBITIONS 1927 Basle etc, 4; 1928 Düsseldorf, 67; Karlsruhe, 2; 1929 Berlin 1, 24; Hamburg, 4; 1930 Amsterdam, 47; 1958 Vienna, 22
PROVENANCE M. de Zwart, Voorburg, Netherlands; H. P. Baron van Tuyll van Serooskerken, Katwijk, Netherlands; Sale Amsterdam [F. Muller] 25-6 November 1913, 129; J. de Vries Art Gallery, Arnhem; Sale Amsterdam [F. Muller] 3 December 1918, 124; Sale The Hague [Kleykamp] 11 November 1919, 60; Otterlo, Rijksmuseum Kröller-Müller, inv nr 189-19, cat van Gogh 1970, nr 78

F 990 PEOPLE UNDER UMBRELLAS
EXHIBITION 1904 Rotterdam, 53
PROVENANCE Oldenzeel Art Gallery, Rotterdam; J. E. van der Meulen, Utrecht; J. E. van der Meulen, Wapenveld, Netherlands [on loan since 1957 to Gemeente

Museum, The Hague, inv nr T 11-X-1957]; The Hague, Wibbina Foundation still on loan to the Gemeente Museum]

F 991 OLD COUPLE: SEEN FROM THE BACK
EXHIBITIONS 1905 Amsterdam, 242; 1914-5 Amsterdam, 23; 1923 Utrecht, Rotterdam, 77; 1932 Manchester, 50; 1954-5 Bern, 82; 1955 Antwerp I, 38; 1955-6 Liverpool etc, 86; 1958-9 San Francisco etc, 93; 1960 Enschede, 9; 1961-2 Baltimore etc, 88; 1965 Charleroi, Ghent, 45; 1966 Paris, Albi, 7; 1967 Lille, Zurich, 8; 1967-8 Dallas etc, 8; 1968 Liège etc, 8; 1968-9 London, 13
PROVENANCE Mrs J. van Gogh-Bonger, Amsterdam; V. W. van Gogh, Laren; Amsterdam, Rijksmuseum Vincent van Gogh [Vincent van Gogh Foundation, inv nr F 991]

F 992 COUPLE WALKING
PROVENANCE Mrs J. van Gogh-Bonger, Amsterdam; V. W. van Gogh, Laren; Amsterdam, Rijksmuseum Vincent van Gogh [Vincent van Gogh Foundation, inv nr F 992]

F 993 PORTRAIT [probably of the bookseller Blok]
EXHIBITION 1961 Amsterdam I, 23
PROVENANCE Oldenzeel Art Gallery, Rotterdam; F. W. R. Wentges, The Hague [acquired 1909]; Wassenaar, R. W. Wentges [acquired 1944; R 1970]

F 994 MINERS' WIVES CARRYING SACKS OF COAL
EXHIBITIONS 1918 The Hague; 1924 Amsterdam, 89; 1928 The Hague; 1929 Hamburg, 145; 1930 Amsterdam, 130; 1952 Milan, 2; 1955 Paris 4, 157; 1956 Eindhoven, 8; Munich, 32; 1957 Essen, 152; 1958 Vienna, 25; Tokyo, Kyoto, 23; 1960-1 Montreal etc, 93; 1962 Warsaw, 4; 1963 Tel Aviv, Haifa, 18; Hamburg, 85; 1966 Belgrade, 2
PROVENANCE J. Hidde Nijland, The Hague [1895-1928]; Dordrechts Museum, Dordrecht [loan Hidde Nijland 1904-1910]; Otterlo, Rijksmuseum Kröller-Müller, inv nr 959-28, cat van Gogh 1970, nr 6

F 995 TRUNK OF A WILLOW
PROVENANCE M. Gieseler, The Hague; M. B. J. Jungman, Noordwijk, Netherlands; Sale Amsterdam [Mak] 11 March 1930, 78; d'Audretsch Art Gallery, The Hague; Neue Galerie, Vienna; The Galerie St Etienne, New York; Kleemann Gallery, New York [acquired 1943]; Sale New York [Parke-Bernet] 19 January 1950, 90; New York, Mrs Julius Joelson [acquired 1950]

F 996 ORPHAN MAN WITH A BROOM
EXHIBITION 1949 Amsterdam I, 23
PROVENANCE M. de Zwart, Voorburg, Netherlands; H. P. Baron van Tuyll van Serooskerken, Katwijk, Netherlands; Sale Amsterdam [F. Muller] 25-26 November 1913, 123; Van Wisselingh Art Gallery, Amsterdam; Knoedler Art Gallery, New York; Geneva, Matthiesen Art Gallery; Present owner unknown

F 996a ORPHAN MAN WITH TOP HAT DRINKING A CUP OF COFFEE
EXHIBITIONS 1947 Basle, 124; 1952 Basle
PROVENANCE H. Tannenbaum Art Gallery, New York; Knoedler Art Gallery, New York; Galerie M. Schulthess, Basle; Basle, F. Hagemann [acquired 1946; R 1970]

F 997 OLD MAN WITH HIS HEAD IN HIS HANDS
EXHIBITIONS 1905 Amsterdam, 246; 1914-5 Amsterdam, 29; 1923 Utrecht, Rotterdam, 78; 1927-8 Berlin etc, 14; 1932 Manchester, 57; 1946 Stockholm etc, 4; 1947-8 London etc, 109; 1948 Bergen, Oslo, 70; 1949-50 New York, Chicago, 24; 1953-4 St Louis etc, 23; 1955 Antwerp I, 26; 1955-6 Liverpool etc, 85; 1957 Marseilles, 3; Breda, 21; Stockholm, 11; 1958-9 San Francisco etc, 94; 1959-60 Utrecht, 68; 1960 Enschede, 10; 1961 San Francisco etc, 94; 1963 Humlebaek, 65; 1964 Washington, New York, 65; 1968-9 London, 14
PROVENANCE Mrs J. van Gogh-Bonger, Amsterdam [R 1905]; V. W. van Gogh, Laren; Amsterdam, Rijksmuseum Vincent van Gogh [Vincent van Gogh Foundation, inv nr F 997]

F 998 A MAN IN SORROW
EXHIBITIONS 1895 The Hague; 1918 The Hague; 1924 Amsterdam, 95; 1928 The Hague; 1929 Hamburg, 156; 1930 Amsterdam, 37; 1935-6 New York etc, 92; 1946-7 Liège etc, 110; 1947 Basle, 122; Paris I, 10; 1947-8 London etc, 110; 1952 Milan, 21
PROVENANCE Oldenzeel Art Gallery, Rotterdam; J. Hidde Nijland, The Hague [1895-1928]; Dordrechts Museum, Dordrecht [loan Hidde Nijland 1904-1910]; Otterlo, Rijksmuseum Kröller-Müller, inv nr 1017-28, cat van Gogh 1970, nr 81

F 999 THE SOWER: FACING RIGHT
PROVENANCE C. M. van Gogh Art Gallery, Amsterdam [R 1909]; Richard Kisling, Zurich; Zurich, Mrs H. Glatt-Kisling

F 1000 THE SOWER: FRONT VIEW
EXHIBITION 1960 Paris, 88
PROVENANCE Oldenzeel Art Gallery, Rotterdam; H. Sijthoff, Wassenaar [1960]; Mrs A. M. Sijthoff-Burger-

hout, Wassenaar; Sale The Hague [Van Marle and Bignell] 21 May 1963, 33 [not sold]; Private collection; Sale London [Sotheby] 5 December 1968, 283; Present owner unknown

F 1001 MAN READING HIS BIBLE
EXHIBITIONS 1904 Rotterdam, 57; 1912 Cologne, 120; 1913 The Hague, 45; 1927 Basle etc, 9; 1928 Dusseldorf, 75; Karlsruhe, 10; 1929 Berlin I, 32; Hamburg, 6; 1930 Amsterdam, 55; 1956 Eindhoven, 9; 1958 Vienna, 26; 1958-9 Schiedam, no cat
PROVENANCE C. M. van Gogh Art Gallery, Amsterdam [R 1911]; Otterlo, Rijksmuseum Kröller-Müller, inv nr 194-11, cat van Gogh 1970, nr 90

F 1002 SAYING GRACE
EXHIBITIONS 1903 Rotterdam I, 40; 1947 Basle, 125
PROVENANCE C. Mouwen jr, Breda; Sale Amsterdam [F. Muller] 3 May 1904, 38; Oldenzeel Art Gallery, Rotterdam [R 1905]; Switzerland, Doyer Family [R 1968]

F 1003 ORPHAN MAN WITH TOP HAT AND BANDAGE OVER HIS EYE
EXHIBITIONS 1929 New York, 98; 1935-6 New York etc, 90; 1948 Cleveland, 39; 1962 Ann Arbor, 80
PRPROVENANCE Paul Rosenberg Art Gallery, Paris; R. Bühler, Winterthur; Kupferstichkabinett, Munich [on loan]; P. J. Sachs, Cambridge, Massachusetts; Cambridge, Massachusetts, The Fogg Museum of Art [on loan since 1928, bequest Meta and Paul J. Sachs 1965], inv nr 1965.289, cat acquisitions 1965, p 31

F 1004 MAN WITH A BANDAGE OVER HIS EYE, SMOKING A GOUDA PIPE
EXHIBITIONS 1912 Cologne, 121; 1913 The Hague, 58; 1927 Basle etc, 22; 1928 Dusseldorf, 88; Karlsruhe, 23; 1929 Berlin I, 26; Hamburg, 18; 1930 Amsterdam, 38; 1956 Nuremberg, 27; 1958 Tokyo, Kyoto, 29; 1961 Munich, 25; 1962 Warsaw, 25; 1963 Tel Aviv, Haifa, 26
PROVENANCE C. M. van Gogh Art Gallery, Amsterdam [1911]; Otterlo, Rijksmuseum Kröller-Müller, inv nr 1004-11, cat van Gogh 1970, nr 93

F 1005 HEAD OF A WOMAN WITH A CAP: LEFT PROFILE
EXHIBITIONS 1905 Amsterdam, 241; 1914-5 Amsterdam, 33; 1953 The Hague, 11; Otterlo, Amsterdam, 14; 1957 Stockholm, 17
PROVENANCE Mrs J. van Gogh-Bonger, Amsterdam; V. W. van Gogh, Laren; Amsterdam, Rijksmuseum Vincent van Gogh [Vincent van Gogh Foundation, inv nr F 1005]

F 1006 BUST OF A WOMAN WITH A CAP: RIGHT PROFILE
EXHIBITIONS 1905 Amsterdam, 464; 1914-5 Amsterdam, 39; 1927-8 Berlin etc, 7
PROVENANCE Mrs J. van Gogh-Bonger, Amsterdam; V. W. van Gogh, Laren; Amsterdam, Rijksmuseum Vincent van Gogh [Vincent van Gogh Foundation, inv nr F 1006]

F 1007 SIEN'S DAUGHTER WITH SHAWL: LEFT PROFILE
EXHIBITIONS 1912 Cologne, 112; 1913 The Hague, 69; 1927 Basle etc, 15; 1928 Dusseldorf, 82; Karlsruhe, 17; 1929 Berlin I, 33; Hamburg, 11; 1930 Amsterdam, 34; 1935-6 New York etc, 91; 1953-4 Saint Louis etc, 18; 1955 Groningen, 9; 1956 Nuremberg, 22; Munich, 33; 1958 Vienna, 27; 1958-9 Washington etc, 143; 1960-1 Montreal etc, 95; 1962 Warsaw, 20; 1963 Tel Aviv, Haifa, 21; 1966 Belgrade, 17
PROVENANCE C. M. van Gogh Art Gallery, Amsterdam [1911]; Otterlo, Rijksmuseum Kröller-Müller, inv nr 200-11, cat van Gogh 1970, nr 71

F 1008 SIEN'S DAUGHTER SEATED: LEFT PROFILE
EXHIBITIONS 1905 Amsterdam, 248; 1907 Berlin, 114; 1914-5 Amsterdam, 34; 1932 Manchester, 58; 1945 Amsterdam, no cat nr; 1946 Stockholm etc, 5; 1947-8 London etc, 111; 1948 Bergen, Oslo, 71; 1955 Antwerp I, 35; 1961-2 Baltimore etc, 89; 1962-3 Pittsburgh etc; 1964 Zundert, 4
PROVENANCE Mrs J. van Gogh-Bonger, Amsterdam; V. W. van Gogh, Laren; Amsterdam, Rijksmuseum Vincent van Gogh [Vincent van Gogh Foundation, inv nr F 1008]

F 1009 PORTRAIT HEAD OF A WOMAN: FULL FACE
EXHIBITIONS 1905 Amsterdam, 236; 1914-5 Amsterdam, 9; 1927-8 Berlin etc, 11
PROVENANCE Mrs J. van Gogh-Bonger, Amsterdam; V. W. van Gogh, Laren; Amsterdam, Rijksmuseum Vincent van Gogh [Vincent van Gogh Foundation, inv nr F 1009]

F 1009a PORTRAIT HEAD OF A WOMAN WITH CAP: FULL FACE
EXHIBITIONS 1960 Paris, 94; 1961 Amsterdam I, 38
PROVENANCE Oldenzeel Art Gallery, Rotterdam; Unknown collection; Wassenaar, Paul Citroen [acquired 1940; on loan to The Hague, Gemeente Museum since 1957, inv nr T 4-X-1957]

F 1010 FISHERMAN WITH PIPE
EXHIBITIONS 1927 Basle etc, 31; 1928 Dusseldorf, 97; Karlsruhe, 32; 1929 Berlin I, 35; Hamburg, 27; 1930 Amsterdam, 145; 1952 Milan, 20; 1956 Eindhoven, 7;

1958-9 Washington etc, 144; 1959 São Paulo, 8; 1960-1 Montreal etc, 94
PROVENANCE F. J. Michelsen, Amsterdam; Sale Amsterdam [F. Muller] 3 December 1918, 306; Otterlo, Rijksmuseum Kröller-Müller, inv nr 1351-18, cat van Gogh 1970, nr 79

F 1011 HEAD OF AN OLD FISHERMAN WITH SOU'WESTER: FULL FACE
EXHIBITIONS 1913 The Hague, 37; 1927 Basle etc, 13; 1928 Düsseldorf, 80; Karlsruhe, 15; 1929 Berlin I, 34; Hamburg, 9; 1930 Amsterdam, 36; 1956 Munich, 34; 1958 Vienna, 28; Tokyo, Kyoto, 30
PROVENANCE C. M. van Gogh Art Gallery, Amsterdam [R 1911]; Otterlo, Rijksmuseum Kröller-Müller, inv nr 198-11, cat van Gogh 1970, nr 80

F 1012 HEAD OF A FISHERMAN: THREE QUARTERS TO THE RIGHT
EXHIBITION 1963 London 4, 39
PROVENANCE H. P. Bremmer, The Hague [until 1956]; Heirs of H. P. Bremmer, The Hague; Van Wisselingh Art Gallery, Amsterdam [R 1969]; Fullerton, California, Norton Simon Foundation

F 1013 FISHERMAN SEATED
PROVENANCE Mrs J. van Gogh-Bonger, Amsterdam; V. W. van Gogh, Laren; Amsterdam, Rijksmuseum Vincent van Gogh [Vincent van Gogh Foundation, inv nr F 1013]

F 1014 HEAD OF A FISHERMAN: THREE QUARTERS TO THE LEFT
EXHIBITIONS 1905 Amsterdam, 458; 1914-5 Amsterdam, 28; 1954-5 Bern, 83; 1955 Antwerp I, 37; 1968-9 London, 17
PROVENANCE Mrs J. van Gogh-Bonger, Amsterdam; V. W. van Gogh, Laren; Amsterdam, Rijksmuseum Vincent van Gogh [Vincent van Gogh Foundation, inv nr F 1014]

F 1015 HEAD OF AN OLD FISHERMAN WITH PIPE
EXHIBITIONS 1905 Amsterdam, 256; 1914-5 Amsterdam, 20
PROVENANCE Mrs J. van Gogh-Bonger, Amsterdam; V. W. van Gogh, Laren; Amsterdam, Rijksmuseum Vincent van Gogh [Vincent van Gogh Foundation, inv nr F 1015]

F 1016 HEAD OF AN ORPHAN MAN WITH PIPE AND COAL PAN: FULL FACE
EXHIBITIONS 1905 Amsterdam, 240; 1914-5 Amsterdam, 21
PROVENANCE Mrs J. van Gogh-Bonger, Amsterdam; V. W. van Gogh, Laren; Amsterdam, Rijksmuseum Vincent van Gogh [Vincent van Gogh Foundation, inv nr F 1016]

F 1017 HEAD OF AN OLD FISHERMAN: FULL FACE
EXHIBITIONS 1905 Amsterdam, 253; 1914-5 Amsterdam, 37
PROVENANCE Mrs J. van Gogh-Bonger, Amsterdam; V. W. van Gogh, Laren; Amsterdam, Rijksmuseum Vincent van Gogh [Vincent van Gogh Foundation, inv nr F 1017]

F 1018 ORPHAN MAN: BUST-LENGTH, FACING LEFT
EXHIBITIONS 1960 Paris, 91; 1961 Amsterdam I, 24
PROVENANCE H. P. Bremmer, The Hague [until 1956]; Heirs of H. P. Bremmer, The Hague; The Hague, F. Bremmer [R 1970]

F 1019 STUDY OF OLD RETERING: FACING FRONT
EXHIBITIONS 1922 Winterthur 2, 122; 1924 Zurich, 78; 1927-8 Berlin etc, 99; 1961 Munich, 26; 1969 Munich, 47
PROVENANCE L. C. Enthoven, Voorburg; Sale Amsterdam [F. Muller] 18 May 1920, 254; A. Hahnloser, Winterthur [R 1927-8]; Bern, H. R. Hahnloser [R 1961, R 1970]

F 1020 THE PUBLIC SOUP KITCHEN
EXHIBITION 1905 Amsterdam, 237
PROVENANCE Mrs J. van Gogh-Bonger, Amsterdam; V. W. van Gogh, Laren; Amsterdam, Rijksmuseum Vincent van Gogh [Vincent van Gogh Foundation, inv nr F 1020]

F 1020a THE PUBLIC SOUP KITCHEN
EXHIBITION 1954 Geneva, 235
PROVENANCE J. H. de Bois Art Gallery, Haarlem; d'Audretsch Art Gallery, The Hague; Unger and van Mens Art Gallery, Rotterdam; Arlesheim-Corseaux, Switzerland, Arthur Stoll [acquired 1953], cat 1961, p 18

F 1020b THE PUBLIC SOUP KITCHEN
EXHIBITIONS 1957 Essen, 156; 1960 Paris, 92
PROVENANCE Private collection, Etten; A. J. van der Goot, Breda; A. Nystad Art Gallery, The Hague [R 1957]; Enschede, A. Menko [R 1960, R 1967]

F 1021 PEASANT WOMAN WITH WHEELBARROW
EXHIBITIONS 1905 Amsterdam, 259; 1919 Haarlem, 20; 1937 Paris, 58; 1938 Amsterdam 3, 34; 1952 Milan, 26; 1953 Berlin, 17; 1956 Amsterdam, 8
PROVENANCE Mrs J. van Gogh-Bonger, Amsterdam, J. H. de Bois Art Gallery, Haarlem; Huinck and Scherjon Art Gallery, Amsterdam; A. M. van Deventer, The Hague [1937]; Oberägeri–De Steeg, S. van Deventer [R 1970]

F1022 VIEW FROM THE WINDOW OF VINCENT'S STUDIO
EXHIBITIONS 1937 Paris, 64; 1950 The Hague, 50; 1955
Antwerp 3,9; 1957 Essen, 158; 1960 Paris, 77;
1961 Munich, 27
PROVENANCE C. van Deinse, The Hague; H. P. Bremmer,
The Hague [1937-56]; Heirs of H. P. Bremmer, The Hague;
The Hague, F. Bremmer [R 1970]

F1023 VIEW FROM THE WINDOW OF VINCENT'S
STUDIO IN THE SNOW
EXHIBITION 1961 Amsterdam1, 25
PROVENANCE A. G. A. van Rappard, Utrecht; Ph. de
Kanter, Delft; Rotterdam, Mrs J. E. Greutert-de Kanter
[R 1968]

F1024 CHILD KNEELING IN FRONT OF THE CRADLE
EXHIBITIONS 1905 Amsterdam; 1914-5 Amsterdam,
8; 1954-5 Bern, 84; 1955 Antwerp 1, 36; 1957 Stockholm,
19; 1960-1 Montreal etc, 98; 1963 Humlebaek, 98; 1964
Washington, New York, 66
PROVENANCE Mrs J. van Gogh-Bonger, Amsterdam;
V. W. van Gogh, Laren; Amsterdam, Rijksmuseum Vincent
van Gogh [Vincent van Gogh Foundation, inv nr F 1024]

F1025 THE SEAMSTRESS [second version]
EXHIBITION 1932 Amsterdam 2, 7
PROVENANCE J. Hageraats Art Gallery, The Hague;
H. P. Bremmer, The Hague; Huinck and Scherjon Art
Gallery, Amsterdam; Rotterdam, Museum Boymans-van
Beuningen [acquired 1949], inv nr MB 1949-T6

F1026 THE SEAMSTRESS [first version]
EXHIBITIONS 1918 The Hague; 1924 Amsterdam, 47; 1928
The Hague; 1929 Hamburg, 83; 1930 Amsterdam, 3;
1949-50 New York, Chicago, 25
PROVENANCE J. Hidde Nijland, The Hague [1905, 1928];
Dordrechts Museum, Dordrecht [loan Hidde Nijland
1904-1910]; Otterlo, Rijksmuseum Kröller-Müller, inv
nr 984-28, cat van Gogh 1970, nr 61

F1026a WOMAN ON HER DEATHBED
EXHIBITIONS 1950 The Hague, 48; 1952 Milan, 25; 1956
Munich, 38; 1961 Amsterdam 1, 40
PROVENANCE Unknown collection, Wassenaar;
H. P. Bremmer, The Hague [acquired about 1945; 1956];
The Hague, Heirs of H. P. Bremmer [R 1970]

F1027 ORPHAN MAN KNEELING IN PRAYER:
FACING RIGHT
EXHIBITIONS 1914 Berlin, 6; 1921 Berlin; 1927-8 Berlin
etc, 98
PROVENANCE W. H. C. Bolleurs, Rotterdam; Sale Amsterdam [F. Muller] 25-26 November 1913, 120 [repr]; Paul
Cassirer Art Gallery, Berlin; Leo Klein-Diephold, Noordwijk; Franz von Mendelssohn-Bartholdy, Berlin- Grunewald [R 1914, R 1927-8]; Present owner unknown

F1028 THE SANDPIT AT DEKKER'S DUNE
PROVENANCE Mrs J. van Gogh-Bonger, Amsterdam;
V. W. van Gogh, Laren; Amsterdam, Rijksmuseum Vincent
van Gogh [Vincent van Gogh Foundation, inv nr F 1028]

F1029 WORKMEN IN THE SANDPIT AT DEKKER'S DUNE
PROVENANCE A. Flechtheim Art Gallery, Düsseldorf; Sale
Berlin [Graupe], cat nr 349 [repr]; Zurich, Private collection
[R 1964]

F1030 THE PEATERY
PROVENANCE Mrs J. van Gogh-Bonger, Amsterdam;
V. W. van Gogh, Laren; Amsterdam, Rijksmuseum
Vincent van Gogh [Vincent vanGogh Foundation,
inv nr F 1030]

F1031 THE PEATERY
EXHIBITION 1904 Rotterdam, 51
PROVENANCE Present owner unknown

F1032 THE WHITE HORSE
EXHIBITIONS 1903 Rotterdam 3, 77; 1910-1 Rotterdam,
24; 1961 Amsterdam 1, 26
PROVENANCE C. Mouwen jr, Breda; S. R. Steinmetz,
Amsterdam [R 1911]; The Hague, R. T. Steinmetz [on loan
to The Hague, Gemeente Museum, inv nr T 17-X-1963]

F1033 WOMAN SEWING: FACING RIGHT
EXHIBITIONS 1905 Amsterdam, 254; 1927 Basle etc, 12;
1928 Düsseldorf, 79; Karlsruhe, 14; 1929 Berlin 1, 36;
Hamburg, 137; 1930 Amsterdam, 140
PROVENANCE Mrs J. van Gogh-Bonger, Amsterdam;
S. Moulijn, Laren; Miedema, Rotterdam [1916]; Otterlo,
Rijksmuseum Kröller-Müller, inv nr 197-16, cat van Gogh
1970, nr 68

F1034 POTATO DIGGERS
PROVENANCE Present owner unknown

F1035 THE SOWER
PROVENANCE Present owner unknown

F1035a PEASANT BURNING WEEDS
EXHIBITIONS 1905 Amsterdam, 267; 1906 Rotterdam, 59
PROVENANCE Mrs J. van Gogh-Bonger, Amsterdam
[R 1905]; O. Reuchlin, Rotterdam; Miss M. C. G. Reuchlin,
Rotterdam; Sale Rotterdam [N.V. Vendu Notarishuis]
18 October 1950, 41; Rotterdam, Private collection [R 1970]

F1036 PEASANT BURNING WEEDS
See lithograph F 1660

F1037 POTATO FIELDS BEHIND THE DUNES
EXHIBITIONS 1918 The Hague; 1924 Amsterdam, 130;
1928 The Hague; 1929 Hamburg, 112; 1930 Amsterdam,
60; 1947 Basle, 128 [2d edition, 129]; 1947-8 London etc,
113; 1949-50 New York, Chicago, 26; 1952 Milan, 12;
1953-4 Saint Louis etc, 11; 1956 Nuremberg, 15; Munich,
39; 1957 Essen, 159; 1961 Munich, 28
PROVENANCE J. Hidde Nijland, The Hague [1895-1928];
Dordrechts Museum, Dordrecht [loan Hidde Nijland
1904-1910]; Otterlo, Rijksmuseum Kröller-Müller, inv
nr 1021-28, cat van Gogh 1970, nr 47

F1038 THE BEACH AT SCHEVENINGEN
EXHIBITIONS 1904 Rotterdam, 50; 1941 Baltimore, p 114;
1949 Baltimore, 18; 1965 Pittsburgh, 29
PROVENANCE Oldenzeel Art Gallery, Rotterdam;
P. Versteeven, The Hague; Sale Amsterdam [A. Mak]
27 October 1925, 121; Goudstikker Art Gallery, Amster-
dam; Thannhauser Art Gallery, New York; Etta Cone,
Baltimore; Baltimore, The Baltimore Museum of Art [The
Cone bequest, 1949], Handbook of the Cone Collection
1955, nr 120 [revised edition 1967, nr 25]

F1039 IN THE WOOD
PROVENANCE Oldenzeel Art Gallery, Rotterdam;
F. W. R. Wentges, The Hague [aquired 1909]; The Hague,
Mrs M. A. R. van der Leeuw-Wentges [acquired 1944]

F1040 A FACTORY
EXHIBITIONS 1914-5 Amsterdam, 27; 1954-5 Bern, 85;
1955 Antwerp 1, 24
PROVENANCE Mrs J. van Gogh-Bonger, Amsterdam;
V. W. van Gogh, Laren; Amsterdam, Rijksmuseum Vincent
van Gogh [Vincent van Gogh Foundation, inv nr F 1040]

F1041 BARNS AND HOUSES AT SCHEVENINGEN
EXHIBITIONS 1905 Amsterdam, 260; 1914-5 Amsterdam,
19; 1923 Utrecht; Rotterdam, 11; 1927-8 Berlin etc, 5; 1949-
50 New York, Chicago, 27; 1953 The Hague, 4; Otterlo,
Amsterdam, 7; 1953-4 Saint Louis etc, 13; 1954-5 Bern, 86;
1955 Antwerp 1, 23; 1957 Stockholm, 6; 1958-9 San
Francisco etc, 95; 1960 Enschede, 11; 1963 Humlebaek, 67;
1964 Washington, New York, 67; 1967 Wolfsburg, 86;
1967-8 Dallas etc, 9; 1968 Liège, 9; 1968-9 London, 9
PROVENANCE Mrs J. van Gogh-Bonger, Amsterdam;
V. W. van Gogh, Laren; Amsterdam, Rijksmuseum Vincent
van Gogh [Vincent van Gogh Foundation, inv nr F 1041]

F1042 THE CARPENTER: SEEN FROM THE BACK
EXHIBITIONS 1919 Haarlem, 19; 1955 New York 2, 88;
1958 London 1, 11
PROVENANCE H. P. Bremmer, The Hague; Mrs van Gent,
Haarlem; J. H. de Bois Art Gallery, Haarlem [acquired
1914]; E. B. Molenaars, Overveen [acquired 1924];
W. Weinberg, Scarsdale; Sale London [Sotheby] 10 July
1957, 56; The Hallsborough Art Gallery, London; England,
H. J. Hyams [R 1968]

F1043 THE CARPENTER: FACING RIGHT
PROVENANCE H. P. Bremmer, The Hague; The Hague,
R. Bremmer [R 1970]

F1044 THE BLACKSMITH: FACING RIGHT
PROVENANCE H. P. Bremmer, The Hague; Heirs of
H. P. Bremmer, The Hague [1956-60]; Unknown collector,
Germany; Sale Bern [Kornfeld] 11-13 June 1969, 494; Zug,
Mayfair Kunst A.G. [R 1969]

F1045 GIRL CARRYING BREAD: FACING RIGHT
PROVENANCE H. P. Bremmer, The Hague; Heirs of
H. P. Bremmer, The Hague [1956-9]; New York,
S. E. Neikrug [acquired 1959]

F1046 OLD SEAMAN SEATED: FULL FACE
EXHIBITION 1958 Amsterdam 2, 18
PROVENANCE C. Mouwen jr, Breda; H. P. Bremmer, The
Hague; Heirs of H. P. Bremmer, The Hague [1956-9]; Van
Wisseling Art Gallery, Amsterdam [acquired 1959];
Winnipeg, Manitoba, S. Kobrinsky [R 1960]

F1047 PEASANT WOMAN SEATED: FACING LEFT
EXHIBITIONS 1932 Amsterdam 2, 4; 1950 The Hague, 49;
1960 Paris, 89
PROVENANCE H. P. Bremmer, The Hague; Heirs of
H. P. Bremmer, The Hague [1956-61]; Van Wisselingh Art
Gallery, Amsterdam [1961]; Winnipeg, Manitoba, S. Sair
[acquired 1961]

F1048 WOMAN AND CHILD UNDER AN UMBRELLA
EXHIBITIONS 1950 The Hague, 47; 1961 Munich, 29

PROVENANCE J. Hageraats Art Gallery, The Hague;
H. P. Bremmer, The Hague; Heirs of H. P. Bremmer, The
Hague [acquired 1956]; The Hague, F. Bremmer [R 1970]

F1049 THE FISHERMAN: FACING RIGHT
PROVENANCE H. P. Bremmer, The Hague; Heirs of
H. P. Bremmer, The Hague [1956-9]; Van Wisselingh Art
Gallery, Amsterdam [1959]; F. A. C. Guépin, Stanmore,
England [1959-66]; London, Heirs of F. A. C. Guépin

F1050 WOMAN IN A LONG CLOAK: FACING LEFT
EXHIBITIONS 1927 Basle etc, 16; 1928 Düsseldorf, 83;
Karlsruhe, 18; 1929 Berlin 1, 23; Hamburg, 12; 1930
Amsterdam, 48; 1956 Nuremberg, 18; Munich, 31; 1958
Tokyo, Kyoto, 24
PROVENANCE M. de Zwart, Voorburg; H. P. Baron van
Tuyll van Serooskerken, Katwijk; Sale Amsterdam
[F. Muller] 25-26 November 1913, 137; Otterlo, Rijks-
museum Kröller-Müller, inv nr 201-13, cat van Gogh 1970,
nr 56

F1051 WOMAN WITH A KETTLE
EXHIBITIONS 1927 Basle etc, 1; 1928 Düsseldorf, 78;
Karlsruhe, 13; 1929 Berlin 1, 21; Hamburg, 8; 1930
Amsterdam, 46; 1935-6 New York etc, 81; 1947 Basle, 126;
1952 Milan, 17; 1953-4 Saint Louis etc, 17; 1956 Nurem-
berg, 21; Munich, 30; 1958 Tokyo, Kyoto, 28; 1966
Belgrade, 16
PROVENANCE C. M. van Gogh Art Gallery, Amsterdam
[1908]; Otterlo, Rijksmuseum Kröller-Müller, inv nr 196-08,
cat van Gogh 1970, nr 66

F1052 SIEN WITH AN UMBRELLA AND A PRAYER BOOK
UNDER HER ARM
EXHIBITIONS 1960 Paris, 90; 1961 Amsterdam 1, 27
PROVENANCE H. P. Bremmer, The Hague [until 1956]; The
Hague, Heirs of H. P. Bremmer

F1053 WOMAN SAYING GRACE
EXHIBITIONS 1912 Cologne, 109; 1913 The Hague, 63;
1927 Basle etc, 18; 1928 Düsseldorf, 85; Karlsruhe, 20; 1929
Berlin 1, 14; Hamburg, 14; 1930 Amsterdam, 43; 1935-6
New York etc, 82; 1956 Nuremberg, 19; Munich, 35; 1958
Vienna, 30; 1959 São Paulo, 7; 1962 Warsaw, 18; 1963 Tel
Aviv, Haifa, 19; 1966 Belgrade, 14
PROVENANCE Bernheim jeune Art Gallery, Paris [1912];
Otterlo, Rijksmuseum Kröller-Müller, inv nr 203-12, cat
van Gogh 1970, nr 57

F1053a WOMAN PEELING POTATOES
EXHIBITIONS 1941 Haarlem, 7; 1960 Paris, 93; 1961
Amsterdam 1, 39
PROVENANCE Mrs J. van Gogh-Bonger, Amsterdam;
Mrs Jordan-Merian, Germany; J. H. de Bois Art Gallery,
Haarlem [R 1938]; Wassenaar, Paul Citroen [on loan since
1957 to The Hague, Gemeente Museum, inv nr T 3-X-1957]

F1054 BUST OF WOMAN WITH HAT: FACING RIGHT
EXHIBITIONS 1946 Bern, 177; 1947 Basle, 127
PROVENANCE Paul Rosenberg Art Gallery, Paris; Richard
Bühler, Winterthur; Bern, Berner Kunstmuseum [acquired
1946]

F1055 SIEN WITH A WHITE BONNET: FACING RIGHT
EXHIBITIONS 1905 Amsterdam, 463; 1914-5 Amsterdam,
40; 1923 Utrecht; Rotterdam, 84
PROVENANCE Mrs J. van Gogh-Bonger, Amsterdam;
V. W. van Gogh, Laren; Amsterdam, Rijksmuseum Vincent
van Gogh [Vincent van Gogh Foundation, inv nr F 1055]

F1056 WOMAN SITTING ON BENCH: FACING LEFT
EXHIBITIONS 1918 The Hague; 1924 Amsterdam, 92
[repr]; 1928 The Hague; 1929 Hamburg, 39; 1930 Amsterdam, 10; 1935-6 New York etc, 83; 1946-7 Geneva, 6;
1947 Paris 1, 6; Geneva, 6; 1956 Nuremberg, 20; Munich, 36
PROVENANCE J. Hidde Nijland, The Hague; Dordrechts
Museum Dordrecht [loan Hidde Nijland 1904-1910];
Otterlo, Rijksmuseum Kröller-Müller, inv nr 935-28, cat
van Gogh 1970, nr 58

F1057 BUST OF A WOMAN: FULL FACE, AGAINST A
DARK BACKGROUND
PROVENANCE H. P. Bremmer, The Hague; W. Moll,
Groningen; W. Moll, The Hague; Groningen, Groninger
Museum voor Stad en Lande [W. Moll bequest], inv
nr 1962-201

F1057a BUST OF A WOMAN: FULL FACE, AGAINST A
LIGHT BACKGROUND
PROVENANCE Albert de Neuville, Liège [acquired 1904];
Freddy Stiennon, Liège; Liège, Mrs L. Stiennon-de
Neuville [1968]

F1058 TWO WOMEN KNEELING IN PRAYER; ONE
WOMAN STANDING IN THE BACKGROUND
EXHIBITIONS 1927 Basle etc, 20; 1928 Düsseldorf, 87;
Karlsruhe, 22; 1929 Berlin 1, 25; Hamburg, 16; 1930
Amsterdam, 27; 1935-6 New York etc, 84; 1949-50 New
York, Chicago, 29; 1952 Milan, 18; 1961 Munich, 30
PROVENANCE M. de Zwart, Voorburg; H. P. Baron van

Tuyll van Serooskerken, Katwijk; Sale Amsterdam
[F. Muller] 25-26 November 1913, 130; Otterlo, Rijksmuseum Kröller-Müller, inv nr 205-13, cat van Gogh 1970,
nr 70

F 1059 HEAD OF A WOMAN
EXHIBITIONS 1955 Antwerp 1, 131; 1957 Essen, 222; 1960
Paris, 101; 1961 Amsterdam 1, 28
PROVENANCE H. P. Bremmer, The Hague; The Hague,
Heirs of H. P. Bremmer [R 1970]

F 1060 WOMAN WITH HER HEAD IN HER HANDS,
SITTING ON AN OVERTURNED BASKET
EXHIBITIONS 1912 Cologne, 110; 1927 Basle etc, 25; 1928
Düsseldorf, 91; Karlsruhe, 26; 1929 Berlin 1, 30; Hamburg,
21; 1930 Amsterdam, 32; 1952 Milan, 16; 1953-4 Saint
Louis etc, 16; 1956 Munich, 37; 1962 Warsaw, 19; 1963 Tel
Aviv, Haifa, 20; 1966 Belgrade, 15
PROVENANCE C. M. van Gogh Art Gallery, Amsterdam
[1911]; Otterlo, Rijksmuseum Kröller-Müller, inv nr 210-11,
cat van Gogh 1970, nr 63

F 1061 SIEN WITH CHILD IN HER RIGHT ARM: FACING
LEFT
EXHIBITIONS 1927 Basle etc, 33; 1928 Düsseldorf, 99;
Karlsruhe, 34; 1929 Berlin 1, 12; Hamburg, 138; 1930
Amsterdam, 131; 1935-6 New York etc, 85
PROVENANCE J. Dona, The Hague [1908]; A. J. G. Verster,
Hilversum; Amsterdam [Mak] 9 March 1920, 23
[repr]; Huinck Art Gallery, Utrecht [1920]; Otterlo, Rijks-
museum Kröller-Müller, inv nr 217-20, cat van Gogh 1970,
nr 73

F 1062 SIEN SUCKLING HER CHILD
EXHIBITIONS 1927 Basle etc, 32; 1928 Düsseldorf, 98;
Karlsruhe, 33; 1929 Berlin 1, 11; Hamburg, 28; 1930
Amsterdam, 42; 1952 Antwerp, 37; 1962 London 1, 7
PROVENANCE M. de Zwart, Voorburg; H. P. Baron van
Tuyll van Serooskerken, Katwijk; Sale Amsterdam
[F. Muller] 25-26 November 1913, 136; J. de Vries Art
Gallery, Arnhem; Sale Amsterdam [F. Muller] 2 February
1918, 125; Sale The Hague [Kleykamp] 11 November 1919,
58; Otterlo, Rijksmuseum Kröller-Müller, inv nr 216-19, cat
van Gogh 1970, nr 69

F 1063 MOTHER IN ARMCHAIR WITH CHILD ON HER
LAP
EXHIBITIONS 1927 Basle etc, 44; 1928 Düsseldorf, 95;
Karlsruhe, 30; 1929 Berlin 1, 7; Hamburg, 25; 1930
Amsterdam, 44; 1935-6 New York etc, 86; 1963 Hamburg, 87
PROVENANCE M. de Zwart, Voorburg; H. P. Baron van
Tuyll van Serooskerken, Katwijk; Sale Amsterdam
[F. Muller] 25-26 November 1913, 128; J. de Vries Art
Gallery, Arnhem; Sale Amsterdam [F. Muller] 3 December
1918, 123; Otterlo, Rijksmuseum Kröller-Müller, inv nr
214-18, cat van Gogh 1970, nr 72

F 1064 SIEN WITH HER CHILD: FACING LEFT
EXHIBITIONS 1939 Amsterdam 2, 15; 1940 Amsterdam, 18
PROVENANCE M. de Zwart, Voorburg; H. P. Baron van
Tuyll van Serooskerken, Katwijk; Sale Amsterdam
[F. Muller] 25-26 November 1913, 135; Sale New York
[Parke-Bernet] 17 May 1945, 29; Present owner unknown

F 1065 SIEN WITH HER CHILD: FACING LEFT
PROVENANCE H. P. Bremmer, The Hague; Mrs H. E. Hannema-de Stuers, The Hague [1919]; H. Hannema, Rotterdam; Huinck and Scherjon Art Gallery, Amsterdam;
Mrs M. Burg, Haarlem; Hugo Perls Art Gallery, New York;
W. Weinberg, Scarsdale; Sale London [Sotheby] 10 July
1957, 55; Present owner unknown

F 1066 WOMAN WITH CHILD ON HER LAP
EXHIBITIONS 1927 Basle etc, 24; 1928 Düsseldorf, 90;
Karlsruhe, 25; 1929 Berlin 1, 29; Hamburg, 20; 1930
Amsterdam, 40
PROVENANCE M. de Zwart, Voorburg; H. P. Baron van
Tuyll van Serooskerken, Katwijk; Sale Amsterdam
[F. Muller] 25-26 November 1913, 134; Otterlo,
Rijksmuseum Kröller-Müller, inv nr 209-13, cat van Gogh
1970, nr 67

F 1067 SIEN WITH CHILD ON HER LAP
EXHIBITIONS 1914-5 Amsterdam, 11; 1923 Utrecht,
Rotterdam, 2; 1927-8 Berlin etc, 12; 1954-5 Bern, 87; 1955
Antwerp 1, 34
PROVENANCE Mrs J. van Gogh-Bonger, Amsterdam;
V. W. van Gogh, Laren; Amsterdam, Rijksmuseum Vincent
van Gogh [Vincent van Gogh Foundation, inv nr F 1067]

F 1068 NURSING MOTHER
EXHIBITION 1961 Amsterdam 1, 29
PROVENANCE L. C. Enthoven, Voorburg; Sale Amsterdam
[F. Muller] 18 May 1920, 257; L. Zélander, Amsterdam;
Mrs R. Zélander-Caffé, Overveen [R 1966]; USA, Private
collection [R 1970]

F 1069 WOMAN WITH HEAD IN HER HANDS, SEATED
ON A BASKET
EXHIBITIONS 1955 New York 2, 89; 1963 New York 3, 130

PROVENANCE Heinemann Art Gallery, Munich;
O. Gerstenberg, Berlin, Grunewald; Chicago, The Art
Institute [gift of Mr Tiffani and Margarete Blake], inv
nr 47.23

F 1070 NURSING MOTHER
EXHIBITIONS 1918 The Hague; 1924 Amsterdam, 45; 1928
The Hague; 1929 Hamburg, 159; 1930 Amsterdam, 143;
1952 Milan, 6
PROVENANCE J. Hidde Nijland, The Hague; Dordrechts
Museum Dordrecht [loan Hidde Nijland 1904-1910];
Otterlo, Rijksmuseum Kröller-Müller, inv nr 1029-28, cat
van Gogh 1970, nr 23

F 1071 SIEN WITH CHILD ON HER LAP: LEFT PROFILE
EXHIBITIONS 1918 The Hague; 1924 Amsterdam, 48; 1928
The Hague; 1929 Hamburg, 89; 1930 Amsterdam, 45
PROVENANCE J. Hidde Nijland, The Hague; Dordrechts
Museum, Dordrecht [loan Hidde Nijland 1904-1910];
Otterlo, Rijksmuseum Kröller-Müller, inv nr 993-28, cat
van Gogh 1970, nr 60

F 1072 SIEN SEWING AND LITTLE GIRL
EXHIBITIONS 1914-5 Amsterdam, 7; 1927-8 Berlin etc, 4;
1955 Antwerp 1, 33; 1957 Stockholm, 18
PROVENANCE Mrs J. van Gogh-Bonger, Amsterdam;
V. W. van Gogh, Laren; Amsterdam, Rijksmuseum Vincent
van Gogh [Vincent van Gogh Foundation, inv nr F 1072]

F 1073 HEAD OF A WOMAN WITH A DARK CAP
EXHIBITIONS 1895 The Hague; 1918 The Hague; 1924
Amsterdam, 33; 1928 The Hague; 1929 Hamburg, 110; 1930
Amsterdam, 123; 1935-6 New York etc, 93; 1950
's-Hertogenbosch, Breda; 1956 Nuremberg, 49; Munich,
47; 1960-1 Montreal etc, 108
PROVENANCE J. Hidde Nijland, The Hague; Dordrechts
Museum, Dordrecht [loan Hidde Nijland 1904-1910];
Otterlo, Rijksmuseum Kröller-Müller, inv nr 1019-28, cat
van Gogh 1970, nr 147

F 1074 WOMAN WITH BROOM: FACING RIGHT
EXHIBITIONS 1905 Amsterdam, 244; 1914-5 Amsterdam,
36; 1927-8 Berlin etc, 8; 1968-9 London, 8
PROVENANCE Mrs J. van Gogh-Bonger, Amsterdam;
V. W. van Gogh, Laren; Amsterdam, Rijksmuseum Vincent
van Gogh [Vincent van Gogh Foundation, inv nr F 1074]

F 1075 WOMAN WITH BROOM: FULL FACE
EXHIBITIONS 1905 Amsterdam, 235; 1914-5 Amsterdam, 6
PROVENANCE Mrs J. van Gogh-Bonger, Amsterdam;
V. W. van Gogh, Laren; Amsterdam, Rijksmuseum Vincent
van Gogh [Vincent van Gogh Foundation, inv nr F 1075]

F 1076 recto BLIND PEASANT
verso STUDY OF A TREE
identical with F 933 recto and verso

F 1077 STUDY OF A MAN AND A BOY SEATED IN A BARN
PROVENANCE L. C. Enthoven, Voorburg; Sale Amsterdam
[F. Muller] 18 May 1920, 255; S. B. Slijper, Blaricum [until
about 1938]; Present owner unknown

F 1078 TWO MEN UNLOADING BRICKS FROM A CART
EXHIBITIONS 1927 Basle etc, 23; 1928 Düsseldorf, 89;
Karlsruhe, 24; 1929 Berlin 1, 28; Hamburg, 19; 1930
Amsterdam, 29
PROVENANCE M. de Zwart, Voorburg; H. P. Baron van
Tuyll van Serooskerken, Katwijk; Sale Amsterdam
[F. Muller] 25-26 November 1913, 131; Otterlo,
Rijksmuseum Kröller-Müller, inv nr 208-13, cat van Gogh
1970, nr 50

F 1078a THE DUSTMAN
PROVENANCE C. A. de Burlet, Berlin; Sale Leipzig
[Boerner] 16 March 1914, 330 [repr]; Leipzig, Museum der
bildenden Künste [The drawing has disappeared since 1948]

F 1079 recto THE DONKEY CART [destroyed]
verso STUDY OF A HORSE [destroyed]
PROVENANCE Oldenzeel Art Gallery, Rotterdam; Mrs
A. J. Kolff-Havelaar, Rotterdam; drawing destroyed by fire
14 May 1940

F 1080 PEASANT WOMAN FEEDING FOWLS
EXHIBITIONS 1918 The Hague; 1924 Amsterdam, 114;
1928 The Hague; 1929 Hamburg, 73; 1930 Amsterdam, 8;
1958 Vienna, 31; 1960-1 Montreal etc, 96; 1966 Belgrade, 5
PROVENANCE J. Hidde Nijland, The Hague; Dordrechts
Museum, Dordrecht [loan Hidde Nijland 1904-1910];
Otterlo, Rijksmuseum Kröller-Müller, inv nr 972-28, cat
van Gogh 1970, nr 10

F 1081 MAN CARRYING A BUNDLE OF BRANCHES
EXHIBITIONS 1955 New York 2, 90; 1961 London, 17
PROVENANCE Oldenzeel Art Gallery, Rotterdam;
F. W. R. Wentges, The Hague [acquired 1909]; Sale Rotter-
dam [Oldenzeel] 30 April 1912, 41; Van Wisselingh Art
Gallery, Amsterdam; J. Blot [1951]; L. Porter [1952];
W. Weinberg, Scarsdale [1955]; Sale London [Sotheby]
10 July 1957, 52; London, The Earl of Inchcape

F 1082 MAN SEATED, DRINKING: FULL FACE
EXHIBITIONS 1949 Amsterdam 1, 22; 1951 Amsterdam 1,
17; 1955 New York 2, 91; 1957 Los Angeles, 30
PROVENANCE M. de Zwart, Voorburg; H. P. Baron van
Tuyll van Serooskerken, Katwijk; Sale Amsterdam
[F. Muller] 25-26 November 1913, 124; J. de Vries Art
Gallery, Arnhem; Sale The Hague [Kleykamp] 11 November
1919, 59; H. P. Baron van Tuyll van Serooskerken, Katwijk
[until 1951]; Van Wisselingh Art Gallery, Amsterdam;
Legatt Art Gallery, The Hague; Knoedler Art Gallery, New
York; M. Frank, New York [1955]; New York, M. Futter
[R 1966]

F 1083 FISHERMAN WITH BASKET ON HIS BACK
PROVENANCE M. de Zwart, Voorburg; H. P. Baron van
Tuyll van Serooskerken, Katwijk; Sale Amsterdam
[F. Muller] 25-26 November 1913, 125 [repr]; D.Mohr-
Friele, The Hague; Sale Amsterdam [F. Muller] 9-10 April
1918, 367; Sale Amsterdam [F. Muller] 3 December 1918,
127; Present owner unknown

F 1084 THE FORGE
EXHIBITIONS 1927 Basle etc, 30; 1928 Düsseldorf, 96;
Karlsruhe, 31; 1929 Berlin 1, 8; Hamburg, 26; 1930
Amsterdam, 63; 1950 's-Hertogenbosch, Breda; 1956
Munich, 7; 1957 Essen, 129; 1958 Vienna, 7; Tokyo, Kyoto,
7; 1960-1 Montreal etc, 81
PROVENANCE W. Dücker, Düsseldorf [1920]; Otterlo,
Rijksmuseum Kröller-Müller, inv nr 215-20, cat van Gogh
1970, nr 151

F 1085 MAN WRITING
PROVENANCE Oldenzeel Art Gallery, Rotterdam;
H. Tutein Noltenius, Delft [until about 1940]; Present
owner unknown

F 1086 OLD MAN WARMING HIMSELF
EXHIBITION 1961 Amsterdam 1, 30
PROVENANCE H. P. Bremmer, The Hague; Mrs
J. E. Crommelin-Tutein Noltenius, Delft [acquired about
1910]; Mrs K. de Kanter-Crommelin, Delft [until 1970];
Santa Ana, California, H. de Kanter

F 1087 THE LAUNDRESS
EXHIBITIONS 1903 Rotterdam 1, 31; 1961 Amsterdam 1, 31
PROVENANCE C. Mouwen jr, Breda; Sale Amsterdam
[F. Muller] 3 May 1904, 29; Sale Amsterdam [F. Muller]
12 May 1908, 140; F. Hennus, Amsterdam; C. H. Guépin,
Santpoort; Sale Amsterdam [Brandt] 15 December 1964,
36; Sale Bern [Kornfeld and Klipstein] 13 June 1968, 398;
Present owner unknown

F 1088 A LANE
PROVENANCE C. Mouwen jr, Breda; Sale Amsterdam
[F. Muller] 3 May 1904, 32; C. H. Guépin, Santpoort [The
drawing has disappeared]

F 1089 ROAD AT LOOSDUINEN
EXHIBITIONS 1905 Amsterdam, 26; 1914-5 Amsterdam,
18; 1920 New York, 18; 1927-8 Berlin etc, 6; 1937 Paris, 59;
1949-50 New York, Chicago, 28; 1951 Lyons etc, 84; 1953
The Hague, 8; Amsterdam, Otterlo, 11; 1953-4 Saint Louis
etc, 14; 1954-5 Bern, 88; 1955 Antwerp 1, 25; 1955-6
Liverpool etc, 84; 1957 Marseilles, 2; Stockholm, 7; 1958-9
San Francisco etc, 96; 1959-60 Utrecht, 67; 1960 Enschede,
12; 1961-2 Baltimore etc, 90; 1963 Sheffield, 16; 1965
Charleroi, Ghent, 46; 1966 Paris, Albi, 8; 1967 Lille, Zurich,
9; 1967-8 Dallas etc, 10; 1968 Liège, 10; 1968-9 London, 7;
1969 Humlebaek, 4
PROVENANCE Mrs J. van Gogh-Bonger, Amsterdam;
V. W. van Gogh, Laren; Amsterdam, Rijksmuseum Vincent
van Gogh [Vincent van Gogh Foundation, inv nr F 1089]

F 1090 PEASANTS WORKING
EXHIBITIONS 1905 Amsterdam, 375; 1914-5 Amsterdam,
167; 1923 Utrecht, Rotterdam, 41; 1945 Amsterdam,
without cat nr; 1946 Stockholm etc, 62; 1947 Basle, 157;
1947-8 London etc, 156; 1948 Bergen, Oslo, 119; 1949-50
New York, Chicago, 154; 1951 Lyons etc, 100; 1954-5 Bern,
137; 1955 Antwerp 1, 270; 1955-6 Liverpool etc, 109; 1957
Stockholm, 73; 1958-9 San Francisco etc, 123; 1961-2
Baltimore etc, 118; 1966 Paris, Albi, 45; 1967 Lille, Zurich,
47; 1967-8 Dallas etc, 44; 1968 Liège, 44; 1968-9 London,
110; 1969 Humlebaek, 45
PROVENANCE Mrs J. van Gogh-Bonger, Amsterdam;
V. W. van Gogh, Laren; Amsterdam, Rijksmuseum Vincent
van Gogh [Vincent van Gogh Foundation, inv nr F 1090]

F 1091 POTATO MARKET
EXHIBITIONS 1903 Rotterdam 3, 66; 1961 Newark, 53
PROVENANCE Oldenzeel Art Gallery, Rotterdam; Mrs
G. Smith-van Stolk, Rotterdam; New York, D. A. Benna-
hum [R 1961, R 1968]

F 1092 WOMAN ON A COUNTRY LANE WITH WILLOWS:
NEAR THE DUNES
EXHIBITIONS 1918 The Hague; 1924 Amsterdam, 112;
1928 The Hague; 1929 Hamburg, 122; 1930 Amsterdam,
21; 1958 Vancouver, 26; 1961 Munich, 31
PROVENANCE J. Hidde Nijland, The Hague; Otterlo,

Rijksmuseum Kröller-Müller, inv nr 1034-28, cat van Gogh 1970, nr 77

F1093 LANDSCAPE WITH FIGURES
EXHIBITION 1953 Zurich, without cat nr
PROVENANCE T. Duret, Paris; Sale Hamburg [H. Rudolph] 5 October 1951, 533; Sale Hamburg [H. Rudolph] 21 April 1952, 322; Galerie du Château d'art, Basle [R 1953]; Sale Bern [Kornfeld and Klipstein] 9-11 June 1966, 350; Present owner unknown

DRENTHE PERIOD

F1094 PEATERY [IN DRENTHE?]
PROVENANCE Oldenzeel Art Gallery, Rotterdam; C. Staib, Rotterdam; P. A. Regnault jr, Laren; Van Wisselingh Art Gallery, Amsterdam; N. J. van Tussenbroek, Haarlem [1953]; P. Citroen, Wassenaar and M. L. de Boer Art Gallery, Amsterdam [1957]; W. Brinkman, Schipluiden; Sale London [Sotheby] 28 June 1961, 79; Amsterdam, Private collection [1969]

F1095 LANDSCAPE WITH BOG TRUNKS
EXHIBITION 1903 Rotterdam 3, 74
PROVENANCE Oldenzeel Art Gallery, Rotterdam; H. Tutein Nolthenius, Delft; Mettes Art Gallery, The Hague; Nieuwenhuizen Segaar Art Gallery, The Hague; M. Frank, New York; Boston, John Goelet [R 1963]

F1096 recto PLOWMAN AND THREE WOMEN
verso FIGURE SKETCHES
EXHIBITIONS 1918 The Hague; 1924 Amsterdam, 77; 1928 The Hague; 1929 Hamburg, 46; 1930 Amsterdam, 70; 1952 Milan, 32; 1958 Vienna, 37; Tokyo, Kyoto, 36; 1966 Belgrade, 22
PROVENANCE J. Hidde Nijland, The Hague; Dordrechts Museum, Dordrecht [loan Hidde Nijland 1904-1910]; Otterlo, Rijksmuseum Kröller-Müller, inv nr 953-28, cat van Gogh 1970, nr 101

F1097 COTTAGE IN THE HEATH
EXHIBITIONS 1918 The Hague; 1924 Amsterdam, 35 [repr]; 1928 The Hague; 1929 Hamburg, 40; 1930 Amsterdam, 67; 1952 Milan, 30; 1953-4 Saint Louis etc, 24; 1956 Nuremberg, 28; Munich, 43; 1958 Tokyo, Kyoto, 35; 1961 Munich, 32
PROVENANCE J. Hidde Nijland, The Hague; Dordrechts Museum, Dordrecht [loan Hidde Nijland 1904-1910]; Otterlo, Rijksmuseum Kröller-Müller, inv nr 936-28, cat van Gogh 1970, nr 99

F1098 THE DRAWBRIDGE AT NIEUW-AMSTERDAM
EXHIBITION 1961 Amsterdam 1, 32
PROVENANCE G. Heymans, Groningen; Miss J. van Binnendijk, Groningen; Groningen, Groninger Museum voor Stad en Lande, inv nr 1961/188

F1099 LANDSCAPE TOWARDS EVENING
EXHIBITION 1932 Amsterdam 2, 9
PROVENANCE Oldenzeel Art Gallery, Rotterdam; M. Gieseler, The Hague; Sale Amsterdam [Mak] 27 November 1925, 28 [repr]; W. van Beuningen, Utrecht; Wassenaar, Mrs C. E. van Beuningen-Fentener van Vlissingen [R 1969]

F1100 THE HEATH: WITH A WHEELBARROW
EXHIBITION 1958 Cleveland, 14
PROVENANCE C. Mouwen jr, Breda; Sale Amsterdam [F. Muller] 4 May 1904, 27; Oldenzeel Art Gallery, Rotterdam; Artz and De Bois Art Gallery, The Hague; E. Schall, Berlin; Lutz Art Gallery, Berlin; F. Kantorowicz, Berlin; J. K. Thannhauser, New York; L. C. Hanna jr, Cleveland; Cleveland, Museum of Art [acquired 1958; bequest of Leonard C. Hanna jr, inv nr 58.30

F1101 LANDSCAPE IN DRENTHE WITH A HUT
PROVENANCE Reckers Art Gallery, Rotterdam; A. Hoynck van Papendrecht, Rotterdam; M. Frank, New York; H. Kaplan, Miami [R 1967]; Fritz and Peter Nathan, Zurich [R 1968]; New York, Private collection [R 1970]

F1102 A HUT IN DRENTHE
EXHIBITIONS 1960 Paris, 95; 1961 Amsterdam 1, 33
PROVENANCE Unger and Van Mens Art Gallery, Rotterdam; J. H. Muntendam, Rotterdam [acquired 1920]; Mrs M. Muntendam-Isebree Moens, The Hague [R 1960]; Galerie Beyeler, Basle [R 1969]; New York, Private collection-courtesy Galerie St. Etienne

F1103 A GROUP OF PEASANT HOUSES IN DRENTHE
EXHIBITIONS 1913 Rotterdam, 28 [probably]; 1946 Stockholm etc, 6; 1947 Basle, 130; 1969 Saint-Etienne, 30
PROVENANCE C. Mouwen jr, Breda; Sale Amsterdam [F. Muller] 4 May 1904, 28; Oldenzeel Art Gallery, Rotterdam; W. H. G. Bolleurs, The Hague; W. G. H. van Houweninge, Sale Rotterdam [Van Marle and De Sille] 21-22 April 1925, 256; d'Audretsch Art Gallery, The Hague; Baron E. von der Heydt, Ascona; Wuppertal, Von der Heydt-Museum der Stadt Wuppertal, inv nr KK 1965/27, cat Handzeichnungen, Pastelle und Aquarelle 1965, nr 62

F1104 LANDSCAPE IN DRENTHE WITH CANAL AND SAILBOAT
EXHIBITIONS 1903 Rotterdam 3, 78; 1953 Amsterdam 1, 9; 1955 New York 2, 92
PROVENANCE C. Mouwen jr, Breda; Sale Amsterdam [F. Muller] 3 May 1905, 34 [repr]; H. Gorter, Bussum; d'Audretsch Art Gallery, The Hague; G. H. F. van Suchtelen, The Hague; Mrs A. L. J. Einthoven-van Suchtelen, The Hague; Huinck and Scherjon Art Gallery, Amsterdam [1953]; W. Weinberg, Scarsdale, New York; Sale London [Sotheby] 10 July 1957, 54; Present owner unknown

F1105 TWO MEN ON A COUNTRY ROAD
PROVENANCE A. G. A. van Rappard, Utrecht; P. de Kanter, Delft; H. E. d'Audretsch, Amerongen; M. Frank, New York; New York, Private collection [R 1968]

F1106 WINTERLANDSCAPE WITH WOMAN AND WHEELBARROWS
EXHIBITIONS 1918 The Hague; 1924 Amsterdam, 57; 1928 The Hague; 1929 Hamburg, 102; 1930 Amsterdam, 126; 1950 's-Hertogenbosch, Breda; 1961 Munich, 33
PROVENANCE J. Hidde Nijland, The Hague; Dordrechts Museum, Dordrecht [loan J. Hidde Nijland 1904-1910]; Otterlo, Rijksmuseum Kröller-Müller, inv nr 1009-28, cat van Gogh 1970, nr 163

NUENEN PERIOD

F1107 THE WEAVER: THE WHOLE LOOM FACING LEFT
EXHIBITIONS 1905 Amsterdam, 338; 1923 Utrecht, Rotterdam, 21; 1924 Amsterdam, 124; Basle, 85; Zurich, 85; Stuttgart, 1; 1925 The Hague, 73; 1926 Munich, 2108; 1927-8 Berlin etc, 23; 1949-50 New York, Chicago, 31; 1954-5 Bern, 89; 1955 Antwerp 1, 78; 1957 Marseilles, 13; Stockholm, 24; 1963 Paris, 28; 1965 Nuenen, without cat nr; Stockholm, 16; 1967 Wolfsburg, 87; 1967-8 Dallas etc, 12; 1968 Liège, 12
PROVENANCE Mrs J. van Gogh-Bonger, Amsterdam; V. W. van Gogh, Laren; Amsterdam, Rijksmuseum Vincent van Gogh [Vincent van Gogh Foundation, inv nr F 1107]

F1108 THE WEAVER: THE WHOLE LOOM, FACING RIGHT
PROVENANCE Druet Art Gallery, Paris; G. Gérard, Limoges [acquired about 1909-1919]; Druet Art Gallery, Paris [1919-20]; Mrs G. Guibert, Limoges [until 1960]; Heirs of Mrs Guibert; Sale Paris [Galliéra] 20 June 1968, 225; Zurich, Fritz and Peter Nathan [R 1970]; Los Angeles, A. Hammer

F1109 THE WEAVER: PART OF THE LOOM, FACING RIGHT
EXHIBITIONS 1895 The Hague; 1918 The Hague; 1924 Amsterdam, 60; 1928 The Hague; 1929 Hamburg, 114; 1930 Amsterdam, 120; 1950 's-Hertogenbosch, Breda; 1952 Milan, 33; 1957 Essen, 167; 1958 Tokyo, Kyoto, 37; 1959 São Paulo, 19; 1962 Warsaw, 29; 1963 Tel Aviv, Haifa, 29
PROVENANCE J. Hidde Nijland, The Hague; Dordrechts Museum, Dordrecht [loan Hidde Nijland 1904-1910]; Otterlo, Rijksmuseum Kröller-Müller, inv nr 1023-28, cat van Gogh 1970, nr 103

F1110 INTERIOR WITH A WEAVER FACING RIGHT
EXHIBITIONS 1918 The Hague; 1924 Amsterdam, 55; 1928 The Hague; 1929 Hamburg, 48; 1930 Amsterdam, 119; 1950 's-Hertogenbosch, Breda; 1956 Munich, 45; 1960-1 Montreal etc, 100
PROVENANCE J. Hidde Nijland, The Hague; Dordrechts Museum, Dordrecht [loan Hidde Nijland 1904-1910]; Otterlo, Rijksmuseum Kröller-Müller, inv nr 945-28, cat van Gogh 1970, nr 102

F1111 FOUR FIGURES WORKING AT A LOOM
EXHIBITIONS 1918 The Hague; 1924 Amsterdam, 111; 1928 The Hague; 1929 Hamburg, 113; 1930 Amsterdam, 124a; 1956 Nuremberg, 52; 1961 Munich, 34
PROVENANCE J. Hidde Nijland, The Hague; Dordrechts Museum, Dordrecht [loan Hidde Nijland 1904-1910]; Otterlo, Rijksmuseum Kröller-Müller, inv nr 1044-28, cat van Gogh 1970, nr 152

F1112 recto STUDIES OF AN AUCTION NEAR NUENEN
verso THE ENTRANCE OF THE OLD CHURCH TOWER AT NUENEN
EXHIBITIONS 1918 The Hague; 1924 Amsterdam, 81; 1928 The Hague; 1929 Hamburg, 116; 1930 Amsterdam, 125; 1950 's-Hertogenbosch, Breda; 1956 Munich, 52; 1957 Essen, 200; 1960-1 Montreal etc, 107; 1962 Warsaw, 41; 1963 Tel Aviv, Haifa, 41
PROVENANCE J. Hidde Nijland, The Hague; Dordrechts Museum, Dordrecht [loan Hidde Nijland 1904-1910]; Otterlo, Rijksmuseum Kröller-Müller, inv nr 1013-28, cat van Gogh 1970, nr 160a, 160b [verso]

F1113 A LUMBER SALE
EXHIBITIONS 1905 Amsterdam, 337; 1914-5 Amsterdam, 52; 1920 New York, 14; 1924 Amsterdam, 127; 1927-8 Berlin etc, 22; 1949-50 New York, Chicago, 30; 1953-4 Saint Louis etc, 34; 1954-5 Bern, 90; 1955 Antwerp 1, 75; 1957 Stockholm, 20; 1958-9 San Francisco etc, 97; 1960

Enschede, 13; 1963 Humlebaek, 69; Paris, 31; 1964 Washington, New York, 69; 1965 Nuenen, no cat nr; 1965-6 Stockholm, Göteborg, 67; 1967 Wolfsburg, 88
PROVENANCE Mrs J. van Gogh-Bonger, Amsterdam; V. W. van Gogh, Laren; Amsterdam, Rijksmuseum Vincent van Gogh [Vincent van Gogh Foundation, inv nr F 1113]

F1114 THE WEAVER: THE WHOLE LOOM, FACING LEFT
EXHIBITIONS 1905 Amsterdam, 335; 1920 New York, 1; 1932 Manchester, 47; 1937 Paris, 63; 1946-7 Liège etc, 18; 1947 Geneva, 18; Paris 1, 18; 1955 Antwerp 1, 80; 1957 Nijmegen, 17; 1961-2 Baltimore etc, 91; 1962-3 Pittsburgh etc; 1967 Tilburg
PROVENANCE Mrs J. van Gogh Bonger, Amsterdam; V. W. van Gogh, Laren; Amsterdam, Rijksmuseum Vincent van Gogh [Vincent van Gogh Foundation, inv nr F 1114]

F1115 THE WEAVER, FACING RIGHT: INTERIOR WITH THREE WINDOWS
EXHIBITIONS 1905 Amsterdam, 323; 1914-5 Amsterdam, 54; 1923 Utrecht, Rotterdam, 70; 1957 Stockholm, 26; 1961-2 Baltimore etc, 92; 1962-3 Pittsburgh etc; 1964 Zundert, 5
PROVENANCE Mrs J. van Gogh-Bonger, Amsterdam; V. W. van Gogh, Laren; Amsterdam, Rijksmuseum Vincent van Gogh [Vincent van Gogh Foundation, inv nr F 1115]

F1116 THE WEAVER, SEEN FROM THE FRONT
EXHIBITIONS 1905 Amsterdam, 301; 1914-5 Amsterdam, 98
PROVENANCE Mrs J. van Gogh-Bonger, Amsterdam; V. W. van Gogh, Laren; Amsterdam, Rijksmuseum Vincent van Gogh [Vincent van Gogh Foundation, inv nr F 1116]

F1116a recto A MAN SEATED BESIDE THE STOVE
verso THE WEAVER: PART OF THE LOOM, THREE QUARTERS TO THE RIGHT
PROVENANCE d'Audretsch Art Gallery, The Hague; H. W. Chr. Nieuwenhuys, Aerdenhout, Netherlands [1959]; New York, P. Rosenberg & Co Art Gallery [R 1960]

F1117 CHAPEL AT NUENEN BETWEEN TREES WITH FIGURE
EXHIBITIONS 1918 The Hague; 1924 Amsterdam, 118; 1928 The Hague; 1929 Hamburg, 125; 1930 Amsterdam, 98; 1935-6 New York etc, 94; 1958 Vienna, 38; Tokyo, Kyoto, 66; 1962 London 1, 16; 1966 Belgrade, 37
PROVENANCE J. Hidde Nijland, The Hague; Otterlo, Rijksmuseum Kröller-Müller, inv nr 1037-28, cat van Gogh 1970, nr 162

F1118 INTERIOR OF A WEAVER'S WORKSHOP WITH BABY CHAIR
EXHIBITIONS 1905 Amsterdam, 303; 1914-5 Amsterdam, 64; 1954-5 Bern, 91; 1955 Antwerp 1, 76; 1955-6 Liverpool etc, 88
PROVENANCE Mrs J. van Gogh-Bonger, Amsterdam; V. W. van Gogh, Laren; Amsterdam, Rijksmuseum Vincent van Gogh [Vincent van Gogh Foundation, inv nr F 1118]

F1119 INTERIOR OF A WEAVER'S WORKSHOP WITH BABY CHAIR
EXHIBITIONS 1903 Rotterdam 3; 1904 Rotterdam, 56; 1928 Paris; 1955 New York 2, 93; 1961 London 1, 8
PROVENANCE C. Mouwen jr, Breda; Sale Amsterdam [F. Muller] 3 May 1904, 30; Oldenzeel Art Gallery, Rotterdam; P. Versteeven, The Hague; Sale Amsterdam [Mak van Waay] 27 October 1925, 122; E. Alexander, Paris; A. Allaire, Crépy en Laonnois, France; Huinck and Scherjon Art Gallery, Amsterdam; W. Weinberg, Scarsdale, New York; Sale London [Sotheby] 10 July 1957, 51; E. Speelman, London; Marlborough Art Gallery, London; Sale London [Sotheby] 31 March 1965, 9; Present owner unknown

F1120 THE WEAVER: THE WHOLE LOOM, FACING LEFT
PROVENANCE Mrs J. van Gogh-Bonger, Amsterdam; V. W. van Gogh, Laren; Amsterdam, Rijksmuseum Vincent van Gogh [Vincent van Gogh Foundation, inv nr F 1120]

F1121 THE WEAVER: THE WHOLE LOOM, FACING RIGHT WITH OIL LAMP
EXHIBITIONS 1905 Amsterdam, 313; 1914-5 Amsterdam, 72; 1923 Utrecht, Rotterdam, 69; 1953 The Hague, 17; Otterlo, Amsterdam, 33; 1953-4 Saint Louis etc, 37; 1954-5 Bern, 92; 1955 Antwerp 1, 79
PROVENANCE Mrs J. van Gogh-Bonger, Amsterdam; V. W. van Gogh, Laren; Amsterdam, Rijksmuseum Vincent van Gogh [Vincent van Gogh Foundation, inv nr F 1121]

F1122 THE WEAVER: HALF LENGTH, FACING RIGHT
EXHIBITIONS 1905 Amsterdam, 295; 1914-5 Amsterdam, 59; 1957 Nijmegen, 18
PROVENANCE Mrs J. van Gogh-Bonger, Amsterdam; V. W. van Gogh, Laren; Amsterdam, Rijksmuseum Vincent van Gogh [Vincent van Gogh Foundation, inv nr F 1122]

F1123 THE WEAVER: THE WHOLE LOOM, FACING LEFT, WITH OIL LAMP
EXHIBITIONS 1905 Amsterdam, 329; 1914-5 Amsterdam,

76; 1946 Stockholm etc, 9; 1955 Antwerp 1, 77; 1957 Stockholm, 25; 1958-9 San Francisco etc, 98; 1959-60 Utrecht, 71; 1960 Enschede, 14; 1961-2 Baltimore etc, 93; 1963 Humlebaek, 70; 1964 Washington, New York, 70; 1965 Charleroi, Ghent, 47; Nuenen, without cat nr; 1966 Paris, Albi, 10; 1967 Lille, Zurich, 11; 1967-8 Dallas etc, 13; 1968-9 London, 21; 1969 Humlebaek, 7
PROVENANCE Mrs J. van Gogh-Bonger, Amsterdam; V. W. van Gogh, Laren; Amsterdam, Rijksmuseum Vincent van Gogh [Vincent van Gogh Foundation, inv nr F 1123]

F 1124 THE WEAVER: THE WHOLE LOOM, FACING LEFT
PROVENANCE Oldenzeel Art Gallery, Rotterdam; J. Hidde Nijland, The Hague; H. P. Bremmer, The Hague [R 1956]; The Hague, Heirs of H. P. Bremmer [R 1970]

F 1125 A WEAVER: THE WHOLE LOOM, FACING RIGHT
EXHIBITIONS 1905 Amsterdam, 325; 1914-5 Amsterdam, 68; 1923 Utrecht, Rotterdam, 4; 1927-8 Berlin etc, 18
PROVENANCE Mrs J. van Gogh-Bonger, Amsterdam; V. W. van Gogh, Laren; Amsterdam, Rijksmuseum Vincent van Gogh [Vincent van Gogh Foundation, inv nr F 1125]

F 1126 WINTER LANDSCAPE WITH FIGURE BEARING WOOD
EXHIBITIONS 1923 Utrecht. Rotterdam. 8; 1924 Amsterdam, 125; 1927-8 Berlin etc, 17; 1955 Antwerp 1, 67
PROVENANCE Mrs J. van Gogh-Bonger, Amsterdam; V. W. van Gogh, Laren; Amsterdam, Rijksmuseum Vincent van Gogh [Vincent van Gogh Foundation, inv nr F 1126]

F 1127 THE VICARAGE GARDEN WITH A VIEW ON THE OLD TOWER OF NUENEN IN WINTER
EXHIBITIONS 1905 Amsterdam, 336; 1914-5 Amsterdam, 43; 1924 Basle, 81; Zurich, 3; Stuttgart, 6; 1925 The Hague, 58; 1927-8 Berlin etc, 42; 1955 Antwerp 1, 65; 1957 Nijmegen, 19; Stockholm, 21; 1962 London 1, 17
PROVENANCE Mrs J. van Gogh-Bonger, Amsterdam; V. W. van Gogh, Laren; Amsterdam, Rijksmuseum Vincent van Gogh [Vincent van Gogh Foundation, inv nr F 1127]

F 1127a GARDEN IN WINTER
EXHIBITION 1969 Stuttgart, 51
PROVENANCE L. van der Loo, Eindhoven [1956]; W. Brinkman, Schipluiden; Stuttgart, Staatsgalerie, Graphische Sammlung [acquired 1963], inv nr C 63/1064

F 1128 THE VICARAGE GARDEN AT NUENEN IN WINTER
EXHIBITIONS 1905 Amsterdam, 306; 1914-5 Amsterdam, 107; 1920 New York, 3; 1923 London, 6; 1925 The Hague, 85; 1927-8 Berlin etc, 28; 1937 Paris, 60; 1946-7 Liège etc, 13; 1947 Geneva, 13; Paris 1, 13; 1947-8 London etc, 114; 1948 Bergen, Oslo, 72; 1949-50 New York, Chicago, 32; 1951 Lyons etc, 85; 1953 The Hague, 16; Otterlo, Amsterdam, 32; 1953-4 Saint Louis etc, 35; 1955 Palm Beach etc, 34; Antwerp 1, 64; 1955-6 Liverpool etc, 89; 1957 Nijmegen, 20; Stockholm, 22; 1958-9 San Francisco etc, 99; 1960 Enschede, 15; 1960-1 Montreal etc, 112; 1961-2 Baltimore etc, 94; 1962-3 Pittsburgh etc, 94; 1964 Zundert, 6; 1965 Nuenen; Stockholm, Göteborg, 68; 1967 Wolfsburg, 89; 1967-8 Dallas etc, 14; 1968 Liège, 14; 1968-9 London, 22; 1969 Humlebaek, 8
PROVENANCE Mrs J. van Gogh-Bonger, Amsterdam; V. W. van Gogh, Laren; Amsterdam, Rijksmuseum Vincent van Gogh [Vincent van Gogh Foundation, inv nr F 1128]

F 1129 ROAD WITH POLLARD WILLOWS AND MAN WITH A WHEELBARROW
EXHIBITIONS 1905 Amsterdam, 286; 1955 Antwerp 1, 63; 1957 Essen; 1959 Recklinghausen, 114; 1960 Paris, 96; 1961 Munich, 36
PROVENANCE Mrs J. van Gogh-Bonger, Amsterdam; Amsterdam, Rijksmuseum [acquired 1906; gift from Mrs Cohen Gosschalk], cat 1934, nr 2926b; on loan to Rijksinspecteur voor roerende monumenten, inv nr B–1148; on loan to Amsterdam, Stedelijk Museum, inv nr B 3093

F 1130 THE VICARAGE GARDEN AT NUENEN IN WINTER
EXHIBITIONS 1959 Budapest, 116; 1967 Vienna, 119
PROVENANCE Paul Majovsky, Budapest; Budapest, Museum of Fine Arts, inv nr 1935-2791, cat 1956, nr 112

F 1131 THE VICARAGE GARDEN AT NUENEN IN WINTER WITH THREE WOMEN
EXHIBITIONS 1905 Amsterdam, 291; 1914 Berlin, 11; 1914-5 Amsterdam, 99; 1923 Utrecht, Rotterdam, 54; 1927-8 Berlin etc, 43; 1932 Manchester, 58; 1949-50 New York, Chicago, 33; 1954-5 Bern, 93; 1955 Antwerp 1, 62; 1965 Nuenen, no cat nr; 1966 Paris, Albi, 11; 1967 Lille, Zurich, 12
PROVENANCE Mrs J. van Gogh-Bonger, Amsterdam; V. W. van Gogh, Laren; Amsterdam, Rijksmuseum Vincent van Gogh [Vincent van Gogh Foundation, inv nr F 1131]

F 1132 THE VICARAGE GARDEN AT NUENEN
EXHIBITIONS 1953-4 Bern, 94; 1955 Antwerp 1, 61
PROVENANCE Mrs J. van Gogh-Bonger, Amsterdam; H. C. Bonger, Amsterdam; Miss E. H. Bonger, Amsterdam; V. W. van Gogh, Laren; Amsterdam, Rijksmuseum Vincent van Gogh [Vincent van Gogh Foundation, inv nr F 1132]

F 1133 LANDSCAPE WITH THE OLD TOWER OF NUENEN WITH BLACK FIGURE
PROVENANCE A. G. A. van Rappard, Utrecht; P. de Kanter, Delft; d'Audretsch Art Gallery, The Hague; W. Walrecht Art Gallery, The Hague [1917]; A. Schwarz, Amsterdam; Sale Amsterdam [P. Brandt] 15-18 November 1954, 40; Present owner unknown

F 1134 THE WEAVER STANDING IN FRONT OF A LOOM: LEFT PROFILE
EXHIBITIONS 1927 Basle etc, 69; 1928 Düsseldorf, 135; Karlsruhe, 70; 1929 Berlin 1, 39; Hamburg, 32; 1930 Amsterdam, 122; 1935-6 New York etc, 95; 1947 Basle, 132 [2d edition, 133]; 1947-8 London etc, 115; 1950 's-Hertogenbosch, Breda; 1952 Milan, 34; 1955 Wormerveer; 1956 Eindhoven, 12; 1958 Vienna, 39; Tokyo, Kyoto, 38; 1961 Munich, 38; 1962 London 1, 21
PROVENANCE W. Walrecht Art Gallery, The Hague [1917]; Otterlo, Rijksmuseum Kröller-Müller, inv nr 252-17, cat van Gogh 1970, nr 104

F 1135 THE POND IN THE VICARAGE GARDEN AT NUENEN, WITH A KINGFISHER
EXHIBITIONS 1905 Amsterdam, 344a; 1947 Basle, 132 [131]; 1947-8 London etc, 118
PROVENANCE J. J. Polak, Rotterdam [1905, until about 1938]; The Netherlands, Private collection [R 1970]

F 1136 WOMAN WINDING BOBBINS
EXHIBITIONS 1918 The Hague; 1924 Amsterdam, 107; 1928 The Hague; 1929 Hamburg, 127; 1930 Amsterdam, 82; 1935-6 New York etc, 96; 1955 Antwerp 1, 21; 1956 Munich, 48
PROVENANCE J. Hidde Nijland, The Hague; Dordrechts Museum, Dordrecht [loan Hidde Nijland 1904-1910]; Otterlo, Rijksmuseum Kröller-Müller, inv nr 1039-28, cat van Gogh 1970, nr 127

F 1137 WOMAN WINDING BOBBINS
EXHIBITIONS 1918 The Hague; 1924 Amsterdam, 117; 1928 The Hague; 1929 Hamburg, 135; 1930 Amsterdam, 96; 1956 Nuremberg, 37; Munich, 48 [repr as drawing F 1136]; 1958 Tokyo, Kyoto, 51; 1961 Munich, 37; 1966 Belgrade, 23
PROVENANCE J. Hidde Nijland, The Hague; Dordrechts Museum, Dordrecht [loan Hidde Nijland 1904-1910]; Otterlo, Rijksmuseum Kröller-Müller, inv nr 1046-28, cat van Gogh 1970, nr 126

F 1138 MAN REELING YARN
EXHIBITIONS 1918 The Hague; 1924 Amsterdam, 108; 1928 The Hague; 1929 Hamburg, 124; 1930 Amsterdam, 121; 1962 Warsaw, 30; 1963 Tel Aviv, Haifa, 30; 1966 Belgrade, 25
PROVENANCE J. Hidde Nijland, The Hague; Otterlo, Rijksmuseum Kröller-Müller, inv nr 1036-28, cat van Gogh 1970, nr 105

F 1139 WOMAN WINDING BOBBINS
EXHIBITIONS 1905 Amsterdam, 275; 1914-5 Amsterdam, 100; 1955 New York 2, 4
PROVENANCE Mrs J. van Gogh-Bonger, Amsterdam; Mrs E. von Mendelssohn-Bartholdy, Leipzig; C. Nicolai Art Gallery, Berlin; W. Streit, Hamburg; Sale Berlin [Graupe] 10 June 1931, 42; Wildenstein Art Gallery, New York; Mr and Mrs Samuel C. Karlan [R 1970]

F 1140 MAN REELING YARN
PROVENANCE Mrs C. Dekker-Fortanier, The Hague; G. J. Dekker, Amersfoort; Bern, Eberhard W. Kornfeld [R 1970]

F 1141 POTATO DIGGERS
PROVENANCE Mrs G. Smith-van Stolk, Rotterdam; Mr and Mrs J. van Hoey Smith, Rockanje; Rockanje, R. W. van Hoey Smith [R 1970]

F 1142 THE PLOW
PROVENANCE Mrs G. Smith-van Stolk, Rotterdam; Mr and Mrs J. van Hoey Smith, Rockanje; Rockanje, R. W. van Hoey Smith [R 1970]

F 1143 THE SOWER
PROVENANCE Mrs G. Smith-van Stolk, Rotterdam; Mr and Mrs J. van Hoey Smith, Rockanje; Rockanje, R. W. van Hoey Smith [R 1970]

F 1144 OX WAGON IN THE SNOW
PROVENANCE Mrs G. Smith-van Stolk, Rotterdam; Mr and Mrs J. van Hoey Smith, Rockanje; Rockanje, R. W. van Hoey Smith [R 1970]

F 1144a MILL AT GENNEP, NEAR NUENEN
PROVENANCE Miss J. A. van den Broek, Eindhoven; A. Houben, Eindhoven; F. E. van der Sommen, Eindhoven [1909-1925]; Miss J. A. van der Sommen, Eindhoven [1925-1949]; Private collection, Netherlands [acquired 1949]; Sale London [Sotheby] 3 July 1969, 211; Present owner unknown

F 1145 HEAD OF A YOUNG PEASANT: RIGHT PROFILE
EXHIBITION 1905 Amsterdam, 462
PROVENANCE Mrs J. van Gogh-Bonger, Amsterdam; V. W. van Gogh, Laren; Amsterdam, Rijksmuseum Vincent van Gogh [Vincent van Gogh Foundation, inv nr F 1145]

F 1146 HEAD OF A YOUNG PEASANT: RIGHT PROFILE
EXHIBITIONS 1905 Amsterdam, 331; 1914-5 Amsterdam, 62; 1927-8 Berlin etc, 33; 1955 Antwerp 1, 101; 1957 Nijmegen, 21; Stockholm, 28; 1958-9 San Francisco etc, 100; 1960 Enschede, 16; 1961-2 Baltimore etc, 95; 1965 Nuenen, without cat nr; 1966 Paris, Albi, 12; 1967 Lille, Zurich, 13; 1967-8 Dallas etc, 15; 1968 Liège, 15
PROVENANCE Mrs J. van Gogh-Bonger, Amsterdam; V. W. van Gogh, Laren; Amsterdam, Rijksmuseum Vincent van Gogh [Vincent van Gogh Foundation, inv nr F 1146]

F 1147 HEAD OF A YOUNG PEASANT: FULL FACE, SMOKING A PIPE
EXHIBITIONS 1905 Amsterdam, 315; 1914-5 Amsterdam, 97; 1923 Utrecht; Rotterdam, 68; 1932 Manchester, 48; 1955 Antwerp 1, 102; 1957 Nijmegen, 22
PROVENANCE Mrs J. van Gogh-Bonger, Amsterdam; V. W. van Gogh, Laren; Amsterdam, Rijksmuseum Vincent van Gogh [Vincent van Gogh Foundation, inv nr F 1147]

F 1148 HEAD OF A PEASANT WOMAN: FULL FACE
PROVENANCE C. M. van Gogh Art Gallery, Amsterdam; Present owner unknown

F 1149 HEAD OF A PEASANT WOMAN WITH DARK CAP: FULL FACE
EXHIBITIONS 1905 Amsterdam, 453; 1914-5 Amsterdam, 73; 1923 Utrecht, Rotterdam, 13
PROVENANCE Mrs J. van Gogh-Bonger, Amsterdam; V. W. van Gogh, Laren; Amsterdam, Rijksmuseum Vincent van Gogh [Vincent van Gogh Foundation, inv nr F 1149]

F 1150 recto HEAD OF A PEASANT WOMAN: FACING LEFT
verso SKETCH OF TWO PERSONS
PROVENANCE Mrs J. van Gogh-Bonger, Amsterdam; V. W. van Gogh, Laren; Amsterdam, Rijksmuseum Vincent van Gogh [Vincent van Gogh Foundation, inv nr F 1150]

F 1151 STUDIES OF THE HEADS OF TWO WOMEN; A PEASANT WALKING
EXHIBITIONS 1918 The Hague; 1924 Amsterdam, 111; 1928 The Hague; 1929 Hamburg, 131; 1930 Amsterdam, 124c; 1956 Nuremberg, 49; Munich, 49; 1958 Tokyo, Kyoto, 60; 1961 Munich, 39
PROVENANCE J. Hidde Nijland, The Hague; Dordrechts Museum, Dordrecht [loan Hidde Nijland 1904-1910]; Otterlo, Rijksmuseum Kröller-Müller, inv nr 1042-28, cat van Gogh 1970, nr 148

F 1152 recto STUDY OF A RIGHT AND LEFT HAND; HEAD OF A PEASANT
verso THATCHED FARM IN THE EVENING
EXHIBITIONS 1914-5 Amsterdam, 122; 1923 Utrecht, Rotterdam, 9; 1927-8 Berlin etc, 31; 1945 Amsterdam, no cat nr; 1965 Nuenen, no cat nr
PROVENANCE Mrs J. van Gogh-Bonger, Amsterdam; V. W. van Gogh, Laren; Amsterdam, Rijksmuseum Vincent van Gogh [Vincent van Gogh Foundation, inv nr F 1152]

F 1153 recto STUDY OF HANDS
verso STILL LIFE WITH HEARTH KETTLE; COTTAGE WITH A PEASANT
EXHIBITIONS 1923, Utrecht, Rotterdam, 72; 1954-5 Bern, 95; 1955 Antwerp 1, 107; 1957 Stockholm, 29
PROVENANCE Mrs J. van Gogh-Bonger, Amsterdam; V. W. van Gogh, Laren; Amsterdam, Rijksmuseum Vincent van Gogh [Vincent van Gogh Foundation, inv nr F 1153]

F 1154 STUDY OF A RIGHT AND A LEFT HAND
PROVENANCE Mrs J. van Gogh-Bonger, Amsterdam; V. W. van Gogh, Laren; Amsterdam, Rijksmuseum Vincent van Gogh [Vincent van Gogh Foundation, inv nr F 1154]

F 1155 STUDY OF HANDS AND ARMS
EXHIBITIONS 1949-50 New York, Chicago, 34; 1954-5 Bern, 96; 1955 Antwerp 1, 108; 1957 Stockholm, 30; Nijmegen, 24; 1958-9 San Francisco etc, 101; 1960 Enschede, 17
PROVENANCE Mrs J. van Gogh-Bonger, Amsterdam; V. W. van Gogh, Laren; Amsterdam, Rijksmuseum Vincent van Gogh [Vincent van Gogh Foundation, inv nr F 1155]

F 1156 recto STUDY OF THREE HANDS, TWO OF THEM HOLDING A STICK
verso HEAD OF A YOUNG PEASANT: FULL FACE
EXHIBITIONS 1954-5 Bern, 97; 1955 Antwerp 1, 100 [verso]
PROVENANCE Mrs J. van Gogh-Bonger, Amsterdam; V. W. van Gogh, Laren; Amsterdam, Rijksmuseum Vincent van Gogh [Vincent van Gogh Foundation, inv nr F 1156]

F 1157 STUDY OF A RIGHT HAND WITH A KETTLE
EXHIBITIONS 1957 Nijmegen, 25; 1958-9 San Francisco etc, 102; 1960 Enschede, 18; 1962 Recklinghausen, 22h; 1963 Humlebaek, 71; 1964 Washington, New York, 71; 1965

Nuenen, no cat nr; 1966 Paris, Albi, 13; 1967 Lille, Zurich, 14
PROVENANCE Mrs J. van Gogh-Bonger, Amsterdam; V. W. van Gogh, Laren; Amsterdam, Rijksmuseum Vincent van Gogh [Vincent van Gogh Foundation, inv nr F 1157]

F 1158 recto STUDY OF FOUR RIGHT HANDS
verso SKETCH OF A LAMP HANGING BEFORE A WINDOW
PROVENANCE Mrs J. van Gogh-Bonger, Amsterdam; V. W. van Gogh, Laren; Amsterdam, Rijksmuseum Vincent van Gogh [Vincent van Gogh Foundation, inv nr F 1158]

F 1159 recto STUDY OF TWO HANDS HOLDING A STICK
verso STUDY OF FOUR HANDS, TWO OF THEM HOLDING A CUP
PROVENANCE Mrs J. van Gogh-Bonger, Amsterdam; V. W. van Gogh, Laren; Amsterdam, Rijksmuseum Vincent van Gogh [Vincent van Gogh Foundation, inv nr F 1159]

F 1160 recto STUDY OF A LEFT ARM
verso STUDY OF A RIGHT ARM
PROVENANCE Mrs J. van Gogh-Bonger, Amsterdam; V. W. van Gogh, Laren; Amsterdam, Rijksmuseum Vincent van Gogh [Vincent van Gogh Foundation, inv nr F 1160]

F 1161 recto STUDY OF THREE HANDS, TWO OF THEM WITH A FORK [for the final version of THE POTATO EATERS]
verso SKETCH OF AN INTERIOR [BACKGROUND FOR THE POTATO EATERS] AND COMPOSITION SKETCH OF THE POTATO EATERS
EXHIBITIONS 1945 Amsterdam, no cat nr; 1953 Otterlo, Amsterdam, 36; The Hague, 21 [verso]; 1953-4 St Louis etc, 38; 1954-5 Bern, 98; 1955 Antwerp I, 109; 1957 Stockholm, 31; Nijmegen, 26; 1958-9 San Francisco etc, 103; 1960 Enschede, 19; 1960-1 Montreal etc, 114; 1961-2 Baltimore etc, 96; 1962 Recklinghausen, 22g; 1963 Humlebaek, 72; 1964 Washington, New York, 72; 1965 Charleroi, Ghent, 48; Nuenen, no cat nr; 1966 Paris, Albi, 14; 1967 Lille, Zurich, 15; 1967-8 Dallas etc, 16; 1968 Liège, 16; 1968-9 London, 31; 1969 Humlebaek, 9
PROVENANCE Mrs J. van Gogh-Bonger, Amsterdam; V. W. van Gogh, Laren; Amsterdam, Rijksmuseum Vincent van Gogh [Vincent van Gogh Foundation, inv nr F 1161]

F 1162 STUDY OF HANDS
EXHIBITION 1954-5 Bern, 99
PROVENANCE Mrs J. van Gogh-Bonger, Amsterdam; V. W. van Gogh, Laren; Amsterdam, Rijksmuseum Vincent van Gogh [Vincent van Gogh Foundation, inv nr F 1162]

F 1163 STUDY OF THREE HANDS
EXHIBITION 1914-5 Amsterdam, 123 [11 studies of hands were exhibited]
PROVENANCE Mrs J. van Gogh-Bonger, Amsterdam; V. W. van Gogh, Laren; Amsterdam, Rijksmuseum Vincent van Gogh [Vincent van Gogh Foundation, inv nr F 1163]

F 1164 recto STUDY OF FOUR HANDS
verso STUDY OF THREE HANDS
EXHIBITIONS 1927-8 Berlin etc, 36; 1954-5 Bern, 100; 1955 Antwerp I, 111
PROVENANCE Mrs J. van Gogh-Bonger, Amsterdam; V. W. van Gogh, Laren; Amsterdam, Rijksmuseum Vincent van Gogh [Vincent van Gogh Foundation, inv nr F 1164]

F 1165 TWO HANDS HOLDING A BOWL
EXHIBITIONS 1955 Antwerp I, 114; 1965 Nuenen, no cat nr; 1965-6 Stockholm, Göteborg, 69; 1967 Wolfsburg, 90
PROVENANCE Mrs J. van Gogh-Bonger, Amsterdam; V. W. van Gogh, Laren; Amsterdam, Rijksmuseum Vincent van Gogh [Vincent van Gogh Foundation, inv nr F 1165]

F 1166 STUDY OF HANDS HOLDING A SHOVEL
EXHIBITIONS 1932 Manchester, 53; 1955 Antwerp I, 112
PROVENANCE Mrs J. van Gogh-Bonger, Amsterdam; V. W. van Gogh, Laren; Amsterdam, Rijksmuseum Vincent van Gogh [Vincent van Gogh Foundation, inv nr F 1166]

F 1167 recto STUDY OF HANDS IN REPOSE
verso STUDY OF THREE HANDS
EXHIBITIONS 1923 Utrecht, Rotterdam, 72; 1954-5 Bern, 101; 1955 Antwerp I, 113; 1967 Lille, Zurich, 16
PROVENANCE Mrs J. van Gogh-Bonger, Amsterdam; V. W. van Gogh, Laren; Amsterdam, Rijksmuseum Vincent van Gogh [Vincent van Gogh Foundation, inv nr F 1167]

F 1168 recto STUDY OF A HAND CLASPING A STICK; AN INTERIOR WITH FOUR PERSONS
verso THREE HANDS HOLDING A STICK
EXHIBITIONS 1954-5 Bern, 102; 1955 Antwerp I, 97; 1957 Stockholm, 32; 1962 Recklinghausen, 22d [erroneously repr F 1227]; 1965 Nuenen, no cat nr; 1966 Paris, Albi, 15
PROVENANCE Mrs J. van Gogh-Bonger, Amsterdam; V. W. van Gogh, Laren; Amsterdam, Rijksmuseum Vincent van Gogh [Vincent van Gogh Foundation, inv nr F 1168]

F 1169 HEAD OF A PEASANT WOMAN: LEFT PROFILE
EXHIBITION 1958 Amsterdam 2, 17
PROVENANCE V. W. van Gogh, Laren; Mrs Visser Omes

[1958]; Van Wisselingh Art Gallery, Amsterdam; Dallas, Texas, L. Pollock [R 1958]

F 1170 HEAD OF A PEASANT WOMAN: FACING RIGHT, AGAINST A DARK BACKGROUND
PROVENANCE Mrs J. van Gogh-Bonger, Amsterdam; V. W. van Gogh, Laren; Amsterdam, Rijksmuseum Vincent van Gogh [Vincent van Gogh Foundation, inv nr F 1170]

F 1171 HEAD OF A PEASANT WOMAN WITH WHITE CAP: THREE QUARTERS TO THE LEFT
PROVENANCE Mrs J. van Gogh-Bonger, Amsterdam; V. W. van Gogh, Laren; Amsterdam, Rijksmuseum Vincent van Gogh [Vincent van Gogh Foundation, inv nr F 1171]

F 1172 HEAD OF A PEASANT WOMAN
PROVENANCE Mrs J. van Gogh-Bonger, Amsterdam; V. W. van Gogh, Laren; Amsterdam, Rijksmuseum Vincent van Gogh [Vincent van Gogh Foundation, inv nr F 1172]

F 1173 HEAD OF A PEASANT WOMAN: THREE QUARTERS TO THE RIGHT
PROVENANCE Mrs J. van Gogh-Bonger, Amsterdam; V. W. van Gogh, Laren; Amsterdam, Rijksmuseum Vincent van Gogh [Vincent van Gogh Foundation, inv nr F 1173]

F 1174 HEAD OF A PEASANT WOMAN: FACING RIGHT
PROVENANCE Mrs J. van Gogh-Bonger, Amsterdam; V. W. van Gogh, Laren; F. Storm, Heemstede; Bentveld, P. D. Sanderse [acquired 1960]

F 1175 HEAD OF A PEASANT WOMAN: FULL FACE
EXHIBITIONS 1926 London 3, 30; 1927-8 Berlin etc, not in cat
PROVENANCE Mrs J. van Gogh-Bonger, Amsterdam; J. H. de Bois Art Gallery, Haarlem; Thannhauser Art Gallery, Berlin [1926]; Mr and Mrs Charles J. Liebman, New York; Sale New York [Parke-Bernet] 7 December 1955, 28; New York, H. Levine

F 1176 HEAD OF A PEASANT WOMAN WITH DARK CAP
PROVENANCE Mrs J. van Gogh-Bonger, Amsterdam; V. W. van Gogh, Laren; Amsterdam, Rijksmuseum Vincent van Gogh [Vincent van Gogh Foundation, inv nr F 1176]

F 1177 HEAD OF A PEASANT WOMAN: FACING LEFT
EXHIBITIONS 1905 Amsterdam, 269; 1914-5 Amsterdam, 47
PROVENANCE Mrs J. van Gogh-Bonger, Amsterdam; V. W. van Gogh, Laren; Amsterdam, Rijksmuseum Vincent van Gogh [Vincent van Gogh Foundation, inv nr F 1177]

F 1178 HEAD OF A PEASANT WOMAN: RIGHT PROFILE
EXHIBITIONS 1918 The Hague; 1924 Amsterdam, 129; 1928 The Hague; 1929 Hamburg, 134; 1930 Hamburg, 80; 1935-6 New York etc, 97; 1956 Nuremberg, 45; Munich, 53
PROVENANCE J. Hidde Nijland, The Hague; Dordrechts Museum, Dordrecht [loan Hidde Nijland 1904-1910]; Otterlo, Rijksmuseum Kröller-Müller, inv nr 1045-28, cat van Gogh 1970, nr 142

F 1179 SIEN WITH SHAWL, AT THE TABLE
EXHIBITIONS 1927 Basle etc, 73; 1928 Düsseldorf, 139; Karlsruhe, 74, 1929 Berlin I, 34; 1930 Amsterdam, 39
PROVENANCE J. R. Tutein Nolthenius, Delft; Otterlo, Rijksmuseum Kröller-Müller, inv nr 256-20, cat van Gogh 1970, nr 59

F 1180 HEAD OF A PEASANT WOMAN WITH WHITE CAP: FULL FACE
PROVENANCE Amélie Dieterle, Paris; Georges Bernheim Art Gallery, Paris; Present owner unknown

F 1181 HEAD OF A PEASANT WOMAN WITH WHITE CAP: FACING RIGHT
EXHIBITIONS 1927 Berlin 2, 120; 1954 Zurich, not in cat; 1958 Zurich, 236
PROVENANCE Mrs J. van Gogh-Bonger, Amsterdam; Caramelli en Tessaro Art Gallery, Amsterdam; Thannhauser Art Gallery, Munich; Mr Wendland, Paris; Sammlung E. G. Bührle, Zurich, [acquired 1942], cat 1958, nr 236; D. Bührle [R 1970]

F 1182 HEAD OF A PEASANT WOMAN: RIGHT PROFILE
EXHIBITIONS 1914-5 Amsterdam, 89; 1920 New York, 24 [repr]; 1926 Munich, 2105; 1927-8 Berlin etc, 21; 1935-6 New York etc, 98; 1947-8 London etc, 119; 1948 Bergen, Oslo, 73; 1949-50 New York, Chicago, 35; 1955 Antwerp I, 104; 1955-6 Liverpool etc, 92; 1958-9 San Francisco etc, 104; 1960 Enschede, 20; 1963 Humlebaek, 73; 1964 Washington, New York, 73; 1965 Nuenen, no cat nr; 1966 Paris, Albi, 16; 1967 Lille, Zurich, 17
PROVENANCE Mrs J. van Gogh-Bonger, Amsterdam; V. W. van Gogh, Laren; Amsterdam, Rijksmuseum Vincent van Gogh [Vincent van Gogh Foundation, inv nr F 1182]

F 1183 HEAD OF A PEASANT WOMAN: FACING RIGHT
EXHIBITIONS 1905 Amsterdam, 279; 1914-5 Amsterdam, 117; 1923 Utrecht, Rotterdam, 18; 1958 Amsterdam 2, 16

PROVENANCE Mrs J. van Gogh-Bonger, Amsterdam; V. W. van Gogh; Mrs Visser Omes [1958]; Van Wisselingh Art Gallery, Amsterdam; Dallas, Texas, L. Pollock [1958]

F 1184 HEAD OF A PEASANT WOMAN: THREE QUARTERS TO THE RIGHT
EXHIBITIONS 1905 Amsterdam, 332; 1914-5 Amsterdam, 67; 1923 Utrecht, Rotterdam, 75; 1954-5 Bern, 103; 1955 Antwerp I, 105; 1964 Zundert, 7; 1966 Paris, Albi, 17; 1967 Lille, Zurich, 18; 1967-8 Dallas etc, 17; 1968 Liège, 17; 1968-9 London, 33; 1969 Humlebaek, 10
PROVENANCE Mrs J. van Gogh-Bonger, Amsterdam; V. W. van Gogh, Laren; Amsterdam, Rijksmuseum Vincent van Gogh [Vincent van Gogh Foundation, inv nr F 1184]

F 1185 HEAD OF A PEASANT WOMAN WITH BONNET: FACING RIGHT
PROVENANCE Mrs J. van Gogh-Bonger, Amsterdam; V. W. van Gogh, Laren; Amsterdam, Rijksmuseum Vincent van Gogh [Vincent van Gogh Foundation, inv nr F 1185]

F 1186 HEAD OF A PEASANT WOMAN
EXHIBITIONS 1905 Amsterdam, 461; 1914-5 Amsterdam, 119; 1923 Utrecht, Rotterdam, 19; 1924 Amsterdam, 128; 1955 Antwerp I, 106
PROVENANCE Mrs J. van Gogh-Bonger, Amsterdam; V. W. van Gogh, Laren; Amsterdam, Rijksmuseum Vincent van Gogh [Vincent van Gogh Foundation, inv nr F 1186]

F 1187 recto PEASANT WOMAN STANDING: SEEN FROM THE BACK
verso PEASANT WOMAN STANDING: FACING RIGHT
EXHIBITIONS 1905 Amsterdam, 272; 1914-5 Amsterdam, 51
PROVENANCE Mrs J. van Gogh-Bonger, Amsterdam; V. W. van Gogh, Laren; Amsterdam, Rijksmuseum Vincent van Gogh [Vincent van Gogh Foundation, inv nr F 1187]

F 1188 PEASANT WOMAN: FACING LEFT
EXHIBITIONS 1953 The Hague, 41; Otterlo, Amsterdam, 24; 1965 Nuenen, no cat nr; 1965-6 Stockholm, Göteborg, 70; 1967 Wolfsburg, 91
PROVENANCE Mrs J. van Gogh-Bonger, Amsterdam; V. W. van Gogh, Laren; Amsterdam, Rijksmuseum Vincent van Gogh [Vincent van Gogh Foundation, inv nr F 1188]

F 1189 PEASANT WOMAN WITH WHITE CAP, SEATED: SEEN FROM THE FRONT
EXHIBITIONS 1927-8 Berlin etc, 39; 1965-6 Stockholm, Göteborg, 71; 1967 Wolfsburg, 92
PROVENANCE Mrs J. van Gogh-Bonger, Amsterdam; V. W. van Gogh, Laren; Amsterdam, Rijksmuseum Vincent van Gogh [Vincent van Gogh Foundation, inv nr F 1189]

F 1190 PEASANT WOMAN WITH WHITE CAP, SEATED: FACING RIGHT
EXHIBITIONS 1905 Amsterdam, 454; 1914-5 Amsterdam, 96; 1957 Stockholm, 27; 1965 Nuenen, no cat nr
PROVENANCE Mrs J. van Gogh-Bonger, Amsterdam; V. W. van Gogh, Laren; Amsterdam, Rijksmuseum Vincent van Gogh [Vincent van Gogh Foundation, inv nr F 1190]

F 1191 PEASANT WOMAN WITH DARK CAP, SEATED: SEEN FROM THE FRONT
PROVENANCE Mrs J. van Gogh-Bonger, Amsterdam; V. W. van Gogh, Laren; Amsterdam, Rijksmuseum Vincent van Gogh [Vincent van Gogh Foundation, inv nr F 1191]

F 1192 PEASANT WOMAN WITH WHITE CAP: FULL FACE
EXHIBITIONS 1905 Amsterdam, 273; 1914-5 Amsterdam, 61
PROVENANCE Mrs J. van Gogh-Bonger, Amsterdam; V. W. van Gogh, Laren; Amsterdam, Rijksmuseum Vincent van Gogh [Vincent van Gogh Foundation, inv nr F 1192]

F 1193 PEASANT WOMAN WITH A WHITE CAP
EXHIBITION 1961 Amsterdam I, 34
PROVENANCE Mrs J. van Gogh-Bonger, Amsterdam; Mrs A. C. van Houten-van Gogh, Dieren; J. Nieweg, Amersfoort; Amersfoort, Miss R. Nieweg [R 1970]

F 1193a HEAD OF A PEASANT WOMAN
PROVENANCE Mrs J. van Gogh-Bonger, Amsterdam; F. Storm, Heemstede [acquired 1923]; A. Storm, Göteborg [acquired 1960]; M. Knoedler Art Gallery, New York; Southampton, New York, Mr and Mrs Clifford Michel

F 1194 PEASANT WOMAN: FACING RIGHT
PROVENANCE Oldenzeel Art Gallery, Rotterdam; J. Willebeek le Mair, Rotterdam; d'Audretsch Art Gallery, The Hague; Sale Amsterdam [Brandt] 15 June 1964, 38; Sale Geneva [Galerie Motte] 28 June 1968, 81; London, Jacques O'Hana Ltd Collection [R 1969]

F 1194a HEAD OF A PEASANT WOMAN
PROVENANCE Van der Boom, 's Hertogenbosch [1944-57]; M. L. de Boer Art Gallery, Amsterdam [until 1959]; Present owner unknown

F 1195 recto STUDY OF A WOMAN WITH A SHAWL
verso WOMAN WITH SHAWL, BEARING A SACK:
WALKING TO THE LEFT
EXHIBITIONS 1918 The Hague; 1924 Amsterdam, 64; 1928
The Hague; 1929 Hamburg, 41; 1930 Amsterdam, 81; 1956
Nuremberg, 47; Munich, 66; 1958 Vienna, 51; Tokyo,
Kyoto, 59
PROVENANCE J. Hidde Nijland, The Hague [1895-1928];
Dordrechts Museum, Dordrecht [loan Hidde Nijland
1904-1910]; Otterlo, Rijksmuseum Kröller-Müller, inv
nr 1006-28, cat van Gogh 1970, nr 146a, 146b [verso]

F 1196 STUDY OF A WOMAN WITH SKIRT OVER HER
HEAD
EXHIBITIONS 1918 The Hague; 1924 Amsterdam, 63; 1928
The Hague; 1929 Hamburg, 96; 1930 Amsterdam, 76; 1952
Milan, 41; 1956 Nuremberg, 43; Munich, 67; 1957 Essen,
172; 1958 Tokyo, Kyoto, 56; 1962 Warsaw, 37; 1963 Tel
Aviv, Haifa, 37; 1966 Belgrade, 34
PROVENANCE J. Hidde Nijland, The Hague [1895-1928];
Dordrechts Museum, Dordrecht [loan Hidde Nijland
1904-1910]; Otterlo, Rijksmuseum Kröller-Müller, inv
nr 1003-28, cat van Gogh 1970, nr 135

F 1197 OLD WOMAN WITH A SHAWL
EXHIBITIONS 1905 Amsterdam, 321; 1920 New York, 20
PROVENANCE Mrs J. van Gogh-Bonger, Amsterdam;
V. W. van Gogh, Laren; Amsterdam, Rijksmuseum Vincent
van Gogh [Vincent van Gogh Foundation, inv nr F 1197]

F 1198 HEAD OF A PEASANT
EXHIBITIONS 1905 Amsterdam, 270; 1914-5 Amsterdam,
110; 1963 Humlebaek, 74; 1964 Washington, New York,
74; 1965 Charleroi, Ghent, 49; Nuenen, no cat nr; 1966
Paris, Albi, 18; 1967 Lille, Zurich, 19
PROVENANCE Mrs J. van Gogh-Bonger, Amsterdam;
V. W. van Gogh, Laren; Amsterdam, Rijksmuseum Vincent
van Gogh [Vincent van Gogh Foundation, inv nr F 1198]

F 1199 YOUNG PEASANT WITH A PIPE: FACING LEFT
EXHIBITIONS 1905 Amsterdam, 315; 1914-5 Amsterdam,
63; 1923 Utrecht, Rotterdam, 68; 1954-5 Bern, 104; 1955
Antwerp 1, 103; 1968-9 London, 32
PROVENANCE Mrs J. van Gogh-Bonger, Amsterdam;
V. W. van Gogh, Laren; Amsterdam, Rijksmuseum Vincent
van Gogh [Vincent van Gogh Foundation, inv nr F 1199]

F 1200 HEAD OF A MAN WITH HAT: FACING RIGHT
PROVENANCE Mrs J. van Gogh-Bonger, Amsterdam;
V. W. van Gogh, Laren; Amsterdam, Rijksmuseum Vincent
van Gogh [Vincent van Gogh Foundation, inv nr F 1200]

F 1201 recto PEASANT SEATED: FULL FACE
verso PEASANT DIGGING: FACING LEFT
EXHIBITION 1961 Amsterdam 1, 35
PROVENANCE J. Hidde Nijland, The Hague; Oldenzeel Art
Gallery, Rotterdam [1909]; F. W. R. Wentges, The Hague
[1909]; Wassenaar, R. W. Wentges [R 1970]

F 1202 WINTER LANDSCAPE WITH FIGURES
PROVENANCE Mrs J. van Gogh-Bonger, Amsterdam;
V. W. van Gogh, Laren; Amsterdam, Rijksmuseum Vincent
van Gogh [Vincent van Gogh Foundation, inv nr F 1202]

F 1203 INTERIOR WITH A PEASANT WOMAN SEWING:
FACING LEFT
EXHIBITIONS 1918 The Hague; 1924 Amsterdam, 105;
1928 The Hague; 1929 Hamburg, 69; 1930 Amsterdam,
116; 1961 Munich, 40
PROVENANCE J. Hidde Nijland, The Hague; Dordrechts
Museum, Dordrecht [loan Hidde Nijland 1904-1910];
Otterlo, Rijksmuseum Kröller-Müller, inv nr 968-28, cat
van Gogh 1970, nr 144

F 1204 INTERIOR WITH A PEASANT WOMAN SEWING:
FACING LEFT
PROVENANCE Mrs J. van Gogh-Bonger, Amsterdam;
V. W. van Gogh, Laren; Amsterdam, Rijksmuseum Vincent
van Gogh [Vincent van Gogh Foundation, inv nr F 1204]

F 1205 PEASANT WOMAN SEWING: FACING LEFT
EXHIBITIONS 1905 Amsterdam, 281; 1914-5 Amsterdam,
69; 1923 Utrecht, Rotterdam, 74; 1927-8 Berlin etc, 40;
1965-6 Stockholm, Göteborg, 72; 1967 Wolfsburg, 93
PROVENANCE Mrs J. van Gogh-Bonger, Amsterdam;
V. W. van Gogh, Laren; Amsterdam, Rijksmuseum Vincent
van Gogh [Vincent van Gogh Foundation, inv nr F 1205]

F 1206 INTERIOR WITH PEASANT WOMAN SEWING:
FACING RIGHT
EXHIBITIONS 1918 The Hague; 1924 Amsterdam, 44; 1928
The Hague; 1929 Hamburg, 58; 1930 Amsterdam, 115; 1950
's Hertogenbosch, Breda; 1958 Tokyo, Kyoto, 64
PROVENANCE J. Hidde Nijland, The Hague; Dordrechts
Museum, Dordrecht [loan Hidde Nijland 1904-1910];
Otterlo, Rijksmuseum Kröller-Müller, inv nr 955-28, cat
van Gogh 1970, nr 157

F 1207 INTERIOR WITH A PEASANT WOMAN KNITTING:
SEEN FROM THE FRONT
EXHIBITIONS 1918 The Hague; 1924 Amsterdam, 52; 1928
The Hague; 1929 Hamburg, 75; 1930 Amsterdam, 112
PROVENANCE J. Hidde Nijland, The Hague; Dordrechts
Museum, Dordrecht [loan Hidde Nijland 1904-1910];
Otterlo, Rijksmuseum Kröller-Müller, inv nr 974-28, cat
van Gogh 1970, nr 158

F 1207a INTERIOR WITH A PEASANT WOMAN KNITTING:
SEEN FROM THE FRONT
EXHIBITION 1959 Budapest, 114
PROVENANCE Paul Majovsky, Budapest; Budapest,
Museum of Fine Arts, inv nr Ltsz 1935-2793

F 1208 INTERIOR WITH A PEASANT WOMAN PEELING
POTATOES: SEEN FROM THE FRONT
EXHIBITIONS 1905 Amsterdam, 328; 1914-5 Amsterdam, 65
PROVENANCE Mrs J. van Gogh-Bonger, Amsterdam;
V. W. van Gogh, Laren; Amsterdam, Rijksmuseum Vincent
van Gogh [Vincent van Gogh Foundation, inv nr F 1208]

F 1209 PEASANT WOMAN PEELING POTATOES
EXHIBITIONS 1918 The Hague; 1924 Amsterdam, 120;
1928 The Hague; 1929 Hamburg, 74; 1930 Amsterdam,
138; 1958 Vienna, 9
PROVENANCE J. Hidde Nijland, The Hague; Dordrechts
Museum, Dordrecht [loan Hidde Nijland 1904-1910];
Otterlo, Rijksmuseum Kröller-Müller, inv nr 973-28, cat
van Gogh 1970, nr 39

F 1210 INTERIOR WITH A PEASANT WOMAN PEELING
POTATOES: FACING LEFT
EXHIBITIONS 1945 Amsterdam, no cat nr; 1954-5 Bern,
105; 1955 Antwerp 1, 92
PROVENANCE Mrs J. van Gogh-Bonger, Amsterdam;
V. W. van Gogh, Laren; Amsterdam, Rijksmuseum Vincent
van Gogh [Vincent van Gogh Foundation, inv nr F 1210]

F 1211 PEASANT WOMAN BY THE FIRE PEELING
POTATOES
EXHIBITIONS 1903 Rotterdam 3, 65; 1927 Basle etc, 74;
1928 Düsseldorf, 140; Karlsruhe, 75; 1929 Berlin 1, 64;
Hamburg, 35; 1930 Amsterdam, 117; 1950 's Hertogenbosch, Breda; 1958 Vienna, 54; 1960-1 Montreal etc, 101;
1962 Warsaw, 36; 1963 Tel Aviv, Haifa, 36
PROVENANCE Mrs A. Müller-Abeken, Scheveningen; Sale
Amsterdam [F. Muller] 19 May 1920, 88; Otterlo, Rijksmuseum Kröller-Müller, inv nr 257-20, cat van Gogh 1970,
nr 125

F 1212 PEASANT WOMAN BY THE FIRE FEELING
POTATOES
PROVENANCE A. van Buuren, Brussels [R 1928]; Present
owner unknown

F 1213 PEASANT WOMAN PEELING POTATOES
EXHIBITIONS 1927 Basle etc, 70; 1928 Düsseldorf, 128;
Karlsruhe, 71; 1929 Berlin 1, 65; Hamburg, 33; 1930
Amsterdam, 134
PROVENANCE Sale The Hague [Oldenzeel] 26-27 June
1917, 41; Otterlo, Rijksmuseum Kröller-Müller, inv
nr 253-17, cat van Gogh 1970, nr 38

F 1214 INTERIOR WITH A PEASANT WOMAN SHELLING
PEAS: THREE QUARTERS TO THE RIGHT
EXHIBITIONS 1905 Amsterdam, 304; 1914-5 Amsterdam,
105; 1923 Utrecht, Rotterdam; 1937 Paris, 131; 1945
Amsterdam, no cat nr; 1946 Stockholm etc, 14; 1946-7
Liège etc, 17; 1947 Geneva, 17; Paris 1, 17; 1949-50 New
York, Chicago, 36; 1953 The Hague, 27; Otterlo, Amster-
dam, 45; 1954-5 Bern, 106; 1955 Antwerp 1, 93; 1955-6
Liverpool etc, 96; 1957 Nijmegen, 31; Stockholm, 41;
1958-9 San Francisco etc, 105; 1960 Enschede, 21; 1961-2
Baltimore etc, 97; 1962 Pittsburgh etc, 75; 1963 Humlebaek, 75;
1964 Washington, New York, 75; 1966 Paris, Albi, 19; 1967
Lille, Zurich, 20; 1967-8 Dallas etc, 18; 1968 Liège, 18;
1968-9 London, 48
PROVENANCE Mrs J. van Gogh-Bonger, Amsterdam;
V. W. van Gogh, Laren; Amsterdam, Rijksmuseum Vincent
van Gogh [Vincent van Gogh Foundation, inv nr F 1214]

F 1215 INTERIOR WITH A PEASANT WOMAN MAKING
PANCAKES
EXHIBITIONS 1905 Amsterdam, 300; 1914-5 Amsterdam,
108; 1924 Amsterdam, 122; 1926 Munich, 2107; 1927-8
Berlin etc, 19; 1932 Manchester, 79; 1946 Stockholm etc, 7;
1954-5 Bern, 107; 1955 Antwerp 1, 94; 1961 Scarborough
PROVENANCE Mrs J. van Gogh-Bonger, Amsterdam;
V. W. van Gogh, Laren; Amsterdam, Rijksmuseum Vincent
van Gogh [Vincent van Gogh Foundation, inv nr F 1215]

F 1216 WOMAN BY THE HEARTH
EXHIBITIONS 1927 Basle etc, 72; 1928 Düsseldorf, 138;
Karlsruhe, 73; 1929 Berlin 1, 67; Hamburg, 150; 1930
Amsterdam, 139; 1956 Eindhoven, 4
PROVENANCE L. C. Enthoven, Voorburg, Netherlands;
Sale Enthoven, Amsterdam [F. Muller] 18 May 1920, 251;
Otterlo, Rijksmuseum Kröller-Müller, inv nr 255-20, cat
van Gogh 1970, nr 29

F 1217 INTERIOR WITH A WOMAN BY THE FIREPLACE:
FACING RIGHT
EXHIBITIONS 1918 The Hague; 1924 Amsterdam, 61; 1928
The Hague; 1929 Hamburg, 113; 1930 Amsterdam, 113;
1950 's Hertogenbosch, Breda; 1958 Tokyo, Kyoto, 63;
1959 São Paulo, 12; 1966 Belgrade, 36
PROVENANCE J. Hidde Nijland, The Hague; Dordrechts
Museum, Dordrecht [loan Hidde Nijland 1904-1910];
Otterlo, Rijksmuseum Kröller-Müller, inv nr 1022-28, cat
van Gogh 1970, nr 156

F 1218 INTERIOR WITH A WOMAN BY THE FIREPLACE:
FACING RIGHT
EXHIBITIONS 1918 The Hague; 1924 Amsterdam, 56; 1928
The Hague; 1929 Hamburg, 64; 1930 Amsterdam, 114; 1947
Basle, 144; 1952 Milan, 44; 1956 Nuremberg, 54; 1958
Vienna, 55; Tokyo, Kyoto, 62; 1961 Munich, 41; 1962
Warsaw, 40; 1963 Tel Aviv, Haifa, 40
PROVENANCE J. Hidde Nijland, The Hague; Dordrechts
Museum, Dordrecht [loan Hidde Nijland 1904-1910];
Otterlo, Rijksmuseum Kröller-Müller, inv nr 963-28, cat
van Gogh 1970, nr 155

F 1219 recto INTERIOR WITH A STANDING WOMAN
SLICING BREAD: SEEN FROM THE BACK
verso WOMAN SLICING BREAD
EXHIBITION 1965 Nuenen, no cat nr
PROVENANCE Mrs J. van Gogh-Bonger, Amsterdam;
V. W. van Gogh, Laren; Amsterdam, Rijksmuseum Vincent
van Gogh [Vincent van Gogh Foundation, inv nr F 1219]

F 1220 INTERIOR WITH PEASANT WOMAN SEWING:
SEEN FROM THE FRONT
EXHIBITIONS 1918 The Hague; 1924 Amsterdam, 86; 1928
The Hague; 1929 Hamburg, 119; 1930 Amsterdam, 118;
1956 Nuremberg, 53; 1962 Warsaw, 39; 1963 Tel Aviv,
Haifa, 39
PROVENANCE J. Hidde Nijland, The Hague; Dordrechts
Museum, Dordrecht [loan Hidde Nijland 1904-1910];
Otterlo, Rijksmuseum Kröller-Müller, inv nr 1031-28, cat
van Gogh 1970, nr 154

F 1221 OLD PEASANT WOMAN MENDING A MAN'S SHIRT
EXHIBITIONS 1927 Basle etc, 71; 1928 Düsseldorf, 137;
Karlsruhe, 72; 1929 Berlin 1, 66; Hamburg, 140; 1930
Amsterdam, 148; 1935-6 New York etc, 99; 1946-7 Liège
etc, 5; 1947 Paris 1, 5; Geneva, 5; 1950 's Hertogenbosch,
Breda; 1956 Nuremberg, 5; Munich, 18; 1958 Tokyo,
Kyoto, 9; 1961 Munich, 10; 1962 Warsaw, 10; 1963 Tel
Aviv, Haifa, 9
PROVENANCE L. C. Enthoven, Voorburg, Netherlands;
Sale Enthoven, Amsterdam [F. Muller] 18 May 1920, 250;
Otterlo, Rijksmuseum Kröller-Müller, inv nr 254-20, cat
van Gogh 1970, nr 22

F 1222 INTERIOR WITH A PEASANT WOMAN BY THE
FIREPLACE
EXHIBITIONS 1905 Amsterdam, 326; 1914-5 Amsterdam,
46; 1920 New York, 15; 1949-50 New York, Chicago, 37;
1963 Paris, 29; 1964 Zundert
PROVENANCE Mrs J. van Gogh-Bonger, Amsterdam;
V. W. van Gogh, Laren; Amsterdam, Rijksmuseum Vincent
van Gogh [Vincent van Gogh Foundation, inv nr F 1222]

F 1223 INTERIOR WITH A WOMAN AT THE LEFT BY THE
FIREPLACE
PROVENANCE Oldenzeel Art Gallery, Rotterdam;
F. W. R. Wentges, The Hague [acquired 1909];
F. P. O. Wentges, Rotterdam; E. Weye Art Gallery, New
York; L. Herring, New York; R. W. Wentges, Rotterdam;
Sale London [Sotheby] 1 July 1959, 72; C. Kalmann; Sale
Amsterdam [Mak van Waay] 4 February 1964, 141; Sale
London [Christie] 19 June 1964, 9; Present owner unknown

F 1224 PEASANT WOMAN WITH A WHITE CAP: FULL
FACE
EXHIBITIONS 1905 Amsterdam, 278; 1914-5 Amsterdam,
75; 1932 Manchester, 46; 1964
Zundert, 9
PROVENANCE Mrs J. van Gogh-Bonger, Amsterdam;
V. W. van Gogh, Laren; Amsterdam, Rijksmuseum Vincent
van Gogh [Vincent van Gogh Foundation, inv nr F 1224]

F 1225 TWO PEASANTS PLANTING POTATOES
PROVENANCE Mrs J. van Gogh-Bonger, Amsterdam;
V. W. van Gogh, Laren; Amsterdam, Rijksmuseum Vincent
van Gogh [Vincent van Gogh Foundation, inv nr F 1225]

F 1226 THE POTATO EATERS
EXHIBITION 1951 Houston, 1
PROVENANCE Miss W. van Gogh, Dieren; E. Alexandre,
Paris; O. Wacker Art Gallery, Berlin; New York,
J. K. Thannhauser Art Gallery, [R 1951]

F 1227 recto STUDY FOR THE POTATO EATERS
verso PEASANT WOMAN STANDING: SEEN FROM
THE FRONT
EXHIBITIONS 1905 Amsterdam, 459; 1914-5 Amsterdam,
50; 1923 Utrecht, Rotterdam, 15; 1927-8 Berlin etc, 30;
1953 The Hague, 20; Otterlo, Amsterdam, 37; 1953-4

St Louis etc, 40; 1954-5 Bern, 108; 1955 Antwerp 1, 96
PROVENANCE Mrs J. van Gogh-Bonger, Amsterdam;
V. W. van Gogh, Laren; Amsterdam, Rijksmuseum Vincent
van Gogh [Vincent van Gogh Foundation, inv nr F 1227]

F 1228 TWO PEASANT WOMEN, WORKING IN THE
FIELDS
PROVENANCE Mrs J. van Gogh-Bonger, Amsterdam;
V. W. van Gogh, Laren; Amsterdam, Rijksmuseum Vincent
van Gogh [Vincent van Gogh Foundation, inv nr F 1228]

F 1229 recto STUDY OF A HAND HOLDING A CUP;
STUDY OF A CAT
verso MAN AND TWO WOMEN AROUND A TABLE
EXHIBITIONS 1953 The Hague, 22; Otterlo, Amsterdam,
39; 1953-4 St Louis etc, 39; 1962 Recklinghausen, 22f
PROVENANCE Mrs J. van Gogh-Bonger, Amsterdam;
V. W. van Gogh, Laren; Amsterdam, Rijksmuseum Vincent
van Gogh [Vincent van Gogh Foundation, inv nr F 1229]

F 1230 PUBLIC SALE OF CROSSES OF THE CEMETERY
AT NUENEN
EXHIBITIONS 1905 Amsterdam, 334; 1914-5 Amsterdam,
44; 1923 Utrecht, Rotterdam, 3; 1927-8 Berlin etc, 27;
1954-5 Bern, 109; 1955 Antwerp 1, 72; 1955-6 Liverpool
etc, 93; 1957 Stockholm, 34; 1958-9 San Francisco etc, 106;
1960 Enschede, 22; 1961-2 Baltimore etc, 99; 1962 Pittsburgh
etc; 1963 Humlebaek, 76; 1964 Washington, New York, 76;
1965 Charleroi, Ghent, 50; Nuenen, no cat nr; 1966 Paris,
Albi, 20; 1967 Lille, Zurich, 21; 1967-8 Dallas etc, 19; 1968
Liège, 19; 1968-9 London, 40
PROVENANCE Mrs J. van Gogh-Bonger, Amsterdam;
V. W. van Gogh, Laren; Amsterdam, Rijksmuseum Vincent
van Gogh [Vincent van Gogh Foundation, inv nr F 1230]

F 1231 recto STUDY FOR THE PUBLIC SALE OF CROSSES
OF THE CEMETERY AT NUENEN
verso STUDY FOR THE PUBLIC SALE OF CROSSES
OF THE CEMETERY AT NUENEN
EXHIBITIONS 1905 Amsterdam, 314; 1914-5 Amsterdam,
48; 1923 Utrecht, Rotterdam, 17; 1957 Stockholm, 35; 1965
Nuenen, no cat nr
PROVENANCE Mrs J. van Gogh-Bonger, Amsterdam;
V. W. van Gogh, Laren; Amsterdam, Rijksmuseum Vincent
van Gogh [Vincent van Gogh Foundation, inv nr F 1231]

F 1232 WINTER LANDSCAPE
EXHIBITIONS 1918 The Hague; 1924 Amsterdam, 34
[repr]; 1928 The Hague; 1929 Hamburg, 111; 1930 Amsterdam, 84; 1950 's Hertogenbosch, Breda; 1956 Nuremberg,
56; 1958 Vienna, 42; Tokyo, Kyoto, 65
PROVENANCE J. Hidde Nijland, The Hague; Dordrechts
Museum, Dordrecht [loan Hidde Nijland 1904-1910];
Otterlo, Rijksmuseum Kröller-Müller, inv nr 1020-28, cat
van Gogh 1970, nr 161

F 1233 recto SNOW LANDSCAPE
verso SKETCH OF FIGURES IN A LANDSCAPE; SKETCH
OF A WOMAN WITH A BASKET ON HER BACK
EXHIBITIONS 1905 Amsterdam, 293; 1914-5 Amsterdam,
118; 1923 Utrecht, Rotterdam, 83
PROVENANCE Mrs J. van Gogh-Bonger, Amsterdam;
V. W. van Gogh, Laren; Amsterdam, Rijksmuseum Vincent
van Gogh [Vincent van Gogh Foundation, inv nr F 1233]

F 1234 THE VICARAGE GARDEN WITH FIGURES
EXHIBITIONS 1932 Amsterdam 2, 16; 1950 The Hague, 53;
1952 Milan, 46; 1955 New York 2, 94; 1956 Munich, 72;
1957 Essen, 206; 1958 Vancouver, 29; 1960 Paris, 100; 1961
Munich, 46
PROVENANCE C. Mouwen jr, Breda; H. P. Bremmer, The
Hague; Heirs of H. P. Bremmer, The Hague; Wassenaar,
B. Meijer [R 1969]

F 1235 WINTER
EXHIBITIONS 1950 The Hague, 51; 1961 Amsterdam 1, 36;
Munich, 42
PROVENANCE H. P. Bremmer, The Hague; F. Bremmer,
The Hague [R 1970]

F 1236 recto THE CHURCHYARD AND THE OLD TOWER
AT NUENEN IN WINTER
verso SKETCH OF A CHURCH
EXHIBITIONS 1905 Amsterdam, 460; 1914-5 Amsterdam,
58; 1914 Berlin, 10; 1920 New York, 19; 1925 The Hague,
82; 1927-8 Berlin etc, 29; 1955 Antwerp 1, 71; 1964
Zundert, 10; 1965-6 Stockholm, Göteborg, 73; 1967
Wolfsburg, 94
PROVENANCE Mrs J. van Gogh-Bonger, Amsterdam,
V. W. van Gogh, Laren; Amsterdam, Rijksmuseum Vincent
van Gogh [Vincent van Gogh Foundation, inv nr F 1236]

F 1237 THE CHURCHYARD AND THE OLD TOWER AT
NUENEN IN WINTER
EXHIBITION 1914-5 Amsterdam, 121
PROVENANCE Mrs J. van Gogh-Bonger, Amsterdam;
V. W. van Gogh, Laren; Amsterdam, Rijksmuseum Vincent
van Gogh [Vincent van Gogh Foundation, inv nr F 1237]

F 1238 THE CHURCH AT TONGERLE IN WINTER
EXHIBITIONS 1905 Amsterdam, 330; 1914-5 Amsterdam,
57; 1923 Utrecht, Rotterdam, 16; 1924 Amsterdam, 126;
1926 Munich, 211; 1927-8 Berlin etc, 16; 1932 Manchester,
49; 1949-50 New York, Chicago, 39; 1953 The Hague, 19;
Otterlo, Amsterdam, 35; 1954-5 Bern, 110; 1955 Antwerp 1,
70; 1964 Zundert, 11; 1966 Paris, Albi, 21; 1967 Lille,
Zurich, 22
PROVENANCE Mrs J. van Gogh-Bonger, Amsterdam;
V. W. van Gogh, Laren; Amsterdam, Rijksmuseum Vincent
van Gogh [Vincent van Gogh Foundation, inv nr F 1238]

F 1239 AVENUE OF POPLARS WITH FIGURE
EXHIBITIONS 1914-5 Amsterdam, 2; 1927-8 Berlin etc, 38a;
1932 Manchester, 51; 1949-50 New York, 40; 1953-4
St Louis etc, 36; 1954-5 Bern, 111; 1955 Antwerp 1, 66;
1955-6 Liverpool etc, 90; 1957 Marseilles, 12; Stockholm,
23; 1958-9 San Francisco etc, 107; 1959-60 Utrecht, 70;
1960-1 Montreal etc, 113; 1961-2 Baltimore etc, 100; 1962
Pittsburgh etc; 1965 Nuenen, no cat nr; 1967 Lille, Zurich,
24; 1968-9 London, 24
PROVENANCE Mrs J. van Gogh-Bonger, Amsterdam;
V. W. van Gogh, Laren; Amsterdam, Rijksmuseum Vincent
van Gogh [Vincent van Gogh Foundation, inv nr F 1239]

F 1240 ALLEY OF WILLOWS WITH SHEPHERD AND
PEASANT WOMAN
EXHIBITIONS 1958-9 Washington etc, 145; 1963 Humle-
baek, 77; 1964 Washington, New York, 77; 1965 Charleroi,
Ghent, 51; 1966 Paris, Albi, 22; 1967 Lille, Zurich, 23;
1967-8 Dallas etc, 20; 1968 Liège, 20; 1968-9 London, 23
PROVENANCE Mrs A. C. van Houten-van Gogh, Dieren;
Mr and Mrs H. J. Calkoen, Driehuis [1958]; Amsterdam,
Rijksmuseum Vincent van Gogh [Vincent van Gogh
Foundation, acquired 1963, inv nr F 1240]

F 1240a LANDSCAPE WITH WILLOWS AND SUN
SHINING THROUGH CLOUDS
EXHIBITIONS 1950 The Hague, 52; 1960 Paris, 98; 1960-1
Eindhoven, Schiedam, 144; 1961 Munich, 35
PROVENANCE H. P. Bremmer, The Hague; H. Bremmer,
Zeist; Chicago, The Art Institute [acquired 1969], inv
nr 69.268

F 1241 AVENUE OF TREES IN WINTER
PROVENANCE A. G. A. van Rappard, Utrecht; Mrs
Spanjaard-Keller, The Hague; W. B. Tholen, The Hague;
d'Audretsch Art Gallery, The Hague [1940]; F. C. d'Audretsch, Wassenaar; New York, Mrs M. Frank [R 1970]

F 1242 HUTS WITH THATCHED ROOFS
EXHIBITION 1930 Amsterdam, 112
PROVENANCE Mrs J. van Gogh-Bonger, Amsterdam;
C. Frank Stoop, London [1930]; London, Tate Gallery,
[acquired 1933; bequest of C. Frank Stoop], inv nr 4715, cat
1959, p 274

F 1243 THE DITCH
EXHIBITIONS 1905 Amsterdam, 342; 1914-5 Amsterdam,
41; 1947-8 London etc, 116; 1949-50 New York, Chicago,
38; 1953-4 St Louis etc, 2; 1955 Antwerp 1, 68; 1957
Nijmegen, 33; Stockholm, 3; 1958-9 San Francisco etc, 86;
1960 Enschede, 3; 1963 Humlebaek, 63; 1964 Washington,
New York, 63; 1965-6 Stockholm, Göteborg 61; 1967
Wolfsburg, 82
PROVENANCE Mrs J. van Gogh-Bonger, Amsterdam;
H. C. Bonger, Amsterdam [R 1905]; Miss E. H. Bonger,
Amsterdam; V. W. van Gogh, Laren; Amsterdam,
Rijksmuseum Vincent van Gogh [Vincent van Gogh
Foundation, inv nr F 1243]

F 1244 recto STUDY OF FOUR FLYING SWALLOWS
verso SKETCH OF ONE SWALLOW
EXHIBITIONS 1953 The Hague, 50; Otterlo, Amsterdam,
88; 1954-5 Bern, 112; 1957 Stockholm, 75
PROVENANCE Mrs J. van Gogh-Bonger, Amsterdam;
V. W. van Gogh, Laren; Amsterdam, Rijksmuseum Vincent
van Gogh [Vincent van Gogh Foundation, inv nr F 1244]

F 1244a recto THE VIOLINIST
verso THE VIOLINIST
EXHIBITIONS 1955-6 Liverpool etc, 99; 1967 Wolfsburg,
103; 1968-9 London, 63
PROVENANCE Mrs J. van Gogh-Bonger, Amsterdam;
V. W. van Gogh, Laren; Amsterdam, Rijksmuseum Vincent
van Gogh [Vincent van Gogh Foundation, inv nr F 1244a]

F 1244b recto THE CLARINETTIST; THE FLUTIST
verso PORTRAIT OF A WOMAN SITTING
EXHIBITION 1968-9 London, 62
PROVENANCE Mrs J. van Gogh-Bonger, Amsterdam;
V. W. van Gogh, Laren; Amsterdam, Rijksmuseum Vincent
van Gogh [Vincent van Gogh Foundation, inv nr F 1244b]

F 1244c recto THE CONTRABASSPLAYER
verso THE PIANIST
EXHIBITION 1955-6 Liverpool etc, 98
PROVENANCE Mrs J. van Gogh-Bonger, Amsterdam;
V. W. van Gogh, Laren; Amsterdam, Rijksmuseum Vincent
van Gogh [Vincent van Gogh Foundation, inv nr F 1244c]

F 1244d recto HEAD OF A MAN
verso MAN WITH A TALL HAT
EXHIBITION 1955-6 Liverpool etc, 100
PROVENANCE Mrs J. van Gogh-Bonger, Amsterdam;
V. W. van Gogh, Laren; Amsterdam, Rijksmuseum Vincent
van Gogh [Vincent van Gogh Foundation, inv nr F 1244d]

F 1245 THE ORCHARD
PROVENANCE Mrs J. van Gogh-Bonger, Amsterdam;
V. W. van Gogh, Laren; Amsterdam, Rijksmuseum Vincent
van Gogh [Vincent van Gogh Foundation, inv nr F 1245]

F 1246 AVENUE OF TREES WITH FIGURES
EXHIBITION 1956 Amsterdam, 13
PROVENANCE H. P. Bremmer, The Hague; Mrs Pet,
Groningen [R 1905]; Mrs W. C. Pet-Meiners, Amsterdam;
Amsterdam, S. Polak

F 1247 WILLOWS
EXHIBITIONS 1905 Amsterdam, 469; 1914-5 Amsterdam,
165; 1926 London 3, 21; 1936 Gloucester
PROVENANCE Mrs J. van Gogh-Bonger, Amsterdam;
V. W. van Gogh, Laren; Lord Sandwich, Huntingdon; Sale
London [Christie] 30 November 1962, 43; Amiya, Countess
of Sandwich, Huntingdon; Sale London [Christie]
27 November 1964, 100; Present owner unknown

F 1248 COTTAGES IN THE HEATHER
EXHIBITIONS 1924 Amsterdam, 110; 1952 Milan, 31;
1960-1 Montreal etc, 99; 1966 Belgrade, 21
PROVENANCE J. Hidde Nijland, The Hague; Otterlo,
Rijksmuseum Kröller-Müller, inv nr 1033-28, cat van Gogh
1970, nr 100

F 1249 PINE TREES IN THE FEN
EXHIBITIONS 1905 Amsterdam, 305; 1906 Rotterdam, 60;
1914-5 Amsterdam, 124; 1924 New York, 10; 1925 The
Hague, 86; 1926 Munich, 2108; 1927-8 Berlin etc, 24;
1947-8 London etc, 117; 1948 Bergen, Oslo, 74; 1953 The
Hague, 18; Otterlo, Amsterdam, 34; 1955 Antwerp 1, 69;
1955-6 Liverpool etc, 91; 1957 Stockholm, 4; 1961-2
Baltimore etc, 83; 1963 Humlebaek, 62; 1964 Washington,
New York, 62; 1965 Charleroi, Ghent, 43; 1966 Paris, Albi,
2; 1967 Lille, Zurich, 1; 1967-8 Dallas etc, 2; 1968 Liège, 2;
1968-9 London, 25
PROVENANCE Mrs J. van Gogh-Bonger, Amsterdam;
V. W. van Gogh, Laren; Amsterdam, Rijksmuseum Vincent
van Gogh [Vincent van Gogh Foundation, inv nr F 1249]

F 1250 PEASANT WOMAN WITH A SPADE: FACING
RIGHT
EXHIBITIONS 1905 Amsterdam, 311; 1914-5 Amsterdam,
102; 1957 Nijmegen, 35; Stockholm, 36
PROVENANCE Mrs J. van Gogh-Bonger, Amsterdam;
V. W. van Gogh, Laren; Amsterdam, Rijksmuseum Vincent
van Gogh [Vincent van Gogh Foundation, inv nr F 1250]

F 1251 PEASANT WOMAN WITH A PITCHFORK: FACING
RIGHT
EXHIBITIONS 1905 Amsterdam, 285; 1914-5 Amsterdam,
86; 1923 Utrecht, Rotterdam, 59; 1924 Basle, Zurich, 82;
Stuttgart, 3; 1925 The Hague, 59; 1927-8 Berlin etc, 35;
1947-8 London etc, 123; 1948 Bergen, Oslo, 75; 1954-5
Bern, 113; 1955 Antwerp 1, 88; 1955-6 Liverpool etc, 94;
1961 Scarborough; 1966 Paris, Albi, 23; 1967 Lille,
Zurich, 24; 1967-8 Dallas etc, 21; 1968 Liège, 21; 1968-9
London, 44
PROVENANCE Mrs J. van Gogh-Bonger, Amsterdam;
V. W. van Gogh, Laren; Amsterdam, Rijksmuseum Vincent
van Gogh [Vincent van Gogh Foundation, inv nr F 1251]

F 1252 PEASANT WOMAN DIGGING: FACING RIGHT
EXHIBITIONS 1924 Amsterdam, 50; 1955 New York 2, 95
PROVENANCE J. Hidde Nijland, The Hague; New York,
Mr and Mrs H. Lawrence Herring [R 1955 and 1970]

F 1253 PEASANT WOMAN DIGGING: FACING LEFT
EXHIBITIONS 1918 The Hague; 1924 Amsterdam, 53; 1928
The Hague; 1929 Hamburg, 71; 1930 Amsterdam, 89
PROVENANCE J. Hidde Nijland, The Hague; Dordrechts
Museum, Dordrecht [loan Hidde Nijland 1904-10]; Otterlo,
Rijksmuseum Kröller-Müller, inv nr 988-28, cat van Gogh
1970, nr 124

F 1254 PEASANT WOMAN DIGGING: SEEN FROM THE
FRONT
EXHIBITIONS 1918 The Hague; 1924 Amsterdam, 103;
1928 The Hague; 1929 Hamburg, 81; 1930 Amsterdam, 91;
1956 Nuremberg, 31; Munich, 59; 1958 Tokyo, Kyoto, 42;
1966 Belgrade, 25
PROVENANCE J. Hidde Nijland, The Hague; Dordrechts
Museum, Dordrecht [loan Hidde Nijland 1904-10]; Otterlo,
Rijksmuseum Kröller-Müller, inv nr 982-28, cat van Gogh
1970, nr 109

F 1255 PEASANT WOMAN DIGGING: SEEN FROM BEHIND
EXHIBITIONS 1905 Amsterdam, 294; 1914-5 Amsterdam,
83; 1923 Utrecht, Rotterdam, 56; 1945 Amsterdam, no cat
nr; 1946 Stockholm etc, 16; 1955 Antwerp 1, 82; 1957
Marseilles, 14; Stockholm, 37; 1958-9 San Francisco etc,

108; 1959 Utrecht; 1960 Enschede, 24; 1961-2 Baltimore etc, 101; 1962 Pittsburgh etc; 1963 Humlebaek, 78; 1964 Washington etc, 78; 1965 Charleroi, Ghent, 52; 1965 Nuenen, no cat nr; 1966 Paris, Albi, 24; 1967 Lille, Zurich, 26; 1967-8 Dallas etc, 22; 1968 Liège, 22; 1968-9 London, 43
PROVENANCE Mrs J. van Gogh-Bonger, Amsterdam; V. W. van Gogh, Laren; Amsterdam, Rijksmuseum Vincent van Gogh [Vincent van Gogh Foundation, inv nr F 1255]

F 1256 PEASANT WOMAN WITH A FORK: SEEN FROM BEHIND, A WINDMILL IN THE BACKGROUND
EXHIBITIONS 1905 Amsterdam, 277; 1914-5 Amsterdam, 66; 1923 Utrecht, Rotterdam, 62; 1955 Antwerp 1, 81
PROVENANCE Mrs J. van Gogh-Bonger, Amsterdam; V. W. van Gogh, Laren; Amsterdam, Rijksmuseum Vincent van Gogh [Vincent van Gogh Foundation, inv nr F 1256]

F 1257 recto PEASANT WOMAN DIGGING POTATOES: SEEN FROM THE FRONT
verso PEASANT WOMAN: SEEN FROM BEHIND
EXHIBITIONS 1905 Amsterdam, 451; 1914-5 Amsterdam, 91
PROVENANCE Mrs J. van Gogh-Bonger, Amsterdam; V. W. van Gogh, Laren; Amsterdam, Rijksmuseum Vincent van Gogh [Vincent van Gogh Foundation, inv nr F 1257]

F 1258 PEASANT WOMAN DIGGING: SEEN FROM BEHIND
EXHIBITIONS 1905 Amsterdam, 455; 1914-5 Amsterdam, 88
PROVENANCE Mrs J. van Gogh-Bonger, Amsterdam; V. W. van Gogh, Laren; Amsterdam, Rijksmuseum Vincent van Gogh [Vincent van Gogh Foundation, inv nr F 1258]

F 1259 PEASANT WOMAN TOSSING HAY: SEEN FROM BEHIND
PROVENANCE J. Hidde Nijland, The Hague; Dordrecht, Dordrechts Museum [acquired 1914; bequest of J. Hidde Nijland], cat 1928, nr 276

F 1260 PEASANT WOMAN TOSSING HAY: SEEN FROM THE FRONT
EXHIBITIONS 1918 The Hague; 1924 Amsterdam, 70; 1928 The Hague; 1929 Hamburg, 44; 1930 Amsterdam, 73; 1947 Basle, 134 [2d edition 135]; 1956 Eindhoven, 15; 1958 Tokyo, Kyoto, 44; 1966 Belgrade, 2
PROVENANCE J. Hidde Nijland, The Hague; Dordrechts Museum, Dordrecht [loan Hidde Nijland 1904-10]; Otterlo, Rijksmuseum Kröller-Müller, inv nr 941-28, cat van Gogh 1970, nr 117

F 1261 PEASANT WOMAN TOSSING HAY: FACING RIGHT
EXHIBITIONS 1918 The Hague; 1924 Amsterdam, 31; 1928 The Hague; 1929 Hamburg, 93; 1930 Amsterdam, 83; 1950 's-Hertogenbosch etc; 1952 Antwerp, 37b; 1953-4 Saint Louis etc, 42; 1955 Groningen, 10; 1956 Nuremberg, 32; 1958 Tokyo, Kyoto, 43; 1963 Amsterdam, 98
PROVENANCE J. Hidde Nijland, The Hague; Dordrechts Museum, Dordrecht [loan Hidde Nijland 1904-10]; Otterlo, Rijksmuseum Kröller-Müller, inv nr 998-28, cat van Gogh 1970, nr 113

F 1262 PEASANT WOMAN BINDING SHEAVES: FACING RIGHT
EXHIBITIONS 1918 The Hague; 1924 Amsterdam, 72; 1928 The Hague; 1929 Hamburg, 98; 1930 Amsterdam, 100; 1935-6 New York etc, 100; 1955 Wormerveer; 1956 Eindhoven, 14; 1958 Vienna, 43
PROVENANCE J. Hidde Nijland, The Hague; Dordrechts Museum, Dordrecht [loan Hidde Nijland 1904-10]; Otterlo, Rijksmuseum Kröller-Müller, inv nr 1005-28, cat van Gogh 1970, nr 112

F 1262a PEASANT WOMAN KNEELING: FACING LEFT
EXHIBITION 1926 London 3, 33
PROVENANCE B. Jonzen, Caterham; Sale London [Sotheby] 4 May 1960, 183; Present owner unknown

F 1262b PEASANT WOMAN KNEELING AND PULLING OUT CARROTS
PROVENANCE J. Hidde Nijland, The Hague; D. Nijland, Santpoort; G. J. Nieuwenhuizen Segaar Art Gallery, The Hague; Charles Vidor, Beverly Hills, California; New York, Mrs Doris Vidor [R 1970]

F 1263 PEASANT WOMAN BINDING WHEAT: FACING RIGHT
EXHIBITIONS 1918 The Hague; 1924 Amsterdam, 69; 1928 The Hague; 1929 Hamburg, 84; 1930 Amsterdam, 75; 1947 Basle, 43; 1947-8 London etc, 121; 1958 Vienna, 46; Tokyo Kyoto, 47; 1966 Belgrade, 27
PROVENANCE J. Hidde Nijland, The Hague; Dordrechts Museum, Dordrecht [loan Hidde Nijland 1904-10]; Otterlo, Rijksmuseum Kröller-Müller, inv nr 985-28, cat van Gogh 1970, nr 120

F 1264 PEASANT WOMAN BINDING WHEAT: STOOPING
EXHIBITIONS 1918 The Hague; 1924 Amsterdam, 79; 1928 The Hague; 1929 Hamburg, 105; 1930 Amsterdam, 93; 1935-6 New York etc, 103; 1950 's-Hertogenbosch etc; 1956 Nuremberg, 34; Munich, 60; 1958 Vienna, 45; 1958-9

Schiedam; 1960-1 Montreal etc, 109; 1962 Warsaw, 34; 1963 Hamburg, 88; Tel Aviv, Haifa, 34
PROVENANCE J. Hidde Nijland, The Hague; Dordrechts Museum, Dordrecht [loan Hidde Nijland 1904-10]; Otterlo, Rijksmuseum Kröller-Müller, inv nr 1014-28, cat van Gogh 1970, nr 116

F 1265 PEASANT WOMAN GLEANING GRAIN: SEEN FROM THE FRONT
EXHIBITIONS 1927 Basle etc, 67; 1928 Düsseldorf, 113; Karlsruhe, 68; 1929 Berlin 1, 37; Hamburg, 30; 1930 Amsterdam, 79; 1952 Antwerp, 37d; 1956 Munich, 58; 1958 Vienna, 47; Tokyo, Kyoto, 50
PROVENANCE C. Hoogendijk, The Hague; Sale Amsterdam [F. Muller] 21-22 May 1912, 112; Otterlo, Rijksmuseum Kröller-Müller, inv nr 250-12, cat van Gogh 1970, nr 122

F 1265a PEASANT WOMAN GLEANING GRAIN: FACING LEFT
EXHIBITIONS 1905 Paris, 28; 1960 London 1, 84
PROVENANCE A. Vollard Art Gallery, Paris; F. Jourdain, Paris [R 1905]; Marlborough Art Gallery, London [R 1962]; London, Charles Clore [R 1970]

F 1266 PEASANT WOMAN PICKING UP A SHEAF OF GRAIN: SEEN FROM THE FRONT
EXHIBITIONS 1905 Amsterdam, 316; 1914-5 Amsterdam, 80
PROVENANCE Mrs J. van Gogh-Bonger, Amsterdam; V. W. van Gogh, Laren; Amsterdam, Rijksmuseum Vincent van Gogh [Vincent van Gogh Foundation, inv nr F 1266]

F 1267 PEASANT WOMAN CARRYING A SHEAF OF GRAIN: SEEN FROM THE FRONT
PROVENANCE W. Halvorsen, Paris; Thorwald Hellesen, Paris; Halvor Schon and G. Jebsen, Oslo; Oslo, Nasjonal-galleriet [acquired 1919]

F 1268 PEASANT WOMAN CARRYING HAY: FACING LEFT
EXHIBITIONS 1918 The Hague; 1924 Amsterdam, 30 [repr]; 1928 The Hague; 1929 Hamburg, 43; 1930 Amsterdam, 97; 1935-6 New York etc, 104; 1946-7 Liège etc, 15; 1947 Paris 1, 15; Geneva, 15; Basle, 138; 1947-8 London etc, 120; 1956 Nuremberg, 50; Munich, 54; 1957 Essen, 170; 1958 Vienna, 52; Tokyo, Kyoto, 61; 1961 Munich, 43; 1963 Hamburg, 89; 1966 Belgrade, 35
PROVENANCE J. Hidde Nijland, The Hague; Dordrechts Museum, Dordrecht [loan Hidde Nijland 1904-10; Otterlo, Rijksmuseum Kröller-Müller, inv nr 939-28, cat van Gogh 1970, nr 150

F 1269 PEASANT WOMAN STOOPING: SEEN FROM THE BACK AND THE SIDE; SKETCHES OF FIGURES HARVESTING
EXHIBITIONS 1927 Basle etc, 68; 1928 Düsseldorf, 134; Karlsruhe, 69; 1929 Berlin 1, 77; Hamburg, 31; 1930 Amsterdam, 87; 1946-7 Liège etc, 16; 1947 Paris 1, 15; Geneva, 16; 1953 Otterlo, Amsterdam, 42; 1953-4 St Louis etc, 49; 1956 Nuremberg, 36; Munich, 57; 1958 Tokyo, Kyoto, 49; 1962 Warsaw, 35; 1963 Tel Aviv, Haifa, 35
PROVENANCE Bing, Paris; Sale Paris [Drouot] 17 May 1900, 115; Bernheim jeune Art Gallery, Paris; Otterlo, Rijksmuseum Kröller-Müller, inv nr 251-00, cat van Gogh 1970, nr 123

F 1270 PEASANT WOMAN PLANTING BEETS
PROVENANCE J. Hidde Nijland, The Hague; Rotterdam, Museum Boymans-van Beuningen [acquired 1899; gift of J. Hidde Nijland], inv nr VvG 2, cat 1928, nr 789

F 1271 PEASANT WOMAN PULLING OUT BEETS
See REJECTED WORKS

F 1272 PEASANT WOMAN PLANTING POTATOES: SEEN FROM THE FRONT
PROVENANCE Frankfurt, Städelsches Kunstinstitut

F 1272a PEASANT WOMAN PLANTING BEETS
EXHIBITION 1953 Amsterdam 1, 10
PROVENANCE J. Hidde Nijland, The Hague; D. Nijland, Santpoort; Huinck and Scherjon Art Gallery, Amsterdam; Coleman Art Gallery, Philadelphia; Easton, Pennsylvania, E. R. Schaible

F 1273 PEASANT WOMAN DIGGING UP POTATOES
EXHIBITIONS 1905 Amsterdam, 319 [?]; 1920 New York, 2; 1923 London, 2; 1927-8 Berlin etc, 26; 1947-8 London etc, 129; 1954-5 Bern, 114; 1955 Antwerp 1, 89; 1957 Stockholm, 42; Marseilles, 16; Breda, 33; 1958-9 San Francisco etc, 109; 1959-60 Utrecht, 74; 1960 Enschede, 25; 1961-2 Baltimore etc, 102; 1962-3 Pittsburgh etc; 1963 Sheffield, 17; 1964 Zundert, 12; 1965 Nuenen, no cat nr; 1965-6 Stockholm, 74; 1967 Wolfsburg, 95
PROVENANCE Mrs J. van Gogh-Bonger, Amsterdam; V. W. van Gogh, Laren; Amsterdam, Rijksmuseum Vincent van Gogh [Vincent van Gogh Foundation, inv nr F 1273]

F 1274 PEASANT WOMAN WORKING
EXHIBITIONS 1905 Amsterdam, 317; 1914-5 Amsterdam,

79; 1923 Utrecht, Rotterdam, 79
PROVENANCE Mrs J. van Gogh-Bonger, Amsterdam; V. W. van Gogh, Laren; Amsterdam, Rijksmuseum Vincent van Gogh [Vincent van Gogh Foundation, inv nr F 1274]

F 1275 PEASANT WOMAN DIGGING UP POTATOES
EXHIBITIONS 1905 Amsterdam, 319; 1914-5 Amsterdam, 116
PROVENANCE Mrs J. van Gogh-Bonger, Amsterdam; V. W. van Gogh, Laren; Amsterdam, Rijksmuseum Vincent van Gogh [Vincent van Gogh Foundation, inv nr F 1275]

F 1275a PEASANT WOMAN GLEANING GRAIN: FACING LEFT
PROVENANCE J. Hidde Nijland, The Hague; The Hague, G. J. Nieuwenhuizen Segaar Art Gallery [R 1970]

F 1276 recto WOMAN DIGGING: FULL FACE
verso PEASANT WOMAN: SEEN FROM BEHIND
EXHIBITIONS 1918 The Hague; 1924 Amsterdam, 75; 1928 The Hague; 1929 Hamburg, 65; 1930 Amsterdam, 109; 1952 Milan, 36; 1956 Eindhoven, 13; Munich, 64; 1957 Essen, 175; 1958 Tokyo, Kyoto, 41; 1961 Munich, 44
PROVENANCE J. Hidde Nijland, The Hague; Dordrechts Museum, Dordrecht [loan Hidde Nijland 1904-10]; Otterlo, Rijksmuseum Kröller-Müller, inv nr 964-28, cat van Gogh 1970, nr 108

F 1277 PEASANT WOMAN WORKING: FACING LEFT
EXHIBITIONS 1918 The Hague; 1924 Amsterdam, 71; 1928 The Hague; 1929 Hamburg, 54; 1930 Amsterdam, 77; 1947 Basle, 137; 1953-4 St Louis etc, 44; 1956 Nuremberg, 39; Munich, 56; 1966 Belgrade, 31
PROVENANCE J. Hidde Nijland, The Hague; Dordrechts Museum, Dordrecht [loan Hidde Nijland 1904-10]; Otterlo, Rijksmuseum Kröller-Müller, inv nr 951-28, cat van Gogh 1970, nr 129

F 1278 WOMAN WITH BROOM: FULL FACE
EXHIBITIONS 1918 The Hague; 1924 Amsterdam, 41; 1928 The Hague; 1929 Hamburg, 86; 1930 Amsterdam, 111; 1952 Antwerp, 37c; 1958 Tokyo, Kyoto, 48; 1966 Belgrade, 29
PROVENANCE J. Hidde Nijland, The Hague; Otterlo, Rijksmuseum Kröller-Müller, inv nr 970-28, cat van Gogh 1970, nr 121

F 1279 PEASANT WOMAN GLEANING GRAIN: FACING LEFT
EXHIBITION 1957 Essen, 201
PROVENANCE K. Osthaus, Hagen; Folkwang Museum, Hagen [1910]; Essen, Folkwang Museum, cat 1929, nr 439

F 1280 PEASANT WOMAN KNEELING: SEEN FROM THE BACK
PROVENANCE C. Hoogendijk, The Hague; Sale Amsterdam [F. Muller] 21-22 May 1912, 113; A. Kann, Saint-Germain-en Laye; W. Halvorsen, Paris; Thorwald Hellesen, Paris; Halvor Schon and G. Jebsen, Oslo [acquired 1916]; Oslo, Nasjonal Galleriet [acquired 1919]

F 1281 WOMAN WITH AN AX: FACING LEFT
EXHIBITIONS 1918 The Hague; 1924 Amsterdam, 42; 1928 The Hague; 1929 Hamburg, 115; 1930 Amsterdam, 85; 1947 Basle, 141; 1950 's-Hertogenbosch etc; 1956 Nuremberg, 38; Munich, 65; 1958 Vienna, 48; Tokyo, Kyoto, 52; 1960-1 Montreal etc, 102
PROVENANCE J. Hidde Nijland, The Hague; Dordrechts Museum, Dordrecht [loan Hidde Nijland 1904-10]; Otterlo, Rijksmuseum Kröller-Müller, inv nr 1024-28, cat van Gogh 1970, nr 128

F 1282 WOMAN SCOURING A CALDRON
EXHIBITIONS 1918 The Hague; 1924 Amsterdam, 29 [repr]; 1928 The Hague; 1929 Hamburg, 82; 1930 Amsterdam, 102; 1947 Basle, 139; 1947-8 London etc, 122; 1949-50 New York, Chicago, 42; 1952 Milan, 42; 1953-4 St Louis etc, 50; 1956 Nuremberg, 42; Munich, 55; 1958 Vienna, 50; Tokyo, Kyoto, 55; 1960-1 Montreal etc, 104; 1966 Belgrade, 33
PROVENANCE J. Hidde Nijland, The Hague; Dordrechts Museum, Dordrecht [loan Hidde Nijland 1904-10]; Otterlo, Rijksmuseum Kröller-Müller, inv nr 983-28, cat van Gogh 1970, nr 134

F 1283 recto WOMAN WITH A WOODEN PAIL: FACING LEFT
verso PEASANT WOMAN SWEEPING: FACING LEFT
EXHIBITIONS 1924 Amsterdam, 67; 1928 The Hague; 1929 Hamburg, 92; 1930 Amsterdam, 74
PROVENANCE J. Hidde Nijland, The Hague; Dordrechts Museum, Dordrecht [loan Hidde Nijland 1904-10]; Otterlo, Rijksmuseum Kröller-Müller, inv nr 997-28, cat van Gogh 1970, nr 136

F 1284 WOMAN BY THE WASH TUB, IN A GARDEN
EXHIBITION 1947 Basle, 145
PROVENANCE J. W. Böhler, Lucerne [bought in New York]; Basle, R. von Hirsch [R 1970]

F 1285 PEASANT WOMAN SCRUBBING AN IRON POT
See REJECTED WORKS

F 1286 PEASANT WOMAN PEELING POTATOES
See REJECTED WORKS

F 1287 SKETCH OF A WOMAN STOOPING BY THE
FIREPLACE
EXHIBITIONS 1905 Amsterdam, 322; 1914-5 Amsterdam, 56
PROVENANCE Mrs J. van Gogh-Bonger, Amsterdam;
V. W. van Gogh, Laren; Amsterdam, Rijksmuseum Vincent
van Gogh [Vincent van Gogh Foundation, inv nr F 1287]

F 1288 PEASANT WOMAN SEATED BY THE FIREPLACE:
FACING LEFT
EXHIBITIONS 1920 New York, 22 [repr]; 1924 Amsterdam,
123; 1925 The Hague, 79; 1927-8 Berlin etc, 20; 1955
Antwerp 1, 95; 1964 Zundert, 13
PROVENANCE Mrs J. van Gogh-Bonger, Amsterdam;
V. W. van Gogh, Laren; Amsterdam, Rijksmuseum Vincent
van Gogh [Vincent van Gogh Foundation, inv nr F 1288]

F 1289 recto PEASANT WOMAN: WALKING TO THE LEFT
verso PEASANT WOMAN CARRYING SOMETHING
IN HER APRON: SEEN FROM THE FRONT
EXHIBITIONS 1918 The Hague; 1924 Amsterdam, 36; 1928
The Hague; 1929 Hamburg, 99; 1930 Amsterdam, 78; 1947
Basle, 140; 1947-8 London etc, 124; 1952 Milan, 43; 1953-4
St Louis etc, 47; 1958 Tokyo, Kyoto, 58
PROVENANCE J. Hidde Nijland, The Hague; Dordrechts
Museum, Dordrecht [loan Hidde Nijland 1904-10]; Otterlo,
Rijksmuseum Kröller-Müller, inv nr 937-28, cat van Gogh
1970, nr 145

F 1290 PEASANT WOMAN AT THE SPINNING WHEEL:
FACING LEFT
EXHIBITION 1905 Amsterdam, 456
PROVENANCE Mrs J. van Gogh-Bonger; V. W. van Gogh,
Laren; Amsterdam, Rijksmuseum Vincent van Gogh
[Vincent van Gogh Foundation, inv nr F 1290]

F 1290a THE SPINNER
EXHIBITIONS 1905 Amsterdam, 302; 1965 Leiden, 32
PROVENANCE Mrs J. van Gogh-Bonger, Amsterdam;
H. Stinnes, Cologne; J. H. de Bois Art Gallery, Haarlem;
H. E. d'Audretsch Art Gallery, The Hague; H. E. van Gel-
der, The Hague; Wassenaar, H. J. de Koster [R 1970]

F 1291 WOMAN ON A BENCH BY THE HEARTH: FACING
LEFT
EXHIBITIONS 1918 The Hague; 1924 Amsterdam, 111;
1928 The Hague; 1929 Hamburg, 129; 1953 The Hague, 23;
Otterlo, Amsterdam, 40; 1956 Nuremberg, 46; 1961 Munich
48
PROVENANCE J. Hidde Nijland, The Hague; Dordrechts
Museum, Dordrecht [loan Hidde Nijland 1904-10]; Otterlo,
Rijksmuseum Kröller-Müller, inv nr 1040-28, cat van Gogh
1970, nr 143

F 1292 PEASANT WOMAN BY A POOL
EXHIBITIONS 1918 The Hague; 1924 Amsterdam, 111 (?);
1928 The Hague; 1929 Hamburg, 130; 1930 Amsterdam,
124b; 1950 's-Hertogenbosch etc; 1956 Eindhoven, 19; 1961
Munich, 49
PROVENANCE J. Hidde Nijland, The Hague; Dordrechts
Museum, Dordrecht [loan Hidde Nijland 1904-10]; Otterlo,
Rijksmuseum Kröller-Müller, inv nr 1041-28, cat van Gogh
1970, nr 149

F 1293 PEASANT WOMAN WITH A KETTLE, STANDING
NEAR A FIREPLACE
EXHIBITIONS 1905 Amsterdam, 324; 1906 Rotterdam, 61;
1969 Stuttgart, 50
PROVENANCE Mrs J. van Gogh-Bonger, Amsterdam
[1905]; Mr Haspels [1906]; Mrs C. C. Haspels-Kleyn van
Brandes; Sale Amsterdam [F. Muller] 26 January
1944, 282; Unknown collection; Stuttgart, Graphische
Sammlung Staatsgalerie Stuttgart [acquired 1967] inv
nr C 67/1470

F 1294 WOMAN SEWING, SITTING ON A BASKET:
FACING RIGHT
PROVENANCE H. P. Bremmer, The Hague; N. E. Kröller,
The Hague; Otterlo, Rijksmuseum Kröller-Müller, inv
nr 192-00, cat van Gogh 1970, nr 64

F 1295 TWO WOMEN DIGGING
EXHIBITIONS 1918 The Hague; 1924 Amsterdam, 99; 1928
The Hague; 1929 Hamburg, 107; 1930 Amsterdam, 92; 1956
Nuremberg, 30; 1958 Vienna, 53; Tokyo, Kyoto, 40
PROVENANCE J. Hidde Nijland, The Hague; Dordrechts
Museum, Dordrecht [loan Hidde Nijland 1904-10]; Otterlo,
Rijksmuseum Kröller-Müller, inv nr 1015-28, cat van Gogh
1970, nr 107

F 1296 TWO PEASANT WOMEN DIGGING
EXHIBITION 1904 Rotterdam, 58
PROVENANCE C. Mouwen jr, Breda; Sale Amsterdam
[F. Muller] 3 May 1904, 26; Oldenzeel Art Gallery, Rotter-
dam; Switzerland, Doyer Family

F 1297 recto SKETCH OF THE HEAD OF A MAN
verso STUDY OF TWO WOMEN; STUDY OF A MAN
CARRYING A BUNDLE OF BRANCHES ON HIS BACK
EXHIBITION 1905 Amsterdam, 77 [verso]
PROVENANCE Mrs J. van Gogh-Bonger, Amsterdam;
V. W. van Gogh, Laren; Amsterdam, Rijksmuseum Vincent
van Gogh [Vincent van Gogh Foundation, inv nr F 1297]

F 1297a recto HEAD OF A PEASANT WOMAN
verso WOMAN SWEEPING: FACING LEFT
PROVENANCE A. Wirtz, Breda; J. C. Wirtz, Eindhoven;
Sale Rotterdam [Van Marle] 21 December 1954, 100 [repr];
Sale Amsterdam [P. Brandt] 27 June 1955, 43; J. C. Wirtz,
Son, Noord-Brabant; Wassenaar, Paul Citroen [R 1965]

F 1298 recto THREE PEASANT WOMEN
verso PEASANT WOMAN: FACING LEFT
EXHIBITIONS 1905 Amsterdam, 327; 1914-5 Amsterdam,
103; 1945 Amsterdam, no cat nr
PROVENANCE Mrs J. van Gogh-Bonger, Amsterdam;
V. W. van Gogh, Laren; Amsterdam, Rijksmuseum Vincent
van Gogh [Vincent van Gogh Foundation, inv nr F 1298]

F 1299 PEASANT AND PEASANT WOMAN DIGGING
EXHIBITIONS 1927 Basle etc, 76; 1928 Düsseldorf, 142;
Karlsruhe, 77; 1929 Berlin 1, 68; Hamburg, 142; 1930
Amsterdam, 216; 1949 Gouda; 1949-50 New York, Chicago
42; 1952 Milan, 35; 1956 Nuremberg, 29; Munich, 63; 1958
Tokyo, Kyoto, 39; 1960-1 Montreal etc, 110; 1966 Belgrade,
24
PROVENANCE L. C. Enthoven, Voorburg; Sale Amsterdam
[F. Muller] 18 May 1920, 258; Otterlo, Rijksmuseum
Kröller-Müller, inv nr 259-20, cat van Gogh 1970, nr 106

F 1300 DIGGING UP POTATOES
See REJECTED WORKS

F 1301 recto HARVEST: PEASANT WOMAN STOOPING
AND PEASANT REAPING WHEAT
verso STUDY OF A PEASANT WORKING
EXHIBITIONS 1918 The Hague; 1924 Amsterdam, 78; 1928
The Hague; 1929 Hamburg, 62; 1930 Amsterdam, 110;
1935-6 New York etc; 1950 's-Hertogenbosch etc; 1962
Warsaw, 33; 1963 Tel Aviv, Haifa, 33
PROVENANCE J. Hidde Nijland, The Hague; Dordrechts
Museum, Dordrecht [loan Hidde Nijland 1904-10]; Otterlo,
Rijksmuseum Kröller-Müller, inv nr 960-28, cat van Gogh
1970, nr 115

F 1302 PEASANT DIGGING: SEEN FROM THE BACK
EXHIBITIONS 1905 Amsterdam, 310; 1914-5 Amsterdam,
85; 1927-8 Berlin etc, 32; 1949-50 New York, Chicago, 41;
1951 Lyons etc, 86; 1955 Antwerp 1, 83; 1957 Nijmegen, 36;
Stockholm, 39; 1958-9 San Francisco etc, 110; 1960
Enschede, 26; 1961-2 Baltimore etc, 103; 1965-6 Stockholm,
Göteborg, 75; 1967 Wolfsburg, 96; 1967-8 Dallas etc, 23;
1968 Liège, 23; 1968-9 London, 45; 1969 Humlebaek, 11
PROVENANCE Mrs J. van Gogh-Bonger, Amsterdam;
V. W. van Gogh, Laren; Amsterdam, Rijksmuseum Vincent
van Gogh [Vincent van Gogh Foundation, inv nr F 1302]

F 1303 PEASANT DIGGING: SEEN FROM THE BACK
EXHIBITIONS 1905 Amsterdam, 287; 1914-5 Amsterdam,
92
PROVENANCE Mrs J. van Gogh-Bonger, Amsterdam;
V. W. van Gogh, Laren; Amsterdam, Rijksmuseum Vincent
van Gogh [Vincent van Gogh Foundation, inv nr F 1303]

F 1304 PEASANT DIGGING UP POTATOES: SEEN FROM
THE FRONT
EXHIBITION 1961 Amsterdam 1, 37
PROVENANCE H. P. Bremmer, The Hague [until 1956];
Heirs of H. P. Bremmer, The Hague; John Streep Art
Dealer, New York [acquired 1957]; Knoedler Art Gallery,
New York [1962]; Sale London [Sotheby] 23 October 1963,
73; Present owner unknown

F 1305 PEASANT DIGGING: FACING LEFT
EXHIBITIONS 1905 Amsterdam, 320; 1914-5 Amsterdam,
112; 1923 Utrecht, Rotterdam, 1; 1937 Paris, 61; 1965
Nuenen, no cat nr
PROVENANCE Mrs J. van Gogh-Bonger, Amsterdam;
V. W. van Gogh, Laren; Amsterdam, Rijksmuseum Vincent
van Gogh [Vincent van Gogh Foundation, inv nr F 1305]

F 1306 YOUNG PEASANT, DIGGING: FACING RIGHT
PROVENANCE W. Halvorsen, Paris; Thorwald Hellesen,
Paris; Halvor Schon and G. Jebsen, Oslo [acquired 1916];
Oslo, Nasjonal Galleriet [acquired 1919]

F 1307 YOUNG PEASANT DIGGING: FACING LEFT
EXHIBITIONS 1905 Amsterdam, 296; 1914-5 Amsterdam,
92; 1926 Munich, 2106; 1927-8 Berlin etc, 37; 1955 Antwerp
1, 85
PROVENANCE Mrs J. van Gogh-Bonger, Amsterdam;
V. W. van Gogh, Laren; Amsterdam, Rijksmuseum Vincent
van Gogh [Vincent van Gogh Foundation, inv nr F 1307]

F 1308 PEASANT DIGGING: FACING RIGHT
EXHIBITIONS 1905 Amsterdam, 318; 1914-5 Amsterdam,
94; 1955 Antwerp 1, 84
PROVENANCE Mrs J. van Gogh-Bonger, Amsterdam;
V. W. van Gogh, Laren; Amsterdam, Rijksmuseum Vincent
van Gogh [Vincent van Gogh Foundation, inv nr F 1308]

F 1309 PEASANT DIGGING: SEEN FROM THE FRONT
EXHIBITIONS 1905 Amsterdam, 333; 1914-5 Amsterdam,
81; 1927-8 Berlin etc, 38; 1953 The Hague, 26; Otterlo,
Amtserdam, 44
PROVENANCE Mrs J. van Gogh-Bonger, Amsterdam;
V. W. van Gogh, Laren; Amsterdam, Rijksmuseum Vincent
van Gogh [Vincent van Gogh Foundation, inv nr F 1309]

F 1310 PEASANT DIGGING: FACING RIGHT
EXHIBITION 1914-5 Amsterdam, 114
PROVENANCE Mrs J. van Gogh-Bonger, Amsterdam;
V. W. van Gogh, Laren; Amsterdam, Rijksmuseum Vincent
van Gogh [Vincent van Gogh Foundation, inv nr F 1310]

F 1311 SKETCH OF A PEASANT WORKING: FACING
RIGHT
EXHIBITIONS 1918 The Hague; 1924 Amsterdam, 66; 1928
The Hague; 1929 Hamburg, 94; 1930 Amsterdam, 88; 1952
Antwerp, 37e; 1958 Tokyo, Kyoto, 54; 1960-1 Montreal
etc, 103
PROVENANCE J. Hidde Nijland, The Hague; Dordrechts
Museum, Dordrecht [loan Hidde Nijland 1904-10]; Otterlo,
Rijksmuseum Kröller-Müller, inv nr 999-28, cat van Gogh
1970, nr 131

F 1312 THE REAPER WITH HAT: SEEN FROM THE BACK
EXHIBITIONS 1957 Essen, 202; 1960 Paris, 97
PROVENANCE J. Hidde Nijland, The Hague; Amsterdam,
Rijksmuseum [acquired 1906; gift of J. Hidde Nijland], cat
1911, nr 2926a [on loan since 1960 to Stedelijk Museum,
Amsterdam]

F 1313 THE REAPER WITH HAT: SEEN FROM THE BACK
EXHIBITIONS 1924 Amsterdam, 87; 1928
The Hague; 1929 Hamburg, 90; 1930 Amsterdam, 106; 1947
Basle, 133 [2d edition 134]; 1950 's-Hertogenbosch etc;
1953-4 St Louis etc, 43; 1956 Nuremberg, 35; Munich, 61;
1957 Essen, 73; 1958 Tokyo, Kyoto, 45
PROVENANCE J. Hidde Nijland, The Hague; Dordrechts
Museum, Dordrecht [loan Hidde Nijland 1904-10]; Otterlo,
Rijksmuseum Kröller-Müller, inv nr 992-28, cat van Gogh
1970, nr 118

F 1314 THE REAPER WITH HAT: FACING RIGHT
EXHIBITIONS 1918 The Hague; 1924 Amsterdam, 109;
1928 The Hague; 1929 Hamburg, 70; 1930 Amsterdam, 99;
1961 Munich, 45; 1962 Warsaw, 32; 1963 Tel Aviv, Haifa,
32
PROVENANCE J. Hidde Nijland, The Hague; Dordrechts
Museum, Dordrecht [loan Hidde Nijland 1904-10]; Otterlo,
Rijksmuseum Kröller-Müller, inv nr 969-28, cat van Gogh
1970, nr 111

F 1315 THE REAPER WITH HAT: SEEN FROM THE BACK
EXHIBITIONS 1918 The Hague; 1924 Amsterdam, 32
[repr]; 1928 The Hague; 1929 Hamburg, 95; 1930 Amster-
dam, 104; 1947 Basle, 136; 1955 Wormerveer; 1956
Nuremberg, 23; Munich, 62; 1958 Vienna, 44; 1959 São
Paulo, 13; 1966 Belgrade, 26
PROVENANCE J. Hidde Nijland, The Hague; Dordrechts
Museum, Dordrecht [loan Hidde Nijland 1904-10]; Otterlo,
Rijksmuseum Kröller-Müller, inv nr 1001-28, cat van Gogh
1970, nr 114

F 1316 THE REAPER WITH HAT: FACING RIGHT
EXHIBITIONS 1905 Amsterdam, 344; 1914-5 Amsterdam,
115; 1945 Amsterdam, no cat nr; 1946 Stockholm etc, 15;
1946-7 Liège etc, 14; 1947 Paris 1, 14; Geneva, 14; 1954-5
Bern, 115; 1955 Antwerp 1, 86; 1961-2 Baltimore etc, 104;
1968-9 London, 47
PROVENANCE Mrs J. van Gogh-Bonger, Amsterdam;
V. W. van Gogh, Laren; Amsterdam, Rijksmuseum Vincent
van Gogh [Vincent van Gogh Foundation, inv nr F 1316]

F 1317 THE REAPER WITH CAP: MOVING TO THE RIGHT
EXHIBITIONS 1905 Amsterdam, 339; 1914-5 Amsterdam,
82; 1923 Utrecht, Rotterdam, 60; 1924 Basle, 83; Zurich,
83; Stuttgart, 4; 1925 Paris 1; The Hague, 60; 1926 Munich,
2108; 1947-8 London etc, 125; 1948 Bergen, Oslo, 75; 1955
Antwerp 1, 87; 1955-6 Liverpool etc, 95; 1957 Breda, 32;
Marseilles, 15; Stockholm, 38
PROVENANCE Mrs J. van Gogh-Bonger, Amsterdam;
V. W. van Gogh, Laren; Amsterdam, Rijksmuseum Vincent
van Gogh [Vincent van Gogh Foundation, inv nr F 1317]

F 1318 THE REAPER WITH CAP: MOVING TO THE RIGHT
EXHIBITIONS 1905 Amsterdam, 289; 1920 New York, 32;
1923 London, 4; 1925 The Hague, 83; 1926 Munich, 2099;
1927-8 Berlin etc, 15; 1932 Manchester, 56; 1947-8 London
etc, 126; 1948 Bergen, Oslo, 77; 1953-4 St Louis etc, 48;
1955 Palm Beach etc, 35; 1959-60 Utrecht, 72; 1960
Enschede, 27; 1961-2 Baltimore etc, 105; 1964 Washington,
New York, 79; 1965 Charleroi, Ghent, 53; 1966 Paris, Albi,
25; 1967 Lille, Zurich, 27; 1967-8 Dallas etc, 24; 1968 Liège,
24; 1968-9 London, 46; 1969 Humlebaek, 12

PROVENANCE Mrs J. van Gogh-Bonger, Amsterdam; V. W. van Gogh, Laren; Amsterdam, Rijksmuseum Vincent van Gogh [Vincent van Gogh Foundation, inv nr F 1318]

F 1319 recto THE REAPER WITH CAP: SEEN FROM THE FRONT
verso LANDSCAPE WITH SHEAVES OF WHEAT AND A WIND MILL
EXHIBITIONS 1905 Amsterdam, 290; 1914-5 Amsterdam, 71
PROVENANCE Mrs J. van Gogh-Bonger, Amsterdam; V. W. van Gogh, Laren; Amsterdam, Rijksmuseum Vincent van Gogh [Vincent van Gogh Foundation, inv nr F 1319]

F 1320 THE REAPER WITH HAT: MOVING TO THE RIGHT
PROVENANCE E. Hahnloser, Zurich; Zurich, Mrs D. Hahnloser-Gassmann

F 1321 recto A REAPER AND A WOMAN BINDING SHEAVES: A WIND MILL IN THE BACKGROUND
verso FIGURE OF A MAN WITH A HAT
EXHIBITIONS 1905 Amsterdam, 284; 1914-5 Amsterdam, 95; 1923 Utrecht, Rotterdam, 60
PROVENANCE Mrs J. van Gogh-Bonger, Amsterdam; V. W. van Gogh, Laren; Amsterdam, Rijksmuseum Vincent van Gogh [Vincent van Gogh Foundation, inv nr F 1321]

F 1322 recto PEASANT REAPING WHEAT IN A LANDSCAPE WITH TREES AND A LITTLE HOUSE
verso THE REAPER WITH HAT: SEEN FROM THE BACK
EXHIBITIONS 1918 The Hague; 1924 Amsterdam, 74; 1928 The Hague; 1929 Hamburg, 104; 1930 Amsterdam, 107; 1957 Essen, 174; 1958 Vancouver, 28; 1960-1 Montreal etc, 111; 1962 Warsaw, 31; 1962 London 1, 18; 1963 Tel Aviv, Haifa, 31
PROVENANCE J. Hidde Nijland, The Hague; Dordrechts Museum, Dordrecht [loan Hidde Nijland 1904-10]; Otterlo, Rijksmuseum Kröller-Müller, inv nr 1011-28, cat van Gogh 1970, nr 110

F 1323 THE REAPER WITH HAT: SEEN FROM THE BACK
EXHIBITIONS 1918 The Hague; 1924 Amsterdam, 59; 1928 The Hague; 1929 Hamburg, 78; 1930 Amsterdam, 71; 1958 Tokyo, Kyoto, 46
PROVENANCE J. Hidde Nijland, The Hague; Dordrechts Museum, Dordrecht [loan Hidde Nijland 1904-10]; Otterlo, Rijksmuseum Kröller-Müller, inv nr 979-28, cat van Gogh 1970, nr 119

F 1324 PEASANT REAPING WHEAT
See REJECTED WORKS

F 1325 PEASANT WORKING: FACING RIGHT, TWO COTTAGES IN THE BACKGROUND
EXHIBITIONS 1918 The Hague; 1924 Amsterdam, 83; 1928 The Hague; 1929 Hamburg, 76; 1930 Amsterdam, 108; 1950-1 Leiden etc, 59; 1952 Milan, 38; 1956 Eindhoven, 16; Munich, 69; 1958 Vienna, 49; 1959 São Paulo, 11
PROVENANCE J. Hidde Nijland, The Hague; Dordrechts Museum, Dordrecht [loan Hidde Nijland 1904-10]; Otterlo, Rijksmuseum Kröller-Müller, inv nr 976-28, cat van Gogh 1970, nr 132

F 1326 A PEASANT WORKING: FACING RIGHT, TWO COTTAGES IN THE BACKGROUND
EXHIBITIONS 1918 The Hague; 1924 Amsterdam, 113; 1928 The Hague; 1929 Hamburg, 120; 1930 Amsterdam, 95; 1950 's-Hertogenbosch etc; 1953-4 St Louis etc, 45; 1956 Nuremberg, 40; Munich, 68; 1957 Geneva, 130; 1958 Tokyo, Kyoto, 53
PROVENANCE J. Hidde Nijland, The Hague; Otterlo, Rijksmuseum Kröller-Müller, inv nr 1032-28, cat van Gogh 1970, nr 130

F 1327 THE WOODCUTTER: FACING RIGHT
EXHIBITIONS 1905 Amsterdam, 288; 1914-5 Amsterdam, 106; 1921 New York, 33; 1924 Basle, 84; Zurich, 84; Stuttgart, 2; 1925 The Hague, 72; 1926 Munich, 2108; 1927-8 Berlin etc, 25; 1932 Manchester, 55; 1947-8 London etc, 127; 1948 Bergen, Oslo, 98; 1954-5 Bern, 117; 1955 Antwerp 1, 90; 1957 Stockholm, 40; 1966 Paris, Albi, 26; 1967 Lille, Zurich, 28; 1967-8 Dallas etc, 25; 1968 Liège, 25; 1968-9 London, 42
PROVENANCE Mrs J. van Gogh-Bonger, Amsterdam; V. W. van Gogh, Laren; Amsterdam, Rijksmuseum Vincent van Gogh [Vincent van Gogh Foundation, inv nr F 1327]

F 1328 recto PEASANT: FACING RIGHT
verso THREE STUDIES OF A PEASANT; A HEAD: SEEN FROM THE BACK
EXHIBITIONS 1918 The Hague; 1924 Amsterdam, 40; 1928 The Hague; 1929 Hamburg, 87; 1930 Amsterdam, 101; 1956 Eindhoven, 17; Munich, 71; 1957 Essen, 171; 1963 Hamburg, 90
PROVENANCE J. Hidde Nijland, The Hague; Dordrechts Museum, Dordrecht [loan Hidde Nijland 1904-1910]; Otterlo, Rijksmuseum Kröller-Müller, inv nr 989-28, cat van Gogh 1970, nr 137

F 1329 recto PEASANT WALKING TO THE LEFT
verso STUDIES OF FOUR FIGURES
EXHIBITIONS 1918 The Hague; 1924 Amsterdam, 102; 1928 The Hague; 1929 Hamburg, 47; 1930 Amsterdam, 90; 1952 Milan, 39; 1953-4 St Louis etc, 46; 1956 Munich, 70; 1960-1 Montreal etc, 105; 1962 Warsaw, 38; 1963 Tel Aviv, Haifa, 38
PROVENANCE J. Hidde Nijland, The Hague; Dordrechts Museum, Dordrecht [loan Hidde Nijland 1904-10]; Otterlo, Rijksmuseum Kröller-Müller, inv nr 944-28, cat van Gogh 1970, nr 140

F 1330 recto PEASANT WALKING: SEEN FROM THE FRONT
verso STUDY FOR A PEASANT: THREE HANDS HOLDING A STICK
EXHIBITIONS 1918 The Hague; 1924 Amsterdam, 104; 1928 The Hague; 1929 Hamburg, 68; 1930 Amsterdam, 103; 1947 Basle, 142; London, 128; 1952 Milan, 39; 1953-4 St Louis etc, 46; 1965 Nuremberg, 41; Munich, 70; 1960-1 Montreal etc, 105
PROVENANCE J. Hidde Nijland, The Hague; Dordrechts Museum, Dordrecht [loan Hidde Nijland 1904-10]; Otterlo, Rijksmuseum Kröller-Müller, inv nr 967-28, cat van Gogh 1970, nr 133

F 1331 SHORT-LEGGED OLD MAN WITH A BALD HEAD: SEEN FROM THE FRONT
EXHIBITIONS 1905 Amsterdam, 274; 1914-5 Amsterdam, 74; 1923 Utrecht, Rotterdam, 66; 1926 London 3, 41; 1955 Antwerp 1, 91
PROVENANCE Mrs J. van Gogh-Bonger, Amsterdam; V. W. van Gogh, Laren; Amsterdam, Rijksmuseum Vincent van Gogh [Vincent van Gogh Foundation, inv nr F 1331]

F 1332 recto SHORT-LEGGED OLD MAN WITH A BALD HEAD: SEEN FROM THE FRONT
verso PEASANT AND PEASANT WOMAN WITH BABY
EXHIBITIONS 1905 Amsterdam, 312; 1914-5 Amsterdam, 90
PROVENANCE Mrs J. van Gogh-Bonger, Amsterdam; V. W. van Gogh, Laren; Amsterdam, Rijksmuseum Vincent van Gogh [Vincent van Gogh Foundation, inv nr F 1332]

F 1333 recto STUDY OF TWO PEASANTS
verso STUDY OF TWO PEASANTS
EXHIBITIONS 1918 The Hague; 1924 Amsterdam, 82; 1928 The Hague; 1929 Hamburg, 109; 1930 Amsterdam, 105; 1958 Tokyo, Kyoto, 57
PROVENANCE J. Hidde Nijland, The Hague; Dordrechts Museum, Dordrecht [loan Hidde Nijland 1904-10]; Otterlo, Rijksmuseum Kröller-Müller, inv nr 1018-28, cat van Gogh 1970, nr 141

F 1334 PEASANT RESTING IN A CHAIR
See REJECTED WORKS

F 1335 MAN LOADING A CART
EXHIBITIONS 1918 The Hague; 1924 Amsterdam, 111; 1928 The Hague; 1929 Hamburg, 132; 1930 Amsterdam, 124; 1956 Eindhoven, 18; 1961 Munich, 50
PROVENANCE J. Hidde Nijland, The Hague, Dordrechts Museum, Dordrecht [loan Hidde Nijland 1904-10]; Otterlo, Rijksmuseum Kröller-Müller, inv nr 1043-28, cat van Gogh 1970, nr 139

F 1336 recto THE OLD TOWER AT NUENEN; STUDIES OF FIGURES
verso MAN WITH LADDER ON HIS SHOULDER AND A GROUP OF FIGURES; CEMETERY WITH WOODEN CROSSES
EXHIBITIONS 1918 The Hague; 1924 Amsterdam, 80; 1928 The Hague; 1929 Hamburg, 106; 1930 Amsterdam, 72; 1949-50 New York, Chicago, 44; 1952 Milan, 42; 1956 Nuremberg, 44; Munich, 51; 1958 Vienna, 41
PROVENANCE J. Hidde Nijland, The Hague; Dordrechts Museum, Dordrecht [loan Hidde Nijland 1904-10]; Otterlo, Rijksmuseum Kröller-Müller, inv nr 1035-28, cat van Gogh 1970, nr 138

F 1337 MANGLE WITH TWO WOMEN AND A MAN
EXHIBITIONS 1918 The Hague; 1924 Amsterdam, 76; 1928 The Hague; 1929 Hamburg, 60; 1930 Amsterdam, 23
PROVENANCE J. Hidde Nijland, The Hague; Dordrechts Museum, Dordrecht [loan Hidde Nijland 1904-10]; Otterlo, Rijksmuseum Kröller-Müller, inv nr 957-28, cat van Gogh 1970, nr 153

F 1338 PEASANT AND PEASANT WOMAN WALKING ON A ROAD
EXHIBITIONS 1924 Amsterdam, 111; 1956 Almelo, 47
PROVENANCE J. Hidde Nijland, The Hague; Mrs H. Kröller-Müller, The Hague; Netherlands, Private collection [R 1970]

F 1339 FIELD WITH A MAN BINDING SHEAVES
EXHIBITIONS 1905 Amsterdam, 308; 1914-5 Amsterdam, 104; 1927-8 Berlin etc, 34
PROVENANCE Mrs J. van Gogh-Bonger, Amsterdam; V. W. van Gogh, Laren; Amsterdam, Rijksmuseum Vincent van Gogh [Vincent van Gogh Foundation, inv nr F 1339]

F 1340 FIELD WITH SHEAVES: WINDMILL IN THE LEFT BACKGROUND
EXHIBITIONS 1920 New York, 31; 1924 Amsterdam, 121; 1953 The Hague, 25; Otterlo, Amsterdam, 43; 1955 Antwerp 1, 73; 1965 Nuenen, no cat nr
PROVENANCE Mrs J. van Gogh-Bonger, Amsterdam; V. W. van Gogh, Laren; Amsterdam, Rijksmuseum Vincent van Gogh [Vincent van Gogh Foundation, inv nr F 1340]

F 1341 FIELD WITH ONE SHEAF: WINDMILL IN THE RIGHT BACKGROUND
EXHIBITIONS 1905 Amsterdam, 452; 1955 Antwerp 1, 74
PROVENANCE Mrs J. van Gogh-Bonger, Amsterdam; V. W. van Gogh, Laren; Amsterdam, Rijksmuseum Vincent van Gogh [Vincent van Gogh Foundation, inv nr F 1341]

F 1342 SHEAVES: WINDMILL IN THE RIGHT BACKGROUND
EXHIBITIONS 1905 Amsterdam, 292; 1914-5 Amsterdam, 49
PROVENANCE Mrs J. van Gogh-Bonger, Amsterdam; V. W. van Gogh, Laren; Amsterdam, Rijksmuseum Vincent van Gogh [Vincent van Gogh Foundation, inv nr F 1342]

F 1343 THE VICARAGE AT NUENEN: SEEN FROM THE BACK, WITH THE ARTIST'S STUDIO ON THE RIGHT
PROVENANCE Mrs E. H. du Quesne-van Gogh, Baarn; Probably De Bois Art Gallery, Haarlem [R 1928]; Canada, Private collection

F 1343a THE VICARAGE AT NUENEN: SEEN FROM THE FRONT
EXHIBITIONS 1956 Amsterdam, 14; 1957 Essen, 203; 1960 Paris, 99
PROVENANCE J. P. Scholte, Lochem; Mrs J. P. Scholte-van Houten, Lochem; Oegstgeest, Netherlands, collection Scholte-van Houten [R 1969]

F 1344 THE FARM
PROVENANCE Mrs J. van Gogh-Bonger, Amsterdam; V. W. van Gogh, Laren; Amsterdam, Rijksmuseum Vincent van Gogh [Vincent van Gogh Foundation, inv nr F 1344]

F 1345 FARM WITH WINDMILL IN THE BACKGROUND
EXHIBITIONS 1905 Amsterdam, 341; 1914-5 Amsterdam, 60; 1920 New York, 35; 1923 London, 12; 1945 Amsterdam, no cat nr
PROVENANCE Mrs J. van Gogh-Bonger, Amsterdam; V. W. van Gogh, Laren; Amsterdam, Rijksmuseum Vincent van Gogh [Vincent van Gogh Foundation, inv nr F 1345]

F 1346 TWO ISOLATED TREES UNDER STORM CLOUDS: A WINDMILL IN THE BACKGROUND
EXHIBITIONS 1905 Amsterdam, 340; 1914-5 Amsterdam, 53; 1920 New York, 26
PROVENANCE Mrs J. van Gogh-Bonger, Amsterdam; V. W. van Gogh, Laren; Amsterdam, Rijksmuseum Vincent van Gogh [Vincent van Gogh Foundation, inv nr F 1346]

F 1347 LANDSCAPE WITH A BRIDGE
EXHIBITIONS 1924 Amsterdam, 62; 1947 Basle, 131 [2d edition 135]; 1958 Vienna, 33; 1960-1 Montreal etc, 97
PROVENANCE J. Hidde Nijland, The Hague; Dordrechts Museum, Dordrecht [loan Hidde Nijland 1904-10]; Otterlo, Rijksmuseum Kröller-Müller, inv nr 954-28, cat van Gogh 1970, nr 55

F 1348 STREET IN RAINY WEATHER [IN EINDHOVEN]
PROVENANCE Mrs J. van Gogh-Bonger, Amsterdam; V. W. van Gogh, Laren; Amsterdam, Rijksmuseum Vincent van Gogh [Vincent van Gogh Foundation, inv nr F 1348]

F 1349 recto STUDIES OF A CLOCK, A SPOON RACK AND A WOODEN SHOE
verso STUDIES OF A PLATE, TWO KNIVES AND A WATER KETTLE
EXHIBITION 1955 Antwerp 1, 98
PROVENANCE Mrs J. van Gogh-Bonger, Amsterdam; V. W. van Gogh, Laren; Amsterdam, Rijksmuseum Vincent van Gogh [Vincent van Gogh Foundation, inv nr F 1349]

ANTWERP PERIOD

F 1350 recto THE STEEN AT ANTWERP
verso TWO SKETCHES OF A WOMAN SEATED IN A BOX AT A THEATER
EXHIBITIONS 1946-7 Liège etc, 37; 1947 Paris 1, 37; Geneva, 38; 1955 Antwerp 1, 134, 127 [verso]; 1962 London 1, 22; 1963 Humlebaek, 80 [verso]; 1964 Washington, New York, 80 [verso]
PROVENANCE Mrs J. van Gogh-Bonger, Amsterdam; V. W. van Gogh, Laren; Amsterdam, Rijksmuseum Vincent van Gogh [Vincent van Gogh Foundation, inv nr F 1350]

F 1350a DANCING HALL
EXHIBITIONS 1960-1 Montreal etc, 116; 1962 London 1, 25
PROVENANCE Mrs J. van Gogh-Bonger, Amsterdam; V. W. van Gogh, Laren; Amsterdam, Rijksmuseum Vincent van Gogh [Vincent van Gogh Foundation, inv nr F 1350a]

F 1350b WOMEN DANCING
EXHIBITION 1962 London I, 26
PROVENANCE Mrs J. van Gogh-Bonger, Amsterdam;
V. W. van Gogh, Laren; Amsterdam, Rijksmuseum Vincent
van Gogh [Vincent van Gogh Foundation, inv nr F 1350b]

F 1351 THE STEEN AT ANTWERP
EXHIBITIONS 1905 Amsterdam, 465; 1946-7 Liège etc, 36;
1947 Paris, 36; Geneva, 37; 1955 Antwerp I, 135; 1957
Stockholm, 44; 1960-1 Montreal etc, 115; 1963 Humlebaek,
81; 1964 Washington, New York, 81
PROVENANCE Mrs J. van Gogh-Bonger, Amsterdam;
V. W. van Gogh, Laren; Amsterdam, Rijksmuseum Vincent
van Gogh [Vincent van Gogh Foundation, inv nr F 1351]

F 1352 THE GROTE MARKT IN ANTWERP
EXHIBITIONS 1945 Amsterdam, no cat nr; 1946 Stockholm
etc, 19; 1946-7 Liège etc, 35; 1947 Paris I, 35; Geneva, 36;
1953 The Hague, 44; Otterlo, Amsterdam, 51; 1953-4
St Louis etc, 57; 1954-5 Bern, 118; 1955 Antwerp I, 136;
1955-6 Liverpool etc, 97; 1961-2 Baltimore etc, 107; 1963
Humlebaek, 82; 1964 Washington, New York, 82; 1966
Paris, Albi, 28; 1967 Lille, Zurich, 30; 1967-8 Dallas etc, 27;
1968 Liège, 27; 1968-9 London, 55
PROVENANCE Mrs J. van Gogh-Bonger, Amsterdam;
V. W. van Gogh, Laren; Amsterdam, Rijksmuseum Vincent
van Gogh [Vincent van Gogh Foundation, inv nr F 1352]

F 1353 NUDE WOMAN
EXHIBITIONS 1955 Antwerp I, 139; 1962 London I, 28
PROVENANCE Mrs J. van Gogh-Bonger, Amsterdam;
V. W. van Gogh, Laren; Amsterdam, Rijksmuseum Vincent
van Gogh [Vincent van Gogh Foundation, inv nr F 1353]

F 1354 SQUARE IN ANTWERP
EXHIBITIONS 1962 London I, 23; 1964 Zundert, 14
PROVENANCE Mrs J. Gogh-Bonger, Amsterdam;
V. W. van Gogh, Laren; Amsterdam, Rijksmuseum Vincent
van Gogh [Vincent van Gogh Foundation, inv nr F 1354]

F 1354a recto SELF PORTRAIT; SKETCH OF A FLOWER
verso SELF PORTRAIT; FIGURE SKETCHES
EXHIBITION 1955 Antwerp I, 141, 142 [verso]
PROVENANCE Mrs J. van Gogh-Bonger, Amsterdam;
V. W. van Gogh, Laren; Amsterdam, Rijksmuseum Vincent
van Gogh [Vincent van Gogh Foundation, inv nr F 1354a]

F 1355 TOWN VIEW IN ANTWERP
PROVENANCE Mrs J. van Gogh-Bonger, Amsterdam;
V. W. van Gogh, Laren; Amsterdam, Rijksmuseum Vincent
van Gogh [Vincent van Gogh Foundation, inv nr F 1355]

F 1356 SPIRE OF THE CHURCH OF OUR LADY IN
ANTWERP
EXHIBITIONS 1905 Amsterdam, 466; 1945 Amsterdam, no
cat nr; 1954-5 Bern, 119; 1955 Antwerp I, 137; 1957
Marseilles, 21; Stockholm, 45; 1958-9 San Francisco etc,
112; 1959-60 Utrecht, 75; 1960 Enschede, 28; 1961-2
Baltimore etc, 106; 1963 Humlebaek, 83; 1964 Washington,
New York, 83; 1965 Charleroi, Ghent, 54; 1965-6 Stock-
holm, Göteborg, 76; 1967 Wolfsburg, 97
PROVENANCE Mrs J. van Gogh-Bonger, Amsterdam;
V. W. van Gogh, Laren; Amsterdam, Rijksmuseum Vincent
van Gogh [Vincent van Gogh Foundation, inv nr F 1356]

F 1357 PORTRAIT OF A WOMAN
EXHIBITIONS 1927-8 Berlin etc, 44; 1955 Antwerp I, 126;
1957 Stockholm, 43
PROVENANCE Mrs J. van Gogh-Bonger, Amsterdam;
V. W. van Gogh, Laren; Amsterdam, Rijksmuseum Vincent
van Gogh [Vincent van Gogh Foundation, inv nr F 1357]

F 1357a PORTRAIT OF A WOMAN WITH HAT
EXHIBITIONS 1955 Antwerp I, 140; 1957 Essen, 211
PROVENANCE Mrs E. H. du Quesne-van Gogh, Baarn; Jos
Verwiel; H. Wiegersma, Deurne [1957]; Sale London
[Sotheby] 25 November 1959, 79; Deurne, Netherlands,
Heirs of J. Wiegersma

F 1358 HEAD OF A MAN
PROVENANCE Mrs J. van Gogh-Bonger, Amsterdam;
V. W. van Gogh, Laren; Amsterdam, Rijksmuseum Vincent
van Gogh [Vincent van Gogh Foundation, inv nr F 1358]

F 1359 HEAD OF A MAN WITH PIPE: LEFT PROFILE
EXHIBITION 1955 Antwerp I, 130
PROVENANCE Mrs J. van Gogh-Bonger, Amsterdam;
V. W. van Gogh, Laren; Amsterdam, Rijksmuseum Vincent
van Gogh [Vincent van Gogh Foundation, inv nr F 1359]

F 1360 recto STUDY OF SEVEN HANDS
verso STUDY OF THREE SPARROWS
EXHIBITIONS 1955 Antwerp I, 155, 160 [verso]; 1964
Zundert, 15
PROVENANCE Mrs J. van Gogh-Bonger, Amsterdam;
V. W. van Gogh, Laren; Amsterdam, Rijksmuseum Vincent
van Gogh [Vincent van Gogh Foundation, inv nr F 1360]

F 1361 HANGING SKELETON
EXHIBITIONS 1955 Antwerp I, 154; 1962 London I, 27
PROVENANCE Mrs J. van Gogh-Bonger, Amsterdam;
V. W. van Gogh, Laren; Amsterdam, Rijksmuseum Vincent
van Gogh [Vincent van Gogh Foundation, inv nr F 1361]

PARIS PERIOD

F 1362 recto NUDE MAN STANDING
below PEASANT DIGGING, SEEN FROM THE BACK
verso HEADS
EXHIBITION 1962 London I, 29
PROVENANCE Mrs J. van Gogh-Bonger, Amsterdam;
V. W. van Gogh, Laren; Amsterdam, Rijksmuseum Vincent
van Gogh [Vincent van Gogh Foundation, inv nr F 1362]
EDITORS' COMMENT verso not by Vincent van Gogh

F 1363 STUDIES AFTER PLASTER STATUETTES
See under F 1363a, b, c etc

F 1363a recto STUDY AFTER LIVING MODEL: STANDING
MAN AND SITTING WOMAN
verso STUDY AFTER PLASTER STATUETTE:
FEMALE TORSO ON ROUND PEDESTAL,
SEEN FROM THE BACK
EXHIBITION 1962 London I, 30
PROVENANCE Mrs. J. van Gogh-Bonger, Amsterdam;
V. W. van Gogh, Laren; Amsterdam, Rijksmuseum Vincent
van Gogh [Vincent van Gogh Foundation, inv nr F 1363a]

F 1363b STUDY AFTER PLASTER STATUETTE: FEMALE
TORSO ON PEDESTAL, SEEN FROM THE BACK
PROVENANCE Mrs J. van Gogh-Bonger, Amsterdam;
V. W. van Gogh, Laren; Amsterdam, Rijksmuseum Vincent
van Gogh [Vincent van Gogh Foundation, inv nr F 1363b]

F 1363c recto STUDY AFTER PLASTER STATUETTE:
FEMALE TORSO WITH ONE THIGH
verso STUDIES AFTER PLASTER STATUETTE:
TWO STUDIES OF THE SAME NUDE ON A
PEDESTAL, LEFT HAND BEFORE THE EYES
PROVENANCE Mrs J. van Gogh-Bonger, Amsterdam;
V. W. van Gogh, Laren; Amsterdam, Rijksmuseum Vincent
van Gogh [Vincent van Gogh Foundation, inv nr F 1363c]

F 1363d STUDY AFTER PLASTER STATUETTE: MAN
KNEELING
PROVENANCE Mrs J. van Gogh-Bonger, Amsterdam;
V. W. van Gogh, Laren; Amsterdam, Rijksmuseum Vincent
van Gogh [Vincent van Gogh Foundation, inv nr F 1363d]

F 1363e STUDY AFTER PLASTER STATUETTE: FEMALE
TORSO WITH ONE LEG, SEEN FROM THE RIGHT
PROVENANCE Mrs J. van Gogh-Bonger, Amsterdam;
V. W. van Gogh, Laren; Amsterdam, Rijksmuseum Vincent
van Gogh [Vincent van Gogh Foundation, inv nr F 1363e]

F 1363f recto STUDY AFTER PLASTER STATUETTE:
FEMALE TORSO WITH ONE LEG AND TOP HAT
verso STUDY OF BARE LEGS
EXHIBITION 1962 London I, 32
PROVENANCE Mrs J. van Gogh-Bonger, Amsterdam;
V. W. van Gogh, Laren; Amsterdam, Rijksmuseum Vincent
van Gogh [Vincent van Gogh Foundation, inv nr F 1363f]

F 1363g STUDY AFTER PLASTER STATUETTE: FEMALE
TORSO WITH ONE LEG, SEEN FROM THE BACK
PROVENANCE Mrs J. van Gogh-Bonger, Amsterdam;
V. W. van Gogh, Laren; Amsterdam, Rijksmuseum Vincent
van Gogh [Vincent van Gogh Foundation, inv nr F 1363g]

F 1364 STUDIES AFTER LIVING MODELS, STUDIES OF
FEET, etc
See under F 1364-1, 1364-2 etc

F 1364-1 STUDY AFTER LIVING MODEL: MALE NUDE
EXHIBITION 1955 Antwerp I, 214
PROVENANCE Mrs J. van Gogh-Bonger, Amsterdam;
V. W. van Gogh, Laren; Amsterdam, Rijksmuseum Vincent
van Gogh [Vincent van Gogh Foundation, inv nr F 1364-1]

F 1364-2 MALE NUDE
PROVENANCE See under F 1364-1; Amsterdam, Rijksmuseum Vincent van Gogh [Vincent van Gogh Foundation,
inv nr F 1364-2]

F 1364a STUDY AFTER LIVING MODEL: NUDE BOY,
SEEN FROM THE BACK
PROVENANCE Mrs J. van Gogh-Bonger, Amsterdam;
V. W. van Gogh, Laren; Amsterdam, Rijksmuseum Vincent
van Gogh [Vincent van Gogh Foundation, inv nr F 1364a]

F 1364b recto STUDY AFTER LIVING MODEL: STANDING
NUDE BOY
verso STUDY AFTER LIVING MODEL:
NUDE BOY, SEEN FROM THE BACK
PROVENANCE Mrs J. van Gogh-Bonger, Amsterdam;
V. W. van Gogh, Laren; Amsterdam, Rijksmuseum Vincent
van Gogh [Vincent van Gogh Foundation, inv nr F 1364b]

F 1364c STUDY AFTER LIVING MODEL: MALE NUDE
WITH RAISED RIGHT ARM, IN RIGHT PROFILE
PROVENANCE Mrs J. van Gogh-Bonger, Amsterdam;
V. W. van Gogh, Laren; Amsterdam, Rijksmuseum Vincent
van Gogh [Vincent van Gogh Foundation, inv nr F 1364c]

F 1364d recto STUDY AFTER LIVING MODEL: TWO
VIEWS OF A NUDE BOY, SEEN FROM THE
BACK
verso STUDY AFTER LIVING MODEL: STANDING
NUDE BOY, SEEN FROM THE FRONT
PROVENANCE Mrs J. van Gogh-Bonger, Amsterdam;
V. W. van Gogh, Laren; Amsterdam, Rijksmuseum Vincent
van Gogh [Vincent van Gogh Foundation, inv nr F 1364d]

F 1364e STUDY AFTER PLASTER STATUETTE: THE
DISCUS THROWER, SEEN FROM THE BACK
PROVENANCE Mrs J. van Gogh-Bonger, Amsterdam;
V. W. van Gogh, Laren; Amsterdam, Rijksmuseum Vincent
van Gogh [Vincent van Gogh Foundation, inv nr F 1364e]

F 1365 STUDY AFTER LIVING MODEL: STANDING
FEMALE NUDE
To the right SEVEN FIGURES SEATED AT A TABLE
EXHIBITION 1962 London I, 37
PROVENANCE Mrs J. van Gogh-Bonger, Amsterdam;
V. W. van Gogh, Laren; Amsterdam, Rijksmuseum Vincent
van Gogh [Vincent van Gogh Foundation, inv nr F 1365]

F 1366 recto Left half FIVE SKETCHES OF A SITTING
NUDE GIRL
Right half STUDIES AFTER PLASTER
STATUETTES: STANDING MAN WITH ONE
ARM, SEEN FROM THE FRONT
Below FEMALE TORSO WITH ONE LEG, SEEN
FROM THE BACK
verso Left half TWO STUDIES AFTER PLASTER
STATUETTES: FEMALE TORSO WITH ONE
LEG, SEEN FROM THE BACK
Below MAN BOXING, SEEN FROM THE BACK
Right half NUDE GIRL SITTING, SEEN FROM
THE LEFT
EXHIBITIONS 1947-8 London etc, 130; 1948 Bergen, Oslo,
79; 1953 The Hague, 51; Otterlo, Amsterdam, 89; 1953-4
St Louis etc, 58; 1954-5 Bern, 121; 1955 Antwerp I, 212
PROVENANCE Mrs J. van Gogh-Bonger, Amsterdam;
V. W. van Gogh, Laren; Amsterdam, Rijksmuseum Vincent
van Gogh [Vincent van Gogh Foundation, inv nr F 1366]

F 1367 NUDE GIRL SITTING
EXHIBITIONS 1905 Amsterdam, 348; 1914-5 Amsterdam,
139; 1920 New York, 17 [repr]; 1954-5 Bern, 122; 1955
Antwerp I, 213; 1964 Zundert, 16; 1966 Paris, Albi, 29;
1967 Lille, Zurich, 31; 1967-8 Dallas etc, 28; 1968 Liège, 28;
1968-9 London, 61
PROVENANCE Mrs J. van Gogh-Bonger, Amsterdam;
V. W. van Gogh, Laren; Amsterdam, Rijksmuseum Vincent
van Gogh [Vincent van Gogh Foundation, inv nr F 1367]

F 1368 NUDE: YOUNG WOMAN
EXHIBITIONS 1955 Antwerp I, 215; 1960-1 Montreal etc,
117
PROVENANCE Mrs J. van Gogh-Bonger, Amsterdam;
V. W. van Gogh, Laren; Amsterdam, Rijksmuseum Vincent
van Gogh [Vincent van Gogh Foundation, inv nr F 1368]

F 1369 recto SEATED WORKER WITH A CAP: SEEN FROM
THE FRONT
verso SEATED WORKER, WITH BEARD
EXHIBITIONS 1957 Stockholm, 47; 1963 Humlebaek, 84
[verso]; 1964 Washington, New York, 84 [verso]
PROVENANCE Mrs J. van Gogh-Bonger, Amsterdam;
V. W. van Gogh, Laren; Amsterdam, Rijksmuseum Vincent
van Gogh [Vincent van Gogh Foundation, inv nr F 1369]

F 1370 MAN SEATED, FACING LEFT
PROVENANCE Mrs J. van Gogh-Bonger, Amsterdam;
V. W. van Gogh, Laren; Amsterdam, Rijksmuseum Vincent
van Gogh [Vincent van Gogh Foundation, inv nr F 1370]

F 1371 recto STUDY AFTER PLASTER STATUETTE:
FEMALE TORSO ON PEDESTAL, THREE
QUARTERS TO THE RIGHT
verso VENUS DE MILO [first sketch for a study]
PROVENANCE Mrs J. van Gogh-Bonger, Amsterdam;
V. W.van Gogh, Laren; Amsterdam, Rijksmuseum Vincent
van Gogh [Vincent van Gogh Foundation, inv nr F 1371]

F 1372 recto HEAD OF A MAN WITH HAT AND PIPE
verso HEAD OF A MAN: FULL FACE
EXHIBITION 1955 Antwerp I, 144, 145 [verso]
PROVENANCE Mrs J. van Gogh-Bonger, Amsterdam;
V. W. van Gogh, Laren; Amsterdam, Rijksmuseum Vincent
van Gogh [Vincent van Gogh Foundation, inv nr F 1372]

F 1373 recto OWL SEEN IN PROFILE
verso OWL SEEN FROM THE FRONT
EXHIBITION 1914-5 Amsterdam, 137
PROVENANCE Mrs J. van Gogh-Bonger, Amsterdam;
V. W. van Gogh, Laren; Amsterdam, Rijksmuseum Vincent
van Gogh [Vincent van Gogh Foundation, inv nr F 1373]

F 1374 STUDY OF HOUSES
PROVENANCE Mrs J. van Gogh-Bonger, Amsterdam; V. W. van Gogh, Laren; Amsterdam, Rijksmuseum Vincent van Gogh [Vincent van Gogh Foundation, inv nr F 1374]

F 1375 STUDIES: FIGURE, LANDSCAPE AND OTHER SKETCHES
PROVENANCE Mrs J. van Gogh-Bonger, Amsterdam; V. W. van Gogh, Laren; Amsterdam, Rijksmuseum Vincent van Gogh [Vincent van Gogh Foundation, inv nr F 1375]

F 1376 NUDE WOMAN SQUATTING
EXHIBITION 1962 London 1, 33
PROVENANCE Mrs J. van Gogh-Bonger, Amsterdam; V. W. van Gogh, Laren; Amsterdam, Rijksmuseum Vincent van Gogh [Vincent van Gogh Foundation, inv nr F 1376]

F 1377 PEOPLE WALKING IN A WOOD
EXHIBITION 1962 London 1, 45
PROVENANCE Mrs J. van Gogh-Bonger, Amsterdam; V. W. van Gogh, Laren; Amsterdam, Rijksmuseum Vincent van Gogh [Vincent van Gogh Foundation, inv nr F 1377]

F 1378 recto TWO SELF PORTRAITS [with fragments of a third]
verso SKETCH OF A SITTING WOMAN
EXHIBITIONS 1961-2 Baltimore etc, 108; 1963 Humlebaek, 85; 1964 Washington, New York, 85; 1966 Paris, Albi, 30; 1967 Lille, Zurich, 32; 1967-8 Dallas etc, 29; 1968 Liège, 29; 1968-9 London, 92; 1969 Humlebaek, 14
PROVENANCE Mrs J. van Gogh-Bonger, Amsterdam; V. W. van Gogh, Laren; Amsterdam, Rijksmuseum Vincent van Gogh [Vincent van Gogh Foundation, inv nr F 1378]

F 1379 SELF PORTRAIT
EXHIBITIONS 1964 Zundert, 19; 1966 Paris, Albi, 31; 1967 Lille, Zurich, 33; 1967-8 Dallas etc, 30; 1968 Liège, 30; 1968-9 London, 91
PROVENANCE Mrs J. van Gogh-Bonger, Amsterdam; V. W. van Gogh, Laren; Amsterdam, Rijksmuseum Vincent van Gogh [Vincent van Gogh Foundation, inv nr F 1379]

F 1380 recto THE STREET
verso MAN ON A BENCH; SKETCH OF A HORSE
EXHIBITION 1962 London 1, 41
PROVENANCE Mrs J. van Gogh-Bonger, Amsterdam; V. W. van Gogh, Laren; Amsterdam, Rijksmuseum Vincent van Gogh [Vincent van Gogh Foundation, inv nr F 1380]

F 1381 recto A RAINY DAY
verso SKETCH OF A FEMALE FIGURE
PROVENANCE Mrs J. van Gogh-Bonger, Amsterdam; V. W. van Gogh, Laren; Amsterdam, Rijksmuseum Vincent van Gogh [Vincent van Gogh Foundation, inv nr F 1381]

F 1382 THE FOREST BROOK
PROVENANCE Mrs J. van Gogh-Bonger, Amsterdam; V. W. van Gogh, Laren; Amsterdam, Rijksmuseum Vincent van Gogh [Vincent van Gogh Foundation, inv nr F 1382]

F 1383 THE TERRACE OF THE TUILERIES
PROVENANCE Mrs J. van Gogh-Bonger, Amsterdam; V. W. van Gogh, Laren; Amsterdam, Rijksmuseum Vincent van Gogh [Vincent van Gogh Foundation, inv nr F 1383]

F 1384 THE GARDEN OF THE TUILERIES
PROVENANCE Mrs J. van Gogh-Bonger, Amsterdam; V. W. van Gogh, Laren; Amsterdam, Rijksmuseum Vincent van Gogh [Vincent van Gogh Foundation, inv nr F 1384]

F 1385 THE BANKS OF THE SEINE AT PARIS
EXHIBITION 1962 London 1, 42 [erroneously mentioned as F 1354]
PROVENANCE Mrs J. van Gogh-Bonger, Amsterdam; V. W. van Gogh, Laren; Amsterdam, Rijksmuseum Vincent van Gogh [Vincent van Gogh Foundation, inv nr F 1385]

F 1386 PARK IN PARIS
PROVENANCE Mrs J. van Gogh-Bonger, Amsterdam; V. W. van Gogh, Laren; Amsterdam, Rijksmuseum Vincent van Gogh [Vincent van Gogh Foundation, inv nr F 1386]

F 1387 VIEW OF PARIS ROOFTOPS, WITH THE PANTHEON
EXHIBITIONS 1945 Amsterdam, no cat nr; 1946 Stockholm etc, 21; 1954-5 Bern, 124; 1955 Antwerp 1, 227; 1957 Marseilles, 39; 1958-9 San Francisco etc, 113; 1960 Enschede, 29; 1966 Paris, Albi, 32; 1967 Lille, Zurich, 34; 1967-8 Dallas etc, 31; 1968 Liège, 31; 1968-9 London, 64
PROVENANCE Mrs J. van Gogh-Bonger, Amsterdam; V. W. van Gogh, Laren; Amsterdam, Rijksmuseum Vincent van Gogh [Vincent van Gogh Foundation, inv nr F 1387]

F 1388 VIEW OF PARIS FROM THE HILL OF MONTMARTRE
EXHIBITIONS 1905 Amsterdam, 467; 1914-5 Amsterdam, 134; 1954-5 Bern, 125; 1955 Antwerp 1, 228; 1957 Stockholm, 46; 1965-6 Stockholm, Göteborg, 77; 1967 Wolfsburg, 98
PROVENANCE Mrs J. van Gogh-Bonger, Amsterdam; V. W. van Gogh, Laren; Amsterdam, Rijksmuseum Vincent van Gogh [Vincent van Gogh Foundation, inv nr F 1388]

F 1389 VIEW OF PARIS WITH NOTRE DAME AND TOUR SAINT JACQUES
EXHIBITION 1926 London 3, 34
PROVENANCE Mrs J. van Gogh-Bonger, Amsterdam; V. W. van Gogh, Laren; V. Rienaecker, London; Present owner unknown

F 1390 VIEW ON PARIS WITH THE OPERA
EXHIBITIONS 1905 Amsterdam, 352; 1914-5 Amsterdam, 128; 1961-2 Baltimore etc, 109; 1965-6 Stockholm, Göteborg, 78; 1967 Wolfsburg, 99; 1967-8 Dallas etc, 32; 1968 Liège, 32; 1968-9 London, 65
PROVENANCE Mrs J. van Gogh-Bonger, Amsterdam; V. W. van Gogh, Laren; Amsterdam, Rijksmuseum Vincent van Gogh [Vincent van Gogh Foundation, inv nr F 1390]

F 1391 VIEW FROM VINCENT'S ROOM IN THE RUE LEPIC
EXHIBITIONS 1905 Amsterdam, 346; 1914-5 Amsterdam, 131; 1923 Utrecht, Rotterdam, 80; 1927-8 Berlin etc, 54; 1945 Amsterdam, no cat nr; 1946-7 Liège etc, 40; 1947 Paris 1, 40; Geneva, 41; 1948 Bergen, Oslo, 80; 1957 Stockholm, 53; 1958-9 San Francisco etc, 114; 1960 Enschede, 30; 1963 Humlebaek, 86; 1964 Washington, New York, 86; 1965 Charleroi, Ghent, 55; 1966 Paris, Albi, 33; 1967 Lille, Zurich, 35; Glasgow, 43
PROVENANCE Mrs J. van Gogh-Bonger, Amsterdam; V. W. van Gogh, Laren; Amsterdam, Rijksmuseum Vincent van Gogh [Vincent van Gogh Foundation, inv nr F 1391]

F 1392 THE WINDOW AT THE RESTAURANT CHEZ BATAILLE
EXHIBITIONS 1905 Amsterdam, 347; 1914-5 Amsterdam, 129; 1926 Munich, 2101; 1927-8 Berlin etc, 55; 1932 Manchester, 63; 1945 Amsterdam, no cat nr; 1946 Stockholm etc, 31; 1946-7 Liège etc, 41; 1947 Paris 1, 41; Basle, 148; Geneva, 42; 1947-8 London etc, 132; 1948 Bergen, Oslo, 81; 1953 The Hague, 52; Otterlo, Amsterdam, 91; 1953-4 St Louis etc, 86; 1954-5 Bern, 126; 1955 Antwerp 1, 230; 1957 Stockholm, 52; 1958-9 San Francisco etc, 115; 1960 Enschede, 31; 1960-1 Montreal etc, 118; 1961-2 Baltimore etc, 110; 1964 Zundert, 20; 1966 Paris, Albi, 34; 1967 Lille, Zurich, 36; 1967-8 Dallas etc, 33; 1968 Liège, 33; 1968-9 London, 75
PROVENANCE Mrs J. van Gogh-Bonger, Amsterdam; V. W. van Gogh, Laren; Amsterdam, Rijksmuseum Vincent van Gogh [Vincent van Gogh Foundation, inv nr F 1392]

F 1393 THE BOULEVARD DE CLICHY
EXHIBITIONS 1920 New York, 6; 1927-8 Berlin etc, 49; 1945 Amsterdam, no cat nr; 1946 Stockholm etc, 36; 1946-7 Liège etc, 42; 1947 Geneva, 43; Paris 1, 42; 1947-8 London etc, 133; 1948 Bergen, Oslo, 82; 1949-50 New York, Chicago, 62; 1954-5 Bern, 127; 1955 Antwerp 1, 234; 1955-6 Liverpool etc, 102; 1957 Stockholm, 54; 1960-1 Montreal etc, 119; 1961-2 Baltimore etc, 111; 1963 Humlebaek, 87; 1964 Washington, New York, 87; 1965-6 Stockholm, Göteborg, 80; 1967 Wolfsburg, 100; 1967-8 Dallas etc, 34; 1968 Liège, 34; 1968-9 London, 69
PROVENANCE Mrs J. van Gogh-Bonger, Amsterdam; V. W. van Gogh, Laren; Amsterdam, Rijksmuseum Vincent van Gogh [Vincent van Gogh Foundation, inv nr F 1393]

F 1394 A VIEW OF THE HILL OF MONTMARTRE
PROVENANCE Mrs J. van Gogh-Bonger, Amsterdam; V. W. van Gogh, Laren; Amsterdam, Rijksmuseum Vincent van Gogh [Vincent van Gogh Foundation, inv nr F 1394]

F 1395 THE MOULIN DE LA GALETTE
EXHIBITIONS 1955 Antwerp 1, 232; 1957 Stockholm, 49
PROVENANCE Mrs J. van Gogh-Bonger, Amsterdam; V. W. van Gogh, Laren; Amsterdam, Rijksmuseum Vincent van Gogh [Vincent van Gogh Foundation, inv nr F 1395]

F 1396 THE MOULIN DE LA GALETTE
EXHIBITIONS 1905 Amsterdam, 348; 1914-5 Amsterdam, 130; 1946-7 Liège etc, 43; 1947 Geneva, 44; Paris 1, 43; 1947-8 London etc, 134; 1948 Bergen, Oslo, 83; 1954-5 Bern, 128; 1965-6 Stockholm, Göteborg; 1967 Wolfsburg, 101
PROVENANCE Mrs J. van Gogh-Bonger, Amsterdam; V. W. van Gogh, Laren; Amsterdam, Rijksmuseum Vincent van Gogh [Vincent van Gogh Foundation, inv nr F 1396]

F 1396a THE MOULIN DE LA GALETTE
EXHIBITIONS 1917 Amsterdam, 6; 1942 Baltimore, Worcester, 3; 1951 Houston, 2
PROVENANCE Mrs J. van Gogh-Bonger, Amsterdam; H. Stinnes, Cologne; Mrs J. van Gogh-Bonger, Amsterdam; J. H. de Bois Art Gallery, Haarlem [R 1917]; Syracuse, N.Y., Miss E. Hudson [acquired 1934; R 1951]

F 1397 THE MOULIN DE LA GALETTE
EXHIBITIONS 1905 Amsterdam, 354; 1914-5 Amsterdam, 136; 1923 Utrecht, Rotterdam, 10; 1956 Munich, 105; 1964 Laren, 29; 1966 Laren, 92
PROVENANCE Mrs J. van Gogh-Bonger, Amsterdam; V. W. van Gogh, Laren; Buffa Art Gallery, Amsterdam; H. Nijgh, Rotterdam [cat collection H. Nijgh 1933, nr 86]; Mrs P. de Boer, Amsterdam [R 1956]; Amsterdam, P. and N. de Boer Foundation

F 1398 VIEW FROM MONTMARTRE
EXHIBITIONS 1905 Amsterdam, 345; 1914-5 Amsterdam, 133; 1923 Utrecht, Rotterdam, 5; 1926 Munich, 2100; 1927-8 Berlin etc, 48; 1955 Antwerp 1, 229; 1957 Stockholm, 50; 1964 Zundert, 21; 1966 Paris, Albi, 35; 1967 Lille, Zurich, 37
PROVENANCE Mrs J. van Gogh-Bonger, Amsterdam [R 1905]; V. W. van Gogh, Laren; Amsterdam, Rijksmuseum Vincent van Gogh [Vincent van Gogh Foundation, inv nr F 1398]

F 1399 THE GRAVEYARD
EXHIBITIONS 1905 Amsterdam, 282; 1936 Haarlem, 16; 1958 Vienna, 68a; 1961 Munich, 52
PROVENANCE Mrs J. van Gogh-Bonger, Amsterdam; J. H. de Bois Art Gallery, Haarlem [R 1935-6]; Private collection, Vienna; Vienna, Albertina [acquired 1937], inv nr 27.791

F 1399a THE GRAVEYARD
EXHIBITIONS 1905 Amsterdam, 283; 1935 Haarlem, 12; 1941 Haarlem, 8; 1947 Basle, 146; 1949-50 New York, Chicago, 63; 1952 Milan, 63; 1953-4 St Louis etc, 85; 1956 Nuremberg, 58; Munich, 95; 1957 Essen, 232; 1958 Vienna, 68; Tokyo, Kyoto, 83; 1959 São Paulo, 1; 1961 Munich, 51; 1962 Warsaw, 53; 1963 Tel Aviv, Haifa, 55
PROVENANCE Mrs J. van Gogh-Bonger, Amsterdam [R 1905]; J. H. de Bois Art Gallery, Haarlem; M. J. van Tussenbroek, Haarlem; Huinck and Scherjon Art Gallery, Amsterdam [R 1942]; Otterlo, Rijksmuseum Kröller-Müller, inv nr 1121-42, cat van Gogh 1970, nr 193

F 1400 SUBURB OF PARIS [LA BARRIÈRE]
EXHIBITIONS 1905 Amsterdam, 350; 1914-5 Amsterdam, 127; 1923 Utrecht, Rotterdam, 81; 1927-8 Berlin etc, 51; 1937 Paris, 67; 1945 Amsterdam, no cat nr; 1946-7 Liège etc, 44; 1947 Paris 1, 44; Geneva, 45; 1949-50 New York, Chicago, 64; 1953 The Hague, 53; Otterlo, Amsterdam, 92; 1953-4 St Louis etc, 89; 1954-5 Bern, 129; 1955 Antwerp 1, 236; 1955-6 Liverpool etc, 104; 1957 Marseilles, 41; Stockholm, 55; 1960-1 Montreal etc, 121; 1963 Humlebaek, 88; Paris, 30; 1964 Washington, New York, 88; 1965-6 Stockholm, Göteborg, 82; 1967 Wolfsburg, 102
PROVENANCE Mrs J. van Gogh-Bonger, Amsterdam; V. W. van Gogh, Laren; Amsterdam, Rijksmuseum Vincent van Gogh [Vincent van Gogh Foundation, inv nr F 1400]

F 1401 LA BARRIÈRE WITH HORSE-TRAMWAY
EXHIBITIONS 1923 Utrecht, Rotterdam, 28; 1926 Munich, 2103; 1927-8 Berlin etc, 47; 1932 Manchester, 64; 1945 Amsterdam, no cat nr; 1946-7 Liège etc, 45; 1947 Paris 1, 46; Geneva, 47; 1947-8 London etc, 135; 1948 Bergen, Oslo, 84; 1953 The Hague, 54; Otterlo, Amsterdam, 93; 1953-4 St Louis etc, 90; 1954-5 Bern, 130; 1955 Antwerp 1, 237; 1957 Stockholm, 56; 1958-9 San Francisco etc, 116; 1959-60 Utrecht, 78; 1960 Enschede, 32; 1961-2 Baltimore etc, 112; 1963 Humlebaek, 89; 1964 Washington, New York, 89; 1965 Charleroi, Ghent, 56; 1966 Paris, Albi, 36; 1967 Lille, Zurich, 38; 1967-8 Dallas etc, 35; 1968 Liège, 35; 1968-9 London, 85; 1969 Humlebaek, 15
PROVENANCE Mrs J. van Gogh-Bonger, Amsterdam; V. W. van Gogh, Laren; Amsterdam, Rijksmuseum Vincent van Gogh [Vincent van Gogh Foundation, inv nr F 1401]

F 1402 THE RAMPARTS OF PARIS
PROVENANCE Artz and De Bois Art Gallery, The Hague; J. Th. Schall, Berlin [acquired 1912]; Sale collection Schall a o, Berlin [Cassirer] 26 October 1926, 8 [repr]; W. C. Regendanz; Sale collection W. C. Regendanz a o, London [Christie] 16 July 1948, 45; Lefèvre Galleries, London [1948]; London, Private collection [R 1969]

F 1403 THE RAMPARTS OF PARIS WITH HOUSES
EXHIBITIONS 1905 Amsterdam, 351; 1914-5 Amsterdam, 126; 1923 Utrecht, Rotterdam, 82; 1926 London 3, 38; 1952 London, 27; 1960 London 5, 103; 1962 London 5, 243; 1967 Glasgow, 44
PROVENANCE Mrs J. van Gogh-Bonger, Amsterdam; V. W. van Gogh, Laren; Sir Thomas Barlow; Manchester, The Whitworth Institute, Whitworth Art Gallery [acquired 1927; gift of Sir Thomas Barlow]

F 1404 NUDE WOMAN RECLINING
EXHIBITION 1957 Stockholm, 51
PROVENANCE Mrs J. van Gogh-Bonger, Amsterdam; V. W. van Gogh, Laren; Amsterdam, Rijksmuseum Vincent van Gogh [Vincent van Gogh Foundation, inv nr F 1404]

F 1405 THE BOULEVARD DE CLICHY [?] IN PARIS
EXHIBITIONS 1905 Amsterdam, 349; 1914-5 Amsterdam, 135; 1962 London 1, 46
PROVENANCE Mrs J. van Gogh-Bonger, Amsterdam; V. W. van Gogh, Laren; Amsterdam, Rijksmuseum Vincent van Gogh [Vincent van Gogh Foundation, inv nr F 1405]

F 1406 GARDEN ENTRANCE ON A SUNNY DAY
EXHIBITIONS 1905 Amsterdam, 364; 1923 Utrecht, Rotterdam, 30; 1927-8 Berlin etc, 50; 1945 Amsterdam, no cat nr; 1946-7 Liège etc, 46; 1947 Paris 1, 47; Geneva, 48; 1947-8 London etc, 136; 1948 Bergen, Oslo, 85; 1953 The

Hague, 55; Otterlo, Amsterdam, 97; 1953-4 St Louis etc, 92; 1954-5 Bern, 131; 1955 Antwerp 1, 238; 1955-6 Liverpool etc, 105; 1957 Stockholm, 58; 1958-9 San Francisco etc, 118; 1959-60 Utrecht, 79; 1960 Enschede, 33; 1960-1 Montreal etc, 122; 1961-2 Baltimore etc, 113; 1963 Humlebaek, 90; 1964 Washington, New York, 90; 1965 Charleroi, Ghent, 57; 1967 Lille, Zurich, 39; 1967-8 Dallas etc, 36; 1968 Liège, 36; 1968-9 London, 84; 1969 Humlebaek, 16
PROVENANCE Mrs J. van Gogh-Bonger, Amsterdam; V.W. van Gogh, Laren; Amsterdam, Rijksmuseum Vincent van Gogh [Vincent van Gogh Foundation, inv nr F 1406]

F1407 LA GUINGUETTE
EXHIBITIONS 1927-8 Berlin etc, 45; 1945 Amsterdam, no cat nr; 1946 Stockholm etc, 23; 1946-7 Liège etc, 47; 1947 Paris 1, 48; Geneva, 49; 1947-8 London etc, 137; 1948 Bergen, Oslo, 86; 1949-50 New York, Chicago, 65; 1951 Lyons etc, 87; 1953 The Hague, 56; Otterlo, Amsterdam, 90; 1953-4 St Louis etc, 84; 1955 Antwerp 1, 231; 1955-6 Liverpool etc, 101; 1957 Marseilles, 48; Liège, 37; 1958-9 San Francisco etc, 117; 1959-60 Utrecht, 76; 1960 Enschede, 34; 1961-2 Baltimore etc, 114; 1963 Sheffield, 18; Humlebaek, 91; 1964 Washington, New York, 91; 1965 Charleroi, Ghent, 58; 1966 Paris, Albi, 38; 1967 Lille, Zurich, 40; 1967-8 Dallas etc, 37; 1968-9 London, 59; 1969 Humlebaek, 17
PROVENANCE Mrs J. van Gogh-Bonger, Amsterdam; V.W. van Gogh, Laren; Amsterdam, Rijksmuseum Vincent van Gogh [Vincent van Gogh Foundation, inv nr F 1407]

F1408 THE RESTAURANT DE LA SIRÈNE AT ASNIÈRES
EXHIBITIONS 1914-5 Amsterdam, 132; 1927-8 Berlin etc, 53; 1945 Amsterdam, no cat nr; 1946 Stockholm etc, 38; 1953 The Hague, 57; Otterlo, Amsterdam, 94; 1953-4 St Louis etc, 87; 1954-5 Bern, 132; 1955 Antwerp 1, 233; 1958-9 San Francisco etc, 119; 1960 Enschede, 35; 1965-6 Stockholm, Göteborg, 81
PROVENANCE Mrs J. van Gogh-Bonger, Amsterdam; V.W. van Gogh, Laren; Amsterdam, Rijksmuseum Vincent van Gogh [Vincent van Gogh Foundation, inv nr F 1408]

F1409 SAILING BOAT AT ASNIÈRES
EXHIBITIONS 1914-5 Amsterdam, 161; 1927-8 Berlin etc, 52; 1953 The Hague, 58; Otterlo, Amsterdam, 96; 1953-4 St Louis etc, 88; 1954-5 Bern, 133; 1955 Antwerp 1, 235; 1955-6 Liverpool etc, 103; 1957 Marseilles, 40; Stockholm, 57; 1958-9 San Francisco etc, 120; 1959-60 Utrecht, 77; 1960 Enschede, 36; 1960-1 Montreal etc, 120; 1961-2 Baltimore etc, 115; 1963 Humlebaek, 92; 1965 Charleroi, Ghent, 59; 1966 Paris, Albi, 39; 1967 Lille, Zurich, 41; 1967-8 Dallas etc, 38; 1968 Liège, 9; 1968-9 London, 81
PROVENANCE Mrs J. van Gogh-Bonger, Amsterdam; V.W. van Gogh, Laren; Amsterdam, Rijksmuseum Vincent van Gogh [Vincent van Gogh Foundation, inv nr F 1409]

F1410 OUTSKIRTS OF PARIS NEAR MONTMARTRE
EXHIBITIONS 1930 Amsterdam, 113; 1937 Paris, 65; 1941 New York, 151; 1946-7 Liège etc, 48; 1947 Paris 1, 49; Geneva, 50; Basle, 147; 1953 The Hague, 59; Otterlo, Amsterdam, 95; 1953-4 St Louis etc, 91; 1956 Munich, 96; 1957 Essen, 233; 1959 Recklinghausen, 113; 1960 Paris, 102; 1961 Munich, 53; 1963 Tel Aviv, Haifa, 56
PROVENANCE Artz and De Bois Art Gallery, The Hague [until 1912]; Amsterdam, Stedelijk Museum [acquired 1912; gift of Vereniging van Hedendaagse Kunst]

F1411 SHELTER ON THE HILL OF MONTMARTRE, WITH SUNFLOWERS
EXHIBITIONS 1905 Amsterdam, 353; 1914-5 Amsterdam, 153; 1923 Utrecht, Rotterdam, 24; 1927-8 Berlin etc, 46; 1945 Amsterdam, no cat nr; 1946 Stockholm etc, 34; 1946-7 Liège etc, 49; 1947 Paris 1, 50; Geneva, 51; 1947-8 London etc, 138; 1948 Bergen, Oslo, 87; 1955 Antwerp 1, 239; 1958-9 Washington etc, 146; 1963 Paris, 33; 1966 Paris, Albi, 40; 1967 Lille, Zurich, 42; 1967-8 Dallas etc, 39; 1968 Liège, 39; 1968-9 London, 86
PROVENANCE Mrs J. van Gogh-Bonger, Amsterdam [R 1905]; V.W. van Gogh, Laren; Amsterdam, Rijksmuseum Vincent van Gogh [Vincent van Gogh Foundation, inv nr F 1411]

F1412 LE PÈRE TANGUY
EXHIBITIONS 1914-5 Amsterdam, 138; 1954-5 Bern, 134; 1955 Antwerp 1, 240; 1957 Stockholm, 57; 1962 London 1, 48
PROVENANCE Mrs J. van Gogh-Bonger, Amsterdam; V.W. van Gogh, Laren; Amsterdam, Rijksmuseum Vincent van Gogh [Vincent van Gogh Foundation, inv nr F 1412]

ARLES PERIOD

F1413 VINCENT'S HOUSE AT ARLES
EXHIBITIONS 1905 Amsterdam, 474; 1914-5 Amsterdam, 181; 1937 Paris, 73; 1945 Amsterdam, no cat nr; 1946 Stockholm etc, 70; 1946-7 Liège etc, 84; 1947 Paris 1, 85; Geneva, 85; 1947-8 London etc, 141; 1948 Bergen, Oslo, 89; 1949-50 New York, Chicago, 98; 1953 The Hague, 99; Otterlo, Amsterdam, 119; 1954-5 Bern, 135; 1955 Antwerp 1, 274; 1955-6 Liverpool etc, 116; 1957 Marseilles, 56; Stockholm, 62; 1958-9 San Francisco etc, 121; 1959-60 Utrecht, 80; 1960 Enschede, 37; 1961 Arles; 1962 London 1, 53; 1963 Paris, 32; Humlebaek, 99; 1964 Washington, New York, 99; 1966 Paris, Albi, 41; 1967 Zurich, Lille, 43; 1967-8 Dallas etc, 40; 1968 Liège, 40; 1968-9 London, 127; 1969 Humlebaek, 18
PROVENANCE Mrs J. van Gogh-Bonger, Amsterdam [R 1905]; V.W. van Gogh, Laren; Amsterdam, Rijksmuseum Vincent van Gogh [Vincent van Gogh Foundation, inv nr F 1413]

F1414 ORCHARD IN THE PROVENCE
EXHIBITIONS 1905 Amsterdam, 397; 1914-5 Amsterdam, 174; 1923 Utrecht, Rotterdam, 31; 1925 The Hague, 78; 1927-8 Berlin etc, 58; 1932 Manchester, 60; 1937 Paris, 68; 1945 Amsterdam, no cat nr; 1946 Stockholm etc, 48; 1946-7 Liège etc, 82; 1947 Paris 1, 83; Geneva, 83; 1947-8 London etc, 140; 1948 Bergen, Oslo, 90; 1949-50 New York, Chicago, 96; 1953 The Hague, 98; Otterlo, Amsterdam, 118; 1953-4 St Louis etc, 116; 1955 Antwerp 1, 275; 1955-6 Liverpool etc, 111; 1957 Marseilles, 57; Stockholm, 60; 1958-9 San Francisco etc, 122; 1959-60 Utrecht, 81; 1960 Enschede, 38; 1961 Arles; 1961-2 Baltimore etc, 116; 1962-3 Pittsburgh etc; 1963 Sheffield, 19; Humlebaek, 94; 1964 Washington, New York, 94; 1965 Charleroi, Ghent, 61; 1966 Paris, Albi, 42; 1967 Lille, Zurich, 44; 1967-8 Dallas etc, 41; 1968 Liège, 41; 1968-9 London, 107; 1969 Humlebaek, 19
PROVENANCE Mrs J. van Gogh-Bonger, Amsterdam; V.W. van Gogh, Laren; Amsterdam, Rijksmuseum Vincent van Gogh [Vincent van Gogh Foundation, inv nr F 1414]

F1415 THE FARMHOUSE IN THE WHEATFIELD
EXHIBITIONS 1905 Amsterdam, 473; 1914-5 Amsterdam, 166; 1923 Utrecht, Rotterdam, 63; 1925 The Hague, 64; 1927-8 Berlin etc, 71; 1932 Manchester, 67; 1953 The Hague, 100; Otterlo, Amsterdam, 120; 1953-4 St Louis etc, 117; 1961 Scarborough; 1966 Paris, Albi, 43; 1967 Lille, Zurich, 45; 1967-8 Dallas etc, 42; 1968 Liège, 42; 1968-9 London, 109; 1969 Humlebaek, 20
PROVENANCE Mrs J. van Gogh-Bonger, Amsterdam [R 1905]; V.W. van Gogh, Laren; Amsterdam, Rijksmuseum Vincent van Gogh [Vincent van Gogh Foundation, inv nr F 1415]

F1416 recto VIEW OF ARLES
verso DRAWBRIDGE IN ARLES
EXHIBITIONS 1905 Amsterdam, 386; 1906 Berlin, 77; 1921 Berlin; 1927-8 Berlin etc, not mentioned in catalogue; 1934 Cambridge, 36; 1935 Buffalo, 127; 1935-6 New York etc, 107; 1939 Boston, 168; 1943 New York 2, 70; 1944 New York 1, p 91; 1948 Cleveland, 41; 1955 New York 2, 97
PROVENANCE Mrs J. van Gogh-Bonger, Amsterdam [R 1905]; Paul Cassirer Art Gallery, Berlin; H. Freudenberg, Nikolassee; Mrs Murray S. Danforth, Providence, Rhode Island [R 1935]; Collection Danforth, Newport, Rhode Island; Providence, Rhode Island, Museum of Art, Rhode Island School of Design, inv nr 42.212

F1417 THE RUINS OF MONTMAJOUR
EXHIBITIONS 1905 Amsterdam, 405; 1914 Berlin, 56; 1914-5 Amsterdam, 163; 1923 Utrecht, Rotterdam, 27; 1924 Basle, 89; Zurich, 89; Stuttgart, 11; 1925 The Hague, 69; 1926 Munich, 2109; 1954-5 Bern, 136; 1955 Antwerp 1, 276; 1960-1 Montreal etc, 123
PROVENANCE Mrs J. van Gogh-Bonger, Amsterdam [R 1905]; V.W. van Gogh, Laren; Amsterdam, Rijksmuseum Vincent van Gogh [Vincent van Gogh Foundation, inv nr F 1417]

F1418 VIEW OF LA CRAU
PROVENANCE Mrs J. van Gogh-Bonger, Amsterdam; Mrs R. Spanjaard-Spanjaard, The Hague; Rosengart Art Gallery, Lucerne; San Francisco, Nicol Smith

F1419 VIEW OF LA CRAU
EXHIBITIONS 1957 Essen, 275; 1958 Amsterdam 1, 244
PROVENANCE Karl Osthaus, Hagen; Folkwang Museum, Hagen [until 1922]; Essen, Folkwang Museum [acquired 1922], cat 1929, nr 436

F1420 LA CRAU SEEN FROM MONTMAJOUR
EXHIBITIONS 1898 The Hague [repr]; 1905 Amsterdam, 413; 1906 Berlin; 1915 Amsterdam, 26; 1924 Basle, 88; Zurich, 88; Stuttgart, 12; 1925 The Hague, 71; 1926 Munich, 2108; London 3, 22; 1927-8 Berlin etc, 60; 1937 Paris, 72; 1945 Amsterdam, no cat nr; 1946 Stockholm etc, 51; 1946-7 Liège etc, 85; 1947 Paris 1, 86; Geneva, 86; Basle, 150; 1947-8 London etc, 142; 1948 Bergen, Oslo, 91; 1949-50 New York, Chicago, 97; 1951 Lyons etc, 88; 1953 The Hague, 101; Otterlo, Amsterdam, 122; 1953-4 St Louis etc, 119; 1955 Antwerp 1, 277; 1955-6 Liverpool etc, 113; 1957 Los Angeles, 39; Marseilles, 58; Stockholm, 63; 1958-9 San Francisco etc, 124; 1959 Aix-en-Provence, 26; 1959-60 Utrecht; 1960 Enschede, 39; 1960-1 Montreal etc, 124; 1961 Arles; 1961-2 Baltimore etc, 117; 1962-3 Pittsburgh etc; 1964 Zundert, 22; 1966 Paris, Albi, 44; 1967 Lille, Zurich, 46; 1967-8 Dallas etc, 43; 1968 Liège, 43; 1968-9 London, 115; 1969 Humlebaek, 21
PROVENANCE Mrs J. van Gogh-Bonger, Amsterdam [R 1905]; V.W. van Gogh, Laren; Amsterdam, Rijksmuseum Vincent van Gogh [Vincent van Gogh Foundation, inv nr F 1420]

F1421 THE PARK OPPOSITE THE YELLOW HOUSE
EXHIBITIONS 1905 Amsterdam, 400; 1914-5 Amsterdam, 158; 1923 Utrecht, Rotterdam, 50; 1927-8 Berlin etc, 77; 1932 Manchester, 59; 1946-7 Liège etc, 87; 1947 Paris 1, 88; Geneva, 88; 1947-8 London etc, 143; 1948 Bergen, Oslo, 92; 1955 Antwerp 1, 278; 1955-6 Liverpool etc, 112; 1957 Stockholm, 64; 1958-9 San Francisco etc, 125; 1960 Enschede, 41; 1961 Arles; 1961-2 Baltimore etc, 119; 1962-3 Pittsburgh etc; 1963-4 Amsterdam; 1964 Zundert, 23; 1965-6 Stockholm, Göteborg, 83; 1967 Wolfsburg, 104; 1968-9 London, 128
PROVENANCE Mrs J. van Gogh-Bonger, Amsterdam [R 1905]; V.W. van Gogh, Laren; Amsterdam, Rijksmuseum Vincent van Gogh [Vincent van Gogh Foundation, inv nr F 1421]

F1422 BRETON WOMEN IN THE PLAIN OF PONT-AVEN [after Emile Bernard]
EXHIBITIONS 1927 Paris; 1930 Amsterdam, 114
PROVENANCE Druet Art Gallery, Paris [R 1905]; Paul Rosenberg Art Gallery, Paris [R 1909]; P. Molinard, Paris [before 1928]; A. Gold Art Gallery, Berlin [R 1930]; Milan, Civica Galleria d'Arte Moderna di Milano [Grassi collection]

F1423 THE RUINS OF MONTMAJOUR
EXHIBITIONS 1905 Amsterdam, 416; 1914-5 Amsterdam, 173; 1920 New York, 11; 1945 Amsterdam, no cat nr; 1958 Amsterdam 1, 250; 1959 Aix-en-Provence, 27; 1965-6 Stockholm, Göteborg, 84
PROVENANCE Mrs J. van Gogh-Bonger, Amsterdam [R 1905]; V.W. van Gogh, Laren; Amsterdam, Rijksmuseum Vincent van Gogh [Vincent van Gogh Foundation, inv nr F 1423]

F1424 LANDSCAPE NEAR MONTMAJOUR
EXHIBITIONS 1898 The Hague [repr]; 1945 Basle, 21; 1948-9 Cambridge, 68; 1968-9 London, 116
PROVENANCE Mrs H. Mauve-Carbentus; Anton Mauve, Laren; Rudolf Mauve, Scheveningen; d'Audretsch Art Gallery, The Hague; A. van Hoboken, Vienna; Private collection, Lausanne, Ascona [R 1945]; César Mange de Hauke, Paris, New York [R 1948]; London, The British Museum [The César Mange de Hauke bequest], inv nr 1968-2-10-20, cat C. M. de Hauke bequest 1968, nr 14

F1425 HAYRICKS
PROVENANCE G. Fayet, Igny; E. Druet Art Gallery, Paris; Berlin, M. Meirowsky [acquired 1913]

F1426 HAYRICKS
EXHIBITION 1959 Budapest, 115
PROVENANCE Paul Majovsky, Budapest; Budapest, Museum of Fine Arts, inv nr Ltsz 1935-2792

F1427 HAYRICKS
EXHIBITIONS 1905 Paris, 31; 1935-6 New York etc, 105; 1942 Baltimore, Worcester, 13; 1943 New York, 71; 1944 New York 1, p 91
PROVENANCE John Russell, Belle-Isle-en-Mer; Henri Matisse, Paris [acquired 1897; R 1905]; Pierre Matisse Art Gallery, New York [R 1935 and 1943]; Philadelphia, Pa., Philadelphia Museum of Art, inv nr 62-229-1

F1428 BOATS ON THE BEACH AT SAINTES-MARIES
EXHIBITION 1905 Amsterdam, 376
PROVENANCE Mrs J. van Gogh-Bonger, Amsterdam [R 1905]; Paul Cassirer, Berlin; Munich, Mrs Hugo von Tschudi [on loan at the Museum in Breslau]; Heirs of H. von Tschudi

F1429 BOATS ON THE BEACH AT SAINTES-MARIES
EXHIBITIONS 1900-1 Rotterdam, 60; 1913 Düsseldorf, no cat nr [repr]; 1914 Berlin, 88; 1927-8 Berlin etc, not mentioned in the cat; 1929 Berlin 3, 122; 1937 Paris, 224
PROVENANCE Mrs J. van Gogh-Bonger, Amsterdam; de Bois Art Gallery, Haarlem; A. Flechtheim Art Gallery, Düsseldorf [acquired 1913]; Sale Flechtheim, Berlin [Cassirer] 5 June 1917, 139 [repr]; Berlin, Bernhard Köhler [acquired 1937]

F1430 SAILING BOATS COMING ASHORE
EXHIBITIONS 1924 Stuttgart; 1958 East-Berlin, K34; 1961 Munich, 55
PROVENANCE East Berlin, National Galerie [acquired 1906], inv nr F 923, cat 2

F1430a SAILING BOATS COMING ASHORE
EXHIBITIONS 1939 Adelaide etc., 138
PROVENANCE John Russell, Belle-Isle-en Mer; Thannhauser Art Gallery, New York; New York, J.K. Thannhauser, courtesy Thannhauser Foundation, cat The Thannhauser Foundation 1965, nr 14 [loan to Guggenheim Museum, New York]

F1430b SAILING BOATS COMING ASHORE
EXHIBITIONS 1891 Brussels, 10; 1957 Essen, 284; 1960 Paris, 104; 1961 Munich, 56; 1962 Brussels, Otterlo, 48; 1964 Brussels, 40; Kassel, 8; 1966 Brussels, 16; 1967 Ostende, 130

PROVENANCE Mrs J. van Gogh-Bonger, Amsterdam; Octave Maus, Brussels [acquired 1891]; Mrs Madeleine Octave Maus, Brussels; Brussels, Musée d'Art Moderne, [acquired 1955], inv nr 6743

F 1431 SEA WITH SAILING BOATS
EXHIBITIONS 1927-8 Berlin etc, 105
PROVENANCE Mrs H. Mauve-Carbentus; Anton Mauve, Laren; A. R. Mauve, Laren; d'Audretsch Art Gallery, The Hague; F. Vowinckel, Cologne-Marienburg; Cologne-Marienburg, Werner Vowinckel

F 1432 DUNES, BEACH AND SEA WITH SAILINGBOATS
EXHIBITIONS 1905 Amsterdam, 399; 1914-5 Amsterdam, 150; 1923 Utrecht, Rotterdam, 38; 1927-8 Berlin etc, 65; 1932 Manchester, 66; 1945 Amsterdam, no cat nr; 1946 Stockholm etc, 54; 1946-7 Liège etc, 94; 1947 Paris 1, 95; Geneva, 95; 1947-8 London etc, 146; 1948 Bergen, Oslo, 95; 1954-5 Bern, 138; 1955 Antwerp 1, 279; 1957 Stockholm, 65; 1958-9 San Francisco etc, 126; 1959 Amsterdam; Aix-en-Provence, 28; 1960 Enschede, 42; Amsterdam, 39; Amsterdam, 37; 1961 Arles; 1961-2 Baltimore etc, 120; 1962-3 Pittsburgh etc; 1966 Paris, Albi, 46; 1967 Lille, Zurich, 48; 1967-8 Dallas etc, 45; 1968 Liège, 45; 1968-9 London, 120; 1969 Humlebaek, 23
PROVENANCE Mrs J. van Gogh-Bonger, Amsterdam; V. W. van Gogh, Laren; Amsterdam, Rijksmuseum Vincent van Gogh [Vincent van Gogh Foundation, inv nr F 1432]

F 1433 SEA WITH SAILING BOATS NEAR SAINTES-MARIES
EXHIBITIONS 1929-30 Berlin, 63; 1931 Providence; 1935-6 New York etc, 109; 1937 Paris, 69; 1939 Oakland, 119; 1940 San Francisco 3, 42; 1943 New York 2, 72; 1944 Montreal, 123; 1948 St Louis, 64; Cleveland, 42; 1951 Houston, 12; 1955 New York 2, 98; 1957 Milwaukee, 80
PROVENANCE John Russell, Belle-Isle-en-Mer; Sale Paris [Drouot] 31 March 1920, 66; Maurice Gobin Art Gallery, Paris; J. W. Böhler, Lucerne; Paul Cassirer Art Gallery, Berlin [R 1929]; Paul Cassirer Art Gallery, Berlin [R 1929]; Jacques Seligmann & Co Art Gallery, Paris and New York [R 1935 and 1944]; Fine Art Associates Galleries, New York; St Louis, Joseph Pulitzer Jr [R 1955]

F 1434 STREET AT SAINTES-MARIES
EXHIBITIONS 1905 Amsterdam, 378; 1914 Berlin, 97; 1927-8 Berlin etc, 104; 1943 Basle, 160; 1945 Basle, 22; 1946-7 Liège etc, 92; 1947 Basle, 151; Paris 1, 93; Geneva, 93
PROVENANCE Mrs J. van Gogh-Bonger, Amsterdam; Paul Cassirer Art Gallery, Berlin; J. Zimmermann, Mittelschreiberhau; Private collection, Switzerland; Basle, R. von Hirsch [R 1970]

F 1435 STREET AT SAINTES-MARIES
EXHIBITIONS 1935-6 New York etc, 110; 1956 Munich, 113; 1957 Los Angeles, 32
PROVENANCE Druet Art Gallery, Paris; Thannhauser Art Gallery, Munich; M. Goldschmidt, Frankfurt; A. Ronde, Mayence; Private collection, New York [R 1935]; New York, Museum of Modern Art [Abby Aldrich Rockefeller Bequest], inv nr 243.48

F 1436 ROAD WITH MAS AT SAINTES-MARIES
EXHIBITIONS 1905 Amsterdam, 379; 1927-8 Berlin etc, 103; 1935-6 New York etc, 111; 1943 New York 2, 73; 1947 San Francisco, 131; 1948 Cleveland, 43; 1955 New York 2, 99
PROVENANCE Mrs J. van Gogh-Bonger [R 1905]; Paul Cassirer Art Gallery, Berlin; H. Simon, Frankfurt [R 1928]; Wildenstein Art Gallery, New York; F. H. Hirschland, Harrison, New York; Mr and Mrs H. Hirschland, Berkeley Heights [R 1965]; Paris, H. Berggruen [R 1970]

F 1437 ROAD AT SAINTES-MARIES IN SUNSHINE
EXHIBITIONS 1905 Amsterdam, 381; 1914-5 Amsterdam, 141; 1920 New York, 13; 1925 The Hague, 62; 1926 Munich, 2109; 1927-8 Berlin etc, 64; 1932 Manchester, 69; 1945 Amsterdam, no cat nr; 1946 Stockholm etc, 55; 1947-8 London etc, 144; 1948 Bergen, Oslo, 93; 1949-50 New York, Chicago, 101; 1951 Lyons etc, 89; 1953 The Hague, 102; Otterlo, Amsterdam, 123; 1953-4 St Louis etc, 120; 1959 Amsterdam, 38; Amsterdam, 36; 1961-2 Baltimore etc, 121; 1962-3 Pittsburgh etc; 1963 Humlebaek, 95; 1964 Washington, New York, 95; 1965 Charleroi, Ghent, 62; 1966 Paris, Albi, 47; 1967 Lille, Zurich, 49; 1967-8 Dallas etc, 46; 1968 Liège, 46; 1968-9 London, 121; 1969 Humlebaek, 24
PROVENANCE Mrs J. van Gogh-Bonger, Amsterdam [R 1905]; V. W. van Gogh, Laren; Amsterdam, Rijksmuseum Vincent van Gogh [Vincent van Gogh Foundation, inv nr F 1437]

F 1438 THREE HUTS AT SAINTES-MARIES
EXHIBITIONS 1905 Amsterdam, 382; 1914-5 Amsterdam, 142; 1923 Utrecht, Rotterdam, 52; 1927-8 Berlin etc, 66; 1947 Basle, 153; 1947-8 London etc, 145; 1948 Bergen, Oslo, 94; 1949-50 New York, Chicago, 100; 1954-5 Bern, 139; 1955 Antwerp 1, 280; 1955-6 Liverpool etc, 114; 1957 Marseilles, 59; Stockholm, 66; 1958-9 San Francisco etc, 127; 1959 Amsterdam; Aix-en-Provence, 29; 1959-60 Utrecht, 84; 1960 Enschede, 43; 1960-1 Montreal etc, 125; 1961 Arles; 1965-6 Stockholm, Göteborg, 85; 1967 Wolfsburg, 105
PROVENANCE Mrs J. van Gogh-Bonger, Amsterdam [R 1905]; V. W. van Gogh, Laren; Amsterdam, Rijksmuseum Vincent van Gogh [Vincent van Gogh Foundation, inv nr F 1438]

F 1439 VIEW ON SAINTES-MARIES WITH CHURCH AND RAMPARTS
EXHIBITIONS 1905 Amsterdam, 386, 381 or 387; 1912 Cologne, 123; 1914 Berlin, 93; 1921 Berlin; 1935 Basle, 240; 1955 Winterthur 2, 159
PROVENANCE Mrs J. van Gogh-Bonger, Amsterdam [R 1905]; Paul Cassirer Art Gallery, Berlin; Mrs M. Mauthner, Berlin [R 1912]; Winterthur, O. Reinhart

F 1440 TWO HUTS AT SAINTES-MARIES
EXHIBITIONS 1905 Amsterdam, 380; 1955 New York 2, 100; 1957 Los Angeles, 33; 1959 New York 3, 15; 1966 New York 2, 9
PROVENANCE Mrs J. van Gogh-Bonger, Amsterdam [R 1905]; Miss E. Bonger, Amsterdam; W. Mengelberg, Amsterdam; Sale Amsterdam [Mak van Waay] 25 March 1952, 78; Mr and Mrs Louis Ritter, Scarsdale, New York [R 1955]; Scarsdale, New York, Ritter Foundation Inc. [R 1966]

F 1441 THE SOWER IN A WHEATFIELD WITH THE SETTING SUN
EXHIBITIONS 1905 Amsterdam, 384; 1920 New York, 34; 1937 Paris, 173; 1945 Amsterdam, no cat nr; 1946-7 Liège etc, 89; 1947 Paris 1, 90; Geneva, 90; 1947-8 London etc, 147; 1948 Bergen, Oslo, 96; 1949-50 New York, Chicago, 99; 1951 Lyons etc, 90; 1953 The Hague, 103; Otterlo, Amsterdam, 124; 1953-4 St Louis etc, 121; 1957 Stockholm, 67; 1959 Amsterdam; 1961 Scarborough; 1962 London 1, 54; 1963 Humlebaek, 96; 1964 Washington, New York, 96; 1965 Charleroi, Ghent, 63; 1966 Paris, Albi, 48; 1967 Lille, Zurich, 50; 1967-8 Dallas etc, 47; 1968 Liège, 47; 1968-9 London, 123; 1969 Humlebaek, 25
PROVENANCE Mrs J. van Gogh-Bonger, Amsterdam [R 1905]; V. W. van Gogh, Laren; Amsterdam, Rijksmuseum Vincent van Gogh [Vincent van Gogh Foundation, inv nr F 1441]

F 1442 THE SOWER IN A WHEATFIELD WITH THE SETTING SUN
PROVENANCE Th. Duret, Paris; Sale Paris [Drouot] 1 March 1928, 41 [repr]; Emile Bernheim Art Gallery, Paris; Thannhauser Art Gallery, Berlin; Present owner unknown

F 1443 THE ZOUAVE SEATED: FULL FACE
EXHIBITIONS 1905 Amsterdam, 383; 1913 Düsseldorf, no cat nr [repr]; 1962 Cambridge, USA, 37
PROVENANCE Mrs J. van Gogh-Bonger, Amsterdam [R 1905]; Hugo Moser Art Gallery, Berlin; Max Lewin, Breslau; Paul Cassirer Art Gallery, Berlin; Providence, Rhode Island, John Nicholas Brown [R 1962]

F 1444 THE CANAL LA ROUBINE DU ROI WITH WASHERWOMEN
EXHIBITIONS 1927 Basle etc, 127; 1928 Düsseldorf, 195; Karlsruhe, 130; 1929 Berlin 1, 99; Hamburg, 37; 1930 Amsterdam, 127; 1935-6 New York etc, 112; 1946-7 Liège etc, 91; 1947 Paris 1, 92; Geneva, 92; Basle, 152; 1949-50 New York, Chicago, 102; 1952 Milan, 97; 1956 Munich, 115; 1957 Essen, 285; 1958 Vienna, 89; 1959 Aix-en-Provence, 25; 1961 Munich, 58; 1962 Warsaw, 71; 1963 Tel-Aviv, Haifa, 80
PROVENANCE Werner Dücker, Düsseldorf; Otterlo, Rijksmuseum Kröller-Müller, inv nr 306-20, cat van Gogh 1970, nr 231

F 1445 STUDY OF THREE CICADAS
EXHIBITION 1962 London 1, 51
PROVENANCE Mrs J. van Gogh-Bonger, Amsterdam; V. W. van Gogh, Laren; Amsterdam, Rijksmuseum Vincent van Gogh [Vincent van Gogh Foundation, inv nr F 1445]

F 1446 MONTMAJOUR
EXHIBITIONS 1905 Amsterdam, 406; 1914-5 Amsterdam, 172; 1962 Warsaw, 99; 1964 Kassel, 6
PROVENANCE Mrs J. van Gogh-Bonger, Amsterdam; W. A. Bonger, Amsterdam [R 1905]; Mrs M. Bonger- Van Heteren, Haarlem; Amsterdam, Rijksmuseum [acquired 1962], inv nr 1962: 65

F 1447 THE ROCK: MONTMAJOUR
EXHIBITIONS 1905 Amsterdam, 396; 1914-5 Amsterdam, 175; 1915 Amsterdam, 27; 1920 New York, 5; 1926 London 3, 20; 1927-8 Berlin etc, 61; 1935-6 New York etc, 108; 1937 Paris, 75; 1945 Amsterdam, no cat nr; 1946 Stockholm etc, 61; 1946-7 Liège etc, 93; 1947 Paris 1, 94; Geneva, 94; 1947-8 London etc, 148; 1948 Bergen, Oslo, 97; 1949-50 New York, Chicago, 103; 1951 Lyons etc, 91; 1953 The Hague, 104; Otterlo, Amsterdam, 125; 1953-4 St Louis etc, 122; 1954-5 Bern, 140; 1955 Antwerp 1, 281; 1955-6 Liverpool etc, 115; 1957 Marseilles, 60; Stockholm, 69; 1958 Amsterdam 1, 252; 1958-9 San Francisco etc, 128; 1959 Aix-en-Provence, 30; 1959-60 Utrecht; 1960 Enschede, 44; 1960-1 Montreal etc, 126; 1961 Arles; 1961-2 Baltimore etc, 122; 1962-3 Pittsburgh etc; 1966 Paris, Albi, 49; 1967 Lille, Zurich, 51; 1967-8 Dallas etc, 48; 1968 Liège, 48; 1968-9 London, 129; 1969 Humlebaek, 26
PROVENANCE Mrs J. van Gogh-Bonger, Amsterdam [R 1905]; V. W. van Gogh, Laren; Amsterdam, Rijksmuseum Vincent van Gogh [Vincent van Gogh Foundation, inv nr F 1447]

F 1448 THE PLAIN OP LA CRAU
EXHIBITIONS 1914 Berlin, 102; 1952 Milan, 98; 1953 Zurich, not in cat
PROVENANCE Mrs J. van Gogh-Bonger, Amsterdam; Paul Cassirer Art Gallery, Berlin; A. Walter von Heymel, Munich; Mrs A. Heye, Bremen; Fritz Nathan, Zurich; Sale Bern [Kornfeld and Klipstein] 24 November 1955, nr 11; Present owner unknown

F 1449 VIEW IN THE PARK
EXHIBITION 1927 Hamburg 2, 53
PROVENANCE John Russell, Belle-Isle-en-Mer; Sale Paris [Drouot] 31 March 1920, 65; Le Garrec Art Gallery, Paris; d'Audretsch Art Gallery, The Hague; Lutz Art Gallery, Berlin; Sale Berlin [Amsler & Ruthardt] 29 October 1925, 247 [repr]; Van Diemen Art Gallery, Berlin; Thannhauser Art Gallery, New York; Josef von Sternberg, Hollywood; Sale New York [Parke-Bernet] 22 November 1949, 28; Present owner unknown

F 1450 A PARK IN ARLES
EXHIBITION 1893 Copenhagen, 197
PROVENANCE Julien Tanguy, Paris; Johan Rohde, Copenhagen [acquired 1892]; Sale London [Sotheby] 6 July 1960, 160; M. Knoedler Art Gallery, London; Toronto, M. F. Feheley [R 1970]

F 1451 A PARK IN ARLES
EXHIBITION 1938 London 1, 24
PROVENANCE J. H. de Bois Art Gallery, Haarlem; Thannhauser Art Gallery, New York; USA, Private collection

F 1452 VIEW OF ARLES FROM MONTMAJOUR
EXHIBITIONS 1893 Copenhagen, 193; 1961 Munich, 59
PROVENANCE Oslo, Nasjonalgalleriet [acquired 1893]

F 1453 VINCENT'S HOUSE AT ARLES
EXHIBITION 1924 Zurich, 99
PROVENANCE Tanner Art Gallery, Zurich; Brienz, Switzerland, N. Dreher [acquired 1918]

F 1454 A GARDEN
PROVENANCE John Russell, Belle-Isle-en-Mer; Sale Paris [Drouot] 31 March 1920, 67; Maurice Gobin Art Gallery, Paris; Lausanne, A. Strölin Art Gallery

F 1455 A GARDEN
EXHIBITIONS 1905 Amsterdam, 395; 1906 Berlin, 78; 1914 Berlin, 94; 1914-5 Amsterdam, 164; 1921 Berlin; 1955 Winterthur 2, 160
PROVENANCE Mrs J. van Gogh-Bonger, Amsterdam [R 1905]; Paul Cassirer Art Gallery, Berlin; Mrs M. Mauthner, Berlin; Winterthur, Oscar Reinhart [R 1955]

F 1456 A GARDEN
EXHIBITION 1967 Lille, Zurich, 95
PROVENANCE Mrs J. van Gogh-Bonger, Amsterdam; Mrs Hugo von Tschudi, Munich [on loan at the Museum in Breslau]; Zurich, Fritz Nathan [R 1970]

F 1457 FLOWERBED WITH SUNFLOWERS
EXHIBITIONS 1905 Amsterdam, 390; 1923 Utrecht, Rotterdam, 47; 1924 Basle, 97; Zurich, 97; Stuttgart, 16; 1925 The Hague, 70; 1927-8 Berlin etc, 68; 1932 Manchester, 70; 1945 Amsterdam, no cat nr; 1946 Stockholm etc, 63; 1946-7 Liège etc, 90; 1947 Paris 1, 91; Geneva, 91; 1947-8 London etc, 149; 1948 Bergen, Oslo, 98; 1949-50 New York, Chicago, 104; 1953 The Hague, 105; Otterlo, Amsterdam, 129; 1953-4 St Louis etc, 125; 1955 Antwerp 1, 291; 1955-6 Liverpool etc, 117; 1957 Stockholm, 70; 1958 Liège, 49; 1958-9 San Francisco etc, 129; 1960 Enschede, 45; 1962 London 1, 55; 1963 Humlebaek, 97; 1964 Washington, New York, 97; 1965 Charleroi, Ghent, 64; 1966 Paris, Albi, 50; 1967 Lille, Zurich, 52; 1967-8 Dallas etc, 49; 1968 Liège, 49; 1968-9 London, 130
PROVENANCE Mrs J. van Gogh-Bonger, Amsterdam [R 1905]; V. W. van Gogh, Laren; Amsterdam, Rijksmuseum Vincent van Gogh [Vincent van Gogh Foundation, inv nr F 1457]

F 1458 THE POSTMAN ROULIN
EXHIBITIONS 1922 Winterthur 2, 124; 1924 Zurich, 79; 1927-8 Berlin etc, 101; 1929 Winterthur, 60; 1947 Basle, 155; 1952 Milan, 99; 1953 Zurich, not listed in cat
PROVENANCE John Russell, Belle-Isle-en-Mer; Sale Paris [Drouot] 31 March 1920, 70; A. Hahnloser, Winterthur; Mrs H. Hahnloser-Bühler, Winterthur; Bern, H. R. Hahnloser [R 1970]

F1459 THE POSTMAN ROULIN
EXHIBITIONS 1905 Amsterdam, 415; 1921 Berlin, 64; 1927-8 Berlin etc, not listed in cat; 1932 Buffalo; 1935-6 New York etc, 117A; 1937 Paris, 70; 1947 San Francisco, 133; 1948 Cleveland, 46; 1950 Los Angeles, 22; 1955 Paris 2, 78; 1957 Los Angeles, 36; 1961 Newark [N.J.], 55; 1962 Minneapolis, New York, 120; 1964 Kassel, 7
PROVENANCE Mrs J. van Gogh-Bonger, Amsterdam [R 1905]; Paul Cassirer Art Gallery, Berlin; H. Freudenberg, Nikolassee; Jacques Seligmann & Co. Art Gallery, Paris and New York [R 1935 and 1937]; George Gard de Sylva, Los Angeles [acquired 1938]; Los Angeles, County Museum of Art [George Gard de Sylva Collection], inv nr M. 49.17.1, cat The George Gard de Sylva Collection 1950, nr 22

F1460 PORTRAIT OF PATIENCE ESCALIER
EXHIBITIONS 1900-1 Rotterdam, 54; 1927-8 Berlin etc, 102; 1969 Cambridge, USA, 125
PROVENANCE Mrs J. van Gogh-Bonger, Amsterdam; K. Fahraeus, Lidingö-Brevik [acquired 1911]; Thorsten Laurin, Stockholm [R 1927-8]; Paris, Art Dealer; G. L. Winthrop, New York [acquired 1931]; Cambridge, USA, Fogg Art Museum [G. L. Winthrop bequest], inv nr 1943.515, cat 1969, nr 125

F1461 PORTRAIT OF PATIENCE ESCALIER
EXHIBITIONS 1905 Paris, 29; 1935-6 New York etc, 106; 1948 Cleveland, 45
PROVENANCE A. Vollard Art Gallery, Paris; Thorsten Laurin, Stockholm; Henri Matisse, Paris [R 1905]; Pierre Matisse Art Gallery, New York; Mrs Henry Goldman, New York [R 1935]; Sale New York [Parke-Bernet] 28 February 1948, 91; Edward Bragaline, New York; Switzerland, Private collection

F1462 RIVER WITH TWO BOATS
EXHIBITIONS 1905 Amsterdam, 417; 1927-8 Berlin etc, 106; 1935 Buffalo, 128; 1935-6 New York etc, 113; 1948 New York 2, 72
PROVENANCE Mrs J. van Gogh-Bonger, Amsterdam [R 1905]; Klas Fahraeus, Stockholm [acquired 1911]; August T. Levinson, Copenhagen; Hugo Perls Art Gallery, Berlin [R 1927-8]; New York, Miss Edith Wetmore [R 1935; 1948]

F1463 INTERIOR OF THE NIGHT CAFÉ IN ARLES
EXHIBITIONS 1904 Rotterdam, 77; 1924 Zurich, 34; 1940 Lucerne, 55
PROVENANCE A. C. van Blommenstein, the Netherlands [R 1904]; L. C. Enthoven, Voorburg; Sale Enthoven, Amsterdam [F. Muller] 18 May 1920, 243; A. Hahnloser, Winterthur; Bern, H. R. Hahnloser [R 1970]

F1464 THE MILL
PROVENANCE Artz & de Bois Art Gallery, The Hague; Erich Schall, Baden-Baden; Heinrich Stinnes, Cologne-Lindenthal; Western Germany, Private collection [R 1970]

F1465 A PARK IN ARLES
EXHIBITION 1936 London 3, 165
PROVENANCE Theo van Gogh, Paris; Lutz Art Gallery, Berlin; G. F. Reber, Barmen; Max Silberberg, Breslau; W. A. Coolidge, London; Mrs Edward Gage, London; Sale London [Sotheby] 3 December 1958, 47; Present owner unknown

F1466 THISTLES ALONG THE ROADSIDE
EXHIBITIONS 1905 Amsterdam, 366; 1914-5 Amsterdam, 147; 1923 Utrecht, Amsterdam, 67; 1927-8 Berlin etc, 69; 1932 Manchester, 61; 1945 Amsterdam, no cat nr; 1946 Stockholm etc, 64; 1947 Basle, 156; 1947-8 London etc, 150; 1948 Bergen, Oslo, 100; 1949-50 New York, Chicago, 105; 1951 Lyons etc, 92; 1953 The Hague, 106; Otterlo, Amsterdam, 130; 1953-4 St Louis etc, 128; 1954-5 Bern, 141; 1955 Antwerp 1, 282; 1955-6 Liverpool etc, 121; 1958-9 San Francisco etc, 130; 1960 Enschede, 46; 1961 Arles; 1961-2 Baltimore etc, 123; 1926-3 Pittsburgh etc; 1964 Zundert, 24; 1966 Paris, Albi, 51; 1967 Lille, Zurich, 53; 1967-8 Dallas etc, 50; 1968 Liège, 50; 1968-9 London, 138; 1969 Humlebaek, 27
PROVENANCE Mrs J. van Gogh-Bonger, Amsterdam [R 1905]; V. W. van Gogh, Laren; Amsterdam, Rijksmuseum Vincent van Gogh [Vincent van Gogh Foundation, inv nr F 1466]

F1467 THE COURTYARD OF THE HOSPITAL IN ARLES
EXHIBITIONS 1891 Brussels; 1900-1 Rotterdam, 12; 1905 Amsterdam, 393; 1914-5 Amsterdam, 144; 1915 Amsterdam, 25; 1923 Utrecht, Rotterdam, 35; 1925 The Hague, 77; 1926 London 3, 27; 1927-8 Berlin etc, 59; 1945 Amsterdam, no cat nr; 1946 Stockholm etc, 75; 1946-7 Liège etc, 86; 1947 Geneva, 87; Paris 1, 87; 1947-8 London etc, 158; 1948 Bergen, Oslo, 100; 1949-50 New York, Chicago, 106; 1951 Lyons etc, 93; 1953 The Hague, 107; Otterlo, Amsterdam, 135; 1953-4 St Louis etc, 131; 1954-5 Curaçao; 1955 Palm Beach etc, 36; Antwerp 1, 283; Amsterdam 1, 178; 1955-6 Liverpool etc, 122; 1957 Nijmegen; Stockholm, 76; 1958-9 San Francisco etc, 131; 1959 Aix-en-Provence, 35; 1960 Enschede, 54; 1961 Arles; 1961-2 Baltimore etc, 128; 1962-3 Pittsburgh etc; 1963 Humlebaek, 98; 1964 Washington, New York, 98; 1965 Charleroi, Ghent, 65; 1966 Paris, Albi, 52; 1967 Lille, Zurich, 54; 1967-8 Dallas etc, 51; 1968 Liège, 51; 1968-9 London, 144a; 1969 Humlebaek, 28
PROVENANCE Mrs J. van Gogh-Bonger, Amsterdam [R 1905]; V. W. van Gogh, Laren; Amsterdam, Rijksmuseum Vincent van Gogh [Vincent van Gogh Foundation, inv nr F 1467]

F1468 VIEW IN THE PARK IN ARLES
EXHIBITIONS 1905 Amsterdam, 412; 1935-6 New York etc, 114; 1946 Chicago, 26; 1963 New York 3, 131
PROVENANCE Mrs J. van Gogh-Bonger, Amsterdam [R 1905]; J. Veth, Amsterdam; Mrs C. Veth, San Francisco [R 1935]; Chicago, The Art Institute [gift of Tiffany and Margaret Blake], inv nr 45.31

F1469 THE FLOWERING TREE
EXHIBITIONS 1900-1 Rotterdam, 37; 1905 Amsterdam, 152; 1920 New York, 16; 1927 Paris; 1945 Amsterdam, no cat nr; 1946 Stockholm etc, 47; 1946-7 Liège etc, 95; 1947 Paris 1, 96; Geneva, 96; 1949-50 New York, Chicago, 107; 1953 The Hague, 108; Otterlo, Amsterdam, 121; 1953-4 St Louis etc, 118; 1955 Antwerp 1, 284; 1955-6 Liverpool etc, 110; 1957 Stockholm, 61; 1961 Arles; 1961-2 Liège, Breda; 1963 Humlebaek, 93; 1964 Washington, New York, 93; 1965 Charleroi, Ghent, 60; 1966 Paris, Albi, 53; 1967 Lille, Zurich, 55; 1967-8 Dallas etc, 52; 1968 Liège, 52; 1968-9 London, 103
PROVENANCE Mrs J. van Gogh-Bonger, Amsterdam; V. W. van Gogh, Laren; Amsterdam, Rijksmuseum Vincent van Gogh [Vincent van Gogh Foundation, inv nr F 1469]

F1470 THE LANGLOIS BRIDGE SEEN FROM THE ROAD
EXHIBITIONS 1905 Amsterdam, 369 [?]; 1914 Berlin, 101; 1921 Berlin; 1927-8 Berlin etc, no cat nr [repr]; 1969 Stuttgart, 52
PROVENANCE Mrs J. van Gogh-Bonger, Amsterdam [R 1905]; Hugo Cassirer, Berlin; The Hague, Gemeente Museum [on loan 1933-1939, cat 1935, p 77]; Mrs L. Fuerstenberg-Cassirer, Johannesburg; R. Cassirer, Johannesburg; J. K. Thannhauser Art Gallery, New York; A. Goldschmidt, Paris; Private collection; Stuttgart, Graphische Sammlung Staatsgalerie, inv nr C 67/1491

F1471 THE LANGLOIS BRIDGE WITH A WOMAN CARRYING AN UMBRELLA
EXHIBITIONS 1914 Berlin, 72; 1927-8 Berlin etc, no cat nr; 1935 Basle, 241; 1935-6 New York etc, 115; 1947 San Francisco, 134; 1951 Houston, 13; 1957 Los Angeles, 37
PROVENANCE Mrs J. van Gogh-Bonger, Amsterdam; Paul Cassirer Art Gallery, Berlin; Mrs T. Durieux-Cassirer, Berlin; Mrs Paret, Berlin; Jacques Seligmann & Co. Art Gallery, New York [R 1935]; George Gard de Sylva, Los Angeles [acquired 1938]; Los Angeles, County Museum, [George Gard de Sylva Collection], inv nr M. 49.17.2, cat The Gard de Sylva Collection 1950, nr 21

F1472 THE RHÔNE
EXHIBITIONS 1905 Amsterdam, 407; 1906 Berlin, 76; 1953 Berlin, 20; 1956 Nuremberg, 59; Munich, 116a; 1957 Essen, 288; 1958 Vienna, 90; Amsterdam 1, 266; 1961 Munich, 61; 1963 Hamburg, 92; 1968 Munich, 27
PROVENANCE Mrs J. van Gogh-Bonger, Amsterdam [R 1905]; Mrs Hugo von Tschudi, Munich; Munich, Neue Staatsgalerie [acquired 1912], inv nr 10036; Munich, Staatliche Graphische Sammlung, inv nr 44329

F1472a THE RHÔNE SEEN FROM THE TRINQUETAILLE BRIDGE
EXHIBITIONS 1930 Amsterdam, 116; 1937 Paris, 74; 1956 Munich, 116; Nuremberg, 64; 1957 Essen, 289
PROVENANCE Mrs P. F. Fentener van Vlissingen, Helmond; Van Wisselingh Art Gallery, Amsterdam; Rotterdam, Museum Boymans-van Beuningen [gift of Mr H. van Beek and Mr H. Nygh 1929], inv nr VvG 3

F1473 THE BANK OF THE CANAL LA ROUBINE DU ROI
EXHIBITIONS 1905 Amsterdam, 401; 1906 Berlin, 67; 1953 Berlin, 19; 1956 Nuremberg, 60; Munich, 115a; 1957 Essen, 286; 1958 Vienna, 91; Amsterdam 1, 264; 1961 Munich, 60; 1963 Hamburg, 91; 1968 Munich, 28
PROVENANCE Mrs J. van Gogh-Bonger, Amsterdam [R 1905]; Mrs Hugo von Tschudi, Berlijn; Munich, Neue Staatsgalerie [acquired 1912], inv nr 10035; Munich, Staatliche Graphische Sammlung, inv nr 44330, cat 1955, p 61

F1474 MEADOW WITH FLOWERS
EXHIBITIONS 1905 Amsterdam, 414; 1914-5 Amsterdam, 140; 1923 Utrecht, Rotterdam, 36; 1924 Basle, 86; Zurich, 86; Stuttgart, 9; 1925 The Hague, 61; 1927-8 Berlin etc, 70; 1945 Amsterdam, no cat nr; 1946 Stockholm etc, 60; 1946-7 Liège etc, 88; 1947 Paris 1, 89; Geneva, 89; 1947-8 London etc, 151; 1952 Paris 2, 159; 1954-5 Bern, 142; 1955 Antwerp 1, 285; 1955-6 Liverpool etc, 118; 1957 Stockholm, 68; 1958-9 San Francisco etc, 132; 1959 Aix-en-Provence, 32; 1960 Enschede, 47; 1961 Arles; 1965-6 Stockholm, Göteborg, 86; 1967 Wolfsburg, 106; 1967-8 Dallas etc, 53; 1968 Liège, 53; 1968-9 London, 113; 1969 Humlebaek, 29
PROVENANCE Mrs J. van Gogh-Bonger, Amsterdam [R 1905]; V. W. van Gogh, Laren; Amsterdam, Rijksmuseum Vincent van Gogh [Vincent van Gogh Foundation, inv nr F 1474]

F1475 VIEW OF ARLES SEEN FROM A HILL
PROVENANCE Mrs J. van Gogh-Bonger, Amsterdam [R 1905]; R. N. Roland Holst, Amsterdam [1892?]; J. H. de Bois Art Gallery, Haarlem; F. W. Koenigs, Haarlem; Rotterdam, Museum Boymans-van Beuningen [acquired 1940; Collection F. W. Koenigs, gift of D. G. van Beuningen], inv nr F II 198

F1476 PARK IN ARLES WITH A CORNER OF THE YELLOW HOUSE
PROVENANCE Mrs J. van Gogh-Bonger, Amsterdam; V. W. van Gogh, Laren; Amsterdam, Rijksmuseum Vincent van Gogh [Vincent van Gogh Foundation, inv nr F 1476]

F1477 PARK ALONG THE FENCE
EXHIBITIONS 1905 Amsterdam, 402; 1923 Utrecht, Rotterdam, 53; 1927-8 Berlin etc, 76; 1946-7 Liège etc, 78; 1947 Paris 1, 79; Geneva, 79; 1947-8 London etc, 153; 1948 Bergen, Oslo, 102; 1953 The Hague, 109; Otterlo, Amsterdam, 132; 1953-4 St Louis etc, 127; 1955 Antwerp 1, 286; 1957 Marseilles, 61; Stockholm, 72; 1958-9 San Francisco etc, 133; 1959-60 Utrecht, 86; 1960 Enschede, 48; 1960-1 Montreal etc, 127; 1961-2 Baltimore etc, 124; 1962-3 Pittsburgh etc; 1963 Humlebaek, 100; 1964 Washington, New York, 100; 1965 Charleroi, Ghent, 66; 1966 Paris, Albi, 54; 1967 Lille, Zurich, 56; 1968-9 London, 135
PROVENANCE Mrs J. van Gogh-Bonger, Amsterdam [R 1905]; V.W. van Gogh, Laren; Amsterdam, Rijksmuseum Vincent van Gogh [Vincent van Gogh Foundation, inv nr F 1477]

F1478 MAS IN THE PROVENCE
EXHIBITIONS 1905 Amsterdam, 385; 1937 Paris, 71; 1946-7 Liège etc, 79; 1947 Paris 1, 80; Geneva, 80; 1948 Bergen, Oslo, 101; 1952 Milan, 101; 1953 The Hague, 110; Otterlo, Amsterdam, 126; 1955-6 Liverpool etc, 119; 1956 Munich, 117; 1957 Essen, 293; 1959 Recklinghausen, 115; 1960 Paris, 103; 1961 Munich, 62; 1962 Warsaw, 98; 1963 Haifa, Tel Aviv, 81; 1964 Kassel, 5
PROVENANCE Mrs J. van Gogh-Bonger, Amsterdam [R 1905]; Amsterdam, Rijksmuseum [acquired 1906; gift from Mrs J. van Gogh-Bongers; on loan to Stedelijk Museum, Amsterdam], cat 1911, nr 2926c

F1478a DWELLING AND GARDEN BEHIND A WALL
EXHIBITIONS 1949 New York 2, 87; 1955 New York 2, 104; 1960 Buffalo, 29; 1961 New York 1, 118; 1967 New York, Philadelphia, no cat nr
PROVENANCE Comtesse de Cumont, Avignon; Miss M. de Gaigneron, Paris; Wildenstein Art Gallery, New York; Bradford, Mr and Mrs T. Edward Hanley [R 1970]

F1479 FIELD WITH THE CEMETERY OF SAINTES-MARIES IN THE BACKGROUND
EXHIBITIONS 1905 Amsterdam, 377; 1914 Berlin, 66; 1929-30 Berlin, 64; 1945 Basle, 23; 1947 Basle, 154
PROVENANCE Mrs J. van Gogh-Bonger, Amsterdam [R 1905]; Paul Cassirer, Berlin; Mrs Tilla Durieux-Cassirer, Berlin; Mrs Paret, Berlin; Alfred Cassirer, Berlin; Switzerland, Private collection

F1480 THE LANGLOIS BRIDGE
EXHIBITIONS 1905 Amsterdam, 360; 1906 Rotterdam, 64; 1909-10 Berlin, 220; 1914-5 Amsterdam, 180; 1927-8 Berlin etc, 108; 1953 Zurich, not listed in cat
PROVENANCE Mrs J. van Gogh-Bonger, Amsterdam [R 1905]; Rothermundt, Dresden [acquired 1910]; Hugo Perls Art Gallery, Berlin; Baron von Simolin, Berlin; Private collection [1952, 1953 on loan to Kunsthaus, Zurich]

F1480a VIEW OF ROOFS WITH THE TOWER OF ST JULIEN AT ARLES
EXHIBITIONS 1955 New York 2, 96; 1957 Essen, 264; 1957 Los Angeles, 31; 1961 Munich, 54; 1963 Hamburg, 94
PROVENANCE Paul Poiret, Paris; Otto Wertheim, Paris; John Rewald, New York; Sale London [Sotheby] 7 July 1960, 47; Paris, Heinz Berggruen Gallery [R 1963]

F1481 WHEATFIELD WITH THE ALPILLES IN THE BACKGROUND
EXHIBITIONS 1908 Paris 2; 1929-30 Berlin, 65; 1955 New York 2, 101; 1957 Los Angeles, 34
PROVENANCE A. Schuffenecker, Clamart [R 1893]; E. Druet Art Gallery, Paris; Tanner Art Gallery, Zurich; J. W. Böhler, Lucerne; New York, Mrs Max J. J. Rossbach [R 1955]

F1482 THE ZOUAVE: HALF LENGTH
EXHIBITIONS 1929 New York, 96; 1943 New York 2, 74
PROVENANCE Raoul de Gunzbourg, Geneva; C. Moos Art Gallery, Geneva; Paul A. Adamidé Bey, Geneva; Walter E. Sachs, New York [R 1929]; Mrs E. N. Arling, New York; Emanie Philips, New York; New York, The Metropolitan Museum of Art [acquired 1962; gift of Emanie Philips], inv nr 62.151

F 1482a THE ZOUAVE: HEAD AND SHOULDERS
EXHIBITION 1939 Adelaide etc, 137
PROVENANCE John Russell, Belle-Isle-en-Mer; Thannhauser Art Gallery, New York; New York, J. K. Thannhauser, Courtesy of Thannhauser Foundation, cat The Thannhauser Foundation 1965, nr 17 [on loan to Guggenheim Museum, New York]

F 1483 HARVEST IN THE PROVENCE, AT THE LEFT MONTMAJOUR
EXHIBITIONS 1930 London 3, 15; 1948 London 2, 30
PROVENANCE J. Meier-Graefe, Paris; Bernheim Art Gallery, Paris; Aghion, Paris; P. Rosenberg Art Gallery, Paris; Jos. Hessel Art Gallery, Paris; Georges Bernheim Art Gallery, Paris; Flechtheim Art Gallery, Düsseldorf; F. Haniel, Wistinghausen; Alex Reid and Lefevre Art Gallery, London; London, Mrs J. B. A. Kessler [R 1948]

F 1484 HARVEST IN THE PROVENCE, WITH MONTMAJOUR AT THE LEFT
EXHIBITIONS 1909-10 Berlin, 218; 1969 Cambridge, USA, 124
PROVENANCE Artz & de Bois Art Gallery, The Hague; Erich Schall, Berlin; P. Seligmann, Cologne; F. Haniel, Wistinghausen; Wildenstein Art Gallery, New York; Scott & Fowles Art Gallery, New York; G. L. Winthrop, New York [acquired 1932]; Cambridge, USA, Fogg Art Museum, [acquired 1943; Winthrop bequest], inv nr 1943.279

F 1485 HARVEST IN THE PROVENCE, AT THE LEFT MONTMAJOUR
EXHIBITIONS 1924 Stuttgart; 1958 Berlin East, K 33; 1961 Munich, 63
PROVENANCE Mrs J. van Gogh-Bonger, Amsterdam; Paul Cassirer Art Gallery, Berlin; East Berlin, National Galerie [acquired 1906], inv nr F 923, cat 1

F 1486 HARVEST IN THE PROVENCE, WITH MONTMAJOUR AT THE LEFT
EXHIBITIONS 1943 New York 2, 75; 1944 Montreal, 122; 1947 San Francisco, 136; 1948 Cleveland, 49; 1951 Houston 14; 1955 New York 2, 102; 1957 Los Angeles, 35; 1959 New York 4, 61; 1966 Washington, 239
PROVENANCE J. Russell, Belle-Isle-en-Mer; Sale Paris [Drouot] 31 March 1920, 63 [repr]; Le Garrec Art Gallery, Paris; d'Audretsch Art Gallery, The Hague; Lutz Art Gallery, Berlin; George Hirschland, Werden on the Ruhr; Richard S. Hirschland, Englewood, N.J.; Upperville, Virginia, Mr and Mrs Paul Mellon [R 1970]

F 1487 THE PARK
PROVENANCE J. H. de Bois Art Gallery, Haarlem; Heinrich Stinnes, Cologne-Lindenthal; Sale Stuttgart [Stuttgarter Kunstkabinett] 25 April 1951, nr 1345; Private collection, New York; Sale Basle [Auctiones] 24 January 1970, 81; Paris, Heinz Berggruen [R 1970]

F 1488 SHEAVES
EXHIBITIONS 1924 Stuttgart, 20; 1958 Berlin East, K 35; 1961 Munich, 64
PROVENANCE East Berlin, National Galerie [acquired 1906], inv nr F 923, cat 3

F 1489 SHEAVES
EXHIBITIONS 1922 Winterthur 2, 123; 1924 Zurich, 77; 1927-8 Berlin etc, 107; 1961 Munich, 65
PROVENANCE John Russell, Belle-Isle-en-Mer; Sale Paris [Drouot] 31 March 1920, 68; A. Hahnloser, Winterthur [R 1927-8]; Bern, Hans R. Hahnloser [R 1970]

F 1490 ARLES: VIEW FROM THE WHEATFIELDS
EXHIBITIONS 1935-6 New York etc, 116; 1947 San Francisco, 135; 1948 New York 2, 73; Cleveland, 47; 1949 New York 2, 88; 1967 Washington, Los Angeles, 76
PROVENANCE John Russell, Belle-Isle-en-Mer; Sale Paris [Drouot] 31 March 1920, 64; H. J. Laroche, Paris; Wildenstein Art Gallery, New York; Chicago, Mr and Mrs Leigh B. Block [R 1967]

F 1491 ARLES: VIEW FROM THE WHEATFIELDS
EXHIBITIONS 1905 Paris, 30; 1942 Baltimore, Worcester, 14
PROVENANCE Ambroise Vollard Art Gallery, Paris; Henri Matisse, Paris [R 1905, 1942]; Present owner unknown
EDITORS' COMMENT: In his manuscript Faille notes the last owner Pierre Matisse Art Gallery, New York, who denies however, ever having owned or handled this particular work.

F 1492 ARLES: VIEW FROM THE WHEATFIELDS
EXHIBITIONS 1927-8 Berlin etc, not listed in cat; 1943 Basle, 162; 1945 Basle, 24; 1947 Basle, 151
PROVENANCE Mrs J. Van Gogh-Bunger, Amsterdam; G. Engelbrecht, Hamburg; J. Freund, Berlin; Basle, Robert von Hirsch [R 1970]

F 1493 SLOPE OF A HILL WITH BUSHES
EXHIBITIONS 1905 Amsterdam, 392; 1914-5 Amsterdam, 176; 1920 New York, 12; 1927-8 Berlin etc, 56; 1932 Manchester, 62; 1946-7 Liège etc, 80; 1947 Paris 1, 81; Geneva, 81; 1955 Antwerp 1, 271; 1959 Aix-en-Provence, 36; 1965-6 Stockholm, Göteborg, 87; 1967 Wolfsburg, 107
PROVENANCE Mrs J. van Gogh-Bonger, Amsterdam [R 1905]; V. W. van Gogh, Laren; Amsterdam, Rijksmuseum Vincent van Gogh [Vincent van Gogh Foundation, inv nr F 1493]

F 1494 FIELD WITH POPPIES
EXHIBITIONS 1905 Amsterdam, 389; 1929-30 Berlin, 66; 1934 Bern, 63; 1955 New York 2, 103; 1957 Milwaukee, 74
PROVENANCE Mrs J. van Gogh-Bonger, Amsterdam; C. M. van Gogh Art Gallery, Amsterdam [about 1919-20]; H. van de Velde, Wassenaar [acquired 1894]; Caspari Art Gallery, Munich; J. W. Böhler, Lucerne; Paul Cassirer Art Gallery, Berlin [R 1929-30]; Sale Berlin [Graupe] 27 May 1935, 69; Wildenstein Art Galleries, New York; Fine Arts Associates, New York; Ralph H. Booth, Detroit; William D. Vogel, Milwaukee [R 1955]; Mr and Mrs Richard S. Davis, Wayzata [Minnesota] [R 1957]; Myrtil Frank, New York; Fritz Nathan, Zurich; St Louis, Missouri, Mrs Mark C. Steinberg [R 1970]

F 1495 ROAD WITH TELEGRAPH-POLE AND CRANE
EXHIBITIONS 1905 Amsterdam, 372; 1909-10 Berlin, 214; 1914-5 Amsterdam, 151; 1923 Utrecht, Rotterdam, 40; 1927-8 Berlin etc, 74; 1946-7 Liège etc, 81; 1947 Paris 1, 82; Geneva, 82; 1947-8 London etc, 152; 1948 Bergen, Oslo, 103; 1949-50 New York, Chicago, 108; 1953 The Hague, 111; Otterlo, Amsterdam, 134; 1953-4 St Louis etc, 126; 1954-5 Bern, 143; 1955 Antwerp 1, 287; 1955-6 Liverpool etc, 120; 1957 Marseilles, 62; Stockholm, 71; 1958-9 San Francisco etc, 134; 1959 Aix-en-Provence, 33; 1959-60 Utrecht, 85; 1960 Enschede, 49; 1960-1 Montreal etc, 128; 1961 Arles; 1961-2 Baltimore etc, 125; 1962-3 Pittsburgh etc; 1964 Zundert, 25; 1965-6 Stockholm, Göteborg, 88; 1967 Wolfsburg, 108; 1967-8 Dallas etc, 54; 1968 Liège, 54; 1968-9 London, 131; 1969 Humlebaek, 30
PROVENANCE Mrs J. van Gogh-Bonger, Amsterdam; V. W. van Gogh, Laren; Amsterdam, Rijksmuseum Vincent van Gogh [Vincent van Gogh Foundation, inv nr F 1495]

F 1496 LANDSCAPE WITH THE WINDMILL OF ALPHONSE DAUDET [FONTVIEILLE]
EXHIBITIONS 1905 Amsterdam, 398; 1914-5 Amsterdam, 149; 1923 Utrecht, Rotterdam, 61; 1924 Basle, 90; Zurich, 90; Stuttgart, 8; 1925 The Hague, 63; 1927-8 Berlin etc, 73; 1955 Antwerp 1, 272; 1955-6 Liverpool etc, 106; 1958-9 San Francisco etc, 135; 1959 Aix-en-Provence, 81; 1960 Enschede, 50; 1961 Arles; 1962 London; 1965-6 Stockholm, Göteborg, 89; 1967 Wolfsburg, 109; 1968-9 London, 111
PROVENANCE Mrs J. van Gogh-Bonger, Amsterdam; V. W. van Gogh, Laren; Amsterdam, Rijksmuseum Vincent van Gogh [Vincent van Gogh Foundation, inv nr F 1496]

F 1497 CORNER OF THE GARDEN OF SAINT PAUL'S HOSPITAL
EXHIBITIONS 1905 Amsterdam, 470; 1930 Amsterdam, 115; 1947-8 London etc, 169
PROVENANCE Mrs J. van Gogh-Bonger, Amsterdam [R 1905]; Frank C. Stoop, London [R 1930]; London, Tate Gallery [acquired 1933; gift of Mr. Stoop], inv nr 4716

F 1498 recto FIELD WITH THE GUARDIAN'S HUT, CAMARGUE
verso AVENUE IN THE PARK IN ARLES
EXHIBITIONS 1905 Amsterdam, 370; 1927-8 Berlin etc, 67; 1945 Amsterdam, no cat nr; 1946 Stockholm etc, 67; 1954-5 Bern, 144; 1955 Antwerp 1, 288; 1958-9 San Francisco etc, 136; 1959-60 Utrecht, 88; 1960 Enschede, 51; 1961 Arles; 1966 Paris, Albi, 55; 1967 Lille, Zurich, 57; 1967-8 Dallas etc, 55; 1968 Liège, 55; 1968-9 London, 117
PROVENANCE Mrs J. van Gogh-Bonger, Amsterdam [R 1905]; V. W. van Gogh, Laren; Amsterdam, Rijksmuseum Vincent van Gogh [Vincent van Gogh Foundation, inv nr F 1498]

F 1499 PATH THROUGH A FIELD WITH WILLOWS
EXHIBITIONS 1905 Amsterdam, 404; 1923 Utrecht, Rotterdam, 51; 1927-8 Berlin etc, 62; 1932 Manchester, 65; 1947 Basle, 149; 1947-8 London etc, 139; 1948 Bergen, Oslo, 88; 1949-50 New York, Chicago, 95; 1955 Antwerp 1, 273; 1955-6 Liverpool etc, 107; 1958-9 San Francisco etc, 137; 1960 Enschede, 52; 1961 Arles; 1961-2 Baltimore etc, 126; 1962-3 Pittsburgh etc; 1966 Paris, Albi, 56; 1967 Lille, Zurich, 58; 1967-8 Dallas etc, 56; 1968 Liège, 56; 1968-9 London, 102; 1969 Humlebaek, 31
PROVENANCE Mrs J. van Gogh-Bonger, Amsterdam [R 1905]; V. W. van Gogh, Laren; Amsterdam, Rijksmuseum Vincent van Gogh [Vincent van Gogh Foundation, inv nr F 1499]

F 1500 THE FACTORY
EXHIBITIONS 1905 Amsterdam, 408; 1914-5 Amsterdam, 169; 1923 Utrecht, Rotterdam, 48; 1926 London 3, 37; 1948 London 1, 100; 1955 Paris 3, 92; 1959-60 London, 23; 1962 Manchester, 21
PROVENANCE Mrs J. van Gogh-Bonger, Amsterdam [R 1905]; V. W. van Gogh, Laren; Leicester Galleries, London [R 1923]; S. Courtauld, London [R 1927]; London, The Home House Trustees [The Courtauld Institute], cat 1954, nr 155 [loan to the Tate Gallery, London 1954-5]

F 1501 LANDSCAPE WITH TREES
EXHIBITIONS 1905 Amsterdam, 471; 1924 Basle, 92; Zurich, 92; Stuttgart, 14; 1925 The Hague, 68; 1946-7 Liège etc, 83; 1947 Paris 1, 84; Geneva, 84; 1947-8 London etc, 154; 1948 Bergen, Oslo, 104; 1953 The Hague, 112; Otterlo, Amsterdam, 138; 1953-4 St Louis etc, 130; 1954-5 Bern, 145; 1955 Antwerp 1, 327; 1957 Stockholm, 86; 1958-9 Washington etc, 147; 1963-4 Amsterdam, 65; 1965-6 Stockholm, Göteborg, 91; 1967 Wolfsburg, 110
PROVENANCE Mrs J. van Gogh-Bonger, Amsterdam [R 1905]; V. W. van Gogh, Laren; Amsterdam, Rijksmuseum Vincent van Gogh [Vincent van Gogh Foundation, inv nr F 1501]

F 1502 THE ROAD TO TARASCON WITH FIGURE
EXHIBITIONS 1919 Haarlem, 18 [repr]; 1926 London 3, 28; 1927-8 Berlin etc, 63; 1947 Basle, 162; 1952 Milan, 102; 1953 Zurich, not listed in cat; 1956 Munich, 118; 1957 Essen, 294; 1961 Munich, 66; 1963 Hamburg, 93; 1967 Zurich, 96
PROVENANCE J. H. de Bois Art Gallery, Haarlem [R 1913 and 1917]; Private collection, England; Otto Wacker Art Gallery, Berlin [R 1926]; Zurich, Kunsthaus

F 1502a THE ROAD TO TARASCON: SKY WITH SUN
EXHIBITION 1939 Adelaide etc, 139
PROVENANCE John Russell, Belle-Isle-en-Mer; Thannhauser Art Gallery, New York; New York, J. K. Thannhauser, courtesy Thannhauser Foundation, cat The Thannhauser Foundation 1965, nr 18 [on loan to Guggenheim Museum, New York]

F 1503 PORTRAIT OF LA MOUSMÉ: BUST
EXHIBITIONS 1952 Milan, 100; 1953 The Hague, 113; Otterlo, Amsterdam, 128
PROVENANCE John Russell, Belle-Isle-en-Mer; Sale Paris [Drouot] 31 March 1920, 69; Le Garrec Art Gallery, Paris; d'Audretsch Art Gallery, The Hague; Lutz Art Gallery, Berlin; Amsterdam, Stedelijk Museum [R 1947 and 1953]; New York, Mrs K. Hirschland [R 1965]; New York, Paul M. Hirschland [R 1970]

F 1504 LA MOUSMÉ SITTING IN AN ARMCHAIR
EXHIBITION 1960 Moscow, no cat nr
PROVENANCE Possibly Sale Paris [Drouot] 16 May 1908, 54; Moscow, Pushkin Museum

F 1505 CORNER OF THE GARDEN OF ST PAUL'S HOSPITAL
EXHIBITIONS 1927 Basle etc, 118; 1928 Düsseldorf, 168; Karlsruhe, 121; 1929 Berlin 1, 104; Hamburg, 36; 1930 Amsterdam, 128; 1947 Basle, 158; 1952 Milan, 96; 1953 The Hague, 114; Otterlo, Amsterdam, 127; 1953-4 St Louis etc, 123; 1956 Nuremberg, 62; Munich, 119; 1958 Vienna, 92; Tokyo, Kyoto, 110; 1959 São Paulo, 2; 1961 Munich, 68; 1962 Warsaw, 70; 1963 Tel Aviv, Haifa, 79; 1966 Belgrade, 40
PROVENANCE J. J. Hanken, The Hague; Sale Amsterdam [F. Muller] 19 June 1917, 62; Otterlo, Rijksmuseum Kröller-Müller, inv nr 297-17, cat van Gogh 1970, nr 230

F 1506 FIELD WITH HOUSES AND SKY WITH SUN
EXHIBITIONS 1905 Amsterdam, 373; 1914-5 Amsterdam, 145; 1923 Utrecht, Rotterdam, 39; 1927-8 Berlin etc, 75; 1945 Amsterdam, no cat nr; 1946 Stockholm etc, 59; 1947 Basle, 159; 1947-8 London etc, 155; 1948 Bergen, Oslo, 105; 1953 The Hague, 115; Otterlo, Amsterdam, 139; 1953-4 St Louis etc, 124; 1954-5 Bern, 146; 1955 Antwerp 1, 289; 1955-6 Liverpool etc, 108; 1958-9 San Francisco etc, 138; 1959-60 Utrecht, 87; 1960 Enschede, 53; 1960-1 Montreal etc, 129; 1961 Arles; 1961-2 Baltimore etc, 127; 1962-3 Pittsburgh etc; 1963 Humlebaek, 114; 1964 Washington, New York, 101; 1965 Charleroi, Ghent, 67; 1966 Paris, Albi, 57; 1967 Lille, Zurich, 59; 1967-8 Dallas etc, 57; 1968 Liège, 57; 1968-9 London, 112; 1969 Humlebaek, 33
PROVENANCE Mrs J. van Gogh-Bonger, Amsterdam; V. W. van Gogh, Laren; Amsterdam, Rijksmuseum Vincent van Gogh [Vincent van Gogh Foundation, inv nr F 1506]

F 1507 THE BRIDGE AT TRINQUETAILLE
EXHIBITION 1959 Cincinnati, 311
PROVENANCE J. Hessel Art Gallery, Paris; R. Lehman, New York; New York, Estate of R. Lehman [bequeathed to the Metropolitan Museum, New York 1969]

F 1507a HEAD OF A GIRL [THE MUDLARK]
PROVENANCE John Russell, Belle-Isle-en-Mer; Thannhauser Art Gallery, New York; New York, J. K. Thannhauser, courtesy Thannhauser Foundation, cat The Thannhauser Foundation 1965, nr 15 [on loan to Guggenheim Museum, New York]

F 1508 recto STANDING MALE: NUDE
verso THE INTERIOR OF A RESTAURANT
EXHIBITIONS 1914-5 Amsterdam, 178; 1953 The Hague, 116; Otterlo, Amsterdam, 131; 1954-5 Bern, 147; 1955 Antwerp 1, 292; 1957 Stockholm, 74; 1962 London 1, 65;

1965-6 Stockholm, Göteborg, 90; 1967 Wolfsburg, 111
PROVENANCE Mrs J. van Gogh-Bonger, Amsterdam; V.W. van Gogh, Laren; Amsterdam, Rijksmuseum Vincent van Gogh [Vincent van Gogh Foundation, inv nr F 1508]

F 1509 A TRUNK OF A TREE
EXHIBITIONS 1947 San Francisco, 130; 1948 New York 2, 74; Cleveland, 48; 1949 New York 2, 89
PROVENANCE J. H. de Bois Art Gallery, Haarlem; New York, Wildenstein Art Gallery [R 1947 and 1948]; New York, Mrs George F. Baker [R 1970]

F 1510 CHAIR AT THE LEFT SIDE OF A FIREPLACE
EXHIBITIONS 1965-6 Stockholm, Göteborg, 92; 1967 Wolfsburg, 112; 1968-9 London, 151
PROVENANCE Mrs J. van Gogh-Bonger, Amsterdam; V.W. van Gogh, Laren; Amsterdam, Rijksmuseum Vincent van Gogh [Vincent van Gogh Foundation, inv nr F 1510]

F 1511 CHAIR ON THE RIGHT SIDE OF A FIREPLACE
EXHIBITION 1955 Antwerp 1, 293
PROVENANCE Mrs J. van Gogh-Bonger, Amsterdam; V.W. van Gogh, Laren; Amsterdam, Rijksmuseum Vincent van Gogh [Vincent van Gogh Foundation, inv nr F 1511]

F 1512 recto THE CANE-BOTTOMED CHAIR [sketched over an erased landscape]
verso SKETCHES OF PLOUGHING HORSES
EXHIBITIONS 1947-8 London etc, 157; 1948 Bergen, Oslo, 106; 1953 The Hague, 117; Otterlo, Amsterdam, 133; 1955 Antwerp 1, 294; 1963 Humlebaek, 102; 1964 Washington, New York, 102; 1965 Charleroi, Ghent, 68; 1966 Paris, Albi, 58; 1967 Lille, Zurich, 60; 1967-8 Dallas etc, 58; 1968 Liège, 58; 1969 Humlebaek, 32
PROVENANCE Mrs J. van Gogh-Bonger, Amsterdam; V.W. van Gogh, Laren; Amsterdam, Rijksmuseum Vincent van Gogh [Vincent van Gogh Foundation, inv nr F 1512]

F 1513 THE POND IN THE PARK, THE YELLOW HOUSE IN THE BACKGROUND
EXHIBITIONS 1905 Amsterdam, 409; 1914-5 Amsterdam, 160; 1924 Basle, 95; Zurich, 95; Stuttgart, 18; 1926 London 3, 26; 1927-8 Berlin etc, 97; 1945 Amsterdam, no cat nr; 1946 Stockholm etc, 49; 1953 The Hague, 118; Otterlo, Amsterdam, 137; 1953-4 St Louis etc, 129; 1954-5 Bern, 148; 1955 Antwerp 1, 290; 1959 Aix-en-Provence, 34; 1960 Arles; 1963 Humlebaek, 103; 1964 Washington, New York, 103; 1965 Charleroi, Ghent, 69; 1966 Paris, Albi, 59; 1967 Lille, Zurich, 61; 1967-8 Dallas etc, 59; 1968 Liège, 59; 1968-9 London, 134
PROVENANCE Mrs J. van Gogh-Bonger, Amsterdam [R 1905]; V.W. van Gogh, Laren; Amsterdam, Rijksmuseum Vincent van Gogh [Vincent van Gogh Foundation, inv nr F 1513]

F 1514 ARLES SEEN FROM THE FIELDS: SUMMER EVENING
EXHIBITIONS 1905 Amsterdam, 387; 1929 Winterthur, 59; 1937 Paris, 172; 1947 Basle, 160; 1952 Milan, 104; 1956 Munich, 114; 1961 Munich, 57
PROVENANCE Mrs J. van Gogh-Bonger, Amsterdam [R 1905]; Paul Majovsky, Budapest; E. Hahnloser, Zurich; Winterthur, Kunstmuseum [acquired 1928; gift E. Hahnloser]

F 1515 RHÔNE BANK, STARRY NIGHT
PROVENANCE Present owner unknown

F 1516 AN ORCHARD WITH THE TOWERS OF ARLES IN THE BACKGROUND
EXHIBITIONS 1905 Amsterdam, 365; 1923 Utrecht, Rotterdam, 65; London, 10; 1935-6 New York etc, 117
PROVENANCE Mrs J. van Gogh-Bonger, Amsterdam [R 1905]; M.J. Sadler, Oxford; Mrs Cornelius J. Sullivan, New York [R 1935]; Sale Sullivan, New York [Parke-Bernet] 6-7 December 1939, nr 157; Mrs Louis F. Hyde, Glens Falls, N.Y.; Glens Falls, N.Y., The Hyde Collection [acquired 1952]

F 1517 LANDSCAPE WITH FARM AND TWO TREES
EXHIBITIONS 1914-5 Amsterdam, 146; 1957 Essen, 270; 1960 Paris, 105; 1966 Washington, 240
PROVENANCE Mrs J. van Gogh-Bonger, Amsterdam; J. H. de Bois Art Gallery, Haarlem; H. Wiegersma, Deurne [R 1933]; Sale London [Sotheby] 25 November 1959, nr 80; Bryan L. Hunter, London; Sale London [Sotheby] 23 November 1960, nr 23; Upperville, Virginia, Mr and Mrs Paul Mellon [R 1966]

F 1518 THREE TREES, ROUTE DE TARASCON
EXHIBITIONS 1905 Amsterdam, 411; 1914-5 Amsterdam, 159; 1923 Utrecht, Rotterdam, 37; 1948 Cleveland, 44
PROVENANCE Mrs J. van Gogh-Bonger, Amsterdam; V.W. van Gogh, Laren; W. Pach, New York; Sale New York [Parke-Bernet] 6 January 1949, 29; Present owner unknown

F 1518a ROAD WITH TREES NEAR A HOUSE
EXHIBITIONS 1935 Haarlem 2, 15; 1958 Vienna, 92a
PROVENANCE Mrs J. van Gogh-Bonger, Amsterdam; Frederik van Eeden, Bussum; J. H. de Bois Art Gallery, Haarlem [R 1935]; Würthle Art Gallery, Vienna; Vienna, Albertina [acquired 1936], inv nr 26.871

F 1519 CAFÉ IN ARLES: PLACE DU FORUM
EXHIBITIONS 1905 Amsterdam, 388; 1906 Berlin, 71
PROVENANCE Mrs J. van Gogh-Bonger, Amsterdam [R 1905]; Mrs Hugo von Tschudi, Munich [on loan at the Museum in Breslau]; Fritz Nathan Art Gallery, Zurich; Cabbé-Roquebrune, France, Emery Reves [R 1970]

F 1520 recto MASK OF AN EGYPTIAN MUMMY
verso MASK OF AN EGYPTIAN MUMMY
PROVENANCE Mrs J. van Gogh-Bonger, Amsterdam; V.W. van Gogh, Laren; Amsterdam, Rijksmuseum Vincent van Gogh [Vincent van Gogh Foundation, inv nr F 1520]

F 1521 recto MASK OF AN EGYPTIAN MUMMY
verso MASK OF AN EGYPTIAN MUMMY
PROVENANCE Mrs J. van Gogh-Bonger, Amsterdam; V.W. van Gogh, Laren; Amsterdam, Rijksmuseum Vincent van Gogh [Vincent van Gogh Foundation, inv nr F 1521]

SAINT RÉMY PERIOD

F 1522 TREE WITH IVY AND A STONE BENCH IN THE GARDEN OF ST PAUL'S HOSPITAL
EXHIBITIONS 1905 Amsterdam, 403; 1914-5 Amsterdam, 189; 1923 Utrecht, Rotterdam, 45; 1924 Basle, 94; Zurich, 94; Stuttgart, 7; 1925 The Hague, 65; 1926 London 3; 1927-8 Berlin etc, 91; 1932 Manchester, 76; 1947 Basle, 164; 1947-8 London etc, 159; 1948 Bergen, Oslo, 107; 1949-50 New York, Chicago, 147; 1953 The Hague, 141; Otterlo, Amsterdam, 171; 1953-4 St Louis etc, 156; 1954-5 Bern, 149; 1955 Antwerp 1, 328; 1955-6 Liverpool etc, 123; 1957 Marseilles, 77; Stockholm, 77; 1958-9 San Francisco etc, 139; 1959-60 Utrecht, 89; 1960 Enschede, 55; 1960-1 Montreal etc, 130; 1961-2 Baltimore etc, 129; 1962-3 Pittsburgh etc; 1963 Humlebaek, 104; 1964 Washington, New York, 104; 1965 Charleroi, Ghent, 70; 1966 Paris, Albi, 60; 1967 Lille, Zurich, 62; 1967-8 Dallas etc, 60; 1968 Liège, 60; 1968-9 London, 146
PROVENANCE Mrs J. van Gogh-Bonger, Amsterdam [R 1905]; V.W. van Gogh, Laren; Amsterdam, Rijksmuseum Vincent van Gogh [Vincent van Gogh Foundation, inv nr F 1522]

F 1523 DEATH'S-HEAD MOTH
EXHIBITIONS 1947-8 London etc, 160; 1948 Bergen, Oslo, 108; 1949-50 New York, Chicago, 135; 1955 Antwerp 1, 357; 1966 Paris, Albi, 61; 1967 Lille, Zurich, 63; 1967-8 Dallas etc, 61; 1968 Liège, 61
PROVENANCE Mrs J. van Gogh-Bonger, Amsterdam; V.W. van Gogh, Laren; Amsterdam, Rijksmuseum Vincent van Gogh [Vincent van Gogh Foundation, inv nr F 1523]

F 1524 CYPRESSES
EXHIBITIONS 1905 Amsterdam, 421; 1935-6 New York etc, 118; 1943 New York 2, 76; 1944 New York 1, 91; 1946 Chicago, 24; 1955 New York 2, 105; 1963 New York 3, 132
PROVENANCE Mrs J. van Gogh-Bonger, Amsterdam [R 1905]; M. K. Fahraeus, Lidingö-Brevik [acquired 1911]; M. Gösta Olson, Svensk-Franska Konst Galleriet, Stockholm; N. Eisenlöffel Art Gallery, Amsterdam; Otto Wacker Art Gallery, Berlin; Thannhauser Art Gallery, New York; Robert Allerton, USA; Chicago, The Art Institute of Chicago [R. Allerton bequest], inv nr 27.543

F 1525 CYPRESSES
EXHIBITIONS 1905 Amsterdam, 420; 1914-5 Amsterdam, 186; 1923 Utrecht, Rotterdam, 43; London, 5; 1935-6 New York etc, 119; 1940 San Francisco 3, 43; 1943 New York 2, 77; 1947 San Francisco, 137; 1948 Cleveland, 50; 1949-50 New York, Chicago, 136; 1951 Houston, 16; 1953 New York, 80; 1955 Paris 2, 79; 1963 Hamburg, 95
PROVENANCE Mrs J. van Gogh-Bonger, Amsterdam [R 1905]; M. E. Sadler, Oxford; Private collection, Germany; M. Knoedler Art Galllery, New York [R 1935]; Brooklyn, The Brooklyn Museum [acquired 1938], inv nr 38.123.19, cat 1967, p 402

F 1525a CYPRESSES, WITH TWO WOMEN IN THE FOREGROUND
EXHIBITIONS 1905 Amsterdam, 422; 1947 Basle, 163; 1952 Milan, 122; 1956 Nuremberg, 67; Munich, 140; 1958 Vienna, 108; Tokyo, Kyoto, 112; 1959 São Paulo, 3; 1961 Munich, 70; 1962 Warsaw, 86; London 1, 61; 1963 Tel Aviv, Haifa, 96; 1963-4 Amsterdam, 67; 1964 Kassel, 3
PROVENANCE Mrs J. van Gogh-Bonger, Amsterdam [R 1905]; Miss J. A. van Hasselt, Amsterdam; Fréquin Art Gallery, The Hague [R 1942]; Otterlo, Rijksmuseum Kröller-Müller, inv nr 1110-42, cat van Gogh 1970, nr 252

F 1526 OLEANDERS IN THE HOSPITAL GARDEN AT SAINT RÉMY
EXHIBITION 1908 Paris 2, 14
PROVENANCE G. Fayet, Igny [R 1908]; E. Druet Art Gallery, Paris; Sacha Guitry, Paris; Present owner unknown

F 1527 FLOWERS IN THE GARDEN OF THE HOSPITAL AT SAINT RÉMY
EXHIBITIONS 1905 Amsterdam, 362; 1927 Basle etc, 102; 1928 Düsseldorf, 169; Karlsruhe, 104; 1929 Berlin 1, 131; Hamburg, 143; 1930 Amsterdam, 129; 1935-6 New York etc, 121; 1947 Basle, 165; 1950-1 Leiden etc, 60; 1952 Milan, 95; 1953 The Hague, 119; Otterlo, Amsterdam, 136; 1953-4 St Louis etc, 159; 1956 Munich, 139; 1957 Essen, 332; 1958 Vienna, 106; Tokyo, Kyoto, 111; 1959 Aix-en-Provence, 52; 1961 Munich, 69; 1962 Warsaw, 69; 1963 Tel Aviv, Haifa, 97; 1966 Belgrade, 39
PROVENANCE Mrs J. van Gogh-Bonger, Amsterdam; Sale Amsterdam [F. Muller] 29 April 1914, 406; Sale Amsterdam [F. Muller] 6 July 1915, 54; Otterlo, Rijksmuseum Kröller-Müller, inv nr 281-15, cat van Gogh 1970, nr 229

F 1528 WINDOW OF THE ROOM USED BY VINCENT AS STUDIO AT ST PAUL'S HOSPITAL
EXHIBITIONS 1905 Amsterdam, 155; 1927 Paris; 1930 Amsterdam, 117; 1945 Amsterdam, no cat nr; 1946 Stockholm etc, 76; 1947-8 London etc, 161; 1948 Bergen, Oslo, 109; 1949-50 New York, Chicago, 145; 1953 The Hague, 142; Otterlo, Amsterdam, 168; 1953-4 St Louis etc, 154; 1954-5 Bern, 150; 1955 Antwerp 1, 354; 1955-6 Liverpool etc, 128; 1957 Stockholm, 80; 1958-9 San Francisco etc, 142; 1959 Aix-en-Provence, 56; 1960 Enschede, 56; 1960-1 Montreal etc, 134; 1961-2 Baltimore etc, 130; 1962-3 Pittsburgh etc; 1963 Humlebaek, 105; 1964 Washington, New York, 105; 1965 Charleroi, Ghent, 72; 1966 Paris, Albi, 62; 1967 Lille, Zurich, 64; 1967-8 Dallas etc, 62; 1968 Liège, 62; 1968-9 London, 154; 1969 Humlebaek, 34
PROVENANCE Mrs J. van Gogh-Bonger, Amsterdam; V.W. van Gogh, Laren; Amsterdam, Rijksmuseum Vincent van Gogh [Vincent van Gogh Foundation, inv nr F 1528]

F 1529 A PASSAGE AT ST PAUL'S HOSPITAL
EXHIBITIONS 1905 Amsterdam, 363; 1914-5 Amsterdam, 156; 1920 New York, 7; 1926 Munich, 2102; 1929 New York, 97; 1934-5 New York, 18; 1935-6 New York etc, 120; 1951 Houston, 19; 1955 New York 2, 53
PROVENANCE Mrs J. van Gogh-Bonger, Amsterdam [R 1905]; V.W. van Gogh, Laren; John D. Rockefeller, New York [R 1929]; New York, Museum of Modern Art [acquired 1948; Mrs Abby Aldrich Rockefeller bequest], inv nr 242-48

F 1530 THE VESTIBULE OF ST PAUL'S HOSPITAL
EXHIBITIONS 1914-5 Amsterdam, 154; 1923 Utrecht, Rotterdam, 25; 1926 London 3, 1; 1927-8 Berlin etc, 81; 1937 Paris, 77; 1945 Amsterdam, no cat nr; 1946 Stockholm etc, 77; 1946-7 Liège etc, 128; 1947 Paris 1, 129; Geneva, 129; 1947-8 London etc, 163; 1948 Bergen, Oslo, 116; 1953 The Hague, 143; Otterlo, Amsterdam, 169; 1953-4 St Louis etc, 153; 1954-5 Bern, 151; 1955 Antwerp 1, 353; 1955-6 Liverpool etc, 127; 1957 Marseilles, 81; Stockholm, 81; 1958-9 San Francisco etc, 143; 1959 Aix-en-Provence, 57; 1960 Enschede, 57; 1961-2 Baltimore etc, 131; 1962-3 Pittsburgh etc; 1963 Humlebaek, 106; 1964 Washington, New York, 106; 1966 Paris, Albi, 63; 1967 Lille, Zurich, 65; 1967-8 Dallas etc, 63; 1968 Liège, 63; 1968-9 London, 155; 1969 Humlebaek, 35
PROVENANCE Mrs J. van Gogh-Bonger, Amsterdam; V.W. van Gogh, Laren; Amsterdam, Rijksmuseum Vincent van Gogh [Vincent van Gogh Foundation, inv nr F 1530]

F 1531 THE FOUNTAIN IN THE GARDEN OF ST PAUL'S HOSPITAL
EXHIBITIONS 1891 Bruxelles; 1892 Antwerp, 10; 1893 Copenhagen, 195; 1905 Amsterdam, 394; 1914 Berlin, 78; 1914-5 Amsterdam, 143; 1915 Amsterdam, 24; 1923 Utrecht, Rotterdam, 34; 1925 The Hague, 76; 1926 Munich, 2108; 1927-8 Berlin etc, 82; 1935-6 New York etc, 122; 1937 Paris, 189; 1945 Amsterdam, no cat nr; 1946 Stockholm etc, 78; 1946-7 Liège etc, 130; 1947 Paris 1, 131; Geneva, 131; 1947-8 London etc, 162; 1948 Bergen, Oslo, 110; 1949-50 New York, Chicago, 137; 1951 Lyons etc, 94; 1953 The Hague, 144; Otterlo, Amsterdam, 170; 1953-4 St Louis etc, 155; 1954-5 Curaçao; 1955 Palm Beach etc, 37; Antwerp 1, 329; 1955-6 Liverpool etc, 124; 1957 Nijmegen; Stockholm, 79; 1958-9 San Francisco etc, 140; 1959 Aix-en-Provence, 55; 1960 Enschede, 58; 1960-1 Montreal etc, 131; 1961-2 Baltimore etc, 132; 1962-3 Pittsburgh etc; 1963 Sheffield, 20; Humlebaek, 107; 1964 Washington, New York, 107; 1965 Charleroi, Ghent, 71; 1966 Paris, Albi, 64; 1967 Lille, Zurich, 66; 1967-8 Dallas etc, 64; 1968 Liège, 64; 1968-9 London, 148; 1969 Humlebaek, 36
PROVENANCE Mrs J. van Gogh-Bonger, Amsterdam [R 1905]; V.W. van Gogh, Laren; Amsterdam, Rijksmuseum Vincent van Gogh [Vincent van Gogh Foundation, inv nr F 1531]

F 1532 TREE WITH IVY IN THE GARDEN OF ST PAUL'S HOSPITAL
EXHIBITIONS 1905 Amsterdam, 357; 1914-5 Amsterdam, 188; 1926 London 3, 40; 1927-8 Berlin etc, 85; 1932 Manchester, 73; 1946-7 Liège etc, 129; 1947 Paris 1, 130; Geneva, 130; 1947-8 London etc, 164; 1948 Bergen, Oslo, 111; 1962 London 1, 63; 1964 Zundert, 26; 1966 Paris, Albi, 65; 1967 Lille, Zurich, 67; 1967-8 Dallas etc, 65; 1968 Liège, 65; 1968-9 London, 147

PROVENANCE Mrs J. van Gogh-Bonger, Amsterdam [R 1905]; V. W. van Gogh, Laren; Amsterdam, Rijksmuseum Vincent van Gogh [Vincent van Gogh Foundation, inv nr F 1532]

F 1533 A TREE IN THE GARDEN OF ST PAUL'S HOSPITAL, WITH A FIGURE IN THE BACKGROUND
EXHIBITIONS 1905 Amsterdam, 418; 1914 Berlin, 60; 1914-5 Amsterdam, 170; 1926 London 3, 2; 1927-8 Berlin etc, 57; 1930 Amsterdam, 118; 1945 Amsterdam, no cat nr; 1946 Stockholm etc, 68; 1946-7 Liège etc, 131; 1947 Paris 1, 132; Geneva, 132; 1947-8 London etc, 165; 1948 Bergen, Oslo, 112; 1949-50 New York, Chicago, 138; 1953 The Hague, 145; Otterlo, Amsterdam, 172; 1953-4 St Louis etc, 157; 1954-5 Bern, 152; 1955 Antwerp 1, 330; 1955-6 Liverpool etc, 126; 1957 Stockholm, 82; 1958-9 San Francisco etc, 141; 1960 Enschede, 62; 1965-6 Stockholm, Göteborg, 93; 1967 Wolfsburg, 113; 1967-8 Dallas etc, 66; 1968 Liège, 66; 1968-9 London, 157; 1969 Humlebaek, 37
PROVENANCE Mrs J. van Gogh-Bonger, Amsterdam [R 1905]; V. W. van Gogh, Laren; Amsterdam, Rijksmuseum Vincent van Gogh [Vincent van Gogh Foundation, inv nr F 1533]

F 1534 A TREE IN THE GARDEN OF ST PAUL'S HOSPITAL
EXHIBITION 1927-8 Berlin etc, not listed in cat
PROVENANCE Thannhauser Art Gallery, Berlin; Present owner unknown

F 1535 THE GARDEN OF ST PAUL'S HOSPITAL
EXHIBITIONS 1905 Amsterdam, 356; 1914 Berlin, 59; 1914-5 Amsterdam, 162; 1926 Munich, 2098; 1930 Amsterdam, 119; 1945 Amsterdam, no cat nr; 1946 Stockholm etc, 69; 1946-7 Liège etc, 132; 1947 Paris 1, 133; Geneva, 133; 1947-8 London etc, 166; 1948 Bergen, Oslo, 113; 1953 The Hague, 146; Otterlo, Amsterdam, 173; 1953-4 St Louis etc, 158; 1954-5 Bern, 153; 1955 Antwerp 1, 331; 1955-6 Liverpool etc, 129; 1957 Stockholm, 83; 1959 Aix-en-Provence, 58; 1961-2 Baltimore etc, 133; 1962-3 Pittsburgh etc; 1963 Humlebaek, 108; 1964 Washington, New York, 108; 1966 Paris, Albi, 66; 1967 Lille, Zurich, 68; 1967-8 Dallas etc, 67; 1968 Liège, 67; 1968-9 London, 156; 1969 Humlebaek, 38
PROVENANCE Mrs J. van Gogh-Bonger, Amsterdam [R 1905]; V. W. van Gogh, Laren; Amsterdam, Rijksmuseum Vincent van Gogh [Vincent van Gogh Foundation, inv nr F 1535]

F 1536 THE GARDEN OF ST PAUL'S HOSPITAL IN SUMMER
EXHIBITIONS 1905 Amsterdam, 358; 1912 Cologne, 70; 1914 Berlin, 68
PROVENANCE Mrs J. van Gogh-Bonger, Amsterdam [R 1905]; Paul Cassirer Art Gallery, Berlin [acquired 1907]; Mrs Tilla Durieux-Cassirer, Berlin [R 1912]; Mrs Paret, Berlin [R 1914]; Present owner unknown

F 1537 STONE BENCH IN THE GARDEN OF ST PAUL'S HOSPITAL
EXHIBITIONS 1954-5 Bern, 154; 1955 Antwerp 1, 332
PROVENANCE Mrs J. van Gogh-Bonger, Amsterdam; V. W. van Gogh, Laren; Amsterdam, Rijksmuseum Vincent van Gogh [Vincent van Gogh Foundation, inv nr F 1537]

F 1538 WHEATFIELDS AND CYPRESSES
EXHIBITIONS 1905 Amsterdam, 428; 1914-5 Amsterdam, 185; 1923 Utrecht, Rotterdam, 58; 1927-8 Berlin etc, 92; 1932 Manchester, 74; 1937 Paris, 179; 1946-7 Liège etc, 133; 1947 Paris 1, 134; Geneva, 134; 1947-8 London etc, 167; 1948 Bergen, Oslo, 114; 1949-50 New York, Chicago, 139; 1951 Lyons etc, 95; 1953 The Hague, 147; Otterlo, Amsterdam, 174; 1953-4 St Louis etc, 160; 1955 Antwerp 1, 333; 1955-6 Liverpool etc, 130; 1957 Marseilles, 78; Stockholm, 85; 1958-9 San Francisco etc, 144; 1959 Aix-en-Provence, 59; 1959-60 Utrecht, 92; 1960 Enschede, 60; 1961-2 Baltimore etc, 134; 1962-3 Pittsburgh etc; 1963 Humlebaek, 109; 1964 Washington, New York 109; 1965 Charleroi, Ghent, 73; 1966 Paris, Albi, 67; 1967 Lille, Zurich, 69; 1967-8 Dallas etc, 68; 1968 Liège, 68; 1968-9 London, 160; 1969 Humlebaek, 39
PROVENANCE Mrs J. van Gogh-Bonger, Amsterdam [R 1905]; V. W. van Gogh, Laren; Amsterdam, Rijksmuseum Vincent van Gogh [Vincent van Gogh Foundation, inv nr F 1538]

F 1539 recto LANDSCAPE WITH CYPRESSES WITH FOUR FIGURES
verso SIX SKETCHES OF FIGURES, AMONG OTHERS A MAN SOWING WHEAT
EXHIBITIONS 1905 Amsterdam, 423; 1953 Berlin, 21; 1957 Essen, 333; 1961 Munich, 71; 1964 Kassel, 4
PROVENANCE Mrs J. van Gogh-Bonger, Amsterdam [R 1905]; Karl Osthaus, Hagen; Essen, Folkwangmuseum, cat 1929, nr 438

F 1540 CYPRESSES IN STARRY NIGHT [lost]
EXHIBITIONS 1905 Amsterdam, 429; 1914 Berlin, 103; 1927-8 Berlin etc, 109; 1937 Paris, 78
PROVENANCE Mrs J. van Gogh-Bonger, Amsterdam [R 1905]; Alfred Walter von Heymel, Munich; Mrs A. Heye, Bremen; Bremen, Kunsthalle [acquired 1918]; The drawing disappeared during World War II

F 1541 recto LANDSCAPE WITH CYPRESSES
verso VIEW OF A TOWN WITH A SPIRE
PROVENANCE Mrs J. van Gogh-Bonger, Amsterdam; V. W. van Gogh, Laren; Amsterdam, Rijksmuseum Vincent van Gogh [Vincent van Gogh Foundation, inv nr F 1541]

F 1542 WILD VEGETATION IN THE HILLS
EXHIBITIONS 1924 Basle, 96; Zurich, 96; Stuttgart, 15; 1927-8 Berlin etc, 87; 1932 Manchester, 71; 1937 Paris, 166; 1953 The Hague, 148; Otterlo, Amsterdam, 175; 1953-4 St Louis etc, 162; 1954-5 Bern, 155; 1955 Antwerp 1, 334; 1957 Stockholm, 78; 1959 Aix-en-Provence, 54; 1965 Stockholm, Göteborg, 94; 1967 Wolfsburg, 114; 1967-8 Dallas etc, 69; 1968 Liège, 69; 1968-9 London, 161
PROVENANCE Mrs J. van Gogh-Bonger, Amsterdam; V. W. van Gogh, Laren; Amsterdam, Rijksmuseum Vincent van Gogh [Vincent van Gogh Foundation, inv nr F 1542]

F 1543 OLIVE TREES IN THE MOUNTAINS
EXHIBITION 1914-5 Amsterdam, 183
PROVENANCE Mrs J. van Gogh-Bonger, Amsterdam; V. W. van Gogh, Laren; Amsterdam, Rijksmuseum Vincent van Gogh [Vincent van Gogh Foundation, inv nr F 1543]

F 1544 OLIVE TREES IN LANDSCAPE WITH MOUNT GAUSSIER AND THE ROCK WITH TWO HOLES
EXHIBITIONS 1923 Utrecht, Rotterdam, 46; London, 9
PROVENANCE Mrs J. van Gogh-Bonger, Amsterdam; M. E. Sadler, Oxford; Sale Paris [Petit] 9 May 1932, 7; Paul Cassirer Art Gallery, Amsterdam; Max Silberberg, Breslau; Sale Berlin [Graupe] 23 March 1935, 37; East Berlin, National Galerie [acquired 1935], inv nr F IV 721, cat 6

F 1545 THE PARK OF ST PAUL'S HOSPITAL
EXHIBITION 1927-8 Berlin etc, not listed in cat
PROVENANCE Mrs S. Paret, Berlin; Sale Berlin [Cassirer] 17 May 1927, 40 [repr]; M. Fahrenhorst, Düsseldorf; Sale Cologne [Lempertz] 6 December 1968, 3724; Mrs M. Feilchenfeldt Gallery, Zurich; Fullerton, California, Norton Simon Foundation [R 1970]

F 1546 REAPER IN A WHEAT FIELD WITH RISING SUN
EXHIBITIONS 1905 Amsterdam, 424; 1927-8 Berlin etc, 93; 1958 East Berlin, K 36
PROVENANCE Mrs J. van Gogh-Bonger, Amsterdam [R 1905]; F. M. Wibaut, Amsterdam; Otto Wacker Art Gallery, Berlin; East Berlin, National Galerie [acquired 1928], inv nr F III 1639, cat 4

F 1547 WHEATFIELD BEHIND ST PAUL'S HOSPITAL
EXHIBITIONS 1898 The Hague; 1905 Amsterdam, 425; 1914-5 Amsterdam, 182; 1923 Utrecht, Rotterdam, 57; 1924 Basle, 91; Zurich, 91; Stuttgart, 13; 1927-8 Berlin etc, 89; 1945 Amsterdam, no cat nr; 1946 Stockholm etc, 80; 1946-7 Liège etc, 134; 1947 Paris 1, 135; Geneva, 135; 1947-8 London etc, 168; 1948 Bergen, Oslo, 115; 1953 The Hague, 149; Otterlo, Amsterdam, 176; 1953-4 St Louis etc, 161; 1955 Antwerp 1, 335; 1957 Stockholm, 84; 1958-9 San Francisco etc, 145; 1960 Enschede, 61; 1960-1 Montreal etc, 132; 1965-6 Stockholm, Göteborg, 95; 1967 Wolfsburg, 115
PROVENANCE Mrs J. van Gogh-Bonger, Amsterdam; V. W. van Gogh, Laren; Amsterdam, Rijksmuseum Vincent van Gogh [Vincent van Gogh Foundation, inv nr F 1547]

F 1548 WHEATFIELD WITH CYPRESS
EXHIBITIONS 1905 Amsterdam, 374; 1935-6 New York etc, 123; 1943 New York 2, 78
PROVENANCE Mrs J. van Gogh-Bonger, Amsterdam [R 1905]; G. Sérigiers, Antwerp; Bernard Wacker, Düsseldorf; Thannhauser Art Gallery, New York; James W. Barney, New York [R 1935]; Sale New York [Parke-Bernet] 26 October 1944, 77; New York, J. K. Thannhauser Art Gallery; Present owner unknown

F 1549 recto STUDY OF A CHAIR AND A LEFT HAND
verso FIELD BEHIND ST PAUL'S HOSPITAL
EXHIBITIONS [verso] 1927-8 Berlin etc, 84; 1945 Amsterdam, no cat nr; 1955 Antwerp 1, 336; 1966 Paris, Albi, 68; 1967 Lille, Zurich, 70; 1967-8 Dallas etc, 70; 1968 Liège, 70; 1968-9 London, 159
PROVENANCE Mrs J. van Gogh-Bonger, Amsterdam; V. W. van Gogh, Laren; Amsterdam, Rijksmuseum Vincent van Gogh [Vincent van Gogh Foundation, inv nr F 1549]

F 1550 SOWER IN THE RAIN
EXHIBITIONS 1957 Essen, 337; 1961 Munich, 72
PROVENANCE Karl Osthaus, Hagen; Essen, Folkwangmuseum, cat 1929, nr 437

F 1551 recto SOWER IN THE RAIN
verso PEASANT WORKING
EXHIBITIONS 1905 Amsterdam, 430; 1932 Manchester, 68; 1945 Amsterdam, no cat nr; 1962 London 1, 66; 1965-6 Stockholm, Göteborg, 96; 1967 Wolfsburg, 116; 1967-8 Dallas etc, 71; 1968 Liège, 71; 1968-9 London, 179; 1969 Humlebaek, 40
PROVENANCE Mrs J. van Gogh-Bonger, Amsterdam [R 1905]; V. W. van Gogh, Laren; Amsterdam, Rijksmuseum Vincent van Gogh [Vincent van Gogh Foundation, inv nr F 1551]

F 1552 ENCLOSURE BEHIND ST PAUL'S HOSPITAL: RISING SUN
EXHIBITIONS 1937 Paris, 76; 1956 Nuremberg, 65; Munich, 140a; 1957 Essen, 336; 1958 Vienna, 107; Amsterdam 1, 320; 1961 Munich, 73; 1968 Munich, 29
PROVENANCE Mrs Hugo von Tschudi, Munich; Munich, Neue Staatsgalerie, inv nr 10037, cat Bayerische Staatsgemäldesammlungen, 1955, p 71; Munich, Staatliche Graphische Sammlung, inv nr 44336

F 1553 LANDSCAPE WITH SUN AND TWO PEASANTS
EXHIBITIONS 1905 Amsterdam, 427; 1927-8 Berlin etc, 110
PROVENANCE Mrs J. van Gogh-Bonger, Amsterdam [R 1905]; J. H. de Bois Art Gallery, Haarlem; G. Schweitzer, Berlin [R 1927-8]; Present owner unknown

F 1554 ROCKY GROUND: MONTMAJOUR
PROVENANCE Jacques Doucet, Paris; Sale Paris [Drouot] 28/29 December 1917, 335 [reproduced]; Paul Cassirer Art Gallery, Berlin; Madrid, Mrs M. L. Caturla

F 1555 OLIVE TREES
EXHIBITIONS 1924 Basle, Zurich, 93; Stuttgart, 17; 1925 The Hague, 74; 1927-8 Berlin etc, 72; 1932 Manchester, 72; 1953-4 St Louis etc, 163
PROVENANCE Mrs J. van Gogh-Bonger, Amsterdam; V. W. van Gogh, Laren; Amsterdam, Rijksmuseum Vincent van Gogh [Vincent van Gogh Foundation, inv nr F 1555]

F 1556 CORNER OF THE ENCLOSURE BEHIND ST PAUL'S HOSPITAL
PROVENANCE Mrs J. van Gogh-Bonger, Amsterdam; V. W. van Gogh, Laren; Amsterdam, Rijksmuseum Vincent van Gogh [Vincent van Gogh Foundation, inv nr F 1556]

F 1557 CORNER OF THE ENCLOSURE BEHIND ST PAUL'S HOSPITAL
PROVENANCE Mrs J. van Gogh-Bonger, Amsterdam; V. W. van Gogh, Laren; Amsterdam, Rijksmuseum Vincent van Gogh [Vincent van Gogh Foundation, inv nr F 1557]

F 1558 CORNER OF THE ENCLOSURE BEHIND ST PAUL'S HOSPITAL
PROVENANCE Mrs J. van Gogh-Bonger, Amsterdam; V. W. van Gogh, Laren; Amsterdam, Rijksmuseum Vincent van Gogh [Vincent van Gogh Foundation, inv nr F 1558]

F 1559 CORNER OF THE ENCLOSURE BEHIND ST PAUL'S HOSPITAL
PROVENANCE Mrs J. van Gogh-Bonger, Amsterdam; V. W. van Gogh, Laren; Amsterdam, Rijksmuseum Vincent van Gogh [Vincent van Gogh Foundation, inv nr F 1559]

F 1560 CORNER OF THE ENCLOSURE BEHIND ST PAUL'S HOSPITAL
PROVENANCE Mrs J. van Gogh-Bonger, Amsterdam; V. W. van Gogh, Laren; Amsterdam, Rijksmuseum Vincent van Gogh [Vincent van Gogh Foundation, inv nr F 1560]

F 1561 CORNER OF THE ENCLOSURE BEHIND ST PAUL'S HOSPITAL
PROVENANCE Mrs J. van Gogh-Bonger, Amsterdam; V. W. van Gogh, Laren; Amsterdam, Rijksmuseum Vincent van Gogh [Vincent van Gogh Foundation, inv nr F 1561]

F 1562 TREE IN THE ENCLOSURE BEHIND ST PAUL'S HOSPITAL
EXHIBITIONS 1955 Antwerp 1, 337; 1962 London 1, 62
PROVENANCE Mrs J. van Gogh-Bonger, Amsterdam; V. W. van Gogh, Laren; Amsterdam, Rijksmuseum Vincent van Gogh [Vincent van Gogh Foundation, inv nr F 1562]

F 1563 ENCLOSURE WITH PINE TREES
PROVENANCE Mrs J. van Gogh-Bonger, Amsterdam; V. W. van Gogh, Laren; Amsterdam, Rijksmuseum Vincent van Gogh [Vincent van Gogh Foundation, inv nr F 1563]

F 1564 SIX PINES NEAR THE ENCLOSURE WALL
PROVENANCE Mrs J. van Gogh-Bonger, Amsterdam; V. W. van Gogh, Laren; Bergen, Netherlands, D. de Wolff Peereboom [acquired 1943]

F 1565 PINE TREES IN THE GARDEN OF ST PAUL'S HOSPITAL
EXHIBITIONS 1955 Antwerp 1, 338; 1957 Marseilles, 79; Stockholm, 89
PROVENANCE Mrs J. van Gogh-Bonger, Amsterdam; V. W. van Gogh, Laren; Amsterdam, Rijksmuseum Vincent van Gogh [Vincent van Gogh Foundation, inv nr F 1565]

F 1566 THREE PINE TREES IN THE ENCLOSURE
PROVENANCE Mrs J. van Gogh-Bonger, Amsterdam; V. W. van Gogh, Laren; Amsterdam, Private collection [R 1970]

F1567 A CLUSTER OF PINE TREES
PROVENANCE Mrs J. van Gogh-Bonger, Amsterdam;
V. W. van Gogh, Laren; Amsterdam, Rijksmuseum Vincent
van Gogh [Vincent van Gogh Foundation, inv nr F1567]

F1568 PINE TREES NEAR THE ENCLOSURE
PROVENANCE Mrs J. van Gogh-Bonger, Amsterdam;
V. W. van Gogh, Laren; Amsterdam, Rijksmuseum Vincent
van Gogh [Vincent van Gogh Foundation, inv nr F1568]

F1569 ROAD WITH PINE TREES
EXHIBITION 1962 London 1, 58
PROVENANCE Mrs J. van Gogh-Bonger, Amsterdam;
V. W. van Gogh, Laren; Amsterdam, Rijksmuseum Vincent
van Gogh [Vincent van Gogh Foundation, inv nr F1569]

F1570 PINE TREES IN THE GARDEN OF ST PAUL'S
HOSPITAL
EXHIBITIONS 1962 London 1, 59; 1964 Zundert, 27;
1965-6 Stockholm, Göteborg, 97; 1967 Wolfsburg, 117;
1967-8 Dallas etc, 72; 1968 Liège, 72; 1968-9 London, 149
PROVENANCE Mrs J. van Gogh-Bonger, Amsterdam;
V. W. van Gogh, Laren; Amsterdam, Rijksmuseum Vincent
van Gogh [Vincent van Gogh Foundation, inv nr F1570]

F1571 CORNER OF THE ENCLOSURE WITH PINE TREES
EXHIBITIONS 1952 Paris 2, 160; 1954-5 Bern, 156; 1955
Antwerp 1, 339
PROVENANCE Mrs J. van Gogh-Bonger, Amsterdam;
V. W. van Gogh, Laren; Amsterdam, Rijksmuseum Vincent
van Gogh [Vincent van Gogh Foundation, inv nr F1571]

F1572 recto FOUR PINE TREES WITH WALL OF THE
ENCLOSURE
verso STONE BENCH IN THE GARDEN OF ST PAUL'S
HOSPITAL
EXHIBITIONS 1945 Amsterdam, no cat nr; 1954-5 Bern,
157; 1955 Antwerp 1, 340; 1966 Paris, Albi, 69; 1967 Lille,
Zurich, 71
PROVENANCE Mrs J. van Gogh-Bonger, Amsterdam;
V. W. van Gogh, Laren; Amsterdam, Rijksmuseum Vincent
van Gogh [Vincent van Gogh Foundation, inv nr F1572]

F1573 GROUP OF PINES
PROVENANCE Mrs J. van Gogh-Bonger, Amsterdam;
V. W. van Gogh, Laren; Amsterdam, Rijksmuseum Vincent
van Gogh [Vincent van Gogh Foundation, inv nr F1573]

F1574 THE GARDEN OF ST PAUL'S HOSPITAL
EXHIBITIONS 1953 The Hague, 150; Otterlo, Amsterdam,
177
PROVENANCE Mrs J. van Gogh-Bonger, Amsterdam;
V. W. van Gogh, Laren; Amsterdam, H. M. Wezelaar
[acquired about 1944]

F1575 A STORM-BROKEN PINE TREE
PROVENANCE Mrs J. van Gogh-Bonger, Amsterdam;
V. W. van Gogh, Laren; Amsterdam, Rijksmuseum Vincent
van Gogh [Vincent van Gogh Foundation, inv nr F1575]

F1576 recto DEAD TREE IN THE GARDEN OF ST PAUL'S
HOSPITAL
verso ENCLOSURE WITH TREES
EXHIBITIONS 1955 Antwerp 1, 341; 1958-9 San Francisco
etc, 146; 1960 Enschede, 62; 1965-6 Stockholm, Göteborg,
98; 1967 Wolfsburg, 118
PROVENANCE Mrs J. van Gogh-Bonger, Amsterdam;
V. W. van Gogh, Laren; Amsterdam, Rijksmuseum Vincent
van Gogh [Vincent van Gogh Foundation, inv nr F1576]

F1577 GARDEN WITH STONE BENCH AND ST PAUL'S
HOSPITAL IN THE BACKGROUND
EXHIBITIONS 1954-5 Bern, 158; 1955 Antwerp 1, 342; 1966
Paris, Albi, 70; 1967 Lille, Zurich, 72; 1967-8 Dallas etc, 73;
1968 Liège, 73; 1968-9 London, 150
PROVENANCE Mrs J. van Gogh-Bonger, Amsterdam;
V. W. van Gogh, Laren; Amsterdam, Rijksmuseum Vincent
van Gogh [Vincent van Gogh Foundation, inv nr F1577]

F1578 ENCLOSURE WITH PINE TREES
EXHIBITIONS 1954-5 Bern, 159; 1955 Antwerp 1, 343
PROVENANCE Mrs J. van Gogh-Bonger, Amsterdam;
V. W. van Gogh, Laren; Amsterdam, Rijksmuseum Vincent
van Gogh [Vincent van Gogh Foundation, inv nr F1578]

F1578a TWO TREES
PROVENANCE Mrs von Hoeltzke, Egypt [bought 1892, The
Hague, according to a notice on Faille's photograph];
Julius Spencer, Pasadena, Cal; Sale New York [Parke-
Bernet] 26 May 1949, 87; Present owner unknown

F1579 TRUNKS OF TWO PINE TREES
EXHIBITIONS 1954-5 Bern, 160; 1955 Antwerp 1, 344
PROVENANCE Mrs J. van Gogh-Bonger, Amsterdam;
V. W. van Gogh, Laren; Amsterdam, Rijksmuseum Vincent
van Gogh [Vincent van Gogh Foundation, inv nr F1579]

F1580 A TREE WITH A BRICK WALL IN THE
BACKGROUND
EXHIBITIONS 1945 Amsterdam, no cat nr; 1946 Stockholm
etc, 87; 1966 Paris, Albi, 71; 1967 Lille, Zurich, 73
PROVENANCE Mrs J. van Gogh-Bonger, Amsterdam;
V. W. van Gogh, Laren; Amsterdam, Rijksmuseum Vincent
van Gogh [Vincent van Gogh Foundation, inv nr F1580]

F1581 PINE TREES IN THE GARDEN OF ST PAUL'S
HOSPITAL
PROVENANCE Mrs J. van Gogh-Bonger, Amsterdam;
V. W. van Gogh, Laren; Amsterdam, Rijksmuseum Vincent
van Gogh [Vincent van Gogh Foundation, inv nr F1581]

F1582 PATH IN THE PINES
EXHIBITIONS 1945 Amsterdam, no cat nr; 1946 Stockholm
etc, 90; 1949-50 New York, Chicago, 140; 1951 Lyons etc,
99; 1955 Antwerp 1, 345; 1965-6 Stockholm, Göteborg, 99;
1967 Wolfsburg, 119
PROVENANCE Mrs J. van Gogh-Bonger, Amsterdam;
V. W. van Gogh, Laren; Amsterdam, Rijksmuseum Vincent
van Gogh [Vincent van Gogh Foundation, inv nr F1582]

F1583 SKETCH OF A FIELD WITH THE TRUNK OF A PINE
EXHIBITIONS 1955 Antwerp 1, 346; 1966 Paris, Albi, 72;
1967 Lille, Zurich, 74; 1967-8 Dallas etc, 74; 1968 Liège, 74;
1968-9 London, 162
PROVENANCE Mrs J. van Gogh-Bonger, Amsterdam;
V. W. van Gogh, Laren; Amsterdam, Rijksmuseum Vincent
van Gogh [Vincent van Gogh Foundation, inv nr F1583]

F1584 STUDY OF CLOUDS
EXHIBITIONS 1965-6 Stockholm, Göteborg, 100; 1967
Wolfsburg, 120; 1967-8 Dallas etc, 75; 1968 Liège, 75
PROVENANCE Mrs J. van Gogh-Bonger, Amsterdam;
V. W. van Gogh, Laren; Amsterdam, Rijksmuseum Vincent
van Gogh [Vincent van Gogh Foundation, inv nr F1584]

F1585 recto COUPLE ARM IN ARM: WINTER
verso INTERIOR OF A FARMHOUSE WITH TWO
PEASANTS AROUND A TABLE
EXHIBITIONS 1958-9 San Francisco etc, 147; 1960
Enschede, 63; 1963 Humlebaek, 110; 1964 Washington,
New York, 110; 1965 Charleroi, Ghent, 74; [verso] 1966
Paris, Albi, 73; 1967 Lille, Zurich, 75; 1967-8 Dallas etc, 75;
1968 Liège, 76; 1968-9 London, 180
PROVENANCE Mrs J. van Gogh-Bonger, Amsterdam;
V. W. van Gogh, Laren; Amsterdam, Rijksmuseum Vincent
van Gogh [Vincent van Gogh Foundation, inv nr F1585]

F1586 recto TWO MEN ON A ROAD WITH PINE TREES
verso STOOPING PEASANT WOMEN
EXHIBITIONS [verso] 1965-6 Stockholm, Göteborg, 101;
1967 Wolfsburg, 121
PROVENANCE Mrs J. van Gogh-Bonger, Amsterdam;
V. W. van Gogh, Laren; Amsterdam, Rijksmuseum Vincent
van Gogh [Vincent van Gogh Foundation, inv nr F1586]

F1587 recto THE CARRIAGE AND TWO FIGURES ON
THE ROAD
verso PEASANT SHOVELING
EXHIBITIONS [recto] 1945 Amsterdam, no cat nr; 1946
Stockholm etc, 91; 1949-50 New York, Chicago, 141; 1951
Lyons etc, 98; 1953 The Hague, 151; Otterlo, Amsterdam,
178; 1954-5 Bern, 161; 1955 Antwerp 1, 358; 1957 Stockholm, 91; 1959 Aix-en-Provence, 62; [verso] 1963 Humlebaek, 111; 1964 Washington, New York, 111; 1965 Charleroi, Ghent, 75; 1966 Paris, Albi, 74; 1967 Lille, Zurich, 76
PROVENANCE V. W. van Gogh, Laren; Amsterdam, Rijksmuseum Vincent van Gogh [Vincent van Gogh Foundation,
inv nr F1587]

F1588 PEASANTS AT A MEAL
EXHIBITIONS 1914-5 Amsterdam, 190; 1927-8 Berlin etc,
86; 1945 Amsterdam, no cat nr; 1946 Stockholm etc, 95;
1949-50 New York, Chicago, 142; 1955 Antwerp 1, 359;
1957 Stockholm, 92; 1959 Aix-en-Provence, 60; 1961-2
Baltimore etc, 135; 1962 Recklinghausen, 22e; 1962-3
Pittsburgh etc; 1965-6 Stockholm, Göteborg, 102; 1967
Wolfsburg, 122; 1967-8 Dallas etc, 77; 1968 Liège, 77;
1968-9 London, 181

F1589 recto FAMILY: THREE FIGURES ON A ROAD
verso PEASANT INTERIOR WITH THREE FIGURES
PROVENANCE Mrs J. van Gogh-Bonger, Amsterdam;
V. W. van Gogh, Laren; Amsterdam, Rijksmuseum Vincent
van Gogh [Vincent van Gogh Foundation, inv nr F1589]

F1589a PATH BETWEEN GARDEN WALLS
PROVENANCE Comtesse de Cumont, Avignon; Miss M. de
Gaigneron, Paris; Tony Mayer, Paris; Marcel Guiot Art
Gallery, Paris; Burlingame, Cal., Mr and Mrs Philip
N. Lilienthal [R 1970]

F1590 recto SKETCH OF TWO TREES
verso FOUR MEN ON THE ROAD
EXHIBITIONS [verso] 1954-5 Bern, 162; 1955 Antwerp 1,
347; 1958-9 San Francisco etc, 148; 1959 Aix-en-Provence,
61; 1959-60 Utrecht, 93; 1960 Enschede, 64; 1964 Zundert,
28; 1966 Paris, Albi, 75; 1967 Lille, Zurich, 77
PROVENANCE Mrs J. van Gogh-Bonger, Amsterdam;
V. W. van Gogh, Laren; Amsterdam, Rijksmuseum Vincent
van Gogh [Vincent van Gogh Foundation, inv nr F1590]

F1591 recto WINTERLANDSCAPE WITH PEOPLE ON
THE ROAD
verso LANDSCAPE WITH FARMS AND PEASANTS
EXHIBITIONS 1914-5 Amsterdam, 192; 1927-8 Berlin etc,
83; 1957 Stockholm, 94; 1961-2 Baltimore etc, 136; 1962-3
Pittsburgh etc; 1963 Humlebaek, 112; 1964 Washington,
New York, 112; 1965 Charleroi, Ghent, 76; 1965-6 Stockholm, Göteborg, 103; 1967 Wolfsburg, 123; 1967-8 Dallas
etc, 78; 1968 Liège, 78; 1968-9 London, 183; 1969 Humlebaek, 41
PROVENANCE Mrs J. van Gogh-Bonger, Amsterdam;
V. W. van Gogh, Laren; Amsterdam, Rijksmuseum Vincent
van Gogh [Vincent van Gogh Foundation, inv nr F1591]

F1592 recto WINTER LANDSCAPE WITH MANY FIGURES
verso A MAN SOWING
EXHIBITIONS 1914-5 Amsterdam, 184; 1923 Utrecht,
Rotterdam, 23; 1927-8 Berlin etc, 78; 1932 Manchester, 78;
1945 Amsterdam, no cat nr; 1946 Stockholm etc, 94;
1949-50 New York, Chicago, 143; 1966 Paris, Albi, 76; 1967
Lille, Zurich, 78
PROVENANCE Mrs J. van Gogh-Bonger, Amsterdam;
V. W. van Gogh, Laren; Amsterdam, Rijksmuseum Vincent
van Gogh [Vincent van Gogh Foundation, inv nr F1592]

F1593 recto HUT WITH CYPRESSES IN WINTER: THREE
PEASANTS WORKING
verso SKETCHES OF PEASANT AND HOUSES
EXHIBITIONS [recto] 1920 New York, 21; 1925 The Hague,
80; 1926 Munich, 2109; 1927-8 Berlin etc, 80; 1935-6 New
York etc, 124; 1946-7 Liège etc, 135; 1947 Paris 1, 136;
Geneva, 136; 1947-8 London etc, 170; 1948 Bergen, Oslo,
117; 1949-50 New York, Chicago, 144; 1951 Lyons etc, 96;
1954-5 Bern, 163; 1955 Antwerp 1, 348; 1957 Marseilles, 80;
Stockholm, 93; 1958-9 San Francisco etc, 149; 1959-60
Utrecht, 94; 1960 Enschede, 65; 1961-2 Baltimore etc, 137;
1962-3 Pittsburgh etc; 1963 Humlebaek, 113; 1964
Washington, New York, 113; 1965-6 Stockholm, Göteborg,
104; 1967 Wolfsburg, 124
PROVENANCE Mrs J. van Gogh-Bonger, Amsterdam;
V. W. van Gogh, Laren; Amsterdam, Rijksmuseum Vincent
van Gogh [Vincent van Gogh Foundation, inv nr F1593]

F1594 recto FARMS WITH DIGGING PEASANTS
verso FAMILY AROUND THE TABLE
EXHIBITIONS [recto] 1945 Amsterdam, no cat nr; 1946
Stockholm etc, 93; [verso] 1965 Nuenen, no cat nr; 1966
Paris, Albi, 77; 1967 Lille, Zurich, 79; 1967-8 Dallas etc, 79;
1968 Liège, 79; 1968-9 London, 182
PROVENANCE Mrs J. van Gogh-Bonger, Amsterdam;
V. W. van Gogh, Laren; Amsterdam, Rijksmuseum Vincent
van Gogh [Vincent van Gogh Foundation, inv nr F1594]

F1595 recto STREET, LINED WITH FARMHOUSES
verso PEASANTS AT TABLE; BUSTS OF TWO PEASANTS
PROVENANCE V. W. van Gogh, Laren; Private collection,
USA [R 1952]; Bier Art Gallery, Haarlem; Legat Art Gallery,
The Hague; Sidney Janis, New York; Present owner
unknown

F1596 recto ON THE ROAD
verso PEASANTS AT TABLE
EXHIBITIONS [verso] 1965-6 Stockholm, Göteborg, 105;
1967 Wolfsburg, 125
PROVENANCE Mrs J. van Gogh-Bonger, Amsterdam;
V. W. van Gogh, Laren; Amsterdam, Rijksmuseum Vincent
van Gogh [Vincent van Gogh Foundation, inv nr F1596]

F1596a recto MASK OF AN EGYPTIAN MUMMY; SKETCH
OF A GIRL STANDING
verso A PEASANT STOOPING
PROVENANCE Mrs J. van Gogh-Bonger, Amsterdam;
V. W. van Gogh, Laren; Amsterdam, Rijksmuseum Vincent
van Gogh [Vincent van Gogh Foundation, inv nr F1596a]

F1597 recto RETURN OF THE FIELD-WORKERS IN THE
RAIN
verso LANDSCAPE WITH HUT AND TWO PEASANTS
WITH WHEELBARROW
EXHIBITIONS 1945 Amsterdam, no cat nr; 1946 Stockholm
etc, 89; 1946-7 Liège etc, 136; 1947 Paris 1, 137; Geneva,
137; 1947-8 London etc, 171; 1948 Bergen, Oslo, 118;
1954-5 Bern, 164; 1955 Antwerp 1, 349; 1960 Paris, 106, 107
[verso]; 1960-1 Montreal etc, 133; 1961-2 Baltimore etc,
138; 1962-3 Pittsburgh etc; 1963 Humlebaek, 114; 1964
Washington, New York, 114; 1965 Charleroi, Ghent, 77
PROVENANCE Mrs J. van Gogh-Bonger, Amsterdam;
V. W. van Gogh, Laren; Amsterdam, Rijksmuseum Vincent
van Gogh [Vincent van Gogh Foundation, inv nr F1597]

F1598 recto LANDSCAPE WITH FOUR FIGURES AND
WHEELBARROWS
verso STUDIES OF PEASANTS AT WORK
EXHIBITIONS [verso] 1966 Paris, Albi, 78; 1967 Lille,
Zurich, 80; 1967-8 Dallas etc, 80; 1968 Liège, 80; 1968-9
London, 185
PROVENANCE Mrs J. van Gogh-Bonger, Amsterdam;
V. W. van Gogh, Laren; Amsterdam, Rijksmuseum Vincent
van Gogh [Vincent van Gogh Foundation, inv nr F1598]

F 1599 recto STUDIES OF PEASANTS; MAN WITH A WHEELBARROW; WOMAN WITH A WHEELBARROW
verso A MAN SEATED AT TABLE AND OTHER STUDIES OF PEASANTS WORKING
EXHIBITIONS 1945 Amsterdam, no cat nr; 1965-6 Stockholm, Göteborg, 106; 1967 Wolfsburg, 126
PROVENANCE Mrs J. van Gogh-Bonger, Amsterdam; V.W. van Gogh, Laren; Amsterdam, Rijksmuseum Vincent van Gogh [Vincent van Gogh Foundation, inv nr F 1599]

F 1600 recto SKETCHES OF MEN DIGGING
verso SKETCHES OF DIGGING PEASANTS AND HOUSES
EXHIBITIONS 1965-6 Stockholm, Göteborg, 107; 1967 Wolfsburg, 127
PROVENANCE Mrs J. van Gogh-Bonger, Amsterdam; V.W. van Gogh, Laren; Amsterdam, Rijksmuseum Vincent van Gogh [Vincent van Gogh Foundation, inv nr F 1600]

F 1601 recto SKETCHES OF A FIGURE SITTING AT A TABLE
verso STUDIES OF SEATED FIGURES
EXHIBITIONS [verso] 1966 Paris, Albi, 79; 1967 Lille, Zurich, 81; 1967-8 Dallas etc, 81; 1968 Liège, 81
PROVENANCE Mrs J. van Gogh-Bonger, Amsterdam; V.W. van Gogh, Laren; Amsterdam, Rijksmuseum Vincent van Gogh [Vincent van Gogh Foundation, inv nr F 1601]

F 1602 recto THE ENCLOSURE BEHIND ST PAUL'S HOSPITAL
verso SIX SKETCHES OF PEASANTS DIGGING
EXHIBITIONS [verso] 1962 London 1, 60 [erroneoulsy cited as F 1602 recto]; 1966 Paris, Albi, 80; 1967 Lille, Zurich, 82; 1967-8 Dallas etc, 82; 1968 Liège, 82; 1968-9 London, 184
PROVENANCE Mrs J. van Gogh-Bonger, Amsterdam; V.W. van Gogh, Laren; Amsterdam, Rijksmuseum Vincent van Gogh [Vincent van Gogh Foundation, inv nr F 1602]

F 1603 recto TWO STUDIES OF A SOWER AND SIX STUDIES OF RIGHT HANDS SOWING
verso STUDIES OF PEASANTS AND HANDS
EXHIBITIONS 1945 Amsterdam, no cat nr; 1946 Stockholm etc, 85; 1955-6 Liverpool etc, 125; 1957 Stockholm, 90; 1958-9 San Francisco etc, 150; 1960 Enschede, 66; 1961-2 Baltimore etc, 139; 1962-3 Pittsburgh etc; 1966 Paris, Albi, 81; 1967 Zurich, 83; 1967-8 Dallas etc, 83; 1968 Liège, 83; 1968-9 London, 187; 1969 Humlebaek, 42
PROVENANCE Mrs J. van Gogh-Bonger, Amsterdam; V.W. van Gogh, Laren; Amsterdam, Rijksmuseum Vincent van Gogh [Vincent van Gogh Foundation, inv nr F 1603]

F 1604 recto FIGURES IN A LANDSCAPE
verso A GROUP OF FIGURES ON THE BEACH
PROVENANCE Mrs J. van Gogh-Bonger, Amsterdam; V.W. van Gogh, Laren; Amsterdam, Rijksmuseum Vincent van Gogh [Vincent van Gogh Foundation, inv nr F 1604]

F 1605 recto PEASANTS WORKING OUTDOORS
verso TWO WINDOWS WITH IRON BARS IN ST PAUL'S HOSPITAL
PROVENANCE Mrs J. van Gogh-Bonger, Amsterdam; V.W. van Gogh, Laren; Amsterdam, Rijksmuseum Vincent van Gogh [Vincent van Gogh Foundation, inv nr F 1605]

F 1606 recto STUDIES OF A WOMAN AT THE TABLE AND A WOMAN STANDING
verso A MAN AT WORK; A DOG
PROVENANCE Mrs J. van Gogh-Bonger, Amsterdam; V.W. van Gogh, Laren; Amsterdam, Rijksmuseum Vincent van Gogh [Vincent van Gogh Foundation, inv nr F 1606]

F 1607 recto STUDIES OF A WOMAN ON THE ROAD AND A MAN ON THE ROAD
verso TWO WOMEN BLEACHING LAUNDRY
PROVENANCE Mrs J. van Gogh-Bonger, Amsterdam; V.W. van Gogh, Laren; Amsterdam, Rijksmuseum Vincent van Gogh [Vincent van Gogh Foundation, inv nr F 1607]

F 1608 recto PEASANT FAMILY NEAR THE FIREPLACE
verso SKETCHES OF HANDS; A PEASANT DIGGING
EXHIBITIONS 1923 Utrecht, Rotterdam, 26; 1925 The Hague, 81; 1927-8 Berlin etc, 79; 1945 Amsterdam, no cat nr; 1955 Antwerp 1, 352; 1966 Paris, Albi, 82; 1967 Lille, Zurich, 84; 1967-8 Dallas etc, 84; 1968 Liège, 84; 1968-9 London, 186
PROVENANCE Mrs J. van Gogh-Bonger, Amsterdam; V.W. van Gogh, Laren; Amsterdam, Rijksmuseum Vincent van Gogh [Vincent van Gogh Foundation, inv nr F 1608]

F 1609 recto HORSE AND CARRIAGE
verso SEATED NUDE [after Bargue]
EXHIBITIONS 1914-5 Amsterdam, 177; 1955 Antwerp 1, 350
PROVENANCE Mrs J. van Gogh-Bonger, Amsterdam; V.W. van Gogh, Laren; Amsterdam, Rijksmuseum Vincent van Gogh [Vincent van Gogh Foundation, inv nr F 1609]

F 1610 recto HORSE AND CARRIAGE
verso SKETCH OF TWO WOMEN WORKING
PROVENANCE Mrs J. van Gogh-Bonger, Amsterdam; V.W. van Gogh, Laren; Amsterdam, Rijksmuseum Vincent van Gogh [Vincent van Gogh Foundation, inv nr F 1610]

F 1611 recto LEAF AND POD OF A CHESTNUT TREE
verso SKETCHES OF A PERSPECTIVE FRAME
EXHIBITIONS 1955 Antwerp 1, 356; 1957 Stockholm, 87
PROVENANCE Mrs J. van Gogh-Bonger, Amsterdam; V.W. van Gogh, Laren; Amsterdam, Rijksmuseum Vincent van Gogh [Vincent van Gogh Foundation, inv nr F 1611]

F 1612 BRANCHES OF FEATHER HYACINTH
EXHIBITIONS 1905 Amsterdam, 371; 1914-5 Amsterdam, 168; 1927-8 Berlin etc, 88; 1949-50 New York, Chicago, 146; 1951 Lyons etc, 97; 1953 The Hague, 152; Otterlo, Amsterdam, 179; 1953-4 St Louis etc, 164; 1954-5 Bern, 165; 1955 Antwerp 1, 359; 1955-6 Liverpool etc, 131; 1957 Marseilles, 82; Stockholm, 88; 1958-9 San Francisco etc, 151; 1959 Aix-en-Provence, 53; 1960 Enschede, 67; 1960-1 Montreal etc, 135; 1961-2 Baltimore etc, 140; 1966 Paris, Albi, 83; 1967 Lille, Zurich, 85; 1967-8 Dallas etc, 85; 1968 Liège, 85; 1968-9 London, 188
PROVENANCE Mrs J. van Gogh-Bonger, Amsterdam; V.W. van Gogh, Laren; Amsterdam, Rijksmuseum Vincent van Gogh [Vincent van Gogh Foundation, inv nr F 1612]

F 1613 STUDY OF ARUM
EXHIBITIONS 1900-1 Rotterdam, 27; 1905 Amsterdam, 368; 1923 Utrecht, Rotterdam, 49; 1926 London 3, 23; 1927-8 Berlin etc, 90; 1932 Manchester, 77; 1945 Amsterdam, no cat nr; 1946 Stockholm etc, 98; 1955 Antwerp 1, 360; 1955-6 Liverpool etc, 132; 1958-9 San Francisco etc, 152; 1960 Enschede, 68; 1960-1 Montreal etc, 136; 1966 Paris, Albi, 84; 1967 Lille, Zurich, 86; 1967-8 Dallas etc, 86; 1968 Liège, 86; 1968-9 London, 189; 1969 Humlebaek, 43
PROVENANCE Mrs J. van Gogh-Bonger, Amsterdam; V.W. van Gogh, Laren; Amsterdam, Rijksmuseum Vincent van Gogh [Vincent van Gogh Foundation, inv nr F 1613]

F 1614 BRANCHES OF PERIWINKLE
EXHIBITIONS 1914-5 Amsterdam, 193; 1954-5 Bern, 166; 1963 Humlebaek, 115; 1964 Washington, New York, 115; 1965 Charleroi, Ghent, 78; 1966 Paris, Albi, 85; 1967 Lille, Zurich, 87
PROVENANCE Mrs J. van Gogh-Bonger, Amsterdam; V.W. van Gogh, Laren; Amsterdam, Rijksmuseum Vincent van Gogh [Vincent van Gogh Foundation, inv nr F 1614]

F 1615 recto HARVESTING HAY
verso HILLY LANDSCAPE WITH HARVESTERS
EXHIBITIONS 1914-5 Amsterdam, 191; 1955 Antwerp 1, 351; 1967 Wolfsburg, 128 [verso]
PROVENANCE Mrs J. van Gogh-Bonger, Amsterdam; V.W. van Gogh, Laren; Amsterdam, Rijksmuseum Vincent van Gogh [Vincent van Gogh Foundation, inv nr F 1615]

F 1616 A MAN, A WOMAN AND A CHILD
PROVENANCE Paul Ferd. Gachet, Auvers [1890-1909]; Paul Gachet, Auvers; Mrs E. Walter, Paris; Paris, Musée National du Louvre, inv nr RF 29.886

F 1617 WOMAN SEATED WITH A CHILD ON HER KNEES
PROVENANCE Paul Ferd. Gachet, Auvers [1890-1909]; Paul Gachet, Auvers; Mrs E. Walter, Paris; Paris, Musée National du Louvre inv nr RF 29.885

F 1618 THE SOWERS
EXHIBITION 1956 New York, 169
PROVENANCE Paul Ferd. Gachet, Auvers [1890-1909]; Paul Gachet, Auvers; New York, Wildenstein Art Gallery; Mr and Mrs Joram Piatigorski [R 1970]

F 1619 recto STUDY OF TWO WOMEN
verso STUDY OF A WOMAN STANDING, TWO HEADS AND ANOTHER FIGURE
EXHIBITION 1955 New York 2, 106
PROVENANCE Paul Ferd. Gachet, Auvers [1890-1909]; Paul Gachet, Auvers; J.K. Thannhauser Art Gallery, New York; Alastair B. Martin; Poughkeepsie, New York, Vassar College Art Gallery [acquired 1959; gift of Alastair B. Martin], inv nr 59.10

F 1620 recto WORK IN THE FIELDS
verso A MAN DIGGING, TWO SEATED CHILDREN AND OTHER SKETCHES
EXHIBITIONS 1937 Paris, 81; 1960 Buffalo, 30; 1967 New York, Philadelphia, no cat nr
PROVENANCE Paul Ferd. Gachet, Auvers [1890-1909]; Paul Gachet, Auvers [R 1937]; Wildenstein Art Gallery, New York; Bradford, Pa., T. Edw. Hanley

F 1621 recto STUDY
verso SKETCH OF A LANDSCAPE WITH TREES
PROVENANCE Paul Ferd. Gachet, Auvers [1890-1909]; Paul Gachet, Auvers; Present owner unknown

F 1622 recto THE HINDLEGS OF A HORSE
verso HEAD OF A YOUNG MAN WITH HAT
PROVENANCE Paul Ferd. Gachet, Auvers [1890-1909]; Paul Gachet, Auvers; Mrs E. Walter, Paris; Paris, Musée National du Louvre, inv. nr RF 29.884

AUVERS PERIOD

F 1623 recto MISS GACHET AT THE PIANO
verso STUDY OF A FRUIT TREE AND OF TWO PEOPLE AT WORK
EXHIBITIONS 1945 Amsterdam, no cat nr; 1946 Stockholm etc, 101; 1947 Basle, 166; 1947-8 London etc, 172; 1948 Bergen, Oslo, 120; 1953 The Hague, 180; Otterlo, Amsterdam, 191; 1953-4 St Louis etc, 175; 1954-5 Paris, 62; 1955 Antwerp 1, 368; 1955-6 Liverpool etc, 133; 1957 Stockholm, 98; 1958-9 San Francisco etc, 153; 1960 Enschede, 69; 1960-1 Montreal etc, 137; 1962 London 1, 69; 1963 Humlebaek, 116; 1964 Washington, New York, 116; 1968-9 London, 199
PROVENANCE Mrs J. van Gogh-Bonger, Amsterdam; V.W. van Gogh, Laren; Amsterdam, Rijksmuseum Vincent van Gogh [Vincent van Gogh Foundation, inv nr F 1623]

F 1624 OLD VINEYARD WITH PEASANT WOMAN
EXHIBITIONS 1905 Amsterdam, 472; 1923 Utrecht, Rotterdam, 29; 1924 Basle, 98; Zurich, 98; Stuttgart, 19; 1925 The Hague, 75; 1927-8 Berlin etc, 94; 1937 Paris, 82; 1945 Amsterdam, no cat nr; 1946 Stockholm etc, 99; 1946-7 Liège etc, 137; 1947 Paris 1, 138; Geneva, 138; 1947-8 London etc, 174; 1948 Bergen, Oslo, 121; 1949-50 New York, Chicago, 158; 1953 The Hague, 181; Otterlo, Amsterdam, 192; 1953-4 St Louis etc, 176; 1954-5 Paris, 60; 1955 Antwerp 1, 369; 1955-6 Liverpool etc, 135; 1957 Stockholm, 95; 1958-9 San Francisco etc, 154; 1960 Enschede, 70; 1960-1 Montreal etc, 140; 1961-2 Liège, Breda, 59; 1963 Humlebaek, 117; 1964 Washington, New York, 117; 1965 Charleroi, Ghent, 79; 1966 Paris, Albi, 87; 1967 Lille, Zurich, 88; 1967-8 Dallas etc, 87; 1968 Liège, 87; 1968-9 London, 191; 1969 Humlebaek, 44
PROVENANCE Mrs J. van Gogh-Bonger, Amsterdam; V.W. van Gogh, Laren; Amsterdam, Rijksmuseum Vincent van Gogh [Vincent van Gogh Foundation, inv nr F 1624]

F 1625 LANDSCAPE
EXHIBITIONS 1935-6 New York etc, 126; 1943 New York 2, 79; 1948 Cleveland, 38
PROVENANCE Mrs Jeanne Guillaumin, Paris; New York, Metropolitan Museum of Art [acquired 1924; Rogers Fund], inv nr 24.196

F 1626 recto PEASANT WOMAN IN A WHEATFIELD
verso TWO PEASANT WOMEN BINDING SHEAVES
EXHIBITIONS 1954-5 Bern, 167; 1955 Antwerp 1, 370; 1960 Paris, 108; 1964 Zundert, 29
PROVENANCE Mrs J. van Gogh-Bonger, Amsterdam; V.W. van Gogh, Laren; Amsterdam, Rijksmuseum Vincent van Gogh [Vincent van Gogh Foundation, inv nr F 1626]

F 1627 WOODED SHORE OF THE OISE
EXHIBITION 1955 Antwerp 1, 371
PROVENANCE Mrs J. van Gogh-Bonger, Amsterdam; V.W. van Gogh, Laren; Amsterdam, Rijksmuseum Vincent van Gogh [Vincent van Gogh Foundation, inv nr F 1627]

F 1628 PATH IN THE FIELDS
PROVENANCE Mrs J. van Gogh-Bonger, Amsterdam; V.W. van Gogh, Laren; Amsterdam, Rijksmuseum Vincent van Gogh [Vincent van Gogh Foundation, inv nr F 1628]

F 1629 WOODED SHORE OF THE OISE
PROVENANCE Mrs J. van Gogh-Bonger, Amsterdam; V.W. van Gogh, Laren; Amsterdam, Rijksmuseum Vincent van Gogh [Vincent van Gogh Foundation, inv nr F 1629]

F 1630 recto Above THE TOWN HALL IN AUVERS
Below SKETCH OF A MAN'S HEAD
verso above MONTCEL: HOUSES BEHIND TREES
Below A HUT; OTHER SKETCHES
EXHIBITIONS 1946-7 Liège etc, 139; 1947 Paris 1, 140; Geneva, 140; 1947-8 London etc, 173; 1948 Bergen, Oslo, 122; 1949-50 New York, Chicago, 157; 1953 The Hague, 182; Otterlo, Amsterdam, 193; 1953-4 St Louis etc, 177; 1954-5 Paris, 62; 1955 Antwerp 1, 372; 1955-6 Liverpool etc, 134; 1957 Marseilles, 88; Stockholm, 96; 1958-9 San Francisco etc, 155; 1959-60 Utrecht, 95; 1960 Enschede, 71; 1960-1 Montreal etc, 138; 1961-2 Baltimore etc, 141; 1962-3 Pittsburgh etc; 1963 Humlebaek, 118; 1964 Washington, New York, 118; 1965 Charleroi, Ghent, 80; 1966 Paris, Albi, 88; 1967 Lille, Zurich, 89; 1967-8 Dallas etc, 88; 1968 Liège, 88; 1968-9 London, 200; 1969 Humlebaek, 45
PROVENANCE Mrs J. van Gogh-Bonger, Amsterdam; V.W. van Gogh, Laren; Amsterdam, Rijksmuseum Vincent van Gogh [Vincent van Gogh Foundation, inv nr F 1630]

F 1631 recto SKETCH OF A MULE
verso SKETCH OF FIVE LAUNDRESSES
PROVENANCE Mrs J. van Gogh-Bonger, Amsterdam; V.W. van Gogh, Laren; Amsterdam, Rijksmuseum Vincent van Gogh [Vincent van Gogh Foundation, inv nr F 1631]

F 1632 SKETCH OF THREE COWS AND TWO CHILDREN
PROVENANCE Mrs J. van Gogh-Bonger, Amsterdam; V.W. van Gogh, Laren; Amsterdam, Rijksmuseum Vincent van Gogh [Vincent van Gogh Foundation, inv nr F 1632]

F 1633 SKETCH OF A CHILD IN A PERAMBULATOR
PROVENANCE Mrs J. van Gogh-Bonger, Amsterdam;
V. W. van Gogh, Laren; Amsterdam, Rijksmuseum Vincent
van Gogh [Vincent van Gogh Foundation, inv nr F 1633]

F 1634 recto STUDIES OF A STANDING WOMAN AND A
PEASANT WOMAN WITH A RAKE
verso SKETCH OF ROOFS
PROVENANCE Mrs J. van Gogh-Bonger, Amsterdam;
V. W. van Gogh, Laren; Amsterdam, Rijksmuseum Vincent
van Gogh [Vincent van Gogh Foundation, inv nr F 1634]

F 1635 recto SKETCH OF AN EGYPTIAN HEAD AND
SKETCH OF A WOMAN
verso MAN WITH A SCYTHE
PROVENANCE Mrs J. van Gogh-Bonger, Amsterdam;
V. W. van Gogh, Laren; Amsterdam, Rijksmuseum Vincent
van Gogh [Vincent van Gogh Foundation, inv nr F 1635]

F 1636 HOUSES AT AUVERS WITH PEASANT WOMAN
IN THE FOREGROUND
EXHIBITIONS 1947 Basle, 167; 1947-8 London etc, 175;
1948 Bergen, Oslo, 123; 1953 The Hague, 183; Otterlo,
Amsterdam, 194; 1953-4 St Louis etc, 178; 1954-5 Paris, 64;
1957 Stockholm, 97; 1961 Scarborough; 1962 London 1,
70; 1966 Paris, Albi, 89; 1967 Lille, Zurich, 90; 1967-8
Dallas etc, 89; 1968 Liège, 89; 1968-9 London, 198
PROVENANCE Mrs J. van Gogh-Bonger, Amsterdam;
V. W. van Gogh, Laren; Amsterdam, Rijksmuseum Vincent
van Gogh [Vincent van Gogh Foundation, inv nr F 1636]

F 1637 recto MONTCEL: HOUSES BEHIND TREES
[Identical with F 1630 verso]
verso SKETCH OF A MAN'S HEAD [Identical with F 1630
recto]
PROVENANCE Mrs J. van Gogh-Bonger, Amsterdam;
V. W. van Gogh, Laren; Amsterdam, Rijksmuseum Vincent
van Gogh [Vincent van Gogh Foundation, inv nr F 1630]

F 1638 recto STREET IN AUVERS: THE HOUSE OF
PÈRE PILON
verso SKETCH OF A VILLAGE STREET WITH HOUSES
EXHIBITIONS 1914-5 Amsterdam, 195; 1923 Utrecht,
Rotterdam, 44; 1927-8 Berlin etc, 96; 1953-4 St Louis etc,
180; 1963 Humlebaek, 119; 1964 Washington, New York, 119
PROVENANCE Mrs J. van Gogh-Bonger, Amsterdam;
V. W. van Gogh, Laren; Amsterdam, Rijksmuseum Vincent
van Gogh [Vincent van Gogh Foundation, inv nr F 1638]

F 1639 VIEW ACROSS THE OISE TOWARDS MÉRY
EXHIBITIONS 1914-5 Amsterdam, 197; 1930 Amsterdam,
120; 1947-8 London etc, 176
PROVENANCE Mrs J. van Gogh-Bonger, Amsterdam;
Frank C. Stoop, London [R 1930]; London, Tate Gallery
[acquired 1933; bequest of Frank C. Stoop], inv nr 4714

F 1640 recto WOODED LANDSCAPE WITH HOUSES
verso HOUSE AND CHESTNUT TREES
EXHIBITIONS 1905 Amsterdam, 431; 1914-5 Amsterdam,
196; 1923 Utrecht, Rotterdam, 42; 1927-8 Berlin etc, 95;
1932 Manchester, 75; 1935-6 New York etc, 125; 1937
Paris, 79; 1945 Amsterdam, no cat nr; 1946 Stockholm etc,
100; 1946-7 Liège etc, 138; 1947 Paris 1, 139; Geneva, 139;
1947-8 London etc, 177; 1948 Bergen, Oslo, 124; 1949-50
New York, Chicago, 156; 1951 Lyons etc, 101; 1953 The
Hague, 184; Otterlo, Amsterdam, 195; 1953-4 St Louis etc,
179; 1954-5 Paris, 63; 1955 Antwerp 1, 373; 1955-6 Liverpool etc, 136; 1961-2 Baltimore etc, 142; 1962-3 Pittsburgh
etc; 1963 Humlebaek, 120; 1964 Washington, New York,
120; 1965 Charleroi, Ghent, 81; 1965-6 Stockholm, Göteborg, 108; 1967 Wolfsburg, 129; 1967-8 Dallas etc, 90; 1968
Liège, 90; 1968-9 London, 192; 1969 Humlebaek, 46
PROVENANCE Mrs J. van Gogh-Bonger, Amsterdam
[R 1905]; V. W. van Gogh, Laren; Amsterdam, Rijksmuseum Vincent van Gogh [Vincent van Gogh Foundation,
inv nr F 1640]

F 1640a VIEW OF A VILLAGE WITH TWO WOMEN IN
THE FOREGROUND
PROVENANCE Mrs J. van Gogh-Bonger, Amsterdam;
Mrs von Hoeltzke, Egypt [acquired 1892]; Julius Spencer,
Pasadena, California; Sale New York [Parke-Bernet]
26 May 1949, nr 86; Present owner unknown

F 1641 SHEAVES
EXHIBITIONS 1949-50 New York, Chicago, 155; 1954-5
Bern, 168; 1955 Antwerp 1, 374; 1960-1 Montreal etc, 139;
1966 Paris, Albi, 90; 1967 Lille, Zurich, 91
PROVENANCE Mrs J. van Gogh-Bonger, Amsterdam;
V. W. van Gogh, Laren; Amsterdam, Rijksmuseum Vincent
van Gogh [Vincent van Gogh Foundation, inv nr F 1641]

F 1642 LANDSCAPE WITH HOUSES AND A WOMAN
WORKING IN THE FIELD
EXHIBITIONS 1926 London 3, 31; 1943 New York 2, 80
PROVENANCE Mrs J. van Gogh-Bonger, Amsterdam;
J. H. de Bois Art Gallery, Haarlem; The Leicester Galleries,
London; Walter S. Brewster, USA [R 1943]; Chicago,
The Art Institute [acquired 1949; bequest of Kate
L. Brewster], inv nr 49.382

F 1643 HAYRICKS
EXHIBITIONS 1914-5 Amsterdam, 194; 1926 London 3, 25
PROVENANCE Mrs J. van Gogh-Bonger, Amsterdam;
V. W. van Gogh, Laren; Manchester, Whitworth Institute
[acquired 1926]

F 1644 recto PEASANT WOMAN WALKING TO THE
RIGHT
verso WOMAN WITH HAT IN CHECKED COAT
PROVENANCE Paul Ferd. Gachet, Auvers [1890-1909];
Paul Gachet, Auvers; Mrs E. Walter, Paris; Paris, Musée
National du Louvre, inv nr RF 29.883

F 1645 recto STUDY OF A SOWER AND A MAN WITH A
SPADE
verso STUDY OF TWO SOWERS
PROVENANCE Paul Ferd. Gachet, Auvers [1890-1909];
Paul Gachet, Auvers; Paris, Jacques Dubourg [R 1965]

F 1646 recto THREE STUDIES
verso A STEAMER WITH SEVERAL PEOPLE
PROVENANCE Paul Ferd. Gachet, Auvers [1890-1909];
Paul Gachet, Auvers; Present owner unknown

F 1647 recto LANDSCAPE WITH TWO FIGURES
verso FIGURES ON A ROAD
EXHIBITION 1955 New York 2, 107
PROVENANCE Paul Ferd. Gachet, Auvers [1890-1909];
Paul Gachet, Auvers; Wildenstein Art Gallery, New York;
St Louis, Mr and Mrs Sydney M. Shoenberg

F 1648 recto SNOW LANDSCAPE
verso PEASANT COTTAGES SEEN FROM THE FIELDS
EXHIBITIONS 1905 Paris, 23; 1955 New York 2, 108; 1956
New York, 170
PROVENANCE Paul Ferd. Gachet, Auvers [1890-1909];
Paul Gachet, Auvers [R 1905]; Wildenstein Art Gallery,
New York; Caracas, Ernesto Blohm [R 1970]

F 1649 recto STUDIES OF PEASANTS WORKING: SOWERS
AND DIGGERS
verso A MAN IN FRONT OF A FARMSTEAD; OTHER
SKETCHES
PROVENANCE Paul Ferd. Gachet, Auvers [1890-1909];
Paul Gachet, Auvers; Zurich, W. Feilchenfeldt; Present
owner unknown

F 1650 recto STILL LIFE: CAN, BOOKS, WINEGLASS,
BREAD AND ARUM; SKETCH OF TWO WOMEN AND
A GIRL
verso A MAN AND A WOMAN; OUTLINES OF LANDSCAPE
WITH FIGURES
EXHIBITIONS 1955 New York 2, 109; 1956 New York, 171;
1960 New York 3, 80
PROVENANCE Paul Ferd. Gachet, Auvers [1890-1909];
Paul Gachet, Auvers; Wildenstein Art Gallery, New York;
Sale London [Sotheby] 22 June 1966, nr 4; Present owner
unknown

F 1651 recto STUDIES OF FIGURES AND WOODEN SHOES
verso SKETCHES OF FIGURES AND HANDS
PROVENANCE Paul Ferd. Gachet, Auvers [1890-1909];
Paul Gachet, Auvers; New York, Private collection

F 1652 recto FIGURE SKETCHES
verso SKETCH OF A YOUNG WOMAN AND OTHER
SKETCHES
EXHIBITIONS 1959 Santa Barbara, California, 124
PROVENANCE Paul Ferd. Gachet, Auvers [1890-1909];
Paul Gachet, Auvers; Wildenstein Art Gallery, New York
[R 1959]; New York, Mr and Mrs Harry M. Goldblatt
[acquired 1960]

F 1653 THE FARM OF PÈRE ELOI, IN THE FOREGROUND
A WOMAN WORKING
EXHIBITIONS 1937 Paris, 80; 1954-5 Paris, 59; 1967-8
Paris, 522; 1968 Paris, 88
PROVENANCE Paul Ferd. Gachet, Auvers [1890-1909];
Paul Gachet, Auvers [R 1937]; Paris, Musée national du
Louvre, Cabinet des dessins [acquired 1954; gift Paul
Gachet], inv nr RF 30.271 [L. Suppl. 1886a]

F 1654 recto COUNTER AT RAVOUX' INN
verso COCK; HEN
PROVENANCE Paul Ferd. Gachet, Auvers [1890-1909];
Paul Gachet, Auvers; Richmond, Virginia, Ed. Buckman
[gift of P. Gachet]

LITHOGRAPHS

F 1655 SORROW
EXHIBITIONS [Impressions I or III] 1914-5 Amsterdam, 13;
1927-8 Berlin etc, 13; 1937 Paris, 133; 1945 Amsterdam, no
cat nr; 1946 Stockholm etc, 3; 1946-7 Liège etc, 11; 1947
Paris 1, 11; Geneva, 11; 1947-8 London etc, 108; 1948
Bergen, Oslo, 69; 1957 Stockholm, 12; 1966 Paris, 9; 1967
Lille, Zurich, 10; 1967-8 Dallas etc, 11; 1968 Liège, 11;
1968-9 London, 15
PROVENANCE I Mrs J. van Gogh-Bonger, Amsterdam;
V. W. van Gogh, Laren; Amsterdam, Rijksmuseum Vincent
van Gogh [Vincent van Gogh Foundation, inv nr F 1655/I]
PROVENANCE II Ph. de Kanter, Delft; H. E. d'Audretsch,
Amerongen; New York, The Museum of Modern Art
PROVENANCE III Mrs J. van Gogh-Bonger, Amsterdam;
V. W. van Gogh, Laren; Amsterdam, Rijksmuseum Vincent
van Gogh [Vincent van Gogh Foundation, inv nr F 1655/III]

F 1656 THE DIGGER
EXHIBITIONS I 1935-6, New York etc, 101; 1954-5 Bern,
169
PROVENANCE I Mrs J. van Gogh-Bonger, Amsterdam;
V. W. van Gogh, Laren; Amsterdam, Rijksmuseum Vincent
van Gogh [Vincent van Gogh Foundation, inv nr F 1656/I]
EXHIBITIONS II 1914 Haarlem; 1969 Stuttgart, 48
PROVENANCE II H. P. Bremmer, The Hague; Sale Bern
[Kornfeld and Klipstein] 9-11 June 1966, 351; Stuttgart,
Staatsgalerie [acquired 1966], inv nr A 66/4444

F 1657 OLD MAN DRINKING COFFEE
EXHIBITION I 1914-5 Amsterdam, 26a
PROVENANCE I Mrs J. van Gogh-Bonger, Amsterdam;
V. W. van Gogh, Laren; Amsterdam, Rijksmuseum Vincent
van Gogh [Vincent van Gogh Foundation, inv nr F 1657/I]
PROVENANCE II Ph. de Kanter, Delft; H. E. d'Audretsch,
Amerongen; Amerongen, Mrs d'Audretsch-Krop [R 1968]
EXHIBITION III 1947 Basle, 124
PROVENANCE III Switzerland, Private collection

F 1658 ORPHAN MAN, STANDING
EXHIBITIONS [impressions I or III] 1914-5 Amsterdam, 14;
1924 Amsterdam, 18; 1954-5 Bern, 170
PROVENANCE I Mrs J. van Gogh-Bonger, Amsterdam;
V. W. van Gogh, Laren; Amsterdam, Rijksmuseum Vincent
van Gogh [Vincent van Gogh Foundation, inv nr F 1658/I]
PROVENANCE II Ph. de Kanter, Delft; H. E. d'Audretsch,
Amerongen; Philadelphia, Lessing Rosenwald
PROVENANCE III Mrs J. van Gogh-Bonger, Amsterdam;
V. W. van Gogh, Laren; Amsterdam, Rijksmuseum Vincent
van Gogh [Vincent van Gogh Foundation, inv nr F 1658/III]
PROVENANCE IV Vincent van Gogh [The Hague]; Sale
Amsterdam [de Vries] 5-6 November 1912, nr 450;
Amsterdam, Houthakker Art Gallery; Present
owner unknown [Note: pedigree not clear]

F 1659 MAN DIGGING IN THE ORCHARD
EXHIBITION I 1914-5 Amsterdam, 55
PROVENANCE I Mrs J. van Gogh-Bonger, Amsterdam;
V. W. van Gogh, Laren; Amsterdam, Rijksmuseum Vincent
van Gogh [Vincent van Gogh Foundation, inv nr F 1659/I]
PROVENANCE II Ph. de Kanter, Delft; H. E. d'Audretsch,
Amerongen; Amerongen, Mrs d'Audretsch-Krop [R 1968]
EXHIBITION III 1969 Stuttgart, 49
PROVENANCE III C. M. van Gogh Art Gallery, Amster-
dam; Vincent van Gogh Art Gallery, [Amsterdam]; Sale
Amsterdam [de Vries] 16-17 July 1930, nr 479; De Bois Art
Gallery, Haarlem; W. F. Arntz; Sale Stuttgart [Stuttgarter
Kunstkabinett] 24 November 1953, nr 1082; Stuttgart,
Staatsgalerie [acquired 1954], inv nr GVL 32 [A 54/1529]
[Note: Pedigree is based upon the sale cat Stuttgart
[Stuttgarter Kunstkabinett] 24 November 1953, nr 1082]
PROVENANCE IV Proof formerly in the collection of Paul
Gachet [according to Vanbeselaere 1937]; Present owner
unknown

F 1660 MAN BURNING WEEDS AND A WOMAN SITTING
ON A WHEELBARROW
EXHIBITIONS I 1905 Amsterdam, 268; 1914-5 Amsterdam,
125
PROVENANCE I Mrs J. van Gogh-Bonger, Amsterdam;
V. W. van Gogh, Laren; Amsterdam, Rijksmuseum Vincent
van Gogh [Vincent van Gogh Foundation, inv nr F 1660/I]
PROVENANCE II C. M. van Gogh Art Gallery, Amsterdam;
Vincent van Gogh Art Gallery, [Amsterdam]; Sale Bern
[Gutekunst und Klipstein] 20 June 1938, nr 271; Present
owner unknown
EXHIBITIONS III 1918 The Hague; 1924 Amsterdam, 58;
1928 The Hague; 1929 Hamburg, 103; 1930 Amsterdam,
94; 1956 Nuremberg, 55
PROVENANCE III J. Hidde Nijland, The Hague; Dordrecht,
Dordrechts Museum [loan Hidde Nijland 1904-10]; Otterlo,
Rijksmuseum Kröller-Müller, inv nr 1010-28, cat van Gogh
1970, nr 159 [classified as F 1036]

F 1661 POTATO EATERS
EXHIBITIONS I or II 1904 Rotterdam, 62; 1914-5 Amster-
dam, 113; 1928 Vienna, 41; 1953 Otterlo, Amsterdam, 38;
1953-4 Saint Louis etc, 36; 1957 Stockholm, 33; 1966 Paris,
Albi, 27; 1967 Lille, Zurich, 29; 1967-8 Dallas etc, 26; 1968
Liège, 26; 1968-9 London, 39; 1969 Humlebaek, 13
PROVENANCE I Mrs J. van Gogh-Bonger, Amsterdam;
V. W. van Gogh, Laren; Amsterdam, Rijksmuseum Vincent
van Gogh [Vincent van Gogh Foundation, inv nr F 1661/I]
PROVENANCE II Mrs J. van Gogh-Bonger, Amsterdam;
V. W. van Gogh, Laren; Amsterdam, Rijksmuseum Vincent
van Gogh [Vincent van Gogh Foundation, inv nr F 1661/II]
PROVENANCE III Ph. de Kanter, Delft; Philadelphia,
Lessing Rosenwald
EXHIBITIONS IV 1952 Milan, 45; 1956 Nuremberg, 57;
Munich, 50; 1958 Vienna, 40; Tokyo, Kyoto, 67; 1966
Belgrade, 38

PROVENANCE IV Unknown provenance; Otterlo, Rijks-
museum Kröller-Müller, inv nr A 17-kl. I-00, cat van Gogh
1970, nr 167a
PROVENANCE V Rockanje, R. van Hoey Smith
PROVENANCE VI The Hague, d'Audretsch Art Gallery;
Present owner unknown
PROVENANCE VII Moreover a proof on sale Stuttgart
[Stuttgarter Kunstkabinett] 7-9 November 1951, nr 1058

F 1662 WORN OUT: AT ETERNITY'S GATE
EXHIBITIONS Impressions I or II 1905 Amsterdam, 247;
1914-5 Amsterdam, 32; 1954-5 Bern, 171
PROVENANCE I Mrs J. van Gogh-Bonger, Amsterdam;
V. W. van Gogh, Laren; Amsterdam, Rijksmuseum Vincent
van Gogh [Vincent van Gogh Foundation, inv nr F 1662/I]
PROVENANCE II Mrs J. van Gogh-Bonger, Amsterdam;
V. W. van Gogh, Laren; Amsterdam, Rijksmuseum Vincent
van Gogh [Vincent van Gogh Foundation, inv nr F 1662/II]
PROVENANCE III Ph. de Kanter, Delft; Private collection
PROVENANCE IV J. Hidde Nijland, The Hague; Sale The
Hague [Pulchri] 5-6 October 1937, nr 49; Present owner
unknown
EXHIBITION V 1947 Basle, 123
PROVENANCE V Arlesheim, Arthur Stoll [cat Sammlung
Stoll, Zurich/Stuttgart 1961, nr 73]
PROVENANCE VI Vincent van Gogh, [Amsterdam]; Sale
Amsterdam [de Vries] 5-6 November 1912, nr 451; Hout-
hakker Art Gallery, Amsterdam
PROVENANCE VII Proof mentioned Sale Paris [Drouot]
31 March 1920, nr 71: Le vieil ouvrier pleurant.
Lithographie. Fort rare. Present owner unknown

F 1663 MAN SITTING ON A BASKET CUTTING HIS BREAD
EXHIBITIONS 1904 Rotterdam, 63 [not sure which
impression]; 1914-5 Amsterdam, 17 [impressions I or II];
1926 Munich, 2104 [not sure which impression]
PROVENANCE I Mrs J. van Gogh-Bonger, Amsterdam;
V. W. van Gogh, Laren; Amsterdam, Rijksmuseum Vincent
van Gogh [Vincent van Gogh Foundation, inv nr F 1663/I]
PROVENANCE II Mrs J. van Gogh-Bonger, Amsterdam;
V. W. van Gogh, Laren; Amsterdam, Rijksmuseum Vincent
van Gogh [Vincent van Gogh Foundation, inv nr F 1663/II]
EXHIBITIONS III 1914 Haarlem, 17; 1915 Rotterdam, 35;
1935 Haarlem, 39; 1938 Haarlem, 21; 1942 Rotterdam, 43
[probably impression de Bois]
PROVENANCE III Haarlem, J. H. de Bois Art Gallery;
Present owner unknown
PROVENANCE IV Delft, Ph. de Kanter; Present owner
unknown

ETCHING

F 1664 PORTRAIT OF DR GACHET: L'HOMME À LA PIPE
EXHIBITIONS I 1905 Paris, 26; 1914-5 Amsterdam, 200;
1935-6 New York etc, 127; 1953-4 St Louis etc, 181; 1954-5
Bern, 172; 1962 London I, 71 [impression I or II]
PROVENANCE I Mrs. J. van Gogh-Bonger, Amsterdam;
V. W. van Gogh, Laren; Amsterdam, Rijksmuseum Vincent
van Gogh [Vincent van Gogh Foundation, inv nr F 1664/I]
EXHIBITIONS II 1952 Milan, 127; 1953-4 St Louis etc, 181;
1956 Nuremberg, 70; Munich, 166; 1958 Vienna, 112;
Tokyo, Kyoto, 128; 1962 Warsaw, 88; 1963 Tel Aviv, Haifa,
100; 1966 Belgrade, 41
PROVENANCE II Unknown provenance; Otterlo, Rijks-
museum Kröller-Müller, inv nr C 23-kl. I-00, cat van Gogh
1970, nr 255
EXHIBITIONS III 1946-7 Liège etc, 140; 1947 Paris I, 141;
Geneva, 141
PROVENANCE III Amsterdam, Rijksprentenkabinet
PROVENANCE IV Cincinnati, Ohio, Cincinnati Museum of
Art [The Albert P. Strietmann collection], inv nr 1960.699
EXHIBITION V 1930 Amsterdam, 311
PROVENANCE V J. B. de la Faille, Heemstede; Heemstede,
Heirs of J. B. de la Faille
EXHIBITION VI 1912 Cologne, 125
PROVENANCE VI Düsseldorf, A. Flechtheim [R 1912];
Present owner unknown
EXHIBITIONS VII 1937 Paris, 206; 1960 Paris, 109
PROVENANCE VII Paul Gachet, Auvers; Heirs of Paul
Gachet
EXHIBITIONS VIII 1953 Berlin, 22
PROVENANCE VIII Sale Amsterdam [Mak] 27 October
1925, nr 182; The Hague, Gemeentemuseum, inv nr I/1926
EXHIBITION IX 1963 Hamburg, 96
PROVENANCE IX Hamburg, Kunsthalle
EXHIBITION X 1961 Munich, 74
PROVENANCE X Munich, Staatliche Graphische Sammlung
PROVENANCE XI New York, Museum of Modern Art
PROVENANCE XII Rotterdam, Museum Boymans-van
Beuningen
EXHIBITION XIII 1929 Cambridge, USA, 124
PROVENANCE XIII W. G. Russell Allen
EXHIBITION XIV 1955 New York I, p 7
PROVENANCE XIV New York, Galerie St Etienne
PROVENANCE XV Toledo, USA, Toledo Museum, inv
nr 1940.98
PROVENANCE XVI Washington, Phillips Gallery
See moreover cat under F 1664

SUPPLEMENTARY PAINTINGS

SP 1665 TWO FEMALE FIGURES IN THE WOOD
EXHIBITION 1960 Paris, 3
PROVENANCE H. P. Bremmer, The Hague; Private
collection; Paris, Private collection [R 1960]

SP 1666 THREE FIGURES WALKING ALONG A CANAL
PROVENANCE Present owner unknown

SP 1667 HEAD OF A PEASANT WOMAN: THREE
QUARTERS TO THE LEFT
EXHIBITIONS 1903 Rotterdam 3, 39; 1962 Amsterdam, 24
PROVENANCE W. van Bakel, Breda; H. D. Pierson,
Scheveningen [acquired 1903]; Scheveningen, Mrs E. de
Ridder-Pierson

SP 1668 HEAD OF A PEASANT WOMAN WITH WHITE
CAP: FULL FACE
EXHIBITION 1903 Rotterdam 3, 58
PROVENANCE W. van Bakel, Breda; H. D. Pierson,
Scheveningen [acquired 1903]; Zurich, Mrs A. M. Pierson
[R 1964]

SP 1669 PEASANT HUT WITH BARNS
EXHIBITION 1969 London, hors cat
PROVENANCE Unknown dealer, Hampstead; London,
Luigi Grosso [acquired 1969]

SP 1670 STILL LIFE: MEAT, CELERY AND POTS
PROVENANCE Unknown dealer, Paris; Hastings-on-
Hudson, New York, J. Lipchitz

SP 1671 STILL LIFE: TWO HERRINGS, TOWEL AND
GLASS
PROVENANCE Family of Mrs Scharenguival, USA; USA, Mr
and Mrs Scharenguival [R 1968]

SP 1672 TWILIGHT, BEFORE THE STORM:
MONTMARTRE
PROVENANCE Paris, G. Darrieutort [R 1969]

SP 1672a SELF PORTRAIT
PROVENANCE Family von Steiger, Switzerland; Private
collection, Bregenz; Vienna, Gemäldegalerie des Kunsthistorischen Museums [acquired 1964], inv nr MG 319, cat
Neuerworben 1955 bis 1966, nr 12 [illustration p 24]

SUPPLEMENTARY DRAWINGS

SD 1673 FRENCH PEASANT WOMAN [after Dalou]
PROVENANCE Mrs J. van Gogh-Bonger, Amsterdam;
V. W. van Gogh, Laren; Amsterdam, Rijksmuseum Vincent
van Gogh [Vincent van Gogh Foundation, inv nr SD 1673]

SD 1674 A MOWER
PROVENANCE Miss W. M. D. van der Linden [from
Oldenzeel 1892]; Mrs W. M. D. Spies-van der Linden,
Transvaal; P. Spies and/or M. Spies, Eindhoven; V. W. van
Gogh, Laren; Amsterdam, Rijksmuseum Vincent van Gogh
[Vincent van Gogh Foundation, inv nr SD 1674]

SD 1675 MAN WITH BASKET, SOWING
PROVENANCE J. Hageraats Art Gallery, The Hague
[bought from a private owner at Nuenen]; Mrs van
Velthuysen-Treybits, The Hague [gift from Hageraats
1906]; The Hague, Heirs of Mrs van Velthuysen [R 1964]

SD 1676 FIELD OF STUBBLE WITH A THUNDERSTORM
OVERHEAD
PROVENANCE J. B. [Minus] Oostrijck, Etten; Sale Rotter-
dam [van Marle and de Sille] 15-17 December 1948, nr 40;
L. van Zanten Art Gallery, Rotterdam [R 1940]; Mainz and
Legat Art Gallery, The Hague; P. Citroen, Wassenaar;
Private collection; Netherlands, Private collection [R 1969]

SD 1677 DONKEY CART
EXHIBITIONS 1966 Paris, Albi, 2a; 1967 Lille, Zurich, 3;
1967-8 Dallas etc, 3; 1968 Liège, 3; 1968-9 London, 4
PROVENANCE Miss W. M. D. van der Linden [from
Oldenzeel 1892]; Mrs W. M. D. Spies-van der Linden,
Transvaal; P. Spies and/or M. Spies, Eindhoven; V. W. van
Gogh, Laren; Amsterdam, Rijksmuseum Vincent van Gogh
[Vincent van Gogh Foundation, inv nr SD 1677]

SD 1678 THE STATIONSSTRAAT AT ETTEN
EXHIBITION 1960 Paris, 74b
PROVENANCE L. Oostrijck, Etten; J. Oostrijck, Etten;
J. B. [Minus] Oostrijck, Etten; J. de Visser, Etten; Private
collection [R 1960]; F. Nathan, Zurich; R. Lehman, New
York [R 1964]; New York, Estate of Robert Lehman
[bequeathed to the Metropolitan Museum, 1969]

SD 1679 CORNER OF HERENGRACHT AND PRINSESSE-
GRACHT IN THE HAGUE
EXHIBITION 1969 Humlebaek, 5 [repr]
PROVENANCE C. M. van Gogh Art Gallery, Amsterdam;
The Hague [de Vries] 13 May 1902, nr 437 [not sold];
Amsterdam, Rijksmuseum Vincent van Gogh [Vincent van
Gogh Foundation, inv nr SD 1679]

SD 1680 VIEW IN THE HAGUE
PROVENANCE Unknown collection; Sale The Hague
[Venduhuis] June 1960; Private collection

SD 1681 BOY WITH WOODEN SHOES, STANDING:
FULL FACE
EXHIBITION 1968-9 London, 26
PROVENANCE Mrs J. van Gogh-Bonger, Amsterdam;
Mr and Mrs Hamburger, Groningen [gift from Mrs van
Gogh about 1900]; Mrs Leopold-Hamburger; Amsterdam,
Rijksmuseum Vincent van Gogh [Vincent van Gogh
Foundation, inv nr SD 1681]

SD 1682 ORPHAN MAN DRINKING COFFEE
EXHIBITIONS 1968-9 London, 16; 1969 Humlebaek, 6
PROVENANCE A. Sirkissian, Paris; V. W. van Gogh, Laren
[R 1964]; Amsterdam, Rijksmuseum Vincent van Gogh
[Vincent van Gogh Foundation, inv nr SD 1682]

SD 1683 MAN STANDING, READING A BOOK
PROVENANCE Present owner unknown
EDITORS' COMMENT In the files of the Rijksbureau voor
Kunsthistorische Documentatie in The Hague is a
reproduction of SD 1683 that comes from the archives of
F. Muller & Co, Amsterdam, indicating with great
likelihood that the drawing was once auctioned by Muller

SD 1684 SIEN: FACING LEFT
EXHIBITION 1948 Bergen, Oslo, not in cat
PROVENANCE M. de Zwart, Voorburg, Netherlands;
H. P. Baron van Tuyll van Serooskerken, Katwijk; Sale
Amsterdam [F. Muller] 25-26 November 1913, nr 122; Sale
Amsterdam [F. Muller] 9-10 April 1918, nr 368; Sale
Amsterdam [F. Muller] 3 December 1918, nr 128; D. Mohr
Friele, Bergen, Norway [R 1937]; E. B. Hjertholm, Bergen,
Norway; Bergen, Norway, H. Claussen [R 1970]

SD 1685 YOUNG GIRL: HALF FIGURE, RIGHT PROFILE
PROVENANCE Oldenzeel Art Gallery, Rotterdam;
Anonymous owner, Netherlands; Sale Amsterdam [Mak]
15 April 1969, nr 204 [repr]; New York/Amsterdam, John
Streep Art Dealer [acquired 1969]

SD 1686 FUNERAL AT NUENEN IN WINTER
PROVENANCE J. Kalff, Zwolle; Munich, Mrs F. von Werz
[R 1970]

SD 1687 WINTER LANDSCAPE WITH THE OLD TOWER
OF NUENEN IN THE BACKGROUND
PROVENANCE J. Kalff, Zwolle; Stockholm, A. M. Ober-
mayer [R 1968]

SD 1688 THE WEAVER STANDING IN FRONT OF A LOOM
PROVENANCE Present owner unknown

SD 1689 WOMAN WITH A BUNDLE OF BRANCHES,
STUDIES OF HANDS
PROVENANCE Mrs J. van Gogh-Bonger, Amsterdam;
V. W. van Gogh, Laren; Amsterdam, Rijksmuseum Vincent
van Gogh [Vincent van Gogh Foundation, inv nr SD 1689]

SD 1690 PEASANT WOMAN DIGGING UP CARROTS
PROVENANCE A. Vollard, Paris; Hebrard, Paris [acquired
1906]; Present owner unknown

SD 1691 PEASANT WOMAN DIGGING UP CARROTS
PROVENANCE A. Slatineanu [bought in Paris before 1908];
B. Slatineanu [acquired 1908]; Bucharest, Colectia de Arte
Comparata

SD 1692 THE ANTWERP MARKET AT NIGHT
EXHIBITION 1962 London I, 24
PROVENANCE Mrs J. van Gogh-Bonger, Amsterdam;
V. W. van Gogh, Laren; Amsterdam, Rijksmuseum Vincent
van Gogh [Vincent van Gogh Foundation, inv nr SD 1692]

SD 1693a FIELD WITH WAGON AND RABBITS
EXHIBITION 1955 Antwerp I, 133
PROVENANCE Mrs J. van Gogh-Bonger, Amsterdam;
V. W. van Gogh, Laren; Amsterdam, Rijksmuseum Vincent
van Gogh [Vincent van Gogh Foundation, inv nr SD 1693a]

SD 1693b WOMEN ON THE BEACH
EXHIBITION 1955 Antwerp I, 132
PROVENANCE Mrs J. van Gogh-Bonger, Amsterdam;
V. W. van Gogh, Laren; Amsterdam, Rijksmuseum Vincent
van Gogh [Vincent van Gogh Foundation, inv nr SD 1693b]

SD 1693c STUDY OF A KNEE
EXHIBITION 1955 Antwerp I, 149
PROVENANCE Mrs J. van Gogh-Bonger, Amsterdam;
V. W. van Gogh, Laren; Amsterdam, Rijksmuseum Vincent
van Gogh [Vincent van Gogh Foundation, inv nr SD 1693c]

SD 1693d STUDY OF A KNEE
EXHIBITION 1955 Antwerp I, 150
PROVENANCE Mrs J. van Gogh-Bonger, Amsterdam;
V. W. van Gogh, Laren; Amsterdam, Rijksmuseum Vincent
van Gogh [Vincent van Gogh Foundation, inv nr SD 1693d]

SD 1693e HEAD OF A WOMAN: RIGHT PROFILE
EXHIBITION 1955 Antwerp I, 138
PROVENANCE Mrs J. van Gogh-Bonger, Amsterdam;
V. W. van Gogh, Laren; Amsterdam, Rijksmuseum Vincent
van Gogh [Vincent van Gogh Foundation, inv nr SD 1693e]

SD 1693f STUDY OF A RIGHT HAND
EXHIBITION 1955 Antwerp I, 147
PROVENANCE Mrs J. van Gogh-Bonger, Amsterdam;
V. W. van Gogh, Laren; Amsterdam, Rijksmuseum Vincent
van Gogh [Vincent van Gogh Foundation, inv nr SD 1693f]

SD 1693g STUDY OF A LEFT HAND
EXHIBITION 1955 Antwerp I, 146
PROVENANCE Mrs J. van Gogh-Bonger, Amsterdam;
V. W. van Gogh, Laren; Amsterdam, Rijksmuseum Vincent
van Gogh [Vincent van Gogh Foundation, inv nr SD 1693g]

SD 1693h STUDY AFTER PLASTER STATUETTE: FEMALE
TORSO, SEEN FROM THE FRONT
EXHIBITION 1955 Antwerp I, 151
PROVENANCE Mrs J. van Gogh-Bonger, Amsterdam;
V. W. van Gogh, Laren; Amsterdam, Rijksmuseum Vincent
van Gogh [Vincent van Gogh Foundation, inv nr SD 1693h]

SD 1693i STUDY AFTER PLASTER STATUETTE: FEMALE
TORSO, SEEN FROM THE SIDE
EXHIBITION 1955 Antwerp I, 152
PROVENANCE Mrs J. van Gogh-Bonger, Amsterdam;
V. W. van Gogh, Laren; Amsterdam, Rijksmuseum Vincent
van Gogh [Vincent van Gogh Foundation, inv nr SD 1693i]

SD 1693j STUDY OF A FOREARM
EXHIBITION 1955 Antwerp I, 148
PROVENANCE Mrs J. van Gogh-Bonger, Amsterdam;
V. W. van Gogh, Laren; Amsterdam, Rijksmuseum Vincent
van Gogh [Vincent van Gogh Foundation, inv nr SD 1693j]

SD 1694 HEAD OF A MAN: LEFT PROFILE
EXHIBITION 1955 Antwerp I, 143
PROVENANCE Mrs J. van Gogh-Bonger, Amsterdam;
V. W. van Gogh, Laren; Amsterdam, Rijksmuseum Vincent
van Gogh [Vincent van Gogh Foundation, inv nr SD 1694]

SD 1695 HEAD OF A WOMAN: FACING RIGHT
EXHIBITION 1955 Antwerp I, 153
PROVENANCE Mrs J. van Gogh-Bonger, Amsterdam;
V. W. van Gogh, Laren; Amsterdam, Rijksmuseum Vincent
van Gogh [Vincent van Gogh Foundation, inv nr SD 1695]

SD 1696 STUDY AFTER LIVING MODEL: FEMALE NUDE
WITH RAISED ARMS
PROVENANCE Mrs J. van Gogh-Bonger, Amsterdam;
V. W. van Gogh, Laren; Amsterdam, Rijksmuseum Vincent
van Gogh [Vincent van Gogh Foundation, inv nr SD 1696]

SD 1697 recto FOUR STUDIES OF FEET
verso STUDY OF A FOOT
PROVENANCE Mrs J. van Gogh-Bonger, Amsterdam;
V. W. van Gogh, Laren; Amsterdam, Rijksmuseum Vincent
van Gogh [Vincent van Gogh Foundation, inv nr SD 1697]

SD 1698 STUDY AFTER LIVING MODEL: STANDING
FEMALE NUDE, FACING RIGHT
PROVENANCE Mrs J. van Gogh-Bonger, Amsterdam;
V. W. van Gogh, Laren; Amsterdam, Rijksmuseum Vincent
van Gogh [Vincent van Gogh Foundation, inv nr SD 1698]

SD 1699 STUDY AFTER LIVING MODEL: STANDING
FEMALE NUDE IN RIGHT PROFILE
EXHIBITION 1962 London I, 31 [erroneously listed as
F 1363]
PROVENANCE Mrs J. van Gogh-Bonger, Amsterdam;
V. W. van Gogh, Laren; Amsterdam, Rijksmuseum Vincent
van Gogh [Vincent van Gogh Foundation, inv nr SD 1699]

SD 1700 STUDY AFTER LIVING MODEL: SITTING
FEMALE NUDE, THREE QUARTERS TO THE RIGHT;
TRACES OF A MALE NUDE
PROVENANCE Mrs J. van Gogh-Bonger, Amsterdam;
V. W. van Gogh, Laren; Amsterdam, Rijksmuseum Vincent
van Gogh [Vincent van Gogh Foundation, inv nr SD 1700]

SD 1701 recto STUDY AFTER PLASTER STATUETTE:
BUST BY ANTONIO DEL POLLAIUOLO IN THE
BARGELLO IN FLORENCE
verso STUDY AFTER LIVING MODEL: NUDE MAN
SITTING ON A STOOL, SEEN FROM THE BACK
PROVENANCE Mrs J. van Gogh-Bonger, Amsterdam;
V. W. van Gogh, Laren; Amsterdam, Rijksmuseum Vincent
van Gogh [Vincent van Gogh Foundation, inv nr SD 1701]

SD 1702 recto STUDIES AFTER PLASTER STATUETTES
Left STANDING MALE WITH ONE ARM, SEEN FROM THE
BACK; STANDING MALE WITHOUT ARMS, SEEN FROM
THE FRONT
Right STANDING MALE WITH ONE ARM, SEEN FROM
THE BACK
verso STUDY AFTER PLASTER STATUETTE: STANDING
MALE WITH ONE ARM, SEEN FROM THE BACK

PROVENANCE Mrs J. van Gogh-Bonger, Amsterdam;
V. W. van Gogh, Laren; Amsterdam, Rijksmuseum Vincent
van Gogh [Vincent van Gogh Foundation, inv nr SD 1702]

SD 1703 recto THREE STUDIES OF FEET
verso PART OF A CANAL BORDERED BY TREES
PROVENANCE Mrs J. van Gogh-Bonger, Amsterdam;
V. W. van Gogh, Laren; Amsterdam, Rijksmuseum Vincent van Gogh [Vincent van Gogh Foundation,
inv nr SD 1703]

SD 1704 WOMAN AND DOG: IN THE BACKGROUND THE
ENTRANCE OF THE BAL BOULE NOIR
EXHIBITION 1962 London I, 43 [repr]
PROVENANCE Mrs J. van Gogh-Bonger, Amsterdam;
V. W. van Gogh, Laren; Amsterdam, Rijksmuseum Vincent
van Gogh [Vincent van Gogh Foundation, inv nr SD 1704]

SD 1705 recto TWO LOVERS
verso SKETCH OF A HOUSE
EXHIBITION 1962 London I, 40 [repr]
PROVENANCE Mrs J. van Gogh-Bonger, Amsterdam;
V. W. van Gogh, Laren; Amsterdam, Rijksmuseum Vincent
van Gogh [Vincent van Gogh Foundation, inv nr SD 1705]

SD 1706 STUDY AFTER LIVING MODEL: A MAN WITH
HIS RIGHT ARM RAISED
PROVENANCE Mrs J. van Gogh-Bonger, Amsterdam;
V. W. van Gogh, Laren; Amsterdam, Rijksmuseum Vincent
van Gogh [Vincent van Gogh Foundation, inv nr SD 1706]

SD 1707 STUDY AFTER PLASTER STATUETTE: FEMALE
TORSO ON PEDESTAL, FACING RIGHT
PROVENANCE Mrs J. van Gogh-Bonger, Amsterdam;
V. W. van Gogh, Laren; Amsterdam, Rijksmuseum Vincent
van Gogh [Vincent van Gogh Foundation, inv nr SD 1707]

SD 1708 recto STUDY AFTER PLASTER STATUETTE:
FEMALE TORSO ON ROUND PEDESTAL, SEEN FROM
THE BACK
verso STUDY AFTER PLASTER STATUETTE: FEMALE
TORSO ON ROUND PEDESTAL, FACING RIGHT
PROVENANCE Mrs J. van Gogh-Bonger, Amsterdam;
V. W. van Gogh, Laren; Amsterdam, Rijksmuseum Vincent
van Gogh [Vincent van Gogh Foundation, inv nr SD 1708]

SD 1709 recto STUDY AFTER PLASTER STATUETTE:
FEMALE TORSO ON ROUND PEDESTAL, FACING RIGHT
verso STUDY AFTER PLASTER STATUETTE: FEMALE
TORSO WITH ONE LEG, RIGHT PROFILE
PROVENANCE Mrs J. van Gogh-Bonger, Amsterdam;
V. W. van Gogh, Laren; Amsterdam, Rijksmuseum Vincent
van Gogh [Vincent van Gogh Foundation, inv nr SD 1709]

SD 1710 recto STUDY AFTER LIVING MODEL: STANDING
FEMALE NUDE, FROM THE THIGHS UP
verso STUDY AFTER THE LIVING MODEL: STANDING
MALE NUDE, SEEN FROM THE BACK; THREE STUDIES
AFTER A PLASTER STATUETTE: FEMALE TORSO WITH
ONE LEG, FACING RIGHT
EXHIBITION 1954-5 Bern, 123
PROVENANCE Mrs J. van Gogh-Bonger, Amsterdam;
V. W. van Gogh, Laren; Amsterdam, Rijksmuseum Vincent
van Gogh [Vincent van Gogh Foundation, inv nr SD 1710]

SD 1711 recto STUDY AFTER PLASTER STATUETTE:
FEMALE TORSO ON ROUND PEDESTAL, SEEN FROM
THE FRONT
verso STUDY AFTER PLASTER STATUETTE: FEMALE
TORSO, FACING LEFT
PROVENANCE Mrs J. van Gogh-Bonger, Amsterdam;
V. W. van Gogh, Laren; Amsterdam, Rijksmuseum Vincent
van Gogh [Vincent van Gogh Foundation, inv nr SD 1711]

SD 1712 recto STUDY AFTER PLASTER STATUETTE:
FEMALE TORSO, FACING RIGHT
verso STUDY AFTER PLASTER STATUETTE: FEMALE
TORSO, SEEN FROM ABOVE AND TO THE RIGHT
PROVENANCE Mrs J. van Gogh-Bonger, Amsterdam;
V. W. van Gogh, Laren; Amsterdam, Rijksmuseum Vincent
van Gogh [Vincent van Gogh Foundation, inv nr SD 1712]

SD 1713 recto STUDY AFTER PLASTER STATUETTE:
FEMALE TORSO, SEEN FROM THE FRONT
verso STUDY AFTER PLASTER STATUETTE: MALE
TORSO, SEEN FROM THE FRONT; SITTING WOMAN
PROVENANCE Mrs J. van Gogh-Bonger, Amsterdam;
V. W. van Gogh, Laren; Amsterdam, Rijksmuseum Vincent
van Gogh [Vincent van Gogh Foundation, inv nr SD 1713]

SD 1714 SKETCH OF A VIOLINIST AND A LADY PIANIST
EXHIBITION 1962 London I, 39
PROVENANCE Mrs J. van Gogh-Bonger, Amsterdam;
V. W. van Gogh, Laren; Amsterdam, Rijksmuseum Vincent
van Gogh [Vincent van Gogh Foundation, inv nr SD 1714]

SD 1715 SKETCH OF A MAN'S HEAD
PROVENANCE Present owner unknown

SD 1716 recto STUDY AFTER PLASTER STATUETTE:
FEMALE TORSO WITH ONE LEG
verso STUDY AFTER PLASTER STATUETTE: FEMALE
TORSO WITH ONE LEG
Lower left RIVER LANDSCAPE
EXHIBITION 1962 London I, 34
PROVENANCE Mrs J. van Gogh-Bonger, Amsterdam;
V. W. van Gogh, Laren; Amsterdam, Rijksmuseum Vincent
van Gogh [Vincent van Gogh Foundation, inv nr SD 1716]

SD 1717 SKETCH OF A SITTING FEMALE NUDE
EXHIBITION 1962 London I, 35
PROVENANCE Mrs J. van Gogh-Bonger, Amsterdam;
V. W. van Gogh, Laren; Amsterdam, Rijksmuseum Vincent
van Gogh [Vincent van Gogh Foundation, inv nr SD 1717]

SD 1718 SKETCH OF A SEATED WOMAN DRESSING
EXHIBITION 1962 London I, 36 [repr]
PROVENANCE Mrs J. van Gogh-Bonger, Amsterdam;
V. W. van Gogh, Laren; Amsterdam, Rijksmuseum Vincent
van Gogh [Vincent van Gogh Foundation, inv nr SD 1718]

SD 1719 recto Above SKETCH OF A ROAD WITH
BUILDINGS
Below RAMPARTS WITH THREE FIGURES
verso SKETCH OF A BUILDING
PROVENANCE Mrs J. van Gogh-Bonger, Amsterdam;
V. W. van Gogh, Laren; Amsterdam, Rijksmuseum Vincent
van Gogh [Vincent van Gogh Foundation, inv nr SD 1719]

SD 1720 COUPLE STROLLING UNDER SUNFLOWERS ON
A HILL OVERLOOKING THE CITY
PROVENANCE Mrs J. van Gogh-Bonger, Amsterdam;
V. W. van Gogh, Laren; Amsterdam, Rijksmuseum Vincent
van Gogh [Vincent van Gogh Foundation, inv nr SD 1720]

SD 1721 GYPSIES AT SAINTES-MARIES
PROVENANCE Present owner unknown

SD 1722 LA MOUSMÉ
PROVENANCE Paul Gauguin, Paris; Paris, Musée National
du Louvre [ms Noa-Noa-Paul Gauigun]

SD 1723 THE POSTMAN ROULIN
PROVENANCE Sale Paris [Drouot] 27 February 1919,
nr 144 [repr]; Present owner unknown

SD 1724 recto STUDY OF TWO LEFT FEET
verso SKETCHES OF PEASANT PLOWING WITH HORSES
PROVENANCE Mrs J. van Gogh-Bonger, Amsterdam;
V. W. van Gogh, Laren; Amsterdam, Rijksmuseum Vincent
van Gogh [Vincent van Gogh Foundation, inv nr SD 1724]

SD 1725 STUDY OF SIX HANDS
PROVENANCE Mrs J. van Gogh-Bonger, Amsterdam;
V. W. van Gogh, Laren; Amsterdam, Rijksmuseum Vincent
van Gogh [Vincent van Gogh Foundation, inv nr SD 1725]

SD 1726 STUDY OF EIGHT HANDS
PROVENANCE Mrs J. van Gogh-Bonger, Amsterdam;
V. W. van Gogh, Laren; Amsterdam, Rijksmuseum Vincent
van Gogh [Vincent van Gogh Foundation, inv nr SD 1726]

SD 1727 STUDY OF A LEFT HAND
PROVENANCE Mrs J. van Gogh-Bonger, Amsterdam;
V. W. van Gogh, Laren; Amsterdam, Rijksmuseum Vincent
van Gogh [Vincent van Gogh Foundation, inv nr SD 1727]

SD 1728 WHEATFIELD SEEN FROM THE WINDOW OF
VINCENT'S ROOM IN ST PAUL'S HOSPITAL
EXHIBITIONS 1898 The Hague, 29; 1966 Paris, 86
PROVENANCE Miss E. D. van den Broecke, Oostkapelle,
Netherlands [Miss A. P. Ogtrop, Middelburg enjoyed the
usufruct]; Middelburg, Zeeuws Museum, inv nr M 67-54;
Otterlo, Rijksmuseum Kröller-Müller [acquired 1970], inv
nr 1517-70

SD 1729 LES OLIVEUSES
PROVENANCE Mrs J. van Gogh-Bonger, Amsterdam;
V. W. van Gogh, Laren; Amsterdam, Rijksmuseum Vincent
van Gogh [Vincent van Gogh Foundation, inv nr SD 1729]

SD 1730 HORSE AND CART
PROVENANCE Mrs J. van Gogh-Bonger, Amsterdam;
V. W. van Gogh, Laren; Amsterdam, Rijksmuseum Vincent
van Gogh [Vincent van Gogh Foundation, inv nr SD 1730]

SD 1731 HEN
PROVENANCE Mrs J. van Gogh-Bonger, Amsterdam;
V. W. van Gogh, Laren; Amsterdam, Rijksmuseum Vincent
van Gogh [Vincent van Gogh Foundation, inv nr SD 1731]

SD 1732 STOOPING WOMAN ON ROAD WITH TREES
PROVENANCE Mrs. J. van Gogh-Bonger, Amsterdam;
V. W. van Gogh, Laren; Amsterdam, Rijksmuseum Vincent
van Gogh [Vincent van Gogh Foundation, inv nr SD 1732]

List of Redated Works

PAINTINGS

F	redated from	to	by
14	The Hague	Nuenen	Faille
16	Drenthe	The Hague	Faille
28	Nuenen	Paris	the editors
61 verso	Nuenen	Paris	Faille
68	Nuenen	Nuenen (drawings)	the editors
77 verso	Nuenen	Paris	Faille
109 verso	Nuenen	Paris	Faille
174	Nuenen	Antwerp	Faille
177a	Nuenen	Paris	the editors
178 verso	Nuenen	Paris	the editors
179 verso	Nuenen	Paris	Faille
180	Nuenen	Paris	the editors
181	Nuenen	Paris	the editors
186	Nuenen	The Hague	Faille
188	Nuenen	Drenthe	Faille
189	Nuenen	The Hague	the editors
192	Nuenen	The Hague	Faille
197	Nuenen	Paris	the editors
201	Nuenen	Paris	Faille
203	Nuenen	Paris	Faille
203a	Nuenen	Antwerp	Faille
204	Antwerp	The Hague	the editors
207a	Antwerp	Paris	the editors
208	Antwerp	Paris	the editors
208a	Antwerp	Paris	the editors
209	Antwerp	Paris	the editors
210	Antwerp	Nuenen	Faille
212a	Antwerp	Nuenen	Faille
260	Paris	Antwerp	Faille
269 recto	Paris	Nuenen	Faille
280	Paris	Auvers	the editors
290	Paris	Arles	Faille
365 recto	Paris	Nuenen	Faille
384	Paris	Arles	Faille
386	Paris	Arles	Faille
402	Arles	Saint Rémy	Faille
452	Arles	Paris	Faille
469	Arles	Paris	Faille
483	Arles	Saint Rémy	Faille
484	Arles	Saint Rémy	the editors
522	Arles	Paris	Faille
526	Arles	Paris	Faille
528	Arles	Saint Rémy	Faille
531	Arles	Saint Rémy	Faille
540	Arles	Saint Rémy	Faille
541	Arles	Saint Rémy	Faille
542	Arles	Saint Rémy	Faille
543	Arles	Saint Rémy	Faille
581	Arles	Saint Rémy	Faille
583	Arles	Paris	Faille
585	Arles	Saint Rémy	Faille
586	Arles	Saint Rémy	Faille
587	Arles	Saint Rémy	Faille
589	Arles	Auvers	the editors
595	Arles	Auvers	the editors
596	Arles	Paris	Faille
597	Arles	Auvers	the editors
598	Arles	Auvers	the editors
599	Arles	Auvers	the editors
603	Arles	Paris	Faille
636	Saint Rémy	Auvers	Faille
666	Saint Rémy	Paris	the editors
666a	Saint Rémy	Paris	the editors
740	Saint Rémy	Auvers	the editors
748	Saint Rémy	Auvers	the editors
749	Saint Rémy	Auvers	the editors
818	Auvers	Saint Rémy	Faille

DRAWINGS

F	redated from	to	by
830	Cuesmes-Brussels	Etten	Faille
833	Cuesmes-Brussels	Etten	Faille
835	Cuesmes-Brussels	Juvenilia	the editors
836	Cuesmes-Brussels	Juvenilia	Faille
837	Cuesmes-Brussels	Juvenilia	Faille
838	Cuesmes-Brussels	Juvenilia	Faille
839	Cuesmes-Brussels	Juvenilia	Faille
840	Cuesmes-Brussels	The Hague	Faille
841	Cuesmes-Brussels	The Hague	Faille
847	Etten	Cuesmes-Brussels	the editors
848	Etten	Cuesmes-Brussels	the editors
852	Etten	The Hague	Faille
853	Etten	The Hague	Faille
872	Etten	The Hague	Faille
874 recto	Etten	Cuesmes-Brussels	the editors
877	Etten	Drenthe	the editors
882	Etten	The Hague	Faille
898	Etten	The Hague	Faille
899	Etten	The Hague	Faille
901	Etten	The Hague	Faille
904	Etten	The Hague	Faille
905	Etten	Juvenilia	the editors
992	The Hague	Arles	Faille
995	The Hague	Etten	the editors
1070	The Hague	Etten	Faille
1073	The Hague	Drenthe	Faille
1081	The Hague	Nuenen	Faille
1085	The Hague	Etten	the editors
1086	The Hague	Etten	the editors
1090	The Hague	Arles	Faille
1093	The Hague	Antwerp	the editors
1105	Drenthe	Cuesmes-Brussels	Faille
1106	Drenthe	Nuenen	Faille
1116a recto	Nuenen	Etten	the editors
1160 recto	Nuenen	Antwerp	the editors
1160 verso	Nuenen	Antwerp	the editors
1179	Nuenen	The Hague	Faille
1209	Nuenen	Etten	Faille
1213	Nuenen	Etten	Faille
1216	Nuenen	Etten	Faille
1221	Nuenen	Etten	Faille
1235	Nuenen	Etten	the editors
1244 recto	Nuenen	Paris	Faille
1244 verso	Nuenen	Paris	Faille

1244a recto and verso, 1244b recto and verso, 1244c recto and verso and 1244d recto and verso were not in Faille 1928. Faille marked the photographs with numbers of the Nuenen period, but filed these drawings in his manuscript as belonging to the Paris period

F	redated from	to	by
1248	Nuenen	Drenthe	Faille
1294	Nuenen	The Hague	Faille
1338	Nuenen	Antwerp	Faille
1347	Nuenen	Drenthe	Faille
1360 recto	Antwerp	Saint Rémy	the editors
1360 verso	Antwerp	Saint Rémy	the editors
1362 recto	Paris	Antwerp	the editors
1363a recto	Paris	Antwerp	the editors
1364-1	Paris	Antwerp	the editors
1364-2	Paris	Antwerp	the editors
1368	Paris	Antwerp	the editors
1369 recto	Paris	Antwerp	the editors
1369 verso	Paris	Antwerp	the editors
1372 recto	Paris	Antwerp	the editors
1372 verso	Paris	Antwerp	the editors
1375	Paris	Saint Rémy	the editors
1494	Arles	Saint Rémy	the editors
1497	Arles	Saint Rémy	Faille
1501	Arles	Saint Rémy	the editors
1505	Arles	Saint Rémy	the editors
1508 recto	Arles	Paris	Faille
1520 recto	Arles	Saint Rémy	the editors
1520 verso	Arles	Saint Rémy	the editors
1521 recto	Arles	Saint Rémy	the editors
1521 verso	Arles	Saint Rémy	the editors
1549 recto	Saint Rémy	Arles	the editors
1554	Saint Rémy	Arles	Faille
1589a	Saint Rémy	Auvers	the editors
1609 recto	Saint Rémy	Auvers	the editors
1609 verso	Saint Rémy	Auvers	the editors
1610 recto	Saint Rémy	Auvers	the editors
1610 verso	Saint Rémy	Auvers	the editors
1611 recto	Saint Rémy	Auvers	the editors
1611 verso	Saint Rémy	Auvers	the editors
1612	Saint Rémy	Auvers	the editors
1613	Saint Rémy	Auvers	the editors
1614	Saint Rémy	Auvers	the editors
1615 recto	Saint Rémy	Auvers	Faille
1615 verso	Saint Rémy	Auvers	Faille
1616	Saint Rémy	Auvers	the editors
1619 recto	Saint Rémy	Auvers	the editors
1619 verso	Saint Rémy	Auvers	the editors
1635 recto	Auvers	Saint Rémy	the editors
1641	Auvers	Arles	the editors
1645 recto	Auvers	Saint Rémy	the editors
1645 verso	Auvers	Saint Rémy	the editors
1647 recto	Auvers	Saint Rémy	Faille
1647 verso	Auvers	Saint Rémy	Faille
1648 recto	Auvers	Saint Rémy	Faille
1648 verso	Auvers	Saint Rémy	Faille
1649 recto	Auvers	Saint Rémy	the editors
1649 verso	Auvers	Saint Rémy	the editors
1651 recto	Auvers	Arles	the editors
1651 verso	Auvers	Saint Rémy	the editors

List of Works with Signature and Date

The following numbers are signed [dated or otherwise inscribed] by Vincent or others. [For comments see corresponding numbers in the catalogue]. Unless otherwise indicated, the inscription reads simply: Vincent.

PAINTINGS

1c, 3, 13, 28, 34, 45, 47, 82, 83, 84, 88, 92, 104a, 106, 107, 111, 112, 114, 117, 130, 141, 170, 180, 201, 203, 212a, 213, 215a, 224, 229, 234, 235, 237: *Vincent 86*, 238, 241, 244, 245, 246, 247, 248, 248b, 249, 250, 251, 252, 255, 258: *V*, 262, 263: *Tanguy Vincent janvier 87*, 263a: *Vincent 87*, 265, 271, 273, 274, 278, 282, 283a, 283b, 285, 286b, 288, 322, 324, 324a, 328: *Vincent 87*, 329, 331, 332a, 333: *Vincent 87*, 334, 335: *87*, 340: *Vincent 87*, 343, 346, 347, 357: *Vincent 87*, 375: *Vincent 87*, 376: *Vincent 87*, 378: *à l'ami Lucien Pissaro Vincent*, 379: *Vincent 87*, 383: *Vincent 87 A mon frère Theo*, 392, 393, 394: *Souvenir de Mauve Vincent*, 395, 396, 397, 398, 400, 403, 405, 406, 410, 412, 413, 415, 417, 422, 425, 435, 443, 446, 449, 450, 454, 455, 456, 458, 461, 463: *Vincent le café de nuit*, 465, 476: *Vincent, A mon ami Paul G.*, 498, 500: *Vincent Arles 89*, 501: *à l'ami Laval Vincent*, 502: *Vincent Arles 89*, 504: *Vincent la Berceuse*, 505: *Vincent Arles 89 La Berceuse*, 506: *Vincent Arles 89 La Berceuse*, 508: *La Berceuse*, 522: *Vincent 88*, 550, 552, 553, 555, 556, 571: *Vincent Pont de l'Anglois*, 578, 579, 585, 591, 594, 596, 608, 609, 652, 664, 666a: *Vincent 89*, 734, 757: *d'après Eug. Delacroix a appartenu à Diaz. Vincent*, 768, 777: *le jardin de Daubigny*

DRAWINGS

828, 829: *Vincent d'après J. F. Millet les Bêcheurs*, 832: *the Bearers of the Burden*, 834: *d'après J. F. Millet l'Angelus du Soir, Atel. Vincent*, 840, 841: *atelier Vincent*, 843: *At. Vincent*, 845, 847: *d'après Hans Holbein la fille du bourgmestre Jacques Meyer*, 850, 851, 853, 854, 855: *V v G*, 856: *port. Vincent*, 857: *Zaayer*, 858, 860, 860a, 861, 863: *Worn out. Vincent*, 864: *Worn out*, 866, 868: *Atelier Vincent*, 869, 870, 871, 872: *aventurier en voyage*, 873: *atelier Vincent*, 875, 877: *kerkje te Zweeloo*, 881: 43: 120 *Vincent v. Gogh*, 885:

atelier Vincent, 887, 889: *Atelier Vincent*, 896: *V v G*, 897, 898: *Port. Vincent*, 900: *Atelier Vincent*, 901, 902: *Atelier Vincent*, 903: *atelier Vincent*, 913, 914, 917, 918, 919, 920, 921, on the reverse: *Gronde nabij de Rijnspoor*, 922, 922a, 923, 924, 925, 928, 929: *Vincent. Sorrow*, 929a: *Vincent del. Sorrow. Comment se fait-il qu'il y ait sur la terre une femme seule – délaissée Michelet*, 930, 930a, 931, 933: *Atelier Vincent*, 934, 938: *Vincent del. Scharrendroogerij te Scheveningen*, 939: *Vincent – 82*, 940: *Scharrendroogerij in de duinen Scheveningen. Vincent*, 941, 942: *Vincent del.*, 944, 946a, 951, 952 recto: *Bezuidenhout*, 955, 959: *Port. Vincent*, 964b, 965, 975, 978a, 980, 985, 986: *Vincent feci*, 987, 988a, 997, 998a: *atelier Vincent*, 1000, 1003, 1006, 1008, 1009, 1010, 1019, 1020a, 1024, 1025, 1026: *At. Vincent*, 1036, 1037, 1047, 1048, 1049, 1052, 1055, 1056: *Port. Vincent*, 1057, 1059, 1067, 1068, 1070: *Atelier Vincent*, 1072, 1076: *port. Vincent Hidde Nijland*, 1078a: *Vincent. The Dustman*, 1086, 1089, 1092: *At. Vincent*, 1106: *port. Vincent. Hidde Nijland*, 1107, 1110: *Port. Vincent*, 1113, 1114, 1115, 1118, 1119, 1121, 1122, 1123, 1125, 1127: *Mélancolie*, 1128, 1129, 1130, 1131: *Jardin d'hiver*, 1132, 1134, 1135, 1136, 1138, 1139, 1171, 1173, 1177, 1180, 1195 verso: *verz. H.N*, 1198, 1199, 1201 verso: *Port. Vincent. Hidde Nijland*, 1202, 1203, 1206, 1207a: *dessin de Vincent van Gogh*, 1209: *Vincent verz. Hidde Nijland*, 1212, 1214: *Vincent [Ecosseuse de pois]*, 1216, 1218, 1221, 1222, 1230, 1235, 1240, 1245, 1246, 1252, 1259, 1261, 1262, 1262a, 1262b, 1263 [twice], 1270: *Planteuse de betteraves. juin*, 1272: *Vincent Planteuse de pommes de terre*, 1272a: *Planteuse de betteraves, juin, Vincent*, 1273: *Vincent arracheuse de pommes de terre*, 1275a, 1277, 1281, 1282, 1284, 1293, 1295: *Port Vincent*, 1301 recto, verso: *eig. Hidde Nijland*, 1302: *Bêcheur dans un champ de pommes de terre février*, 1303: *betterave*, 1314, 1315, 1322 recto: [*Port. Vincent*], verso: *Port. Vincent Hidde Nijland*, 1323 [twice], 1325, 1326, 1329 verso: *verz. Hidde Nijland*, 1330 verso: *Hidde Nijland*, 1333 verso: *Vincent. Verz. Hidde Nijland*, 1336 verso: *V.v.G. verz. Hidde Nijland*, 1347, 1348: *Un dimanche à Eindhoven, Vincent*, 1392: *la fenêtre chez Bataille Vincent 87*, 1414: *Verger de Provence Vincent*, 1416: *vue d'Arles Vincent*, 1417: *ruine de Montmajour*, 1418,

1419: *vue de la Crau*, 1420: *la Crau vue prise à Mont Major*, 1422: *d'après un tableau d'E. Bernard. Vincent*, 1424, 1427, 1428: *Vincent Souvenir de Saintes-Maries Méditerranée*, 1430b, 1435, 1442, 1443, 1446, 1447, 1448: *Vincent vue prise à...*, 1449, 1450, 1452, 1454, 1455, 1456, 1457, 1460, 1467, 1472a: *Bords du Rhône Vincent*, 1475: *vue d'Arles*, 1478: *Vincent un mas de Provence*, 1479: *cimetière de Stes Maries*, 1480: *Vincent le pont de l'Anglais Arles*, 1482: *A mon cher copain Emile Bernard. Vincent*, 1482a, 1483: *Vincent. La moisson en Provence*, 1486: *Vincent. La moisson en Provence*, 1488, 1489, 1490, 1492, 1493: *Bruyère*, 1495, 1499: *Arles Mars 88*, 1503, 1527: on the reverse: *geteekend door Vincent van Gogh. 1890. wed. Th. van Gogh-Bonger*

LITHOGRAPHS

1655: *Vincent Sorrow*, 1656, 1657, 1658, 1659, 1660, 1661, 1662, 1663

ETCHING

1664: *15 [25?] Mai 90* [on the reverse *l'homme à la pipe. Portrait de mon père, le docteur Gachet. Eau forte de Vincent van Gogh. Auvers sur Oise. Mai 1890*]

SUPPLEMENTARY PAINTINGS

1669, 1671: *V*, 1672: on the reverse: *8 heures soir 27 Juillet pour le crépuscule orage*

SUPPLEMENTARY DRAWINGS

1673: *paysanne française d'après la terre cuite de Dalou*, 1675, 1679: *Vincent*, verso: *Hoek Heerengracht en Prinsengracht en Boschbrug*, 1680, 1681, 1682: *Vincent del.*, 1690: *arracheuse de carottes [hiver]*, 1691: *arracheuse de carottes [hiver]*, 1693: *Place de Meir Florens: Louizenstrotje*, 1697: *l'tiaple n'egsisde boind*, 1704: *de son métier elle ne faisait rien. Le soir elle baladait son chien. La Vilette.*, 1715, 1721: *Saintes Maries V*, 1722: *du regretté Vincent van Gogh*

List of Subjects

composed under responsibility of G. D. Schwartz

The Rejected works and Juvenilia are not included in this list. Abbreviations used to identify technique and period are:

d	drawing	An	Antwerp	E	Etten
e	etching	Ar	Arles	N	Nuenen
g	gouache	Au	Auvers	P	Paris
l	lithograph	C-B	Cuesmes-Brussels	SR	Saint Rémy
p	painting			TH	The Hague
wc	water color	D	Drenthe		

SINGLE FIGURES AT WORK

MEN

F 5 Fisherman on the beach	p TH
F 11 The sower	p TH
F 12 Man at work	p TH
F 20 Peasant burning weeds	p D
F 24 Weaver with a view of the Nuenen tower	p N
F 26 Weaver: figure apart	p N
F 27 Weaver: facing front	p N
F 29 Weaver with loom and spinning wheel	p N
F 30 The weaver: the whole loom, facing front	p N
F 32 Weaver facing left standing	p N
F 33 Weaver standing: seen from the back	p N
F 35 Weaver facing left: whole figure	p N
F 37 The weaver: interior with three windows	p N
F 42 Shepherd: storm effect	p N
F 162 Weaver: the whole loom, facing right	p N
F 166 Peasant digging	p N
F 171 The basket maker	p N
F 171a The basket maker	p N
F 450 The sower	p Ar
F 451 The sower	p Ar
F 827 Coal shoveler	d C-B
F 851 Young peasant with sickle	d-wc E
F 852 The sower: facing right	d TH
F 855 Young peasant digging: facing right	d-wc E
F 856 Peasant sowing: facing right	d E
F 857 The sower: full face	d E
F 858 The sower: facing right	d E
F 859 Young peasant digging: facing right	d-wc E
F 860 Peasant digging: facing left	d E
F 860a Peasant digging: facing right	d E
F 861 The gardener leaning on a spade: three quarters to the left	d-wc E
F 862 Peasant sowing	d E
F 865 Man with basket, sowing	d-wc E
F 866 Peasant digging: facing left	d-wc E
F 866a The sower	d-wc E
F 878 The carpenter	d E
F 879 A kneeling man planting	d E
F 882 A man sowing: facing left	d TH
F 890 Man sweeping	d-wc E
F 891 Peasant sieving grain	d-wc E
F 893 Man with a stick	d E
F 894 Man chopping wood	d E
F 895 Peasant with hatchet	d E
F 906 Man digging: seen from the back	d TH
F 907 Man digging: seen from the back	d TH
F 908 Man digging: three quarters to the left	d TH
F 965 Old man carrying a basket: facing right	d TH
F 964a Man with a spade, resting	d TH
F 969 Orphan man cleaning boots	d TH
F 979 Man with a rake: facing right	d TH
F 979a Young man with a broom	d TH
F 987 Man with an axe on his shoulder	d TH
F 996 Orphan man with a broom	d TH
F 999 The sower: facing right	d TH
F 1000 The sower: front view	d TH
F 1035 The sower	TH
F 1042 The carpenter: seen from the back	d TH
F 1043 The carpenter: full face	d TH
F 1044 The blacksmith: facing right	d TH
F 1081 Man carrying a bundle of branches	wc N
F 1083 Fisherman with basket on his back	d TH
F 1107 The weaver: the whole loom, facing left	wc N
F 1108 The weaver: the whole loom, facing right	wc N
F 1109 The weaver: part of the loom, facing right	d N
F 1110 Interior with a weaver facing right	d-wc N
F 1114 The weaver: the whole loom, facing left	d-wc N
F 1115 The weaver, facing right: interior with three windows	d-wc N
F 1116 The weaver, seen from the front	d N
F 1116a verso The weaver: part of the loom, three quarters to the left	wc N
F 1118 Interior of a weaver's workshop with baby chair	d N
F 1119 Interior of a weaver's workshop with baby chair	wc N
F 1120 The weaver: the whole loom, facing left	d N
F 1121 The weaver: the whole loom, facing right, with oil lamp	d N
F 1122 The weaver: half length, facing right	d N
F 1123 The weaver: the whole loom, facing left, with oil lamp	d N
F 1124 The weaver: the whole loom, facing left	d N
F 1125 The weaver: the whole loom, facing right	d-wc N
F 1134 The weaver standing in front of a loom: left profile	d N
F 1138 Man reeling yarn	d N
F 1140 Man reeling yarn	wc N
F 1142 The plow	d N
F 1143 The sower	d N
F 1201 verso Peasant digging: facing left	d N
F 1301 verso Study of a peasant working [*the lower part of a drawing torn in half; the upper part is* F 1321 *verso*]	d N
F 1302 Peasant digging: seen from the back	d N
F 1303 Peasant digging: seen from the back	d N
F 1304 Peasant digging up potatoes: seen from the front	d N
F 1305 Peasant digging: facing left	d N
F 1306 Young peasant, digging: facing right	d N
F 1307 Young peasant digging: facing left	d N
F 1308 Peasant digging: facing right	d N
F 1309 Peasant digging: seen from the front	d N
F 1310 Peasant digging: facing right	d N
F 1311 Sketch of a peasant working: facing right	d N
F 1312 The reaper with hat: seen from the back	d N
F 1313 The reaper with hat: seen from the back	d N
F 1314 The reaper with hat: facing right	d N
F 1315 The reaper with hat: seen from the back	d N
F 1316 The reaper with hat: facing right	d N
F 1317 The reaper with cap: moving to the right	d N
F 1318 The reaper with cap: moving to the right	d N
F 1319 recto The reaper with cap: seen from the front	d N
F 1320 The reaper with hat: moving to the right	d N
F 1321 verso Figure of a man with a hat [*the upper part of a drawing torn in half; the lower part is* F 1301 *verso*]	d N
F 1322 recto Peasant reaping wheat in a landscape with trees and a little house	d N
F 1322 verso The reaper with hat: seen from the back	d N
F 1323 The reaper with hat: seen from the back	d N
F 1325 Peasant working: facing right, two cottages in the background	d N
F 1326 A peasant working: facing right, two cottages in the background	d N
F 1327 The woodcutter: facing right	d N
F 1441 The sower in a wheatfield with the setting sun	d Ar
F 1442 The sower in a wheatfield with the setting sun	d Ar
F 1550 Sower in the rain	d SR
F 1551 recto Sower in the rain	d SR
F 1551 verso Peasant working	d SR
F 1587 verso Peasant shoveling	d SR
F 1592 verso A man sowing	d SR
F 1635 verso Man with a scythe	d A
F 1656 The digger	l H
F 1659 Man digging in the orchard	l H
SD 1675 Man with basket, sowing	d E
SD 1688 The weaver standing in front of a loom	wc N

WOMEN

F 6 Fisherman's wife on the beach	p TH
F 36 The spinner	p N
F 68 Peasant woman winding bobbins	wc N
F 71 Peasant woman sewing	p N
F 73 Woman seated before an open door, peeling potatoes	p N
F 94 Peasant woman digging: seen from the back	p N
F 95 Peasant woman digging	p N
F 95a Peasant woman digging	p N
F 98 Peasant woman digging potatoes: left profile	p N
F 126a Peasant woman sewing	p N
F 139 Peasant woman raking	p N
F 145 Peasant woman peeling potatoes	p N
F 147 Peasant woman digging potatoes	p N
F 148 Peasant woman laundering	p N
F 152 Peasant woman sweeping	p N
F 157 Peasant woman darning stockings	p N
F 158 Peasant woman by the fireplace	p N
F 176 Peasant woman by the fireplace	p N
F 365 recto Peasant woman seated	p N
F 854 Peasant woman peeling potatoes	d E
F 867 Peasant woman sewing	d E
F 869 Young Scheveningen woman, seated: facing left	wc E
F 870 Young Scheveningen woman, knitting: facing right	wc E
F 881 Peasant girl gathering potatoes	d E
F 883 A woman sowing, with basket	d E
F 884 Young girl gardening	d-wc E
F 885 Interior with woman sewing: facing left	d-wc E
F 886 Woman, sewing by the window: facing right	wc E
F 887 A young woman sewing, with white cat	d-wc E
F 888 recto Woman mending stockings	d-wc E
F 889 Woman grinding coffee	d-wc E
F 892 Woman churning butter	d-wc E
F 910a Woman knitting near a window	wc TH
F 911 verso Stooping woman, picking up a net	TH
F 932 Sien sewing: whole figure in right profile	d TH
F 937 verso Sien sewing [*unfinished sketch*]	d TH
F 983 Standing girl, knitting: facing right	d TH
F 984 Seated girl, knitting: facing left	d TH
F 1021 Peasant woman with wheelbarrow	d-wc TH
F 1025 The seamstress [*second version*]	d TH
F 1026 The seamstress [*first version*]	d TH
F 1033 Woman sewing: facing right	d-wc TH
F 1053a Woman peeling potatoes	d TH
F 1074 Woman with broom: facing right	d-wc TH
F 1075 Woman with broom: full face	d-wc TH
F 1080 Peasant woman feeding fowls	d TH
F 1087 The laundress	wc TH
F 1106 Winter landscape with woman and wheelbarrow	d N
F 1136 Woman winding bobbins	d N
F 1137 Woman winding bobbins	d N
F 1139 Woman winding bobbins	g N
F 1203 Interior with a peasant woman sewing: facing left	d N
F 1204 Interior with a peasant woman sewing: facing left	d N
F 1205 Peasant woman sewing: facing left	d N
F 1206 Interior with a peasant woman sewing: facing right	d N
F 1207 Interior with a peasant woman knitting: seen from the front	d N
F 1207a Interior with a peasant woman knitting: seen from the front	d N
F 1208 Interior with a peasant woman peeling potatoes: seen from the front	d N
F 1209 Peasant woman peeling potatoes: facing left	d-wc E
F 1210 Interior with a peasant woman peeling potatoes: facing left	d N
F 1212 Peasant woman by the fire peeling potatoes	d-wc N
F 1213 Peasant woman peeling potatoes: facing left	d-wc E
F 1214 Interior with a peasant woman shelling peas: three quarters to the right	d N
F 1215 Interior with a peasant woman making pancakes	d N
F 1219 recto Interior with a standing woman slicing bread: facing right	d N
F 1219 verso Woman slicing bread	d N
F 1220 Interior with peasant woman sewing: seen from the front	d N
F 1221 Old peasant woman, sewing: facing right	d-wc E
F 1232 Winter landscape	d N
F 1233 recto Snow landscape	d N
F 1250 Peasant woman with a spade: facing right	d N
F 1251 Peasant woman with a pitchfork: facing right	d N
F 1252 Peasant woman digging: facing right	d N
F 1253 Peasant woman digging: facing left	d N
F 1254 Peasant woman digging: seen from the front	d N
F 1255 Peasant woman digging: seen from behind	d N
F 1256 Peasant woman with a fork: seen from behind, a windmill in the background	d N
F 1257 recto Peasant woman digging potatoes: seen from the front	d N
F 1257 verso Peasant woman: seen from behind	d N
F 1258 Peasant woman digging: seen from behind	d N
F 1259 Peasant woman tossing hay: seen from behind	d N
F 1260 Peasant woman tossing hay: seen from the front	d N
F 1261 Peasant woman tossing hay: facing right	d N
F 1262 Peasant woman binding sheaves: facing right	d N
F 1262a Peasant woman kneeling: facing right	d N
F 1262b Peasant woman kneeling and pulling out carrots	d N
F 1263 Peasant woman binding wheat: facing right	d N
F 1264 Peasant woman binding wheat: stooping, seen from the front	d N
F 1265 Peasant woman cleaning grain: seen from the front	d N
F 1265a Peasant woman gleaning grain: facing left	d N
F 1266 Peasant woman picking up a sheaf of grain: seen from the front	d N
F 1267 Peasant women carrying a sheaf of grain: seen from the front	d N
F 1268 Peasant woman carrying hay: facing left	d N
F 1270 Peasant woman planting beets	d N
F 1272 Peasant woman planting potatoes: seen from the front	d N
F 1272a Peasant woman planting beets	d N
F 1273 Peasant woman digging up potatoes	d N
F 1274 Peasant woman working	d N
F 1275 Peasant woman digging up potatoes	d N
F 1275a Peasant woman gleaning grain: facing left	d N
F 1276 recto Woman digging: full face	d N
F 1276 verso Peasant woman stooping: facing left	d N
F 1277 Peasant woman working: facing left	d N
F 1278 Woman with broom: full face	d N
F 1279 Peasant woman gleaning grain: facing left	d N
F 1280 Peasant woman kneeling: seen from the back	d N
F 1281 Woman with an ax: facing left	d N
F 1282 Woman scouring a caldron	d N
F 1283 recto Woman with a wooden pail: facing left	d N
F 1283 verso Peasant woman sweeping: facing left	d N
F 1287 Sketch of a woman stooping by the fireplace	d N
F 1289 verso Peasant woman carrying something in her apron: seen from the front	d N

F 1290 Peasant woman at the spinning wheel: facing left — d N
F 1290a The spinner — d N
F 1291 Woman on a bench by the hearth: facing left — d N
F 1292 Peasant woman by a pool — d N
F 1293 Peasant woman with a kettle, standing near a fireplace — wc N
F 1294 Woman sewing, sitting on a basket: facing right — d T H
F 1297a verso Woman sweeping: facing left — d N
F 1626 recto Peasant woman in a wheatfield — d Au
F 1642 Landscape with houses and a woman working in the field — d Au
F 1653 The farm of Pierre Eloi, in the foreground a woman working — d Au
SD 1690 Peasant woman digging up carrots — d N
SD 1691 Peasant woman digging up carrots — d N

MORE THAN ONE FIGURE AT WORK

F 7 Mending the nets — p T H
F 9 Potato digging — p T H
F 19 Two men digging, and a wheelbarrow — p D
F 21 The peat boat — p D
F 41 Potato planting — p N
F 43 Wood gatherers in the snow — p N
F 96 Two peasant women digging, facing each other — p N
F 97 Two peasant women digging potatoes, facing right — p N
F 129a Potato planting: a man and a woman — p N
F 172 The plower — p N
F 695 Women digging in field with snow — p S R
F 701 The diggers — p S R

F 831 Miners — d C-B
F 832 Miners' women carrying sacks [the bearers of the burden] — d C-B
F 853 Two sowers — d T H
F 922 Sand diggers in the dunes — d T H
F 927 Work in the fields — wc T H
F 930a The road workers — d T H
F 948 Three wood cutters — wc T H
F 950 Four wood cutters — d-wc T H
F 1028 The sand pit at Dekker's Dune — d T H
F 1029 Workmen in the sand pit at Dekker's Dune — d T H
F 1030 The peatery — d T H
F 1031 The peatery — T H
F 1034 Potato diggers — T H
F 1035a Peasant burning weeds — wc T H
F 1036 Peasant burning weeds — i-d T H
F 1078 Two men unloading bricks from a cart — d T H
F 1078a The dustman — d T H
F 1084 The forge — d T H
F 1090 Peasants working — d Ar
F 1096 recto Plowman and three women — d D
F 1111 Four figures working at a loom — d N
F 1114i Potato diggers — d N
F 1202 Winter landscape with figures — wc N
F 1225 Two peasants planting potatoes — d N
F 1228 Two peasant women, working in the fields — d N
F 1284 Woman by the wash tub, in a garden — d N
F 1295 Two women digging — d N
F 1296 Two peasant women digging — wc N
F 1299 Peasant and peasant woman digging — d-wc N
F 1301 recto Harvest: peasant women stooping and peasant reaping wheat — d N
F 1321 recto A reaper and a woman binding sheaves: a windmill in the background — d N
F 1333 recto Study of two peasants — d N
F 1337 Mangle with two women and a man — d N
F 1399 The graveyard — d P
F 1399a The graveyard — d P
F 1539 recto Landscape with cypresses and four figures — d S R
F 1586 verso Stooping peasant women — d S R
F 1593 recto Hut with cypresses in winter: three peasants working — d S R
F 1594 recto Farms with digging peasants — d S R
F 1597 verso Landscape with hut and two peasants with wheelbarrow — d S R
F 1598 recto Landscape with four figures and wheelbarrows — d S R
F 1598 verso Studies of peasants at work — d S R
F 1599 recto Studies of peasants; man with a wheelbarrow; woman with a wheelbarrow — d S R
F 1600 recto Sketches of men digging — d S R
F 1602 verso Six sketches of peasants digging — d S R
F 1605 recto Peasants working outdoors — d S R
F 1607 verso Two women bleaching laundry — d S R
F 1610 verso Sketch of two women working — d Au
F 1615 recto Hay harvest — d Au
F 1615 verso Hilly landscape with harvesters — d Au
F 1618 The sowers — d S R
F 1620 recto Work in the fields — d S R
F 1626 verso Two peasant women binding sheaves — d Au
F 1631 verso Sketch of five laundresses — d Au
F 1634 recto Studies of a standing woman and a peasant woman with a rake — d Au

F 1645 recto Study of a sower and a man with a spade — d S R
F 1645 verso Study of two sowers — d S R
F 1649 recto Studies of peasants working: sowers and diggers — d S R
F 1660 Man burning weeds and a woman sitting on a wheelbarrow — i T H
SD 1729 Les Oliveuses — d S R

SELF PORTRAITS

F 61 verso Self portrait with straw hat — p P
F 77 verso Self portrait: full face — p P
F 109 verso Self portrait: full face — p P
F 178 verso Self portrait — p P
F 179 verso Self portrait — p P
F 180 Self portrait — p P
F 181 Self portrait in front of the easel — p P
F 208 Self portrait with pipe: three quarters to the right — p P
F 208a Self portrait with felt hat — p P
F 263a Self portrait with pipe and glass — p P
F 267 Self portrait: three quarters to the left — p P
268 Self portrait: three quarters to the right — p P
258 verso Self portrait: full face — p P
F 294 Self portrait with straw hat: three quarters to the left — p P
F 295 Self portrait with gray felt hat: bust, full face — p P
F 296 Self portrait with gray felt hat: full face — p P
F 319 Self portrait with a Japanese print — p P
F 320 Self portrait: three quarters to the left — p P
F 344 Self portrait in a gray felt hat: three quarters to the left — p P
F 345 Self portrait: three quarters to the left — p P
F 356 Self portrait: three quarters to the right — p P
F 365 verso Self portrait with straw hat — p P
F 366 Self portrait: nearly full face — p P
F 380 Self portrait: three quarters to the left — p P
F 448 The painter on the road to Tarascon [destroyed] — p Ar
F 559 Self portrait with straw hat — p P
F 476 Self portrait [dedicated to Paul Gauguin] — p Ar
F 501 Self portrait — p Ar
F 522 Self portrait in front of the easel — p P
F 524 Self portrait with pipe and straw hat — p Ar
F 525 Self portrait without beard — p Ar
F 526 Self portrait with straw hat — p P
F 527 Self portrait with bandaged ear — p Ar
F 528 Self portrait — p S R
F 529 Self portrait with bandaged ear and pipe — p Ar
F 626 Self portrait — p S R
F 627 Self portrait — p S R

F 1378 recto Two self portraits; fragments of a third — d P
F 1379 Self portrait — d P
SP 1672a Self portrait — p P

HEADS AND HALF-LENGTHS

MEN

F 160a Portrait of a peasant — p N
F 163 Head of a peasant — p N
F 164 Head of a young peasant with a pipe — p N
F 165 Portrait of a peasant — p N
F 168 Head of a peasant: right profile — p N
F 169 Head of a peasant with a pipe: half profile to the right — p N
F 169a Head of a peasant — p N
F 179 recto Portrait of a farmer — p N
F 205 Head of an old man: left profile — p An
F 209 Head of a man: three quarters to the left — p P
F 263 Portrait of Père Tanguy — p P
F 288 Portrait of a man — p P
F 289 Man in a skull cap — p P
F 343 Portrait of Alexander Reid — p P
F 363 Portrait of Père Tanguy — p P
F 364 Portrait of Père Tanguy — p P
F 423 A bugler of the Zouave regiment — p Ar
F 432 The postman Joseph Roulin: half-length, sitting at a table — p Ar
F 433 Head of the postman Joseph Roulin — p Ar
F 434 Head of the postman Joseph Roulin — p Ar
F 435 Head of the postman Joseph Roulin against a flowery background — p Ar
F 436 Head of the postman Joseph Roulin against a flowery background — p Ar
F 439 Head of the postman Joseph Roulin against a flowery background — p Ar
F 443 Portrait of Patience Escalier, shepherd in the Provence — p Ar
F 444 Portrait of Patience Escalier, shepherd in the Provence — p Ar
F 462 Portrait of Eugène Boch, a Belgian painter — p Ar
F 473 Portrait of Milliet — p Ar
F 492 Portrait of Armand Roulin — p Ar
F 493 Portrait of Armand Roulin: facing left — p Ar
F 500 Portrait of Doctor Félix Rey — p Ar
F 531 The peasant — p S R
F 532 The one-eyed man — p Ar
F 533 Portrait of a man — p Ar

F 534 The smoker — p Ar
F 536 Young man in a cap — p Ar
F 537 Portrait of Camille Roulin — p Ar
F 538 Portrait of Camille Roulin — p Ar
F 629 Portrait of Trabu, an attendant of Saint Paul's Hospital — p S R
F 703 Head of a patient in Saint Paul's Hospital — p S R
F 753 Portrait of Dr Gachet — p Au
F 754 Portrait of Dr Gachet — p Au
F 787 Young man with cornflower — p Au
F 876 The artist's father Theodorus van Gogh [after a photograph] — d E
F 954 Head of an orphan man with top hat: right profile — d T H
F 954a Head of an orphan man with top hat — d T H
F 955 Bald-headed orphan man facing right — d T H
F 961 Orphan man with top hat — d T H
F 964b Man seated drinking a cup of coffee — d T H
F 986 Orphan man with top hat: half figure — d T H
F 993 Portrait [probably of the bookseller Blok] — d-wc T H
F 998 A man in sorrow — d T H
F 1003 Orphan man with top hat and bandage over his eye — d T H
F 1004 Man with a bandage over his eye, smoking a Gouda pipe — d T H
F 1011 Head of an old fisherman with sou'wester: full face — d T H
F 1012 Head of a fisherman: three quarters to the right — d T H
F 1014 Head of a fisherman: three quarters to the left — d T H
F 1015 Head of an old fisherman with pipe — d T H
F 1016 Head of an orphan man with pipe and coal pan: full face — d T H
F 1017 Head of an old fisherman: full face — d T H
F 1018 Orphan man: bust-length, facing left — d T H
F 1019 Study of Old Retering: facing front — d T H
F 1145 Head of a young peasant: right profile — d N
F 1146 Head of a young peasant: right profile — d N
F 1147 Head of a young peasant: full face, smoking a pipe — d N
F 1156 verso Head of a young peasant: full face — d N
F 1198 Head of a peasant — d N
F 1199 Young peasant with a pipe: facing left — d N
F 1200 Head of a man with hat: facing right — d N
F 1244a recto The violinist — d P
F 1244a verso The violinist — d P
F 1244c recto The pianist — d P
F 1244c verso The contrabass player — d P
F 1244 recto A man seen in left profile — d P
F 1244 verso Man with top hat — d P
F 1297 recto Sketch of a man's head [fragment: upper part] — d T H
F 1328 recto Peasant: facing right — d N
F 1358 Head of a man — d An
F 1359 Head of a man with pipe: left profile — d An
F 1372 recto Head of a man with hat and pipe — d An
F 1372 verso Head of a man: full face — d An
F 1412 Le Père Tanguy — d P
F 1458 The postman Roulin — d Ar
F 1459 The postman Roulin: half-length, sitting at a table — d Ar
F 1460 Portrait of Patience Escalier — d Ar
F 1461 Portrait of Patience Escalier — d Ar
F 1482 The Zouave: half-length — d-wc Ar
F 1482a The Zouave: head and shoulders — d Ar
F 1622 verso Head of a young man with a hat: full face — d Au
F 1664 Portrait of Dr Gachet: l'homme à la pipe — e Au
SD 1694a Head of a man: left profile — d An
SD 1715 Sketch of a man's head — d P
SD 1734 verso Head of a young man with a hat: full face — d Au

WOMEN

F 65 Peasant woman with white cap: head, three quarters left — p N
F 69 Head of a peasant woman: full face — p N
F 70 Head of a peasant woman: right profile against a window — p N
F 70a Study of a peasant woman: full face, half length against a window — p N
F 74 Head of an old peasant woman: full face, with dark cap — p N
F 75 Head of an old peasant woman: full face, with white cap — p N
F 80 Head of a peasant woman with white cap: facing right — p N
F 80a Head of a peasant woman with white cap: facing right — p N
F 81 Head of a peasant woman with a white cap: full face — p N
F 85 Head of a peasant woman with white cap: full face — p N
F 85a Head of a peasant woman with white cap: full face — p N
F 86 Head of a peasant woman: left profile — p N
F 127 Peasant woman: half figure — p N
F 130 Head of a peasant woman with white cap: front view — p N

F 131 Head of a peasant woman: left profile — p N
F 132 Head of a peasant woman: left profile — p N
F 132 Head of a peasant woman: left profile — p N
F 133 Head of a peasant woman: right profile — p N
F 134 Head of a peasant woman: half profile to the left — p N
F 135 Head of a peasant woman: right profile — p N
F 136 Head of a peasant woman: right profile — p N
F 136a Head of a peasant woman with dark cap: full face — p N
F 137 Bust of a peasant woman: full face, light background — p N
F 138 Head of a peasant woman: full face, light background — p N
F 140 Peasant woman with a white cap: left three-quarter view — p N
F 141 Head of a peasant woman with a white cap: left three-quarter view — p N
F 143 Peasant woman seated with arms crossed — p N
F 144 Head of a peasant woman: right profile — p N
F 144a Peasant woman seated: right profile — p N
F 146 Head of an old peasant woman with white cap: full face — p N
F 146a Head of a peasant woman with white cap: full face — p N
F 150 Head of a peasant woman: left half-profile, light background — p N
F 151 Head of a peasant woman: three quarters to the left — p N
F 153 Head of a peasant woman: right profile, light background — p N
F 153a Head of a peasant woman: left profile, light background — p N
F 154 Head of a peasant woman: three quarters to the right — p N
F 155 Peasant woman in a moss-green shawl — p N
F 156 Peasant woman in a white cap: bust, three quarters to the right — p N
F 159 Sketch of the head of a peasant woman: full face, light background — p N
F 160 Peasant woman in a red bonnet — p N
F 161 Hooded peasant woman: half length — p N
F 174 The midwife: head with white bonnet — p An
F 206 Head of a woman: nearly full face — p An
F 207 Portrait of a woman: bust, left profile — p An
F 207a Portrait of a woman in blue: three quarters to the right — p P
F 215a Study of a young woman: half-length, left profile — p P
F 215b Portrait of a woman: facing right — p P
F 215c Portrait of a woman with hat — p P
F 215d Portrait of a woman seated — p P
F 269 recto Study of a peasant woman — p N
F 357 Head of a woman — p P
F 367 Woman seated in the grass — p P
F 369 Woman with cradle — p P
F 370 Woman sitting in the Café du Tambourin [Avenue de Clichy, Paris] — p P
F 381 The italian woman with carnations [La Segatori?] — p P
F 388 recto Head of a peasant woman — p N
F 390 An old Arlesian woman — p Ar
F 431 La Mousmé — p Ar
F 477 Portrait of the artist's mother [after a photograph] — p Ar
F 488 L'Arlésienne: Madame Ginoux with books — p Ar
F 489 L'Arlésienne: Madame Ginoux with gloves and umbrella — p Ar
F 497 The novel reader — p Ar
F 503 Mme Augustine Roulin — p Ar
F 504 La Berceuse: Mme Augustine Roulin — p Ar
F 505 La Berceuse: Mme Augustine Roulin — p Ar
F 506 La Berceuse: Mme Augustine Roulin — p Ar
F 507 La Berceuse: Mme Augustine Roulin — p Ar
F 508 La Berceuse: Mme Augustine Roulin — p Ar
F 518 Portrait of a young girl against a pink background — p Ar
F 535 The girl with the ruffled hair — p Ar
F 631 Portrait of the wife of the attendant Trabu — p SR
F 768 Portrait of Miss Adeline Ravoux, the innkeeper's daughter — p Au
F 769 Portrait of Miss Adeline Ravoux, the innkeeper's daughter — p Au
F 774 Peasant woman against a background of wheat — p Au
F 786 Portrait of Miss Adeline Ravoux, the innkeeper's daughter — p Au
F 788 Young girl standing against background of wheat — p Au

F 840 Half figure of standing woman: facing left — d-wc T H
F 849 Portrait of Vincent's sister, Willemina van Gogh [after a photograph] — d E
F 931 Sien in white bonnet: left profile — d T H
F 946 verso Woman from Scheveningen, seated — wc T H
F 1005 Head of a woman with cap: left profile — d T H
F 1006 Bust of a woman with a cap: right profile — d T H
F 1009 Portrait head of a woman: full face — d T H
F 1009a Portrait head of a woman with a cap: full face — d T H

F 1047 Peasant woman seated: facing left — d T H
F 1148 Head of a peasant woman: full face — d N
F 1149 Head of a peasant woman with dark cap: full face — d N
F 1150 recto Head of a peasant woman: facing left — d N
F 1054 Bust of woman with hat: facing right — d T H
F 1055 Sien with a white bonnet: facing right — d T H
F 1057 Bust of a woman: full face, against a dark background — d-wc T H
F 1057a Bust of a woman: full face, against a light background — d T H
F 1059 Head of a woman — d T H
F 1073 Head of a woman with dark cap — d D
F 1169 Head of a peasant woman: left profile — d N
F 1170 Head of a peasant woman: facing right, against a dark background — d N
F 1171 Head of a peasant woman with white cap: three quarters to the left — d N
F 1172 Head of a peasant woman — d N
F 1173 Head of a peasant woman: three quarters to the right — d N
F 1174 Head of a peasant woman: facing right — d N
F 1175 Head of a peasant woman: full face — d N
F 1176 Head of a peasant woman with dark cap — d N
F 1177 Head of a peasant woman: facing left — d N
F 1178 Head of a peasant woman: right profile — d N
F 1180 Head of a peasant woman with white cap: full face — d N
F 1181 Head of a peasant woman with white cap: facing right — d N
F 1182 Head of a peasant woman: right profile — d N
F 1183 Head of a peasant woman: facing right — d N
F 1184 Head of a peasant woman: three quarters to the left — d N
F 1185 Head of a peasant woman with bonnet: facing right — d N
F 1186 Head of a peasant woman — d N
F 1188 Peasant woman: facing left — d N
F 1189 Peasant woman with white cap, seated: seen from the front — d N
F 1190 Peasant woman with white cap, seated: facing right — d N
F 1191 Peasant woman with dark cap, seated: seen from the front — d N
F 1192 Peasant woman with white cap: full face — d N
F 1193 Peasant woman with a white cap — d N
F 1193a Head of a peasant woman — d N
F 1194 Peasant woman: facing right — wc N
F 1194a Head of a peasant woman — d N
F 1224 Peasant woman with a white cap: full face — d N
F 1297a recto Head of a peasant woman — d N
F 1357 Portrait of a woman — d An
F 1357a Portrait of a woman with hat — d An
F 1503 Portrait of La Mousmé: bust — d Ar
F 1504 La Mousmé sitting in an armchair — d Ar
SP 1667 Head of a peasant woman: three quarters to the left — p N
SP 1668 Head of a peasant woman with white cap: full face — p N
SD 1784 Sien: facing left — d T H
SD 1693e Head of a woman: right profile — d An
SD 1695a Head of a woman: facing right — d An
SD 1722 La Mousmé — d Ar

WHOLE FIGURES

MEN
F 167 Peasant seated at table — p N
F 280 Portrait of Alexander Reid — p P
F 424 The Zouave — p Ar
F 702 Old man weeping — p SR

F 863 Worn out — d-wc E
F 864 Worn out — wc E
F 868 Old peasant by the fireplace — d E
F 897 Peasant reading by the fireplace — d-wc E
F 933 verso Blind man — d T H
F 953 Orphan man holding a top hat in his left hand — d T H
F 956 Orphan man with top hat eating — d T H
F 956a Orphan man with cap eating — d T H
F 957 Orphan man holding a cup — d T H
F 958 Orphan man with walking stick — d T H
F 959 Orphan man with glass and handkerchief — d T H
F 960 Orphan man with walking stick: seen from the back — d T H
F 962 Orphan man with walking stick — d T H
F 963 Orphan man with walking stick: facing right — d T H
F 965 Orphan man seen from the back — d T H
F 966 Orphan man reading- facing right — d T H
F 968 Orphan man with umbrella: seen from the back — d T H
F 972 Orphan man with an umbrella under his arm — d T H
F 972a Orphan man with umbrella: seen from behind — d T H
F 973 Orphan man standing, top hat in his right hand: full face — d T H
F 974 Orphan man warming himself: seen from the back — d T H
F 975 Orphan man with top hat and crossed hands — d T H

F 976 Orphan man drinking a cup of coffee — d T H
F 977 Orphan man with top hat and walking stick: full face — d T H
F 978 Orphan man looking at his watch — d T H
F 978a Orphan man — d T H
F 996a Orphan man with top hat drinking a cup of coffee — d T H
F 997 Old man with his head in his hands — d T H
F 1001 Man reading his bible — d T H
F 1002 Saying grace — d T H
F 1010 Fisherman with pipe — d T H
F 1013 Fisherman seated — d T H
F 1027 Orphan man kneeling in prayer: facing right — d T H
F 1046 Old seaman seated: full face — d T H
F 1049 The fisherman: facing right — d T H
F 1082 Man seated, drinking: full face — d T H
F 1085 Man writing: facing left — d E
F 1086 Old man warming himself — d E
F 1116a recto Man seated beside stove — d E
F 1202 recto Peasant seated: full face — d N
F 1329 recto Peasant walking to the left — d N
F 1330 recto Peasant walking: seen from the front — d N
F 1331 Short-legged old man with a bald head: seen from the front — d N
F 1332 recto Short-legged old man with a bald head: seen from the front — d N
F 1369 recto Seated worker with a cap: seen from the front — d An
F 1369 verso Seated worker, with beard — d An
F 1370 Man seated, facing left — d P
F 1443 The Zouave seated: full face — d Ar
F 1596a verso A peasant stooping — d SR
F 1657 Old man drinking coffee — l T H
F 1658 Orphan man, seated — l T H
F 1662 Worn out: at Eternity's Gate — l T H
F 1663 Man sitting on a basket cutting his bread — l T H
SD 1682 Orphan man drinking coffee — d T H
SD 1683 Man standing, reading a book — d T H
SD 1723 The postman Roulin — d Ar

WOMEN
F 72 Peasant woman taking her meal — p N
F 126 Peasant woman seated — p N
F 128 Peasant woman standing indoors — p N
F 699a Peasant woman walking in the fields — p SR
F 772 Marguerite Gachet at the piano — p Au

F 841 Woman on het deathbed — d-wc T H
F 871 Young fisherwoman from Scheveningen, standing: facing left — wc T H
F 873 Girl with black cap, on the ground by the fire: facing left — d-wc E
F 880 Girl kneeling in front of bucket — d E
F 896 Girl standing: facing right — d E
F 898 Sien with a cigar, sitting on the ground by the stove — d T H
F 899 A stooping woman — d T H
F 913 Woman walking with a stick — d T H
F 934 Old woman, standing: right profile — wc T H
F 935 Sien resting head on left hand, seated: right profile — d T H
F 936 Sien's mother sitting: right profile — d T H
F 937 recto Sien resting her head on her left hand, seated: Left profile — d T H
F 949 Woman in a wood — wc T H
F 1050 Woman in a long cloak: facing left — d T H
F 1051 Woman with a kettle — d T H
F 1052 Sien with an umbrella and a prayer book under her arm — d T H
F 1053 Woman saying grace — d T H
F 1056 Woman sitting on bench: facing left — d T H
F 1060 Woman with her head in her hands, sitting on an overturned basket — d T H
F 1069 Woman with her head in her hands, seated on a basket — d T H
F 1179 Sien with shawl, at the table — d-wc T H
F 1187 recto Peasant woman standing: seen from the back — d N
F 1187 verso Peasant woman standing: facing right — d N
F 1195 recto Study of a woman with a shawl — d N
F 1195 verso Woman with shawl, bearing a sack: walking to the left — d N
F 1196 Study of a woman with skirt over her head — d N
F 1197 Old woman with a shawl — d N
F 1216 Woman by the hearth — d-wc E
F 1217 Interior with a woman by the fireplace: facing right — d N
F 1218 Interior with a woman by the fireplace: facing right — d N
F 1222 Interior with a peasant woman by the fireplace — wc N
F 1223 Interior with a woman at the left by the fireplace — wc N
F 1227 verso Peasant woman standing: seen from the front — d N
F 1288 Peasant woman seated by the fireplace: facing left — d N
F 1289 recto Peasant woman: walking to the left — d N
F 1298 verso Peasant woman: facing left — d N
F 1623 recto Miss Gachet at the piano — d Au

F 1644 recto Peasant woman walking to the right   d Au
F 1644 verso A standing woman: seen from behind   d Au
S D 1732 Stooping woman on road with trees   d Au
S D 1733 recto Peasant woman walking to the right   d Au
S D 1733 verso Woman with hat in checked coat   d Au

MORE THAN ONE FIGURE

F 77 recto Interior of a peasant's house with four   p N
persons
F 78 The potato eaters   p N
F 82 The potato eaters   p N
F 149 Woman with a boy on her lap   p N
F 445 Encampment of gypsies with caravans   p Ar
F 463 The night café [now 'Café de l'Alcazar'] on   p Ar
the place Lamartine, Arles
F 478 The brothel   p Ar
F 485 The lovers: the poet's garden   p Ar
F 490 Mother Roulin with her baby   p Ar
F 491 Mother Roulin [in profile] with her baby   p Ar
F 544 A pair of lovers [fragment]   p Ar
F 547 The dance hall   p Ar
F 549 Interior of a restaurant in Arles   p Ar
F 549a Interior of a restaurant in Arles   p Ar
F 819 Women walking along the fields   p Au

F 909 Third-class waiting room   wc T H
F 967 In the church   d-wc T H
F 970 The state lottery office   wc T H
F 971 Orphan man with a child standing between   d T H
his knees
F 981 Orphan man holding a child   d T H
F 988 Two women standing talking   d T H
F 988a Two women strolling, one of them carrying   d T H
a kettle
F 989 Orphan man conversing with a woman   d T H
F 990 People under umbrellas   wc T H
F 991 Old couple: seen from the back   d T H
F 992 Couple walking   d Ar
F 1020 The public soup kitchen   d T H
F 1020a The public soup kitchen   d T H
F 1020b The public soup kitchen   d-wc T H
F 1048 Woman and child under an umbrella   d T H
[probably Sien and her daughter]
F 1058 Two women kneeling in prayer; one   d T H
woman standing in the background
F 1061 Sien with child in her right arm, facing left   d-wc T H
F 1062 Sien suckling her child   d T H
F 1063 Mother in armchair with child on her lap   d T H
F 1064 Sien with her child: facing left   d T H
F 1065 Sien with her child: facing left   d T H
F 1066 Woman with child on her lap   d T H
F 1067 Sien with child on her lap   d T H
F 1068 Nursing mother   d-wc T H
F 1070 Nursing mother and a child on the floor   d-wc E
F 1071 Sien with child on her lap: left profile   d T H
F 1072 Sien sewing and little girl   d T H
F 1077 Study of a man and a boy seated in a barn   d T H
F 1091 Potato market   wc T H
F 1096 Figure sketches   D
F 1105 Two men on a country road   d C-B
F 1112 recto Studies of an auction near Nuenen   d N
F 1113 A lumber sale   wc-N
F 1150 verso Sketch of two persons   d N
F 1226 The potato eaters   d N
F 1227 recto Study for the potato eaters   d N
F 1229 verso Man and two women around a table   d N
F 1230 Public sale of crosses of the cemetery at   wc N
Nuenen
F 1231 recto Study for the public sale of crosses of   d N
the cemetery at Nuenen
F 1231 verso Study for the public sale of crosses of   d N
the cemetery at Nuenen
F 1244b recto The clarinettist and flutist   d P
F 1298 recto Three peasant women   d N
F 1329 verso Studies of four figures   d N
F 1332 verso Peasant and peasant woman with baby   d N
F 1333 verso Study of two peasants   d N
F 1338 A couple on the road   d An
F 1350 verso Two sketches of a woman seated in   d An
a box at the theater
F 1350a Dancing hall   d An
F 1350b Women dancing   d An
F 1377 People walking in a wood   d P
F 1380 recto The street   d P
F 1381 recto A rainy day   d P
F 1463 Interior of the night café in Arles   wc Ar
F 1585 recto Couple arm in arm in winter   d S R
F 1585 verso Interior of a farmhouse with two   d S R
peasants at the table
F 1586 recto Two men on a road with pine trees   d S R
F 1587 recto The carriage and two figures on the   d S R
road
F 1588 Peasants at a meal   d S R
F 1589 recto Family: three figures on a road   d S R
F 1589 verso Peasant interior with three figures   d S R
F 1590 verso Four men on the road   d S R
F 1591 recto Winter landscape with people on the   d S R
road
F 1592 recto Winter landscape with many figures   d S R

F 1594 verso Family around the table   d S R
F 1596 recto On the road   d S R
F 1596 verso Peasants at table   d S R
F 1597 recto Return of the field-workers in the rain   d S R
F 1601 recto Sketches of a figure sitting at a table   d S R
F 1601 verso Studies of seated figures   d S R
F 1604 recto Figures in a landscape   d S R
F 1604 verso A group of figures on the beach   d S R
F 1606 recto Studies of a woman at the table and a   d S R
woman standing
F 1607 recto Studies of a woman on the road and a   d S R
man on the road
F 1608 recto Peasant family near the fireplace   d S R
F 1616 A man, a woman and a child   d S R
F 1617 Woman seated with a child on her knees   d S R
F 1619 recto Study of two women   d Au
F 1632 Sketch of three cows and two children   d Au
F 1647 recto Landscape with two figures   d S R
F 1647 verso Figures on a road   d S R
F 1652 recto Figure sketches   d Au
F 1654 recto Counter at Ravoux' Inn   d Au
F 1661 Potato eaters   I N
S P 1665 Two women in the woods   p T H
S P 1666 Three figures walking along a canal   p T H
S D 1693b Women on the beach   d An
S D 1705 recto Two lovers   d P
S D 1714 Sketch of a violinist and a lady pianist   d P
S D 1720 Couple strolling under sunflowers on a   d P
hill overlooking the city
S D 1721 Gypsies at Saintes-Maries   d Ar

CHILDREN

F 440 The baby Marcelle Roulin   p Ar
F 441 The baby Marcelle Roulin   p Ar
F 441a The baby Marcelle Roulin   p Ar
F 665 The schoolboy   p S R
F 783 Two children   p Au
F 784 Two children   p Au
F 785 Levert's daughter with orange   p Au

F 872 An adventurer setting out   d T H
F 911 recto Little child: facing left   d T H
F 912 Portrait of little child: facing left   d T H
F 986 Boy with spade, seated on a barrel   d T H
F 1007 Sien's daughter with shawl: left profile   d T H
F 1008 Sien's daughter seated: left profile   d T H
F 1024 Child kneeling in front of the cradle   d T H
F 1045 Girl carrying bread: facing right   d T H
F 1507a Head of a girl [the mudlark]   d Ar
F 1633 Sketch of a child in a perambulator   d Au
S D 1681 Boy with wooden shoes, standing: full face   d T H
S D 1685 Young girl: half figures, right profile   d T H

INTERIORS

F 342 Interior of a restaurant   p P
F 482 Vincent's bedroom in Arles   p Ar
F 483 Vincent's bedroom in Arles   p S R
F 484 Vincent's bedroom in Arles   p S R

F 888 verso Part of an interior with fireplace   d E
[unfinished sketch]
F 1508 verso The interior of a restaurant   d Ar
F 1510 Chair at the left side of a fireplace   d Ar
F 1511 Chair on the right side of a fireplace   d Ar
F 1512 recto The cane-bottomed chair [sketched   d Ar
over an erased landscape]

NUDES

F 215 Nude study: little girl seated   p P
F 328 Nude woman reclining: seen from the back   p P
F 329 Nude woman reclining   p P
F 330 Nude woman on a bed   p P

F 929 Sorrow   d T H
F 929a Sorrow   d T H
F 1353 Nude woman   d An
F 1363a recto Study after living models: standing   d An
male and sitting female nudes
F 1364-1 Study after living model- standing male   d An
nude
F 1364-2 Study after living model: standing male   d An
nude
F 1364a Study after living model- standing nude   d P
boy, seen from the back
F 1364b recto Study after living model: standing   d P
nude boy
F 1364b verso Study after living model: nude boy,   d P
seen from the back
F 1364c Study after living model: male nude with   d P
raised right arm, in right profile
F 1364d recto Study after living model: two views   d P
of a nude boy, seen from the back
F 1364d verso Study after living model: standing   d P
nude boy, seen from the front
F 1367 Nude girl sitting   d P
F 1368 Study after living model: seated female nude   d An
F 1376 Nude woman squatting   d P

F 1378 verso Sketch of a sitting woman   d P
F 1381 verso Sketch of a female figure   d P
F 1404 Nude woman reclining   d P
F 1655 Sorrow   I T H
S D 1696 Study after living model: female nude   d An
with raised arms
S D 1698 Study after living model: standing female   d An
nude, facing right
S D 1699 Study after living model: standing female   d An
nude in right profile
S D 1700 Study after living model: sitting female   d An
nude, three quarters to the right; traces of a male
nude
S D 1701 verso Study after living model: nude man   d P
sitting on a stool, seen from the back
S D 1706 Study after living model: a man with his   d P
right arm raised
S D 1710 recto Study after living model: standing   d P
female nude, from the thighs up
S D 1717 Sketch of a sitting female nude   d P
S D 1718 Sketch of a seated woman dressing   d P

LIMBS

F 66 Study of hands   p N

F 1153 recto Study of hands   d N
F 1154 Study of a right and a left hand   d N
F 1155 Study of hands and arms   d N
F 1156 recto Study of three hands, two of them   d N
holding a stick
F 1158 recto Study of four right hands   d N
F 1159 recto Study of two hands holding a   d N
stick
F 1159 verso Study of four hands, two of them   d N
holding a cup
F 1160 recto Study of a left arm   d An
F 1160 verso Study of a right arm   d An
F 1161 recto Study of three hands, two of them   d N
with a fork
F 1162 Study of hands   d N
F 1163 Study of three hands   d N
F 1164 recto Study of four hands   d N
F 1164 verso Study of three hands   d N
F 1165 Two hands holding a bowl   d N
F 1166 Study of hands holding a shovel   d N
F 1167 recto Study of hands in repose   d N
F 1167 verso Study of three hands   d N
F 1168 verso Three hands holding a stick   d N
F 1360 recto Study of seven hands   d S R
F 1363f verso Study of bare legs   d P
S D 1693c Study of a knee   d An
S D 1693d Study of a knee   d An
S D 1693 f Study of a right hand   d An
S D 1693g Study of a left hand   d An
S D 1693j Study of a forearm   d An
S D 1697 recto Four studies of feet   d An
S D 1697 verso Study of a foot   d An
S D 1703 recto Three studies of feet   d P
S D 1724 recto Study of two left feet   d S R
S D 1725 Study of six hands   d S R
S D 1726 Study of eight hands   d S R
S D 1727 study of a left hand   d S R

IDENTIFIED SITES

AMSTERDAM
F 113 View in Amsterdam from Central Station   p N
F 114 Landing stage at Amsterdam   p N

ANTWERP
F 211 The Antwerp quay   p An
F 260 Houses in Antwerp   p An

F 1350 recto The Steen at Antwerp   d An
F 1351 The Steen at Antwerp   d An
F 1352 The Grote Markt in Antwerp   d An
F 1354 Square in Antwerp   d An
F 1355 Town view in Antwerp   d An
F 1356 Spire of the church of Our Lady in Antwerp   d An
S D 1692 The Antwerp market at night   d An

ARLES
F 389 A pork butcher's shop   p Ar
F 391 Snowy landscape with Arles in the   p Ar
background
F 396 The Gleize bridge over the Vigueyret canal   p Ar
F 397 The Langlois bridge with women washing   p Ar
F 398 Avenue of plane trees near the station   p Ar
F 400 The Langlois bridge with road alongside the   p Ar
canal
F 409 View of Arles with irises in the foreground   p Ar
F 464 Vincent's house on the Place Lamartine   p Ar
F 465 Summer evening   p Ar
F 467 The café terrace on the Place du Forum,   p Ar
Arles, at night
F 468 Sunshine in the park: the poet's garden   p Ar
F 471 The park with the entrance seen through the   p Ar
trees
F 472 The public park   p Ar

F 1235 Winter	d E
F 1236 verso Sketch of a church	d N
F 1242 Huts with thatched roofs	d N
F 1243 The ditch	d N
F 1248 Cottages in the heather	d D
F 1344 The farm	d N
F 1345 Farm with windmill in the background	d N
F 1347 Landscape with a bridge	d D
F 1374 Study of houses	d P
F 1464 The mill	d-wc Ar
F 1474 Meadow with flowers	d Ar
F 1478 Mas in the Provence	d Ar
F 1478a Dwelling and garden behind a wall	d Ar
F 1493 Slope of a hill with bushes	d Ar
F 1495 Road with telegraph-pole and crane	d Ar
F 1498 recto Field with guardian's hut, Camargue	d Ar
F 1499 Path through a field with willows	d Ar
F 1500 The factory	d Ar
F 1506 Field with houses and sky with sun	d Ar
F 1517 Landscape with farm and two trees	d Ar
F 1541 verso View of a town with a spire	d SR
F 1584 Study of clouds	d SR
F 1542 Wild vegetation in the hills	d SR
F 1591 verso Landscape with farms and peasants	d SR
F 1595 recto Street lined with farmhouses	d SR
F 1621 verso Sketch of a landscape with trees	d SR
F 1625 Landscape	wc Au
F 1638 verso Sketch of a village street with houses	d Au
F 1640 recto Wooded landscape with houses	d-wc Au
F 1640 verso House and chestnut trees	d Au
F 1640a View of a village with two women in the foreground	d Au
F 1642 Landscape with houses and a woman working in the field	d Au
F 1648 recto Snow landscape	d SR
F 1648 verso Peasant cottages seen from the fields	d SR
SP 1669 Peasant hut with barns	p N
SD 1676 Field of stubble with a thunderstorm overhead	d E
SD 1693a Field with wagon and rabbits	d An
SD 1705 verso Sketch of a house	d P
SD 1719 verso Sketch of a building	d P

STILL LIFE

KITCHEN OBJECTS

F 1Still life with cabbage	p E
F 1a Still life with beer mug and fruit	p E
F 49 Still life with three beer mugs	p N
F 50 Still life with five bottles and cup	p N
F 51 Still life with brass bowl	p N
F 52 Still life with coffee mill, pipe case and jug	p N
F 53 Still life with cups, bowls and three bottles	p N
F 54 Still life with clogs and pots	p N
F 55 Still life with a bottle and two bags	p N
F 56 Still life with five bottles	p N
F 57 Still life with pottery and two bottles	p N
F 58 Still life with pottery, beer glass and bottles	p N
F 59 Still life with two jars and two pumpkins	p N
F 61 recto Still life with box and other objects	p N
F 99 Still life: basket with apples	p N
F 100 Still life: basket of potatoes	p N
F 101 Still life: basket of apples	p N
F 102 Still life: cabbages, potatoes and leaves	p N
F 103 Still life: vegetables and fruits	p N
F 104 Still life: ginger pot and apples	p N
F 104a Still life: ginger pot and onions	p N
F 105 Still life: bown with pears	p N
F 106 Still life: apples and two pumpkins	p N
F 107 Still life: two baskets with potatoes	p N
F 115 Still life: basket with potatoes	p N
F 116 Still life: basket with potatoes	p N
F 118 Still life: earthen bowe with potatoes	p N
F 178 recto Still life with pottery, beerglass and bottles	p N
F 202 Still life: copper coffeepot and two white bowls	p N
F 203 Still life: herrings	p P
F 203a Still life: lemons	p An
F 212a Still life: vegetables	p N
F 219 Still life: basket with apples, meat and a breadroll	p P
F 253 Still life: a bottle, two glasses and a plate of bread	p P
F 253a Still life: plate with rolls	p P
F 254 Still life: apples	p P
F 256 Mussels and shrimps	p P
F 283 Still life: red herrings	p P
F 283a Still life: two herrings	p P
F 283b Still life: herrings with a garlic	p P
F 285 Still life: herrings, lemons and tomatoes	p P
F 337 Still life: pot with chive	p P
F 338 Still life: lemons on a plate	p P
F 339 Still life: absinthe	p P
F 340 Still life: decanter and lemons on a plate	p P
F 374 Still life: red cabbages and onions	p P
F 378 Still life: basket of apples	p P
F 379 Still life: basket of apples	p P
F 382 Still life: apples, grapes and pears	p P
F 383 Still life: lemons, pears and grapes	p P
F 384 Still life: basket of lemons	p Ar
F 386 Still life: potatoes	p Ar
F 395 Still life: basket with six oranges	p Ar
F 410 Still life: blue enamel coffeepot, earthenware and fruit	p Ar
F 502 Still life with oranges, lemons and blue gloves	p Ar
F 510 Bloaters on a piece of yellow paper	p Ar
F 602 Still life: quince pears	p Ar
F 603 Still life: grapes	p P
F 604 Still life: drawing board with onions etc	p Ar
SP 1670 Still life: meat, celery and pots	p P
SP 1671 Still life: two herrings, towel and glass	p P

FLOWERS AND STUDIES OF NATURE

F 76 Still life: satin flowers and a bowl with leaves and flowers	p N
F 197 Still life: bouquet of daisies	p P
F 198 Still life: ginger pot filled with chrysanthemums	p N
F 199 Still life: hellebores	p N
F 200 Still life: dead leaves	p N
F 201 Still life: geranium in a pot	p P
F 213 Still life: fritillaries in a copper vase	p P
F 214 Still life with fritillaries	p P
F 217 Still life: bowl with chrysanthemums	p P
F 218 Still life: vase with roses	p P
F 220 Still life: vase with carnations	p P
F 234 Still life: one-eared vase with asters and phlox	p P
F 235 Still life: one-eared vase with hollyhocks	p P
F 236 Still life: one-eared vase with dianthus	p P
F 237 Still life: one-eared vase with physostegia, gladiolus and lychnis	p P
F 241 Still life: vase with zinnias and geranium	p P
F 242 Still life: vase with onoethera and alstroemeria	p P
F 243 Still life: vase with carnations	p P
F 243a Still life: vase with myosotis and peonies	p P
F 244 Still life: bowl with pansies	p P
F 245 Still life: vase with carnations	p P
F 246 Still life: one-eared vase with carnations and roses and a bottle	p P
F 247 Still life: vase with gladioli	p P
F 248 Still life: vase with red gladioli	p P
F 248a Still life: vase with gladioli	p P
F 248b Still life: one-eared vase with red gladioli	p P
F 249 Still life: bowl with peonies and roses	p P
F 250 Still life: bowl with sunflowers and other flowers	p P
F 251 Still life: bowl with summer flowers [heliopsis and gypsophila?]	p P
F 252 Still life: bowl with zinnias	p P
F 258 Still live: white vase with roses and other flowers	p P
F 259 Still life: vase with carnations and zinnias	p P
F 278 Still life: vase with daisies and dahlias	p P
F 279 Still life: red poppies	p P
F 280 Still life: vase with daisies and poppies	p Au
F 281 Still life: coleus plant in a flower pot	p P
F 282 Still life: cineraria in a flowerpot	p P
F 286 Still life: vase with delphinium, aster, salvia and spiraea	p P
F 286a Still life: vase with gladioli and lilacs	p P
F 286b Still life: lilacs	p P
F 287 Still life: vase with flowers, coffeepot and fruit	p P
F 322 Still life: vase with lilacs, daisies and anemones	p P
F 323 Still life: vase with daisies and anemones	p P
F 324 Still life: vase with cornflowers and poppies	p P
F 324a Still life: vase with viscaria	p P
F 327 Still life: one-eared vase with carnations	p P
F 334 Still life: a basket of crocuses	p P
F 336 Still life: basket of bulbs	p P
F 337 Still life: pot with chife	p P
F 375 Still life: sunflowers	p P
F 376 Still life: sunflowers	p P
F 377 Still life: sunflowers	p P
F 392 Still life: blossoming almond branch in a glass	p Ar
F 447 The thistles	p Ar
F 447a Two thistles	p Ar
F 452 Sunflowers	p P
F 453 Still life: vase with three sunflowers	p Ar
F 454 Still life: vase with fourteen sunflowers	p Ar
F 455 Still life: vase with twelve sunflowers	p Ar
F 456 Still life: vase with twelve sunflowers	p Ar
F 457 Still life: vase with fourteen sunflowers	p Ar
F 458 Still life: vase with fourteen sunflowers	p Ar
F 459 Still life: vase with five sunflowers [*destroyed*]	p Ar
F 588 Still life: wild flowers in a vase	p Ar
F 589 Still life: flowers in a vase	p Au
F 591 Still life: basket with daisies	p Ar
F 592 Still life: one-eared vase with zinnias	p Ar
F 593 Still life: one-eared vase with oleanders and books	p Ar
F 594 Still life: vase with oleanders	p Ar
F 595 Still life: roses	p Au
F 596 Still life: pink roses	p Au
F 597 Dog-roses or branches of wild briar	p Au
F 598 Still life: vase with carnations and stock-gilliflowers	p Au
F 599 Still life: vase with thistles	p Au
F 600 Still life: one-eared vase with wild flowers	p Ar
F 601 Still life: the iris	p Ar
F 608 Irises	p SR
F 666 Still life: scabiosa and ranunculus	p P
F 666a Still life: peonies	p P
F 678 Still life: irises against a yellow background	p SR
F 680 Still life: vase with irises against a pink background	p SR
F 681 Still life: roses in a terracotta pot	p SR
F 682 Still life: roses in green pot	p SR
F 763 Still life: vase with field flowers and thistles	p Au
F 764 Still life: japanese vase with roses and anemones	p Au
F 764a Still life: vase with rosemallows	p Au
F 748 Butterflies and poppies	p Au
F 749 Roses and a beetle	p Au
F 767 Ears of wheat	p Au
F 820 Blossoming chestnut branches	p Au
F 821 Branches of a white flowering acacia tree	p Au
F 1466 Thistles along the roadside	d Ar
F 1611 recto Chestnut leaf and husk	d Au
F 1612 Branches of feather hyacinth [Muscari Comosum]	d Au
F 1613 Study of arum	d Au
F 1614 Branches of periwinkle	d Au

OTHER STILL LIFE OBJECTS

F 60 Still life with paintbrushes in a pot	p N
F 62 Still life with straw hat and pipe	p N
F 63 Still life with bottle, clogs and pot with brushes	p N
F 64 Still life with mantelpiece ornament, cowrie shell, ink bottles and smoking set	p N
F 108 Three birds' nests	p N
F 109 recto Two birds' nests	p N
F 110 Three birds' nests with tree trunks and leaves	p N
F 111 Four birds' nests against a light background	p N
G 112 Three birds' nests	p N
F 117 Still life with open bible, extinguished candle and Zola's Joie de vivre	p N
F 175 The spinning wheel	p N
F 212 Skull with burning cigarette	p An
F 255 A pair of shoes	p P
F 297 The skull	p P
F 297a The skull	p P
F 331 A pair of shoes	p P
F 332 Three pairs of shoes	p P
F 332a A pair of shoes	p P
F 333 A pair of shoes	p P
F 335 Still life: three books [*Émile Zola, 'Au Bonheur des Dames'; Jean Richepin, 'Braves Gens'; Jules and Edmond de Goncourt, 'Fille Élisa'*]	p P
F 358 Still life: romans parisiens	p P
F 359 Still life: romans parisiens with a rose	p P
F 360 Still life: plaster statuette and books [*G. de Maupassant, 'Bel Ami'; Jules and Edmond de Goncourt, 'Germinie Lacerteux'*]	p P
F 393 Still life: book and blossoming almond branch in a glass	p Ar
F 461 Still life: a pair of shoes	p Ar
F 498 Vincent's chair with his pipe	p Ar
F 499 Gauguin's armchair, candle and books [his empty chair]	p Ar
F 607 A pair of wooden shoes	p Ar

F 1158 verso Sketch of a lamp hanging behore a window	d N
F 1361 Hanging skeleton	d An
F 1520 verso Mask of an egyptian mummy	d SR
F 1521 reco Mask of an egyptian mummy	d SR
F 1521 verso Mask of an egyptian mummy	d SR
F 1611 verso Sketches of a perspective frame	d Au
F 1635 recto Mask of an egyptian mummy	d SR

ANIMALS

F 1b Lying cow	p TH
F 1c Lying cow	p TH
F 14 The green parrot	p N
F 15 Cows in the meadow	p TH
F 28 The kingfisher	p P
F 38 The ox cart: red and white ox	p N
F 39 Ox cart: spotted black ox	p N
F 177 Two rats	p N
F 177a Stuffed kalong	p P
F 402 Two white butterflies	p SR
F 605 A crab upside down	p Ar
F 606 Two crabs [*probably one crab, seen from above and below*]	p Ar
F 610 Death's-head moth	p SR
F 739 Landscape with rabbits	p SR

F 1032 The white horse	d TH
F 1079 recto The donkey cart [*destroyed*]	d TH
F 1079 verso Study of a horse [*destroyed*]	
F 1244 recto Study of four flying swallows	d P
F 1335 Man loading a cart	d N

Index of Selected Subjects

List of Collections

Rosenberg, P., Art Gallery 867, 1116a
Rossbach, Mrs Max J. H. 1481
Schmolka, Paul 146a
Schweitzer, Mr & Mrs P. 139
Spiro, Harry 216
Starr, Heirs C. V. 740
Stralem, Mr & Mrs Donald B. 153a
Streep, Art Gallery, John 953, SD 1685
Thannhauser, J. K. 81
Thannhauser, Mrs J. K. 909
Thannhauser Foundation 239, 622, 694, 1226, 1430a, 1482a, 1502a, 1507a, 1548
Vidor, Mrs Doris 1262b
Vogel, Mr & Mrs Edwin C. 568
Wetmore, Miss Edith 1462
Whitney, Mr & Mrs John Hay 626, 712
Wildenstein Art Galleries 68
Wyler, Alfred 207
Zimmerman, F. A. P. 964
Private Collections 367, 427, 551, 608, 864, 870, 939a, 1101, 1102, 1105, 1651
NORWALK [Connecticut] Hays, Mr & Mrs Mortimer 176
OKLAHOMA CITY [Oklahoma] Weitzenhoffer, A. M. 270
PHILADELPHIA [Pennsylvania] Philadelphia Museum of Art 455, 490, 1427
McIlhenny, Henry P. 650
Wright, Mr and Mrs William Coxe 197
PITTSBURGH [Pennsylvania] Museum of Art Carnegie Institute 348a, 781
POUGHKEEPSIE [New York] Vassar College Art Gallery 1619
PRINCETON [New Jersey] Oppenheimer, Mrs J. Robert 737
PROVIDENCE [Rhode Island] Museum of Art, Rhode Island School of Design 800, 1416

Danforth Jr., Murray S. 549
RICHMOND [Virginia] Buckman, Ed. 1654
ST. LOUIS [Missouri] City Art Museum of Saint Louis 317, 762, 795, 874
Johnstone, Mr & Mrs Edwin McClellan 286a
Pulitzer Jr., Joseph 1433
Shoenberg, Mr & Mrs Sydney M. 379, 1647
Steinberg, Mrs Marck C. 1494
SAN ANTONIO [Texas] Marion Koogler McNay Art Institute 819
SAN FRANCISCO [California] California Palace of the Legion of Honor The Mr & Mrs Frederick J. Hellman Collection 264a
San Francisco Museum of Art 768
Magnin, Mr & Mrs Grover A. 252
Russell, Henry P. 419
Smith, Nicol 1418
SANTA ANA [California] Kanter, H. de 1086
SCARSDALE [New York] Ritter Foundation Inc. 1440
Schocken, Mrs Salman 351
SHORT HILLS [New York] Blum, Albert B. 247
SYRACUSE [New York] Hudson, Miss Elisabeth 1396a
TOLEDO [Ohio] Toledo Museum of Art 559, 759, 1664
UPPERVILLE [Virginia] Mellon, Paul 186, 311, 502, 573, 591, 1486, 1517
WASHINGTON DC National Gallery of Art 431, 440, 656, 788
Brown, John Nicholas 1443
Kreeger, Mr & Mrs David Lloyd 596
Phillips Collection 566, 658, 804, 1664
WEST CHESTER [Pennsylvania] Taylor, William H. 803
WORCESTER [Massachusetts] Worcester Art Museum 954
Riley, Mr & Mrs Chapin 957

OWNER'S ADDRESS UNKNOWN

Goldschmidt, A. E. 968
Milton, S. 1262a
Piatigorski, Dr & Mrs Joram 1618
Scharenguival, Mr & Mrs SP 1671
Wolf, Mrs L 696

ANONYMOUS PRIVATE COLLECTIONS

47, 396, 624, 808, 965, 1646

DESTROYED WORKS

124, 202, 271, 448, 459, 471, 1078a, 1079, 1540

WHEREABOUTS UNKNOWN

1c, 10, 11, 15, 42, 60, 64, 65, 67, 92, 92a, 96, 132, 157, 171a, 185a, 187, 191a, 196, 199, 204, 214, 223, 235a, 236, 248, 259, 264, 288, 312, 315, 319, 324, 407, 420, 446, 447a, 474, 479, 485, 567, 582, 584, 589, 594, 606, 609, 623, 631, 644, 663, 664, 666a, 684, 698, 699a, 718, 722, 727, 743, 766, 769, 787, 794, 796, 825, 828, 849a, 883, 895, 899, 904, 910a, 916, 926, 984, 986, 988, 996, 1000, 1027, 1031, 1034, 1035, 1044, 1064, 1077, 1083, 1085, 1087, 1093, 1119, 1133, 1144a, 1148, 1180, 1194, 1194a, 1212, 1223, 1247, 1357a, 1389, 1425, 1428, 1442, 1448, 1449, 1465, 1483, 1491, 1515, 1526, 1534, 1536, 1553, 1578a, 1595, 1621, 1640a, 1650, 1659, 1660, 1661, 1662, 1663, 1664, SP 1666, SD 1683, SD 1688, SD 1690, SD 1721, SD 1723, SD 1729. Juvenilia V, XIX, XXII

List of Exhibitions

The details of the individual exhibitions are listed in the following order:
    town
    title
    institute or locality housing the exhibition
    date
    number of entries under van Gogh.
Where this number could not be verified, it was taken either from references in daily or weekly papers, or it was the total of numbers as mentioned by de la Faille.
Where data are not known, this is indicated by –.
All exhibition catalogues mentioned in this list can be consulted at the Rijksbureau voor Kunsthistorische Documentatie, The Hague, either in the original or in photocopy, except for those marked *.

—, 1888 [?]
* PARIS, Rétrospective organisée par la Société Nationale aux Champs-de-Mars, 1 nr

1888
PARIS, Salon des Artistes Indépendants, Pavillon de la Ville, 22 March-3 May, 3 nrs

1889
PARIS, Salon des Artistes Indépendants, Salle de la Sté d'Horticulture, 3 September-4 October, 2 nrs

1890
PARIS, Salon des Artistes Indépendants, Pavillon de la Ville, 20 March-27 April, 10 nrs
BRUSSELS, Les XX, 7ième exposition annuelle, —, 6 nrs

1891
BRUSSELS, Les XX, 8ième exposition annuelle, February, 15 nrs
* THE HAGUE, VvG teekeningen, Kunstbeschouwing, Pulchri Studio, 19 December, —
PARIS, Salon des Artistes Indépendants, Pavillon de la Ville, 20 March-27 April, 10 nrs

1892
* AMSTERDAM 1, VvG werken van, Firma Buffa, February, 10 paintings, — drawings
* AMSTERDAM 2, VvG teekeningen, Kunstbeschouwing, Arti et Amicitiae, 25 February, —
* AMSTERDAM 3, Keuze-tentoonstelling, ter gelegenheid van de Lustrum-feesten, Amsterdamsche Universiteit, Arti et Amicitiae, July, 2 nrs [F 404, F 650]
ANTWERP, Kunst van Heden, Art d'Aujourd'hui, 1ière exposition annuelle, May-June, 12 nrs [9 paintings, 3 drawings]
THE HAGUE, VvG werken van, Haagsche Kunstkring [Buitenhof], 16 May-6 June, 89 nrs [45 paintings, 44 drawings]
PARIS, VvG 16 toiles peintes [organized by Émile Bernard], Galerie Le Barc de Bouteville, April, 16 nrs
* ROTTERDAM 1, VvG schilderijen en teekeningen, Kunsthandel Oldenzeel, March, 20 paintings, — drawings
* ROTTERDAM 2, VvG teekeningen [drawings Dutch period], Kunsthandel Oldenzeel, October-November, —

1892-93
AMSTERDAM, VvG nagelaten werken, Kunstzaal Panorama-gebouw, 17 December-5 February, 112 nrs [87 paintings, 25 drawings, some letters]

1893
AMSTERDAM, Zesde tentoonstelling Nederlandsche Ets-club, Arti et Amicitiae, February-March, 5 nrs [1 lithography]
COPENHAGEN, Frie udstilling, Halmtorv, 26 March-end of May, 29 nrs
* LEIDEN, VvG teekeningen, De Lakenhal, 25 April-1 May, 60 nrs

1894
NIJMEGEN, Schilder- en beeldhouwkunst, Sociëteit 'De Vereeniging', 20 June-20 July, 3 nrs

1895
* THE HAGUE, VvG collection Hidde Nijland, Haagsche Kunstkring, February-March, —

1896
* GRONINGEN, VvG, Schilderyen en teekeningen, Groningsch Museum, February, —
ROTTERDAM, VvG [French period], Kunstzalen Oldenzeel, March, 78 nrs

1898
THE HAGUE, VvG Arts and Crafts Art Gallery, [November], 44 nrs
OSLO, ETC, Oslo [Kristiania], [Modern French Art], —, —
Stockholm, Sveriges almänna konstförening, February, —
Gothenburg —, —, 5 nrs

1900-01
ROTTERDAM, VvG teekeningen, Rotterdamsche Kunst-kring, 23 December-10 February, 76 nrs

1901
THE HAGUE, Eerste Internationale Tentoonstelling, Boschoord [Bezuidenhout], 9 May-12 June, 3 nrs
BERLIN, 3rd Secession, 8 May-[?], 5 nrs
PARIS, VvG, Bernheim Jeune, 15-31 March, 71 nrs

1902-03
* VIENNA, Secession, Impressionisten, —, —,

1903
MUNICH, Secession, Kgl. Kunstausstellungsgebäude, Frühjahr [Spring], 7 nrs
* ROTTERDAM 1, VvG, Kunstzalen Oldenzeel, January, 30 nrs or more
* ROTTERDAM 2, VvG, Kunstzalen Oldenzeel, May, —
* ROTTERDAM 3, VvG, Kunstzalen Oldenzeel, November, —

1904
BRUSSELS, Peintres Impressionnistes, La Libre Esthétique, 25 February-29 March, 7 nrs
* GRONINGEN, VvG, —, —, —
PARIS, Tableaux par Paul Cirou et quelques autres des écoles françaises et anglaises du XVIII siècle et de Corot… van Gogh, Galerie L. Soullié, 18 February-5 March, 4 nrs
ROTTERDAM, VvG, Kunstzalen Oldenzeel, 10 November-15 December, 77 nrs
* VIENNA, Secession, —, January-February, —

1905
AMSTERDAM, VvG, Stedelijk Museum, July-August, 474 nrs
* BERLIN, VvG, Paul Cassirer [Art Gallery], Frühjahr [Spring], 32 nrs or more
HAMBURG, VvG, Paul Cassirer [Art Gallery], I. Ausstellung, September-October, 54 nrs
PARIS, VvG exposition rétrospective, Salon des Artistes Indépendants, 24 March-30 April, 45 nrs
* ROTTERDAM, Mentioned in sale catalogue Amsterdam [A. Mak], 10 February 1919, note p. 18; the exhibition could not be checked
UTRECHT, VvG [paintings], Vereeniging voor de Kunst, 10 September-1 October, 59 nrs

1906
* BASLE [?], Wanderausstellung Pariser Künstler, —, —, 1 nr
BERLIN, 12th Secession, Zeichnende Künste, 1 December-[?], 30 nrs
* MIDDELBURG, VvG, Vereeniging voor de Kunst, 25 March-1 April, —
ROTTERDAM, VvG, Kunstzalen Oldenzeel, 26 January-28 February, 65 nrs

1907
BERLIN, 13th Secession, Ausstellungshaus am Kurfürstendamm, —, 10 nrs
* MANNHEIM, Internationale Kunstausstellung, —, 1 May-20 October, 14 nrs
ROTTERDAM, Keuze-tentoonstelling van Ned. Portretkunst der laatste 50 jaren, Rotterdamsche Kunstkring, 16 March-14 April, 4 nrs
ZURICH, Zürcher Kunstgesellschaft IV. Serie [2. Abteilung], Künstlerhaus, 11 April-12 May, 1 nr

1908
AMSTERDAM, VvG, C. M. van Gogh Kunsthandel, September, 125 nrs
BERLIN, 14th Secession, Ausstellungshaus am Kurfürstendamm, 14 April-[?], 1 nr
BERLIN, 15th Secession, Ausstellungshaus am Kurfürstendamm, December, 2 nrs
* MOSCOW, Exp. 'Toison d'or', —, —, 1 nr
* MUNICH 1, —, Moderne Kunsthandlung [F. J. Brakl], [March], —
MUNICH 2, Van Gogh-Gauguin, Galerie W. Zimmerman, [?]-15 April, 13 nrs
PARIS 1, Cent tableaux de Vincent van Gogh, Bernheim Jeune, January, 100 nrs
PARIS 2, VvG, Galerie E. Druet, 6-18 January, 35 nrs
ROTTERDAM 1, Tent. van hedendaagsche Hollandse Schilderkunst, Rotterdamsche Kunstkring, 12 July-2 August, 4 nrs
* ROTTERDAM 2, —, Kunstzalen Oldenzeel, September, 1 nr
ZURICH, VvG, VI. Serie, Künstlerhaus, 10-26 July, 41 nrs [paintings]

1909
BERLIN, 18th Secession, Ausstellungshaus am Kurfürstendamm, —, 10 nrs or more
BREMEN, Gemälde, Zeichnungen und Bildwerke aus Bremischem Privatbesitz, Kunsthalle, 11 April-8 May, 3 nrs
* LONDON, Impressionist painters, New Gallery, —, 1 nr
MUNICH, VvG [French period], Moderne Kunsthandlung [F. J. Brakl], December [?], 55 nrs
PARIS, VvG, Galerie E. Druet, 8-20 November, 60 nrs
ROTTERDAM, Het Hollandsche Stilleven in den loop der tijden, Rotterdamsche Kunstkring, 11 September-10 October, 4 nrs
VIENNA, Internationale Kunstschau, —, —, 11 nrs

1909-10
BERLIN, 19th Secession, Paul Cassirer [Art Gallery], 27 November-9 January, 19 nrs

1910
BERLIN 1, VvG, Paul Cassirer [Art Gallery], 25-October-20 November, 74 nrs
BERLIN 2, 20th Secession, Ausstellungshaus am Kurfürstendamm, without date, 1 nr
BRUSSELS, L'évolution du Paysage, La Libre Esthétique, 12 March-17 April, 3 nrs
* FRANKFURT/M, Frankfurter Kunstverein, —, —, —
ROTTERDAM, VvG werken uit Fransche tijd, Rotterdamsche Kunstkring, 11 June-10 July, 35 nrs

1910-11
LONDON, Manet and the Post-Impressionists, Grafton Galleries, 8 November-16 January, 22 nrs
* ROTTERDAM, Het dier in de beeldende kunst, Kunsthandel A. M. Reckers, 17 December-15 January, —

1911
AMSTERDAM, VvG, Larensche Kunsthandel, June, 69 nrs
BUDAPEST, Collection Marczell de Nemes, Musée des Beaux-Arts, — 2 nrs
* PARIS, —, Bernheim Jeune, August, 1 nr

1912
BERLIN, 24th Secession, April-May, 4 nrs
COLOGNE, Internationale Kunstausstellung des Sonderbundes westdeutscher Kunstfreunde und Künstler zu Köln, 25 May-30 September, 125 nrs
DÜSSELDORF, Sammlung Marczell von Nemes [Budapest], Städt. Kunsthalle, July-December, 3 nrs
THE HAGUE, VvG [drawings], Artz & De Bois [Art Gallery], July-August, 40 nrs
PARIS, Exposition des portraits du XIXe siècle, 10th Salon d'Automne, 1 October-8 November, 3 nrs

1912-13
* BARMEN, ETC Sammlung G. F. Reber, Ruhmeshalle, September, —
Berlin, Paul Cassirer [Art Gallery], Spring, —
Darmstadt, Mathildenhöhe, April, —

1913
* BARMEN, —, Kunstverein, January, 1 nr
* BERLIN 1, VvG [?], Paul Cassirer [Art Gallery], March [?], 1 nr
BERLIN 2, 26th Secession, without date, 8 nrs
BERLIN 3, Sammlung Reber, see Barmen etc.
BRUSSELS, Interprétations du Midi, La Libre Esthétique, 8 March-13 April, 7 nrs
DARMSTADT, Sammlung Reber, see Barmen etc, 1912-1913
DÜSSELDORF, Beiträge zur Kunst des XIX. Jahrhunderts und unserer Zeit, Galerie Alfred Flechtheim, without date, 7 nrs
FRANKFURT/M, Frankfurter Kunstschätze, Frankfurter Kunstverein, 20 July-30 September, 3 nrs
THE HAGUE, VvG Paintings and Drawings, Lange Voorhout, July-September, 152 nrs
HAARLEM, J. H. de Bois [Art Gallery], Catalogus I, —, 8 nrs
NEW YORK, ETC The Armory Show, International Exhibition of Modern Art, New York, —, 17 February-15 March
Chicago, Art Institute of Chicago, 24 March-15 April
Boston, Copley Hall, 28 April-18 May, 18 nrs
ROTTERDAM, Moderne schilderijen, aquarellen…, Rotterdamsche Kunstkring, 15 September-5 October, 4 nrs

1914
ANTWERP, Kunst van Heden–L'art contemporain, 7 March-5 April, 96 nrs
BERLIN, VvG, Paul Cassirer [Art Gallery], 10. Ausstellung, May-June, 146 nrs
DRESDEN, Französischer Malerei des XIX. Jahrhunderts, Galerie Ernst Arnold, April-May, 8 nrs
LONDON, Art français, exposition d'art décoratif contemporain, 1800-1885, [August], 2 nrs
* MUNICH, —, Galerie Gaspari, July-September, 1 nr

1914-15
AMSTERDAM, VvG Teekeningen uit de verzameling mevr. J. v. Gogh-Bonger en V. W. v. Gogh, Stedelijk Museum, 22 December-12 January, 201 nrs

1915
AMSTERDAM, VvG Werken van Genooten, Schilderijen, teekeningen en Beeldhouwwerken, Gebouw van het Genootschap van kunstenaren moderne Kunstkring, 26 September-30 November, 81 nrs [28 nrs VvG]
ARNHEM, VvG Teekeningen uit de verzameling mevr. J. van Gogh-Bonger en V. W. van Gogh, Gymnasium-gebouw, March-April, 200 nrs
SAN FRANCISCO, Panama-Pacific International Exposition 20 February-4 December, 1 nr

1916
* MUNICH, —, Galerie Gaspari, August, 1 nr
* PARIS, —, Salon des Artistes Indépendants, —, 1 nr

1917
AMSTERDAM, J. H. de Bois Art Gallery, Haarlem, —,
16 April-31 May, 3 nrs
* ZURICH I, —, —, —, 4 nrs
ZURICH 2, Französische Kunst des XIX. und XX. Jahrhunderts, Zürcher Kunsthaus, 5 October-4 November,
9 nrs

1918
* CHEMNITZ, Ausstellung privater Sammlungen, König
Albert Museum, —, 1 nr
* COPENHAGEN, —, Winkel & Magnussen, November,
1 nr
THE HAGUE, VvG Aquarellen, teekeningen en schetsen,
verzameling Hidde Nijland, Haagsche Kunstkring, 6-29
April, 84 nrs
* OSLO, —, —, June, 1 nr

1919
HAARLEM, Moderne schilderijen en teekeningen, J. H. de
Bois Kunsthandel, April, catalogue in J. H. de Bois' Twee-
maandelijksch Bulletin April, II, nr 2, 5 nrs

1920
* KREFELD, Exhibition of the Art Society 'Neue Kunst'
[French and German Artists], Kaiser-Wilhelm Museum,
probably December, —
NEW YORK, VvG Montross Gallery, 23 October-[?],
67 nrs
* VENICE, 12th Biennale, Esposizione Internazionale
d'Arte della Città di Venezia, —, 9 nrs

1921
* BERLIN, Van Gogh-Matisse, Kronprinzenpalais,
Nationalgalerie, — 9 nrs
NEW YORK, Loan exhibition of impressionist and post-
impressionist paintings, Metropolitan Museum of Art,
3 May-15 September, 7 nrs
PARIS, Exposition hollandaise, tableaux, aquarelles et
dessins anciens et modernes, —, April-May, 8 nrs
* TOKYO, Shirabaka group, Hoshi pharmaceutical
company's building [3rd floor], 5-13 March, 1 nr

1922
* COLOGNE, —, —, —, 1 nr
COPENHAGEN, Udstilling af aeldre og nyere hollandsk
Malerkunst, June, 3 nrs
* PARIS, —, Bernheim Jeune, 20 June-2 July, 1 nr
* ROTTERDAM, —, Museum Boymans, Christmas, 1 nr
WINTERTHUR I, Meisterwerke aus Privatsammlungen im
Museum, Kunstverein Winterthur, 20 August-8 October,
9 nrs
WINTERTHUR 2, 60 Zeichnungen und Aquarelle als
Ergänzung der Ausstellung von Meisterwerken aus Privat-
sammlungen im Museum, Graphisches Kabinett,
20 August-1 October, 3 nrs

1923
AMSTERDAM 2, Nederlandsche beeldende Kunsten,
Stedelijk Museum, September, 13 nrs
* HAARLEM, —, Museum Teyler, 26 April-26 May, 2 nrs
LONDON, VvG, Leicester Galleries, December, 40 nrs
MANCHESTER, Masterpieces of French art of the 19th
century in aid of the Lord Mayor's appeal for the hospitals,
Thos. Agnew & Sons, — 2 nrs
* PARIS, Peintres de l'école post-impressionniste, —,
November, 1 nr
PRAGUE, Výstava Francouzského Umení XIX. a XX. Stoleti
[Franco-Tchèque Art of the XIXth-XX th Century], Town-
hall, 22 May-15 July, 5 nrs
ROTTERDAM, UTRECHT, VvG Teekeningencollectie van
mevr. J. van Gogh-Bonger
Rotterdam, Rotterdamsche Kunstkring, 15 March-2 April,
Utrecht, Vereeniging Voor de Kunst, January-March,
85 nrs

1924
AMSTERDAM, VvG, Gebouw voor Beeldende Kunst,
Vondelstraat, [March-April 1924], 132 nrs [Dutch period]
BASLE, VvG, Kunsthalle, 27 March-21 April, 98 nrs
* BERLIN, —, Paul Cassirer [Art Gallery], May-June, 1 nr
THE HAGUE, Tentoonstelling van Kunstwerken uit het
bezit van werkende leden van het genootschap Pulchri
Studio, April, 2 nrs
* HAARLEM, J. H. de Bois [Art Gallery], [August 1924?],
2 nrs
* LONDON I, —, Tate Gallery, — 1 nr
* LONDON 2, Post-Impressionist Masters, The Lefèvre
Galleries, —, 3 nrs
PARIS, Peintres de l'école française du XIXe siècle,
M. Knoedler & Cie, 12 May — [?], 2 nrs
* PRAGUE, —, —, January, 1 nr
STUTTGART, VvG, Württembergische Kunstverein,
Kunstgebäude, October-November, 42 nrs
ZURICH VvG, Kunsthaus, 3 July-10 August, 99 nrs

1925
BERLIN, —, Paul Cassirer [Art Gallery], September-Octo-
ber, 1 nr
THE HAGUE, VvG, Pulchri Studio, March-April, 86 nrs

PARIS I, VvG exp. rétrospective des oeuvres..., Galerie
Marcel Bernheim, 5-24 January, 56 nrs
PARIS 2, Les grandes influences au dix-neuvième siècle
d'Ingres à Cézanne, Paul Rosenberg [Art gallery],
15 January-7 February, 1 nr
PARIS 3, Cinquante ans de peinture française, 1875-1925,
Musée des Arts décoratifs, 28 May-12 July, 4 nrs
POTSDAM, 50 Jahre holländischer Malerei, —, summer,
10 nrs
VIENNA, 82. Ausstellung der Secession, die führenden
Meister der französischen Kunst im XIX. Jahrhundert, —
March-April, 9 nrs

1926
AMSTERDAM, VvG, Stedelijk Museum, 15 May-15 June,
144 nrs
DRESDEN, Internationale Kunstausstellung, —, June-
September, 10 nrs
* LONDON I, —, French Gallery, February-March, 2 nrs
LONDON 2, List of loans at the opening exhibition of the
Modern Foreign Gallery, Tate Gallery, June-October, 6 nrs
LONDON 3, VvG, The Leicester Galleries, November-
December, 43 nrs
* MOSCOU, —, Musée de l'Art Moderne, —, 2 nrs
MUNICH, I. Allgemeine Kunst-Ausstellung, Glaspalast,
1 June-October, 47 nrs
* NORWICH, Exposition centenaire au Musée de Norwich,
—, 1 nr
PARIS, Trente ans d'art indépendant rétrospective
1884-1914, Société des Artistes Indépendants, 20 February-
21 March, 10 nrs
VENICE, Biennale, XV Esposizione Internazionale d'Arte
della città di Venezia, April-October, 5 nrs

1927
BASLE, ETC, VvG 143 Werke aus der Sammlung Kröller
im Haag, Basle, Kunsthalle, June-August
Bern, Kunsthalle, September-October
Brussels, 150 [sic] Werken der Verzameling Kröller,
's-Gravenhage Museum voor Moderne Kunst, November-
December
BERLIN I, Französische Malerei des XIX. Jahrhunderts,
Hugo Perls, January-February, 5 nrs
BERLIN 2, Erste Sonderausstellung in Berlin, Galerien
Thannhauser [München-Luzern], 9 January-mid February,
20 nrs
* BERLIN 3, —, Galerie Matthiesen, February-March,
6 nrs
* DÜSSELDORF I, Unbekannte Bilder von Van Gogh,
Galerie Hans Bammann, — 6 nrs
DÜSSELDORF 2, Alte Meister deutscher und französischer
Kunst des 19. Jahrhunderts, Galerie Hans Bammann,
Autumn, 2 nrs
* THE HAGUE, Fransche Schilders der 19e eeuw, Kunstzaal
Kleykamp, March-April, 2 nrs
* HAMBURG I, Europäische Kunst der Gegenwart,
Zentenärausstellung des Kunstvereins Hamburg, —, 1 nr
* HAMBURG 2, Französische Malerei des 19. und 20. Jahr-
hunderts, Commeter Art Gallery, March-April, 1 nr
NEW YORK, Loan exhibition of paintings from El Greco
and Rembrandt to Cézanne and Matisse, Reinhardt
Galleries, 15 January-5 February, 1 nr
PARIS, VvG l'époque française, Bernheim Jeune,
20 June-2 July, 57 nrs
* ROTTERDAM, —, Kunsthandel Unger en van Mens,
April, 2 nrs

1927-28
BERLIN, ETC, VvG, Otto Wacker Art Gallery, Berlin,
6 December-1 February, 119 nrs [nrs 1-97 lent anonymously
by the Van Gogh family; 98-118 by various owners]
Vienna, Neue Galerie, February-March, first 97 nrs
Hanover, Kestner Gesellschaft, 3-30 April, 97 nrs
ROTTERDAM, Kersttentoonstelling, Museum Boymans,
23 December-16 January, 17 nrs

1928
AMSTERDAM, Cent ans de Peinture Française, E. J. van
Wisselingh & Co, 16 April-5 May, 1st part, 1 nr
* BASLE, —, Society of Fine Arts [Künstlerverein?], —, 1 nr
BERLIN, VvG, Paul Cassirer [Art Gallery], 15 January-
1 March, 92 nrs
DÜSSELDORF, Ausgewählte Kunstwerke aus der Sammlung
Frau H. Kröller-Müller, Den Haag, Kunsthalle, August-
September, 555 nrs [143 nrs VvG]
FRANKFURT/M, VvG, Galerie M. Goldschmidt, 15 March-
15 April, 16 nrs
THE HAGUE, VvG verzameling Hidde Nijland, Kunstzaal
Kleykamp, —, 102 nrs
HANOVER I, VvG, 35 Gemälde, [Autumn], probably the
same exhibition as Munich 1928
HANOVER 2, VvG, see Berlin etc. 1927-28
KARLSRUHE, VvG, 150 Werke aus der Sammlung Kröller-
Müller im Haag, Badische Kunsthalle, October-November
* MOSCOW, —, Museum of Modern Art, —, 1 nr
MUNICH, VvG, 35 unbekannte Gemälde aus Privatbesitz,
Graphisches Kabinett [Art Gallery, Dir. Günther Franke],
22 November-end of December, 35 nrs
NEW YORK I, Loan exhibition of paintings from Memling,
Holbein and Titian to Renoir and Picasso, Reinhardt

Galleries, 27 February-17 March, 1 nr
* NEW YORK 2, A century of French painting,
M. Knoedler & Co, 12 November-8 December, 3 nrs
* PARIS, —, L. Dru Art Gallery, 23 June-12 July, 1 nr
VIENNA-HANOVER, See Berlin etc. 1927-28
VIENNA, VvG, Neue Galerie, May-June, 49 nrs

1929
AMSTERDAM, VvG teekeningen en aquarellen ingericht
door de Vereeniging 'Vrienden van Vincent van Gogh en
zijn tijd', Stedelijk Museum, 19 October-17 November,
87 nrs
BERLIN I, VvG 143 Werke aus dem Besitz von Frau
Kröller-Müller im Haag, National-Galerie, January,
143 nrs
BERLIN 2, [Dubious Van Gogh paintings in the Wacker
collection], Nationalgalerie, January-[?], 16 nrs [no
catalogue edited]
BERLIN 3, Seit Cézanne in Paris, Galerie Alfred Flecht-
heim, 23 November-Christmas, 10 nrs
CAMBRIDGE [MASS.], French Painting of the nineteenth
and twentieth centuries, Fogg Art Museum, 6 March-
6 April, 10 nrs
* CLEVELAND, French Art since 1800, Cleveland Museum,
—, 1 nr
* HAMBURG, VvG Sammlung Kröller-Müller im Haag,
Kunstverein, February?-March?, 257 nrs
LONDON I, Dutch Art 1450-1900, Royal Academy of Arts,
4 January-9 March, 20 nrs
LONDON 2, Ten Masterpieces by nineteenth century
French painters, Alex Reid & Lefèvre, June-July, 2 nrs
* LUCERNE, Exposition de peintures de l'École
Impressionniste et Néo-Impressionniste, —, February, 1 nr
NEW YORK, First Loan Exhibition Cézanne-Gauguin-
Seurat-van Gogh, Museum of Modern Art, November,
28 nrs
UTRECHT, VvG, Vereeniging voor de Kunst, May-June, —
WINTERTHUR, Moderne Aquarelle und Zeichnungen,
Kunstverein Winterthur, 22 September-20 October,
4 nrs

1929-30
BERLIN, Ein Jahrhundert französischer Zeichnung, Paul
Cassirer [Art Gallery], December-January, 4 nrs

1930
AMSTERDAM, Vincent van Gogh en zijn tijdgenooten,
Stedelijk Museum, 6 September-2 November, 121 nrs
* GLASGOW, 19th and 20th Century French Paintings,
Alex Reid. & Lefèvre, —, 1 nr
LONDON I, An exhibition of pictures by Modern French
Masters, Arthur Tooth and Sons Galleries, 2 April-3 May,
1 nr
LONDON 2, VvG, Leicester Galleries, June, 31 nrs
LONDON 3, Renoir and the Post-Impressionists, Alex
Reid & Lefèvre, June-July, 4 nrs
* NEW YORK I, —, Museum of Modern Art, —, 1 nr
NEW YORK 2, Masterpieces by nineteenth century French
painters, M. Knoedler & Co, October-November, 1 nr
* PARIS, —, Galerie Georges Petit, June, 1 nr
PROVIDENCE, Modern French Art, Rhode Island School
of Design, 11-31 March, 4 nrs

1931
BASLE, Meister des 19. Jahrhunderts, Kunsthalle,
27 September-25 October, 5 nrs
* BOSTON, —, Museum of Fine Arts, —, —
FRANKFURT/M, Vom Abbild zum Sinnbild, Städelsches
Kunstinstitut, 3 June-3 July, 1 nr
NEW YORK, The Landscape in French Painting XIX-XX
centuries, M. Knoedler & Co, October-November, 1 nr
PARIS, Oeuvres importantes de grands maîtres du dix-
neuvième siècle, Galerie Paul Rosenberg, 18 May-27 June,
6 nrs
* PROVIDENCE, —, Rhode Island School of Design,
April, —
* WILMINGTON, ETC, A Century of French painting,
Wilmington, Wilmington Society of Fine Arts, 2-16
February
Chicago, M. Knoedler & Co, 24 February-14 March
Minneapolis, Minneapolis Institute of Fine Arts, 19 March-
2 April. 1 nr

1932
* AMSTERDAM I, Hollandsche en Fransche schilderkunst
der XIXe en XXe eeuw, E. J. van Wisselingh & Co, 27 April-
28 May, 2 nrs
AMSTERDAM 2, Schilderijen door Vincent van Gogh,
J. B. Jongkind, Floris Verster, Kunsthandel Huinck en
Scherjon, 14 May-18 June, 22 nrs
* BUFFALO, French 19th century Paintings and Drawings,
Buffalo Fine Arts Academy, — 1 nr
* CHICAGO, —, Art Institute of Chicago, —, 1 nr
MANCHESTER, VvG, Collection Ir. van Gogh [mainly coll.
van Gogh-Bonger], Art Gallery, 13 October-27 November,
79 nrs
NEW YORK, Flowers by French painters XIX-XX centuries,
M. Knoedler & Co, November, 2 nrs
PARIS, Quelques oeuvres importantes de Manet à van Gogh
Durand-Ruel, February-March, 1 nr

1933
AMSTERDAM 1, Exposition d'art français peinture du XIX et XX siècle, E.J. van Wisselingh & Co., 7 January-4 February, 1 nr
AMSTERDAM 2, Het Stilleven, Kunsthandel J. Goudstikker, 18 February-19 March, 9 nrs
AMSTERDAM 3, Hollandsche en Fransche schilderkunst der XIX en XX eeuw, E.J. van Wisselingh & Co, July-August, 2 nrs
CHICAGO, A Century of Progress of Paintings and Sculpture, The Art Institute of Chicago, 1 June-1 November, 15 nrs
* CINCINNATI, French nineteenth century masterpieces, Cincinnati Art Museum, —,
* LOS ANGELES, Five centuries of European painting, The Los Angeles County Museum, 25 November-31 December, —
ROTTERDAM 1, 115 Stillevens, 1480-1933, Museum Boymans, 1-23 April, 3 nrs
ROTTERDAM 2, Schilderijen door Nederlandsche en Fransche Meesters, Kunstzalen Unger & Van Mens, 24 September-22 October, 1 nr

1933-34
ROTTERDAM, Schilderijen van Delacroix tot Cézanne en Vincent van Gogh, Museum Boymans, 20 December-21 January, 10 nrs

1934
* AMSTERDAM 1, —, E.J. van Wisselingh & Co, 28 Maart-[?] 1 nr
AMSTERDAM 2, Schilderijen door Nederlandsche en Fransche Meesters, Kunsthandel Huinck en Scherjon, 7 April-5 May, 3 nrs
BERN, Französische Meister des 19. Jahrhunderts und van Gogh, Kunsthalle, 18 February-2 April, 11 nrs
* CAMBRIDGE [MASS.], French drawings and prints, Fogg Art Museum, —,
CHICAGO, A Century of Progress, Paintings and Sculpture, The Art Institute of Chicago, 1 June-1 November, 7 nrs
* EDINBURGH, —, Royal Scottish Academy, —, 1 nr
LONDON, Renoir, Cézanne and their contemporaries, Alex Reid & Lefèvre, June, 2 nrs
MONTREAL, French paintings by the Impressionists and modern artists, W. Scott & Sons, December, 1 nr
NEW YORK 1, Important paintings by great French Masters of the Nineteenth century, organized by Paul Rosenberg and Durand-Ruel, Durand-Ruel Galleries, 12 February-10 March, 3 nrs
NEW YORK 2, Landscape paintings, Metropolitan Museum of Art, 14 May-30 September, 1 nr
* OTTAWA, French painting of the 19th century, National Gallery of Canada, March, 3 nrs
* PARIS, Gauguin, ses amis, l'école de Pont-Aven et l'Académie Julian, Galerie des Beaux-Arts, February-March, 1 nr
SAN FRANCISCO, French Painting, The California Palace of the Legion of Honor, 8 June-8 July, 8 nrs
TOLEDO, French Impressionists and Post-Impressionists, Toledo Museum of Art, November, 3 nrs

1934-35
BALTIMORE, A survey of French painting, Baltimore Museum of Art, 23 November-1 January, 1 nr
NEW YORK, Modern Work of Art, Museum of Modern Art, 20 November-20 January, 5 nrs

1935
* AMSTERDAM 1, —, Kunsthandel Huinck en Scherjon, May-June, 1 nr
AMSTERDAM 2, Peinture française XIXme siècle, E.J. van Wisselingh & Co, 15 July-17 August, 5 nrs
AMSTERDAM 3, Hollandsche en Fransche meesters der XIXe eeuw, E.J. van Wisselingh & Co, 2 November-7 December, 1 nr
BASLE, Meisterzeichnungen französischer Künstler von Ingres bis Cézanne, Kunsthalle, 29 June-18 August, 3 nrs
BRUSSELS, L'Impressionnisme, Palais des Beaux-Arts, 15 June-29 September, 11 nrs
* BUDAPEST, —, Musée des Beaux-Arts, —, 1 nr
BUFFALO, Master Drawings, Albright Art Gallery, January, 2 nrs
HAARLEM 1, Moderne prentkunst en Hollandsche aquarellen, J. H. de Bois [Art Gallery], July-August, 2 nrs
HAARLEM 2, Moderne schilderijen, J. H. de Bois [Art Gallery], November-December, 1 nr, see J. H. de Bois' Bulletin, nr 146
KANSAS CITY, One Hundred Years French Painting 1820-1920, The William Rockhill Nelson Gallery of Art, 31 March-28 April, 3 nrs
LONDON, Nineteenth century Masterpieces, Wildenstein & Co 9 May-15 June, 1 nr
* MONTEVIDEO, Exp. organisée par les Amigos del Arte, — September, 1 nr
NEW YORK, A nineteenth century selection French paintings, Bignou Gallery, March, 1 nr

1935-36
NEW YORK, ETC, VvG New York, Museum of Modern
Art, December-January, 127 nrs
Chicago, The Art Institute of Chicago, —
Boston, Museum of Fine Arts, 19 February-15 March
Cleveland, Museum of Art, 25 March-19 April
Detroit, Institute of Arts, 6-28 October
Kansas City, The William Rockhill Nelson Gallery of Art, —
Minneapolis, The Minneapolis Institute of Arts, —
Philadelphia, Pennsylvania Museum of Art, —
San Francisco, —,
ROTTERDAM, Fransche schilderijen uit de negentiende eeuw, benevens Jongkind, Vincent van Gogh, Kröller-Müller Stichting, Museum Boymans, December-January, 7 nrs

1936
AMSTERDAM, Bloemenstillevens, Kunsthandel Huinck en Scherjon, 22 February-21 March, 1 nr
CLEVELAND, The twentieth anniversary exhibition, Cleveland Museum of Art, 26 June-4 October, 3 nrs
* GLOUCESTER, —, —, —, 1 nr
* HAARLEM, —, J. H. de Bois [Art Gallery], 7 November-7 December, 2 nrs
* LONDON 1, Corot to Cézanne, Alex Reid & Lefèvre, 1 nr
LONDON 2, Collection of a Collector, Modern French Paintings from Ingres to Matisse, Wildenstein & Co, July, 2 nrs
LONDON 3, Paintings, Drawings, Sculpture and Prints by modern Artists, The Leicester Galleries, Summer, 1 nr
LONDON 4, Masters of French 19th century paintings, New Burlington Galleries, 1-31 October, 6 nrs
PARIS 1, Cinquantenaire du Symbolisme, Bibliothèque Nationale, —, 1 nr
PARIS 2, Le Grand Siècle, Paul Rosenberg, 15 June-11 July, 2 nrs
SAN DIEGO, California Pacific International Exhibition, The Palace of Fine Arts, 12 February-9 September, 1 nr [exhibited until 31 May]

1936-37
* ROTTERDAM, Kersttentoonstelling, Museum Boymans, December-January, 4 nrs

1937
* CHICAGO, French nineteenth century paintings, The Art Institute of Chicago, 3-15 May, 2 nrs
HARTFORD, Forty-three Portraits, The Wadsworth Atheneum, [January], 1 nr
LONDON, An exhibition of Works by Ingres to Van Gogh, Rosenberg & Helft, 25 February-25 March, 1 nr
* NEW YORK, French Masters from Courbet to Seurat, Seligmann & Co, 22 March-17 April, 1 nr
PARIS, VvG Sa vie et son oeuvre, Exposition internationale groupe 1, classe 3, Nouveaux Musées, Quai de Tokio, June-October, 226 nrs, catalogue édité par l'Amour de l'Art

1937-38
AMSTERDAM, Kersttentoonstelling, Kunsthandel Huinck en Scherjon, 22 December-31 January, 1 nr

1938
AMSTERDAM 1, Exposition de peinture, E.J. van Wisselingh, 25 June-23 July, 1 nr
AMSTERDAM 2, Nederlandsche Schilderkunst, Meesterwerken uit de 19e eeuw, E.J. van Wisselingh & Co, 10 August-10 September, 1 nr
AMSTERDAM 3, Nederlandsche en Fransche Kunst, Kunsthandel Huinck & Scherjon, 15 October-15 November, 3 nrs
HARTFORD, The painters of still life, Wadsworth Atheneum 25 January-15 February, 1 nr
LONDON 1, Artists who died young, Leicester Galleries, March-April, 6 nrs
LONDON 2, The Tragic Painters, Alex. Reid & Lefèvre, June, 3 nrs
* NEW YORK 1, The Tragic Painters, Bignou Gallery, February-March, 3 nrs
NEW YORK 2, Great Portraits from Impressionism to Modernism, Wildenstein & Co, 1-29 March, 4 nrs
PARIS 1, La peinture française du XIXe siècle en Suisse, organisée par La Gazette des Beaux-Arts, —, 2 nrs
PARIS 2, La rose dans l'art, Château de Bagatelle, —, 1 nr
VENICE, 21st Biennale Esposizione Internazionale d'Arte della Città di Venezia, 3 nrs
* WASHINGTON, Flowers and Fruits, Museum of Modern Art Gallery of Washington, 29 March-24 April, 1 nr

1938-39
AMSTERDAM, Kersttentoonstelling, Kunsthandel Huinck en Scherjon, 24 December-31 January, 1 nr
* ROTTERDAM, Schilderijen, Teekeningen en Beeldhouwwerken uit particuliere Nederlandsche Verzamelingen, Museum Boymans, December-January, 1 nr

1939
* ADELAIDE, ETC, French and British Contemporary Art [Herald exhibition], National Art Gallery [and other State Galleries], 21 August — [?], 8 nrs
* AMSTERDAM 1, —, Kunsthandel Huinck en Scherjon, 27 May-15 June, 1 nr
AMSTERDAM 2, Maîtres français et hollandais du XIXme siècle, E.J. van Wisselingh & Co, 1 June-1 July, 2 nrs

BELGRADE, Peinture française XIXe siècle, Musée de Prince Paul, —, 4 nrs
BOSTON, Paintings, drawings and prints from private collections in New England, Museum of Fine Arts, 9 June-10 September, 7 nrs
LONDON 1, Milestones in French painting, Alex. Reid & Lefèvre, June, 2 nrs
* LONDON 2, Renoir to Cézanne, Alex. Reid & Lefèvre, —, 1 nr
* MOSCOW, [French landscape 19th-20th century], — — —
NEW YORK, Small masterpieces of late 19th century French art, Durand-Ruel Galleries, 2-31 December, 1 nr
* OAKLAND, Modern Master Drawings, Miller Cottage Art Gallery, —, —
PARIS, —, Galerie Thannhauser, —, 1 nr
SAN FRANCISCO, Golden Gate International Exhibition, Masterworks of five Centuries, — 14 nrs

1939-40
* BUENOS AIRES, ETC, Pintura Francesa, —, —, —
ROTTERDAM, Kersttentoonstelling schilderijen, beeldhouwwerken en teekeningen, Museum Boymans, 23 December-29 January, 2 nrs
SAN FRANCISCO, Seven Centuries of Painting, The California Palace of the Legion of Honor and the M. H. de Young Memorial Museum, 29-December-28 January, 6 nrs

1940
AMSTERDAM, Peinture française, E.J. van Wisselingh & Co., 6 March-6 April, 3 nrs
CHICAGO, Origins of Modern Art, The Arts Club, —, 1 nr
DETROIT, The Age of Impressionism and objective Realism, Detroit Institute of Arts, 3 May-2 June, 6 nrs
LUCERNE, Die Hauptwerke der Sammlung Hahnloser, Winterthur, Kunstmuseum, —, 12 nrs
NEW YORK 1, Modern Masters, Museum of Modern Art, —, 2 nrs
NEW YORK 2, Masterpieces of Art, New York World's Fair, May-October, 7 nrs
NEW YORK 3, VvG collection Ir. V. W. van Gogh, Paintings, Holland House, 6-28 June, 14 nrs
NEW YORK 4, Modern French Paintings, Knoedler Art Gallery, [?] — 16 March, 1 nr
SAN FRANCISCO 1, Contemporary Art, Museum of Art, 18 January-5 February, 1 nr
SAN FRANCISCO 2, Golden Gate International Exposition Art, Palace of Fine Arts, —, 2 nrs
SAN FRANCISCO 3, Golden Gate International Exposition, Master Drawings, Palace of Fine Arts, —, 2 nrs

1941
* ALBI, —, —, —, [mentioned in Louvre catalogue, Impressionnistes, 1959], 2 nrs
* BALTIMORE, A century of Baltimore collecting 1840-1940 Museum of Art, —, 1 nr
CHICAGO, Masterpieces of French Art, The Art Institute, 10 April-20 May, 3 nrs
* HAARLEM, Moderne Schilderijen 19e en 20ste eeuw, J. H. de Bois, Spring, 2 nrs
* LOS ANGELES, Aspects of French Painting from Cézanne to Picasso, Los Angeles County Museum, 15 January-2 March, 1 nr
NEW YORK, French Painting from David to Toulouse-Lautrec, Metropolitan Museum of Art, 6 February-26 March, 6 nrs
WORCESTER, The Art of the Third Republic, French painting 1870-1940, Worcester Art Museum, 22 February-16 March, 2 nrs

1942
BALTIMORE, WORCESTER, VvG paintings by, Baltimore, The Baltimore Museum of Art, 18 September-18 October, 38 nrs
Worcester, The Worcester Art Museum, 28 October-28 November, 38 nrs
NEW YORK, VvG Masterpieces, Paul Rosenberg, 5-31 January, 11 nrs
PARIS, Le paysage français de Corot à nos jours, Galerie Charpentier, [about June], 1 nr

1943
BASLE, Kunstwerke des 19. Jahrhunderts aus Basler Privatbesitz, Kunsthalle, 1 May-4 July, 3 nrs
* GLASGOW, Spirit of France, Glasgow Art Gallery, —, —
NEW YORK 1, From Paris to the Sea Down the River Seine, Wildenstein & Co, 28 January-27 February, 1 nr
NEW YORK 2, VvG The art and life of —, Wildenstein & Co, October-November, 80 nrs
NEW YORK 3, Loan exhibition of the collection of pictures of Erich Maria Remarque, M. Knoedler & Co, 18 October-13 November, 1 nr
* PARIS, Fleurs et Fruit, Galerie Charpentier, — 1 nr
ZURICH, Ausländische Kunst in Zürich, Kunsthaus, 25 July-26 September, 11 nrs

1943-44
INDIANAPOLIS, ETC, VvG 14 paintings by — and work by contemporary Dutch artists, Indianapolis, John Herron Art Institute, November-December
Cincinnati, Cincinnati Art Museum, January

Ottawa, National Gallery, February
Fort Wayne, Fort Wayne Art School and Museum, May,
14 nrs

1944
MONTREAL, Five centuries of Dutch Art, Art Association
of Montreal, 9 March-9 April, 30 nrs
NEW YORK 1, Modern drawings, Museum of Modern Art,
—, 3 nrs
NEW YORK 2, Art in progress, fifteenth anniversary
exhibition, Museum of Modern Art, —, 2 nrs
* NEW YORK 3, The Coordination Council of French
Relief Societies, Jardin d'été, 3-31 May, 1 nr

1945
AMSTERDAM, V v G Een documentaire tentoonstelling,
Stedelijk Museum, —, 153 nrs
BASLE, V v G 25 Werke, Hollandhilfe, Galerie Schulthess,
23 June-19 August, 25 nrs
* COPENHAGEN, —, Glyptotek, —, —
THE HAGUE, Den Haag eert de Nederlandse Schilders van
de 19e eeuw, Pulchri Studio, 25 August-30 September,
13 nrs
PARIS, Paysages de France, Galerie Charpentier, without
date, 1 nr

1945-46
* AMSTERDAM, Exposition de peinture, E.J. van Wisselingh & Co, 17 December-26 January, 2 nrs

1946
AMSTERDAM, Meesterwerken van 1800 tot heden, Stedelijk
Museum, —, —, [no catalogue]
* BERN, Peinture contemporaine, École de Paris, Kunst-
halle, 27 February-28 March, 4 nrs
* CAMBRIDGE [MASS.], Collection M. Wertheim, Fogg Art
Museum, —, 1 nr
* CHICAGO, Drawings old and new, The Art Institute, —,
2 nrs
PARIS, Les chefs-d'oeuvre des collections privées
françaises retrouvées en Allemagne, Orangerie des Tuileries,
June-August, 1 nr
STOCKHOLM, ETC, V v G, *Stockholm*, Nationalmuseum,
March-June
Göteborg, Konstmuseum, —
Malmö, Malmö Museum, —, 104 nrs
WASHINGTON, French Paintings from the Chester Dale
Collection, National Gallery of Art, —, 3 nrs

1946-47
LIÈGE, ETC, V v G *Liège*, Musée des Beaux-Arts, October
Brussels, Palais des Beaux-Arts, 9 November-19 December
Mons, Musée des Beaux-Arts, January, 171 nrs

1947
* ALBUQUERQUE, The Harwood Foundation, The
University of New Mexico, — 1 nr
BASLE, V v G, Kunsthalle, 11 October-23 November, 167 nrs
GENEVA, V v G, 172 oeuvres de —, Musée Rath, 22 March-
20 April, 172 nrs
GRONINGEN 1, V v G, tekeningen en aquarellen van —,
Kunstlievend Genootschap Pictura, 25 May-15 June, 86 nrs
GRONINGEN 2, V v G [paintings] collection V. W. van Gogh
Museum van Oudheden, 18 October-9 November, 106 nrs
* LONDON, 19th century French Masters, Alex. Reid &
Lefèvre, — 1 nr
* MUNICH, Moderne französische Malerei, —, —, —
PARIS 1, V v G, Musée de l'Orangerie, January-March,
173 nrs
PARIS 2, Beautés de la Provence, Galerie Charpentier, —,
6 nrs
PARIS 3, Cinquantenaire des Amis du Louvre, Orangerie
des Tuileries, —, 1 nr
ROTTERDAM, V v G Drawings from the collection of
Ir. V. W. van Gogh, Museum Boymans, July-August,
115 nrs
SAN FRANCISCO, 19th century French Drawings,
California Palace of the Legion of Honor, 8 March-6 April,
9 nrs
WINTERTHUR, Grosse Maler des 19. Jahrhunderts aus den
Münchener Museen, Kunstmuseum, 17 August-16 Novem-
ber, 3 nrs

1947-48
LONDON, ETC, V v G, *London*, Tate Gallery, December-
January
Birmingham, City Art Gallery, January-February
Glasgow, City Art Gallery, 21 February-14 March, 178 nrs

1948
AMSTERDAM 1, Peinture française école XIXme siècle,
E.J. van Wisselingh & Co, 22 June-31 July, 1 nr
AMSTERDAM 2, V v G en zijn nederlandse tijdgenoten,
Stedelijk Museum, Summer, 4 ill., c. 50 nrs
BERGEN-OSLO, V v G Malerier Tegninger, *Bergen*, Kunst-
forening, 23 March-15 May, 124 nrs
Oslo, Kunstnernes Hus, 24 April-15 May, 125 nrs
CLEVELAND, V v G, Cleveland Museum of Art, 3 Novem-
ber-12 December, 50 nrs
THE HAGUE, V v G collection Ir. V. W. van Gogh,

Gemeentemuseum, 12 October-12 December, 303 nrs
LONDON 1, Samuel Courtauld Memorial exhibition, Tate
Gallery, — 7 nrs
LONDON 2, The Kessler Collection 19th and 20th Century
French Masters, Wildenstein & Co, October-November,
1 nr
NEW YORK 1, V v G 14 Masterpieces, M. Knoedler & Co,
30 March-17 April, 14 nrs
NEW YORK 2, [Loan exhib.] Six masters of Post-
Impressionism, Wildenstein & Co, 8 April-8 May, 11 nrs
PARIS, La Douceur de vivre, Bernheim-Jeune,
20 September-20 October, 1 nr
ST. LOUIS, St. Louis Collections, an exhibition of 20th
century Art, The City Art Museum of St. Louis,
20 September-25 October, 1 nr

1948-49
CAMBRIDGE [MASS.] Seventy Master Drawings, Fogg Art
Museum, 27 November-6 January, 1 nr

1949
AMSTERDAM 1, Peinture française XIXme et XXme siècle,
E.J. van Wisselingh & Co, 19 April-25 May, 2 nrs
AMSTERDAM 2, Maîtres français XIXme et XXme siècle,
E.J. van Wisselingh & Co, 10 October-12 November, 2 nrs
BALTIMORE, Selections from the Cone Collection,
Baltimore Museum of Art, October, 1 nr
* BEVERLEY HILLS [CAL.], —, Associated American
Artists Galleries, February —
BUENOS AIRES, De Manet à nos jours, National Museum,
—, 1 nr
* GOUDA, V v G, Het Catharina Gasthuis, April-May, —
* HANNOVER, Französische Malerei im 19. Jahrhundert,
—, Landesgalerie, —
LYONS, Les grands courants de la peinture contemporaine,
Musée de Lyon, —, 4 nrs
NEW YORK 1, Trends in European Painting 1680-1930, The
century Association, 2 February-31 March, 2 nrs
NEW YORK 2, Drawings through 4 centuries, Wildenstein
& Co, Summer, 3 nrs
NEW YORK 3, What they said – Postscript to art criticism,
Durand-Ruel Galleries, 28 November-17 December, 1 nr
* PHILADELPHIA, The Henry P. Mc Ilhenny Collection,
Philadelphia Museum of Art, —, 1 nr

1949-50
NEW YORK, CHICAGO, V v G, *New York*, Metropolitan
Museum of Art, without date
Chicago, The Art Institute of Chicago, without date, 158 nrs

1950
* COLUMBUS [OHIO] Masterpieces of Painting, Columbus
Gallery of Fine Arts, Fall, 1 nr
THE HAGUE, Verzameling H. P. Bremmer, Gemeente-
museum, 9 March-23 April, 25 nrs
's-HERTOGENBOSCH, BREDA, V v G, *'s-Hertogenbosch*,
Centraal Noord-Brabants Museum, March, —
Breda, Stedelijk Museum De Beyerd, April, —
LONDON, XIX th century French Masters, Lefèvre
Gallery, July, 1 nr
* LOS ANGELES, —, —, —, —
NEW HAVEN, French Paintings of the Latter Half of the
Nineteenth Century, Yale University Art Gallery, 17 April-
21 May, 1 nr
PARIS 1, La Peinture française au Musée Municipal
d'Amsterdam, Galerie Bignou, 21 April-12 May, 2 nrs
PARIS 2, Oeuvres choisies du XIXe siècle, Galerie Max
Kaganovitch, 22 May-5 July, 6 nrs
* PHILADELPHIA, Masterpieces of Philadelphia private
collectors, Part II, —, —, 1 nr
ZURICH, Europäische Kunst des 13.-20. Jahrhunderts,
Kunsthaus, 6 June-3 September, 9 nrs

1950-51
LEIDEN, ETC, Van Fantin Latour tot Picasso [from the
collection of the Rijksmuseum Kröller-Müller], *Leiden*, de
Lakenhal, 14 October-26 November, 4 nrs
Enschede, Rijksmuseum Twenthe, 6 January-11 February,
—,
Groningen, Museum voor Oudheden, 17 February-11 March
Leeuwarden, Friesch Museum, 17 March-8 April
PARIS, Art Sacré, Oeuvres françaises du XIX et XX siècles,
Musée National d'Art Moderne, 29 November-21 January,
1 nr
PHILADELPHIA, Masterpieces of painting, Diamond
Jubilee Exhibition, Philadelphia Museum of Art, 4 Novem-
ber-11 February, 2 nrs

1951
ABERDEEN, Paintings from North-East Homes, Aberdeen
Art Gallery, — 1 nr
ALBI, Toulouse Lautrec, ses amis et ses maîtres,
Cinquantenaire de la mort de Toulouse-Lautrec, Musée
d'Albi, 11 August-28 October, 4 nrs
AMSTERDAM 1, Maîtres français XIXme et XXme siècles,
E.J. van Wisselingh & Co, 24 September-27 October, 1 nr
AMSTERDAM 2, Rembrandt, Hokusai, van Gogh [drawings]
Stedelijk Museum, cat. 83, October-November, 31 nrs
HOUSTON, V v G, Contemporary Arts Museum, 4-25
February, 21 nrs

LONDON, Géricault to Renoir, The Lefèvre Galleries, May,
1 nr
LYONS, ETC, V v G collection V. W. van Gogh and other
owners, *Lyons*, Musée de Lyon, February-March, 101 nrs
Arles, Vincent van Gogh en Provence, Musée Réattu, May
St. Rémy, Hotel de Sade, May, 101 nrs
NEWCASTLE-UPON-TYNE, Pictures from collections in
Northumberland, Hatton Gallery, Kings College, 8 May-
15 June, 1 nr
NEW YORK, The Lewisohn collection. The Metropolitan
Museum of Art, 2 November-2 December, 1 nr
PARIS 1, Impressionnistes et romantiques français dans les
musées allemands, Musée de l'Orangerie, — 6 nrs
PARIS 2, Gauguin et ses Amis, Galerie A. Weill, 1-20 June,
3 nrs
* PITTSBURGH [PENN.], French painting 1100-1900,
Carnegie Institute, 18 October-2 December, 1 nr

1952
* AMSTERDAM, Aquarellen en tekeningen, Kunsthandel
Huinck en Scherjon, 6 October-15 November, 2 nrs
ANTWERP, De Arbeid in de Kunst, Van Meunier tot
Permeke, Koninklijk Museum voor Schone Kunsten,
26 April-30 June, 9 nrs
* BASLE, Rembrandt, Hokusai, van Gogh [drawings],
Kunstmuseum, — [31] nrs, see 1951 Amsterdam 2, 1952
Groningen
EINDHOVEN, V v G, collection Ir. V. W. van Gogh,
Stedelijk van Abbe Museum, 22 March-4 May, 81 nrs
ENSCHEDE, V v G collection Ir. V. W. van Gogh, Rijks-
museum Twenthe, 20 February-16 March, 81 nrs
GRONINGEN, Rembrandt, Hokusai, van Gogh [drawings],
Pictura, 12 April-12 May, 22 nrs
LONDON 1, Some aspects of modern Dutch painting, The
Redfern Gallery, March-April, 2 nrs
LONDON 2, French paintings of the XIX th and XX th
century, Matthiesen Gallery, Summer, 2 nrs
LONDON 3, French masters XIX and XX century, The
Lefèvre Gallery, June-July, 1 nr
LONDON 4, XXth Century Masterpieces, Tate Gallery,
15 July-17 August, 2 nrs
MANCHESTER, Contemporary Watercolours and Drawings
from the Whitworth Art Gallery, Arts Council of Great
Britain, without date, 1 nr
MILAN, V v G Dipinti e disegni, Palazzo Reale, February-
April, 127 nrs
PARIS 1, La Nature morte de l'antiquité à nos jours,
Orangerie des Tuileries, April-June, 1 nr
PARIS 2, Cent-cinquante ans de dessin 1800-1950,
M M Bernheim-Jeune, from 20 December, 2 nrs
PARIS 3, Émile Zola, Bibliothèque Nationale, 1 nr
ZURICH, Um 1900 – Art Nouveau und Jugendstil, Kunst-
gewerbemuseum, June-September, 1 nr

1952-53
NEW YORK, ETC., Les Fauves, *New York*, Museum of
Modern Art, 8 October-4 January
Minneapolis, The Minneapolis Institute of Arts,
21 January-22 February
San Francisco, San Francisco Museum of Art, 13 March-
12 April
Toronto, The Art Gallery of Toronto, 1-31 May, 1 nr

1953
AMSTERDAM 1, Schilderijen, etc, Kunsthandel Huinck en
Scherjon, June-July, 3 nrs
AMSTERDAM 2, Van Gogh en zijn Franse tijdgenoten,
Stedelijk Museum, —, 1 nr
ASSEN, V v G from the collection of Ir. V. W. van Gogh, —
6-21 November, 50 nrs
BERLIN, V v G Gemälde und Zeichnungen, Berliner Fest-
wochen, Bezirksamt Tiergarten, Amt für Kunst, 22 nrs
BERN, Europäische Kunst in Berner Privatbesitz, Kunst-
halle, 31 July-20 September, 3 nrs
* BRUSSELS, —, Palais des Beaux-Arts, May, 1 nr
THE HAGUE, V v G, Gemeente Museum, 30 March-17 May,
198 nrs
HOENSBROEK, V v G from the collection of Ir. V. W. van
Gogh, Kasteel Hoensbroek, 23 May-27 July, 110 nrs
LONDON 1, European Masters, Marlborough Fine Art Ltd,
November-December, 1 nr
LONDON 2, Recent acquisitions VIII, Arthur Tooth & Sons
Ltd, 17 November-13 December, 1 nr
NEW YORK 1, Landscape Drawings and Watercolors,
Pierpont Morgan Library, 31 January-11 April, 2 nrs
* NEW YORK 2, Collector's Choice, Paul Rosenberg,
17 March-18 April, 1 nr
NEW YORK 3, French Art around 1900, Fine Arts
Associates, 26 October-21 November, 1 nr
OTTERLO, AMSTERDAM, V v G Eeuwfeest [Centenary],
Otterlo, Rijksmuseum Kröller-Müller, 24 May-19 July
Amsterdam, Stedelijk Museum, 23 July-20 September, 195 nrs
PARIS, Figures nues d'école française, Galerie Charpentier,
— 1 nr
* TORONTO, —, Laing Gallery, December, 2 nrs
* VLAARDINGEN, V v G, De Visbank, 27 March-19 April,
—
WASHINGTON [DC], Forty paintings from the Edward
G. Robinson collection, National Gallery of Art, 10 May-
24 June, 1 nr

ZUNDERT, VvG from the collection of Ir. V.W. van Gogh, Parochiehuis, 30 March-20 April, 59 nrs
ZURICH, VvG Zeichnungen und Aquarelle, Kunsthaus, 24 January-1 March, 139 nrs

1953-54
* NEW YORK, —, Museum of Modern Art, October-January, 1 nr
PARIS, Chefs-d'oeuvre du Musée d'Art de São Paulo, Musée de l'Orangerie, October-January, 3 nrs
ST. LOUIS [MISS.], ETC, VvG, *St. Louis*, City Art Museum of Saint Louis, 17 October-13 December
Philadelphia [Penn.], Philadelphia Museum of Art, 2 January-28 February
Toledo [Ohio], Toledo Museum of Art, 7 March-30 April, 181 nrs

1954
CHICAGO, Masterpieces of Religious Art, Art Institute of Chicago, 15 July-31 August, 1 nr
DETROIT, The two sides of the medal, French painting from Gérôme to Gauguin, Detroit Institute of Arts, without date, 4 nrs
DORDRECHT, Nederlandse stillevens uit vier eeuwen, Dordrechts Museum, 17 July-31 August, 3 nrs
EDINBURGH, Loan exhibition Maitland Collection, National Gallery of Scotland, April, 1 nr
EINDHOVEN, Luik [Liège] verzamelt kunst, coll. Graindorge, coll. Musée des Beaux-Arts, Stedelijk Van Abbe Museum, 20 February-31 March, 1 nr
GENEVA, Trésors des collections Romandes, Musée Rath, 26 June-3 October, 2 nrs
NEW YORK, Magic of Flowers in Painting, Wildenstein & Co, 13 April-15 May, 3 nrs
OTTAWA, Paintings from the collection of John A. Mac Aulay [Winnipeg] National Gallery of Canada, without date, —, —
* RECKLINGHAUSEN, Zeugnisse europäischer Gemeinsamkeit, Meisterwerke der Malerei und Plastik aus europäischen Museen und Privatsammlungen, Ruhrfestspiele, Städtische Kunsthalle, 18 June-30 July, 1 nr
ROTTERDAM, Vier Eeuwen Stilleven in Frankrijk, Museum Boymans, 10 July-20 September, 6 nrs
STOCKHOLM, Cézanne till Picasso, Fransk Konst i svenske ägo, Liljevachs Konsthall, September, 2 nrs
UTRECHT, Meesterwerken uit São Paulo, Centraal Museum 6 March-2 May, 3 nrs
ZURICH, VvG, Kunsthaus, 9 October-21 November, 79 nrs

1954-55
BERN, VvG, Berner Kunstmuseum, 27 November-30 January, 4 nrs
PARIS, Van Gogh et les Peintres d'Auvers-sur-Oise, l'Orangerie des Tuileries, 26 November-28 February, 25 nrs

1955
AMSTERDAM 1, VvG collection Ir. V.W. van Gogh paintings and drawings, Stedelijk Museum, Summer, 243 nrs
AMSTERDAM 2, Maîtres français XIXme et XXme siècle, E.J. van Wisselingh & Co, 10 October-12 November, 2 nrs
ANTWERP 1, VvG, Feestzaal Meir, 7 May-19 June, 358 nrs [152 paintings, 206 drawings]
ANTWERP 2, Kunst van Heden, Koninklijk Museum voor Schone Kunsten, 14 May-12 June, 5 nrs
ANTWERP 3, Vincent van Gogh en zijn Hollandse tijdgenoten, Zaal Comité voor Artistieke Werking, 15 May-9 June, 15 nrs
CHICAGO, Great French Paintings, an exhibition in memory of Chauncey McCormick, Art Institute of Chicago, 20 January-20 February, 2 nrs
DORDRECHT, Boom, Bloem en Plant, Dordrechts Museum, 16 July-31 August, 4 nrs
* GRONINGEN, Tekeningen en Aquarellen van 19de eeuwse Nederlandse Schilders, Pictura, — —
LONDON, XIX and XX century French Masters, Marlborough Fine Art Ltd, November-December, 1 nr
MARSEILLES, Les impressionnistes français, Musée Cantini, July, 1 nr
NEW YORK 1, Masters of the nineteenth century, Galerie St. Etienne, 18 January-12 February, 2 nrs
NEW YORK 2, VvG loan exhibition, Wildenstein & Co, 24 March-30 April, 109 nrs
NEW YORK 3, Paintings from private collections, Museum of Modern Art 31 May-5 September, 7 nrs
NEW YORK 4, An exhibition of paintings, E. and A. Silberman Galleries, 12 October-1 November, 1 nr
PALM BEACH [FLA.] ETC, VvG *Palm Beach* [*Fla.*], Society of the Four Arts, 21 January-13 February
Miami [*Fla.*], Lowe Gallery of the University of Miami [Fla.], 24 February-20 March
New Orleans [*Louisiana*], —, 27 March-20 April, 37 nrs
* PARIS 1, Tableaux de collections parisiennes 1850-1950, Galerie Beaux-Arts, 22 April-31 May, 1 nr
PARIS 2, De David à Toulouse-Lautrec, chefs-d'oeuvre des coll. américaines, Musée de l'Orangerie, May-July, 6 nrs
PARIS 3, Impressionnistes de la Collection Courtauld de Londres, Musée de l'Orangerie, November, 7 nrs
* PARIS 4, Exposition internationale d'Industrie minérale, Musée des Travaux-Publics, —, —

ROTTERDAM, Kunstschatten uit Nederlandse verzamelingen, Museum Boymans, 19 June-25 September, 6 nrs
WINTERTHUR 1, Europäische Meister 1790-1910, Kunstmuseum, 12 June-24 July, 8 nrs
WINTERTHUR 2, Die Privatsammlung Oskar Reinhart, Kunstmuseum, 21 August-20 November, 6 nrs
* WORMERVEER, Ons Huis, Arbeid in de Kunst, —, —, —

1955-56
LIVERPOOL, ETC, VvG, *Liverpool*, The Walker Art Gallery 29 October-10 December
Manchester, The City Art Gallery, 17 December-4 February
Newcastle-upon-Tyne, The Laing Art Gallery, 11 February-24 March, arranged by the Arts Council of Great Britain, 137 nrs
* MOSCOW, LENINGRAD, [French Art XIIth-XXth Century], Museum of Modern Art -, Hermitage, —, —
PARIS, Un siècle de chemin de fer et d'art, Galerie Charpentier, —, 1 nr

1956
ALMELO, Van Daumier tot Picasso, Kunstkring de Waag, 17 March-30 April, 2 nrs
AMSTERDAM, VvG Quelques oeuvres de l'époque 1881-1886, provenant de collections particulières néerlandaises, E.J. van Wisselingh & Co, 20 February-17 March, 34 nrs
CINCINNATI, The Mary E. Johnston collection, Contemporary Arts Center in the Cincinnati Art Museum, 20 April-12 May, 1 nr
EINDHOVEN, VvG from the collection of Rijksmuseum Kröller-Müller, Stedelijk van Abbemuseum, 28 January-12 March, 51 nrs
HAARLEM, VvG collection Ir. V.W. van Gogh [drawings], Vishal, 21 July-27 August, 86 nrs
LEEUWARDEN, VvG from the collection Ir. V.W. van Gogh [Paintings], Fries Museum, 14 April-13 May, 47 nrs
LONDON, XIXth and XXth century French Masters, Marlborough Fine Art Ltd, October-November, 1 nr
MILWAUKEE, CINCINNATI, Still life painting since 1470, *Milwaukee* Milwaukee Art Institute, September
Cincinnati, Cincinnati Art Museum, October, 1 nr
MUNICH, VvG Haus der Kunst, October-December, 166 nrs and 5 supplement nrs
NEW HAVEN, Pictures collected by Yale Alumni, Yale University, 8 May-18 June, 5 nrs
NEW YORK, French paintings of the XIXth and XXth centuries, E.J. van Wisselingh & Co, 15 November-15 December, 1 nr
NUREMBERG, VvG Zeichnungen und Aquarelle von Vincent van Gogh, aus dem Besitz des Rijksmuseum Kröller-Müller [From the Kröller-Müller Museum] und von anderen Leihgebern, Fränkische Galerie, 12 February-11 March, 70 nrs
RALEIGH [NC], French painting of the last half of the nineteenth century, North Carolina Museum of Art, 15 June-29 July, 3 nrs
WASHINGTON, Visionaries and dreamers, The Corcoran Gallery of Art, 7 April-27 May, 1 nr

1956-57
LOS ANGELES, SAN FRANCISCO, The Gladys Lloyd Robinson and Edward G. Robinson collection, *Los Angeles*, Los Angeles County Museum, 11 September-11 November
San Francisco, California Palace of the Legion of Honor, 30 November-13 January, 2 nrs
ROTTERDAM, VvG Vincent in Arles, Collection Ir. V.W. v. Gogh [paintings French period], Volks Universiteit, 21 December-3 January, 15 nrs
VIENNA, Die Moderne Galerie des Kunsthistorischen Museums, Akademie der bildenden Künste, December-January, 1 nr

1957
BREDA, VvG collection Ir. V.W. van Gogh, Stedelijk Museum De Beyerd, 2-24 February, 90 nrs
COLOGNE, Park und Garten in der Malerei, Wallraf-Richartz-Museum, —, 2 nrs
DUBLIN, Paintings from Irish Collections, Municipal Gallery of Modern Art, May-August, 1 nr
ESSEN, VvG Leben und Schaffen, Dokumentation, Gemälde, Zeichnungen, Villa Hügel, 16 October-15 December, 385 nrs [Dokumentation 244, Paintings 56, Drawings 84 nrs]
GENEVA, Art et Travail, Musée d'Art et d'Histoire, 14 June-22 September, 3 nrs
* LIÈGE —, —, —, —
LONDON, XIX and XX Century European Masters, Marlborough Fine Art Ltd, October-December, 1 nr
LOS ANGELES, VvG Loan exhibition of paintings and drawings, Municipal Art Gallery, 3 July-4 August, 39 nrs
MARSEILLES, VvG collection Ir. V.W. van Gogh, Musée Cantini, 12 March-28 April, 88 nrs
MILWAUKEE, An inaugural exhibition, Milwaukee Art Institute, 12 September-20 October, 9 nrs
NEW YORK, The Richard L. Feigen collection, World House Galleries, 18 September-2 November, 1 nr
NIJMEGEN, VvG tekeningen en aquarellen uit de collectie Ir. V.W. van Gogh, De Waag, 13 March-15 April, 78 nrs
PARIS 1, Cent chefs-d'oeuvre de l'art français 1750-1950,

Galerie Charpentier, without date, 1 nr
PARIS 2, Voici des fruits, des fleurs, des feuilles et des branches..., Bernheim-Jeune, without date, 2 nrs
PARIS 3, Exposition de la collection Lehman de New York, Musée de l'Orangerie, [May], 1 nr
RECKLINGHAUSEN, Verkannte Kunst, Städtische Kunsthalle, 16 June-31 July, 4 nrs
STOCKHOLM, VvG Akvareller, teckningar, oljestudier, brev [from the collection of Ir V.W. van Gogh], Nationalmuseum, cat nr 242, October-November, 119 nrs [98 drawings, 21 paintings]

1957-58
* COPENHAGEN, — Statens Museum for Kunst, — —
LEIDEN, SCHIEDAM, VvG collection Ir. V.W. van Gogh, *Leiden*, Stedelijk Museum De Lakenhal, 9 November-16 December
Schiedam, Stedelijk Museum, 21 December-27 January, 80 nrs
NEW YORK, ETC, The Niarchos Collection of Paintings, *New York*, M. Knoedler & Co, 3 December-18 January
Ottawa, National Gallery of Canada, 5 February-2 March
Boston [Mass.], Museum of Fine Arts, 15 March-20 April 7 nrs — see also London 2, 1958

1958
AMSTERDAM 1, VvG Documentaire tentoonstelling [paintings, drawings and documents], Stedelijk Museum, cat nr 187, 16 May-30 June, 390 nrs
AMSTERDAM 2, Maîtres français XIXme et XXme siècle, E.J. van Wisselingh & Co, June-August, 5 nrs
BERLIN-OST, Schätze der Weltkultur von der USSR gerettet, National Galerie, — 5 nrs
* BERLIN-WEST, Von Manet bis Matisse, National Galerie, — 1 nr
CLEVELAND, In Memoriam Leonard C. Hanna, Jr., Cleveland Museum of Art, —, 4 nrs
* LIÈGE, —, —, —, —
LONDON 1, Exhibition of fine paintings and drawings of four centuries, Hallsborough Gallery, 14 April-24 May, 1 nr
LONDON 2, The Niarchos collection of paintings, Tate Gallery, 23 May-29 June, 7 nrs
LONDON 3, XIX and XX Century European Masters, Marlborough Fine Art Ltd, Summer, 1 nr
MONS, VvG son art et ses amis, collection Ir. V.W. van Gogh, Musée des Beaux-Arts, 22 March-5 May, 81 nrs [51 nrs van Gogh, 30 nrs friends v. Gogh]
NEW YORK, Paintings from private collections, Summer loan exhibition, Metropolitan Museum of Art, Summer, 8 nrs
* PROVINCETOWN [MASS.], Inaugural Exhibition, Chrysler Art Museum of Provincetown, —, —
TOKYO, KYOTO, VvG collection Kröller-Müller Museum Otterlo,
Tokyo, The Tokyo National Museum, 15 October-25 November,
Kyoto, The Art Municipal Museum, 3-27 December, 130 nrs
VANCOUVER, The changing Landscape of Holland, The Fine Arts Gallery, University of British Columbia, 23 July-29 August, 4 nrs
VEVEY, Monet à Chagall, Rosensaft collection, Musée Jenisch, 28 June-14 September, 1 nr
VIENNA, VvG from the Kröller-Müller collection, Otterlo [except a few items], Oesterreichische Galerie, February-March, 112 nrs
ZURICH, Sammlung Emil G. Bührle, Kunsthaus, 7 June-end of September, 14 nrs

1958-59
* MUNICH, Hauptwerke der Sammlung Emil Georg Bührle, Haus der Kunst, —, 14 nrs
SAN FRANCISCO, ETC, VvG collection Ir. V.W. van Gogh, *San Francisco*, The M.H. de Young Memorial Museum,
Los Angeles, The Los Angeles County Museum, —
Portland, The Portland Art Museum,
Seattle, Seattle Art Museum, October-April 155 nrs [84 paintings, 71 drawings]
* SCHIEDAM, Op een Blad Papier. Tekeningen en Aquarellen uit het Rijksmuseum Kröller-Müller, Stedelijk Museum, December 1958-January 1959, [no cat]
WASHINGTON, ETC, Dutch Drawings, Masterpieces of five centuries, *Washington*, National Gallery of Art,
New York [*NY*], The Pierpont Morgan Library
Minneapolis [*Minn.*], The Minneapolis Institute of Arts,
Boston [*Mass.*] Museum of Fine Arts,
Cleveland [*Ohio*], Cleveland Museum of Arts,
Chicago [*Ill.*], Art Institute of Chicago, —, 6 nrs

1959
AIX-EN-PROVENCE, VvG en Provence, Pavillon de Vendôme, 3 October-30 November, 62 nrs
* BUDAPEST, Drawings from the Majovsky collection, National Museum, — 3 nrs
CINCINNATI, The Lehman collection, New York, Cincinnati Art Museum, 8 May-5 July, 3 nrs
LONDON, XIXth and XXth century European Masters, Marlborough Fine Art Ltd, Summer, 2 nrs
NEW YORK 1, Paintings, Watercolors and Sculptures, from the Collection of Mr and Mrs Henry Pearlman, M. Knoedler & Co, 27 January-21 February, 1 nr

NEW YORK 2, Paintings from private collections, Summer Loan Exhibition, Metropolitan Museum of Art, 7 July-6 September, 6 nrs
NEW YORK 3, Paintings from the Ritter Foundation, Fine Arts Associates, 13-31 October, 1 nr
NEW YORK 4, Great Master Drawings of seven centuries, M. Knoedler & Co, 13 October-7 November, 1 nr
PARIS, De Géricault à Matisse, Petit Palais, March-May, 5 nrs
RECKLINGHAUSEN, Die Handschrift des Künstlers, Kunsthalle, 23 May-5 July, 6 nrs
SANTA BARBARA, Drawings of Five Centuries, Santa Barbara Museum of Art, 21 April-17 May, 1 nr
SAN FRANCISCO, The Collection of Mr & Mrs William Goetz, California Palace of the Legion of Honor, 18 April-31 May, 1 nr
SÃO PAULO, 5 a Bienal de S. Paulo, Museu de Arte Moderna, September-December, p 241-242, 30 nrs
WASHINGTON, Masterpieces of Impressionist and post-Impressionist Painting, National Gallery of Art, 25 April-24 May, 5 nrs

1959-60
LONDON, Drawings and Engravings from the Courtauld Collection, Courtauld Institute, December-April, 1 nr
* PLYMOUTH, BRISTOL, The Morris Loan Collection
Plymouth, City Art Museum, —, —
Bristol, City Art Gallery, —, 1 nr
UTRECHT, VvG schilderijen en tekeningen, verzameling Ir. V. W. van Gogh, Centraal Museum, 18 December-1 February, 95 nrs [65 paintings, 30 drawings]

1960
* ARLES, —, —, —, —,
BASLE, La Femme, Galerie Beyeler, May-June, 1 nr
BUFFALO, The T. Edward Hanley collection, Drawings, Watercolors, Pastels, Bradford [Pa.], Albright Art Gallery, 6 January-14 February, 2 nrs
CUESMES, VvG, Borinage, 1-20 October, 75 nrs
DAYTON [OHIO], French paintings 1789-1929 from the collection of W. P. Chrysler, Dayton Art Institute, 25 March 22 May, 1 nr
ENSCHEDE, VvG collectie Ir. V. W. van Gogh, [drawings], Rijksmuseum Twenthe, 6 February-20 March, 71 nrs
* HOUSTON, From Gauguin to Gorky, Museum of Fine Arts, —, —
LONDON 1, XIX and XX Century drawings and Watercolours and XX Century sculpture, Marlborough Fine Art Ltd, February-March, 1 nr
LONDON 2, Flower and Still Life Paintings of 4 Centuries from the Hallsborough Gallery, 2 May-17 June, 1 nr
LONDON 3, Masters of Modern Art, Marlborough Fine Art Ltd, June-August, 1 nr
LONDON 4, VvG Selfportraits, Marlborough Fine Art Ltd, October, 18 nrs
LONDON 5, Drawings and Watercolours from the Whitworth Art Gallery [University of Manchester], — 1 nr
MINNEAPOLIS, Drawings, Paintings & Sculpture from Three private collections, David Daniels, Mr and Mrs Samuel H. Maslon, and Mr and Mrs Donald Winston, Institute of Arts, 13 July-14 August, 1 nr [coll. of Mr David Daniels, New York]
MONTREAL, Canada collects: European Painting 1860-1960, Museum of Fine Arts, 19 January-21 February, 1 nr
MOSCOW, French Art second half 19th century from the Collection of Paintings in the Museums of the USSR, Pushkin Museum, without date, 3 nrs
NEW HAVEN, Paintings, Drawings and Sculpture, collected by Yale Alumni, Yale University, 19 May-26 June, 4 nrs
NEW YORK 1, The Walter C. Baker Collection of Drawings, Metropolitan Museum of Art, 2 June-4 September, 1 nr
NEW YORK 2, Paintings from private collections, Summer Loan Exhibition Metropolitan Museum of Art, 6 July-4 September, 7 nrs
NEW YORK 3, Drawings by the Masters, Wildenstein, October, 1 nr
PARIS 1, VvG, Musée Jacquemart-André, February-March, 112 nrs
PARIS 2, Les Amis de Van Gogh, Institut Néerlandais, 9 November-17 December, 4 nrs and 2 letters
* PHILADELPHIA, Summer Loan, Philadelphia Museum of Art, —, —
RALEIGH, The Maurice Wertheim Collection, Modern French Art, Monet to Picasso, North Carolina Museum of Art, 17 June-4 September, 2 nrs
SAN FRANCISCO, Modern Masters in West Coast Collections, San Francisco Museum of Art, 18 October-27 November, 2 nrs
* SYRACUSE, —, —, —, —
TOKYO, Masterpieces of the ex-Matsukata collection, National Museum of Western Art, 14 May-10 July, nr

1960-61
EINDHOVEN, SCHIEDAM, Eindhoven verzamelt, van Jongkind tot Jorn,
Eindhoven, Stedelijk Van Abbe Museum, 5 November-13 December
Schiedam, Stedelijk Museum, 17 December-30 January, 2 nrs
LONDON, The John Hay Whitney Collection, The Tate Gallery, 16 December-29 January, 2 nrs
MONTREAL, ETC, VvG Paintings-Drawings
Montreal, The Montreal Museum of Fine Arts, 6 October-6 November
Ottawa [Ont,], The National Gallery of Canada, 17 November-18 December
Winnipeg [Manitoba], The Winnipeg Art Gallery, 29 December-31 January
Toronto [Ont.], The Art Gallery of Toronto, 10 February-12 March, 140 nrs
PARIS 1, Les sources du XX siècle, les arts en Europe 1884-1914, Musée national d'Art Moderne, 4 November-23 January, 12 nrs

1961
AMSTERDAM 1, VvG Aquarelles & dessins de l'époque 1881-1885 provenant de collections particulières néerlandaises, Kunsthandel E. J. van Wisselingh, 19 April-18 May, 40 nrs
AMSTERDAM 2, Polariteit, Stedelijk Museum, 22 July-18 September, 2 nrs [see Recklinghausen]
ARLES, VvG, Musée Réattu, 20 Mai-18 June, 24 nrs
* DALLAS, Impressionists and their Forebears from Barbizon, Museum for contemporary Art, March-April, 1 nr
EDINBURGH, LONDON, Masterpieces of French painting from the Bührle Collection,
Edinburgh, Royal Scottish Academy, 19 August-17 September, 7 nrs
London, National Gallery, 29 September-5 November, 8 nrs
THE HAGUE, Collection Thompson, Gemeentemuseum, 17 February-9 April, 1 nr
LONDON 1, 19th and 20th century drawings, watercolours, sculpture, Marlborough Fine Art Ltd, February-March, 1 nr
LONDON 2, French Landscapes, Marlborough Fine Art Ltd, October-December, 1 nr
LONDON 3, Collection of the Earl of Inchcape, Leggatt Brothers, Autumn, 1 nr
MUNICH, VvG Zeichnungen und Aquarelle, Städtische Galerie, 23 May-25 June, 74 nrs
NEWARK [N.J.] Nineteenth Century Master Drawings, The Newark Museum, 16 March-30 April, 3 nrs
NEW YORK 1, Masterpieces, Loan Exhibition of Paintings and Drawings, A Memorial Exhibition for Adele R. Levy, Wildenstein, 6 April-7 May, 1 nr
NEW YORK 2, Paintings from private collections, Summer Loan Exhibition Metropolitan Museum of Art, Summer, 4 nrs
* PARIS 1, Paris vu par les maîtres de Corot à Utrillo, Musée Carnavalet, March-May, 5 nrs
PARIS 2, Cent chefs-d'oeuvre prêtés par les plus grands amateurs de Paris, Musée Jacquemart-André, Summer, 1 nr
RECKLINGHAUSEN, Polarität, Das Apollinische und das Dionysische, Städtische Kunsthalle, June-July, 2 nrs
SAN FRANCISCO, French paintings of the 19th century from the Collection of Mrs Mellon Bruce, The California Palace of the Legion of Honor, 15 June-30 July, 1 nr
* SCARBOROUGH, —, —, —, —
WOLFSBURG, Französische Malerei von Delacroix bis Picasso, Stadthalle, 8 April-31 May, 8 nrs

1961-62
BALTIMORE, ETC, VvG Paintings, watercolors and drawings, *Baltimore*, The Baltimore Museum of Art, 18 October-26 November
Cleveland, The Cleveland Museum of Art, 5 December-14 January
Buffalo [N.Y.], Albright Art Gallery, 30 January-1 March
Boston [Mass.], Museum of Fine Arts, 22 March-29 April, 142 nrs [81 paintings, 61 drawings]
LIÈGE, BREDA, Aquarelles et gouaches hollandaises de 1850 à nos jours, *Liège*, Musée des Beaux-Arts, 24 November-8 January
Breda, Nederlandse aquarellen en gouaches, etc., De Beyerd, Cultureel Centrum, 26 January-4 March, 4 nrs
TOKYO, KYOTO, Exposition d'Art français 1840-1940, *Tokyo*, Musée National de Tokyo, 3 November-15 January
Kyoto, Musée Municipal à Kyoto, 26 January-15 March, 1 nr

1962
AMSTERDAM, Maîtres français XIX-XX siècle, Kunsthandel E. J. van Wisselingh, 14 May-9 June, 3 nrs
* ANN ARBOR, A generation of draughtsmen, University of Michigan, Museum of Art, 25 April-29 May, 29 nrs
BRUSSELS, OTTERLO, Les XX 1883-1893, *Brussels*, Koninklijke Musea voor Schone Kunsten, 17 February-8 April
Otterlo, Rijksmuseum Kröller-Müller, 15 April-17 June, 4 nrs
CAMBRIDGE, Forty master drawings from the collection of John Nicholas Brown, Fogg Art Museum, Harvard University, Summer, 1 nr
* FORT WORTH, —, Fort Worth Art Center, May, —
LONDON 1, VvG Van Gogh's life in his Drawings, Van Gogh's Relations with Signac, Marlborough Fine Art Ltd, May-June, 71 nrs and 19 documents
LONDON 2, French Masters, Marlborough Fine Art Ltd, June-July, 1 nr
LONDON 3, Recent Acquisitions XVII, Arthur Tooth & Sons Ltd, 14 November-15 December, 1 nr
LONDON 4, XIX and XX Century French Paintings, drawings and bronzes, The Lefèvre Gallery, November-December, 1 nr
LONDON 5, Primitives to Picasso, Royal Academy of Arts, Winter, 2 nrs
MANCHESTER, Master drawings from the Witt and Courtauld Collections, Whitworth Art Gallery of the University, 17 November-22 December, 1 nr
MINNEAPOLIS, NEW YORK, The Nineteenth Century: 125 Master Drawings, *Minneapolis*, University Gallery, University of Minnesota, 26 March-23 April
New York, The Solomon R. Guggenheim Museum, 15 May-1 July, 3 nrs
NEW YORK, Loan Exhibition of Paintings from private collections, Metropolitan Museum of Art, Summer, 2 nrs
PROVINCETOWN [MASS.], OTTAWA, The Controversial Century 1850-1950, Paintings from the Collection of Walter P. Chrysler Jr, Chrysler Art
Provincetown [Mass.], Chrysler Art Museum of Provincetown, —, 5 nrs
Ottawa, —, —, 5 nrs
RECKLINGHAUSEN, Idee und Vollendung, Kunsthalle, 19 May-15 July, 10 nrs
SAN FRANCISCO, The Henry P. McIlhenny Collection, The California Palace of the Legion of Honor, 15 June-31 July, 1 nr
WARSAW, VvG Paintings, drawings, etching [National Museum], 8-18 October, 100 nrs, collection Kröller-Müller Museum, Otterlo
WASHINGTON, Exhibition of the collection of Mr and Mrs André Meyer, National Gallery of Art, 9 June-8 July, 3 nrs

1962-63
PITTSBURGH, ETC, VvG, *Pittsburgh*, Carnegie Institute, 18 October-4 November,
Detroit, Detroit Institute of Arts, 11 December-29 January
Kansas City, William Rockhill Nelson Gallery of Art and Mary Atkins Museum of Fine Arts, 7 February-26 March, 142 nrs

1963
AMSTERDAM, Maîtres français XIXme et XXme siècle, E. J. van Wisselingh, 18 November-20 December, 1 nr
EDINBURGH, The Maitland gift and related pictures, National Gallery of Scotland, — 3 nrs
HAMBURG, Wegbereiter der modernen Malerei Cézanne-Gauguin-Van Gogh-Seurat, Kunstverein, 4 May-14 July, 29 nrs [17 paintings, 12 drawings]
HARTFORD [CONN.], Harvest of Plenty, Wadsworth Atheneum, 24 October-1 December, 1 nr
HUMLEBAEK [DENMARK], VvG collection Vincent van Gogh Stichting, Louisiana Museum, 24 October-8 December, 120 nrs
LONDON 1, Private views, works from the collection of 20 friends of the Tate Gallery, Tate Gallery, 18 April-19 May, 1 nr
LONDON 2, A Loan Exhibition of the French Impressionists and some of their contemporaries, Wildenstein, 24 April-18 May, 2 nrs
LONDON 3, A great period of French Painting, Marlborough Fine Art Ltd, June-July, 1 nr
LONDON 4, XIX and XX Century French Paintings and Drawings, The Lefèvre Gallery, November-December, 3 nrs
* MIAMI, Renoir to Picasso 1914, Joe and Emily Lowe Art Gallery, University of Miami, —, —
NEW YORK 1, Reader's Digest collection, M. Knoedler & Co, 15 May-8 June, 1 nr
NEW YORK 2, Loan Exhibition Paintings from Private collections, Metropolitan Museum of Art, Summer, 1 nr
NEW YORK 3, Master drawings from the Art Institute of Chicago, Wildenstein, 17 October-30 November, 3 nrs
PARIS, L'Aquarelle néerlandaise au siècle dernier, Institut néerlandais, 28 February-31 March, 7 nrs
PHILADELPHIA, A world of Flowers, Philadelphia Museum of Art, 2 May-9 June, 2 nrs
SCHAFFHAUSEN, Die Welt des Impressionismus, Museum zu Allerheiligen, 29 June-29 September, 5 nrs
SHEFFIELD, VvG Paintings and drawings lent by Ir V. W. van Gogh, Graves Art Gallery, 20 April-12 May, 20 nrs
TEL AVIV, HAIFA, VvG, *Tel Aviv*, Tel Aviv Museum, Helena Rubinstein Pavilion, January-February
Haifa, Municipal Museum of Modern Art, February-March, 101 nrs, collection Kröller-Müller Museum, Otterlo
UTICA, NEW YORK, Armory Show, 50th Anniversary Exhibition, *Utica*, Munson Williams Proctor Institute, 17 February-31 March
New York, Armory of the 69th Regiment, 6-28 April, 5 nrs

1963-64
AMSTERDAM, Hollandse kunstenaars in hun ontboezemingen, Rijksmuseum, 2 December-2 February, letters

1964
BRUSSELS, Aquarellen, Gouaches en Pastellen van de 19de eeuw tot heden, Koninklijke Musea voor Schone Kunsten van België, 25 January-19 April, 1 nr
KASSEL, Internationale Ausstellung Documenta III, Alte

Galerie, 27 June-5 October, 8 nrs [drawings]
LAREN, Schilderkunst uit la Belle Époque, Singer Museum, 4 July-16 September, 3 nrs and 1 supplement nr
LAUSANNE, Chefs-d'oeuvre des collections suisses de Manet à Picasso, Palais de Beaulieu, —, 6 nrs
NEW YORK 1, The Educated Eye, Perls Galleries, 4-23 May, 1 nr
NEW YORK 2, VvG Van Gogh and Expressionism, The Solomon R. Guggenheim Foundation, 1 July-13 September, 98 nrs [33 paintings by v. Gogh; 65 paintings by 28 other artists]
NEW YORK 3, Important European Paintings from Texas Private Collections, Marlborough-Gerson Gallery Inc., November-December, 1 nr
PARIS 1, Fondation Rodolphe Staechelin, de Corot à Picasso, Musée National d'Art Moderne, 10 April-28 June, 4 nrs
PARIS 2, l'Héritage de Delacroix, M. Knoedler & Co, 8-30 June, 1 nr
WASHINGTON, NEW YORK, VvG paintings, watercolors and drawings, *Washington*, The Washington Gallery of Modern Art, 2 February-19 March
New York, The Solomon R. Guggenheim Museum, 2 April-28 June 120 nrs
ZEIST, Kunstbezit uit Zeist en omgeving, Het Slot, 15 May-21 June, 1 nr
ZUNDERT, VvG Tekeningen van Vincent van Gogh, Parochiehuis, 28 May-8 June, 30 nrs

1964-65
DELFT, ANTWERP, De schilder in zijn wereld, *Delft*, Stedelijk Museum 'Het Prinsenhof', 19 December-24 January, 5 nrs
Antwerp, Koninklijk Museum voor Schone Kunsten, 6 February-14 March, 5 nrs

1965
AMSTERDAM, Maîtres français XIXme et XXme siècle, E.J. van Wisselingh, 25 November-20 December, 1 nr
BERLIN, Von Delacroix bis Picasso Ein Jahrhundert französischer Malerei, National-Galerie, Staatliche Museen zu Berlin, September-October, 2 nrs
BORDEAUX, Chefs-d'oeuvre de la Peinture française dans les Musées de l'Ermitage et de Moscou, Musée des Beaux-Arts, 14 May-6 September, 3 nrs
BUDAPEST, French Paintings from Delacroix-Picasso, Musée des Beaux-Arts, [Prague-Berlin-Budapest], —, 1 nr
CHARLEROI, GHENT, VvG Peintures-aquarelles-dessins, *Charleroi*, Palais des Beaux-Arts, 9 January-9 February
Ghent, Museum voor Schone Kunsten, 19 February-21 March, 81 nrs [41 paintings, 40 drawings]
GUILDFORD, 19th and 20th century French paintings and drawings, Reid Gallery, 4-23 December, 1 nr
THE HAGUE, —, Galerie Nova Spectra, January [handwritten exhibition list], 1 nr
LEIDEN, Uit het kunstbezit van de leden van de Vereniging van Belangstellenden in de Lakenhal, De Lakenhal, 25 February-29 March, 1 nr
LONDON, Nineteenth and Twentieth Century French paintings from English Private collections, Marlborough Fine Art Ltd, June-July, 1 nr
NEW YORK 1, Masterpieces of Modern Art, arranged by courtesy of the Thannhauser Foundation, Guggenheim Museum, April-September, 9 nrs including 3 original letters
NEW YORK 2, Olympia's Progene, French Impressionist and Post-Impressionist Paintings, Wildenstein, 28 October-27 November, 11 nrs
NUENEN, VvG, Townhall, 8-29 May, 41 nrs
PITTSBURGH [PENN.], The Seashore paintings of the 19th and 20th centuries, Museum of Art, 22 October-5 December, 1 nr
PRAGUE, French paintings from Delacroix-Picasso, National Museum, April-May, 1 nr [see Budapest]
SAN FRANCISCO, The San Francisco collector, M.H. de Young Memorial Museum, 21 September-17 October, 1 nr

1965-66
PARIS, Chefs-d'oeuvre de la Peinture française dans les Musées de Leningrad et de Moscou, Musée du Louvre, September-January, 3 nrs
STOCKHOLM, GÖTEBORG, VvG Tentoongestelde werken uit de collectie Vincent van Gogh Stichting, Amsterdam, *Stockholm*, Moderna Museet, 22 October-19 December
Göteborg, Göteborgs Konstmuseum, 30 December-20 February, 108 nrs [60 paintings, 48 drawings]

1966
AMSTERDAM, Maîtres français XIXme et XXme siècle, E.J. van Wisselingh & Co, 21 November-23 December, 1 nr

ARNHEM, VvG Loan works from the Kröller-Müller Museum, Gemeente Museum, 19 January-28 February, 61 nrs [42 paintings, 19 drawings]
BASLE, Autour de l'Impressionnisme, Galerie Beyeler, June-July, 4 nrs
BELGRADE, VvG collection Kröller-Müller Otterlo, Narodni Muzej, 30 October-20 December, 83 nrs
BORDEAUX, La peinture française, collections américaines, —, — 13 May-15 September, 1 nr
BRUSSELS, Van en over de 'xx' en 'La Libre Esthétique', Koninklijk Museum voor Schone Kunsten, 29 April-10 July, 1 nr
GOUDA, Collectie Van Baaren [Utrecht], Catharina Gasthuis, 4 June-2 October, 6 nrs
LAREN, De Kunst van het Verzamelen, Singer Museum, 18 June-18 September, 7 nrs
LONDON, XIX and XX century French Paintings and Drawings, The Lefèvre Gallery, November-December, 1 nr
NEW YORK 1, Impressionist Treasures from private collections New York, M. Knoedler & Co, 12-29 January, 3 nrs
NEW YORK 2, Summer Loan Exhibition, Paintings, Drawings and Sculpture from private collections, The Metropolitan Museum of Art, Summer, 7 nrs [5 paintings, 2 drawings]
PARIS, ALBI, VvG dessinateur, [Fondation VvG] *Paris*, Institut néerlandais, 28 January-20 March
Albi, Musée-Toulouse-Lautrec, 27 May-31 August, 90 nrs [drawings]
WASHINGTON, French Paintings from the collection of Mr and Mrs Paul Mellon and Mrs Mellon Bruce, National Gallery of Art, without date, 9 nrs
ZURICH, Die neue Galerie des Kunsthistorischen Museums Wien, Von Caspar David Friedrich bis Edvard Munch, Kunsthaus, February-March, 2 nrs

1966-67
JERUSALEM, ETC, Paintings from the collection of Joseph H. Hazen, *Jerusalem*, The Israel Museum, Summer, 1 nr
Cambridge [Mass.], Fogg Art Museum, Harvard University
Honolulu [Hawaii], Honoluly Academy of Arts
Berkeley [Cal.], University Art Museum, University of California
Houston [Texas], Museum of Fine Arts of Houston
Los Angeles [Cal.], The Art Galleries, University of California, 1 nr

1967
GLASGOW, A Man of Influence: Alex Reid, The Scottish Arts Council, 21 October-11 November, 4 nrs
LILLE, ZURICH, VvG Dessins, Aquarelles, *Lille*, Palais des Beaux-Arts, 14 January-13 March, 91 nrs
Zurich, Kunsthaus, 5 April-4 June, with 5 supplement nrs
MONTREAL, Man and His World, International Fine Arts Exhibition, Expo '67, 28 April-27 October, 3 nrs
NEW YORK, PHILADELPHIA —, *New York*, Gallery of Modern Art, 3 January-12 March
Philadelphia, Selections from the collection of Dr and Mrs T. Edward Hanley, Bradford [Pa.], Philadelphia Museum of Art, 6 April-28 May, 2 nrs
OSTEND, Europa 1900, Musée des Beaux-Arts, 3 June-30 September, 1 nr
PARIS, Chefs-d'oeuvre des collections suisses de Manet à Picasso, Orangerie des Tuileries, — 7 nrs
RALEIGH, North Carolina collects, North Carolina Museum of Art, 10-29 October, 1 nr
TILBURG, Textielambacht in de schilderkunst 16e-20e eeuw, Nederlands Textielmuseum, 21 April-1 August, 3 nrs
WASHINGTON, LOS ANGELES, 100 European paintings & drawings from the collection Mr and Mrs Leigh B. Block, Chicago, *Washington*, National Gallery of Art, 4 May-11 June,
Los Angeles, County Museum of Art, 21 September-2 November, 4 nrs
VIENNA, Meisterzeichnungen aus dem Museum der Schönen Künste in Budapest, Graphische Sammlung Albertina, 22 May-9 July, 1 nr
WOLFSBURG, VvG Gemälde, Aquarelle, Zeichnungen, [VvG Foundation], Stadthalle, 18 February-2 April, 129 nrs

1967-68
DALLAS, ETC, VvG Drawings, Watercolors, *Dallas*, Dallas Museum of Fine Arts, 6 October-4 November
Philadelphia, Philadelphia Museum of Art, 17 November-31 December
Toledo, The Toledo Museum of Art, 20 January-3 March
Ottawa, The National Gallery of Canada, 14 March-15 April, 90 nrs
PARIS, Vingt ans d'acquisitions au Musée du Louvre

1947-1967, Orangerie des Tuileries, 16 December-March, 4 nrs
STUTTGART, Gemälde, Graphik, Plastik Katalog Nr 1, Galerie Valentien, 9 December-17 February, 1 nr

1968
THE HAGUE, Enkele aspecten van het stilleven, Galerie Nova Spectra, 20 March-14 April, 1 nr
LIÈGE, VvG, Musée des Beaux-Arts, 3-30 September, 90 nrs
MINNEAPOLIS, Etc, Loan exhibition selections from the drawing collection of David Daniels, *Minneapolis*, The Minneapolis Institute of Arts, 22 February-21 April
Chicago, Art Institute of Chicago, 3 May-23 June
Kansas City, Nelson Gallery-Atkins Museum, 11 July-29 September
Cambridge [Mass.], Fogg Art Museum, 16 October-25 November, 1 nr
MUNICH, Deutsche und französische Aquarelle und Zeichnungen 1870-1930, Staatliche Graphische Sammlung, 26 April-17 July, 3 nrs
NEW YORK, Neo-Impressionism, The Solomon R. Guggenheim Museum, February-April, 1 nr
PARIS, Maîtres du blanc et noir au XIXe siècle, Musée du Louvre [Cabinet des Dessins], summer, 1 nr

1968-69
LONDON, VvG Paintings and Drawings of the VvG Foundation, Hayward Gallery, 23 October-12 January, 204 nrs

1969
BASLE, Watercolors, drawings, gouaches, Galerie Beyeler, January-March, 1 nr
CAMBRIDGE [MASS.], Grenville L. Winthrop Retrospective for a collector, Fogg Museum of Art, 23 January-31 March, 2 nrs
HUMLEBAEK, VvG Tegninger og akvareller, [VvG Foundation] Louisiana Museum, 25 January-16 March, 46 nrs
LONDON 1, Art detection, painting and the x-ray, Thos. Agnew & Sons, 4-28 March, 1 nr
LONDON 2, European drawings from the National Gallery of Canada, Colnaghi's, 3 July-1 August, 1 nr
MEMPHIS, The Armand Hammer Collection, Brooks Memorial Art Gallery, 2 October-30 December, 1 nr
MUNICH Europäische Meisterwerke aus Schweizer Sammlungen, Staatliche Graphische Sammlung, 8 August-19 October, 4 nrs
ST. ÉTIENNE, Cent dessins du Musée de Wuppertal, Musée d'Art et d'Industrie de Saint Étienne, 18 March-28 April, 1 nr
STUTTGART, Von Ingres bis Picasso, Französische Zeichnungen des 19. Jahrhunderts aus dem Besitz der Graphischen Sammlung der Staatsgalerie Stuttgart, Staatsgalerie Stuttgart, 16 April-6 July, 5 nrs

1969-70
LOS ANGELES, ETC, VvG Paintings and drawings [VvG Foundation], *Los Angeles*, Los Angeles County Museum of Art, 14 October-1 December
St. Louis, City Art Museum of St. Louis, 20 December-1 February, 114 nrs [68 paintings, 45 drawings, 1 lithography]
Philadelphia, Philadelphia Museum of Art, 28 February-5 April, 69 nrs [paintings only]
Columbus, The Columbus Gallery of Fine Arts, 5 March-5 April, 46 nrs [45 drawings and 1 lithography]
PARIS, De Raphaël à Picasso, Dessins de la Galerie Nationale du Canada, Musée du Louvre, 28 November-2 February, 1 nr

1970
FRANKFURT/M, VvG Zeichnungen und Aquarelle, Frankfurter Kunstverein, 30 April-21 June, 65 nrs
LONDON, Summer Exhibition, French Paintings and Sculpture of the Nineteenth and Twentieth Centuries, O'Hana Gallery, 13 May-19 September, 2 nrs
MUNICH, PARIS, VvG Europäischer Expressionismus, *Munich*, Haus der Kunst, 7 March-10 May, 2 nrs
Paris, l'Expressionisme Européen, Musée National d'Art Moderne, 26 May-27 July, 1 nr [F 462]
OSAKA, Expo 70, Museum of Fine Arts, 13 March-13 September, 1 nr [F 429]
PARIS, Maurice Denis, Orangerie des Tuileries, 3 June-31 August, 1 nr [F 319]
WASHINGTON, The Armand Hammer Collection, Smithsonian Institution, —, 1 nr [see Memphis 1969]

Selected Bibliography

I. BIBLIOGRAPHIES [arranged chronologically]

SCHEIWILLER, GIOVANNI. Nota bibliografica. 476 References. Included in Lamberto Vitali. Vincent van Gogh. Arte moderna straniera no 6, Milano, 1936, and in: Marco Valsecchi. Disegni di Vincent van Gogh. Arte Moderna straniera no 8, Milano, 1942.
BROOKS JR., CHARLES MATTOON. Vincent van Gogh a Bibliography. From 1890 through 1940. Introduction and Notes by the author. 777 References. New York, 1942.
BUCKMAN, EDUARD. Bibliography Vincent van Gogh. From 1940 through July 1951. 273 References. Supplement: 1940 through June 1953, 35 pp. Type-Script. Richmond [Virginia], 1954.

II. LETTERS [arranged chronologically]

GOGH, VINCENT WILLEM VAN. Extraits des lettres de Vincent [van] Gogh à E. Bernard [1887-90]. Mercure de France 7, 1893, 333-39; 8, 1893, 1-22, 112-22, 211-17, 303-15; 9, 1893, 69-76, 109-19, 263-72; 10, 1894, 28-35, 221-29; 11, 1894, 248-61; 12, 1894, 17-25; 13, 1895, 208-19.
— [A collection of Van Gogh letters] Van Nu en Straks 3, 1895, 3-36.
— Vincent van Gogh, Briefe. [Deutsche Ausgabe von Margarete Mauthner]. Berlin, 1906.
— Iz perepiski s druz'yami. Zolotye Runo 7-9, 1908, XIII-XVI.
— Pisma van-Goga. Zolotoye Runo 2-3, 1909, 80-86.
— Lettres de Vincent van Gogh à Emile Bernard, publiées par Ambroise Vollard. Paris, 1911.
— Vincent van Gogh, Briefe. [Deutsche Ausgabe von Margarete Mauthner]. Sechste Auflage. [Berlin], [1913].
— [Vincent van Gogh] pis'ma... E. Bernard. Apollon 7, 1913, 30-37; 8, 1913, 22-35; 9, 1913, 42-52; 10, 1913, 51-64.
— The letters of a Post-Impressionist; being the familiar correspondence of Vincent van Gogh. Boston and New York, 1913.
— Brieven aan zijn broeder. [Preface and notes by J. van Gogh-Bonger]. Amsterdam, Sloterdijk, 1914.
— ... Briefe an seinen Bruder; zusammengestellt von seiner Schwägerin Johanna van Gogh-Bonger. Die Übertragung der holländischen Briefe besorgte Leo Klein-Diepold, die der französischen Carl Einstein. Berlin, 1914.
— Predisloviye k 'pis'mam van Goga'. Moskwa, 1919.
— ... Briefe an Emile Bernard und Paul Gauguin. Basel, 1921.
— ... Brieven aan zijn broeder; uitgegeven en toegelicht door zijn schoonzuster J. van Gogh-Bonger, tweede druk. Amsterdam-Sloterdijk, 1923.
— Vincent van Gogh; Briefe, mit zwölf Abbildungen. Berlin, [1924].
— Briefe an Emile Bernard, Paul Gauguin, Paul Signac und andere. Herausgegeben und aus dem französischen neu übertragen von Hans Graber. Basel, 1924.
— [Letters], edited by Eber László. Budapest, 1924.
— Vier unveröffentlichte Briefe an die Familie der 'Arleserin'. Das Kunstblatt 10, 1926, 449-55.
— Recueil des lettres à Emile Bernard. Tonnerre, 1926.
— Neue Briefe von Van Gogh, Antiquitäten-Rundschau 25, 1926.
— The letters of Vincent van Gogh to his brother, 1872-1886; with a memoir by his sister-in-law, Johanna van Gogh-Bonger. London, 1927.
— ... Briefe an seinen Bruder. Berlin, 1928.
— ... Briefe an Emile Bernard, Paul Gauguin, Paul Signac und andere, mit fünfzehn Reproduktionen. 2. berichtigte und erweiterte Ausgabe. Basel, 1929.
— Further letters of Vincent van Gogh to his brother, 1886-1889. London, 1929.
— ... 'Pisma'. [Translation of letters with comment by N. M. Sjtsjokotow]. Moscow and Leningrad, 1935.
— ... Breve i udvalg og oversaettelse ved Kai Flor. København, 1936.
— ... Letters to an artist; from Vincent van Gogh to Anton Ridder van Rappard, 1881-1885. Translated from the Dutch by Rela van Messel, with an introduction by Walter Pach. New York, 1937.
— ... Lettres de Vincent van Gogh à son frère Théo; comprenant un choix de lettres françaises originales et de lettres traduites du hollandais par Georges Philippart et précédées d'une notice biographique par Charles Terrasse. Paris, 1937.
— ... Brieven aan A. G. A. Ridder van Rappard, 1881-1885. Amsterdam, 1937.
— ... Briefe an den Maler Anthon van Rappard, 1881-1885. Wien, 1937.
— ... Briefe an Emile Bernard, Paul Gauguin, Paul Signac und andere, herausgegeben von Hans Graber, mit zwanzig Reproduktionen. Dritte vermehrte Auflage. Basel, 1938.
— ... [Letters translated into Bulgarian by K. Tzonev. 1939].
— Lettere al Fratello di Vincent van Gogh a cura di Marco Valsecchi, Milano, 1946.
— Verzamelde Brieven van Vincent van Gogh [Preface and Notes Ir V. W. van Gogh]. 4 Vol., 3rd edition, Amsterdam, Antwerpen, 1952.
— Verzamelde Brieven van Vincent van Gogh [Preface and Notes Ir V. W. van Gogh]. 2 Vol., 4th edition, Amsterdam, Antwerpen, 1955.
— Correspondance complète de Vincent van Gogh [Preface and Notes by Georges Charensol]. 3 Vol., Paris, 1960.
— Briefe an die jüngste Schwester und an die Mutter [Introduction by Eugen Skasa-Weisz]. München, 1961.
— The letters of Vincent van Gogh, Selected, Edited and Introduced by Mark Roskill. London, Glasgow, 1963.
— The Complete Letters of Vincent van Gogh. Introduction by V. W. van Gogh. Preface and Memoir by Mrs J. van Gogh-Bonger. 3 Vol.. Greenwich [Connecticut], 1966.
— Van Gogh. Pisma. [Preface P. V. Melkovoy. Redaction J. I. Kusnetsov]. Leningrad, Moscow, 1966.

III. CATALOGUES [arranged chronologically]

FAILLE, JACOB-BAART DE LA. L'Oeuvre de Vincent van Gogh. Catalogue Raisonné. 4 vol., 1664 Nos. Paris, Brussels, 1928.
FAILLE, JACOB-BAART DE LA. Les Faux Van Gogh. 174 Nos. Brussels, 1930.
FAILLE, JACOB-BAART DE LA. Vincent van Gogh. Préface de Charles Terrasse. 817 Nos. Paris, London, New York, 1939 [Hypérion].
SCHERJON, W. Catalogue des Tableaux par Vincent van Gogh décrits dans ses lettres. Périodes St Rémy et Auvers sur Oise. 149 Nos. Utrecht, 1932.
SCHERJON, W. and GRUYTER, W. JOS. DE. Vincent van Gogh's Great Period. Arles, St Rémy and Auvers sur Oise [complete catalogue]. 2 Vol., 227 Nos. Amsterdam, 1937.
VANBESELAERE, W. De Hollandsche periode [1880-1885] in het werk van Vincent van Gogh [Preface, August Vermeylen]. Amsterdam, Antwerpen, 1937. [French edition in the same year].

IV. ARTICLES, BULLETINS AND PUBLISHED LECTURES [arranged alphabetically].

AIGRISSE, GILBERTE. l'Evolution du symbole chez Van Gogh. *Psyche*, 92, 1954.
— La ronde des prisonniers. *De Tafelronde*, II, 8, 9, 1955, 18-22.
— Psychoanalyse de Vincent van Gogh. *de Nevelvlek*, May 1955, 56-60.
ANFRAY, LOUIS. Les mangeurs de Pommes de Terre dans l'oeuvre de Vincent van Gogh. *Art Documents*, 31, 1953.
— Méthode d'examen d'un tableau. *Art Documents*, 39, 1953.
— Une énigme Van Gogh. *Art Documents*, 39, 1953.
— Les Mangeurs de pommes de terre dans l'oeuvre de Vincent van Gogh. Réponse à l'article de M. L. Gans. *Art Documents*, 40, 1954, 6, 7.
— Le cuivre gravé 'Portrait de l'homme à la pipe'. *Art Documents*, 42, 1954.
— Vincent van Gogh à Auvers-sur-Oise. *Art Documents*, 43, 1954.
— La Vérité torturée. *Art Documents*, 44, 1954.
— Le cuivre gravé par Vincent van Gogh serait un 'Portrait d'Arlésienne'. *Arts Documents*, 45, 1954.
— Les Mangeurs de pommes de terre dans l'oeuvre de Vincent van Gogh. *Museumjournaal* I, 1955, 177-83.
— l'Identité des Mangeurs de pommes de terre. *Les Cahiers de Van Gogh*, 3, 1958, 11-17, 20.
APPLETON, MARG. An unnoticed drawing by Vincent van Gogh. *Museum News*, V, 4, 1947, 2-3.
BAZIN, G. La méridienne de Van Gogh, aquarelle du Louvre. *Revue du Louvre*, XIV, 1, 1964, 45-46.
BERNARD, EMILE. Souvenirs sur Van Gogh. *l'Amour de l'Art*, V, 1924, 393-400.
BERNARD, MICHEL-ANGE. Emile Bernard et Vincent van Gogh. *Art Documents*, 16, 17, 18, 21, 27, 1952; 29, 1953.
BEVER, AD VAN. Les Ainés. Un peintre maudit. Vincent van Gogh [1853-1890]. *La Plume* XVII, 373, 1905, 532-45, 596-609.
BLUM, HÉLÈNE P. Les chaises de Van Gogh. *Revue française de Psychoanalyse*, XXI, 1, 1958, 82-93.
BOIME, ALBERT. A source for van Gogh's Potato-eaters. *Gazette des Beaux Arts*, LXVII, 1167, 1966, 249-53.
BONGER, F. Vincent van Gogh als lezer. *Maandblad voor Beeldende Kunsten*, XXVI, March 1950, 53-66.
BRAUMANN, M. Bei Freunden Van Gogh's in Arles. *Kunst und Künstler*, XXVI, 1928, 451-54.
BREKELMANS, F.A. Vincent van Gogh en Zundert. *Jaarboek* [Breda], 1953.
BREMMER, H.P. Openingsrede. *Mededelingen*, The Hague, VIII, 5-6, 1953, 71-73.
BUCARELLI, PALMA. Acquisti della Galleria Nazionale d'Arte Moderna. *Bolletino d'Arte*, Roma, 1962.
BUCKMAN, EDW. Een onbekende brief van Van Gogh. *Kroniek van Kunst en Kultuur*, XV, 2, 1955, 44.
CARRIÈRE-RAVOUX, ADELINE. Les Souvenirs d'Adeline Ravoux sur le séjour de Vincent van Gogh à Auvers-sur-Oise. *Les Cahiers de Van Gogh*, 1, 1956, 7-17.
CARROY, CHRISTIAN. Een Panoramalandschap van Van Gogh. *Bull. Rijksmuseum*, Amsterdam, X, 4, 1962, 139-42.
CHARENSOL, GEORGES. Van Gogh à Marseille. *Revue des Deux Mondes*, 3, 1957, 144-51.
— Van Gogh en Provence. *Revue des Deux Mondes*, 6, 1959, 336-44.
COHEN GOSSCHALK, JOHAN. Vincent van Gogh. *Elsevier's Geïllustreerd Maandschrift*, XXX, 1905, 219-34.
COOPER, DOUGLAS. The Yellow house and its Significance. *Mededelingen*, The Hague, VIII, 5-6, 1953, 94-106.
CUNNINGHAM, CHARLES. Roulin the Postman, by Vincent van Gogh. *Bull. Museum of Fine Arts*, Boston, XXXIV, 201, 1936, 2-3.
— A selfportrait by Van Gogh. *Wadsworth Atheneum Bulletin*, II, 53, 1955, 2.
DERKERT, CARLO. Theory and Practice in Van Gogh's Dutch Painting. And: Landscape with Cornshocks. *Konsthistorisk Tidskrift*, XV, 3-4, 1946, 97-120, and 121-130.
DOITEAU, VICTOR. La curieuse figure du dr Gachet. *Aesculape*, XIII, 1923 and XIV, 1924.
DOITEAU, VICTOR et LEROY, EDGAR. Van Gogh et le portrait du dr Rey. *Aesculape*, XXIX, 1939, 42-47, 50-55.
EBBINGE WUBBEN, J.C. Een schenking aan de Stichting Museum Boymans. *Bull. Museum Boymans*, Rotterdam, II, 2, 1951. 21-26.
FAILLE, JACOB-BAART DE LA. Unbekannte Bilder von Vincent van Gogh. *Cicerone*, XIX, 1927, 101-02.
— Een merkwaardig zelfportret van Vincent van Gogh. *Phoenix*, III, 9, 1948, 215.
— Een onbekende brief van Vincent. *Kroniek van Kunst en Kultuur*, XIV, 3, 1954, 52-54.
— Le mystère du cuivre gravé: portrait à la pipe du docteur Gachet. *Les Cahiers de Van Gogh*, 3, 1958, 4-7.
— Un portrait de Théo par Vincent. *Les Cahiers de Van Gogh*, 4, 1958, 3-4.
FIERENS, PAUL. Un dessin de Vincent van Gogh. *Bull. Musées Royaux des Beaux Arts*, Brussels, 1, 1956, 40-47.
— Les Faux van Gogh. *Journal des Débats*, XXXVII, 25, 1930, 679-81.
FLORISOONE, MICHEL. Van Gogh et Guillaumin. *Bull. des Musées de France*, I, 1950, 8-10.
— Deux grands chefs-d'oeuvre de Van Gogh entrent au Musée du Louvre. *Bull. des Musées de France*, VI, 1949, 139-50.
FRY, ROGER. Van Gogh. *The Burlington Magazine*, XLIII, 1923, 306-08.
GACHET, PAUL. Vincent van Gogh aux Indépendants. Paris, *Les Beaux Arts*, 1953.
— Van Gogh à Auvers, Histoire d'un tableau. Paris, *Les Beaux Arts*, 1953.
— A propos de quelques erreurs sur Vincent van Gogh. *La Revue des Arts*, Musées de France, IX, 2, 1959, 85-86.
GANS, LOUIS. Een vermeende versie van de 'aardappeleters'. Onjuiste interpretatie van Van Gogh's brieven. *Museumjournaal*, I, 4, 1955, 98-102.
— Twee onbekende tekeningen uit Van Gogh's Hollandse Tijd. *Museumjournaal*, II, 7-8, 1957, 117-18.
— Vincent van Gogh en de Schilders van de Petit Boulevard *Museumjournaal*, IV, 5-6, 1958, 85-93.
GARNIER, CHR. Auvers-sur-Oise et Van Gogh. *Revue des deux Mondes*, I, 1959.
GAUGUIN, P. Vincent van Gogh. *Kunst und Künstler*, VIII, 1910, 579-86.
GAUNT, W. a.o. *Art News Annual* [New York] XIX, 48, 1950, special Van Gogh issue.
GAUTHIER, M. La Femme en bleu. *Les Nouvelles Littéraires*, April, 1-6, 1953, Febr.-April, 5, 1954.
GELDER, J.G. VAN. Vincent van Gogh: pentekening 1883. *Leven en werken*, XIX, 1934, 653.
— De Genesis van de Aardappeleters, [1885], *Beeldende Kunst* XXCIII, I, 1942, 1-8. English edition: Gallery Books 17, London, 1947.
— Vincent's Begin. *De Tafelronde*, II, 8-9, 1955, 23-28.
GIAVANOLA W. VAN. Bibliografia su Van Gogh. *Le Arte*, 3, Jan.-Febr. 1952, 37-41.
GOGH, VINCENT W. VAN. Aesthetic Exercise III and: Portrait of Alexander Reid Esq. *the Scottish Art Review*, II, 2, 1948, 13-16; and 21-22.
— Tralbaut over Van Gogh. *Museumjournaal*, I, 5, 1955, 118-22.
— Madame Roulin – La Berceuse door Vincent en P. Gauguin. *Museumjournaal*, I, 2, 1955, 46-48.
— Vincent van Gogh en andere Nederlandse en Franse schilders beoordeeld door een Deense tijdgenoot. *Museumjournaal*, II, 3-4, 1956, 52-58.
— Vincent van Gogh: twee tekeningen uit de Borinage. *Museumjournaal* V, 4, 1959, 80-81.
— Van Gogh publicaties I. *Museumjournaal*, XIII, I, 1968, 271-73.
— Van Gogh publicaties 5. *Museumjournaal* XIII, 5, 1968, 42-45.
GOULINAT, J.G. Les collections Gustave Fayet. *l'Amour de l'Art*, VI, 4, 1925, 131-42.
GRUYTER W. JOS DE. Echt of Vals? Van Gogh's twee populieren bij Huinck & Scherjon, Amsterdam. *Elsevier's Geïllustreerd Maandschrift*, LXXX, 1930, 65-67.
— Theo and Vincent van Gogh. *Mededelingen*. The Hague, IX, 1-2, 1954, 2-5.
HAMMACHER, A.M. De lusten en de onlusten in de cultus van Vincent van Gogh. *De Gids*, XCV, 1931, II, 98-121.
— Van Gogh Centenary. *Scottish Art Review*, IV, 4, 1953.
— Van Gogh en de Maatschappij. *Mededelingen*, The Hague, VIII, 5-6, 1953, 74-79.
— Einige Betrachtungen zur Niederländischen Van Gogh Gedenkausstellung. *Schweizer Monatshefte*, Aug. 1953.
— Vincent van Gogh und sein Bruch mit der Gesellschaft. Lecture. Cologne, 1957.
HAVERKAMP BEGEMANN, E. Vroege tekeningen van Breitner en Van Gogh. *Bull. Museum Boymans*, Rotterdam, I, 4, 1950, 58-61.

HENNUS, M.F. Een portretje van Vincent van Gogh. *Maandblad voor Beeldende Kunsten*, X, Sept. 1936, 265-66.

HENTZEN, ALFRED. Der Garten Daubigny's von Vincent van Gogh. *Zeitschrift für Kunstgeschichte*, IV, 1935, 325-33.

— Nochmals 'der Garten Daubigny's' von Vincent van Gogh. *Zeitschrift für Kunstgeschichte*, V, 1936, 87-88.

HONEYMAN, T.J. Van Gogh a link with Glasgow. *Scottish Art Review*, II, 2, 1948, 16-20.

HULSKER, JAN. Van Gogh. *Maatstaf*, 1958-1961.

— Van Gogh's Dutch Years, *Delta*, III, 1, Spring 1960, 31-46.

— Zijn Naam Vincent is voor het Nageslacht. 150 Jaar Koninkrijk der Nederlanden. Amsterdam, 1963, 148-55.

— The Houses where van Gogh lived in The Hague. *Bull. Rijksmuseum Van Gogh*, Amsterdam, I, 1, 1969.

HUTTER, A. De vijf diagnoses van de ziekte van Vincent van Gogh. *Nederlandsch Tijdschrift voor Geneeskunde*, Febr. 1931.

JAFFE, HANS L.C. Vincent van Gogh en Hugo von Hofmannsthal. *De Tafelronde*, II, 8-9, 1955, 66-72.

— Een onbekende aquarel van Vincent van Gogh. *Museumjournaal*, II, 1, 2, 1956, 5-6.

— Vincent van Gogh en G.H. Breitner, een parallel? *Miscellanea*. Joseph Duverger. Bijdragen tot de kunstgeschiedenis der Nederlanden, I, Gent, 1968, 383-87.

JOOSTEN, ELLEN. De Berceuse uit de Kröller-Müller collectie. *Museumjournaal*, III, 2, 1957, 36-37.

— Het rijke begrip 'invloed'. *Museumjournaal*, V, 4, 1959, 73-76.

— De verzameling van Theo van Gogh. *Museumjournaal*, V, 8-9, 1959, 155-57.

JOOSTEN, JOOP M. Van Gogh publicaties 9-15. *Museumjournaal*, XIV, 3-5, 1969, 154-58, 216-20, 269-74; XV, 1-3, 1970, 47-50, 100-04.

JOURDAIN, F.A. A propos de Van Gogh. *Arts de France*, 11-12, 1947, 78, 103-06.

— Les Van Gogh du Père Tanguy. *Connaissance des Arts*, 90, 1959, 18-21.

KNUTTEL, G.WZN. Van Gogh der Holländer. Resumée XIII, *Congrès International de l'Histoire de l'Art*, 1932.

KOKOSCHKA, OSKAR. Van Gogh's Influence on Modern Painting. *Mededelingen*, the Hague, VIII, 5, 6, 1953, 79-81.

KRAUS, GERARD. Vincent van Gogh en de Psychiatrie. *Psychiatrische en Neurologische Bladen*, XLV, 1941, 985-1034.

— The relation of Theo and Vincent van Gogh. Lecture, Otterlo, 1953.

— De relatie tussen mens en kunstenaar. *Mededelingen*, the Hague, VIII, 5-6, 1953, 82-93.

KURZ, OTTO. Recent Research. *The Burlington Magazine*, XCII, 569, 1950, 239-40.

LANGUI, EMILE. Vincent van Gogh. La technique. *Les Arts Plastiques*, I, 1947, 29-38.

LEPROHON, PIERRE. Le Pont d'Asnières, inspirateur des peintres, *La Vie du Rail*, 9, Febr. 1964, 22-23.

LEYMARIE, JEAN. Symbole et Réalité chez Van Gogh. *Mededelingen*, the Hague, IX, 1-2, 1954, 41-49.

LOVGREN, SVEN. Van Gogh's 'Stjernenatt'. *Paletten*, 1957, 101-05.

LWOFF, NICOLAS. Buenos Aires, promenade du soir. *Arts*, 6, Oct. 1950, 3.

MAGRITTE, RENE. Van Gogh et la Liberté. *De Nevelvlek*, May 1955, 54-56.

MALRAUX, ANDRÉ. Van Gogh et les Peintres d'Auvers chez le Docteur Gachet. *l'Amour de l'Art*, XXXIII, 1952.

MAROIS, PIERRE. Le secret de Van Gogh, II, *France Illustration*, 138, 139, 1953.

MAURON, CHARLES. Vincent et Théo van Gogh, une symbiose. Lecture, Amsterdam, 1953.

— Notes sur la structure de l'Inconscient chez Van Gogh. *Psyche*, 75-78, Jan.-April 1953.

— Vincent et Théo. *l'Arc*, II, 8, 1959, 3-12.

MEERLOO, J.A.M. Een diagnostische strijd over Vincent van Gogh, *Psychiatrische en Neurologische Bladen*, 34, 1931.

— Three Artists. *The American Imago*, X, 3, 1953.

— Vincent van Gogh's quest for identity, *Nederlands Kunsthistorisch Jaarboek*, 14, 1963, 183-97.

MEYERSON, AKE. Van Gogh and the School of Pont-Aven. *Konsthistorisk Tidskrift*, XV, 1946, 97-120.

MINKOWSKA, FR. Notes sur Van Gogh. *Revue esthétique*, 1951, 151-57.

MÖBIUS, M.R. Vincent van Gogh. Zum Selbstbildnis von 1889. *Cicerone*, XVIII, 1926, 512-22.

MOTTE, DANIEL. l'Eglise d'Auvers. *Peintre*, 40, 1952, 5-6.

NAVRATIL, L. Aan welke ziekte leed van Gogh? *CIBA*, 1959, 209-16.

NORDENFALK, CARL. Van Gogh and Sweden. *Konsthistorisk Tidskrift*, XV, 1946, 85-98.

— Van Gogh and Literature. *Journal of Warburg and Courtauld Institutes*, London, X, 1947, 132-47.

NOVOTNY, FRITZ. Die Bilder Van Goghs nach fremden Vorbildern. *Festschrift* Kurt Badt, Berlin, 1961, 213-30.

— Zu einem unbekannten Selbstbildnis von Van Gogh. *Alte und Moderne Kunst*, VII, Sept., Oct. 1962.

— Die Zeichnungen van Gogh's in der Albertina. *Albertina Studien*, I, 1963, 15-20.

OP DE COUL, MARTHA. Van Gogh publicaties 7. *Museumjournaal* XIV, 1, 1969, 42-45.

PACH, WALTER. Vincent van Gogh. *International Studio*, 72, 284, 1920, 13-20.

PICA, A. Giudici Italiani su Van Gogh. *Le Arte*, 3, 1952, 7-12.

PFANNSTIEL, A. and SCHRETLEN, M. Van Gogh's Jardin de Daubigny. *Maandblad voor Beeldende Kunsten*, XIII, 1935, 140-145.

PLÜSS, EDUARD. Ungemalte Bilder von Vincent van Gogh. *Festschrift* Kurt Badt, Berlin, 1961, 231-59.

POLLACK, PETER J. What Vincent saw. *Bull. Art Institute of Chicago*, XLIV, 1, Febr. 1950, 5-9.

PRINZHORN, HANS. Genius and Madness. *Parnassus*, II, 1930, 19-20, 44.

PRIOU, J.-N. Van Gogh et la Famille Roulin. *Revue des P.T.T. de France*, X, 3, 1955, 26-33.

REWALD, JOHN. Van Gogh en Provence. *l'Amour de l'Art*, XVII, 1936, 289-98.

— Précisions sur Van Gogh. *l'Amour de l'Art*, XIX, 1938, 256-57.

— the Artist and the Land. *Art News Annual*, XIX, 48, 1950, 64-73.

RIESE, WALTHER. De ziekte van Vincent van Gogh. *CIBA*, VI, 5, 1958, 198-206.

ROBERT, MARTHE. Vincent van Gogh. Le Génie et son Double. *Preuves*, 204, 1968, 3-16.

ROSKILL, MARK. Van Gogh's blue cart and his creative process. *Oud Holland*, LXXXI, 1, 1966, 3-19.

SABLONIÈRE, MARGRIT DE. Een onbekende schets van Vincent van Gogh. *Museumjournaal*, I, 4, 1955, 68-69; and: *De Nevelvlek*. May 1955, 46-47.

— Sien. *De Tafelronde*, II, 8-9, 1955, 54-65.

— The biographical particulars about Vincent van Gogh. *Museumjournaal*, II, 1-2, 1956, 21-25.

— Een boek over Pictologie? *Museumjournaal*, II, 7-8, 1957, 118-20.

SCHERJON, WILLEM. Van Gogh traced by his letters. Letter to Chester Dale. *Art News*, XXVII, April 1929, 1-2.

— Proof of Genuineness of disputed Van Gogh. *Art News*, XXVIII, July 1930, 14-15.

SCHEYER, E. Far Eastern Art and French Impressionism. *The Art Quarterly*, VI, 2, 1943, 117-43.

SCHRETLEN, M.J. De Jardin de Daubigny van Vincent van Gogh. *Maandblad voor Beeldende Kunsten*, X, 1933, 44-48.

— Zie Pfannstiel, A.

SCHWARZ, HEINRICH. An unnoticed Drawing by Vincent van Gogh. *Museum Notes*, Rhode Island IV, April 1946.

SEUPHOR, MICHEL. Vincent van Gogh. Esquisse pour un portrait spiriteul. *Tout Dire*, 1945, 195-210.

SEZNEC, JEAN. Literary inspiration in Van Gogh. *Magazine of Art*, 43, 8, 1950, 282-88, 306-07.

SHAPIRO, MEYER. Un Tableau de Van Gogh. *Profils*, I, Oct. 1952.

TELLEGEN, ANNET. Geen Panorama landschap bij Van Gogh. *Bull. Rijksmuseum*. Amsterdam, XII, 2, 1964, 57-61.

— Vincent en Gauguin. *Museumjournaal*, XI, 1-2, 1966, 42-44.

— Vincent van Gogh's Appelboomgaard. De populierenlaan bij Vincent van Gogh, Van Gogh en Montmajour. *Bull. Museum Boymans-van Beuningen*, Rotterdam, XVIII, 1, 1967, 2-33.

— Van Gogh publicaties 2, *Museumjournaal*, XIII, 2, 1968, 117-22.

THANNHAUSER, HENRY. Van Gogh et John Russell. Documents Inédits. *L'Amour de l'Art*, XIX, 7, 1938, 281-86.

TRALBAUT, MARK E. Van Gogh's Japanisme. *Mededelingen*. The Hague, IX, 1-2, 1954, 6-40.

— Vincent Theo Johanna. Lecture. Amsterdam, 1953.

— Twee onuitgegeven Documenten. *De Tafelronde*, II, 8-9, 1955, 6-9.

— In Van Gogh's voetspoor te Nuenen. *De Toerist*, XXXIV, 8, 9, 11, 1955, 210-18ff.

— In Van Gogh's voetspoor te Antwerpen. *De Toerist*, XXXIV, 12, 1955, 361-71.

— Over de duurzaamheid van de huidige Van Gogh Cultus. *C.A.W.*, Antwerp, May-June 1955.

— Vincent van Gogh in het caf'conc op het raakpunt met Raffaëlli. Amsterdam, 1955.

— Vincent van Gogh en de Keramiek. *Mededelingen* Vrienden van de Nederlandse Ceramiek. Amsterdam, 2, 1955, 2-40.

— and LEURS, STAN. De verdwenen kerk van Nuenen. *Brabantia*, 1-2, 1957, 29-68.

— Archives Internationales de Van Gogh I, II, 1967-68.

VISSER, H.F.E. De literatuur over Vincent van Gogh. *De Beweging*, XIII, 1, 2, 1917, 322-40, 378-401.

WEISBACH. W. Der Stil Vincent van Goghs. *Universitas*, Stuttgart IX, 1955, 233-239.

WESTERMAN HOLSTIJN, A.J. Die psychologische Entwicklung Vincent van Goghs. *Imago*, X, 4, 1924, 389-417.

V. BOOKS [arranged alphabetically]

AURIER, G.-ALBERT. Oeuvres Posthumes. Paris, 1898.

BAARD, H.P. Gesprekken met Vincent. Haarlem, 1951.

BADER, ALFRED. Künstler-Tragik: Karl Stauffer, Vincent van Gogh. Basel, 1932.

BADT, KURT. Die Farbenlehre Van Goghs, Cologne, 1961.

BEER, JOACHIM. Essai sur les rapport de l'art et de la maladie de Vincent van Gogh. Thesis. Straatsbourg, 1936.

BEUCKEN, JEAN DE. Un portrait de Vincent van Gogh. Liège, [1939].

BOURNIQUEL, CAMILLE, a.o. Van Gogh. Coll. Génies et Réalités. Paris, 1968.

BREMMER, H.P. Vincent van Gogh, Inleidende beschouwingen. Amsterdam, 1911.

— Vincent van Gogh, 24 tekeningen uit zijn 'Hollandsche periode' verzameling Hidde Nijland. Amsterdam undated.

BROMIG-KOLLERITZ, K. Die Selbstbildnisse Vincent van Goghs, Versuch einer kunsthistorischen Erfassung der Darstellungen. Thesis [typescript] München, 1955.

BUCKMANN, MARK. Die Farbe bei Vincent van Gogh. Zürich, 1948.

CABANNE, PIERRE. Van Gogh, l'homme et son oeuvre. Paris, undated.

CHETHAM, CHARLES. The role of Vincent van Gogh's copies in the development of his art. Thesis [typescript] Cambridge, Mass. 1960.

COGNIAT, RAYMOND. Van Gogh. Paris, 1959.

COLIN, PIERRE. Van Gogh. Maîtres de l'art moderne. Paris, 1925.

COOPER, DOUGLAS. Zeichnungen und Aquarelle von Vincent van Gogh. Intro: Hugo von Hofmannsthal. Basel, 1954.

COQUIOT, GUSTAVE. Vincent van Gogh. Paris, 1923.

COURTHION, PIERRE. Van Gogh raconté par lui-même et par ses amis, ses contemporains, sa postérité. Genève, 1947.

DANTZIG, M.M. VAN. Vincent? a new method of identifying the artist and his work... Amsterdam, undated.

DOITEAU, VICTOR and LEROY, EDG. La Folie de Vincent van Gogh, Préface de Paul Gachet. Paris, 1928.

DOUWES, W.F. Vincent van Gogh. Amsterdam, [1930].

DURET, THÉODORE. Van Gogh. Paris, 1924.

DUTHUIT, GEORGES. Van Gogh, Lausanne, 1948.

ECKHARDT, WOLFGANG Van Gogh und Deutschland. Ein Beitrag zum Thema: Künstler und Publikum. Thesis. Berlin, 1956.

ELGAR, FRANK. Van Gogh. The Drawbridge. Paris, London, 1948.

— Van Gogh. Paris, 1958.

ERPEL, FRITZ. Die Selbstbildnisse Vincent van Goghs. Berlin, 1963.

ESTIENNE, C. Van Gogh. Genève, 1953.

FAILLE, J.-B. DE LA. l'Epoque française de Van Gogh. Paris, [1927].

FELS, FLORENT. Vincent van Gogh. Paris, 1928.

FLORISOONE, MICHEL. Van Gogh. Paris, 1937.

GACHET, PAUL. Souvenirs de Cézanne et de Van Gogh–Auvers 1873-1890. Paris, 1953.

— Paul van Rijssel, le docteur Gachet graveur. Paris, 1954.

— Deux Amis des Impressionistes, Le docteur Gachet et Murer. Paris, 1956.

GOGH, THÉO VAN. Lettres à son Frère Vincent. Intro. by V.W. van Gogh. Amsterdam, 1932.

GOGH, VINCENT W. VAN. Vincent van Gogh in England Compiled from his letters. Amsterdam, 1968.

GOLDSCHEIDER, L. Van Gogh. Paintings and Drawings. Oxford, London, 1947.

GRAETZ, HEINZ. The symbolic Language of Vincent van Gogh. London, 1963.

GRUYTER, W. JOS DE. Tekeningen van Vincent van Gogh Nederlands Kunstbezit, [1961].

HAMMACHER, A.M. Vincent van Gogh. Deventer, 1947.

— Vincent van Gogh. Amsterdam, [1948].

— Van Gogh. Les grands maîtres du dessin, Milano, 1953.

— Vincent van Gogh. Selbstbildnisse. Reklambücher. Stuttgart, 1960.

— Van Gogh. London, 1961, revised: 1967.

— Vincent van Gogh. New York, 1968.

HAMMACHER, ARNO. Van Gogh. The land where he was born and raised. The Hague, 1953.

HARTLAUB, G.F. Vincent van Gogh. Leipzig, 1922.

— Vincent van Gogh. Berlin, 1930.

HARTRICK, A.S. A Painter's Pilgrimage through fifty years Cambridge, 1939.

HAVELAAR, JUST. Vincent van Gogh. Amsterdam, 1915.

HOLMER, FOLKE. Vincent van Gogh. Stockholm, 1948.

HUISMAN, PH. Van Gogh Portraits. Lausanne, 1960.

HULSKER, JAN. Wie was Vincent van Gogh? The Hague, 1958.

HUYGHE, RENÉ. Vincent van Gogh. Paris, 1958.

ISAÄCSON, J.J. Een nieuw standpunt in Kunst; Vincent van Gogh en D.B. Nanninga. Amsterdam, 1906.

JAMES, PHILIP. Van Gogh, 1853-1890. London, 1949.

JASPERS, KARL. Strindberg und Van Gogh, Versuch einer pathographischen Analyse unter vergleichender Heranziehung von Swedenborg und Hölderlin. Leipzig, 1922.

JEWELL, EDWARD ALDEN. Vincent van Gogh. New York, [1946].

KELLER, HORST. Vincent van Gogh, die Jahre der Vollendung. Cologne, 1969.

KNUTTEL, G. Vincent van Gogh. Deventer, 1960.

LELJ, C. Fiori di Vincent. Carotto, 1945.

LEPROHON, PIERRE. Tel fut Van Gogh. Paris, 1964.

LEYMARIE, JEAN. Van Gogh. Paris, 1952.

— Qui était van Gogh? Genève, 1968.

LONGSTREET, STEPHEN. The Drawings of Van Gogh. Los Angeles, 1963.

MAROIS, PIERRE. Le secret de Van Gogh. Paris, 1957.

MAURON, CHARLES. Van Gogh au seuil de la Provence. Marseille, 1959.

MEIER-GRAEFE, J. Vincent van Gogh. München, 1910.

— Vincent. München, 1921.

— Vincent van Gogh, a biographical study. New York, 1922.

— Vincent van Gogh. Der Zeichner. Berlin, 1928.

MEURIS, JACQUES. Van Gogh, Aujourd'hui. Paris, 1958.

MINKOWSKA, DR F. Van Gogh, sa Vie, sa Maladie et son Oeuvre suivi de deux autres Etudes avec préface de dr E. Minkowski. Paris, 1963.

MÜNSTERBERGER, W. Vincent van Gogh, Tekeningen, Studiën. Schetsen. Bussum, 1940.

NAGERA, HUMB. Vincent van Gogh. London, 1967.

NIZON, PAUL. Die Anfänge Vincent van Goghs, der Zeichnungsstil der holländischen Zeit. Thesis. Bern, 1960.

NORDENFALK, C. Vincent van Gogh. En livsväg. Stockholm, 1943.

NOVOTNY, FRITZ. Über das 'Elementare' in der Kunstgeschichte und andere Aufsätze. Wien, 1968.

NIJLAND, HIDDE J. Vincent van Gogh, 100 tekeningen uit de verzameling Hidde Nijland in het museum te Dordrecht. Amsterdam, 1905.

PACH, WALTER. Vincent van Gogh. A Study of the Artist and his Work in Relation to His Times. New York, 1936.

PARRONCHI, ALESSANDRO. Van Gogh. Firenze, 1949.

PERRUCHOT, HENRI. La Vie de Van Gogh. Paris, 1955.

PIÉRARD. L. La Vie tragique de Vincent van Gogh. Paris, 1924.

PLASSCHAERT, ALBERT. Vincent van Gogh. Haarlem, 1898.

QUESNE-VAN GOGH, E.H. DU. Vincent van Gogh, persoonlijke herinneringen. Intro. Benno J. Stokvis. Baarn, 1910.

REWALD, JOHN. Post-Impressionism. From Van Gogh to Gauguin. New York, 1956.

ROHDE, M.P. Van Gogh's Verden. Stockholm, 1969.

ROSE, M. AND MANNHEIM, M.J. Vincent van Gogh im Spiegel seiner Handschrift. Basel–Leipzig, 1938.

ROSSET, A.M. Van Gogh. Paris, 1941.

RÜDLINGER, ARNOLD. 24 Zeichnungen, Lithographien und Auszüge aus Briefe Vincent van Goghs. Bern, 1947.

SABLONIÈRE, M. DE. Vincent van Gogh. Amsterdam, [1954].

— Een studie bij kaarslicht [étude à la bougie]. Leiden, 1954.

— Inleiding tot de kunst van Vincent van Gogh. Amsterdam, 1958.

SCHERJON, W. De zelfportretten van Vincent van Gogh uit St Rémy. Utrecht, [1929].

SHAPIRO, MEYER. Vincent van Gogh. New York, 1951.

SHIKIBA, RYNZABURO. [Vincent van Gogh. His life and psychosis]. Tokyô, 1932.

— A century of Vincent van Gogh. Tokyô, 1954.

— Vincent van Gogh. Tokyô, 1955.

SIDOROWA, W. Vincent van Gogh [1853-90]. Moskwa, 1926.

STEENHOFF, W. Vincent van Gogh. Amsterdam, 1905.

STELLINGWERF, J. Werkelijkheid en Grondmotief bij Vincent Willem van Gogh. Thesis. Amsterdam, 1959.

STERNHEIM, C. Gauguin und Van Gogh, Berlin, 1924.

STOKVIS, B.J. Nasporingen omtrent Vincent van Gogh in Brabant. Amsterdam, 1926.

SZYMANSKA, ANNA. Unbekannte Jugendzeichnungen Vincent van Goghs. Berlin, 1967.

TERRASSE, CHARLES. Van Gogh, peintre. Paris, 1935.

THURLER, JEAN. A propos de Van Gogh. Thesis. Genève, 1927.

TRALBAUT, M.E. Vincent van Gogh in zijn Antwerpse periode. Amsterdam, 1948.

— Vincent van Gogh en Charles Degroux. Gent, 1953.

— Van Gogh reflecties op Van Ostayen. Deurne, 1956.

— Van Gogh, début et évolution. Amsterdam, 1957.

— Van Gogh, eine Bildbibliographie. München, 1958.

— Van Gogh te Antwerpen. Antwerp, 1958.

— Vincent van Gogh in Drenthe. Assen, 1959.

— 8 × Vincent van Gogh. Antwerp, 1962.

— Van Goghiana I, II, III, IV, V, VI, VII. Antwerp, 1963-1970.

— De Gebroeders Van Gogh. Zundert, 1964.

— Vincent van Gogh, le Mal Aimé. Lausanne, 1969.

ÜBERWASSER, WALTER. Le Jardin de Daubigny, das letzte Hauptwerk Van Goghs. Basel, 1936.

VALSECCHI, MARCO. Disegni di Vincent van Gogh. Milano, 1942.

— Van Gogh. Milano, 1957.

VITALI, LAMBERTO. Vincent van Gogh pittore. Milano, 1936.

— Vincent van Gogh, Milano, 1952.

VETH, CORNELIS. Falsche Expertisen–Falsche Experten. Berlin, 1932.

WALLACE, ROBERT. The world of Van Gogh 1853-1890. Time-Life Books. New York, 1969.

WEISBACH, WERNER. Vincent van Gogh, Kunst und Schicksal. 2 Vol. Basel, 1949.

Photographic Acknowledgements

All the COLOR REPRODUCTIONS in this book are made after original ektachromes taken expressly for this edition by André Held of Lausanne, with the following exceptions:

Amsterdam, Kunsthandel Gebroeders Douwes NV, p 112, F 177a
Bremen, Kunsthalle, p 409, F 581
Chicago, The Art Institute of Chicago, p 182, F 354; p 358, F 529
Dallas, Dallas Museum of Fine Arts, p 181, F 352
Moscow, The State Hermitage Museum, p 376, F 579
New Haven, Yale University Art Gallery, p 288, F 463
New York, Paulus Leeser, p 146, F 207
—, The Museum of Modern Art, p 428, F 612; p 590; F 1529
—, Taylor and Dull Inc., p 93, F 48a
Vienna, Photo Meyer KG, p 518, F 775
Photographer unknown, p 463, F 626

BLACK-AND-WHITE REPRODUCTIONS were made after photographs supplied by the Netherlands Institute for Art History in the Hague [among which the photographs from the legacy of the late Dr J.-B. de la Faille], The Municipal Museum in Amsterdam and the State Museum Kröller-Müller in Otterlo, unless otherwise specified below.

Amsterdam, Kunstveilingen Paul Brandt, 1194
—, Bern. F. Eilers, 943, 1077, 1247, 1389, 1536, 1589 recto, 1589 verso
—, Kunsthandel Huinck & Scherjon NV, 636, 1025
—, Nauta, 1087
—, Rijksmuseum, 190, 863, 1446
—, E. J. van Wisselingh & Co, 125, 195, 564, 844, 880, 953, 969, 982, 1032, 1053a, 1472a
—, W. Zimmerman, 1088
Antwerp, Foto t' Felt, 98
Arles, Bibliothèque d'Arles, 507
Baltimore, The Baltimore Museum of Art, 333
Berlin East, National-Galerie, 489, 930a, 1430, 1485, 1488, 1544, 1546
Berlin West, von Dühren und Henschel, 736
Bern, Gerhard Kowald, 1463
—, Albert Winkler, 964b
Birmingham, Barber Institute of Fine Arts, 95a
Bolton, Manor Photographic Services, 1403, 1643
Boston, Museum of Fine Arts, 508, 805
Bremen, Stickelmann, 581, 1540
Bristol, City Art Gallery, 170
Brussels, Koninklijke Bibliotheek, p 17
—, Paul Bijtebier, p 23
Budapest, Musée des Beaux Arts, 1130
Cambridge, Mass., The Fogg Art Museum, 332, 1003
Chicago, The Art Institute of Chicago, 272, 1069, 1468, 1524, 1642
Cincinnati, Cincinnati Art Museum, 135, 948
Cleveland, The Cleveland Museum of Art, 657, 786, 1100
Coburg, Städtisches Fremdenverkehrsamt, 567
Cologne, Kölnisches Stadtmuseum, 570
Copenhagen, Kunsthistorisk Pladearkiv, 796

Dallas, Hence Griffith, 1169, 1183
Denver, Robert Berkeley's Lainson Studio, p 24
Detroit, The Detroit Institute of Arts, 526
Dordrecht, Foto Stijns, 1259
Eindhoven, Philips' Persbureau, 278
Essen, Folkwang Museum, 449, 492, 1279, 1539 recto, 1550
—, Foto Witzel, 1419
Essen-Stadtwald, Foto Liselotte Witze, 1539 verso
Geneva, Musée d'Art et d'Histoire, 284
Glasgow, Annan Photographer, 140, 553, 714
Glens Falls, The Hyde Collection, 1516
Göteborg, Konstmuseum, 586
Groningen, Fotobedrijf 'Piet Boonstra', 185, 946a, 1057, 1098
The Hague, A. Dingjan, 473, 893, 952 verso, 973, 989, 1026a, 1061, 1095, 1111, 1136, 1137, 1151, 1240a, 1290a, 1292, 1328 verso, 1335, 1336 verso, 1337, 1399a, 1505, 1527, 1676, 1678, 1680
—, A. Frequin, 85, 86, 108, 113, 133, 136a, 146, 151, 177, 203, 227, 246, 249, 266a, 291, 342, 378, 397, 416, 425, 439, 467, 470, 475, 541, 583, 585, 587, 604, 617, 620, 633, 683, 689, 722, 723, 724, 735, 747, 763, 826, 849, 857, 872, 877, 881, 894, 901, 912, 913, 914, 915, 917, 920, 922, 924, 929, 939, 941, 946 verso, 949, 964, 975, 981, 984, 993, 1000, 1023, 1035a, 1039, 1048, 1052, 1058, 1068, 1078, 1086, 1099, 1124, 1135, 1141, 1144, 1144a, 1174, 1193, 1201 recto, 1201 verso, 1234, 1235, 1248, 1294, 1295, 1314, 1338, 1347, 1397, 1475, 1574, 1675, 1687
—, Gemeente Museum, 162, 178 recto, 178 verso, 979a, 990, 1470
Johannesburg, Johannesburg Art Gallery, 399
Kansas City, William Rockhill Nelson Gallery of Art, 165, 715
Leningrad, State Hermitage Museum, 548
London, The British Museum, 1424
—, Christie's, 575a
—, Courtauld Institute of Art, 527, 1500
—, A. C. Cooper Ltd., 325, 558, 562
—, Marlborough Fine Art Ltd., 153a, 1119
—, National Gallery, 454, 672
—, Sotheby & Co, 85a, 757, 801, 803, 1480a, 1517
—, Tate Gallery, 498, 615, 1242, 1639, p 12
Los Angeles, Henry Kahn Custom Photo Lab., 864
—, Los Angeles County Museum of Art, 1459, 1471
Lugano, Foto Brunel, 191
Mannheim, Kunsthalle Mannheim, 250
Merion, The Barnes Foundation, 435, 674
Middelburg, Ies Lamain, 1728
Minneapolis, The Minneapolis Institute of Arts, 710
Moscow, Pushkin Museum of Fine Arts, 1504
Munich, Bayerische Staatsgemäldesammlungen, 456, 516, 762, 782, 1472, 1552
New Britain, E. Irving Blomstrann, 268, 279
New Haven, Yale University Art Gallery, 276
New Orleans, Industrial Photographers, 216
New York, Brenwasser, 361, 501, 1193a, 1418
—, Rudolph Buckhardt, 1105
—, Galerie St. Etienne, 939a

—, Findlay Associates, Inc., 270
—, Henry Grossman ASMP, 1091
—, M. Knoedler & Co. Inc., 257, 317, 502, 608, 1324, 1440
—, The Metropolitan Museum of Art, 552, 613, 654, 680, 817, 1482, 1625
—, O. E. Nelson Photographer, 145
—, Parke-Bernet Galleries Inc., 240, 710a
—, Paul Rosenberg & Co., 598
—, John D. Schiff, 139
—, E. & A. Silberman Galleries, Inc., 142, 273, 592
—, The Solomon R. Guggenheim Museum, 622
—, Adolph Studly, 930
—, Taylor and Dull Inc., 203a, 995
—, Wildenstein & Co, Inc., 252, 488, 529, 640, 688, 812, 1620 recto, 1620 verso, 1652 verso
Oslo, O. Vaering, 528, 1267, 1280, 1306, 1452
Ottawa, The National Gallery of Canada, 601, 846
Paris, Galerie Bernheim-Jeune, 324a
—, Photographie Giraudon, 785, 822
—, Musée Jacquemart-André, 1020b, 1665
—, Art Gallery Jos Hessel, 298
—, Musées Nationaux, 381, 1616, 1617, 1622 recto, 1622 verso, 1644 recto, 1644 verso, 1653
—, Presses Universitaires de France, p 26
—, Musée Rodin, 363, 545
—, Marc Vaux, 1670
Philadelphia, Philadelphia Museum of Art, 490
Providence, Museum of Art, 1416 recto, 1416 verso
Raleigh, North Carolina Museum of Art, 971
Richmond, The Virginia Museum of Fine Arts, 1654 recto, 1654 verso
Rotterdam, Museum Boymans-van Beuningen, 842
—, Vennootschap 'Brinio', 961, 1065
Saint Louis, City Art Museum, 874 recto
San Antonio, Patteson Photographers, 819
São Paulo, Museu de Arte, 542, 732
Stockholm, Nationalmuseum, 821
Tokyo, Bridgestone Gallery, 283b
Toledo, The Toledo Museum of Art, 759
Utrecht, Museum Van Baaren, 306
—, Centraal Museum, 121
—, Kunsthistorisch Instituut Rijksuniversiteit, 234
Vienna, Albertina, 1399
—, Kunsthistorisches Museum, 775
Washington, National Gallery of Art, 426, 523, 565, 573, 788
Winnipeg, Brigdens Photographers, 89, 141, 599
Winterthur, Kunstmuseum Winterthur, 434, 1514
—, Kunstverein Winterthur, 536
—, Michael Speich, 494
Wuppertal-Elberfeld, Foto-Studio M. Abel-Menne, 172, 287, 1103
Zurich, Collection E. Bührle, 450, 556
—, Foto Hänssler, 1029
—, Kunsthaus Zurich, 1502
—, Dr. Fritz Nathan und Dr. Peter Nathan, 286b, 1456
Charles Uht, 1662

Errata and Addenda

XII a

ERRATA

page 41: Instructions for the use of the catalogue: 2nd column, 6th line from the bottom: the passage 'the work bis' should read 'the word bis'

F 185a EDITORS' COMMENT The editors consider the attribution to van Gogh not altogether convincing. The touch and the weak structure both of the whole composition and of several details are features reminiscent of certain painters of the schools of The Hague and Laren. The picture has formerly been in the possession of the Laren painter J. S. H. Kever

F 212a EDITORS' COMMENT Faille gave this painting a number which implicates that it should be dated to the Antwerp period; in his manuscript for the present edition, however, he dated the painting correctly to Nuenen

F 748a EDITORS' COMMENT Erroneously reproduced under this number on Plate CCXXXI in Faille 1928, but described under F 681a [see REJECTED WORKS]

F 791 EDITORS' COMMENT 'Père Pilon' should read Pierre Pilon, a painter who worked at Auvers [see Paul Gachet, Un peintre méconnu – Pierre Pilon; brochure, December 1953]

F 860a LITERATURE Expertised under the auspices of the Expertise Institute, Amsterdam 1968

F 911 verso: technique: Pen

F 949 should read: F 949 recto

F 949 verso: see addenda

F 1132 Period should be: Nuenen

F 1161 verso: technique: Black crayon

F 1236 Period should be: Nuenen

F 1244a recto and verso: redated to Paris: see after F 1412

F 1660 III ex coll Hidde Nijland F 1036 and F 1660 [vol IV pl LIII and pl CCX]

F 157 COLLECTION Edgware, M. Azulai and L. Lipton [acquired 1970]

ADDENDA

F 67 COLLECTION Los Angeles, Armand Hammer

F 94 COLLECTION Sale London [Sotheby] 1 July 1970, 32

F 95 COLLECTION Utrecht, Stichting G. Ribbius Peletier jr tot behoud van het Landgoed Linschoten

F 144 COLLECTION Montreal, John H. Shuter

F 145 EXHIBITION 1970 London, 83

F 149 EXHIBITION 1970 London, 82

F 160a COLLECTION Sale London [Sotheby], 1 July 1970, 23 [dimensions 39.5 × 30 cms]

F 201 COLLECTION Collection Scholte-van Houten

F 213 EDITORS' COMMENT The picture has been restored after an accident in February 1963

F 240 COLLECTION Private collection

F 242 COLLECTION Sale London [Sotheby] 1 July 1970, 8

F 246a COLLECTION Obbach, Sammlung Georg Schäfer

F 258 COLLECTION Prien-Chiemsee [DBR], Baronin von Varnbüler

F 326 COLLECTION Property of Trustees under the Will of the late Georg S. Hirschland

F 357 COLLECTION Foundation Rudolf Staechelin [1970]

F 384 EDITORS' COMMENT The background is more greenish than yellow

F 399 COLLECTION Collection late Hugo Cassirer

F 495 EDITORS' COMMENT About the problem which picture was sold in Brussels in February 1890 for 400 francs to Anna Boch and which for 350 francs in May 1891 [from Tanguy], the editors suggested one of the two might have been one of the Sunflowers. However, a recent communication of Mrs Claudine Lemaire [Brussels] to A. M. Hammacher cites a catalogue, 'de l'Exposition des peintres impressionnistes à la Libre Esthétique', 28 February-29 March 1904 Brussels, where under

numbers 176 and 178 are mentioned as belonging to Mrs Anna Boch: La Vigne Rouge and La Vallée du Rhône. It is uncertain, since obviously the title changed after 1904, which picture is identical with nr 178 in the 1904 exhibition. Anyhow La Vallée du Rhône was not for sale at the 'Vente Druet' of 1909, but in 1935 no van Gogh was left in the collection Anna Boch. The painter Boch, brother of Anna, bought for a 'comparitively big price' [letter 644] directly from the van Goghs in June-July 1890 a picture and made an exchange [being in Paris with Theo] with F 622 [letter T 38]

F 575a EXHIBITION 1970 Washington, DC, 60

F 625 COLLECTION Basle, Galerie Beyeler [1970]

F 627 EDITORS' COMMENT The painting had to be relined in 1969 and just as was the case with F 754, it could be x-rayed before the restoration. The documents of the 'Centre des recherches du Louvre', shown to A. M. Hammacher, revealed once more the impressive coherence of figure and background, with repeated curving lines and no retouches in the succession of curves of the background

F 630 EDITORS' COMMENT Reference to A. Robaut L'oeuvre complet de Eugène Delacroix, Paris, nr 1173

F 633 EDITORS' COMMENT Reference to A. Robaut, L'oeuvre complet de Eugène Delacroix, Paris, nr 1168

F 677 LITERATURE Reference to A. Bartsch, Catalogue raisonné des estampes de Rembrandt [1797] ed 1880, nr 73

F 699 EDITORS' COMMENT Reference to L. Delteil, le peintre graveur, vol. I, Paris 1906, nr 33

F 754 EDITORS' COMMENT The difference in expression and conception of the two Gachet portraits F 753 and F 754 not only caused different interpretations but gave rise to doubts about the authenticity of F 754. Thus the author H. R. Graetz who had interpreted and analysed the state of mind of the painter and his model in his book 'The Symbolic Language of Vincent van Gogh' 1963, pp 259-268, only accepted F 753 as a work by van Gogh. In an unpublished letter of 1970 to two of the editors [Hammacher and Hulsker] Mr Graetz explains his reasons for denying the authenticity of F 754 in which among other defects he misses the psychological expression of F 753 he had stressed in his book. F 754 was relined in 1969. Before the restoration a great number of macrophotos, infra-red, ultra-violet and x-ray photos of several details were made at the 'Centre des recherches du Louvre', permitting a close examination of the brush strokes and construction of the picture. The documents resulting from this research, shown to A. M. Hammacher, provided proof of a striking continuity of the brush strokes, no retouches, a direct rythmical handwriting, with the alternations and other particularities, characteristic for van Gogh. Emile Bernard mentions the existence of two versions in the introduction of a reprint of the 'Lettres à Emile Bernard', Brussels 1942

F 777 COLLECTION Foundation Rudolf Staechelin

F 798 COLLECTION Detroit, Detroit Institute of Arts [1970]

F 902 verso: gekocht van den kunstkooper Oldenzeel te Rotterdam. Teekening van Vincent van Gogh. Dordrecht. Dec. 1892. Hidde Nijland.

F 949 verso BOAT ON THE BEACH WITH FIGURES Pencil and water color
The Hague 1882-1883
COLLECTION Mrs M. Frank, New York [1970]
EDITORS' COMMENT Discovered May 1970
COLLECTION New York, Mrs M. Frank

F 955 COLLECTION Summit, New Jersey, Mr and Mrs Dimitry Jodidio

F 964 COLLECTION Sale London [Sotheby] 2 July 1970, 20

F 998 verso, gekocht van den kunstkooper Oldenzeel te Rotterdam, Smart van Vincent van Gogh. Hidde

Nijland. Dordrecht. Dec. 1892.

F 1002 COLLECTION Switzerland. Private Collection

F 1660, IV, sale London [Sotheby] 2 July 1970. Ex coll H. J. van der Weele, J. H. de Bois, Dr H. Stinnes, sale Leipzig [Boerner] 10-11 November 1932, 114

JUVENILIA XIIa TWO SKETCHES OF A MAN LEANING ON HIS SPADE [after an unknown example]
Pencil on greyish ordinary drawing-paper
22.5 × 28.5 [8¾ × 11¼]
Signed and annotated in lower right V. W. v. Gogh ft 1867
Tilburg 1867
EDITORS' COMMENT Vincent left the boarding-school at Zevenbergen [North Brabant] 31 August 1866 for a boarding-school at Tilburg. He left Tilburg for Zundert 19 March 1868 and he left Zundert for The Hague 30 July 1869. May 1873 Vincent arrived at London.
COLLECTION E. H. Held, The Hague [1970]

The following numbers [65 drawings] were exhibited in the Frankfurter Kunstverein at Frankfurt/M., 21 April-21 June 1970:
F 848, 872, 877, 886, 893, 901, 902a, 912, 922a, 925, 926, 946, 946a, 958, 961, 972a, 990, 996a, 1019, 1020a, 1021, 1025, 1038, 1054, 1057, 1098, 1103, 1127a, 1140, 1242, 1270, 1272, 1312, 1320, 1367, 1380, 1399, 1410, 1430b, 1436, 1451, 1452, 1458, 1470, 1471, 1472, 1473, 1478, 1479, 1480a, 1487, 1489, 1497, 1502, 1514, 1529, 1566, 1639, 1645, 1659, 1662, SD 1680, 1684, 1686, 1687.
Furthermore there was exhibited 1 letter with drawing dated 26 September 1888.

COLOPHON: Typesetting in Monotype Times New Roman
with Light Capitals: Van Boekhoven-Bosch NV, Utrecht.
Lithography: L. van Leer & Co. NV, Amsterdam.
Black and white printed by Van Boekhoven-Bosch NV,
Utrecht and de Lange/van Leer NV, Deventer. Color
illustrations printed by de Lange/van Leer NV, Deventer.
Paper: K.N.P., Maastricht/Proost en Brandt NV, Amster-
dam. Ink: Sinclair & Valentine Co. NV, Soest. Bound by
Proost en Brandt NV, Amsterdam.